Advances in Fractional Modeling and Computation

Advances in Fractional Modeling and Computation

Guest Editors

Yuri Mitkov Dimitrov
Venelin Todorov
Slavi Georgiev
Jordan Hristov

MDPI

Basel • Beijing • Wuhan • Barcelona • Belgrade • Novi Sad • Cluj • Manchester

Guest Editors

Yuri Mitkov Dimitrov
Department of Mathematics,
Physics and Informatics
University of Forestry
Sofia
Bulgaria

Venelin Todorov
Department of Parallel
Algorithms and Machine
Learning with a Laboratory in
Neurotechnologies
Bulgarian Academy
of Sciences
Sofia
Bulgaria

Slavi Georgiev
Department of Applied
Mathematics and Statistics
University of Ruse
Ruse
Bulgaria

Jordan Hristov
Department of Chemical
Engineering
University of Chemical
Technology and Metallurgy
Sofia
Bulgaria

Editorial Office

MDPI AG
Grosspeteranlage 5
4052 Basel, Switzerland

This is a reprint of the Special Issue, published open access by the journal *Fractal and Fractional* (ISSN 2504-3110), freely accessible at: https://www.mdpi.com/journal/fractalfract/special_issues/4X6L41Z9X2.

For citation purposes, cite each article independently as indicated on the article page online and as indicated below:

Lastname, A.A.; Lastname, B.B. Article Title. *Journal Name* **Year**, *Volume Number*, Page Range.

ISBN 978-3-7258-7981-6 (Hbk)
ISBN 978-3-7258-7982-3 (PDF)
https://doi.org/10.3390/books978-3-7258-7982-3

Contents

About the Editors

Yuri Mitkov Dimitrov

Yuri Mitkov Dimitrov is an Associate Professor at the University of Forestry in Sofia, Bulgaria. He received a degree in Mathematics from Sofia University and earned doctoral degrees from The Ohio State University and the University of Ruse in 2006 and 2017, respectively. He has published over 40 papers in international journals and conference proceedings. His research interests include scientific computing, Monte Carlo methods, fractional differential equations, and mathematical methods in finance.

Venelin Todorov

Venelin Todorov is an Associate Professor at the Institute of Information and Communication Technologies, Bulgarian Academy of Sciences, Sofia, Bulgaria. He obtained his M.Sc. degree from Sofia University in 2011 and his Ph.D. degree from the Institute of Information and Communication Technologies in 2017. His scientific contributions as a young researcher have been recognized with several prestigious national awards. The main focus of his research is computational mathematics, statistical methods for multidimensional integrals, integral equations, fractional differential equations, and mathematical finance.

Slavi Georgiev

Slavi Georgiev is an Assistant Professor in the Department of Information Modeling at the Institute of Mathematics and Informatics, Bulgarian Academy of Sciences, and in the Department of Applied Mathematics and Statistics at the University of Ruse. He graduated from the High School of Mathematics, Ruse, in 2013 and received his M.Sc. and Ph.D. degrees in Applied Mathematics from the University of Ruse in 2018 and 2022, respectively. His research interests include numerical methods for integer- and fractional-order differential equations, mathematical and stochastical modeling, and quantitative finance.

Jordan Hristov

Jordan Hristov is a Professor of Chemical Engineering. He graduated with an M.Sc. in Electrical Engineering from the Technical University of Sofia in 1979. He was awarded a Ph.D. in Chemical Engineering by the University of Chemical Technology and Metallurgy, Sofia, Bulgaria, in 1994, and a D.Sc. in Chemical Engineering by the same university in 2018. His research interests include transport phenomena, mathematical modelling, fractional calculus, heat transfer, approximate analytical methods, and dimensional analysis. The principal direction of his research over the last decade has focused on approximate analytical solutions of nonlinear and fractional problems, applications of non-singular fractional operators to nonlocal problems, fractional viscoelasticity, heat conduction, and nonlinear diffusion.

fractal and fractional

MDPI

ditorial

Advances in Fractional Modeling and Computation

Yuri Dimitrov [1,2,*], Slavi Georgiev [2,3], Venelin Todorov [4,5] and Jordan Hristov [6,*]

1 Department of Mathematics, Physics and Informatics, University of Forestry, 1756 Sofia, Bulgaria
2 Department of Informational Modeling, Institute of Mathematics and Informatics, Bulgarian Academy of Sciences, 1113 Sofia, Bulgaria; sggeorgiev@math.bas.bg
3 Department of Applied Mathematics and Statistics, University of Ruse, 7017 Ruse, Bulgaria
4 Department of Parallel Algorithms and Machine Learning with a Laboratory in Neurotechnologies, Institute of Information and Communication Technologies, Bulgarian Academy of Sciences, 1113 Sofia, Bulgaria; venelin@parallel.bas.bg
5 Centre of Excellence in Informatics and Information and Communication Technologies, Institute of Information and Communication Technologies, Bulgarian Academy of Sciences, 1113 Sofia, Bulgaria
6 Department of Chemical Engineering, University of Chemical Technology and Metallurgy, 1756 Sofia, Bulgaria
* Correspondence: yuri.dimitrov@ltu.bg (Y.D.); jordan.hristov@mail.bg (J.H.)

1. Introduction

Fractional calculus, the study of derivatives and integrals of arbitrary order [1–3], has a history dating back to Leibniz in 1695, who first considered a half-order derivative. Over time, mathematicians such as Liouville, Riemann, and Grünwald formalized fractional operators. Today, commonly used definitions include the Riemann–Liouville, Caputo, and Grünwald–Letnikov derivatives [4], while other important definitions, such as Weyl, Hadamard, Marchaud, and Riesz fractional derivatives, are widely applied in mathematical physics and engineering.

In the third quarter of the 20th century, fractional calculus experienced renewed interest due to its ability to model systems with memory and nonlocal effects. Applications emerged in viscoelasticity, anomalous diffusion, and control theory, supported by advances in analytical and numerical methods. Theoretical foundations, including stability, existence, and uniqueness of solutions, were also developed.

The 21st century has seen rapid expansion in fractional calculus, driven by the introduction of novel operators such as the Caputo–Fabrizio (2015) and Atangana–Baleanu–Caputo (2016) derivatives [5,6]. These definitions utilize nonsingular kernels to overcome the limitations of classical formulations and offer improved modeling of memory effects. Among these, the Hilfer fractional derivative has garnered significant attention for providing greater flexibility in capturing intermediate and mixed memory behaviors [7]. Collectively, these advances have significantly expanded the applicability of fractional calculus across various disciplines including physics, biology, finance, and engineering [8–12].

This Special Issue on 'Advances in Fractional Modeling and Computation' reflects current trends in the rapid development of fractional calculus as a powerful framework for modeling complex, memory-dependent, and nonlocal phenomena. Out of 64 received submissions, 21 high-quality papers were accepted for publication, resulting in an acceptance rate of 37.5%. The collected papers address recent theoretical advances, efficient numerical and computational methods, and diverse applications of fractional differential equations in science and engineering. Emphasis is placed on modern fractional operators and high-accuracy algorithms, highlighting the role of fractional models in anomalous diffusion, viscoelasticity, control theory, and applied physics. Together, these contributions demonstrate how fractional modeling and computation continue to evolve in response to contemporary scientific and technological challenges.

2. An Overview of Published Articles

This volume presents recent advances in both analytical and numerical approaches to fractional differential equations, emphasizing their role in modeling real-world phenomena and demonstrating the practical value of fractional calculus for addressing challenges in science and engineering. The contributions in this reprint are organized into three main themes, reflecting the scope of the Special Issue.

2.1. Theoretical Analysis of Fractional Operators and Systems

The theoretical properties of fractional operators and systems are explored in the following papers. Contribution 1 study a class of boundary value problems for impulsive fractional integro-differential equations involving the Caputo–Hadamard fractional derivative. Sufficient conditions for the existence and uniqueness of solutions are established using the Banach contraction principle and Krasnoselskii's fixed-point theorem. Contribution 2 introduce a fractional order chaotic system with nonlinear terms and study its dynamic behavior. Various characteristics such as stability of equilibrum points, phase portraits, bifurcation diagrams and Lyapunov exponents are examined to illistrate the behavior of the system and design a feedback control scheme to stabilize the system. Contribution 3 propose a fully intuitionistic fuzzy multi-objective, multi-item solid fractional transportation model with fractional objective functions to handle imprecision in logistical parameters. The proposed model is linearized and reduced to a crisp multi-objective problem, which is then solved using three types of membership functions. Contribution 4 analyze neutral fractional systems with Riemann–Liouville derivatives and distributed delays, proving the existence and uniqueness of solutions when the initial functions are discontinuous. In addition, they introduce a new concept of weighted stability in the Lyapunov, Ulam–Hyers, and Ulam–Hyers–Rassias senses, extending classical stability notions to systems with Riemann–Liouville derivatives and establishing key stability results. Contribution 5 introduce a generalized degenerate version of two-dimensional Appell polynomials using tools from fractional calculus. Several fundamental properties of these new polynomials are established, including their generating function, explicit series representation, recurrence relations, and determinant form, showing that well-known two-dimensional and classical Appell polynomials arise as special cases. Contribution 6 investigate a tempered fractional sub-diffusion model with a changing-sign perturbation and weak singularity, which is relevant to anomalous diffusion phenomena. A novel power factor is introduced into the Green function, ensuring that the associated linear operator has a positive lower bound. By applying a priori estimates and Schauder's fixed-point theorem, the authors establish the existence of a positive solution.

2.2. Numerical Methods for Fractional Differential Equations

Numerical methods for solving fractional differential equations are discussed in the following six papers. Contribution 7 develop a new compact difference–Galerkin spectral method for solving multi-dimensional fourth-order partial differential equations with a time-fractional derivative of order $\alpha \in (1,2)$ under complex boundary conditions. The stability, convergence, and solvability of the proposed numerical scheme are rigorously established. Contribution 8 develop a numerical approach for solving a class of fractional nonlinear mixed integro-differential equations that model various physical phenomena. This work introduces a quadrature Nyström method to numerically treat this challenging class of equations. The study provides a rigorous theoretical analysis, including proofs of existence, uniqueness,

https://doi.org/10.3390/fractalfract10010045

convergence, and error bounds for the solution. Contributions 9 and 10 construct expansion formulas of order $2-\alpha$ for approximations of the Caputo fractional derivative, parameter-dependent discretizations of the first derivative, and new approximations of the fractional derivative. The two papers examine applications of the approximations for the numerical solution of classical and fractional differential equations. Proofs of the convergence of the numerical methods and error estimates are presented. Contribution 11 develop a hybrid numerical method for solving fractional mixed diffusion and wave–diffusion equations involving Caputo derivatives of different orders. The approach combines the Laplace transform with a local radial basis function (RBF) scheme and the Stehfest algorithm, which circumvent traditional time-stepping procedures, thereby reducing computational complexity and improving efficiency. Contribution 12 introduce a Genocchi polynomial method to numerically solve a class of nonlinear fractional integral equations. The paper establishes the existence and uniqueness of solutions in a Hilbert space setting and analyzes the stability and error of the numerical approximations.

2.3. Fractional Models of Memory-Based Systems

Applications of fractional calculus to epidemiology, physics, and materials science are studied in the following nine papers. Contribution 13 propose a novel fractional discrete reaction–diffusion model to study the spread of infectious diseases. The linear stability of the equilibrium solutions and the global asymptotic stability of the model are analyzed using a specialized Lyapunov function. Contribution 14 develop a sophisticated mathematical model to describe HIV transmission dynamics by incorporating a fractal–fractional operator and three distinct levels of infection. The existence and uniqueness of the solutions are established, and the stability of both disease-free and endemic equilibria is analyzed using tools from fractional calculus. Contribution 15 formulate a fractional order model for measles that captures disease transmission dynamics and assesses the influence of vaccination on the population over time. The study formulates and solves an optimal control problem aimed at minimizing both the disease burden and the economic costs of intervention strategies. Contribution 16 develop a fractional order epidemic model to study the dynamics of a vector-borne disease, incorporating preventive control measures. A rigorous mathematical analysis is conducted to establish the existence, uniqueness, and boundedness of the model's solutions and the stability of the equilibrium states. Contribution 17 investigate an SIR epidemic model that incorporates spatial diffusion and employs a generalized fractional derivative to describe disease dynamics. Rigorous mathematical analysis is presented to establish the existence and uniqueness of solutions to the model, and a numerical scheme is developed for its solution. Simulation results demonstrate the effectiveness of the proposed method and highlight the significant roles that the fractional order and diffusion play in influencing and controlling epidemic dynamics. Contribution 18 propose a fractional order tabu learning neuron model by incorporating fractional calculus into a classical integer-order tabu learning neuron framework. The authors analyze the model's dynamics, including stability, bifurcation behavior, and chaotic phenomena, using both theoretical analysis and numerical simulations. Stability analysis based on the eigenvalues of the Jacobian matrix shows that a Hopf bifurcation occurs in the single-neuron model at a lower memory decay rate than in its integer-order counterpart. Contribution 19 introduce a fractional order viscoelastic creep model that captures the temperature-dependent creep behavior of concrete by employing fractional derivatives to represent its viscoelastic response. Experimental creep data obtained at various temperatures are used to validate the model, indicating that the fractional order approach provides a more accurate and parameter-efficient description of creep behavior than traditional empirical models. Contribution 20 integrate fractional calculus into cosmology to study scalar field

https://doi.org/10.3390/fractalfract10010045

models with conformal and nonminimal couplings to gravity. The study analyzes both exact and numerical solutions for different coupling forms, demonstrating that fractional order dynamics can reproduce accelerated cosmic expansion and provide a generalized framework for investigating the interplay between gravity and scalar fields in the evolution of the universe. Contribution 21 derive a new general fractional calculus model for time-dependent nuclear reactor neutron diffusion that incorporates the effects of delayed neutrons. Numerical studies for slab, cylindrical, and spherical reactor geometries are carried out using two analytical approximation techniques, the Temimi–Ansari method (TAM) and the Sumudu residual power series method (SRPSM), confirming that both methods yield consistent and physically realistic neutron diffusion results.

3. Concluding Remarks

In conclusion, the works presented here affirm that fractional calculus has evolved from a well-established mathematical field into an essential cross-disciplinary framework for modeling complex systems. Its growing impact across physics, engineering, biology, and the applied sciences demonstrates its unique effectiveness in capturing memory-dependent, nonlocal, and multiscale phenomena/features often inadequately described by classical integer-order approaches. We extend our deepest gratitude to the authors for their outstanding contributions, to the reviewers for their thorough and diligent work, and to the editorial staff of *Fractal and Fractional* for their support in making this Special Issue a valuable resource for the scientific community and for future research.

Conflicts of Interest: The authors declare no conflict of interest.

List of Contributions

1. Alruwaily, Y.; Venkatachalam, K.; El-hady, E. Some Results on Fractional Boundary Value Problem for Caputo-Hadamard Fractional Impulsive Integro Differential Equations. *Fractal Fract.* **2023**, *7*, 884. https://doi.org/10.3390/fractalfract7120884.
2. Ren, L.; Muhsen, S.; Shateyi, S.; Saberi-Nik, H. Dynamical Behaviour, Control, and Boundedness of a Fractional-Order Chaotic System. *Fractal Fract.* **2023**, *7*, 492. https://doi.org/10.3390/fractalfract7070492.
3. Almotairi, S.; Badr, E.; Elsisy, M.; Farahat, F.; El Sayed, M. Performance Analysis of Fully Intuitionistic Fuzzy Multi-Objective Multi-Item Solid Fractional Transportation Model. *Fractal Fract.* **2024**, *8*, 404. https://doi.org/10.3390/fractalfract8070404.
4. Kiskinov, H.; Milev, M.; Cholakov, S.; Zahariev, A. Fundamental Matrix, Integral Representation and Stability Analysis of the Solutions of Neutral Fractional Systems with Derivatives in the Riemann—Liouville Sense. *Fractal Fract.* **2024**, *8*, 195. https://doi.org/10.3390/fractalfract8040195.
5. Zayed, M.; Wani, S. A Study on Generalized Degenerate Form of 2D Appell Polynomials via Fractional Operators. *Fractal Fract.* **2023**, *7*, 723. https://doi.org/10.3390/fractalfract7100723.
6. Zhang, X.; Chen, J.; Chen, P.; Li, L.; Wu, Y. Nonlocal Changing-Sign Perturbation Tempered Fractional Sub-Diffusion Model with Weak Singularity. *Fractal Fract.* **2024**, *8*, 337. https://doi.org/10.3390/fractalfract8060337.
7. Wang, Y.; Yi, S. A Compact Difference-Galerkin Spectral Method of the Fourth-Order Equation with a Time-Fractional Derivative. *Fractal Fract.* **2025**, *9*, 155. https://doi.org/10.3390/fractalfract9030155.
8. Jan, A.; Abdou, M.; Basseem, M. A Physical Phenomenon for the Fractional Nonlinear Mixed Integro-Differential Equation Using a Quadrature Nystrom Method. *Fractal Fract.* **2023**, *7*, 656. https://doi.org/10.3390/fractalfract7090656.
9. Dimitrov, Y.; Georgiev, S.; Todorov, V. Approximation of Caputo Fractional Derivative and Numerical Solutions of Fractional Differential Equations. *Fractal Fract.* **2023**, *7*, 750. https://doi.org/10.3390/fractalfract7100750.

https://doi.org/10.3390/fractalfract1001004

10. Dimitrov, Y.; Georgiev, S.; Todorov, V. First Derivative Approximations and Applications. *Fractal Fract.* **2024**, *8*, 608. https://doi.org/10.3390/fractalfract8100608.
11. Kamal, R.; Kamran; Alzahrani, S.; Alzahrani, T. A Hybrid Local Radial Basis Function Method for the Numerical Modeling of Mixed Diffusion and Wave-Diffusion Equations of Fractional Order Using Caputo's Derivatives. *Fractal Fract.* **2023**, *7*, 381. https://doi.org/10.3390/fractalfract7050381.
12. Matoog, R.; Mahdy, A.; Abdou, M.; Mohamed, D. A Computational Method for Solving Nonlinear Fractional Integral Equations. *Fractal Fract.* **2024**, *8*, 663. https://doi.org/10.3390/fractalfract8110663.
13. Alsayyed, O.; Hioual, A.; Gharib, G.; Abualhomos, M.; Al-Tarawneh, H.; Alsauodi, M.; Abu-Alkishik, N.; Al-Husban, A.; Ouannas, A. On Stability of a Fractional Discrete Reaction–Diffusion Epidemic Model. *Fractal Fract.* **2023**, *7*, 729. https://doi.org/10.3390/fractalfract7100729.
14. Anjam, Y.; Turki Alqahtani, R.; Alharthi, N.; Tabassum, S. Unveiling the Complexity of HIV Transmission: Integrating Multi-Level Infections via Fractal-Fractional Analysis. *Fractal Fract.* **2024**, *8*, 299. https://doi.org/10.3390/fractalfract8050299.
15. Chatterjee, A.; Sharma, S.; Al Basir, F. A Compartmental Approach to Modeling the Measles Disease: A Fractional Order Optimal Control Model. *Fractal Fract.* **2024**, *8*, 446. https://doi.org/10.3390/fractalfract8080446.
16. Jan, R.; Boulaaras, S.; Alharbi, A.; Abdul Razak, N. Fractional-Calculus Analysis of the Dynamics of a Vector-Borne Infection with Preventive Measures. *Fractal Fract.* **2024**, *8*, 691. https://doi.org/10.3390/fractalfract8120691.
17. Alazman, I.; Mishra, M.; Alkahtani, B.; Dubey, R. Analysis of Infection and Diffusion Coefficient in an SIR Model by Using Generalized Fractional Derivative. *Fractal Fract.* **2024**, *8*, 537. https://doi.org/10.3390/fractalfract8090537.
18. Yu, Y.; Gu, Z.; Shi, M.; Wang, F. Fractional-Order Tabu Learning Neuron Models and Their Dynamics. *Fractal Fract.* **2024**, *8*, 428. https://doi.org/10.3390/fractalfract8070428.
19. Chen, J.; Gong, L.; Meng, R. Application of Fractional Calculus in Predicting the Temperature-Dependent Creep Behavior of Concrete. *Fractal Fract.* **2024**, *8*, 482. https://doi.org/10.3390/fractalfract8080482.
20. Marroquín, K.; Leon, G.; Millano, A.; Michea, C.; Paliathanasis, A. Conformal and Non-Minimal Couplings in Fractional Cosmology. *Fractal Fract.* **2024**, *8*, 253. https://doi.org/10.3390/fractalfract8050253.
21. Shqair, M.; Alqahtani, Z.; Hagag, A. Applying Two Fractional Methods for Studying a Novel General Formula of Delayed-Neutron-Affected Nuclear Reactor Equations. *Fractal Fract.* **2025**, *9*, 246. https://doi.org/10.3390/fractalfract9040246.

References

1. Oldham, K.B.; Spanier, J. *The Fractional Calculus: Theory and Applications of Differentiation and Integration to Arbitrary Order*; Academic Press: New York, NY, USA, 1974.
2. Samko, S.G.; Kilbas, A.A.; Marichev, O.I. *Fractional Integrals and Derivatives: Theory and Applications*; Gordon and Breach Science Publishers: Amsterdam, The Netherlands, 1993.
3. Podlubny, I. *Fractional Differential Equations*; Academic Press: San Diego, CA, USA, 1999.
4. Diethelm, K. *The Analysis of Fractional Differential Equations: An Application-Oriented Exposition Using Differential Operators of Caputo Type*; Lecture Notes in Mathematics; Springer: Berlin/Heidelberg, Germany, 2010; Volume 2004. [CrossRef]
5. Caputo, M.; Fabrizio, M. A new definition of fractional derivative without singular kernel. *Prog. Fract. Differ. Appl.* **2015**, *1*, 73–85.
6. Atangana, A.; Baleanu, D. New fractional derivatives with nonlocal and non-singular kernel: Theory and application to heat transfer model. *Therm. Sci.* **2016**, *20*, 763–769. [CrossRef]
7. Sousa, J.V.C.d.; Capelas de Oliveira, E. On the ψ-Hilfer fractional derivative. *Commun. Nonlinear Sci. Numer. Simul.* **2018**, *60*, 72–91. [CrossRef]
8. Baleanu, D.; Diethelm, K.; Scalas, E.; Trujillo, J.J. *Fractional Calculus: Models and Numerical Methods*; Series on Complexity, Nonlinearity and Chaos; World Scientific: Singapore, 2012.

https://doi.org/10.3390/fractalfract10010045

9. Gómez-Aguilar, J.F.; Atangana, A. (Eds.) *Applications of Fractional Calculus to Modeling in Dynamics and Chaos*; Routledge: London, UK, 2021; ISBN 9780367438876.
10. West, B.J.; Chen, Y. *Fractional Calculus for Skeptics I: The Fractal Paradigm*; CRC Press: Boca Raton, FL, USA, 2024.
11. Jiang, S.D.; Zhang, J.W.; Zhang, Q.; Zhang, Z.M. Fast Evaluation of the Caputo Fractional Derivative and Its Applications to Fractional Diffusion Equations. *Commun. Comput. Phys.* **2017**, *21*, 650–678. [CrossRef]
12. Yan, Y.G.; Sun, Z.Z.; Zhang, J.W. Fast Evaluation of the Caputo Fractional Derivative and Its Applications to Fractional Diffusion Equations: A Second-Order Scheme. *Commun. Comput. Phys.* **2017**, *22*, 1028–1048. [CrossRef]

https://doi.org/10.3390/fractalfract10010045

fractal and fractional

rticle

Applying Two Fractional Methods for Studying a Novel General Formula of Delayed-Neutron-Affected Nuclear Reactor Equations

Mohammed Shqair [1], Zuhur Alqahtani [2,*] and Ahmed Hagag [3]

1 Department of Physics, College of Science, Zarqa University, Zarqa 13110, Jordan; mshqair@zu.edu.jo
2 Department of Mathematical Sciences, College of Science, Princess Nourah bint Abdulrahman University, P.O. Box 84428, Riyadh 11671, Saudi Arabia
3 Department of Basic Science, Faculty of Engineering, Sinai University (Kantara Branch), Ismailia 41636, Egypt; ahmed.shehata@su.edu.eg
* Correspondence: zumalqahtani@pnu.edu.sa

Abstract: In this work, the novel general formula for a time-dependent nuclear reactor system of equations with delayed neutron effect has been formulated using a fractional calculus model. We explore the properties of this model, including two analytical approximation methods, the Temimi–Ansari method (TAM) and the Sumudu residual power series method (SRPSM), for solving the equation. These methods allow for the computation of approximate solutions at specific points. This is particularly useful for partial differential equations (PDEs) arising in various fields like physics, engineering, and finance. This work is hoped to improve the advancement of nuclear modeling and simulation, providing researchers and engineers with a powerful mathematical tool for studying the complex dynamics of these critical energy systems.

Keywords: nuclear reactor equations; fractional calculus; TAM; SRPSM; delayed neutrons

1. Introduction

The study of nuclear reactors and the neutron behavior inside them is a critical area of research, with important implications for energy production, nuclear safety, and waste management. Traditional approaches to modeling nuclear dynamics have relied on classical partial differential equations (PDEs) and their associated numerical solutions, where fractional partial differential equations express the effect of delayed neutrons.

Finding new sources of energy is increasingly being considered. Nuclear energy can be considered one of the important energy sources, where the nuclear fission in the nuclear reactor creates energy when the mass is annihilated [1–4]. Expressing the behavior of the neutron during nuclear reactions is modeled as a neutron transport equation; this equation is simplified to the diffusion equation. More interest in studying equation models is considered when Cassell et al. find the neutron distribution in the hemispherical reactors using mixed boundary conditions [5]. Williams studies the nuclear reactor transport equation in two interacting cylinder faces [6]. Khasawneh et al. used the homotopy perturbation method (HPM) in finding the solution of the nuclear reactor equation when neutrons diffuse in hemispherical and cylindrical reactors in two different works where (HPM) was used for the first time in nuclear reactor theory [7,8]. El-Ajou et al. used the residual power series (RPSM) in studying neutron distribution in one-dimensional spherical reactors and two-dimensional hemispherical reactors [9]. Fractional derivatives are employed due to their ability to model anomalous diffusion, which occurs in systems with non-standard transport properties.

One step forward in studying these models is to investigate neutron diffusion equations with delayed neutron presence, where the fractional calculus can assist researchers in studying different cases of nuclear reactor diffusion equations with delayed neutrons. Filali et al. used fractional calculus to solve time-dependent neutron diffusion equations [10]. Roul et al. studied a numerical approximation of considering a dynamic neutron diffusion system numerically [11]. Aboanber studied the matrix representation of two-group nuclear reactor dynamics using fractional analysis [12]. Sardar et al. solved the effect of delayed neutrons on coupled neutron diffusion equations using fractional analysis [13]. Khaled et al. solved the behavior of anomalous neutrons under the effect of delayed neutrons [14]. Vázquez-Rodríguez R. et al. studied the fractional neutron point kinetics model for reactivity transients of the NuScale and compared it with the classical kinetics approach [15]. Yin, D., Xie, Y., and Mei, L. considered the stability and convergence analysis of finite difference methods for the fractional neutron diffusion equation [16]. Burqan A. solved a novel scheme of the ARA transform for systems of partial fractional neutron diffusion equations [17].

Alia et al. found an iterative scheme to study the anomalous neutron diffusion system [18]. Momani et al. studied a spherical-reactor two-group neutron diffusion system [19].

This work considers the generalized comprehensive system of the neutron diffusion equation in different geometries with delayed neutrons. This generalization includes the spherical system for the first time in addition to the slab and cylindrical reactors studied throughout history. One additional novel point is that this system can study all essential geometries simultaneously; moreover, it can easily simplify it for each case. The contribution of this work in scientific research is studying the system of three essential reactor geometries (slab, cylindrical, and spherical reactors), simultaneously using the same formula and solving using two different methods, then comparing them.

The use of fractional calculus helps to address sub-diffusion and super-diffusion behaviors that have been observed in various physical systems, including nuclear reactors [20–22]. In this work, two powerful analytical techniques, the Temimi–Ansari method (TAM) and the Sumudu residual power series method (SRPSM), are employed to solve the generalized comprehensive system of neutron diffusion equations in various reactor geometries with delayed neutrons. TAM [23–25] is an iterative method known for its simplicity and efficiency in handling both linear and nonlinear fractional differential equations. It generates successive approximations that converge toward the exact solution, making it highly suitable for complex systems like neutron diffusion. SRPSM [26,27], on the other hand, combines the Sumudu transform with a residual power series, allowing for a structured approach to solving fractional differential equations while maintaining computational efficiency. By applying these methods, the study addresses the neutron diffusion problem in slab, cylindrical, and spherical geometries, providing solutions that capture the effects of delayed neutrons and fractional dynamics, thereby improving the accuracy and generality of the nuclear reactor models.

The present work is arranged as follows. The nuclear reactor theory principles are considered in Section 2. The TAM and SRPSM are presented in Section 3. Finding analytical results for the nuclear reactor equations fractionally using both proposed methods is considered in Section 4. The numerical implementations are presented in Section 5. The conclusion of this study is presented in Section 6.

2. The Physical Phenomena

The neutrons are distributed as the solute dissolves in the solution. In chemistry, the original equation is called the diffusion equation whereas, in nuclear reactor theory, it is specified as the time-dependent nuclear reactor equation [1–4]:

$$\frac{1}{v_c}\frac{\partial \varphi(\boldsymbol{r},t)}{\partial t} = s(\boldsymbol{r},t) - \Sigma_a \varphi(\boldsymbol{r},t) - \boldsymbol{\nabla} \cdot \boldsymbol{J}(\boldsymbol{r},t), \tag{1}$$

Concepts in Equation (1) are represented as the following: $\varphi(r,t)$, $\boldsymbol{J}(r,t)$, Σ_a, v_c, and $s(\boldsymbol{r},t)$ are the flux, the current density, the cross-section for the absorption process on a macroscopic scale, the velocity of neutrons, and the source term, respectively.

Fick's law can simplify the $\varphi(r,t)$ and $\boldsymbol{J}(\boldsymbol{r},t)$ relationship as

$$\boldsymbol{J}(\boldsymbol{r},t) = -D\boldsymbol{\nabla}\varphi(\boldsymbol{r},t), \tag{2}$$

so

$$\frac{1}{v_c}\frac{\partial \varphi(\boldsymbol{r},t)}{\partial t} = s(\boldsymbol{r},t) - \Sigma_a \varphi(\boldsymbol{r},t) + D\nabla^2 \varphi(\boldsymbol{r},t), \tag{3}$$

Here, the neutron diffusion coefficient is known as D.

In nuclear reactor physics, $s(\boldsymbol{r},t)$ is represented as $v\Sigma_f \varphi(\boldsymbol{r},t)$, where Σ_f and v are the macroscopic fission cross-section and the number of neutrons produced per fission, respectively.

As we study the three essential nuclear reactor geometries—the slab, cylindrical, and spherical reactors—the Laplacian $\nabla^2\varphi(\boldsymbol{r},t)$ term needs to be simplified to deal with each coordinate system (Cartesian for the slab reactor, cylindrical for the cylinder reactor, and spherical for the sphere reactor). In one dimension, the Laplacian can be simplified to $\frac{\partial^2}{\partial x^2}\varphi(x,t) + \frac{a}{x}\frac{\partial \varphi(x,t)}{\partial x}$; the Laplacian determines the reactor geometry, where $a = 0$, $a = 1$, and $a = 2$ represent the slab reactor, cylindrical reactor, and spherical reactor, respectively.

The study of the effect of delayed neutrons, which result from some minor reactions, is manipulated fractionally; the delayed neutrons control the neutrons lifespan in nuclear reactors.

The time-dependent system of neutron diffusion equations, where delayed neutrons affect the source term, is

$$s(r,t) = \gamma_f \sum_f \varphi(r,t) + \lambda\omega(r,t). \tag{4}$$

The general form of a one-dimensional time-dependent nuclear reactor system is

$$\begin{aligned} &\frac{1}{v_c}\frac{\partial}{\partial t}\varphi(x,t) = D\frac{\partial^2}{\partial x^2}\varphi(x,t) + \frac{a}{x}\frac{\partial \varphi(x,t)}{\partial x} + \left(-\sum_a + \gamma_f \sum_f\right)\varphi(x,t) + \lambda\omega(x,t), \\ &\frac{\partial}{\partial t}\omega(x,t) = \beta v \sum_f \varphi(x,t) - \lambda\omega(x,t). \end{aligned} \tag{5}$$

In the studied system, the initial conditions are presented as

$$\varphi(x,0) = \varphi_0(x), \quad \omega(x,0) = \frac{\beta\gamma_f \sum_f}{\lambda}\varphi_0(x). \tag{6}$$

The symbols in Equation (6), $\varphi(x,t)$,γ_f,β, and λ, are the neutron intensity, fission average neutrons, delayed fission neutrons proportion, and constant of decay, respectively. The overall cross-section Σ is considered as $v\Sigma_f\varphi(\boldsymbol{r},t) - \Sigma_a$. In Equation (3), physically, the anomalous neutron diffusion when the delayed neutrons are considered instead of Gaussian neutron diffusion, which can represent this work equation and, mathematically, the fractional diffusion equations represent the case.

The anomalous diffusion changes the representation of the system from regular diffusion in the Gaussian neutron distribution to irregular diffusion; the power-law pattern represents the mean-squared displacement time relation.:

$$\left\langle x^2(t) \right\rangle \sim t^\alpha, \tag{7}$$

where α is the fractional nuclear equation for the diffused neutrons factor, the value of $\alpha > 1$ determines diffusion (the super-diffusion happens when $\alpha > 1$, while sub-diffusion happens when $\alpha > 1$; it is straightforward to show that the classical diffusion occurs when $\alpha = 1$) [13].

The general system of time-dependent neutron diffusion equations in fractional form—this system is suitable for all three essential nuclear reactors—is written for the first time in this work as the following:

$$\begin{aligned} &\frac{1}{v_c}\mathfrak{D}_t^\alpha \varphi(x,t) = D\nabla^2\varphi(x,t) + \frac{a}{x}\frac{\partial\varphi(x,t)}{\partial x} + \left(\gamma_f \sum_f - \sum_a\right)\varphi(x,t) + \lambda\omega(x,t), \\ &\mathfrak{D}_t^\alpha \omega(x,t) = \beta\gamma_f \sum_f \varphi(x,t) - \lambda\omega(x,t), \\ &\varphi(x,0) = \varphi_0(x), \quad \omega(x,0) = \frac{\beta\gamma_f \sum_f}{\lambda}\varphi_0(x). \end{aligned} \tag{8}$$

It must be noted that the simpler forms of this system are considered in soon-to-be published works, where all studied special cases of this formula show an improvement [7–14].

3. Preliminaries

Fractional calculus extends classical calculus by introducing derivatives and integrals of non-integer order, offering a powerful framework to model systems with memory effects and anomalous behavior. In this study, fractional derivatives are employed to capture the complex dynamics of neutron diffusion in nuclear reactors, particularly under the influence of delayed neutrons. Among the various definitions of fractional derivatives, the Caputo fractional derivative is a cornerstone of our analysis due to its practical advantages in physical modeling and its compatibility with initial value problems.

Fractional derivatives, unlike their integer-order counterparts, are non-local operators defined through integrals that account for the history of the function. This non-locality introduces a "memory effect", making them particularly suited for describing phenomena such as anomalous diffusion—where the mean-squared displacement follows a power-law pattern ($\langle x^2(t)\rangle \sim t^\alpha$) rather than the linear relationship of classical diffusion ($\alpha = 1$). In the context of nuclear reactors, this property allows us to model the sub-diffusion ($\alpha < 1$) and super-diffusion ($\alpha > 1$) behaviors observed due to delayed neutron effects.

In this section, we present the foundational concepts of the Caputo fractional derivative and the Sumudu transform, which are critical to the development of our analytical methods—the Temimi–Ansari Method (TAM) and the Sumudu Residual Power Series Method (SRPSM)—for solving the fractional neutron diffusion equations with delayed neutrons.

Definition 1. *Caputo Fractional Derivative.*

The Caputo fractional derivative of order ε for a function $\theta(x,t)$ is defined as [26]

$$\mathfrak{D}_t^\varepsilon \theta(x,t) = \mathfrak{J}_t^{n-\varepsilon}\partial_t^n \theta(x,t), \quad n-1 < \varepsilon \leq n,\, x \in I,\, t > 0, \tag{9}$$

where $\mathfrak{D}_t^\varepsilon$ denotes the Caputo derivative operator, $\mathfrak{J}_t^{n-\varepsilon}$ is the Riemann–Liouville fractional integral of order $n-\varepsilon$, ∂_t^n is the n-th integer-order derivative with respect to time t, n is a positive integer such that $n-1<\varepsilon\leq n$, and I is a spatial interval. The Riemann–Liouville fractional integral is given by

$$\mathfrak{J}_t^\alpha\theta(x,t)=\frac{1}{\Gamma(\alpha)}\int_0^t(t-\tau)^{\alpha-1}\theta(x,\tau)\,d\tau,\quad \alpha>0, \tag{10}$$

where Γ is the Gamma function.

The Caputo definition is particularly advantageous in physical applications because it allows the initial conditions to be specified in terms of integer-order derivatives (e.g., $\theta(x,0)$, $\partial_t\theta(x,0)$), which align naturally with measurable quantities like neutron flux and precursor concentrations in nuclear reactor systems. This contrasts with other fractional derivatives, such as the Riemann–Liouville derivative, which require fractional-order initial conditions that are less intuitive in a physical context. Furthermore, the Caputo derivative of a constant is zero, which is consistent with classical calculus and simplifies the modeling of steady-state behaviors.

In our study, the Caputo derivative is applied to the time-dependent neutron diffusion equations to reflect the memory-dependent dynamics introduced by delayed neutrons. This fractional approach enhances the representation of neutron transport, capturing both Gaussian ($\varepsilon=1$) and anomalous ($\varepsilon\neq1$) diffusion regimes, as detailed in Section 2.

Definition 2. *Sumudu Transform.*

For a function $\theta(t)$ over a set $\mathbb{A}$, the Sumudu transform is defined as [27]

$$\Theta(\zeta)=S[\theta(t)]=\int_0^\infty\theta(\zeta t)e^{-t}\,dt,\quad \zeta\in(-\varepsilon_1,\varepsilon_2), \tag{11}$$

where $\theta(t)$ is a continuous function and the set $\mathbb{A}$ is defined as

$$\mathbb{A}=\left\{\theta(t)\mid \text{there exists } \Delta,\varepsilon_1,\varepsilon_2>0, |\theta(t)|<\Delta e^{\frac{|t|}{\varepsilon_i}}, t\in(-1)^i\times[0,\infty)\right\}. \tag{12}$$

The Sumudu transform of the Caputo derivative is given by

$$S[\mathfrak{D}_t^\varepsilon\theta(t)]=\zeta^{-\varepsilon}S[\theta(t)]-\sum_{\lambda=0}^{n-1}\zeta^{-\varepsilon+\lambda}\theta^{(\lambda)}(0),\quad n-1<\varepsilon\leq n,\ \varepsilon>0,\ n\in\mathbb{N}. \tag{13}$$

The Sumudu transform is a key tool in the SRPSM, as it converts fractional differential equations into algebraic equations, facilitating the construction of series solutions. Its properties, outlined in the subsequent lemma, further support its application in our analytical framework.

Lemma 1. *Let $\theta(t)$ and $\vartheta(t)$ be piecewise continuous functions of exponential order on $[0,\infty)$, with $\Theta(\zeta)=S[\theta(t)]$, $\Upsilon(\zeta)=S[\vartheta(t)]$, and u,v,w,a constants [27]. Then the following apply:*

(i) $S[u\theta(t)+v\vartheta(t)]=uS[\theta(t)]+vS[\vartheta(t)]=u\Theta(\zeta)+v\Upsilon(\zeta)$;

(ii) $S^{-1}[u\Theta(\zeta)+v\Upsilon(\zeta)]=u\theta(t)+v\vartheta(t)$;

(iii) $S[e^{wt}\theta(t)]=\frac{1}{(1-w\zeta)}\Theta\left(\frac{\zeta}{1-w\zeta}\right)$;

(iv) $\lim_{\zeta\to0}\Theta(\zeta)=\theta(0)$;

(v) $S[\theta(at)]=a\Theta(\zeta), a>0$, *and* $\lim_{t\to0}\theta(t)=\lim_{\zeta\to0}\Theta(\zeta)$.

These definitions and properties underpin the analytical solutions derived in Sections 4 and 5, enabling us to address the fractional neutron diffusion system effectively.

4. Methods Principal Ideas

4.1. The Fractional TAM

The TAM is an iterative technique that has been successfully applied to solve nonlinear fractional differential equations. It is particularly advantageous for problems involving linear and nonlinear components. In our work, we applied TAM to the fractional neutron diffusion equations for various geometries (slab, cylindrical, and spherical). The method's strength lies in its ability to handle both linear and nonlinear terms iteratively, making it suitable for solving complex fractional differential equations like those encountered in nuclear reactor physics. TAM has previously been applied to fractional systems in other fields, but its use in fractional nuclear reactor equations, especially with delayed neutrons, is novel and provides new insights into reactor dynamics.

To elaborate on the principal concept of this method, we make the following assumptions about the generic non-homogeneous fractional differential equation (FPDE) [23–25]:

$$\Upsilon(\theta(x,t)) = \Theta(\theta(x,t)) + p(x,t), \quad m-1 < \epsilon \leq m, \tag{14}$$

under the boundary conditions

$$\mathscr{B}\left(\theta, \frac{\partial \theta}{\partial x}\right) = 0, \tag{15}$$

where $\Upsilon = \mathscr{D}_t^{\epsilon} = \frac{\partial^{\epsilon}}{\partial t^{\epsilon}}$ is the fractional operator, Θ is the standard differential operators, $\theta(x,t)$ is depicting the anonymous function, $p(x,t)$ is the representation of the acknowledged continuous functions, and the symbol B indicates the boundary operator. The primary requirement in this case is Υ, which is the generic fractional differential operator. However, we can set down several linear expressions in addition to the nonlinear expressions as needed. The first step in the proposed technique is to derive the initial condition by removing the nonlinear component as follows:

$$\mathfrak{D}_t^{\epsilon}\theta_0(x,t) = p(x,t), \mathfrak{B}\left(\theta_0, \frac{\partial \theta_0}{\partial x}\right) = 0. \tag{16}$$

To obtain the subsequent iteration, we solve the following equation:

$$\mathfrak{D}_t^{\epsilon}\theta_1(x,t) = \Theta(\theta_0(x,t)) + p(x,t), \mathfrak{B}\left(\theta_1, \frac{\partial \theta_1}{\partial x}\right) = 0. \tag{17}$$

This gives us a straightforward iterative stride $\theta_{m+1}(x,t)$, which is the appropriate method for handling a set of linear and nonlinear problems.

$$\mathfrak{D}_t^{\epsilon}\theta_{m+1}(x,t) = \Theta(\theta_m(x,t)) + p(x,t), \mathfrak{B}\left(\theta_{m+1}, \frac{\partial \theta_{m+1}}{\partial x}\right) = 0. \tag{18}$$

It is crucial to remember that, in this method, $\theta_{m+1}(x,t)$ solves the issue in (1) independently.

Applying the iterative strategy is simple, and each iteration improves the previous one. By using this approach further, it is possible to obtain an ideal approximation that matches the exact solution. Thus, the solution to Equation (14) is shown as

$$\theta(x,t) = \lim_{m\to\infty} \theta_m(x,t). \tag{19}$$

The addition of the fractional derivative $\mathfrak{D}_t^{\varepsilon}$ to TAM profoundly changes the iterative process by incorporating a memory effect that accounts for the historical behavior of the neutron flux $\theta(x,t)$. In contrast to integer-order derivatives, which represent immediate rates of change, the fractional derivative $(0 < \varepsilon \leq 1)$ describes long-term dependence caused by delayed neutrons, as stated in Section 3. This effect manifests in each iteration, where the fractional operator $\mathfrak{D}_t^{\varepsilon}$ integrates the past states of $\varepsilon < 1$ via the convolution with a power-law kernel. As a result, the solutions exhibit anomalous diffusion characteristics: subdiffusion for $\varepsilon < 1$ and classical diffusion for $\varepsilon = 1$, reflecting the physical reality of neutron transport in reactors with delayed neutron contributions. In our work, this allows TAM to more correctly represent the progressive development of neutron populations, with the fractional-order ε functioning as a tuning parameter to change the memory strength and diffusion type, hence influencing the convergence and stability of the iterative approximations.

4.2. The Fractional SRPSM

The SRPSM combines the Sumudu transform with a residual power series, allowing for efficient series solutions to fractional differential equations. This method is especially useful for obtaining analytical solutions to problems with fractional operators due to its ability to transform complex fractional terms into simpler algebraic forms. SRPSM has been applied to fractional neutron diffusion equations in this work, providing solutions that converge quickly and accurately. The novelty of this method in our research lies in its application to the neutron diffusion equations of time-dependent fractional order with delayed neutrons, which had not been explored previously in nuclear reactor studies.

Now, the approach for applying SRPSM to solve the fractional nuclear reactor system of equations with delayed neutrons consists of the following steps [26,27]:

Step 1: Applying Sumudu transform on Equation (14) as

$$\mathcal{S}(\Upsilon(\theta(x,t))) = \mathcal{S}(\Theta(\theta(x,t)) + p(x,t)). \tag{20}$$

Applying the differentiation property of Sumudu transform, $\mathcal{S}[\mathfrak{D}_t^{\epsilon}\theta(x,t)] = \frac{1}{s^{\epsilon}}\{\mathcal{S}(\theta(x,t)) - \theta_0(x)\}$ on Equation (4), we get

$$\frac{1}{s^{\epsilon}}\{\mathcal{S}(\theta(x,t)) - \theta_0(x)\} \quad = \quad \mathcal{S}\{\Theta(\theta(x,t)) + p(x,t)\}, \tag{21}$$

i.e.,

$$\mathcal{S}(\theta(x,t)) \quad = \quad \theta_0(x) + s^{\epsilon}\mathcal{S}\{\Theta(\theta(x,t)) + p(x,t)\}. \tag{22}$$

Step 2: Applying Sumudu transform inverse function in Equation (22) to have

$$\theta(x,t) = \theta_0(x) + \mathcal{S}^{-1}[s^{\epsilon}\mathcal{S}\{\Theta(\theta(x,s)) + p(x,s)\}], \tag{23}$$

here, $\theta_0(x)$ is the initial condition.

Step 3: Thus, the algorithm of $\theta(x,t)$ can be considered in the form

$$\theta(x,t) = \sum_{n=0}^{\infty} f_n(x,t)\frac{t^{n\epsilon}}{\Gamma(1+n\epsilon)}. \tag{24}$$

Step 4: The function of Sumudu residual is

$$\mathcal{S}Res(\Theta(x,s)) = \Theta(x,s) - \frac{1}{s}\theta_0(x) - \frac{1}{s^{\epsilon}}\{\Theta(\theta(x,s)) + p(x,s)\}. \tag{25}$$

In SRPSM, the fractional derivative $\mathfrak{D}_t^{\varepsilon}$ affects the solution via power-series expansion, where the fractional-order ε determines the time-scaling of the terms $t^{n\varepsilon}/\Gamma(1+n\varepsilon)$. This scaling captures the fractional operator's non-local character and embeds delayed neutrons' memory effect into the series coefficients $f_n(x,t)$. As ε deviates from 1, the series records anomalous diffusion, with lower ε values highlighting slower, sub-diffusive behavior due to increased historical reliance and $\varepsilon > 1$ potentially revealing super-diffusive tendencies. The Sumudu transform accentuates this impact by transforming the fractional derivative into an algebraic form ($\zeta^{-\varepsilon}$), allowing for the rapid calculation of the series terms. In our nuclear reactor model, this results in a solution that accurately represents the delayed neutron dynamics, with the fractional order ε controlling the decay rate and spread of neutron flux over time, as evidenced by the numerical results in Section 6.

5. Neutron Diffusion Equations Analytical Solutions

The nuclear reactor equation is represented fractionally as

$$\begin{gathered}\frac{1}{v_c}\mathfrak{D}_t^{\epsilon}\theta(x,t) = D\nabla^2\theta(x,t) + \left(\gamma_f\sum_f - \sum_a\right)\theta(x,t) + \left(\frac{a}{x}\right)\frac{\partial\theta(x,t)}{\partial x} + \lambda\vartheta(x,t), \\ \mathfrak{D}_t^{\epsilon}\vartheta(x,t) = \beta\gamma_f\sum_f\theta(x,t) - \lambda\vartheta(x,t),\end{gathered} \tag{26}$$

where the following initial conditions are applied:

$$\theta(x,0) = \theta_0(x), \quad \vartheta(x,0) = \frac{\beta\sum_f}{\lambda}\theta_0(x), \tag{27}$$

For $A = \beta\gamma_f\sum_f$ and $\sum = \gamma_f\sum_f - \sum_a$,

$$\begin{gathered}\mathfrak{D}_t^{\epsilon}\theta(x,t) = v_c D\theta_{xx}(x,t) + v_c\sum\theta(x,t) + \left(\frac{av_c}{x}\right)\theta_x(x,t) + v_c\lambda\vartheta(x,t), \\ \mathfrak{D}_t^{\epsilon}\vartheta(x,t) = A\theta(x,t) - \lambda\vartheta(x,t),\end{gathered} \tag{28}$$

where

$$\theta(x,0) = \theta_0(x), \quad \vartheta(x,0) = \frac{A}{\lambda}\theta_0(x), \tag{29}$$

are the proposed initial conditions.

5.1. Analytical Solution by TAM

By using the fractional TAM, Equation (26) is first rewritten as

$$\begin{cases} \Upsilon_1(\theta(x,t)) = D_t^{\epsilon}\theta(x,t), \Theta_1(\theta(x,t)) = v_c D\theta_{xx}(x,t) + v_c\sum\theta(x,t) + \left(\frac{av_c}{x}\right)\theta_x(x,t) + v_c\lambda\vartheta(x,t), p(x,t) = 0 \\ \Upsilon_2(\vartheta(x,t)) = D_t^{\epsilon}\vartheta(x,t), \quad \Theta_2(\vartheta(x,t)) = A\theta(x,t) - \lambda\vartheta(x,t), \quad q(x,t) = 0. \end{cases} \tag{30}$$

The first problem that has to be handled is

$$\begin{cases} \Upsilon_1(\theta_0(x,t)) = 0, & \theta_0(x,0) = \theta_0 \\ \Upsilon_1(\vartheta_0(x,t)) = 0, & \vartheta_0(x,0) = \frac{A}{\lambda}\theta_0(x) \end{cases} \tag{31}$$

We can solve the above equation using a simple treatment, as follows:

$$\begin{cases} I^{\epsilon}(D_t^{\epsilon}\theta_0(x,t)) = 0, & \theta_0(x,0) = \theta_0 \\ I^{\epsilon}(D_t^{\epsilon}\vartheta_0(x,t)) = 0, & \vartheta_0(x,0) = \frac{A}{\lambda}\theta_0(x). \end{cases} \tag{32}$$

Depending on Definition 2, the primary iteration can be obtained as

$$\begin{cases} \theta_0(x,t) = \theta_0 \\ \vartheta_0(x,t) = \frac{A}{\lambda}\theta_0(x) \end{cases} \tag{33}$$

The next iteration can be computed as

$$\begin{cases} \Upsilon_1(\theta_1(x,t)) = \Theta_1(\theta_0(x,t)) + p(x,t), & \theta_1(x,0) = \theta_0 \\ \Upsilon_1(\vartheta_1(x,t)) = \Theta_2(\vartheta_0(x,t)) + q(x,t), & \vartheta_1(x,0) = \frac{A}{\lambda}\theta_0(x). \end{cases} \tag{34}$$

Next, by integrating both sides of the above equation using Definition 1,

$$\begin{cases} I^{\epsilon}(D_t^{\epsilon}\theta_1(x,t)) = I^{\epsilon}\left(v_c D(\theta_0)_{xx}(x,t) + v_c \sum \theta_0(x,t) + \left(\frac{av_c}{x}\right)(\theta_0)_x(x,t) + v_c\lambda\vartheta_0(x,t)\right), & \theta_1(x,0) = \theta_0 \\ I^{\epsilon}(D_t^{\epsilon}\vartheta_1(x,t)) = I^{\epsilon}(A\theta_0(x,t) - \lambda\vartheta_0(x,t)), & \vartheta_1(x,0) = \frac{A}{\lambda}\theta_0(x). \end{cases} \tag{35}$$

Then, we receive the next iteration as

$$\begin{cases} \theta_1(x,t) = \theta_0 + \frac{t^{\epsilon} v_c[4+2D+(A+\sum)\theta_0]}{\Gamma(\epsilon+1)}, \\ \vartheta_1(x,t) = \frac{A}{\lambda}\theta_0. \end{cases} \tag{36}$$

It is possible to calculate the next iteration, which is provided as

$$\begin{cases} \Upsilon_1(\theta_2(x,t)) = \Theta_1(\theta_1(x,t)) + p(x,t), & \theta_2(x,0) = \theta_0 \\ \Upsilon_2(\vartheta_2(x,t)) = \Theta_2(\vartheta_1(x,t)) + q(x,t), & \vartheta_2(x,0) = \frac{A}{\lambda}\theta_0(x). \end{cases} \tag{37}$$

Next, by integrating both sides of the above equation using Definition 1,

$$\begin{cases} I^{\epsilon}(D_t^{\epsilon}\theta_2(x,t)) = I^{\epsilon}\left(v_c D(\theta_1)_{xx}(x,t) + v_c \sum \theta_1(x,t) + \left(\frac{av_c}{x}\right)(\theta_1)_x(x,t) + v_c\lambda\vartheta_1(x,t)\right), & \theta_2(x,0) = \theta_0, \\ I^{\epsilon}(D_t^{\epsilon}\vartheta_2(x,t)) = I^{\epsilon}(A\theta_1(x,t) - \lambda\vartheta_1(x,t)), & \vartheta_2(x,0) = \frac{A}{\lambda}\theta_0(x). \end{cases} \tag{38}$$

Then, we receive the next iteration as

$$\begin{cases} \theta_2(x,t) = \theta_0 + \frac{t^{\epsilon} v_c[4+2D+(A+\sum)\theta_0]}{\Gamma(\epsilon+1)} + \frac{t^{2\epsilon} v_c^2[2(2+D)(A+2\Sigma)+\sum(A+\sum)\theta_0]}{\Gamma(2\epsilon+1)} \\ \quad + \frac{t^{3\epsilon} v_c^2\left[2(2+D)(A\lambda+\sum(2A+3\sum)v_c)+(A+\Sigma)\left(A\lambda+\sum^2 v_c\right)\theta_0\right]}{\Gamma(3\epsilon+1)} \\ \vartheta_2(x,t) = \frac{A}{\lambda}\theta_0 + \frac{At^{2\epsilon} v_c[4+2D+(A+\Sigma)\theta_0]}{\Gamma(2\epsilon+1)} + \frac{At^{3\epsilon} v_c[-2(2+D)(\lambda-(A+2\sum)v_c)+(A+\Sigma)(-\lambda+\Sigma v_c)\theta_0]}{\Gamma(3\epsilon+1)}. \end{cases} \tag{39}$$

Every time $\theta_m(x,t)$ and $\vartheta_m(x,t)$ are repeated, an approximate solution to Equation (26) is found, according to Equation (19).

As iterations grow in number, our results become closer to the exact results. Using this approach, we can complete the following series template for approximate solutions as

$$\begin{cases} \theta(x,t) = \lim_{m\to\infty}\theta_m(x,t) \simeq \theta_2(x,t) \\ \vartheta(x,t) = \lim_{m\to\infty}\vartheta_m(x,t) \simeq \vartheta_2(x,t). \end{cases} \tag{40}$$

5.2. Analytical Solution by SRPSM

The objective in this step is to construct a series solution for the fractional nuclear reactor system of equations fractionally using the Sumudu Residual Power Series Method (SRPSM).

Upon applying the Sumudu transform to the coupled Equation (26), we see that

$$\begin{gathered} \mathcal{S}[\mathfrak{D}_t^{\epsilon}\theta(x,t)] = v_c D\mathcal{S}[\theta_{xx}(x,t)] + v_c \sum \mathcal{S}[\theta(x,t)] + \frac{av_c}{x}\mathcal{S}[\theta_x(x,t)] + v_c\lambda\mathcal{S}[\vartheta(x,t)], \\ \mathcal{S}[\mathfrak{D}_t^{\epsilon}\vartheta(x,t)] = A[\theta(x,t)] - \lambda\mathcal{S}[\vartheta(x,t)]. \end{gathered} \tag{41}$$

Lemma 1 and the initial conditions in Equation (27) allow us to create Equation (28) in the following way:

$$
\begin{aligned}
s^{\epsilon}\Theta(x,s) - s^{\epsilon-1}\theta_0(x) &= v_c D\Theta_{xx}(x,s) + v_c \sum \Theta(x,s) + \frac{a v_c}{x}\Theta_x(x,s) + v_c\lambda\Xi(x,s) \\
s^{\epsilon}\Xi(x,s) - s^{\epsilon-1}\frac{A}{\lambda}\theta_0(x) &= A\Theta(x,s) - \lambda\Xi(x,s),
\end{aligned}
\tag{42}
$$

where $\Theta(x,s) = \mathcal{S}[\theta(x,t)], \Xi(x,s) = \mathcal{S}[\vartheta(x,t)]$. Equation (42) may be rewritten as

$$
\begin{aligned}
\Theta(x,s) - \frac{1}{s}\theta_0(x) - \frac{v_c D}{s^{\epsilon}}\Theta_{xx}(x,s) - \frac{v_c\sum}{s^{\epsilon}}\Theta(x,s) - \frac{a v_c}{x s^{\epsilon}}\Theta_x(x,s) - \frac{v_c\lambda}{s^{\epsilon}}\Xi(x,s) &= 0, \\
\Xi(x,s) - \frac{A}{\lambda s}\theta_0(x) - \frac{A}{s^{\epsilon}}\Theta(x,s) + \frac{\lambda}{s^{\epsilon}}\Xi(x,s) &= 0.
\end{aligned}
\tag{43}
$$

The linked Equation (43) forms a system of linear partial differential equations with derivatives for the variable x.

As per the SRPS methodology, the System (43) series solution needs to possess the subsequent configuration:

$$
\begin{aligned}
\Theta(x,s) &= \sum_{n=0}^{\infty} \frac{u_n(x)}{s^{n\epsilon+1}}, \\
\Xi(x,s) &= \sum_{n=0}^{\infty} \frac{v_n(x)}{s^{n\epsilon+1}}.
\end{aligned}
\tag{44}
$$

We may use Lemma 1 to express the kth truncated series of $\Theta(x,s)$, $\Xi(x,s)$ as follows:

$$
\begin{aligned}
\Theta_k(x,s) &= \frac{\theta_0(x)}{s} + \sum_{n=1}^{k} \frac{u_n(x)}{s^{n\epsilon+1}}, x \in I, s > \delta \geq 0, \\
\Xi_k(x,s) &= \frac{A}{\lambda s}\theta_0(x) + \sum_{n=1}^{k} \frac{v_n(x)}{s^{n\epsilon+1}}, x \in I, s > \delta \geq 0.
\end{aligned}
\tag{45}
$$

In this stage, we obtain the anonymous coefficients of (45) by finding the Sumudu residual functions of Equation (43):

$$
\begin{aligned}
\mathcal{S}Res(\Theta(x,s)) &= \Theta(x,s) - \frac{1}{s}\theta_0(x) - \frac{v_c D}{s^{\epsilon}}\Theta_{xx}(x,s) - \frac{v_c\Sigma}{s^{\epsilon}}\Theta(x,s) - \frac{a v_c}{x s^{\epsilon}}\Theta_x(x,s) - \frac{v_c\lambda}{s^{\epsilon}}\Xi(x,s), \\
\mathcal{S}Res(C(x,s)) &= C(x,s) - \frac{A}{\lambda s}\theta_0(x) - \frac{A}{s^{\epsilon}}\Theta(x,s) + \frac{\lambda}{s^{\epsilon}}\Xi(x,s).
\end{aligned}
\tag{46}
$$

Additionally, the kth Sumudu residual functions are

$$
\begin{aligned}
\mathcal{S}Res_k(\Theta(x,s)) &= \Theta_k(x,s) - \frac{1}{s}\theta_0(x) - \frac{v_c D}{s^{\epsilon}}\Theta_{k_{xx}}(x,s) - \frac{v_c\Sigma}{s^{\epsilon}}\Theta_k(x,s) - \frac{a v_c}{x s^{\epsilon}}\Theta_{k_x}(x,s) - \frac{v_c\lambda}{s^{\epsilon}}\Xi_k(x,s), \\
\mathcal{S}Res_k(\Xi(x,s)) &= \Xi_k(x,s) - \frac{A}{\lambda s}\theta_0(x) - \frac{A}{s^{\epsilon}}\Theta_k(x,s) + \frac{\lambda}{s^{\epsilon}}\Xi_k(x,s).
\end{aligned}
\tag{47}
$$

Since $\mathcal{S}Res(\Theta(x,s)) = 0$ and $\mathcal{S}Res(\Xi(x,s)) = 0$, we see that $s^{k\epsilon+1}\mathcal{S}Res(\Theta(x,s)) = 0$, $s^{k\epsilon+1}\mathcal{S}Res(\Xi(x,s)) = 0$. Therefore,

$$
\lim_{s\to\infty}\left(s^{k\epsilon+1}\mathcal{S}Res_k(\Theta(x,s))\right) = 0, \lim_{s\to\infty}\left(s^{k\epsilon+1}\mathcal{S}Res_k(\Xi(x,s))\right) = 0 \text{ for } k = 0,1,2,\ldots. \tag{48}
$$

Substituting the first Sumudu-residual functions as $\Theta_1(x,s) = \frac{\theta_0(x)}{s} + \frac{u_1(x)}{s^{\epsilon+1}}$ and $\Xi_1(x,s) = \frac{A}{\lambda s}\theta_0(x) + \frac{v_1(x)}{s^{\epsilon+1}}$, we then obtain $u_1(x)$ and $v_1(x)$ in (45):

$$\begin{aligned} \mathcal{S}Res_1(\Theta(x,s)) = {} & \frac{u_1(x)}{s^{\epsilon+1}} - \frac{v_c D}{s^{\epsilon}}\left[\frac{\theta_0''(x)}{s} + \frac{u_1''(x)}{s^{\epsilon+1}}\right] - \frac{v_c \Sigma}{s^{\epsilon}}\left[\frac{\theta_0(x)}{s} + \frac{u_1(x)}{s^{\epsilon+1}}\right] - \\ & \frac{a v_c}{x s^{\epsilon}}\left[\frac{\theta_0'(x)}{s} + \frac{u_1'(x)}{s^{\epsilon+1}}\right] - \frac{v_c\lambda}{s^{\epsilon}}\left[\frac{A}{\lambda s}\theta_0(x) + \frac{v_1(x)}{s^{\epsilon+1}}\right], \\ \mathcal{S}Res_1(\Xi(x,s)) = {} & \frac{v_1(x)}{s^{\epsilon+1}} - \frac{A}{s^{\epsilon}}\left[\frac{\theta_0(x)}{s} + \frac{u_1(x)}{s^{\epsilon+1}}\right] + \frac{\lambda}{s^{\epsilon}}\left[\frac{A}{\lambda s}\theta_0(x) + \frac{v_1(x)}{s^{\epsilon+1}}\right]. \end{aligned} \tag{49}$$

Now, by solving $\lim_{s\to\infty} s^{\epsilon+1}\mathcal{S}Res_1(\Theta(x,s)) = 0$, $\lim_{s\to\infty} s^{\epsilon+1}\mathcal{S}Res_1(\Xi(x,s)) = 0$, we obtain

$$\begin{aligned} u_1(x) &= v_c D\theta_0''(x) + v_c \sum \theta_0(x) + \frac{a v_c}{x}\theta_0'(x) + v_c\lambda\vartheta_0(x), \\ v_1(x) &= 0. \end{aligned} \tag{50}$$

Substituting the second Sumudu residual functions as $\Theta_2(x,s) = \frac{\theta_0(x)}{s} + \frac{u_1(x)}{s^{\epsilon+1}} + \frac{u_2(x)}{s^{2\epsilon+1}}$ and $\Xi_2(x,s) = \frac{A}{\lambda s}\theta_0(x) + \frac{v_2(x)}{s^{2\epsilon+1}}$, we then obtain $u_2(x)$ and $v_2(x)$ in (45):

$$\begin{aligned} \mathcal{S}Res_2(\Theta(x,s)) = {} & \frac{u_1(x)}{s^{\epsilon+1}} + \frac{u_2(x)}{s^{2\epsilon+1}} - \frac{v_c D}{s^{\epsilon}D}\left[\frac{\theta_0''(x)}{s} + \frac{u_1''(x)}{s^{\epsilon+1}} + \frac{u_2''(x)}{s^{2\epsilon+1}}\right] - \frac{v_c\Sigma}{s^{\epsilon}}\left[\frac{\theta_0(x)}{s} + \frac{u_1(x)}{s^{\epsilon+1}} + \frac{u_2(x)}{s^{2\epsilon+1}}\right] - \\ & \frac{a v_c}{x s^{\epsilon}}\left[\frac{\theta_0'(x)}{s} + \frac{u_1'(x)}{s^{\epsilon+1}} + \frac{u_2'(x)}{s^{2\epsilon+1}}\right] - \frac{v_c\lambda}{s^{\epsilon}\epsilon}\left[\frac{A}{\lambda s}\theta_0(x) + \frac{v_2(x)}{s^{2\epsilon+1}}\right]. \\ \mathcal{S}Res_2(\Xi(x,s)) = {} & \frac{v_2(x)}{s^{2\epsilon+1}} - \frac{A}{s^{\epsilon}}\left[\frac{\theta_0(x)}{s} + \frac{u_1(x)}{s^{\epsilon+1}} + \frac{u_2(x)}{s^{2\epsilon+1}}\right] + \frac{\lambda}{s^{\epsilon}}\left[\frac{A}{\lambda s}\theta_0(x) + \frac{v_2(x)}{s^{2\epsilon+1}}\right]. \end{aligned} \tag{51}$$

Now, by solving $\lim_{s\to\infty} s^{2\epsilon+1}\mathcal{S}Res_2(\Theta(x,s)) = 0$, $\lim_{s\to\infty} s^{2\epsilon+1}\mathcal{S}Res_2(\Xi(x,s)) = 0$, we have

$$\begin{aligned} u_2(x) &= v_c D u_1''(x) + v_c \sum u_1^{s\to\infty}(x) + \frac{a v_c}{x}u_1'(x) + v_c\lambda v_1(x), \\ v_2(x) &= A u_1(x). \end{aligned} \tag{52}$$

Substituting the third Sumudu residual functions as $\Theta_2(x,s) = \frac{\theta_0(x)}{s} + \frac{u_1(x)}{s^{\epsilon+1}} + \frac{u_2(x)}{s^{2\epsilon+1}} + \frac{u_3(x)}{s^{3\epsilon+1}}$ and $\Xi_2(x,s) = \frac{A}{\lambda s}\theta_0(x) + \frac{v_2(x)}{s^{2\epsilon+1}} + \frac{v_3(x)}{s^{3\epsilon+1}}$, we then obtain $u_3(x)$ and $v_3(x)$ in (45):

$$\begin{aligned} \mathcal{S}Res_3(\Theta(x,s)) = {} & \frac{u_1(x)}{s^{\epsilon+1}} + \frac{u_2(x)}{s^{2\epsilon+1}} + \frac{u_3(x)}{s^{3\epsilon+1}} - \frac{v_c D}{s^{\epsilon}}\left[\frac{\theta_0''(x)}{s} + \frac{u_1''(x)}{s^{\epsilon+1}} + \frac{u_2''(x)}{s^{2\epsilon+1}} + \frac{u_3''(x)}{s^{3\epsilon+1}}\right] - \\ & \frac{v_c\Sigma}{s^{\epsilon}}\left[\frac{\theta_0'(x)}{s} + \frac{u_1'(x)}{s^{\epsilon+1}} + \frac{u_2'(x)}{s^{2\epsilon+1}} + \frac{u_3'(x)}{s^{3\epsilon+1}}\right] - \frac{a v_c}{x s^{\epsilon}}\left[\frac{\theta_0'(x)}{s} + \frac{u_1'(x)}{s^{\epsilon+1}} + \frac{u_2'(x)}{s^{2\epsilon+1}} + \frac{u_3'(x)}{s^{3\epsilon+1}}\right] \\ & - \frac{v_c\lambda}{s^{\epsilon}}\left[\frac{A}{\lambda s}\theta_0(x) + \frac{v_2(x)}{s^{2\epsilon+1}} + \frac{v_3(x)}{s^{3\epsilon+1}}\right], \\ \mathcal{S}Res_3(\Xi(x,s)) = {} & \frac{v_2(x)}{s^{2\epsilon+1}} + \frac{v_3(x)}{s^{3\epsilon+1}} - \frac{A}{s^{\epsilon}}\left[\frac{\theta_0(x)}{s} + \frac{u_1(x)}{s^{\epsilon+1}} + \frac{u_2(x)}{s^{2\epsilon+1}} + \frac{u_3(x)}{s^{3\epsilon+1}}\right] \\ & + \frac{\lambda}{s^{\epsilon}}\left[\frac{A}{\lambda s}\theta_0(x) + \frac{v_2(x)}{s^{2\epsilon+1}} + \frac{v_3(x)}{s^{3\epsilon+1}}\right]. \end{aligned} \tag{53}$$

Now, by solving $\lim_{s\to\infty} s^{3\epsilon+1}\mathcal{S}Res_3(\Theta(x,s)) = 0$, $\lim_{s\to\infty} s^{3\epsilon+1}\mathcal{S}Res_3(\Xi(x,s)) = 0$, we find that

$$\begin{aligned} u_3(x) &= v_c D u_2''(x) + v_c \sum u_2(x) + \frac{a v_c}{x}u_2'(x) + v_c\lambda v_2(x), \\ v_3(x) &= A u_2(x) - \lambda v_2(x). \end{aligned} \tag{54}$$

In a similar manner, we substitute the kth Sumudu residual function $\mathcal{S}Res_k(\Theta(x,s))$, $\mathcal{S}Res_k(\Xi(x,s))$. For the kth truncated series $\Theta_k(x,s)$, $\Xi_k(x,s)$, multiply the resultant equations by $s^{k\epsilon+1}$, and, when $s \to \infty$, we consider the limit.

To have $u_{k+1}(x), v_{k+1}(x)$ for $k \geq 2$, utilize the recurrence relation displayed below:

$$\begin{aligned} u_n(x) &= v_c D u''_{n-1}(x) + v_c \sum u_{n-1}(x) + \frac{a v_c}{x} u'_{n-1}(x) + v_c \lambda v_{n-1}(x), \\ v_n(x) &= A u_{n-1}(x) - \lambda v_{n-1}(x), n = 1,2,3,\ldots \end{aligned} \tag{55}$$

where $v_0(x) = \frac{A}{\lambda}\theta_0(x)$. As mentioned previously, the System (43) series solution will be

$$\begin{aligned} \Theta(x,s) &= \frac{\theta_0(x)}{s} + \sum_{n=1}^{\infty} \frac{u_n(x)}{s^{n\epsilon+1}}, \\ \Xi(x,s) &= \frac{A}{\lambda s}\theta_0(x) + \sum_{n=1}^{\infty} \frac{v_n(x)}{s^{n\epsilon+1}}. \end{aligned} \tag{56}$$

Here, the system series solution given in (26) is obtained, where the inverse Sumudu transform is applied in (56) as follows:

$$\begin{aligned} \theta(x,t) &= \theta_0(x) + \sum_{n=1}^{\infty} \frac{u_n(x) t^{n\epsilon}}{\Gamma(n\epsilon+1)}, \\ \vartheta(x,t) &= \frac{A}{\lambda}\theta_0(x) + \sum_{n=2}^{\infty} \frac{v_n(x) t^{n\epsilon}}{\Gamma(n\epsilon+1)}, \end{aligned} \tag{57}$$

where

$$\begin{aligned} u_n(x) &= v_c D u''_{n-1}(x) + v_c \sum u_{n-1}(x) + \frac{a v_c}{x} u'_{n-1}(x) + v_c \lambda v_{n-1}(x) \\ v_n(x) &= A u_{n-1}(x) - \lambda v_{n-1}(x), n = 1,2,3,\ldots \end{aligned} \tag{58}$$

6. Numerical Study

Here, the numerical calculations are constructed to improve the theoretical results, built depending on TAM and SRPSM, where the numerical examples compare both methods for each essential reactor's geometries. Three essential geometries are formulated from the general-case theoretical part of the work, where the numerical calculations are stated with the Cartesian coordinates for the slab nuclear reactor ($a = 0$), cylindrical coordinates of the cylindrical reactor ($a = 1$), and spherical coordinates for spherical reactor ($a = 2$).

To perform these calculations, the following important nuclear data, which are obtained using the needed experimental data [10], are tabulated in Table 1.

Table 1. Nuclear reactor cross-section data.

v_c	B	D	λ	Σ
220 cm/s	0.000735 cm^{-1}	0.356 cm^2/s	0.08 s^{-1}	0.005 cm^{-2}

The needed Mathematica code has been written for each case twice, corresponding to TAM and SRPSM.

It must be mentioned that two numerical examples for each reactor geometry are considered, depending on their initial conditions.

6.1. Slab Reactor

To determine the behavior of the neutrons in this reactor, two examples are considered. The neutron flux φ, which represents the population of neutrons, is determined. Figure 1 considers $\varphi(x,0) = 1$ as the initial condition.

In Figure 1a, the flux φ is represented using TAM; in Figure 1b, the flux φ is represented using SRPSM. In Figure 2, φ (x, 0) = x^2 is considered as the initial condition.

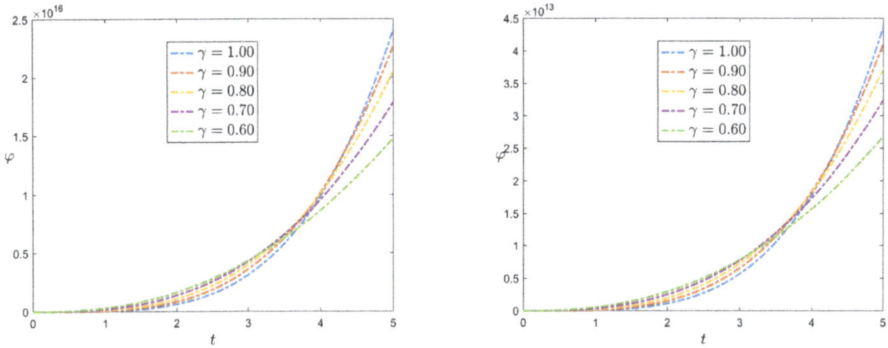

(**a**) TAM solution. (**b**) SRPSM solution.

Figure 1. Slab reactor for $\varphi(x, 0) = 1$.

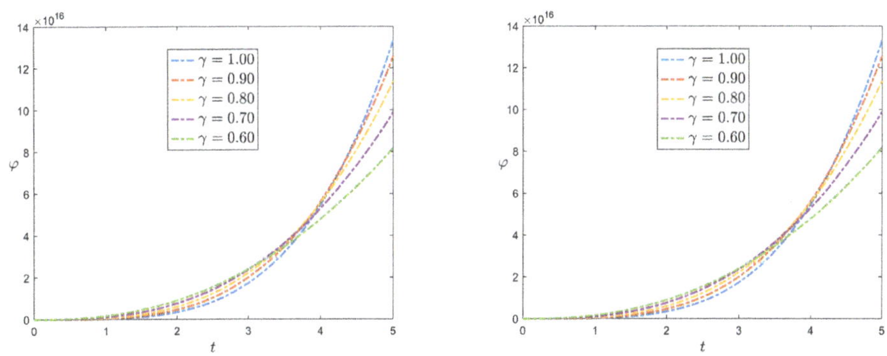

(**a**) TAM solution at $x = 50$. (**b**) SRPSM solution at 50.

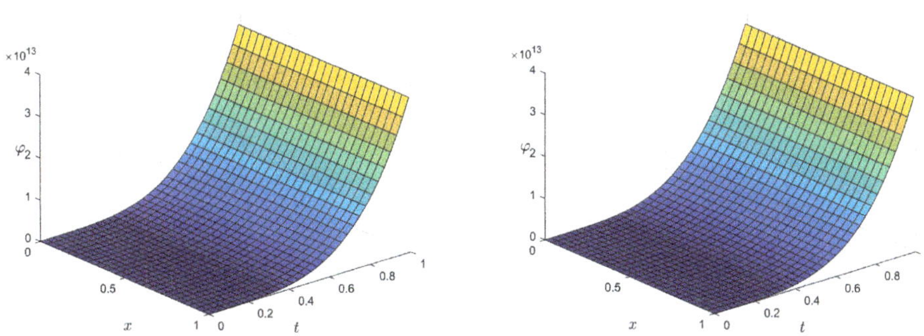

(**c**) TAM solution at $t = 1$. (**d**) SRPSM solution at $t = 1$.

Figure 2. Slab reactor for $\varphi(x, 0) = x^2$.

In Figure 2a, the flux φ is represented using TAM. In Figure 2b, the flux φ as a function of time is represented using SRPSM. In Figure 2c, the flux φ in reactor dimensions is represented using TAM, and, in Figure 2d, the flux φ in the reactor dimension is represented using SRPSM. It is shown in Figures 1 and 2 that the behavior of neutrons is expected; both used methods give results consistent with the historical results [10].

6.2. *Infinite Cylindrical Reactor*

To determine the behavior of the neutrons in this reactor, two examples are considered. The neutron flux φ, which represents the neutron population in the cylindrical reactor, is determined. Figure 3 is based on the initial condition $\varphi(x,0) = 1$.

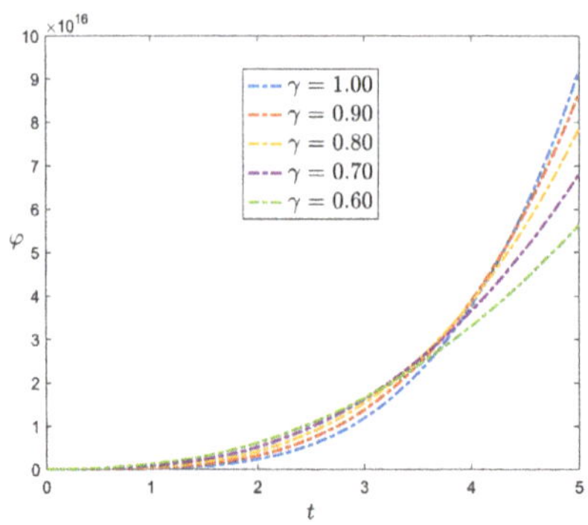

(**a**) TAM solution.

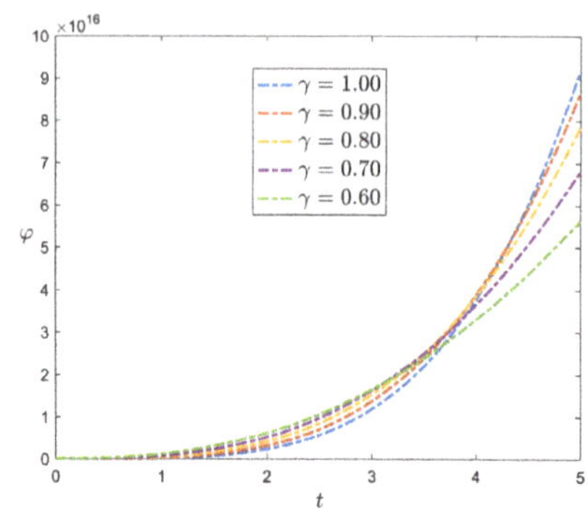

(**b**) SRPSM solution.

Figure 3. Infinite cylindrical reactor for $\varphi(x,0) = 1$.

In Figure 3a, the flux φ is represented using TAM; in Figure 3b, the flux φ is represented using SRPSM. Figure 4 considers the initial condition $\varphi(x,0) = x^2$.

In Figure 4a, the flux φ is represented using TAM. In Figure 4b, the flux φ as a function of time is represented using SRPSM. In Figure 4c, the flux φ in reactor dimensions is represented using TAM, and, in Figure 4d, the flux φ in the reactor dimensions are represented using SRPSM. It is shown in Figures 3 and 4 that the behavior of neutrons is expected; both used methods give results in agreement with the historical results [10].

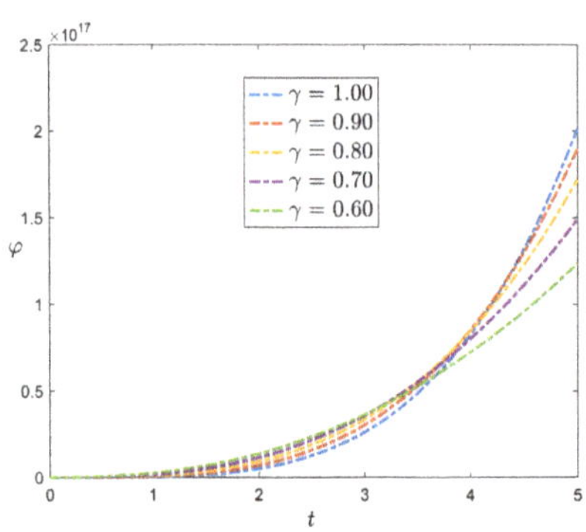

(**a**) TAM solution at $x = 50$.

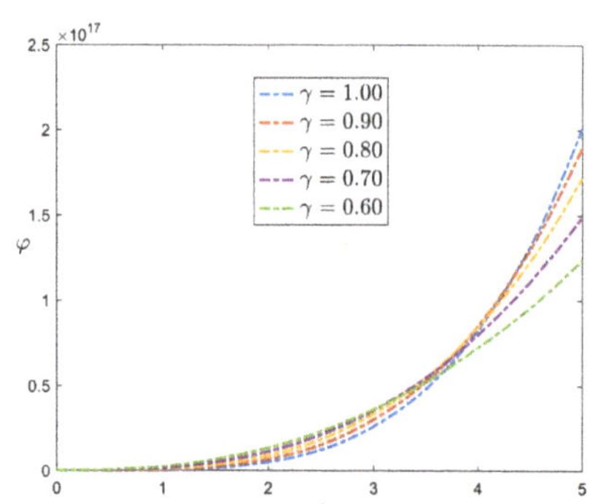

(**b**) SRPSM solution at 50.

Figure 4. *Cont.*

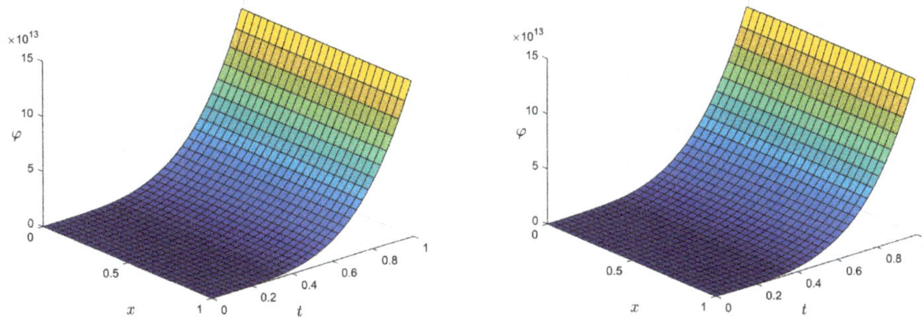

(c) TAM solution at $t = 1$.

(d) SRPSM solution at $t = 1$.

Figure 4. Infinite cylindrical reactor for $\varphi(x,0) = x^2$.

6.3. Spherical Reactor

To determine the behavior of the neutrons in this reactor, two examples are considered the neutron flux φ, which represents the neutron distribution in the cylindrical reactor.

Figure 5 considers the initial condition $\varphi(x,0) = 1$.

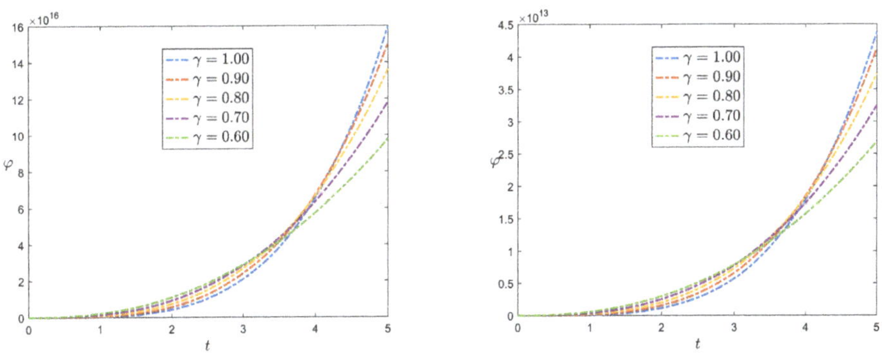

(a) TAM solution.

(b) SRPSM solution.

Figure 5. Spherical reactor for $\varphi(x,0) = 1$.

In Figure 5a, the flux φ is represented using TAM; in Figure 5b, the flux φ as a function of time is represented using SRPSM. Figure 6 considers the initial condition $\varphi(x,0) = x^2$.

In Figure 6a, the flux φ is represented using TAM. In Figure 6b, the flux φ as a function of time is represented using SRPSM. In Figure 6c, the flux φ in reactor dimensions is represented using TAM, and, in Figure 6d, the flux φ in the reactor dimensions is represented using SRPSM. Although the spherical reactor with delayed neutron effect has not been studied in history, for the first time, this system is developed in this work and solved using both TAM and SRPSM methods. The neutron's behavior can be considered as in agreement with other previous geometries studied in this work and in history.

The presented system, considering three reactor geometries, considers anomalous and Gaussian diffusion, where the value of γ determines the type of diffusion. When $\gamma = 1$, the diffusion is Gaussian, but, for $\gamma \neq 1$, the diffusion is anomalous. As γ approaches to unity, the neutron diffusion becomes Gaussian.

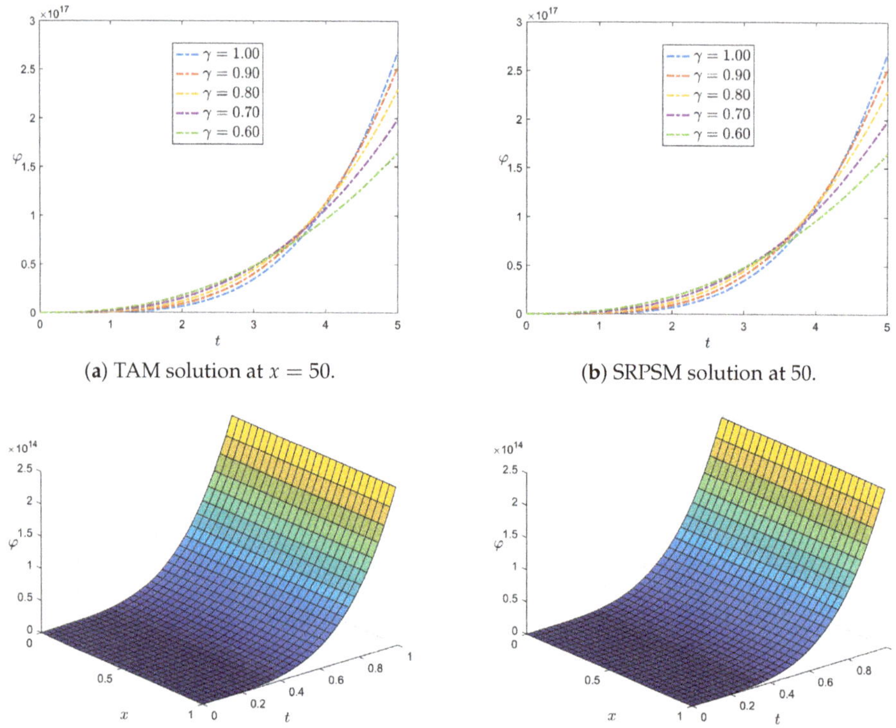

(**a**) TAM solution at $x = 50$.

(**b**) SRPSM solution at 50.

(**c**) TAM solution at $t = 1$.

(**d**) SRPSM solution at $t = 1$.

Figure 6. Spherical reactor for φ (x, 0) = x^2.

In Table 2, the tabulated compassion between the two used methods with different geometries is presented. Moreover, the slab reactor is compared with the work that studied the same reactor using the Laplace transform method (LTM) [28] and the cylindrical reactor is compared with the work that solved the same reactor using the Laplace residual power-series method (LSPSM) [10].

Table 2. Comparison of the methods with different geometries.

	Slab Reactor			Cylindrical Reactor			Spherical Reactor	
x	θ_{TAM}	θ_{SRPSM}	θ_{LTM} [28]	θ_{TAM}	θ_{SRPSM}	θ_{LRPSM} [10]	θ_{TAM}	θ_{SRPSM}
0.0	17.6177	17.6216	17.6212	67.1058	67.1205	67.1205	116.594	116.619
0.1	17.6291	17.6329	17.6253	67.1171	67.1318	67.1318	116.605	116.631
0.2	17.6631	17.6669	17.6677	67.1511	67.1658	67.1658	116.639	116.665
0.3	17.7197	17.7236	17.7227	67.2078	67.2225	67.2225	116.696	116.721
0.4	17.7991	17.8029	17.8011	67.2871	67.3018	67.3018	116.775	116.801
0.5	17.9011	17.9049	17.9035	67.3891	67.4038	67.4038	116.877	116.903
0.6	18.0257	18.0296	18.0290	67.5138	67.5285	67.5285	117.002	117.027
0.7	18.1731	18.1769	18.1766	67.6611	67.6758	67.6758	117.149	117.175
0.8	18.3431	18.3470	18.3398	67.8311	67.8458	67.8458	117.319	117.345
0.9	18.5358	18.5396	18.5412	68.0238	68.0385	68.0385	117.512	117.537
1.0	18.7511	18.7550	18.7495	68.2391	68.2538	68.2538	117.727	117.753

Table 2 assures that the results of our study are perfectly compatible with the used methods for different nuclear reactor geometries.

Finally, both methods have been employed to solve the generalized system of neutron diffusion equations with delayed neutrons across different geometries. TAM is particularly useful for cases requiring iterative improvements to capture nonlinear dynamics, while SRPSM excels in providing fast and accurate series solutions for problems with complex fractional operators. The comparison of both methods demonstrates their compatibility in solving fractional reactor equations while highlighting TAM's suitability for nonlinear problems and SRPSM's efficiency in handling fractional terms.

6.4. Computational Performance of TAM and SRPSM

To thoroughly analyze the suggested approaches, TAM and SRPSM, we measure their computing efficiency in terms of CPU time and computational cost. These metrics are crucial for understanding the approaches' practical application in solving fractional neutron diffusion equations for the three reactor geometries (slab, cylinder, and sphere). All computations were carried out using Mathematica 12.0 on a machine equipped with an Intel Core i5 CPU (3.0 GHz, 8 cores) and 8 GB RAM, assuring uniformity in the computational environment. The CPU time for each technique was assessed as the average time needed to compute the neutron flux $\varphi(x,t)$ for a specified spatial domain $x \in [0,100]$ cm and temporal domain $t \in [0,1]$, using the nuclear data from Table 1 and the initial conditions $\varphi(x,0) = 1$ and $\varphi(x,0) = x^2$. TAM iterations were limited to $m = 3$ (as indicated in Section 5.1), whereas SRPSM truncated the series at $n = 3$ terms (Section 5.2) to balance accuracy and computing effort. The computing cost is measured qualitatively using the memory and algorithmic complexity, considering the iterative nature of TAM and the series expansion of SRPSM.

Table 3 shows that SRPSM consistently beats TAM in terms of CPU time across all geometries and beginning circumstances, with an average savings of 15–20% in calculation time. This improvement is due to SRPSM's series-based method, which uses the Sumudu transform to compute terms algebraically rather than the iterative process of TAM, which requires repetitive fractional integration. For instance, in the slab reactor with Ï(x,0) = 1, SRPSM requires 0.38 s compared to TAM's 0.45 s. The difference becomes more pronounced with the more complex initial condition Ï(x,0) = x^2 , where spatial derivatives increase the computational burden, yet SRPSM maintains its efficiency (e.g., 0.44 s vs. 0.52 s for the slab reactor).

Table 3. CPU time and computational cost comparison.

Geometry	Method	CPU Time (s), $\varphi(x,0) = 1$	CPU Time (s), $\varphi(x,0) = x^2$
Slab Reactor	TAM	0.45	0.52
	SRPSM	0.38	0.44
Cylindrical Reactor	TAM	0.48	0.55
	SRPSM	0.40	0.46
Spherical Reactor	TAM	0.50	0.58
	SRPSM	0.42	0.48

Regarding computational cost, TAM includes iterative evaluations of the fractional operator Dtε; it has a larger memory footprint because intermediate iterates $\theta_m(x,t)$ are stored. In contrast, SRPSM uses less memory and has a computational cost that increases with the number of terms n since it computes a truncated series with coefficients $f_n(x,t)$. However, both approaches are computationally possible for actual applications, with

CPU durations of less than one second for the domain under consideration, making them appropriate for real-time simulations or parametric investigations when implemented on ordinary hardware.

These performance measures supplement the accuracy findings reported in Table 2, revealing that SRPSM provides a good balance of computing efficiency and solution quality, whereas TAM provides resilience for capturing nonlinear dynamics at a slightly higher computational cost.

7. Conclusions

In this work, a general formula for the nuclear reactor system of time-dependent neutron diffusion equations is presented and formulated, which is solved by using a model of fractional calculus that represents the delayed neutron effect. The novelty of our paper is in developing and applying two analytical and numerical methods, TAM and SRPSM, for solving the fractional neutron diffusion equation in nuclear reactors with delayed neutrons. We have demonstrated the application of two analytical methods, TAM and the SRPSM, to analyze a novel formula nuclear reactor equation. These methods allow for a more comprehensive and accurate representation of the complex dynamics governing the nuclear system. Specifically, we have developed analytical approximation methods that enable the computation of approximate solutions. These methods provide a powerful tool for researchers to efficiently analyze and predict nuclear phenomena, without the need for computationally intensive numerical simulations. Overall, this study highlights the importance of interdisciplinary research and the integration of advanced mathematical techniques, such as analytical methods in the pursuit of scientific knowledge and technological innovation.

Author Contributions: Conceptualization, M.S. and Z.A.; Methodology, A.H.; Software, A.H.; Validation, M.S. and Z.A.; Formal analysis, A.H.; Investigation, M.S. and Z.A.; Writing—original draft, A.H.; writing—review and editing, A.H.; Supervision, Z.A. and A.H.; Project administration, M.S.; Funding acquisition, Z.A. All authors have read and agreed to the published version of the manuscript.

Funding: Princess Nourah bint Abdulrahman University Researchers Supporting Project number (PNURSP2025R518), Princess Nourah bint Abdulrahman University, Riyadh, Saudi Arabia. This research is funded partially by Zarqa University, Zarqa, Jordan.

Data Availability Statement: No data were used to support this study.

Conflicts of Interest: The authors declare no conflict of interest.

References

1. Lee, J.C. *Nuclear Reactor: Physics and Engineering*; John Wiley and Sons: Hoboken, NJ, USA, 2020.
2. Stacey, W.M. *Nuclear Reactor Physics*; John Wiley and Sons: Hoboken, NJ, USA, 2018.
3. Almenas, K.; Lee, R. *Nuclear Engineering: An Introduction*; Springer Science and Business Media: Berlin/Heidelberg, Ger many, 2012.
4. Heyde, K. *Basic Ideas and Concepts in Nuclear Physics: An Introductory Approach*; CRC Press: Boca Raton, FL, USA, 2020.
5. Cassell, J.S.; Williams, M.M. A solution of the neutron diffusion equation for a hemisphere with mixed boundary conditions. *Ann. Nucl. Energy* **2004**, *31*, 1987–2004. [CrossRef]
6. Williams, M.M. Neutron transport in two interacting slabs II: The influence of transverse leakage. *Ann. Nucl. Energy* **2002**, *29*, 1551–1596. [CrossRef]
7. Khasawneh, K.; Dababneh, S.; Odibat, Z. A solution of the neutron diffusion equation in hemispherical symmetry using the homotopy perturbation method. *Ann. Nucl. Energy* **2009**, *36*, 1711–1717. [CrossRef]
8. Dababneh, S.; Khasawneh, K.; Odibat, Z. An alternative solution of the neutron diffusion equation in cylindrical symmetry. *Ann. Nucl. Energy* **2011**, *38*, 1140–1143. [CrossRef]

9. El-Ajou, A.; Shqair, M.; Ghabar, I.; Burqan, A.; Saadeh, R. A solution for the neutron diffusion equation in the spherical and hemispherical reactors using the residual power series. *Front. Phys.* **2023**, *11*, 1229142. [CrossRef]
.0. Filali, D.; Shqair, M.; Alghamdi, F.A.; Ismaeel, S.; Hagag, A. Solving a Novel System of Time-Dependent Nuclear Reactor Equations of Fractional Order. *Symmetry* **2024**, *16*, 831. [CrossRef]
.1. Roul, P.; Rohil, V.; Espinosa-Paredes, G.; Obaidurrahman, K. Numerical approximation of a two-dimensional fractional neutron diffusion model describing dynamics of neutron flux in a nuclear reactor. *Prog. Nucl. Energy* **2024**, *172*, 105212. [CrossRef]
.2. Aboanber, A.E.; Nahla, A.A.; Aljawazneh, S.M. Fractional two energy groups matrix representation for nuclear reactor dynamics with an external source. *Ann. Nucl. Energy* **2021**, *153*, 108062. [CrossRef]
.3. Sardar, T.; Saha Ray, S.; Bera, R.K.; Biswas, B.B.; Das, S. The solution of coupled fractional neutron diffusion equations with delayed neutrons. *Int. J. Nucl. Energy Sci. Technol.* **2010**, *5*, 105–113. [CrossRef]
.4. Khaled, S.M. Exact solution of the one-dimensional neutron diffusion kinetic equation with one delayed precursor concentration in Cartesian geometry. *AIMS Math.* **2022**, *7*, 12364–12373. [CrossRef]
.5. Vázquez-Rodríguez, R.; Sánchez-Mora, H.; Polo-Labarrios, M.A.; Ortiz-Villafuerte, J.; Lugo-Leyte, R. Fractional neutron point kinetics model for reactivity transients of the NuScale and comparison with the classical kinetics approach. *Prog. Nucl. Energy* **2024**, *105350*, 0149–1970. [CrossRef]
.6. Yin, D.; Xie, Y.; Mei, L. The stability and convergence analysis of finite difference methods for the fractional neutron diffusion equation. *Adv. Comput. Math.* **2023**, *49*, 72. [CrossRef]
.7. Burqan, A. A Novel Scheme of the ARA Transform for Solving Systems of Partial Fractional Differential Equations. *Fractal Fract.* **2023**, *7*, 306. [CrossRef]
.8. Alia, A.; Abbasb, M.; Akramc, T. New group iterative schemes for solving the two-dimensional anomalous fractional sub-diffusion equation. *J. Math. Comp. Sci.* **2021**, *22*, 119–127. [CrossRef]
.9. Momani, S.; Shqair, M.; Batiha, I.; Abu-Sei'leek, M.H.; Alshorm, S.; Abd El-Azeem, S.A. Two Energy groups Neutron Diffusion Model in Spherical Reactors. *Results Nonlinear Anal.* **2024**, *7*, 160–173.
20. Zhang, Q.; Liu, L.; Zhang, C. Compact scheme for fractional diffusion-wave equation with spatial variable coefficient and delays. *Appl. Anal.* **2022**, *101*, 1911–1932. [CrossRef]
21. Ashyralyev, A.; Agirseven, D. On convergence of difference schemes for delay parabolic equations. *Comput. Math. Appl.* **2013**, *66*, 1232–1244. [CrossRef]
22. Xie, J.; Zhang, Z. The high-order multistep ADI solver for two-dimensional nonlinear delayed reaction diffusion equations with variable coefficients. *Comput. Math. Appl.* **2018**, *75*, 3558–3570. [CrossRef]
23. Temimi, H.; Ansari, A.R. A new iterative technique for solving nonlinear second order multi-point boundary value problems. *Appl. Math. Comput.* **2011**, *218*, 1457–1466. [CrossRef]
24. Al-Hanaya, A.; Alotaibi, M.; Shqair, M.; Hagag, A.E. MHD effects on Casson fluid flow squeezing between parallel plates. *AIMS Math.* **2023**, *8*, 29440–29452. [CrossRef]
25. Adwan, M.I.; Al-Jawary, M.A.; Tibaut, J.; Ravnik, J. Analytic and numerical solutions for linear and nonlinear multidimensional wave equations. *Arab. J. Basic Appl. Sci.* **2020**, *27*, 166–182. [CrossRef]
26. Rao, A.; Vats, R.K.; Yadav, S. Numerical study of nonlinear time-fractional Caudrey Dodd Gibbon Sawada Kotera equation arising in propagation of waves. *Chaos Solitons Fractals* **2024**, *184*, 114941. [CrossRef]
27. Nadeem, M.; Alsayaad, Y. Analytical study of one dimensional time fractional Schrodinger problems arising in quantum mechanics. *Sci. Rep.* **2024**, *14*, 12503. [CrossRef] [PubMed]
28. Burqan, A.; Shqair, M.; El-Ajou, A.; Ismaeel, S.M.; Al-Zhour, Z. Analytical solutions to the coupled fractional neutron diffusion equations with delayed neutrons system using Laplace transform method. *AIMS Math.* **2023**, *8*, 19297–192312. [CrossRef]

fractal and fractional

MDPI

Article

A Compact Difference-Galerkin Spectral Method of the Fourth-Order Equation with a Time-Fractional Derivative

Yujie Wang [1] and Shichao Yi [1,2,3,*]

[1] School of Science, Jiangsu University of Science and Technology, Zhenjiang 212003, China; 222210504116@stu.just.edu.cn
[2] Zhenjiang Jizhi Ship Technology Co., Ltd., Zhenjiang 212003, China
[3] Yangzijiang Shipbuilding Group, Taizhou 212299, China
* Correspondence: shichaoyi@just.edu.cn

Abstract: In this article, we proposed a compact difference-Galerkin spectral method for the fourth-order equation in multi-dimensional space with the time-fractional derivative order $\alpha \in (1,2)$. The novel compact difference-Galerkin spectral method can effectively address the issue of high-order derivative accuracy and handle complex boundary problems. Simultaneously, the main conclusions of this article, including the stability, convergence, and solvability of the method, are derived. Finally, some computational experiments are illustrated to demonstrate the superiority of the compact difference-Galerkin spectral method.

Keywords: Galerkin spectral method; time-fractional order; variable coefficient fourth-order equation

1. Introduction

Fractional calculus is generally the generalization of integer-order derivatives and integrals to the case of arbitrary non-integer orders. However, the concept of fractional calculus emerged almost simultaneously with integer-order calculus. The concept of fractional calculus was first proposed by L'Hospital and Leibniz [1]. Historically, Leibniz, Euler, Laplace, Lacroix, and Fourier all noticed derivatives of arbitrary orders. A series of articles published by Liouville from 1832 to 1837 made him the de facto founder of the theory of fractional calculus. After Liouville, Riemann, Fourier, Willian Center, Morgan, Bernhard Riemann, Cayley, and Weyl also conducted work of great significance. After more than 300 years of development, fractional calculus and fractional differential equations have been deeply studied and widely applied in many fields of science and engineering, including fluid mechanics, electronic networks, electromagnetics, probability theory, statistics, viscoelasticity theory, electrochemistry, quantum mechanics, plasma physics, superconductivity, materials science, turbulence, economics and finance, etc. [2–9].

In 1965, Professor Mandelbrot of Yale University in the United States proposed the concept of fractals and believed that there are a large number of phenomena with fractional dimensions in nature and engineering, and their essence is the self-similarity between the whole and the part [10]. It is believed that there is a close internal connection between fractional Brownian motion and the definition of fractional calculus proposed by Riemann-Liouville. Since then, as the basis of fractal geometry and fractal dynamics, the research on fractional operator theory and fractional differential equations has begun to receive extensive attention, and the focus of fractional calculus research has gradually shifted from the pure mathematical field to other disciplinary fields.

Geophysicists Caputo [11] and Mainardi [12] used the fractional calculus method to study complex viscoelastic and rheological media and developed several new mechanical models. Moreover, more importantly, Caputo [11] developed a new definition different from the traditional Riemann-Liouville fractional-derivative definition, which overcame the strong singularity of the former and naturally included the initial conditions in the definition, and has been widely applied in solving practical problems. The first doctoral dissertation on fractional-order viscoelastic material modeling was completed by Bagley under the guidance of Torvik [13]. After that, the application of fractional calculus to the modeling of viscoelastic materials and other complex mechanical processes began to receive increasing attention.

Here, we will consider the following fourth-order equation with a time-fractional derivative in multi-dimensional space:

$$ {}_0^c\mathfrak{D}_t^\alpha u(\mathbf{x},t) - {}_0^c\mathfrak{D}_t^\alpha \Delta u(\mathbf{x},t) = -\Delta^2 u(\mathbf{x},t) + \Delta u(\mathbf{x},t) + f(\mathbf{x},t), \ \mathbf{x} \in \Omega, t \in (0,T], \tag{1} $$

with the following initial and boundary conditions:

$$ \begin{aligned} &u(\mathbf{x},0) = u_0(\mathbf{x}), u_t(\mathbf{x},0) = v_0(\mathbf{x}), \mathbf{x} \in \Omega, \\ &u(\mathbf{x},t) = \Delta u(\mathbf{x},t) = 0, \mathbf{x} \in \Gamma, t \in (0,T], \end{aligned} \tag{2} $$

where $u(\mathbf{x},t)$ is an unknown function and $f(\mathbf{x},t)$ is the source term. Here, ${}_0^c\mathfrak{D}_t^\beta$ denotes the Caputo fractional derivative of order β and it is defined by [2,11,12]

$$ {}_0^c\mathfrak{D}_t^\beta u(\mathbf{x},t) = \frac{1}{\Gamma(2-\beta)} \int_0^t \frac{\partial^2 u(\mathbf{x},\eta)}{\partial \eta^2} \frac{d\eta}{(t-\eta)^{\beta-1}}, 1 \leq \beta \leq 2, \tag{3} $$

where $\Gamma(\cdot)$ is the Gamma function.

In recent decades, the fourth-order model system [14,15] constitutes a significant element of the fractional-order system. It is widely present in diverse domains such as physics, engineering, and statistics. For instance, it can be found in wave equations of beam systems [16], a system of flat surface furnished with grooves [17,18], and several formations in mathematical modeling pertaining to fourth-order subdiffusion systems [18–21], among others. Owing to the circumstance that most fractional partial differential equations lack an analytical solution, a substantial number of researchers have focused their efforts on approximation or numerical techniques applicable to these fractional-order systems. A significant portion of the research community has centered on the strong format. This particular model is directly derived from the original discrete equation and is thus also known as the collocation method. The strong formulation proves to be reliable, exhibits a simple structure, and expedites the establishment of the algebraic system. The homotopy analysis method has been employed to obtain approximations for specific fractional partial differential equations, as reported in relevant references [22,23]. A finite difference approximation in the time direction and a finite element method in the spatial direction are presented and deliberated to seek the numerical solutions of a time-fractional fourth-order reaction–diffusion problem. Furthermore, certain fractional differential equations which are applied in the modeling of dynamical systems have been explored by means of an implicit difference format, as documented in reference [24]. Parvizi et al. have effectively harnessed the Jacobi collocation method in reference [25] to acquire the numerical resolution of the fractional equation accompanied by a nonlinear source term, and comparable research undertakings are still in progress.

Nearly all of these schemes need to take into account the strong form (collocation method). In the strong form, it demands that the analytic function possesses a relatively high degree of smoothness. Meanwhile, the Galerkin weak form is more convenient for dealing with complex boundary conditions. For complex geometric shapes and boundary conditions, the strong form may lead to great difficulties in solving the equations. The Galerkin weak form is capable of handling boundary conditions more flexibly. Meanwhile, this article employs the time derivative scenario of the unknown function as it is convenient for obtaining the representations of the second-order derivative situation and facilitating the integration process. By combining the advantages mentioned above, the new scheme we obtain is more stable. The remainder of this paper is structured in the following manner: In Sections 2 and 3, a compact difference-Galerkin method is deduced and several preliminary concepts as well as lemmas are introduced. In Section 4, the principal conclusions of this article, which encompass the stability, convergence, and solvability of the method, are verified. In Section 5, a number of computational experiments are exemplified to exhibit the superiority of the difference-Galerkin method. Eventually, certain conclusions are provided in Section 6.

2. Algebraic Equation and Preliminaries

2.1. Variational Equations for the Fourth-Order Equation

Denote the inner product as follows:

$$(u,w) = \int_{\Omega} uwd\Omega,\ \forall u,w \in\ L^2(\Omega). \tag{4}$$

Then, the variable formulation of (1) is restated in the following manner:

$$({}_0^C\mathfrak{D}_t^{\alpha}u,w) + ({}_0^C\mathfrak{D}_t^{\alpha}\nabla u,\nabla w) = (\nabla(\triangle u),\nabla w) - (\nabla u,\nabla w) + (f,w),\ \forall w \in H^1(\Omega). \tag{5}$$

Let $\{t_n | n \geq 0\}$ denote the equidistant time interval, with $t_n = n\tau, \tau > 0$. Moreover, suppose

$$\partial v(t_{i+1})/\partial t = (v^{i+1} - v^i)/\tau,\quad u^n = u^0 + \tau\sum_{k=1}^{n}(v^{k-1} + v^k)/2, \tag{6}$$

where u^n, v^n represent the values of the function and its first derivative function at the time t_n.

The difference scheme of (1) and (5) is presented as follows:

$$\begin{aligned} &\frac{1}{\tau\Gamma(2-\alpha)}\left(\left[a_0v^n - \sum_{k=1}^{n-1}(a_{n-k-1} - a_{n-k})v^n - a_{n-1}v_0\right],w\right) \\ &+ \frac{1}{\tau\Gamma(2-\alpha)}\left(\nabla\left[a_0v^n - \sum_{k=1}^{n-1}(a_{n-k-1} - a_{n-k})v^n - a_{n-1}v_0\right],\nabla w\right) \\ &= \left(\nabla\left(\Delta\left(u^{n-1} + \tau\frac{v^{n-1}+v^n}{2}\right)\right),\nabla w\right) - \left(\nabla\left(u^{n-1} + \tau\frac{v^{n-1}+v^n}{2}\right),\nabla w\right) \\ &+ (f^n,w) + (R_\tau^n,w), w \in\ H_0^1(\Omega), \end{aligned} \tag{7}$$

where $a_l = \int_{t_l}^{t_{l+1}}\frac{dt}{t^{\alpha-1}} = \frac{\tau^{3-\alpha}}{2-\alpha}\left[(l+1)^{2-\alpha} - l^{2-\alpha}\right], b_l = a_{n-l}$. It is easy to verify that a_l is a monotone decreasing sequence for each n with $a_0 = \tau^{2-\alpha}/(2-\alpha)$.

2.2. Galerkin–Legendre Scheme

Let $\{L_i\}_{j=0}^{p}$ be a set of orthogonal Legendre polynomial bases in one-dimensional space:

$$L_0 = 1, L_1 = x, (j+2)L_{j+2} = (2j+3)xL_{j+1} - (j+1)L_j, j = 2,\cdots$$

such that

$$(L_i, L_j) = (i + 1/2)^{-1}\delta_{ij}, 0 \leq i, j < \infty.$$

Here, δ represents the delta function. From [26], two kinds of the best basis functions in $H_0^1(\Omega)$ and $H_0^2(\Omega)$ are

$$H_0^1(\Omega) = span\{\phi_i(x), 0 \leq i < \infty\}, H_0^2(\Omega) = span\{\psi_i(x), 0 \leq i < \infty\},$$

where

$$\phi_i(x) = L_i(x) - L_{i+2}(x), \psi_i(x) = L_i(x) - \frac{2(2i+5)}{2i+7}L_{i+2}(x) + \frac{2i+3}{2i+7}L_{i+4}(x), i = 0, 1, \cdots$$

such that

$$(\phi_i', \phi_j') = (4i+6)^{-1}\delta_{ij}, (\psi_i'', \psi_j'') = (2(2i+3)^2(2i+5))^{-1}\delta_{ij}, 0 \leq i, j < \infty.$$

2.3. Algebraic Equation of Weak form with the Boundary Conditions

Take a one-dimensional problem as an example, assuming a column vector

$$\mathbf{U} = [u_0, u_1, u_2, \cdots, u_M]^T, \mathbf{V} = [v_0, v_1, v_2, \cdots, v_M]^T, \tag{8}$$

where $u(x_i), v(x_i), and\ w(x_i)$ represent the i-st node function value, derivative value of u, and w function value, respectively, and M represents the number of nodes.

Using the spectral method, the r-th derivative of U can be discretized as

$$\mathbf{U}^{(r)} = \mathbf{A}^r\mathbf{U}, \tag{9}$$

where $\mathbf{A}$ is the first-order differential matrix.

In general, we also have

$$\int_\Omega g(\mathbf{x})d(\Omega) = \sum_{i=1}^{M} g(\mathbf{x}_i)\omega_i. \tag{10}$$

ω_i is called the volume element on the node $\mathbf{x}_i$ in physics, and it is also named the weight for the corresponding numerical integration in mathematics.

To facilitate the application of boundary conditions, the variables v^n and Δu^n are used simultaneously with the following supplementary equation:

$$(\Delta u^n, w) + \left(\nabla\left(u^{n-1} + \tau\frac{v^{n-1} + v^n}{2}\right), \nabla w\right) = 0. \tag{11}$$

We multiply both sides of the above equation by $-\frac{2}{\tau}$ and considering the arbitrariness of w, and we use Equations (7) and (11) to obtain the following system of equations in matrix form:

$$\begin{bmatrix} \frac{a_0}{\tau\Gamma(2-\alpha)}(\mathbf{\Omega} + \mathbf{A}^{\mathrm{T}}\mathbf{\Omega}\mathbf{A}) + \frac{\tau}{2}\mathbf{A}^{\mathrm{T}}\mathbf{\Omega}\mathbf{A} & -\mathbf{A}^{\mathrm{T}}\mathbf{\Omega}\mathbf{A} \\ -\mathbf{A}^{\mathrm{T}}\mathbf{\Omega}\mathbf{A} & -\frac{2}{\tau}\mathbf{\Omega} \end{bmatrix} \begin{bmatrix} \mathbf{V}^{\mathrm{n}} \\ \mathbf{\Delta U}^{\mathrm{n}} \end{bmatrix} = \begin{bmatrix} \mathbf{P} \\ \mathbf{A}^{\mathrm{T}}\mathbf{\Omega}\mathbf{A}(\frac{2}{\tau}\mathbf{U}^{n-1} + \mathbf{V}^{n-1}) \end{bmatrix}, \tag{12}$$

where $\mathbf{P} = \mathbf{P_1} + \mathbf{P_2} + \Omega\mathbf{F}$, $\mathbf{P_1} = \frac{\mathbf{\Omega}(\mathbf{I}-\mathbf{\Delta})}{\tau\Gamma(2-\alpha)}\left[\sum_{k=1}^{n-1}(a_{n-k-1} - a_{n-k})\mathbf{V}^n + a_{n-1}\mathbf{V}_0\right]$, $\mathbf{P_2} = \tau(\Omega - \mathbf{A}^{\mathrm{T}}\Omega\mathbf{A})\left(\mathbf{\Delta U}^{n-1} + \frac{\mathbf{\Delta V}^{n-1}}{2}\right)$, $\mathbf{\Omega}$ is a diagonal matrix composed of weight vectors ω_i and $\mathbf{F}$ is composed of the source terms of each node.

Further, we introduce the following boundary conditions: $\mathbf{BV^n} = -\mathbf{BV^{n-1}}$, $\mathbf{B}(\mathbf{\Delta U^n}) = 0$, where $\mathbf{B}$ is the matrix assembled from all boundary points.

2.4. Preliminary Lemmas

We also define

$$\|g^n\|_\infty = \max_{0\le i\le M} |g_i^n|, |\nabla g^n| = \sqrt{h\sum_{i=1}^{M}(g_{i-1}^n)^2}, h = \prod_{x\in\mathbf{x}} h_x. \tag{13}$$

Furthermore, in the case where $g(\Gamma) = 0$, we obtain

$$\|g^n\|_\infty \le \frac{\sqrt{D}}{2}|\nabla g^n|, \tag{14}$$

where D represents the measure of the spatial domain Ω.

Next, the following theorem offers an error estimation for the Galerkin method:

Theorem 1. *If u, w, u_p and $w_p \in C^{n+1}(\Omega)$, where Ω has a nonempty, open bounded set with a Lipschitz continuous boundary, then the following error estimates hold:*

$$\|u^{(k)} - u_p^{(k)}\|_\infty \le c_1\|u^{n+1}\|_\infty h^{\min\{p,n+1\}-2-k},$$

and

$$\|(u^{(k_1)}, w^{(k_2)}) - \sum_{i=1}^{M} g(\mathbf{x}_i)u_p^{(k_1)}w_p^{(k_2)}\|_\infty \le c_1^* h^{2\min\{p,n+1\}-4-k_1-k_2}.$$

For the high-dimensional case, the above corresponding properties also hold with a small change of the coefficient (see [26]).

3. Some Lemmas

Regarding the fractional derivative of the proposed scheme, upon setting w equal to v, some lemmas [27,28] are required:

Lemma 1. *For $n \ge 1$ and $t_k = k\tau, 0 \le k \le n$, we have*

$$0 \le \sum_{k=1}^{n}\int_{t_{k-1}}^{t_k}\left[(t_n-t)^{2-\alpha} - \frac{(t_{n-1}-t)^{2-\alpha}+(t_n-t)^{2-\alpha}}{2}\right]dt \le \left[\frac{2-\alpha}{12}+\frac{2^{3-\alpha}}{3-\alpha}-(1+2^{1-\alpha})\right]\tau^{3-\alpha}. \tag{15}$$

Lemma 2. *Suppose $v(t) \in C^2([0,t_n])$. Then,*

$$\begin{aligned}&\left|\int_0^{t_n} v'(t)\frac{dt}{(t_n-t)^{\alpha-1}} - \sum_{k=1}^{n}\frac{v^k-v^{k-1}}{\tau}\int_{t_{k-1}}^{t_k}\frac{dt}{(t_n-t)^{\alpha-1}}\right|\\ &\le \frac{\tau^{3-\alpha}}{2-\alpha}\left[\frac{2-\alpha}{12}+\frac{2^{3-\alpha}}{3-\alpha}-(1+2^{1-\alpha})\right]\|v(t)\|_{L^{2,\infty}([0,t_n])}.\end{aligned} \tag{16}$$

Lemma 3. *Suppose $v(t) \in C^2[0,t_n]$. Then,*

$$\left|\int_0^{t_n} v'(t)\frac{dt}{(t_n-t)^{\alpha-1}} - \frac{1}{\tau}\left[a_0v^n - \sum_{k=1}^{n-1}(a_{n-k-1}-a_{n-k})v^k - a_{n-1}v^0\right]\right| \\ \le \frac{\tau^{3-\alpha}}{2-\alpha}\left[\frac{2-\alpha}{12}+\frac{2^{3-\alpha}}{3-\alpha}-(1+2^{1-\alpha})\right]\|g(t)\|_{L^{1,\infty}([0,t_n])}. \tag{17}$$

where a_l^n is defined in (7) *and* $1<\alpha<2$.

Based on Lemma 3 and by introducing Equation (17), we have

$$\begin{aligned} {}^c\mathfrak{D}_0^\alpha u(x,t) &= \frac{1}{\Gamma(2-\alpha)}\int_0^t \frac{\partial^2 u(x,t)}{\partial t^2}\frac{dt}{(t_n-t)^{\alpha-1}}, \\ &= \frac{1}{\tau\Gamma(2-\alpha)}\left[a_0v^n - \sum_{k=1}^{n-1}(a_{n-k-1}-a_{n-k})v^k - a_{n-1}v^0\right] + (r_1)_i^n, \end{aligned} \tag{18}$$

and

$$\frac{\partial u_i^n}{\partial x} = \sum_{i=1}^{M} L'(x_i)u_i^n + (r_2)_i^n, \frac{\partial^2 u_i^n}{x^2} = \sum_{i=1}^{M} L''(x_i)u_i^n + (r_3)_i^n, \tag{19}$$

where

$$|(r_1)_i^n| \le c_1\tau^{3-\alpha}, |(r_2)_i^n| \le c_2(\tau^2 + h^{\min\{p,n+1\}-3}), |(r_3)_i^n| \le c_3(\tau^2 + h^{\min\{p,n+1\}-4}). \tag{20}$$

By substituting the aforesaid results into (1), taking into account the initial values and setting $w = v^n$, we obtain

$$\begin{aligned} &\frac{1}{\tau\Gamma(2-\alpha)}\sum_i^M \omega_i v_i^n\left(a_0v_i^n \quad \sum_{k=1}^{n-1}(a_{n-k-1}-a_{n-k})v_i^k - a_{n\ 1}v_i^0\right) \\ &+ \frac{1}{\tau\Gamma(2-\alpha)}\sum_i^M \omega_i\nabla v_i^n\nabla\left(a_0v_i^n - \sum_{k=1}^{n-1}(a_{n-k-1}-a_{n-k})v_i^k - a_{n-1}v_i^0\right) \\ &= -\tau\sum_i^M\omega_i\Delta(\sum_{k=1}^{n-1}v_i^k + \frac{v_i^0+v_i^n}{2})\Delta v_i^n - \tau\sum_i^M\omega_i\nabla(\sum_{k=1}^{n-1}v_i^k + \frac{v_i^0+v_i^n}{2})\nabla v_i^n \\ &+ \sum_i^M \omega_i\hat{F}_i^n u_i + (R_i^n, v^n), \end{aligned} \tag{21}$$

where

$$|R^n| \le C(\tau^{3-\alpha} + h^{\min\{p,n+1\}-4}). \tag{22}$$

4. Main Results

Before proving the solvability, stability and convergence, we present the following lemmas:

Lemma 4. *For any $v = \{v(t_0), v(t_1), v(t_2), \cdots\}$, we have*

$$\sum_{n=1}^{N}\left(a_0^nv^n - \sum_{k=1}^{n-1}(a_{n-k-1}^nv^n - a_{n-k}^nv^n)v^k - a_{n-1}^nv^0, v^n\right) \ge \frac{t_N^{1-\alpha}}{2}\tau\sum_{n=1}^{N}\|v^n\|^2 - \frac{t_N^{2-\alpha}}{2(2-\alpha)}\|v^0\|^2. \tag{23}$$

Proof.

$$\begin{aligned}
&\sum_{n=1}^{N}\left(a_0^n v^n-\sum_{k=1}^{n-1}(a_{n-k-1}^n-a_{n-k}^n)v^k-a_{n-1}^n v^0, v^n\right)\\
&=\sum_{n=1}^{N}a_0^n\|v^n\|^2-\sum_{n=1}^{N}\sum_{k=1}^{n-1}(a_{n-k-1}^n-a_{n-k}^n)\left(v^k,v^n\right)-\sum_{n=1}^{N}a_{n-1}^n\left(v^0,v^n\right)\\
&\geq\sum_{n=1}^{N}a_0^n\|v^n\|^2-\frac{1}{2}\sum_{n=1}^{N}\sum_{k=1}^{n-1}(a_{n-k-1}^n-a_{n-k}^n)(\|v^k\|^2+\|v^n\|^2)-\frac{1}{2}\sum_{n=1}^{N}a_{n-1}^n(\|v^0\|^2+\|v^n\|^2)\\
&=\sum_{n=1}^{N}a_0^n\|v^n\|^2-\frac{1}{2}\sum_{n=1}^{N}\sum_{k=1}^{n-1}(a_{n-k-1}^n-a_{n-k}^n)\|v(t_k)\|^2-\frac{1}{2}\sum_{n=1}^{N}\sum_{k=1}^{n-1}(a_{n-k-1}^n-a_{n-k}^n)\|v^n\|^2\\
&-\frac{1}{2}\sum_{n=1}^{N}a_{n-1}^n\|v^0\|^2-\frac{1}{2}\sum_{n=1}^{N}a_{n-1}^n\|v^n\|^2.
\end{aligned}\tag{24}$$

By interchanging the summation order of the third term within the last inequality, we are able to obtain

$$\begin{aligned}
&\sum_{n=1}^{N}\left(a_0^n v^n-\sum_{k=1}^{n-1}(a_{n-k-1}^n-a_{n-k}^n)v^k-a_{n-1}^n v^0, v^n\right)\\
&\geq\sum_{n=1}^{N}a_0^n\|v^n\|^2-\frac{1}{2}\sum_{n=2}^{N}(a_0^n-a_{n-1}^n)\|v^n\|^2-\frac{1}{2}\sum_{n=1}^{N-1}(a_0^n-a_{N-n}^n)\|v^k\|^2-\frac{1}{2}\sum_{n=1}^{N}a_{n-1}^n(\|v^0\|^2+\|v^n\|^2)\\
&=\frac{1}{2}\sum_{n=1}^{N}a_{N-n}(t_n)\|v^n\|^2-\frac{1}{2}\sum_{n=1}^{N}a_{n-1}(t_n)\|v^0\|^2\\
&\geq\frac{1}{2}a_{N-1}\sum_{n=1}^{N}\|v^n\|^2-\frac{t_N^{2-\alpha}}{2(2-\alpha)}\|v^0\|^2\geq\frac{1}{2}t_N^{1-\alpha}\tau\sum_{n=1}^{N}\|v^n\|^2-\frac{t_N^{2-\alpha}}{2(2-\alpha)}\|v^0\|^2,
\end{aligned}\tag{25}$$

where $\{a_l^n\}$ is a strictly decreasing sequence for a fixed n and $\sum_{n=1}^{N}a_{n-1}(t_n)\leq\sum_{n=0}^{N-1}a_n=\int_{t_0}^{t_N}\frac{d\varsigma}{\varsigma^{\alpha-1}}=\frac{t_N^{2-\alpha}}{2-\alpha}, a_l=\int_{t_{l-1}}^{t_l}\varsigma^{1-\alpha}d\varsigma\geq t_{l+1}^{1-\alpha}\tau.$ □

Lemma 5. *Suppose that $\{v^n\}$ is the solution of*

$$\begin{aligned}
&\frac{1}{\tau\Gamma(2-\alpha)}\sum_{i}^{M}\omega_i v_i^n\left(a_0 v_i^n-\sum_{k=1}^{n-1}(a_{n-k-1}-a_{n-k})v_i^k-a_{n-1}v_i^0\right)\\
&+\frac{1}{\tau\Gamma(2-\alpha)}\sum_{i}^{M}\omega_i\nabla v_i^n\nabla\left(a_0 v_i^n-\sum_{k=1}^{n-1}(a_{n-k-1}-a_{n-k})v_i^k-a_{n-1}v_i^0\right)\\
&=-\tau\sum_{i}^{M}\omega_i\Delta(\sum_{k=1}^{n-1}v_i^k+\frac{v_i^0+v_i^n}{2})\Delta v_i^n-\tau\sum_{i}^{M}\omega_i\nabla(\sum_{k=1}^{n-1}v_i^k+\frac{v_i^0+v_i^n}{2})\nabla v_i^n+(R^n,v^n),\\
&u^0=0, u^n(\Gamma)=0, 1\leq i\leq M-1, n=1,2,\cdots
\end{aligned}\tag{26}$$

We have

$$\|\sum_{k=1}^{n}\nabla v^k\|^2\leq\frac{1}{\tau\Gamma(2-\alpha)}\left\{\frac{t_m^{2-\alpha}}{(2-\alpha)}\|v^0\|^2\right\}+h\Gamma(2-\alpha)\tau^{-1}t_m^{\alpha-1}\sum_{n=1}^{m}\|R^n\|^2.\tag{27}$$

Proof. Using Lemma 1, we have

$$\begin{aligned} &\frac{1}{\Gamma(2-\alpha)}\sum_{n=1}^{m}\left(a_0v^n-\sum_{k=1}^{n-1}(a_{n-k-1}-a_{n-k})v^k-a_{n-1}v^0,v\right)\\ &\geq\frac{1}{2\Gamma(2-\alpha)}t_N^{1-\alpha}\tau\sum_{n=1}^{N}\|v^n\|^2-\frac{t_m^{2-\alpha}}{2\Gamma(3-\alpha)}h\sum_{i=1}^{M}\|v_i^0\|^2, \end{aligned} \tag{28}$$

and

$$\begin{aligned} &\frac{-1}{\Gamma(2-\alpha)}\sum_{n=1}^{m}\left(\Delta\left[a_0v^n-\sum_{k=1}^{n-1}(a_{n-k-1}-a_{n-k})v^k-a_{n-1}v^0\right],v\right)\\ &\geq\frac{1}{2\Gamma(2-\alpha)}t_N^{1-\alpha}\tau\sum_{n=1}^{N}\|\nabla v^n\|^2-\frac{t_m^{2-\alpha}}{2\Gamma(3-\alpha)}h\sum_{i=1}^{M}\|\nabla v_i^0\|^2, \end{aligned} \tag{29}$$

Applying the boundary conditions as given in (26), we have $v^n(\Gamma)=\nabla v^n(\Gamma)=0$. Consequently,

$$\tau\sum_{n=1}^{m}\left(\Delta(\sum_{k=1}^{n-1}v^k+\frac{v_0+v_n}{2}),v^n\right)=-\frac{\tau^2}{2}\|\sum_{k=1}^{n}\nabla(v^k)\|^2 \tag{30}$$

$$-\tau\sum_{n=1}^{m}\left(\Delta^2(\sum_{k=1}^{n-1}v^k+\frac{v_0+v_n}{2}),v^n\right)=-\frac{\tau^2}{2}\|\sum_{k=1}^{n}\Delta(v^k)\|^2 \tag{31}$$

In addition,

$$\tau\sum_{n=1}^{m}(R^n,v^n)\leq\frac{1}{2}\sum_{n=1}^{m}\frac{1}{\Gamma(2-\alpha)}\tau t_m^{1-\alpha}\|v^n\|^2+\frac{h}{2}\Gamma(2-\alpha)\tau t_m^{\alpha-1}\|R^n\|^2. \tag{32}$$

By substituting Equations (28)–(32) into (26), we obtain

$$\begin{aligned} &\frac{1}{2\Gamma(2-\alpha)}t_N^{1-\alpha}\tau\sum_{n=1}^{N}\|v^n\|^2-\frac{t_m^{2-\alpha}}{2\Gamma(3-\alpha)}h\sum_{n=1}^{m}(\|v^0\|^2+\|\nabla v^0\|^2)+\frac{t_N^{1-\alpha}\tau}{2\Gamma(2-\alpha)}\sum_{n=1}^{N}\|\nabla v^n\|^2\\ &\leq-\frac{\tau^2}{2}\|\sum_{k=1}^{n}\nabla(v^k)\|^2-\frac{\tau^2}{2}\|\sum_{k=1}^{n}\Delta(v^k)\|^2+\frac{\tau t_m^{1-\alpha}}{2\Gamma(2-\alpha)}\sum_{n=1}^{m}\|v^n\|^2+\frac{h}{2}\Gamma(2-\alpha)\tau t_m^{\alpha-1}\sum_{n=1}^{m}\|R^n\|^2. \end{aligned} \tag{33}$$

Then,

$$\|\sum_{k=1}^{n}\nabla v^k\|^2\leq\frac{1}{\tau\Gamma(2-\alpha)}\left\{\frac{t_m^{2-\alpha}}{(2-\alpha)}\|v^0\|^2\right\}+h\Gamma(2-\alpha)\tau^{-1}t_m^{\alpha-1}\sum_{n=1}^{m}\|R^n\|^2. \tag{34}$$

□

Theorem 2. *The difference scheme given by (7) is uniquely solvable.*

Proof. Since Equation (7) is a system of linear algebraic equations at each iterative process of a different time level, it is sufficient to show that the corresponding homogeneous equations only have zero solutions. By using Lemma 5, we have

$$\nabla v^n=0,\quad n=1,\cdots,N.$$

By combining the above equality with the boundary condition, we obtain

$$v_i^n=0,\quad n\geq 1,1\leq i\leq M.$$

This completes the proof. □

Theorem 3. *Let* $u(x,t) \in C^{4,3}_{\mathbf{x},t}(\Omega \times [0,T])$ *and* $\{v^n | n \geq 0\}$ *be the solution of the difference scheme()-(). Then, for* $n\tau \leq T$, *we have*

$$|u(t_n) - u^n|_\infty \leq \frac{cD}{2}\sqrt{\Gamma(2-\alpha)T^\alpha}(h^{\min\{p,n+1\}-4} + \tau^{3-\alpha}),$$

where c is a constant number.

Proof. Denote

$$\hat{v}^n = v(t_n) - v^n, \hat{u}^n = u(t_n) - u^n, n \geq 0 \tag{35}$$

By subtracting (7) from Equations (21) and (22), respectively, we have the error equations

$$\begin{aligned}
&\frac{1}{\tau\Gamma(2-\alpha)}\sum_i^M \omega_i \hat{v}_i^n \left(a_0 \hat{v}_i^n - \sum_{k=1}^{n-1}(a_{n-k-1} - a_{n-k})\hat{v}_i^k - a_{n-1}\hat{v}_i^0 \right) \\
&+ \frac{1}{\tau\Gamma(2-\alpha)}\sum_i^M \omega_i \nabla \hat{v}_i^n \nabla \left(a_0 \hat{v}_i^n - \sum_{k=1}^{n-1}(a_{n-k-1} - a_{n-k})\hat{v}_i^k - a_{n-1}\hat{v}_i^0 \right) \\
&= -\tau \sum_i^M \omega_i \Delta(\sum_{k=1}^{n-1} \hat{v}_i^k + \frac{\hat{v}_i^0 + \hat{v}_i^n}{2})\Delta \hat{v}_i^n - \tau \sum_i^M \omega_i \nabla(\sum_{k=1}^{n-1} \hat{v}_i^k + \frac{\hat{v}_i^0 + \hat{v}_i^n}{2})\nabla \hat{v}_i^n + (R^n, \hat{v}^n), \\
&\hat{u}^n(\Gamma) = 0, n \geq 1.
\end{aligned} \tag{36}$$

Using Lemma 2, we have

$$\|\nabla \hat{u}^m\|^2 = \frac{\tau^2}{2}\|\sum_{k=1}^{n} \nabla(\hat{v}^k)\|^2 \leq \frac{h}{2}\Gamma(2-\alpha)t_m^{\alpha-1}\tau\sum_{n=1}^{m}\|R_i^n\|^2, n \geq 1. \tag{37}$$

By inserting (21) into the right hand of the above inequality, we obtain

$$\|\nabla \hat{u}^m\| \leq c\sqrt{D\Gamma(2-\alpha)T^\alpha}(h^{\min\{p,n+1\}-4} + \tau^{3-\alpha}), n \geq 1. \tag{38}$$

Noticing (14), we have the following result:

$$|\hat{u}^m|_\infty \leq \frac{cD}{2}\sqrt{\Gamma(2-\alpha)T^\alpha}(h^{\min\{p,n+1\}-4} + \tau^{3-\alpha}), n \geq 1. \tag{39}$$

where c is constant. This completes the proof. □

5. Numerical Experiments

In this section, several numerical experiments are presented to analyze the performance of the proposed difference-Galerkin spectral method. In all numerical experiments, the presented methods are local approximate schemes in spatial dimensions Ω. The numerical results were obtained in MATLAB 2023a on an AMD Ryzen 5 (16G RAM) Windows Win11 system. The L_∞ error, which will be reported in those examples, is defined as

$$E_n = \sqrt{\sum_{i=1}^{m}(u^n(\mathbf{x}_i) - u_i^n)^2} \textit{ and Order} = \frac{\log_2(E_n)}{\log_2(E_{2n})}, \tag{40}$$

where u_i and $u(\mathbf{x}_i)$ denote the numerical and exact solution of the problem, respectively.

5.1. One-Dimensional Time-Fractional Fourth-Order System

Consider that the exact solution to the system is

$$u(x,t) = t^k \sin(\pi x)/k, x \in [0,1], t \in (0,1]. \tag{41}$$

In Figure 1, the two figures at the top depict the present solutions for the fractional-order system, with $M = 21$, $\tau = 10$, $\alpha = 1.7$, and $k = 3.5$. Even though errors are evidently present compared with the analytical solution with $\tau = 1/10$, the complete congruence of the graph shapes vividly attests to the stability of the scheme format.

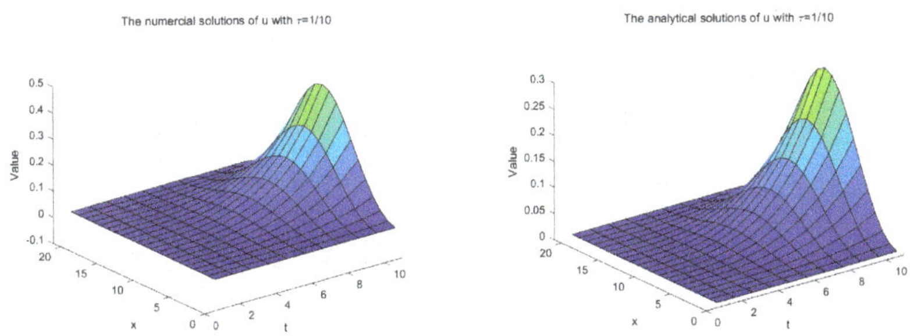

Figure 1. The curved surfaces of the numerical solution u (**left**) and the analytical solution (**right**).

Taking $\alpha = 1.5$ and $k = 3.5$, Table 1 shows some numerical and exact solutions at the points $(0.5, 0.75)$ and $(0.5, 1)$ for diverse mesh sizes while maintaining a fixed temporal step. It is evident from this table that the current scheme converges expeditiously towards the exact solutions.

Table 1. Several numerical outcomes of the diverse space grid schemes ($\tau = 1/320$).

(x,t)	5	7	9	11	13	Exact Solution
$(0.5, 0.75)$	0.1046	0.1044	0.1044	0.1044	0.1044	0.1044
$(0.5, 1)$	0.2863	0.2857	0.2857	0.2857	0.2857	0.2857

Table 2 exhibits the temporal convergence order of the proposed scheme at $t = 1$, which is in proximity to our theoretical values 1.3.

Table 2. Temporal convergence order of the proposed scheme ($M = 21$).

τ	1/10	1/20	1/40	1/80	1/160	1/320	Value
E_n	7.1808×10^{-3}	2.9680×10^{-3}	1.2150×10^{-3}	4.9515×10^{-4}	2.0139×10^{-4}	8.1845×10^{-5}	
Order		1.2746	1.2886	1.2950	1.2979	1.2991	1.3000

5.2. Two-Dimensional Time-Fractional Fourth-Order System

To implement numerical effectiveness, we consider the two-dimensional time-fractional fourth-order system that follows. The exact solution of the system is

$$u(\mathbf{x},t) = t^{3+\alpha} \sin(\pi x)\sin(\pi y) + t\sin(\pi x)\sin(\pi y), \mathbf{x} \in [0,1]^2, t \in (0,1]. \tag{42}$$

Take $M = 21$, and let $\alpha = 1.7, 1.5, 1.3$, respectively. Table 3 presents specific numerical results related to the infinity norm errors and the convergence order for different temporal mesh sizes at t = 1. From these results, it can be observed that the temporal convergence order is approximately and close to $3 - \alpha$.

Table 3. The convergence order in two-dimensional space at t = 1.

τ	$\alpha = 1.7$		$\alpha = 1.5$		$\alpha = 1.3$	
	E_n	**Order**	E_n	**Order**	E_n	**Order**
1/10	5.6317×10^{-3}		2.6130×10^{-3}		1.1484×10^{-3}	
1/20	2.1551×10^{-3}	1.3858	9.3348×10^{-4}	1.4850	3.6085×10^{-4}	1.6701
1/40	8.4851×10^{-4}	1.3448	3.3230×10^{-4}	1.4901	1.1222×10^{-4}	1.6851
1/80	3.3976×10^{-4}	1.3204	1.1790×10^{-4}	1.4949	3.4712×10^{-5}	1.6928
1/160	1.3716×10^{-4}	1.3086	4.1762×10^{-5}	1.4973	1.0711×10^{-5}	1.6964
1/320	5.5570×10^{-5}	1.3035	1.4781×10^{-5}	1.4985	3.3012×10^{-6}	1.6980
1/640	2.2547×10^{-5}	1.3015	5.2290×10^{-6}	1.4991	1.0169×10^{-6}	1.6988
1/1280	9.1538×10^{-6}	1.3005	1.8495×10^{-6}	1.4994	3.1317×10^{-7}	1.6992
1/2560	3.7172×10^{-6}	1.3002	6.5406×10^{-7}	1.4996	9.6428×10^{-8}	1.6994
Theoretical value		1.3000		1.5000		1.7000

In Figure 2, when $\tau = 1/10$ and $\alpha = 1.4$ at $t = 1$, the surfaces of the numerical solution as well as the absolute error of u are depicted. It is readily observable that the numerical solutions are in extremely close proximity to the analytical solutions. By making a comparison between the two surfaces of u, it can be discerned that the surface of the absolute error coincides with that of the numerical results. A comparable conclusion concerning the relationship between the numerical solution and the absolute error of u is derived in Figure 2.

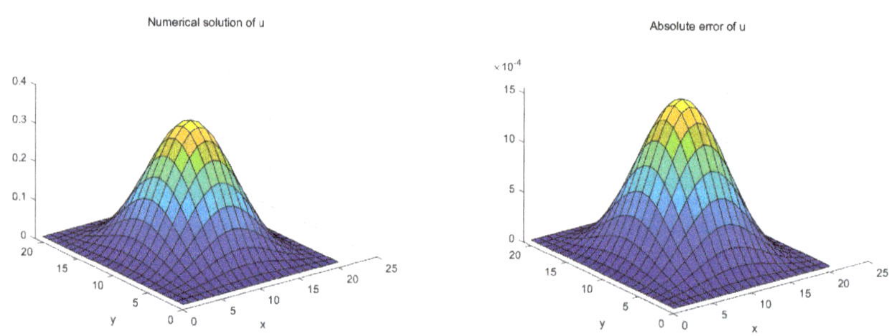

Figure 2. The curved surfaces of the numerical solution u (**left**) and absolute error (**right**).

5.3. Three-Dimensional Time-Fractional Fourth-Order System

To implement the numerical effectiveness, the following fractional fourth-order system is considered. The analytical solution of this system is $u(\mathbf{x}, t) = \frac{t^3}{3}\sin(\pi x)\sin(\pi y)\sin(2\pi z)$, $\mathbf{x} \in [0,1]^3, t \in (0,1]$. By setting $M = 13$ and $\tau = 1/20$, three comparisons of the surfaces between the exact solution and the numerical solution are exhibited, along with the condition $x = 1/2$ at $t = 1$ when taking $\alpha = 1.6$ into account in Figure 3.

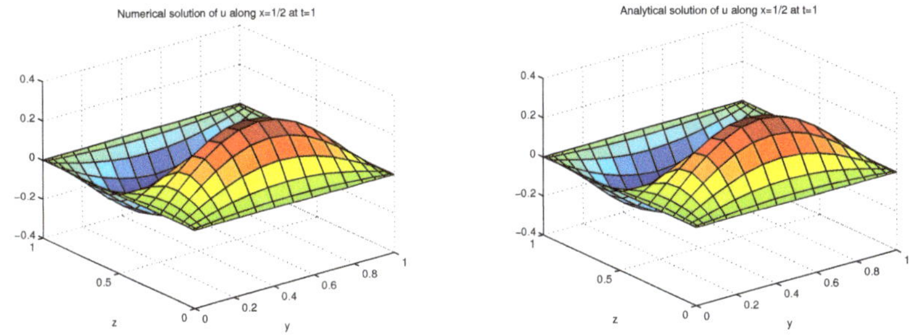

Figure 3. The curved surfaces for the numerical solutions (**left**) and exact solutions (**right**).

Let α assume the values 1.3, 1.5, and 1.7, respectively. Table 4 presents specific numerical results related to the maximum errors and the corresponding temporal convergence order for different temporal mesh sizes at t = 1. From these results, it can be observed that the temporal convergence order is approximately and closely equal to $3-\alpha$.

Table 4. The convergence order in three-dimensional space at t = 1.

τ	$\alpha = 1.3$		$\alpha = 1.5$		$\alpha = 1.7$	
	E_n	Order	E_n	Order	E_n	Order
1/10	2.1249×10^{-4}		4.9392×10^{-3}		9.7883×10^{-3}	
1/20	6.6285×10^{-4}	1.6806	1.7756×10^{-4}	1.4760	3.9602×10^{-3}	1.3055
1/40	2.0573×10^{-5}	1.6979	6.3224×10^{-5}	1.4897	1.6177×10^{-4}	1.2916
1/80	6.3850×10^{-5}	1.6880	2.2444×10^{-5}	1.4942	6.6040×10^{-5}	1.2925
1/160	1.9992×10^{-6}	1.6752	7.9736×10^{-6}	1.4930	2.6878×10^{-5}	1.2946
1/320	6.4637×10^{-7}	1.6291	2.8493×10^{-6}	1.4846	1.0932×10^{-5}	1.2945
Theoretical value		1.7000		1.5000		1.3000

6. Conclusions

In this paper, we present a compact difference-Galerkin spectral scheme for coupledly solving a multi-dimensional variable coefficient time-fractional fourth-order partial differential system. The main conclusions of this article, including the stability, convergence, and solvability of the method, were derived. Finally, some computational experiments are illustrated to demonstrate the superiority of the compact difference-Galerkin method. Lastly, we plan to carry out a multitude of subsequent works, including ones on special boundary conditions, discontinuous solutions, and so on.

Author Contributions: Methodology and formal analysis, S.Y.; writing—original draft preparation, Y.W. All authors have read and agreed to the published version of the manuscript.

Funding: This research received no external funding.

Data Availability Statement: The data will be made available by the authors on request.

Conflicts of Interest: Shichao Yi was employed by the Yangzijiang Shipbuilding Group. The remaining authors declare that this research was conducted in the absence of any commercial or financial relationships that could be construed as a potential conflicts of interest. The Yangzijiang Shipbuilding Group had no role in the design of this study; in the collection, analysis, or interpretation of data; in the writing of this manuscript, or in the decision to publish the results.

References

1. Samko, S.G.; Kilbas, A.A.; Marichev, O.I. *Fractional Integrals and Derivatives: Theory Applications*; Gordon and Breach Science: New York, NY, USA, 1993.
2. Podlubny, I. *Fractional Differential Equations*; Academic Press: New York, NY, USA, 1999.
3. Kilbas, A.A.; Srivastava, H.M.; Trujillo, J.J. *Theory and Applications of Fractional Differential Equations*; North-Holland: New York, NY, USA, 2006.
4. Baleanu, D.; Diethelm, K.; Scalas, E.; Trujillo, J.J. *Fractional Calculus Models and Numerical Methods*; Series on Complexity, Nonlinearity and Chaos; World Scientific: Singapore, 2012.
5. Sun, H.; Zhang, Y.; Baleanu, D.; Chen, W.; Chen, Y. A new collection of real world applications of fractional calculus in science and engineering. *Commun. Nonlinear Sci. Numer. Simul.* **2018**, *64*, 213–231. [CrossRef]
6. Li, X.; Xu, C. A space-time spectral method for the time fractional diffusion equation. *SIAM J. Numer. Anal.* **2009**, *47*, 2108–2131 [CrossRef]
7. Zhao, J.; Xiao, J.; Xu, Y. Stability and convergence of an effective finite element method for multiterm fractional partial differential equations. *Abstr. Appl. Anal.* **2013**, *2013*, 857205. [CrossRef]
8. Zhuang, P.; Gu, Y.T.; Liu, F.; Turner, I.; Yarlagadda, P.K.D.V. Time-dependent fractional advection-diffusion equations by an implicit MLS meshless method. *Int. J. Numer. Methods Eng.* **2011**, *88*, 1346–1362. [CrossRef]
9. Gu, X.M.; Sun, H.W.; Zhao, Y.L.; Zheng, X. An implicit difference scheme for time-fractional diffusion equations with a time-invariant type variable order. *Appl. Math. Lett.* **2021**, *120*, 107270. [CrossRef]
10. Mandelbrot, B.B. *The Fractal Geometry of Nature*; WH Freeman: New York, NY, USA, 1982.
11. Caputo, M. *Elasticitàe Dissipazione*; Zanichelli: Bologna, Italy, 1969.
12. Caputo, M.; Mainardi, F. Linear models of dissipation in an elastic solids. *Riv. Nuevo Clmento (Ser. II)* **1971**, *1*, 161–198.
13. Bagley, R. Applications of Generalized Derivatives of Viscoelasticity. Ph.D. Thesis, Air Force Institute of Technology, Wright-Patterson AFB, OH, USA, 1979.
14. Golbabai, A.; Sayevand, K. Fractional calculus—A new approach to the analysis of generalized fourth-order diffusion-wave equations. *Comput. Math. Appl.* **2011**, *67*, 2227–2231. [CrossRef]
15. Jafari, H.; Dehghan, M.; Sayevand, K. Solving a fourth-order fractional diffusion wave equation in a bounded domain by decomposition method. *Numer. Methods Partial. Differ. Equ.* **2008**, *24*, 1115–1126. [CrossRef]
16. Agrawal, O.P. A general solution for a fourth-order fractional diffusion-wave equation defined in a bounded domain. *Comput. Struct.* **2001**, *79*, 1497–1501. [CrossRef]
17. Oldham, K.B.; Spanier, J. *The Fractional Calculus*; Academic Press: Cambridge, MA, USA, 1974.
18. Vong,S.; Wang,Z. Compact finite difference scheme for the fourth-order fractional subdiffusion system. *Adv. Appl. Math. Mech.* **2014**, *6*, 419–435. [CrossRef]
19. Hu, X.L.; Zhang, L.M. On finite difference methods for fourth-order fractional diffusion-wave and subdiffusion systems. *Appl. Math. Comput.* **2012**, *218*, 5019–5034. [CrossRef]
20. Liu, Y.; Du, Y.W.; Li, H.; Li, J.C.; He, S. A two-grid mixed finite element method for a nonlinear fourth-order reaction diffusion problem with time-fractional derivative. *Comput. Math. Appl.* **2015**, *70*, 2474–2492. [CrossRef]
21. Liu, Y.; Du, Y.W.; Li, H.; He, S.; Gao, W. Finite difference/finite element method for a nonlinear time-fractional fourth-order reaction-diffusion problem. *Comput. Math. Appl.* **2015**, *70*, 573–593. [CrossRef]
22. Dehghan, M.; Manafian, J.; Saadatmandi, A. The solution of the linear fractional partial differential equations using the homotopy analysis method. *Z. Naturforschung-A* **2010**, *65*, 935–949. [CrossRef]
23. Dehghan, M.; Manafian, J.; Saadatmandi, A. Solving nonlinear fractional partial differential equations using the homotopy analysis method. *Numer. Methods Partial. Differ. Equ.* **2010**, *26*, 448–479. [CrossRef]
24. Zhang, H.; Liu, F.; Phanikumar, M.S.; Meerschaert, M.M. A novel numerical method for the time variable fractional order mobile-immobile advection–dispersion model. *Comput. Math. Appl.* **2013**, *66*, 693–701. [CrossRef]
25. WParvizi, M.; Eslahchi, M.R.; Dehghan, M. Numerical solution of fractional advection-diffusion equation with a nonlinear source term. *Numer. Algorithms* **2015**, *68*, 601–629. [CrossRef]
26. Tang, T.; Jie, S. *Spectral and High-Order Methods with Applications*; Science Press: Alexandria, NSW, Australia, 2006.
27. Yi, S.C.; Yao, L.Q. A steady barycentric lagrange interpolation method for the 2d higher order time-fractional telegraph equation with nonlocal boundary condition with error analysis. *Numer. Methods Partial. Differ. Equ.* **2019**, *35*, 1694–1716. [CrossRef]
28. Sun, Z.Z.; Wu, X.N. A fully discrete difference scheme for a diffusion-wave system. *Appl. Numer. Math.* **2006**, *56*, 193–209. [CrossRef]

fractal and fractional

MDPI

Article

Fractional-Calculus Analysis of the Dynamics of a Vector-Borne Infection with Preventive Measures

Rashid Jan [1,2], Salah Boulaaras [3,*], Asma Alharbi [3] and Normy Norfiza Abdul Razak [1]

1 Institute of Energy Infrastructure (IEI), Department of Civil Engineering, College of Engineering, Universiti Tenaga Nasional (UNITEN), Putrajaya Campus, Jalan IKRAM-UNITEN, Kajang 43000, Selangor, Malaysia; rashid_ash2000@yahoo.com (R.J.); normy@uniten.edu.my (N.N.A.R.)
2 Mathematics Research Center, Near East University TRNC, Mersin 10, Nicosia 99138, Turkey
3 Department of Mathematics, College of Science, Qassim University, Buraydah 51452, Saudi Arabia; ao.alharbi@qu.edu.sa
* Correspondence: s.boularas@qu.edu.sa; Tel.: +966-559618327

Abstract: Vector-borne infections pose serious public health challenges due to the complex interplay of biological, environmental, and social factors. Therefore, comprehensive approaches are essential to mitigate the burden of vector-borne infections and minimize their impact on public health. In this research, an epidemic model for the vector-borne disease malaria is structured with a saturated incidence rate via fractional calculus and preventive measures. The essential results and concepts are introduced to examine the proposed model. The solution of the system is examined for some necessary results, and the threshold parameter of the model, indicated by $\mathcal{R}_0$, is calculated. In this paper, the proposed malaria model is analyzed both quantitatively and qualitatively. The fixed-point theorems of Banach and Schaefer are utilized to examine the uniqueness and existence of the solution dynamics. Furthermore, the necessary conditions for the stability of the model have been determined. A numerical approach is offered to visualize the solution pathways of the system and identify its key factors. Through the results, the most influential factors for the control and management of the disease are highlighted.

Keywords: fractional derivatives; disease dynamics; stability analysis; numerical scheme; dynamical behavior; public health

1. Introduction

Vector-borne diseases impose a significant burden on global public health, affecting millions of people in the world each year. Malaria, a health issue of considerable global significance, remains a persistent challenge, with Plasmodium parasites being the causative agents transmitted by the bites of infected mosquitoes, as indicated in [1]. The complex life cycle of the parasites and their interaction with Anopheles mosquitoes contribute to the persistence of this disease. Upon infection, the parasites initially target the liver, undergoing a phase of maturation before entering the bloodstream and infecting red blood cells. A frequent occurrence of flu, chills, and fever-like symptoms that are typical of malaria are caused by this cyclical pattern. The burden of malaria extends beyond individual health impacts, exerting substantial socio-economic effects [2]. Areas with high malaria prevalence often face challenges in economic development, as malaria can contribute to absenteeism, decreased productivity, and increased healthcare expenditures. Policies to address malaria encompass a comprehensive approach, incorporating various elements, including vector control measures and the use of antimalarial medications for both treatment and prevention [3,4]. Furthermore, ongoing research aims to develop more effective vaccines and therapies to further reduce the global incidence of malaria and alleviate its profound public health implications.

Sir Ronald Ross, in his pioneering work, laid the foundation for mathematical epidemiology by developing the first compartmental models to describe the transmission dynamics of malaria, revolutionizing the understanding of infectious disease spread [5]. It is evident that modeling contributes significantly to studying the transmission dynamics of vector-borne infections and to efficiently exploring disease dynamics to guide control interventions [6,7]. By utilizing mathematical analysis, it is possible to identify the main aspects of the transmission process associated with various infections [8,9]. In the literature, numerous researchers have developed models for the management and prevention of malaria, each with different assumptions [10–12]. Researchers looked at how drug resistance and treatment interventions affected malaria dynamics in endemic areas [13]. The study used mathematical modeling to assess how treatment strategies and drug resistance influence the dynamics of the infection. Their results offered valuable insights into the factors affecting disease prevalence and suggested potential strategies for effective control in endemic areas. In another study, researchers explored the dynamics of both drug-resistant and drug-sensitive malaria strains within human populations through a mathematical model [14]. They also applied optimal control theory to assess the potential impact of new preventive policies on the spread of the disease. In the literature, the dynamics of malaria have also been examined in relation to the effects of treatment and vaccination. By applying optimal control methods, they evaluated the effectiveness of treatment and vaccination in reducing the spread of the infection [15].

The dynamics of *Aedes aegypti* with a seasonal population through a mathematical framework have been studied [16]. In this model, the effectiveness of insecticide has been evaluated, and insecticide resistance has been assessed. In [17], the researchers introduced and examined a model to understand temephos resistance within *Aedes aegypti* populations. The issue of insecticide resistance was further explored in [18,19], where the authors introduced new assumptions to examine broader contexts of resistance development. A significant challenge in disease control is the issue of population migration. The movement of infected vectors or hosts from infected areas to non-infected areas can increase the risk of infection. This has been compounded by the rise in resistance to both insecticides and antimalarial drugs [20]. In response to migration-related challenges, scholars have utilized multi-patch models, as demonstrated in [21,22], to explore the dynamics of disease spread across geographically distinct areas. The dynamics of epidemic spread facilitated by carriers have been investigated in the literature [23]. The challenges related to migration, particularly in the context of malaria and general epidemic models, have been explored in [24,25]. To address the aforementioned challenges, it is essential to examine the impact of resistance to antimalarial drugs, insecticides, and population movement as key factors influencing malaria control, especially in the context of a saturated incidence rate.

The associative learning mechanism and early stages of vector-borne disease transmission have been shown to occur [26]. Mosquitoes utilize prior knowledge of a host's location, blood type, appearance, and defensive behaviors to select their feeding targets. Meanwhile, host populations employ memory-based awareness, which can reduce the interaction rate between vectors and hosts [27]. Such behaviors are effectively represented in the mathematical modeling of infectious diseases using a fractional-order system. Therefore, we choose to present the dynamics of malaria through fractional derivatives to demonstrate the impact of memory on infection control and prevention. The concept of the Ulam–Hyers stability is crucial as it provides a mathematical framework that ensures the robustness and reliability of model solutions [28,29]. This stability guarantees that, even with fluctuations in parameters or external conditions, the core insights and predictions of the model remain valid and dependable [30]. It is particularly important for accurately predicting disease dynamics, designing effective control strategies, and evaluating policy interventions. This work aims to establish the Ulam–Hyers stability in a fractional model of malaria, thereby advancing our ability to predict and control malaria transmission.

The current research is ordered as follows: the essential concepts and ideas of fractional theory are delineated in Section 2. An epidemic model is constructed to conceptualize the transmission dynamics of malaria with a saturated incidence rate in Section 3. Section 4 undertakes an in-depth analysis of the model, while Section 5 provides the requisite conditions for the Ulam–Hyers stability. Moreover, we present a computational technique to depict the solutions of the system. Finally, the conclusion of the work is presented in Section 6.

2. Essential Concepts and Theory

Here, we will provide a comprehensive overview of the fundamental concepts and terminology associated with fractional calculus theory. These concepts and theories will be used in the investigation of the malaria model. The essential results are outlined below:

Definition 1 ([31]). *Assume $g(t)$ in a way that $g(t) \in L^1([b,c],R)$, and let ν be the order of the fractional operator; then, the fractional integral is*

$$ {}^{\nu}I^{b}_{b^+}g(t) = \frac{1}{\Gamma(\nu)}\int_0^t (t-s)^{\nu-1}g(s)ds, \quad 0<\nu\le 1. \tag{1}$$

Definition 2 ([31]). *In case that $g(t) \in C^n[b,c]$, then the Caputo operator is*

$$ {}^{LC}D^{\nu}_{0^+}g(t) = \frac{1}{\Gamma(n-\nu)}\int_0^t (t-s)^{n-\nu-1}g^{(n)}(s)ds. \tag{2}$$

Lemma 1 ([31]). *Take the below system for a function $g(t)$:*

$$\begin{cases} {}^{LC}D^{\nu}_{0^+}g(t) = & w(t), \ t\in[0,\tau], \\ g(0) = & w_0, \ \ n-1<\nu<n, \end{cases} \tag{3}$$

in which $w(t) \in C([0,\tau])$ and

$$b(t) = \sum_{i=0}^{n-1} d_i t^i$$

for $i = 0,1,\ldots,n-1$ and $d_i \in R$.

Definition 3 ([32]). *The Laplace transformation for the Caputo operator is given by the following:*

$$\pounds[{}^{LC}D^{\nu}_{0^+}g(t)] = s^{\nu}g(s) - \sum_{k=0}^{n-1} s^{\nu-k-1}g^{(k)}(0), \tag{4}$$

in which $n-1<\hbar<n$.

Theorem 1 ([33]). *Let $G : \mathscr{X} \to \mathscr{X}$ be continuous and compact, where $\mathscr{X}$ is the Banach space. If the following is bounded,*

$$\mathcal{E} = \{g \in \mathscr{X} : b = \lambda G, \lambda \in (0,1)\}; \tag{5}$$

then, G has a fixed point.

3. Evaluation of the Fractional Dynamics

Here, we develop an epidemic model of malaria, categorizing the host strength $\mathscr{N}_h$ into susceptible ($\mathscr{S}_h$), infected ($\mathscr{I}_h$), and recovered ($\mathscr{R}_h$) classes. Simultaneously, the mosquito's strength $\mathscr{N}_v$ is classified into susceptible ($\mathscr{S}_v$) and infectious ($\mathscr{I}_v$) categories. The recruitment of hosts and vectors is denoted by Ξ_h and Ξ_v within this formulation. We represent the natural death rate for the host as μ_h and for the mosquitoes as μ_v. Let $\beta_h b\frac{\mathscr{I}_v}{1+\alpha_1\mathscr{I}_v}$ and $\beta_v b\frac{\mathscr{I}_h}{1+\alpha_2\mathscr{I}_h}$ indicate the force of infection from hosts and vectors. A constant rate of $\epsilon_1\theta_1$ is applied to the population of infected persons, where ϵ_1 indicates the drug's effectiveness and τ_1 indicates the drug-induced recovery. Furthermore, $\epsilon_1\tau_1 p_1\mathscr{I}_h$ represents the proportion of $\mathscr{I}_h$ that exhibits drug resistance, whereas p_1 ranges from 0 to 1 to represent the ratio of resistance acquisition to the drug. Therefore, the proportion of susceptible people impacted by the medicine is shown by the formula $\epsilon_1\tau_1(1-p_1)\mathscr{I}_h$. In addition to this, a part of the $\mathscr{I}_h$ dies from the infection at a rate of ρ, and another part recovers spontaneously at a rate of δ.

The population of vectors undergoes a reduction through natural mortality at a rate of d_v and is further impacted by the application of insecticides at a rate of $\epsilon_2\tau_2$. Here, ϵ_2 denotes the effectiveness of the insecticide, and τ_2 signifies the mortality of mosquitoes resulting from the insecticide application. The quantity of mosquitoes exhibiting resistance to insecticides is denoted as $\epsilon_2\tau_2 p_2$, where $p_2 \in [0,1]$ signifies the ratio of acquiring resistance to insecticides. Consequently, the term $\epsilon_2\tau_2(1-p_2)$ expresses the fraction of mosquitoes that remain sensitive to insecticides. The system of ODEs with the above-mentioned assumptions can be expressed as follows:

$$\begin{cases} \frac{d\mathscr{S}_h}{dt} &= \Xi - \beta_h b \frac{\mathscr{I}_v}{1+\alpha_1\mathscr{I}_v}\mathscr{S}_h + \omega\mathscr{R}_h - d_h\mathscr{S}_h, \\ \frac{d\mathscr{I}_h}{dt} &= \beta_h b \frac{\mathscr{I}_v}{1+\alpha_1\mathscr{I}_v}\mathscr{S}_h - \epsilon_1\tau_1(1-p_1)\mathscr{I}_h - (\delta+\rho+d_h)\mathscr{I}_h, \\ \frac{d\mathscr{R}_h}{dt} &= \epsilon_1\tau_1(1-p_1)\mathscr{I}_h + \delta\mathscr{I}_h - (\omega+d_1)\mathscr{R}_h, \\ \frac{d\mathscr{S}_v}{dt} &= \Xi - \beta_v b \frac{\mathscr{I}_h}{1+\alpha_2\mathscr{I}_h}\mathscr{S}_v - \epsilon_2\tau_2(1-p_2)\mathscr{S}_v - d_v\mathscr{S}_v, \\ \frac{d\mathscr{I}_v}{dt} &= \beta_v b \frac{\mathscr{I}_h}{1+\alpha_2\mathscr{I}_h}\mathscr{S}_v - \epsilon_2\tau_2(1-p_2)\mathscr{I}_v - d_v\mathscr{I}_v, \end{cases} \tag{6}$$

where

$$\mathscr{S}_h(0) \geq 0, \mathscr{I}_h(0) \geq 0, \mathscr{R}_h(0) \geq 0, \mathscr{S}_v(0) \geq 0, \; \textit{and} \; \mathscr{I}_v(0) \geq 0.$$

Additionally, the vector size is

$$\mathscr{N}_v = \mathscr{S}_v + \mathscr{I}_v;$$

similarly, the size of the host population is

$$\mathscr{N}_h = \mathscr{S}_h + \mathscr{I}_h + \mathscr{R}_h.$$

Fractional models provide a more comprehensive framework for vector-borne infection modeling, enhancing our ability to understand and control diseases transmitted by vectors. They capture essential features, making them invaluable tools for researchers and public health practitioners working on vector-borne diseases. For more accurate representation, our model in a fractional framework can be expressed as follows:

$$\begin{cases} {}_0^{LC}\mathrm{D}_t^{\vartheta}\mathscr{S}_h &= \Xi - \beta_h b \frac{\mathscr{I}_v}{1+\alpha_1\mathscr{I}_v}\mathscr{S}_h + \omega\mathscr{R}_h - d_h\mathscr{S}_h, \\ {}_0^{LC}\mathrm{D}_t^{\vartheta}\mathscr{I}_h &= \beta_h b \frac{\mathscr{I}_v}{1+\alpha_1\mathscr{I}_v}\mathscr{S}_h - \epsilon_1\tau_1(1-p_1)\mathscr{I}_h - (\delta+\rho+d_h)\mathscr{I}_h, \\ {}_0^{LC}\mathrm{D}_t^{\vartheta}\mathscr{R}_h &= \epsilon_1\tau_1(1-p_1)\mathscr{I}_h + \delta\mathscr{I}_h - (\omega+d_1)\mathscr{R}_h, \\ {}_0^{LC}\mathrm{D}_t^{\vartheta}\mathscr{S}_v &= \Xi - \beta_v b \frac{\mathscr{I}_h}{1+\alpha_2\mathscr{I}_h}\mathscr{S}_v - \epsilon_2\tau_2(1-p_2)\mathscr{S}_v - d_v\mathscr{S}_v, \\ {}_0^{LC}\mathrm{D}_t^{\vartheta}\mathscr{I}_v &= \beta_v b \frac{\mathscr{I}_h}{1+\alpha_2\mathscr{I}_h}\mathscr{S}_v - \epsilon_2\tau_2(1-p_2)\mathscr{I}_v - d_v\mathscr{I}_v, \end{cases} \tag{7}$$

where ${}_0^{LC}D_t^{\vartheta}$ denotes the Liouville–Caputo's operator, and ϑ is the tfractional order. It has been acknowledged that the findings of fractional systems are more reliable and precise for biological phenomena. In the next step, we will examine the solution of the proposed model of malaria.

Theorem 2. *The solutions* $(\mathscr{S}_h, \mathscr{I}_h, \mathscr{R}_h, \mathscr{S}_v, \mathscr{I}_v)$ *of the proposed model (7) of malaria infection are non-negative and bounded.*

Proof. For the proof, we proceed as follows:

$$\begin{cases} {}_{0}^{LC}D_t^{\vartheta}\mathscr{S}_h\,|_{\mathscr{S}_h=0} &= \Xi_h \geq 0, \\ {}_{0}^{LC}D_t^{\vartheta}\mathscr{I}_h\,|_{\mathscr{I}_h=0} &= \beta_h b.\mathscr{I}_v \geq 0, \\ {}_{0}^{LC}D_t^{\vartheta}\mathscr{R}_h\,|_{\mathscr{R}_h=0} &= \epsilon_1\tau_1(1-p_1).\mathscr{I}_h + \delta\mathscr{I}_h \geq 0, \\ {}_{0}^{LC}D_t^{\vartheta}\mathscr{S}_v\,|_{\mathscr{S}_v=0} &= \Xi_v \geq 0, \\ {}_{0}^{LC}D_t^{\vartheta}\mathscr{I}_v\,|_{\mathscr{I}_v=0} &= \beta_v b.\mathscr{I}_h \geq 0. \end{cases} \tag{8}$$

Thus, the solutions of the fractional dynamics (7) are non-negative. To prove the boundedness, the first three equations of the model imply the following:

$${}_{0}^{LC}D_t^{\vartheta}(\mathscr{S}_h + \mathscr{I}_h + \mathscr{R}_h) \;\leq\; \Xi_h - d_h(\mathscr{S}_h + \mathscr{I}_h + \mathscr{R}_h). \tag{9}$$

Through further simplification, we have

$$\Big((\mathscr{S}_h + \mathscr{I}_h + \mathscr{R}_h)\Big) \leq \left(\mathscr{S}_h(0) + \mathscr{I}_h(0) + \mathscr{R}_h(0) - \frac{\Xi_h}{d_h}\right) E_{\vartheta}(-d_h t^{\vartheta}) + \frac{\Xi_h}{d_h}.$$

Applying the concept of the work [31], the below is obtained:

$$\Big(\mathscr{S}_h + \mathscr{I}_h + \mathscr{R}_h)\Big) \leq \frac{\Xi}{d_h} \cong \mathcal{M}_1.$$

Similarly, the compartments of vector population imply that $\mathscr{S}_v + \mathscr{I}_v \leq \mathcal{M}_2$, in which $\mathcal{M}_2 = \frac{\Xi_v}{d_v}$. As a result, the solutions of the recommended model are bounded and non-negative. Let the infection-free equilibrium of (7) be symbolized by $\mathcal{E}_0(\mathscr{S}_h^0, \mathscr{I}_h^0, \mathscr{R}_h^0, \mathscr{S}_v^0, \mathscr{I}_v^0)$, given by

$$\left(\frac{\Xi}{d_h}, 0, 0, \frac{\Xi_v}{\epsilon_2\tau_2(1-p_2) + d_v}, 0\right).$$

The fundamental reproduction number, commonly symbolized as $\mathscr{R}_0$, stands as a crucial parameter in the field of epidemiology. It signifies the average count of secondary infections produced by an individual who is infected, assuming an entirely susceptible population. It is an important parameter for assessing the potential for an epidemic to spread. We will use the next-generation matrix approach to calculate the $\mathscr{R}_0$ of the proposed system as follows:

$$F = \begin{bmatrix} 0 & \beta_h b.\mathscr{S}_h^0 \\ \beta_v b.\mathscr{S}_v^0 & 0 \end{bmatrix} \text{and } V = \begin{bmatrix} \epsilon_1\tau_1(1-p_1) + \delta + \rho + d_h & 0 \\ 0 & \epsilon_2\tau_2(1-p_2) + \mu_v \end{bmatrix},$$

which implies that

$$F = \begin{bmatrix} 0 & \beta_h b.\mathscr{S}_h^0 \\ \beta_v b.\mathscr{S}_v^0 & 0 \end{bmatrix} \text{and } V = \begin{bmatrix} \frac{1}{\epsilon_1\tau_1(1-p_1)+\delta+\rho+d_h} & 0 \\ 0 & \frac{1}{\epsilon_2\tau_2(1-p_2)+\mu_v} \end{bmatrix}.$$

Further, we have

$$FV^{-1} = \begin{bmatrix} 0 & \frac{\beta_h b.\mathscr{S}_h^0}{\epsilon_1\tau_1(1-p_1)+\delta+\rho+d_h} \\ \frac{\beta_v b.\mathscr{S}_v^0}{\epsilon_2\tau_2(1-p_2)+\mu_v} & 0 \end{bmatrix}.$$

Then, the $\mathscr{R}_0$ of the recommended model (7) of malaria is calculated as follows:

$$\rho(FV^{-1}) = \sqrt{\frac{\beta_h b.\mathscr{S}_h^0}{(\epsilon_1\tau_1(1-p_1) + \delta + \rho + d_h)} \frac{\beta_v b.\mathscr{S}_v^0}{(\epsilon_2\tau_2(1-p_2) + \mu_v)}},$$

which gives

$$\mathscr{R}_0 = \sqrt{\frac{\beta_h b \mathscr{S}_h^0}{(\epsilon_1\tau_1(1-p_1)+\delta+\rho+d_h)} \frac{\beta_v b \mathscr{S}_v^0}{(\epsilon_2\tau_2(1-p_2)+\mu_v)}}.$$

□

Theorem 3. *If $\mathscr{R}_0 < 1$, the infection-free equilibrium in the proposed malaria model exhibits local asymptotic stability; otherwise, it is unstable.*

Proof of Theorem 3. To achieve the desired outcomes, we used the approach of the Jacobian matrix at the DFE, as given below:

$$J(E_0) = \begin{bmatrix} -d_h & 0 & \omega & 0 & -\beta_h b \mathscr{S}_h^0 \\ 0 & -(\epsilon_1\tau_1(1-p_1)+\delta+\rho+d_h) & 0 & 0 & \beta_h b \mathscr{S}_h^0 \\ 0 & (\epsilon_1\tau_1(1-p_1)+\delta) & -(\omega+d_h) & 0 & 0 \\ 0 & -\beta_v b \mathscr{S}_v^0 & 0 & -(\epsilon_2\tau_2(1-p_2)+d_v) & 0 \\ 0 & \beta_v b \mathscr{S}_v^0 & 0 & 0 & -(\epsilon_2\tau_2(1-p_2)+d_v) \end{bmatrix}.$$

Here, the first and second eigenvalues are $-d_h$ and $-(\omega+d_h)$, and the below is as follows:

$$J_1(E_0) = \begin{bmatrix} -(\epsilon_1\tau_1(1-p_1)+\delta+\rho+d_h) & 0 & \beta_h b \mathscr{S}_h^0 \\ -\beta_v b \mathscr{S}_v^0 & -(\epsilon_2\tau_2(1-p_2)+d_v) & 0 \\ \beta_v b \mathscr{S}_v^0 & 0 & -(\epsilon_2\tau_2(1-p_2)+d_v) \end{bmatrix},$$

where the third eigenvalue is given by $-(\epsilon_2\tau_2(1-p_2)+d_v)$. Further, we have

$$J_2(E_0) = \begin{bmatrix} -(\epsilon_1\tau_1(1-p_1)+\delta+\rho+d_h) & \beta_h b \mathscr{S}_h^0 \\ \beta_v b \mathscr{S}_v^0 & -(\epsilon_2\tau_2(1-p_2)+d_v) \end{bmatrix}.$$

Here, the LAS of the disease-free steady state of the suggested model depends on the eigenvalues of matrix J_2. To establish the necessary result, we will prove that $Det(J_2) > 0$ and $Trc(J_2) < 0$ for $\mathscr{R}_0 < 1$. Clearly, both these conditions are satisfied for $\mathscr{R}_0 < 1$. Hence, the Jacobian matrix of our system has negative eigenvalues for $\mathscr{R}_0 < 1$. Thus, the DFE of the proposed model (7) of the disease is LAS for $\mathscr{R}_0 < 1$ and is unstable otherwise. □

4. Existence Theory

In this part of the research, we will probe the qualitative aspects of the model (7) of malaria using the framework of existence theory. We proceed as follows:

$$\begin{cases} \mathscr{C}_1(t,\mathscr{S}_h,\mathscr{I}_h,\mathscr{R}_h,\mathscr{S}_v,\mathscr{I}_v) &= \Xi - \beta_h b \frac{\mathscr{I}_v}{1+\alpha_1\mathscr{I}_v}\mathscr{S}_h + \omega\mathscr{R}_h - d_h\mathscr{S}_h, \\ \mathscr{C}_2(t,\mathscr{S}_h,\mathscr{I}_h,\mathscr{R}_h,\mathscr{S}_v,\mathscr{I}_v) &= \beta_h b \frac{\mathscr{I}_v}{1+\alpha_1\mathscr{I}_v}\mathscr{S}_h - \epsilon_1\tau_1(1-p_1)\mathscr{I}_h - (\delta+\rho+d_h)\mathscr{I}_h, \\ \mathscr{C}_3(t,\mathscr{S}_h,\mathscr{I}_h,\mathscr{R}_h,\mathscr{S}_v,\mathscr{I}_v) &= \epsilon_1\tau_1(1-p_1)\mathscr{I}_h + \delta\mathscr{I}_h - (\omega+d_1)\mathscr{R}_h, \\ \mathscr{C}_4(t,\mathscr{S}_h,\mathscr{I}_h,\mathscr{R}_h,\mathscr{S}_v,\mathscr{I}_v) &= \Xi - \beta_v b \frac{\mathscr{I}_h}{1+\alpha_2\mathscr{I}_h}\mathscr{S}_v - \epsilon_2\tau_2(1-p_2)\mathscr{S}_v - d_v\mathscr{S}_v, \\ \mathscr{C}_5(t,\mathscr{S}_h,\mathscr{I}_h,\mathscr{R}_h,\mathscr{S}_v,\mathscr{I}_v) &= \beta_v b \frac{\mathscr{I}_h}{1+\alpha_2\mathscr{I}_h}\mathscr{S}_v - \epsilon_2\tau_2(1-p_2)\mathscr{I}_v - d_v\mathscr{I}_v. \end{cases} \tag{10}$$

Here, we can generalized the system (10) as given below:

$$\begin{cases} {}^{LC}D_{0^+}^{\vartheta}\mathscr{C}(t) = & \mathscr{H}(t,\mathscr{C}(t)), \; t \in [0,\tau], \\ \mathscr{C}(0) = & \mathscr{C}_0, \; 0 < \vartheta \le 1, \end{cases} \tag{11}$$

with

$$\begin{cases} \mathscr{C}(t) = & \mathscr{S}_h(t), \\ & \mathscr{I}_h(t), \\ & \mathscr{R}_h(t), \\ & \mathscr{S}_v(t), \\ & \mathscr{I}_v(t). \end{cases} \begin{cases} \mathscr{C}_0(t) = & \mathscr{S}_{h0}, \\ & \mathscr{I}_{h0}, \\ & \mathscr{R}_{h0}, \\ & \mathscr{S}_{v0}, \\ & \mathscr{I}_{v0}. \end{cases} \begin{cases} \mathscr{H}(t,\mathscr{C}(t)) = \mathscr{C}_1(t,\mathscr{S}_{h1},\mathscr{I}_h,\mathscr{R}_h,\mathscr{S}_v,\mathscr{I}_v) \\ \mathscr{C}_2(t,\mathscr{S}_{h1},\mathscr{I}_h,\mathscr{R}_h,\mathscr{S}_v,\mathscr{I}_v) \\ \mathscr{C}_3(t,\mathscr{S}_{h1},\mathscr{I}_h,\mathscr{R}_h,\mathscr{S}_v,\mathscr{I}_v) \\ \mathscr{C}_4(t,\mathscr{S}_{h1},\mathscr{I}_h,\mathscr{R}_h,\mathscr{S}_v,\mathscr{I}_v) \\ \mathscr{C}_5(t,\mathscr{S}_{h1},\mathscr{I}_h,\mathscr{R}_h,\mathscr{S}_v,\mathscr{I}_v) \end{cases} \quad (12)$$

The above system (11) can be expressed in the following way through Lemma 1:

$$\mathscr{C}(t) = \mathscr{C}_0(t) + \frac{1}{\Gamma(\vartheta)} \int_0^t (t-s)^{\vartheta-1} \mathscr{H}(s,\mathscr{C}(s))ds. \quad (13)$$

We utilize Lipschitz-condition-based criteria to evaluate the suggested dynamics:

(P1) For q in $[0,1)$, one can find $\mathcal{U}_{\mathscr{H}}$ and $\mathcal{V}_{\mathscr{H}}$ in a manner such that the following holds.

$$|\mathscr{H}(t,\mathscr{C}(t))| \leq \mathcal{U}_{\mathscr{C}}|\mathscr{C}|^q + \mathcal{V}_{\mathscr{H}}. \quad (14)$$

(P2) One can find $M_{\mathscr{H}} > 0$ for all $\mathscr{C}$ and $\bar{\mathscr{C}}$ in $\mathscr{X}$ associated with the following condition:

$$|\mathscr{H}(t,\mathscr{C}) - \mathscr{H}(t,\bar{\mathscr{C}})| \leq M_{\mathscr{H}}[|\mathscr{C} - \bar{\mathscr{C}}|]. \quad (15)$$

In set $\mathscr{X}$, define mapping $\mathscr{B}$ as follows:

$$\mathscr{B}\mathscr{C}(t) = \mathscr{C}_0(t) + \frac{1}{\Gamma(\vartheta)} \int_0^t (t-s)^{\vartheta-1} \mathscr{H}(s,\mathscr{C}(s))ds. \quad (16)$$

If **P1** and **P2** are satisfied, then there is a solution to (11). We take the following actions to investigate the offered model's solution:

Theorem 4. *As long as* **P1** *and* **P2** *are met, there is at least one solution for the system (7) of malaria infection.*

Proof. To establish the necessary findings, we first use Schaefer's fixed point theorem. The following method is used to illustrate this theorem by outlining four distinct stages:

(C1): First, we will validate the continuity of operator $\mathscr{B}$. Assuming $\mathscr{C}_i$ is continuous for $i = 1,2,\ldots,5$, this implies that $\mathscr{H}(t,\mathscr{C}(t))$ is continuous. After that, considering $\mathscr{C}_j$, $\mathscr{C} \in \mathscr{X}$ in a manner that $\mathscr{C}_j \to \mathscr{C}$, we have $\mathscr{B}\mathscr{C}_j \to \mathscr{B}\mathscr{C}$.
Furthermore, let us take

$$\begin{aligned} ||\mathscr{B}\mathscr{C}_j - \mathscr{B}\mathscr{C}|| &= \max_{t\in[0,\tau]} \left| \frac{1}{\Gamma(\vartheta)} \int_0^t (t-r)^{\vartheta-1} Q_j(r,\mathscr{C}_j(r))dr - \frac{1}{\Gamma(\vartheta)} \int_0^t (t-r)^{\vartheta-1} \mathscr{H}(r,\mathscr{C}(r))ds \right| \\ &\leq \max_{t\in[0,\tau]} \int_0^t \left| \frac{(t-r)^{\vartheta-1}}{\Gamma(\vartheta)} \right| |\mathscr{H}_j(r,\mathscr{C}_j(r)) - \mathscr{H}(r,\mathscr{C}(r))|dr \\ &\leq \frac{\tau^{\vartheta} M_{\mathscr{H}}}{\Gamma(\vartheta+1)} ||\mathscr{C}_j - \mathscr{C}|| \to 0 \ \ as \ \ j \to \infty. \end{aligned} \quad (17)$$

Thus, the continuity of $\mathscr{B}\mathscr{C}_j \to \mathscr{B}\mathscr{C}$ is ensured from the continuity of $\mathscr{H}$, which implies that $\mathscr{B}$ is continuous.

(C2): Now, we will verify the bounded nature of $\mathscr{B}$. Let the following conditions be satisfied by operator $\mathscr{B}$ for every $\mathscr{C} \in$ X:

$$\begin{aligned} ||\mathscr{B}\mathscr{C}|| &= \max_{t\in[0,\tau]} \left| \mathscr{C}_0(t) + \frac{1}{\Gamma(\vartheta)} \int_0^t (t-s)^{\vartheta-1} \mathscr{H}(s,\mathscr{C}(s))ds \right| \\ &\leq |\mathscr{C}_0| \max_{t\in[0,\tau]} \frac{1}{\Gamma(\vartheta)} \int_0^t |(t-s)^{\vartheta-1}||\mathscr{H}(s,\mathscr{C}(s))|ds \end{aligned}$$

$$\leq |\mathscr{C}_0| + \frac{\tau^\vartheta}{\Gamma(\vartheta+1)}\{U_Z||\mathscr{C}||^q + V_{\mathscr{H}}\}. \tag{18}$$

Subsequently, we demonstrate the boundedness of $\mathscr{B}(T)$ in subset T of $\mathscr{X}$, where T is bounded. Given $\mathscr{C} \in T$, one may determine a non-negative value U in the following way due to the bounded nature of S:

$$||\mathscr{C}|| \leq U, \forall \mathscr{C} \in T. \tag{19}$$

Accordingly, the outcome for any $\mathscr{C}$ within the set T is derived from the above expression as follows:

$$||\mathscr{B}W|| \leq |\mathscr{C}_0| + \frac{\tau^\vartheta}{\Gamma(\vartheta+1)}[U_{\mathscr{H}}||\mathscr{C}||^q + V_{\mathscr{H}}] \leq |\mathscr{C}_0| + \frac{\tau^\vartheta}{\Gamma(\vartheta+1)}[U_{\mathscr{H}}U^q + V_{\mathscr{H}}]. \tag{20}$$

This implies that $\mathscr{B}(T)$ is a bounded operator.

(C3): For equi-continuity, take t_1 and t_2 in $[0,\tau]$, in which $t_1 \geq t_2$. Subsequently, we obtain the following:

$$\begin{aligned}
|\mathscr{B}\mathscr{C}(t_1) - \mathscr{B}\mathscr{C}(t_1)| &= \Bigg|\frac{1}{\Gamma(\vartheta)}\int_0^{t_1} |(t_1-s)^{\vartheta-1}||\mathscr{H}(s,\mathscr{C}(s))|dr \\
&- \frac{1}{\Gamma(\vartheta)}\int_0^{t_2} |(t_2-s)^{\vartheta-1}||\mathscr{H}(s,\mathscr{C}(s))|dr\Bigg| \\
&\leq \Bigg|\frac{1}{\Gamma(\vartheta)}\int_0^{t_1} |(t_1-s)^{\vartheta-1}| - \frac{1}{\Gamma(\vartheta)}\int_0^{t_2} |(t_2-s)^{\vartheta-1}|\Bigg||\mathscr{H}(s,\mathscr{C}(r))|dr \\
&\leq \frac{\tau^\vartheta}{\Gamma(\vartheta+1)}[U_{\mathscr{H}}||\mathscr{C}||^q + V_{\mathscr{H}}][t_1^\vartheta - t_2^\vartheta] \to 0 \; when \; t_1 \to t_2.
\end{aligned} \tag{21}$$

This uses the Arzelà–Ascoli theorem to guarantee the relative compactness of $\mathscr{B}(T)$.

(C4): For the final stage, take the below set:

$$\mathcal{E} = \{\mathscr{C} \in \mathscr{X} : \mathscr{C} = \lambda B\mathscr{C}, \lambda \in (0,1)\}. \tag{22}$$

To determine the boundedness of $\mathcal{E}$, we assume that $\mathscr{C}$ is a member of $\mathcal{E}$. All t in $[0,\tau]$ satisfy the below:

$$||\mathscr{C}|| = \lambda||B\mathscr{C}|| \leq \lambda\left[|\mathscr{C}_0|\frac{\tau^\vartheta}{\Gamma(\vartheta+1)}[U_{\mathscr{H}}||\mathscr{C}||^q + V_{\mathscr{H}}]\right]. \tag{23}$$

Consequently, the set $\mathcal{E}$ is bounded. The operator B has a fixed point that can be found using Schaefer's theorem. Therefore, the malaria model (11) has at least one solution.

□

Remark 1. *If the condition C1 holds true for $q = 1$, then it is possible to demonstrate Theorem 4 for $\frac{\tau^\vartheta U_Z}{\Gamma(\vartheta+1)} < 1$.*

Theorem 5. *The system (11) of malaria fever possesses a unique solution when the condition $\frac{\tau^\vartheta U_Z}{\Gamma(\vartheta+1)} < 1$ is fulfilled.*

Proof. To achieve this, use Banach's contraction theorem, assuming that $\mathscr{C}$ and $\bar{\mathscr{C}} \in \mathscr{X}$:

$$||B\mathscr{C} - B\bar{\mathscr{C}}|| \leq \max_{t\in[0,\tau]} \frac{1}{\Gamma(\vartheta)}\int_0^t |(t-s)^{\vartheta-1}||\mathscr{H}(s,\mathscr{C}(s)) - \mathscr{H}(s,\bar{\mathscr{C}}(s))|ds$$

$$\leq \frac{\tau^{\vartheta}U_{\mathscr{H}}}{\Gamma(\vartheta+1)}||\mathscr{C}-\bar{\mathscr{C}}||. \tag{24}$$

Thus, there exists a fixed point for B, which implies that model (11) of malaria has a unique solution. □

5. Stability Analysis

In this section of the paper, the Ulam–Hyers stability (UHS) of the system will be examined. This is a foundational concept for ensuring that systems and equations are resilient to small errors, providing both theoretical insight and practical assurance in the analysis of dynamic and functional equations.

Take $\mathscr{L} : \mathscr{X} \to \mathscr{X}$ in such a manner that

$$\mathscr{L}\mathscr{P} = \mathscr{P} \;\; for \;\; \mathscr{P} \in \mathscr{X}. \tag{25}$$

Definition 4. *The above (25) is UHS if $\zeta > 0$, and for any solution $\mathscr{C}$ in $\mathscr{X}$, the below fulfills*

$$||\mathscr{P} - \mathscr{L}\mathscr{P}|| \leq \zeta, \forall t \in [0, \tau]. \tag{26}$$

In addition to this, let $\bar{\mathscr{C}}$ be a unique solution for the above (25) in a manner that $C_q > 0$, and the below holds true as follows:

$$||\bar{\mathscr{P}} - \mathscr{P}|| \leq C_q\zeta, \forall t \in [0, \tau]. \tag{27}$$

Definition 5. *Let $\mathscr{C}$ and $\bar{\mathscr{C}}$ be solutions of (25); then, the solution of (25) is generalized UHS if*

$$||\bar{\mathscr{P}} - \mathscr{P}|| \leq \mathscr{H}(\zeta), \tag{28}$$

in which $\mathscr{H} \in C(R, R)$, and zero is the image of zero.

Remark 2. *Let the solution $\bar{\mathscr{C}}$ belonging to $\mathscr{X}$ fulfill Equation (27), and the below condition is satisfied:*

(a) $|\hbar(t)| \leq \zeta$, *in which* $\hbar \in C([0,\tau]; R)$

(b) $\mathscr{K}\bar{\mathscr{P}}(T) = \bar{\mathscr{P}} + \hbar(T), \forall t \in [0, \tau]$.

After perturbation, the system (11) can be expressed as follows:

$$\begin{cases} {}^{C}D^{\vartheta}_{0+}\mathscr{P}(t) = & \mathscr{C}(t, \mathscr{P}(t)) + \hbar(t), \\ \mathscr{P}(0) = \mathscr{P}_0. \end{cases} \tag{29}$$

Lemma 2. *The system (29) fulfills the following:*

$$|\mathscr{P}(t) - T\mathscr{P}(t)| \leq a\zeta, \;\; in\; which \;\; a = \frac{\tau^{\vartheta}}{\Gamma(\vartheta+1)}. \tag{30}$$

This can be easily proved through Remark 2 and Lemma 1.

Theorem 6. *If $\frac{\tau^{\vartheta}L_{\mathscr{C}}}{\Gamma(\vartheta+1)} < 1$ satisfies Lemma (2), system (11) has a UHS and generalized UHS solution.*

Proof. For the proof, we assume solutions $\mathscr{P} \in X$ and $\bar{\mathscr{P}} \in X$ of the system (11) and take the following:

$$\begin{aligned} |\mathscr{P}(t) - \bar{\mathscr{P}}(t)| &= |\mathscr{P}(t) - \bar{\mathscr{P}}(t)| \\ &\leq |\mathscr{P}(t) - T\bar{\mathscr{P}}(t)| \\ &\leq |\mathscr{P}(t) - T\bar{\mathscr{P}}(t)| \end{aligned}$$

$$\leq \quad a\zeta + \frac{\tau^{\xi} L_{\mathcal{U}}}{\Gamma(\xi+1)} |\mathscr{P}(t) - \bar{\mathscr{P}}(t)|$$
$$\leq \quad \frac{a\zeta}{1 - \frac{\tau^{\xi} L_{\mathcal{U}}}{\Gamma(\xi+1)}}. \tag{31}$$

As a result, the solution of the recommended dynamics (11) of malaria infection is UHS and generalized UHS. □

Definition 6. *For any $\mathscr{P} \in \mathscr{X}$, the solution of (25) is the Ulam–Hyers–Rassias stability (UHS) if the below holds true:*

$$||\mathscr{P} - \mathcal{K}\mathcal{V}|| \leq \Omega(t)\zeta \tag{32}$$

for all $t \in [0, \tau]$. If $0 < C_q$, one can find a unique solution $\bar{\mathscr{P}}$ of (25), satisfying

$$||\bar{\mathscr{P}} - \mathscr{P}|| \leq C_q \Omega(t)\zeta, \ \forall t \in [0, \tau]. \tag{33}$$

Definition 7. *Assume a unique solution $\bar{\mathscr{C}}$, and suppose $\mathscr{C}$ is any other solution to the Equation (25). If*

$$||\bar{\mathscr{P}} - \mathscr{P}|| \leq C_{q,\Omega}\Omega(t)\zeta, \quad for \ t \in [0, \tau], \tag{34}$$

in which $\zeta > 0$ and $\Omega \in D[[0, \tau], R]$ such that $C_{q,\Omega}$. Then, the solution to (25) is generalized UHS.

Remark 3. *Assume $\bar{\mathscr{P}} \in X$, which fulfills (27) and satisfies the following:*
(a) $|\hbar(t)| \leq \zeta\Omega(t), \ in \ which \ \hbar(t) \in C([0, \tau]; R)$
(b) $\mathscr{Z}\bar{\mathscr{P}}(t) = \bar{\mathscr{P}} + \hbar(t)$.

Lemma 3. *The perturbed system in (2) satisfies the subsequent conditions:*

$$|\mathscr{P}(t) - T\mathscr{P}(T)| \leq a\Omega(t)\zeta, \ where \ a = \frac{\tau^{\vartheta}}{\Gamma(\vartheta+1)}. \tag{35}$$

It is easy to show this using Lemma 1 and Remark 3.

Theorem 7. *If $\frac{\tau^{\vartheta} L_{\mathcal{U}}}{\Gamma(\vartheta+1)} < 1$ holds true with Lemma 3, then (11) has a UHS and generalized UHS solution.*

Proof. Let $\mathscr{P} \in \mathscr{X}$ be any solution of (11) and $\bar{\mathscr{P}} \in \mathscr{X}$ be a unique solution; then, the following fulfills

$$\begin{aligned}
|\mathscr{P}(t) - \bar{\mathscr{P}}(t)| &= |\mathscr{P}(t) - \bar{\mathscr{P}}(t)| \\
&\leq |\mathscr{P}(t) - T\bar{\mathscr{P}}(t)| \\
&\leq |\mathscr{P}(t) - T\bar{\mathscr{P}}(t)| \\
&\leq a\Omega(t)\zeta + \frac{\tau^{\vartheta} L_{\mathscr{C}}}{\Gamma(\vartheta+1)} |\mathscr{P}(t) - \bar{\mathscr{P}}(t)| \\
&\leq \frac{a\Omega(t)\zeta}{1 - \frac{\tau^{\vartheta} L_{\mathscr{C}}}{\Gamma(\vartheta+1)}}.
\end{aligned} \tag{36}$$

Thus, system (11) has a UHS and generalized UHS solution. □

These stability results ensure that the model remains reliable and resilient to fluctuations in parameters or external conditions, preserving the validity of its predictions. In this study, we established existing results and stability analysis; however, comparative analysis with existing work and data fitting will be performed in our future work.

6. Numerical Scheme for the Dynamics

Here, an iterative approach is presented to illustrate the dynamical behavior of malaria infection. The scheme is based on the methodology proposed in [34] for fractional model and is described as follows:

$$ {}_0^C D_t^\alpha k(t) = f(t, k(t)), \tag{37} $$

which can be expressed as

$$ k(t) - k(0) = \frac{1}{\Gamma(\alpha)} \int_0^t f(\eta, k(\eta))(t-\eta)^{\alpha-1} d\eta; \tag{38} $$

therefore, at time $t = t_{n+1}$, $n = 0, 1, \ldots$, we have

$$ k(t_{n+1}) - k(0) = \frac{1}{\Gamma(\alpha)} \int_0^{t_{n+1}} (t_{n+1} - t)^{\alpha-1} f(t, k(t)) dt \tag{39} $$

and

$$ f(t_n) - f(0) = \frac{1}{\Gamma(\alpha)} \int_0^{t_n} (t_n - t)^{\alpha-1} f(t, k(t)) dt. \tag{40} $$

From (40) and (39), one can get the following:

$$ \begin{aligned} k(t_{n+1}) &= k(t_n) + \underbrace{\frac{1}{\Gamma(\alpha)} \int_0^{t_{n+1}} (t_{n+1} - t)^{\alpha-1} f(t, k(t)) dt}_{\mathcal{A}_{\alpha,1}} \\ &\quad - \underbrace{\frac{1}{\Gamma(\alpha)} \int_0^{t_n} (t_n - t)^{\alpha-1} f(t, k(t)) dt}_{\mathcal{A}_{\alpha,2}}. \end{aligned} \tag{41} $$

where

$$ \mathcal{A}_{\alpha,1} = \frac{1}{\Gamma(\alpha)} \int_0^{t_{n+1}} (t_{n+1} - t)^{\alpha-1} f(t, k(t)) dt \tag{42} $$

and

$$ \mathcal{A}_{\alpha,2} = \frac{1}{\Gamma(\alpha)} \int_0^{t_n} (t_n - t)^{\alpha-1} f(t, k(t)) dt. \tag{43} $$

Here, the approximation of Lagrange implies

$$ \begin{aligned} \mathbf{P}(t) &\simeq \frac{t - t_{n-1}}{t_n - t_{n-1}} f(t_n, k_n) + \frac{t - t_n}{t_{n-1} - t_n} f(t_{n-1}, k_{n-1}) \\ &= \frac{f(t_n, k_n)}{h}(t - t_{n-1}) - \frac{f(t_{n-1}, k_{n-1})}{h}(t - t_n). \end{aligned} \tag{44} $$

The above yields the following:

$$ \begin{aligned} \mathcal{A}_{\alpha,1} &= \frac{f(t_n, k_n)}{h\Gamma(\alpha)} \int_0^{t_{n+1}} (t_{n+1} - t)^{\alpha-1} (t - t_{n-1}) dt \\ &\quad - \frac{f(t_{n-1}, k_{n-1})}{h\Gamma(\alpha)} \int_0^{t_{n+1}} (t_{n+1} - t)^{\alpha-1} (t - t_n) dt. \end{aligned} \tag{45} $$

After additional simplification,

$$\begin{aligned} \mathcal{A}_{\alpha,1} &= \frac{f(t_n,k_n)}{h\Gamma(\alpha)}\Big[\frac{2h}{\alpha}t_{n+1}^{\alpha} - \frac{t_{n+1}^{\alpha+1}}{\alpha+1}\Big] \\ &\quad -\frac{f(t_{n-1},k_{n-1})}{h\Gamma(\alpha)}\Big[\frac{h}{\alpha}t_{n+1}^{\alpha} - \frac{1}{\alpha+1}t_{n+1}^{\alpha+1}\Big]. \end{aligned} \tag{46}$$

Similarly,

$$\begin{aligned} \mathcal{A}_{\alpha,2} &= \frac{1}{\Gamma(\alpha)}\int_0^{t_n}(t_n-t)^{\alpha-1}\Big[\frac{f(t_n,k_n)}{h}(t-t_{n-1}) \\ &\quad -\frac{f(t_{n-1},k_{n-1})}{h}(t-t_n)\Big]dt. \end{aligned} \tag{47}$$

The below is obtained through simplification:

$$\begin{aligned} \mathcal{A}_{\alpha,2} &= \frac{f(t_n,k_n)}{h\Gamma(\alpha)}\Big[\frac{h}{\alpha}t_n^{\alpha} - \frac{t_n^{\alpha+1}}{\alpha+1}\Big] \\ &\quad +\frac{f(t_{n-1},k_{n-1})}{h\Gamma(\alpha)}\Big[\frac{1}{\alpha+1}t_n^{\alpha+1}\Big]. \end{aligned} \tag{48}$$

Putting (47) and (48) into (41), we have

$$\begin{aligned} k(t_{n+1}) &= k(t_n) + \frac{f(t_n,k_n)}{h\Gamma(\alpha)}\Big[\frac{2ht_{n+1}^{\alpha}}{\alpha} - \frac{t_{n+1}^{\alpha+1}}{\alpha+1} + \frac{h}{\alpha}t_n^{\alpha} - \frac{t_{n+1}^{\alpha+1}}{\alpha+1}\Big] \\ &\quad +\frac{f(t_{n-1},k_{n-1})}{h\Gamma(\alpha)}\Big[-\frac{h}{\alpha}t_{n+1}^{\alpha} + \frac{t_{n+1}^{\alpha+1}}{\alpha+1} + \frac{t_n^{\alpha+1}}{\alpha+1}\Big]. \end{aligned} \tag{49}$$

We examined the time series of our system (7) of malaria using the numerical scheme outlined above. It is important to investigate the dynamical behavior of epidemic models to illustrate the impact of the scenario on the models. We performed several simulations to analyze our model of malaria infection.

We illustrated how the fractional order in the suggested malaria model affects the population of infected people in the first scenario shown in Figures 1 and 2. With a comparison study to the standard system, we assumed different values of ϑ in these figures. The ϑ values in Figure 1 are $\vartheta = 0.85, 0.90, 0.95$, and 1.00. This simulation illustrates the impact of both fractional and classical derivatives, demonstrating the flexibility of fractional systems and the ability to evaluate several values instead of just one. The values of ϑ in Figure 2 are taken to be $\vartheta = 0.70, 0.76, 0.82$, and 0.88. We found that the dynamics of infected persons are significantly and attractively impacted by the index of memory. Moreover, a drop in this system parameter may result in a drop in the prevalence of infections in the community. The memory index can be used to manage the infection level. Policymakers are therefore urged to take the memory index into account as a practical means of managing and mitigating illness.

The influence of the biting rate b on the infection level is depicted in Figure 3. In the second simulation, we assumed that b had the following values: $b = 0.423, 0.523, 0.623$, and 0.723. Evidently, this element is risky and increases the likelihood of infection in the community. In order to stop the virus from spreading across the population, we thus support controlling the bite rate as a preventative approach. The impact of the immunity loss rate on malaria transmission dynamics is depicted in Figure 4. ω was supposed to be 0.0154, 0.0354, 0.0554, and 0.0754. We can observe from this simulation that this input factor raises the risk of infected hosts. We have illustrated the impact of treatment effectiveness on malaria dynamics in Figure 5. This element has a beneficial effect on the system and lowers the level of infection. The impact of pesticide effectiveness on malaria dynamics is depicted in Figure 6. In this simulation, it is assumed that the pesticide efficacy values are 0.531, 0.631, 0.731, and 0.831. This variable lowers the levels of infection by having a positive impact on the system.

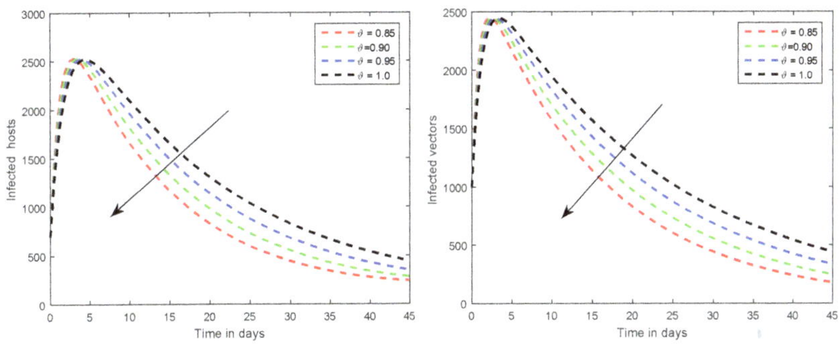

(a) (b)

Figure 1. Illustration of the (**a**) infected hosts and (**b**) infected vectors of our malaria dynamics (7) with various values of ϑ, i.e., $\vartheta = 0.85, 0.90, 0.95, 1.00$.

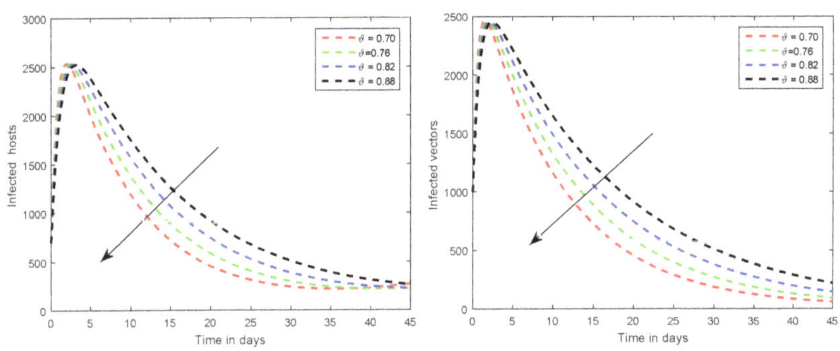

(a) (b)

Figure 2. Representation of the solution series of (**a**) infected hosts and (**b**) infected vectors of malaria dynamics (7) with the variation of ϑ, i.e., $\vartheta = 0.70, 0.76, 0.82, 0.88$.

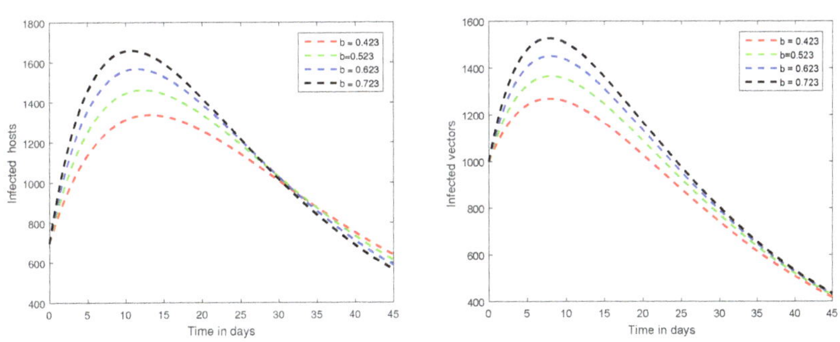

(a) (b)

Figure 3. Graphical view of the (**a**) infected hosts and (**b**) infected vectors of the malaria dynamics (7) with various values of biting rate b, i.e., $b = 0.423, 0.523, 0.623, 0.723$.

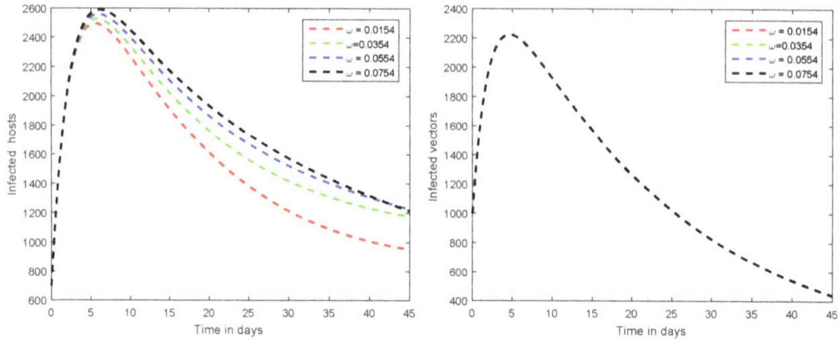

(a) (b)

Figure 4. Plotting the time series of (**a**) infected hosts and (**b**) infected vectors of our malaria dynamics (7) with various values of ω, i.e., $\omega = 0.0154, 0.0354, 0.0554, 0.0754$.

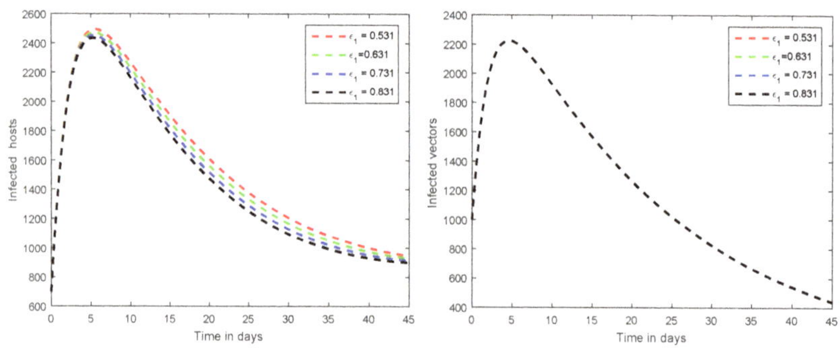

(a) (b)

Figure 5. Plotting the tracking path of (**a**) infected hosts and (**b**) infected vectors of malaria dynamics (7) with the efficacy of drugs in treatment ϵ_1, i.e., $\epsilon_1 = 0.531, 0.631, 0.731, 0.831$.

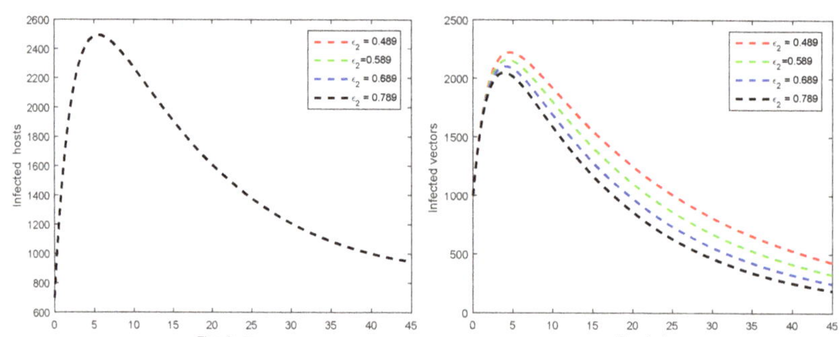

(a) (b)

Figure 6. Illustration of the (**a**) infected hosts and (**b**) infected vectors of our malaria dynamics (7) with the efficacy of insecticides ϵ_2, i.e., $\epsilon_2 = 0.489, 0.589, 0.689, 0.789$.

In this study, our primary focus was on these factors to show their impact on the transmission pathways. Our outcomes emphasize that the index of memory can effectively control the infection level, providing valuable insights for policymakers. We propose that the control of malaria can be significantly enhanced through the implementation of vaccination and treatment. Furthermore, effective infection control measures can be achieved by utilizing bed nets, insecticide spraying, and regulating the memory index.

7. Concluding Remarks

In our work, we structured an epidemic model for the transmission dynamics of malaria with a saturated incidence rate through a fractional framework. We modeled the impact of drug resistance and insecticide on the dynamics of malaria infection. It has been shown that the solutions of the proposed system are non-negative and bounded. The endemic indicator of the system is denoted by $\mathscr{R}_0$ and is determined through the next-generation matrix approach. For the existence and uniqueness of solutions, we applied the Banach and Schaefer frameworks through the fixed-point theorem. We also derived sufficient conditions to guarantee the Ulam–Hyers stability of the model. A numerical method was employed to explore the dynamics of infection, revealing the influence of various input factors on its behavior. Our numerical results identified the most sensitive factors for the effective prevention and management of malaria within the community. Our study highlights the crucial role of memory effects in shaping the complex dynamics of malaria, suggesting its potential as a modifiable control parameter for the management of the infection. Moving forward, our future research will focus on examining the impact of variables such as maturation and incubation delays on malaria dynamics. In future studies, we will investigate the effects of maturation and incubation delay on the dynamics of malaria. Additionally, the impact of pulse vaccination will be analyzed and visualized.

Author Contributions: Conceptualization, methodology, validation, investigation, writing—original draft, R.J.; software, validation, formal analysis, writing—original draft, visualization, S.B.; conceptualization, validation, formal analysis, visualization, supervision, A.A.; conceptualization, software, investigation, resources, writing—review and editing, N.N.A.R. All authors have read and agreed to the published version of the manuscript.

Funding: The researchers would like to thank the Deanship of Graduate Studies and Scientific Research at Qassim University for the financial support (QU-APC-2024-9/1).

Data Availability Statement: No new data were created or analyzed in this study.

Acknowledgments: The researchers would like to thank the Deanship of Graduate Studies and Scientific Research at Qassim University for the financial support (QU-APC-2024-9/1).

Conflicts of Interest: The authors declare no conflicts of interest.

References

1. Sato, S. Plasmodium—A brief introduction to the parasites causing human malaria and their basic biology. *J. Physiol. Anthropol.* **2021**, *40*, 1. [CrossRef] [PubMed]
2. Andrade, M.V.; Noronha, K.; Diniz, B.P.; Guedes, G.; Carvalho, L.R.; Silva, V.A.; Calazans, J.A.; Santos, A.S.; Silva, D.N.; Castro, M.C. The economic burden of malaria: A systematic review. *Malar. J.* **2022**, *21*, 283. [CrossRef] [PubMed]
3. Perera, R.; Wickremasinghe, R.; Newby, G.; Caldera, A.; Fernando, D.; Mendis, K. Malaria control, elimination, and prevention as components of health security: A review. *Am. J. Trop. Med. Hyg.* **2022**, *107*, 747. [CrossRef]
4. Olaniyi, S.; Abimbade, S.F.; Ajala, O.A.; Chuma, F.M. Efficiency and economic analysis of intervention strategies for recurrent malaria transmission. *Qual. Quant.* **2024**, *58*, 627–645. [CrossRef]
5. Smith, D.L.; Battle, K.E.; Hay, S.I.; Barker, C.M.; Scott, T.W.; McKenzie, F.E. Ross, Macdonald, and a theory for the dynamics and control of mosquito-transmitted pathogens. *PLoS Pathog.* **2012**, *8*, e1002588. [CrossRef]
6. Jan, R.; Hinçal, E.; Hosseini, K.; Razak, N.N.A.; Abdeljawad, T.; Osman, M.S. Fractional view analysis of the impact of vaccination on the dynamics of a viral infection. *Alex. Eng. J.* **2024**, *102*, 36–48. [CrossRef]
7. Tchoumi, S.Y.; Diagne, M.L.; Rwezaura, H.; Tchuenche, J.M. Malaria and COVID-19 co-dynamics: A mathematical model and optimal control. *Appl. Math. Model.* **2021**, *99*, 294–327. [CrossRef] [PubMed]
8. Jan, R.; Razak, N.N.A.; Alyobi, S.; Khan, Z.; Hosseini, K.; Park, C.; Salahshour, S.; Paokanta, S. Fractional Dynamics of Chronic Lymphocytic Leukemia with the Effect of Chemoimmunotherapy Treatment. *Fractals* **2024**, *32*, 1–16. [CrossRef]
9. Romero-Leiton, J.P.; Ibargüen-Mondragón, E. Stability analysis and optimal control intervention strategies of a malaria mathematical model. *Appl. Sci.* **2019**, *21*, 184–218.

10. Ozodiegwu, I.D.; Ambrose, M.; Galatas, B.; Runge, M.; Nandi, A.; Okuneye, K.; Dhanoa, N.P.; Maikore, I.; Uhomoibhi, P.; Bever, C.; et al. Application of mathematical modelling to inform national malaria intervention planning in Nigeria. *Malar. J.* **2023**, *22*, 137. [CrossRef]
11. Olaniyi, S.; Ajala, O.A.; Abimbade, S.F. Optimal control analysis of a mathematical model for recurrent malaria dynamics. In *Operations Research Forum*; Springer International Publishing: Cham, Switzerland, 2023; Volume 4, p. 14.
12. Tchoumi, S.Y.; Njintang, N.Y.; Kamgang, J.C.; Tchuenche, J.M. Malaria and malnutrition in children: A mathematical model. *Frankl. Open* **2023**, *3*, 100013. [CrossRef]
13. Chiyaka, C.; Garira, W.; Dube, S. Effects of treatment and drug resistance on the transmission dynamics of malaria in endemic areas. *Theor. Popul. Biol.* **2009**, *75*, 14–29. [CrossRef] [PubMed]
14. Tumwiine, J.; Hove-Musekwa, S.D.; Nyabadza, F. A mathematical model for the transmission and spread of drug sensitive and resistant malaria strains within a human population. *Int. Sch. Res. Not.* **2014**, *2014*, 636973. [CrossRef]
15. Okosun, K.O.; Ouifki, R.; Marcus, N. Optimal control analysis of a malaria disease transmission model that includes treatment and vaccination with waning immunity. *Biosystems* **2011**, *106*, 136–145. [CrossRef]
16. Luz, P.M.; Codeco, C.T.; Medlock, J.; Struchiner, C.J.; Valle, D.; Galvani, A.P. Impact of insecticide interventions on the abundance and resistance profile of Aedes aegypti. *Epidemiol. Infect.* **2009**, *137*, 1203–1215. [CrossRef]
17. Aldila, D.; Nuraini, N.; Soewono, E.; Supriatna, A.K. March. Mathematical model of temephos resistance in Aedes aegypti mosquito population. In *AIP Conference Proceedings*; American Institute of Physics: College Park, MD, USA, 2014; Volume 1589, pp. 460–463.
18. Alphey, N.; Coleman, P.G.; Donnelly, C.A.; Alphey, L. Managing insecticide resistance by mass release of engineered insects. *J. Econ. Entomol.* **2014**, *100*, 1642–1649. [CrossRef]
19. Gourley, S.A.; Liu, R.; Wu, J. Slowing the evolution of insecticide resistance in mosquitoes: A mathematical model. *Proc. R. Soc. A Math. Phys. Eng. Sci.* **2011**, *467*, 2127–2148. [CrossRef]
20. Bloland, P.B.; World Health Organization. *Drug Resistance in Malaria*; No. WHO/CDS/CSR/DRS/2001.4; World Health Organization: Geneva, Switzerland, 2001.
21. Agusto, F.B. Malaria drug resistance: The impact of human movement and spatial heterogeneity. *Bull. Math. Biol.* **2014**, *76*, 1607–1641. [CrossRef]
22. Gao, D.; Ruan, S. A multipatch malaria model with logistic growth populations. *SIAM J. Appl. Math.* **2012**, *72*, 819–841. [CrossRef]
23. Weiss, G.H. On the spread of epidemics by carriers. *Biometrics* **1965**, *21*, 481–490. [CrossRef]
24. Bichara, D.; Iggidr, A. Multi-patch and multi-group epidemic models: A new framework. *J. Math. Biol.* **2018**, *77*, 107–134. [CrossRef] [PubMed]
25. Bock, W.; Jayathunga, Y. Optimal control and basic reproduction numbers for a compartmental spatial multipatch dengue model. *Math. Methods Appl. Sci.* **2018**, *41*, 3231–3245. [CrossRef]
26. Chaves, L.F.; Harrington, L.C.; Keogh, C.L.; Nguyen, A.M.; Kitron, U.D. Blood feeding patterns of mosquitoes: Random or structured? *Front. Zool.* **2010**, *7*, 3. [CrossRef] [PubMed]
27. Vinauger, C.; Buratti, L.; Lazzari, C.R. Learning the way to blood: First evidence of dual olfactory conditioning in a blood-sucking insect, Rhodnius prolixus. I. Appetitive learning. *J. Exp. Biol.* **2011**, *214*, 3032–3038. [CrossRef] [PubMed]
28. Ullam, S.M. *Problems in Modern Mathematics*; Wiley: New York, NY, USA, 1940; Chapter VI.
29. Khalaf, S.L.; Kadhim, M.S.; Khudair, A.R. Studying of COVID-19 fractional model: Stability analysis. *Partial. Differ. Equ. Appl. Math.* **2023**, *7*, 100470. [CrossRef] [PubMed]
30. Usman, M.; Abbas, M.; Omame, A. Analysis of a non-integer order compartmental model for cholera and COVID-19 incorporating human and environmental transmissions. *Phys. Scr.* **2023**, *98*, 125223. [CrossRef]
31. Kilbas, A.A.; Srivastava, H.M.; Trujillo, J.J. *Theory and Applications of Fractional Differential Equations*; Elsevier: Amsterdam, The Netherlands, 2006; Volume 204.
32. Podlubny, I. *Fractional Differential Equations: An Introduction to Fractional Derivatives, Fractional Differential Equations, to Methods of Their Solution and Some of Their Applications*; Elsevier: Amsterdam, The Netherlands, 1998.
33. Granas, A.; Dugundji, J. Elementary fixed point theorems. In *Fixed Point Theory*; Springer: New York, NY, USA, 2003; pp. 9–84.
34. Atangana, A.; Owolabi, K.M. Corrigendum: New numerical approach for fractional differential equations. *Math. Model. Nat. Phenom.* **2021**, *16*, 47. [CrossRef]

fractal and fractional

MDPI

Article

A Computational Method for Solving Nonlinear Fractional Integral Equations

Rajaa T. Matoog [1], Amr M. S. Mahdy [2,3,*], Mohamed A. Abdou [4] and Doaa Sh. Mohamed [2]

1 Mathematics Department, Faculty of Sciences, Umm Al-Qura University, Makkah 24382, Saudi Arabia; rmatoog_777@yahoo.com or rtmatoog@uqu.edu.sa
2 Department of Mathematics, Faculty of Science, Zagazig University, Zagazig 44519, Egypt; doaashokry203@yahoo.com or doaashokry@zu.edu.eg
3 Department of Mathematics & Statistics, College of Science, Taif University, P.O. Box 11099, Taif 21944, Saudi Arabia
4 Department of Mathematics, Faculty of Education, Alexandria University, Alexandria 21526, Egypt; abdella_777@yahoo.com or abdella_777@alexu.edu.eg
* Correspondence: amr_mahdy85@yahoo.com or amr_mahdy85@zu.edu.eg or amattaya@tu.edu.sa

Abstract: This article solves the nonlinear fractional integral equation (NFrIE) using the Genocchi polynomial method (GPM). We have provided proof to demonstrate the existence of a unique solution to the second sort of NFrIE in Hilbert space. The proof of the stability of the error has been described and discussed. These criteria are proven given the spectrum characteristics of a linear self-adjoint operator. Numerous applications, unique conditions, and specific situations are developed. Additionally, numerical examples are constructed to illustrate the efficiency and applicability of the method. Maple 18 software is utilized for the computation of all the numerical outcomes.

Keywords: nonlinear fractional integral equation; Genocchi polynomial method; existence and uniqueness; spectrum relations; stability of error; self adjoint operator

MSC: 45M10; 65R20

1. Introduction

The vast array of applications in pure and applied mathematics, including in physics, fluid mechanics, electrodynamics, nonlinear biological systems, and other scientific and engineering domains, has drawn the interest of numerous researchers in fractional differential (FD) and integral equations (IEs) in recent years. Many different numerical methods have been proposed for solving FD and IEs in recent years. In [1], Hamdan et al. used Haar Wavelet for solving Volterra FIE. In [2], Pu and Fasondini presented Jacobi polynomials to obtain the solution of NFrIE. Bekkouche et al. in [3] introduced the solution to the fractional boundary value problem by using the trapezoidal rule. In [4], Mahdy et al. applied least squares and shifted Legendre methods for solving NFrIE. Alsulaiman et al. [5] used the Bernoulli matrix approach to solve NrIE. In [6], Alharbi et al. used the Haar Wavelet technique to solve FDEs. Mohamed et al., in [7], presented Chebyshev polynomials of the sixth kind for solving fractional mixed nonlinear partial integro-differential problems. Lagrange interpolation was utilized by Zabidiet al. in [8] to solve FDEs. In [9], Yi et al. developed a time-stepping algorithm for solving FDEs. Also, NFrDEs and their applications have been considered in many articles; for example, in [10], Jassim and Hussein presented the Hussein method for solving NFrDEs. In [11], Mohamed et al., the Elzaki transform method and the Homotopy perturbation method were used for solving NFrDEs. Rashid et al. [12], studied the solution of NFrDEs via fixed point theory. Lydia et al. [13] used the Kharrat–Toma iterative method to obtain the solution of NFrDEs. In [14], Yu presented Jumarie-modified Riemann–Liouville fractional calculus for solving NFrDEs.

In the present paper, GPM is applied to solve NFrIE, where GPM converts the problem to a system of algebraic equations that can be solved using numerical techniques. Finally, to demonstrate the applicability and validity of the method, we examine some numerical examples. The GPM is not based on orthogonal functions but belongs to a larger family class of polynomials: the Appell polynomial family. The advantage of GPM is its simplicity, and this method often leads to linear systems, which can be solved using numerical techniques, thus reducing computational costs and improving efficiency. However, the choice of collocation points plays an important role in obtaining accurate results. There are many applications of GPM; for example, in [15], GPM was applied for solving fractional partial integro-differential equations. In [16], GPM was used for solving fractional weakly singular IE. In [17], GPM was introduced to obtain the solution of FIDE. GPM was applied to find the solution of nonlinear Volterra integral equations with weakly singular kernels in [18]. Using the GPM matrix approach, Volterra IEs were solved in [19]. Heydari and Zhagharian [20] used GPM to obtain the solution of fractional Fornberg–Whitham equations. Loh et al. [21] presented the solution of Fredholm–Volterra fractional integro-differential equations via GPM. In [22], Seghiri et al. used GPM to obtain the solution of high-order Fredholm integro-differential equations. In [23], Mustapha used GPM for solving integro-differential equations. In [24], Isah and Phang applied GPM to obtain the solution of NFrDEs.

In this paper's remaining sections are the following. In Section 2, we present some preliminaries and basic information about Riemann –Liouville fractional integrals and Caputo fractional derivatives. In Section 3, applications and special cases of NFrDE are discussed. The existence and uniqueness of the solutions are discussed in Section 4. In Section 5, we studied the stability of error. In Section 6, the Genocchi polynomial method is applied for solving NFrDEs of the second kind. To explain the method in all instances of the error estimated using Maple 18, Section 7 offers a few numerical examples. Finally, a Discussion of the results is presented in Section 8.

In the Hilbert space $L_2(0,a]$, consider the second type of NFrDE:

$$\frac{d^\alpha}{dt^\alpha}[T\varphi(t)-\mu\varphi(t)]-M(t)\gamma(t,\varphi(t))=f(t), \quad (T\varphi(0)=\mu\varphi(0)), \quad (0<\alpha<1, t\in(0,a]). \tag{1}$$

Here, $T:H\to H$ is a linear self-adjoint operator in the Hilbert space, $\varphi:R^+\to H$ is an unknown function, $\gamma(t,\varphi(t))$ is a known function; μ is a constant, may be complex, and has many physical meanings, and $M,f:R^+\to H$ are given functions.

In this article, the convergence and the uniqueness of the solution of Equation (1) will be proved under certain relations. One can deduce several special situations and reach novel outcomes. Error estimate computation is carried out while also taking error stability into account.

The reader is referred to [25] and [26] for the existence of theorems about the FrDE. For reader reference, we direct them to [27] and [28] for descriptions of FI and its derivatives with fundamental characteristics.

2. Preliminaries and Basic Information

The following definitions and characteristics are provided for the reader's convenience.

Definition 1. *The Riemann–Liouville (RL) of order $\alpha>0$ of a function $h:(0,\infty)\to R$ is presented by*

$$I^\alpha_{0^+}h(t)=\frac{1}{\Gamma(\alpha)}\int_0^t(t-s)^{\alpha-1}h(s)ds. \tag{2}$$

under the condition that the R.H.S. is point-wise established on $(0,\infty)$.

Definition 2. *The Caputo fractional derivatives of order $\alpha>0$ of a function $g:(0,\infty)\to R$ provide*

$$D^\alpha_{0^+}g(t)=\frac{1}{\Gamma(n-\alpha)}\int_0^t\frac{g^{(n)}(s)}{(t-s)^{\alpha-n+1}}ds. \tag{3}$$

For the NFrDE (1) after integrating and using RL (2), we have

$$T\varphi(t) - \mu\varphi(t) - \frac{1}{\Gamma(\alpha)}\int_0^t (t-s)^{\alpha-1} M(s)\gamma(s,\varphi(s))ds = F(t), \quad t \in (0,a], \tag{4}$$

$$F(t) = \frac{1}{\Gamma(\alpha)}\int_0^t (t-s)^{\alpha-1} f(s)ds.$$

Formula (4) represents an NFrIE of the second kind.

Definition 3. *We say that $f \in N^{\alpha}(R_+, N), \alpha > 0$ if $f : R_+ \longrightarrow H$ is continuous on the half line $t \geq 0$, $f(0) = 0$ and*

$$\|f\|_{\alpha} = \sup_{t>0}(t^{-\alpha}\|f\|_H),$$

$$\|f\|_{L_2(0,a)} = \left\{\int_0^a f^2(t)dt\right\}^{\frac{1}{2}}.$$

Lemma 1 (Without proof [29]). *In $L_2([0,a])$ space, the self-adjoint compact operator $K\phi$ may be expressed as follows; $K\phi_n = \rho_n\phi_n$, $n > 0$, where the eigenvalues and eigenfunctions are denoted by ρ_n and ϕ_n, respectively.*

3. Applications and Special Cases

Many applications and special cases can be derived from Equation (1) and its corresponding Equation (4).

First application: The following IE is taken into consideration as a significant application in the Hilbert space $L_2(0,a]$.

$$\int_0^t G(\alpha,t,s)\gamma(s,\varphi(s))ds + \int_0^a k(t,z)\varphi(z)dz - \mu\varphi(t) = f(t), \tag{5}$$

with

$$G(\alpha,t,s) = \frac{1}{\Gamma(\alpha)}(t-s)^{\alpha-1}M(s), \quad 0 < z \leq a, t \in (0,a].$$

The equation in Formula (5) is referred to as an IE of the second kind when $\mu =$ constant $\neq 0$, but it is termed the nonlinear Fredholm Volterra IE of the first kind when $\mu = 0$.

In the contact problem and creep theory, the IE (5) emerges in the nonlinear situation $\gamma(t,\varphi(t))$ or the linear status where $\gamma(t,\varphi(t)) = \varphi(t)$. Some elastic material bases are related to the kernels $G(t,s), k(t,z)$ of Fredholm integral terms and Volterra integral terms, respectively. The deformation body's elastic characteristics are described by the value μ. The function $f(t)$ describes this body. Further details about the physical interpretation of Equation (5) and its applications, involving various techniques for solutions, are available in [29].

Second application: The Boltzmann fractional equation

$$G(t)\varphi(t) + \frac{\partial^{\alpha}}{\partial t^{\alpha}}\left(\int_0^1 k(t,z)\varphi(z)dz - \mu\varphi(t)\right) = 0, \tag{6}$$

is derived at $\gamma(t,\varphi(t)) = \varphi(t), f(t) = 0$.

Many applications can be derived from Equation (6) in astrophysics, quantum mechanics, and laser theory.

If the operator T is differentiable, for example, then

$$\left[\frac{d}{dt} - \mu\right]\varphi(t) - I_{0+}^{\alpha} M(t)\gamma(t,\varphi(t)) = f(t), \tag{7}$$

it represents an integro-differential equation of the first order and second kind.

Many special topics can be derived from the principal equation if the operator T is differentiable.

4. Existence and Uniqueness Solution

We shall demonstrate in this section that, under specific circumstances, there exists a unique solution to Equation (1).

The following presumptions are what we established for this goal:

(i) $M(s)$ has a continuous function on R^+ and fulfills

$$A(t) = \sup_{0 \le s \le t} \|M(s)\| < \infty, \quad t \in (0, a].$$

(ii) Characterize $\sigma(T)$ to represent the spectrum of the self-adjoint compact operator T and $\|.\|_t = \sup_{0 \le s \le t} \|.\|$.

(iii) Suppose that the interval $(0, a]$ contains a bounded function $f(t)$.

(iv) The established function $\gamma(t, \varphi(t))$ fulfills

(iv-a) $\|\gamma(t, \varphi(t))\|_t \le F_1 \|\varphi(t)\|_t$;.

(iv-b) $\|\gamma(t, \varphi_1(t)) - \gamma(t, \varphi_2(t))\|_t \le F_2 \|\varphi_1(t) - \varphi_2(t)\|_t$, where F_1 and F_2 are constants with $F > F_1$ and $F > F_2$.

We investigated the existence of a unique solution for NFrIE (1), so we considered

$$\Psi(t) = (T - \mu I)\varphi(t), \tag{8}$$

where I is a unit matrix.

Here, the resolvent, $R_\mu = (T - \mu I)^{-1}$, of T exists. Furthermore, the resolvent has bounds for any $\mu \in T(t)$, and the norm is defined by

$$N(t) = \sup_{\mu \in T(t)} \|R_\mu\|. \tag{9}$$

Theorem 1. *The NFrIE (1) has a convergence and unique solution according to the status*

$$FN(t)A(t)t^\alpha < \Gamma(\alpha + 1), \qquad F > F_2. \tag{10}$$

Furthermore, the norm of the solution to (1) is provided as

$$\|\varphi(t)\|_H \le \frac{\Gamma(\alpha+1)A(t)\|f\|_t}{[\Gamma(\alpha+1) - FN(t)A(t)t^\alpha]}.$$

Proof. First, to prove the convergence of Equation (1), assume that

$$\frac{d^\alpha}{dt^\alpha}[T - \mu I]\varphi(t) = f(t) + M(t)\gamma(t, \varphi(t)),$$

and assume that

$$[T - \mu I]\varphi(t) = \frac{1}{\Gamma(\alpha)} \int_0^t (t-s)^{\alpha-1} M(s)\gamma(s, \varphi(s))ds + \frac{1}{\Gamma(\alpha)} \int_0^t (t-s)^{\alpha-1} f(s)ds.$$

Let

$$(T - \mu I)\varphi(t) = \zeta(t). \tag{11}$$

Hence, we can rewrite Equation (1) in the form

$$\zeta(t)-\frac{1}{\Gamma(\alpha)}\int_0^t (t-s)^{\alpha-1}M(s)\gamma(s,R_\mu\zeta(s))ds=F(t),\qquad F(t)=\frac{1}{\Gamma(\alpha)}\int_0^t (t-s)^{\alpha-1}f(s)ds. \tag{12}$$

Write Equation (12) in the integral operator form

$$\zeta_n(t)=\frac{1}{\Gamma(\alpha)}\int_0^t (t-s)^{\alpha-1}M(s)\gamma(s,R_\mu\zeta_{n-1}(s))ds+F(t), \tag{13}$$

$$\zeta_{n-1}(t)=\frac{1}{\Gamma(\alpha)}\int_0^t (t-s)^{\alpha-1}M(s)\gamma(s,R_\mu\zeta_{n-2}(s))ds+F(t). \tag{14}$$

Then,

$$\zeta_n(t)-\zeta_{n-1}(t)=\frac{1}{\Gamma(\alpha)}\int_0^t (t-s)^{\alpha-1}M(s)\{\gamma(s,R_\mu\zeta_{n-1}(s))-\gamma(s,R_\mu\zeta_{n-2}(s))\}ds.$$

Let

$$\psi_n=\zeta_n(t)-\zeta_{n-1}(t)\Longrightarrow \zeta_n(t)=\sum_{i=0}^{n}\psi_i,\qquad \psi_0=\zeta_0(t)=F(t). \tag{15}$$

Hence, we obtain

$$\|\psi_n\|=\|\frac{1}{\Gamma(\alpha)}\int_0^t (t-s)^{\alpha-1}M(s)\{\gamma(s,R_\mu\zeta_{n-1}(s))-\gamma(s,R_\mu\zeta_{n-2}(s))\}ds\|\leq\frac{F_2N(t)A(t)t^\alpha}{\alpha\Gamma(\alpha)}\|\psi_{n-1}\|,$$

where $N(t)$ is given by Equation (9).

Hence, we obtain

$$\|\psi_n\|\leq\frac{F_2N(t)A(t)t^\alpha}{\alpha\Gamma(\alpha)}\|\psi_{n-1}\|.$$

Applying the Picard technique, followed by the conditions (i)–(v-a), Formula (15) produces

$$\|\psi_n\|_H\leq(\rho)^n\|F(t)\|,\quad \rho=\left(\frac{F_2N(t)A(t)t^\alpha}{\Gamma(\alpha+1)}\right). \tag{16}$$

This constraint causes the series $\{\psi_n\}$ to converge under condition (9), allowing us to write

$$\|\zeta(t)\|_H=\sum_{n=0}^{\infty}\|\psi_n(t)\|_H\leq\sum_{n=0}^{\infty}\|F\|(\rho)^n=\|F\|(1-\rho)^{-1},\rho<1. \tag{17}$$

The above inequality (17) is convergent under the condition (10). In addition, this sequence represents the general solution as $n\to\infty$. Hence, the convergence of the solution is proved. □

Second, to prove the uniqueness of the solution, we can write Equation (12) in the integral operator form

$$\zeta(t)=K\zeta(t)=L\zeta(t)+F(t), \tag{18}$$

where

$$L\zeta(t)=\frac{1}{\Gamma(\alpha)}\int_0^t (t-s)^{\alpha-1}M(s)\gamma(s,R_\mu\zeta(s))ds. \tag{19}$$

Then, we must prove the following two lemmas.

Lemma 2. *The integral operator $K\zeta(t)$, under the conditions (i)–(iv-a) maps the space H into itself.*

Proof. From (19), we can write

$$\|L\zeta(t)\| = \frac{1}{\Gamma(\alpha)}\| \int_0^t (t-s)^{\alpha-1} M(s)\gamma(s, R_\mu\zeta(s))ds\|.$$

After using the Cauchy–Schwartz inequality and conditions (i)–(iv-a), we obtain

$$\|L\zeta(t)\| \leq \rho\|\zeta(t)\|, \quad \rho = \left(\frac{F_2 N(t)A(t)t^\alpha}{\Gamma(\alpha+1)}\right). \tag{20}$$

From inequality (20), we deduce that the integral operator $L\zeta(t)$ is bounded.
After writing (18) in the norm form, and using inequality (20), we obtain

$$\|K\zeta(t)\| \leq \|\rho\zeta(t)\| + \|F(t)\|. \tag{21}$$

Inequality (21) shows that the operator K maps the ball S_σ into itself where the radius of the sphere $\sigma = \frac{\|F(t)\|}{1-\rho} > 0$. Hence, we have

$$\rho = \left(\frac{F_2 N(t)A(t)t^\alpha}{\Gamma(\alpha+1)}\right) < 1.$$

□

Lemma 3. *The integral operator $K\zeta(t)$ under the conditions (i)–(ivb) is continuous.*

Proof. Assuming $\zeta_1(t)$ and $\zeta_2(t)$ have two distinct solutions for Equation (12) in the Hilbert space, the continuity of the solution may be investigated. Thus, we can obtain

$$\|K(\zeta_1-\zeta_2)(t)\| = \frac{1}{\Gamma(\alpha)}\| \int_0^t (t-s)^{\alpha-1} M(s)\{\gamma(s, R_\mu\zeta_1(s)) - \gamma(s, R_\mu\zeta_2(s))\}ds\|.$$

After applying the Cauchy–Schwartz inequality and using conditions (i)–(iv-b), we have

$$\|K(\zeta_1-\zeta_2)(t)\| \leq \rho\|(\zeta_1-\zeta_2)(t)\|.$$

Hence, the integral operator K is continuous and, by extension, the integral operator L is also continuous. Moreover, since $\rho < 1$, then the integral operator K is a contraction mapping. □

5. The Stability of Error

To discuss the stability of error, assume we have a numerical solution in the form

$$\zeta_n(t) - \frac{1}{\Gamma(\alpha)}\int_0^t (t-s)^{\alpha-1} M(s)\gamma(s, R_\mu\zeta_n(s))ds = F_n(t). \tag{22}$$

Then, we have

$$R_n(t) - \frac{1}{\Gamma(\alpha)}\int_0^t (t-s)^{\alpha-1} M(s)[\gamma(s, R_\mu\zeta(s)) - \gamma(s, R_\mu\zeta_n(s))]ds = H_n(t), \tag{23}$$

where

$$R_n(t) = \zeta(t) - \zeta_n(t), \qquad H_n(t) = F(t) - F_n(t).$$

The above formula can be adapted, after applying the conditions (i–iii) and (iv-b) to take the form

$$\|R_n(t)\| \leq \left(\frac{F_2 N(t)A(t)t^\alpha}{\Gamma(\alpha+1)}\right)\|R_n(t)\| + \|H_n(t)\|. \tag{24}$$

The above inequality can be adapted in the form

$$\|R_n(t)\| \leq \frac{\|H_n(t)\|}{\left(1 - \frac{F_2 N(t) A(t) t^\alpha}{\Gamma(\alpha+1)}\right)} = \sigma. \tag{25}$$

Inequality (25) shows that the operator R maps the ball S_σ in the Hilbert space into itself. The radius of the sphere is

$$\sigma = \frac{\|H_n(t)\|}{\left(1 - \frac{F_2 N(t) A(t) t^\alpha}{\Gamma(\alpha+1)}\right)}.$$

Since $\sigma > 0, \|H_n(t)\| > 0$, then $\frac{F_2 N(t) A(t) t^\alpha}{\Gamma(\alpha+1)} < 1$.

Hence, the error $R_n(t)$ is bounded and stable according to the status $F_2 M(t) A(t) t^\alpha < \Gamma(\alpha+1)$.

Furthermore, for the continuity of the error, it is not difficult to prove that for the two functions of error R_{n_1}, R_{n_2}, we have

$$\|R_{n_1}(t) - R_{n_2}(t)\| \leq \left(\frac{F_2 N(t) A(t) t^\alpha}{\Gamma(\alpha+1)}\right) \|R_{n_1}(t) - R_{n_2}(t)\|.$$

The above inequality describes the continuity of the error. Moreover, the operator of error is a contraction according to the status $F_2 N(t) A(t) t^\alpha < \Gamma(\alpha+1)$, so the error has a unique representation.

6. Genocchi Polynomial Method

6.1. Properties of Genocchi Polynomials

The Genocchi numbers G_n and Genocchi polynomials (GPs) $G_n(t)$ are often described using the formulas for exponential generating $S(\zeta)$ and $S(\zeta, t)$, respectively, as follows:

$$S(\xi) = \frac{2\xi}{e^\xi + 1} = \sum_{q=0}^{\infty} G_q \frac{\xi^q}{q!}, \quad (|\xi| < \pi),$$

$$S(\xi, t) = \frac{2\xi e^{\xi t}}{e^\xi + 1} = \sum_{q=0}^{\infty} G_q(t) \frac{\xi^q}{q!}, \quad (|\xi| < \pi),$$

where $G_q(t)$ is GPs of order q. Also, GPs can be determined as follows:

$$G_q(t) = \sum_{k=0}^{q} \binom{q}{k} G_{q-k} t^k = 2B_q(t) - 2^{q+1} B_q(t), \tag{26}$$

and the following relationship yields the Genocchi number G_{q-k}:

$$G_q = 2(1 - 2^q) B_q,$$

where B_q is the famous Bernoulli number and $B_q(t)$ is Bernoulli polynomials.

The generating function for the Bernoulli numbers is

$$\frac{x}{e^x - 1} = \sum_{n=0}^{\infty} \frac{B_n}{n!} x^n = B_0 + xB_1 + \frac{x^2}{2!} B_2 + \ldots + \frac{x^n}{n!} B_n + \ldots.$$

Bernoulli numbers are defined as follows:

$$B_n^- = \sum_{k=0}^{n} \frac{1}{1+k} \sum_{j=0}^{k} (-1)^j \binom{k}{j} j^n, \quad \binom{k}{j} = \frac{k!}{j!(k-j)!},$$

$$B_n^+ = \sum_{k=0}^{n} \frac{1}{1+k} \sum_{j=0}^{k} (-1)^j \binom{k}{j} (j+1)^n,$$

$$B_m = 1 - \sum_{k=0}^{m-1} \binom{m}{k} \frac{B_k}{m-k+1}, \quad B_0 = 1.$$

The Bernoulli polynomials are defined by the generating function

$$G(x,t) = \frac{xe^{xt}}{e^x - 1} = \sum_{n=0}^{\infty} \frac{x^n}{n!} B_n(t).$$

The first few Bernoulli polynomials are defined as

$$B_0(t) = 1, \quad B_1(t) = t - \frac{1}{2}, \quad B_2(t) = t^2 - t + \frac{1}{6}, \quad B_3(t) = t^3 - \frac{3}{2}t^2 + \frac{1}{2}t,$$

$$B_4(t) = t^4 - 2t^3 + t^2 - \frac{1}{30}, \quad B_5(t) = t^5 - \frac{5}{2}t^4 + \frac{5}{3}t^3 - \frac{1}{6}t.$$

The initial group of GPs are listed as follows:

$$G_0(\xi) = 0, \quad G_1(\xi) = 1, \quad G_2(\xi) = 2\xi - 1, \quad G_3(\xi) = 3\xi^2 - 3\xi, \quad G_4(\xi) = 4\xi^3 - 6\xi^2 + 1, \quad G_5(\xi) = 5\xi^4 - 10\xi^3 + 5\xi.$$

Moreover,

$$\int_0^1 G_p(t)G_q(t)dt = \frac{2(-1)^p p!q!}{(p+q)!} G_{p+q}, \quad p,q \geq 1,$$

$$\frac{dG_p(t)}{dt} = pG_{p-1}, \quad p \geq 1,$$

$$G_p(1) + G_p(0) = 0, \quad p > 1,$$

$$G_p(t) = \int_0^t pG_{p-1}(t)dt + G_p, \quad p \geq 1.$$

Liu and Wang [30] studied certain identities of Bernoulli, Euler, and Genocchi polynomials using power sums and alternative power sums. For more details on the relations between Genocchi polynomials and Bernoulli polynomials, please see [30].

6.2. Function Approximation

The unknown function $\varphi(t)$ of Equation (5) can be expanded in terms of GPs as follows,

$$\varphi(t) \simeq \varphi_N(t) = \sum_{n=1}^{N} \varepsilon_n G_n(t), \tag{27}$$

where ε_n are unknown coefficients and $G_n(t)$ is GPs, which are defined by (26).

Substituting from (27) into (5) and using the collocation points

$$t_\ell = \frac{2\ell - 1}{2N}, \quad \ell = 1, 2, \ldots, N, \tag{28}$$

we obtain the next nonlinear system of algebraic equations

$$\int_0^{t_\ell} G(\alpha, t_\ell, s)\gamma\left(s, \sum_{n=1}^{N} \varepsilon_n G_n(s)\right)ds + \int_0^a k(t_\ell, z) \sum_{n=1}^{N} \varepsilon_n G_n(z)dz - \mu \sum_{n=1}^{N} \varepsilon_n G_n(t_\ell) = f(t_\ell). \tag{29}$$

By evaluating the unknown coefficients ε_n and applying the Newton iteration approach [31,32], we may resolve the nonlinear system (29).

Similarly, it is easy to obtain the approximate solution of Equations (6) and (7) in the same manner.

7. Numerical Examples

Two numerical examples with various values of α are provided in this section as an application of the findings above. All of the numerical computations were completed using the Maple 18 program.

Example 1. *Consider the NFrIE of the second kind:*

$$\frac{1}{\Gamma(\alpha)}\int_0^t (t-s)^{\alpha-1}s^5\varphi^2(s)ds+\int_0^1 t^2z^2\varphi(z)dz-\varphi(t)=f(t),\quad T\varphi(0)-\varphi(0)=0, \tag{30}$$

where the known function $f(t)$ is described by putting $\varphi(t)=t^4$ as an exact solution.

After using the value of the unknown function as an exact solution, we have f(t) in the form

$$\frac{\Gamma(10)}{\Gamma(10+\alpha)}t^{9+\alpha}-\frac{4}{5}t^2=f(t).$$

It is clear that the function $f(t)$ is bounded and continuous and $f(0)=0$.

In Example 1, we consider

$$\frac{d^\alpha}{dt^\alpha}\left\{\int_0^1 t^2z^2\varphi(z)dz-\varphi(t)\right\}=g(t)-\left(t^5\varphi^2(t)\right),$$

which is a special case from the general formula

$$\frac{d^\alpha}{dt^\alpha}(T\varphi(t)-\varphi(t))=g(t)-M(t)\gamma(\varphi(t)),\quad (T\varphi(0)-\varphi(0)=0),$$

where $T\varphi(t)-$ is an integral operator.

Now, applying GPM to Equation (30) and using the collocation point (28) for $N=5$, the approximate solution of Equation (30) can be collected in the next forms by varying the value of α:

$$\varphi(t)\simeq\varphi_5(t)=1.50\times10^{-8}-2.47\times10^{-7}t+0.1226\times10^{-5}t^2-0.2280\times10^{-7}t^3+1.000001458t^4,\alpha=0.00001,$$

$$\varphi(t)\simeq\varphi_5(t)=3\times10^{-10}-4\times10^{-9}t+1.4\times10^{-8}t^2-1.7\times10^{-8}t^3+1.000000007t^4,\quad \alpha=\frac{1}{5},$$

$$\varphi(t)\simeq\varphi_5(t)=3\times10^{-10}-4\times10^{-9}t+1.8\times10^{-8}t^2-2.6\times10^{-8}t^3+1.000000012t^4,\alpha=\frac{1}{4},$$

$$\varphi(t)\simeq\varphi_5(t)=2\times10^{-10}-3\times10^{-9}t+8\times10^{-9}t^2-6\times10^{-9}t^3+1.000000002t^4,\alpha=\frac{1}{3},$$

$$\varphi(t)\simeq\varphi_5(t)=1.0\times10^{-9}-7\times10^{-9}t+2.5\times10^{-8}t^2-3.8\times10^{-8}t^3+1.000000020t^4,\alpha=\frac{1}{2},$$

$$\varphi(t)\simeq\varphi_5(t)=1\times10^{-10}-3\times10^{-9}t^2+1.4\times10^{-8}t^3+0.9999999870t^4,\alpha=0.95.$$

Also, absolute errors are shown in Table 1 and Figures 1–8. A comparison between the exact solution and approximate solution of Example 1, $\alpha=1$ is shown in Figure 9.

Example 2. *Consider the integro-differential equation of the first order:*

$$\frac{d\varphi}{dt}-\varphi(t)-\frac{1}{\Gamma(\alpha)}\int_0^t (t-s)^{\alpha-1}s^5\varphi^3(s)ds=f(t),\qquad D\varphi(0)-\varphi(0)=0, \tag{31}$$

where the known function $f(t)$ is described by putting $\varphi(t)=t^2$ as an exact solution.

Table 1. Absolute errors (E) of Example 1.

t	E, α = 0.00001	E, $\alpha = \frac{1}{5}$	E, $\alpha = \frac{1}{4}$	E, $\alpha = \frac{1}{3}$	E, $\alpha = \frac{1}{2}$	E, α = 0.95
0	1.50×10^{-8}	3×10^{-10}	3×10^{-10}	2×10^{-10}	1×10^{-9}	1×10^{-10}
0.1	4.258×10^{-10}	2.37×10^{-11}	5.52×10^{-11}	2.58×10^{-11}	5.14×10^{-10}	8.27×10^{-11}
0.2	1.2672×10^{-9}	6.48×10^{-11}	3.12×10^{-11}	1.248×10^{-10}	3.28×10^{-10}	7.12×10^{-11}
0.3	1.4898×10^{-9}	4.23×10^{-11}	1.152×10^{-10}	1.258×10^{-10}	2.86×10^{-10}	1.027×10^{-10}
0.4	3.7648×10^{-9}	3.12×10^{-11}	2.232×10^{-10}	5.28×10^{-11}	2.8×10^{-10}	1.832×10^{-10}
0.5	4.1250×10^{-9}	1.125×10^{-10}	3.0×10^{-10}	7.50×10^{-11}	2.5×10^{-10}	2.875×10^{-10}
0.6	4.6368×10^{-9}	1.752×10^{-10}	3.192×10^{-10}	2.432×10^{-10}	1.84×10^{-10}	3.592×10^{-10}
0.7	1.08658×10^{-8}	2.097×10^{-10}	2.832×10^{-10}	4.422×10^{-10}	1.18×10^{-10}	3.107×10^{-10}
0.8	3.18768×10^{-8}	2.232×10^{-10}	2.232×10^{-10}	6.672×10^{-10}	1.36×10^{-10}	2.32×10^{-11}
0.9	8.02338×10^{-8}	2.397×10^{-10}	1.992×10^{-10}	9.182×10^{-10}	3.7×10^{-10}	6.533×10^{-10}
1	1.720×10^{-7}	3×10^{-10}	3×10^{-10}	1.2×10^{-9}	1×10^{-9}	1.9×10^{-9}

In Example 2, we consider

$$\frac{d^\alpha}{dt^\alpha}\left\{\frac{d\varphi(t)}{dt} - \varphi(t)\right\} = g(t) - \left(t^5\varphi^3(t)\right),$$

$$\frac{d^\alpha}{dt^\alpha}\{D\varphi(t) - \varphi(t)\} = g(t) - M(t)\gamma(\varphi(t)), \quad (D\varphi(0) - \varphi(0) = 0),$$

where $D\varphi(t)-$ is a differentiable operator.

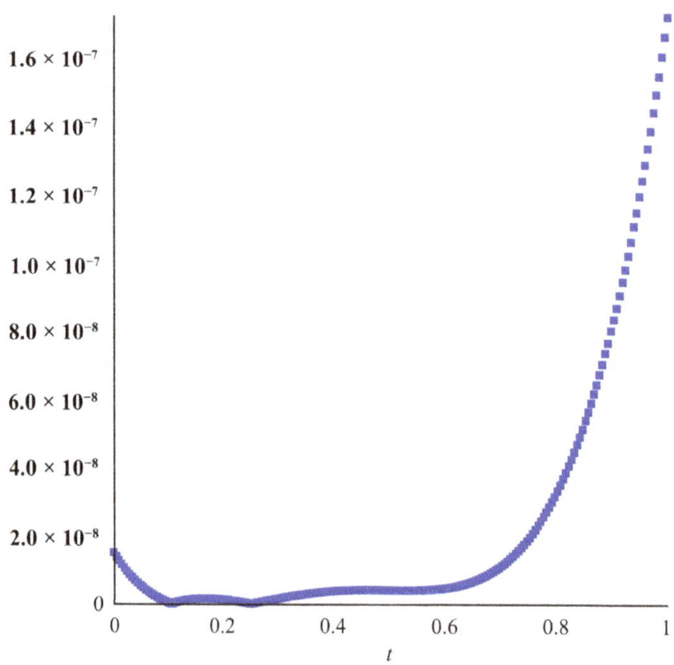

Figure 1. Absolute error of Example 1, $\alpha = 0.00001$.

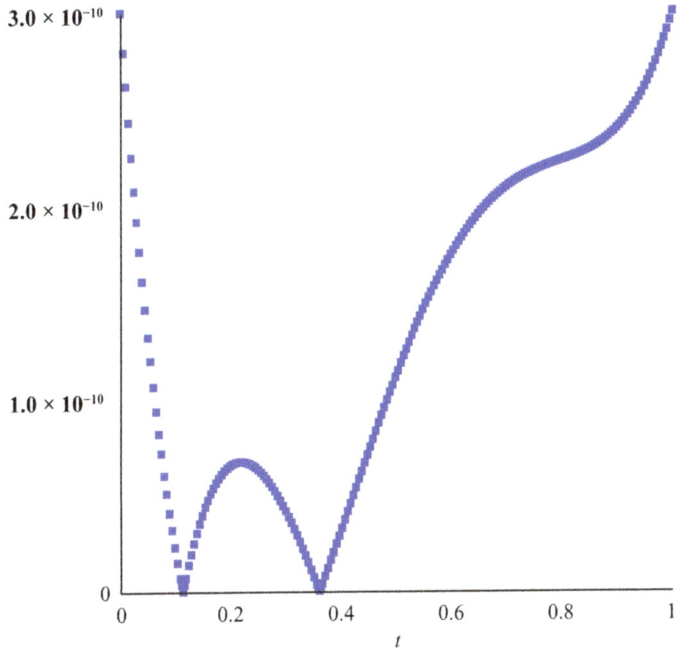

Figure 2. Absolute error of Example 1, $\alpha = \frac{1}{5}$.

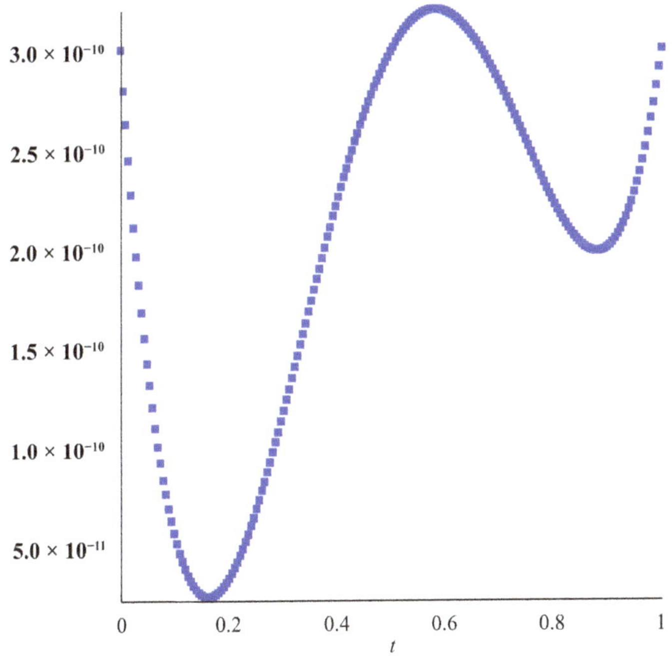

Figure 3. Absolute error of Example 1, $\alpha = \frac{1}{4}$.

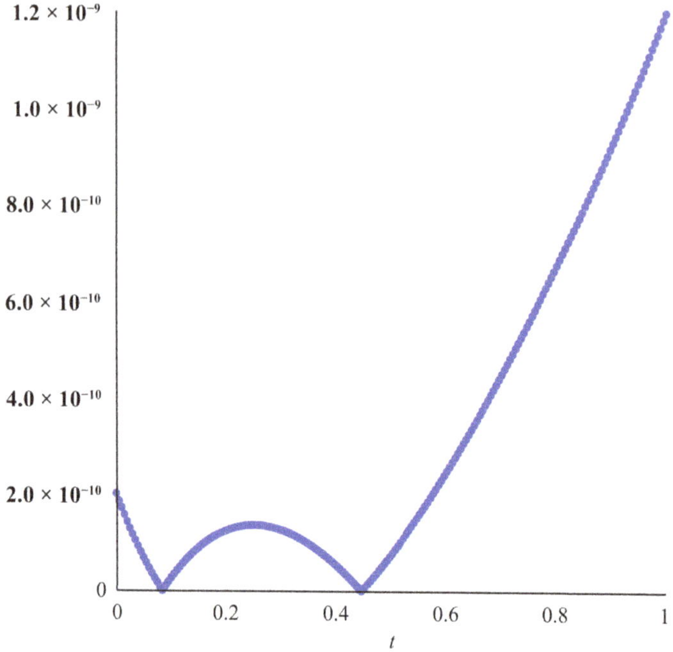

Figure 4. Absolute error of Example 1, $\alpha = \frac{1}{3}$.

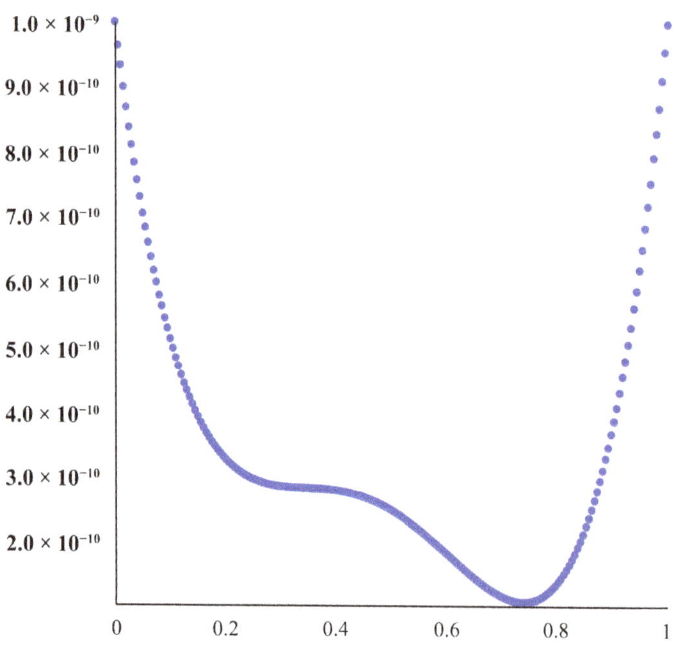

Figure 5. Absolute error of Example 1, $\alpha = \frac{1}{2}$.

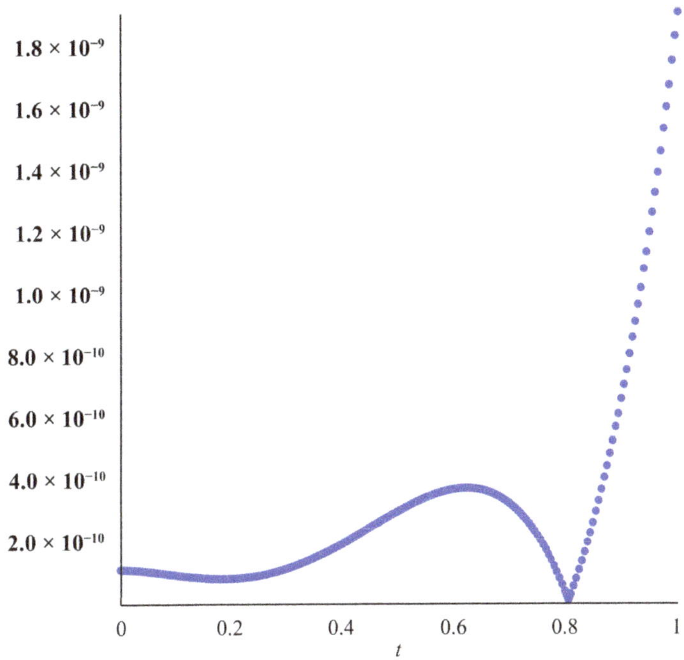

Figure 6. Absolute error of Example 1, $\alpha = 0.95$.

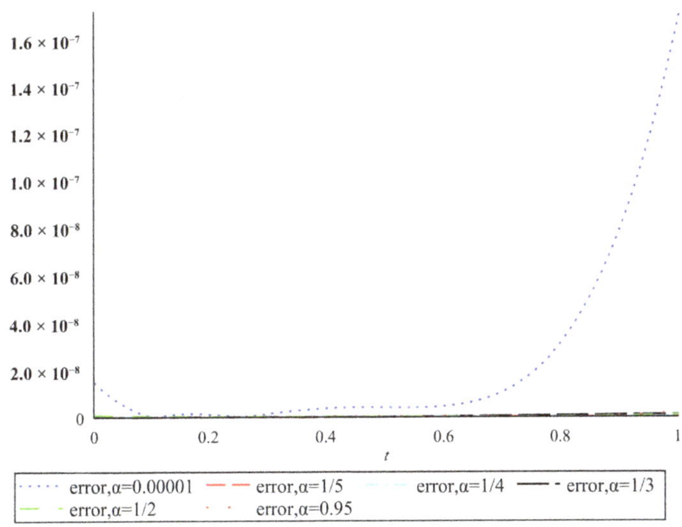

Figure 7. Comparison between the absolute errors of Example 1.

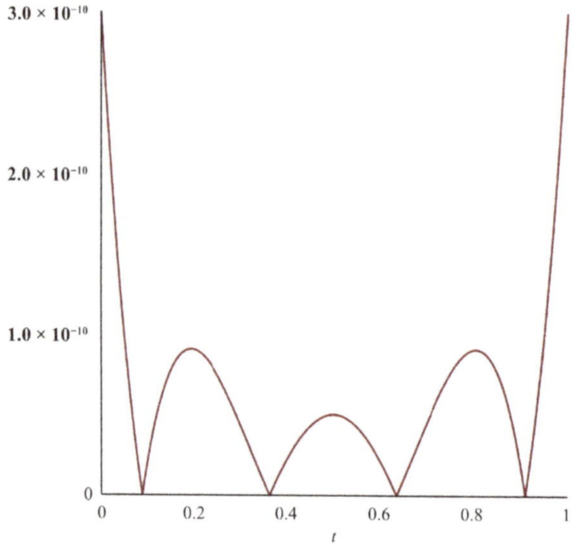

Figure 8. Absolute error of Example 1, $\alpha = 1$.

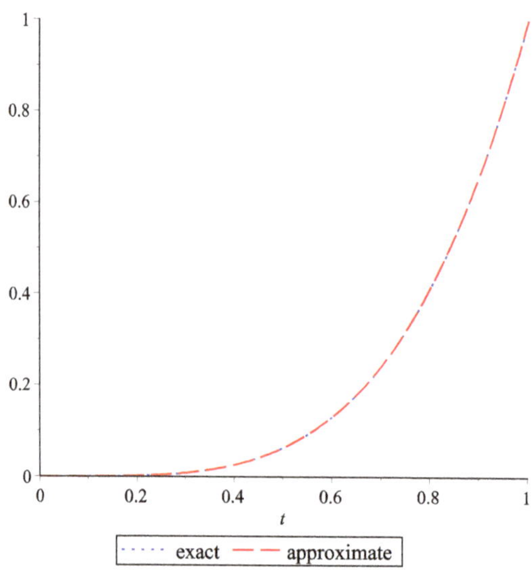

Figure 9. Comparison between exact solution and approximate solution of Example 1, $\alpha = 1$.

Similar to in Example 1, applying GPM to Equation (31) and using the collocation point (28) for $N = 5$, the approximate solution of Equation (31) can be collected in several different formats by varying the value of α:

$$\varphi(t) \simeq \varphi_5(t) = 5.78926571 \times 10^{-11} + 1.000000000 \times t^2 - 6.58944122 \times 10^{-10} t^3 + 8.452573750 \times 10^{-10} t^4, \alpha = 0.00001,$$

$$\varphi(t) \simeq \varphi_5(t) = 1.347313885 \times 10^{-10} + 1 \times 10^{-9} t + 1.000000000 \times t^2 - 9.198107540 \times 10^{-10} t^3$$
$$+7.293681540 \times 10^{-10} t^4, \quad \alpha = \frac{1}{5},$$

$$\varphi(t) \simeq \varphi_5(t) = 2.386554161 \times 10^{-11} + 0.9999999998 \times t^2 + 2.143753015 \times 10^{-10}t^3 - 5.945656755 \times 10^{-11}t^4, \alpha = \frac{1}{4},$$

$$\varphi(t) \simeq \varphi_5(t) = -1.486305278 \times 10^{-11} + 1.000000000 \times t^2 + 1.708136551 \times 10^{-10}t^3 - 1.151329331 \times 10^{-10}t^4, \alpha = \frac{1}{3},$$

$$\varphi(t) \simeq \varphi_5(t) = -5.026134044 \times 10^{-11} - 2 \times 10^{-10}t + 0.9999999999 \times t^2 + 2.168003276 \times 10^{-10}t^3 - 2.089228447 \times 10^{-10}t^4, \alpha = \frac{1}{2},$$

$$\varphi(t) \simeq \varphi_5(t) = -5.747226027 \times 10^{-10} - 4 \times 10^{-10}t + 0.9999999991t^2 + 1.193531824 \times 10^{-9}t^3 - 7.462111175 \times 10^{-10}t^4, \alpha = 0.95.$$

Absolute errors are shown in Table 2 and Figures 10–16.

Table 2. Absolute errors of Example 2.

t	E, α = 0.00001	E, $\alpha = \frac{1}{5}$	E, $\alpha = \frac{1}{4}$	E, $\alpha = \frac{1}{3}$	E, $\alpha = \frac{1}{2}$	E, α = 0.95
0	5.78×10^{-11}	1.34×10^{-10}	2.38×10^{-11}	1.48×10^{-11}	5.02×10^{-11}	5.74×10^{-10}
0.1	5.73×10^{-11}	2.33×10^{-10}	2.20×10^{-11}	1.47×10^{-11}	7.10×10^{-11}	6.22×10^{-10}
0.2	5.39×10^{-11}	3.28×10^{-10}	1.74×10^{-11}	1.36×10^{-11}	9.28×10^{-11}	6.82×10^{-10}
0.3	4.69×10^{-11}	4.15×10^{-10}	1.11×10^{-11}	1.11×10^{-11}	1.15×10^{-10}	7.49×10^{-10}
0.4	3.73×10^{-11}	4.94×10^{-10}	4.06×10^{-12}	6.87×10^{-12}	1.37×10^{-10}	8.21×10^{-10}
0.5	2.83×10^{-11}	5.65×10^{-10}	3.05×10^{-12}	7.07×10^{-13}	1.61×10^{-10}	8.97×10^{-10}
0.6	2.51×10^{-11}	6.30×10^{-10}	9.53×10^{-12}	7.11×10^{-12}	1.86×10^{-10}	9.77×10^{-10}
0.7	3.48×10^{-11}	6.94×10^{-10}	1.48×10^{-11}	1.60×10^{-11}	2.15×10^{-10}	1.06×10^{-9}
0.8	6.67×10^{-11}	7.62×10^{-10}	1.87×10^{-11}	2.54×10^{-11}	2.48×10^{-10}	1.16×10^{-9}
0.9	1.32×10^{-10}	8.42×10^{-10}	2.08×10^{-11}	3.41×10^{-11}	2.90×10^{-10}	1.28×10^{-9}
1	2.44×10^{-10}	9.44×10^{-10}	2.12×10^{-11}	4.08×10^{-11}	3.42×10^{-10}	1.42×10^{-9}

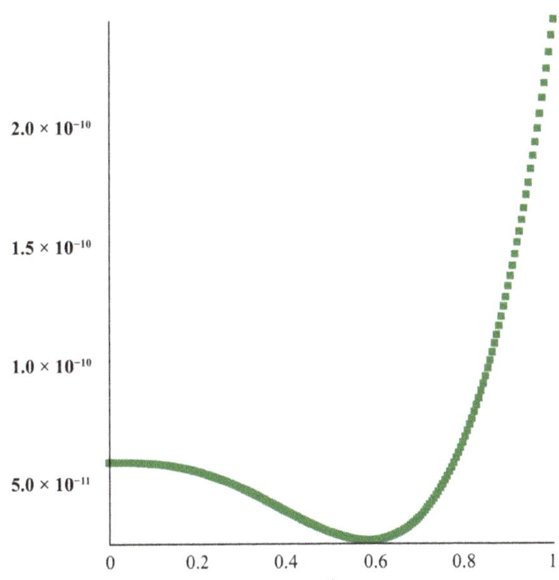

Figure 10. Absolute error of Example 2, $\alpha = 0.00001$.

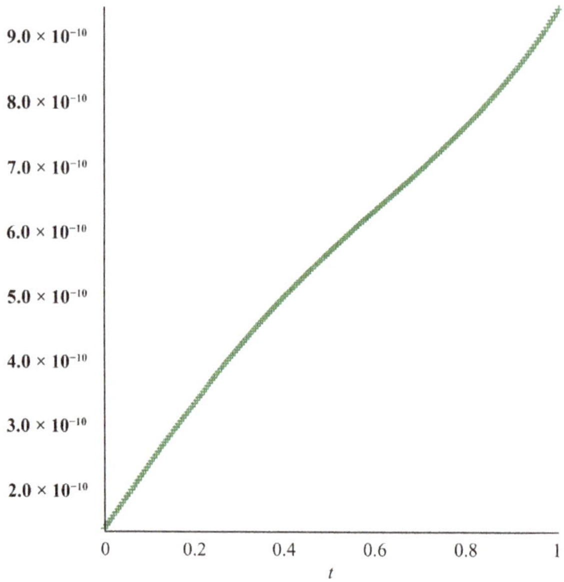

Figure 11. Absolute error of Example 2, $\alpha = \frac{1}{5}$.

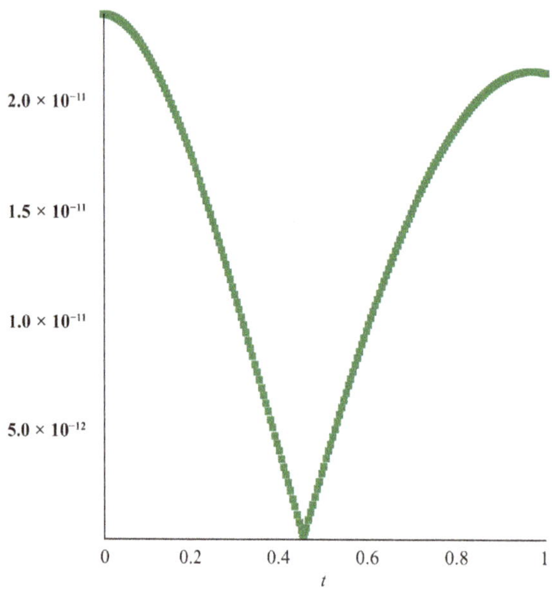

Figure 12. Absolute error of Example 2, $\alpha = \frac{1}{4}$.

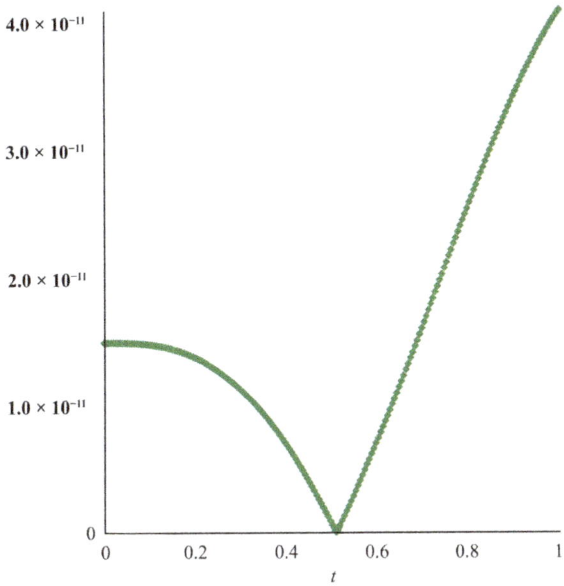

Figure 13. Absolute error of Example 2, $\alpha = \frac{1}{3}$.

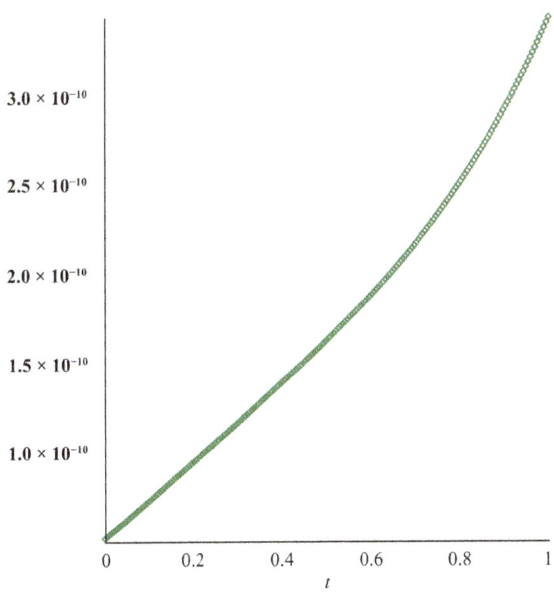

Figure 14. Absolute error of Example 2, $\alpha = \frac{1}{2}$.

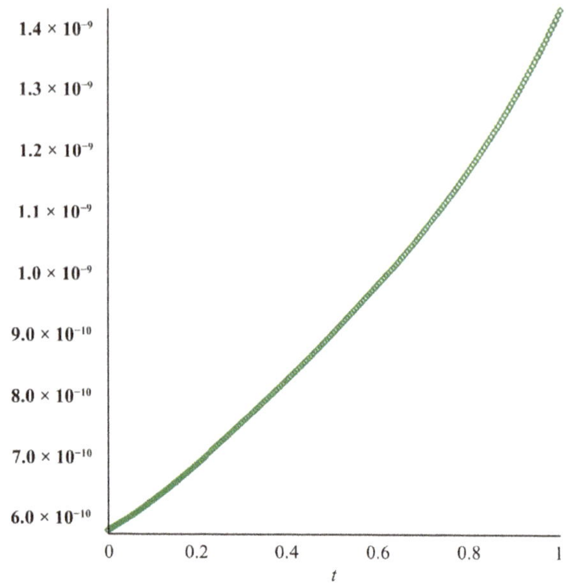

Figure 15. Absolute error of Example 2, $\alpha = 0.95$.

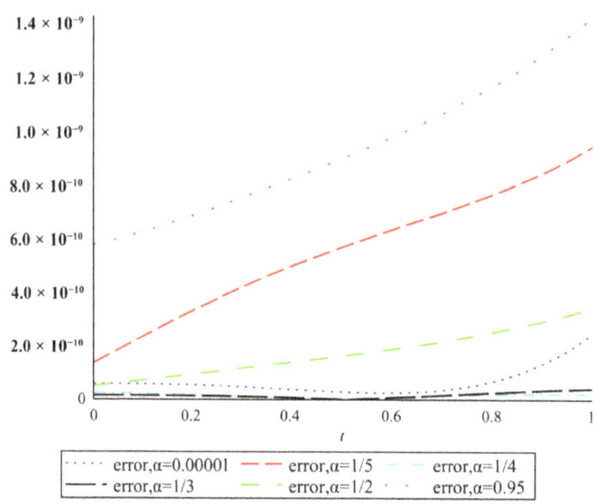

Figure 16. Comparison between the absolute errors of Example 2.

8. Discussion of the Results

Two numerical examples are presented: Example 1, applied to the first application Equation (5), and Example 2, applied to the integro-differential equation of the first order (7) when the operator T is differentiable. We note that

1. In Example 1, the largest error value at $\alpha = 0.00001, t = 1$ is 1.720×10^{-7} but at all different values of α at $t = 1$ the error values equal constant $\times 10^{-9}$ and constant at $\times 10^{-10}$; this is clear in Table 3.

Table 3. The largest error value of example 1.

t	E, α = 0.00001	E, $\alpha = \frac{1}{5}$	E, $\alpha = \frac{1}{4}$	E, $\alpha = \frac{1}{3}$	E, $\alpha = \frac{1}{2}$	E, α = 0.95
1	1.720×10^{-7}	3×10^{-10}	3×10^{-10}	1.2×10^{-9}	1×10^{-9}	1.9×10^{-9}

The lowest value for error at $\alpha = 0.00001, t = 0.1$ is 4.258×10^{-10} but at all different values of α at $t = 0.1$ the error values equal constant $\times 10^{-11}$, except at $\alpha = \frac{1}{2}$ where the error equals 5.14×10^{-10}; this is clear in Table 4.

Table 4. The lowest error value of example 1.

t	E, α = 0.00001	E, $\alpha = \frac{1}{5}$	E, $\alpha = \frac{1}{4}$	E, $\alpha = \frac{1}{3}$	E, $\alpha = \frac{1}{2}$	E, α = 0.95
0.1	4.258×10^{-10}	2.37×10^{-11}	5.52×10^{-11}	2.58×10^{-11}	5.14×10^{-10}	8.27×10^{-11}

In Figure 1, at $\alpha = 0.00001$ the absolute errors equal constant $\times 10^{-7}$ and constant $\times 10^{-8}$, while in Figure 2 at $\alpha = 0.2$ the absolute errors equal constant $\times 10^{-10}$, and also in Figure 3 at $\alpha = 0.25$ the absolute errors equal constant $\times 10^{-10}$ and constant $\times 10^{-11}$, while in Figures 4–6 at $\alpha = \frac{1}{3}, \frac{1}{2}, 0.95$ the absolute errors equal constant $\times 10^{-9}$ and constant $\times 10^{-10}$. A comparison between the absolute errors for different values of α of Example 1 are presented in Figure 7. Figure 8 represents the absolute errors, $\alpha = 1$, and the comparison between the exact solution and approximate solution is represented in Figure 9 at $\alpha = 1$.

2. In example 2, the lowest value for error at $\alpha = \frac{1}{3}, t = 0.5$ is 7.07×10^{-13}.

Table 5. The lowest error value of Example 2.

t	E, α = 0.00001	E, $\alpha = \frac{1}{5}$	E, $\alpha = \frac{1}{4}$	E, $\alpha = \frac{1}{3}$	E, $\alpha = \frac{1}{2}$	E, α = 0.95
0.5	2.83×10^{-11}	5.65×10^{-10}	3.05×10^{-12}	7.07×10^{-13}	1.61×10^{-10}	8.97×10^{10}

Table 6. The largest error value of Example 2.

t	E, α = 0.00001	E, $\alpha = \frac{1}{5}$	E, $\alpha = \frac{1}{4}$	E, $\alpha = \frac{1}{3}$	E, $\alpha = \frac{1}{2}$	E, α = 0.95
1	2.44×10^{-10}	9.44×10^{-10}	2.12×10^{-11}	4.08×10^{-11}	3.42×10^{-10}	1.42×10^{-9}

In Figure 10, at $\alpha = 0.00001$ the absolute errors equal constant $\times 10^{-10}$ and constant $\times 10^{-11}$, while in Figure 11 at $\alpha = 0.2$ the absolute errors equal constant $\times 10^{-10}$, while in Figure 12 at $\alpha = 0.25$ the absolute errors equal constant $\times 10^{-11}$ and constant $\times 10^{-12}$. In Figure 13 at $\alpha = \frac{1}{3}$ the absolute errors equal constant $\times 10^{-11}$, in Figure 14 at $\alpha = \frac{1}{2}$ the absolute errors equal constant $\times 10^{-10}$, while in Figure 15 at $\alpha = 0.95$ the absolute errors equal constant $\times 10^{-9}$ and constant $\times 10^{-10}$. A comparison between the absolute errors of different values of α in Example 2 are presented in Figure 16. In Example 2, we have demonstrated less error value in Table 5, also, we have demonstrated the largest error value in Table 6.

9. Conclusions

In the present paper, the Genocchi polynomial method was applied to solve NFrIEs of the second kind. The Genocchi polynomial method converted the problem to a system of algebraic equations. Finally, two numerical examples were discussed to demonstrate the applicability and validity of the method. We have shown the existence of a unique solution to the second sort of NFrIE in Hilbert space. Furthermore, we have explained and discussed proof of the stability of the error.

Future Works

We will study and extend the work using some different numerical methods and also some semi-analytical methods.

Author Contributions: Conceptualization, A.M.S.M.; Methodology, A.M.S.M., M.A.A. and D.S.M.; Software, R.T.M., A.M.S.M., M.A.A. and D.S.M.; Formal analysis, D.S.M.; Resources, R.T.M., A.M.S.M. and D.S.M.; Data curation, A.M.S.M.; Writing—original draft, R.T.M., A.M.S.M., M.A.A. and D.S.M.; Writing—review & editing, R.T.M., A.M.S.M., M.A.A. and D.S.M.; Supervision, A.M.S.M. and M.A.A.; Funding acquisition, R.T.M. All authors have read and agreed to the published version of the manuscript.

Funding: This research received no external funding.

Institutional Review Board Statement: Not applicable.

Informed Consent Statement: Not applicable.

Data Availability Statement: No new data were created or analyzed in this study. Data sharing is not applicable to this article.

Acknowledgments: The authors express their gratitude to the editor and the anonymous referees for their critical reading of the paper and their insightful remarks, which significantly enhanced it.

Conflicts of Interest: The authors declare no conflict of interest.

References

1. Hamdan, S.; Qatanani, N.; Daraghmeh, A. Numerical techniques for solving linear Volterra fractional integral equation. *J. Appl. Math.* **2019**, *2019*, 5678103. [CrossRef]
2. Pu, T.; Fasondini, M. The numerical solution of fractional integral equations via orthogonal polynomials in fractional powers. *Adv Comput Math.* **2023**, *49*, 1–40. [CrossRef]
3. Bekkouche, M.M.; Mansouri, I.; Azeb Ahmed, A.A. Numerical solution of fractional boundary value problem with caputo-fabrizio and its fractional integral. *J. Appl. Math. Comput.* **2022**, *68*, 4305–4316. [CrossRef] [PubMed]
4. Mahdy, A.M.S.; Nagdy, A.S.; Mohamed, D.S. Solution of fractional integro-differential equations using least squares and shifted legendre methods. *J. Appl. Math. Comput. Mech.* **2024**, *23*, 59–70. [CrossRef]
5. Alsulaiman, R.E.; Abdou, M.A.; Youssef, E.M.; Taha, M. Solvability of a nonlinear integro-differential equation with fractional order using the Bernoulli matrix approach. *AIMS Math.* **2023**, *8*, 7515–7534. [CrossRef]
6. Alharbi, F.M.; Zidan, A.M.; Naeem, M.; Shah, R.; Nonlaopon, K. Numerical investigation of fractional-order differential equations via φ-Haar-Wavelet method. *J. Funct. Spaces* **2021**, *2021*, 3084110. [CrossRef]
7. Mohamed, D.S.; Abdou, M.A.; Mahdy, A.M.S. Dynamical investigation and numerical modeling of a fractional mixed nonlinear partial integro-differential problem in time and space. *J. Appl. Anal. Comput.* **2024**, *14*, 1–21.
8. Zabidi, N.A.; Majid, Z.A.; Kilicman, A.; Ibrahim, Z.B. Numerical solution of fractional differential equations with Caputo derivative by using numerical fractional predict-correct technique. *Adv. Contin. Discret. Model.* **2022**, *2022*, 1–23. [CrossRef]
9. Yi, X.; Liu, C.; Cheong, H.T.; Teo, K.L.; Wang, S. A third-order numerical method for solving fractional ordinary differential equations. *AIMS Math.* **2024**, *9*, 21125–21143. [CrossRef]
10. Jassim, H.K.; Hussein, M.A. A New approach for solving nonlinear fractional ordinary differential equations. *Mathematics* **2023**, *11*, 1565. [CrossRef]
11. Mohamed, M.Z.; Yousif, M.; Hamza, A.E. Solving nonlinear fractional partial differential equations using the elzaki transform method and the homotopy perturbation method. In *Abstract and Applied Analysis*; John Wiley & Sons, Inc.: Hoboken, NJ, USA, 2022; pp. 1–9.
12. Rashid, S.; Ahmad, A.G.; Jarad, F.; Alsaadi, A. Nonlinear fractional differential equations and their existence via fixed point theory concerning to Hilfer generalized proportional fractional derivative. *AIMS Math.* **2022**, *8*, 382–403. [CrossRef]
13. Lydia, S.K.; Jancirani, M.M.; Anitha, A.A. Numerical solution of nonlinear fractional differential equations using kharrat-toma iterative method. *Nat. Volatiles Essent. Oils* **2021**, *8*, 9878–9890.
14. Yu, C. A Study on a nonlinear fractional differential equation. *Int. J. Nov. Res. Comput. Sci. Softw. Eng.* **2023**, *10*, 28–33.
15. Dehestani, H.; Ordokhani, Y.; Razzaghi, M. The novel operational matrices based on 2D-Genocchi polynomials: Solving a general class of variable-order fractional partial integro-differential equations. *Comput. Appl. Math.* **2020**, *39*, 259. [CrossRef]
16. Khajehnasiri, A.; Ebadian, A. Genocchi operational matrix method and their applications for solving fractional weakly singular two-dimensional partial Volterra integral equation. *UPB Sci. Bull. Ser. A* **2023**, *85*, 155–170.
17. Loh, J.R.; Phang, C.; Isah, A. Numerical solution for arbitrary domain of fractional integro-differential equation via the general shifted Genocchi polynomials. *J. Funct. Spaces* **2020**, *2023*, 5921425. [CrossRef]

8. Ebrahimzadeh, A.; Hashemizadeh, E. Optimal control of nonlinear Volterra integral equations with weakly singular kernels based on Genocchi polynomials and collocation method. *J. Nonlinear Math. Phys.* **2023**, *30*, 1758–1773. [CrossRef]
9. Hashemizadeh, E.; Ebadi, M.A.; Noeiaghdam, S. Matrix method by Genocchi polynomials for solving nonlinear Volterra integral equations with weakly singular kernels. *Symmetry* **2020**, *12*, 2105. [CrossRef]
0. Heydari, M.H.; Zhagharian, S. Genocchi polynomials for variable order time fractional Fornberg Whitham type equations. *Partial. Differ. Equ. Appl. Math.* **2023**, *8*, 100554. [CrossRef]
1. Loh, J.R.; Phang, C.; Isah, A. New operational matrix via Genocchi polynomials for solving Fredholm-Volterra fractional integro-differential equations. *Adv. Math. Phys.* **2017**, *2017*, 3821870. [CrossRef]
2. Seghiri, N.; Nadir, M.; Khirani, A. Operational matrices of Genocchi polynomials for solving high-order linear Fredholm integro-differential equations. *Math. Model. Eng. Probl.* **2024**, *11*, 2473–2482. [CrossRef]
3. Mustapha, D. Numerical solution of integro-differential equations of the second kind by using Galerkin's method with Genocchi polynomial. *J. Jilin Univ. (Eng. Technol. Ed.)* **2024**, *43*, 60–70.
4. Isah, A.; Phang, C. New operational matrix of derivative for solving non-linear fractional differential equations via Genocchi polynomials. *J. King Saud Univ. Sci.* **2019**, *31*, 1–7. [CrossRef]
5. Granos, A.; Dugundji, J. *Fixed Point Theorem*; Springer: New York, NY, USA, 2003.
6. Hilfar, R. *Application of Fractional Calculus in Physics*; World Scientific: Singapore, 2000.
7. Kilbas, A.A.; Srivastava, H.M.; Trullo, J.J. *Theory and Applications of Fractional Differential Equations*; Elsevier Science B.V.: Amsterdam, The Netherlands, 2006; North-Holland Mathematics Studies.
8. Abdou, M.A.; Salama, F.A. Fredholm-Volterra integral equation of the first kind and spectral relationships. *Appl. Math. Comput.* **2004**, *153*, 141–153. [CrossRef]
9. Abdou, M.A. Fredholm-Volterra integral equation of the first kind and contact problem. *Appl. Math. Comput.* **2002**, *125*, 177–193. [CrossRef]
0. Liu, H.; Wang, W. Some identities on the Bernoulli, Euler and Genocchi polynomials via power sums and alternate power sums. *Discret. Math.* **2009**, *309*, 3346–3363. [CrossRef]
1. Smith, G.D. *Numerical Solution of Partial Differential Equations: Finite Difference Methods*, 3rd ed.; Oxford University Press: Oxford, UK, 1985.
2. Morton, K.W.; Mayers, D.F. *Numerical Solution of Partial Differential Equations*; Cambridge University Press: Cambridge, UK, 1994.

fractal and fractional

MDPI

Article

First Derivative Approximations and Applications

Yuri Dimitrov [1,2,*], Slavi Georgiev [2,3] and Venelin Todorov [2]

1 Department of Mathematics, Physics and Informatics, University of Forestry, 1756 Sofia, Bulgaria
2 Department of Informational Modeling, Institute of Mathematics and Informatics, Bulgarian Academy of Sciences, 1113 Sofia, Bulgaria; sggeorgiev@math.bas.bg (S.G.); vtodorov@math.bas.bg (V.T.)
3 Department of Applied Mathematics and Statistics, University of Ruse, 7017 Ruse, Bulgaria
* Correspondence: yuri.dimitrov@ltu.bg; Tel.: +359-2-979-28-40

Abstract: In this paper, we consider constructions of first derivative approximations using the generating function. The weights of the approximations contain the powers of a parameter whose modulus is less than one. The values of the initial weights are determined, and the convergence and order of the approximations are proved. The paper discusses applications of approximations of the first derivative for the numerical solution of ordinary and partial differential equations and proposes an algorithm for fast computation of the numerical solution. Proofs of the convergence and accuracy of the numerical solutions are presented and the performance of the numerical methods considered is compared with the Euler method. The main goal of constructing approximations for integer-order derivatives of this type is their application in deriving high-order approximations for fractional derivatives, whose weights have specific properties. The paper proposes the construction of an approximation for the fractional derivative and its application for numerically solving fractional differential equations. The theoretical results for the accuracy and order of the numerical methods are confirmed by the experimental results presented in the paper.

Keywords: fractional derivative; approximation; numerical solution; convergence

1. Introduction

The fractional derivatives are a generalization of the integer-order derivatives and provide powerful tools for analyzing functions and systems. Many of the methods for studying integer-order derivatives also apply to fractional derivatives. The Caputo fractional derivative of order α, where $0 < \alpha < 1$, is defined as

$$f^{(\alpha)}(x) = D^{\alpha} f(x) = \frac{1}{\Gamma(1-\alpha)} \int_l^x \frac{f'(\xi)}{(x-\xi)^{\alpha}} d\xi.$$

Fractional calculus is an active research area and has been used to describe phenomena that cannot be adequately explained by integer-order derivatives. Fractional differential equations have found applications in various fields, including physics, engineering, chemistry and biology [1–6]. Numerical methods are used to analyze models that involve fractional differential equations. The finite difference schemes for solving numerically fractional differential equations use approximations of the fractional derivative. Consider the interval $[l, x]$ and a uniform grid with a step size of $h = (x-l)/N$, where N is a positive integer. Denote $x_n = l + nh$ and $f_n = f(x_n)$. The approximations of fractional derivative $f_n^{(\alpha)}$ have the form $h^{-\alpha} \sum_{k=0}^{n} \sigma_k^{(\alpha)} f_{n-k}$, where $\sigma_k^{(\alpha)}$ are the weights of the approximation and $n = 1, \cdots, N$. The generating function of an approximation of the fractional derivative is defined as $G(x) = \sum_{k=0}^{\infty} \sigma_k^{(\alpha)} x^k$. Two important approximations of the fractional derivative are the Grünwald difference approximation and the L1 approximation. The Grünwald difference approximation of the fractional derivative of order α has a first-order accuracy and a generating function $(1-x)^{\alpha}$. The Grünwald approximation is a second-order shifted approximation of the fractional derivative with a shift parameter $\alpha/2$. L1 approximation has an order $2-\alpha$ and a generating function $(x-1)^2\mathrm{Li}_{\alpha-1}(x)/(x\Gamma(2-\alpha))$. Their weights satisfy

$$\sigma_0^{(\alpha)} > 0, \quad \sigma_1^{(\alpha)} < \sigma_2^{(\alpha)} < \cdots < \sigma_{m-1}^{(\alpha)} < 0, \quad \sum_{k=0}^{m} \sigma_k^{(\alpha)} = 0. \tag{1}$$

The properties of the weights of an approximation of the fractional derivative (1) allow for an effective analysis of the convergence of numerical schemes for fractional differential equations [7–10]. The construction of approximations for the fractional derivative and schemes for numerically solving fractional differential equations is an area of ongoing research. Second-order approximations of the fractional derivative are constructed by Arshad et al. [11], Nasir and Nafa [12]. Approximations of order $3-\alpha$ are constructed by Alikhanov [13], Gao et al. [14], Xing and Yan [15]. High-order approximations and numerical schemes for fractional differential equations are studied in [16–20]. Implicit ADI schemes for fractional differential equations are constructed by Nasrollahzadeh and Hosseini [21], Wang et al. [22]. Denote $s_n = \sum_{k=1}^{n-1} k^{-\alpha} - n^{1-\alpha}/(1-\alpha) - \zeta(\alpha)$. In [23], we obtain an approximation of the fractional derivative and its asymptotic formula

$$\frac{1}{2\Gamma(1-\alpha)h^{\alpha}} \sum_{k=0}^{m} \omega_k^{(\alpha)} f_{n-k} = f_m^{(\alpha)} + \frac{\zeta(\alpha)}{\Gamma(1-\alpha)} f_n' h^{1-\alpha} + O(h^{2-\alpha}), \tag{2}$$

where

$$\omega_0^{(\alpha)} = 1, \quad \omega_1^{(\alpha)} = 2^{-\alpha}, \quad \omega_k^{(\alpha)} = (k+1)^{-\alpha} - (k-1)^{-\alpha},$$
$$\sigma_{m-1}^{(\alpha)} = -(n-1)^{-\alpha} + 2s_n, \quad \sigma_n^{(\alpha)} = -(n-2)^{-\alpha} - 2s_n.$$

Approximation (2) has an order $1-\alpha$ and a generating function $(1-x^2)\mathrm{Li}_{-\alpha}(x)/(2x)$. The main class of approximations of integer-order derivatives is the finite-difference approximations, which have first-order accuracy and second order at the midpoint. Finite-difference approximations are local numerical differentiation methods and are a special case of the Grünwald difference approximation, where the order is an integer. Methods for global numerical differentiation are studied in [24,25]. The methods for constructing approximations of fractional derivatives using a generating function also apply to the construction of integer-order derivative approximations. In [26,27], we construct approximations of the first and second derivatives whose generating functions are transformations of the exponential and logarithmic functions. In [26,28], we construct second-order approximations of the fractional derivative using the asymptotic formula of the L1 approximation and second derivative approximations. In this paper, we apply the method from [26,27] for constructing an approximation of the first derivative and its second-order asymptotic formula

$$\frac{1-a}{h}\left(f_n - (1-a)\sum_{k=1}^{n-2} a^{k-1} f_{n-k} - \frac{a^{n-2}(1-2a)}{1-a} f_1 - \frac{a^{n-1}}{1-a} f_0\right) = f_n' - \frac{C_a}{2} f_n'' h + O(h^2), \tag{3}$$

where the coefficient C_a has a value $C_a = (1+a)/(1-a)$. Approximation (3) has a generating function $G(x) = (1-a)(1-x)/(1-ax)$ and is a global approximation of the first derivative. The structure of the paper is as follows. In Section 2, we construct approximation (3) and the following first-order approximation:

$$\frac{1-a}{h}\left(f_n - (1-a)\sum_{k=1}^{n-1} a^{k-1} f_{n-k} - a^{n-1} f_0\right) = (1-a^n) f_n' + O(h). \tag{4}$$

The weights of approximations (3) and (4) satisfy conditions (1). We consider the application of these approximations for numerically solving an ordinary differential equation and propose an algorithm that computes the numerical solutions using $\mathcal{O}(N)$ arithmetic operations. The computational time and accuracy of the numerical methods are compared with Euler's method. In Section 3, we derive estimates for the errors of approximations (3) and (4) and the corresponding numerical solutions. In Section 4, we construct numerical solutions for first-order ODEs which use approximation (3) of the first derivative. We determine the values of the parameter a such that the numerical methods achieve an arbitrary order of accuracy in the interval $(0, 2]$. In Section 5, we construct a finite difference scheme for the heat diffusion equation which uses approximation (3) for the first partial derivative. The stability and convergence of the scheme are analyzed. In Section 6, we consider an application of approximation (3) for constructing an approximation of the Caputo fractional derivative. By applying approximation (3) with the parameter value $\alpha/2$ to the first derivative f'_n in the asymptotic Formula (2), we obtain the following approximation of a fractional derivative of order $2-\alpha$.

$$\frac{1}{2\Gamma(1-\alpha)h^\alpha}\sum_{k=0}^{n}\sigma_k^{(\alpha)} f_{n-k} = f_n^{(\alpha)} + \mathcal{O}(h^{2-\alpha}), \tag{5}$$

where

$$\sigma_0^{(\alpha)} = 1-(2-\alpha)\zeta(\alpha), \quad \sigma_1^{(\alpha)} = 2^{-\alpha} + 2(1-\alpha/2)^2\zeta(\alpha),$$

$$\sigma_k^{(\alpha)} = (k+1)^{-\alpha} - (k-1)^{-\alpha} + 2(1-\alpha/2)^2(\alpha/2)^{k-1}\zeta(\alpha), \qquad (2 \le k \le n-2),$$

$$\sigma_{n-1}^{(\alpha)} = -(n-1)^{-\alpha} + 2s_n + 2(1-\alpha)(\alpha/2)^{n-2}\zeta(\alpha),$$

$$\sigma_n^{(\alpha)} = -(n-2)^{-\alpha} - 2s_n + 2(\alpha/2)^{n-1}\zeta(\alpha).$$

We prove that the weights of approximation (5) satisfy properties (1). The numerical experiments presented in the paper validate the theoretical results on the accuracy and error of the numerical methods. The main contributions of the paper are the constructions of approximations (3) and (5). The examples in the paper demonstrate that these approximations can be used to construct efficient methods for the numerical solution of differential and fractional differential equations. The method for deriving an approximation (3) can be used to derive approximations of the second derivative and higher-order derivatives [26]. A question for future work is to apply these approximations to the construction of high-order approximations of the fractional derivative that have properties (1) of the weights.

2. Asymptotic Formula

In this section, we use the method from [26,27] to construct an approximation for the first derivative and its asymptotic formula by specifying the generating function of the approximation. Let

$$G(x) = \frac{(1-a)(1-x)}{1-ax},$$

where $|a| < 1$. The generating function $G(x)$ has properties $G(1) = 0, G'(1) = -1$. Denote

$$H(x) = G(e^{-x}) = \frac{(1-a)(1-e^{-x})}{1-ae^{-x}}.$$

The functions $G(x)$ and $H(x)$ have Maclaurin series

$$G(x) = (1-a) - (1-a)^2\sum_{k=1}^{\infty} a^{k-1}x^k, \tag{6}$$

$$H(x) = x - \frac{(1+a)x^2}{2(1-a)} + \frac{(1+4a+a^2)x^3}{6(1-a)^2} + \mathcal{O}(x^4). \tag{7}$$

Consider a uniform grid on the interval $[0, X]$ with step size of $h = X/N$ where N is a positive integer and let $f_n = f(x_n) = f(nh)$. From (6) and (7), we obtain

$$\mathcal{A}_1[f_n] = \frac{1-a}{h}\left(f_n - (1-a)\sum_{k=1}^{n-1} a^{k-1} f_{n-k}\right) = f_n' - \frac{1+a}{2(1-a)} f_n'' h + \mathcal{O}(h^2), \quad (8)$$

where the function $f \in C^2[0, X]$ and satisfies the condition $f(0) = 0$. Now, we extend asymptotic Formula (8) to all functions in the class $C^2[0, X]$. Let

$$\mathcal{A}_2[f_n] = \frac{1-a}{h}\left(f_n - (1-a)\sum_{k=1}^{n-1} a^{k-1} f_{n-k} + c_0 f_0\right) = f_n' + \mathcal{O}(h),$$

where $\mathcal{A}_2$ satisfies the condition $\mathcal{A}_2[1] = 0$.

$$1 - (1-a)\sum_{k=1}^{n-1} a^{k-1} + c_0 = 0, \qquad 1 - (1 - a^{n-1}) + c_0 = 0.$$

The coefficient c_0 has a value $c_0 = -a^{n-1}$ and

$$\mathcal{A}_2[f_n] = \frac{1-a}{h}\left(f_n - (1-a)\sum_{k=1}^{n-1} a^{k-1} f_{n-k} - a^{n-1} f_0\right) = f_n' + \mathcal{O}(h). \quad (9)$$

Asymptotic Formula (9) holds for all functions $f \in C^2[0, X]$. When the parameter a is zero, $\mathcal{A}_2$ is a first-order backward difference approximation of the first derivative. We will consider an application of Formula (9) for the numerical solution of an ordinary differential equation and compare the performance of the method with the Euler method.

Example 1. *Consider the following first-order ordinary differential equation*

$$y'(x) = F(x), \qquad y(0) = y_0, \qquad x \in [0, X]. \quad (10)$$

By approximating the first derivative at the point x_n using a first-order backward difference approximation, we obtain

$$\frac{y_n - y_{n-1}}{h} = F_n + \mathcal{O}(h).$$

The numerical solution of Equation (10) satisfies $u_0 = y_0$ and

$$u_n = u_{n-1} + hF_n. \quad (11)$$

The value of u_n is computed with one addition and one multiplication, assuming that the values F_n of the function F at the nodes x_n of the grid are known. The total number of arithmetic operations of the Euler method is $2N$. Note that in many cases, the computational time required to evaluate the values of F_n exceeds the time needed to compute the numerical solution (11). Now, we construct the numerical solution of Equation (10), which uses asymptotic Formula (9). By substituting y_n' with $\mathcal{A}_2$, we find

$$\frac{1-a}{h}\left(y_n - (1-a)\sum_{k=1}^{n-1} a^{k-1} y_{n-k} - a^{n-1} y_0\right) = F_n + \mathcal{O}(h). \quad (12)$$

The numerical solution obtained from (12) by truncating the error term satisfies

$$\frac{1-a}{h}\left(u_n - (1-a)\sum_{k=1}^{n-1} a^{k-1} u_{n-k} - a^{n-1} u_0\right) = F_n.$$

The sequence $\{u_n\}_{n=0}^N$ has initial conditions $u_0 = y_0, u_1 = u_0 + hF_1$ and satisfies

$$u_n = \frac{hF_n}{1-a} + (1-a)\sum_{k=1}^{n-1} a^{k-1}u_{n-k} + a^{n-1}u_0. \tag{13}$$

Numerical solution (11) is a special case of (13) when the parameter a is zero, $a = 0$. Direct computation of numerical solution (13) using the above formula requires $\mathcal{O}(N^2)$ operations. The weights of $\mathcal{A}_2$ consist of powers of the parameter a, which allows us to compute (13) with $\mathcal{O}(N)$ operations. The sequence u_n satisfies

$$u_n = \frac{hF_n}{1-a} + S_n,$$

where

$$S_n = (1-a)\sum_{k=1}^{n-1} a^{k-1}u_{n-k} + a^{n-1}u_0.$$

The sequence S_n satisfies

$$S_n = (1-a)u_{n-1} + a\left((1-a)\sum_{k=2}^{n-1} a^{k-2}u_{n-k} + a^{n-2}u_0\right),$$

$$S_n = (1-a)u_{n-1} + aS_{n-1}.$$

Both sequences S_n and u_n are computed with $\mathcal{O}(N)$ operations. The pseudocode for calculating the numerical solution (13) is given below.

$A = 1-a;\ H = h/A;\ S = u_0 = y_0;\ u_1 = u_0 + h * F_1;$
for n from 2 to N
$\quad S = A * u_{n-1} + a * S;$
$\quad u_n = H * F_n + S;$

The algorithm uses four operations in Step 1 and five operations for calculating each value of the sequence u_n for $n = 2, \cdots, N$ in Step 2. The total number of operations for computation of the numerical solution (13) is $5N-1$. Consider the ordinary differential equation

$$y'(x) = e^x, \qquad y(0) = 1, \tag{14}$$

where $x \in [0,1]$. The numerical results for the error and order of numerical solutions (11) and (13) of Equation (14) are given in Table 1. The abbreviation NS for numerical solution is used. The calculation of the numerical solutions was performed using Mathematica 13 software. Although Formula (9) holds asymptotically, the experimental results in Table 1 suggest that numerical method (11) has first-order accuracy. This fact is proven in the next section. The time for computation of the values of $F_n = e^{nh}$ is greater than the computational time of the numerical solutions. We observed a small difference in the computational time of the numerical solutions in Table 1, which is a fraction of a second. The finite geometric series satisfies

$$\sum_{k=0}^{n-1} a^k = \frac{1-a^n}{1-a}. \tag{15}$$

By differentiating (15) twice, we find

$$\sum_{k=1}^{n-1} ka^{k-1} = \frac{1+(n-1)a^n - na^{n-1}}{(1-a)^2}, \tag{16}$$

$$\sum_{k=1}^{n-1} k^2 a^{k-1} = \frac{1+a-n^2a^{n-1}+(2n^2-2n-1)a^n-(n-1)^2a^{n+1}}{(1-a)^3}. \qquad (17)$$

Now, we construct an approximation of the first derivative in the form

$$\mathcal{A}_3[f_n] = \frac{1-a}{h}\left(f_n-(1-a)\sum_{k=1}^{n-2} a^{k-1}f_{n-k}-a^{n-2}c_1f_1-a^{n-1}c_0f_0\right) = f'_n + \mathcal{O}(h)$$

which satisfies the conditions $\mathcal{A}_3[1]=0$ and $\mathcal{A}_3[x]=1$. The values of the coefficients c_0 and c_1 are determined from the two conditions.

$$\mathcal{A}_3[1] = \frac{1-a}{h}\left(1-(1-a)\sum_{k=1}^{n-2} a^{k-1}-a^{n-2}c_1-a^{n-1}c_0\right) = 0,$$

$$1-(1-a^{n-2})-a^{n-2}c_1-a^{n-1}c_0=0.$$

The numbers c_0 and c_1 satisfy

$$c_1+ac_0=1. \qquad (18)$$

$$\mathcal{A}_3[x] = (1-a)\left(n-(1-a)\sum_{k=1}^{n-2} a^{k-1}(n-k)-a^{n-2}c_1\right) = 1.$$

Using Formulas (15) and (16), we obtain

$$\sum_{k=1}^{n-2}(n-k)a^{k-1} = -\frac{1+a^{n-2}-2a^{n-1}-n+na}{(1-a)^2}.$$

Then,

$$\begin{aligned}&(1-a)n+1+a^{n-2}-2a^{n-1}-n+na-(1-a)a^{n-2}c_1=1,\\ &a^{n-2}-2a^{n-1}-(1-a)a^{n-2}c_1=1, \qquad (1-a)c_1=1-2a.\end{aligned} \qquad (19)$$

From (18) and (19), we find

$$c_1=\frac{1-2a}{1-a}, \qquad c_0=\frac{1}{1-a}.$$

Approximation $\mathcal{A}_3$ has the form

$$\mathcal{A}_3[f_n] = \frac{1-a}{h}\left(f_n-(1-a)\sum_{k=1}^{n-2} a^{k-1}f_{n-k}-\frac{a^{n-2}(1-2a)}{1-a}f_1-\frac{a^{n-1}}{1-a}f_0\right) = f'_n+\mathcal{O}(h) \quad (20)$$

and holds for every value of n, where $n=2,\cdots,N$. Now, we construct the numerical solution of Equation (10), which uses approximation $\mathcal{A}_3$ for the first derivative. By replacing the first derivative y'_n with $\mathcal{A}_3$, we obtain

$$\frac{1-a}{h}\left(u_n-(1-a)\sum_{k=1}^{n-2} a^{k-1}u_{n-k}-\frac{a^{n-2}(1-2a)}{1-a}u_1-\frac{a^{n-1}}{1-a}u_0\right) = F_n,$$

$$u_n = \frac{hF_n}{1-a}+(1-a)\sum_{k=1}^{n-2} a^{k-1}u_{n-k}+\frac{a^{n-2}(1-2a)}{1-a}u_1+\frac{a^{n-1}}{1-a}u_0. \qquad (21)$$

Numerical solution (21) has initial conditions $u_0=y_0, u_1=u_0+hF_1, u_2=u_1+hF_2$. The algorithm and pseudocode for computing the numerical solution (21) are given below:

$$u_n = \frac{hF_n}{1-a}+S_n,$$

where

$$S_n = (1-a)\sum_{k=1}^{n-1} a^{k-1}u_{n-k} + a^{n-1}u_0.$$

The sequence S_n satisfies

$$S_n = (1-a)u_{n-1} + a\left((1-a)\sum_{k=2}^{n-1} a^{k-2}u_{n-k} + a^{n-2}u_0\right),$$

$$S_n = (1-a)u_{n-1} + aS_{n-1}.$$

The sequences S_n and u_n are calculated in $\mathcal{O}(N)$ time with the following pseudocode.

$u_0 = y_0;\ u_1 = u_0 + h * F_1;\ u_2 = u_1 + h * F_2;$
$A = 1 - a,\ H = h/A;\ S = u_1 + a * (u_0 - u_1)/A;$
for n from 2 to N
    $S = A * u_{n-1} + a * S;$
    $u_n = H * F_n + S;$

The algorithm uses ten operations in Step 1 and five operations for calculating each value of the sequence u_n in Step 2 for $n = 3, \cdots, N$. The total number of operations for calculating numerical solution (21) is $5N$.

From (8), approximation $\mathcal{A}_3$ has a second-order asymptotic expansion formula

$$\frac{1-a}{h}\left(y_n - (1-a)\sum_{k=1}^{n-2} a^{k-1}y_{n-k} - \frac{a^{n-2}(1-2a)}{1-a}y_1 - \frac{a^{n-1}}{1-a}y_0\right) = f'_n - \frac{C_a}{2}f''_n h + \mathcal{O}(h^2), \tag{22}$$

where $C_a = (1+a)/(1-a)$. Approximation $\mathcal{A}_3$ has second-order accuracy, when the coefficient C_a is equal to zero, $C_a = 0$ or $C_a = h$.

$$\frac{1+a}{1-a} = h, \quad 1 + a = h - ah, \quad a = \frac{h-1}{h+1}.$$

Approximation $\mathcal{A}_3$ is second-order accurate when $a = -1$ and $a = (h-1)/(h+1)$. Consider the following ordinary differential equation:

$$y'(x) = \sin x + \cos x, \quad y(0) = -1, \quad x \in [0,1]. \tag{23}$$

Equation (23) has a solution $y(x) = \sin x - \cos x$. The experimental results of numerical solution (21) for Equation (23) and values of the parameter $a = 0.5, a = -1$ and $a = (h-1)/(h+1)$ are given in Table 2.

Table 1. Error and order of numerical methods (11) and (13) of Equation (14).

h	NS(11)		NS(13), $a = -0.1$		NS(13), $a = 0.9$	
	Error	*Order*	*Error*	*Order*	*Error*	*Order*
0.0005	4.2960×10^{-4}	1.00012	3.5607×10^{-4}	1.00025	1.5386×10^{-3}	0.99992
0.00025	2.1479×10^{-4}	1.00006	1.7802×10^{-4}	1.00012	7.6933×10^{-4}	0.99996
0.000125	1.0739×10^{-4}	1.00003	8.9006×10^{-5}	1.00006	3.8467×10^{-4}	0.99998

Table 2. Error and order of numerical method (21) of Equation (23).

h	NS(21), $a = 0.5$		NS(21), $a = -1$		NS(21), $a = (h-1)/(h+1)$	
	Error	*Order*	*Error*	*Order*	*Error*	*Order*
0.0005	3.1026×10^{-4}	0.9982	3.7475×10^{-7}	1.9990	4.0785×10^{-7}	1.9981
0.00025	1.5523×10^{-4}	0.9991	9.3719×10^{-8}	1.9995	1.0203×10^{-7}	1.9991
0.000125	7.7640×10^{-5}	0.9995	2.3433×10^{-8}	1.9997	2.5515×10^{-8}	1.9995

3. Error Estimates and Convergence

In this section, we derive estimates for the errors of approximations $\mathcal{A}_2$ and $\mathcal{A}_3$ of the first derivative and the errors of numerical solutions (13) and (21) of Equation (10). Denote $M = \max_{x\in[0,X]} |f''(x)|$.

Lemma 1. *Let $f \in C^2[0,X]$. Then,*

$$\mathcal{A}_2[f_n] = \frac{1-a}{h}\left(f_n - (1-a)\sum_{k=1}^{n-1} a^{k-1} f_{n-k} - a^{n-1} f_0\right) = (1-a^n)f'_n + E^1_n h, \tag{24}$$

where the coefficient E^1_n satisfies the estimate

$$|E^1_n| < \frac{(1+a)M}{2(1-a)}, \qquad (2 \le n \le N). \tag{25}$$

Proof. From the Taylor theorem,

$$f_{n-k} = f_n - khf'_n + k^2\frac{h^2}{2}f''(\theta_{n-k}) \tag{26}$$

for $k = 1, \cdots, n$ and $\theta_{n-k} \in (x_{n-k}, X)$. By substituting f_{n-k} with (26) in Formula (27) for $\mathcal{A}_2$, we obtain

$$\mathcal{A}_2[f] = K_0 f_n + K_1 f'_n + E^1_n h,$$

where

$$K_0 = 1 - a - (1-a)^2 \sum_{k=1}^{n-1} a^{k-1} - (1-a)a^{n-1} = 0,$$

$$K_1 = (1-a)^2 \sum_{k=1}^{n-1} k a^{k-1} + (1-a)na^{n-1},$$

$$E_n = -\frac{1}{2}\left((1-a)^2 \sum_{k=1}^{n-1} k^2 a^{k-1} f''(\theta_{n-k}) + (1-a)n^2 a^{n-1} f''(\theta_0)\right).$$

From (16) and (17), we obtain

$$K_1 = 1 + (n-1)a^n - na^{n-1} + na^{n-1} - na^n = 1 - a^n,$$

$$|E_n| \le \frac{M}{2}\left((1-a)^2 \sum_{k=1}^{n-1} k^2 a^{k-1} + (1-a)n^2 a^{n-1}\right),$$

$$|E_n| \le \frac{M}{2}\left(\frac{1 + a - n^2 a^{n-1} + (2n^2 - 2n - 1)a^n - (n-1)^2 a^{n+1}}{1-a} + (1-a)n^2 a^{n-1}\right),$$

$$|E_n| \le \frac{M}{2(1-a)}\left(1 + a - (2n+1)a^n + (2n-1)a^{n+1}\right) < \frac{M(1+a)}{2(1-a)}.$$

□

Denote $M_1 = \max_{x\in[0,X]} |f'(x)|$. Now, we prove that (9) holds for $n > \log_{1/a} N$.

Corollary 1. *Let $f \in C^2[0, X]$ and $n > \log_{1/a} N$. Then,*

$$\mathcal{A}_2[f_n] = \frac{1-a}{h}\left(f_n - (1-a)\sum_{k=1}^{n-1} a^{k-1} f_{n-k} - a^{n-1} f_0\right) = f'_n + G_n h, \tag{27}$$

where the coefficient G_n satisfies the estimate

$$|G_n| < \frac{(1+a)M}{2(1-a)} + \frac{M_1}{X} \tag{28}$$

Proof. From (27), it follows that $G_n h = E_n^1 h - a^n f'_n$. Then,

$$|G_n| \le |E_n^1| + \frac{a^n |f'_n| N}{X} < |E_n^1| + \frac{M_1}{X} < \frac{(1+a)M}{2(1-a)} + \frac{M_1}{X}$$

because $a^n < a^{\log_{1/a} N} = 1/N$. □

In the next lemma, we prove that approximation (20) holds for all functions in $C^2[0, X]$.

Lemma 2. *Let $f \in C^2[0, X]$. Then,*

$$\mathcal{A}_3[f_n] = \frac{1}{h}\left((1-a)f_n - (1-a)^2\sum_{k=1}^{n-2} a^{k-1} f_{n-k} - a^{n-2}(1-2a)f_1 - a^{n-1} f_0\right) = f'_n + E_n^2 h,$$

where the coefficient E_n^2 satisfies the estimate

$$|E_n^2| < \frac{(1+a)M}{2(1-a)}, \qquad (2 \le n \le N). \tag{29}$$

Proof. Approximation $\mathcal{A}_3$ is written in the form

$$\mathcal{A}_3[f_n] = K_0 f_n + K_1 f'_n + E_n^2 h,$$

where the coefficients K_0, K_1 and E_n^2 satisfy

$$\begin{aligned} K_0 &= 1 - a - (1-a)^2 \sum_{k=1}^{n-2} a^{k-1} - (1-2a)a^{n-2} - a^{n-1} \\ &= 1 - a - (1-a)(1-a^{n-2}) - (1-2a)a^{n-2} - a^{n-1} = 0, \end{aligned}$$

$$\begin{aligned} K_1 &= (1-a)^2 \sum_{k=1}^{n-2} k a^{k-1} + (1-2a)(n-1)a^{n-2} + n a^{n-1} \\ &= 1 + (n-2)a^{n-1} - (n-1)a^{n-2} + (1-2a)(n-1)a^{n-2} + n a^{n-1} = 1, \end{aligned}$$

$$E_n^2 = -\frac{1}{2}\left((1-a)^2 \sum_{k=1}^{n-2} k^2 a^{k-1} f''(\theta_{n-k}) + (1-2a)(n-1)^2 a^{n-2} f''(\theta_1) + n^2 a^{n-1} f''(\theta_0)\right),$$

$$\begin{aligned} |E_n^2| &\le \frac{M}{2}\left((1-a)^2 \sum_{k=1}^{n-2} k^2 a^{k-1} + (1-2a)(n-1)^2 a^{n-2} + n^2 a^{n-1}\right) \\ &\le \frac{M}{2}\frac{1+a-2a^n}{1-a} < \frac{M(1+a)}{2(1-a)}. \end{aligned}$$

□

The estimate for the coefficients E_n^1 and E_n^2 derived in Lemmas 1 and 2 depends on the step size h, and approximations $\mathcal{A}_2$ and $\mathcal{A}_3$ can be defined for any interval $[l, X]$. Formula $\mathcal{A}_2$ is a first-order approximation of the first derivative for $n > \log_{1/a} N$, while $\mathcal{A}_3$ is an approximation of the first derivative for all $n \geq 2$. The sum of the coefficients of the second derivative in the formula for E_m^2 is

$$\frac{1}{2}\left((1-a)^2\sum_{k=1}^{n-2} k^2 a^{k-1} + (1-2a)(n-1)^2 a^{n-2} + n^2 a^{n-1}\right) = \frac{a+1-2a^n}{2(1-a)}.$$

Therefore, (3) holds for $n > \log_{1/a} N$. Now, we use the bound for the errors of approximations $\mathcal{A}_2$ and $\mathcal{A}_3$ to prove the convergence of numerical methods (13) and (21). Let $e_k = y_k - u_k$ be the error of numerical solution (21) at the point x_k for $k = 1, \cdots, N$. First, we estimate the errors e_1 and e_2. From the Taylor Theorem, the solution of Equation (10) satisfies

$$y_1 = y_0 + hF_1 - \frac{h^2}{2}y''(\theta_1),$$

$$y_2 = y_1 + hF_2 - \frac{h^2}{2}y''(\theta_2).$$

Then,

$$e_1 = -\frac{h^2}{2}y''(\theta_1), \qquad |e_1| \leq \frac{h^2}{2}|y''(\theta_1)| \leq \frac{Mh^2}{2},$$

$$e_2 = e_1 - \frac{h^2}{2}y''(\theta_2), \qquad |e_2| \leq |e_1| + \frac{h^2}{2}|y''(\theta_2)| \leq Mh^2.$$

In Theorems 1 and 2, we derive bounds for the errors of numerical solutions (13) and (21) of Equation (10). The theorems are proved by induction.

Theorem 1. *The errors of numerical solution* (21) *satisfy*

$$|e_n| < \frac{MXh}{(1-a)^2}, \qquad (1 \leq n \leq N). \tag{30}$$

Proof. The estimate (30) for the error of numerical method (21) holds for $n = 1$ and $n = 2$. Suppose that (30) holds for $n = 1, \cdots, m-1$. The solution of Equation (10) and the error of (21) satisfy

$$y_m = \frac{hF_m}{1-a} + (1-a)\sum_{k=1}^{m-2} a^{k-1} y_{m-k} + \frac{a^{m-2}(1-2a)}{1-a}y_1 + \frac{a^{m-1}}{1-a}y_0 + \frac{E_m^2 h^2}{1-a},$$

$$e_m = (1-a)\sum_{k=1}^{m-2} a^{k-1} e_{m-k} + \frac{a^{m-2}(1-2a)}{1-a}e_1 + E_m h^2,$$

where $E_k = E_k^2/(1-a)$ for $k = 1, \cdots, N$. The error e_m is expressed with e_{m-1} as

$$e_m = (1-a)e_{m-1} + a(1-a)\sum_{k=2}^{m-2} a^{k-2} e_{m-k} + \frac{a^{m-2}(1-2a)}{1-a}e_1 + E_m h^2,$$

$$e_m = (1-a)e_{m-1} + a\left(e_{m-1} - \frac{a^{m-3}(1-2a)}{1-a}e_1 - E_{m-1}h^2\right) + \frac{a^{m-2}(1-2a)}{1-a}e_1 + E_m h^2,$$

$$e_m = e_{m-1} + (E_m - aE_{m-1})h^2. \tag{31}$$

By applying (31) successively $m-3$ times, we obtain

$$e_m = e_2 + (E_m - aE_2)h^2 + (1-a)h^2 \sum_{k=3}^{m-1} E_k.$$

Denote

$$E = \max_{1\le k\le N} |E_k| < \frac{M(1+a)}{2(1-a)^2}.$$

The error e_m satisfies the estimate.

$$|e_m| \le |e_2| + (m-2+a)Eh^2 < \frac{Mh^2}{(1-a)^2} + \frac{(1+a)Mh^2}{2(1-a)^2}(m-2+a)$$
$$< \frac{Mh^2}{(1-a)^2} + \frac{Mh^2}{(1-a)^2}(m-2+a) < \frac{Mmh^2}{(1-a)^2} \le \frac{MXh}{(1-a)^2}.$$

□

Now, we estimate the error e_2 of numerical solution (13).

$$y_2 = \frac{f_2 h}{1-a} + (1-a)y_1 + ay_0 + \frac{E_2^1 h^2}{1-a},$$

$$u_2 = \frac{f_2 h}{1-a} + (1-a)u_1 + au_0.$$

The error e_2 satisfies

$$e_2 = (1-a)e_1 + \frac{E_2^1 h^2}{1-a},$$

$$|e_2| \le (1-a)|e_1| + \frac{|E_2^1|h^2}{1-a} \le \frac{M(1-a)h^2}{2} + \frac{M(1+a)h^2}{2(1-a)^2},$$

$$|e_2| \le \frac{Mh^2}{2(1-a)^2}\left(2 - 2a + 3a^2 - a^3\right) < \frac{Mh^2}{(1-a)^2}.$$

Theorem 2. *The error of numerical solution* (13) *satisfies*

$$|e_n| < \left(\frac{2a^2F}{1-a} + \frac{M(1+a)X}{2(1-a)^2}\right)h, \qquad (1 \le n \le N). \tag{32}$$

Proof. The estimate (32) for the error of numerical method (13) holds for $n = 1$ and $n = 2$. Suppose that (32) holds for $n = 1, \cdots, m-1$. The solution of Equation (10) satisfies

$$y_m = \frac{(1-a^m)F_m h}{1-a} + (1-a)\sum_{k=1}^{m-1} a^{k-1} y_{m-k} + a^{m-1}y_0 + \frac{E_m^1 h^2}{1-a}.$$

Then,

$$e_m = -\frac{a^m F_m h}{1-a} + (1-a)\sum_{k=1}^{m-1} a^{k-1} e_{m-k} + E_m h^2,$$

where $E_k = E_k^1/(1-a)$ for $k = 1, \cdots, N$. The error e_m is expressed with e_{m-1} as

$$e_m = -\frac{a^m F_m h}{1-a} + (1-a)e_{m-1} + a(1-a)\sum_{k=2}^{m-1} a^{k-2} e_{m-k} + E_m h^2,$$

$$e_m = -\frac{a^n F_m h}{1-a} + (1-a)e_{m-1} + a\left(e_{m-1} + \frac{a^{m-1}hF_{m-1}}{1-a} - E_{m-2}h^2\right) + E_m h^2,$$

$$e_m = e_{m-1} + \frac{a^n(F_{m-1} - F_m)h}{1-a} + (E_m - aE_{m-1})h^2. \tag{33}$$

By applying (33) successively $m-2$ times, we obtain

$$e_m = e_1 + \left(a^2 F_1 - a^m F_n + (a-1)\sum_{k=2}^{m-1} a^k F_k\right)\frac{h}{1-a} + (E_m - aE_2)h^2 + (1-a)h^2 \sum_{k=3}^{m-1} E_k.$$

Denote $E = \max_{1 \leq k \leq N} |E_k|$ and $F = \max_{x \in [0,X]} |F(x)|$. Then,

$$|e_m| \leq |e_1| + \left(a^2 + a^m + (a-1)\sum_{k=2}^{m-1} a^k\right)\frac{Fh}{1-a} + Eh^2(1+a) + (1-a)(m-3)$$

$$< \frac{Mh^2}{2} + \left(a^2 + a^m + a^2(1-a^{m-2}\right)\frac{Fh}{1-a} + \frac{(1+a)Mh^2}{2(1-a)^2}(m-2+a),$$

$$|e_m| < \left(\frac{2a^2F}{1-a} + \frac{M(1+a)X}{2(1-a)^2}\right)h.$$

□

4. Numerical Solutions of First-Order ODEs

In this section, we construct the numerical methods for first-order ODEs which use approximation $\mathcal{A}_3$ of the first derivative and we obtain recursive formulas for computation of the numerical solution. The performance of the numerical methods is compared with the performance of the corresponding Euler methods. We show that the numerical methods can achieve an arbitrary order in the interval $(0,2]$ by using appropriate choices of the parameter of approximation $\mathcal{A}_3$.

Example 2. *Consider the first-order linear ODE with constant coefficients*

$$y'(x) + Ly(x) = F(x), \qquad y(0) = y_0. \tag{34}$$

By approximating y'_n with first-order backward difference approximation, we obtain

$$\frac{y_n - y_{n-1}}{h} + Ly_n = F_n + O(h).$$

The numerical solution is computed as $u_0 = y_0$ and

$$u_n = \frac{1}{1+Lh}(hF_n + u_{n-1}). \tag{35}$$

By approximating y'_n with approximation $\mathcal{A}_3$, we obtain

$$\frac{1-a}{h}\left(y_n - (1-a)\sum_{k=1}^{n-2} a^{k-1} y_{n-k} - \frac{1-2a}{1-a}a^{n-2}y_1 - \frac{a^{n-1}}{1-a}y_0\right) + Ly_n = y'_n + E_n^2 h,$$

$$\left(1 + \frac{Lh}{1-a}\right)y_n = \frac{hF_n}{1-a} + (1-a)\sum_{k=1}^{n-2} a^{k-1} y_{n-k} + \frac{1-2a}{1-a}a^{n-2}y_1 + \frac{a^{n-1}}{1-a}y_0 + \frac{E_n^2 h^2}{1-a}.$$

Denote $H = h/(1-a)$. The solution of Equation (34) satisfies

$$y_n = \frac{1}{1+LH}\left(F_n H + (1-a)\sum_{k=1}^{n-2} a^{k-1} y_{n-k} + \frac{1-2a}{1-a}a^{n-2}y_1 + \frac{a^{n-1}}{1-a}y_0 + \frac{E_n^2 h^2}{1-a}\right).$$

The numerical solution of Equation (34) is computed as

$$u_n = \frac{1}{1+LH}\left(F_n H + (1-a)\sum_{k=1}^{n-2} a^{k-1} u_{n-k} + \frac{1-2a}{1-a} a^{n-2} u_1 + \frac{a^{n-1}}{1-a} u_0\right). \quad (36)$$

The numerical solution (36) is calculated with $\mathcal{O}(N)$ arithmetic operations using an algorithm that is similar to the algorithms for calculating (13) and (21). From Formula (36), the value of u_n is expressed in terms of u_{n-1} as follows.

$$(1+LH)u_n = F_n H + (1-a)u_{n-1} + a\left((1-a)\sum_{k=2}^{n-2} a^{k-1} u_{n-k} + \frac{1-2a}{1-a} a^{n-2} u_1 + \frac{a^{n-1}}{1-a} u_0\right),$$

$$(1+LH)u_n = F_n H + (1-a)u_{n-1} + a(u_{n-1} - F_{n-1} H).$$

The numerical solution of Equation (34) using the approximation $\mathcal{A}_3$ for the first derivative is computed recursively as $u_0 = y_0$ and

$$u_n = \frac{1}{1+LH}\left((1+aLH)u_{n-1} + H(F_n - aF_{n-1})\right). \quad (37)$$

Consider the following first-order linear ODE:

$$y'(x) + Ly(x) = (1+L)e^x, \qquad y(0) = y_0. \quad (38)$$

Experimental results for the error and order of numerical solutions (35) and (37) of Equation (38) and positive values of L are given in Table 3. Now, we prove the convergence of numerical method (37) when the value of L is positive. Denote by $e_n = y_n - u_n$ the error of (37) at the point x_n. First, we estimate the errors e_1 and e_2. The solution of Equation (34) satisfies

$$y_1 = \frac{1}{1+LH}\left((1+aLH)y_0 + H(F_1 - aF_0)\right) + \varepsilon_1, \quad (39)$$

$$y_2 = \frac{1}{1+LH}\left((1+aLH)y_1 + H(F_2 - aF_1)\right) + \varepsilon_2. \quad (40)$$

From the Taylor theorem, the truncation error ε_1 satisfies

$$\begin{aligned}(1+LH)\varepsilon_1 &= (1+LH)y_1 - HF_1 - (1+aLH)y_0 - aHF_0\\ &= y_1 - Hy_1' - y_0 + aHy_0' = hy_0' - Hy_1' + aHy_0' + \frac{h^2}{2}y''(\theta_1)\\ &= \frac{h}{1-a}(y_0' - y_1') + \frac{h^2}{2}y''(\theta_1) = \frac{h^2}{2}y''(\theta_1) - \frac{h^2}{1-a}y''(\theta_2).\end{aligned}$$

Hence,

$$|\varepsilon_1| \le \frac{h^2}{2}|y''(\theta_1)| + \frac{h^2}{1-a}|y''(\theta_2)| \le \frac{(3-a)Mh^2}{2(1-a)}.$$

In a similar way, we show that $|\varepsilon_2| \le \dfrac{(3-a)Mh^2}{2(1-a)}$. The errors e_1 and e_2 satisfy the estimates

$$e_1 = \varepsilon_1, \quad |e_1| \le \frac{(3-a)Mh^2}{2(1-a)},$$

$$e_2 = \frac{1+aLH}{1+LH}e_1 + \varepsilon_2, \quad |e_2| < |e_1| + |\varepsilon_2| < \frac{(3-a)Mh^2}{1-a}.$$

We will prove the convergence of the numerical method (37) of Equation (38) for positive values of the parameter L and derive an estimate for the error of the method. Denote

$$C = \max\left\{\frac{M(1+a)^2}{2L(1-a)^2}, \frac{(3-a)Mh}{2(1-a)}\right\}.$$

Theorem 3. *Let $L > 0$. Then,*

$$|e_n| < Ch, \qquad (1 \le n \le N). \tag{41}$$

Proof. Inequality (41) is satisfied for $n = 1$ and $n = 2$. Assume that (41) holds for $n \le m-1$. The error e_m satisfies

$$e_m = \frac{1+aLH}{1+LH}e_{m-1} + \frac{(E_m^2 - aE_{m-1}^2)h^2}{(1+LH)(1-a)},$$

$$|e_m| < \frac{1+aLH}{1+LH}|e_{m-1}| + \frac{(|E_m^2| + a|E_{m-1}^2|h^2}{(1+LH)(1-a)}.$$

From Lemma 2

$$|e_m| < \left(1 - \frac{(1-a)LH}{1+LH}\right)|e_{m-1}| + \frac{(1+a)^2Mh^2}{2(1-a)^2(1+LH)}.$$

Using the assumption of induction,

$$|e_m| < Ch - \frac{Lh}{1+LH}Ch + \frac{(1+a)^2Mh^2}{2(1-a)^2(1+LH)} \le Ch.$$

By the principle of induction, the bound (41) holds for all $n = 1, \cdots, N$. □

We will compare the performance of numerical methods (35) and (37) and negative values of the parameter L of Equation (38). Experimental results for the error and order of numerical solutions (35) and (37) and $L = -20, -30, -50$ are given in Tables 4–6. The results of the numerical experiments presented in this section refer to ODSs that are defined in the interval $[0,1]$. The numerical results in Table 4 show that method (35) has a first-order accuracy and its error can be very large for small values of the step size h of the method. In Table 5, the values of the parameter a are fixed numbers close to one. In Table 6, the parameter $a = 1 - h^{0.8}$ and numerical solution (37) has an order 0.2. Although the order of (37) in Tables 5 and 6 is smaller than one, the errors of the method are significantly smaller than the corresponding errors of numerical solution (35) in Table 4.

Example 3. *Consider the first-order linear ODE*

$$y'(x) + G(x)y(x) = F(x), \qquad y(0) = y_0. \tag{42}$$

The numerical solutions (43) and (45) for Equation (42), which use backward difference approximation and approximation $\mathcal{A}_3$ for first derivative, are computed as

$$u_n = \frac{1}{1+hG_n}(hF_n + u_{n-1}), \quad u_0 = y_0, \tag{43}$$

$$u_n = \frac{1}{1-a+hG_n}\left(hF_n + (1-a)^2\sum_{k=1}^{n-2} a^{k-1}u_{n-k} + (1-2a)a^{n-2}u_1 + a^{n-1}u_0\right). \tag{44}$$

In a similar way as in Example 2, a recursive formula for calculating the numerical solution of an Equation (42) is derived from (44)

$$u_n = \frac{1}{1-a+hG_n}\big((1-a+ahG_{n-1})u_{n-1} + h(F_n - aF_{n-1})\big), \quad u_0 = y_0. \tag{45}$$

The first-order liner ODE

$$y'(x) + \tan x\, y(x) = \sec x, \qquad y(0) = -1 \tag{46}$$

has a solution $y(x) = \sin x - \cos x$. The experimental results of numerical solutions (43) and (45) of Equation (46) are given in Table 7.

Numerical solution (45) depends on a parameter a. The method can have any order in the interval $(0,2]$ with a suitable choice of the parameter. The coefficient C_a in an asymptotic Formula (3) has a value $C_a = (1+a)/(1-a)$. The order of NS7 is $1+p$ when the coefficient C_a is equal to sh^p.

$$\frac{1+a}{1-a} = sh^p, \quad 1+a = sh^p - ash^p, \quad a = \frac{sh^p - 1}{sh^p + 1}.$$

When $a = -1 + sh^p$, the coefficient $C_a = sh^p/(2 - sh^p)$ and (45) has an order $1+p$. When $a = 1 - sh^p$, the coefficient C_a satisfies

$$C_a h = \frac{1}{s}(2 - sh^p)h^{1-p} = \frac{2}{s}h^{1-p} - h.$$

Numerical solution (45) has an order $1-p$. A summary of these results is given below.

• Numerical method (45) has an order $1+p$ when $s > 0$ and $-1 < p \leq 1$,

$$a = \frac{sh^p - 1}{sh^p + 1}. \tag{47}$$

Values of the parameter p greater than one, $p > 1$, lead to a second-order method. The experimental results for $p = -0.3$, $p = 0.7$ and $p = 1$ are given in Table 8.

• (45) has an order $1-p$, when $s > 0$ and $0 < p < 1$,

$$a = 1 - sh^p. \tag{48}$$

The experimental results for $p = 0.2$, $p = 0.5$ and $p = 0.7$ are given in Table 9.

• (45) has an order $1+p$, when $s > 0$ and $0 < p \leq 1$,

$$a = -1 + sh^p. \tag{49}$$

When $p > 1$, numerical solution (45) has a second-order accuracy. The experimental results for $p = 0.25$, $p = 0.75$ and $p = 1.5$ are given in Table 10.

The logistic equation is a first-order nonlinear ordinary differential equation used for modeling population dynamics [29–31].

Example 4. *Consider the logistic equation*

$$y'(x) = Ly(x)(1 - y(x)), \qquad y(0) = y_0. \tag{50}$$

Equation (50) has a solution

$$y = \frac{y_0}{y_0 + (1 - y_0)e^{-Lx}}.$$

The explicit schemes of Equation (50) which use first-order backward difference and approximation $\mathcal{A}_3$ of the first derivative satisfy

$$u_n = u_{n-1} + Lhu_{n-1}(1-u_{n-1}), \quad u_0 = y_0, \tag{51}$$

$$u_n = \frac{Lh}{1-a}u_{n-1}(1-u_{n-1}) + (1-a)\sum_{k=1}^{n-2} a^{k-1}u_{n-k} + \frac{(1-2a)a^{n-2}}{1-a}u_1 + \frac{a^{n-1}}{1-a}u_0. \tag{52}$$

Numerical method (52) has initial conditions $u_0 = y_0$, $u_1 = u_0 + Lhu_0(1-u_0)$ and is computed recursively as

$$u_n = u_{n-1} + \frac{Lh}{1-a}\left(u_{n-1}(1-u_{n-1}) - au_{n-2}(1-u_{n-2})\right). \tag{53}$$

Experimental results for the error and order of numerical solutions (51) and (53) of Equation (50) are given in Table 11.

Table 3. Error and order of numerical methods (35) and (37) of Equation (38).

h	NS(35), $L = 2$		NS(37), $L = 2$, $a = -0.9$		NS(37), $L = 20$, $a = 0.5$	
	Error	*Order*	*Error*	*Order*	*Error*	*Order*
0.0005	2.1521×10^{-4}	0.9998	1.1346×10^{-5}	1.0023	9.7015×10^{-5}	0.9990
0.00025	1.0761×10^{-4}	0.9999	5.6688×10^{-6}	1.0011	4.8524×10^{-5}	0.9995
0.000125	5.3809×10^{-5}	0.9999	2.8333×10^{-6}	1.0006	2.4266×10^{-5}	0.9997

Table 4. Error and order of numerical method (35) of Equation (38).

h	NS(35), $L = -20$		NS(35), $L = -30$		NS(35), $L = -50$	
	Error	*Order*	*Error*	*Order*	*Error*	*Order*
1.5625×10^{-5}	200.1160	1.0045	2.8992×10^{6}	1.0101	8.4295×10^{14}	1.0282
7.8125×10^{-6}	99.9028	1.0022	1.4445×10^{6}	1.0051	4.1738×10^{14}	1.0141
3.9062×10^{-6}	49.9120	1.0011	7.2099×10^{5}	1.0025	2.0767×10^{14}	1.0071

Table 5. Error and order of numerical method (37) of Equation (38).

h	NS(37), $L = -20$ $a = 0.99995$		NS(37), $L = -30$ $a = 0.99999$		NS(37), $L = -50$ $a = 0.99997$	
	Error	*Order*	*Error*	*Order*	*Error*	*Order*
1.5625×10^{-5}	0.0333	0.5963	0.0453	0.1657	0.0179	0.4295
7.8125×10^{-6}	0.0192	0.7976	0.0366	0.3072	0.0113	0.6594
3.9062×10^{-6}	0.0103	0.8943	0.0255	0.5211	0.0064	0.8317

Table 6. Error and order of numerical method (37) of Equation (38) and $a = 1 - h^{0.8}$.

h	NS(37), $L = -20$		NS(37), $L = -30$		NS(37), $L = -50$	
	Error	*Order*	*Error*	*Order*	*Error*	*Order*
1.5625×10^{-5}	0.0140	0.1779	0.0092	0.1783	0.0054	0.1785
7.8125×10^{-6}	0.0124	0.1805	0.0081	0.1808	0.0048	0.1811
3.9062×10^{-6}	0.0109	0.1828	0.0071	0.1831	0.0042	0.1833

Table 7. Error and order of numerical methods (43) and (45) of Equation (50).

h	NS(43)		NS(45), $a = -0.3$		NS(45), $a = -0.9$	
	Error	*Order*	*Error*	*Order*	*Error*	*Order*
0.0005	8.4224×10^{-5}	0.9995	4.5348×10^{-5}	0.9994	4.4203×10^{-6}	0.9954
0.00025	4.2119×10^{-5}	0.9997	2.2679×10^{-5}	0.9997	2.2136×10^{-6}	0.9977
0.000125	2.1061×10^{-5}	0.9999	1.1341×10^{-5}	0.9999	1.1077×10^{-6}	0.9989

Table 8. Error and order of numerical method (45) of Equation (50) and $a = (sh^p - 1)/(sh^p + 1)$.

h	NS(45), $s = 1, p = -0.3$		NS(45), $s = 2, p = 0.7$		NS(45), $s = 3, p = 1$	
	Error	*Order*	*Error*	*Order*	*Error*	*Order*
0.0005	8.2264×10^{-4}	0.6986	8.1004×10^{-7}	1.6943	1.1272×10^{-7}	2.0000
0.00025	5.0670×10^{-4}	0.6991	2.5012×10^{-7}	1.6954	2.8180×10^{-8}	2.0000
0.000125	3.1203×10^{-4}	0.6995	7.7183×10^{-8}	1.6962	7.0449×10^{-9}	2.0000

Table 9. Error and order of numerical method (45) of Equation (50) and $a = 1 - sh^p$.

h	NS(45), $s = 1, p = 0.2$		NS(45), $s = 2, p = 0.5$		NS(45), $s = 3, p = 0.7$	
	Error	*Order*	*Error*	*Order*	*Error*	*Order*
0.0005	6.8543×10^{-4}	0.7721	3.6584×10^{-3}	0.4823	1.1166×10^{-2}	0.2866
0.00025	4.0015×10^{-4}	0.7764	2.6093×10^{-3}	0.4875	9.1303×10^{-3}	0.2903
0.000125	2.3303×10^{-4}	0.7800	1.8564×10^{-3}	0.4912	7.4526×10^{-3}	0.2929

Table 10. Error and order of numerical method (45) of Equation (50) and $a = -1 + sh^p$.

h	NS(45), $s = 1, p = 0.25$		NS(45), $s = 2, p = 0.75$		NS(45), $s = 3, p = 1.5$	
	Error	*Order*	*Error*	*Order*	*Error*	*Order*
0.0005	6.7943×10^{-6}	1.2702	2.6885×10^{-7}	1.7395	1.7315×10^{-7}	1.9696
0.00025	2.8227×10^{-6}	1.2672	8.0463×10^{-8}	1.7404	4.3926×10^{-9}	1.9789
0.000125	1.1748×10^{-6}	1.2646	2.4064×10^{-8}	1.7414	1.1094×10^{-9}	1.9853

Table 11. Error and order of numerical methods (51) and (53) of Equation (50) and $L = 1, y_0 = 2$.

h	NS(51)		NS(53), $a = 0.3$		NS(53), $a = 0.5$	
	Error	*Order*	*Error*	*Order*	*Error*	*Order*
0.0005	1.8404×10^{-4}	1.0008	2.6296×10^{-5}	1.0011	1.8392×10^{-4}	0.9998
0.00025	9.1994×10^{-5}	1.0004	1.3143×10^{-5}	1.0005	9.1966×10^{-5}	0.9999
0.000125	4.5991×10^{-5}	1.0002	6.5704×10^{-6}	1.0002	4.5984×10^{-5}	0.9999

5. Numerical Solution of Heat Equation

The heat equation is a partial differential equation that models the distribution of temperature in a one-dimensional object. Heat conduction a classical problem in physics and engineering that can be generalized to higher dimensions and has a wide range of applications. The analytical and numerical solutions of the heat equation are extensively studied in [32–36]. In this section, we construct a finite difference scheme for the heat equation which uses approximation $\mathcal{A}_3$ for the partial derivative in time and second-order difference approximation for the partial derivative in space. The stability and convergence of the method are proved, and experimental results for the error and order of the method are presented.

Example 5. *Consider the following heat equation:*

$$\begin{cases} u_t(x,z) = Du_{xx}(x,t) + F(x,t), & (x,t) \in \mathcal{R}, \\ u(x,0) = u_0(x),\ u(0,t) = u_1(t),\ u(1,t) = u_2(t), \end{cases} \tag{54}$$

where D is the thermal diffusivity of the material and $\mathcal{R} = [0,X] \times [0,T]$. Denote $h = X/N$, $\tau = T/M$, where M and N are positive integers, and $u_n^m = u(nh, m\tau)$, the values of the solution at the nodes $(x_n, y_m) = (nh, m\tau)$ of a rectangular grid $\mathcal{J}$ on $\mathcal{R}$. Now, we construct the finite difference scheme of Equation (54), which uses approximation $\mathcal{A}_3$ for the partial derivative in time and central difference approximation for the partial derivative in space. The solution of heat Equation (54) satisfies

$$\frac{1-a}{\tau}\left(u_n^m - (1-a)\sum_{k=2}^{m-2} a^{k-1}u_n^{m-k} - \frac{1-2a}{1-a}a^{n-2}u_n^1 - \frac{a^{n-1}}{1-a}u_n^0\right)$$
$$= D\frac{u_{n-1}^m - 2u_n^m + u_{n+1}^m}{h^2} + S_n^m\tau + K_n^m h^2 + F_n^m.$$

Denote $\eta = D\tau/((1-a)h^2)$.

$$-\eta u_{n-1}^m + (1+2\eta)u_n^m - \eta u_{n+1}^m = (1-a)\sum_{k=1}^{m-2} a^{k-1}u_n^{m-k} + \frac{1-2a}{1-a}a^{n-2}u_n^1 + \frac{a^{n-1}}{1-a}u_n^0$$
$$+ \frac{\tau F_n^m}{1-a} + \frac{\tau}{1-a}(S_n^m\tau + K_n^m h^2). \tag{55}$$

The coefficient K_n^m satisfies $|K_n^m| < M_4/12$. From Lemma 2 the coefficient S_n^m satisfies the estimate $|S_n^m| < \dfrac{(1+a)M_2}{2(1-a)}$, where

$$M_2 = \max_{(x,t)\in\mathcal{R}}\left|\frac{\partial^2 u(x,t)}{\partial x^2}\right|, \quad M_4 = \max_{(x,t)\in\mathcal{R}}\left|\frac{\partial^4 u(x,t)}{\partial x^4}\right|.$$

Formula (55) is written in the form

$$-\eta u_{n-1}^m + (1+2\eta)u_n^m - \eta u_{n+1}^m = a\left[(1-a)\sum_{k=2}^{m-2} a^{k-2}u_n^{m-k} + \frac{1-2a}{1-a}a^{n-3}u_n^1 + \frac{a^{n-2}}{1-a}u_n^0\right]$$
$$+ (1-a)u_n^{m-1} + \frac{\tau F_n^m}{1-a} + \frac{\tau}{1-a}(S_n^m\tau + K_n^m h^2). \tag{56}$$

From Formulas (55) and (56), we obtain

$$-\eta u_{n-1}^m + (1+2\eta)u_n^m - \eta u_{n+1}^m = a\left[-\eta u_{n-1}^{m-1} + (1+2\eta)u_n^{m-1} - \eta u_{n+1}^{m-1}\right] + (1-a)u_n^{m-1}$$
$$- \frac{a\tau F_n^{m-1}}{1-a} - \frac{a\tau}{1-a}(S_n^{m-1}\tau + K_n^{m-1}h^2) + \frac{\tau F_n^m}{1-a} + \frac{\tau}{1-a}(S_n^m\tau + K_n^m h^2).$$

The solution of heat Equation (54) satisfies

$$-\eta u_{n-1}^m + (1+2\eta)u_n^m - \eta u_{n+1}^m = -a\eta u_{n-1}^{m-1} + (1+2a\eta)u_n^{m-1} - a\eta u_{n+1}^{m-1}$$
$$+ \frac{\tau}{1-a}\left(\bar{F}_n^m + \bar{S}_n^m\tau + \bar{K}_n^m h^2\right), \tag{57}$$

where $\bar{F}_n^m = F_n^m - aF_n^{m-1}$, $\bar{S}_n^m = S_n^m - aS_n^{m-1}$, $\bar{K}_n^m = K_n^m - aK_n^{m-1}$. The numerical solution of heat Equation (54) on row m of the grid $\mathcal{J}$, which corresponds to (57), satisfies

$$-\eta U_{n-1}^m + (1+2\eta)U_n^m - \eta U_{n+1}^m = -a\eta U_{n-1}^{m-1} + (1+2a\eta)U_n^{m-1} - a\eta U_{n+1}^{m-1} + \frac{\tau\bar{F}_n^m}{1-a}. \tag{58}$$

The system of linear Equation (58) is written in matrix form as

$$(I+\eta\Delta)\mathcal{U}_m = (I+a\eta\Delta)\mathcal{U}_{m-1} + \tau\mathcal{F}_m + \eta\mathcal{I}_m, \tag{59}$$

where $\mathcal{U}_m$ and $\mathcal{F}_m$ are vectors of dimension $N-1$ which have entries U_n^m and $\bar{F}_n^m/(1-a)$ for $n = 1, \cdots, N-1$ and $\mathcal{I}_m = \left(u_1(m\tau), 0, \cdots, 0, u_2(m\tau)\right)^T$. The matrix Δ is the tridiagonal matrix of dimension $N-1$ with main diagonal entries equal to 2 and entries above and below the main diagonal equal to -1. Numerical solution (59) is computed with $\mathcal{O}(MN)$ operations because $I+\eta\Delta$ is a tridiagonal M-matrix [37,38].

A Crank–Nicolson scheme for the heat equation has second-order accuracy [39,40]. The convergence of finite difference schemes for the heat equation are studied in [41,42]. Now, we derive a bound for the error of finite difference scheme (59). Let $e_n^m = U_n^m - u_n^m$ be the error of (59) at the point $(nh, m\tau)$ and $\mathcal{E}_m$ be the vector with the errors e_n^m on row m of the grid $\mathcal{J}$, where $n = 1, \cdots, N-1$. The infinity norm of a vector is the maximum absolute value of its components and the infinity norm of a matrix is the maximum of the absolute row sums. In Lemma 3, we estimate the errors of difference scheme (59) on the first row of the grid $\mathcal{J}$.

Lemma 3. *Let $u \in C^4[0,X] \times C^2[0,T]$. Then,*

$$\|\mathcal{E}_1\| < \frac{(1+a)\tau}{12(1-a)}\left(6M_2\tau + M_4h^2\right). \tag{60}$$

Proof. The solution of Equation (54) on the first row of the grid $\mathcal{J}$ satisfies

$$-\eta u_{n-1}^1 + (1+2\eta)u_n^1 - \eta u_{n+1}^1 = -a\eta u_{n-1}^0 + (1+2a\eta)u_n^0 - a\eta u_{n+1}^0 + \frac{\tau}{1-a}\left(F_n^1 - aF_n^0\right) + \varepsilon_n^1,$$

$$\frac{(1-a)(u_n^1 - u_n^0)}{\tau} = \frac{D}{h^2}\left(u_{n-1}^1 - 2u_n^1 + u_{n+1}^1\right) - \frac{aD}{h^2}\left(u_{n-1}^0 - 2u_n^0 + u_{n+1}^0\right) + F_n^1 - aF_n^0 + \frac{1-a}{\tau}\varepsilon_n^1.$$

The first-order difference approximation satisfies

$$\frac{u_n^1 - u_n^0}{\tau} = u_t(x_n, y_1) + C_1\tau = u_t(x_n, y_0) + C_2\tau,$$

where $|C_i| < M_2/2$ for $i = 1, 2$. Then,

$$u_t(x_n, y_1) + C_1\tau - au_t(x_n, y_0) - aC_2\tau = Du_{xx}(x_n, y_1) + C_3h^2 - aDu_{xx}(x_n, y_0) - aC_4h^2 + F(x_n, y_1) - aF(x_n, y_0) + \frac{1-a}{\tau}\varepsilon_n^1,$$

where $|C_i| < M_4/12$ for $i = 3, 4$. The error ε_n^1 satisfies

$$\frac{1-a}{\tau}\varepsilon_n^1 = -C_1\tau + aC_2\tau + C_3h^2 - aC_4h^2,$$

$$|\varepsilon_n^1| \le \frac{\tau}{1-a}\left(|C_1|\tau + a|C_2|\tau + |C_3|h^2 + a|C_4|h^2\right).$$

Hence,

$$|\varepsilon_n^1| < \frac{(1+a)\tau}{12(1-a)}\left(6M_2\tau + M_4h^2\right) \tag{61}$$

for $n = 1, \cdots, N-1$ and $e_0^1 = e_N^1 = 0$. The errors of numerical method (59) on the first row of the grid $\mathcal{J}$ satisfy

$$-\eta e_{n-1}^1 + (1+2\eta)e_n^1 - \eta e_{n+1}^1 = \varepsilon_n^1.$$

The elements of $\mathcal{E}_0$ are equal to zero, $e_n^0 = 0$, and the vector $\mathcal{E}_1$ with the errors of (59) on the first row of the grid $\mathcal{J}$ satisfies

$$(I+\eta\Delta)\mathcal{E}_1 = \mathcal{W}_1, \tag{62}$$

where $\mathcal{W}_1$ is the vector with elements ε_n^1. From (61), the infinity norm of $\mathcal{W}_1$ satisfies

$$||\mathcal{W}_1|| < \frac{(1+a)\tau}{12(1-a)}\left(6M_2\tau + M_4h^2\right).$$

The matrix $I+\eta\Delta$ is a diagonally dominant M-matrix and its infinity norm satisfies [43,44]

$$||(I+\eta\Delta)^{-1}|| < 1.$$

Therefore,

$$||\mathcal{E}_1|| \leq ||(I+\eta\Delta)^{-1}|| \cdot ||\mathcal{W}_1|| < \frac{(1+a)\tau}{12(1-a)}\left(6M_2\tau + M_4h^2\right).$$

□

The vector $\mathcal{E}_m$ with the errors of difference scheme (59) on row m of the grid $\mathcal{J}$ satisfies

$$(I+\eta\Delta)\mathcal{E}_m = (I+a\eta\Delta)\mathcal{E}_{m-1} + \tau\mathcal{W}_m, \tag{63}$$

where $\mathcal{W}_m$ is the vector with entries $\bar{S}_n^m\tau + \bar{K}_n^m h^2$. The infinity norm of $\mathcal{W}_m$ satisfies

$$||\mathcal{W}_m|| \leq M_0(\tau + h^2)$$

where

$$M_0 = \max\left\{\frac{(1+a)^2M_2}{2(1-a)}, \frac{(1+a)M_4}{12}\right\}.$$

The matrix Δ has eigenvalues [45]

$$\lambda_k = 4\sin^2\left(\frac{k\pi}{2N}\right), \quad k = 1, \cdots, N-1$$

and eigenvectors $\mathcal{V}_k$ for $k = 1, \cdots, N-1$, which have components $v_k^i = \sin(k\pi i/N)$, where $i = 1, \cdots, N-1$. Denote by P and Q the following matrices:

$$P = (I+\eta\Delta)^{-1}(I+a\eta\Delta), \quad Q = (I+\eta\Delta)^{-1}.$$

The sequence of vectors $\mathcal{E}_m$ satisfies

$$\mathcal{E}_m = P\mathcal{E}_{m-1} + \tau Q\mathcal{W}_m. \tag{64}$$

The matrix P has eigenvalues $(I+a\eta\lambda_k)/(I+\eta\lambda_k)$ for $k = 1, \cdots, N-1$. The spectral radius of the matrix P is smaller than one, $\rho(P) < 1$, and its powers P^n converge to zero. Therefore, $\lim_{n\to\infty}||P||^n = 0$. Denote

$$p = \max_{n\geq 1}||P||^n, \quad q = ||Q||.$$

In Theorem 4, we prove that finite difference scheme (59) is unconditionally stable and has an accuracy $O(\tau + h^2)$.

Theorem 4. *Let* $u \in C^4[0, X] \times C^2[0, T]$. *Then,*

$$||\mathcal{E}_m|| < C\left(\tau + h^2\right),$$

where $C = p(1 + Tq)M_0$ *and all* $m = 2, \cdots M$.

Proof. By applying (64) successively $m - 1$ times, we obtain

$$\mathcal{E}_m = P^{m-2}\mathcal{E}_1 + \tau \sum_{k=0}^{m-2} P^k Q \mathcal{W}_{m-k}.$$

Then,

$$||\mathcal{E}_m|| \leq ||P^{m-2}|| \cdot ||\mathcal{E}_1|| + \tau \sum_{k=0}^{m-2} ||P^k|| \cdot ||Q|| \cdot ||\mathcal{W}_{m-k}||.$$

From Lemma 3, the norm of the vector $\mathcal{E}_1$ satisfies $||\mathcal{E}_1|| < M_0(\tau + h^2)$. Hence,

$$||\mathcal{E}_m|| < pM_0(\tau + h^2) + pqM_0\tau(\tau + h^2)(m - 1) < p(1 + Tq)M_0(\tau + h^2).$$

□

Consider the following heat equation

$$\begin{cases} u_t(x,z) = 3u_{xx}(x,t) - 4e^{-x-t}, \\ u(x,0) = e^{-x},\ u(0,t) = e^{-t},\ u(1,t) = e^{-1-t}. \end{cases} \tag{65}$$

where $(x,t) \in [0,1] \times [0,1]$. Equation (65) has a solution $u(x,t) = e^{-x-t}$. The graphs of numerical solution (59) and its error for $h = \tau = 0.01$ are shown in Figure 1. Numerical method (59) has an accuracy $\mathcal{O}(\tau + h^2)$ for $a = -0.5$. When the parameter $a = (\tau - 1)/(\tau + 1)$, numerical method (59) has a second-order accuracy $\mathcal{O}(\tau^2 + h^2)$. Experimental results for the error and order of the numerical solution (59) of Equation (65) with $a = -0.5$ and $a = (\tau - 1)/(\tau + 1)$ are given in Tables 12 and 13.

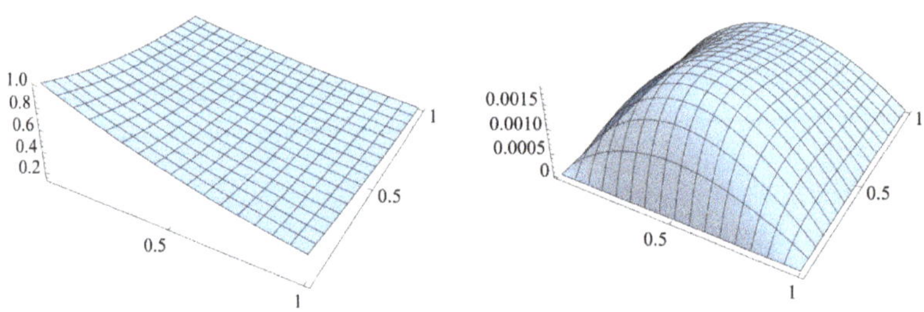

Figure 1. Graphs of numerical solution (59) (**left**) and its error (**right**) for $h = \tau = 0.01$.

Table 12. Error and order of numerical solution (59) and $N = 1000$.

τ	$\alpha = -0.5$		$a = (\tau-1)/(\tau+1)$	
	Error	*Order*	*Error*	*Order*
1/8	5.0573×10^{-4}	–	$18{,}947 \times 10^{-4}$	–
1/16	2.3493×10^{-4}	1.1061	$39{,}067 \times 10^{-5}$	2.2779
1/32	1.1768×10^{-4}	0.9974	9.4822×10^{-6}	2.0427
1/64	5.9357×10^{-5}	0.9873	2.3558×10^{-6}	2.0089
1/128	2.9850×10^{-5}	0.9917	5.9294×10^{-7}	1.9902

Table 13. Error and order of numerical solution (59) and $M = 1000$.

h	$\alpha = -0.5$		$a = (\tau-1)/(\tau+1)$	
	Error	*Order*	*Error*	*Order*
1/5	2.3007×10^{-4}	–	2.2645×10^{-4}	–
1/10	5.8200×10^{-5}	1.9829	5.7235×10^{-5}	1.9842
1/20	1.4924×10^{-5}	1.9633	1.4425×10^{-5}	1.9883
1/40	3.8741×10^{-6}	1.9457	3.6144×10^{-6}	1.9967
1/80	1.0286×10^{-6}	1.9131	9.1106×10^{-7}	1.9881

The order of the numerical method (59) in time is obtained by fixing $N = 1000$ and varying the value of M using the formula $\log_2 |E_\tau / E_{2\tau}|$. Similarly, the order in space is computed as $\log_2 |E_h / E_{2h}|$ with the parameter $M = 1000$ kept fixed.

6. Approximations of the Fractional Derivative

In this section, we discuss the construction of an approximation (5) for the fractional derivative, using the asymptotic Formula (2) and the approximation $\mathcal{A}_3$ for the first derivative. Two approximations of the fractional derivative of order $2-\alpha$ whose weights satisfy (1) are given below. Let $h = (x-l)/N$. The L1 approximation of the Caputo fractional derivative has the form

$$\frac{1}{\Gamma(2-\alpha)h^\alpha} \sum_{k=0}^{n} \sigma_k^{(\alpha)} f_{n-k} = f_n^{(\alpha)} + \mathcal{O}(h^{2-\alpha}), \tag{66}$$

where $\sigma_0^{(\alpha)} = 1, \quad \sigma_n^{(\alpha)} = (n-1)^{1-\alpha} - n^{1-\alpha}$,

$$\sigma_k^{(\alpha)} = (k+1)^{1-\alpha} - 2k^{1-\alpha} + (k-1)^{1-\alpha}, \qquad (1 \le k \le n-1).$$

The L1 approximation and approximation (5) have an order $2-\alpha$ and and their weights satisfy (1). In [7,46], we use the properties of the weights (1) of approximations of the fractional derivative for analyzing the convergence and order of the numerical solutions of two-term ordinary fractional differential equation and the time-fractional Black–Scholes equation. In [26,28], we construct second-order approximations of the Caputo derivative using the asymptotic formula of the L1 approximation. In [23], we obtain an approximation of the Caputo fractional derivative of order $2-\alpha$ by substituting the first derivative in (2) with a first-order backward difference approximation.

$$\frac{1}{2\Gamma(1-\alpha)h^\alpha} \sum_{k=0}^{n} \sigma_k^{(\alpha)} f_{n-k} = f_n^{(\alpha)} + \mathcal{O}(h^{2-\alpha}), \tag{67}$$

where $\sigma_0^{(\alpha)} = 1 - 2\zeta(\alpha), \quad \sigma_1^{(\alpha)} = \frac{1}{2^\alpha} + 2\zeta(\alpha)$,

$$\sigma_k^{(\alpha)} = \frac{1}{(k+1)^\alpha} - \frac{1}{(k-1)^\alpha}, \qquad (2 \le k \le n-2),$$

$$\sigma_{n-1}^{(\alpha)} = -\frac{1}{(n-2)^{\alpha}} - 2s_n, \quad \sigma_n^{(\alpha)} = -\frac{1}{(n-1)^{\alpha}} + 2s_n.$$

and $s_n = \sum_{k=1}^{n-1} k^{-\alpha} - n^{1-\alpha}/(1-\alpha) - \zeta(\alpha)$. Now, we apply approximation $\mathcal{A}_3$ for constructing an approximation of the Caputo derivative. By substituting the first derivative f_n' in Formula (2) with $\mathcal{A}_3$, we obtain an approximation of order $2-\alpha$.

$$\frac{1}{2\Gamma(1-\alpha)h^{\alpha}} \sum_{k=0}^{n} \sigma_k^{(\alpha)} f_{n-k} = f_n^{(\alpha)} + \mathcal{O}(h^{2-\alpha}), \tag{68}$$

where $\sigma_0^{(\alpha)} = 1 - 2(1-b)\zeta(\alpha), \quad \sigma_1^{(\alpha)} = \frac{1}{2^{\alpha}} + 2(1-b)^2\zeta(\alpha),$

$$\sigma_k^{(\alpha)} = \frac{1}{(k+1)^{\alpha}} - \frac{1}{(k-1)^{\alpha}} + 2(1-b)^2 b^{k-1}\zeta(\alpha), \qquad (2 \le k \le n-2),$$

$$\sigma_{n-1}^{(\alpha)} = -\frac{1}{(n-2)^{\alpha}} - 2s_n + 2(1-2b)b^{n-2}\zeta(\alpha),$$

$$\sigma_n^{(\alpha)} = -\frac{1}{(n-1)^{\alpha}} + 2s_n + 2b^{n-1}\zeta(\alpha).$$

The value of zeta function $\zeta(\alpha)$ is negative when $0 < \alpha < 1$ and the parameter b of approximation $\mathcal{A}_3$ has a modulus smaller than one, $|b| < 1$. Therefore, $\sigma_0^{(\alpha)} > 0$ and $\sigma_k^{(\alpha)} < 0$ for $k > 1$. In Lemma 4, we show that the coefficient $\sigma_1^{(\alpha)}$ of approximation (68) is negative when the parameter b has a value $b = \alpha/2$.

Lemma 4. *Let $b = a/2$. Then,*

$$\sigma_1^{(\alpha)} < 0. \tag{69}$$

Proof.

$$\sigma_1^{(\alpha)} = \frac{1}{2^{\alpha}} + 2\left(1 - \frac{\alpha}{2}\right)^2 \zeta(\alpha) = \frac{1}{2^{\alpha}} - \frac{1}{2}(2-a)^2|\zeta(\alpha)|.$$

Inequality (69) holds when

$$\frac{1}{2^{\alpha}} - \frac{1}{2}(2-\alpha)^2|\zeta(\alpha)| < 0,$$

$$|\zeta(\alpha)| > \frac{2}{2^{\alpha}(2-\alpha)^2}.$$

Taking the logarithm of both sides, we obtain

$$\ln|\zeta(\alpha)| > \ln 2 - \alpha \ln 2 - 2\ln(2-\alpha).$$

Let $f(\alpha) = \ln|\zeta(\alpha)| - \ln 2 + \alpha \ln 2 + 2\ln(2-\alpha)$. The function f satisfies $f(0) = 0$ and has first derivative

$$f'(\alpha) = \frac{\zeta'(\alpha)}{\zeta(\alpha)} + \ln 2 - \frac{2}{2-\alpha}.$$

It is sufficient to prove that f' is positive. The zeta function and its derivative have Laurent series expansions

$$\zeta(\alpha) = -\frac{1}{1-a} + \sum_{k=0}^{\infty} \frac{\gamma_k}{k!}(1-a)^k,$$

$$\zeta'(\alpha) = -\frac{1}{(1-\alpha)^2} - \sum_{k=0}^{\infty} \frac{\gamma_{k+1}}{k!}(1-a)^k,$$

where γ_k are Stieltjes constants

$$\gamma_0 = 0.5772,\ \gamma_1 = -0.0728,\ \gamma_2 = -0.0097,\ \gamma_3 = 0.0021,\ \gamma_4 = 0.0023,\ \cdots.$$

Hence,

$$|\zeta(\alpha)| < \frac{1}{1-\alpha}, \quad |\zeta'(\alpha)| > \frac{1}{(1-\alpha)^2} + \gamma_1 + \gamma_2(1-\alpha),$$

$$|\zeta'(\alpha)| > \frac{1}{(1-\alpha)^2} - 0.08 - 0,01(1-\alpha).$$

The derivative of the function f satisfies

$$f'(\alpha) > \frac{1}{1-\alpha} - 0.08(1-\alpha) - 0.01(1-\alpha)^2 + \ln 2 - \frac{2}{2-\alpha}.$$

Denote

$$g(\alpha) = \frac{1}{1-\alpha} - 0.08(1-\alpha) - 0.01(1-\alpha)^2 + \ln 2 - \frac{2}{2-\alpha}.$$

The function g has first-, second- and third-order derivatives

$$g'(\alpha) = \frac{1}{(1-\alpha)^2} + 0.08 + 0.02(1-\alpha) - \frac{2}{(2-\alpha)^2},$$

$$g''(\alpha) = \frac{2}{(1-\alpha)^3} - 0.02 - \frac{4}{(2-\alpha)^3},$$

$$g'''(\alpha) = \frac{6}{(1-\alpha)^4} - \frac{12}{(2-\alpha)^4}.$$

The values of the function g and its derivatives g', g'', g''' at zero are positive:

$$g(0) = \ln 2 - 0.09 > 0, \quad g'(0) = 0.6, \quad g''(0) = 1.48, \quad g'''(0) = 5.25.$$

The third derivative g''' is positive on the interval $[0,1]$ because

$$\left(\frac{2-\alpha}{1-\alpha}\right)^4 > 2, \quad 1 + \frac{1}{1-\alpha} > \sqrt[4]{2}, \quad \frac{1}{1-\alpha} > 1 > \sqrt[4]{2} - 1.$$

Therefore, the functions g, g', g'' are positive and increasing and $f'(\alpha) > g(\alpha) > 0$. The function f is increasing and positive because $f(0) = 0$. □

Approximation (5) of the fractional derivative is obtained from (68) and value of the parameter $b = \alpha/2$. The two-term and multi-term ordinary fractional differential equations are an important class of equations in fractional calculus which generalize the linear ordinary differential equations with constant coefficients. Their analytical and numerical solutions are studied in [47–51]. In the following examples, we will consider an application of approximation (68) for the construction of numerical schemes for the two-term ordinary fractional differential equation and the fractional subdiffusion equation.

Example 6. *Consider the following two-term equation:*

$$y^{(\alpha)}(x) + Ly(x) = F(x), \quad y(0) = y_0. \tag{70}$$

The numerical solution $\{u_n\}_{n=1}^N$ of Equation (70), which uses the L1 approximation (66) of the fractional derivative, is computed as

$$u_m = \frac{1}{\sigma_0^{(\alpha)} + L\Gamma(2-\alpha)h^\alpha}\left(L\Gamma(2-\alpha)h^\alpha F_m - \sum_{k=1}^{m} \sigma_k^{(\alpha)} u_{m-k}\right). \tag{71}$$

The numerical solution of Equation (70), which uses approximations (67) and (68) of the fractional derivative $y_n^{(\alpha)}$, satisfies

$$u_m = \frac{1}{\sigma_0^{(\alpha)} + 2L\Gamma(1-\alpha)h^\alpha}\left(2L\Gamma(1-\alpha)h^\alpha F_m - \sum_{k=1}^{m} \sigma_k^{(\alpha)} u_{m-k}\right) \tag{72}$$

and has initial conditions

$$u_0 = y_0, \quad u_1 = \frac{h^\alpha\Gamma(2-\alpha)F_1 + u_0}{Lh^\alpha\Gamma(2-\alpha)+1}, \quad u_2 = \frac{(2h)^\alpha\Gamma(2-\alpha)F_2 + u_0}{L(2h)^\alpha\Gamma(2-\alpha)+1}. \tag{73}$$

The initial conditions (6) are obtained with the approximation of the fractional derivative

$$\frac{f(\ell)-f(0)}{\Gamma(2-\alpha)\ell^\alpha} = f^{(\alpha)}(\ell) + O(\ell^{2-\alpha}). \tag{74}$$

Consider the two-term equation

$$y^{(\alpha)}(x) + Ly(x) = x^{1-\alpha}E_{1,2-\alpha}(x) + Le^x, \quad y(0) = 1. \tag{75}$$

Equation (75) has a solution $y(x) = e^x$, where $E_{1,2-\alpha}(x)$ is the Mittag–Leffler function

$$E_{1,2-\alpha}(x) = \sum_{k=0}^{\infty} \frac{x^k}{\Gamma(k+2-\alpha)}.$$

The experimental results of numerical solutions (71) and (72) of Equation (75) on the interval $[0,1]$ are given in Tables 14 and 15. The second column of Table 14 pertains to (72) using approximation (67), while the results in the third column relate to (72) using approximation (68) with a parameter $b = -0.5$. The numerical results in Table 15 were obtained using approximation (5) for the fractional derivative. The sequence s_n and the coefficients $\sigma_{n-1}^{(\alpha)}$ and $\sigma_n^{(\alpha)}$ of approximations (67) and (68) for $n = 3,\cdots,N$ are computed recursively in $\mathcal{O}(N)$ arithmetic operations. The (71) and (72) methods have similar computational time and accuracy. The approximation (67) is obtained from Formula (2) by replacing the first derivative f_n' with a first-order difference approximation. Replacing the second derivative and derivatives of higher order with finite difference approximations in the asymptotic formulas leads to approximations whose weights do not satisfy (1). The method of constructing approximation (5) using the approximation $\mathcal{A}_3$ of the first derivative has the advantage that it can be generalized to constructions of high-order fractional derivative approximations, which have properties (1).

The time-fractional subdiffusion equation is a generalization of the heat diffusion equation using a time-fractional derivative of order α with $a \in (0,1)$. The analytical and numerical solutions of fractional subdiffusion equations are studied in [52–56].

Example 7. *Consider the following fractional subdiffusion equation:*

$$\begin{cases} D_t^\alpha u(x,t) = Du_{xx}(x,t) + F(x,t), \\ u(x,0) = u_0(x),\ u(0,t) = u_1(t),\ u(1,t) = u_2(t). \end{cases} \tag{76}$$

where $(x,t) \in [0,1] \times [0,1]$ and $D_t^\alpha u(x,t)$ denotes the Caputo derivative of the solution $u(x,t)$ in time. Let $\tau = 1/M$ and $h = 1/N$, where M and N are positive integers, and let $\mathcal{J}$ be a rectangular grid with nodes $(x_n, y_n) = (nh, mh)$. The numerical solution U_n^m on the first three rows of $\mathcal{J}$ is computed with the approximation (74) of the partial fractional derivative and second-order central difference approximation of the partial derivative in space

$$\frac{U_n^m - U_n^0}{\Gamma(2-\alpha)(m\tau)^\alpha} = \frac{D}{h^2}(U_{n-1}^m - 2U_n^m + U_{n+1}^m) + F_n^m,$$

$$U_n^m - U_n^0 = \frac{D\Gamma(2-\alpha)(m\tau)^\alpha}{h^2}(U_{n-1}^m - 2U_n^m + U_{n+1}^m) + \Gamma(2-\alpha)(m\tau)^\alpha F_n^m.$$

Denote $\eta_m = D\Gamma(2-\alpha)(m\tau)^\alpha/h^2$. The numerical solution satisfies the system of linear equations

$$-\eta_m U_{n-1}^m + (1+2\eta_m)U_n^m - \eta_m U_{n+1}^m = U_n^0 + \Gamma(2-\alpha)(m\tau)^\alpha F_n^m$$

and has initial conditions $U_n^0 = u_0(nh)$ for $n = 0,1,\cdots,N$ and boundary conditions $U_0^m = u_1(m\tau)$, $U_N^m = u_2(m\tau)$ for $m = 1,2,3$. The numerical solution on row m of the grid $\mathcal{J}$, where $m > 3$, which uses approximation (5) of the fractional derivative, satisfies

$$\frac{1}{2\Gamma(1-\alpha)\tau^\alpha}\sum_{k=0}^{m}\sigma_k^{(\alpha)}U_n^{m-k} = \frac{D}{h^2}(U_{n-1}^m - 2U_n^m + U_{n+1}^m) + F_n^m,$$

$$\sigma_0^{(\alpha)}U_n^{m-k} + \sum_{k=1}^{m}\sigma_k^{(\alpha)}U_n^{m-k} = \frac{2D\Gamma(1-a)\tau^\alpha}{h^2}(U_{n-1}^m - 2U_n^m + U_{n+1}^m) + 2\Gamma(1-a)\tau^\alpha F_n^m.$$

Denote $\eta = 2D\Gamma(1-a)\tau^\alpha/h^2$. The numerical solution on row m satisfies the tridiagonal system of linear equations

$$-\eta U_{n-1}^m + (\sigma_0^{(\alpha)} + 2\eta)U_n^m - \eta U_{n+1}^m = \Gamma(2-\alpha)\tau^\alpha F_n^m - \sum_{k=1}^{m}\sigma_k^{(\alpha)}U_n^{m-k}. \tag{77}$$

Consider the fractional subdiffusion equation

$$\begin{cases} D_t^\alpha u(x,t) = Du_{xx}(x,t) + e^x(t^{1-\alpha}E_{1,2-\alpha}(t) - De^t), \\ u(x,0) = e^x,\ u(0,t) = e^t,\ u(1,t) = e^{1+t}. \end{cases} \tag{78}$$

Equation (78) has a solution $u(x,t) = e^{x+t}$. The graphs of numerical solution (77) of Equation (78) and its error for $h = \tau = 0.01$ are shown in Figure 2. Experimental results for the error and order of numerical solution (77) of fractional subdiffusion Equation (78) and $\alpha = 0.5, 0.75$ are given in Tables 16 and 17.

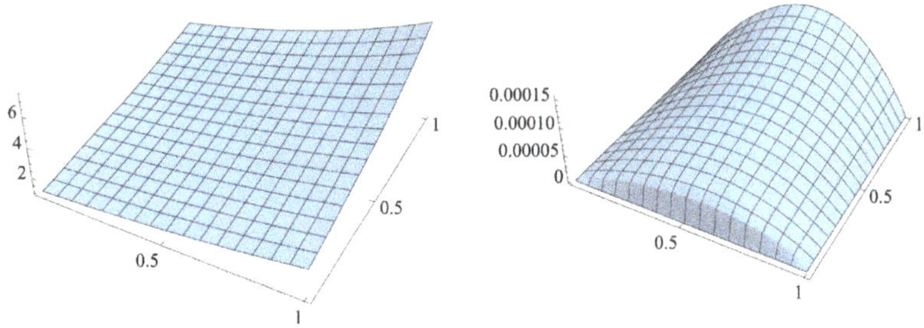

Figure 2. Graphs of numerical solution (77) (**left**) and its error (**right**) for $h = \tau = 0.01$.

Table 14. Error and order of numerical solutions (71) and (72) of Equation (75).

h	NS(71), $\alpha = 0.25, L = 1$		NS(72), $\alpha = 0.5, L = 10$		$\alpha = 0.75, L = 5, b = -0.5$	
	Error	*Order*	*Error*	*Order*	*Error*	*Order*
0.0005	2.9218×10^{-7}	1.7225	7.9883×10^{-7}	1.4919	2.3232×10^{-6}	1.2443
0.00025	8.8244×10^{-7}	1.7273	2.8355×10^{-7}	1.4943	9.7923×10^{-7}	1.2463
0.000125	2.6579×10^{-8}	1.7312	1.0053×10^{-7}	1.4959	4.1236×10^{-7}	1.2477

Table 15. Error and order of numerical solution (72) of Equation (75) and $b = \alpha/2$.

h	NS(72),$\alpha = 0.25, L = 1$		NS(72),$\alpha = 0.5, L = 10$		NS(72),$\alpha = 0.75, L = 5$	
	Error	*Order*	*Error*	*Order*	*Error*	*Order*
0.0005	6.4339×10^{-7}	1.7248	1.5529×10^{-6}	1.4953	3.1981×10^{-5}	1.2487
0.00025	1.9405×10^{-7}	1.7292	5.5026×10^{-7}	1.4968	1.3453×10^{-5}	1.2493
0.000125	5.8383×10^{-8}	1.7328	1.9484×10^{-7}	1.4978	5.6578×10^{-6}	1.2496

Table 16. Error and order of numerical solution (77) and $N = 1000$.

τ	$\alpha = 0.5$		$\alpha = 0.75$	
	Error	*Order*	*Error*	*Order*
1/8	5.6355×10^{-3}	–	1.6687×10^{-2}	–
1/16	2.1509×10^{-3}	1.3896	7.5333×10^{-3}	1.1473
1/32	7.9545×10^{-4}	1.4351	3.2885×10^{-3}	1.1958
1/64	2.8898×10^{-4}	1.4607	1.4105×10^{-3}	1.2213
1/128	1.0393×10^{-4}	1.4753	5.9934×10^{-4}	1.2347

Table 17. Error and order of numerical solution (77) and $N = 1000$.

h	$\alpha = 0.5$		$\alpha = 0.75$	
	Error	*Order*	*Error*	*Order*
1/5	1.6057×10^{-6}	–	1.4085×10^{-6}	–
1/10	3.5567×10^{-4}	1.9845	3.5532×10^{-4}	1.9555
1/20	8.9727×10^{-5}	1.9869	8.9352×10^{-5}	1.9915
1/40	2.2870×10^{-5}	1.9721	2.2487×10^{-5}	1.9903
1/80	6.0154×10^{-6}	1.9267	5.6314×10^{-6}	1.9975

7. Conclusions

In this paper, we construct approximations of the first derivative whose weights contain powers of a parameter a, where $|a| < 1$. The approximations are applied to the numerical solution of ordinary differential equations and the heat equation. The properties of the weights allow the computation of the numerical solution of ordinary differential equations with $\mathcal{O}(N)$ operations. The numerical solutions of partial differential equations are computed with $\mathcal{O}(MN)$ operations, where M is the number of nodes in time and N is the number of nodes in space. The numerical methods are compared with the Euler method using a first-order backward approximation of the first derivative. In the examples given in the paper, we observe similar computational time and accuracy for the numerical methods, with the time difference being less than a second. The numerical methods for ODEs and PDEs using approximation (3) of the first derivative can achieve an arbitrary order in $(0, 2]$ using values of the parameter (47), (48), and (49). The numerical methods constructed in the paper are easy to implement and perform better compared to the Euler method for Equation (38) with negative values of L and values of the parameter a close to one, as shown in Tables 4–6. The main goal of constructing the first derivative approximations (3) and (4) is to use them in constructing fractional derivative approximations, whose weights have property (1). An example of a construction of an approximation of the fractional derivative of order $2-\alpha$ which uses asymptotic Formula (2) and approximation (3) of the first derivative is given in Section 6. The method for constructing the approximation (5) can be generalized to develop high-order approximations of the fractional derivative. In future work, we plan to extend the results presented in this paper. We will present proofs of the convergence of the numerical methods discussed in the paper and apply the method to construct approximations for the second-order and higher-order derivatives. We aim to study the construction of high-order approximations of the fractional derivative with weights that satisfy (1), as well as to investigate the properties and convergence of finite difference schemes for fractional differential equations.

Author Contributions: Conceptualization, Y.D. and S.G.; data curation, V.T.; formal analysis, Y.D. and V.T.; funding acquisition, S.G.; investigation, Y.D.; methodology, V.T. and S.G.; project administration, Y.D. and V.T.; resources, S.G.; software, S.G.; supervision, Y.D.; validation, V.T.; visualization, S.G.; writing—original draft, Y.D. and S.G.; writing—review and editing, Y.D. and V.T. All authors have read and agreed to the published version of the manuscript.

Funding: This study is supported by the Bulgarian National Science Fund under Project KP-06-M62/1 "Numerical deterministic, stochastic, machine and deep learning methods with applications in computational, quantitative, algorithmic finance, biomathematics, ecology and algebra" from 2022.

Data Availability Statement: The data presented in this study are available on request from the corresponding author.

Conflicts of Interest: The authors declare no conflicts of interest.

References

1. Akgül, A.; Conejero, J.A. Fractal fractional derivative models for simulating chemical degradation in a bioreactor. *Axioms* **2024**, *13*, 151. [CrossRef]
2. Akgül, A.; Khoshnaw, S.H.A. Application of fractional derivative on non-linear biochemical reaction models. *Int. J. Intell. Netw.* **2020**, *1*, 2–58. [CrossRef]
3. Baba, I.A.; Rihan, F.A. A fractional–order model with different strains of COVID-19. *Phys. A Stat. Mech. Appl.* **2022**, *603*, 127813. [CrossRef] [PubMed]
4. Gu, Y.; Yu, Z.; Lan, P.; Lu, N. fractional derivative viscosity of ANCF cable element. *Actuators* **2023**, *12*, 64. [CrossRef]
5. Hilfer, R. *Applications of Fractional Calculus in Physics*; World Scientific: Singapore, 2003.
6. Kumar, D.; Singh, J. *Fractional Calculus in Medical and Health Science*; CRC Press: Boca Raton, FL, USA, 2020.
7. Dimitrov, Y.; Georgiev, S.; Miryanov, R.; Todorov, V. Convergence of the L1 two-term equation scheme. *J. Phys. Conf. Ser.* **2023**, *2675*, 012027. [CrossRef]
8. Jin, B.; Lazarov, R.; Zhou, Z. An analysis of the L1 scheme for the subdiffusion equation with nonsmooth data. *IMA J. Numer. Anal.* **2016**, *36*, 197–221. [CrossRef]
9. Li, B.; Xie, X.; Yan, Y. L1 scheme for solving an inverse problem subject to a fractional diffusion equation. *Comput. Math. Appl.* **2023**, *134*, 112–123. [CrossRef]
10. Scherer, R.; Kalla, S.L.; Tang, Y.; Huang, J. The Grünwald—Letnikov method for fractional differential equations. *Comput. Math. Appl.* **2011**, *62*, 902–917. [CrossRef]
11. Arshad, S.; Defterli, O.; Baleanu, D. A second order accurate approximation for fractional derivatives with singular and non-singular kernel applied to a HIV model. *Appl. Math Comput.* **2020**, *374*, 125061. [CrossRef]
12. Nasir, H.M.; Nafa, K. A new second order approximation for fractional derivatives with applications. *Sultan Qaboos Univ. J. Sci.* **2018**, *23*, 43–55. [CrossRef]
13. Alikhanov, A.A. A new difference scheme for the time fractional diffusion equation. *J. Comput. Phys.* **2015**, *280*, 424–438. [CrossRef]
14. Gao, G.-H.; Sun, Z.-Z.; Zhang, H.-W. A new fractional numerical differentiation formula to approximate the Caputo fractional derivative and its applications. *J. Comput. Phys.* **2014**, *259*, 33–50. [CrossRef]
15. Xing, Y.; Yan, Y. A higher order numerical method for time fractional partial differential equations with nonsmooth data. *J. Comput. Phys.* **2018**, *357*, 305–323. [CrossRef]
16. Chen, M.H.; Deng, W.H. Fourth order accurate scheme for the space fractional diffusion equations. *SIAM J. Numer. Anal.* **2014**, *52*, 1418–1438. [CrossRef]
17. Gunarathna, W.A.; Nasir, H.M.; Daundasekera, W.B. An explicit form for higher order approximations of fractional derivatives. *Appl. Numer. Math.* **2019**, *143*, 51–60. [CrossRef]

18. Hao, Z.-P.; Sun, Z.-Z.; Cao, W.-R. A fourth-order approximation of fractional derivatives with its applications. *J. Comput. Phys* **2015**, *281*, 787–805. [CrossRef]
19. Li, L.; Zhao, D.; She, M.; Chen, X. On high order numerical schemes for fractional differential equations by block-by-block approach. *Appl. Math. Comput.* **2022**, *425*, 127098. [CrossRef]
20. Lubich, C. Discretized fractional calculus. *SIAM J. Math. Anal.* **1986**, *17*, 704–719. [CrossRef]
21. Nasrollahzadeh, F.; Hosseini, S.M. An implicit difference ADI method for two-dimensional space-time fractional diffusion equation. *Iran. J. Math. Sci. Inform.* **2016**, *11*, 71–86. [CrossRef]
22. Wang, Z.; Liang, Y.; Mo, Y. A novel high order compact ADI scheme for two dimensional fractional integro-differential equations *Appl. Numer. Math.* **2021**, *167*, 257–272. [CrossRef]
23. Dimitrov, Y. Approximations for the Caputo derivative (I). *J. Fract. Calc. Appl.* **2018**, *9*, 15–44.
24. Ahnert, K.; Abel, M. Numerical differentiation of experimental data: Local versus global methods. *J. Comput. Phys. Commun* **2005**, *177*, 764–774. [CrossRef]
25. Hanke, M.; Scherzer, O. Inverse problems light: Numerical differentiation. *Am. Math. Mon.* **2001**, *108*, 512–521. [CrossRef]
26. Apostolov, S.; Dimitrov, Y.; Todorov, V. Constructions of second order approximations of the Caputo fractional derivative In *Lecture Notes in Computer Science*; Lirkov, I., Margenov, S., Eds.; Large-Scale Scientific Computing. LSSC 2021; Springer Berlin/Heidelberg, Germany, 2022; p. 13127.
27. Todorov, V.; Dimitrov, Y.; Dimov, I. Second order shifted approximations for the first derivative. In *Studies in Computational Intelligence*; Dimov, I., Fidanova, S., Eds.; Advances in High Performance Computing. HPC 2019; Springer: Cham, Switzerland 2011; p. 902.
28. Dimitrov, Y. A second order approximation for the Caputo fractional derivative. *J. Fract. Calc. Appl.* **2016**, *7*, 175–195.
29. Al-Bar, R. On the approximate solution of fractional logistic differential equation using operational matrices of Bernstein polynomials. *Appl. Math.* **2015**, *6*, 2096–2103. [CrossRef]
30. Iannelli, M.; Pugliese, A. *An Introduction to Mathematical Population Dynamics: Along the Trail of Volterra and Lotka*, 4th ed.; Springer Berlin/Heidelberg, Germany, 2014.
31. Kot, M. *Elements of Mathematical Ecology*; Cambridge University Press: Cambridge, UK, 2001.
32. Hahn, D.W.; Özişik, M.N. *Heat Conduction*, 3rd ed.; John Wiley & Sons: Hoboken, NJ, USA, 2012.
33. Incorpera, F.P.; DeWitt, D.P.; Bergman, T.L.; Lavine, A.S. *Fundamentals of Heat and Mass Transfer*, 6th ed.; John Wiley: New York NY, USA, 2006.
34. Majumdar, P. *Computational Methods for Heat and Mass Transfer*; CRC Press: Boca Raton, FL, USA, 2006.
35. Morton, K.W.; Mayers, D.F. *Numerical Solution of Partial Differential Equations: An Introduction*, 2nd ed.; Cambridge University Press: Cambridge, UK, 2005.
36. Zhao, S. A matched alternating direction implicit (ADI) method for solving the heat equation with interfaces. *J. Sci. Comput.* **2015** *63*, 118–137. [CrossRef]
37. Press, W.H.; Teukolsky, S.A.; Vetterling, W.T.; Flannery, B.P. *Numerical Recipes: The Art of Scientific Computing*; Cambridge University Press: Cambridge, UK, 2007.
38. Datta, B.N. *Numerical Linear Algebra and Applications*, 2nd ed.; Society for Industrial and Applied Mathematics: Philadelphia, PA USA, 2010.
39. Suárez-Carreño, F.; Rosales-Romero, L. Convergency and stability of explicit and implicit schemes in the simulation of the heat equation. *Appl. Sci.* **2021**, *11*, 4468. [CrossRef]
40. Sundaram, A. Numerical solution for the heat equation using Crank-Nicolson difference method. *Int. J. Res. Appl. Sci. Eng Technol.* **2023**, *11, 158–164.* . [CrossRef]
41. Ames, W. *Numerical Methods for Partial Differential Equations*; Academic Press: Boston, MA, USA, 1992.
42. Smith, G.D. *Numerical Solution of Partial Differential Equations: Finite Difference Method*; Oxford University Press: Oxford, UK, 1992
43. Kolotilina, L.Y. Bounds for the infinity norm of the inverse for certain M- and H-matrices. *Linear Algebra Appl.* **2009**, *430*, 692–702 [CrossRef]
44. Varah, J.M. A lower bound for the smallest singular value of a matrix. *Linear Algebra Appl.* **1975**, *11*, 3–5. [CrossRef]
45. Kulkarni, D.; Schmidt, D.; Tsui, S.-K. Eigenvalues of tridiagonal pseudo-Toeplitz matrices. *Linear Algebra Appl.* **1999**, *297*, 63–80 [CrossRef]
46. Dimitrov, Y.; Georgiev, S.; Todorov, V. Approximation of Caputo fractional derivative and numerical solutions of fractional differential equations. *Fractal Fract.* **2023**, *7*, 750. [CrossRef]
47. Li, C.; Zeng, F. *Numerical Methods for Fractional Calculus*; Chapman and Hall/CRC: Boca Raton, FL, USA, 2015.
48. Avcı, İ.; Mahmudov, N.I. Numerical solutions for multi-term fractional order differential equations with fractional Taylor operational matrix of fractional integration. *Mathematics* **2020**, *8*, 96. [CrossRef]
49. Diethelm, K.; Ford, N.J. Analysis of fractional differential equations. *J. Math. Anal. Appl.* **2002**, *265*, 229–248. [CrossRef]
50. Edwards, J.T.; Ford, N.J.; Simpson, A.C. The numerical solution of linear multi-term fractional differential equations: Systems of equations. *J. Comput. Appl. Math.* **2002**, *148*, 401–418. [CrossRef]
51. El-Mesiry, A.E.M.; El-Sayed, A.M.A.; El-Saka, H.A.A. Numerical methods for multi-term fractional (arbitrary) orders differential equations. *Appl. Math. Comput.* **2005**, *160*, 683–699. [CrossRef]

52. Ali, U.; Sohail, M.; Abdullah, F.A. An efficient numerical scheme for variable-order fractional sub-diffusion equation. *Symmetry* **2020**, *12*, 1437. [CrossRef]
53. Ashurov, R.; Umarov, S. Determination of the order of fractional derivative for subdiffusion equations. *Fract. Calc. Appl. Anal.* **2020**, *23*, 1647–1662. [CrossRef]
54. Langlands, T.A.M.; Henry, B.I. The accuracy and stability of an implicit solution method for the fractional diffusion equation. *J. Comput. Phys.* **2005**, *205*, 719–736. [CrossRef]
55. Mainardi, F.; Mura, A.; Pagnini, G.; Gorenflo, R. Sub-diffusion equations of fractional order and their fundamental solutions. In *Mathematical Methods in Engineering*; Taş, K., Tenreiro Machado, J.A., Baleanu, D., Eds.; Springer: Berlin/Heidelberg, Germany, 2007; pp. 23–55.
56. Podlubny, I. *Fractional Differential Equations*; Academic Press: Cambridge, MA, USA, 1999.

fractal and fractional

MDPI

Article

Analysis of Infection and Diffusion Coefficient in an SIR Model by Using Generalized Fractional Derivative

Ibtehal Alazman [1], Manvendra Narayan Mishra [2,*], Badr Saad Alkahtani [3] and Ravi Shanker Dubey [4]

[1] Department of Mathematics and Statistics, College of Science, Imam Mohammad Ibn Saud Islamic University (IMSIU), Riyadh 13318, Saudi Arabia; iaazman@imamu.edu.sa
[2] Department of Mathematics, Suresh Gyan Vihar University, Jaipur 302017, India
[3] Department of Mathematics, College of Science, King Saud University, P.O. Box 1142, Riyadh 11989, Saudi Arabia
[4] Department of Mathematics, Amity School of Applied Science, Amity University Rajasthan, Jaipur 303002, India; rsdubey@jpr.amity.edu
* Correspondence: manvendra.mishra22187@gmail.com

Abstract: In this article, a diffusion component in an SIR model is introduced, and its impact is analyzed using fractional calculus. We have included the diffusion component in the SIR model. in order to illustrate the variations. Here, we have applied the general fractional derivative to analyze the impact. The Laplace decomposition technique is employed to obtain the numerical outcomes of the model. In order to observe the effect of the diffusion component in the SIR model, graphical solutions are also displayed.

Keywords: SIR model; general fractional operator; mathematical model; Laplace transform; existence and uniqueness

MSC: 92B05; 92C60; 26A33

1. Introduction

The application of mathematical models to analyze biological systems has captured significant attention in recent decades. Gregor Mendel pioneered this approach by using mathematics to formulate the laws of heredity, and epidemic modeling dates back to the 19th century. Notably, Ronald Ross revolutionized epidemiology by introducing compartmental models such as SIR and SIRS. In [1], Asif et al. offered a comparative study of the SIR model, while the SEIR model was explored in [2] using advanced modeling techniques. Nisar et al. examined the dynamics of whooping cough through the SIR model in [3], and Ergen et al. made predictions regarding disease progression in [4]. Alqarni et al. provided a focused analysis of whooping cough infection in [5]. Today, mathematical modeling is indispensable across nearly every facet of life, valued for its precision and capacity to address complex real-world constraints [6,7].

In recent years, mathematical modeling is becoming more relevant when it comes together with fractional calculus [8–11]. Fractional calculus is one of the most important and impactful areas in mathematics due to various useful operators and some very logical concepts. Fractional calculus gives more precise results due to the memory effect of their kernels [12–16].

In current time, fractional calculus is receiving much more attention from many mathematicians and researchers than the integer order system due to the fact that, in fractional calculus, we have much more freedom to be more accurate than the integer order system, as, in fractional calculus, we can have infinite points at which we can analyze the results, while we have limitations in obtaining the results only at integers in the integer ordered system [17–22]. There has been remarkable work carried out in various fields of our real life like biological fields, epidemiology, engineering, physical problems, medical science, inventory, mechanical problems and many more [23–28].

Now focusing back on our topic, in this paper, we have decided to analyze the effect of diffusion on the system. To be more specific, we have taken the system of an SIR model [4,29–32] of pertussis. This is a very highly contagious bacterial infection. This infection spreads from person to person through social contact. Pertussis has shown extreme growth in the last few decades. As per a report, around 600,000 deaths per year are caused by pertussis around the globe. The main reason of its spread is airborne discharge from the mucous of infected persons. Vaccination has shown some resistance but is not as effective as it should be. Here, we have taken the SIR model given by G. G. Parra et al. [6]. We have added a diffusion factor into the existing model to analyze its effect. We have used the general fractional derivative along with Laplace transformation to achieve our objective. We have used this particular operator (generalized operator) since we can obtain three different results by just changing the kernel of the function, and we can obtain a comparative analytic view by using three different kernels. We have used the generalized operator here because we can compare the results for a classical operator (RL) with non-singular and non-local operators. One more important thing with this paper is the mentioned SIR model is not described by any of the fractional operators till date, so this is a unique problem which we have tried to discuss and analyze. In this paper, we have used the Riemann Liouville derivative (a kind of generalized derivative) rather than Caputo, since our main objective is to analyze the SIR model by generalized fractional derivatives and not only Caputo. We have also presented the existence and uniqueness of our novel approach, and this approach is well supported by the graphical results of the model as well [33–35].

The widespread use of SIR models with fractional derivatives and diffusion coefficients is limited by their complexity, computational costs and difficulty in interpreting parameters, despite the fact that they provide a more sophisticated way to model the spread of disease, especially when memory effects and spatial diffusion are significant.

There are many real world applications of the SIR model which can benefit society. Some examples are as follows: By taking fractional derivatives into account, a fractional SIR model takes the memory component into account and permits the illness to spread based on the system's past as well as its present condition. It is possible to predict disease patterns more precisely in places like urban centers or refugee camps, where they may differ from those in rural regions. The fractional model accounts for differences in the relative contributions of various areas to the transmission of illness. Vaccines frequently produce waning immunity, which is immunity that takes longer to develop or fades over time. This progressive process can be better simulated by a fractional SIR model than by a normal SIR model. The long-term impacts of vaccination efforts can be better understood thanks to the fractional method.

This article is divided into seven parts. Part one consists of the introduction of the article. Section 2 deals with pre-requisites related to the paper. The SIR model [36–39] is briefly discussed in Section 3, while Section 4 presents the existence and uniqueness of the solution. In the next segment, we have found the solution of the SIR model by a general fractional derivative with the help of Laplace transform. Graphical results have been presented in Section 6, while the paper is concluded in Section 7. A list of references is attached at the end to acknowledge the researchers and mathematicians.

2. Pre-Requisites

An overview of the recently defined general fractional operator is given in this section. According to [40], scholars have presented the Caputo ([41]) and Riemann–Liouville (RL) derivatives of the fractional exponent, which are shown by

$$ {}_0^C\mathrm{D}_t^{\gamma} f(t) = \int_0^t \dot{f}(s) \nabla_\iota (t-s) ds, \tag{1} $$

$$ {}_0\mathrm{D}_t^{\gamma} f(t) = \frac{d}{dt}\int_0^t f(s)\nabla_\iota(t-s)ds, \tag{2} $$

where $\gamma \in (0,1)$ is power of derivative, $f : [0,+\infty) \to \mathbb{R}$ is a continuous function with $\dot{f} \in L^1_{\text{loc}}\,(0,+\infty), 0 \leqslant t \leqslant T < +\infty$, ∇_ι is known as kernel. The linear condition is enforced on the operator,

$$ {}_0^C\mathrm{D}_t^{\gamma}(jf(t)+kg(t)) = j{}_0^C\mathrm{D}_t^{\gamma} f(t) + k{}_0^C\mathrm{D}_t^{\gamma} g(t), \tag{3} $$

$$ {}_0\mathrm{D}_t^{\gamma}(jf(t)+kg(t)) = j{}_0\mathrm{D}_t^{\gamma} f(t) + k{}_0\mathrm{D}_t^{\gamma} g(t). \tag{4} $$

It is obvious that for any $t > 0$, $\nabla_\iota(t)$ is met, and a completely function of monotone type $\Im_\iota(t)$ occurs [11],

$$ \nabla_\iota(t) * \Im_\iota(t) = \int_0^\infty \nabla_\iota(s)\Im_\iota(t-s)ds = 1, \tag{5} $$

and further, for $f \in L^1_{\text{loc}}\,(0,+\infty)$, we can rewrite above like

$$ {}_0\mathrm{D}_t^{-\gamma}\left[{}_0^C\mathrm{D}_t^{\gamma} f(t)\right] = f(t) - f(0), \tag{6} $$

where ${}_0\mathrm{D}_t^{-\gamma}$ represents the Riemann–Liouville integral of fractional order ([42]), given as

$$ {}_0\mathrm{D}_t^{-\gamma} f(t) = \int_0^t f(s)\Im_\iota(t-s)ds. \tag{7} $$

The right Caputo and Riemann–Liouville fractional derivatives are

$$ {}_t^C\mathrm{D}_T^{\gamma} f(t) = \int_t^T \dot{f}(s)\nabla_r(s-t)ds, \tag{8} $$

$$ {}_t\mathrm{D}_T^{\gamma} f(t) = \frac{d}{dt}\int_t^T f(s)\nabla_r(s-t)ds \tag{9} $$

and

$$ {}_t\mathrm{D}_T^{-\gamma} f(t) = \int_t^T f(s)\Im_r(s-t)ds. \tag{10} $$

The integration by the component formula is thus satisfied by the aforementioned fractional order operators, according to the results in [43].

$$ \int_0^T f(s){}_0D_s^{\gamma} g(s)ds = \int_0^T g(s){}_s{}^C D_s^{\gamma} f(s)ds, \tag{11} $$

$$ \int_0^T f(s){}_0{}^C D_s^{\gamma} g(s)ds = \int_0^T g(s){}_s D_s^{\gamma} f(s)ds. \tag{12} $$

By changing various kernels into general operator definitions, we can derive three specific cases of the general operator. In the first case when the kernel is $\nabla_\iota(t) = \frac{t^{-\gamma}}{\Gamma(1-\gamma)}$, we have the power function $\Im_\iota(t) = \frac{t^{\gamma-1}}{\Gamma(\gamma)}$ which reforms the integral operator's associated kernel (7).

Further, take kernel $\nabla_\iota(t) = \frac{B(\gamma)}{1-\gamma}\mathrm{E}_\gamma\left(\frac{-\gamma}{1-\gamma}t^\gamma\right)$ where E_γ and $\mathrm{B}(\gamma)$ are Mittag–Leffler and normalization functions. Also, we have

$$ \Im_\iota(t) = \frac{1-\gamma}{B(\gamma)}\delta(t) + \frac{\gamma}{\mathrm{B}(\gamma)\Gamma(\gamma)}t^{\gamma-1}. \tag{13} $$

So, Equations (1) and (2) may be used to obtain the derivatives of Atangana–Baleanu–Caputo (ABC) and Atangana–Baleanu–Riemann–Liouville. The AB type integral is [33]

$$ {}_0\mathrm{D}_t^{-\gamma} f(t) = \frac{1-\gamma}{\mathrm{B}(\gamma)}f(t) + \frac{\gamma}{\mathrm{B}(\gamma)\Gamma(\gamma)}\int_0^t (t-s)^{\gamma-1} f(s)ds. \tag{14} $$

Now, in the last situation, the Caputo–Fabrizio (CF) derivative ([11]) is found by taking kernel $\nabla_{\iota}(t) = \frac{B(\gamma)}{1-\gamma}\exp\left(\frac{-\gamma}{1-\gamma}t\right)$.

2.1. *Riemann–Liouville's Fractional Operator*

Riemann–Liouville's fractional operator ([44]) is explained below:

$$^{RL}D_x^{\alpha}\{f(x)\} = \frac{1}{\Gamma(n-\alpha)}\frac{d^n}{dx^n}\int_0^x (x-y)^{n-\alpha-1}f(y)dy, \quad (15)$$

where α is the order of the derivative, and $0 < \alpha < 1$.

2.2. *Caputo–Fabrizio Fractional Derivative*

Let $h \in H^1(a_1, b_1)$, $b_1 > a_1$, $\beta \in [0,1]$; then, the new Caputo–Fabrizio derivative of fractional order ([45]) is as follows:

$$D_t^{\beta}(\mathrm{h(t)}) = \frac{M(\beta)}{(1-\beta)}\int_a^t h'(x)e^{[-\beta\frac{t-x}{1-\beta}]}\mathrm{dx}. \quad (16)$$

$M(\alpha)$ is a function of normalization such that $M(0) = M(1) = 1$. If the function does not belong to $H^1(a_1, b_1)$, then, the derivative is

$$\mathrm{D}_t^{\beta}(\mathrm{h(t)}) = \frac{N(\rho)}{\rho}\int_a^t h'(x)e^{[-\frac{t-x}{\rho}]}\mathrm{dx},\ N(0) = N(\infty) = 1, \quad (17)$$

and more than that,

$$\lim_{\rho\to 0}\frac{1}{\rho}e^{[-\frac{t-x}{1-\beta}]} - \delta(x-t). \quad (18)$$

2.3. *Atangana–Baleanu Fractional Derivative*

Let $h \in H(0,1)$; then, the Atangana–Baleanu fractional derivative (in Caputo) ([17]) of order α is

$$T_{\alpha}(h)(x) = \frac{B(\alpha)}{1-\alpha}\int_0^x E_{\alpha}\left[-\frac{\alpha}{1-\alpha}(x-s)^{\alpha}\right]h'(s)ds, \quad (19)$$

where $B(\alpha) > 0$ is a normalizing function which agrees to B(0) = B(1) = 1, and E_{α} is the Mittag–Leffler function.

2.4. *Laplace Transform*

The Laplace transformation ([46]) is an important transform in mathematics. It usually converts the system to an algebraic system, which is easily solvable. The Laplace transform of $f(t)$ is represented by $L\{f(t)\}$ and is explained as

$$L\{f(t)\} = \int_0^{\infty} e^{-st}f(t)dt, \quad s > 0. \quad (20)$$

2.4.1. Laplace Transform of Riemann–Liouville Fractional Differential Operator

The Laplace transform of Riemann–Liouville's fractional derivative is explained below:

$$L\left\{{}^{C}D^{\gamma}g(t)\right\} = [sL(g(t)) - g(0)]s^{(\gamma-1)}. \quad (21)$$

2.4.2. Laplace Transform of Caputo–Fabrizio Fractional Differential Operator

The Laplace transformation of CF operator is as follows:

$$L\left\{{}^{CF}D^{\gamma}g(t)\right\} = \frac{1}{2}.\frac{B(\gamma)(2-\gamma)}{1-\gamma}.\frac{sL\{g(t)\}-g(0)}{s+\frac{\gamma}{1-\gamma}}. \tag{22}$$

2.4.3. Laplace Transform of Atangana–Baleanu Fractional Differential Operator

Let ${}^{ABC}D^{\alpha}f(t)$ be the Atangana–Baleanu fractional differential operator of any function $f(t)$; then, the Laplace transform of the Atangana–Baleanu fractional differential operator is defined as follows:

$$L\left\{{}^{ABC}D^{\alpha}f(t)\right\} = \frac{M(\alpha)}{1-\alpha}\frac{p^{\alpha}L\{f(t)\}-p^{\alpha-1}f(0)}{p^{\alpha}+\frac{\alpha}{1-\alpha}}. \tag{23}$$

3. SIR Model

We have considered an SIR model ([1,47,48]) having three compartments or sub classes for the given population, namely, susceptible class $S(t)$, infected class $I(t)$ and recovered class $R(t)$. The total population is represented by N and is defined as $N = S + I + R$.

In this system, to study the effect of diffusion, we added the diffusion term in each equation of the system; hence, the system reduces to

$$\left.\begin{aligned} \frac{dS}{dt} &= \mu - \mu S - N\gamma SI + \alpha\frac{\partial^2 S}{\partial x^2} \\ \frac{dI}{dt} &= N\gamma SI - \mu I - \nu I + \alpha\frac{\partial^2 I}{\partial x^2} \\ \frac{dR}{dt} &= \nu I - \mu R + \alpha\frac{\partial^2 R}{\partial x^2} \end{aligned}\right\}, \tag{24}$$

with the condition that $S + I + R = 1$. In this system, μ is the birth rate, γ is the transmission rate, ν is the recovery rate, and N is the total population and is supposed to be constant. Here, α is the diffusion constant of susceptible, infected and recovered classes, respectively. One important thing to be noted is that we have taken the interval [0, 0.25] as the domain for the given SIR model. Here, the initial conditions for $S(t)$, $I(t)$ and $R(t)$ are given as follows:

$$\begin{aligned} S_0 &= c_1\exp(-10x^2), 0 \le x \le 0.25, \\ I_0 &= c_2\exp(-100x^2), 0 \le x \le 0.25, \\ R_0 &= c_3, \qquad\qquad 0 \le x \le 0.25. \end{aligned} \tag{25}$$

In coming sections, we will use model (25) and set of conditions (25) to achieve our objective.

4. Existence and Uniqueness of Result

Here, we will establish the existence of the result of the model for all three different kernels of the generalized derivative.

4.1. In Caputo–Fabrizio Derivative Case

4.1.1. Theorem 1

Define N_1, N_2, N_3 and their connection to the variables.

Proof. The given system is as follows:

$${}_{0}^{CF}D_t^{\beta}S(t) = \mu - \mu S - N\gamma SI, \tag{26}$$

$${}_{0}^{CF}D_t^{\beta}I(t) = N\gamma SI - \mu I - \nu I, \tag{27}$$

$${}_{0}^{CF}D_t^{\beta}R(t) = \nu I - \mu R. \tag{28}$$

Here, $0 < \beta \leq 1$. Then, converting the above model into integral equations,

$$S(t) - S(0) = {}_{0}^{CF}I_t^{\beta}[\mu - \mu S - N\gamma SI], \tag{29}$$

$$I(t) - I(0) = {}_{0}^{CF}I_t^{\beta}[N\gamma SI - \mu I - \nu I], \tag{30}$$

$$R(t) - R(0) = {}_{0}^{CF}I_t^{\beta}[\nu I - \mu R]. \tag{31}$$

Then, by Nieto's definition, we obtain

$$\begin{aligned} S(t) = S(0) &+ \tfrac{2(1-\beta)}{(2-\beta)B(\beta)}[\mu - \mu S - N\gamma SI] \\ &+ \tfrac{2\beta}{(2-\beta)B(\beta)}\int_0^t [\mu - \mu S - N\gamma SI]ds, \end{aligned}$$

$$I(t) = I(0) + \frac{2(1-\beta)}{(2-\beta)B(\beta)}[N\gamma SI - \mu I - \nu I] + \frac{2\beta}{(2-\beta)B(\beta)}\int_0^t [N\gamma SI - \mu I - \nu I]ds,$$

and

$$R(t) = R(0) + \frac{2(1-\beta)}{(2-\beta)B(\beta)}[\nu I - \mu R] + \frac{2\beta}{(2-\beta)B(\beta)}\int_0^t [\nu I - \mu R]ds.$$

Furthermore, consider the kernels are

$$N_1(t,S) = \mu - \mu S - N\gamma SI,$$

$$N_2(t,I) = N\gamma SI - \mu I - \nu I,$$

$$N_3(t,R) = \nu I - \mu R.$$

□

4.1.2. Theorem 2

Show that N_1, N_2 and N_3 satisfy the Lipschitz condition.

Proof. We shall prove for N_1 at first. Assume S and S_1 are two functions; hence,

$$\begin{aligned} \| N_1(t,S) - N_1(t,S_1) \| &\leq \| \mu - \mu S - N\gamma SI - \{\mu - \mu S_1 - N\gamma S_1 I\} \|, \\ &= \| \mu(S_1 - S) + N\gamma I(S_1 - S) \|, \\ &= \| \mu + N\gamma I \| \| S_1 - S \|, \end{aligned}$$

$$\| N_1(t,S) - N_1(t,S_1) \| \leq H \| S_1(t) - S(t) \|, \\ \textit{where} \| \mu + N\gamma I \| \leq H < 1.$$

Similarly,

$$\begin{aligned} \| N_2(t,I) - N_2(t,I_1) \| &\leq \| N\gamma SI - \mu I - \nu I - \{N\gamma SI_1 - \mu I_1 - \nu I_1\} \|, \\ &\leq \| (\mu + \nu - N\gamma S) \| \| I_1(t) - I(t) \|. \end{aligned}$$

$$\| N_2(t,I) - N_2(t,I_1) \| \leq H_1 \| I_1(t) - I(t) \|, \\ \textit{where} \| (\mu + \nu - N\gamma S) \| \leq H_1 < 1.$$

and

$$\begin{aligned} \| N_3(t,R) - N_3(t,R_1) \| &\leq \| \nu I - \mu R - \{\nu I - \mu R_1\} \|, \\ &\leq \| \mu \| \| R_1(t) - R(t) \|. \end{aligned}$$

$$\| N_3(t,R) - N_3(t,R_1) \| \leq H_2 \| R_1(t) - R(t) \|, \\ \textit{where} \| \mu \| \leq H_2 < 1.$$

Now, by recursive relation,

$$S_n(t) = \frac{2(1-\beta)}{(2-\beta)B(\beta)} N_1(t, S_{n-1}) + \frac{2\beta}{(2-\beta)B(\beta)} \int_0^t N_1(s, S_{n-1}) ds, \quad (32)$$

$$I_n(t) = \frac{2(1-\beta)}{(2-\beta)B(\beta)} N_2(t, I_{n-1}) + \frac{2\beta}{(2-\beta)B(\beta)} \int_0^t N_2(s, I_{n-1}) ds, \quad (33)$$

and

$$R_n(t) = \frac{2(1-\beta)}{(2-\beta)B(\beta)} N_3(t, R_{n-1}) + \frac{2\beta}{(2-\beta)B(\beta)} \int_0^t N_3(s, R_{n-1}) ds. \quad (34)$$

Now, consider the difference between two successive terms is

$$\begin{aligned} U_n(t) &= S_n(t) - S_{n-1}(t) \\ &= \tfrac{2(1-\beta)}{(2-\beta)B(\beta)} N_1(t, S_{n-1}) + \tfrac{2\beta}{(2-\beta)B(\beta)} \int_0^t N_1(s, S_{n-1}) ds \\ &- \tfrac{2(1-\beta)}{(2-\beta)B(\beta)} N_1(t, S_{n-2}) - \tfrac{2\beta}{(2-\beta)B(\beta)} \int_0^t N_1(s, S_{n-2}) ds, \end{aligned}$$

$$\begin{aligned} U_n(t) &= \tfrac{2(1-\beta)}{(2-\beta)B(\beta)} N_1(t, S_{n-1}) - \tfrac{2(1-\beta)}{(2-\beta)B(\beta)} N_1(t, S_{n-2}) \\ &+ \tfrac{2\beta}{(2-\beta)B(\beta)} \int_0^t \{N_1(s, S_{n-1}) - N_1(s, S_{n-2})\} ds. \end{aligned}$$

Now,

$$\begin{aligned} \| U_n(t) \| &= \| S_n(t) - S_{n-1}(t) \| \\ &= \| \tfrac{2(1-\beta)}{(2-\beta)B(\beta)} N_1(t, S_{n-1}) - \tfrac{2(1-\beta)}{(2-\beta)B(\beta)} N_1(t, S_{n-2}) + \tfrac{2\beta}{(2-\beta)B(\beta)} \int_0^t \{N_1(s, S_{n-1}) - N_1(s, S_{n-2})\} ds \|, \\ &\leq \tfrac{2(1-\beta)}{(2-\beta)B(\beta)} \| N_1(t, S_{n-1}) - N_1(t, S_{n-2}) \| + \tfrac{2\beta}{(2-\beta)B(\beta)} \| \int_0^t \{N_1(s, S_{n-1}) - N_1(s, S_{n-2})\} ds \|, \end{aligned}$$

But N_1 satisfies the Lipschitz condition so

$$\| U_n(t) \| \leq \frac{2(1-\beta)}{(2-\beta)B(\beta)} H \| S_{n-1} - S_{n-2} \| + \frac{2\beta}{(2-\beta)B(\beta)} J \int_0^t \| S_{n-1} - S_{n-2} \| ds.$$

Similarly, we can obtain

$$\| W_n(t) \| \leq \frac{2(1-\beta)}{(2-\beta)B(\beta)} H_1 \| I_{n-1} - I_{n-2} \| + \frac{2\beta}{(2-\beta)B(\beta)} J_1 \int_0^t \| I_{n-1} - I_{n-2} \| ds,$$

and

$$\| Q_n(t) \| \leq \frac{2(1-\beta)}{(2-\beta)B(\beta)} H_2 \| R_{n-1} - R_{n-2} \| + \frac{2\beta}{(2-\beta)B(\beta)} J_2 \int_0^t \| R_{n-1} - R_{n-2} \| ds.$$

□

4.1.3. Theorem 3

Show that the SIR system with fractional order is the minimal model of dynamics.

Proof. By the recursive technique, we obtain

$$\| U_n(t) \| \leq \| S(0) \| + \left\{ \frac{2(1-\beta)H}{(2-\beta)B(\beta)} \right\}^n + \left\{ \frac{2\beta Jt}{(2-\beta)B(\beta)} \right\}^n,$$

$$\| W_n(t) \| \leq \| I(0) \| + \left\{ \frac{2(1-\beta)H_1}{(2-\beta)B(\beta)} \right\}^n + \left\{ \frac{2\beta J_1 t}{(2-\beta)B(\beta)} \right\}^n,$$

and

$$\| Q_n(t) \| \leq \| R(0) \| + \left\{ \frac{2(1-\beta)H_2}{(2-\beta)B(\beta)} \right\}^n + \left\{ \frac{2\beta J_2 t}{(2-\beta)B(\beta)} \right\}^n.$$

Hence, the results are validated and found to be continuous as well. So,

$$\begin{aligned} S(t) &= S_n(t) + A_n(t), \\ I(t) &= I_n(t) + C_n(t), \\ R(t) &= R_n(t) + L_n(t), \end{aligned}$$

where A_n, C_n and L_n are remainders of series solution. So,

$$S(t) - S_n(t) = \tfrac{2(1-\beta)}{(2-\beta)B(\beta)} N_1(t, S_n) + \tfrac{2\beta}{(2-\beta)B(\beta)} \int_0^t N_1(s, S_n) ds,$$
$$S(t) - S_n(t) = \tfrac{2(1-\beta)}{(2-\beta)B(\beta)} N_1(t, S - A_n(t)) + \tfrac{2\beta}{(2-\beta)B(\beta)} \int_0^t N_1(s, S - A_n(s)) ds.$$

Similarly, we have

$$I(t) - I_n(t) = \tfrac{2(1-\beta)}{(2-\beta)B(\beta)} N_2(t, I - C_n(t)) + \tfrac{2\beta}{(2-\beta)B(\beta)} \int_0^t N_2(s, I - C_n(s)) ds,$$

and

$$R(t) - R_n(t) = \tfrac{2(1-\beta)}{(2-\beta)B(\beta)} N_3(t, R - L_n(t)) + \tfrac{2\beta}{(2-\beta)B(\beta)} \int_0^t N_3(s, R - L_n(s)) ds.$$

Now, it is clear that,

$$S(t) - S_n(t) = \frac{2(1-\beta)}{(2-\beta)B(\beta)} N_1(t, S - A_n(t)) + \frac{2\beta}{(2-\beta)B(\beta)} \int_0^t N_1(s, S - A_n(s)) ds,$$

$$S(t) - S(0) - \tfrac{2(1-\beta)N_1(t,S)}{(2-\beta)B(\beta)} - \tfrac{2\beta}{(2-\beta)B(\beta)} \int_0^t N_1(s, S) ds = A_n(t)$$
$$+ \tfrac{2(1-\beta)N_1(t,S-A_n(t))}{(2-\beta)B(\beta)} + \tfrac{2\beta}{(2-\beta)B(\beta)} \int_0^t N_1(s, S - A_n(s)) ds.$$

Now,

$$\| S(t) - \tfrac{2(1-\beta)N_1(t,S)}{(2-\beta)B(\beta)} - S(0) - \tfrac{2\beta}{(2-\beta)B(\beta)} \int_0^t N_1(s, S) ds \| \leq \| A_n(t) \|$$
$$+ \left\{ \tfrac{2(1-\beta)H}{(2-\beta)B(\beta)} + \tfrac{2\beta}{(2-\beta)B(\beta)} Jt \right\} \| A_n(t) \|,$$

$$\| I(t) - \tfrac{2(1-\beta)N_2(t,I)}{(2-\beta)B(\beta)} - I(0) - \tfrac{2\beta}{(2-\beta)B(\beta)} \int_0^t N_2(s, I) ds \| \leq \| C_n(t) \|$$
$$+ \left\{ \tfrac{2(1-\beta)H_1}{(2-\beta)B(\beta)} + \tfrac{2\beta}{(2-\beta)B(\beta)} J_1 t \right\} \| C_n(t) \|,$$

and

$$\| R(t) - \tfrac{2(1-\beta)N_3(t,R)}{(2-\beta)B(\beta)} - R(0) - \tfrac{2\beta}{(2-\beta)B(\beta)} \int_0^t N_3(s, R) ds \| \leq \| L_n(t) \|$$
$$+ \left\{ \tfrac{2(1-\beta)H_2}{(2-\beta)B(\beta)} + \tfrac{2\beta}{(2-\beta)B(\beta)} J_2 t \right\} \| L_n(t) \|.$$

Now, making $n \to \infty$, we obtain

$$S(t) = S(0) + \frac{2(1-\beta)N_1(t,S)}{(2-\beta)B(\beta)} + \frac{2\beta}{(2-\beta)B(\beta)} \int_0^t N_1(s,S)ds,$$

$$I(t) = I(0) + \frac{2(1-\beta)N_3(t,I)}{(2-\beta)B(\beta)} + \frac{2\beta}{(2-\beta)B(\beta)} \int_0^t N_2(s,I)ds,$$

and

$$R(t) = R(0) + \frac{2(1-\beta)N_5(t,R)}{(2-\beta)B(\beta)} + \frac{2\beta}{(2-\beta)B(\beta)} \int_0^t N_3(s,R)ds.$$

□

Based on the aforementioned equations, we can state that the system's solution exists. Similarly, when we modify the kernel, we can also demonstrate that the remaining two cases have a solution.

4.2. Uniqueness of Result

Here, we are going to prove that the results mentioned in the above section are totally solitary. For this, we suppose that there exists another set of results for the set up given by Equations (26)–(28), say, $S(t)$, $I(t)$ and $R(t)$. Then, we have

$$\begin{aligned} S(t) - S_1(t) = & \tfrac{2(1-\beta)}{B(\beta)(2-\beta)}[N_1(t,S) - N_1(t,S_1)] \\ & + \tfrac{2(\beta)}{B(\beta)(2-\beta)} \int_0^t [N_1(s,S) - N_1(s,S_1)]\mathrm{ds}, \end{aligned} \tag{35}$$

and on taking norm both sides, we obtain

$$\begin{aligned} \| S - S_1 \| = & \tfrac{2(1-\beta)}{B(\beta)(2-\beta)}[\| N_1(t,S) - N_1(t,S_1) \|] \\ & + \tfrac{2(\beta)}{B(\beta)(2-\beta)} \int_0^t [\| N_1(s,S) - N_1(s,S_1) \|]\mathrm{ds}, \end{aligned} \tag{36}$$

using Lipchitz condition, we obtain

$$\| S - S_1 \| < \frac{2(1-\beta)}{B(\beta)(2-\beta)} HZ + \left(\frac{2(\beta)}{B(\beta)(2-\beta)} J_1 Zt \right)^n, \tag{37}$$

which is true for all n. So,

$$S = S_1, \tag{38}$$

Similarly, $I = I_1$, and $R = R_1$. So, the uniqueness of the solution is proven.

In the same way, we can also show the uniqueness of the solution for the other two cases.

5. Solution of SIR Model Based on General Fractional Derivative by Using Laplace Transform

Here, to study the effect of diffusion, we add the diffusion term in each equation of the system:

$$\left.\begin{aligned} \tfrac{dS}{dt} &= \mu - \mu S - N\gamma SI + \alpha \tfrac{\partial^2 S}{\partial x^2} \\ \tfrac{dI}{dt} &= N\gamma SI - \mu I - \nu I + \alpha \tfrac{\partial^2 I}{\partial x^2} \\ \tfrac{dR}{dt} &= \nu I - \mu R + \alpha \tfrac{\partial^2 R}{\partial x^2} \end{aligned}\right\}. \tag{39}$$

But we are interested in the solution by using the general operator of fractional order. So, we develop another system with the general fractional operator of order β. Hence,

$$\left.\begin{array}{l} {}^{c}D^{\beta}S(t) = \mu - \mu S - N\gamma SI + \alpha\frac{\partial^2 S}{\partial x^2} \\ {}^{c}D^{\beta}I(t) = N\gamma SI - \mu I - \nu I + \alpha\frac{\partial^2 I}{\partial x^2} \\ {}^{c}D^{\beta}R(t) = \nu I - \mu R + \alpha\frac{\partial^2 R}{\partial x^2} \end{array}\right\}, \tag{40}$$

where ${}^{c}D^{\beta}$ represents the general operator of fractional order β. Now, applying Laplace transform on both sides in the first equation of system (40), we obtain

$$L\left\{{}^{c}D^{\beta}S(t)\right\} = L\left\{\mu - \mu S - N\gamma SI + \alpha\frac{\partial^2 S}{\partial x^2}\right\}. \tag{41}$$

By incorporating the various kernels into the various general operator definitions, we may derive three specific cases of the general operator. In the first case, when the kernel is $\nabla_{\iota}(t) = \frac{t^{-\xi}}{\Gamma(1-\xi)}$, we have the power function $\Im_{\iota}(t) = \frac{t^{\xi-1}}{\Gamma(\xi)}$ reforming the integral operator's associated kernel.

In the next condition, take kernel $\nabla_{\iota}(t) = \frac{B(\xi)}{1-\xi}\mathrm{E}_{\xi}\left(\frac{-\xi}{1-\xi}t^{\xi}\right)$, where E_{ξ} and $\mathrm{M}(\xi)$ are Mittag–Leffler and normalization functions. We also have

$$\Im_{\iota}(t) = \frac{1-\xi}{B(\xi)}\delta(t) + \frac{\xi}{\mathrm{B}(\xi)\Gamma(\xi)}t^{\xi-1}. \tag{42}$$

So, this may be used to obtain the derivatives of AB–Caputo and AB–Riemann–Liouville. The AB type integral is

$${}_{0}\mathrm{D}_{t}^{-\xi}f(t) = \frac{1-\xi}{\mathrm{B}(\xi)}f(t) + \frac{\xi}{\mathrm{B}(\xi)\Gamma(\xi)}\int_{0}^{t}(t-s)^{\xi-1}f(s)ds. \tag{43}$$

Now, in the last situation, the CF derivative is found by taking kernel $\nabla_{\iota}(t) = \frac{B(\xi)}{1-\xi}\exp\left(\frac{-\xi}{1-\xi}t\right)$. Since it is clear that the general fractional derivative can be further converted into three different operators, namely Riemann–Liouvilles, Atangana–Baleanu and Caputo–Fabrizio, and we have already discussed their Laplace transform in the pre-requisites section, now, we will obtain the numerical solution of the model in each case:

5.1. Case I: Caputo–Fabrizio Operator

Now, taking Equation (41) and changing the kernel to Caputo–Fabrizio, we obtain

$$L\left\{{}^{CF}D^{\beta}S(t)\right\} = L\left\{\mu - \mu S - N\gamma SI + \alpha\frac{\partial^2 S}{\partial x^2}\right\}. \tag{44}$$

Now, using Equation (22),we have

$$\frac{pL\{S(t)\} - S(0)}{p + \beta(1-p)} = L\left\{\mu - \mu S - N\gamma SI + \alpha\frac{\partial^2 S}{\partial x^2}\right\} \tag{45}$$

or,

$$pL\{S(t)\} - S(0) = \{p + \beta(1-p)\}L\left\{\mu - \mu S - N\gamma SI + \alpha\frac{\partial^2 S}{\partial x^2}\right\} \tag{46}$$

or,

$$pL\{S(t)\} = S(0) + \{p + \beta(1-p)\}L\left\{\mu - \mu S - N\gamma SI + \alpha\frac{\partial^2 S}{\partial x^2}\right\} \tag{47}$$

or,

$$L\{S(t)\} = \frac{S(0)}{p} + \left\{1 + \beta\left(\frac{1}{p} - 1\right)\right\}L\left\{\mu - \mu S - N\gamma SI + \alpha\frac{\partial^2 S}{\partial x^2}\right\}. \tag{48}$$

Now, operating inverse Laplace transform on both sides, we obtain

$$S(t) = S(0) + L^{-1}\left[\left\{1+\beta\left(\frac{1}{p}-1\right)\right\}L\left\{\mu - \mu S - N\gamma SI + \alpha\frac{\partial^2 S}{\partial x^2}\right\}\right], \tag{49}$$

or by the iterative technique, we obtain

$$S_{n+1}(t) = S(0) + L^{-1}\left[\left\{1+\beta\left(\frac{1}{p}-1\right)\right\}L\left\{\mu - \mu S_n - N\gamma S_n I_n + \alpha\frac{\partial^2 S_n}{\partial x^2}\right\}\right]. \tag{50}$$

Similarly, we can have other expressions

$$I_{n+1}(t) = I(0) + L^{-1}\left[\frac{p+\beta(1-p)}{p}L\left\{N\gamma S_n I_n - \mu I_n - \nu I_n + \alpha\frac{\partial^2 I_n}{\partial x^2}\right\}\right], \tag{51}$$

and

$$R_{n+1}(t) = R(0) + L^{-1}\left[\frac{p+\beta(1-p)}{p}L\left\{\nu I_n - \mu R_n + \alpha\frac{\partial^2 R_n}{\partial x^2}\right\}\right]. \tag{52}$$

Equations (50)–(52)denote the required mathematical solution of the model in the CF case.

5.2. Case II: Riemann–Liouville's Operator

Again using the Equation (41) and changing the kernel to the Riemann–Liouville case, we have

$$L\left\{{}^{RL}D^{\beta}S(t)\right\} = L\left\{\mu - \mu S - N\gamma SI + \alpha\frac{\partial^2 S}{\partial x^2}\right\}. \tag{53}$$

Now, using the Equation (21), we obtain

$$p^{\beta}L\{S(t)\} - p^{\beta-1}S(0) = L\left\{\mu - \mu S - N\gamma SI + \alpha\frac{\partial^2 S}{\partial x^2}\right\} \tag{54}$$

or,

$$p^{\beta}L\{S(t)\} = p^{\beta-1}S(0) + L\left\{\mu - \mu S - N\gamma SI + \alpha\frac{\partial^2 S}{\partial x^2}\right\} \tag{55}$$

or,

$$L\{S(t)\} = \frac{S(0)}{p} + \frac{1}{p^{\beta}}L\left\{\mu - \mu S - N\gamma SI + \alpha\frac{\partial^2 S}{\partial x^2}\right\}. \tag{56}$$

Further, taking inverse Laplace transform on both sides, we obtain

$$S(t) = S(0) + L^{-1}\left[\frac{1}{p^{\beta}}L\left\{\mu - \mu S - N\gamma SI + \alpha\frac{\partial^2 S}{\partial x^2}\right\}\right]. \tag{57}$$

Now, by the iterative technique, we obtain

$$S_{n+1}(t) = S(0) + L^{-1}\left[\frac{1}{p^{\beta}}L\left\{\mu - \mu S_n - N\gamma S_n I_n + \alpha\frac{\partial^2 S_n}{\partial x^2}\right\}\right]. \tag{58}$$

Similarly, we can have

$$I_{n+1}(t) = I(0) + L^{-1}\left[\frac{1}{p^{\beta}}L\left\{N\gamma S_n I_n - \mu I_n - \nu I_n + \alpha\frac{\partial^2 I_n}{\partial x^2}\right\}\right], \tag{59}$$

and

$$R_{n+1}(t) = R(0) + L^{-1}\left[\frac{1}{p^{\beta}}L\left\{\nu I_n - \mu R_n + \alpha\frac{\partial^2 R_n}{\partial x^2}\right\}\right]. \tag{60}$$

Equations (58)–(60) denote the required mathematical solution of the model in the RL case.

5.3. Case III: Atangana–Baleanu Operator

Now, taking Equation (41) and changing the kernel to the Atangana–Baleanu case, we obtain

$$L\left\{{}^{ABC}D^{\beta}S(t)\right\} = L\left\{\mu - \mu S - N\gamma SI + \alpha\frac{\partial^2 S}{\partial x^2}\right\}. \tag{61}$$

Now, using the Equation (23), we obtain

$$\frac{M(\beta)}{(1-\beta)}\cdot\frac{p^{\beta}L\{S(t)\} - p^{\beta-1}S(0)}{p^{\beta} + \frac{\beta}{1-\beta}} = L\left\{\mu - \mu S - N\gamma SI + \alpha\frac{\partial^2 S}{\partial x^2}\right\} \tag{62}$$

or,

$$\frac{M(\beta)}{(1-\beta)}.p^{\beta}L\{S(t)\} - p^{\beta-1}S(0) = \left(p^{\beta} + \frac{\beta}{1-\beta}\right)L\left\{\mu - \mu S - N\gamma SI + \alpha\frac{\partial^2 S}{\partial x^2}\right\} \tag{63}$$

or,

$$p^{\beta}L\{S(t)\} - p^{\beta-1}S(0) = \frac{(1-\beta)}{M(\beta)}\left(p^{\beta} + \frac{\beta}{1-\beta}\right)L\left\{\mu - \mu S - N\gamma SI + \alpha\frac{\partial^2 S}{\partial x^2}\right\} \tag{64}$$

or,

$$p^{\beta}L\{S(t)\} = p^{\beta-1}S(0) + \frac{(1-\beta)}{M(\beta)}\left(p^{\beta} + \frac{\beta}{1-\beta}\right)L\left\{\mu - \mu S - N\gamma SI + \alpha\frac{\partial^2 S}{\partial x^2}\right\} \tag{65}$$

or,

$$L\{S(t)\} = \frac{S(0)}{p} + \frac{(1-\beta)}{M(\beta)}\left(1 + \frac{\beta p^{-\beta}}{1-\beta}\right)L\left\{\mu - \mu S - N\gamma SI + \alpha\frac{\partial^2 S}{\partial x^2}\right\}. \tag{66}$$

Furthermore, taking inverse Laplace transform on both sides, we have

$$S(t) = S(0) + L^{-1}\left[\frac{(1-\beta)}{M(\beta)}\left(1 + \frac{\beta p^{-\beta}}{1-\beta}\right)L\left\{\mu - \mu S - N\gamma SI + \alpha\frac{\partial^2 S}{\partial x^2}\right\}\right] \tag{67}$$

or,

$$S(t) = S(0) + L^{-1}\left[\frac{(1-\beta+\beta p^{-\beta})}{M(\beta)}L\left\{\mu - \mu S - N\gamma SI + \alpha\frac{\partial^2 S}{\partial x^2}\right\}\right]. \tag{68}$$

Now, by the iterative technique, we obtain

$$S_{n+1}(t) = S(0) + L^{-1}\left[\frac{(1-\beta+\beta p^{-\beta})}{M(\beta)}L\left\{\mu - \mu S_n - N\gamma S_n I_n + \alpha\frac{\partial^2 S_n}{\partial x^2}\right\}\right] \tag{69}$$

Similarly, we can obtain

$$I_{n+1}(t) = I(0) + L^{-1}\left[\frac{(1-\beta+\beta p^{-\beta})}{M(\beta)}L\left\{N\gamma S_n I_n - \mu I_n - \nu I_n + \alpha\frac{\partial^2 I_n}{\partial x^2}\right\}\right], \tag{70}$$

and

$$R_{n+1}(t) = R(0) + L^{-1}\left[\frac{(1-\beta+\beta p^{-\beta})}{M(\beta)}L\left\{\nu I_n - \mu R_n + \alpha\frac{\partial^2 R_n}{\partial x^2}\right\}\right]. \tag{71}$$

Equations (69)–(71) denote the required mathematical solution of the model in the ABC case.

6. Numerical and Graphical Results

Now, we have also numerically analyzed the SIR model for the better understanding of the diffusion ([6]). During the investigation, we have also used some initial conditions ([1]) and parameter values. To be clear, we have not generated any new data for this research. Our objective is to analyze the model with a new approach and to find something new for society. Here, we have also taken the value of diffusion coefficient α between 0 and 1. The details of the numeric values are explained in Table 1:

Table 1. Table of parameters used.

S.N.	Variable	Symbol	Value
1	Birth rate	μ	0.04
2	Recovery rate	ν	24
3	Transmission rate	γ	123

Using the above mentioned values of parameters, along with $c_1 = 0.0009$, $c_2 = 0.0004$ and $c_3 = 0.7$ in the mathematical results found in the previous section, for time to be fixed as $0 \leq t \leq 2.5$, we can plot the graphs in each case for various factors:

From graphs, we can see that there is a significant impact of the diffusion coefficient of each variable (i.e., susceptible, infected and recovered classes) (Figures 1–13). From Figures 13–21, we can see that infection is going down as we increase the diffusion coefficient in all the cases. Figures 1–9 show the changes in various factors for $\tau = 0.7$, while Figures 10–12 show changes in S, I and in R for x = 0.15, $\alpha = 0.001$ and $\tau = 0.7$. In Figures 22–24, we see an interesting outcome that the Atangana–Baleanu derivative is showing the lowest peak as compared to other two, when discussing the susceptible and infected class, while in recovery, the Riemann–Liouville derivative is showing better results than the other two. Since we have used the presented model with a unique approach, the presented results are better than the results of [1].

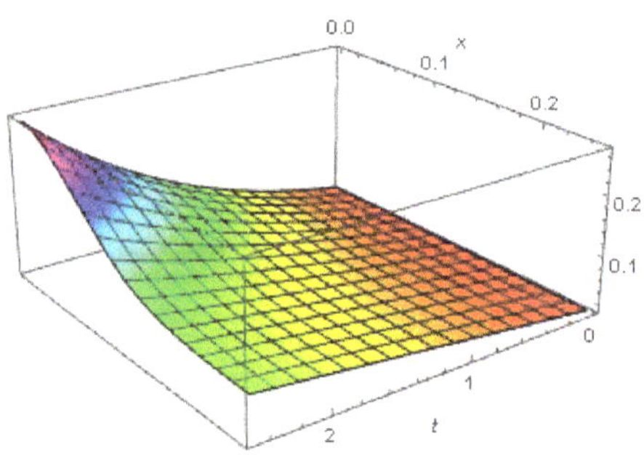

Figure 1. Graph of susceptible against time t, for τ = 0.7 and $\alpha = 0.001$ in Caputo–Fabrizio case.

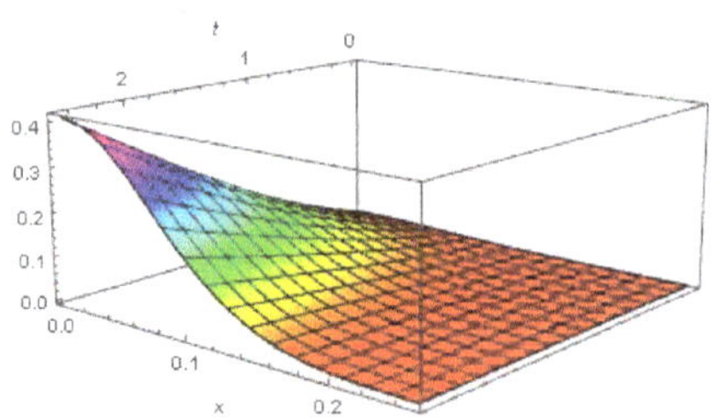

Figure 2. Graph of infected against time t, for τ = 0.7 and $\alpha = 0.001$ in Caputo–Fabrizio case.

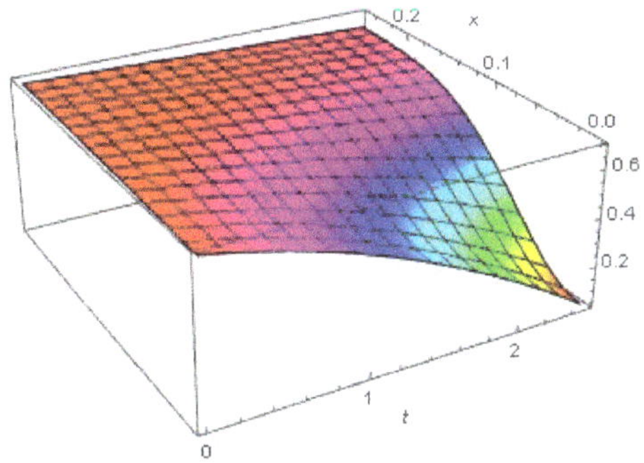

Figure 3. Graph of recovered against time t, for τ = 0.7 and $\alpha = 0.001$ in Caputo–Fabrizio case.

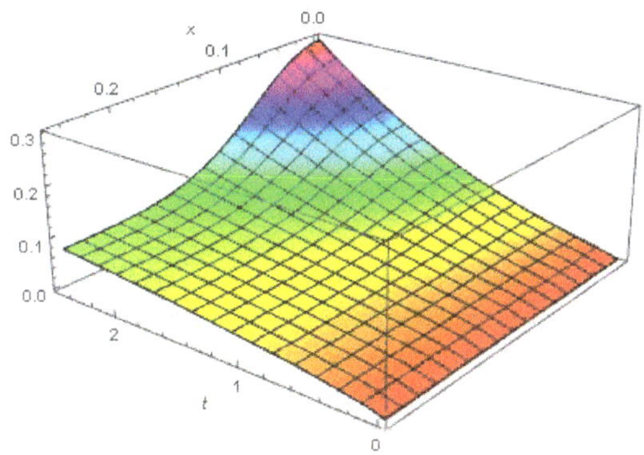

Figure 4. Graph of susceptible with respect to t, for τ = 0.7 and $\alpha = 0.001$ in Riemann–Liouville's case.

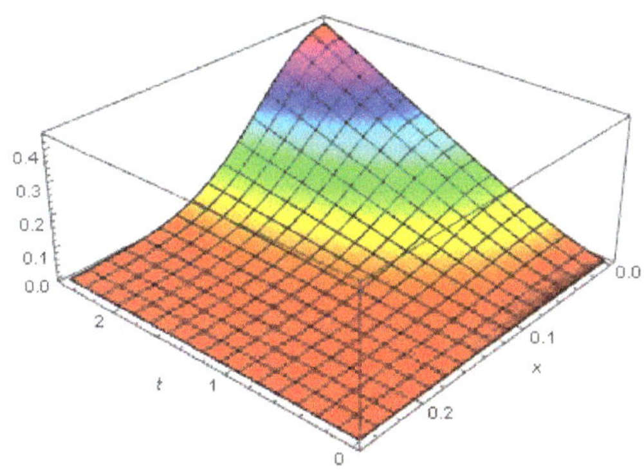

Figure 5. Graph of infected with respect to t, for τ = 0.7 and $\alpha = 0.001$ in Riemann–Liouville's case.

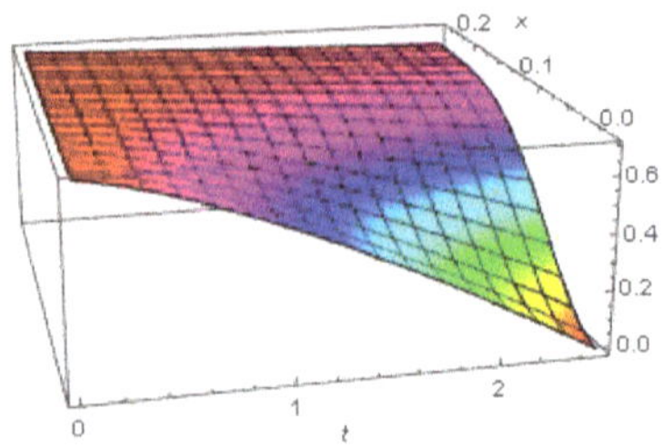

Figure 6. Graph of recovered with respect to t, for τ = 0.7 and $\alpha = 0.001$ in Riemann–Liouville's case.

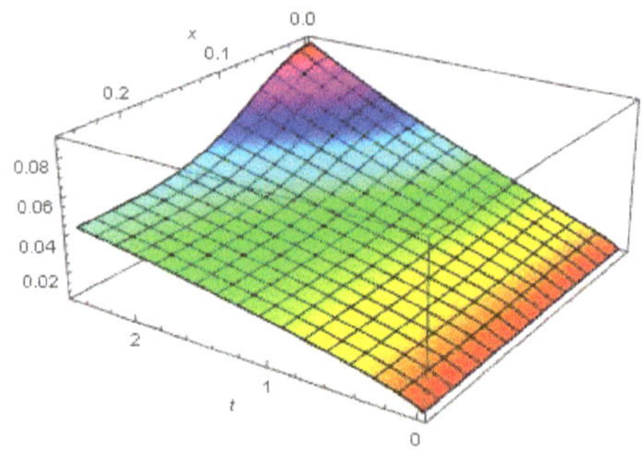

Figure 7. Graph of susceptible with respect to t, for τ = 0.7 and $\alpha = 0.001$ in ABC case.

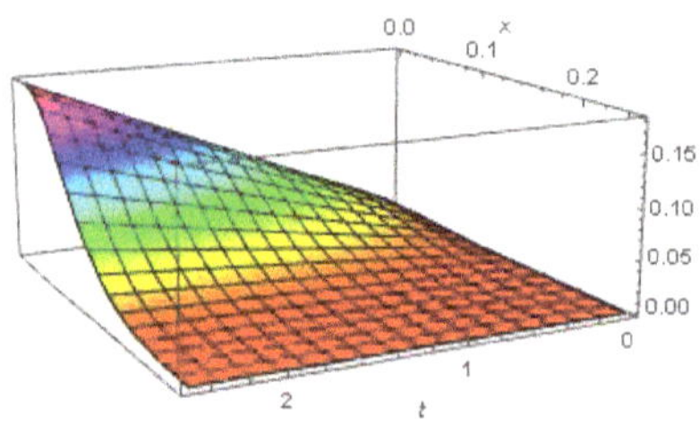

Figure 8. Graph of infected with respect to t, for τ = 0.7 and $\alpha = 0.001$ in ABC case.

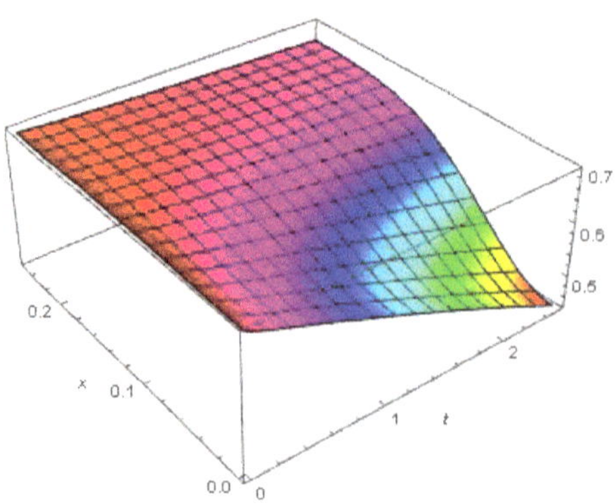

Figure 9. Graph of recovered with respect to t, for τ = 0.7 and $\alpha = 0.001$ in ABC case.

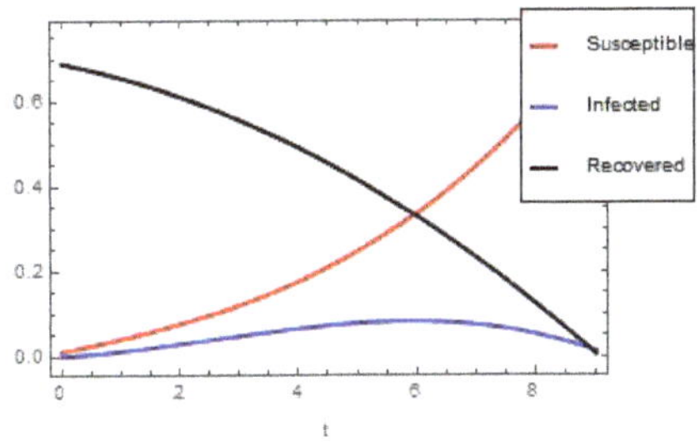

Figure 10. Graph of susceptible, infected and recovered class with respect to t, for x=0.15, $\alpha = 0.001$ and $\tau = 0.7$ in CF case.

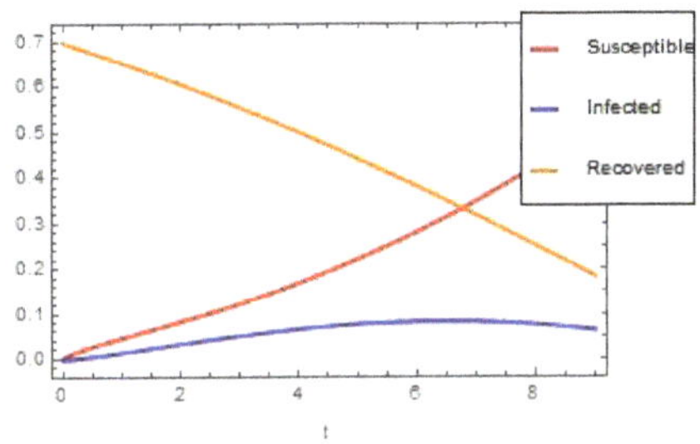

Figure 11. Graph of susceptible, infected and recovered class with respect to t, for x=0.15, $\alpha = 0.001$ and $\tau = 0.7$ in RL case.

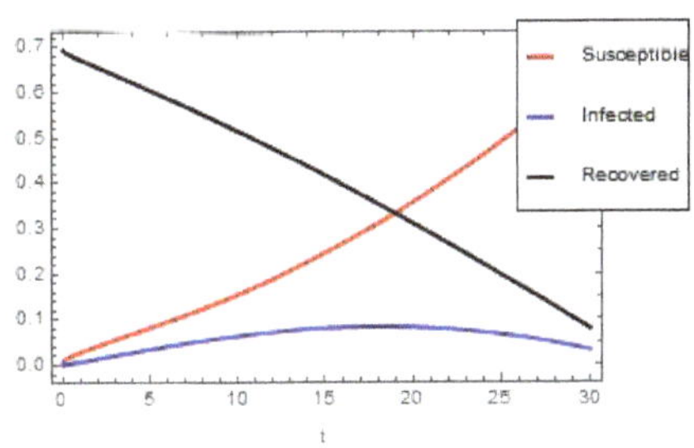

Figure 12. Graph of susceptible, infected and recovered class with respect to t, for x=0.15, $\alpha = 0.001$ and $\tau = 0.7$ in ABC case.

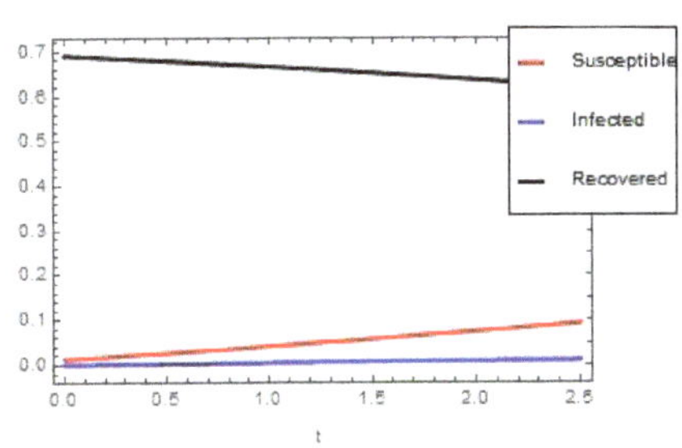

Figure 13. Graph of susceptible, infected and recovered class with respect to t, for diffusion coefficient 0.01 in CF case.

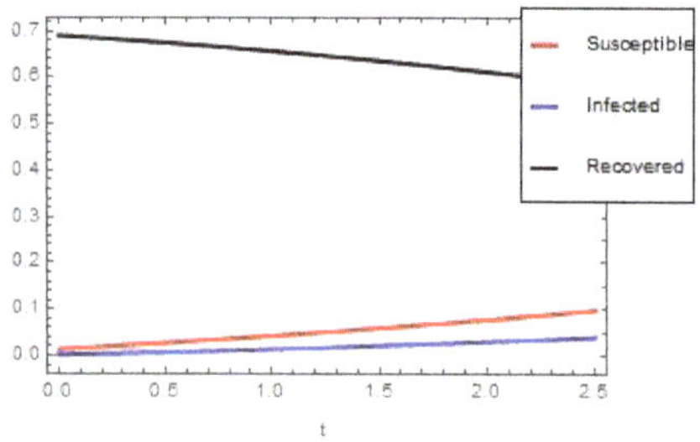

Figure 14. Graph of susceptible, infected and recovered class with respect to t, for diffusion coefficient 0.001 in CF case.

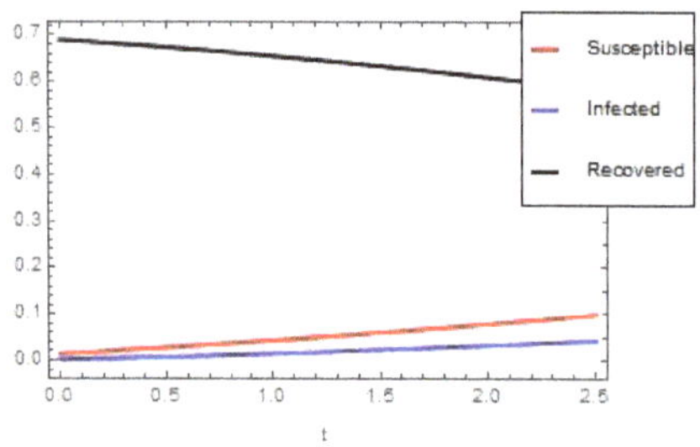

Figure 15. Graph of susceptible, infected and recovered class with respect to t, for diffusion coefficient 0.0001 in CF case.

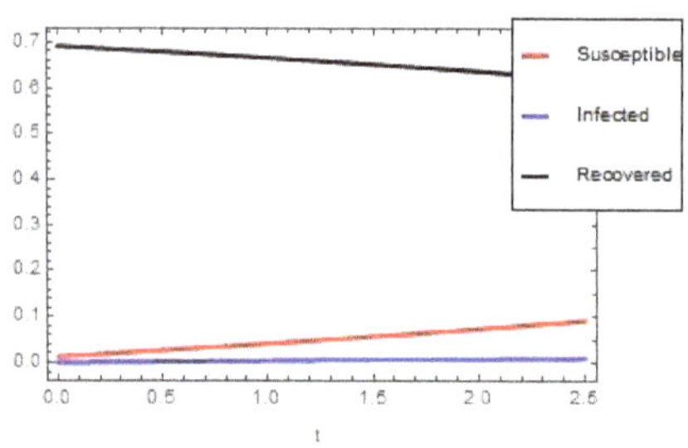

Figure 16. Graph of susceptible, infected and recovered class with respect to t, for diffusion coefficient 0.01 in RL case.

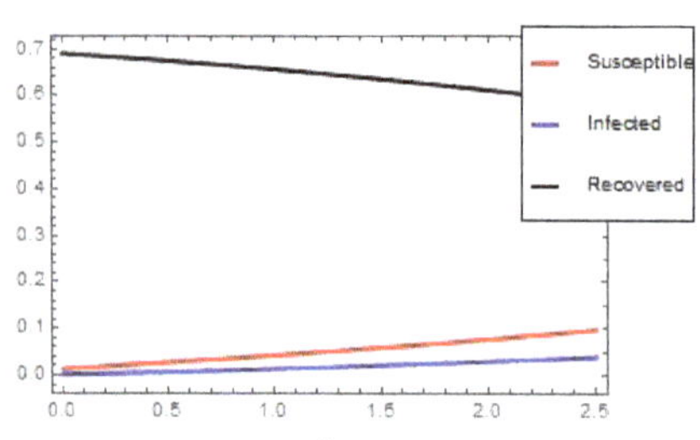

Figure 17. Graph of susceptible, infected and recovered class with respect to t, for diffusion coefficient 0.001 in RL case.

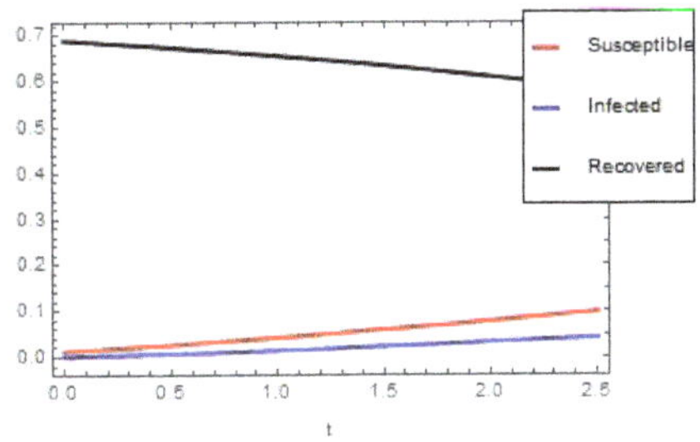

Figure 18. Graph of susceptible, infected and recovered class with respect to t, for diffusion coefficient 0.0001 in RL case.

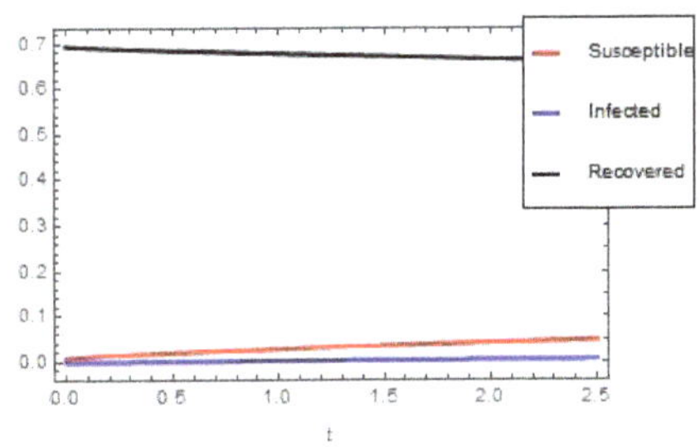

Figure 19. Graph of susceptible, infected and recovered class with respect to t, for diffusion coefficient 0.01 in ABC case.

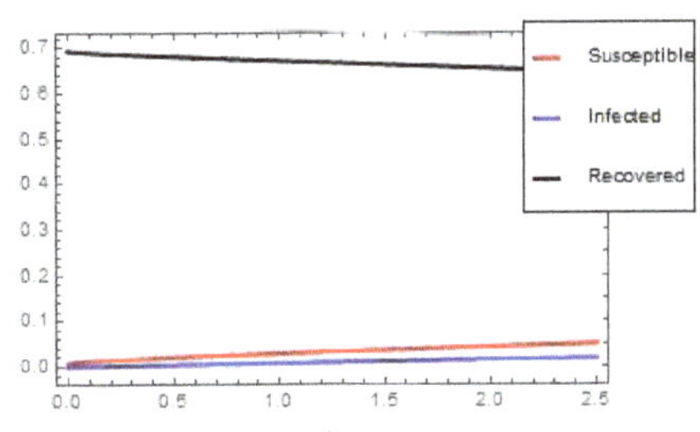

Figure 20. Graph of susceptible, infected and recovered class with respect to t, for diffusion coefficient 0.001 in ABC case.

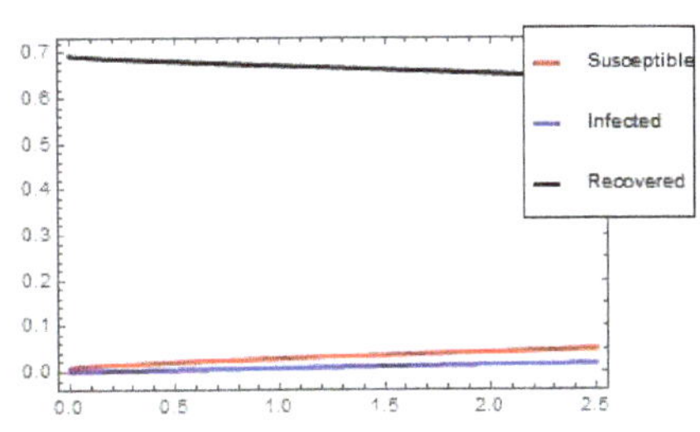

Figure 21. Graph of susceptible, infected and recovered class with respect to t, for diffusion coefficient 0.0001 in ABC case.

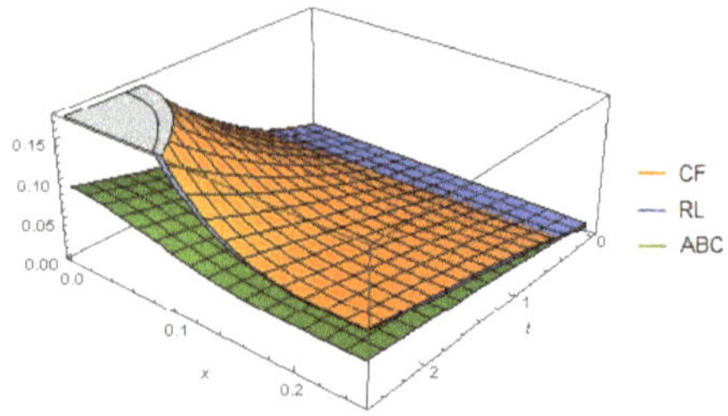

Figure 22. Graph of susceptible with CF, RL and ABC derivative for $\tau = 0.7$ and $\alpha = 0.001$.

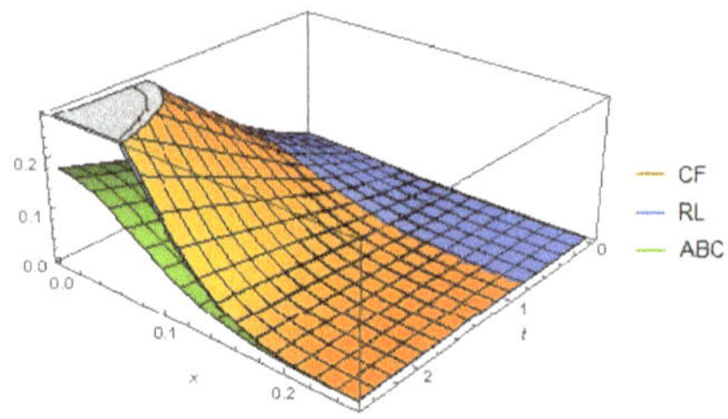

Figure 23. Graph of infected with CF, RL and ABC derivative for $\tau = 0.7$ and $\alpha = 0.001$.

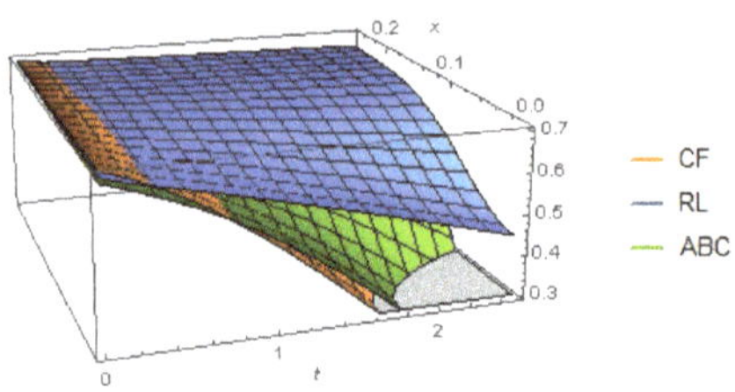

Figure 24. Graph of recovered with CF, RL and ABC derivative for $\tau = 0.7$ and $\alpha = 0.001$.

7. Conclusions

In this study, we analyzed the fractional ordered SIR model under the general fractional derivative using the Laplace transform approach. The presence and uniqueness of outcomes were examined using the fixed point method. Once more, the general derivative technique was used to obtain some numerical results for the suggested model. For various fractional orders and for every general derivative scenario, numerical results have been illustrated. By displaying the relationship between two numbers, the graphical depiction demonstrates the greater significance of the fractional order analysis of mathematical models than integer order analysis. As we all know that there is limited predication available for integer ordered derivatives compared to fractional ordered derivatives, in which we can have a large amount of observations available between two integer points. There may also be significant differences in the susceptible, infected and recovered populations when we change the diffusion coefficient and equation's order.

Now, if we talk about the future research or extending work, then we can also analyze the presented model with the reproduction number, which will certainly give some new and valuable findings for the presented model. There are vast and numerous possibilities in epidemiological modeling using fractional derivatives over integer ordered derivatives, and this will certainly allow for better forecasting and prediction to take more precise corrective steps in the context of real-world situations.

Author Contributions: This study was directed by M.N.M., who also carried out all the mathematical computations. I.A. constructed the study map. R.S.D. summarised the data into tables and drew the figures/graphs. B.S.A. formatted the final paper. The draft was read, corrected and polished by all the authors. All authors have read and agreed to the published version of the manuscript.

Funding: This work was supported and funded by the Deanship of Scientific Research at Imam Mohammad Ibn Saud Islamic University (IMSIU) (grant number IMSIU-RP23002).

Data Availability Statement: Availability of statistics and materials: Availability of statistics is already cited in the article.

Acknowledgments: Authors extend their gratitude to all the reviewers whose suggestations helped to uplift the quality of the article.

Conflicts of Interest: The authors declare no conflicts of interest.

References

1. Asif, M.; Jan, S.U.; Haider, N.; Al-Mdallal, Q.; Abdeljawad, T. Numerical modeling of npz and sir models with and without diffusion. *Results Phys.* **2020**, *19*, 103512. [CrossRef]
2. Asif, M.; Khan, Z.A.; Haider, N.; Al-Mdallal, Q. Numerical simulation for solution of SEIR models by meshless and finite difference methods. *Chaos Solitons Fractals* **2020**, *141*, 110340. [CrossRef]
3. Ahmed, N.; Ali, M.; Rafiq, M.; Khan, I.; Nisar, K.S.; Rehman, M.A.; Ahmad, M.O. A numerical efficient splitting method for the solution of two dimensional susceptible infected recovered epidemic model of whooping cough dynamics: Applications in bio-medical engineering. *Comput. Methods Programs Biomed.* **2020**, *190*, 105350. [CrossRef] [PubMed]
4. Ergen, K.; Çilli, A.; Yahnıoğlu, N. Predicting epidemic diseases using mathematical modelling of SIR. *Acta Phys. Pol.* **2015**, *128*. [CrossRef]
5. Alqarni, M.M.; Nasir, A.; Alyami, M.A.; Raza, A.; Awrejcewicz, J.; Rafiq, M.; Ahmed, N.; Shaikh, T.S.; Mahmoud, E.E. A SEIR Epidemic Model of Whooping Cough-Like Infections and Its Dynamically Consistent Approximation. *Complexity* **2022**, *2022*, 3642444. [CrossRef]
6. González-Parra, G.; Arenas, A.J.; Chen-Charpentier, B.M. Combination of nonstandard schemes and Richardson's extrapolation to improve the numerical solution of population models. *Math. Comput. Model.* **2010**, *52*, 1030–1036. [CrossRef]
7. Dang, Q.A.; Hoang, M.T. Nonstandard finite difference schemes for a general predator–prey system. *J. Comput. Sci.* **2019**, *36*, 101015. [CrossRef]
8. Kilbas, A.A.; Srivastava, H.M.; Trujillo, J.J. *Theory and Applications of Fractional Differential Equations*; Elsevier: Amsterdam, The Netherlands, 2006.
9. Koca, I. Analysis of rubella disease model with non-local and non-singular fractional derivatives. *Int. J. Optim. Control. Theor. Appl. (IJOCTA)* **2018**, *8*, 17–25. [CrossRef]
10. Yavuz, M.; Özdemir, N. Analysis of an epidemic spreading model with exponential decay law. *Math. Sci. Appl.-Notes* **2020**, *8*, 142–154. [CrossRef]
11. Caputo, M.; Fabrizio, M. A new definition of fractional derivative without singular kernel. *Prog. Fract. Differ. Appl.* **2015**, *1*, 73–85.
12. Yadav, S.K.; Purohit, M.; Gour, M.M.; Yadav, L.K.; Mishra, M.N. Hybrid technique for multi-dimensional fractional diffusion problems involving Caputo–Fabrizio derivative. *Int. J. Math. Ind.* **2024**, 2450020. [CrossRef]
13. El-Dessoky, M.M.; Khan, M.A. Modeling and analysis of an epidemic model with fractal-fractional Atangana-Baleanu derivative. *Alex. Eng. J.* **2022**, *61*, 729–746. [CrossRef]
14. Khan, M.A.; Ullah, S.; Kumar, S. A robust study on 2019-nCOV outbreaks through non-singular derivative. *Eur. Phys. J. Plus.* **2021**, *136*, 1–20. [CrossRef] [PubMed]
15. Alazman, I.; Mishra, M.N.; Alkahtani, B.S.; Goswami, P. Computational analysis of rabies and its solution by applying fractional operator. *Appl. Math. Sci. Eng.* **2024**, *32*, 2340607. [CrossRef]
16. Owolabi, K.M.; Atangana, A. Mathematical modelling and analysis of fractional epidemic models using derivative with exponential kernel. In *Fractional Calculus in Medical and Health Science*; CRC Press: Boca Raton, FL, USA, 2020; pp. 109–128.
17. Nisar, K.S.; Farman, M.; Abdel-Aty, M.; Cao, J. A review on epidemic models in sight of fractional calculus. *Alex. Eng. J.* **2023**, *75*, 81–113. [CrossRef]
18. Djennadi, S.; Shawagfeh, N.; Osman, M.S.; Gómez-Aguilar, J.F.; Arqub, O.A. The Tikhonov regularization method for the inverse source problem of time fractional heat equation in the view of ABC-fractional technique. *Phys. Scr.* **2021**, *96*, 094006. [CrossRef]
19. Alzahrani, E.O.; Khan, M.A. Comparison of numerical techniques for the solution of a fractional epidemic model. *Eur. Phys. J. Plus* **2020**, *135*, 110. [CrossRef]
20. Dhandapani, P.B.; Thippan, J.; Baleanu, D.; Sivakumar, V. On a novel fuzzy fractional retarded delay epidemic model. *AIMS Math.* **2022**, *7*, 10122–10142. [CrossRef]
21. Areshi, M.; Goswami, P.; Mishra, M.N. Comparative study of blood sugar–insulin model using fractional derivatives. *J. Taibah Univ. Sci.* **2024**, *18*, 2339009. [CrossRef]

22. Taghvaei, A.; Georgiou, T.T.; Norton, L.; Tannenbaum, A. Fractional SIR epidemiological models. *Sci. Rep.* **2020**, *10*, 20882. [CrossRef]
23. Dubey, R.S.; Mishra, M.N.; Goswami, P. Systematic Analysis of Oxygen Diffusion Problem having Local Fractional Derivative.
24. Baleanu, D.; Mohammadi, H.; Rezapour, S. Analysis of the model of HIV-1 infection of $CD4^{+}$ T-cell with a new approach of fractional derivative. *Adv. Differ. Equations* **2020**, *2020*, 71. [CrossRef]
25. Kumawat, N.; Shukla, A.; Mishra, M.N.; Sharma, R.; Dubey, R.S. Khalouta Transform and Applications to Caputo-Fractional Differential Equations. *Front. Appl. Math. Stat.* **2024**, *10*, 1351526. [CrossRef]
26. Liu, X.; ur Rahmamn, M.; Ahmad, S.; Baleanu, D.; Nadeem Anjam, Y. A new fractional infectious disease model under the non-singular Mittag–Leffler derivative. *Waves Random Complex Media* **2022**, 1–27. [CrossRef]
27. Yang, X.J.; Baleanu, D.; Srivastava, H.M. *Local Fractional Integral Transforms and Their Applications*; Academic Press: Cambridge, MA, USA, 2015.
28. Alazman, I.; Alkahtani, B.S.T.; Rahman, M.U.; Mishra, M.N. Nonlinear complex dynamical analysis and solitary waves for the (3+1)-D nonlinear extended Quantum Zakharov–Kuznetsov equation. *Results Phys.* **2024**, *58*, 107432. [CrossRef]
29. Ammi, M.R.S.; Tahiri, M.; Torres, D.F. Necessary optimality conditions of a reaction-diffusion SIR model with ABC fractional derivatives. *arXiv* **2021**, arXiv:2106.15055. [CrossRef]
30. Losada, J.; Nieto, J.J. Properties of a new fractional derivative without singular kernel. *Progr. Fract. Differ. Appl* **2015**, *1*, 87–92.
31. Zhenzhen, L.; Yongguang, Y.; Weiyi, X.; Guojian, R.; Xiangyun, M. Global dynamics for a class of discrete fractional epidemic model with reaction-diffusion. *arXiv* **2022**, arXiv:2208.06548.
32. Sidi Ammi, M.R.; Tahiri, M.; Tilioua, M.; Zeb, A.; Khan, I.; Andualem, M. Global analysis of a time fractional order spatio-temporal SIR model. *Sci. Rep.* **2022**, *12*, 5751. [CrossRef]
33. İlhan, Ö.; Şahin, G. A numerical approach for an epidemic SIR model via Morgan-Voyce series. *Int. J. Math. Comput. Eng.* **2024**, *2*, 125–140. [CrossRef]
34. Kumar, M.; Jhinga, A.; Daftardar-Gejji, V. New algorithm for solving non-linear functional equations. *Int. J. Appl. Comput. Math.* **2020**, *6*, 26. [CrossRef]
35. Daftardar-Gejji, V.; Jafari, H. An iterative method for solving nonlinear functional equations. *J. Math. Anal. Appl.* **2006**, *316*, 753–763. [CrossRef]
36. Angstmann, C.N.; Henry, B.I.; McGann, A.V. A fractional-order infectivity and recovery SIR model. *Fractal Fract.* **2017**, *1*, 11. [CrossRef]
37. Alòs, E.; Mancino, M.E.; Merino, R.; Sanfelici, S. A fractional model for the COVID-19 pandemic: Application to Italian data. *Stoch. Anal. Appl.* **2021**, *39*, 842–860. [CrossRef]
38. Angstmann, C.N.; Henry, B.I.; McGann, A.V. A fractional-order infectivity SIR model. *Phys. A Stat. Mech. Appl.* **2016**, *452*, 86–93. [CrossRef]
39. Singh, A.K.; Mehra, M.; Gulyani, S. A modified variable-order fractional SIR model to predict the spread of COVID-19 in India. *Math. Methods Appl. Sci.* **2023**, *46*, 8208–8222. [CrossRef]
40. Singh, R.; Mishra, J.; Gupta, V.K. Dynamical analysis of a Tumor Growth model under the effect of fractal fractional Caputo-Fabrizio derivative. *Int. J. Math. Comput. Eng.* **2023**, *1*, 115–126. [CrossRef]
41. Agarwal, H.; Mishra, M.N.; Dubey, R.S. On fractional Caputo operator for the generalized glucose supply model via incomplete Aleph function. *Int. J. Math. Ind.* **2024**, *2024*, 2450003. [CrossRef]
42. Alqahtani, A.M.; Mishra, M.N. Mathematical Analysis of Streptococcus Suis Infection in Pig- Human Population by Riemann-Liouville Fractional Operator. *Prog. Fract. Differ. Appl.* **2024**, *10*, 119–135.
43. Sabir, Z.; Umar, M. Levenberg-Marquardt backpropagation neural network procedures for the consumption of hard water-based kidney function. *Int. J. Math. Comput. Eng.* **2023**, *1*, 127–138. [CrossRef]
44. Alqahtani, A.M.; Shukla, A. Computational analysis of multi-layered Navier–Stokes system by Atangana–Baleanu derivative. *Appl. Math. Sci. Eng.* **2024**, *32*, 2290723. [CrossRef]
45. Moore, E.J.; Sirisubtawee, S.; Koonprasert, S. A Caputo–Fabrizio fractional differential equation model for HIV/AIDS with treatment compartment. *Adv. Differ. Equ.* **2019**, *2019*, 200. [CrossRef]
46. Luchko, Y.; Yamamoto, M. General time-fractional diffusion equation: Some uniqueness and existence results for the initial-boundary-value problems. *Fract. Calc. Appl. Anal.* **2016**, *19*, 676–695. [CrossRef]
47. Yasin, M.W.; Ahmed, N.; Iqbal, M.S.; Rafiq, M.; Raza, A.; Akgül, A. Reliable numerical analysis for stochastic reaction-diffusion system. *Phys. Scr.* **2022**, *98*, 015209. [CrossRef]
48. Phaijoo, G.R.; Gurung, D.B. Sensitivity analysis of SEIR-SEI model of dengue disease. *Gams J. Math. Math. Biosci.* **2018**, *6*, 41–50.

fractal and fractional

MDPI

Article

Application of Fractional Calculus in Predicting the Temperature-Dependent Creep Behavior of Concrete

Jiecheng Chen, Lingwei Gong and Ruifan Meng *

School of Mechanical and Electrical Engineering, Guangzhou University, Guangzhou 510006, China; 2112307104@e.gzhu.edu.cn (J.C.); novygong@gmail.com (L.G.)
* Correspondence: rfmeng@gzhu.edu.cn

Abstract: Creep is an essential aspect of the durability and longevity of concrete structures. Based on fractional-order viscoelastic theory, this study investigated a creep model for predicting the temperature-dependent creep behavior of concrete. The order of the proposed fractional-order creep model can intuitively reflect the evolution of the material characteristics between solids and fluids, which provides a quantitative way to directly reveal the influence of loading conditions on the temperature-dependent mechanical properties of concrete during creep. The effectiveness of the model was verified using the experimental data of lightweight expansive shale concrete under various temperature and stress conditions, and the comparison of the results with those of the model in the literature showed that the proposed model has good accuracy while maintaining simplicity. Further analysis of the fractional order showed that temperature, not stress level, is the key factor affecting the creep process of concrete. At the same temperature, the fractional order is almost a fixed value and increases with the increase in temperature, reflecting the gradual softening of the mechanical properties of concrete at higher temperature. Finally, a novel prediction formula containing the average fractional-order value at each temperature was established, and the creep deformation of concrete can be predicted only by changing the applied stress, which provides a simple and practical method for predicting the temperature-dependent creep behavior of concrete.

Keywords: fractional calculus; creep; temperature dependence; concrete

1. Introduction

Concrete is widely used in the fields of construction engineering and road materials, and its durability and sustainable stability are essential for the safety of infrastructure [1]. However, creep deformation occurs in concrete with time under long-term loading, which results in pavement damage and foundational settlement [2,3]. Therefore, experimental research as well as theoretical modeling of the creep behavior of concrete have long been research concerns [4,5].

To date, a great deal of research has been devoted to establishing theoretical models to accurately predict the creep deformation of various concretes. Li et al. [6] developed a constitutive model for polypropylene concrete based on high-temperature dynamic experimental data to improve the predictability of mechanical behavior under varying thermal conditions. By including the transient creep explicitly in a uniaxial constitutive model, Gernay and Franssen [7] described the complex, unsteady temperature–stress relationship of concrete materials. Furthermore, Li et al. [8] proposed a thermodynamically coupled constitutive model for concrete derived from the Drucker–Prager strength criterion to predict creep behavior at various temperatures. Despite these advances, the existing concrete creep models are often too complex to be applied under different stresses and temperatures [9]. Therefore, developing a simple and effective model for predicting the creep behavior of concrete under various environmental conditions remains a key task, which is crucial for predicting the creep deformation of concrete in practical engineering applications.

In recent decades, more and more researchers have recognized fractal and fractional differential operators as alternative approaches for characterizing the properties of viscoelastic materials [10]. Among them, the fractal models are particularly suitable for predicting the effective thermal conductivity of porous materials because they have multiscale pores that are statistically self-similar [11]. In the field of concrete, Qu et al. [12] established a thermal resistance network model based on the Sierpinski carpet in parallel and series to model the effective thermal conductivity of novel autoclaved aerated concrete (AAC)-based composites. Jiang et al. [13] constructed a hybrid fractal model by mixing an n-stage Sierpinski carpet to reproduce the multiscale pore structure, which can be used for heat transfer as well as ion and gas transport simulations in porous cement-based materials. Fractal derivative constitutive models have also been applied to investigate the creep behavior of concrete [14]. In a recent study, Bouras and Vrcelj [15] developed linear creep models for reinforced and prestressed concrete by adopting fractal-derivative-based viscoelastic laws.

The key feature of fractional differential operators is the inherent long-term memory effect, which makes them particularly suitable for modeling phenomena with significant time dependence, damage progression, and microstructural changes [16,17]. The utility of fractional calculus in modeling viscoelastic materials is particularly notable due to its ability to reveal the evolution of the mechanical properties of materials between ideal solids and fluids [18]. For example, Bonfanti et al. [19] applied fractional viscoelastic models to power-law materials, effectively capturing the viscoelastic response of soft materials across a broad range of time scales and revealing the connection between the complex internal structure of soft materials and their macroscopic mechanical responses. Katicha et al. [20] developed a fractional viscoelastic model by simplifying the parameter settings of the generalized fractional Maxwell model, which can accurately predict the linear viscoelastic properties of asphalt concrete. Zatar et al. [21] applied fractional calculus to study the viscoelasticity of piles and soils, accurately identifying these properties in structural dynamics. The application of fractional-order calculus in these works significantly improved the practicability and adaptability of the models and more effectively reflected the complex viscoelastic behavior of materials with the change of fractional order.

As a typical viscoelastic behavior, creep is one of the domains where fractional calculus has been extensively applied [22,23]. For instance, Sapora et al. [24] proposed a method based on fractional calculus for simulating the creep recovery of modified asphalt binders, accurately describing their viscoelastic behaviors at different temperatures. Tang et al. [25] proposed a new geotechnical creep model based on variable-order fractional derivatives and continuum damage mechanics, which can simulate the creep behavior of rocks under long-term loading with greater accuracy, especially during the accelerated creep stage. Zhou et al. [26] applied fractional calculus to enhance the elasto-viscoplastic model to better describe and predict the creep behavior of soft soil and clay. Therefore, the present studies have proven that the use of fractional calculus can provide a rapid and reliable approach for describing creep behavior.

Fractional-order models have also been successfully applied to describe the creep behavior of concrete. Bouras et al. [27] developed a nonlinear thermoviscoelastic model using fractional derivatives to effectively simulate the creep behavior of concrete under different stresses and temperatures with very few parameters. Zhang et al. [28] developed a constitutive model for the nonlinear creep damage of concrete based on fractional calculus, improving the prediction of creep and fracture behavior at different stress levels. In addition, Ribeiro et al. [29] used fractional calculus to more accurately simulate the creep behavior of concrete and polymers with fewer rheological elements than traditional models, effectively characterizing the long-term creep in complex materials.

Although significant progress has been made in capturing the creep behavior of concrete with fractional calculus methods, existing models rarely consider the law of order variation, especially for the prediction of concrete creep, by establishing a quantitative relationship between order and environmental parameters. Therefore, the motivation of this study was not only to use fractional calculus to characterize the creep behavior of concrete but also to further analyze the relationship between the fractional order and the factors affecting the creep of concrete, including temperature and applied stress. Consequently, the innovation of this study is establishing a novel prediction formula considering the influence of environmental parameters on the value of the fractional order, providing a simple and practical method for predicting the temperature-dependent creep behavior of concrete.

In the following, Section 2 is dedicated to the derivation of a fractional creep model based on fractional viscoelastic theory. The model is capable of characterizing creep behavior under various conditions with simple parameters. In Section 3, the proposed model is fitted to the experimental data of lightweight expansive shale concrete to validate its effectiveness and obtain the model parameters. Section 4 provides a quantitative analysis of the relationship between order and different applied stress and temperature loading conditions to effectively predict the temperature-dependent creep behavior of concrete. Finally, the conclusions are drawn in Section 5.

2. Fractional Creep Model

In the conventional mechanical theories, the linear elastic behavior of ideal solids is typically characterized by Hooke's law, $\sigma(t) = E\varepsilon(t) = ED_t^0\varepsilon(t)$, which illustrates that stress σ and strain ε are proportional, with the modulus of elasticity E serving as the constant of proportionality. The viscous behavior of ideal fluids is governed by Newton's law, $\sigma(t) = \frac{\eta d\varepsilon(t)}{dt} = \eta D_t^1\varepsilon(t)$, where stress is a linear function of the strain rate, with the viscosity coefficient η being the proportionality constant. This behavior is illustrated in the fractional "spring-pot" element depicted in Figure 1.

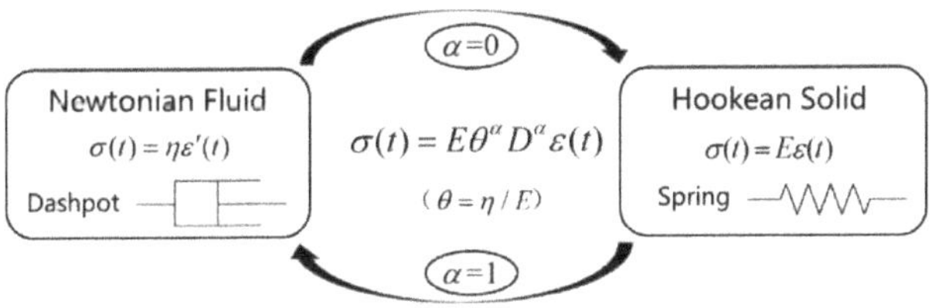

Figure 1. Fractional "spring-pot" element.

Therefore, by substituting the derivative order with the fractional order α, the stress–strain equation can express the intermediate mechanical behavior of viscoelastic materials between ideal solids and ideal fluids [30]:

$$\sigma(t) = E\theta^{\alpha} D_t^{\alpha}\varepsilon(t)\ 0 < \alpha < 1, \tag{1}$$

where E denotes the elastic modulus at $\alpha = 0$, and θ is defined as η/E, representing the relaxation time parameter. On this basis, considering the creep behavior of concrete under constant stress, Equation (1) can be rewritten as follows:

$$\varepsilon(t) = \frac{1}{E}\theta^{-\alpha} D_t^{-\alpha}\sigma(t)\ 0 < \alpha < 1. \tag{2}$$

Throughout the development of fractional calculus, numerous definitions have been proposed. For instance, the left-sided Riemann–Liouville fractional derivative of a function $f(t)$ for order $0 < \alpha < 1$ is defined as follows [31]:

$$D_t^{\alpha} f(t) = \frac{1}{\Gamma(1-\alpha)} D_t^1 \int_0^t \frac{f(\tau)}{(t-\tau)^{\alpha}} d\tau, \tag{3}$$

where Γ denotes the Gamma function:

$$\Gamma(t) = \int_0^t e^{-t}\tau^{t-1}d\tau. \tag{4}$$

The Gamma function has the following properties:

$$\Gamma(x+1) = x\Gamma(x). \tag{5}$$

The definition of the fractional integral operator [32] is expressed as

$$D_t^{-\alpha} f(t) = \int_0^t \frac{(t-\tau)^{\alpha-1}}{\Gamma[\alpha]} f(\tau)d\tau. \tag{6}$$

By substituting the fractional integral operator from Equation (6) and constant stress $\sigma(t) = \sigma_0$ into Equation (2), the expression of the creep model is obtained:

$$\varepsilon(t) = \frac{1}{E}\theta^{-\alpha} \int_0^t \frac{(t-\tau)^{\alpha-1}}{\Gamma[\alpha]} \sigma_0 d\tau. \tag{7}$$

The integration of the right side of Equation (7), along with the use of the property of the Gamma function of Equation (5), allows for a further formulation to be deduced:

$$\varepsilon(t) = \frac{\sigma_0}{E\theta^\alpha\Gamma[\alpha]} \frac{-(t-\tau)^\alpha}{\alpha(t)}|_0^t = \frac{\sigma_0}{E\theta^\alpha} \frac{t^\alpha}{\Gamma[1+\alpha]}. \tag{8}$$

Hence, it is evident that the fractional creep model represented by Equation (8) involves only three parameters: E, θ, and α, offering the advantage of easy data fitting. Theoretically, E and θ are material constants, while the fractional-order derivative α dictates the variation in the creep model's response. Therefore, by simply adjusting the value of α, one can satisfy the creep curves of concrete under different stresses and temperatures.

In summary, the fractional creep model shows the ability to accurately characterize the creep behavior of concrete. In the following sections, the effectiveness of the fractional creep model is validated by fitting to the experimental data, and the law of the fractional order with experimental conditions is discussed in detail.

3. Results and Discussion

To evaluate the effectiveness of the proposed fractional creep model when applied to concrete, experimental data from the literature were used. Bouras et al. [27] conducted a series of creep loading tests on lightweight expansive shale concrete. In terms of temperature conditions, the experimental data under temperatures of 22 °C, 204 °C, and 316 °C were chosen for data fitting. The levels of applied stress (σ/f_c') contained 0.3, 0.45, and 0.6, where f_c' denotes the compressive strength, which was 24.0 MPa. Therefore, the selected applied stresses σ_0 corresponded to 7.2 MPa, 10.8 MPa, and 14.4 MPa, respectively.

In order to accurately describe the experimental data, the least squares fitting method was used to determine the parameter values of the fractional-order creep model. The calibration process was performed using MATLAB (MathWorks) to minimize the root mean square error (RMSE) and to maximize the coefficient of determination (R-squared), thus providing a quantitative measure of the goodness of fit. The RMSE and R-squared formulas used are as follows [33]:

$$\text{RMSE} = \sqrt{\frac{1}{n}\sum_{i=1}^{n}(y_i - \hat{y}_i)^2} \tag{9}$$

$$R^2 = 1 - \frac{\sum_{i=1}^{n}(y_i - \hat{y}_i)^2}{\sum_{i=1}^{n}(y_i - \overline{y})^2} \tag{10}$$

where n represents the number of observations, y_i is the observed value, $\hat{y}_i$ is the predicted value, and $\overline{y}$ is the mean of the observed values. The RMSE measures the average magnitude of prediction errors, providing an absolute measure of fit. A lower RMSE value indicates a better fit. The R-squared indicates the proportion of variance explained by the model, with a value closer to one indicating a better fit.

The RMSE is often more relevant for precise engineering predictions due to its direct reflection of prediction errors. Meanwhile, the R-squared is vital for understanding the explanatory power of a model [34]. MATLAB can produce a negative R-squared if the model fit is worse than a horizontal mean line, indicating poor model performance.

Throughout the process, the material constants E and θ were kept constant at the same temperature, while the values of the parameters were variably adjusted within a certain range to achieve an optimal fit for varying stress levels.

Based on the above methods, the model parameters for the expansive shale light concrete test data were obtained, as presented in Table 1. It can be observed that the values of the material constants E and θ remain within a certain range at each temperature, regardless of the change in the applied stress. This shows that the model has the robustness to accurately represent material behavior under the influence of environmental factors without deviating from these effective parameter ranges. The model fitting results for lightweight expansive shale concrete at 22 °C, 204 °C, and 316 °C are demonstrated in Figures 2–4. These figures show that the creep characteristics of concrete are significantly affected by the loading conditions and that the creep strain increases significantly at higher temperatures or greater stress levels. It is worth noting that under each loading condition, the fitting curve of the fractional order creep model has a strong correlation with the experimental data.

Table 1. Model parameters and fitting results for lightweight expansive shale concrete.

T (°C)		**22**			**204**			**316**	
σ_0 (MPa)	**7.2**	**10.8**	**14.4**	**7.2**	**10.8**	**14.4**	**7.2**	**10.8**	**14.4**
E (MPa)	20,841	20,345	18,570	11,720	11,458	11,298	4811	4390	4652
θ (s)	3.34×10^6	1.70×10^6	1.73×10^6	1.09×10^5	1.04×10^5	8.64×10^4	4.14×10^5	3.68×10^5	3.91×10^5
α	0.3078	0.2993	0.2977	0.3683	0.3630	0.3629	0.4028	0.4059	0.3948

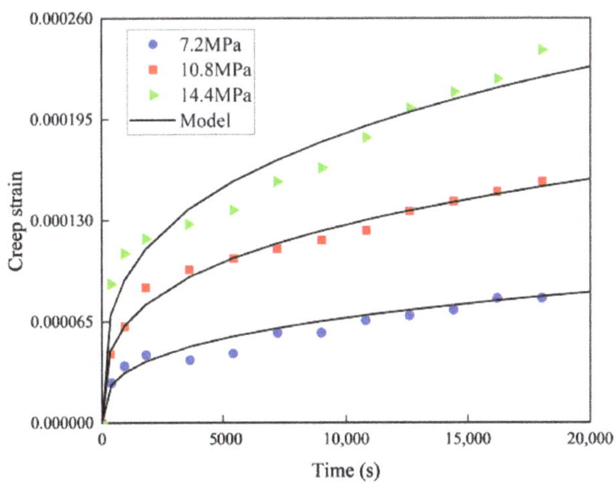

Figure 2. Model fitting results of the fractional creep model versus the experimental data for lightweight expansive shale concrete at 22 °C.

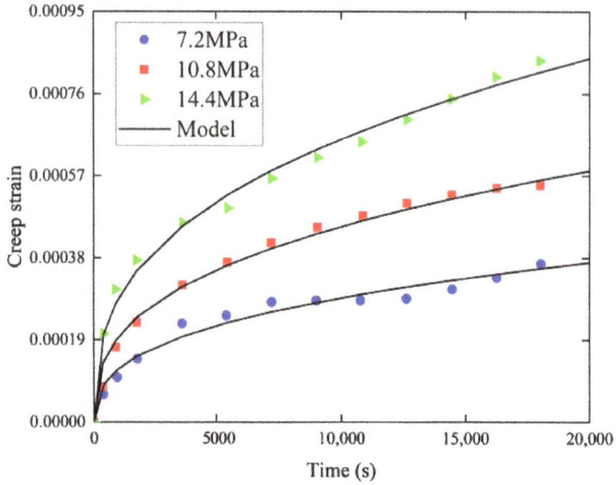

Figure 3. Model fitting results of the fractional creep model versus the experimental data for lightweight expansive shale concrete at 204 °C.

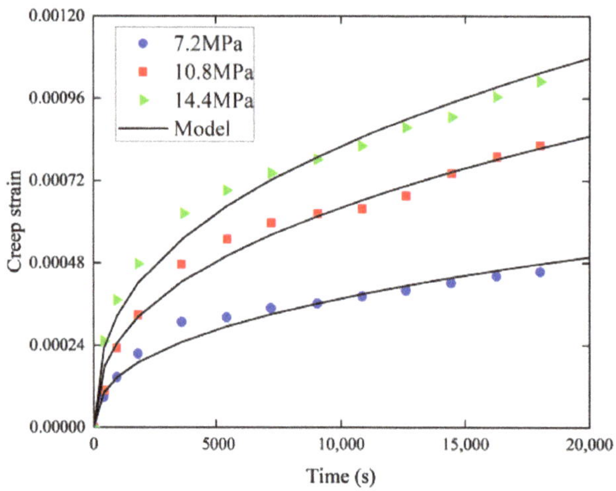

Figure 4. Model fitting results of the fractional creep model versus the experimental data for lightweight expansive shale concrete at 316 °C.

For the experimental data at temperatures of 22 °C, 204 °C, and 316 °C, comparisons of the model proposed in this paper with the model proposed by Bouras et al. [27] are depicted in Figures 5–7, which prove that the proposed fractional creep model can more accurately match the experimental data. In the cases of low temperatures and low loading stresses, for example, when the temperature is 22 °C and the applied stresses are 7.2 MPa and 10.8 MPa, there is a large deviation between the results obtained by the model in the literature and the experimental data, but the proposed fractional order creep model accurately describes the experimental results. Table 2 presents the RMSE and R-squared comparisons between the proposed fractional creep model and the previous model at these three temperatures, further validating that the model proposed in this paper has higher accuracy. Moreover, it can be observed that within the strain–time curves, the order of the fractional derivative lies between 0 and 1, covering the range from pure elasticity to Newtonian viscosity. In addition, it should be emphasized that during all fitting processes, the fractional order was strictly between 0 and 1 across various stress levels and temperatures, which conforms to the range from pure elasticity to Newtonian viscosity in the fractional viscoelastic spectrum.

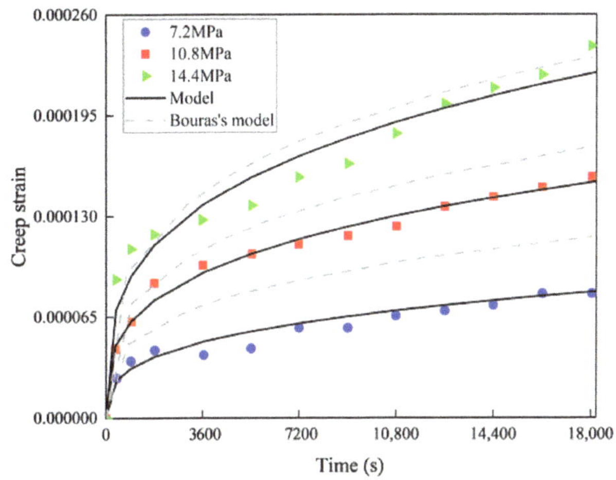

Figure 5. Comparison of fitting effectiveness of the fractional creep model and nonlinear thermo-viscoelastic rheological model for concrete creep at 22 °C.

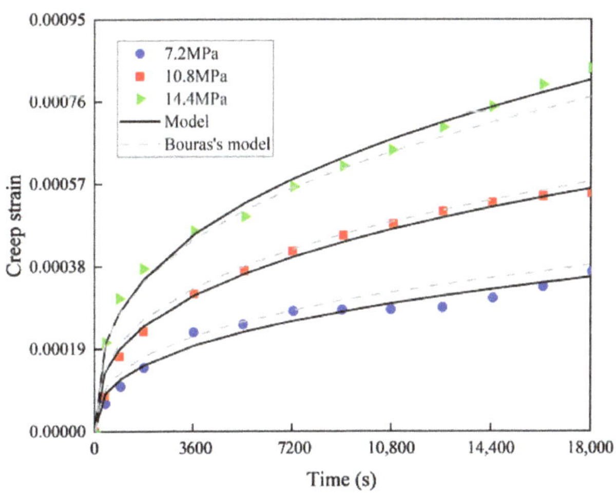

Figure 6. Comparison of fitting effectiveness of the fractional creep model and nonlinear thermo-viscoelastic rheological model for concrete creep at 204 °C.

In summary, according to the data fitting and model comparison procedure, it was proven that the proposed fractional model can effectively describe the creep behavior of concrete, and the fractional order can directly reflect the evolution of the mechanical properties of concrete. In the next section, the relationship between the value of fractional order α and the loading conditions is discussed in detail to finally achieve the prediction of concrete creep.

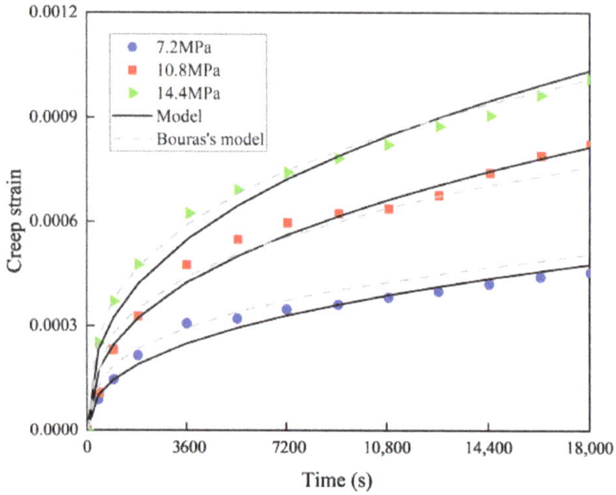

Figure 7. Comparative fitting effectiveness of the fractional creep model and nonlinear thermo-viscoelastic rheological model for concrete creep at 316 °C.

Table 2. Comparison of fitting parameters between the fractional creep model and the nonlinear thermo-viscoelastic rheological model.

T (°C)		22			204			316		
σ_0 (MPa)		7.2	10.8	14.4	7.2	10.8	14.4	7.2	10.8	14.4
Bouras's model	RMSE	3.20×10^{-5}	1.81×10^{-5}	2.54×10^{-5}	3.29×10^{-5}	2.68×10^{-5}	3.57×10^{-5}	3.96×10^{-5}	5.01×10^{-5}	2.10×10^{-5}
	R^2	−0.8034	0.8222	0.9395	0.9132	0.9787	0.9831	0.9235	0.9636	0.9951
Proposed Model	RMSE	5.80×10^{-6}	5.19×10^{-6}	1.44×10^{-5}	2.03×10^{-5}	2.14×10^{-5}	2.31×10^{-5}	2.56×10^{-5}	3.63×10^{-5}	4.25×10^{-5}
	R^2	0.9477	0.9889	0.9593	0.9724	0.9890	0.9927	0.9734	0.9841	0.9835

4. Prediction of Concrete Creep

The variation in the fractional order between 0 and 1 can reflect the hardness or softness of a material; therefore, the numerical value of the fractional order can intuitively reveal the influences of external environmental factors on the mechanical properties of a material.

During the data fitting process for lightweight expansive shale concrete, it is worth noting that the material constants E and θ changed little at a given temperature. The relationship between the fractional order α and applied stress levels is graphically depicted in Figure 8. It can be clearly seen that the numerical values of the fractional order α are basically consistent at the same temperature, regardless of the changes in the applied stress levels. Therefore, it is illustrated that the mechanical properties of lightweight expansive concrete and the law of the corresponding fractional order are principally governed by temperature.

The variation in the fractional order α with the experimental temperature is further plotted in Figure 9. It is shown that under the constant applied stress condition, the fractional order α demonstrates an upward trend with increasing temperature. This trend is consistent with the effect of temperature on creep behavior; that is, an increase in temperature tends to accelerate the creep phenomenon, thus making the material gradually softer. Therefore, the numerical variation in fractional-order values intuitively reflects the dominant impact of temperature on the creep behavior of lightweight expansive concrete. More importantly, Figures 8 and 9 clearly show that the order curves are almost the same at all three temperatures, which provides a method of achieving the prediction of concrete creep.

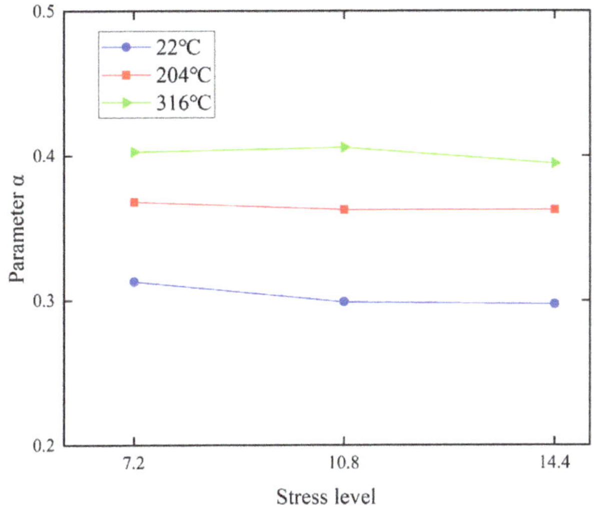

Figure 8. Relationship between fractional order and applied stress for lightweight expansive shale concrete.

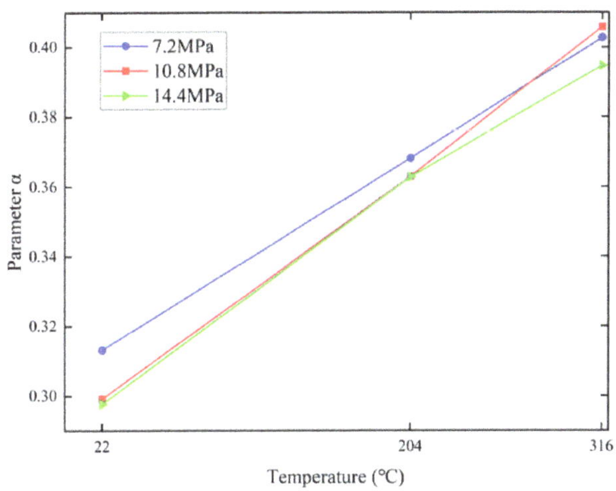

Figure 9. Relationship between fractional order and temperature of lightweight expansive shale concrete.

At the same temperature, the average values of the material's parameters and the fractional order under different stress levels are as presented in Table 3. The model predictions employing the averaged parameters for the creep behavior of lightweight expansive shale concrete are depicted in Figures 10–12. The results illustrate that the fractional-order creep model can effectively describe the creep behavior of concrete under different applied stress levels through the average parameter values at each temperature. This means that the temperature-dependent creep deformation of concrete can be directly predicted only by changing the applied stress values in the fitting formula. This is of great significance for the design and application of concrete in the fields of construction and road engineering.

Table 3. Average values of material parameters E, θ, and α at the same temperature.

T (°C)	22	204	316
E (MPa)	20,712	11,492	4618
θ (s)	1.76×10^6	9.98×10^4	3.91×10^5
α	0.3034	0.3647	0.4012

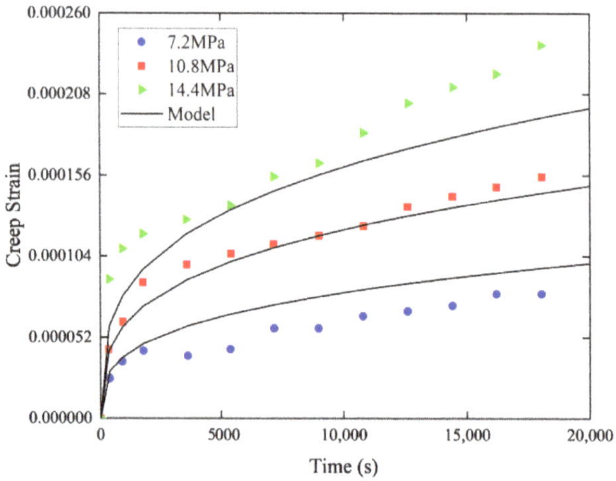

Figure 10. Model prediction of the average order value for lightweight expansive shale concrete at different stress levels at 22 °C.

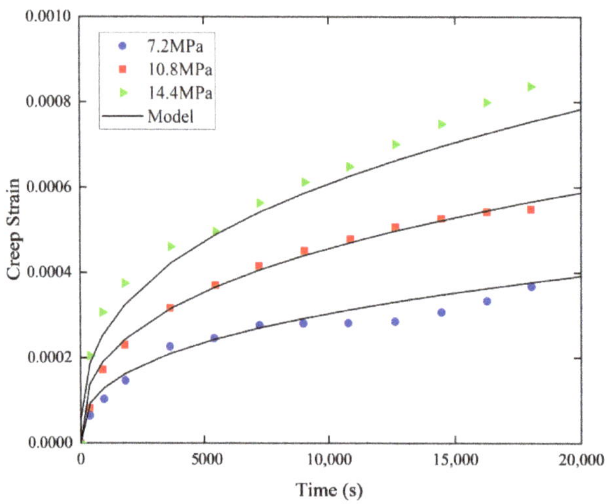

Figure 11. Model prediction of the average order value for lightweight expansive shale concrete at different stress levels at 204 °C.

In conclusion, the analysis of the rule of the fractional order shows that the value of the fractional order is mainly affected by temperature, and the creep deformation of concrete can be successfully predicted using the average fractional order value at different temperatures. In addition, the numerical value of the fractional order intuitively reflects the evolution of the mechanical properties of concrete with the variation in temperature.

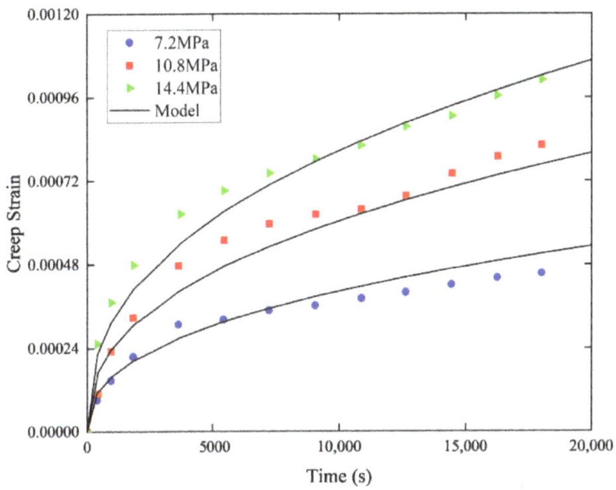

Figure 12. Model prediction of the average order value for lightweight expansive shale concrete at different stress levels at 316 °C.

5. Conclusions

In this work, a fractional creep model was derived from fractional viscoelastic theory to describe the temperature-dependent creep behavior of concrete, in which the fractional order has the ability to reveal the transition in mechanical properties from hard to soft. The effectiveness of the model was verified via data fitting and comparison with a lightweight expansive shale concrete model in the literature. The conclusions are summarized as follows:

(i) The fractional creep model can accurately describe the experimental data and has good adaptability as well as robustness under different temperatures and applied stresses.
(ii) The value of the fractional order tends to increase with the increase in temperature. This intuitively reflects that high temperatures accelerate the creep process of concrete, making its mechanical properties gradually softer.
(iii) The prediction formula containing the average fractional-order value at each temperature was established, and the creep deformation of concrete was predicted only by changing the applied stress, which provides an innovative and practical method for predicting the temperature-dependent creep behavior of concrete.

Author Contributions: Conceptualization, R.M.; methodology, L.G.; validation, J.C.; investigation, L.G.; data curation, J.C. and L.G.; writing—original draft preparation, J.C.; writing—review and editing, R.M.; visualization, J.C.; supervision, R.M.; funding acquisition, R.M. All authors have read and agreed to the published version of the manuscript.

Funding: This research was funded by the Regional Joint Fund-Youth Fund Projects of the Guangdong Basic and Applied Basic Research Foundation (grant No. 2022A1515110003) and the Basic and Applied Basic Research Project of Guangzhou Basic Research Program (grant No. 202201010260).

Data Availability Statement: The raw data supporting the conclusions of this article will be made available by the authors on request.

Acknowledgments: The authors gratefully acknowledge the financial support from the Regional Joint Fund-Youth Fund Projects of the Guangdong Basic and Applied Basic Research Foundation (grant No. 2022A1515110003) and the Basic and Applied Basic Research Project of Guangzhou Basic Research Program (grant No. 202201010260).

Conflicts of Interest: The authors declare no conflict of interest.

References

1. Wang, Y.; Xu, Q.; Chen, S. Approaches of concrete creep using micromechanics: Numerical simulation and predictive model. *Model. Simul. Mater. Sci. Eng.* **2019**, *27*, 055012. [CrossRef]
2. Liu, W.; Zhang, S.; Sun, B.; Chen, L. Creep characteristics and time-dependent creep model of tunnel lining structure concrete. *Mech. Time-Depend. Mater.* **2021**, *25*, 365–382. [CrossRef]
3. Mussabayev, T.T.; Nuguzhinov, Z.S.; Nemova, D.; Kayupov, T.; Tolkynbaev, T.A.; Akmakanova, A.Z.; Khafizova, G.S. Creep of Concrete in Shell Structures: Nonlinear Theory. *Materials* **2023**, *16*, 5587. [CrossRef] [PubMed]
4. Houhou, N.; Benzarti, K.; Quiertant, M.; Chataigner, S.; Fléty, A.; Marty, C. Analysis of the nonlinear creep behavior of concrete/FRP-bonded assemblies. *J. Adhes. Sci. Technol.* **2014**, *28*, 1345–1366. [CrossRef]
5. Baktheer, A.; Chudoba, R. Experimental and theoretical evidence for the load sequence effect in the compressive fatigue behavior of concrete. *Mater. Struct.* **2021**, *54*, 1–23. [CrossRef]
6. Li, R.; Liu, L.; An, H.; Wang, Y. Study on Dynamic Constitutive Model of Polypropylene Concrete under Real-Time High-Temperature Conditions. *Appl. Sci.* **2022**, *12*, 1482. [CrossRef]
7. Gernay, T.; Franssen, J.-M. A formulation of the Eurocode 2 concrete model at elevated temperature that includes an explicit term for transient creep. *Fire Saf. J.* **2012**, *51*, 1–9. [CrossRef]
8. Li, L.; Wang, H.; Wu, J.; Jiang, W. A thermomechanical coupling constitutive model of concrete including elastoplastic damage. *Appl. Sci.* **2021**, *11*, 604. [CrossRef]
9. Liang, M.; Chang, Z.; Wan, Z.; Gan, Y.; Schlangen, E.; Šavija, B. Interpretable Ensemble-Machine-Learning models for predicting creep behavior of concrete. *Cem. Concr. Compos.* **2022**, *125*, 104295. [CrossRef]
10. Stanisauskis, E.; Mashayekhi, S.; Pahari, B.; Mehnert, M.; Steinmann, P.; Oates, W. Fractional and fractal order effects in soft elastomers: Strain rate and temperature dependent nonlinear mechanics. *Mech. Mater.* **2022**, *172*, 104390. [CrossRef]
11. Qin, X.; Yin, W. A novel fractal model for effective thermal conductivity in granular porous media. *Geothermics* **2023**, *108*, 102625. [CrossRef]
12. Qu, M.L.; Tian, S.Q.; Fan, L.W.; Yu, Z.T.; Ge, J. An experimental investigation and fractal modeling on the effective thermal conductivity of novel autoclaved aerated concrete (AAC)-based composites with silica aerogels (SA). *Appl. Therm. Eng.* **2020**, *179*, 115770. [CrossRef]
13. Jiang, J.; Zheng, L.; Jones, M.R.; Lu, Z.; Li, J. Estimating thermal conductivity of lightweight nanoporous cement pastes using a hybrid fractal model. *Constr. Build. Mater.* **2022**, *327*, 126941. [CrossRef]
14. Li, T.; Hou, R.; Liu, G.; Han, Q.; Li, D. Investigations on Creep Behavior and Fractal Derivative Constitutive Model of Sandstone under Different Drying-Wetting Cycles. *KSCE J. Civ. Eng.* **2022**, *26*, 69–78. [CrossRef]
15. Bouras, Y.; Vrcelj, Z. Fractional and fractal derivative-based creep models for concrete under constant and time-varying loading. *Constr. Build. Mater.* **2023**, *367*, 130324. [CrossRef]
16. Wu, F.; Gao, R.; Liu, J.; Li, C. New fractional variable-order creep model with short memory. *Appl. Math. Comput.* **2020**, *380*, 125278. [CrossRef]
17. Shitikova, M.V. Fractional operator viscoelastic models in dynamic problems of mechanics of solids: A Review. *Mech. Solids* **2022**, *57*, 1–33. [CrossRef]
18. Mainardi, F.; Spada, G. Creep, relaxation and viscosity properties for basic fractional models in rheology. *Eur. Phys. J. Spéc. Top.* **2011**, *193*, 133–160. [CrossRef]
19. Bonfanti, A.; Kaplan, J.L.; Charras, G.; Kabla, A. Fractional viscoelastic models for power-law materials. *Soft Matter* **2020**, *16*, 6002–6020. [CrossRef]
20. Katicha, S.W.; Apeagyei, A.K.; Flintsch, G.W.; Loulizi, A. Universal linear viscoelastic approximation property of fractional viscoelastic models with application to asphalt concrete. *Mech. Time-Depend. Mater.* **2014**, *18*, 555–571. [CrossRef]
21. Zatar, W.; Xiao, F.; Chen, G.S.; Hulsey, J.L. Identification of viscoelastic property of pile-soil interactions with fractional derivative model. *J. Low Freq. Noise, Vib. Act. Control.* **2021**, *40*, 1392–1400. [CrossRef]
22. Huang, Y.; Xiao, L.; Bao, T.; Liu, Y. Fractional order creep model for dam concrete considering degree of hydration. *Mech. Time-Depend. Mater.* **2019**, *23*, 361–372. [CrossRef]
23. Xu, H.; Jiang, X. Creep constitutive models for viscoelastic materials based on fractional derivatives. *Comput. Math. Appl.* **2017**, *73*, 1377–1384. [CrossRef]
24. Sapora, A.; Cornetti, P.; Carpinteri, A.; Baglieri, O.; Santagata, E. The use of fractional calculus to model the experimental creep-recovery behavior of modified bituminous binders. *Mater. Struct.* **2016**, *49*, 45–55. [CrossRef]
25. Tang, H.; Wang, D.; Huang, R.; Pei, X.; Chen, W. A new rock creep model based on variable-order fractional derivatives and continuum damage mechanics. *Bull. Eng. Geol. Environ.* **2018**, *77*, 375–383. [CrossRef]
26. Zhou, F.; Wang, L.; Liu, H. A fractional elasto-viscoplastic model for describing creep behavior of soft soil. *Acta Geotech.* **2021**, *16*, 67–76. [CrossRef]
27. Bouras, Y.; Zorica, D.; Atanacković, T.M.; Vrcelj, Z. A non-linear thermo-viscoelastic rheological model based on fractional derivatives for high temperature creep in concrete. *Appl. Math. Model.* **2018**, *55*, 551–568. [CrossRef]
28. Zhang, C.; Zhu, Z.; Zhu, S.; He, Z.; Zhu, D.; Liu, J.; Meng, S. Nonlinear creep damage constitutive model of concrete based on fractional calculus theory. *Materials* **2019**, *12*, 1505. [CrossRef] [PubMed]

29. Ribeiro, J.G.T.; de Castro, J.T.P.; Meggiolaro, M.A. Modeling concrete and polymer creep using fractional calculus. *J. Mater. Res. Technol.* **2021**, *12*, 1184–1193. [CrossRef]
30. Smit, W.; de Vries, H. Rheological models containing fractional derivatives. *Rheol. Acta* **1970**, *9*, 525–534. [CrossRef]
31. Diethelm, K.; Ford, N.; Freed, A.; Luchko, Y. Algorithms for the fractional calculus: A selection of numerical methods. *Comput. Methods Appl. Mech. Eng.* **2005**, *194*, 743–773. [CrossRef]
32. Lorenzo, C.F.; Hartley, T.T. Variable order and distributed order fractional operators. *Nonlinear Dyn.* **2002**, *29*, 57–98. [CrossRef]
33. Yang, C.; Huang, R.; Liu, D.; Qiu, W.; Zhang, R.; Tang, Y. Analysis and warning prediction of tunnel deformation based on multifractal theory. *Fractal Fract.* **2024**, *8*, 108. [CrossRef]
34. Kati, N.; Ucar, F. An Intelligent Model for Supercapacitors with a Graphene-Based Fractal Electrode to Investigate the Cyclic Voltammetry. *Fractal Fract.* **2023**, *7*, 218. [CrossRef]

fractal and fractional

MDPI

Article

A Compartmental Approach to Modeling the Measles Disease: A Fractional Order Optimal Control Model

Amar Nath Chatterjee [1], Santosh Kumar Sharma [1] and Fahad Al Basir [2,*]

[1] Department of Mathematics, K.L.S. College, Magadh University, Bodhgaya, Nawada 805110, Bihar, India; amarnc@klscollege.ac.in (A.N.C.); santoshmumath@gmail.com (S.K.S.)
[2] Department of Mathematics, Asansol Girls' College, Asansol 713304, West Bengal, India
* Correspondence: fahadbasir@gmail.com or fahadalbasir@agc.ac.in

Abstract: Measles is the most infectious disease with a high basic reproduction number (R_0). For measles, it is reported that R_0 lies between 12 and 18 in an endemic situation. In this paper, a fractional order mathematical model for measles disease is proposed to identify the dynamics of disease transmission following a declining memory process. In the proposed model, a fractional order differential operator is used to justify the effect and success rate of vaccination. The total population of the model is subdivided into five sub-compartments: susceptible (S), exposed (E), infected (I), vaccinated (V), and recovered (R). Here, we consider the first dose of measles vaccination and convert the model to a controlled system. Finally, we transform the control-induced model to an optimal control model using control theory. Both models are analyzed to find the stability of the system, the basic reproduction number, the optimal control input, and the adjoint equations with the boundary conditions. Also, the numerical simulation of the model is presented along with using the analytical findings. We also verify the effective role of the fractional order parameter alpha on the model dynamics and changes in the dynamical behavior of the model with $R_0 = 1$.

Keywords: measles; basic reproduction number; fractional calculus; optimal control system

1. Introduction

Measles is an infectious disease that causes respiratory illness. Cough, coryza, and conjunctivitis are major symptoms of measles. Also, the maculopapular rash is observed after two weeks of infection, and it spreads rapidly all over the body. After four days of infection, the patients are considered contagious to before four days after the rash appears. The *morbillivirus* in the *Paramyxoviridae* family is known as the measles virus. It is a single-stranded RNA virus with one serotype. The measles virus can only be found in humans.

The infection rate of measles through person-to-person transmission is very high, and its attack rate is over 90%. It is the first infectious disease that humans can ever face in their childhood [1]. The basic symptom is a red rash, and sometimes it leads to serious fetal complications like pneumonia, diarrhea, and encephalitis. Some children suffer from blindness, deafness, or vision impairment. But measles infection creates lifelong immunity from future attacks [2]. In the wild, more than 30 to 40 million children suffer from measles, and over 1 million face complications like pneumonia, diarrhea, and malnutrition [3]. It has been reported that measles is the major cause of child death worldwide in spite of control measures [4].

The only efficient and safe method of protecting against measles infection is vaccination [5]. Without immunization, pregnant women and small children are at significant risk. As per WHO, the measles vaccine has been found to last for at least 20 years and is typically maintained for life in the majority of people. The efficacy of the measles vaccination is around 85% for children aged nine to eleven months, and it rises to 95% following a second dose given after a year [6].

Except for vaccination, there is no specific medicine for the treatment of measles. Complete bed rest and an intake of plenty of healthy fluids helps to reduce the fever and pains, as well as antibiotic use [7,8].

Since the previous decade, mathematical modeling has been used as one of the most essential tools for understanding the dynamics of human or animal disease [9]. For measles disease dynamics, Momoh et al. [10] proposed and analyzed an SEIR measles model to look at how the latent period affected the dynamics of the disease. In 2014, Adewale et al. [11] explained the impact of distance between infected and uninfected people. Ochoche and Gwervina [12] explored the SIR model of measles with two stages of vaccination. They conducted research to show that a full course of immunization can eradicate the illness. Edward [13] has researched the mathematical model for control dynamics in measles infection. Smith [14] conducted a quantitative analysis of the effectiveness of vaccination in avoiding measles. Raymond researched the stochastic measles model with vaccination impact [15]. Garba et al. [16] studied the role of vaccines on measles infection. Christopher et al. [17] studied the dynamics of the measles epidemic under the influence of vaccination combinations. The control and transmission dynamics of measles were used by Mitku et al. [18] to study the SEIR mathematical model of the disease. A stochastic differential equation model with double-dose vaccination was developed by Tilahun in 2020 [8]. In order to estimate the frequency of measles in Bangladesh, Kuddus [19] studied a compartmental mathematical model of the measles disease. In [20], a generalized SVEIR epidemic model with a general nonlinear incidence rate was proposed as a candidate model for measles virus dynamics.

The above-mentioned models are based on ordinary differential equations. But the deterministic technique for ordinary differential equations has several limitations. Thus, our motivation is to explore the fractional order differential problem (FODE) in measles disease dynamics.

Optimal control theory is useful for managing a disease in cost-effective way. In [7], an optimal control of measles was explored with vaccination using a mathematical model of integer order. Here, we formulated fractional optimal control (FOC) to combat the measles infection.

In this study, we derived a fractional order differential equation model of the dynamics of measles transmission with vaccines in optimal control approach. Five compartments were used in this model to separate the entire population: vulnerable, exposed, infected, immunized, and recovered. The model was put forth using the fractional method, which is recognized to be important since it adds more realism than the deterministic approach. We are aware that in nonlinear mathematical modeling, fractional order differential equations (FODE) are crucial [21–24].

To determine the efficacy of immunization, multiple analyses of the suggested model were conducted. Positiveness, existence, basic reproduction number, and model stability analysis made up the qualitative study of the model. Additionally, we looked at the model's optimum control theory method. MATLAB software version R2018a was utilized to carry out numerical solutions.

The arrangement of the article is as follows: A fractional order mathematical model of measles in the presence of vaccination is proposed and the uniqueness and positivity of solutions are examined in Section 2. The model analysis (equilibria and stability) and the basic reproduction number are determined in Section 3. The fractional optimal control problem is formulated and analyzed in Section 4. Numerical results of the analytical discoveries are presented in Section 5. Finally, the discussion in Section 6 and the conclusions in Section 7 complete the paper.

2. The Basic Assumptions and the Mathematical Model

Here, we consider S, V, E, I, and R as the concentrations of the susceptible population, vaccination populations, exposed population but not infections, infected population, and recovered population, with some basic assumptions. The schematic diagram is represented in Figure 1. To construct the mathematical model, we consider the following assumptions:

$(A1)$ p is the probability of a susceptible population, and λ is the birth rate of populations. μ is the death rate of populations, and ν is the vaccination rate from S,
$(A2)$ β is the disease transmission rate,
$(A3)$ ρ is the rate of infection,
$(A4)$ θ is the decay rate for the first doses of the vaccine to the susceptible population, and b is the rate at which the vaccinated population moves to the recover class. η is the death rate for the infected class due to infection, and ω is the natural recovery rate of the infected population. ϕ is the rate at which the first dose of the vaccine is administered. Thus, our model based on $(A1)$–$(A4)$ is constructed.

The above assumptions, $(A1)$–$(A4)$, lead us to formulate the model equations as follows:

$$\begin{aligned} D^{\alpha}S &= p\lambda - \beta SI + \theta V - (\nu + \mu)S, \\ D^{\alpha}V &= (1-p)\lambda + \nu S - (\theta + b + \mu)V, \\ D^{\alpha}E &= \beta SI - (\rho + \mu)E, \\ D^{\alpha}I &= \rho E - (\phi + \eta + \mu)I, \\ D^{\alpha}R &= \omega I + bV - \mu R \end{aligned} \tag{1}$$

with initial conditions

$$S(t_0) = S_0, V(t_0) = V_0, E(t_0) = E_0, I(t_0) = I_0, R(t_0) = R_0. \tag{2}$$

All the parameters are taken from Table 1.

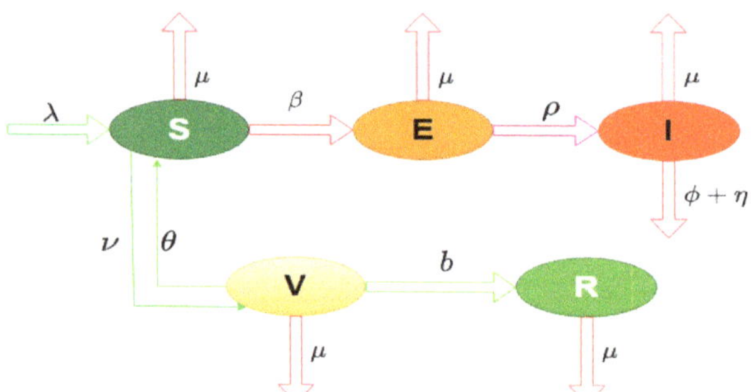

Figure 1. Diagram of fractional Model (1).

2.1. Mathematical Analysis

To determine the existence and uniqueness of the model, we rewrite Model (1) as

$$D_t^{\alpha} g(t) = f(t, g(t)), 0 < \alpha \leq 1, \tag{3}$$

where

$$f(t, g) = [f_1, f_2, f_3, f_4, f_5]^T; \text{ here, } T \text{ denotes the transpose}$$

with initial values

$$g(0) = [S(0), V(0), E(0), I(0), R(0)]$$

as the initial condition, where the derivative is in the left Caputo sense. Here, f_1, f_2, f_3, f_4, f_5 are right-hand-side of System (1). For Model (1), we have

$$\begin{aligned} f_1 &= p\lambda - \beta SI + \theta V - (\nu + \mu)S, \\ f_2 &= (1-p)\lambda + \nu S - (\theta + b + \mu)V, \\ f_3 &= \beta SI - (\rho + \mu)E, \\ f_4 &= \rho E - (\phi + \eta + \mu)I, \\ f_5 &= \omega I + bV - \mu R. \end{aligned} \tag{4}$$

Function $f(t,.g) : R \times R^d \to R^d$ with $d \geq 1$.

Table 1. Parameters and their values for (1).

Parameter	Definition	Value	Reference
p	Proportion of the successively vaccinated at birth	0.1	Assumed
λ	Birth rate	200	[25]
β	Contact rate	0.09091	[26]
θ	Efficacy rate of 1st dose of vaccine to susceptible rate	0.167	Assumed
ν	Vaccination rate from S	0.008754	Assumed
μ	Natural death rate	0.00875	[25]
b	Received 2nd dose of vaccine to recovery rate	0.5	Assumed
ρ	Recovered form the infected class at rate	0.003	[25]
ϕ	Receive 1st dose of vaccine to susceptibility rate	0.2	[25]
η	Disease death rate for infected class	0.09	Assumed
ω	Natural rate of progression	0.0013	[25]

2.2. Local Existence and Uniqueness of Solutions

Let us consider $R^5_+ = \left[g \in R^5 | g \geq 0\right]$ and $g(t) = (S, V, E, I, R)^T$ and the rational field $Q[p,q]$. We have the following theorem.

Theorem 1. *For $h(x) \in Q[p,q]$ and $D^\alpha_t h(x) \in Q[p,q]$; then, $0 < \alpha \leq 1$,*

$$h(g) = h(p) + \frac{1}{\Gamma(\alpha)}\left(D^\alpha_p f\right)(\phi)(g-p)^\alpha,$$

Here , $p \leq \phi \leq l, \forall l \in (p,q]$ [27]. Let $g(x) \in Q[p,q]$ and $D^\alpha_p h(g) \in Q[p,q]$, for $0 < \eta \leq 1$. If $D^\alpha_p h(g) \geq 0$, for all $g \in (p,q)$,$h(g)$ is non-decreasing for each $g \in (p,q)$ if $D^\alpha_p h(g) \leq 0$, $\forall g \in (p,q)$; then, $h(g)$ is non-increasing for each $g \in (p,q)$.

We consider $M(t)$ such that $M(t) : R_{0,+} \to R_{0,+}$ as follows:.

$$M(t) = f_1 + f_2 + f_3 + f_4 + f_5, \forall t \geq t_0. \tag{5}$$

where $f_i, i = 1,2,3,4,5$. Function $M(t)$ is defined and differentiable for $\left[0, t_f\right]$, and we have

$$M(t) \leq p\lambda - \delta(S + V + E + I + R). \tag{6}$$

From (6), we have

$$f(t) \leq p\lambda - \delta[S(t) + V(t) + E(t) + I(t) + R(t)], \forall t \in \left(0, t_f\right). \tag{7}$$

The local existence of the solution of fractional ordered System (1) can be proved using the following theorem [28].

Theorem 2. *For $Q = [t_0 - b, t_0 + b], W = g \in R^d || g - g_0 || \leq b, U = \{(t,g) \in R \times R^d | t \in Q, Q \in W\}$.*

And $f : U \to R^d$ satisfies the following three properties:

(a) $f(t,g)$ is Lebesgue measurable with $t \in Q$ with t,
(b) $f(t,g)$ is continuous on W,
(c) $m(t) \in L^5(Q)$ is a real function satisfying $f(t,g) \leq m(t)$ for $t \in Q$ with $g \in W$.

Now, $\alpha > \frac{1}{2}$; we have only one solution of $D_t^\alpha g(t) = f(t,g(t)), 0 < \alpha < 1$ within $[t_0 - s, t_0 + s], s > 0$. Now, the $(f_1, f_2, f_3, f_4, f_5)$ of Model (1) are measurable $\forall t \in [t_0 - s, t_0 + s]$. Thus, $f(g,t)$ satisfies Theorem 3 with $m(t) = \lambda - \delta g(t)$, with $g = S + V + E + I + R$. Hence, there exists a solution for Model (1) in $\left(0, t_f\right)$.

Theorem 3. *Suppose the conditions of Theorem 2 hold. Now, consider a real-valued function $\kappa(t) \in L^5(Q)$ for which*

$$||f(t,g) - f(t,\kappa)|| \leq \kappa(t)||g - \kappa||, \tag{8}$$

with $t \in Q$ and $g, k \in W$; then, system $D_t^\alpha g(t) = f(t,g(t)), 0 < \alpha \leq 1$ possesses a unique solution on the interval $[t_0 - s, t_0 + s]$ for some $s > 0$. From Equations (1) and (6), we have

$$||f(t,g) - f(t,\kappa)|| \leq \kappa(t)||g - \kappa||, \tag{9}$$

with $\kappa(t) \leq \frac{\lambda}{\delta}$, thus satisfying fractional ordered System (1) with the uniqueness of the solution. With the help of Theorem 3.1 [28], we verify the global existence of the solution.

Theorem 4. *Vector filed $V(t,g)$ exists along with the conditions for Theorems (2) and (3) in the global space and $||f(t,g)|| \leq \omega + l||x||$ for almost every $t \in R$ and $g \in R^d$ with $\omega, l > 0$. Then, function $g(t)$ can be defined on $(-\infty, +\infty)$ by solving (1) with an initial condition. Using (6) along with the norm property, we have $||f(g(t))|| \leq \lambda + \delta||g||$. Thus, the global existence condition is satisfied with $\omega = \lambda$ and $l = \delta$.*

2.3. Basic Reproduction Ratio

To calculate the basic reproduction number for System (1), we consider F and G to be two three-dimensional matrices corresponding to vectors $\mathcal{F}$ and $\mathcal{G}$ defined. To formulate the matrix, we only consider the infected compartments of the system, which are E, I, R. At the infection-free state, we have

$$\mathcal{F} = \begin{pmatrix} \beta S I \\ 0 \\ 0 \end{pmatrix}, \mathcal{G} = \begin{pmatrix} (\rho + \mu)E \\ (\phi + \eta + \mu)I - \rho E \\ -\omega I - bV + \mu R \end{pmatrix}. \tag{10}$$

Then, we have

$$F = \begin{pmatrix} 0 & \beta S & 0 \\ 0 & 0 & 0 \\ 0 & 0 & 0 \end{pmatrix}, G = \begin{pmatrix} (\rho + \mu) & 0 & 0 \\ -\rho & (\phi + \eta + \mu) & 0 \\ 0 & -\omega & \mu \end{pmatrix},$$

Now,

$$G^{-1} = \begin{pmatrix} \frac{1}{(\rho+\mu)} & 0 & 0 \\ \frac{\rho}{(\rho+\mu)(\phi+\eta+\mu)} & \frac{1}{(\phi+\eta+\mu)} & 0 \\ \frac{\rho\omega}{\mu(\rho+\mu)(\phi+\eta+\mu)} & \frac{\omega}{\mu(\phi+\eta+\mu)} & \frac{1}{\mu} \end{pmatrix},$$

which is a non-singular matrix.

Then, FG^{-1} at E^0 is also a non-negative next-generation matrix, which provides the estimated number of the new infection,

$$FG^{-1} = \begin{bmatrix} 0 & \beta S^0 & 0 \\ 0 & 0 & 0 \\ 0 & 0 & 0 \end{bmatrix} \times \begin{bmatrix} \frac{1}{(\rho+\mu)} & 0 & 0 \\ \frac{\rho}{(\rho+\mu)(\phi+\eta+\mu)} & \frac{1}{(\phi+\eta+\mu)} & 0 \\ \frac{\rho\omega}{\mu(\rho+\mu)(\phi+\eta+\mu)} & \frac{\omega}{\mu(\phi+\eta+\mu)} & \frac{1}{\mu} \end{bmatrix},$$

$$= \begin{bmatrix} \frac{\beta S^0 \rho}{(\rho+\mu)(\phi+\eta+\mu)} & \frac{\beta S^0}{(\phi+\eta+\mu)} & 0 \\ 0 & 0 & 0 \\ 0 & 0 & 0 \end{bmatrix}. \quad (11)$$

According to [29,30], we obtain the basic reproduction number R_0 as

$$\mathcal{R}_0 = \frac{\beta S^0 \rho}{(\rho+\mu)(\phi+\eta+\mu)}. \quad (12)$$

Theorem 5. *System (1) of measles infection has a threshold parameter basic reproduction number $R_0 = \frac{\beta S^0 \rho}{(\rho+\mu)(\phi+\eta+\mu)}$ at E^0. For $R_0 > 1$, Model (1) switches to the endemic state.*

3. Model Analysis

In this model, (1), we have two equilibrium points.

1. $E^0(S^0, V^0, 0, 0, 0)$ represents no infection.

$$\begin{aligned} S^0 &= \frac{\lambda(\nu+\mu+p\mu)}{[\mu^2+\mu(\theta+b)+\nu(\mu+b)]} > 0, \\ V^0 &= \frac{\lambda(\mu+\nu-\mu p)}{[\mu^2+\mu(\theta+b)+\nu(\mu+b)]} > 0, \end{aligned} \quad (13)$$

and V^0 exist when $p < \frac{\mu+\nu}{\mu}$.

2. With the endemic equilibrium point $E^*(S^*, V^*, E^*, I^*, R^*)$, we obtain

$$\begin{aligned} S^* &= \frac{(\rho+\mu)(\phi+\eta+\mu)}{\beta\rho}, \\ V^* &= \frac{\beta(1-\rho)\lambda+\nu(\mu+\rho)(\phi+\eta+\mu)}{\beta\rho(\theta+b+\mu)}, \\ E^* &= \frac{(\phi+\eta+\mu)I^*}{\rho}, \\ I^* &= \frac{p\lambda+(\nu+\mu)S^*-0V^*}{\beta S^*}, \\ R^* &= \frac{\omega I^*+bV^*}{\mu}. \end{aligned} \quad (14)$$

E^* exits when $\theta < \frac{p\lambda+(\nu+\mu)S^*}{\beta S^* V^*}$.

Stability Analysis

At E^0, we have the Theorem stated below.

Theorem 6. *When $R_0 < 1$, disease-free equilibrium E^0 for (1) is locally asymptotically stable if $R_0 < 1$ and unstable if $R_0 > 1$*

To verify the local stability of System (1) at E^0, we have

$$J = \begin{pmatrix} -(\beta I+\nu+\mu) & \theta & 0 & -\beta S & 0 \\ \nu & -(\theta+b+\mu) & 0 & 0 & 0 \\ 0 & 0 & -(\rho+\mu) & \beta S & 0 \\ 0 & 0 & \rho & -(\phi+\eta+\mu) & 0 \\ 0 & b & 0 & \omega & -\mu \end{pmatrix}, \quad (15)$$

Now,

$$|J - \xi I_{4\times4}|_{E^0} = \begin{pmatrix} -(\nu+\mu)-\xi & \theta & 0 & -\beta S & 0 \\ \nu & -(\theta+b+\mu)-\xi & 0 & 0 & 0 \\ 0 & 0 & -(\rho+\mu)-\xi & \beta S & 0 \\ 0 & 0 & \rho & -(\phi+\eta+\mu)-\xi & 0 \\ 0 & b & 0 & \omega & -\mu-\xi \end{pmatrix}, \quad (16)$$

and the characteristic equation for (16) is

$$\xi^4 + A_{11}\xi^3 + A_{22}\xi^2 + A_{33}\xi + A_{44} = 0 \tag{17}$$

where

$$\begin{aligned} A_{11} &= (a_1 + a_2 + a_3 + a_4), \\ A_{22} &= (a_3a_4 - \beta\nu S) + (a_1 + a_2)(a_3 + a_4) + (a_1a_2 - \theta\nu), \\ A_{33} &= (a_1 + a_2)(a_3a_4 - \beta\nu S)(a_2a_1 - \theta\nu)(a_3 + a_4), \\ A_{44} &= (a_1a_2 - \theta\nu)(a_3a_4 - \beta\nu S), \end{aligned}$$

and

$$a_1 = (\theta + b + \mu), a_2 = (\mu + \nu), a_3 = (\mu + \rho), a_4 = (\phi + \eta + \mu),$$

Now, the characteristic polynomial $D(\epsilon)$ with

$$\epsilon(\xi) = \xi^4 + A_{11}\xi^3 + A_{22}\xi^2 + A_{33}\xi^2 + A_{44} = 0 \tag{18}$$

is

$$D(\epsilon) = \begin{pmatrix} 1 & A_{11} & A_{22} & A_{33} & A_{44} & 0 & 0 \\ 0 & 1 & A_{11} & A_{22} & A_{33} & A_{44} & 0 \\ 0 & 0 & 1 & A_{11} & A_{22} & A_{33} & A_{44} \\ 4 & 3A_{11} & 2A_{22} & A_{33} & 0 & 0 & 0 \\ 0 & 4 & 3A_{11} & 2A_{22} & A_{33} & 0 & 0 \\ 0 & 0 & 4 & 3A_{11} & 2A_{22} & A_{33} & 0 \\ 0 & 0 & 0 & 4 & 3A_{11} & 2A_{22} & A_{33} \end{pmatrix}. \tag{19}$$

We have the following properties.

Proposition 1. *At equilibrium point E^* for the system in R^4_+, we have the following.*

(i) *There exist κ_1, κ_2, and κ_3 where $\kappa_1 = A_{11}; \kappa_2 = A_{11}A_{22} - A_{33}$ and*

$$\kappa_3 = \begin{pmatrix} A_{11} & 1 & 0 \\ A_{33} & A_{22} & A_{11} \\ 0 & A_{44} & A_{33} \end{pmatrix}.$$

When $\alpha = 1$, then it satisfies the following condition:

$$\kappa_1 > 0, \kappa_2 > 0, \kappa_3 = 0 and \kappa_4 > 0,$$

which shows the locally asymptotically stable condition for E^*.

(ii) *E^* is unstable when $D(\epsilon) > 0$, $A_{11}, A_{22} < 0$, and $\alpha > \frac{2}{3}$.*

(iii) *E^* is locally asymptotically stable when $D(\epsilon) < 0, A_{11} > 0, A_{22} > 0, A_{33}, A_{44}$, and $\alpha < \frac{1}{3}$ exist. Also at E^*, the system is unstable. When $D(\epsilon) < 0, A_{11} < 0, A_{22} > 0, A_{33} < 0$, and $A_{44} > 0$.*

(iv) *E^* is locally asymptotically stable for $\alpha \in (0,1)$ along with condition $D(\epsilon) < 0$, $A_{11} > 0, A_{22} > 0, A_{33} > 0, A_{44} > 0$, and $A_{22} = \frac{A_{11}A_{44}}{A_{33}} + \frac{A_{33}}{A_{11}}$.*

(v) *The necessary condition for locally asymptotically stable E^* is $A_{44} > 0$.*

Remark 1. *Endemic equilibrium E^* is locally asymptotically stable for $\alpha = 1$ when it satisfies the R-H conditions. But this condition is not sufficient when $\alpha \in [0,1)$.*

4. The Fractional Optimal Control Problem

This section deals with control strategies. Here, our main aim is to reduce the side effects of the vaccine and the cost of treatment. The control input is defined as $u(t) = \{u_1(t), u_2(t)\}$. Here, we assume $u_1(t)$ as the first dose and $u_2(t)$ as the second dose of the vaccine.

We take the objective function as

$$J[u(t)] = \int_0^T \left[Au_1^2 + Bu_2^2 + CE^2 + DI^2\right]dt, \tag{20}$$

where C and D represent the penalty multipliers on the benefit of the cost, and A and B stand for weighting constants on the profit of the price of making. We take a quadratic cost functional on the control factors as an approximation to the real nonlinear functional that depends on the fact that the cost takes a nonlinear form to overcome the bang-bang or singular optimal control cases.

Here, the aim is to minimize the above functional equations. Thus, the problem can be represented as follows:

$$\min J[u(t)] = \int_0^T \left[Au_1^2 + Bu_2^2 + CE^2 + DI^2\right]dt, \tag{21}$$

subject to state System (22),

$$\begin{aligned} D^\alpha S &= p\lambda - (1-u_1)\beta SI + \theta V - (\nu+\mu)S, \\ D^\alpha V &= (1-p)\lambda + \nu S - (\theta + b + \mu)V, \\ D^\alpha E &= (1-u_1)\beta SI - (1-u_2)(\rho+\mu)E, \\ D^\alpha I &= (1-u_2)\rho E - (\phi + \eta + \mu)I, \\ D^\alpha R &= \omega I + bV - \mu R \end{aligned} \tag{22}$$

with the following initial conditions:

$$S(0) = S_0, V(0) = V_0, E(0) = E_0, I(0) = I_0, R(0) = R_0. \tag{23}$$

The objective functional is described by $D_t^\alpha = (S, V, E, I, R)$. The weight constants C and D are associated to the infected class, while A and B are related to control variables $u_1(t)$ and $u_2(t)$. Eradication of the disease by minimizing the infected population is our main focusing area. Control input (u_1^*, u_2^*) is derived from

$$\mathcal{J}(u_1^*, u_2^*) = \min\{\mathcal{J}(u_1, u_2), u_i \in \mathcal{U}, fori = 1,2\}, \tag{24}$$

where control function $\mathcal{U}$ is defined as

$$\mathcal{U} = \{(u_1, u_2)|u_i \text{ is the Lebesgue measurable on}[0,T], 0 \le u_i(t) \le 1, i = 1,2\}. \tag{25}$$

Conditions for Optimalilty

The fractional order control problem is defined as

$$D_t^\alpha x = f(x,u,t), withx(0) = x_0. \tag{26}$$

Here, state vector $x(t) = [S(t), V(t), E(t), I(t), R(t)]^T$ and control vector $u(t) = [u_1(t), u_2(t)]^T$. J is given as

$$J(u) = \int_0^t g(x,u,t)dt. \tag{27}$$

Thus, we have

$$infJ(u(.)) = J(u^*(.)), \tag{28}$$

with state system

$$D_t^\alpha = f(x,u,v), x(0) = x_0. \tag{29}$$

Here, $V(t)$ is the co-vector satisfy

$$D_{tf}^\alpha V = \frac{\partial g}{\partial x} + V^T \frac{\partial f}{\partial x}, V\left(t_f\right) = 0. \tag{30}$$

Thus, u^* is calculated with the help of

$$\frac{\partial g}{\partial x} + V^T \frac{\partial f}{\partial u^*} \quad = \quad 0. \tag{31}$$

Equations (29)–(31) represent the Euler–Lagrange optimally condition.

To determine the solution, we construct the Hamiltonian function as

$$H \quad = \quad g + V^T f \tag{32}$$

where

$$\begin{aligned} g &= (Au_1^2 + Bu_2^2 + CE^2 + DI^2), \\ V &= (v_1, v_2, v_3, v_4, v_5)^T, \\ f &= (f_1, f_2, f_3, f_4, f_5)^T. \end{aligned}$$

By the help of the Euler–Lagrange property, we can minimize (14).

The adjoint system for the control input $(u_1(t), u_2(t))$ for Model (22) is given by

$$\begin{aligned} D^{\alpha}_{tf}\xi_1 &= -[(1-u_1)\beta I(\xi_3 - \xi_1) + \xi_2\nu - \xi_1(\nu+\mu)], \\ D^{\alpha}_{tf}\xi_2 &= -[\theta(\xi_1 - \xi_2) + b(\xi_5 - \xi_2) - \xi_2\mu], \\ D^{\alpha}_{tf}\xi_3 &= -(1-u_2)[\xi_4\rho - \xi_3(\rho+\mu)], \\ D^{\alpha}_{tf}\xi_4 &= -[\beta S(1-u_1)(\xi_3 - \xi_1) - \xi_4(\phi+\eta+\mu) + \xi_5\omega], \\ D^{\alpha}_{tf}\xi_5 &= \xi_5\mu. \end{aligned} \tag{33}$$

Thus, we have

$$\begin{aligned} u_1^*(t) &= \frac{(\xi_3-\xi_1)\beta SI}{2A}, \\ u_2^*(t) &= -\frac{\xi_3(\mu E)}{2B}. \end{aligned} \tag{34}$$

The standard form of control is given below:

$$u_1^*(t) \quad = \quad \begin{cases} 0, & \frac{(\xi_3-\xi_1)\beta SI}{2A} < 0, \\ \frac{(\xi_3-\xi_1)\beta SI}{2A}, & 0 < \frac{(\xi_3-\xi_1)\beta SI}{2A} < 1, \\ 1, & \frac{(\xi_3-\xi_1)\beta SI}{2A} > 1. \end{cases} \tag{35}$$

$$u_2^*(t) \quad = \quad \begin{cases} 0, & -\frac{\xi_3(\mu E)}{2B} < 0, \\ -\frac{\xi_3(\mu E)}{2B}, & 0 < -\frac{\xi_3(\mu E)}{2B} < 1, \\ 1, & -\frac{\xi_3(\mu E)}{2B} > 1. \end{cases} \tag{36}$$

The compact form of $u_1^*(t)$ is

$$u_1^*(t) \quad = \quad max\Big(min\Big(1, \frac{(\xi_3-\xi_1)\beta SI}{2A}\Big), 0\Big). \tag{37}$$

Similarly, for $u_2^*(t)$, we have

$$u_2^*(t) \quad = \quad max\Big(min\Big(1, -\frac{\xi_3(\mu E)}{2B}\Big), 0\Big). \tag{38}$$

5. Numerical Findings

This section deals with numerical findings based on our analytical results. We follow the iterative schemes as established by Cao et al. [31] for numerically solving the proposed Model (1) and the optimal system (i.e., state System (33) together with adjoint System (22)).

In order to solve Model (1), the iterative scheme is developed:

$$
\begin{aligned}
S(n) &= [p\lambda - (1-u_1)\beta S(n-1)I(n-1) + \theta V(n-1) - (\nu+\mu)S(n-1)]h^{\eta} - \sum_{r=1}^{n} l(r)S(n-r), \\
V(n) &= [(1-p)\lambda + \nu S(n-1) - (\theta+b+\mu)V(n-1)]h^{\eta} - \sum_{r=1}^{m} l(r)V(n-r), \\
E(n) &= [(1-u_1)\beta S(n-1)I(n-1) - (1-u_2)(\rho+\mu)E(n-1)]h^{\eta} - \sum_{r=1}^{n} l(r)E(n-r), \\
I(n) &= [(1-u_2)\rho E(m-1) - (\phi+\eta+\mu)I(n-1)]h^{\eta} - \sum_{r=1}^{n} l(r)I(n-r), \\
R(n) &= [\omega I(n-1) + bV(n-1) - \mu R(n-1)]h^{\eta} - \sum_{r=1}^{n} l(r)R(n-r).
\end{aligned} \tag{39}
$$

The last term of the above set of equations is the memory term. Here, $l(0) = 1$ and $l(m) = \frac{1-\eta}{r} l_{r-1}, n \geq 0$, and all the model variables are all positive. The system behaviors are represented by different values of α in Figure 2. Here, we demonstrate an integer order system with $\alpha = 1$ and a fractional order system for $\alpha = 0.98$. The figure clearly shows that the linear order system converges to its steady state in a shorter time. Figure 3 shows the effect of β on model dynamics. Here, we consider $\beta = 0.0002, 0.00002$. This figure shows that decreasing the value of the infection rate is useful for controlling the disease.

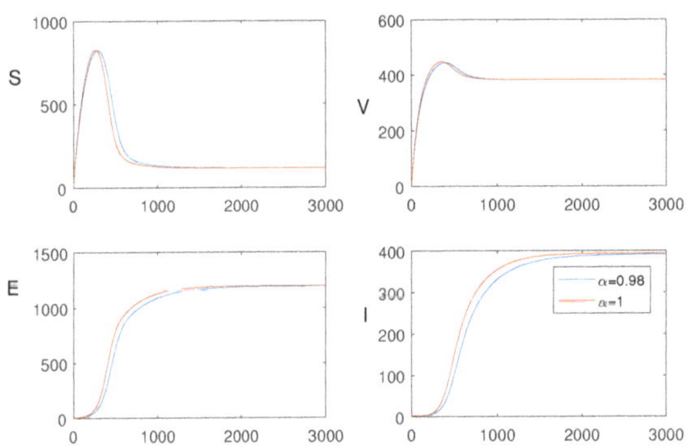

Figure 2. System trajectories (1) are plotted as functions of time for different values of parameter α (order of derivative) as in Table 1.

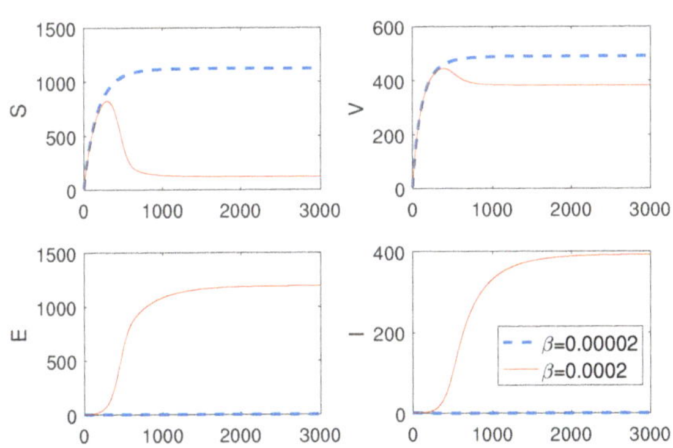

Figure 3. System trajectories (1) are shown in the figure for different values of parameter β (infection rate). The rest of the parameters are taken from Table 1.

To analyze fractional order Model (22), we follow the algorithm from the article of Cao et al. [32]. To solve optimal System (22), we consider (33). Here, we use the forward iteration method to solve (22), and for (33), we use the backward iteration method.

The numerical solution of Model (22) is represented in Figures 4 and 5 in the presence of control. Figure 4 shows the system behavior when control is incorporated, and the optimal control input is represented by Figure 5. From this simulation, we observe that control reduces the infected population and increases the susceptible population.

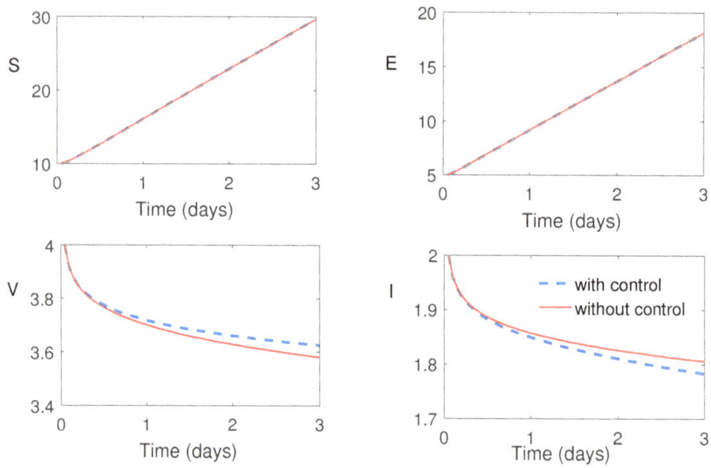

Figure 4. Numerical comparison of Models (1) and (22).

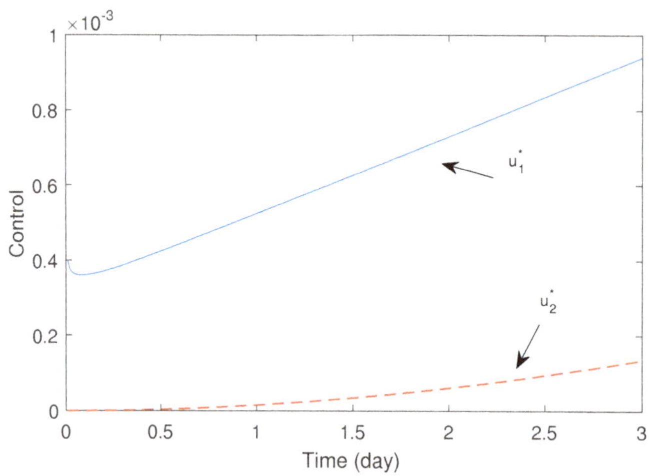

Figure 5. Double optimal control variables.

6. Discussion

This work deals with the study of measles disease infection in the presence of vaccination. We formulated an SVEIR-type compartmental model. The model is extended to the SEIR model to gat an idea of the effect of vaccination. In the model with vaccination, we studied the effectiveness of the first dose of vaccination to control the infection in a cost-effective way.

Analytical and numerical analyses confirm that the system has a disease-free state when the basic reproduction number is $R_0 < 1$, but when $R_0 > 1$, the system switches its state to an endemic state (Figures 3 and 6). An endemic equilibrium point exists for $R_0 > 1$ and is asymptotically stable. Also, optimal control therapy can improve the susceptible population and reduce the infection level (Figures 4 and 5) in a cost-effective way.

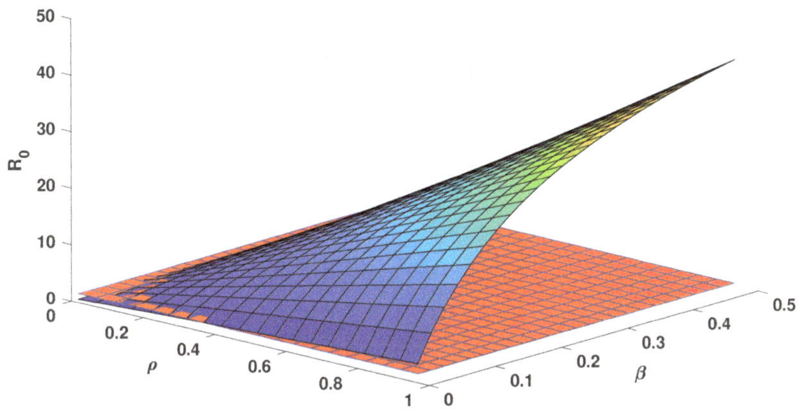

Figure 6. Phase plan of R_0 with respect to β and ρ for Model (1) showing the stable and unstable regions.

In summary, the stability analysis shows that the disease is endemic when the basic reproduction number is greater than unity. The optimal control problem is solved using an iterative method. Simulation results show that the role of fractional order parameter α is effective on model dynamics. The FOCP shows that the vaccination is administered in an optimal order.

7. Conclusions

In this article, the focus is to formulate a fractional order mathematical model for the dynamics of the measles disease.

The physical–dynamical problem consists of memory or aftereffects. Also, we know that the fractional order differential equation model plays a more significant role and has more advantages compared to the integer-order mathematical model in handling such problems. Thus, we incorporate a FODE model to study the vaccination effect on the measles infection. Here, we extend our model based on control input. Non-medical interventions (like self-isolation and contact tracing) and medical interventions (like vaccination) are considered control inputs, and we try to optimize the control effect on model dynamics.

In a nutshell, it can be concluded that the fractional order mathematical model is more realistic than the integer order model. The control measures through vaccination have a significant impact on the disease when applied in an optimal way.

The present work can be extended using impulse drug dosing [33]. This method will enable us to apply the two consecutive doses one by one with an interval.

Author Contributions: Methodology, A.N.C. and S.K.S.; Validation, F.A.B.; Formal analysis, S.K.S.; Writing—original draft, A.N.C.; writing—review and editing, F.A.B.; Visualization, A.N.C.; Supervision, F.A.B. All authors have read and agreed to the published version of the manuscript.

Funding: This research received no external funding.

Data Availability Statement: Data are contained within the article.

Conflicts of Interest: The authors declare no conflicts of interest.

References

1. Atkinson, W.L.; Kaplan, J.M.; Clover, R. Measles: Virology, epidemiology, disease, and prevention. *Am. J. Prev. Med.* **1994**, *10*, 22–30. [CrossRef] [PubMed]
2. Thar, A.M.C.; Wai, K.T.; Harries, A.D.; Show, K.L.; Mon, L.L.; Lin, H.H. Reported measles cases, measles-related deaths and measles vaccination coverage in Myanmar from 2014 to 2018. *Trop. Med. Health* **2020**, *48*, 4. [CrossRef] [PubMed]
3. Michael, B.; Oldstone, A. *Viruses, Plagues and History*; Oxford University Press: Oxford, UK, 1998.
4. Rubin, R. Despite Safe and Effective Vaccine, Measles Cases and Deaths Increased Worldwide From 2021 to 2022. *JAMA* **2024**, *331*, 188–189. [CrossRef] [PubMed]
5. Plans-Rubió, P. Vaccination coverage for routine vaccines and herd immunity levels against measles and pertussis in the world in 2019. *Vaccines* **2021**, *9*, 256. [CrossRef] [PubMed]
6. UNICEF; WHO; The World Bank Group Joint Child Malnutrition Estimates. *Levels and Trends in Child Malnutrition: Key findings of the 2019 Edition of the Joint Child Malnutrition Estimates*; World Health Organization: Geneva, Switzerland, 2020.
7. Viriyapong, R.; Ridbamroong, W. Global stability analysis and optimal control of measles model with vaccination and treatment. *J. Appl. Math. Comput.* **2020**, *62*, 207–237. [CrossRef]
8. Tilahun, G.T.; Demie, S.; Eyob, A. Stochastic model of measles transmission dynamics with double dose vaccination. *Infect. Dis. Model.* **2020**, *5*, 478–494. [CrossRef]
9. Sowole, S.O.; Ibrahim, A.; Sangare, D.; Lukman, A.O. Mathematical model for measles disease with control on the susceptible and exposed compartments. *Open J. Math. Anal.* **2020**, *4*, 60–75. [CrossRef]
10. Momoh, A.; Ibrahim, M.; Uwanta, I.; Manga, S. Mathematical model for control of measles epidemiology. *Int. J. Pure Appl. Math.* **2013**, *87*, 707–718. [CrossRef]
11. Adewale, S.; Mohammed, I.; Olopade, I. Mathematical analysis of effect of area on the dynamical spread of measles. *IOSR J. Eng.* **2014**, *2*, 43–57. [CrossRef]
12. Ochoche, J.; Gweryina, R. A mathematical model of measles with vaccination and two phases of infectiousness. *IOSR J. Math.* **2014**, *10*, 95–105.
13. Edward, S.; Raymond, K.; Gabriel, K.; Nestory, F.; Godfrey, M.; Arbogast, M. A mathematical model for control and elimination of the transmission dynamics of measles. *Appl. Comput. Math.* **2015**, *4*, 396–408. [CrossRef]
14. Smith, R.K.; Archibald, A.; MacCarthy, E.; Liu, L.; Luke, N.S. A mathematical investigation of vaccination strategies to prevent a measles epidemic. *North Carol. J. Math. Stat.* **2016**, *2*, 29–44.
15. Kitengeso, R. Stochastic modelling of the transmission dynamics of measles with vaccination control. *Int. J. Theor. Appl. Math.* **2016**, *2*, 60–73.
16. Garba, S.; Safi, M.; Usaini, S. Mathematical model for assessing the impact of vaccination and treatment on measles transmission dynamics. *Math. Methods Appl. Sci.* **2017**, *40*, 6371–6388. [CrossRef]
17. Obumneke, C.; Adamu, I.I.; Ado, S.T. Mathematical model for the dynamics of measles under the combined effect of vaccination and measles therapy. *Int. J. Sci. Technol.* **2017**, *6*, 862–874.
18. Mitku, S.N.; Koya, P.R. Mathematical modeling and simulation study for the control and transmission dynamics of measles. *Am. J. Appl. Math.* **2017**, *5*, 99–107. [CrossRef]
19. Kuddus, M.A.; Mohiuddin, M.; Rahman, A. Mathematical analysis of a measles transmission dynamics model in Bangladesh with double dose vaccination. *Sci. Rep.* **2021**, *11*, 16571. [CrossRef] [PubMed]
20. El Hajji, M.; Albargi, A.H. A mathematical investigation of an "SVEIR" epidemic model for the measles transmission. *Math. Biosci. Eng* **2022**, *19*, 2853–2875. [CrossRef] [PubMed]
21. Naik, P.A.; Zu, J.; Owolabi, K.M. Global dynamics of a fractional order model for the transmission of HIV epidemic with optimal control. *Chaos Solitons Fractals* **2020**, *138*, 109826. [CrossRef]
22. Atangana, A. On the new fractional derivative and application to nonlinear Fisher's reaction–diffusion equation. *Appl. Math. Comput.* **2016**, *273*, 948–956. [CrossRef]
23. Samui, P.; Mondal, J.; Ahmad, B.; Chatterjee, A.N. Clinical effects of 2-DG drug restraining SARS-CoV-2 infection: A fractional order optimal control study. *J. Biol. Phys.* **2022**, *48*, 415–438. [CrossRef] [PubMed]
24. Chatterjee, A.N.; Al Basir, F.; Almuqrin, M.A.; Mondal, J.; Khan, I. SARS-CoV-2 infection with lytic and non-lytic immune responses: A fractional order optimal control theoretical study. *Results Phys.* **2021**, *26*, 104260. [CrossRef] [PubMed]
25. Peter, O.; Afolabi, O.; Victor, A.; Akpan, C.; Oguntolu, F. Mathematical model for the control of measles. *J. Appl. Sci. Environ. Manag.* **2018**, *22*, 571–576. [CrossRef]
26. Anes, T. Modeling and Control of Measles Transmission in Ghana. Ph.D. Thesis, Kwame Nkrumah University of Science and Technology, Kumasi, Ghana, 2012.
27. Odibat, Z.M.; Shawagfeh, N.T. Generalized Taylor's formula. *Appl. Math. Comput.* **2007**, *186*, 286–293. [CrossRef]
28. Lin, W. Global existence theory and chaos control of fractional differential equations. *J. Math. Anal. Appl.* **2007**, *332*, 709–726. [CrossRef]
29. Van den Driessche, P.; Watmough, J. Reproduction numbers and sub-threshold endemic equilibria for compartmental models of disease transmission. *Math. Biosci.* **2002**, *180*, 29–48. [CrossRef] [PubMed]
30. Heffernan, J.M.; Smith, R.J.; Wahl, L.M. Perspectives on the basic reproductive ratio. *J. R. Soc. Interface* **2005**, *2*, 281–293. [CrossRef] [PubMed]

31. Sardar, T.; Rana, S.; Chattopadhyay, J. A mathematical model of dengue transmission with memory. *Commun. Nonlinear Sci. Numer. Simul.* **2015**, *22*, 511–525. [CrossRef]
32. Cao, X.; Datta, A.; Al Basir, F.; Roy, P.K. Fractional-order model of the disease psoriasis: A control based mathematical approach. *J. Syst. Sci. Complex.* **2016**, *29*, 1565–1584. [CrossRef]
33. Chatterjee, A.; Basir, F.; Biswas, D.; Abraha, T. Global Dynamics of SARS-CoV-2 Infection with Antibody Response and the Impact of Impulsive Drug Therapy. *Vaccines* **2022**, *10*, 1846. [CrossRef]

fractal and fractional

MDPI

Article

Fractional-Order Tabu Learning Neuron Models and Their Dynamics

Yajuan Yu [1,*], Zhenhua Gu [2], Min Shi [3] and Feng Wang [1,*]

[1] Department of Mathematics, Changzhou University, Changzhou 213164, China
[2] School of Computer Science and Artificial Intelligence, Changzhou University, Changzhou 213159, China; s22150812016@smail.cczu.edu.cn
[3] College of Automation, Nanjing University of Posts and Telecommunications, Nanjing 210023, China; 20130562@njupt.edu.cn
* Correspondence: yyjxye@cczu.edu.cn (Y.Y.); fengwang@cczu.edu.cn (F.W.)

Abstract: In this paper, by replacing the exponential memory kernel function of a tabu learning single-neuron model with the power-law memory kernel function, a novel Caputo's fractional-order tabu learning single-neuron model and a network of two interacting fractional-order tabu learning neurons are constructed firstly. Different from the integer-order tabu learning model, the order of the fractional-order derivative is used to measure the neuron's memory decay rate and then the stabilities of the models are evaluated by the eigenvalues of the Jacobian matrix at the equilibrium point of the fractional-order models. By choosing the memory decay rate (or the order of the fractional-order derivative) as the bifurcation parameter, it is proved that Hopf bifurcation occurs in the fractional-order tabu learning single-neuron model where the value of bifurcation point in the fractional-order model is smaller than the integer-order model's. By numerical simulations, it is shown that the fractional-order network with a lower memory decay rate is capable of producing tangent bifurcation as the learning rate increases from 0 to 0.4. When the learning rate is fixed and the memory decay increases, the fractional-order network enters into frequency synchronization firstly and then enters into amplitude synchronization. During the synchronization process, the oscillation frequency of the fractional-order tabu learning two-neuron network increases with an increase in the memory decay rate. This implies that the higher the memory decay rate of neurons, the higher the learning frequency will be.

Keywords: tabu learning; memory kernel function; fractional-order derivative; Hopf bifurcation; synchronization

1. Introduction

The human brain is a network connected by billions of neurons through synapses. Excited by external stimuli, the response of the brain is transmitted through the network in the form of electrical signals. It is therefore of significant importance to study neurons firing to disclose the function of the brain. To date, based on plenty of experiments and the experimental data, many classical neuron models have been constructed, such as the Hodgkin–Huxley (H-H) model [1,2], FitzHugh–Nagumo (FHN) model [3–5], Morris–Lecar (ML)model [6,7], Hindmarsh–Rose (HR) model [8,9], Chay model [10], Rulkov model [11], and Izhikevich model [12]. These models can emulate different neurons and display different neurodynamics, such as resting states, periodic oscillations, and chaos. The different neurodynamics, as mentioned earlier, play important roles in neural information encoding.

Tabu learning is the method of applying tabu search in neural networks to solve optimization problems [13]. Based on the energy distribution around the current state, tabu learning can avoid searched states and find new ones that are not searched, and then the search efficiency can be improved. In tabu learning searches, the neurons need some judgment and selection. This implies that the tabu learning neuron owns the memory. In existing models about tabu learning, the memory is described by the integration of state variable [13,14].

Tabu learning single-neuron models are two-dimensional [13] and are studied widely because of their simple mathematical structure [14–21]. Choosing the memory decay rate as the bifurcation parameter, Hopf bifurcations are shown in tabu learning neurons [14,15,17,19]. In [20], by replacing the resistive self-connection synaptic weight with a memristive self-connection synaptic weight, a memristive synaptic weight-based tabu learning neuron model is proposed. In the memristive synaptic weight-based tabu learning neuron model, there are infinitely many nonchaotic attractors composed of mono-periodic, multi-periodic, and quasi-periodic orbits. Additionally, in [18], hidden attractors are discovered in a non-autonomous tabu learning model with sinusoidal external excitation. Recently, based on the sinusoidal activation function, reference [21] proposed a two-dimensional non-autonomous tabu learning single-neuron model which can generate a class of multi-scroll chaotic attractors with parameters controlling the number of scrolls.

In the tabu learning single neuron models mentioned above, the exponential memory kernel function $e^{-\alpha t}$ is applied. Compared to the power-law memory kernel function $t^{-\alpha}$, the exponential memory kernel function limits to zero more quickly as $t \rightarrow +\infty$. Therefore, the exponential memory kernel function results in a lower memory capacity for the states. As stated in [22], memory capacity is limited if the memory states are not truly persistent over time. For improving memory capacity, it is reasonable to replace the exponential memory kernel function of the neuron by the power-law memory kernel function. In fact, the fractional-order derivative is defined in the power-law memory kernel function. And it has been proven that the fractional-order derivative owns the memory effect and is not a strictly local operator [23]. The order of the fractional-order derivative is related to the memory loss or the "proximity effect" of some characteristics [24]. Then, in the following discussion, the exponential memory kernel function of the neuron was replaced by the power-law memory kernel function, and a novel Caputo's fractional-order tabu learning single-neuron model and a network of two interacting Caputo fractional-order tabu learning neurons are proposed. In these new fractional-order models, the physical meaning of the order of the fractional-order derivatives is the memory decay rate of the neuron.

To begin with, by choosing the memory decay rate (i.e., the order of the fractional-order derivative) as a bifurcation parameter, it is proved that Hopf bifurcation occurs in the Caputo's fractional-order tabu leaning single-neuron model. Secondly, the dynamics of the network of two interacting Caputo's fractional-order tabu learning neurons is discussed. With a lower memory decay rate, the fractional-order network showed tangent bifurcation as the learning rate increased from 0 to 0.4. Then, when the learning rate was fixed, the network entered into frequency synchronization firstly and then the amplitudes of two neurons gradually became consistent as the memory decay rate increased from 0 to 1. This study shows that the memory decay rate, i.e., the order of the fractional-order derivative, has a significant impact on the dynamics of fractional-order tabu learning neuron models.

The paper is organized as follows. The Caputo's fractional-order tabu learning single-neuron model and the network of two interacting Caputo's fractional-order tabu learning neurons are proposed in Section 2. In Section 3, the stabilities of the models are evaluated by the eigenvalues of the Jacobian matrix at the equilibrium point. In Section 4, numerical simulations of the fractional-order models are shown. Finally, conclusions are drawn in Section 5.

2. Preliminaries and Fractional-Order Tabu Learning Models

2.1. Preliminaries on Fractional-Order Systems

First, the α-order ($0 < \alpha < 1$) integral is defined by [23] as

$$ {}_0I_t^{\alpha} x(t) = \frac{1}{\Gamma(\alpha)} \int_0^t \frac{x(\tau)}{(t-\tau)^{1-\alpha}} d\tau \tag{1} $$

where $\Gamma(z) = \int_0^\infty e^{-s} s^{z-1} ds$ is the Gamma function. Corresponding to the fractional-order integral, there is a fractional-order derivative which has several different definitions such as Grunwald–Letnikov's derivative, Caputo's derivative, and Riemann-Liouville's derivative. In this study, Caputo's derivative is employed. The $\alpha-$order $(0 < \alpha < 1)$ derivative is defined as

$$ {}_0^C D_t^\alpha f(t) = \frac{1}{\Gamma(1-\alpha)} \int_0^t \frac{f'(\tau)}{(t-\tau)^\alpha} d\tau \tag{2}$$

where $f'(\tau)$ is the first-order derivative of function $f(\tau)$. The integration in Equation (2) indicates that the Caputo's derivative is non-local. Consequently, a fractional-order mathematical model can contain the memory of system variables.

For the stability analysis of a fractional-order mathematical model, the following lemma is needed [25].

Lemma 1. *The fractional-order system*

$$ {}_0^C D_t^\alpha X = f(X) \tag{3}$$

is asymptotically stable at the equilibrium point $E_0 = (x_1^0, x_2^0, \cdots, x_n^0)$ if all the eigenvalues λ of the Jacobian matrix M_{E_0} satisfy the condition:

$$ |\arg(\lambda)| > (\alpha\pi)/2 \tag{4}$$

where $\arg(\lambda)$ is the argument of λ, $X = (x_1, x_2, \cdots, x_n)^T$, $f(X) = (f_1(X), f_2(X), \cdots, f_n(X))^T$ and $f_i(X) = f_i(x_1, x_2, \cdots, x_n)$, $i = 1, 2, \cdots, n$.

2.2. A Fractional-Order Tabu Learning Single-Neuron Model

A classical tabu learning single-neuron model is described by [15] as

$$\begin{cases} \dot{u} = -x + af(u) + J, \\ \dot{J} = -\alpha J - \beta f(u). \end{cases} \tag{5}$$

where u is the action potential of the neuron, J is the tabu learning variable, $f(u)$ is the activation function, and a is the self-connection strength of the neuron. In model (5), the tabu learning variable J is computed by

$$ J(t) = -\beta \int_0^t e^{\alpha(\tau-t)} f(u(\tau)) d\tau \tag{6}$$

where $\alpha > 0$ is the memory decay rate and $\beta > 0$ is the learning rate. As $t \to +\infty$, the exponential memory kernel function e^{-t} limits to zero more quickly than the power-law memory kernel function $t^{-\alpha}$. That is to say, with the exponential memory kernel function e^{-t}, the memory capacity of the neuron is not truly persistent over time and so neurons will begin to relearn states that have been learned but forgotten. To make the memory time long enough, the exponential kernel function e^{-t} in Equation (6) is replaced by the power-law kernel function $t^{-\alpha}$. By doing so, the tabu learning variable J is computed by

$$ J(t) = -\beta \int_0^t (\tau - t)^\alpha f(u(\tau)) d\tau = -\beta \int_0^t (t-\tau)^{-\alpha} f(u(\tau)) d\tau \tag{7}$$

Equation (7) can be rewritten as

$$ J(t) = -\beta \int_0^t \frac{f(u(\tau))}{(t-\tau)^{1-(1-\alpha)}} d\tau = -\beta\Gamma(1-\alpha) \frac{1}{\Gamma(1-\alpha)} \int_0^t \frac{f(u(\tau))}{(t-\tau)^{1-(1-\alpha)}} d\tau \tag{8}$$

Referring to Equation (1), the tabu learning variable J can be described as

$$J(t) = -\beta\Gamma(1-\alpha)_0 I_t^{(1-\alpha)} f(u(t)) \tag{9}$$

Based on the following relationship,

$${}_0^C D_t^\alpha ({}_0 I_t^\alpha x(t)) = x(t) \tag{10}$$

we can obtain

$${}_0^C D_t^{1-\alpha} J(t) = -\beta\Gamma(1-\alpha) f(u(t)) \tag{11}$$

Then, a novel fractional-order tabu learning single neuron model is proposed as follows:

$$\begin{cases} {}_0^C D_t^{1-\alpha} u = -u + af(u) + J, \\ {}_0^C D_t^{1-\alpha} J = -\beta\Gamma(1-\alpha) f(u). \end{cases} \tag{12}$$

where $\alpha (0 < \alpha < 1)$ is the memory decay rate and $\beta > 0$ is the learning rate.

2.3. A Fractional-Order Coupled Tabu Learning Two-Neuron Model

In this section, a network of two interacting fractional-order tabu learning neurons with the lower memory decay rate α is constructed as follows:

$$\begin{cases} {}_0^C D_t^{1-\alpha} u_1 = -0.1u_1 + T_{11} f(u_1) + T_{12} f(u_2) + J_1, \\ {}_0^C D_t^{1-\alpha} u_2 = -0.1u_2 + T_{21} f(u_1) + T_{22} f(u_2) + J_2, \\ {}_0^C D_t^{1-\alpha} J_1 = -\beta\Gamma(1-\alpha) f(u_1), \\ {}_0^C D_t^{1-\alpha} J_2 = -\beta\Gamma(1-\alpha) f(u_2). \end{cases} \tag{13}$$

where the learning rate $\beta > 0$ is changed in the interval $(0, 1]$, the activation function $f(u_i) = \tanh(5u_i), i = 1, 2$, and the weight matrix Q between two neurons is

$$Q = \begin{pmatrix} T_{11} & T_{12} \\ T_{21} & T_{22} \end{pmatrix} = \begin{pmatrix} 0.1 & 0.5 \\ -1 & 2 \end{pmatrix} \tag{14}$$

The classical integer-order model corresponding to model (13) is displayed in [15].

3. Dynamics of the Fractional-Order Models

3.1. Stability Analysis of Model (12)

If $f(u) = 0$ has the root of $u = u_0$, model (12) has an equilibrium point $E = (u_0, u_0)$. The Jacobian matrix M at E is

$$M = \begin{bmatrix} af'(u_0) - 1 & 1 \\ -\beta\Gamma(1-\alpha) f'(u_0) & 0 \end{bmatrix} \tag{15}$$

The characteristic equation of matrix M is

$$\lambda^2 - m_1\lambda + m_2 = 0$$

where $m_1 = af'(u_0) - 1, m_2 = \beta\Gamma(1-\alpha) f'(u_0)$. The eigenvalues of matrix M are

$$\lambda_1 = \frac{1}{2}(m_1 + \sqrt{m_1^2 - 4m_2}), \quad \lambda_2 = \frac{1}{2}(m_1 - \sqrt{m_1^2 - 4m_2})$$

The eigenvalues $\lambda_i (i = 1, 2)$ changed with the parameters m_1, m_2 are displayed in Table 1, where $\Re(\lambda)$ is the real part of the eigenvalue λ.

Table 1. The eigenvalue λ.

Parameters	$m_1 < 0$	$m_1 = 0$	$m_1 > 0$
$m_2 < 0$	$\lambda_1 < 0, \lambda_2 > 0$	$\lambda_1 > 0, \lambda_2 < 0$	$\lambda_1 > 0, \lambda_2 < 0$
$m_2 = 0$	$\lambda_1 = 0, \lambda_2 = m_1 < 0$	$\lambda_1 = \lambda_2 = 0$	$\lambda_1 = m_1 > 0, \lambda_2 = 0$
$m_2 > 0, m_1^2 - 4m_2 \geq 0$	$\lambda_1 < 0, \lambda_2 < 0$	/	$\lambda_1 > 0, \lambda_2 > 0$
$m_2 > 0, m_1^2 - 4m_2 \leq 0$	$\Re(\lambda_1) = \Re(\lambda_2) = (1/2)m_1$	$\Re(\lambda_1) = \Re(\lambda_2) = 0$	$\Re(\lambda_1) = \Re(\lambda_2) = (1/2)m_1$

Remark 1. *(1) If $\Im(\lambda) = 0$ ($\Im(\lambda)$ is the imaginary part of λ), λ is a real number. As $\lambda < 0$, one has $|\arg(\lambda)| = \pi > \pi/2 > (\alpha\pi)/2$ $(0 < \alpha < 1)$; as $\lambda > 0$, one has $|\arg(\lambda)| = 0 < (\alpha\pi)/2$ $(0 < \alpha < 1)$.*
(2) If $\Im(\lambda) \neq 0$, it is easy to know $\tan(\arg(\lambda)) = \Im(\lambda)/\Re(\lambda)$. Then as $\Re(\lambda) < 0$, one has $|\arg(\lambda)| > \pi/2 > (\alpha\pi)/2$ $(0 < \alpha < 1)$; as $\Re(\lambda) > 0$, one has $|\arg(\lambda)| < \pi/2$.

By the location of eigenvalue λ on the complex plain, the stability of model (12) can be evaluated as following:
Case 1. As $m_2 < 0$, shown in Table 1, two eigenvalues are real numbers and one of them is in the positive real axis of the complex plane, i.e., there is $|\arg(\lambda)| = 0 < (\alpha\pi)/2$ $(0 < \alpha < 1)$. So as $m_2 < 0$, model (12) at the equilibrium point E is unstable for any m_1.
Case 2. As $m_2 = \beta\Gamma(1-\alpha)f'(u_0) = 0$, due to $\alpha > 0$ and $\beta > 0$, one has $f'(u_0) = 0$. Thus, $m_1 = af'(u_0) - 1 = -1 < 0$, $\lambda_1 = 0$ and $\lambda_2 = -1 < 0$. So, as $m_2 = 0$, model (12) at the equilibrium point E is stable.
Case 3. As $m_2 > 0$ and $m_1 < 0$, two eigenvalues are negative real numbers. And $|\arg(\lambda)| = \pi > (\alpha\pi)/2$ $(0 < \alpha < 1)$. In this case, model (12) at the equilibrium point E is stable.
Case 4. As $m_2 > 0, m_1 > 0$ and $m_1^2 - 4m_2 \geq 0$, two eigenvalues are positive real numbers. Then, $|\arg(\lambda)| = 0 < (\alpha\pi)/2$ $(0 < \alpha < 1)$. Model (12) at the equilibrium point E is unstable.
Case 5. As $m_2 > 0, m_1 > 0$ and $m_1^2 - 4m_2 < 0$, both eigenvalues have positive real parts. The argument of the eigenvalue is $\arg(\lambda) = \arctan(\Im(\lambda)/\Re(\lambda))$. Referring to Lemma 1, model (12) at the equilibrium point E is stable if $|\arg(\lambda)| > (\alpha\pi)/2$ and is unstable if $|\arg(\lambda)| < (\alpha\pi)/2$.
Therefore, the following conclusions can be drawn:

Theorem 1. *The stability of model (12) at the equilibrium E depends on the parameters m_1 and m_2. It is stated as:*
(1) If $m_2 < 0$ or $m_2 > 0, m_1 > 0, m_1^2 - 4m_2 \geq 0$, model (12) is unstable;
(2) If $m_2 > 0, m_1 \leq 0$ or $m_2 = 0$, model (12) is stable;
(3) As $m_2 > 0, m_1 > 0, m_1^2 - 4m_2 < 0$, model (12) is stable if $\sqrt{4m_2 - m_1^2}/m_1 > \tan((1-\alpha)\pi/2)$ and is unstable if $\sqrt{4m_2 - m_1^2}/m_1 < \tan((1-\alpha)\pi/2)$. In this case, when increasing order α from 0 to 1, model (12) experiences Hopf bifurcation at $\alpha_0 = 1 - (2/\pi)\arctan(\sqrt{4m_2 - m_1^2}/m_1)$.

3.2. Stabilty Analysis of Model (13) with the Decay Rate $\alpha = 0.01$

The Jacobian matrix corresponding to model (13) at the equilibrium point $(0,0,0,0)$ is

$$M^* = \begin{pmatrix} 5T_{11} - 0.1 & 5T_{12} & 1 & 0 \\ 5T_{21} & 5T_{22} - 0.1 & 0 & 1 \\ -5\beta\Gamma(0.99) & 0 & 0 & 0 \\ 0 & -5\beta\Gamma(0.99) & 0 & 0 \end{pmatrix} \quad (16)$$

Thus, the eigenpolynomial for discriminating the stability of equilibrium point $(0,0,0,0)$ can be yielded as

$$det(\lambda I - M^*) = (\lambda^2 - m_1\lambda + m_0)(\lambda^2 - m_2\lambda + m_0) - 25T_{12}T_{21}\lambda^2 = 0 \tag{17}$$

where $m_0 = 5\beta\Gamma(0.99), m_1 = 5T_{11} - 0.1 = 0.4, m_2 = 5T_{22} - 0.1 = 9.9, T_{12}T_{21} = -0.5$. Due to $\beta > 0$, $\lambda = 0$ is not the root of Equation (17). Then, Equation (17) can be changed into

$$(\lambda + \frac{m_0}{\lambda})^2 - (m_1 + m_2)(\lambda + \frac{m_0}{\lambda}) + m_1 m_2 + 12.5 = 0 \tag{18}$$

Thus,

$$\lambda + \frac{m_0}{\lambda} = \frac{(m_1 + m_2) \pm \sqrt{(m_1 - m_2)^2 - 50}}{2} \tag{19}$$

When substituting $m_1 = 0.4, m_2 = 9.9$ into Equation (19), we obtain

$$\lambda + \frac{m_0}{\lambda} = 5.15 - \frac{\sqrt{161}}{4} = k_1, \lambda + \frac{m_0}{\lambda} = 5.15 + \frac{\sqrt{161}}{4} = k_2$$

where $k_1 \approx 1.9779, k_2 \approx 8.3221$. Furthermore, we can obtain

$$\lambda^2 - k_1\lambda + m_0 = 0, \lambda^2 - k_2\lambda + m_0 = 0$$

Then, the roots of Equation (17) are

$$\lambda_{1,2} = (k_1 \pm \sqrt{k_1^2 - 4m_0})/2,\ \lambda_{3,4} = (k_2 \pm \sqrt{k_2^2 - 4m_0})/2 \tag{20}$$

If $k_1^2 - 4m_0 \geq 0$ and $k_2^2 - 4m_0 \geq 0$, the eigenvalues $\lambda_i \geq 0 (i = 1,2,3,4)$.
If $k_1^2 - 4m_0 < 0, k_2^2 - 4m_0 < 0$ and $0 < \beta \leq 1$, there are

$$\frac{\sqrt{4m_0 - k_i^2}}{k_i} < \tan(\frac{0.99\pi}{2}), i = 1,2 \tag{21}$$

This implies that the eigenvalues lie in an unstable zone.
Due to $k_1 < k_2$, with $k_1^2 - 4m_0 < 0, k_2^2 - 4m_0 > 0$ and $0 < \beta \leq 1$, we obtain

$$|\arg(\lambda_{1,2})| = \frac{\sqrt{4m_0 - k_1^2}}{k_1} < \tan(\frac{0.99\pi}{2}),\ \lambda_3 > 0, \lambda_4 > 0 \tag{22}$$

In summary, the equilibrium point $(0,0,0,0)$ of model (13) is unstable for any β $(0 < \beta \leq 1)$.

4. Numerical Simulations of the Fraction-Order Models

4.1. Numerical Simulations of Model (12)

In this section, the numerical simulations of model (12) are shown with $a = 1.6, \beta = 0.5$, $f(u) = \tanh(u)$. In this case, the equilibrium $E = (0,0), m_1 = 0.6$, and $m_2 = 0.5\Gamma(1-\alpha) > 0$. As $0 < \alpha < 1$, one has $\Gamma(1-\alpha) > 1$ and $m_1^2 - 4m_2 = 0.36 - 2\Gamma(1-\alpha) < 0$. Referring to Theorem 1, the bifurcation point α_0 can be calculated by

$$\alpha_0 = 1 - \frac{2}{\pi}\arctan\frac{\sqrt{2\Gamma(1-\alpha_0) - 0.36}}{0.6} \tag{23}$$

By using Matlab, Equation (23) has the root $\alpha_0 \approx 0.2504$. Figure 1 is the time history of the action potential u. As $\alpha = 0.24$, the action potential u is periodic spiking; while $\alpha = 0.26$, the action potential u convergences to the quiescent state. These numerical results are consistent with the third conclusion shown in Theorem 1.

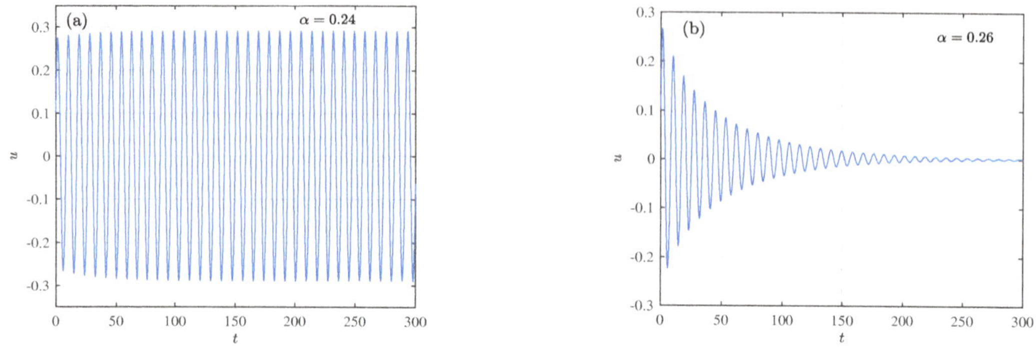

Figure 1. The time history of u. (**a**) $\alpha = 0.24$; (**b**) $\alpha = 0.26$.

Remark 2. *It is shown in [15] that model (5) shows Hopf Bifurcation when the memory decay rate* $\alpha = 0.6$ *, while in the fractional-order model (12), Hopf Bifurcation occurs when the memory decay rate* $\alpha = 0.2504$*. This implies that the memory kernel function has heavy effects on the dynamics of the tabu learning single-neuron model.*

4.2. Dynamics of Model (13) with $\alpha = 0.01$ Induced by the Learning Rate β

As shown in Section 3.2, model (13) is unstable for all $\beta > 0$. In this case, periodic spiking and chaotic spiking occur in model (13). Figure 2 is the bifurcation diagram of the local maxima of the variable u_1. It is found that model (13) changes between the periodic spiking and the chaotic spiking as β increases from 0 to 0.4. While $\beta > 0.4$, model (13) goes into chaotic spiking. Figure 3 is the time history of state u_1 for different β values. There is periodic spiking when $\beta = 0.05$, $\beta = 0.305$, and $\beta = 0.35$, and then there is chaotic spiking when $\beta = 0.301$, $\beta = 0.31$, $\beta = 0.32$, $\beta = 0.4$, and $\beta = 0.5$. This implies that model (13) shows that tangent bifurcation increased β from 0 to 0.4 and shows only chaotic spiking when $\beta > 0.4$.

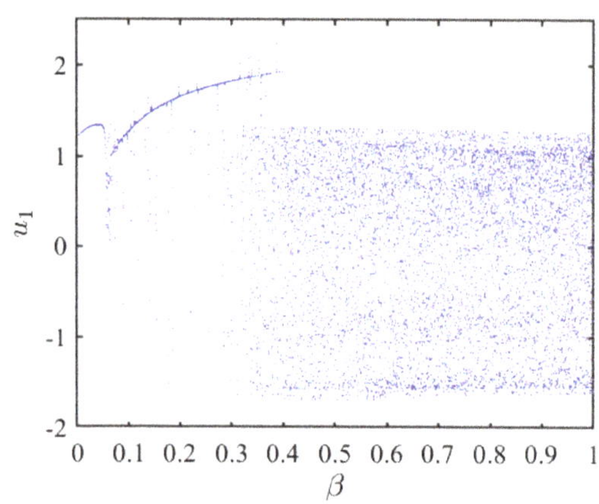

Figure 2. Bifurcation diagram of the local maxima of the variable u_1 of model (13) regarding β.

4.3. Dynamic Transitions of Model (13) Induced by the Memory Decay Rate α

In Section 4.1, model (12) with different memory decay rates α shows different dynamics. Taking this into account, we chose a different memory decay rate α for model (13) with $\beta = 0.5$.

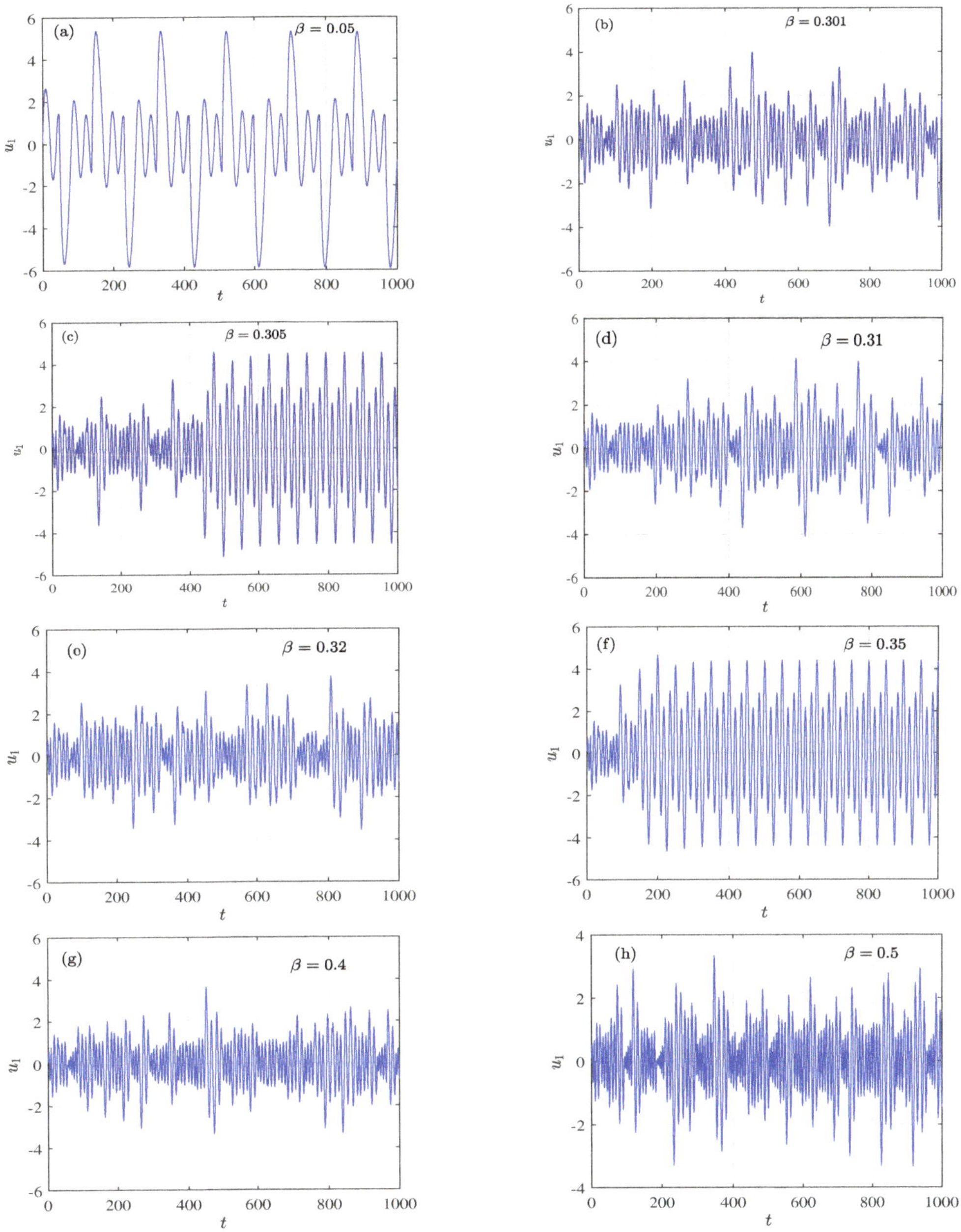

Figure 3. The time history of u_1. (**a**) $\beta = 0.05$; (**b**) $\beta = 0.301$; (**c**) $\beta = 0.305$; (**d**) $\beta = 0.31$; (**e**) $\beta = 0.32$; (**f**) $\beta = 0.35$; (**g**) $\beta = 0.4$; (**h**) $\beta = 0.5$.

When $\alpha = 0.01$ and $\alpha = 0.1$, model (13) is chaotic (Figure 4a$_1$,b$_1$). When $\alpha = 0.5$ or $\alpha = 0.9$, model (13) goes into periodic spiking (Figure 4c$_1$,d$_1$), and it is found that the frequency of the oscillation increases as the order α increases. This implies that the learning frequency of tabu learning neurons is very high when the memory decay rate is high. In theory, this is quite consistent with the actual phenomenon. In addition, when the memory decay rate α increased from 0.01 to 0.9, Figure 4a$_2$,b$_2$,c$_2$,d$_2$ show that model (13) enters frequency synchronization firstly and then the amplitudes of two neurons gradually become consistent. This implies that the memory decay rate α has a significant impact on the synchronization of the neurons connected by model (13).

Remark 3. *When $\beta = 0.5$, the classical integer-order model with the memory decay rate $\alpha = 0.1$ corresponding to model (13) produces periodic spiking [15], while the fractional-order model (13) with $\alpha = 0.1$ shows chaotic spiking (Figure 4b$_2$). The conclusion is drawn that the fractional-order model (13) has stronger nonlinearity than the corresponding classical integer-order model.*

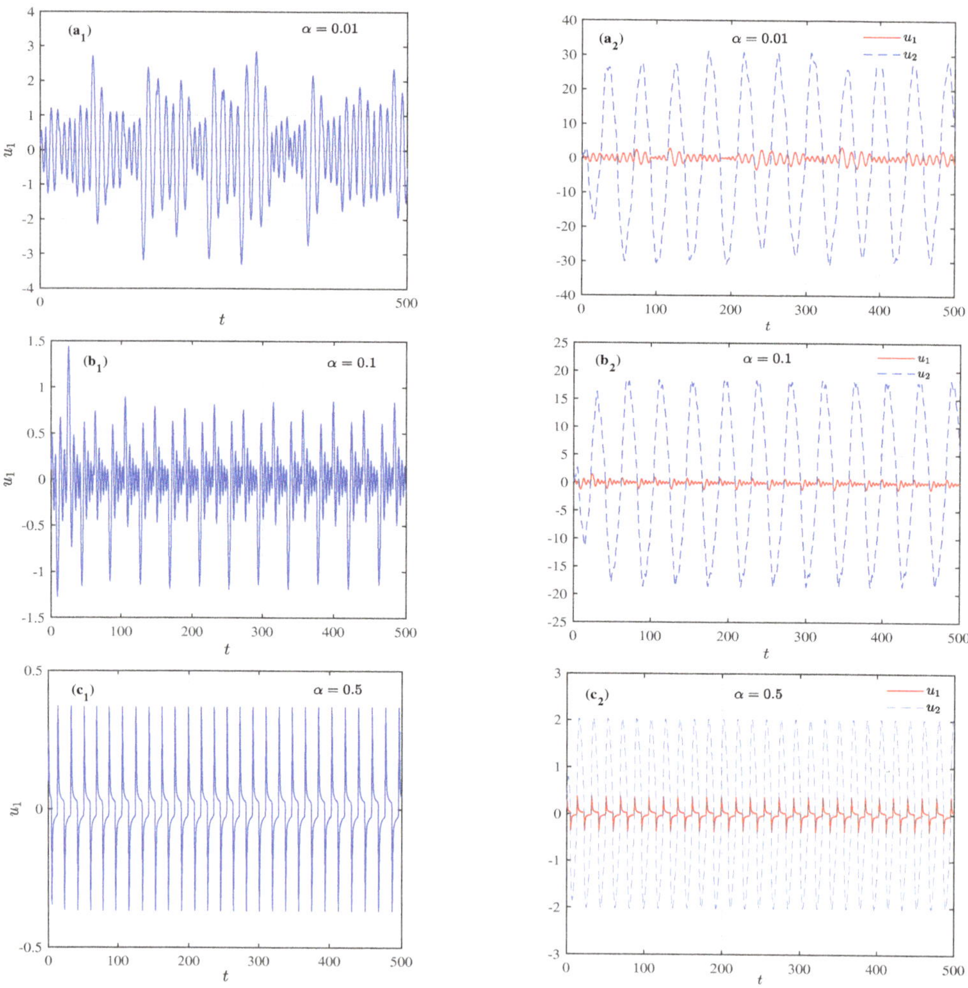

Figure 4. *Cont.*

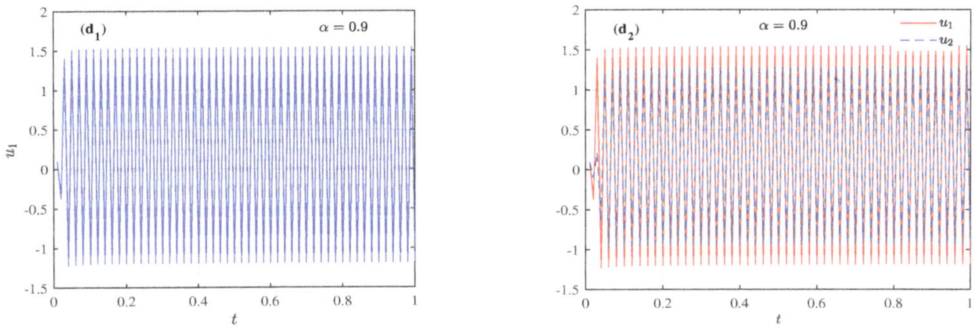

Figure 4. The time histories of model (13): ($\mathbf{a_1}$–$\mathbf{c_1}$,$\mathbf{d_1}$) are the time histories of u_1; ($\mathbf{a_2}$–$\mathbf{d_2}$) are the time histories of u_1 and u_2.

5. Conclusions

In this paper, a novel fractional-order tabu learning single-neuron mathematical model is proposed by introducing the exponential memory kernel function to the tabu learning variable. In the new model, the memory decay rate is measured by the order of the fractional-order derivative. Similar to the integer-order tabu learning neuron, the fractional-order tabu learning neuron model showed Hopf bifurcation as the memory decay rate increased from 0 to 1. It is interesting that the memory decay rate at which the fractional-order model showed Hopf bifurcation is numerically smaller than that of the integer-order tabu learning model. This indicates that the memory capacity has a significant impact on the neuron behavior. Based on this new fractional-order tabu learning model, the network of two interacting fractional-order tabu learning neurons is displayed. It is found that the network with a lower memory decay rate of 0.01 is unstable and shows tangent bifurcation as the learning rate increases from 0 to 1. However, when fixing the learning rate at 0.5 and increasing the memory decay from 0 to 1, the network enters into frequency synchronization firstly and then the amplitudes of two neurons gradually become consistent. At the same time, the numerical simulation shows that the bigger the memory decay rate is, the higher the learning frequency of the fractional-order tabu learning neuron network is, which coincides with the rule of fast forgetting and fast learning. This indicates that the memory decay rate takes an important role in the synchronization of a network connected by two fractional-order tabu learning neurons.

Of course, all results stated above are based only on mathematical models and theoretical analysis. In future research, it is needed to confirm that the actual firing of neurons matches our model.

Author Contributions: Conceptualization, Y.Y. and F.W.; methodology, Y.Y.; software, M.S.; validation, Z.G.; formal analysis, Y.Y.; investigation, Y.Y.; writing—original draft preparation, Y.Y.; supervision, F.W. All authors have read and agreed to the published version of the manuscript.

Funding: This research was supported by the grants from the National Natural Science Foundation of China under 11602035, 12172066, the Natural Science Foundation of Jiangsu Province, China under BK20201447, and the Science and Technology Innovation Talent Support Project of Jiangsu Advanced Catalysis and Green Manufacturing Collaborative Innovation Center under ACGM2022-10-02.

Data Availability Statement: All data were contained in the main text.

Conflicts of Interest: The authors declare no conflicts of interest.

References

1. Hodgkin, A.; Huxley, A. A quantitative description of membrane current and its application to conduction and excitation in nerve. *J. Physiol.* **1952**, *117*, 500–544. [CrossRef] [PubMed]
2. Xu, Q.; Wang, Y.; Chen, B.; Li, Z.; Wang, N. Firing pattern in a memristive Hodgkin-Huxley circuit: Numerical simulation and analog circuit validation. *Chaos Solitons Fractals* **2023**, *172*, 113627. [CrossRef]

3. Nagumo, J.; Arimoto, S.; Yoshizawa, S. An Active Pulse Transmission Line Simulating Nerve Axon. *Proc. IRE* **1962**, *50*, 2061–2070. [CrossRef]
4. Njitacke, Z.T.; Ramadoss, J.; Takembo, C.N.; Rajagopal, K.; Awrejcewicz, J. An enhanced FitzHugh–Nagumo neuron circuit microcontroller-based hardware implementation: Light illumination and magnetic field effects on information patterns. *Chaos Solitons Fractals* **2023**, *167*, 113014. [CrossRef]
5. Yao, Z.; Sun, K.; He, S. Firing patterns in a fractional-order FithzHugh-Nagumo neuron model. *Nonlinear Dyn.* **2022**, *110*, 1807–1822. [CrossRef]
6. Morris, C.; Lecar, H. Voltage oscillations in the barnacle giant muscle fiber. *Biophys. J.* **1981**, *35*, 193–213. [CrossRef]
7. Fan, W.; Chen, X.; Wu, H.; Li, Z.; Xu, Q. Firing patterns and synchronization of Morris-Lecar neuron model with memristive autapse. *Int. J. Electron. Commun. (AEÜ)* **2023**, *158*, 154454. [CrossRef]
8. Hindmarsh, J.; Rose, M. A model of neuronal bursting using three coupled first order differential equations. *Proc. R. Soc. B* **1984**, *221*, 87–102.
9. Xie, Y.; Yao, Z.; Ren, G.; Ma, J. Estimate physical reliability in Hindmarsh-Rose neuron. *Phys. Lett. A* **2023**, *464*, 128693. [CrossRef]
10. Chay, T.R. Chaos in a three-variable model of an excitable cell. *Physica D* **1985**, *16*, 233–242. [CrossRef]
11. Bao, H.; Li, K.; Ma, J.; Hua, Z.; Xu, Q.; Bao, B. Memristive effects on an improved discrete Rulkov neuron model. *Sci. China Technol. Sci.* **2023**, *66*, 3153–3163. [CrossRef]
12. Izhikevich, E.M. Simple model of spiking neurons. *IEEE Trans. Neural Netw.* **2015**, *14*, 1569–1572. [CrossRef]
13. Beyer, D.A.; Ogier, R.G. Tabu learning: A neural network search method for solving nonconvex optimization problems. In Proceedings of the IEEE International Joint Conference on Neural Networks, Singapore, 18–21 November 1991; pp. 953–961.
14. Bao, B.; Hou, L.; Zhu, Y.; Wu, H.; Chen, M. Bifurcation analysis and circuit implementation for a tabu learning neuron model. *Int J. Electron. Commun. (AEÜ)* **2020**, *121*, 153235. [CrossRef]
15. Li, C.G.; Chen, G.R.; Liao, X.F.; Yu, J. Hopf bifurcation and Chaos in tabu learning neuron models. *Int. J. Bifurc. Chaos* **2005**, *15*, 2633–2642. [CrossRef]
16. Xiao, M.; Cao, J. Bifurcation analysis on a discrete-time tabu learning model. *J. Comput. Appl. Math.* **2008**, *220*, 725–738. [CrossRef]
17. Li, Y.G. Hopf bifurcation analysis in a tabu learning neuron model with two delays. *ISRN Appl. Math.* **2011**, *2011*, 636732. [CrossRef]
18. Bao, B.; Luo, J.; Bao, H.; Chen, C.; Wu, H.; Xu, Q. A simple non-autonomous hidden chaotic system with a switchable stable node-focus. *Int. J. Bifurc. Chaos* **2019**, *29*, 1950168. [CrossRef]
19. Li, Y.; Zhou, X.; Wu, Y.; Zhou, M. Hopf bifurcation analysis of a tabu learning two-neuron model. *Chaos Soliton Fract.* **2006**, *29*, 190–197. [CrossRef]
20. Hou, L.P.; Bao, H.; Xu, Q.; Chen, M.; Bao, B.C. Coexisting infinitely many nonchaotic attractors in a memristive weight-based tabu learning neuron. *Int. J. Bifurc. Chaos* **2021**, *12*, 2150189. [CrossRef]
21. Bao, H.; Ding, R.Y.; Chen, B.; Xu, Q.; Bao, B.C. Two-dimensional non-autonomous neuron model with parameter-controlled multi-scroll chaotic attractors. *Chaos Soliton Fract.* **2023**, *169*, 113228. [CrossRef]
22. Chaudhuri, R.; Fiete, I. Computational principles of memory. *Nat. Neurosci.* **2016**, *19*, 394–403. [CrossRef] [PubMed]
23. Podlubny, I. *Fractional Differential Equations*; Academic Press: Cambridge, MA, USA, 1999.
24. Petras, I. Fractional-order memristor-based Chua's circuit. *IEEE T. Circuits-II* **2010**, *57*, 975–979. [CrossRef]
25. Matignon, D. Stability results for fractional differential equations with applications to control processing. In Proceedings of the IMACS, IEEE-SMC, Lille, France, 9–12 July 1996; pp. 963–968.

fractal and fractional

Article

Performance Analysis of Fully Intuitionistic Fuzzy Multi-Objective Multi-Item Solid Fractional Transportation Model

Sultan Almotairi [1,2,*], Elsayed Badr [3,4], M. A. Elsisy [5], F. A. Farahat [6] and M. A. El Sayed [5,7,*]

1 Department of Computer Science, Faculty of College of Computer and Information Sciences, Majmaah University, Majmaah 11952, Saudi Arabia
2 Department of Computer Science, Faculty of Computer and Information Systems, Islamic University of Madinah, Medinah 42351, Saudi Arabia
3 Scientific Computing Department, Faculty of Computers and Artificial Intelligence, Benha University, Benha 13511, Egypt; alsayed.badr@fci.bu.edu.eg
4 The Egyptian School of Data Science (ESDS), Benha, Egypt
5 Department of Basic Engineering Sciences, Faculty of Engineering, Benha University, ElQalyoubia 13511, Egypt; mohamed.alseisy@bhit.bu.edu.eg
6 Higher Technological Institute, Tenth of Ramadan City, Cairo 10116, Egypt; farhat_math@hti.edu.eg
7 Basic Sciences Department, Faculty of Engineering, BADR University in Cairo BUC, Cairo 11829, Egypt
* Correspondence: almotairi@mu.edu.sa (S.A.); mohamedali20008@yahoo.com or mohamed.ali@bhit.bu.edu.eg (M.A.E.S.)

Abstract: An investigation is conducted in this paper into a performance analysis of fully intuitionistic fuzzy multi-objective multi-item solid fractional transport model (FIF-MMSFTM). It is to be anticipated that the parameters of the conveyance model will be imprecise by virtue of numerous uncontrollable factors. The model under consideration incorporates intuitionistic fuzzy (IF) quantities of shipments, costs and profit coefficients, supplies, demands, and transport. The FIF-MMSFTM that has been devised is transformed into a linear form through a series of operations. The accuracy function and ordering relations of IF sets are then used to reduce the linearized model to a concise multi-objective multi-item solid transportation model (MMSTM). Furthermore, an examination is conducted on several theorems that illustrate the correlation between the FIF-MMSFTM and its corresponding crisp model, which is founded upon linear, hyperbolic, and parabolic membership functions. A numerical example was furnished to showcase the efficacy and feasibility of the suggested methodology. The numerical data acquired indicates that the linear, hyperbolic, and parabolic models require fewer computational resources to achieve the optimal solution. The parabolic model has the greatest number of iterations, in contrast to the hyperbolic model which has the fewest. Additionally, the elapsed run time for the three models is a negligible amount of time: 0.2, 0.15, and 1.37 s, respectively. In conclusion, suggestions for future research are provided.

Keywords: intuitionistic fuzzy set; multi-objective optimization; accuracy function fractional transportation problem

1. Introduction

Transportation issues (TP) have been the subject of considerable scholarly attention [1–7] due to their critical significance in supply chain management and logistics (e.g., cost reduction and service quality improvement) [4]. Hitchcock first introduced the classic Transportation Problems (TPs) [8], which Shell subsequently expanded to Solid Transportation Problems (STPs) [9], which integrated a novel set of conveyances. This development resulted in three-dimensional TPs that more closely resemble real-world applications. Subsequently, scholars investigated STPs through various lenses. Haley [10] proposed a solution procedure for STPs using a modified distribution method. Patel and Tripathy [11] examined a computationally preferable approach for STPs with mixed constraints. Baidya et al. [12] introduced the concept of a safety factor in TPs and scrutinized an STP that utilized fuzzy numbers to represent imprecise parameters. Chen et al. [13] addressed STPs in fuzzy and interval environments. In addition, Chen et al. [14] provided STPs with an entropy function implemented in an ambiguous circumstance.

A multi-objective transportation problem (MOTP), which evaluates distinct objectives at various dimensions and is inherently contradictory, frequently reflects the practical situation. The task of simultaneously optimizing all objectives while adhering to specified constraints presents a formidable obstacle. Numerous disciplines, including engineering, economics, and logistics, use MOTP to balance competing objectives through trade-offs in order to achieve optimal outcomes. Bit et al. [3] were the first to apply fuzzy linear programming to multi-objective STP solutions. Also, Kundu et al. [15] looked into multi-objective STP in uncertain settings and the vagueness of parameters related to problems like this that can happen when there is not enough information or when the financial markets are unstable. This entailed representing unit transportation costs as random, fuzzy, and hybrid variables, respectively.

Practically speaking, it is common for businesses to manufacture multiple products in an effort to maximize profits. Afterwards, businesses distribute these products to various destinations using diverse modes of conveyance. Multiple elements are therefore typically required to solve STPs. The STP with multiple items has been the subject of extensive research, including that of Liu et al. [16], who examined a single-objective, multi-item fixed-charge STP having ambiguous inputs.

At this time, decision-makers (DMs) are primarily concerned with the accurate determination of parameter values [4]. Given the intrinsic ambiguity, it is imperative to establish clear parameters for the model, such as the objective function coefficients and constraints [17,18]. As a result, it is logical to solicit a variety of descriptive perspectives from authorities and thought leaders regarding these parameters, which may be considered imprecise data [18,19]. Uncertainty can be caused by a variety of uncontrollable factors. For example, DMs' initial omission of transportation costs could result in unpredictability regarding cost estimation [19]. As a result of fierce competition, market conditions in the contemporary business landscape are inherently volatile, generating erratic demand for recently introduced products. Furthermore, there may be uncertainties concerning the accessibility of resources at the origin as a result of a multitude of factors. It is possible that the necessary quantity of resources will not be available for transportation [19,20]. Moreover, when a requester requires additional resources, the supplier's resource allocation becomes uncertain. Requesters' rapid modification of demands via email or mobile communication contributes to the inherent uncertainty [19].

Substantial advancements in the domain of network design have led to a multitude of approaches in managing uncertainty. Researchers have classified various approaches into three categories: intuitionistic, imprecise, and uncertain. The works cited in the text are as follows: Ghosh et al. [21], Rizk-Allah et al. [22], Biswas et al. [23], and Si-faoui and Aïder [24]. A TP denotes itself as "fully fuzzy" when every parameter, including decision variables, is fuzzy. Several researchers, including Jalil et al. [25] and Ebrahimnejad [26], have investigated entirely fuzzy TPs with respect to individual items. Ziqan et al. [27] investigated completely fuzzy linear systems using fuzzy numbers. When faced with imprecise constraints such as availability, demand, and conveyance capacity, fuzzy numbers are frequently employed to represent them. On the contrary, traditional Fuzzy Set (FS) theory only considers gratification in relation to fuzziness, neglecting to consider dissatisfaction. To get around this problem, Atanassov came up with a better framework called the Intuitionistic Fuzzy Set (IFS). This framework combined levels of membership and non-membership, which made it easier to handle uncertainty [28]. Prior scholars such as Ebrahimnejad and Verdegay [29], Midya et al. [30], and Roy and Midya [31] have integrated IFS into the formulations of TP. Among the various forms of IFNs, we frequently use triangular or trapezoidal IFNs to control ambiguity.

A number of scholars have emphasized seminal articles concerning TPs and their possible uses. FST has become a fundamental principle in improving transportation frameworks, specifically with regard to their operational implementations [32,33]. Ammar and Youness [2] conducted an investigation into MOTPs using imprecise numbers. Fuzzy programming techniques have tackled MOTPs with a variety of non-linear membership functions [18]. Lee and Abd Elwahed [1] presented an implementation of Fuzzy Goal Programming (FGP) for MOTPs. We employed FGP in conjunction with non-linear membership to address MOTPs [34,35]. Gupta and Kumar [36] proposed a method for handling linear MOTPs with ambiguous characteristics. Roy and Mahapatra [37] introduced MOTPs utilizing interval and formula within the stochastic environment. Roy et al. [19] investigated multi-choice TPs with exponential distribution. Mahapatra et al. [38] exhibited an extremist value distribution incorporating multi-choice stochastic TPs. Maity and Roy [39] utilized the utility function approach to analyze MOTPs under multi-decision conditions. Maity and Roy [40] also proposed an alternative method for dealing with MOTPs in the presence of nonlinear demand and cost variables. All of the parameters in the method for solving MOTPs proposed by Gupta and Kumar [36] are interval fuzzy numbers. Kocken et al. [41] introduced a compensatory fuzzy method for fuzzy parameter MOTP resolution. Roy et al. [42] examined an innovative method for resolving IF MOTPs. In their work, Mahajan and Gupta [17] put forth an entirely IF MOTP that features a multitude of membership functions.

In various practical scenarios, such as analyzing the economic aspects of transportation projects and management situations, TPs with ratio objective functions often serve as performance metrics. Some ratio goals in TPs are to obtain the best overall statistical transportation charges to overall average transportation charges, the best gross returns to gross operations, the best project resources to principal, and the best overall tariffs to overall general costs on leech [43]. Cetin and Tiryaki proposed a fuzzy approach for fractional MOTPs, utilizing a generalized version of Dinkelbach's algorithm. In a setting with fuzzy random hybridized ambiguity, Nasseri and Bavandi demonstrated multi-choice linear programming, as well as its application to a multicommodity TP [44]. El Sayed and Abo-Sinna presented an innovative method for a fully IF fractional MOTP, representing all parameters and variables as IFNs [45]. El Sayed and Baky presented a multi-choice fractional stochastic MOTP [46]. Additionally, Devnath et al. introduced a fully fuzzy multi-item, fixed charge in dimensions with breakability during transport [47]. Mondal et al. considered an IF sustainable multi-objective multi-item multi-choice step fixed-charge STP [48]. Chhibber et al. [49] presented a literature review on fuzzy TPs, which are non-linear IF multi-objective problems. Malik et al. exhibited a method for dealing with fully interval-valued via goal programming IF MOTPs [50]. In their paper [51], Bind et al. described a means of solving an enduring multi-objective multi-item 4D STP that uses triangular intuitionistic fuzzy numbers (TIFN).

A thorough review of the literature reveals a potentially effective approach in the quest for solutions to the complex issues presented by nonlinear TPs: the use of global optimization techniques. Scholars have investigated a variety of approaches to address the inherent complexity of nonlinear TPs in this domain. After conducting a thorough examination and synthesis of prior research, it becomes indisputable that the implementation of global optimization strategies has considerable capacity to provide efficacious resolutions. Researchers have devised various global optimization methods to resolve non-linear TPs, including the branch and reduce method, the branch and cut method, and a hybrid approach that combines local and global search strategies [52]. We have implemented mixed integer nonlinear programming methods, such as the extended cutting plane, branch and reduce, branch and cut, and simple branch and bound, to address nonlinear discrete TPs [53]. This methodology not only acknowledges the nonlinear characteristics of TPs, but it also surpasses the constraints of traditional optimization techniques by incorporating sophisticated algorithms and expanding the search space. Through the integration of knowledge from multiple fields, the proposed methodology emerges as a strong contender, providing notable benefits in comparison to conventional optimization methods, including improved precision, scalability, and resilience.

This study aims to introduce the FIF-MMSFTM, a model that has not previously been described in the literature. We have developed a model that optimizes the profit-to-cost ratio of a product shipment unit quantity from its source to its destination through a specific mode. An IFN represents each coefficient and parameter to mitigate the challenges associated with data acquisition during the modeling phase of real-world TPs. Additionally, we construct three distinct solution models using linear, parabolic, and hyperbolic functions, respectively, to equip the DM with the ability to distinguish among various solutions. Furthermore, the FIF-MMSFTM provides the solution in the form of IFNs with considerably fewer computational efforts, a considerably shorter runtime, and less precise numbers. Ultimately, we can expand the present framework to include a large-scale FIF-MMSFTM.

Although a multitude of studies have investigated STPs in a variety of contexts, it is apparent that linear and single-objective STPs may not be adequate to tackle the intricacies of the real world. In light of this constraint, we proposed a FIF-MMSFTM to bridge this void. This model integrates IF factors, including supplies, demands, transportation, and shipped quantity, profit, and cost coefficients. Firstly, we conceptualize a transformation procedure that converts the model into a linear format. Subsequently, we employ the ordering relations and accuracy function of IFS to further simplify the linearized model and generate a crisp MSTM. In our solution model, we build upon Zimmerman's approach [54] in order to optimize membership functions while minimizing non-membership functions. We incorporate linear, hyperbolic, and parabolic membership into the solution model. We provide a numeric illustration to showcase the practicality and effectiveness of the proposed methodology.

This article is structured as follows: After the introduction, Section 2 provides key ideas and preliminary work. Section 3 establishes the creation of the FIF-MMSFTM. Section 4 outlines the technique of linearizing the FIF-MMSFTM. Sections 5 and 6 elaborate on the development of the suggested strategy and an algorithm for solution procedures, respectively. Section 7 presents an example to demonstrate the applicability of the suggested methodology. Lastly, the paper concludes with some key insights.

2. Preliminaries and Notions

This section outlines the main concepts of IFSs and IFNs [17,28,55,56]. Table 1 displays the abbreviations and nomenclature used in the current study.

Table 1. Abbreviations and nomenclature.

FIF-MMSFTM	Fully intuitionistic fuzzy multi-objective multi-item solid fractional transportation model
IF	Intuitionistic fuzzy
MMSTM	Multi-objective multi-item solid transportation model
TP	Transportation problems
STP	Solid transportation problems
MOTP	Multi-objective transportation problem
DM	Decision-makers
FS	Fuzzy set
IFS	Intuitionistic fuzzy set
FGP	Fuzzy goal programming
IFN	Intuitionistic fuzzy numbers
TIFN	Triangular intuitionistic fuzzy number
AF	Accuracy function
LMF	Linear membership functions
HMF	Hyperbolic membership functions
PMF	Parabolic membership functions

Definition 1. *An IFS $\overset{\sim I}{A}$ in X is a set of ordered triples $\overset{\sim I}{A} = \left\{ \left(x, \mu_{\underset{A}{\sim I}}(x), v_{\underset{A}{\sim I}}(x) \right) \middle| x \in X \right\}$, where $\mu_{\underset{A}{\sim I}}(x)$, $v_{\underset{A}{\sim I}}(x) : X \to [0,\ 1]$ are functions such that $0 \le \mu_{\underset{A}{\sim I}}(x) + v_{\underset{A}{\sim I}}(x) \le 1,\ \forall x \in X$. The value of $\mu_{\underset{A}{\sim I}}(x)$ acts as the grade of membership and $v_{\underset{A}{\sim I}}(x)$ acts as the grade of non-membership*

of the element $x \in X$ *being in* $\overset{\sim I}{A}$. $h(x) = 1 - \mu_{\overset{\sim I}{A}}(x) - v_{\overset{\sim I}{A}}(x)$ *represents the grade of hesitation for the element* x *in* $\overset{\sim I}{A}$ *[28].*

Definition 2. *A TIFN* $\overset{\sim I}{A} = (a_1, a_2, a_3; a'_1, a_2, a'_3)$ *(Figure 1) is an IFS with membership and non-membership as follows [17]:*

$$\mu_{\overset{\sim I}{A}}(x) = \begin{cases} \frac{x-a_1}{a_2-a_1}, & a_1 < x \le a_2, \\ 1, & x = a_2, \\ \frac{a_3-x}{a_3-a_2}, & a_2 \le x \le a_3, \\ 0, & otherwise, \end{cases} \tag{1}$$

$$\mu_{\overset{\sim I}{v}}(x) = \begin{cases} \frac{a_2-x}{a_2-a'_1}, & a'_1 < x \le a_2, \\ 0, & x = a_2, \\ \frac{x-a_2}{a'_3-a_2}, & a_2 \le x \le a'_3, \\ 1, & otherwise, \end{cases} \tag{2}$$

where $a'_1 \le a_1 \le a_2 \le a_3 \le a'_3$.

Definition 3. *A TIFNs* $\overset{\sim I}{A} = (a_1, a_2, a_3; a'_1, a_2, a'_3)$ *is thought to be a positive TIFN iff,* $a'_1 \ge 0$ *[17,42,56].*

Definition 4. *Arithmetic operations on TIFNs [42,56]*

Let $\overset{\sim I}{A} = (a_1, a_2, a_3; a'_1, a_2, a'_3)$ *and* $\overset{\sim I}{B} = (b_1, b_2, b_3; b'_1, b_2, b'_3)$ *be a positive TIFN then;*
Addition: $\overset{\sim I}{A} + \overset{\sim I}{B} = (a_1 + b_1, a_2 + b_2, a_3 + b_3; a'_1 + b'_1, a_2 + b_2, a'_3 + b'_3)$;
Subtraction: $\overset{\sim I}{A} - \overset{\sim I}{B} = (a_1 - b_3, a_2 + b_2, a_3 + b_1; a'_1 - b'_3, a_2 + b_2, a'_3 - b'_1)$;
Multiplication: $\overset{\sim I}{A} \times \overset{\sim I}{B} = (a_1b_1, a_2b_2, a_3b_3; a'_1b'_1, a'_2b'_2, a'_3b'_3)$.

Definition 5. *(The Accuracy function) (AF) Let* $\overset{\sim I}{A} = (a_1, a_2, a_3; a'_1, a_2, a'_3)$ *be TIFN. The score function for the membership* $\mu_{\overset{\sim I}{A}}$ *and non-membership* $v_{\overset{\sim I}{A}}$ *function is indicated by* $S\left(\mu_{\overset{\sim I}{A}}\right)$ $S\left(v_{\overset{\sim I}{A}}\right)$ *and obtained as* $S\left(\mu_{\overset{\sim I}{A}}\right) = \frac{a_1+2a_2+a_3}{4}$, $S\left(v_{\overset{\sim I}{A}}\right) = \frac{a'_1+2a_2+a'_3}{4}$. *The AF of* $\overset{\sim I}{A}$ *is symbolized by* $\Re\left(\overset{\sim I}{A}\right)$ *and established as follows [42,56,57]:*

$$\Re\left(\overset{\sim I}{A}\right) = \frac{S\left(\mu_{\overset{\sim I}{A}}\right) + S\left(v_{\overset{\sim I}{A}}\right)}{2} = \frac{a_1 + 2a_2 + a_3 + a'_1 + 2a_2 + a'_3}{8}$$

Theorem 1. *Let* $\overset{\sim I}{A}$ *and* $\overset{\sim I}{B}$ *be two TIFNs. Then* $\Re\left(\overset{\sim I}{A} + t\overset{\sim I}{B}\right) = \Re\left(\overset{\sim I}{A}\right) + t\Re\left(\overset{\sim I}{B}\right)$ *for all* $t \in R$ *[55].*

The Proof of Theorem 1 can be easily found in [45,55].

Definition 6. *Ordering of TIFNs, consider* $\overset{\sim I}{A} = (a_1, a_2, a_3; a'_1, a_2, a'_3)$ *and* $\overset{\sim I}{B} = (b_1, b_2, b_3; b'_1, b_2, b'_3)$ *then [29,31,40]*

(a) $\Re\left(\overset{\sim I}{A}\right) \ge \Re\left(\overset{\sim I}{B}\right)$ iff $\overset{\sim I}{A} \ge \overset{\sim I}{B}$;

(b) $\Re\left(\overset{\sim I}{A}\right) \leq \Re\left(\overset{\sim I}{B}\right)\ iff\ \overset{\sim I}{A} \leq \overset{\sim I}{B}$;

(c) $\Re\left(\overset{\sim I}{A}\right) = \Re\left(\overset{\sim I}{B}\right)\ iff\ \overset{\sim I}{A} = \overset{\sim I}{B}$;

(d) $min\left(\overset{\sim I}{A}, \overset{\sim I}{B}\right) = \overset{\sim I}{A},\ if\ \overset{\sim I}{A} \leq \overset{\sim I}{B}\ or\ \overset{\sim I}{B} \geq \overset{\sim I}{A}$;

(e) $max\left(\overset{\sim I}{A}, \overset{\sim I}{B}\right) = \overset{\sim I}{A},\ if\ \overset{\sim I}{A} \geq \overset{\sim I}{B}\ or\ \overset{\sim I}{B} \leq \overset{\sim I}{A}$.

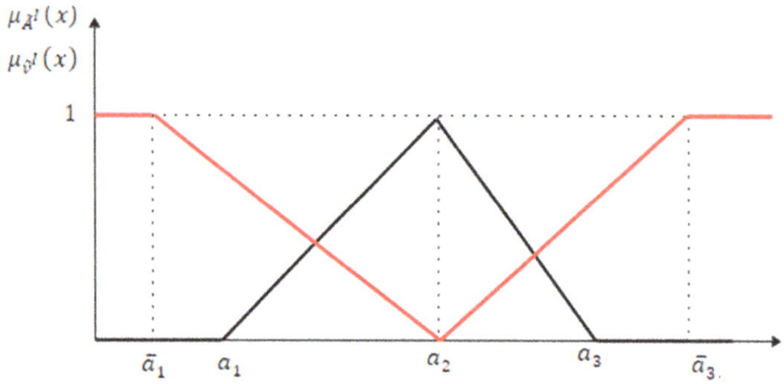

Figure 1. Triangular intuitionistic fuzzy number.

3. Problem Formulation

In real-world TPs, the constructing phase often encounters inaccuracies in transportation parameters due to incomplete data and market fluctuations. We employ a FIF-MMSFTM, where TINFs represent IFNs, to address this quantitatively. Suppose there are sources, destinations, and conveyances. This paper uses the following notations in the mathematical model development for the proposed FIF-MMSFTM, as shown in Table 2. We can express the FIF-MMSFTM's mathematical formulation as follows [4,47,51]:

$$max\ \overset{\sim I}{Z}_q\left(\overset{\sim I}{x}\right) = \frac{\overset{\sim I}{N}_q\left(\overset{\sim I}{x}\right)}{\overset{\sim I}{D}_q\left(\overset{\sim I}{x}\right)} = \frac{\sum_{i=1}^{m}\sum_{j=1}^{n}\sum_{k=1}^{k}\sum_{p=1}^{l} \overset{\sim(q)I}{c}_{ijkp}\overset{\sim I}{x}_{ijkp} + \overset{\sim(q)I}{\alpha}_0}{\sum_{i=1}^{m}\sum_{j=1}^{n}\sum_{k=1}^{k}\sum_{p=1}^{l} \overset{\sim(q)I}{d}_{ijkp}\overset{\sim I}{x}_{ijkp} + \overset{\sim(q)I}{\beta}_0}, \quad q = 12,\ldots,Q \tag{3}$$

subject to

$$\sum_{j=1}^{n}\sum_{k=1}^{k} \overset{\sim I}{x}_{ijkp} \leq \overset{\sim I}{a}_{ip}, \quad i = 1,2,\ldots,m, \quad p = 1,2,\ldots,l, \tag{4}$$

$$\sum_{i=1}^{m}\sum_{k=1}^{k} \overset{\sim I}{x}_{ijkp} \geq \overset{\sim I}{b}_{jp}, \quad j = 1,2,\ldots,n, \quad p = 1,2,\ldots,l, \tag{5}$$

$$\sum_{p=1}^{l}\sum_{i=1}^{m}\sum_{j=1}^{n} \overset{\sim I}{x}_{ijkp} \leq \overset{\sim I}{e}_{k}, \quad k = 1,2,\ldots,k, \tag{6}$$

$$\overset{\sim I}{x}_{ijkp} \geq \overset{\sim I}{0}, \quad \forall\ i,\ j,\ k,\ p. \tag{7}$$

Table 2. Notations.

Index	i	Index for the ith-source;
	j	Index for the jth-destinations;
	k	Index for the kth-conveyances;
	p	Index for the pth-item;
	q	Index for the qth- objective function;

Table 2. *Cont.*

Sets	m	Number of sources;
	n	Number of destinations;
	k	Number of conveyances;
	l	Number of items.
Parameters	$\overset{\sim(q)I}{c}_{ijkp}$	IF profit gained from shipment unit quantity of pth product from i^{th} source to j^{th} destination via k^{th} conveyance;
	$\overset{\sim(q)I}{d}_{ijkp}$	IF cost per unit of shipment of pth product from i^{th} source to j^{th} destination via k^{th} conveyance;
	$\overset{\sim(q)I}{\alpha_0}$	IF fixed profit associated with p^{th} product;
	$\overset{\sim(q)I}{\beta_0}$	IF fixed cost associated with p^{th} product;
	$\overset{\sim I}{a}_{ip}$	IF supply of pth product at source i;
	$\overset{\sim I}{b}_{jp}$	IF demand of pth product at destination j;
	$\overset{\sim I}{e}_{k}$	IF capacity of kth conveyance.
Decision variables	$\overset{\sim I}{x}_{ijkp}$	IF quantity shipped of pth product from i^{th} source to j^{th} destination by k^{th} conveyance;
Optimization objectives	$\overset{\sim I}{Z}_q\left(\overset{\sim I}{x}\right)$	Objective function with IF parameters.

where $\overset{\sim(q)I}{c}_{ijkp} = \left(c^{1(q)}_{ijkp}, c^{2(q)}_{ijkp}, c^{3(q)}_{ijkp}; c'^{1(q)}_{ijkp}, c^{2(q)}_{ijkp}, c'^{3(q)}_{ijkp}\right)$ is a TIFN that represents the revenue from shipping unit amount of pth goods via k^{th} conveyance from i^{th} source to j^{th} destination. Also, $\overset{\sim(q)I}{d}_{ijkp} = \left(d^{1(q)}_{ijkp}, d^{2(q)}_{ijkp}, d^{3(q)}_{ijkp}; d'^{1(q)}_{ijkp}, d^{2(q)}_{ijkp}, d'^{3(q)}_{ij}\right)$ is a TIFN that indicates the cost of shipping a unit of pth product from i^{th} source to j^{th} destination via k^{th} conveyance. $\overset{\sim(q)I}{\alpha_0}$, $\overset{\sim(q)I}{\beta_0}$ are assumed to be TIFNs that denote the fixed profit and cost associated with p^{th} product, i^{th} source, j^{th} destination, and k^{th} conveyance, respectively. $\overset{\sim I}{x}_{ijkp} = \left(x^1_{ijkp}, x^2_{ijkp}, x^3_{ijkp}; x'^1_{ijkp}, x^2_{ijkp}, x'^3_{ijkp}\right)$ denotes a TIFN quantity shipped of pth product from i^{th} source to j^{th} destination via k^{th} conveyance. $\overset{\sim I}{a}_{ip} = \left(a^1_{ip}, a^2_{ip}, a^3_{ip}; a'^1_{ip}, a^2_{ip}, a'^3_{ip}\right)$ represents the accessible TIF supply at i^{th} source, and $\overset{\sim I}{b}_{jp} = \left(b^1_{jp}, b^2_{jp}, b^3_{jp}; b'^1_{jp}, b^2_{jp}, b'^3_{jp}\right)$ alludes to the accessible TIF demand at j^{th} destination for p^{th} product. $\overset{\sim I}{e}_{k} = \left(e^1_{k}, e^2_{k}, e^3_{k}; e'^1_{k}, e^2_{k}, e'^3_{k}\right)$ is the total TIF capacity of kth conveyance. Additionally, we hypothesize that $\overset{\sim I}{D}_q\left(\overset{\sim I}{x}\right) > \overset{\sim I}{0}, q = 1, 2, .., Q, \overset{\sim I}{a}_{ip} > \overset{\sim I}{0}, \forall i, p; \overset{\sim I}{b}_{jp} > \overset{\sim I}{0}, \forall j, p; \overset{\sim(q)I}{c}_{ijkp} > \overset{\sim I}{0}, \overset{\sim(q)I}{\alpha_0} > \overset{\sim I}{0}, \overset{\sim(q)I}{\beta_0} > \overset{\sim I}{0}, \forall i, j, k, p$, and the gross supply is equivalent to or above the value of the gross demand as well as overall conveyance capacities that are higher than or comparable to overall needs.

$$\sum_{i=1}^{m} \overset{\sim I}{a}_{ip} \geq \sum_{j=1}^{n} \overset{\sim I}{b}_{jp}, \quad \forall\, i,\ p \quad and \qquad \sum_{k=1}^{p} \overset{\sim I}{e}_{k} \geq \sum_{p=1}^{l} \sum_{j=1}^{n} \overset{\sim I}{b}_{jp}, \tag{8}$$

As a necessary and sufficient condition for the existence of a feasible solution to the FIF-MMSFTM, the discrepancy (8) is thought to exist. Let S be a convex, compact, and feasible set that is described with Equations (4)–(7), and $S \neq \varnothing$.

Definition 7. *A point $\overset{\sim *I}{x}_{ijkp} \in S$ is claimed to be an IF weakly efficient solution iff there is no $\overset{\sim I}{x}_{ijkp} \in S$ such that*

$$\frac{\overset{\sim I}{N}_q\left(\overset{\sim I}{x}_{ijkp}\right)}{\overset{\sim I}{D}_q\left(\overset{\sim I}{x}_{ijkp}\right)} > \frac{\overset{\sim I}{N}_q\left(\overset{\sim *I}{x}_{ijkp}\right)}{\overset{\sim I}{D}_q\left(\overset{\sim *I}{x}_{ijkp}\right)}, \qquad q = 1, 2, \ldots, Q.$$

Definition 8. *A point $\overset{\sim *I}{x}_{ijkp} \in S$ is claimed to be an IF strongly efficient solution iff there is no $\overset{\sim I}{x}_{ijkp} \in S$ such that*

$$\frac{\overset{\sim I}{N}_q\left(\overset{\sim I}{x}_{ijkp}\right)}{\overset{\sim I}{D}_q\left(\overset{\sim I}{x}_{ijkp}\right)} \geq \frac{\overset{\sim I}{N}_q\left(\overset{\sim *I}{x}_{ijkp}\right)}{\overset{\sim I}{D}_q\left(\overset{\sim *I}{x}_{ijkp}\right)}, \qquad q = 1, 2, \ldots, Q.$$

4. Linearization Procedure

The FIF-MMSFTM can be converted into FIF-MMSTM based on Charnes and Cooper [6] strategy by introducing a new variable $\tilde{w}^I = \tilde{t}^I\tilde{x}^I;\ \tilde{t}^I > 0^I$, [6,58,59] since $\tilde{D}^I_q\left(\tilde{x}^I\right) > 0^I;\ \tilde{c}^{(q)I}_{ijkp} > 0^I;$ $q = 1,2,\ldots,Q$, and $\tilde{x}^I_{ijkp} \geq 0^I$. Thus, we take into account the lowest value of $\frac{\tilde{1}^I}{\tilde{D}^I_q\left(\tilde{x}^I\right)} = \tilde{t}^I$, i.e.,

$$\bigcap \frac{\tilde{1}^I}{\sum_{i=1}^{m}\sum_{j=1}^{n}\sum_{k=1}^{k}\sum_{p=1}^{l} \tilde{d}^{(q)I}_{ijkp}\tilde{x}^I_{ijkp} + \tilde{\beta}^{(q)I}_0} = \tilde{t}^I, \qquad q = 1,2,\ldots,Q, \tag{9}$$

In general, it can be formulated as follows:

$$\frac{\tilde{1}^I}{\sum_{i=1}^{m}\sum_{j=1}^{n}\sum_{k=1}^{k}\sum_{p=1}^{l} \tilde{d}^{(q)I}_{ijkp}\tilde{x}^I_{ijkp} + \tilde{\beta}^{(q)I}_0} \geq \tilde{t}^I, \qquad q = 1,2,\ldots,Q, \tag{10}$$

Following the stratification of the change $\tilde{w}^I = \tilde{t}^I\tilde{x}^I;\ \tilde{t}^I > 0^I$, and using Equation (10), FIF-MMSFTM transforms into a comparable FIF-MMSTM as follows [47,58,59]:

$$max\ \tilde{Z}^I_q\left(\tilde{x}^I\right) = \tilde{t}^I\tilde{N}^I_q\left(\frac{\tilde{w}^I_{ijkp}}{\tilde{t}^I}\right), \qquad q = 12,\ldots,Q \tag{11}$$

subject to

$$\tilde{t}^I\tilde{D}^I_q\left(\frac{\tilde{w}^I_{ijkp}}{\tilde{t}^I}\right) \leq \tilde{1}^I, \qquad \forall i,\ j,k,p; \qquad q = 12,\ldots,Q \tag{12}$$

$$\sum_{j=1}^{n}\sum_{k=1}^{k}\left(\frac{\tilde{w}^I_{ijkp}}{\tilde{t}^I}\right) \leq \tilde{a}^I_{ip}, \qquad i = 1,2,\ldots,m, \quad p = 1,2,\ldots,l, \tag{13}$$

$$\sum_{i=1}^{m}\sum_{k=1}^{k}\left(\frac{\tilde{w}^I_{ijkp}}{\tilde{t}^I}\right) \geq \tilde{b}^I_{jp}, \qquad j = 1,2,\ldots,n, \quad p = 1,2,\ldots,l, \tag{14}$$

$$\sum_{p=1}^{l}\sum_{i=1}^{m}\sum_{j=1}^{n}\left(\frac{\tilde{w}^I_{ijkp}}{\tilde{t}^I}\right) \leq \tilde{e}^I_k, \qquad k = 1,2,\ldots,k, \tag{15}$$

$$\tilde{w}^I_{ijkp} \geq 0^I, \quad \tilde{t}^I > 0^I, \qquad i = 1,2,\ldots,m, \qquad j = 1,2,\ldots,n. \tag{16}$$

Remark 1. *The IF efficient solution for the model* (11) − (16) $\left(\frac{\tilde{w}^{*I}_{ijkp}}{\tilde{t}^{*I}}\right) = \left(\left(\frac{w^*_{ijkp}}{t^*}\right)^1, \left(\frac{w^*_{ijkp}}{t^*}\right)^2, \left(\frac{w^*_{ijkp}}{t^*}\right)^3; \left(\frac{w^*_{ijkp}}{t^*}\right)'^1, \left(\frac{w^*_{ijkp}}{t^*}\right)^2, \left(\frac{w^*_{ijkp}}{t^*}\right)'^3\right) \in G$, *where G is the collection of constraints* (12) − (16), *meets the following conditions:*

1. $\sum_{j=1}^{n}\sum_{k=1}^{k}\left(\frac{\tilde{w}^I_{ijkp}}{\tilde{t}^I}\right) \leq \tilde{a}^I_{ip}, i = 1,2,\ldots,m, p = 1,2,\ldots,l;$
2. $\sum_{i=1}^{m}\sum_{k=1}^{k}\left(\frac{\tilde{w}^I_{ijkp}}{\tilde{t}^I}\right) \geq \tilde{b}^I_{jp}, j = 1,2,\ldots,n, p = 1,2,\ldots,l;$
3. $\sum_{p=1}^{l}\sum_{i=1}^{m}\sum_{j=1}^{n}\left(\frac{\tilde{w}^I_{ijkp}}{\tilde{t}^I}\right) \leq \tilde{e}^I_k, k = 1,2,\ldots,k;$
4. $\tilde{w}^{*I}_{ijkp} \geq 0^I; \tilde{t}^{*I} > 0^I\ i = 1,2,\ldots,m; j = 1,2,\ldots,n; k = 1,2,\ldots,k; p = 1,2,\ldots,l;$
5. $\forall\left(\frac{\tilde{w}^I_{ijkp}}{\tilde{t}^I}\right) \in S$, *we have that* $\frac{\tilde{N}^I_q\left(\frac{\tilde{w}^I_{ijkp}}{\tilde{t}^I}\right)}{\tilde{D}^I_q\left(\frac{\tilde{w}^I_{ijkp}}{\tilde{t}^I}\right)} \leq \frac{\tilde{N}^I_q\left(\frac{\tilde{w}^{*I}_{ijkp}}{\tilde{t}^{*I}}\right)}{\tilde{D}^I_q\left(\frac{\tilde{w}^{*I}_{ijkp}}{\tilde{t}^{*I}}\right)}$.

Theorem 2. *The solution* $\overset{\sim *I}{x}$ *for the Equations* $(3)-(7)$ *is an IF efficient solution iff the solution* $\left(\overset{\sim *I}{w}, \overset{\sim *I}{t}\right)$ *for the Equations* $(11)-(16)$ *is also an IF efficient solution.*

Proof. Contrariwise, suppose that $\overset{\sim *I}{x}_{ijkp} = \frac{\overset{\sim *I}{w}_{ijkp}}{\overset{\sim *I}{t}}$ is a solution which is a fuzzy efficient solution for Equations (3)–(7), but $\left(\overset{\sim *I}{w}_{ijkp}, \overset{\sim *I}{t}\right)$ is a solution that is not a fuzzy efficient solution for Equations (11)–(16). Therefore, there should be $\overset{\sim I}{w}_{ijkp} \in S$ such that the following is true:

$$\overset{\sim I}{t}\,\overset{\sim I}{N_q}\left(\frac{\overset{\sim *I}{w}_{ijkp}}{\overset{\sim *I}{t}}\right) \leq \overset{\sim I}{t}\,\overset{\sim I}{N_q}\left(\frac{\overset{\sim I}{w}_{ijkp}}{\overset{\sim I}{t}}\right), \qquad q = 1,2,\ldots,Q; \quad \text{and} \tag{17}$$

$$\overset{\sim I}{t}\,\overset{\sim I}{N_v}\left(\frac{\overset{\sim *I}{w}_{ijkp}}{\overset{\sim *I}{t}}\right) < \overset{\sim I}{t}\,\overset{\sim I}{N_v}\left(\frac{\overset{\sim I}{w}_{ijkp}}{\overset{\sim I}{t}}\right), \qquad \text{for at least one } v, \quad v \in \{1,2,\ldots,Q\} \tag{18}$$

Making use of Chakraborty and Gupta's innovation [47,59], based on information provided by Arya et al., [58], we infer the following:

$$\overset{\sim I}{t}\,\overset{\sim I}{N_q}\left(\overset{\sim *I}{x}_{ijkp}\right) \leq \overset{\sim I}{t}\,\overset{\sim I}{N_q}\left(\frac{\overset{\sim I}{w}_{ijkp}}{\overset{\sim I}{t}}\right), \qquad q = 1,2,\ldots,Q; \quad \text{and} \tag{19}$$

$$\overset{\sim I}{t}\,\overset{\sim I}{N_v}\left(\overset{\sim *I}{x}_{ijkp}\right) < \overset{\sim I}{t}\,\overset{\sim I}{N_v}\left(\frac{\overset{\sim I}{w}_{ijkp}}{\overset{\sim I}{t}}\right), \qquad \text{for at least one } v, \; v \in \{1,2,\ldots,Q\} \tag{20}$$

This deduces that

$$\frac{\overset{\sim I}{N_q}\left(\overset{\sim *I}{x}_{ijkp}\right)}{\overset{\sim I}{D_q}\left(\overset{\sim *I}{x}_{ijkp}\right)} \leq \frac{\overset{\sim I}{N_q}\left(\overset{\sim I}{x}_{ijkp}\right)}{\overset{\sim I}{D_q}\left(\overset{\sim I}{x}_{ijkp}\right)}, \qquad q = 1,2,\ldots,Q; \tag{21}$$

$$\text{and} \quad \frac{\overset{\sim I}{N_v}\left(\overset{\sim *I}{x}_{ijkp}\right)}{\overset{\sim I}{D_v}\left(\overset{\sim *I}{x}_{ijkp}\right)} \leq \frac{\overset{\sim I}{N_v}\left(\overset{\sim I}{x}_{ijkp}\right)}{\overset{\sim I}{D_v}\left(\overset{\sim I}{x}_{ijkp}\right)}, \qquad \textit{for at least one } v, \quad v \in \{1,2,\ldots,Q\} \tag{22}$$

This demonstrates that $\overset{\sim *I}{x}_{ijkp}$ is not an IF efficient solution for the Equations (3)–(7). This disproves our hypothesis and therefore assumes that $\left(\overset{\sim *I}{w}_{ijkp}, \overset{\sim *I}{t}\right)$ is an IF efficient solution for the Equations (11)–(16).

Conversely, suppose that $\left(\overset{\sim *I}{w}_{ijkp}, \overset{\sim *I}{t}\right)$ is an IF efficient solution to Equations (11)–(16) and $\overset{\sim *I}{x}_{ijkp}$ is not an IF efficient solution to Equations (3)–(7). Then, there need to $\overset{\sim I}{x}_{ijkp} \in S$

$$\frac{\overset{\sim I}{N_q}\left(\overset{\sim *I}{x}_{ijkp}\right)}{\overset{\sim I}{D_q}\left(\overset{\sim *I}{x}_{ijkp}\right)} \leq \frac{\overset{\sim I}{N_q}\left(\overset{\sim I}{x}_{ijkp}\right)}{\overset{\sim I}{D_q}\left(\overset{\sim I}{x}_{ijkp}\right)}, \qquad q = 1,2,\ldots,Q; \tag{23}$$

$$\text{and} \quad \frac{\overset{\sim I}{N_v}\left(\overset{\sim *I}{x}_{ijkp}\right)}{\overset{\sim I}{D_v}\left(\overset{\sim *I}{x}_{ijkp}\right)} \leq \frac{\overset{\sim I}{N_v}\left(\overset{\sim I}{x}_{ijkp}\right)}{\overset{\sim I}{D_v}\left(\overset{\sim I}{x}_{ijkp}\right)}, \qquad \text{for at least one } v, \quad v \in \{1,2,\ldots,Q\} \tag{24}$$

Applying the conversion $\overset{\sim *I}{w}_{ijkp} = \overset{\sim *I}{t} \overset{\sim *I}{x}_{ijkp}$, we conclude the following:

$$\overset{\sim I}{t} \overset{\sim I}{N}_q \left(\frac{\overset{\sim *I}{w}_{ijkp}}{\overset{\sim *I}{t}} \right) \leq \frac{\overset{\sim I}{N}_q \left(\overset{\sim I}{x}_{ijkp} \right)}{\overset{\sim I}{D}_q \left(\overset{\sim I}{x}_{ijkp} \right)}, \qquad q = 1, 2, \ldots, Q; \quad \text{and} \tag{25}$$

$$\overset{\sim I}{t} \overset{\sim I}{N}_v \left(\frac{\overset{\sim *I}{w}_{ijkp}}{\overset{\sim *I}{t}} \right) < \frac{\overset{\sim I}{N}_v \left(\overset{\sim I}{x}_{ijkp} \right)}{\overset{\sim I}{D}_v \left(\overset{\sim I}{x}_{ijkp} \right)}, \qquad \text{for at least one } v, \ v \in \{1, 2, \ldots, Q\} \tag{26}$$

It contradicts the fact that the solution $\left(\overset{\sim *I}{w}_{ijkp}, \overset{\sim *I}{t} \right)$ of Equations (11)–(16) is an IF efficient solution. Hence, the solution $\overset{\sim *I}{x}_{ijkp}$ of Equations (3)–(7) is an IF efficient solution. This proves the theorem. □

5. Conception of a Suggested Strategy

Upon developing the real-world FIF-MMSFTM (3)–(7), we proceed to linearize the issue using the transformation outlined in the preceding section. This necessitates the introduction of a novel IF variable. We can reform the crisp model as follows [47] by applying the AF to each objective function, employing arithmetic operations, and using the order of TIFN.

$$max\ \Re\left(\overset{\sim I}{Z}_q \right) = \begin{Bmatrix} \Re\left(\left(t^1, t^2, t^3; t'^1, t^2, t'^3 \right) \left[\overset{\sim I}{N}_1 \left(\frac{w^1_{ijkp}}{t^1}, \frac{w^2_{ijkp}}{t^2}, \frac{w^3_{ijkp}}{t^3}; \frac{w'^1_{ijkp}}{t'^1}, \frac{w^2_{ijkp}}{t^2}, \frac{w'^3_{ijkp}}{t'^3} \right) \right] \right) \\ \Re\left(\left(t^1, t^2, t^3; t'^1, t^2, t'^3 \right) \left[\overset{\sim I}{N}_2 \left(\frac{w^1_{ijkp}}{t^1}, \frac{w^2_{ijkp}}{t^2}, \frac{w^3_{ijkp}}{t^3}; \frac{w'^1_{ijkp}}{t'^1}, \frac{w^2_{ijkp}}{t^2}, \frac{w'^3_{ijkp}}{t'^3} \right) \right] \right) \\ \vdots \\ \Re\left(\left(t^1, t^2, t^3; t'^1, t^2, t'^3 \right) \left[\overset{\sim I}{N}_q \left(\frac{w^1_{ijkp}}{t^1}, \frac{w^2_{ijkp}}{t^2}, \frac{w^3_{ijkp}}{t^3}; \frac{w'^1_{ijkp}}{t'^1}, \frac{w^2_{ijkp}}{t^2}, \frac{w'^3_{ijkp}}{t'^3} \right) \right] \right) \end{Bmatrix}$$

subject to

$$\Re\left(\sum_{i=1}^{m} \sum_{j=1}^{n} \sum_{k=1}^{k} \sum_{p=1}^{l} d^{1(q)}_{ijkp} w^1_{ijkp} + \beta_0^{1(q)} t^1 \right) \leq 1; \qquad \Re\left(\sum_{i=1}^{m} \sum_{j=1}^{n} \sum_{k=1}^{k} \sum_{p=1}^{l} d^{2(q)}_{ijkp} w^2_{ijkp} + \beta_0^{2(q)} t^2 \right) \leq 1$$

$$\Re\left(\sum_{i=1}^{m} \sum_{j=1}^{n} \sum_{k=1}^{k} \sum_{p=1}^{l} d^{3(q)}_{ijkp} w^3_{ijkp} + \beta_0^{3(q)} t^3 \right) \leq 1, \qquad q = 1, 2, \ldots, Q$$

$$\Re\left(\sum_{i=1}^{m} \sum_{j=1}^{n} \sum_{k=1}^{k} \sum_{p=1}^{l} d'^{1(q)}_{ijkp} w'^1_{ijkp} + \beta_0'^{1(q)} t'^1 \right) \leq 1; \quad \Re\left(\sum_{i=1}^{m} \sum_{j=1}^{n} \sum_{k=1}^{k} \sum_{p=1}^{l} d^{2(q)}_{ijkp} w^2_{ijkp} + \beta_0^{2(q)} t^2 \right) \leq 1$$

$$\Re\left(\sum_{i=1}^{m} \sum_{j=1}^{n} \sum_{k=1}^{k} \sum_{p=1}^{l} d'^{3(q)}_{ijkp} w'^3_{ijkp} + \beta_0'^{3(q)} t'^3 \right) \leq 1, \qquad q = 1, 2, \ldots, Q$$

$$\Re\left(\sum_{j=1}^{n} \sum_{k=1}^{k} w^1_{ijkp} - a^1_{ip} t^1 \right) \leq 0; \qquad \Re\left(\sum_{j=1}^{n} \sum_{k=1}^{k} w^2_{ijkp} - a^2_{ip} t^2 \right) \leq 0; \quad \forall\ i,\ p$$

$$\Re\left(\sum_{j=1}^{n} \sum_{k=1}^{k} w^3_{ijkp} - a^3_{ip} t^3 \right) \leq 0; \qquad i = 1, 2, \ldots, m, \quad p = 1, 2, \ldots, l, \tag{27}$$

$$\Re\left(\sum_{j=1}^{n} \sum_{k=1}^{k} w'^1_{ijkp} - a'^1_{ip} t'^1 \right) \leq 0; \qquad \Re\left(\sum_{j=1}^{n} \sum_{k=1}^{k} w^2_{ijkp} - a^2_{ip} t^2 \right) \leq 0; \quad \forall\ i,\ p$$

$$\Re\left(\sum_{j=1}^{n} \sum_{k=1}^{k} w'^3_{ijkp} - a'^3_{ip} t'^3 \right) \leq 0; \qquad i = 1, 2, \ldots, m, \quad p = 1, 2, \ldots, l,$$

$$\Re\left(\sum_{i=1}^{m}\sum_{k=1}^{k} w_{ijkp}^{1} - b_{jp}^{1}t^{1}\right) \geq 1; \quad \Re\left(\sum_{i=1}^{m}\sum_{k=1}^{k} w_{ijkp}^{2} - b_{jp}^{2}t^{2}\right) \geq 1, \quad j = 1,2,\ldots,n, \quad p = 1,2,\ldots,l,$$

$$\Re\left(\sum_{i=1}^{m}\sum_{k=1}^{k} w_{ijkp}^{3} - b_{jp}^{3}t^{3}\right) \geq 1; \quad j = 1,2,\ldots,n, \quad p = 1,2,\ldots,l,$$

$$\Re\left(\sum_{i=1}^{m}\sum_{k=1}^{k} w_{ijkp}^{\prime 1} - b_{jp}^{\prime 1}t^{\prime 1}\right) \geq 1; \quad \Re\left(\sum_{i=1}^{m}\sum_{k=1}^{k} w_{ijkp}^{2} - b_{jp}^{2}t^{2}\right) \geq 1, \quad j = 1,2,\ldots,n, \quad p = 1,2,\ldots,l,$$

$$\Re\left(\sum_{i=1}^{m}\sum_{k=1}^{k} w_{ijkp}^{\prime 3} - b_{jp}^{\prime 3}t^{\prime 3}\right) \geq 1; \quad j = 1,2,\ldots,n, \quad p = 1,2,\ldots,l,$$

$$\Re\left(\sum_{p=1}^{l}\sum_{i=1}^{m}\sum_{j=1}^{n} w_{ijkp}^{1} - e_{k}^{1}t^{1}\right) \leq 1; \quad \Re\left(\sum_{p=1}^{l}\sum_{i=1}^{m}\sum_{j=1}^{n} w_{ijkp}^{2} - e_{k}^{2}t^{2}\right) \leq 1 \quad k = 1,2,\ldots,k,$$

$$\Re\left(\sum_{p=1}^{l}\sum_{i=1}^{m}\sum_{j=1}^{n} w_{ijkp}^{3} - e_{k}^{3}t^{3}\right) \leq 1; \quad k = 1,2,\ldots,k,$$

$$\Re\left(\sum_{p=1}^{l}\sum_{i=1}^{m}\sum_{j=1}^{n} w_{ijkp}^{\prime 1} - e_{k}^{\prime 1}t^{\prime 1}\right) \leq 1; \quad \Re\left(\sum_{p=1}^{l}\sum_{i=1}^{m}\sum_{j=1}^{n} w_{ijkp}^{2} - e_{k}^{2}t^{2}\right) \leq 1 \quad k = 1,2,\ldots,k,$$

$$\Re\left(\sum_{p=1}^{l}\sum_{i=1}^{m}\sum_{j=1}^{n} w_{ijkp}^{\prime 3} - e_{k}^{\prime 3}t^{\prime 3}\right) \leq 1; \quad k = 1,2,\ldots,k,$$

$$w_{ijkp}^{\prime 1} \geq 0; \ w_{ijkp}^{1} - w_{ijkp}^{\prime 1} \geq 0; \ w_{ijkp}^{\prime 2} - w_{ijkp}^{1} \geq 0; \ w_{ijkp}^{2} - w_{ijkp}^{\prime 2} = 0; \ w_{ijkp}^{3} - w_{ijkp}^{2} \geq 0;$$
$$w_{ijkp}^{\prime 3} - w_{ijkp}^{3} \geq 0, \ t^{\prime 1} > 0, t^{1} - t^{\prime 1} > 0; \ t^{\prime 2} - t^{1} > 0; \ t^{2} - t^{\prime 2} = 0; \ t^{3} - t^{2} > 0; \ t^{\prime 3} - t^{3} > 0,$$

The model (27) represents the linearized form of the FIF-MMSFTM. Consequently, various techniques can address the resulting FIF-MMSTM to derive an efficient solution. Examining the collection of limitations in model (27) indicated by G_1, we first define the appropriate objective for the single objective function. The optimal value for each objective is determined and referred to as the desired or most satisfactory level denoted by U_q. Let $U_q = max\,\Re\left(\overset{\sim I}{Z_q}\right)$; $L_q = min\,\Re\left(\overset{\sim I}{Z_q}\right)$ $q = 1,2,\ldots,Q$, L_q represent the least desirable level of satisfaction for the qth objective. Subsequently, model (27) is transformed to a FGP model, with the objective of attaining the single optimum U_q. However, some flexibility is allowed, and this degree of indulgence is determined by the minimal value L_q. The FGP model is formulated as follows [17]:

$$Find \quad \left\{w_{ijkp},\ t;\ i = 12,\ldots,m;\ j = 1,2,\ldots,n;\quad p = 1,2,\ldots,l;\ \ k = 1,2,\ldots,k\ \right\} \tag{28}$$

subject to

$$w_{ijkp}, \quad t \in G_1 \tag{29}$$

$$\Re\left(\overset{\sim I}{Z_q}\left(w_{ijkp},\ t\right)\right) \approx U_q, \qquad q = 1,2,\ldots,Q \tag{30}$$

where the constraint $\Re\left(\overset{\sim I}{Z_q}\left(w_{ijkp},\ t\right)\right) \approx U_q$, $q = 1,2,\ldots,Q$ is an IF constraint that includes IF parity that may be addressed by using a membership role. This membership role can be linear, parabolic, or hyperbolic according to the DM's preferences. Assuming that $\Re\left(\overset{\sim I}{Z_q}\left(\boldsymbol{w_{ijkp}},\boldsymbol{t}\right)\right)$ denoted by $Z_q\left(\boldsymbol{w_{ijkp}},\boldsymbol{t}\right)$ [17,20].

5.1. Linear Membership Function Model

In the literature on solving fuzzy mathematical programming problems, a key assumption is often made about applying a linear membership function (LMF) in the decision-making method. People primarily favor this choice because of its simplicity and ease of implementation. It involves defining the upper and lower bounds of respect for decision parameters. Typically, refs. [17,20,42] represent linear membership and non-membership functions, as illustrated in Figure 2.

$$\mu^L\left(Z_q\left(w_{ijkp}, t\right)\right) = \begin{cases} 0, & Z_q\left(w_{ijkp}, t\right) \le L_q, \\ \frac{Z_q\left(w_{ijkp}, t\right) - L_q}{U_q - L_q}, & L_q \le Z_q\left(w_{ijkp}, t\right) \le U_q, \\ 1, & Z_q\left(w_{ijkp}, t\right) \ge U_q, \end{cases} \tag{31}$$

$$v^L\left(Z_q\left(w_{ijkp}, t\right)\right) = \begin{cases} 1, & Z_q\left(w_{ijkp}, t\right) \le L_q, \\ \frac{U_q - Z_q\left(w_{ijkp}, t\right)}{U_q - L_q}, & L_q \le Z_q\left(w_{ijkp}, t\right) \le U_q, \\ 0, & Z_q\left(w_{ijkp}, t\right) \ge U_q, \end{cases} \tag{32}$$

Let $\gamma = min\left\{\mu^L\left(Z_q\left(w_{ijkp}, t\right)\right), q = 1, 2, \ldots, Q\right\}$ and $\vartheta = max\left\{v^L\left(Z_q\left(w_{ijkp}, t\right)\right), q = 1, 2, \ldots, Q\right\}$. Stated differently, $\mu^L\left(Z_q\left(w_{ijkp}, t\right)\right) \ge \gamma$ and $v^L\left(Z_q\left(w_{ijkp}, t\right)\right) \le \vartheta, \forall q$. Based on Zimmerman's method [54], which offers to maximize the lowest acceptance grade while simultaneously minimizing the greatest rejection degree, we use LMF to develop the model as follows:

$$\begin{array}{l} max \quad \gamma - \vartheta \\ subject\ to \\ Z_1\left(w_{ijkp}, t\right) - \gamma(U_1 - L_1) \ge L_1, \\ Z_2\left(w_{ijkp}, t\right) - \gamma(U_2 - L_2) \ge L_2, \\ \vdots \\ Z_q\left(w_{ijkp}, t\right) - \gamma(U_q - L_q) \ge L_q, \\ Z_1\left(w_{ijkp}, t\right) + \vartheta(U_1 - L_1) \ge U_1, \\ Z_2\left(w_{ijkp}, t\right) + \vartheta(U_2 - L_2) \ge U_2, \\ \vdots \\ Z_q\left(w_{ijkp}, t\right) + \vartheta(U_q - L_q) \ge U_q, \\ \gamma \ge \vartheta, \quad \gamma + \vartheta \le 1, \qquad \gamma, \vartheta \in [0,\ 1] \\ w_{ijkp}, \ t \in G_1 \end{array} \tag{33}$$

Theorem 3. *A unique optimal solution of the LMF model is an efficient solution of the model (33).*

Proof. Allow $\left(\hat{w}_{ijkp}, \ \hat{t}, \hat{\gamma}, \ \hat{\vartheta}\right)$ to represent the singular best solution for LMF. Then, for any feasible $\left(w_{ijkp}, \ t, \gamma, \ \vartheta\right)$ of the LMF problem, $(\hat{\gamma} - \hat{\vartheta}) > (\gamma - \vartheta)$. On the other hand, assume that the model (33), with respect to $\left(\hat{w}_{ijkp}, \ \hat{t}, \hat{\gamma}, \ \hat{\vartheta}\right)$, is not efficiently solved. Then, there exists $w^*_{ijkp}, \quad t^*\left(w^*_{ijkp} \ne \hat{w}_{ijkp} \ and\ t^* \ne \hat{t}\right)$ feasible to model (33), such that $Z_q\left(\hat{w}_{ijkp}, \ \hat{t}\right) \le Z_q\left(w^*_{ijkp}, t^*\right); \ \forall\, q = 12, \ldots, Q$, and $Z_q\left(\hat{w}_{ijkp}, \ \hat{t}\right) < Z_q\left(w^*_{ijkp}, t^*\right)$ for a minimum of one q. Therefore,

$$\frac{U_q - Z_q\left(\hat{w}_{ijkp}, \ \hat{t}\right)}{U_q - L_q} \ge \frac{U_q - Z_q\left(w^*_{ijkp}, t^*\right)}{U_q - L_q}, \qquad \forall\, q = 12, \ldots, Q \quad \text{and}$$

$$\frac{U_q - Z_q\left(\hat{w}_{ijkp}, \ \hat{t}\right)}{U_q - L_q} > \frac{U_q - Z_q\left(w^*_{ijkp}, t^*\right)}{U_q - L_q}, \qquad \text{for at least one } q.$$

$$\text{Thus,} \quad \max_q\left(\frac{U_q - Z_q\left(\hat{w}_{ijkp}, \ \hat{t}\right)}{U_q - L_q}\right) > (\ge) \max_q\left(\frac{U_q - Z_q\left(w^*_{ijkp}, t^*\right)}{U_q - L_q}\right).$$

$$\text{Let } \vartheta^* = \max_q\left(\frac{U_q - Z_q\left(w^*_{ijkp}, t^*\right)}{U_q - L_q}\right), \ \text{then} \quad \hat{\vartheta} > (\ge)\vartheta^*.$$

$$\text{Similarly,} \quad \frac{Z_q\left(\hat{w}_{ijkp}, \ \hat{t}\right) - L_q}{U_q - L_q} \le \frac{Z_q\left(w^*_{ijkp}, t^*\right) - L_q}{U_q - L_q}, \qquad \forall\, q = 12, \ldots, Q \quad \text{and}$$

$$\frac{Z_q\left(\hat{w}_{ijkp}, \hat{t}\right) - L_q}{U_q - L_q} < \frac{Z_q\left(w^*_{ijkp}, t^*\right) - L_q}{U_q - L_q}, \qquad \text{for at least one } q.$$

$$\text{Thus,} \quad \min_q \left(\frac{Z_q\left(\hat{w}_{ijkp}, \hat{t}\right) - L_q}{U_q - L_q} \right) \leq (<) \min_q \left(\frac{Z_q\left(w^*_{ijkp}, t^*\right) - L_q}{U_q - L_q} \right).$$

$$\text{Suppose } \gamma^* = \min_q \left(\frac{Z_q\left(w^*_{ijkp}, t^*\right) - L_q}{U_q - L_q} \right), \text{ which means } \quad \hat{\gamma} - \hat{\vartheta} < \gamma^* - \vartheta^*.$$

There is no unique ideal solution. It is an efficient solution of model (33), as it contradicts the truth that $\left(\hat{w}_{ijkp}, \hat{t}, \hat{\gamma}, \hat{\vartheta}\right)$ is the single optimal solution of LMF. □

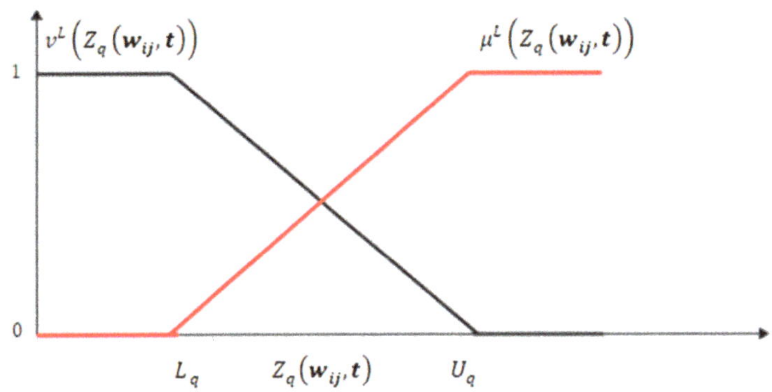

Figure 2. Linear membership and non-membership functions.

5.2. Hyperbolic Membership Function Model

The LMF may not adequately capture decision-making in many real-world situations, as the degree of approval or opposition for a given target may vary non-constantly. Nonlinear membership functions offer a more precise representation of DMs' behavior under certain conditions. Drawing from references [17,20,42], we can express the hyperbolic membership and non-membership function (HMF) (Figure 3) as follows:

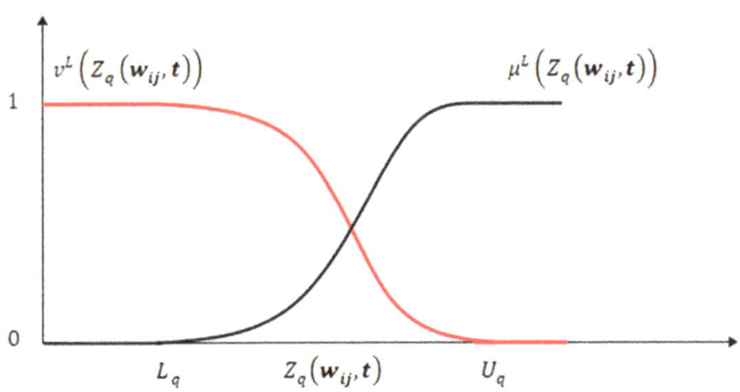

Figure 3. Hyperbolic membership and non-membership functions.

$$\mu^H\left(Z_q\left(w_{ijkp}, t\right)\right) = \begin{cases} 0, & Z_q\left(w_{ijkp}, t\right) \leq L_q, \\ \frac{1}{2}\tanh\left(\alpha_q\left(Z_q\left(w_{ijkp}, t\right) - \frac{U_q + L_q}{2}\right)\right) + \frac{1}{2}, & L_q \leq Z_q\left(w_{ijkp}, t\right) \leq U_q, \\ 1, & Z_q\left(w_{ijkp}, t\right) \geq U_q, \end{cases} \quad (34)$$

$$v^H\left(Z_q\left(w_{ijkp},t\right)\right)=\begin{cases}1, & Z_q\left(w_{ijkp},t\right)\le L_q,\\ \frac{1}{2}\tanh\left(\alpha_q\left(\frac{U_q+L_q}{2}-Z_q\left(w_{ijkp},t\right)\right)\right)+\frac{1}{2}, & L_q\le Z_q\left(w_{ijkp},t\right)\le U_q,\\ 0, & Z_q\left(w_{ijkp},t\right)\ge U_q,\end{cases} \tag{35}$$

where $\alpha_q = \frac{6}{U_q-L_q}, q = 1,2,..,Q$. Let $\gamma = min\left\{\mu^H\left(Z_q\left(w_{ijkp},t\right)\right), q=1,2,\ldots,Q\right\}$ and $\vartheta = max\left\{v^H\left(Z_q\left(w_{ijkp},t\right)\right), q=1,2,\ldots,Q\right\}$. Consequently, we create the crisp model utilizing the HMF as follows:

$$\begin{aligned}
&max\ \ \gamma-\vartheta\\
&subject\ to\\
&\alpha_1\, Z_1\left(w_{ijkp},t\right)-\tanh^{-1}(2\gamma-1)\ge\tfrac{\alpha_1}{2}(U_1+L_1),\\
&\alpha_2\, Z_2\left(w_{ijkp},t\right)-\tanh^{-1}(2\gamma-1)\ge\tfrac{\alpha_2}{2}(U_2+L_2),\\
&\vdots\\
&\alpha_q\, Z_q\left(w_{ijkp},t\right)-\tanh^{-1}(2\gamma-1)\ge\tfrac{\alpha_q}{2}(U_q+L_q),\\
&\alpha_1\, Z_1\left(w_{ijkp},t\right)+\tanh^{-1}(2\vartheta-1)\ge\tfrac{\alpha_1}{2}(U_1+L_1),\\
&\alpha_2\, Z_2\left(w_{ijkp},t\right)+\tanh^{-1}(2\vartheta-1)\ge\tfrac{\alpha_2}{2}(U_2+L_2),\\
&\vdots\\
&\alpha_q\, Z_q\left(w_{ijkp},t\right)+\tanh^{-1}(2\vartheta-1)\ge\tfrac{\alpha_q}{2}(U_q+L_q),\\
&\gamma\ge\vartheta,\quad \gamma+\vartheta\le 1,\qquad \gamma,\vartheta\in[0,\ 1]\\
&w_{ijkp},\ t\ \in \boldsymbol{G}_1
\end{aligned}\tag{36}$$

The HMF exhibits a concave segment at one end and a convex segment at the other. The convex shape typically represents scenarios where the DM requires a higher level of satisfaction margin. Conversely, the concave portion signifies situations where a smaller margin of fulfillment suffices.

The preceding model is comparable to:

$$\begin{aligned}
&max\ \ \delta-\beta\\
&subject\ to\\
&\alpha_1\, Z_1\left(w_{ijkp},t\right)-\delta\ge\tfrac{\alpha_1}{2}(U_1+L_1),\\
&\alpha_2\, Z_2\left(w_{ijkp},t\right)-\delta\ge\tfrac{\alpha_2}{2}(U_2+L_2),\\
&\vdots\\
&\alpha_q\, Z_q\left(w_{ijkp},t\right)-\delta\ge\tfrac{\alpha_q}{2}(U_q+L_q),\\
&\alpha_1\, Z_1\left(w_{ijkp},t\right)+\beta\ge\tfrac{\alpha_1}{2}(U_1+L_1),\\
&\alpha_2\, Z_2\left(w_{ijkp},t\right)+\beta\ge\tfrac{\alpha_2}{2}(U_2+L_2),\\
&\vdots\\
&\alpha_q\, Z_q\left(w_{ijkp},t\right)+\beta\ge\tfrac{\alpha_q}{2}(U_q+L_q),\\
&\delta\ge\beta,\ \ \beta\ge 0,\ \ \delta\ge 0,\ \ \text{and}\ \ \alpha_q=\tfrac{6}{U_q-L_q},\quad q=1,2,\ldots,Q,\\
&w_{ijkp},\ t\ \in \boldsymbol{G}_1
\end{aligned}\tag{37}$$

where $\delta=\tanh^{-1}(2\gamma-1);\beta=\tanh^{-1}(2\vartheta-1)$, as γ and ϑ are proportional to $tanh^{-1}(2\gamma-1)$ and $\tanh^{-1}(2\vartheta-1)$. The aforementioned approach is more applicable to real-world scenarios because it addresses uncertain fractional MOTPs. Additionally, the model keeps costs and non-negative variables, making it applicable in real-world scenarios.

Theorem 4. *A unique optimal solution of the HMF model is an efficient solution of the model (37).*

Proof. Consider $\left(\hat{w}_{ijkp},\ \hat{t},\hat{\gamma},\ \hat{\vartheta}\right)$ the unique optimal solution of HMF. By paradox, postulate that $\left(\hat{w}_{ijkp},\ \hat{t},\hat{\gamma},\ \hat{\vartheta}\right)$ is not an efficient solution to the model (37). Then, there exist $w^*_{ijkp},\quad t^*\left(w^*_{ijkp}\neq\hat{w}_{ijkp}\ and\ t^*\neq\hat{t}\right)$ feasible to model (37), such that

$Z_q\left(\hat{w}_{ijkp}, \hat{t}\right) \leq Z_q\left(w^*_{ijkp}, t^*\right)$; $\forall\, q = 12, \ldots, Q$, and $Z_q\left(\hat{w}_{ijkp}, \hat{t}\right) < Z_q\left(w^*_{ijkp}, t^*\right)$ for a minimum of one q. So,

$$\tanh\left(\alpha_q\left(Z_q\left(w^*_{ijkp}, t^*\right) - \frac{U_q + L_q}{2}\right)\right) \geq \tanh\left(\alpha_q\left(Z_q\left(\hat{w}_{ijkp}, \hat{t}\right) - \frac{U_q + L_q}{2}\right)\right), \quad q = 1, 2, \ldots, Q,$$

$$\tanh\left(\alpha_q\left(Z_q\left(w^*_{ijkp}, t^*\right) - \frac{U_q + L_q}{2}\right)\right) > \tanh\left(\alpha_q\left(Z_q\left(\hat{w}_{ijkp}, \hat{t}\right) - \frac{U_q + L_q}{2}\right)\right), \quad q = 1, 2, \ldots, Q,$$

So,

$$\min_q\left(\tanh\left(\alpha_q\left(Z_q\left(w^*_{ijkp}, t^*\right) - \frac{U_q + L_q}{2}\right)\right)\right) > (\geq) \min_q\left(\tanh\left(\alpha_q\left(Z_q\left(\hat{w}_{ijkp}, \hat{t}\right) - \frac{U_q + L_q}{2}\right)\right)\right).$$

$$\text{If } \gamma^* = \min_q\left(\frac{1}{2}\tanh\left(\alpha_q\left(Z_q\left(w^*_{ijkp}, t^*\right) - \frac{U_q + L_q}{2}\right)\right) + \frac{1}{2}\right), \quad \text{then} \quad \gamma^* > (\geq)\hat{\gamma}.$$

In a similar manner, we obtain

$$\vartheta^* = \max_q\left(\tanh\left(\alpha_q\left(\frac{U_q + L_q}{2} - Z_q\left(w^*_{ijkp}, t^*\right)\right)\right)\right), \quad \text{then} \quad \hat{\vartheta} > (\geq)\vartheta^*.$$

Hence, $\hat{\gamma} - \hat{\vartheta} < \gamma^* - \vartheta^*$. This runs counter to the fact that $\left(\hat{w}_{ijkp}, \hat{t}, \hat{\gamma}, \hat{\vartheta}\right)$ is the unique optimal solution of HMF. □

5.3. Parabolic Membership Function Model

The parabolic membership and non-membership functions (PMF) (Figure 4) are expressed as follows [17,20,42]:

$$\mu^P\left(Z_q\left(w_{ijkp}, t\right)\right) = \begin{cases} 0, & Z_q\left(w_{ijkp}, t\right) \leq L_q, \\ 1 - \left(\frac{U_q - Z_q\left(w_{ijkp}, t\right)}{U_q - L_q}\right)^2, & L_q \leq Z_q\left(w_{ijkp}, t\right) \leq U_q, \\ 1, & Z_q\left(w_{ijkp}, t\right) \geq U_q, \end{cases} \tag{38}$$

$$v^P\left(Z_q\left(w_{ijkp}, t\right)\right) = \begin{cases} 1, & Z_q\left(w_{ijkp}, t\right) \leq L_q, \\ 1 - \left(\frac{Z_q\left(w_{ijkp}, t\right) - L_q}{U_q - L_q}\right)^2, & L_q \leq Z_q\left(w_{ijkp}, t\right) \leq U_q, \\ 0, & Z_q\left(w_{ijkp}, t\right) \geq U_q, \end{cases} \tag{39}$$

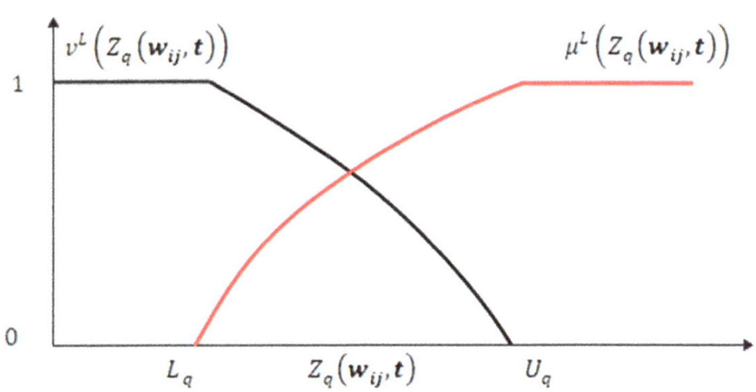

Figure 4. Parabolic membership and non-membership functions.

Let $\gamma = min\left\{\mu^P\left(Z_q\left(\boldsymbol{w_{ijkp}}, \boldsymbol{t}\right)\right), q = 1, 2, \ldots, Q\right\}$ and $\vartheta = max\left\{v^P\left(Z_q\left(\boldsymbol{w_{ijkp}}, \boldsymbol{t}\right)\right), q = 1, 2, \ldots, Q\right\}$. Consequently, we formulate the crisp model utilizing the PMF in accordance with Zimmerman technique [58] as follows:

$$
\begin{aligned}
& max \ \ \gamma - \vartheta \\
& subject\ to \\
& \quad \left(U_1 - Z_1\left(\boldsymbol{w_{ijkp}}, \boldsymbol{t}\right)\right)^2 \leq (1-\gamma)\,(U_1 - L_1)^2 \\
& \quad \left(U_2 - Z_2\left(\boldsymbol{w_{ijkp}}, \boldsymbol{t}\right)\right)^2 \leq (1-\gamma)\,(U_2 - L_2)^2 \\
& \quad \vdots \\
& \quad \left(U_q - Z_q\left(\boldsymbol{w_{ijkp}}, \boldsymbol{t}\right)\right)^2 \leq (1-\gamma)\,(U_q - L_q)^2 \\
& \quad \left(Z_1\left(\boldsymbol{w_{ijkp}}, \boldsymbol{t}\right) - L_1\right)^2 \geq (1-\vartheta)(U_1 - L_1)^2 \\
& \quad \left(Z_2\left(\boldsymbol{w_{ijkp}}, \boldsymbol{t}\right) - L_2\right)^2 \geq (1-\vartheta)(U_2 - L_2)^2 \\
& \quad \vdots \\
& \quad \left(Z_q\left(\boldsymbol{w_{ijkp}}, \boldsymbol{t}\right) - L_q\right)^2 \geq (1-\vartheta)(U_q - L_q)^2 \\
& \quad \gamma \geq \vartheta, \quad \gamma + \vartheta \leq 1, \qquad \gamma, \vartheta \in [0,\ 1] \\
& \quad w_{ijkp}, \ t \ \in \boldsymbol{G_1}
\end{aligned}
\tag{40}
$$

The model described above relies on the PMF, as linear membership and non-membership functions are often inadequate for representing real-world scenarios accurately. Moreover, the model maintains constraints on costs and ensures non-negative variables, thereby enhancing its applicability to real-world problems.

Theorem 5. *A unique optimal solution of the PMF model is an efficient solution of the model (40).*

Proof. Consider $\left(\hat{w}_{ijkp}, \ \hat{t}, \hat{\gamma}, \ \hat{\vartheta}\right)$ the unique optimal solution of PMF. By paradox, assume $\left(\hat{w}_{ijkp}, \ \hat{t}, \hat{\gamma}, \ \hat{\vartheta}\right)$ is not an efficient solution to the model (40). Next, there are $w^*_{ijkp}, \quad t^*\left(w^*_{ijkp} \neq \hat{w}_{ijkp}\ and\ t^* \neq \hat{t}\right)$ feasible to model (40), such that $Z_q\left(\hat{w}_{ijkp}, \ \hat{t}\right) \leq Z_q\left(w^*_{ijkp}, t^*\right); \ \ \forall\, q = 12, \ldots, Q$, and $Z_q\left(\hat{w}_{ijkp}, \ \hat{t}\right) < Z_q\left(w^*_{ijkp}, t^*\right)$ for a minimum of one q. Thus,

$$1 - \left(\frac{U_q - Z_q\left(w^*_{ijkp}, t^*\right)}{U_q - L_q}\right)^2 \geq 1 - \left(\frac{U_q - Z_q\left(\hat{w}_{ijkp}, \ \hat{t}\right)}{U_q - L_q}\right)^2, \qquad q = 1, 2, \ldots, Q,$$

$$1 - \left(\frac{U_q - Z_q\left(w^*_{ijkp}, t^*\right)}{U_q - L_q}\right)^2 > 1 - \left(\frac{U_q - Z_q\left(\hat{w}_{ijkp}, \ \hat{t}\right)}{U_q - L_q}\right)^2, \qquad q = 1, 2, \ldots, Q,$$

$$\min_q\left(1 - \left(\frac{U_q - Z_q\left(w^*_{ijkp}, t^*\right)}{U_q - L_q}\right)^2\right) > (\geq) \min_q\left(1 - \left(\frac{U_q - Z_q\left(\hat{w}_{ijkp}, \ \hat{t}\right)}{U_q - L_q}\right)^2\right).$$

$$\text{If } \gamma^* = \min_q\left(1 - \left(\frac{U_q - Z_q\left(w^*_{ijkp}, t^*\right)}{U_q - L_q}\right)^2\right), \quad \text{then} \ \ \gamma^* > (\geq)\hat{\gamma}.$$

In a similar manner, we obtain

$$\vartheta^* = \max_q\left(1 - \left(\frac{Z_q\left(w^*_{ijkp}, t^*\right) - L_q}{U_q - L_q}\right)^2\right), \ \text{then} \quad \hat{\vartheta} > (\geq)\vartheta^*.$$

Hence, $\hat{\gamma} - \hat{\vartheta} < \gamma^* - \vartheta^*$. This runs counter to the fact that $\left(\hat{w}_{ijkp}, \ \hat{t}, \hat{\gamma}, \ \hat{\vartheta}\right)$ is the unique optimal solution of PMF. □

6. An Algorithm for Solving the FIF-MMSFTM via Various Membership Functions

The following Algorithm 1 describes the FIF-MMSFTM solution procedures as outlined in Section 5:

Algorithm 1: Solving the FIF-MMSFTM via Various Membership Functions

Input: IF parameters
Output: IF solution.

Step 1.	Set up the IF parameter-based issue, referred to as FIF-MMSFTM;
Step 2.	Execute the linearization strategy to obtain FIF-MMSFTM. Model (30)–(34);
Step 3.	Formulate the crisp model (45) using the AF $\Re\left(\overset{\sim I}{Z}_q\left(w_{ijkp}, t\right)\right) q = 1, 2, \ldots, Q,$ and arithmetic operations;
Step 4.	Develop the FGP version of the FIF-MMSFTM as in models (46)–(48);
Step 5.	Use Zimmerman's technique to define and solve the LHF (51). If the DM is fulfilled, proceed to Step 8; Otherwise, proceed to the Following Step;
Step 6.	Evaluate the HMF model (55). If the DM meets their requirements, proceed to Step 8, otherwise advance to the next step;
Step 7.	Go to the following step after resolving the PMF model (58);
Step 8.	End with the acquired IF solution.

7. Numerical Illustration

Consider a TP with 2 origins, 2 destinations, and 2 conveyances between supply and demand. Every parameter was considered as TIFN. Here, the emblems $\overset{\sim I}{a}_{ip}$, $\overset{\sim I}{b}_{jp}$, and $\overset{\sim I}{e}_k$ are employed to indicate the IF power of supply, the IF demand prerequisite, and the IF capacity of transportation, respectively. The details for the FIF-MMSFTP are provided in Tables 3–10.

Table 3. $C_{ijk1}^{(1)}$ profit gained from shipment unit quantity.

i	j		j	
	1	2	1	2
1	$(1,2,4;0,2,6)$	$(2,3,5;1,3,7)$	$(7,9,11;6,9,12)$	$(2,5,7;1,5,8)$
2	$(3,5,8;1,5,10)$	$(4,5,7;2,5,9)$	$(3,5,8;1,5,10)$	$(5,7,9;4,7,12)$
k	1		2	

Table 4. $C_{ijk2}^{(1)}$ profit gained from shipment unit quantity.

i	j		j	
	1	2	1	2
1	$(6,8,10;5,8,12)$	$(4,5,7;2,5,9)$	$(3,5,8;1,5,10)$	$(3,5,8;1,5,10)$
2	$(7,9,11;6,9,12)$	$(2,3,5;1,3,7)$	$(6,8,10;5,8,12)$	$(4,5,7;2,5,9)$
k	1		2	

Table 5. $d_{ijk1}^{(1)}$ the expense per unit of shipment.

i	j		j	
	1	2	1	2
1	$(1,2,3;0,2,4)$	$(2,3,5;1,3,6)$	$(2,3,5;1,3,6)$	$(2,4,6;1,4,7)$
2	$(3,5,6;2,5,7)$	$(1,2,3;0,2,4)$	$(3,5,8;1,5,10)$	$(1,3,5;0,3,6)$
k	1		2	

Table 6. $d_{ijk2}^{(1)}$ the expense per unit of shipment.

i	j		j	
	1	2	1	2
1	(2,3,5;1,3,6)	(1,2,3;0,2,4)	(3,5,8;1,5,10)	(1,3,5;0,3,6)
2	(4,5,6;3,5,7)	(3,5,8;1,5,10)	(1,2,3;0,2,4)	(1,2,3;0,2,4)
k	1		2	

Table 7. $C_{ijk1}^{(2)}$ profit gained from shipment unit quantity.

i	j		j	
	1	2	1	2
1	(3,5,8;1,5,10)	(4,5,7;2,5,9)	(6,8,10;5,8,12)	(3,5,8;1,5,10)
2	(7,9,11;6,9,12)	(7,9,11;6,9,14)	(5,7,9;4,7,12)	(8,10,12;7,10,15)
k	1		2	

Table 8. $C_{ijk2}^{(2)}$ profit gained from shipment unit quantity.

i	j		j	
	1	2	1	2
1	(7,8,9;5,8,10)	(1,3,5;0,3,7)	(3,5,8;1,5,10)	(8,10,12;7,10,13)
2	(6,9,11;5,9,12)	(7,9,11;6,9,14)	(10,11,12;9,11,13)	(1,3,5;0,3,7)
k	1		2	

Table 9. $d_{ijk1}^{(2)}$ the expense per unit of shipment.

i	j		j	
	1	2	1	2
1	(1,2,3;0,2,4)	(2,3,4;1,3,5)	(2,3,4;1,3,5)	(4,5,6;3,5,7)
2	(3,5,7;1,5,8)	(1,2,3;0,2,4)	(3,5,6;2,5,7)	(1,2,3;0,2,4)
k	1		2	

Table 10. $d_{ijk2}^{(2)}$ the expense per unit of shipment.

i	j		j	
	1	2	1	2
1	(2,3,4;1,3,5)	(2,3,4;1,3,5)	(5,6,7;3,5,8)	(1,2,3;0,2,4)
2	(4,5,6;3,5,7)	(1,2,3;0,2,4)	(4,5,6;3,5,7)	(2,3,4;1,3,5)
k	1		2	

$\overset{\sim I}{a}_{11} = (15, 20, 30; 10, 20, 40)$; $\overset{\sim I}{a}_{12} = (5, 18, 25; 1, 18, 28)$; $\overset{\sim I}{a}_{21} = (4, 15, 20; 2, 15, 40)$
$\overset{\sim I}{a}_{22} = (10, 30, 40; 5, 30, 50)$; $\overset{\sim I}{b}_{11} = (1, 8, 12; 0, 8, 14)$; $\overset{\sim I}{b}_{12} = (2, 5, 10; 1, 5, 15)$
$\overset{\sim I}{b}_{21} = (3, 7, 15; 1, 7, 16)$; $\overset{\sim I}{b}_{22} = (4, 8, 10; 2, 8, 12)$; $\overset{\sim I}{e}_{1} = (15, 20, 25; 10, 20, 30)$
$\overset{\sim I}{e}_{1} = (18, 25, 30; 15, 25, 40)$

Solution: First, predicated on the suggested modification $\overset{\sim I}{w} = \overset{\sim I}{t}\overset{\sim I}{x}$, the FIF-MMSFTM is transformed into the FIF-MMSTM as follows:

$$
\begin{aligned}
max\ \overset{\sim I}{Z}_1\left(\overset{\sim I}{w},\overset{\sim I}{t}\right) = {} & \overset{\sim I(1)}{c}_{1111}\overset{\sim I}{w}_{1111} + \overset{\sim I(1)}{c}_{1211}\overset{\sim I}{w}_{1211} + \overset{\sim I(1)}{c}_{2111}\overset{\sim I}{w}_{2111} + \overset{\sim I(1)}{c}_{2211}\overset{\sim I}{w}_{2211} \\
& + \overset{\sim I(1)}{c}_{1121}\overset{\sim I}{w}_{1121} + \overset{\sim I(1)}{c}_{1221}\overset{\sim I}{w}_{1221} + \overset{\sim I(1)}{c}_{2121}\overset{\sim I}{w}_{2121} + \overset{\sim I(1)}{c}_{2221}\overset{\sim I}{w}_{2221} + \overset{\sim I(1)}{c}_{1112}\overset{\sim I}{w}_{1112} \\
& + \overset{\sim I(1)}{c}_{1212}\overset{\sim I}{w}_{1212} + \overset{\sim I(1)}{c}_{2112}\overset{\sim I}{w}_{2112} + \overset{\sim I(1)}{c}_{2212}\overset{\sim I}{w}_{2212} + \overset{\sim I(1)}{c}_{1122}\overset{\sim I}{w}_{1122} + \overset{\sim I(1)}{c}_{1222}\overset{\sim I}{w}_{1222} \\
& + \overset{\sim I(1)}{c}_{2122}\overset{\sim I}{w}_{2122} + \overset{\sim I(1)}{c}_{2222}\overset{\sim I}{w}_{2222} + \overset{\sim I(1)}{\alpha_0}\overset{\sim I}{t},
\end{aligned}
$$

$$
\begin{aligned}
max\ \overset{\sim I}{Z}_2\left(\overset{\sim I}{w},\overset{\sim I}{t}\right) = {} & \overset{\sim I(2)}{c}_{1111}\overset{\sim I}{w}_{1111} + \overset{\sim I(2)}{c}_{1211}\overset{\sim I}{w}_{1211} + \overset{\sim I(2)}{c}_{2111}\overset{\sim I}{w}_{2111} + \overset{\sim I(2)}{c}_{2211}\overset{\sim I}{w}_{2211} \\
& + \overset{\sim I(2)}{c}_{1121}\overset{\sim I}{w}_{1121} + \overset{\sim I(2)}{c}_{1221}\overset{\sim I}{w}_{1221} + \overset{\sim I(2)}{c}_{2121}\overset{\sim I}{w}_{2121} + \overset{\sim I(2)}{c}_{2221}\overset{\sim I}{w}_{2221} + \overset{\sim I(2)}{c}_{1112}\overset{\sim I}{w}_{1112} \\
& + \overset{\sim I(2)}{c}_{1212}\overset{\sim I}{w}_{1212} + \overset{\sim I(2)}{c}_{2112}\overset{\sim I}{w}_{2112} + \overset{\sim I(2)}{c}_{2212}\overset{\sim I}{w}_{2212} + \overset{\sim I(2)}{c}_{1122}\overset{\sim I}{w}_{1122} + \overset{\sim I(2)}{c}_{1222}\overset{\sim I}{w}_{1222} \\
& + \overset{\sim I(2)}{c}_{2122}\overset{\sim I}{w}_{2122} + \overset{\sim I(2)}{c}_{2222}\overset{\sim I}{w}_{2222} + \overset{\sim I(2)}{\alpha_0}\overset{\sim I}{t},
\end{aligned}
$$

Subject to

$$
\begin{aligned}
& \overset{\sim I(1)}{d}_{1111}\overset{\sim I}{w}_{1111} + \overset{\sim I(1)}{d}_{1211}\overset{\sim I}{w}_{1211} + \overset{\sim I(1)}{d}_{2111}\overset{\sim I}{w}_{2111} + \overset{\sim I(1)}{d}_{2211}\overset{\sim I}{w}_{2211} + \overset{\sim I(1)}{d}_{1121}\overset{\sim I}{w}_{1121} + \overset{\sim I(1)}{d}_{1221}\overset{\sim I}{w}_{1221} \\
& + \overset{\sim I(1)}{d}_{2121}\overset{\sim I}{w}_{2121} + \overset{\sim I(1)}{d}_{2221}\overset{\sim I}{w}_{2221} + \overset{\sim I(1)}{d}_{1112}\overset{\sim I}{w}_{1112} + \overset{\sim I(1)}{d}_{1212}\overset{\sim I}{w}_{1212} + \overset{\sim I(1)}{d}_{2112}\overset{\sim I}{w}_{2112} + \overset{\sim I(1)}{d}_{2212}\overset{\sim I}{w}_{2212} \\
& + \overset{\sim I(1)}{d}_{1122}\overset{\sim I}{w}_{1122} + \overset{\sim I(1)}{d}_{1222}\overset{\sim I}{w}_{1222} + \overset{\sim I(1)}{d}_{2122}\overset{\sim I}{w}_{2122} + \overset{I(1)}{d}_{2222}\overset{\sim I}{w}_{2222} + \overset{\sim I(1)}{\beta_0}\overset{\sim I}{t} \le 1,
\end{aligned}
$$

$$
\begin{aligned}
& \overset{\sim I(2)}{d}_{1111}\overset{\sim I}{w}_{1111} + \overset{\sim I(2)}{d}_{1211}\overset{\sim I}{w}_{1211} + \overset{\sim I(2)}{d}_{2111}\overset{\sim I}{w}_{2111} + \overset{\sim I(2)}{d}_{2211}\overset{\sim I}{w}_{2211} + \overset{\sim I(2)}{d}_{1121}\overset{\sim I}{w}_{1121} + \overset{\sim I(2)}{d}_{1221}\overset{\sim I}{w}_{1221} \\
& + \overset{\sim I(2)}{d}_{2121}\overset{\sim I}{w}_{2121} + \overset{\sim I(2)}{d}_{2221}\overset{\sim I}{w}_{2221} + \overset{\sim I(2)}{d}_{1112}\overset{\sim I}{w}_{1112} + \overset{\sim I(2)}{d}_{1212}\overset{\sim I}{w}_{1212} + \overset{\sim I(2)}{d}_{2112}\overset{\sim I}{w}_{2112} + \overset{\sim I(2)}{d}_{2212}\overset{\sim I}{w}_{2212} \\
& + \overset{\sim I(2)}{d}_{1122}\overset{\sim I}{w}_{1122} + \overset{\sim I(2)}{d}_{1222}\overset{\sim I}{w}_{1222} + \overset{\sim I(2)}{d}_{2122}\overset{\sim I}{w}_{2122} + \overset{I(2)}{d}_{2222}\overset{\sim I}{w}_{2222} + \overset{\sim I(2)}{\beta_0}\overset{\sim I}{t} \le 1,
\end{aligned}
$$

$$
\begin{aligned}
& \overset{\sim I}{w}_{1111} + \overset{\sim I}{w}_{1121} + \overset{\sim I}{w}_{1211} + \overset{\sim I}{w}_{1221} - \overset{\sim I}{a}_{11}\overset{\sim I}{t} \le \overset{\sim I}{0} \\
& \overset{\sim I}{w}_{1112} + \overset{\sim I}{w}_{1122} + \overset{\sim I}{w}_{1212} + \overset{\sim I}{w}_{1222} - \overset{\sim I}{a}_{12}\overset{\sim I}{t} \le \overset{\sim I}{0} \\
& \overset{\sim I}{w}_{2111} + \overset{\sim I}{w}_{2121} + \overset{\sim I}{w}_{2211} + \overset{\sim I}{w}_{2221} - \overset{\sim I}{a}_{21}\overset{\sim I}{t} \le \overset{\sim I}{0} \\
& \overset{\sim I}{w}_{2112} + \overset{\sim I}{w}_{2122} + \overset{\sim I}{w}_{2212} + \overset{\sim I}{w}_{2222} - \overset{\sim I}{a}_{22}\overset{\sim I}{t} \le \overset{\sim I}{0} \\
& \overset{\sim I}{w}_{1111} + \overset{\sim I}{w}_{1112} + \overset{\sim I}{w}_{2111} + \overset{\sim I}{w}_{2112} - \overset{\sim I}{b}_{11}\overset{\sim I}{t} \ge \overset{\sim I}{0} \\
& \overset{\sim I}{w}_{1121} + \overset{\sim I}{w}_{1122} + \overset{\sim I}{w}_{2121} + \overset{\sim I}{w}_{2122} - \overset{\sim I}{b}_{12}\overset{\sim I}{t} \ge \overset{\sim I}{0} \\
& \overset{\sim I}{w}_{1211} + \overset{\sim I}{w}_{1212} + \overset{\sim I}{w}_{2211} + \overset{\sim I}{w}_{2212} - \overset{\sim I}{b}_{21}\overset{\sim I}{t} \ge \overset{\sim I}{0} \\
& \overset{\sim I}{w}_{1221} + \overset{\sim I}{w}_{1222} + \overset{\sim I}{w}_{2221} + \overset{\sim I}{w}_{2222} - \overset{\sim I}{b}_{22}\overset{\sim I}{t} \ge \overset{\sim I}{0} \\
& \overset{\sim I}{w}_{1111} + \overset{\sim I}{w}_{1211} + \overset{\sim I}{w}_{2111} + \overset{\sim I}{w}_{2211} + \overset{\sim I}{w}_{1112} + \overset{\sim I}{w}_{1212} + \overset{\sim I}{w}_{2112} + \overset{\sim I}{w}_{2212} - \overset{\sim I}{e}_{1}\overset{\sim I}{t} \le \overset{\sim I}{0} \\
& \overset{\sim I}{w}_{1121} + \overset{\sim I}{w}_{1221} + \overset{\sim I}{w}_{2121} + \overset{\sim I}{w}_{2221} + \overset{\sim I}{w}_{1122} + \overset{\sim I}{w}_{1222} + \overset{\sim I}{w}_{2122} + \overset{\sim I}{w}_{2222} - \overset{\sim I}{e}_{2}\overset{\sim I}{t} \le \overset{\sim I}{0} \\
& \overset{\sim I}{w}_{ijkp} \ge \overset{\sim I}{0}, \quad \forall\, i,j,k,p; \quad \overset{\sim I}{t} > \overset{\sim I}{0},
\end{aligned}
$$

Then, the crisp model was obtained by applying the AF, ordering relation and arithmetic operations as follows:

$$max\ \Re\left(\tilde{Z}_1^{I}\left(w_{ijkp},\ t\right)\right) = \frac{1}{8}\left[\begin{array}{l}
w^{1}_{1111} + 4w^{2}_{1111} + 4w^{3}_{1111} + 0w^{\prime 1}_{1111} + 4w^{\prime 2}_{1111} + 6w^{\prime 3}_{1111} + 2w^{1}_{1211} + 6w^{2}_{1211} + 5w^{3}_{1211} \\
+w^{\prime 1}_{1211} + 6w^{\prime 2}_{1211} + 7w^{\prime 3}_{1211} + 3w^{1}_{2111} + 10w^{2}_{2111} + 8w^{3}_{2111} + w^{\prime 1}_{2111} + 10w^{\prime 2}_{2111} + 10w^{\prime 3}_{2111} \\
+4w^{1}_{2211} + 10w^{2}_{2211} + 7w^{3}_{2211} + 2w^{\prime 1}_{2211} + 10w^{\prime 2}_{2211} + 9w^{\prime 3}_{2211} + 7w^{1}_{1121} + 18w^{2}_{1121} \\
+11w^{3}_{1121} + 6w^{\prime 1}_{1121} + 18w^{\prime 2}_{1121} + 12w^{\prime 3}_{1121} + 2w^{1}_{1221} + 10w^{2}_{1221} + 7w^{3}_{1221} + w^{\prime 1}_{1221} \\
+10w^{\prime 2}_{1221} + 8w^{\prime 3}_{1221} + 3w^{1}_{2121} + 10w^{2}_{2121} + 8w^{3}_{2121} + w^{\prime 1}_{2121} + 10w^{\prime 2}_{2121} + 10w^{\prime 3}_{2121} \\
+5w^{1}_{2221} + 14w^{2}_{2221} + 9w^{3}_{2221} + 4w^{\prime 1}_{2221} + 14w^{\prime 2}_{2221} + 12w^{\prime 3}_{2221} 6w^{1}_{1112} + 16w^{2}_{1112} + 10w^{3}_{1112} \\
+5w^{\prime 1}_{1112} + 16w^{\prime 2}_{1112} + 12w^{\prime 3}_{1112} + 4w^{1}_{1212} + 10w^{2}_{1212} + 7w^{3}_{1212} + 2w^{\prime 1}_{1212} + 10w^{\prime 2}_{1212} + 9w^{\prime 3}_{1212} \\
+7w^{1}_{2112} + 18w^{2}_{2112} + 11w^{3}_{2112} + 6w^{\prime 1}_{2112} + 18w^{\prime 2}_{2112} + 12w^{\prime 3}_{2112} + 2w^{1}_{2212} + 6w^{2}_{2212} + 5w^{3}_{2212} \\
+1w^{\prime 1}_{2212} + 6w^{\prime 2}_{2212} + 7w^{\prime 3}_{2212} + 3w^{1}_{1122} + 10w^{2}_{1122} + 8w^{3}_{1122} + w^{\prime 1}_{1122} + 10w^{\prime 2}_{1122} + 10w^{\prime 3}_{1122} \\
+3w^{1}_{1222} + 10w^{2}_{1222} + 8w^{3}_{1222} + w^{\prime 1}_{1222} + 10w^{\prime 2}_{1222} + 10w^{\prime 3}_{1222} + 6w^{1}_{2122} + 16w^{2}_{2122} + 10w^{3}_{2122} \\
+5w^{\prime 1}_{2122} + 16w^{\prime 2}_{2122} + 12w^{\prime 3}_{2122} + 4w^{1}_{2222} + 10w^{2}_{2222} + 7w^{3}_{2222} + 2w^{\prime 1}_{2222} + 10w^{\prime 2}_{2222} + 9w^{\prime 3}_{2222} \\
+150t^{1} + 200t^{2} + 250t^{3} + 100t^{\prime 1} + 200t^{\prime 2} + 300t^{\prime 3}
\end{array}\right]$$

$$max\ \Re\left(\tilde{Z}_2^{I}\left(w_{ijkp},\ t\right)\right) = \frac{1}{8}\left[\begin{array}{l}
3w^{1}_{1111} + 10w^{2}_{1111} + 8w^{3}_{1111} + w^{\prime 1}_{1111} + 10w^{\prime 2}_{1111} + 10w^{\prime 3}_{1111} + 4w^{1}_{1211} + 10w^{2}_{1211} + 7w^{3}_{1211} \\
+2w^{\prime 1}_{1211} + 10w^{\prime 2}_{1211} + 9w^{\prime 3}_{1211} + 7w^{1}_{2111} + 18w^{2}_{2111} + 11w^{3}_{2111} + 6w^{\prime 1}_{2111} + 18w^{\prime 2}_{2111} + 12w^{\prime 3}_{2111} \\
+7w^{1}_{2211} + 18w^{2}_{2211} + 11w^{3}_{2211} + 6w^{\prime 1}_{2211} + 18w^{\prime 2}_{2211} + 14w^{\prime 3}_{2211} + 6w^{1}_{1121} + 16w^{2}_{1121} \\
+10w^{3}_{1121} + 5w^{\prime 1}_{1121} + 16w^{\prime 2}_{1121} + 12w^{\prime 3}_{1121} + 3w^{1}_{1221} + 10w^{2}_{1221} + 8w^{3}_{1221} + w^{\prime 1}_{1221} \\
+10w^{\prime 2}_{1221} + 10w^{\prime 3}_{1221} + 5w^{1}_{2121} + 14w^{2}_{2121} + 9w^{3}_{2121} + 4w^{\prime 1}_{2121} + 14w^{\prime 2}_{2121} + 12w^{\prime 3}_{2121} \\
+8w^{1}_{2221} + 20w^{2}_{2221} + 12w^{3}_{2221} + 7w^{\prime 1}_{2221} + 20w^{\prime 2}_{2221} + 15w^{\prime 3}_{2221} + 7w^{1}_{1112} + 16w^{2}_{1112} + 9w^{3}_{1112} \\
+5w^{\prime 1}_{1112} + 16w^{\prime 2}_{1112} + 10w^{\prime 3}_{1112} + w^{1}_{1212} + 6w^{2}_{1212} + 5w^{3}_{1212} + 0w^{\prime 1}_{1212} + 6w^{\prime 2}_{1212} + 7w^{\prime 3}_{1212} \\
+6w^{1}_{2112} + 18w^{2}_{2112} + 11w^{3}_{2112} + 5w^{\prime 1}_{2112} + 18w^{\prime 2}_{2112} + 12w^{\prime 3}_{2112} + 7w^{1}_{2212} + 18w^{2}_{2212} + 11w^{3}_{2212} \\
+6w^{\prime 1}_{2212} + 18w^{\prime 2}_{2212} + 14w^{\prime 3}_{2212} + 3w^{1}_{1122} + 10w^{2}_{1122} + 8w^{3}_{1122} + w^{\prime 1}_{1122} + 10w^{\prime 2}_{1122} + 10w^{\prime 3}_{1122} \\
+8w^{1}_{1222} + 20w^{2}_{1222} + 12w^{3}_{1222} + 7w^{\prime 1}_{1222} + 20w^{\prime 2}_{1222} + 13w^{\prime 3}_{1222} + 10w^{1}_{2122} + 22w^{2}_{2122} + 12w^{3}_{2122} \\
+9w^{\prime 1}_{2122} + 22w^{\prime 2}_{2122} + 13w^{\prime 3}_{2122} + w^{1}_{2222} + 6w^{2}_{2222} + 5w^{3}_{2222} + 0w^{\prime 1}_{2222} + 6w^{\prime 2}_{2222} + 7w^{\prime 3}_{2222} \\
+250t^{1} + 300t^{2} + 350t^{3} + 200t^{\prime 1} + 300t^{\prime 2} + 400t^{\prime 3}
\end{array}\right]$$

Subject to

$$\frac{1}{8}\left[\begin{array}{l}
w^{1}_{1111} + 4w^{2}_{1111} + 3w^{3}_{1111} + 0w^{\prime 1}_{1111} + 4w^{\prime 2}_{1111} + 4w^{\prime 3}_{1111} + 2w^{1}_{1211} + 6w^{2}_{1211} + 5w^{3}_{1211} \\
+w^{\prime 1}_{1211} + 6w^{\prime 2}_{1211} + 6w^{\prime 3}_{1211} + 3w^{1}_{2111} + 10w^{2}_{2111} + 6w^{3}_{2111} + 2w^{\prime 1}_{2111} + 10w^{\prime 2}_{2111} + 7w^{\prime 3}_{2111} \\
+w^{1}_{2211} + 4w^{2}_{2211} + 3w^{3}_{2211} + 0w^{\prime 1}_{2211} + 4w^{\prime 2}_{2211} + 4w^{\prime 3}_{2211} + 2w^{1}_{1121} + 6w^{2}_{1121} \\
+5w^{3}_{1121} + w^{\prime 1}_{1121} + 6w^{\prime 2}_{1121} + 6w^{\prime 3}_{1121} + 2w^{1}_{1221} + 8w^{2}_{1221} + 6w^{3}_{1221} + w^{\prime 1}_{1221} \\
+8w^{\prime 2}_{1221} + 7w^{\prime 3}_{1221} + 3w^{1}_{2121} + 10w^{2}_{2121} + 8w^{3}_{2121} + w^{\prime 1}_{2121} + 10w^{\prime 2}_{2121} + 10w^{\prime 3}_{2121} \\
+w^{1}_{2221} + 6w^{2}_{2221} + 5w^{3}_{2221} + 0w^{\prime 1}_{2221} + 6w^{\prime 2}_{2221} + 6w^{\prime 3}_{2221} + 2w^{1}_{1112} + 6w^{2}_{1112} + 5w^{3}_{1112} \\
+w^{\prime 1}_{1112} + 6w^{\prime 2}_{1112} + 6w^{\prime 3}_{1112} + w^{1}_{1212} + 4w^{2}_{1212} + 3w^{3}_{1212} + 0w^{\prime 1}_{1212} + 4w^{\prime 2}_{1212} + 4w^{\prime 3}_{1212} \\
+4w^{1}_{2112} + 10w^{2}_{2112} + 6w^{3}_{2112} + 3w^{\prime 1}_{2112} + 10w^{\prime 2}_{2112} + 7w^{\prime 3}_{2112} + 3w^{1}_{2212} + 10w^{2}_{2212} + 8w^{3}_{2212} \\
+1w^{\prime 1}_{2212} + 10w^{\prime 2}_{2212} + 10w^{\prime 3}_{2212} + 3w^{1}_{1122} + 10w^{2}_{1122} + 8w^{3}_{1122} + w^{\prime 1}_{1122} + 10w^{\prime 2}_{1122} + 10w^{\prime 3}_{1122} \\
+w^{1}_{1222} + 6w^{2}_{1222} + 5w^{3}_{1222} + 0w^{\prime 1}_{1222} + 6w^{\prime 2}_{1222} + 6w^{\prime 3}_{1222} + w^{1}_{2122} + 4w^{2}_{2122} + 3w^{3}_{2122} \\
+0w^{\prime 1}_{2122} + 4w^{\prime 2}_{2122} + 4w^{\prime 3}_{2122} + w^{1}_{2222} + 4w^{2}_{2222} + 3w^{3}_{2222} + 0w^{\prime 1}_{2222} + 4w^{\prime 2}_{2222} + 4w^{\prime 3}_{2222} \\
+50t^{1} + 100t^{2} + 150t^{3} + 20t^{\prime 1} + 100t^{\prime 2} + 200t^{\prime 3}
\end{array}\right] \leq 1$$

$$\frac{1}{8}\left[\begin{array}{l}
w^{1}_{1111} + 4w^{2}_{1111} + 3w^{3}_{1111} + 0w^{\prime 1}_{1111} + 4w^{\prime 2}_{1111} + 4w^{\prime 3}_{1111} + 2w^{1}_{1211} + 6w^{2}_{1211} + 4w^{3}_{1211} \\
+w^{\prime 1}_{1211} + 6w^{\prime 2}_{1211} + 5w^{\prime 3}_{1211} + 3w^{1}_{2111} + 10w^{2}_{2111} + 7w^{3}_{2111} + w^{\prime 1}_{2111} + 10w^{\prime 2}_{2111} + 8w^{\prime 3}_{2111} \\
+w^{1}_{2211} + 4w^{2}_{2211} + 3w^{3}_{2211} + 0w^{\prime 1}_{2211} + 4w^{\prime 2}_{2211} + 4w^{\prime 3}_{2211} + 2w^{1}_{1121} + 6w^{2}_{1121} \\
+4w^{3}_{1121} + w^{\prime 1}_{1121} + 6w^{\prime 2}_{1121} + 5w^{\prime 3}_{1121} + 4w^{1}_{1221} + 10w^{2}_{1221} + 6w^{3}_{1221} + 3w^{\prime 1}_{1221} \\
+10w^{\prime 2}_{1221} + 7w^{\prime 3}_{1221} + 3w^{1}_{2121} + 10w^{2}_{2121} + 6w^{3}_{2121} + 2w^{\prime 1}_{2121} + 10w^{\prime 2}_{2121} + 7w^{\prime 3}_{2121} \\
+w^{1}_{2221} + 4w^{2}_{2221} + 3w^{3}_{2221} + 0w^{\prime 1}_{2221} + 4w^{\prime 2}_{2221} + 4w^{\prime 3}_{2221} + 2w^{1}_{1112} + 6w^{2}_{1112} + 4w^{3}_{1112} \\
+w^{\prime 1}_{1112} + 6w^{\prime 2}_{1112} + 5w^{\prime 3}_{1112} + 2w^{1}_{1212} + 6w^{2}_{1212} + 4w^{3}_{1212} + w^{\prime 1}_{1212} + 6w^{\prime 2}_{1212} + 5w^{\prime 3}_{1212} \\
+4w^{1}_{2112} + 10w^{2}_{2112} + 6w^{3}_{2112} + 3w^{\prime 1}_{2112} + 10w^{\prime 2}_{2112} + 7w^{\prime 3}_{2112} + w^{1}_{2212} + 4w^{2}_{2212} + 3w^{3}_{2212} \\
+0w^{\prime 1}_{2212} + 4w^{\prime 2}_{2212} + 4w^{\prime 3}_{2212} + 5w^{1}_{1122} + 12w^{2}_{1122} + 7w^{3}_{1122} + 3w^{\prime 1}_{1122} + 12w^{\prime 2}_{1122} + 8w^{\prime 3}_{1122} \\
+w^{1}_{1222} + 4w^{2}_{1222} + 3w^{3}_{1222} + 0w^{\prime 1}_{1222} + 4w^{\prime 2}_{1222} + 4w^{\prime 3}_{1222} + 4w^{1}_{2122} + 10w^{2}_{2122} + 6w^{3}_{2122} \\
+3w^{\prime 1}_{2122} + 10w^{\prime 2}_{2122} + 7w^{\prime 3}_{2122} + 2w^{1}_{2222} + 6w^{2}_{2222} + 4w^{3}_{2222} + w^{\prime 1}_{2222} + 6w^{\prime 2}_{2222} + 5w^{\prime 3}_{2222} \\
+150t^{1} + 200t^{2} + 250t^{3} + 100t^{\prime 1} + 200t^{\prime 2} + 300t^{\prime 3}
\end{array}\right] \leq 1$$

$$\left[\begin{array}{l}
w^{1}_{1111} + 2w^{2}_{1111} + w^{3}_{1111} + w^{\prime 1}_{1111} + 2w^{\prime 2}_{1111} + w^{\prime 3}_{1111} + w^{1}_{1121} + 2w^{2}_{1121} + w^{3}_{1121} + w^{\prime 1}_{1121} \\
+2w^{\prime 2}_{1121} + w^{\prime 3}_{1121} + w^{1}_{1211} + 2w^{2}_{1211} + w^{3}_{1211} + w^{\prime 1}_{1211} + 2w^{\prime 2}_{1211} + w^{\prime 3}_{1211} + w^{1}_{1221} + 2w^{2}_{1221} \\
+w^{3}_{1221} + w^{\prime 1}_{1221} + 2w^{\prime 2}_{1221} + w^{\prime 3}_{1221} - 15t^{1} - 40t^{2} - 30t^{3} - 10t^{\prime 1} - 40t^{\prime 2} - 40t^{\prime 3}
\end{array}\right] \leq 0$$

$$\left[\begin{array}{l}
w^{1}_{1112} + 2w^{2}_{1112} + w^{3}_{1112} + w^{\prime 1}_{1112} + 2w^{\prime 2}_{1112} + w^{\prime 3}_{1112} + w^{1}_{1122} + 2w^{2}_{1122} + w^{3}_{1122} + w^{\prime 1}_{1122} \\
+2w^{\prime 2}_{1122} + w^{\prime 3}_{1122} + w^{1}_{1212} + 2w^{2}_{1212} + w^{3}_{1212} + w^{\prime 1}_{1212} + 2w^{\prime 2}_{1212} + w^{\prime 3}_{1212} + w^{1}_{1222} + 2w^{2}_{1222} \\
+w^{3}_{1222} + w^{\prime 1}_{1222} + 2w^{\prime 2}_{1222} + w^{\prime 3}_{1222} - 5t^{1} - 36t^{2} - 25t^{3} - 1t^{\prime 1} - 36t^{\prime 2} - 28t^{\prime 3}
\end{array}\right] \leq 0$$

$$\begin{bmatrix} w^1_{2111} + 2w^2_{2111} + w^3_{2111} + w'^1_{2111} + 2w'^2_{2111} + w'^3_{2111} + w^1_{2121} + 2w^2_{2121} + w^3_{2121} + w'^1_{2121} \\ +2w'^2_{2121} + w'^3_{2121} + w^1_{2211} + 2w^2_{2211} + w^3_{2211} + w'^1_{2211} + 2w'^2_{2211} + w'^3_{2211} + w^1_{2221} + 2w^2_{2221} \\ +w^3_{2221} + w'^1_{2221} + 2w'^2_{2221} + w'^3_{2221} - 4t^1 - 30t^2 - 20t^3 - 2t'^1 - 30t'^2 - 40t'^3 \end{bmatrix} \leq 0$$

$$\begin{bmatrix} w^1_{2112} + 2w^2_{2112} + w^3_{2112} + w'^1_{2112} + 2w'^2_{2112} + w'^3_{2112} + w^1_{2122} + 2w^2_{2122} + w^3_{2122} + w'^1_{2122} \\ +2w'^2_{2122} + w'^3_{2122} + w^1_{2212} + 2w^2_{2212} + w^3_{2212} + w'^1_{2212} + 2w'^2_{2212} + w'^3_{2212} + w^1_{2222} + 2w^2_{2222} \\ +w^3_{2222} + w'^1_{2222} + 2w'^2_{2222} + w'^3_{2222} - 10t^1 - 60t^2 - 40t^3 - 5t'^1 - 60t'^2 - 50t'^3 \end{bmatrix} \leq 0$$

$$\begin{bmatrix} w^1_{1111} + 2w^2_{1111} + w^3_{1111} + w'^1_{1111} + 2w'^2_{1111} + w'^3_{1111} + w^1_{1121} + 2w^2_{1121} + w^3_{1121} + w'^1_{1121} \\ +2w'^2_{1121} + w'^3_{1121} + w^1_{2111} + 2w^2_{2111} + w^3_{2111} + w'^1_{2111} + 2w'^2_{2111} + w'^3_{2111} + w^1_{2121} + 2w^2_{2121} \\ +w^3_{2121} + w'^1_{2121} + 2w'^2_{2121} + w'^3_{2121} - 1t^1 - 16t^2 - 12t^3 - 0t'^1 - 16t'^2 - 14t'^3 \end{bmatrix} \geq 0$$

$$\begin{bmatrix} w^1_{1112} + 2w^2_{1112} + w^3_{1112} + w'^1_{1112} + 2w'^2_{1112} + w'^3_{1112} + w^1_{1122} + 2w^2_{1122} + w^3_{1122} + w'^1_{1122} \\ +2w'^2_{1122} + w'^3_{1122} + w^1_{2112} + 2w^2_{2112} + w^3_{2112} + w'^1_{2112} + 2w'^2_{2112} + w'^3_{2112} + w^1_{2122} + 2w^2_{2122} \\ +w^3_{2122} + w'^1_{2122} + 2w'^2_{2122} + w'^3_{2122} - 2t^1 - 10t^2 - 10t^3 - 1t'^1 - 10t'^2 - 15t'^3 \end{bmatrix} \geq 0$$

$$\begin{bmatrix} w^1_{1211} + 2w^2_{1211} + w^3_{1211} + w'^1_{1211} + 2w'^2_{1211} + w'^3_{1211} + w^1_{1221} + 2w^2_{1221} + w^3_{1221} + w'^1_{1221} \\ +2w'^2_{1221} + w'^3_{1221} + w^1_{2211} + 2w^2_{2211} + w^3_{2211} + w'^1_{2211} + 2w'^2_{2211} + w'^3_{2211} + w^1_{2221} + 2w^2_{2221} \\ +w^3_{2221} + w'^1_{2221} + 2w'^2_{2221} + w'^3_{2221} - 3t^1 - 14t^2 - 15t^3 - 1t'^1 - 14t'^2 - 16t'^3 \end{bmatrix} \geq 0$$

$$\begin{bmatrix} w^1_{1212} + 2w^2_{1212} + w^3_{1212} + w'^1_{1212} + 2w'^2_{1212} + w'^3_{1212} + w^1_{1222} + 2w^2_{1222} + w^3_{1222} + w'^1_{1222} \\ +2w'^2_{1222} + w'^3_{1222} + w^1_{2212} + 2w^2_{2212} + w^3_{2212} + w'^1_{2212} + 2w'^2_{2212} + w'^3_{2212} + w^1_{2222} + 2w^2_{2222} \\ +w^3_{2222} + w'^1_{2222} + 2w'^2_{2222} + w'^3_{2222} - 4t^1 - 16t^2 - 10t^3 - 2t'^1 - 16t'^2 - 12t'^3 \end{bmatrix} \geq 0$$

$$\begin{bmatrix} w^1_{1111} + 2w^2_{1111} + w^3_{1111} + w'^1_{1111} + 2w'^2_{1111} + w'^3_{1111} + w^1_{1211} + 2w^2_{1211} + w^3_{1211} + w'^1_{1211} + 2w'^2_{1211} \\ +w'^3_{1211} + w^1_{2111} + 2w^2_{2111} + w^3_{2111} + w'^1_{2111} + 2w'^2_{2111} + w'^3_{2111} + w^1_{2211} + 2w^2_{2211} + w^3_{2211} + w'^1_{2211} \\ +2w'^2_{2211} + w'^3_{2211} + w^1_{1112} + 2w^2_{1112} + w^3_{1112} + w'^1_{1112} + 2w'^2_{1112} + w'^3_{1112} + w^1_{1212} + 2w^2_{1212} + w^3_{1212} \\ +w'^1_{1212} + 2w'^2_{1212} + w'^3_{1212} + w^1_{2112} + 2w^2_{2112} + w^3_{2112} + w'^1_{2112} + 2w'^2_{2112} + w'^3_{2112} + w^1_{2212} + 2w^2_{2212} \\ +w^3_{2212} + w'^1_{2212} + 2w'^2_{2212} + w'^3_{2212} - 15t^1 - 40t^2 - 25t^3 - 10t'^1 - 40t'^2 - 30t'^3 \end{bmatrix} \leq 0$$

$$\begin{bmatrix} w^1_{1121} + 2w^2_{1121} + w^3_{1121} + w'^1_{1121} + 2w'^2_{1121} + w'^3_{1121} + w^1_{1221} + 2w^2_{1221} + w^3_{1221} + w'^1_{1221} + 2w'^2_{1221} \\ +w'^3_{1221} + w^1_{2121} + 2w^2_{2121} + w^3_{2121} + w'^1_{2121} + 2w'^2_{2121} + w'^3_{2121} + w^1_{2221} + 2w^2_{2221} + w^3_{2221} + w'^1_{2221} \\ +2w'^2_{2221} + w'^3_{2221} + w^1_{1122} + 2w^2_{1122} + w^3_{1122} + w'^1_{1122} + 2w'^2_{1122} + w'^3_{1122} + w^1_{1222} + 2w^2_{1222} + w^3_{1222} \\ +w'^1_{1222} + 2w'^2_{1222} + w'^3_{1222} + w^1_{2122} + 2w^2_{2122} + w^3_{2122} + w'^1_{2122} + 2w'^2_{2122} + w'^3_{2122} + w^1_{2222} + 2w^2_{2222} \\ +w^3_{2222} + w'^1_{2222} + 2w'^2_{2222} + w'^3_{2222} - 18t^1 - 50t^2 - 30t^3 - 15t'^1 - 50t'^2 - 40t'^3 \end{bmatrix} < 0$$

$$w'^1_{ijkp} \geq 0;\ w^1_{ijkp} - w'^1_{ijkp} \geq 0;\ w^2_{ijkp} - w^1_{ijkp} \geq 0;\ w^2_{ijkp} - w'^2_{ijkp} = 0;\ w^3_{ijkp} - w^2_{ijkp} \geq 0;$$

$$w'^3_{ij} - w^3_{ij} \geq 0; \quad i = 1,2; \quad j = 1,2; \quad k = 1,2; \quad p = 1,2.$$

$$t'^1 > 0;\ t^1 - t'^1 > 0; \quad t^2 - t^1 > 0; \quad t^2 - t'^2 = 0; \quad t^3 - t^2 > 0; \quad t'^3 - t^3 > 0;$$

Then, the individual maximum $U_q = max\Re\left(\overset{\sim I}{Z_q}\left(w_{ij}, t\right)\right), q = 1,2$ and personal minimal $L_q = min\Re\left(\overset{\sim I}{Z_q}\left(w_{ij}, t\right)\right), q = 1,2$ are obtained as in Table 11.

Table 11. Individual minimum and maximum values.

Objective Function	$\Re\left(\overset{\sim I}{Z_1}\left(w_{ijkp}, t\right)\right)$	$\Re\left(\overset{\sim I}{Z_2}\left(w_{ijkp}, t\right)\right)$
$U_q = max$	1.806118	2.37213
$L_q = min$	0.002937	0.00389

The following formulation of precise identical structures with various membership functions can be made based on Zimmerman's methodology:

LMF:

$max\gamma - \vartheta$
subject to

$$\frac{1}{8}\left[\begin{array}{l}
w^1_{1111}+4w^2_{1111}+4w^3_{1111}+0w'^1_{1111}+4w'^2_{1111}+6w'^3_{1111}+2w^1_{1211}+6w^2_{1211}+5w^3_{1211}\\
+w'^1_{1211}+6w'^2_{1211}+7w'^3_{1211}+3w^1_{2111}+10w^2_{2111}+8w^3_{2111}+w'^1_{2111}+10w'^2_{2111}+10w'^3_{2111}\\
+4w^1_{2211}+10w^2_{2211}+7w^3_{2211}+2w'^1_{2211}+10w'^2_{2211}+9w'^3_{2211}+7w^1_{1121}+18w^2_{1121}\\
+11w^3_{1121}+6w'^1_{1121}+18w'^2_{1121}+12w'^3_{1121}+2w^1_{1221}+10w^2_{1221}+7w^3_{1221}+w'^1_{1221}\\
+10w'^2_{1221}+8w'^3_{1221}+3w^1_{2121}+10w^2_{2121}+8w^3_{2121}+w'^1_{2121}+10w'^2_{2121}+10w'^3_{2121}\\
+5w^1_{2221}+14w^2_{2221}+9w^3_{2221}+4w'^1_{2221}+14w'^2_{2221}+12w'^3_{2221}6w^1_{1112}+16w^2_{1112}+10w^3_{1112}\\
+5w'^1_{1112}+16w'^2_{1112}+12w'^3_{1112}+4w^1_{1212}+10w^2_{1212}+7w^3_{1212}+2w'^1_{1212}+10w'^2_{1212}+9w'^3_{1212}\\
+7w^1_{2112}+18w^2_{2112}+11w^3_{2112}+6w'^1_{2112}+18w'^2_{2112}+12w'^3_{2112}+2w^1_{2212}+6w^2_{2212}+5w^3_{2212}\\
+1w'^1_{2212}+6w'^2_{2212}+7w'^3_{2212}+3w^1_{1122}+10w^2_{1122}+8w^3_{1122}+w'^1_{1122}+10w'^2_{1122}+10w'^3_{1122}\\
+3w^1_{1222}+10w^2_{1222}+8w^3_{1222}+w'^1_{1222}+10w'^2_{1222}+10w'^3_{1222}+6w^1_{2122}+16w^2_{2122}+10w^3_{2122}\\
+5w'^1_{2122}+16w'^2_{2122}+12w'^3_{2122}+4w^1_{2222}+10w^2_{2222}+7w^3_{2222}+2w'^1_{2222}+10w'^2_{2222}+9w'^3_{2222}\\
+150t^1+200t^2+250t^3+100t'^1+200t'^2+300t'^3
\end{array}\right]-1.803\gamma\geq 0.002937,$$

$$\frac{1}{8}\left[\begin{array}{l}
3w^1_{1111}+10w^2_{1111}+8w^3_{1111}+w'^1_{1111}+10w'^2_{1111}+10w'^3_{1111}+4w^1_{1211}+10w^2_{1211}+7w^3_{1211}\\
+2w'^1_{1211}+10w'^2_{1211}+9w'^3_{1211}+7w^1_{2111}+18w^2_{2111}+11w^3_{2111}+6w'^1_{2111}+18w'^2_{2111}+12w'^3_{2111}\\
+7w^1_{2211}+18w^2_{2211}+11w^3_{2211}+6w'^1_{2211}+18w'^2_{2211}+14w'^3_{2211}+6w^1_{1121}+16w^2_{1121}\\
+10w^3_{1121}+5w'^1_{1121}+16w'^2_{1121}+12w'^3_{1121}+3w^1_{1221}+10w^2_{1221}+8w^3_{1221}+w'^1_{1221}\\
+10w'^2_{1221}+10w'^3_{1221}+5w^1_{2121}+14w^2_{2121}+9w^3_{2121}+4w'^1_{2121}+14w'^2_{2121}+12w'^3_{2121}\\
+8w^1_{2221}+20w^2_{2221}+12w^3_{2221}+7w'^1_{2221}+20w'^2_{2221}+15w'^3_{2221}+7w^1_{1112}+16w^2_{1112}+9w^3_{1112}\\
+5w'^1_{1112}+16w'^2_{1112}+10w'^3_{1112}+w^1_{1212}+6w^2_{1212}+5w^3_{1212}+0w'^1_{1212}+6w'^2_{1212}+7w'^3_{1212}\\
+6w^1_{2112}+18w^2_{2112}+11w^3_{2112}+5w'^1_{2112}+18w'^2_{2112}+12w'^3_{2112}+7w^1_{2212}+18w^2_{2212}+11w^3_{2212}\\
+6w'^1_{2212}+18w'^2_{2212}+14w'^3_{2212}+3w^1_{1122}+10w^2_{1122}+8w^3_{1122}+w'^1_{1122}+10w'^2_{1122}+10w'^3_{1122}\\
+8w^1_{1222}+20w^2_{1222}+12w^3_{1222}+7w'^1_{1222}+20w'^2_{1222}+13w'^3_{1222}+10w^1_{2122}+22w^2_{2122}+12w^3_{2122}\\
+9w'^1_{2122}+22w'^2_{2122}+13w'^3_{2122}+w^1_{2222}+6w^2_{2222}+5w^3_{2222}+0w'^1_{2222}+6w'^2_{2222}+7w'^3_{2222}\\
+250t^1+300t^2+350t^3+200t'^1+300t'^2+400t'^3
\end{array}\right]-2.36824\gamma\geq 0.00389,$$

$$\frac{1}{8}\left[\begin{array}{l}
w^1_{1111}+4w^2_{1111}+4w^3_{1111}+0w'^1_{1111}+4w'^2_{1111}+6w'^3_{1111}+2w^1_{1211}+6w^2_{1211}+5w^3_{1211}\\
+w'^1_{1211}+6w'^2_{1211}+7w'^3_{1211}+3w^1_{2111}+10w^2_{2111}+8w^3_{2111}+w'^1_{2111}+10w'^2_{2111}+10w'^3_{2111}\\
+4w^1_{2211}+10w^2_{2211}+7w^3_{2211}+2w'^1_{2211}+10w'^2_{2211}+9w'^3_{2211}+7w^1_{1121}+18w^2_{1121}\\
+11w^3_{1121}+6w'^1_{1121}+18w'^2_{1121}+12w'^3_{1121}+2w^1_{1221}+10w^2_{1221}+7w^3_{1221}+w'^1_{1221}\\
+10w'^2_{1221}+8w'^3_{1221}+3w^1_{2121}+10w^2_{2121}+8w^3_{2121}+w'^1_{2121}+10w'^2_{2121}+10w'^3_{2121}\\
+5w^1_{2221}+14w^2_{2221}+9w^3_{2221}+4w'^1_{2221}+14w'^2_{2221}+12w'^3_{2221}6w^1_{1112}+16w^2_{1112}+10w^3_{1112}\\
+5w'^1_{1112}+16w'^2_{1112}+12w'^3_{1112}+4w^1_{1212}+10w^2_{1212}+7w^3_{1212}+2w'^1_{1212}+10w'^2_{1212}+9w'^3_{1212}\\
+7w^1_{2112}+18w^2_{2112}+11w^3_{2112}+6w'^1_{2112}+18w'^2_{2112}+12w'^3_{2112}+2w^1_{2212}+6w^2_{2212}+5w^3_{2212}\\
+1w'^1_{2212}+6w'^2_{2212}+7w'^3_{2212}+3w^1_{1122}+10w^2_{1122}+8w^3_{1122}+w'^1_{1122}+10w'^2_{1122}+10w'^3_{1122}\\
+3w^1_{1222}+10w^2_{1222}+8w^3_{1222}+w'^1_{1222}+10w'^2_{1222}+10w'^3_{1222}+6w^1_{2122}+16w^2_{2122}+10w^3_{2122}\\
+5w'^1_{2122}+16w'^2_{2122}+12w'^3_{2122}+4w^1_{2222}+10w^2_{2222}+7w^3_{2222}+2w'^1_{2222}+10w'^2_{2222}+9w'^3_{2222}\\
+150t^1+200t^2+250t^3+100t'^1+200t'^2+300t'^3
\end{array}\right]+1.803\vartheta\geq 1.806118,$$

$$\frac{1}{8}\left[\begin{array}{l}
3w^1_{1111}+10w^2_{1111}+8w^3_{1111}+w'^1_{1111}+10w'^2_{1111}+10w'^3_{1111}+4w^1_{1211}+10w^2_{1211}+7w^3_{1211}\\
+2w'^1_{1211}+10w'^2_{1211}+9w'^3_{1211}+7w^1_{2111}+18w^2_{2111}+11w^3_{2111}+6w'^1_{2111}+18w'^2_{2111}+12w'^3_{2111}\\
+7w^1_{2211}+18w^2_{2211}+11w^3_{2211}+6w'^1_{2211}+18w'^2_{2211}+14w'^3_{2211}+6w^1_{1121}+16w^2_{1121}\\
+10w^3_{1121}+5w'^1_{1121}+16w'^2_{1121}+12w'^3_{1121}+3w^1_{1221}+10w^2_{1221}+8w^3_{1221}+w'^1_{1221}\\
+10w'^2_{1221}+10w'^3_{1221}+5w^1_{2121}+14w^2_{2121}+9w^3_{2121}+4w'^1_{2121}+14w'^2_{2121}+12w'^3_{2121}\\
+8w^1_{2221}+20w^2_{2221}+12w^3_{2221}+7w'^1_{2221}+20w'^2_{2221}+15w'^3_{2221}+7w^1_{1112}+16w^2_{1112}+9w^3_{1112}\\
+5w'^1_{1112}+16w'^2_{1112}+10w'^3_{1112}+w^1_{1212}+6w^2_{1212}+5w^3_{1212}+0w'^1_{1212}+6w'^2_{1212}+7w'^3_{1212}\\
+6w^1_{2112}+18w^2_{2112}+11w^3_{2112}+5w'^1_{2112}+18w'^2_{2112}+12w'^3_{2112}+7w^1_{2212}+18w^2_{2212}+11w^3_{2212}\\
+6w'^1_{2212}+18w'^2_{2212}+14w'^3_{2212}+3w^1_{1122}+10w^2_{1122}+8w^3_{1122}+w'^1_{1122}+10w'^2_{1122}+10w'^3_{1122}\\
+8w^1_{1222}+20w^2_{1222}+12w^3_{1222}+7w'^1_{1222}+20w'^2_{1222}+13w'^3_{1222}+10w^1_{2122}+22w^2_{2122}+12w^3_{2122}\\
+9w'^1_{2122}+22w'^2_{2122}+13w'^3_{2122}+w^1_{2222}+6w^2_{2222}+5w^3_{2222}+0w'^1_{2222}+6w'^2_{2222}+7w'^3_{2222}\\
+250t^1+300t^2+350t^3+200t'^1+300t'^2+400t'^3
\end{array}\right]+2.36824\vartheta\geq 2.37213,$$

$$\gamma\geq\vartheta,\quad \gamma+\vartheta\leq 1,\qquad \gamma,\vartheta\in[0,\ 1]$$

and all the constraints in the

HMF model:

max$\delta-\beta$

subject to

$$\frac{3.32745}{8}\left[\begin{array}{l} w^1_{1111} + 4w^2_{1111} + 4w^3_{1111} + 0w'^1_{1111} + 4w'^2_{1111} + 6w'^3_{1111} + 2w^1_{1211} + 6w^2_{1211} + 5w^3_{1211} \\ +w'^1_{1211} + 6w'^2_{1211} + 7w'^3_{1211} + 3w^1_{2111} + 10w^2_{2111} + 8w^3_{2111} + w'^1_{2111} + 10w'^2_{2111} + 10w'^3_{2111} \\ +4w^1_{2211} + 10w^2_{2211} + 7w^3_{2211} + 2w'^1_{2211} + 10w'^2_{2211} + 9w'^3_{2211} + 7w^1_{1121} + 18w^2_{1121} \\ +11w^3_{1121} + 6w'^1_{1121} + 18w'^2_{1121} + 12w'^3_{1121} + 2w^1_{1221} + 10w^2_{1221} + 7w^3_{1221} + w'^1_{1221} \\ +10w'^2_{1221} + 8w'^3_{1221} + 3w^1_{2121} + 10w^2_{2121} + 8w^3_{2121} + w'^1_{2121} + 10w'^2_{2121} + 10w'^3_{2121} \\ +5w^1_{2221} + 14w^2_{2221} + 9w^3_{2221} + 4w'^1_{2221} + 14w'^2_{2221} + 12w'^3_{2221} 6w^1_{1112} + 16w^2_{1112} + 10w^3_{1112} \\ +5w'^1_{1112} + 16w'^2_{1112} + 12w'^3_{1112} + 4w^1_{1212} + 10w^2_{1212} + 7w^3_{1212} + 2w'^1_{1212} + 10w'^2_{1212} + 9w'^3_{1212} \\ +7w^1_{2112} + 18w^2_{2112} + 11w^3_{2112} + 6w'^1_{2112} + 18w'^2_{2112} + 12w'^3_{2112} + 2w^1_{2212} + 6w^2_{2212} + 5w^3_{2212} \\ +1w'^1_{2212} + 6w'^2_{2212} + 7w'^3_{2212} + 3w^1_{1122} + 10w^2_{1122} + 8w^3_{1122} + w'^1_{1122} + 10w'^2_{1122} + 10w'^3_{1122} \\ +3w^1_{1222} + 10w^2_{1222} + 8w^3_{1222} + w'^1_{1222} + 10w'^2_{1222} + 10w'^3_{1222} + 6w^1_{2122} + 16w^2_{2122} + 10w^3_{2122} \\ +5w'^1_{2122} + 16w'^2_{2122} + 12w'^3_{2122} + 4w^1_{2222} + 10w^2_{2222} + 7w^3_{2222} + 2w'^1_{2222} + 10w'^2_{2222} + 9w'^3_{2222} \\ +150t^1 + 200t^2 + 250t^3 + 100t'^1 + 200t'^2 + 300t'^3 \end{array}\right] - \delta \geq 3,$$

$$\frac{2.534}{8}\left[\begin{array}{l} 3w^1_{1111} + 10w^2_{1111} + 8w^3_{1111} + w'^1_{1111} + 10w'^2_{1111} + 10w'^3_{1111} + 4w^1_{1211} + 10w^2_{1211} + 7w^3_{1211} \\ +2w'^1_{1211} + 10w'^2_{1211} + 9w'^3_{1211} + 7w^1_{2111} + 18w^2_{2111} + 11w^3_{2111} + 6w'^1_{2111} + 18w'^2_{2111} + 12w'^3_{2111} \\ +7w^1_{2211} + 18w^2_{2211} + 11w^3_{2211} + 6w'^1_{2211} + 18w'^2_{2211} + 14w'^3_{2211} + 6w^1_{1121} + 16w^2_{1121} \\ +10w^3_{1121} + 5w'^1_{1121} + 16w'^2_{1121} + 12w'^3_{1121} + 3w^1_{1221} + 10w^2_{1221} + 8w^3_{1221} + w'^1_{1221} \\ +10w'^2_{1221} + 10w'^3_{1221} + 5w^1_{2121} + 14w^2_{2121} + 9w^3_{2121} + 4w'^1_{2121} + 14w'^2_{2121} + 12w'^3_{2121} \\ +8w^1_{2221} + 20w^2_{2221} + 12w^3_{2221} + 7w'^1_{2221} + 20w'^2_{2221} + 15w'^3_{2221} + 7w^1_{1112} + 16w^2_{1112} + 9w^3_{1112} \\ +5w'^1_{1112} + 16w'^2_{1112} + 10w'^3_{1112} + w^1_{1212} + 6w^2_{1212} + 5w^3_{1212} + 0w'^1_{1212} + 6w'^2_{1212} + 7w'^3_{1212} \\ +6w^1_{2112} + 18w^2_{2112} + 11w^3_{2112} + 5w'^1_{2112} + 18w'^2_{2112} + 12w'^3_{2112} + 7w^1_{2212} + 18w^2_{2212} + 11w^3_{2212} \\ +6w'^1_{2212} + 18w'^2_{2212} + 14w'^3_{2212} + 3w^1_{1122} + 10w^2_{1122} + 8w^3_{1122} + w'^1_{1122} + 10w'^2_{1122} + 10w'^3_{1122} \\ +8w^1_{1222} + 20w^2_{1222} + 12w^3_{1222} + 7w'^1_{1222} + 20w'^2_{1222} + 13w'^3_{1222} + 10w^1_{2122} + 22w^2_{2122} + 12w^3_{2122} \\ +9w'^1_{2122} + 22w'^2_{2122} + 13w'^3_{2122} + w^1_{2222} + 6w^2_{2222} + 5w^3_{2222} + 0w'^1_{2222} + 6w'^2_{2222} + 7w'^3_{2222} \\ +250t^1 + 300t^2 + 350t^3 + 200t'^1 + 300t'^2 + 400t'^3 \end{array}\right] - \delta \geq 3,$$

$$\frac{3.32745}{8}\left[\begin{array}{l} w^1_{1111} + 4w^2_{1111} + 4w^3_{1111} + 0w'^1_{1111} + 4w'^2_{1111} + 6w'^3_{1111} + 2w^1_{1211} + 6w^2_{1211} + 5w^3_{1211} \\ +w'^1_{1211} + 6w'^2_{1211} + 7w'^3_{1211} + 3w^1_{2111} + 10w^2_{2111} + 8w^3_{2111} + w'^1_{2111} + 10w'^2_{2111} + 10w'^3_{2111} \\ +4w^1_{2211} + 10w^2_{2211} + 7w^3_{2211} + 2w'^1_{2211} + 10w'^2_{2211} + 9w'^3_{2211} + 7w^1_{1121} + 18w^2_{1121} \\ +11w^3_{1121} + 6w'^1_{1121} + 18w'^2_{1121} + 12w'^3_{1121} + 2w^1_{1221} + 10w^2_{1221} + 7w^3_{1221} + w'^1_{1221} \\ +10w'^2_{1221} + 8w'^3_{1221} + 3w^1_{2121} + 10w^2_{2121} + 8w^3_{2121} + w'^1_{2121} + 10w'^2_{2121} + 10w'^3_{2121} \\ +5w^1_{2221} + 14w^2_{2221} + 9w^3_{2221} + 4w'^1_{2221} + 14w'^2_{2221} + 12w'^3_{2221} 6w^1_{1112} + 16w^2_{1112} + 10w^3_{1112} \\ +5w'^1_{1112} + 16w'^2_{1112} + 12w'^3_{1112} + 4w^1_{1212} + 10w^2_{1212} + 7w^3_{1212} + 2w'^1_{1212} + 10w'^2_{1212} + 9w'^3_{1212} \\ +7w^1_{2112} + 18w^2_{2112} + 11w^3_{2112} + 6w'^1_{2112} + 18w'^2_{2112} + 12w'^3_{2112} + 2w^1_{2212} + 6w^2_{2212} + 5w^3_{2212} \\ +1w'^1_{2212} + 6w'^2_{2212} + 7w'^3_{2212} + 3w^1_{1122} + 10w^2_{1122} + 8w^3_{1122} + w'^1_{1122} + 10w'^2_{1122} + 10w'^3_{1122} \\ +3w^1_{1222} + 10w^2_{1222} + 8w^3_{1222} + w'^1_{1222} + 10w'^2_{1222} + 10w'^3_{1222} + 6w^1_{2122} + 16w^2_{2122} + 10w^3_{2122} \\ +5w'^1_{2122} + 16w'^2_{2122} + 12w'^3_{2122} + 4w^1_{2222} + 10w^2_{2222} + 7w^3_{2222} + 2w'^1_{2222} + 10w'^2_{2222} + 9w'^3_{2222} \\ +150t^1 + 200t^2 + 250t^3 + 100t'^1 + 200t'^2 + 300t'^3 \end{array}\right] + \beta \geq 3,$$

$$\frac{2.534}{8}\left[\begin{array}{l} 3w^1_{1111} + 10w^2_{1111} + 8w^3_{1111} + w'^1_{1111} + 10w'^2_{1111} + 10w'^3_{1111} + 4w^1_{1211} + 10w^2_{1211} + 7w^3_{1211} \\ +2w'^1_{1211} + 10w'^2_{1211} + 9w'^3_{1211} + 7w^1_{2111} + 18w^2_{2111} + 11w^3_{2111} + 6w'^1_{2111} + 18w'^2_{2111} + 12w'^3_{2111} \\ +7w^1_{2211} + 18w^2_{2211} + 11w^3_{2211} + 6w'^1_{2211} + 18w'^2_{2211} + 14w'^3_{2211} + 6w^1_{1121} + 16w^2_{1121} \\ +10w^3_{1121} + 5w'^1_{1121} + 16w'^2_{1121} + 12w'^3_{1121} + 3w^1_{1221} + 10w^2_{1221} + 8w^3_{1221} + w'^1_{1221} \\ +10w'^2_{1221} + 10w'^3_{1221} + 5w^1_{2121} + 14w^2_{2121} + 9w^3_{2121} + 4w'^1_{2121} + 14w'^2_{2121} + 12w'^3_{2121} \\ +8w^1_{2221} + 20w^2_{2221} + 12w^3_{2221} + 7w'^1_{2221} + 20w'^2_{2221} + 15w'^3_{2221} + 7w^1_{1112} + 16w^2_{1112} + 9w^3_{1112} \\ +5w'^1_{1112} + 16w'^2_{1112} + 10w'^3_{1112} + w^1_{1212} + 6w^2_{1212} + 5w^3_{1212} + 0w'^1_{1212} + 6w'^2_{1212} + 7w'^3_{1212} \\ +6w^1_{2112} + 18w^2_{2112} + 11w^3_{2112} + 5w'^1_{2112} + 18w'^2_{2112} + 12w'^3_{2112} + 7w^1_{2212} + 18w^2_{2212} + 11w^3_{2212} \\ +6w'^1_{2212} + 18w'^2_{2212} + 14w'^3_{2212} + 3w^1_{1122} + 10w^2_{1122} + 8w^3_{1122} + w'^1_{1122} + 10w'^2_{1122} + 10w'^3_{1122} \\ +8w^1_{1222} + 20w^2_{1222} + 12w^3_{1222} + 7w'^1_{1222} + 20w'^2_{1222} + 13w'^3_{1222} + 10w^1_{2122} + 22w^2_{2122} + 12w^3_{2122} \\ +9w'^1_{2122} + 22w'^2_{2122} + 13w'^3_{2122} + w^1_{2222} + 6w^2_{2222} + 5w^3_{2222} + 0w'^1_{2222} + 6w'^2_{2222} + 7w'^3_{2222} \\ +250t^1 + 300t^2 + 350t^3 + 200t'^1 + 300t'^2 + 400t'^3 \end{array}\right] + \beta \geq 3,$$

$$\delta \geq \beta, \quad \beta \geq 0, \quad \delta \geq 0,$$

and all the constraints

where $\delta = \tanh^{-1}(2\gamma - 1)$; and$\beta = \tanh^{-1}(2\vartheta - 1)$.

PMF model:

max$\gamma - \vartheta$
subject to

$$\left[1.806118-\frac{1}{8}\left[\begin{array}{l} w^{1}_{1111}+4w^{2}_{1111}+4w^{3}_{1111}+0w'^{1}_{1111}+4w'^{2}_{1111}+6w'^{3}_{1111}+2w^{1}_{1211}+6w^{2}_{1211}+5w^{3}_{1211} \\ +w'^{1}_{1211}+6w'^{2}_{1211}+7w'^{3}_{1211}+3w^{1}_{2111}+10w^{2}_{2111}+8w^{3}_{2111}+w'^{1}_{2111}+10w'^{2}_{2111}+10w'^{3}_{2111} \\ +4w^{1}_{2211}+10w^{2}_{2211}+7w^{3}_{2211}+2w'^{1}_{2211}+10w'^{2}_{2211}+9w'^{3}_{2211}+7w^{1}_{1121}+18w^{2}_{1121} \\ +11w^{3}_{1121}+6w'^{1}_{1121}+18w'^{2}_{1121}+12w'^{3}_{1121}+2w^{1}_{1221}+10w^{2}_{1221}+7w^{3}_{1221}+w'^{1}_{1221} \\ +10w'^{2}_{1221}+8w'^{3}_{1221}+3w^{1}_{2121}+10w^{2}_{2121}+8w^{3}_{2121}+w'^{1}_{2121}+10w'^{2}_{2121}+10w'^{3}_{2121} \\ +5w^{1}_{2221}+14w^{2}_{2221}+9w^{3}_{2221}+4w'^{1}_{2221}+14w'^{2}_{2221}+12w'^{3}_{2221}6w^{1}_{1112}+16w^{2}_{1112}+10w^{3}_{1112} \\ +5w'^{1}_{1112}+16w'^{2}_{1112}+12w'^{3}_{1112}+4w^{1}_{1212}+10w^{2}_{1212}+7w^{3}_{1212}+2w'^{1}_{1212}+10w'^{2}_{1212}+9w'^{3}_{1212} \\ +7w^{1}_{2112}+18w^{2}_{2112}+11w^{3}_{2112}+6w'^{1}_{2112}+18w'^{2}_{2112}+12w'^{3}_{2112}+2w^{1}_{2212}+6w^{2}_{2212}+5w^{3}_{2212} \\ +1w'^{1}_{2212}+6w'^{2}_{2212}+7w'^{3}_{2212}+3w^{1}_{1122}+10w^{2}_{1122}+8w^{3}_{1122}+w'^{1}_{1122}+10w'^{2}_{1122}+10w'^{3}_{1122} \\ +3w^{1}_{1222}+10w^{2}_{1222}+8w^{3}_{1222}+w'^{1}_{1222}+10w'^{2}_{1222}+10w'^{3}_{1222}+6w^{1}_{2122}+16w^{2}_{2122}+10w^{3}_{2122} \\ +5w'^{1}_{2122}+16w'^{2}_{2122}+12w'^{3}_{2122}+4w^{1}_{2222}+10w^{2}_{2222}+7w^{3}_{2222}+2w'^{1}_{2222}+10w'^{2}_{2222}+9w'^{3}_{2222} \\ +150t^{1}+200t^{2}+250t^{3}+100t'^{1}+200t'^{2}+300t'^{3} \end{array}\right]\right]^{2} \le 3.2515(1-\gamma)$$

$$\left[2.3721-\frac{1}{8}\left[\begin{array}{l} 3w^{1}_{1111}+10w^{2}_{1111}+8w^{3}_{1111}+w'^{1}_{1111}+10w'^{2}_{1111}+10w'^{3}_{1111}+4w^{1}_{1211}+10w^{2}_{1211}+7w^{3}_{1211} \\ +2w'^{1}_{1211}+10w'^{2}_{1211}+9w'^{3}_{1211}+7w^{1}_{2111}+18w^{2}_{2111}+11w^{3}_{2111}+6w'^{1}_{2111}+18w'^{2}_{2111}+12w'^{3}_{2111} \\ +7w^{1}_{2211}+18w^{2}_{2211}+11w^{3}_{2211}+6w'^{1}_{2211}+18w'^{2}_{2211}+14w'^{3}_{2211}+6w^{1}_{1121}+16w^{2}_{1121} \\ +10w^{3}_{1121}+5w'^{1}_{1121}+16w'^{2}_{1121}+12w'^{3}_{1121}+3w^{1}_{1221}+10w^{2}_{1221}+8w^{3}_{1221}+w'^{1}_{1221} \\ +10w'^{2}_{1221}+10w'^{3}_{1221}+5w^{1}_{2121}+14w^{2}_{2121}+9w^{3}_{2121}+4w'^{1}_{2121}+14w'^{2}_{2121}+12w'^{3}_{2121} \\ +8w^{1}_{2221}+20w^{2}_{2221}+12w^{3}_{2221}+7w'^{1}_{2221}+20w'^{2}_{2221}+15w'^{3}_{2221}+7w^{1}_{1112}+16w^{2}_{1112}+9w^{3}_{1112} \\ +5w'^{1}_{1112}+16w'^{2}_{1112}+10w'^{3}_{1112}+w^{1}_{1212}+6w^{2}_{1212}+5w^{3}_{1212}+0w'^{1}_{1212}+6w'^{2}_{1212}+7w'^{3}_{1212} \\ +6w^{1}_{2112}+18w^{2}_{2112}+11w^{3}_{2112}+5w'^{1}_{2112}+18w'^{2}_{2112}+12w'^{3}_{2112}+7w^{1}_{2212}+18w^{2}_{2212}+11w^{3}_{2212} \\ +6w'^{1}_{2212}+18w'^{2}_{2212}+14w'^{3}_{2212}+3w^{1}_{1122}+10w^{2}_{1122}+8w^{3}_{1122}+w'^{1}_{1122}+10w'^{2}_{1122}+10w'^{3}_{1122} \\ +8w^{1}_{1222}+20w^{2}_{1222}+12w^{3}_{1222}+7w'^{1}_{1222}+20w'^{2}_{1222}+13w'^{3}_{1222}+10w^{1}_{2122}+22w^{2}_{2122}+12w^{3}_{2122} \\ +9w'^{1}_{2122}+22w'^{2}_{2122}+13w'^{3}_{2122}+w^{1}_{2222}+6w^{2}_{2222}+5w^{3}_{2222}+0w'^{1}_{2222}+6w'^{2}_{2222}+7w'^{3}_{2222} \\ +250t^{1}+300t^{2}+350t^{3}+200t'^{1}+300t'^{2}+400t'^{3} \end{array}\right]\right]^{2} \le 5.61(1-\gamma)$$

$$\left[\frac{1}{8}\left[\begin{array}{l} w^{1}_{1111}+4w^{2}_{1111}+4w^{3}_{1111}+0w'^{1}_{1111}+4w'^{2}_{1111}+6w'^{3}_{1111}+2w^{1}_{1211}+6w^{2}_{1211}+5w^{3}_{1211} \\ +w'^{1}_{1211}+6w'^{2}_{1211}+7w'^{3}_{1211}+3w^{1}_{2111}+10w^{2}_{2111}+8w^{3}_{2111}+w'^{1}_{2111}+10w'^{2}_{2111}+10w'^{3}_{2111} \\ +4w^{1}_{2211}+10w^{2}_{2211}+7w^{3}_{2211}+2w'^{1}_{2211}+10w'^{2}_{2211}+9w'^{3}_{2211}+7w^{1}_{1121}+18w^{2}_{1121} \\ +11w^{3}_{1121}+6w'^{1}_{1121}+18w'^{2}_{1121}+12w'^{3}_{1121}+2w^{1}_{1221}+10w^{2}_{1221}+7w^{3}_{1221}+w'^{1}_{1221} \\ +10w'^{2}_{1221}+8w'^{3}_{1221}+3w^{1}_{2121}+10w^{2}_{2121}+8w^{3}_{2121}+w'^{1}_{2121}+10w'^{2}_{2121}+10w'^{3}_{2121} \\ +5w^{1}_{2221}+14w^{2}_{2221}+9w^{3}_{2221}+4w'^{1}_{2221}+14w'^{2}_{2221}+12w'^{3}_{2221}6w^{1}_{1112}+16w^{2}_{1112}+10w^{3}_{1112} \\ +5w'^{1}_{1112}+16w'^{2}_{1112}+12w'^{3}_{1112}+4w^{1}_{1212}+10w^{2}_{1212}+7w^{3}_{1212}+2w'^{1}_{1212}+10w'^{2}_{1212}+9w'^{3}_{1212} \\ +7w^{1}_{2112}+18w^{2}_{2112}+11w^{3}_{2112}+6w'^{1}_{2112}+18w'^{2}_{2112}+12w'^{3}_{2112}+2w^{1}_{2212}+6w^{2}_{2212}+5w^{3}_{2212} \\ +1w'^{1}_{2212}+6w'^{2}_{2212}+7w'^{3}_{2212}+3w^{1}_{1122}+10w^{2}_{1122}+8w^{3}_{1122}+w'^{1}_{1122}+10w'^{2}_{1122}+10w'^{3}_{1122} \\ +3w^{1}_{1222}+10w^{2}_{1222}+8w^{3}_{1222}+w'^{1}_{1222}+10w'^{2}_{1222}+10w'^{3}_{1222}+6w^{1}_{2122}+16w^{2}_{2122}+10w^{3}_{2122} \\ +5w'^{1}_{2122}+16w'^{2}_{2122}+12w'^{3}_{2122}+4w^{1}_{2222}+10w^{2}_{2222}+7w^{3}_{2222}+2w'^{1}_{2222}+10w'^{2}_{2222}+9w'^{3}_{2222} \\ +150t^{1}+200t^{2}+250t^{3}+100t'^{1}+200t'^{2}+300t'^{3} \end{array}\right]\right]^{2} \ge 3.2515(1-\vartheta)$$

$$\left[\frac{1}{8}\left[\begin{array}{l} 3w^{1}_{1111}+10w^{2}_{1111}+8w^{3}_{1111}+w'^{1}_{1111}+10w'^{2}_{1111}+10w'^{3}_{1111}+4w^{1}_{1211}+10w^{2}_{1211}+7w^{3}_{1211} \\ +2w'^{1}_{1211}+10w'^{2}_{1211}+9w'^{3}_{1211}+7w^{1}_{2111}+18w^{2}_{2111}+11w^{3}_{2111}+6w'^{1}_{2111}+18w'^{2}_{2111}+12w'^{3}_{2111} \\ +7w^{1}_{2211}+18w^{2}_{2211}+11w^{3}_{2211}+6w'^{1}_{2211}+18w'^{2}_{2211}+14w'^{3}_{2211}+6w^{1}_{1121}+16w^{2}_{1121} \\ +10w^{3}_{1121}+5w'^{1}_{1121}+16w'^{2}_{1121}+12w'^{3}_{1121}+3w^{1}_{1221}+10w^{2}_{1221}+8w^{3}_{1221}+w'^{1}_{1221} \\ +10w'^{2}_{1221}+10w'^{3}_{1221}+5w^{1}_{2121}+14w^{2}_{2121}+9w^{3}_{2121}+4w'^{1}_{2121}+14w'^{2}_{2121}+12w'^{3}_{2121} \\ +8w^{1}_{2221}+20w^{2}_{2221}+12w^{3}_{2221}+7w'^{1}_{2221}+20w'^{2}_{2221}+15w'^{3}_{2221}+7w^{1}_{1112}+16w^{2}_{1112}+9w^{3}_{1112} \\ +5w'^{1}_{1112}+16w'^{2}_{1112}+10w'^{3}_{1112}+w^{1}_{1212}+6w^{2}_{1212}+5w^{3}_{1212}+0w'^{1}_{1212}+6w'^{2}_{1212}+7w'^{3}_{1212} \\ +6w^{1}_{2112}+18w^{2}_{2112}+11w^{3}_{2112}+5w'^{1}_{2112}+18w'^{2}_{2112}+12w'^{3}_{2112}+7w^{1}_{2212}+18w^{2}_{2212}+11w^{3}_{2212} \\ +6w'^{1}_{2212}+18w'^{2}_{2212}+14w'^{3}_{2212}+3w^{1}_{1122}+10w^{2}_{1122}+8w^{3}_{1122}+w'^{1}_{1122}+10w'^{2}_{1122}+10w'^{3}_{1122} \\ +8w^{1}_{1222}+20w^{2}_{1222}+12w^{3}_{1222}+7w'^{1}_{1222}+20w'^{2}_{1222}+13w'^{3}_{1222}+10w^{1}_{2122}+22w^{2}_{2122}+12w^{3}_{2122} \\ +9w'^{1}_{2122}+22w'^{2}_{2122}+13w'^{3}_{2122}+w^{1}_{2222}+6w^{2}_{2222}+5w^{3}_{2222}+0w'^{1}_{2222}+6w'^{2}_{2222}+7w'^{3}_{2222} \\ +250t^{1}+300t^{2}+350t^{3}+200t'^{1}+300t'^{2}+400t'^{3} \end{array}\right]\right]^{2} \ge 5.61(1-\vartheta)$$

$$\gamma \ge \vartheta, \quad \gamma+\vartheta \le 1, \qquad \gamma, \vartheta \in [0,\ 1]$$

and all the constraints.

The membership and non-membership values for any model are obtained by resolving the three crisp issues. Additionally, as shown in Table 12, IF solutions and intuitionistic objective values are also achieved. The numerical models are carried with a PC having a Core i5 CPU@2.8 GH, 8 GB of RAM and a 64-bit operating system. The numerical models are solved using Lingo programming software: LINGO 19.

Table 12. The IF solutions and intuitionistic objective values.

Membership Function Type	Intuitionistic Fuzzy Solution	Intuitionistic Objective Value
Linear	$\tilde{x}^{I}_{1111}=\begin{pmatrix}0,0,0;\\0,0,0\end{pmatrix}$; $\tilde{x}^{I}_{1121}=\begin{pmatrix}9.655,9.655,9.655;\\9.655,9.655,3.283\end{pmatrix}$ $\tilde{x}^{I}_{2111}=\begin{pmatrix}0,0,0;\\0,0,0\end{pmatrix}$; $\tilde{x}^{I}_{2211}=\begin{pmatrix}0,0,0;\\0,0,0\end{pmatrix}$ $\tilde{x}^{I}_{1211}=\begin{pmatrix}0,0,0;\\0,0,0,\end{pmatrix}$; $\tilde{x}^{I}_{1221}=\begin{pmatrix}0,0,0;\\0,0,0\end{pmatrix}$ $\tilde{x}^{I}_{2121}=\begin{pmatrix}0,0,0;\\0,0,0\end{pmatrix}$ $\tilde{x}^{I}_{2221}=\begin{pmatrix}0,0,0;\\0,0,69.37\end{pmatrix}$ $\tilde{x}^{I}_{1112}=\begin{pmatrix}15.158,15.158,15.158;\\15.158,15.158,5.154\end{pmatrix}$ $\tilde{x}^{I}_{1212}=\begin{pmatrix}0,0,0;\\0,0,0\end{pmatrix}$ $\tilde{x}^{I}_{2112}=\begin{pmatrix}0,0,0;\\0,0,0\end{pmatrix}$ $\tilde{x}^{I}_{2212}=\begin{pmatrix}2.99,2.99,2.99;\\2.99,2.99,26.02\end{pmatrix}$ $\tilde{x}^{I}_{1122}=\begin{pmatrix}0,0,0;\\0,0,0\end{pmatrix}$ $\tilde{x}^{I}_{1222}=\begin{pmatrix}0,0,0;\\0,0,0\end{pmatrix}$ $\tilde{x}^{I}_{2122}=\begin{pmatrix}0,0,0;\\0,0,0\end{pmatrix}$ $\tilde{x}^{I}_{2222}=\begin{pmatrix}0,0,0;\\0,0,0\end{pmatrix}$	$\tilde{Z}^{I}_{1}=\begin{pmatrix}1.055,2.202,4.814;\\0.255,2.202,29.618\end{pmatrix}$ $\tilde{Z}^{I}_{2}=\begin{pmatrix}1.34,\ 2.095,\ 3.476;\\0.473,\ 2.095,\ 15.566\end{pmatrix}$
Hyperbolic	$\tilde{x}^{I}_{1111}=\begin{pmatrix}0,0,0;\\0,0,0\end{pmatrix}$; $\tilde{x}^{I}_{1121}=\begin{pmatrix}6.857,6.857,6.857;\\0,6.857,6.857\end{pmatrix}$ $\tilde{x}^{I}_{2111}=\begin{pmatrix}0.429,0.429,0.429;\\0,0.429,0.429\end{pmatrix}$; $\tilde{x}^{I}_{1221}=\begin{pmatrix}0,0,0;\\0,0,0\end{pmatrix}$ $\tilde{x}^{I}_{1211}=\begin{pmatrix}0,0,0;\\0,0,0,\end{pmatrix}$; $\tilde{x}^{I}_{2211}=\begin{pmatrix}0,0,31.5;\\0,0,31.5\end{pmatrix}$ $\tilde{x}^{I}_{2121}=\begin{pmatrix}0,0,0;\\0,0,0\end{pmatrix}$ $\tilde{x}^{I}_{2221}=\begin{pmatrix}0,0,30;\\0,0,30\end{pmatrix}$ $\tilde{x}^{I}_{1112}=\begin{pmatrix}0,0,0;\\0,0,0\end{pmatrix}$ $\tilde{x}^{I}_{1212}=\begin{pmatrix}0,0,0;\\0,0,0\end{pmatrix}$ $\tilde{x}^{I}_{2112}=\begin{pmatrix}0,0,31.755;\\0,0,31.755\end{pmatrix}$ $\tilde{x}^{I}_{2212}=\begin{pmatrix}0,0,0;\\0,0,0\end{pmatrix}$ $\tilde{x}^{I}_{1122}=\begin{pmatrix}0,0,0;\\0,0,0\end{pmatrix}$ $\tilde{x}^{I}_{1222}=\begin{pmatrix}0,0,0;\\0,0,0\end{pmatrix}$ $\tilde{x}^{I}_{2122}=\begin{pmatrix}0,0,0;\\0,0,0\end{pmatrix}$ $\tilde{x}^{I}_{2222}=\begin{pmatrix}0,0,0;\\0,0,0\end{pmatrix}$	$\tilde{Z}^{I}_{1}=\begin{pmatrix}0.32,\ 2.15,17.98;\\0.129,\ 2.15,\ 70.55\end{pmatrix}$ $\tilde{Z}^{I}_{2}=\begin{pmatrix}0.449,\ 1.611,\ 8.964;\\0.248,\ 1.611,\ 17.594\end{pmatrix}$
Parabolic	$\tilde{x}^{I}_{1111}=\begin{pmatrix}0,0,0;\\0,0,0\end{pmatrix}$; $\tilde{x}^{I}_{1121}=\begin{pmatrix}9.655,9.655,9.655;\\9.655,9.655,3.283\end{pmatrix}$ $\tilde{x}^{I}_{2111}=\begin{pmatrix}0,0,0;\\0,0,0\end{pmatrix}$; $\tilde{x}^{I}_{2211}=\begin{pmatrix}0,0,0;\\0,0,0\end{pmatrix}$ $\tilde{x}^{I}_{1211}=\begin{pmatrix}0,0,0;\\0,0,0,\end{pmatrix}$; $\tilde{x}^{I}_{1221}=\begin{pmatrix}0,0,0;\\0,0,0\end{pmatrix}$ $\tilde{x}^{I}_{2121}=\begin{pmatrix}0,0,0;\\0,0,0\end{pmatrix}$ $\tilde{x}^{I}_{2221}=\begin{pmatrix}0,0,0;\\0,0,69.37\end{pmatrix}$ $\tilde{x}^{I}_{1112}=\begin{pmatrix}15.158,15.158,15.158;\\15.158,15.158,5.154\end{pmatrix}$ $\tilde{x}^{I}_{1212}=\begin{pmatrix}0,0,0;\\0,0,0\end{pmatrix}$ $\tilde{x}^{I}_{2112}=\begin{pmatrix}0,0,0;\\0,0,0\end{pmatrix}$ $\tilde{x}^{I}_{2212}=\begin{pmatrix}2.99,2.99,2.99;\\2.99,2.99,26.02\end{pmatrix}$ $\tilde{x}^{I}_{1122}=\begin{pmatrix}0,0,0;\\0,0,0\end{pmatrix}$ $\tilde{x}^{I}_{1222}=\begin{pmatrix}0,0,0;\\0,0,0\end{pmatrix}$ $\tilde{x}^{I}_{2122}=\begin{pmatrix}0,0,0;\\0,0,0\end{pmatrix}$ $\tilde{x}^{I}_{2222}=\begin{pmatrix}0,0,0;\\0,0,0\end{pmatrix}$	$\tilde{Z}^{I}_{1}=\begin{pmatrix}1.055,2.202,4.814;\\0.255,2.202,29.618;\end{pmatrix}$ $\tilde{Z}^{I}_{2}=\begin{pmatrix}1.34,\ 2.095,\ 3.476;\\0.473,\ 2.095,\ 15.566\end{pmatrix}$

Thus, for the LMF, HMF, and PMF structures, $\mu_{\underset{Z_1}{\sim}^{I}}(x)$ and $v_{\underset{Z_1}{\sim}^{I}}(x)$ may be constructed.

$$\mu_{\underset{Z_1}{\sim}^{I}}(x) = \begin{cases} \frac{x-1.055}{2.202-1.055} & 1.055 < x \leq 2.202, \\ 1 & x = 2.202, \\ \frac{4.814-x}{4.814-2.202}, & 2.202 \leq x \leq 4.814, \\ 0, & otherwise, \end{cases}$$

$$v_{\underset{Z_1}{\sim}^{I}}(x) = \begin{cases} \frac{2.202-x}{2.202-0.255} & 0.255 < x \leq 2.202, \\ 0 & x = 2.202 \\ \frac{x-2.202}{29.618-2.202}, & 2.202 \leq x \leq 29.618, \\ 1, & otherwise, \end{cases}$$

$$\mu_{\underset{Z_2}{\sim}^{I}}(x) = \begin{cases} \frac{x-1.34}{2.095-1.34} & 1.34 < x \leq 2.095, \\ 1 & x = 2.095, \\ \frac{3.476-x}{3.476-2.095}, & 2.095 \leq x \leq 3.476, \\ 0, & otherwise, \end{cases}$$

$$v_{\underset{Z_2}{\sim}^{I}}(x) = \begin{cases} \frac{2.095-x}{2.095-0.473} & 0.473 < x \leq 2.095, \\ 0 & x = 2.095, \\ \frac{x-2.095}{15.566-2.095}, & 2.095 \leq x \leq 15.566, \\ 1, & otherwise, \end{cases}$$

Also, for the HMF models

$$\mu_{\underset{Z_1}{\sim}^{I}}(x) = \begin{cases} \frac{x-0.32}{2.15-0.32} & 0.32 < x \leq 2.15, \\ 1 & x = 2.15, \\ \frac{17.98-x}{17.98-2.15}, & 2.15 \leq x \leq 17.98, \\ 0, & otherwise, \end{cases}$$

$$v_{\underset{Z_1}{\sim}^{I}}(x) = \begin{cases} \frac{2.15-x}{2.15-0.129} & 0.129 < x \leq 2.15, \\ 0 & x = 2.15, \\ \frac{x-2.15}{70.55-2.15}, & 2.15 \leq x \leq 70.55, \\ 1, & otherwise, \end{cases}$$

$$\mu_{\underset{Z_2}{\sim}^{I}}(x) = \begin{cases} \frac{x-0.449}{1.611-0.449} & 0.449 < x \leq 1.611, \\ 1 & x = 1.611, \\ \frac{8.964-x}{8.964-1.611}, & 1.611 \leq x \leq 8.964, \\ 0, & otherwise, \end{cases}$$

$$v_{\underset{Z_2}{\sim}^{I}}(x) = \begin{cases} \frac{1.611-x}{1.611-0.248} & 0.248 < x \leq 1.611, \\ 0 & x = 1.611, \\ \frac{x-1.611}{17.594-1.611}, & 1.611 \leq x \leq 17.594, \\ 1, & otherwise, \end{cases}$$

Table 13 provides an evaluation of the various membership models. The HMF is greater than the parabolic and linear ones. In the three presented solution models, both degrees of refusal and acceptance were considered. Numerical data for the LMF, HMF, and PMF models were exhibited in Table 14 to ensure the applicability and computational efficiency of the proposed models for solving FIF-MMSFTM. The total solver iteration and elapsed run time per second were exhibited. The HMF model has the smallest number of iterations, while the PMF model has the largest number of iterations. It is clear that the elapsed runtime of the HMF model is smaller than that of the LMF and PMF models. Also, the model class, nonlinear variables, integer variables, and a total number of constraints were provided. This study that is being presented has broad applications in a variety of logistical and supply chain management organizations. When single-type ambiguity is insufficient to describe specific parameters during any logistic operation, the suggested approach can be beneficial in handling two-fold ambiguity (multi-choice and IFN).

Table 13. Comparison of the different membership approaches.

Membership Function	γ	ϑ	$\gamma-\vartheta$
Linear	0.971	0.029	0.942
Hyperbolic	1	0	1
Parabolic	0.9428	0.0572	0.8856

Table 14. Numerical data of LMF, HMF, and PMF models.

	LMF Model	HMF Model	PMF Model
Total solver iteration	26	10	103
Elapsed runtime seconds	0.2	0.15	1.37
Model class	LP	LP	QP
Total variables	104	104	104
Nonlinear variables	0	0	102
Integer variables	0	0	0
Total constraints	129	133	135

8. Conclusions

Through this research, the FIF-MMSFTM was formed. Given the evolving market policies, we anticipate the quantities shipped, profits, cost coefficients, supplies, demands, and transportation parameters to exhibit TIFNs. Analyzing TPs within the IF domain is becoming increasingly relevant and practically applicable compared to conventional fuzzy domains. To address this, the developed FIF-MMSFTM is transformed into a linear model by introducing a new variable to tackle the nonlinearity of fractional objective functions. Subsequently, the model is converted into a crisp version using the AF and ordering relations of the IFS. Extending Zimmerman's approach is realized to maximize membership and minimize non-membership functions within the solution model. In many real-world situations, the degree of approval or opposition to a given target may vary non-constantly. Nonlinear membership (HMF and PMF) functions offer a more precise representation of DMs' behavior under certain conditions. Furthermore, in the proposed solution model, three different membership functions, namely LMF, PMF, and HMF, were utilized. For the presented LMF, HMF, and PMF models, the proof is that the unique optimal solution of each model is an efficient solution of the original transportation model. The main advantage of the proposed model is that it can easily be applied in various uncertain domains, requiring less computational effort to obtain the optimal solution. The elapsed run time is very short, at 0.2, 0.15, and 1.37 s for the presented LMF, HMF, and PMF models, respectively. Also, each model has 104 variables and 129 constraints.

Numerous unexplored areas to investigate in the field of solid fraction transportation, in our opinion, will be investigated in the future. The following lists a few of these points:

- Multi-choice multi-objective multi-item solid fractional transportation models.
- Fully IF multi-objective fractional programming problems;
- Bi-level supply chain model under an IF environment.

Author Contributions: Conceptualization, M.A.E.S.; Methodology, E.B. and M.A.E.S.; Software, S.A. and M.A.E.S.; Validation, M.A.E.; Formal analysis, F.A.F.; Investigation, S.A.; Data curation, M.A.E.; Writing – original draft, F.A.F. and M.A.E.S.; Writing – review & editing, M.A.E.S.; Supervision, E.B.; Funding acquisition, S.A. All authors have read and agreed to the published version of the manuscript.

Funding: The author would like to thank the Deanship of Scientific Research at Majmaah University for supporting this work under Project Number No. R-2024-888.

Data Availability Statement: The data used to support the findings of this study are available from the corresponding author upon request.

Conflicts of Interest: The authors declare no conflicts of interest.

References

1. Abd El-Wahed, W.F.; Lee, S.M. Interactive fuzzy goal programming for multi-objective transportation problems. *Int. J. Manag. Sci.* **2006**, *34*, 158–166. [CrossRef]
2. Ammar, E.E.; Youness, E.A. Study on multi-objective transportation problem with fuzzy numbers. *Appl. Math. Comput.* **2005**, *166*, 241–253.
3. Bit, A.K.; Biswal, M.P.; Alam, S.S. Fuzzy programming approach to multi-criteria decision-making transportation problem. *Fuzzy Sets Syst.* **1992**, *50*, 135–141. [CrossRef]
4. Cetin, N.; Tiryaki, F. A Fuzzy Approach Using Generalized Dinkelbach's Algorithm for Multi-objective Linear Fractional Transportation Problem. *Math. Probl. Eng.* **2014**, *2014*, 702319. [CrossRef]
5. Chanas, S.; Kuchta, D. A concept of the optimal solution of the transportation problem with fuzzy cost coefficients. *Fuzzy Sets Syst.* **1996**, *82*, 299–305. [CrossRef]
6. Charnes, A.; Cooper, W.W. Programming with linear fractional functional. *Nav. Res. Logist. Q.* **1962**, *9*, 181–186. [CrossRef]
7. Diaz, J.A. Finding a complete description of all efficient solutions to a multi-objective transportation problem. *Ekon. Mat. Obz.* **1979**, *15*, 62–73.
8. Hitchcock, F.L. The distribution of a product from several sources to numerous localities. *J. Math. Phys.* **1941**, *20*, 224–230. [CrossRef]
9. Shell, E. Distribution of a product by several properties, directorate of management analysis. In Proceedings of the Second Symposium in Linear Programming, Washington, DC, USA, 27–29 January 1955; Volume 2, pp. 615–642.
10. Haley, K. New methods in mathematical programming—The solid transportation problem. *Oper. Res.* **1962**, *10*, 448–463. [CrossRef]
11. Patel, G.; Tripathy, J. The solid transportation problem and its variants. *Int. J. Manag. Syst.* **1989**, *5*, 17–36.
12. Baidya, A.; Bera, U.K.; Maiti, M. A solid transportation problem with safety factor under different uncertainty environments. *J. Uncertain. Anal. Appl.* **2013**, *1*, 18. [CrossRef]
13. Chen, S.M.; Phuong, B.D.H. Fuzzy time series forecasting based on optimal partitions of intervals and optimal weighting vectors. *Knowl. Based Syst.* **2017**, *118*, 204–216. [CrossRef]
14. Chen, B.; Liu, Y.; Zhou, T. An entropy based solid transportation problem in uncertain environment. *J. Ambient. Intell. Hum. Comput.* **2019**, *10*, 357–363. [CrossRef]
15. Kundu, P.; Kar, S.; Maiti, M. Multi-objective solid transportation problems with budget constraint in uncertain environment. *Int. J. Syst. Sci.* **2014**, *45*, 1668–1682. [CrossRef]
16. Liu, L.; Zhang, B.; Ma, W. Uncertain programming models for fixed charge multi-item solid transportation problem. *Soft Comput.* **2018**, *22*, 5825–5833. [CrossRef]
17. Mahajan, S.; Gupta, K.S. On fully intuitionistic fuzzy multi-objective transportation problems using different membership functions. *Ann. Oper. Res.* **2019**, *296*, 211–241. [CrossRef]
18. Verma, R.; Biswal, M.P.; Biswas, A. Fuzzy programming technique to solve multi-objective transportation problems with some non-linear membership functions. *Fuzzy Sets Syst.* **1997**, *91*, 37–43. [CrossRef]
19. Roy, S.K.; Mahapatra, D.R.; Biswal, M.P. Multi-choice stochastic transportation problem with exponential distribution. *J. Uncertain Syst.* **2012**, *6*, 200–213.
20. Singh, S.K.; Yadav, S.P. Intuitionistic fuzzy multi-objective linear programming problem with various membership functions. *Ann. Oper. Res.* **2018**, *269*, 693–707. [CrossRef]
21. Ghosh, S.; Roy, S.K.; Ebrahimnejad, A.; Verdegay, J.L. Multi-objective fully intuitionistic fuzzy fixed-charge solid transportation problem. *Complex Intell. Syst.* **2021**, *7*, 1009–1023. [CrossRef]
22. Rizk-Allah, R.M.; Hassanien, A.E.; Elhoseny, M. A multi-objective transportation model under neutrosophic environment. *Comput. Electr. Eng.* **2018**, *69*, 705–719. [CrossRef]
23. Biswas, A.; Shaikh, A.A.; Niaki, S.T.A. Multi-objective non-linear fixed charge transportation problem with multiple modes of transportation in crisp and interval environments. *Appl. Soft Comput.* **2019**, *80*, 628–649. [CrossRef]
24. Sifaoui, T.; Aïder, M. Uncertain interval programming model for multi-objective multi-item fixed charge solid transportation problem with budget constraint and safety measure. *Soft Comput.* **2019**, *24*, 10123–10147. [CrossRef]
25. Jalil, S.A.; Sadia, S.; Javaid, S.; Ali, Q. A solution approach for solving fully fuzzy multiobjective solid transportation problem. *Int. J. Agric. Stat. Sci.* **2017**, *13*, 75–84.
26. Ebrahimnejad, A. An effective computational attempt for solving fully fuzzy linear programming using Molp problem. *J. Ind. Prod. Eng.* **2019**, *36*, 59–69. [CrossRef]
27. Ziqan, A.; Ibrahim, S.; Marabeh, M.; Qarariyah, A. Fully fuzzy linear systems with trapezoidal and hexagonal fuzzy numbers. *Granul. Comput.* **2021**, *7*, 229–238. [CrossRef]
28. Atanassov, K.T. Intuitionistic fuzzy sets. *Fuzzy Sets Syst.* **1986**, *20*, 87–96. [CrossRef]
29. Ebrahimnejad, A.; Verdegay, J.L. A new approach for solving fully intuitionistic fuzzy transportation problems. *Fuzzy Optim. Decis. Mak.* **2018**, *17*, 447–474. [CrossRef]
30. Midya, S.; Roy, S.K.; Vincent, F.Y. Intuitionistic fuzzy multi-stage multi-objective fixed-charge solid transportation problem in a green supply chain. *Int. J. Mach. Learn. Cybern.* **2021**, *12*, 699–717. [CrossRef]

31. Roy, S.K.; Midya, S. Multi-objective fixed-charge solid transportation problem with product blending under intuitionistic fuzzy environment. *Appl. Intell.* **2019**, *49*, 3524–3538. [CrossRef]
32. Zadeh, L.A. Toward a generalized theory of uncertainty (GTU)—An outline. *Inf. Sci.* **2005**, *172*, 1–40. [CrossRef]
33. Zadeh, L.A. Is there a need for fuzzy logic? *Inf. Sci.* **2008**, *178*, 2751–2779. [CrossRef]
34. Zangiabadi, M.; Maleki, H.R. Fuzzy goal programming for multi-objective transportation problems. *J. Appl. Math. Comput.* **2007**, *24*, 449–460. [CrossRef]
35. Zangiabadi, M.; Maleki, H.R. Fuzzy goal programming technique to solve multi-objective transportation problems with some non-linear membership functions. *Iran. J. Fuzzy Syst.* **2013**, *10*, 61–74.
36. Gupta, A.; Kumar, A. A new method for solving linear multi-objective transportation problems with fuzzy parameters. *Appl. Math. Model.* **2012**, *36*, 1421–1430. [CrossRef]
37. Roy, S.K.; Mahapatra, D.R. Multi-objective interval valued transportation probabilistic problem involving lognormal. *Int. J. Math. Sci. Comput.* **2011**, *1*, 14–21.
38. Mahapatra, D.R.; Roy, S.K.; Biswal, M.P. Multi-choice stochastic transportation problem involving extreme value distribution. *Appl. Math. Model.* **2013**, *37*, 2230–2240. [CrossRef]
39. Maity, G.; Roy, S.K. Solving multi-choice multi-objective transportation problem: A utility function approach. *J. Uncertain. Anal. Appl.* **2014**, *2*, 11. [CrossRef]
40. Maity, G.; Roy, S.K. Solving a multi-objective transportation problem with nonlinear cost and multi-choice demand. *Int. J. Manag. Sci. Eng. Manag.* **2016**, *11*, 62–70. [CrossRef]
41. Kocken, H.G.; Ozlok, B.A.; Tiryaki, F. A compensatory fuzzy approach to multi-objective transportation problems with fuzzy parameters. *Eur. J. Pure Appl. Math.* **2014**, *7*, 369–386.
42. Roy, S.K.; Ebrahimnejad, A.; Verdegay, J.L.; Das, S. New approach for solving intuitionistic fuzzy multi-objective transportation problem. *Sadhana* **2018**, *43*, 3. [CrossRef]
43. Mahmoodirad, A.; Allahviranloo, T.; Niroomand, S. A new effective solution method for fully intuitionistic fuzzy transportation problem. *Soft Comput.* **2018**, *23*, 4521–4530. [CrossRef]
44. Nasseri, S.H.; Bavandi, S. Multi-choice Linear Programming in Fuzzy Random Hybrid Uncertainty Environment and Their Application in Multi-commodity Transportation Problem. *Fuzzy Inf. Eng.* **2020**, *12*, 109–122. [CrossRef]
45. El Sayed, M.A.; Abo-Sinna, M.A. A novel Approach for Fully Intuitionistic Fuzzy Multi-Objective Fractional Transportation Problem. *Alex. Eng. J.* **2021**, *60*, 1447–1463. [CrossRef]
46. El Sayed, M.A.; Baky, I.A. Multi-choice fractional stochastic multi-objective transportation problem. *Soft Comput.* **2023**, *27*, 11551–11567. [CrossRef]
47. Devnath, S.; Giri, P.K.; Mondal, S.S.; Maiti, M. Fully fuzzy multi-item two-stage fixed charge four dimensional transportation problems with flexible constraints. *Granul. Comput.* **2022**, *7*, 779–797. [CrossRef]
48. Mondal, A.; Roy, S.K.; Midya, S. Intuitionistic fuzzy sustainable multi-objective multi-item multi-choice step fixed-charge solid transportation problem. *J. Ambient. Intell. Humaniz. Comput.* **2023**, *14*, 6975–6999. [CrossRef]
49. Chhibber, D.; Srivastava, P.K.; Bisht, D.C. From fuzzy transportation problem to non-linear intuitionistic fuzzy multi-objective transportation problem: A literature review. *Int. J. Model. Simul.* **2021**, *41*, 335–350. [CrossRef]
50. Malik, M.; Gupta, S.K. Goal programming technique for solving fully interval-valued intuitionistic fuzzy multiple objective transportation problems. *Soft Comput.* **2020**, *24*, 13955–13977. [CrossRef]
51. Bind, A.B.; Rani, D.; Goyal, K.K.; Ebrahimnejad, A. A solution approach for sustainable multi-objective multi-item 4D solid transportation problem involving triangular intuitionistic fuzzy parameters. *J. Clean. Prod.* **2023**, *414*, 137661. [CrossRef]
52. Klanšek, U.; Pšunder, M. solving the nonlinear transportation problem by global optimization. *Transport* **2010**, *25*, 314–324. [CrossRef]
53. Klanšek, U. solving the nonlinear discrete transportation problem MINLP optimization. *Transport* **2013**, *29*, 1–11. [CrossRef]
54. Zimmermann, H.J. *Fuzzy Set Theory and Its Applications*; Springer: Berlin/Heidelberg, Germany, 2001.
55. Gong, Z.; Zhangc, N.; Chiclanad, F. The optimization ordering model for intuitionistic fuzzy preference relations with utility functions. *Knowl.-Based Syst.* **2018**, *162*, 174–184. [CrossRef]
56. Mahapatra, G.S.; Roy, T.K. Intuitionistic Fuzzy Number and Its Arithmetic Operation with Application on System Failure. *J. Uncertain. Syst.* **2013**, *7*, 92–107.
57. Singh, V.P.; Sharma, K.; Chakraborty, D.; Ebrahimnejad, A. A novel multi objective bi-level programming problem under intuitionistic fuzzy environment and its application in production planning problem. *Complex Intell. Syst.* **2022**, *8*, 3263–3278. [CrossRef]
58. Arya, R.; Singh, P.; Kumari, S.; Obaidat, M.S. An approach for solving fully fuzzy multi-objective linear fractional optimization problems. *Soft Comput.* **2020**, *24*, 9105–9119. [CrossRef]
59. Chakraborty, M.; Gupta, S. Fuzzy mathematical programming for multi-objective linear fractional programming problem. *Fuzzy Sets Syst.* **2002**, *125*, 335–342. [CrossRef]

fractal and fractional

MDPI

Article

Nonlocal Changing-Sign Perturbation Tempered Fractional Sub-Diffusion Model with Weak Singularity

Xinguang Zhang [1,2,*], Jingsong Chen [3,*], Peng Chen [1], Lishuang Li [1] and Yonghong Wu [2]

[1] School of Mathematical and Informational Sciences, Yantai University, Yantai 264005, China; chenpeng06072022@163.com (P.C.); lls748264@163.com (L.L.)
[2] Department of Mathematics and Statistics, Curtin University, Perth, WA 6845, Australia; y.wu@curtin.edu.au
[3] School of Statistics and Mathematics, Zhongnan University of Economics and Law, Wuhan 430073, China
* Correspondence: zxg123242@163.com (X.Z.); kingson_chen@163.com (J.C.)

Abstract: In this paper, we study the existence of positive solutions for a changing-sign perturbation tempered fractional model with weak singularity which arises from the sub-diffusion study of anomalous diffusion in Brownian motion. By two-step substitution, we first transform the higher-order sub-diffusion model to a lower-order mixed integro-differential sub-diffusion model, and then introduce a power factor to the non-negative Green function such that the linear integral operator has a positive infimum. This innovative technique is introduced for the first time in the literature and it is critical for controlling the influence of changing-sign perturbation. Finally, an a priori estimate and Schauder's fixed point theorem are applied to show that the sub-diffusion model has at least one positive solution whether the perturbation is positive, negative or changing-sign, and also the main nonlinear term is allowed to have singularity for some space variables.

Keywords: nonlocal boundary condition; tempered fractional equation; sign-changing perturbation; Schauder's fixed point theorem

MSC: 34A08; 34A25; 47H14

1. Introduction

The particle's random walks in Brownian motion is governed by the following diffusion equation [1]:

$$\partial_t f(z,t) = \partial_z^2 f(z,t),$$

where $f(z,t)$ is the particle jump density function. In anomalous diffusion, the mean square variance sometimes grows faster to create a super-diffusion and sometimes spreads slower to form sub-diffusion than in the Gaussian process; thus, anomalous diffusion in Brownian motion exhibits a long-range dependence characteristic, which can be modeled by the fractional diffusion equation

$$\partial_t^\alpha f(z,t) = \partial_z^\beta f(z,t),$$

where the fractional space derivative of order $0 < \beta < 2$ corresponds to heavy-tailed power law particle jumps $P[J > z] \approx z^{-\beta}$ in the Lèvy flight, and the fractional time derivative of order $0 < \alpha \leq 1$ describes the heavy-tailed power law waiting time $P[W > t] \approx t^{-\alpha}$ between jumps. This indicates that the solution of the anomalous diffusion equation exhibits a feature of heavy tails, that is, it falls off like a power law decay at infinity with a time lag. However, in most cases, a more rapid exponential decay is much more favored. In order to find a strategy to temper the power law decay, Sabzikar et al. [2] introduced an exponential factor $e^{-\lambda|z|}$ into the particle jump density, and gave a Fourier transform form for the tempered probability density function $f(z,t)$ and tempered fractional derivative operators $\partial^{\beta,\lambda}_{\pm,z} f(z,t)$

$$\mathcal{F}[f](z,t) = e^{-[pB^{\beta,\lambda}_{+}(z)+qB^{\beta,\lambda}_{-}(z)]\mu t}, \quad \mathcal{F}[\partial^{\beta,\lambda}_{\pm,z} f](z,t) = B^{\beta,\lambda}_{\pm}(z)\mathcal{F}[f](z,t),$$

where $p = 1-q, 0 \le p \le 1$, μ is constant and

$$B^{\beta,\lambda}_{\pm}(z) = \begin{cases} (\lambda \pm zi)^{\beta} - \lambda^{\beta}, & 0 < \beta < 1, \\ (\lambda \pm zi)^{\beta} - \lambda^{\beta} - \pm\beta\lambda^{\beta-1} zi, & 1 < \beta < 2, \end{cases} \tag{1}$$

which leads to the following tempered fractional equation in anomalous diffusion:

$$\partial_t f(z,t) = (-1)^k C_T \{p\partial^{\beta,\lambda}_{+,z} + q\partial^{\beta,\lambda}_{-,z}\} f(z,t), \beta \in (k-1,k), k = 1,2.$$

The point source of solutions for this equation is tempered stable probability densities satisfying semi-heavy tails with transition from power law to Gaussian. This flexible model with an exponential decay over long time scales has many advantages, for example, in the real physical system, a Gaussian stochastic process without sharp cutoff can be captured by a tempered Lévy flight [3]. The probability densities of the tempered Lévy flight can be controlled by the tempered fractional diffusion model [4]. In addition, the tempered diffusion model has been shown to have important applications in geophysics [5,6], finance [7] and Laguerre polynomials [8]. In finance, the price fluctuations with semi-heavy tails can be simulated by the tempered stable process, which resemble a power law over a moderate time but converge to a Gaussian process over a long time [9]. In other words, the decay follows a power law over short time scales, but eventually follows the exponential rule over long time scales. In the following, we give the strictly mathematical definition of the tempered fractional:

Definition 1 ([10]). *Let $x : (0,+\infty) \to \mathbb{R}$, then the tempered fractional derivative is defined by*

$$\mathbb{D}^{\alpha,\lambda}_t x(t) = e^{-\lambda t} \mathscr{D}_t{}^{\alpha} (e^{\lambda t} x(t)),$$

where

$$\mathscr{D}_t{}^{\alpha} x(t) = \frac{d^n}{dt^n} ({}_0 I^{n-\alpha}_t x(t)) = \frac{1}{\Gamma(n-\alpha)} \left(\frac{d}{dt}\right)^n \int_0^t (t-s)^{n-\alpha-1} x(s) ds, \ n = [\alpha] + 1$$

is the Riemann–Liouville fractional derivative and

$${}_0 I^{n-\alpha}_t x(t) = \frac{1}{\Gamma(\alpha)} \int_0^t (t-s)^{\alpha-1} x(s) ds$$

denotes the Riemann–Liouville fractional integral operator.

On the other hand, we also notice that, if $\lambda = 0$, the tempered fractional derivative reduces to the Riemann–Liouville and Caputo fractional derivatives, which implies that the tempered fractional derivative is one of the generalized forms of the fractional derivatives, that is, in a mathematical sense, tempered fractional calculus extends the theory of classical fractional calculus such as the Riemann–Liouville, Caputo fractional derivatives, etc. [11–24] to a more general case. In a recent work [10], the existence of a positive solution for a singular tempered fractional turbulent flow model for a porous medium with order $\alpha \in (0,1]$, $\beta \in (1,2]$ was established.

$$\begin{cases} \mathbb{D}_t^{\alpha,\lambda}\left(\varphi_p\left(\mathbb{D}_t^{\beta,\lambda}z(t)\right)\right) = f(t,z(t)), \ t \in (0,1), \\ z(0) = 0, \ \mathbb{D}_t^{\beta,\lambda}z(0) = 0, \ z(1) = \int_0^1 e^{-\lambda(1-t)}z(t)dt. \end{cases} \tag{2}$$

It has been proven that the tempered turbulent flow model (2) has at least one positive solution satisfying

$$k_1 e^{-\lambda t}t^{\beta-1} \le w(t) \le k_2 e^{-\lambda t}t^{\beta-1},$$

where $k_1, k_2 > 0$ are constants. Ledesma et al. [25] considered a boundary value problem with tempered fractional derivatives and oscillating term

$$\begin{cases} \mathbb{D}_{b^-}^{\alpha,\lambda}\left({}^C\mathbb{D}_{a^+}^{\alpha,\lambda}z(t)\right) = \mu\varrho(t)f(z(t)), \ t \in (a,b), \\ z(a) = z(b) = 0, \end{cases} \tag{3}$$

where $\frac{1}{2} < \alpha < 1$, $\lambda > 0$ and $\mu \in \mathbb{R}$; $\varrho \in L^\infty(a,b)$, $\mathbb{D}_{b^-}^{\alpha,\lambda}$ and ${}^C\mathbb{D}_{a^+}^{\alpha,\lambda}$ are tempered left Riemann–Liouville and right Caputo fractional derivatives, respectively. By using a variational principle due to Ricceri, the existence of infinitely many weak solutions was established provided that the nonlinear term f has a suitable oscillating behavior either at the origin or at infinity.

In this paper, we focus on a sub-diffusion model in anomalous diffusion which possesses a changing-sign perturbation

$$\begin{cases} -\mathbb{D}_t^{\alpha,\lambda}z(t) = f\left(t, e^{\lambda t}z(t), \mathbb{D}_t{}^{\beta,\lambda}z(t)\right) + \kappa(t) \\ \mathbb{D}_t{}^{\beta,\lambda}z(0) = 0, \ \mathbb{D}_t{}^{\beta,\lambda}z(1) = \int_0^1 e^{-\lambda(1-t)}\mathbb{D}_t{}^{\beta,\lambda}z(t)dt, \end{cases} \tag{4}$$

where $1 < \alpha \le 2, 0 < \beta < 1$ and $1 < \alpha - \beta \le \beta + 1$, $f : [0,1] \times (0,\infty) \times (0,\infty) \to (0,\infty)$ is continuous which implies that the nonlinearity may be singular in some space variables; $\kappa \in C([0,1], R)$ may be sign-changing.

As far as we know, although many analysis methods, such as the spaces theories [26–31], iterative techniques [32–34], smooth theories [35–37], operator methods [38–41], upper–lower solution methods [42–44], the moving sphere method [45] and critical point theories [46–49], have been employed to study various nonlinear problems, little work has been carried out for changing-sign problems except for [50,51]. In particular, no work has been carried out for the changing-sign perturbation tempered fractional equation with singularity for space variables and a nonlocal boundary condition. The present paper is the first work for the sub-diffusion model in anomalous diffusion processes with a changing-sign perturbation.

2. Basic Definitions and Preliminaries

Firstly, we recall some properties of the Riemann–Liouville fractional calculus.

Lemma 1 ([10]).

(1) *Let $g(t) \in L^1[0,1] \cap C[0,1], \gamma > 0$, then*

$${}_0I_t^{\gamma}\mathscr{D}_t{}^{\gamma}(g(t)) = g(t) + b_1 t^{\gamma-1} + b_2 t^{\gamma-2} + \cdots + b_m t^{\gamma-m},$$

where $b_i \in R, i = 1,2,3,\ldots,m, (m = [\gamma]+1)$.

(2) *If $u \in L^1(0,1), \alpha > \beta > 0$, then*

$${}_0I_t^{\alpha}{}_0I_t^{\beta}u(t) = {}_0I_t^{\alpha+\beta}u(t), \ \mathscr{D}_t{}^{\beta}{}_0I_t^{\alpha}u(t) = {}_0I_t^{\alpha-\beta}u(t), \ \mathscr{D}_t{}^{\beta}{}_0I_t^{\beta}u(t) = u(t).$$

(3) *If* $\rho > 0, \mu > 0$, *then*

$$\mathscr{D}_t^{\rho} t^{\mu-1} = \frac{\Gamma(\mu)}{\Gamma(\mu-\rho)} t^{\mu-\rho-1}.$$

The work space of this paper is the Banach space $E = C[0,1]$ which is equipped with the usual maximum norm $||x|| = \max_{0\le t\le 1} |x(t)|$. Let

$$P = \{x \in E : x(t) \geq 0, t \in [0,1]\},$$

then, P is a normal cone.

Lemma 2. *Suppose* $\kappa(t)$ *is a positive continuous function in* $[0,1]$*; then, the linear tempered fractional equation*

$$\begin{cases} -\mathbb{D}_t^{\alpha-\beta,\lambda} z(t) = \kappa(t), \\ z(0) = 0, \;\; z(1) = \displaystyle\int_0^1 e^{-\lambda(1-t)} z(t)dt, \end{cases} \tag{5}$$

has the unique positive solution

$$\varphi(t) = \int_0^1 H(t,s)\kappa(s)ds, \tag{6}$$

where

$$H(t,s) = \begin{cases} \dfrac{[(\alpha-\beta)(1-s)^{\alpha-\beta-1}(\alpha-\beta-1+s)t^{\alpha-\beta-1} - (\alpha-\beta)(\alpha-\beta-1)(t-s)^{\alpha-\beta-1}]e^{-\lambda(t-s)}}{(\alpha-\beta-1)\Gamma(\alpha-\beta+1)}, \\ \qquad s \leq t; \\ \dfrac{(\alpha-\beta)(1-s)^{\alpha-\beta-1}(\alpha-\beta-1+s)}{(\alpha-\beta-1)\Gamma(\alpha-\beta+1)} t^{\alpha-\beta-1}e^{-\lambda(t-s)}, \; t \leq s, \end{cases} \tag{7}$$

is the Green function of (5).

Clearly, $H(t,s)$ is non-negative and continuous for $(t,s) \in [0,1] \times [0,1]$.
Make the transformation

$$z(t) = e^{-\lambda t} I^{\beta}(e^{\lambda t} y(t)), \;\; y(t) \in C[0,1],$$

then, by [10], the singular perturbation tempered fractional Equation (4) can be converted to the following equivalent mixed integro-differential tempered fractional equation:

$$\begin{cases} -\mathbb{D}_t^{\alpha-\beta,\lambda} y(t) = f(t, I^{\beta}(e^{\lambda t} y(t)), y(t)) + \kappa(t), \\ y(0) = 0, \;\; y(1) = \displaystyle\int_0^1 e^{-\lambda(1-t)} y(t)dt. \end{cases} \tag{8}$$

As a result, a function y is a solution of (8) if and only if it is a solution of the following integral equation:

$$y(t) = \int_0^1 H(t,s)\Big[f(s, I^{\beta}(e^{\lambda s} y(s)), y(s)) + \kappa(s)\Big]ds.$$

Now, let $y(t) = t^{\alpha-\beta-1}x(t)$; then, we can rewrite the above integral equation:

$$x(t) = \int_0^1 t^{\beta+1-\alpha} H(t,s)\Big[f(s, I^{\beta}(e^{\lambda s} s^{\alpha-\beta-1} x(s)), s^{\alpha-\beta-1}x(s)) + \kappa(s)\Big]ds.$$

Let

$$H^*(t,s) = t^{\beta+1-\alpha} H(t,s),$$

then, we consider the fixed point of the following operator:

$$(Tx)(t) = \int_0^1 H^*(t,s)\Big[f(s, I^\beta(e^{\lambda s}s^{\alpha-\beta-1}x(s)), s^{\alpha-\beta-1}x(s)) + \kappa(s)\Big]ds.$$

We use the following hypothesis in this paper.

(**C1**) There exist a constant $\theta \in (0, \frac{\beta}{\alpha-\beta-1})$ and $\omega_1, \omega_2 \in P, \omega_1 \not\equiv 0, \omega_2 \not\equiv 0$ such that

$$\frac{t^{\theta(\alpha-\beta-1)}\omega_1(t)}{(x+y)^\theta} \leq f(t,x,y) \leq \frac{t^{\theta(\alpha-\beta-1)}\omega_2(t)}{(x+y)^\theta}, \ (x,y) \in [0,\infty) \times (0,\infty), \ t \in (0,1).$$

Let $\varphi(t)$ be the unique solution of Equation (5) and rewrite $\varphi(t)$ as

$$\varphi(t) = \int_0^1 H^*(t,s)\kappa(s)ds,$$

and define functions

$$\phi(t) = \int_0^1 H^*(t,s)\omega_1(s)ds, \ \psi(t) = \int_0^1 H^*(t,s)\omega_2(s)ds.$$

For the above the functions φ, ϕ and ψ, we denote

$$\begin{aligned}
\varphi_* &= \min_{0\leq t\leq 1} \varphi(t), \quad \varphi^* = \sup_{0\leq t\leq 1} \varphi(t), \\
\phi_* &= \min_{0\leq t\leq 1} \phi(t), \quad \phi^* = \max_{0\leq t\leq 1} \phi(t), \\
\psi_* &= \min_{0\leq t\leq 1} \psi(t), \quad \psi^* = \max_{0\leq t\leq 1} \psi(t).
\end{aligned}$$

Noticing

$$\phi(t) = \int_0^1 H^*(t,s)\omega_1(s)ds \geq \int_0^1 \frac{(\alpha-\beta)(1-s)^{\alpha-\beta-1}(\alpha-\beta-1+s)}{(\alpha-\beta-1)\Gamma(\alpha-\beta+1)} e^{-\lambda}\omega_1(s)ds,$$

then, it follows from (**C1**) that $0 < \phi_* \leq \phi^* \leq \psi_* \leq \psi^*$.

Our main tool used in deriving our results is the following Schauder fixed point theorem.

Lemma 3 (Schauder fixed point theorem). *Let Ω be a closed bounded convex subset of a Banach space E. Assume that $T : \Omega \to \Omega$ is compact. Then, T has at least one fixed point in Ω.*

3. Positive Case for $\varphi(t)$

Theorem 1. *Assume that (**C1**) holds and $\varphi_* \geq 0$. Then, the singular perturbation tempered fractional equation with nonlocal boundary condition (4) has at least one positive solution.*

Proof. Firstly, choose a constant

$$R > \max\left\{1, \phi_*^{-\frac{1}{1-\theta}}\left(1 + \frac{e^\lambda}{\Gamma(\beta+1)}\right)^{\frac{\theta}{1-\theta}}, (\psi^* + \varphi^*)^{\frac{1}{1-\theta}}\right\}$$

and take the closed convex set of P

$$\Omega = \{x \in P : \frac{1}{R} \leq x(t) \leq R, \ t \in [0,1]\}.$$

Noticing that $1 < \alpha - \beta \leq \beta + 1$, we have

$$\begin{aligned}\frac{\Gamma(\alpha-\beta)t^{\alpha-1}}{\Gamma(\alpha)R} &\leq I^{\beta}(e^{\lambda s}s^{\alpha-\beta-1}x(s)) = \int_0^t \frac{(t-s)^{\beta-1}}{\Gamma(\beta)}s^{\alpha-\beta-1}e^{\lambda s}x(s)ds \\ &\leq \frac{e^{\lambda}Rt^{\beta}}{\Gamma(\beta+1)} \leq \frac{e^{\lambda}Rt^{\alpha-\beta-1}}{\Gamma(\beta+1)} \leq \frac{e^{\lambda}R}{\Gamma(\beta+1)},\end{aligned} \tag{9}$$

for $\theta \in (0, \frac{\beta}{\alpha-\beta-1})$ and $s \in (0,1)$; it follows from (**C1**) and (9) that

$$\begin{aligned}&\frac{\omega_1(s)}{R^{\theta}\left(1+\frac{e^{\lambda}}{\Gamma(\beta+1)}\right)^{\theta}} \\ &\leq \frac{s^{\theta(\alpha-\beta-1)}\omega_1(s)}{(s^{\alpha-\beta-1}x(s)+I^{\beta}(e^{\lambda s}s^{\alpha-\beta-1}x(s)))^{\theta}} \\ &\leq f(s, I^{\beta}(e^{\lambda s}s^{\alpha-\beta-1}x(s)), s^{\alpha-\beta-1}x(s)) \\ &\leq \frac{s^{\theta(\alpha-\beta-1)}\omega_2(s)}{(s^{\alpha-\beta-1}x(s)+I^{\beta}(e^{\lambda s}s^{\alpha-\beta-1}x(s)))^{\theta}} \leq \omega_2(s)R^{\theta}.\end{aligned} \tag{10}$$

Consequently, by (9) and (10), one has

$$\begin{aligned}(Tx)(t) &= \int_0^1 H^*(t,s)\left[f(s, I^{\beta}(e^{\lambda s}s^{\alpha-\beta-1}x(s)), s^{\alpha-\beta-1}x(s)) + \kappa(s)\right]ds \\ &= \int_0^1 H^*(t,s)f(s, I^{\beta}(e^{\lambda s}s^{\alpha-\beta-1}x(s)), s^{\alpha-\beta-1}x(s))ds + \varphi(t).\end{aligned} \tag{11}$$

Thus, $T : \Omega \to E$ is a completely continuous operator.

In what follows, we show that T maps the closed convex set Ω into Ω. In fact, for any given $x \in \Omega$ and $t \in [0,1]$, from (9)–(11), one has

$$\begin{aligned}(Tx)(t) &= \int_0^1 H^*(t,s)f(s, I^{\beta}(e^{\lambda s}s^{\alpha-\beta-1}x(s)), s^{\alpha-\beta-1}x(s))ds + \varphi(t) \\ &\geq \frac{1}{R^{\theta}\left(1+\frac{e^{\lambda}}{\Gamma(\beta+1)}\right)^{\theta}}\int_0^1 H^*(t,s)\omega_1(s)ds \\ &\geq \frac{\phi_*}{R^{\theta}\left(1+\frac{e^{\lambda}}{\Gamma(\beta+1)}\right)^{\theta}} \\ &= \frac{\phi_* R^{1-\theta}}{R\left(1+\frac{e^{\lambda}}{\Gamma(\beta+1)}\right)^{\theta}} \\ &\geq \frac{1}{R},\end{aligned}$$

and

$$\begin{aligned}(Tx)(t) &= \int_0^1 H^*(t,s)f(s, I^{\beta}(e^{\lambda s}s^{\alpha-\beta-1}x(s)), s^{\alpha-\beta-1}x(s))ds + \varphi(t) \\ &\leq R^{\theta}\int_0^1 H^*(t,s)\omega_2(s)ds + \varphi^* \\ &\leq \psi^* R^{\theta} + \varphi^* \leq (\psi^* + \varphi^*)R^{\theta} \leq R.\end{aligned}$$

Thus, T maps the closed convex set Ω into Ω. According to Schauder's fixed point theorem, T has a fixed point $x^* \in \Omega$ and, hence, the singular perturbation tempered fractional equation with a nonlocal boundary condition (4) has at least one positive solution. □

4. Negative Case for $\varphi(t)$

Theorem 2. *Assume that* (**C1**) *holds and* $\varphi^* \leq 0$. *If*

$$\varphi_* \geq \left(\frac{\phi_* \theta^2}{\psi^{*\theta} \left(1 + \frac{1}{\Gamma(\beta+1)}\right)^\theta} \right)^{\frac{1}{1-\theta^2}} \left(1 - \frac{1}{\theta^2}\right), \tag{12}$$

then, the singular perturbation tempered fractional equation with nonlocal boundary condition (4) *has at least one positive solution.*

Proof. For this case, we only need to find the suitable $0 < r < R$ such that $T : \Omega \to \Omega$, where

$$\Omega = \{x \in P : r \leq x(t) \leq R, \ \ t \in [0,1]\}.$$

Similar to (9), we have

$$\begin{aligned} &\frac{\Gamma(\alpha-\beta)t^{\alpha-1}r}{\Gamma(\alpha)} \\ &\leq I^\beta(e^{\lambda s} s^{\alpha-\beta-1} x(s)) \\ &\leq \frac{e^\lambda R t^\beta}{\Gamma(\beta+1)} \\ &\leq \frac{e^\lambda R}{\Gamma(\beta+1)}, \end{aligned} \tag{13}$$

and then

$$\begin{aligned} &\frac{\omega_1(s)}{R^\theta \left(1 + \frac{e^\lambda}{\Gamma(\beta+1)}\right)^\theta} \\ &\leq f(s, I^\beta(e^{\lambda s} s^{\alpha-\beta-1} x(s)), s^{\alpha-\beta-1} x(s)) \\ &\leq \frac{\omega_2(s)}{r^\theta}. \end{aligned} \tag{14}$$

Consequently, for any given $x \in \Omega$ and $t \in [0,1]$, from (14), one has

$$\begin{aligned} (Tx)(t) &= \int_0^1 H^*(t,s) f(s, I^\beta(e^{\lambda s} s^{\alpha-\beta-1} x(s)), s^{\alpha-\beta-1} x(s)) ds + \varphi(t) \\ &\geq \frac{1}{R^\theta \left(1 + \frac{e^\lambda}{\Gamma(\beta+1)}\right)^\theta} \int_0^1 H^*(t,s) \omega_1(s) ds + \varphi_* \\ &\geq \frac{\phi_*}{R^\theta \left(1 + \frac{e^\lambda}{\Gamma(\beta+1)}\right)^\theta} + \varphi_*, \end{aligned} \tag{15}$$

and

$$\begin{aligned} (Tx)(t) &= \int_0^1 H^*(t,s) f(s, I^\beta(e^{\lambda s} s^{\alpha-\beta-1} x(s)), s^{\alpha-\beta-1} x(s)) ds + \varphi(t) \\ &\leq \frac{1}{r^\theta} \int_0^1 H^*(t,s) \omega_2(s) ds \\ &\leq \frac{\psi^*}{r^\theta}. \end{aligned} \tag{16}$$

From (15) and (16), $T : \Omega \to \Omega$ holds provided that the following inequalities are valid:

$$\frac{\phi_*}{R^\theta \left(1 + \frac{1}{\Gamma(\beta+1)}\right)^\theta} + \varphi_* \geq r, \ \ \frac{\psi^*}{r^\theta} \leq R. \tag{17}$$

In order to show that (17) holds, let

$$R = \frac{\psi^*}{r^\theta}.$$

Clearly, to ensure that the inequalities (17) are true, we only need to find a suitable $r > 0$ such that

$$R = \frac{\psi^*}{r^\theta} > r, \quad \frac{\phi_* r^{\theta^2}}{\psi^{*\theta}\left(1 + \frac{1}{\Gamma(\beta+1)}\right)^\theta} + \varphi_* \geq r,$$

i.e.,

$$0 < r < \psi^{*\frac{1}{1+\theta}}, \quad \varphi_* \geq r - \frac{\phi_*}{\psi^{*\theta}\left(1 + \frac{1}{\Gamma(\beta+1)}\right)^\theta} r^{\theta^2}. \tag{18}$$

Now, let

$$h(x) = x - \frac{\phi_*}{\psi^{*\theta}\left(1 + \frac{1}{\Gamma(\beta+1)}\right)^\theta} x^{\theta^2}, \quad x \in (0, \infty).$$

Obviously,

$$h'(x) = 1 - \frac{\theta^2 \phi_*}{\psi^{*\theta}\left(1 + \frac{1}{\Gamma(\beta+1)}\right)^\theta x^{1-\theta^2}},$$

which implies that $h(x)$ takes the minimum value

$$h(\vartheta) = \left(\frac{\phi_* \theta^2}{\psi^{*\theta}\left(1 + \frac{1}{\Gamma(\beta+1)}\right)^\theta}\right)^{\frac{1}{1-\theta^2}} \left(1 - \frac{1}{\theta^2}\right),$$

when

$$\vartheta = \left(\frac{\theta^2 \phi_*}{\psi^{*\theta}\left(1 + \frac{1}{\Gamma(\beta+1)}\right)^\theta}\right)^{\frac{1}{1-\theta^2}}.$$

Let $r = \vartheta$; since $\phi_* \leq \psi^*, 0 < \theta^2 < 1, 1 + \frac{1}{\Gamma(\beta+1)} > 1$, from (12), we obtain

$$\begin{aligned} r = \vartheta &= \left(\frac{\theta^2 \phi_*}{\psi^{*\theta}\left(1 + \frac{1}{\Gamma(\beta+1)}\right)^\theta}\right)^{\frac{1}{1-\theta^2}} \\ &< \left(\frac{\psi^*}{\psi^{*\theta}}\right)^{\frac{1}{1-\theta^2}} \\ &= \psi^{*\frac{1}{1+\theta}}, \end{aligned}$$

and

$$\begin{aligned} \varphi_* &\geq \left(\frac{\phi_* \theta^2}{\psi^{*\theta}\left(1 + \frac{1}{\alpha\Gamma(\alpha)}\right)^\theta}\right)^{\frac{1}{1-\theta^2}} \left(1 - \frac{1}{\theta^2}\right) \\ &= r - \frac{\phi_*}{\psi^{*\theta}\left(1 + \frac{1}{\Gamma(\beta+1)}\right)^\theta} r^{\theta^2}. \end{aligned}$$

Therefore, if

$$r = \vartheta, \; R = \frac{\psi^*}{\vartheta^\theta},$$

then (18) is true. Thus, by mean of Schauder's fixed point theorem, T has a fixed point $x^* \in \Omega$ and, hence, the singular perturbation tempered fractional Equation (4) with nonlocal boundary condition has at least one positive solution. □

5. Changing-Sign Case for $\varphi(t)$

In order to establish the existence of a positive solution for the changing-sign case, we firstly consider the following equation:

$$x^{1-\theta^2}(\psi^* + \varphi^* x^\theta)^{1+\theta} = \frac{\theta^2 \psi^* \phi_*}{\left(1 + \frac{1}{\Gamma(\beta+1)}\right)^\theta}. \tag{19}$$

Lemma 4. *If $0 < \theta < 1$, then Equation (19) possesses a unique positive solution ϑ in $(0, \infty)$. Moreover,*

$$\vartheta \in \left(0, \left(\frac{\theta^2 \psi^* \phi_*}{\left(1 + \frac{1}{\Gamma(\beta+1)}\right)^\theta}\right)^{\frac{1}{2+2\theta}}\right).$$

Proof. Let

$$\mu := \left(\frac{\theta^2 \psi^* \phi_*}{\left(1 + \frac{1}{\Gamma(\beta+1)}\right)^\theta}\right)^{\frac{1}{2+2\theta}}, \quad h(x) = \frac{\theta^2 \psi^* \phi_*}{\left(1 + \frac{1}{\Gamma(\beta+1)}\right)^\theta} - x^{1-\theta^2}(\psi^* + \varphi^* x^\theta)^{1+\theta},$$

then

$$h(0) = \lim_{x \to 0} h(x) = \frac{\theta^2 \psi^* \phi_*}{\left(1 + \frac{1}{\Gamma(\beta+1)}\right)^\theta} > 0. \tag{20}$$

Since $0 < \theta < 1, \ \psi^* \geq \phi_*$, one has

$$0 < \mu = \left(\frac{\theta^2 \psi^* \phi_*}{\left(1 + \frac{1}{\Gamma(\beta+1)}\right)^\theta}\right)^{\frac{1}{2+2\theta}} < \psi^{*\frac{1}{1+\theta}},$$

which yields

$$\mu^{(1+\theta)^2} < \psi^{*1+\theta}.$$

Hence,

$$\begin{aligned} h(\mu) &= \mu^{2+2\theta} - \mu^{1-\theta^2}(\psi^* + \varphi^* \mu^\theta)^{1+\theta} \\ &= \mu^{1-\theta^2}\left[\mu^{(1+\theta)^2} - (\psi^* + \varphi^* \mu^\theta)^{1+\theta}\right] \\ &< \mu^{1-\theta^2}\left[\mu^{(1+\theta)^2} - \psi^{*1+\theta}\right] < 0, \end{aligned} \tag{21}$$

Moreover,

$$\begin{aligned} h'(x) &= -(1-\theta^2)x^{-\theta^2}(\psi^* + \varphi^* x^\theta)^{1+\theta} - \varphi^* \theta x^{1-\theta^2}(\psi^* + \varphi^* x^\theta)^\theta x^{\theta-1} \\ &< 0, \ x \in (0, \infty), \end{aligned} \tag{22}$$

which implies that $h(x)$ is strictly decreasing in $(0, \infty)$. Thus, it follows from (20)–(22) that Equation (19) possesses a unique positive solution $\vartheta \in (0, \mu)$. □

Theorem 3. *Suppose that* (**C1**) *holds and* $\varphi_* \leq 0, \ \ \varphi^* \geq 0$. *If*

$$\varphi_* \geq \vartheta - \frac{\phi_* \vartheta^{2\theta}}{(\psi^* + \varphi^* \vartheta^\theta)^\theta \left(1 + \frac{1}{\Gamma(\beta+1)}\right)^\theta}, \tag{23}$$

where ϑ *is the solution of Equation* (19), *then the singular perturbation tempered fractional Equation* (4) *with nonlocal boundary condition has at least one positive solution.*

Proof. If $\varphi_* \leq 0, \ \ \varphi^* \geq 0$, we still need to seek for suitable $0 < r < R$ such that $T : \Omega \to \Omega$, where

$$\Omega = \{x \in P : r \leq x(t) \leq R, \ \ t \in [0,1]\}.$$

For any given $x \in \Omega$, it follows from (13) and (14), $\varphi_* \leq 0, \ \ \varphi^* \geq 0$ that

$$\begin{aligned} (Tx)(t) &= \int_0^1 H^*(t,s) f(s, I^\beta(e^{\lambda s} s^{\alpha-\beta-1} x(s)), s^{\alpha-\beta-1} x(s)) ds + \varphi(t) \\ &\geq \frac{1}{R^\theta \left(1 + \frac{e^\lambda}{\Gamma(\beta+1)}\right)^\theta} \int_0^1 H^*(t,s) \omega_1(s) ds + \varphi_* \\ &\geq \frac{\phi_*}{R^\theta \left(1 + \frac{e^\lambda}{\Gamma(\beta+1)}\right)^\theta} + \varphi_*, \end{aligned} \tag{24}$$

and

$$\begin{aligned} (Tx)(t) &= \int_0^1 H^*(t,s) f(s, I^\beta(e^{\lambda s} s^{\alpha-\beta-1} x(s)), s^{\alpha-\beta-1} x(s)) ds + \varphi(t) \\ &\leq \frac{1}{r^\theta} \int_0^1 H^*(t,s) \omega_2(s) ds \leq \frac{\psi^*}{r^\theta} + \varphi^*. \end{aligned} \tag{25}$$

By (24) and (25), to guarantee $T : \Omega \to \Omega$, it is sufficient to find $0 < r < R$ such that

$$\frac{\phi_*}{R^\theta \left(1 + \frac{1}{\Gamma(\beta+1)}\right)^\theta} + \varphi_* \geq r, \quad \frac{\psi^*}{r^\theta} + \varphi^* \leq R. \tag{26}$$

To perform this, take

$$R = \frac{\psi^*}{r^\theta} + \varphi^*.$$

This is equivalent to finding an $r > 0$ satisfying

$$\frac{\psi^*}{r^\theta} + \varphi^* > r, \ \ \varphi_* \geq r - \frac{\phi_* r^{2\theta}}{(\psi^* + \varphi^* r^\theta)^\theta \left(1 + \frac{1}{\Gamma(\beta+1)}\right)^\theta}. \tag{27}$$

Let

$$h(x) = x - \frac{\phi_* x^{2\theta}}{(\psi^* + \varphi^* x^\theta)^\theta \left(1 + \frac{1}{\Gamma(\beta+1)}\right)^\theta}.$$

Then

$$\begin{aligned} h'(x) &= 1 - \frac{\phi_* \left[\theta^2 x^{\theta^2 - 1} (\psi^* + \theta^2 \varphi^* x^\theta)^\theta - \varphi^* x^{\theta^2} (\psi^* + \varphi^* x^\theta)^{\theta-1} x^{\theta-1}\right]}{(\psi^* + \varphi^* x^\theta)^{2\theta} \left(1 + \frac{1}{\Gamma(\beta+1)}\right)^\theta} \\ &= 1 - \frac{\phi_* \theta^2 x^{\theta^2 - 1}}{(\psi^* + \varphi^* x^\theta)^\theta \left(1 + \frac{1}{\Gamma(\beta+1)}\right)^\theta} \left[1 - \frac{\varphi^* x^\theta}{\psi^* + \varphi^* x^\theta}\right] \\ &= 1 - \frac{\phi_* \psi^* \theta^2 x^{\theta^2 - 1}}{(\psi^* + \varphi^* x^\theta)^{\theta+1} \left(1 + \frac{1}{\Gamma(\beta+1)}\right)^\theta}, \end{aligned}$$

and, hence,

$$\lim_{x\to 0} h'(x) = -\infty, \quad \lim_{x\to\infty} h'(x) = 1.$$

Thus, there exists ϑ such that

$$h'(\vartheta) = 1 - \frac{\phi_* \psi^* \theta^2 \vartheta^{\theta^2 - 1}}{(\psi^* + \varphi^* \vartheta^\theta)^{\theta+1} \left(1 + \frac{1}{\Gamma(\beta+1)}\right)^\theta} = 0,$$

i.e., ϑ solves Equation (19).

$$x^{1-\theta^2} (\psi^* + \varphi^* x^\theta)^{1+\theta} = \frac{\theta^2 \psi^* \phi_*}{\left(1 + \frac{1}{\Gamma(\beta+1)}\right)^\theta}.$$

It follows from Lemma 4 that ϑ is unique and

$$\vartheta \in \left(0, \left(\frac{\theta^2 \psi^* \phi_*}{\left(1 + \frac{1}{\Gamma(\beta+1)}\right)^\theta}\right)^{\frac{1}{2+2\theta}}\right).$$

On the other hand,

$$h''(r) = \frac{(1-\theta^2)\theta^2 \phi_* \psi^* r^{\theta^2 - 2}}{(\psi^* + \varphi^* r^\theta)^{\theta+1} \left(1 + \frac{1}{\Gamma(\beta+1)}\right)^\theta} + \frac{(1+\theta)\theta^3 \varphi^* \phi_* \psi^* r^{\theta^2 + \theta - 2}}{(\psi^* + \varphi^* r^\theta)^{\theta+2} \left(1 + \frac{1}{\Gamma(\beta+1)}\right)^\theta} > 0,$$

which implies that $h(r)$ reaches its minimum value at ϑ, that is

$$h(\vartheta) = \min_{r \in (0,\infty)} h(r).$$

Take $r = \vartheta$, assumption (23) ensures the following inequality holds:

$$\varphi_* \geq r - \frac{\phi_* r^{2\theta}}{(\psi^* + \varphi^* r^\theta)^\theta \left(1 + \frac{1}{\Gamma(\beta+1)}\right)^\theta}.$$

Next, we verify the inequality $R > r$. It follows from

$$R = \frac{\psi^*}{\vartheta^\theta} + \varphi^*, \quad \vartheta^{1-\theta^2} (\psi^* + \varphi^* \vartheta^\theta)^{1+\theta} = \frac{\theta^2 \psi^* \phi_*}{\left(1 + \frac{1}{\Gamma(\beta+1)}\right)^\theta},$$

that

$$\vartheta^{1+\theta} R^{1+\theta} = \frac{\theta^2 \psi^* \phi_*}{\left(1 + \frac{1}{\Gamma(\beta+1)}\right)^\theta},$$

that is

$$R = \frac{1}{\vartheta} \left(\frac{\theta^2 \psi^* \phi_*}{\left(1 + \frac{1}{\Gamma(\beta+1)}\right)^\theta}\right)^{\frac{1}{1+\theta}}.$$

Since

$$0 < \vartheta < \left(\frac{\theta^2 \psi^* \phi_*}{\left(1 + \frac{1}{\Gamma(\beta+1)}\right)^\theta}\right)^{\frac{1}{2+2\theta}},$$

one has

$$R > \left(\frac{\theta^2 \psi^* \phi_*}{\left(1 + \frac{1}{\Gamma(\beta+1)}\right)^{\theta}} \right)^{\frac{1}{2+2\theta}} > \vartheta = r.$$

Hence, we have found a constant $r = \vartheta$ such that (26) holds. According to Schauder's fixed point theorem, the singular perturbation tempered fractional Equation (4) with nonlocal boundary condition has at least one positive solution. □

6. Example

In anomalous diffusion, the mean square variance sometimes grows slower than Gaussian to form a sub-diffusion which can be modeled by the time tempered fractional diffusion equation. In this section, we only give an example for the most complex case, i.e., with uncertain changing-sign perturbations, to demonstrate the application of our main results.

Example 1. *Consider the sub-diffusion model* (4) *in anomalous diffusion with a changing-sign perturbation* $\kappa(t)$ *for the case* $\alpha = \frac{3}{2}, \beta = \frac{1}{4}, \lambda = 2$,

$$\begin{cases} -\mathbb{D}_t^{\frac{3}{2},2} z(t) = \dfrac{100.5t^{\frac{1}{12}}}{e^{2t}\left(e^{2t}z(t) + |\mathbb{D}_t^{\frac{1}{4},2} z(t)|\right)^{\frac{1}{3}}} + \kappa(t) \\ \mathbb{D}_t^{\frac{1}{4},2} z(0) = 0, \ \mathbb{D}_t^{\frac{1}{4},2} z(1) = \displaystyle\int_0^1 e^{-2(1-t)} \mathbb{D}_t^{\frac{1}{4},2} z(t) dt, \end{cases} \tag{28}$$

where

$$\kappa(t) = \begin{cases} -\dfrac{1}{5} e^{-2t}, & t \in \left[0, \dfrac{1}{2}\right), \\ \dfrac{1}{5} e^{-2t+1}, & t \in \left[\dfrac{1}{2}, 1\right]. \end{cases}$$

Conclusion The sub-diffusion model (28) has at least one positive solution.

Proof. Let $\omega_1(t) = 100e^{-2t}, \ \omega_2(t) = 101e^{-2t}$ and

$$f(t,x,y) = \frac{100.5t^{\frac{1}{12}}}{e^{2t}(x+y)^{\frac{1}{3}}}, \ (x,y) \in [0,\infty) \times (0,\infty), \ t \in (0,1),$$

then

$$\frac{100t^{\frac{1}{12}}e^{-2t}}{(x+y)^{\frac{1}{3}}} \le f(t,x,y) \le \frac{101t^{\frac{1}{12}}e^{-2t}}{(x+y)^{\frac{1}{3}}}, (x,y) \in [0,\infty) \times (0,\infty), \ t \in (0,1).$$

Thus, **(C1)** holds. On the other hand, by Lemma 2, we obtain

$$H(t,s) = \begin{cases} \dfrac{5\left[(1-s)^{\frac{1}{4}}(\frac{1}{4}+s)t^{\frac{1}{4}} - \frac{1}{4}(t-s)^{\frac{1}{4}}\right]e^{-2(t-s)}}{\Gamma(\frac{9}{4})}, & s \le t; \\ \dfrac{5(1-s)^{\frac{1}{4}}(\frac{1}{4}+s)}{\Gamma(\frac{9}{4})} t^{\frac{1}{4}} e^{-2(t-s)}, & t \le s, \end{cases} \tag{29}$$

then

$$H^*(t,s)=\begin{cases}\dfrac{5\Big[(1-s)^{\frac{1}{4}}(\frac{1}{4}+s)-\frac{1}{4}t^{-\frac{1}{4}}(t-s)^{\frac{1}{4}}\Big]e^{-2(t-s)}}{\Gamma(\frac{9}{4})}, & s\le t;\\ \dfrac{5(1-s)^{\frac{1}{4}}(\frac{1}{4}+s)}{\Gamma(\frac{9}{4})}e^{-2(t-s)}, & t\le s.\end{cases} \tag{30}$$

Now, we compute φ^*, φ_* and ϕ_*, ψ^*. Note that

$$\varphi(t)=\int_0^1 H^*(t,s)\kappa(s)ds=\frac{1}{\Gamma(\frac{9}{4})}\begin{cases}-\dfrac{5}{9}e^{-2t}+\dfrac{1}{25}e^{-2t}t, & 0\le t<\dfrac{1}{2},\\ \dfrac{5}{9}e^{-2t+1}+\dfrac{1}{25}e^{-2t+1}t, & \dfrac{1}{2}\le t\le 1,\end{cases}$$

and, hence,

$$\varphi_*=\frac{-\frac{5}{9}}{\Gamma(\frac{9}{4})}=-0.4903,\ \ \varphi^*=\frac{5}{9\Gamma(\frac{9}{4})}+\frac{1}{50\Gamma(\frac{9}{4})}=0.5080.$$

Similarly, we have

$$\phi(t)=\int_0^1 H^*(t,s)\omega_1(s)ds=\frac{2500}{9\Gamma(\frac{9}{4})}e^{-2t}-\frac{20}{\Gamma(\frac{9}{4})}e^{-2t}t,$$

$$\psi(t)=\int_0^1 H^*(t,s)\omega_2(s)ds=\frac{2525}{9\Gamma(\frac{9}{4})}e^{-2t}-\frac{101}{5\Gamma(\frac{9}{4})}e^{-2t}t,$$

and, consequently,

$$\phi_*=\min_{0\le t\le 1}\phi(t)=30.8,\ \ \phi^*=\max_{0\le t\le 1}\phi(t)=245.2,$$
$$\psi_*=\min_{0\le t\le 1}\psi(t)=27.472,\ \ \psi^*=\max_{0\le t\le 1}\phi(t)=247.6.$$

Thus, Equation (19) becomes

$$x^{\frac{8}{9}}(247.6+0.5080x^{\frac{1}{3}})^{\frac{4}{3}}=\frac{\frac{1}{9}\times 247.6\times 30.8}{(1+1.1033)^{\frac{1}{3}}}=661.3405. \tag{31}$$

which has a unique solution $\vartheta=0.3814$. Hence,

$$\vartheta-\frac{\phi_*\vartheta^{2\theta}}{(\psi^*+\varphi^*\vartheta^\theta)^\theta\Big(1+\frac{1}{\Gamma(\beta+1)}\Big)^\theta}=0.3814-\frac{0.3814^{\frac{2}{3}}\times 30.8}{(247.6+0.5080\times 0.3814^{\frac{1}{3}})^{\frac{1}{3}}(1+1.1033)^{\frac{1}{3}}}$$
$$=-1.6310<\varphi_*=-0.4903.$$

It follows from Theorem 3 that the sub-diffusion model (28) has at least one positive solution. □

7. Conclusions

The tempered fractional derivative is a more flexible alternative to classical fractional derivatives, which can model random walks with semi-heavy tails and stable probability densities for the particle jumps, i.e., the transition has a semi-long-range dependence in a long time range as a power law but is like the Gaussian in a short time range. In this paper, by using the technique of two-step substitution, the higher-order sub-diffusion model is converted to a lower-order mixed integro-differential sub-diffusion model, and then, by introducing a power factor, we derive that the linear integral operator we define has a positive infimum; this innovative technique is introduced for the first time in the literature and it is critical for controlling the influence of changing-sign perturbation. Then, an a priori estimate and Schauder's fixed point theorem are applied to prove that the sub-diffusion model has at least one positive solution whether the perturbation is positive, negative or changing-sign. In particular, the main nonlinear term is allowed to have singularity for some space variables. In the end, we shall also address that the perturbation in this paper only depends on a time variable; if it relies on both time variables and space variables, then further study will become more challenging and interesting.

Author Contributions: Investigation, P.C. and L.L.; Writing—original draft, X.Z. and J.C.; Writing—review & editing, Y.W. All authors have read and agreed to the published version of the manuscript.

Funding: The authors are supported financially by the Natural Science Foundation of Shandong Province of China (ZR2022AM015), and an ARC Discovery Project Grant.

Data Availability Statement: Data are contained within the article.

Conflicts of Interest: The authors declare that there is no conflict of interest regarding the publication of this paper.

References

1. Einstein, A. On the movement of small particles suspended in a stationary liquid demanded by the molecular kinetic theory of heat. *Ann. Phys.* **1905**, *17*, 549–560. [CrossRef]
2. Sabzikar, F.; Meerschaert, M.; Chen, J. Tempered fractional calculus. *J. Comput. Phys.* **2015**, *293*, 14–28. [CrossRef]
3. Koponen, I. Analytic approach to the problem of convergence of truncated Lévy flights towards the Gaussian stochastic process. *Phys. Rev. E* **1995**, *52*, 1197–1199. [CrossRef]
4. Cartea, Á.; Negrete, D. Fluid limit of the continuous-time random walk with general Lévy jump distribution functions. *Phys. Rev. E* **2007**, *76*, 041105. [CrossRef]
5. Meerschaert, M.; Zhang, Y.; Baeumer, B. Tempered anomalous diffusion in heterogeneous systems. *Geophys. Res. Lett.* **2008**, *35*, L17403. [CrossRef]
6. Zhang, Y.; Meerschaert, M. Gaussian setting time for solute transport in fluvial systems. *Water Resour. Res.* **2011**, *47*, W08601. [CrossRef]
7. Carr, P.; Geman, H.; Madan, D.; Yor, M. The fine structure of asset returns: An empirical investigation. *J. Bus.* **2002**, *75*, 305–333. [CrossRef]
8. Chen, S.; Shen, J.; Wang, L. Laguerre functions and their applications to tempered fractional differential equations on infinite intervals. *J. Sci. Comput.* **2018**, *74*, 1286–1313. [CrossRef]
9. Nielsen, O. Processes of normal inverse Gaussian type. *Financ. Stoch.* **1998**, *2*, 41–68. [CrossRef]
10. Zhang, X.; Chen, P.; Tian, H.; Wu, Y. Upper and lower solution method for a singular tempered fractional equation with a p-Laplacian operator. *Fractal Fract.* **2023**, *7*, 522. [CrossRef]
11. Chen, W.; Fu, Z.; Grafakos, L.; Wu, Y. Fractional Fourier transforms on L^p and applications. *Appl. Comput. Harmon. Anal.* **2021**, *55*, 71–96. [CrossRef]
12. Dong, B.; Fu, Z.; Xu, J. Riesz-Kolmogorov theorem in variable exponent Lebesgue spaces and its applications to Riemann-Liouville fractional differential equations. *Sci. China Math.* **2018**, *61*, 1807–1824. [CrossRef]
13. Guo, X.; Fu, Z. An initial and boundary value problem of fractional Jeffreys' fluid in a porous half spaces. *Comput. Math. Appl.* **2019**, *78*, 1801–1810. [CrossRef]
14. Shi, S. Some notes on supersolutions of fractional p-Laplace equation. *J. Math. Anal. Appl.* **2018**, *463*, 10521074. [CrossRef]
15. Shi, S.; Zhang, L. Dual characterization of fractional capacity via solution of fractional p-Laplace equation. *Math. Nachr.* **2020**, *293*, 2233–2247. [CrossRef]
16. Shi, S.; Zhai, Z.; Zhang, L. Characterizations of the viscosity solution of a nonlocal and nonlinear equation induced by the fractional p-Laplace and the fractional p-convexity. *Adv. Calc. Var.* **2024**, *17*, 195–207. . [CrossRef]
17. Tang, H.; Wang, G. Limiting weak type behavior for multilinear fractional integrals. *Nonlinear Anal.* **2020**, *2020*, 197. [CrossRef]
18. Shi, S.; Xiao, J. Fractional capacities relative to bounded open Lipschitz sets complemented. *Calc. Var. Partial. Differ. Eq.* **2017**, *56*, 3. [CrossRef]
19. Yang, Y.; Wu, Q.; Jhang, S.; Kang, Q. Approximation theorems associated with multidimensional fractional fouried reansform and applications in Laplace and heat equations. *Fractal. Fract.* **2022**, *6*, 625. [CrossRef]
20. Shi, S.; Xiao, J. On Fractional Capacities Relative to Bounded Open Lipschitz Sets. *Potential Anal.* **2016**, *45*, 261–298. [CrossRef]
21. Zhang, X.; Yu, L.; Jiang, J.; Wu, Y.; Cui, Y. Solutions for a singular Hadamard-type fractional differential equation by the spectral construct analysis. *J. Funct. Spaces* **2020**, *2020*, 8392397. [CrossRef]
22. Shi, S.; Zhang, L.; Wang, G. Fractional Non-linear Regularity, Potential and Balayage. *J. Geom. Anal.* **2022**, *32*, 221. [CrossRef]
23. Xu, H.; Zhang, L.; Wang, G. Some new inequalities and extremal solutions of a Caputo-Fabrizio fractional Bagley-Torvik differential equation. *Fractal Fract.* **2022**, *6*, 488. [CrossRef]
24. Shi, S.; Xiao, J. A tracing of the fractional temperature field. *Sci. China Math.* **2017**, *60*, 23032320. [CrossRef]

25. Ledesma, C.; Cuti, H.; Rodríguez, J.; Bonilla, M. Boundary value problem with tempered fractional derivatives and oscillating term. *J.-Pseudo-Differ. Oper. Appl.* **2023**, *14*, 62. [CrossRef]
26. Chang, D.; Duong, X.; Li, J.; Wang, W.; Wu, Q. An explicit formula of Cauchy-Szegö kernel for quaternionic Siegel upper half space and applications. *Indiana Univ. Math. J.* **2021**, *70*, 2451–2477. [CrossRef]
27. Yang, M.; Fu, Z.; Liu, S. Analyticity and existence of the Keller-Segel-Navier-Stokes equations in critical Besov spaces. *Adv. Nonlinear Stud.* **2018**, *18*, 517–535. [CrossRef]
28. Gong, R.; Vempati, M.; Wu, Q.; Xie, P. Boundedness and compactness of Cauchy-type integral commutator on weighted Morrey spaces. *J. Aust. Math. Soc.* **2022**, *113*, 3656. [CrossRef]
29. Yang, M.; Fu, Z.; Sun, J. Existence and Gevrey regularity for a two-species chemotaxis system in homogeneous Besov spaces. *Sci. China Math.* **2017**, *60*, 1837–1856. [CrossRef]
30. Cao, J.; Chang, D.; Fu, Z.; Yang, D. Real interpolation of weighted tent spaces. *Appl. Anal.* **2016**, *59*, 2415–2443. [CrossRef]
31. Chang, D.; Fu, Z.; Yang, D.; Yang, S. Real-variable characterizations of Musielak-Orlicz-Hardy spaces associated with Schrödinger operators on domains. *Math. Methods Appl. Sci.* **2016**, *39*, 533–569. [CrossRef]
32. Zhang, X.; Liu, L.; Wu, Y.; Cui, Y. A sufficient and necessary condition of existence of blow-up radial solutions for a k-Hessian equation with a nonlinear operator. *Nonlinear Anal. Model. Control.* **2020**, *25*, 126–143. [CrossRef]
33. Zhang, X.; Xu, P.; Wu, Y.; Wiwatanapataphe, B. The uniqueness and iterative properties of solutions for a general Hadamard-type singular fractional turbulent flow model. *Nonlinear Anal. Model. Control.* **2022**, *27*, 428–444. [CrossRef]
34. Zhang, X.; Jiang, J.; Wu, Y.; Wiwatanapataphee, B. Iterative properties of solution for a general singular n-Hessian equation with decreasing nonlinearity. *Appl. Math. Lett.* **2021**, *112*, 106826. [CrossRef]
35. Chen, P.; Duong, X.; Li, J.; Wu, Q. Compactness of Riesz transform commutator on stratified Lie groups. *J. Funct. Anal.* **2019**, *277*, 1639–1676. [CrossRef]
36. Shi, S.; Fu, Z.; Lu, S. On the compactness of commutators of Hardy operators. *Pac. J. Math.* **2020**, *307*, 239–256. [CrossRef]
37. Duong, X.; Lacey, M.; Li, J.; Wick, B.; Wu, Q. Commutators of Cauchy-Szego type integrals for domains in C^n with minimal smoothness. *Indiana Univ. Math. J.* **2021**, *70*, 1505–1541. [CrossRef]
38. Fu, Z.; Gong, S.; Lu, S.; Yuan, W. Weighted multilinear Hardy operators and commutators. *Forum Math.* **2015**, *27*, 2825–2852. [CrossRef]
39. Shi, S.; Lu, S. Characterization of the central Campanato space via the commutator operator of Hardy type. *J. Math. Anal. Appl.* **2015**, *429*, 713732. [CrossRef]
40. Wu, Q.; Fu, Z. Boundedness of Hausdorff operators on Hardy spaces in the Heisen-berg group. *Banach J. Math. Anal.* **2018**, *12*, 909–934. [CrossRef]
41. Gu, L.; Ma, D. Dirac, Operators with gradient potentials and related monogenic functions. *Complex Anal. Oper. Theory* **2020**, *14*, 53. [CrossRef]
42. Zhang, X.; Kong, D.; Tian, H.; Wu, Y.; Wiwatanapataphee, B. An upper-lower solution method for the eigenvalue problem of Hadamard-type singular fractional differential equation. *Nonlinear Anal. Model. Control.* **2022**, *27*, 789–802. [CrossRef]
43. Zhang, X.; Tain, H.; Wu, Y.; Wiwatanapataphee, B. The radial solution for an eigenvalue problem of singular augmented Hessian equation. *Appl. Math. Lett.* **2022**, *134*, 108330. [CrossRef]
44. Zhang, X.; Xu, P.; Wu, Y. The eigenvalue problem of a singular k-Hessian equation. *Appl. Math. Lett.* **2022**, *124*, 107666. [CrossRef]
45. Wang, G.; Liu, Z.; Chen, L. Classification of solutions for an integral system with negative exponents. *Complex Var. Elliptic Equ.* **2019**, *64*, 204–222. [CrossRef]
46. Wu, Y.; Chen, W. On strong indefinite Schrödinger equations with non-periodic potential. *J. Appl. Anal. Comput.* **2023**, *13*, 1–10.
47. Yang, M.; Fu, Z.; Sun, J. Existence and large time behavior to coupled chemotaxis-fluid equations in Besov-Morrey spaces. *J. Differ. Equ.* **2019**, *266*, 5867–5894. [CrossRef]
48. Yang, S.; Chang, D.; Yang, D.; Fu, Z. Gradient estimates via rearrangements for solutions of some Schrödinger equations. *Anal. Appl.* **2018**, *16*, 339–361. [CrossRef]
49. Chen, W.; Fu, Z.; Wu, Y. Positive solutions for nonlinear Schrodinger Kirchhoff equation in R^3. *Appl. Math. Lett.* **2020**, *104*, 10627[illegible] [CrossRef]
50. Zhang, X.; Yu, L.; Jiang, J.; Wu, Y.; Cui, Y. Positive solutions for a weakly singular Hadamard-type fractional differential equation with changing-sign nonlinearity. *J. Funct. Spaces* **2020**, *2020*, 5623589. [CrossRef]
51. Zhang, X.;Tain, H.; Wu, Y.; Wiwatanapataphee, B. Existence of positive solutions for third-order semipositone boundary value problems on time scales. *Nonlinear Anal. Model. Control.* **2023**, *28*, 133–151. [CrossRef]

fractal and fractional

MDPI

Article

Unveiling the Complexity of HIV Transmission: Integrating Multi-Level Infections via Fractal-Fractional Analysis

Yasir Nadeem Anjam [1,*], Rubayyi Turki Alqahtani [2], Nadiyah Hussain Alharthi [2] and Saira Tabassum [1]

1 Department of Applied Sciences, National Textile University, Faisalabad 37610, Pakistan; tabassumsaira92@gmail.com

2 Department of Mathematics and Statistics, College of Science, Imam Mohammad Ibn Saud Islamic University (IMSIU), Riyadh 11623, Saudi Arabia; rtalqahtani@imamu.edu.sa (R.T.A.); nhalharthi@imamu.edu.sa (N.H.A.)

* Correspondence: ynanjam@ntu.edu.pk

Abstract: This article presents a non-linear deterministic mathematical model that captures the evolving dynamics of HIV disease spread, considering three levels of infection in a population. The model integrates fractal-fractional order derivatives using the Caputo operator and undergoes qualitative analysis to establish the existence and uniqueness of solutions via fixed-point theory. Ulam-Hyer stability is confirmed through nonlinear functional analysis, accounting for small perturbations. Numerical solutions are obtained using the fractional Adam-Bashforth iterative scheme and corroborated through MATLAB simulations. The results, plotted across various fractional orders and fractal dimensions, are compared with integer orders, revealing trends towards HIV disease-free equilibrium points for infective and recovered populations. Meanwhile, susceptible individuals decrease towards this equilibrium state, indicating stability in HIV exposure. The study emphasizes the critical role of controlling transmission rates to mitigate fatalities, curb HIV transmission, and enhance recovery rates. This proposed strategy offers a competitive advantage, enhancing comprehension of the model's intricate dynamics.

Keywords: HIV model; fractal-fractional derivative; existence and uniqueness; Ulam-Hyers stability; fractional Adams-Bashforth method; numerical simulation

1. Introduction

HIV, the human immunodeficiency virus, gradually weakens the immune system, leading to Acquired Immune Deficiency Syndrome (AIDS), where the immune system is compromised [1]. Transmission occurs through various modes such as sexual contact, needle sharing among drug users, vertical transmission from mother to child, and contaminated blood transfusions [2,3]. Understanding the dynamics of HIV transmission is crucial for developing effective prevention and treatment strategies. Mathematical modeling plays a key role in providing insights into virus epidemiology, forecasting trends, evaluating interventions, and addressing critical social issues. While traditional epidemiological compartmental models demonstrate regularity, global challenges often show quasi-linear characteristics, necessitating non-linear mathematical models for precise explanations [4,5]. Studies on HIV transmission dynamics have explored factors like viral load, transmission routes, and demographics, integrating pre-exposure prophylaxis and treatment strategies [6,7]. Mathematical methods also inform clinical guidelines for HIV/AIDS diagnosis, monitoring, and treatment [8]. Furthermore, research has focused on modeling and controlling HIV/AIDS transmission in China using real data from 2004 to 2016 [9], analyzing the stability of infection-age structured HIV-1 models that connect within-host and between-host dynamics [10], developing peptide inhibitors for HIV transmission [11], creating mathematical models of HIV transmission and infection dynamics [12], understanding the dynamics of HIV/AIDS transmission concerning protection awareness and fluctuations [13], conducting numerical investigations of stochastic HIV/AIDS infection models [14], exploring global dynamics of age-infection HIV models with a nonlinear infection rate [15], and modeling epidemic dynamics of HIV/AIDS transmission with different latent stages based on treatment [16]. Additionally, [17] developed an epidemic model for HBV infection, incorporating vaccination and medication administered through hospitalization.

Recent studies have introduced fractional calculus as a powerful tool for dealing with derivatives and integrals of any positive real order, enhancing models with non-local characteristics and memory dependencies [18]. Fractional techniques like Riemann-Liouville, Hadamard, Katugampola, and Caputo derivatives have significantly improved the accuracy of simulating real-world phenomena. The concept of fractional derivatives was first introduced by Riemann-Liouville in 1832, with Caputo later refining it in 1967 to incorporate boundary and initial conditions for more practical problem-solving in real-world contexts [19,20]. Numerical, computational, and iterative methods have been used to investigate fractional-order mathematical models. Caputo and Fabrizio invented the Caputo-Fabrizio (CF) derivative to overcome the limitations of the classic Caputo operator. This derivative increases exactness under specific situations and resolves problems with singular kernels [21–23]. Caputo further extended Atangana-Baleanu fractional derivatives and incorporated the Mittag-Leffler function from the Caputo-Fabrizio derivative [24]. They developed a fractional mathematical model for Atangana-Baleanu Caputo derivatives based on the Caputo-Fabrizio operator. Conversely, [25] explored the mathematical modeling of COVID-19 with the Caputo-Fabrizio operator. Each operator is tailored to specific systems based on their features and the desired degree of flexibility.

Atangana's recent research delves into the intricate relationship between fractional and fractal mathematics, introducing a novel fractal-fractional operator characterized by both self-similarity and fractional calculus properties [24]. An operator with a degree of self-similarity or fractal-like behavior combined with operations exhibiting fractional calculus qualities is called a fractal-fractional operator. These operators find utility in mathematical models aimed at describing complex and non-linear phenomena characterized by memory effects or patterns that repeat at varying scales. This field of research holds great potential for addressing a variety of challenging issues in diverse settings. Interestingly, this operator offers a more efficient method for extracting fractal fractions compared to conventional techniques, as it captures both the fractional order and the fractal dimension [26,27]. Fractal-fractional derivatives offer a unique approach to exploring fractional operators and fractal dimensions concurrently, enabling the development of models that effectively capture memory effects in dynamic systems. Moreover, researchers have leveraged alternative kernels and fractal-fractional differential equations to address challenges within the domain of fractal-fractional differential equations [28]. Fractional calculus has garnered significant attention from the global scientific community, thanks to its diverse features and practical applications across physics and engineering. It is essential to use a fractional-order system model to observe memory, crossover behavior, and hereditary features in systems [29]. This operator enables more effective modeling of complex systems with memory-dependent dynamics, finding applications in health surveillance and COVID-19 modeling. Studies by Qureshi [30], Li [31], Owolabi [32], Ahmad [33], Anjam [34], Liu [35], and Ahmad [36] demonstrate the utility of fractal-fractional operators across diverse fields. Qureshi and Atangana [37] have investigated models of nonlinear diarrhea transmission dynamics employing fractal-fractional operators. Furthermore, novel fractal-fractional operators have been applied to study the propagation of COVID-19, examining the effectiveness of lockdowns and vaccination strategies in controlling disease transmission [38]. Farman [39] suggests a compound-fractal methodology for modeling plant virus dynamics.

The choice of a fractional operator, coupled with its specific kernel type, plays a critical role in accurately portraying the memory effects, crossover behavior, and long-term dynamics inherent in models of HIV disease transmission. Selecting the Caputo operator with a power law kernel is particularly essential due to its capacity to effectively capture these memory effects and long-range dependencies within the system. These attributes are vital for modeling the intricate transmission dynamics of HIV disease, as they allow for a detailed depiction of the multifaceted interactions among various factors influencing the virus's spread. These factors encompass healthcare policies, societal perceptions, individual behaviors, and the efficacy of interventions, all of which significantly contribute to understanding and managing HIV transmission dynamics. These insights have guided the research in highlighting the broad significance of its discoveries.

This study explores the dynamics of HIV disease transmission, focusing on three infection levels within a population. The developed model incorporates a fractal-fractional order derivative with a power law kernel and conducts stability analysis through a nonlinear deterministic HIV transmission model. The model classifies the population into five mutually inclusive classes: susceptible individuals, different stages of infection, and recovered individuals. The analysis includes a thorough examination to validate the model's reliability, confirming the existence and uniqueness of solutions within the fixed-point theory framework. Subsequently, Ulam-Hyres stability is applied using nonlinear functional analysis to verify solution stability. Recognizing the significance of the topic, a novel fractional Adam-Bashforth iterative numerical scheme is employed for numerical simulations, with results validated through MATLAB simulations. The numerical results are graphically represented for various fractional orders and fractal dimensions, facilitating comparisons with integer orders. The study highlights the sensitivity of adjusting the fractional order and fractal dimension, emphasizing the practicality of the fractional approach.

The structure of the work is delineated as follows: Section 2 provides an overview of the model's development and rationale. Section 3 delves into the analytical foundations of the techniques employed. The fractional representation of the developed model is expounded upon in Section 4. Section 5 is dedicated to establishing the existence and uniqueness within the fixed-point theory framework, alongside addressing stability analysis. Details of the numerical simulations conducted using the fractional Adams-Bashforth method to validate the theoretical findings are presented in Section 6. MATLAB (ver. 2023b) is also leveraged for numerical simulations to visually represent the results. Lastly, the concluding section encapsulates the key findings of the proposed model.

2. Development of the Model

Model Description

Mathematical models are essential for comprehending the dynamics of HIV transmission and for crafting efficient prevention and treatment strategies. Employing epidemiological methods in constructing these models is crucial to illuminating the underlying mechanisms of HIV transmission. Identifying key determinants is essential for controlling the spread of HIV. Various HIV transmission models, grounded in infectious mechanisms, have been developed and documented, significantly contributing to the design of prevention and treatment strategies. These models play a pivotal role in addressing the HIV epidemic [7,8].

This study is centered on investigating a mathematical model to understand the transmission dynamics of HIV disease within a population, encompassing three levels of infection. The mathematical model divides the whole population $\mathcal{N}(\xi)$ into five subsets: susceptible individuals $\mathcal{S}(\xi)$, individuals at infective stage 1 $\mathcal{I}_1(\xi)$, individuals at infective stage 2 $\mathcal{I}_2(\xi)$, individuals under treatment $\mathcal{Q}(\xi)$, and recovered individuals $\mathcal{R}(\xi)$. Thus, the total human population at any time ξ is represented as:

$$\mathcal{N}(\xi) = \mathcal{S}(\xi) + \mathcal{I}_1(\xi) + \mathcal{I}_2(\xi) + \mathcal{Q}(\xi) + \mathcal{R}(\xi).$$

This arrangement enables us to capture the dynamics of the HIV model by integrating three levels of infection. This is achieved by monitoring the transitions between these distinct states within the population over time. Thus, the fundamental transmission dynamic model of HIV spread in the human population can be summarized as follows:

$$\begin{aligned}
\frac{d\mathcal{S}}{d\xi} &= \Lambda - \mu\mathcal{S} - (\beta_1\mathcal{I}_1 + \beta_2\mathcal{I}_2)\mathcal{S}, \\
\frac{d\mathcal{I}_1}{d\xi} &= \beta_1\mathcal{I}_1\mathcal{S} + \delta_2\mathcal{I}_2 - \delta_1\mathcal{I}_1 - \gamma_1\mathcal{I}_1 - \mu\mathcal{I}_1 - \sigma_1\mathcal{I}_1, \\
\frac{d\mathcal{I}_2}{d\xi} &= \beta_2\mathcal{I}_2\mathcal{S} + \delta_4\mathcal{Q} + \delta_1\mathcal{I}_1 - \gamma_2\mathcal{I}_2 - \delta_2\mathcal{I}_2 - \delta_3\mathcal{I}_2 - \mu\mathcal{I}_2 - \sigma_2\mathcal{I}_2, \\
\frac{d\mathcal{Q}}{d\xi} &= \delta_3\mathcal{I}_2 - \gamma_3\mathcal{Q} - \delta_4\mathcal{Q} - \mu\mathcal{Q} - \sigma_3\mathcal{Q}, \\
\frac{d\mathcal{R}}{d\xi} &= \sigma_1\mathcal{I}_1 + \sigma_2\mathcal{I}_2 + \sigma_3\mathcal{Q} - \mu\mathcal{R},
\end{aligned} \tag{1}$$

regarding the initial data set:

$$\mathcal{S}(0) \geq 0,\ \mathcal{I}_1(0) \geq 0,\ \mathcal{I}_2(0) \geq 0,\ \mathcal{Q}(0) \geq 0,\ \mathcal{R}(0) \geq 0.$$

The system (1) comprises several dependent parameters, each with detailed descriptions as follows: Λ denotes the recruitment rate of the population, β_1 represents the transmission coefficient from susceptible individuals to infected individuals in stage 1, β_2 is the transmission coefficient from susceptible individuals to infected individuals in stage 2, μ is the natural death rate for each compartment, δ_1 measures the rate of transmission from infected individuals in stage 1 to those in stage 2, δ_2 denotes the rate of transmission from infected individuals in stage 2 to those in stage 1, δ_3 represents the rate of transmission from infected individuals in stage 2 to those hospitalized, and δ_4 is the rate at which hospitalized patients transition to infected individuals in stage 2. Additionally, σ_1, σ_2 and σ_3 are the coefficients of transmission for infected individuals in stage 1, stage 2, and hospitalized cases transitioning to recovered cases, respectively. Finally, γ_1, γ_2, and γ_3 indicate the death rate of infected individuals in stage 1, stage 2, and hospitalized cases, respectively.

3. Basic Preliminaries

In this section, our objective is to explore our proposed model further by revisiting various essential concepts, definitions, and lemmas.

Definition 1 ([24]). *Suppose $\eta(\xi)$ is a function that is differentiable. The expression for the fractal-fractional derivative with fractional order $0 < \alpha \leq 1$ and fractal dimension $0 < \beta \leq 1$ can be formulated as follows:*

$$^{\mathcal{FF}}\mathbf{D}_{\xi}^{\alpha,\beta}(\eta(\xi)) = \frac{1}{(q-\alpha)}\frac{d}{d\xi^{\beta}}\int_0^{\xi}(\xi - x)^{q-\alpha-1}\eta(x)dx,$$

including $q - 1 < \alpha,\ \beta \leq q$, where $q \in \mathbb{N}$ and $\frac{d\eta(x)}{dx^{\beta}} = \lim_{\xi\to 0}\frac{\eta(\xi)-\eta(x)}{\xi^{\beta}-x^{\beta}}$.

Definition 2 ([24]). *If $\eta(\xi)$ is a continuous function, the integral of fractal-fractional order incorporating the function $\eta(\xi)$ with order α can be represented as follows:*

$$^{\mathcal{FF}}\mathbf{I}^{\alpha}\eta(\xi) = \frac{\beta}{\Gamma(\alpha)}\int_0^{\xi}(\xi - x)^{\alpha-1}x^{\beta-1}\eta(x)dx.$$

Definition 3. *The integral with a fractional order, specifically the Caputo derivative, associated with the function η, can be described as follows:*

$$\mathbf{I}_{\xi}^{\alpha}\eta(\xi) = \frac{1}{\Gamma(\alpha)}\int_0^{\xi}(\xi - x)^{1-\alpha}\eta(x)dx, \quad \xi > 0.$$

Definition 4 ([40] Contraction Mapping). *Suppose $\mathcal{B}$ is a Banach space. The operator $\mathcal{P}$, which maps from $\mathbf{X}$ to $\mathbf{X}$, is a contraction if and only if:*

$$\|\mathcal{P}(x) - \mathcal{P}(y)\| \leq \mathcal{W}\|x - y\|, \quad \forall x, y, \in \mathbf{X}, 0 < \mathcal{W} < 1.$$

Lemma 1 ([40] Banach's Fixed Point Theorem). *In a Banach space $\mathcal{B}$, when considering a non-empty open subset Ω, a contraction mapping q onto Ω has a unique fixed point.*

Lemma 2 ([40] Krasnoselskii's Fixed Points Theorem). *Within the Banach space $\mathcal{B}$, there is a non-empty, closed, convex subset Ω. Let's consider two operators, denoted as $\mathcal{P}_1$ and $\mathcal{P}_2$, which satisfy the following conditions:*

(i) $\mathcal{P}_1 x + \mathcal{P}_2 y \in \Omega, \forall x, y \in \Omega,$
(ii) *There is a compact and continuous operator $\mathcal{P}_1$,*
(iii) *A contraction mapping is defined by $\mathcal{P}_2$.*

Then, there exists $z \in \Omega$ which is equal to $\mathcal{P}_1 z + \mathcal{P}_2 z = z$.

Corollary 1 ([41]). *Suppose $\mathcal{Y}(\xi) \in \mathbb{C}(r_1, r_2)$ and ${}^{\mathcal{FF}}\mathbf{D}^{\alpha}_{\xi}(\eta(\xi)) \in \mathbb{C}(r_1, r_2)$ where $\alpha \in (0, 1]$. If:*

(i) ${}^{\mathcal{FF}}\mathbf{D}^{\alpha}_{\xi}(\eta(\xi)) \geq 0$ *for all $\xi \in (r_1, r_2)$, hence, $\mathcal{Y}(\xi)$ does not decrease.*
(ii) ${}^{\mathcal{FF}}\mathbf{D}^{\alpha}_{\xi}(\eta(\xi)) \leq 0$ *for all $\xi \in (r_1, r_2)$, hence $\mathcal{Y}(\xi)$ does not increase.*

Theorem 1 ([42]). *In a metric space that is complete, every sequence that contracts converges as a Cauchy sequence within that space.*

Theorem 2 ([42]). *Suppose $A \subseteq \mathbb{R}$ and $\varsigma : A \to \mathbb{R}^n$ are mappings that are continuously differentiable, with s belonging to A. For every compact subset $\mathcal{A}$ of A, the mapping ς obeys a Lipschitz condition with a Lipschitz constant denoted as L, where $L > 0$ signifies the supremum of the derivative of ς over $\mathcal{A}$, expressed as:*

$$L = \sup_{s \in \mathcal{A}} \left| \frac{d\varsigma}{ds} \right|.$$

4. Fractional Formulation of the Proposed Model

Traditional models using integer-order derivatives often struggle to capture the intricate and dynamic behavior of disease propagation with the robustness and efficiency required for accurate analysis. In contrast, fractional-order models offer a more suitable framework for analyzing real-world data and providing a detailed description of complex occurrences. In the modeling of HIV spread as outlined in system (1), we opted to replace the traditional integer-order time derivative D_t with the fractal-fractional order derivative ${}^{\mathcal{FF}}\mathbf{D}$. This choice of fractional order allows us to capture memory effects and gain a more profound understanding of the disease dynamics.

Additionally, the integer-order model (1) for HIV transmission dynamics is inherently complex and nonlinear, lacking memory effects common in many complex biological systems. This memory effect is crucial for capturing the lasting impact of past infections on the current spread of the virus. To address this limitation, we employ the concept of general fractional operators (as discussed in Section 3) in the HIV spreading model. Fractional derivatives inherently possess a hereditary property, making them suitable for modeling a wider range of real-world phenomena beyond classical integer-order systems with derivatives ranging between 0 and 1. In this study, we employ a system of nonlinear fractional-order equations utilizing the fractal-fractional derivative in the Caputo sense. Previous research indicates that the Caputo derivative, utilizing the power-law kernel, is adept at modeling power-law processes encountered in real-world scenarios. By replacing the time derivative with the Caputo derivative and utilizing a numerical scheme, we incorporate the power law effect inherent in fractional calculus. This methodology enables the model to generate numerical results for different fractional values, depicting the system's dynamics near the steady-state condition. Integrating fractional-order derivatives ensures that the resulting model accurately reflects the underlying dynamics of HIV transmission, including both short-term and long-term infection rate effects. This adaptability enables a closer alignment with observed data and a more nuanced understanding of the fundamental mechanisms driving HIV transmission. Therefore, these modifications and extensions are applied to the deterministic mathematical model (1) for the HIV epidemic, incorporating various infection stages. Consequently, the revised fractional HIV epidemic model is expressed as follows:

$$\begin{aligned}
&{}^{\mathcal{FF}}\mathbf{D}^{\alpha,\,\beta}\mathcal{S} = \Lambda - \mu\mathcal{S} - (\beta_1\mathcal{I}_1 + \beta_2\mathcal{I}_2)\mathcal{S},\\
&{}^{\mathcal{FF}}\mathbf{D}^{\alpha,\,\beta}\mathcal{I}_1 = \beta_1\mathcal{I}_1\mathcal{S} + \delta_2\mathcal{I}_2 - \delta_1\mathcal{I}_1 - \gamma_1\mathcal{I}_1 - \mu\mathcal{I}_1 - \sigma_1\mathcal{I}_1,\\
&{}^{\mathcal{FF}}\mathbf{D}^{\alpha,\,\beta}\mathcal{I}_2 = \beta_2\mathcal{I}_2\mathcal{S} + \delta_4\mathcal{Q} + \delta_1\mathcal{I}_1 - \gamma_2\mathcal{I}_2 - \delta_2\mathcal{I}_2 - \delta_3\mathcal{I}_2 - \mu\mathcal{I}_2 - \sigma_2\mathcal{I}_2,\\
&{}^{\mathcal{FF}}\mathbf{D}^{\alpha,\,\beta}\mathcal{Q} = \delta_3\mathcal{I}_2 - \gamma_3\mathcal{Q} - \delta_4\mathcal{Q} - \mu\mathcal{Q} - \sigma_3\mathcal{Q},\\
&{}^{\mathcal{FF}}\mathbf{D}^{\alpha,\,\beta}\mathcal{R} = \sigma_1\mathcal{I}_1 + \sigma_2\mathcal{I}_2 + \sigma_3\mathcal{Q} - \mu\mathcal{R},
\end{aligned} \tag{2}$$

with the initial condition

$$\mathcal{S}(0) = \mathcal{S}_0 \geq 0,\ \ \mathcal{I}_1(0) = \mathcal{I}_{10} \geq 0,\ \ \mathcal{I}_2(0) = \mathcal{I}_{20} \geq 0,\ \ \mathcal{Q}(0) = \mathcal{Q}_0 \geq 0,\ \ \mathcal{R}(0) = \mathcal{R}_0 \geq 0.$$

5. Exploring Theoretical Aspects of the Proposed Model

In this section, we conduct a comprehensive examination of the formulated model, delving into its fundamental characteristics and confirming its appropriateness for numerical approximations. To ensure the model's reliability, we validate the existence and uniqueness of its solution using the definitions and theorems referenced in [24]. This rigorous theoretical analysis provides insights into the model's behavior and confirms the feasibility of conducting rigorous numerical experiments.

Let's consider the existence of model (1). We define a Banach space $\mathcal{B} = \mathbf{X} \times \mathbf{X} \times \mathbf{X} \times \mathbf{X} \times \mathbf{X}$, where $\mathbf{X} = (\mathcal{C}[0,T],\mathbb{R})$, with a norm defined as a set of values representing a function space. The function space is denoted by $\|\Xi\| = \max_{\xi\in[0,T]} |\Xi(\xi)|$. Specifically,

$$\|\Xi\| = \|\mathcal{S},\mathcal{I}_1,\mathcal{I}_2,\mathcal{Q},\mathcal{R}\| = \max_{\xi\in[0,T]} \Big\{|\mathcal{S}(\xi)| + |\mathcal{I}_1(\xi)| + |\mathcal{I}_2(\xi)| + |\mathcal{Q}(\xi)| + |\mathcal{R}(\xi)|\Big\}.$$

Next, it is essential to compute the specified integral. This leads to the following expression for the right-hand side of model (1):

$$\begin{aligned}
&{}^{\mathcal{RL}}\mathbf{D}^{\alpha}\mathcal{S}(\xi) = \beta\xi^{\beta-1}\mathcal{G}_1(\mathcal{S},\mathcal{I}_1,\mathcal{I}_2,\mathcal{Q},\mathcal{R},\xi) = \Lambda - \mu\mathcal{S} - (\beta_1\mathcal{I}_1 + \beta_2\mathcal{I}_2)\mathcal{S},\\
&{}^{\mathcal{RL}}\mathbf{D}^{\alpha}\mathcal{I}_1(\xi) = \beta\xi^{\beta-1}\mathcal{G}_2(\mathcal{S},\mathcal{I}_1,\mathcal{I}_2,\mathcal{Q},\mathcal{R},\xi) = \beta_1\mathcal{I}_1\mathcal{S} + \delta_2\mathcal{I}_2 - \delta_1\mathcal{I}_1 - \gamma_1\mathcal{I}_1 - \mu\mathcal{I}_1 - \sigma_1\mathcal{I}_1,\\
&{}^{\mathcal{RL}}\mathbf{D}^{\alpha}\mathcal{I}_2(\xi) = \beta\xi^{\beta-1}\mathcal{G}_3(\mathcal{S},\mathcal{I}_1,\mathcal{I}_2,\mathcal{Q},\mathcal{R},\xi) = \beta_2\mathcal{I}_2\mathcal{S} + \delta_4\mathcal{Q} + \delta_1\mathcal{I}_1 - \gamma_2\mathcal{I}_2 - \delta_2\mathcal{I}_2 - \delta_3\mathcal{I}_2 - \mu\mathcal{I}_2 - \sigma_2\mathcal{I}_2,\\
&{}^{\mathcal{RL}}\mathbf{D}^{\alpha}\mathcal{Q}(\xi) = \beta\xi^{\beta-1}\mathcal{G}_4(\mathcal{S},\mathcal{I}_1,\mathcal{I}_2,\mathcal{Q},\mathcal{R},\xi) = \delta_3\mathcal{I}_2 - \gamma_3\mathcal{Q} - \delta_4\mathcal{Q} - \mu\mathcal{Q} - \sigma_3\mathcal{Q},\\
&{}^{\mathcal{RL}}\mathbf{D}^{\alpha}\mathcal{R}(\xi) = \beta\xi^{\beta-1}\mathcal{G}_5(\mathcal{S},\mathcal{I}_1,\mathcal{I}_2,\mathcal{Q},\mathcal{R},\xi) = \sigma_1\mathcal{I}_1 + \sigma_2\mathcal{I}_2 + \sigma_3\mathcal{Q} - \mu\mathcal{R}.
\end{aligned} \tag{3}$$

The self-contained system (3) can be condensed into a compact framework as follows:

$$\begin{cases} {}^{\mathcal{RL}}\mathbf{D}^{\alpha}\Xi(\xi) = \beta\xi^{\beta-1}\chi(\xi,\Xi(\xi)),\ 0 < \alpha,\ \beta \leq 1,\\ \Xi(0) = \Xi_0. \end{cases} \tag{4}$$

By substituting ${}^{\mathcal{RL}}\mathbf{D}^{\alpha,\beta}$ with ${}^{C}\mathbf{D}^{\alpha,\beta}$ and utilizing the Riemann-Liouville integral, the solution to Equation (4) will take on the following form:

$$\Xi(\xi) = \Xi_0(\xi) + \frac{\beta}{\Gamma(\alpha)}\int_0^{\xi}(\xi - x)^{\alpha-1}x^{\beta-1}\chi(x,\Xi(x))dx, \tag{5}$$

where

$$\Xi(\xi) = \begin{pmatrix} \mathcal{S}(\xi) \\ \mathcal{I}_1(\xi) \\ \mathcal{I}_2(\xi) \\ \mathcal{Q}(\xi) \\ \mathcal{R}(\xi) \end{pmatrix}, \quad \Xi_0(\xi) = \begin{pmatrix} \mathcal{S}_0 \\ \mathcal{I}_{10} \\ \mathcal{I}_{20} \\ \mathcal{Q}_0 \\ \mathcal{R}_0 \end{pmatrix}, \quad \chi(\xi, \Xi(\xi)) = \begin{pmatrix} \mathcal{G}_5(\mathcal{S}, \mathcal{I}_1, \mathcal{I}_2, \mathcal{Q}, \mathcal{R}, \xi) \\ \mathcal{G}_5(\mathcal{S}, \mathcal{I}_1, \mathcal{I}_2, \mathcal{Q}, \mathcal{R}, \xi) \\ \mathcal{G}_5(\mathcal{S}, \mathcal{I}_1, \mathcal{I}_2, \mathcal{Q}, \mathcal{R}, \xi) \\ \mathcal{G}_5(\mathcal{S}, \mathcal{I}_1, \mathcal{I}_2, \mathcal{Q}, \mathcal{R}, \xi) \\ \mathcal{G}_5(\mathcal{S}, \mathcal{I}_1, \mathcal{I}_2, \mathcal{Q}, \mathcal{R}, \xi) \end{pmatrix}.$$

To transform system (1) into a fixed-point problem, we define the operator $\mathcal{P} : \mathbb{B} \to \mathbb{B}$ as follows:

$$\mathcal{P}(\Xi)(\xi) = \Xi_0(\xi) + \frac{\beta}{\Gamma(\alpha)} \int_0^{\xi} x^{\beta-1}(\xi - x)^{\alpha-1} \chi(x, \Xi(x)) dx. \tag{6}$$

5.1. Existence and Uniqueness Results

Using the theorems derived from the referenced source, we establish the existence results derived from the devised model [40].

Theorem 3. *A mapping that is completely continuous can be defined as $\mathcal{P} : \mathbb{B} \to \mathbb{B}$*

$$\upsilon(\mathcal{P}) = \{\Xi \in \mathbb{B} : \Xi = \zeta\mathcal{P}(\Xi),\ \zeta \in [0,1]\}.$$

The boundedness of the operator $\mathcal{P}$ implies the existence of at least one fixed point in $\mathbb{B}$.

To verify the existence and stability analysis of the solution for the formulated model, we will examine the resulting propositions:

$(\mathcal{C})$For any Ξ and $\overline{\Xi}$ in $\mathcal{B}$, there exists a positive constant $\mathbb{M}_\chi$ such that the following condition holds:

$$|\chi(\xi, \Xi) - \chi(\xi, \overline{\Xi})| \leq \mathbb{M}_\chi |\Xi - \overline{\Xi}|.$$

The representation described below can be utilized in several ways to achieve the desired results:

$$\Delta = \frac{\beta \mathbb{P}^{\alpha+\beta-1} \mathbf{B}(\alpha, \beta)}{\Gamma(\alpha)}.$$

In this scenario, the symbol $\mathbf{B}(\alpha, \beta)$ denotes the beta function.

Theorem 4. *If the operator χ, defined as $\chi : C[0,T] \times \mathbb{B} \to \mathbb{R}$, is continuous and condition $(\mathcal{C})$ can be satisfied, then there must be at least one solution to problem (2) for the system.*

Proof. Our initial objective is to show that the operator $\mathcal{P} : \mathbb{B} \to \mathbb{B}$ defined in (6) is completely continuous. Let's take a sequence Ξ_n such that Ξ_n converges to Ξ in $\mathbb{B}$, where $\xi \in [0, T]$. This sequence can be represented as:

$$\begin{aligned} \|\mathcal{P}(\Xi_n) - \mathcal{P}(\Xi)\| &\leq \frac{\beta}{\Gamma(\alpha)} \max_{\xi \in [0,T]} \int_0^{\xi} x^{\beta-1}(\xi - x)^{\alpha-1} |\chi(x, \Xi_n(x)) - \chi(x, \Xi(x))| dx, \\ &\leq \frac{\beta \mathcal{K}_\chi}{\Gamma(\alpha)} \|\Xi_n - \Xi\| \max_{\xi \in [0,T]} \int_0^{\xi} x^{\alpha-1}(1 - x)^{\beta-1} \xi^{\alpha+\beta-1} dx, \\ &\leq \Delta \mathcal{K}_\chi \| \Xi_n - \Xi\|. \end{aligned} \tag{7}$$

Consequently, since Ξ_n converges to Ξ, it follows that $\|\mathcal{P}(\Xi_n) - \mathcal{P}(\Xi)\|$ tends to zero as n approaches zero. Therefore, the operator is continuous.

Suppose $\mathfrak{T}$ is a bounded set in $\mathbb{B}$. Then, there exists a constant $C_\chi > 0$ such that $|\chi(\xi, \Xi(\xi))| \leq C_\chi$ holds for all $\Xi \in \mathcal{B}$, and for any $\Xi \in \mathfrak{T}$, we can express this as:

$$\begin{aligned}
&\|\mathcal{P}(\Xi)\| \leq \frac{\beta C_\chi}{\Gamma(\alpha)} \max_{\xi\in[0,T]} \left| \int_0^\xi (\xi - x)^{\alpha-1} x^{\beta-1} dx \right|, \\
&\leq \frac{\beta C_\chi}{\Gamma(\alpha)} \max_{\xi\in[0,T]} \int_0^\xi (1 - x)^{\beta-1} x^{\alpha-1} \xi^{\alpha+\beta-1} dx, \\
&\leq \Delta C_\chi.
\end{aligned} \tag{8}$$

Thus, Equation (8) signifies that the operator $\mathcal{P}$ is uniformly bounded.

Additionally, to confirm the equi-continuity of the operator $\mathcal{P}$, let's consider $0 \leq \xi_2 \leq \xi_1 \leq T$. We deduce the following outcome:

$$\begin{aligned}
&\|\mathcal{P}(\Xi(\xi_1)) - \mathcal{P}(\Xi(\xi_2))\| \leq \frac{\beta C_\chi}{\Gamma(\alpha)} \max_{\xi\in[0,T]} \left| \int_0^{\xi_1} (\xi_1 - x)^{\alpha-1} x^{\beta-1} dx - \int_0^{\xi_2} (\xi_2 - x)^{\alpha-1} x^{\beta-1} dx \right|, \\
&\leq \frac{\beta C_\chi \mathbf{B}(\alpha,\beta)}{\Gamma(\alpha)} (\xi_1^{\alpha+\beta-1} - \xi_2^{\alpha+\beta-1}) \to 0 \ as\ \xi_1 \to \xi_2.
\end{aligned} \tag{9}$$

Hence, the operator $\mathcal{P}$ exhibits equi-continuity, boundedness, and continuity simultaneously. Therefore, by invoking the Arzela-Ascoli theorem, we can demonstrate that the operator $\mathcal{P}$ is relatively compact and completely continuous.

Consider the set v, defined as $v = \{\Xi \in \mathbb{B} : \Xi = \zeta, \mathcal{P}(\Xi), \zeta \in [0,1]\}$. Let's now confirm the boundedness of v. Take $\Xi \in v$; for $\xi \in [0, T]$, we find $\|\Xi\| = \Delta C_\chi$.

Thus, v is bounded. By Theorem (3), system (2) has at least one solution. □

We will utilize the fixed-point technique outlined in [40] to establish the uniqueness of the solution for model (2).

Theorem 5. *Given proposition $(\mathcal{C})$ and under the condition $\mathbf{H}_\chi \leq 1$, problem (2) can be uniquely resolved as follows:*

$$\mathbf{H}_\chi = \Delta \mathbb{M}_\chi. \tag{10}$$

Proof. Let's define $\max_{\xi\in[0,T]} |\chi(\xi, 0)| = \mathcal{K}_\chi < \infty$, such that $\varrho \geq \frac{\Delta \mathcal{K}_\chi}{1-\Delta \mathbb{M}_\chi}$. Our objective is to prove that $\mathcal{P}(\mathcal{B}\varrho) \subset \mathcal{B}\varrho$, where $\mathcal{B}\varrho = \{\Xi \in \mathbb{B} : \|\Xi\| \leq \varrho\}$ and $\Xi \in \mathcal{B}_\varrho$. We have:

$$\begin{aligned}
&\|\mathcal{P}(\Xi)\| \leq \frac{\beta}{\Gamma(\alpha)} \max_{\xi\in[0,T]} \int_0^\xi (\xi - x)^{\alpha-1} x^{\beta-1} \Big(|\chi(\xi, \Xi(\xi)) - \chi(\xi, 0)| + |\chi(\xi, 0)| \Big) dx, \\
&\leq \frac{\beta \mathbb{P}^{\alpha+\beta-1} \mathbf{B}(\alpha,\beta)(\mathbb{M}_\chi \|\Xi\| + \mathcal{K}_\chi)}{\Gamma(\alpha)}, \\
&\leq \Delta(\mathbb{M}_\chi \varrho + \mathcal{K}_\chi), \\
&\leq \varrho.
\end{aligned} \tag{11}$$

The operator $\mathcal{P} : \mathbb{B} \to \mathbb{B}$ described in (6) is subject to proposition $(\mathcal{C})$, which asserts the following condition for all $\xi \in [0, T]$, Ξ, and $\overline{\Xi} \in \mathbb{B}$:

$$\begin{aligned}
&\|\mathcal{P}(\Xi) - \mathcal{P}(\overline{\Xi})\| \leq \frac{\beta}{\Gamma(\alpha)} \max_{\xi\in[0,T]} \left| \int_0^\xi (\xi - x)^{\alpha-1} x^{\beta-1} \chi(x, \Xi(x)) dx - \int_0^\xi (\xi - x)^{\alpha-1} x^{\beta-1} \chi(x, \overline{\Xi}(x)) dx \right|, \\
&\leq \mathbf{H}_\chi \|\Xi - \overline{\Xi}\|.
\end{aligned} \tag{12}$$

Thus, due to the contraction property of the operator $\mathcal{P}$, the formulated model (2) has a unique solution. □

5.2. Ulam-Hyers Stability Analysis

This section is dedicated to conducting Ulam-Hyers (UH) stability analysis to confirm the stability of the formulated model (2).

Definition 5. *For the formulated model to be considered Ulam-Hyers (UH) stable, it must satisfy a condition where there exists a $\Re_{\alpha,\beta} > 0$ such that for any $\rho > 0$ and every $\Xi \in C([0,T],\mathbb{R})$, the subsequent condition holds:*

$$|{}^{\mathcal{FF}}\mathbf{D}_{\xi}^{\alpha,\,\beta}\Xi(\xi) - \chi(\xi,\Xi(\xi))| \leq \rho,\ \xi \in [0,T], \tag{13}$$

and there exists a unique solution $\Phi \in C([0,T],\mathbb{R})$ such that

$$|\Xi(\xi) - \Phi(\xi)| \leq \Re_{\alpha,\beta}\,\rho,\ \xi \in [0,T]. \tag{14}$$

Suppose there exists a small perturbation $\chi \in C([0,T],\mathbb{R})$ such that $\chi(0) = 0$. We will observe:

- $|\chi(\xi)| \leq \rho$, for $\rho > 0$;
- ${}^{\mathcal{FF}}\mathbf{D}_{\xi}^{\alpha,\,\beta}\Xi(\xi) = \chi(\xi,\Xi(\xi)) + \chi(\xi)$.

Lemma 3. *The solution to the perturbed equation*

$$\begin{aligned} &{}^{\mathcal{FF}}\mathbf{D}_{\xi}^{\alpha,\,\beta}\Xi(\xi) = \chi(\xi,\Xi(\xi)) + \chi(\xi),\\ &\Xi(0) = \Xi_0, \end{aligned} \tag{15}$$

fulfills the following relation:

$$\left|\Xi(\xi) - \left(\Xi_0(\xi) + \frac{\beta}{\Gamma(\alpha)}\int_0^{\xi} x^{\beta-1}(\xi - x)^{\alpha-1}\chi(x,\Xi(x))dx\right)\right| \leq \mathbb{C}_{\alpha,\,\beta}\,\rho, \tag{16}$$

where $\left(\frac{\beta}{\Gamma(\alpha)}\mathbb{P}^{\alpha+\beta-1}\mathbf{B}(\alpha,\beta)\right) = \mathbb{C}_{\alpha,\,\beta}\,\rho$.

Proof. For simplicity, we will refrain from delving into the proof. □

Theorem 6. *Given Proposition ($\mathcal{C}$) and Lemma 3, the solution to integral Equation (2) is deemed Ulam-Hyers stable, provided that the condition $\mathbf{H}_{\chi} < 1$ is satisfied.*

Proof. Let $Z \in \mathbb{B}$ denote the unique solution to the proposed model, and consider $\Xi \in \mathbb{B}$ as any solution that satisfies Equation (5). By employing fractal-fractional integration, we derive the following expression:

$$\begin{aligned} |\Xi(\xi) - Z(\xi)| &= \left|\Xi(\xi) - \left(Z_0(\xi) + \frac{\beta}{\Gamma(\alpha)}\int_0^{\xi}(\xi - x)^{\alpha-1}x^{\beta-1}\chi(x,Z(x))dx\right)\right|,\\ &\leq \left|\Xi(\xi) - \left(\Xi_0(\xi) + \frac{\beta}{\Gamma(\alpha)}\int_0^{\xi}(\xi - x)^{\alpha-1}x^{\beta-1}\chi(x,\Xi(x))dx\right)\right|\\ &+ \left|\left(\Xi_0(\xi) + \frac{\beta}{\Gamma(\alpha)}\int_0^{\xi}(\xi - x)^{\alpha-1}x^{\beta-1}\chi(x,\Xi(x))dx\right) - \left(Z_0(\xi) + \frac{\beta}{\Gamma(\alpha)}\int_0^{\xi}(\xi - x)^{\alpha-1}x^{\beta-1}\chi(x,Z(x))dx\right)\right|,\\ &\leq \mathbb{C}_{\alpha,\beta}\,\rho + \frac{\beta}{\Gamma(\alpha)}\mathbb{P}^{\alpha+\beta-1}\mathbb{M}_{\chi}\mathbf{B}(\alpha,\beta)\|\Xi(\xi) - Z(\xi)\|,\\ &\leq \mathbb{C}_{\alpha,\,\beta}\rho + \mathbf{H}_{\chi}\|\Xi(\xi) - Z(\xi)\|. \end{aligned} \tag{17}$$

Hence, we can state:

$$\|\Xi - Z\| \leq \mathbb{C}_{\alpha,\,\beta}\rho + \mathbf{H}_{\chi}\|\Xi - Z\|. \tag{18}$$

The Equation (18) can be expressed as follows:

$$\|\Xi - Z\| \leq \Re_{\alpha,\,\beta}\,\rho. \tag{19}$$

Therefore, $\Re_{\alpha,\beta} = \left(\frac{\mathbb{C}\alpha,\beta}{1-\mathbf{H}\chi}\right)$. This indicates that the solution to Equation (5) demonstrates UH stability, thus confirming the Ulam-Hyers stability of the solution to the proposed model (2). □

6. Numerical Method for Fractal-Fractional Model

In this section, our goal is to delineate a numerical method for simulating the formulated model using computational techniques. To achieve this, we will employ the Caputo derivative and its corresponding integral to convert the model (5) into the following format:

$$\begin{aligned}
\mathcal{S}(\xi) &= \mathcal{S}(0) + \frac{\beta}{\Gamma(\alpha)} \int_0^{\xi} x^{\beta-1}(\xi - x)^{\alpha-1} \mathcal{G}_1(\mathcal{S}, \mathcal{I}_1, \mathcal{I}_2, \mathcal{Q}, \mathcal{R}, x)dx, \\
\mathcal{I}_1(\xi) &= \mathcal{I}_1(0) + \frac{\beta}{\Gamma(\alpha)} \int_0^{\xi} x^{\beta-1}(\xi - x)^{\alpha-1} \mathcal{G}_2(\mathcal{S}, \mathcal{I}_1, \mathcal{I}_2, \mathcal{Q}, \mathcal{R}, x)dx, \\
\mathcal{I}_2(\xi) &= \mathcal{I}_2(0) + \frac{\beta}{\Gamma(\alpha)} \int_0^{\xi} x^{\beta-1}(\xi - x)^{\alpha-1} \mathcal{G}_3(\mathcal{S}, \mathcal{I}_1, \mathcal{I}_2, \mathcal{Q}, \mathcal{R}, x)dx, \\
\mathcal{Q}(\xi) &= \mathcal{Q}(0) + \frac{\beta}{\Gamma(\alpha)} \int_0^{\xi} x^{\beta-1}(\xi - x)^{\alpha-1} \mathcal{G}_4(\mathcal{S}, \mathcal{I}_1, \mathcal{I}_2, \mathcal{Q}, \mathcal{R}, x)dx, \\
\mathcal{R}(\xi) &= \mathcal{R}(0) + \frac{\beta}{\Gamma(\alpha)} \int_0^{\xi} x^{\beta-1}(\xi - x)^{\alpha-1} \mathcal{G}_5(\mathcal{S}, \mathcal{I}_1, \mathcal{I}_2, \mathcal{Q}, \mathcal{R}, x)dx.
\end{aligned} \tag{20}$$

Next, we will demonstrate the numerical solution of Equation (20) at discrete-time instances $\xi = \xi_{m+1}$ for $m = 0, 1, 2, \ldots$ using the new approach. This enables us to illustrate the first equation of the system outlined above.

$$\mathcal{S}_{m+1}(\xi) = \mathcal{S}(0) + \frac{\beta}{\Gamma(\alpha)} \int_0^{\xi_{m+1}} x^{\beta-1}(\xi_{m+1} - x)^{\alpha-1} \mathcal{G}_1(\mathcal{S}, \mathcal{I}_1, \mathcal{I}_2, \mathcal{Q}, \mathcal{R}, x)\, dx, \tag{21}$$

and

$$\mathcal{S}_{m}(\xi) = \mathcal{S}(0) + \frac{\beta}{\Gamma(\alpha)} \int_0^{\xi_{m}} x^{\beta-1}(\xi_{m} - x)^{\alpha-1} \mathcal{G}_1(\mathcal{S}, \mathcal{I}_1, \mathcal{I}_2, \mathcal{Q}, \mathcal{R}, x)\, dx. \tag{22}$$

Additionally, it's important to note that the approximate integral form obtained from the equation above can be succinctly summarized as follows:

$$\mathcal{S}_{m+1}(\xi) = \mathcal{S}(0) + \frac{\beta}{\Gamma(\alpha)} \sum_{i=0}^{m} \int_{\xi_i}^{\xi_{i+1}} x^{\beta-1}(\xi_{m+1} - x)^{\alpha-1} \mathcal{G}_1(\mathcal{S}, \mathcal{I}_1, \mathcal{I}_2, \mathcal{Q}, \mathcal{R}, x)\, dx. \tag{23}$$

In the infinite interval $[\xi_i, \xi_{i+1}]$, the function $\mathcal{G}_1(\mathcal{S}, \mathcal{I}_1, \mathcal{I}_2, \mathcal{Q}, \mathcal{R}, x)$ approximates the step size of the interpolation by employing Lagrange interpolation with $h = [\xi_i - \xi_{i-1}]$. This is expressed as:

$$\mathcal{S}_m^*(\xi) \approx \frac{1}{h}\Big[(\xi - \xi_{i-1})\xi_i^{\beta-1} \mathcal{G}_1(\mathcal{S}_i, \mathcal{I}_{1(i)}, \mathcal{I}_{2(i)}, \mathcal{Q}_i, \mathcal{R}_i, \xi_i) - (\xi - \xi_i)\xi_{i-1}^{\beta-1} \mathcal{G}_1(\mathcal{S}_{i-1}, \mathcal{I}_{1(i-1)}, \mathcal{I}_{2(i-1)}, \mathcal{Q}_{i-1}, \mathcal{R}_{i-1}, \xi_{i-1})\Big]. \tag{24}$$

Replacing Equation (24) with Equation (23) results in the following expression:

$$\mathcal{S}_{m+1}(\xi) = \mathcal{S}(0) + \frac{\beta}{\Gamma(\alpha)} \sum_{i=0}^{m} \int_{\xi_i}^{\xi_{i+1}} x^{\beta-1}(\xi_{m+1} - x)^{\alpha-1} \mathcal{G}_1(\mathcal{S}, \mathcal{I}_1, \mathcal{I}_2, \mathcal{Q}, \mathcal{R}, x)\, \mathcal{S}_m^*(\xi)\, dx. \tag{25}$$

The numerical iterative solution for the $\mathcal{S}$ class of the formulated model using the Caputo operator with fractal-fractional derivative requires evaluating the integral on the right-hand side of Equation (25) as follows:

$$\mathcal{S}_{m+1} = \begin{cases} \mathcal{S}_0 + \frac{\beta h^\alpha}{\Gamma(\alpha+2)} \sum_{i=0}^{m} \Big[(\xi_i^{\beta-1}) \mathcal{G}_1(\mathcal{S}_i, \mathcal{I}_{1(i)}, \mathcal{I}_{2(i)}, \mathcal{Q}_i, \mathcal{R}_i, \xi_i) \times \Big((m+1-i)^\beta (m-i+2+\beta) - (m-i)^\beta (m-i+2+2\beta) \Big) \\ -\xi_{i-1}^{\beta-1} \mathcal{G}_1(\mathcal{S}_{i-1}, \mathcal{I}_{1(i-1)}, \mathcal{I}_{2(i-1)}, \mathcal{Q}_{i-1}, \mathcal{R}_{i-1}, \xi_{i-1}) \times \Big((m+1-i)^\beta + 1 - (m-i)^\beta (m-i+1+\beta) \Big) \Big]. \end{cases} \quad (26)$$

Consequently, the remaining terms in the formulated model concerning the respective compartments can be articulated as follows:

$$\mathcal{I}_{1(m+1)} = \begin{cases} \mathcal{I}_1(0) + \frac{\beta h^\alpha}{\Gamma(\alpha+2)} \sum_{i=0}^{m} \Big[(\xi_i^{\beta-1}) \mathcal{G}_2(\mathcal{S}_i, \mathcal{I}_{1(i)}, \mathcal{I}_{2(i)}, \mathcal{Q}_i, \mathcal{R}_i, \xi_i) \times \Big((m+1-i)^\beta (m-i+2+\beta) - (m-i)^\beta (m-i+2+2\beta) \Big) \\ -\xi_{i-1}^{\beta-1} \mathcal{G}_2(\mathcal{S}_{i-1}, \mathcal{I}_{1(i-1)}, \mathcal{I}_{2(i-1)}, \mathcal{Q}_{i-1}, \mathcal{R}_{i-1}, \xi_{i-1}) \times \Big((m+1-i)^\beta + 1 - (m-i)^\beta (m-i+1+\beta) \Big) \Big]. \end{cases} \quad (27)$$

$$\mathcal{I}_{2(m+1)} = \begin{cases} \mathcal{I}_2(0) + \frac{\beta h^\alpha}{\Gamma(\alpha+2)} \sum_{i=0}^{m} \Big[(\xi_i^{\beta-1}) \mathcal{G}_3(\mathcal{S}_i, \mathcal{I}_{1(i)}, \mathcal{I}_{2(i)}, \mathcal{Q}_i, \mathcal{R}_i, \xi_i) \times \Big((m+1-i)^\beta (m-i+2+\beta) - (m-i)^\beta (m-i+2+2\beta) \Big) \\ -\xi_{i-1}^{\beta-1} \mathcal{G}_3(\mathcal{S}_{i-1}, \mathcal{I}_{1(i-1)}, \mathcal{I}_{2(i-1)}, \mathcal{Q}_{i-1}, \mathcal{R}_{i-1}, \xi_{i-1}) \times \Big((m+1-i)^\beta + 1 - (m-i)^\beta (m-i+1+\beta) \Big) \Big]. \end{cases} \quad (28)$$

$$\mathcal{Q}_{m+1} = \begin{cases} \mathcal{Q}_0 + \frac{\beta h^\alpha}{\Gamma(\alpha+2)} \sum_{i=0}^{m} \Big[(\xi_i^{\beta-1}) \mathcal{G}_4(\mathcal{S}_i, \mathcal{I}_{1(i)}, \mathcal{I}_{2(i)}, \mathcal{Q}_i, \mathcal{R}_i, \xi_i) \times \Big((m+1-i)^\beta (m-i+2+\beta) - (m-i)^\beta (m-i+2+2\beta) \Big) \\ -\xi_{i-1}^{\beta-1} \mathcal{G}_4(\mathcal{S}_{i-1}, \mathcal{I}_{1(i-1)}, \mathcal{I}_{2(i-1)}, \mathcal{Q}_{i-1}, \mathcal{R}_{i-1}, \xi_{i-1}) \times \Big((m+1-i)^\beta + 1 - (m-i)^\beta (m-i+1+\beta) \Big) \Big]. \end{cases} \quad (29)$$

$$\mathcal{R}_{m+1} = \begin{cases} \mathcal{R}_0 + \frac{\beta h^\alpha}{\Gamma(\alpha+2)} \sum_{i=0}^{m} \Big[(\xi_i^{\beta-1}) \mathcal{G}_5(\mathcal{S}_i, \mathcal{I}_{1(i)}, \mathcal{I}_{2(i)}, \mathcal{Q}_i, \mathcal{R}_i, \xi_i) \times \Big((m+1-i)^\beta (m-i+2+\beta) - (m-i)^\beta (m-i+2+2\beta) \Big) \\ -\xi_{i-1}^{\beta-1} \mathcal{G}_5(\mathcal{S}_{i-1}, \mathcal{I}_{1(i-1)}, \mathcal{I}_{2(i-1)}, \mathcal{Q}_{i-1}, \mathcal{R}_{i-1}, \xi_{i-1}) \times \Big((m+1-i)^\beta + 1 - (m-i)^\beta (m-i+1+\beta) \Big) \Big]. \end{cases} \quad (30)$$

Numerical Experimentation and Discussion

In this section, we delve into the numerical simulation of our proposed scheme using a fractal-fractional approach to model HIV disease dynamics. We emphasize the intricate relationships among model parameters and their combined impact on HIV transmission across three infection levels within the community. Our HIV fractional-order model is designed to analyze disease transmission through simulations, employing fractal-fractional derivatives with a power-law representation. The initial compartmental conditions, as detailed in [2], are set as follows: $\mathcal{S}(0) = 5726$, $\mathcal{I}_1(0) = 70$, $\mathcal{I}_2(0) = 40$, $\mathcal{Q}(0) = 10$, and $\mathcal{R}(0) = 0$. Fractional values are instrumental in discerning outcomes within this nonlinear system. To ensure the study's robustness, we adopt parameter values from Table 1 based on established literature. Our model yields compelling results by incorporating non-integer parameter values. Adjusting fractional values with precision enables us to derive solutions for variables $\mathcal{S}$, $\mathcal{I}_1$, $\mathcal{I}_2$, $\mathcal{Q}$, and $\mathcal{R}$, as depicted in Figures 1–5. We utilize MATLAB for numerical simulations spanning 500 days with a time step of $h = 0.03$. Our exploration encompasses five distinct cases where we vary the fractional orders (α) and dimensions (β) of the independent variable ξ, aiming to deepen our understanding of the model's behavior.

Moreover, by employing the fractal-fractional derivative with the Caputo operator, our model generates numerical outputs for various fractional values, focusing on the steady-state point. The graphical representation of the HIV transmission model using our proposed numerical method and the comparison between fractal-fractional and integer orders are illustrated in Figures 1–5. All trajectories demonstrate a consistent pattern, converging to the true endemic equilibrium point. Initially, we maintain a proportional relationship between the fractal order (α) and fractional dimension (β) of the independent variable ξ, ensuring $\alpha = \beta$. We then explore variations in these values, setting $\alpha = 0.80, 0.85, 0.90, 0.95, 1.00$ and $\beta = 0.80, 0.85, 0.90, 0.95, 1.00$, over a time span of $\xi \in [0, 500]$ units (days) with a time step of $h = 0.03$. This exploration elucidates the impact of different fractal orders and dimensions on the trajectories of compartmental classes in the HIV transmission model. Each combination of α and β unveils distinct patterns and behaviors, as depicted in Figure 1a–e. Each trajectory, corresponding to a specific fractional order α and fractal dimension β, represents the disease dynamics within the modeled population. Notably, each graph exhibits varying rates of convergence based on fractal order and dimension, while all converge to a steady state.

Table 1. Parameters and its values.

Parameters	Values	Source	Parameters	Values	Source
Λ	$200.88\,\text{day}^{-1}$	[43]	β_1	$0.0000405\,\text{day}^{-1}$	[44]
β_2	$0.0000483\,\text{day}^{-1}$	[44]	γ_1	$0.01\,\text{day}^{-1}$	[45]
γ_2	$0.02\,\text{day}^{-1}$	[45]	γ_3	$0.04\,\text{day}^{-1}$	[46]
δ_1	$9.2274 \times 10^{-3}\,\text{day}^{-1}$	[47] and estimate	δ_2	$8.0037 \times 10^{-3}\,\text{day}^{-1}$	[47] and estimate
δ_3	$2.8595 \times 10^{-3}\,\text{day}^{-1}$	[47] and estimate	δ_4	$1.8595 \times 10^{-3}\,\text{day}^{-1}$	[47] and estimate
σ_1	$0.1\,\text{day}^{-1}$	[2] and estimate	σ_2	$0.2\,\text{day}^{-1}$	[2] and estimate
σ_3	$0.2\,\text{day}^{-1}$	[2] and estimate	μ	$0.01\,\text{day}^{-1}$	[45]

Figure 1a illustrates the evolution of the susceptible class $\mathcal{S}$ over time, considering constant fractional orders and dimensions. Different fractional orders exhibit varying slopes, impacting the dynamics of susceptibility in HIV transmission. Initially, the susceptible population experiences a rapid reduction at lower fractional orders but stabilizes to a steady state over time. This demonstrates how varying levels of memory and complexity influence the rate of change in susceptibility over time. Fractal dimensions remain stable, indicating a consistent transmission pattern, while varying slopes for the same fractional orders highlight the nuanced effects of memory. The initial decline followed by stabilization reflects a balance between exposure and immunity, akin to real-world scenarios where populations reach a stable risk level due to HIV exposure. Higher fractional orders suggest a more intricate interplay of factors affecting susceptibility, implying a more efficient utilization of historical data or long-term memory in the transmission process.

In Figure 1b, we present the dynamic behavior of the infective population at stage 1, denoted as $\mathcal{I}_1(\xi)$. The infected population demonstrates rapid growth as the fractional order α increases. Subsequently, decreasing the fractional order leads to a decline in the infected population. This trend stabilizes over time, indicating a more established state of infection within the population. The initial rapid increase followed by a gradual decrease in the infective population mirrors the dynamic nature of HIV transmission, as observed in real-world scenarios. This pattern reflects the early surge in infections as the virus spreads, followed by a period during which interventions, immunity, or other factors contribute to a reduction in new infections. Figure 1c illustrates the dynamics of the HIV-infected population at stage 2, denoted as $\mathcal{I}_2(\xi)$. The initial increase in the infected population is observed for higher fractional orders, followed by a decrease for lower fractional orders. These dynamics are influenced by various factors, including intervention strategies, transmission rates, and the interaction between different stages of infection.

Figure 1d illustrates the dynamic behavior of populations undergoing treatment, denoted as $\mathcal{Q}(\xi)$. This figure illustrates an increasing number of individuals recovering from HIV infection, reflecting the dynamic response of infective populations to treatment interventions. The decline in infected individuals is gradual as fractional orders increase, highlighting the sensitivity of dynamics to different parameter settings. Such dynamics mirror real-world scenarios where treatment plays a critical role in reducing infection rates and improving outcomes for individuals affected by HIV.

On the other hand, Figure 1e delves into the behavior of the recovered population, $\mathcal{R}(\xi)$. It depicts how HIV-recovered populations engage in treatment-seeking behavior, initially surging and then gradually declining. Notably, the recovered population increases quickly with lower fractional orders, with the decline being more pronounced for higher fractional orders. These findings underscore the significant influence of fractional orders and fractal dimensions on HIV transmission dynamics and treatment decisions, providing valuable insights into the complex interplay between these parameters and HIV dynamics.

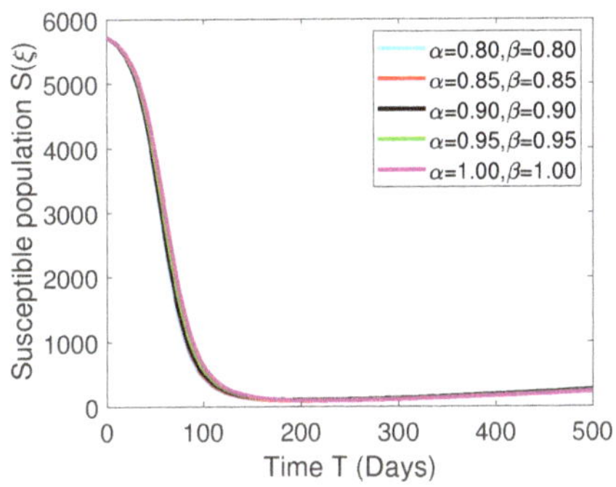

(**a**) Dynamical simulation of $\mathcal{S}(\xi)$

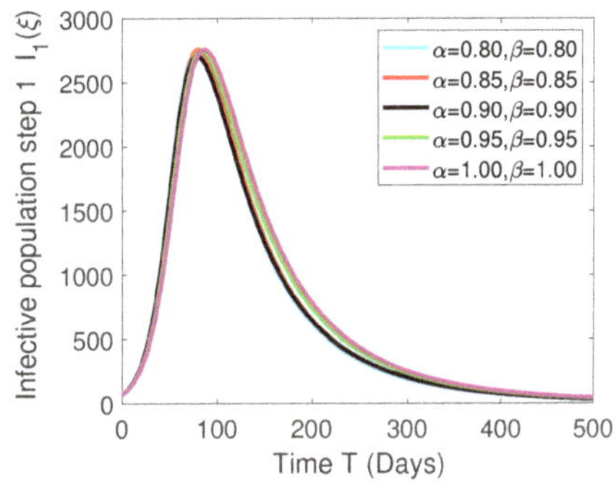

(**b**) Dynamical simulation of $\mathcal{I}_1(\xi)$

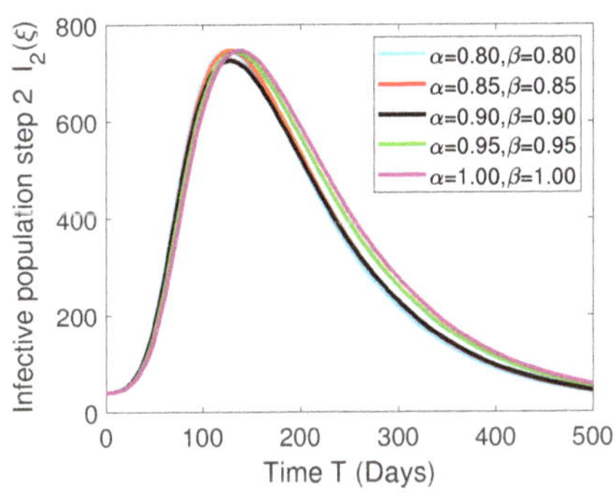

(**c**) Dynamical simulation of $\mathcal{I}_2(\xi)$

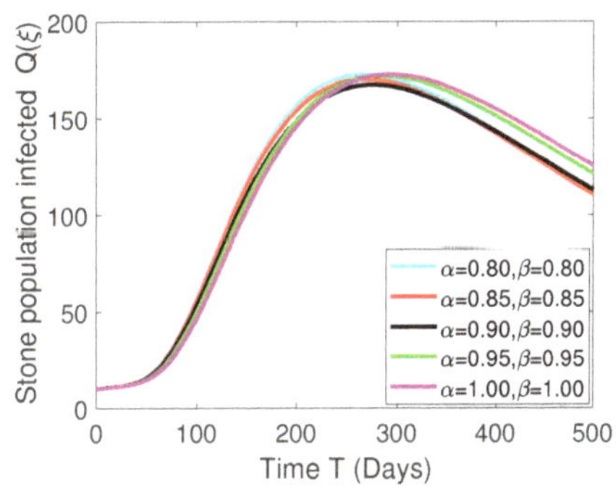

(**d**) Dynamical simulation of $\mathcal{Q}(\xi)$

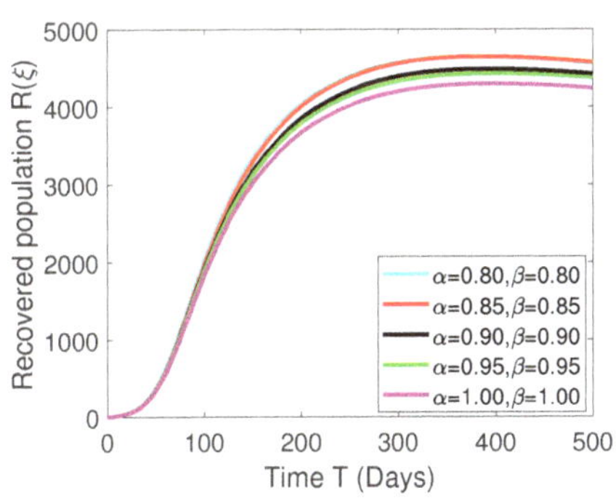

(**e**) Dynamical simulation of $\mathcal{R}(\xi)$

Figure 1. The numerical simulation results show the behaviors of all compartments in the devised model under uniform fractional orders and fractal dimensions, specifically when $\alpha = \beta$.

In the second case, the analysis focuses solely on the fractional order α while keeping the fractal dimension β fixed at $\beta = 1$. The study examines a range of α values, specifically

($\alpha = 0.80, 0.85, 0.90, 0.95$, and 1.00), to explore how variations in fractional orders impact the dynamics of the HIV model across different infection levels, recovery stages, and treatment decisions. Figure 2a–e depict each trajectory against a specific value of fractional order α at fractal dimension $\beta = 1$, illustrating the disease dynamics of the HIV model population. It is evident that each graph exhibits a different rate of convergence (based on fractional order α), but each curve ultimately reaches a steady state.

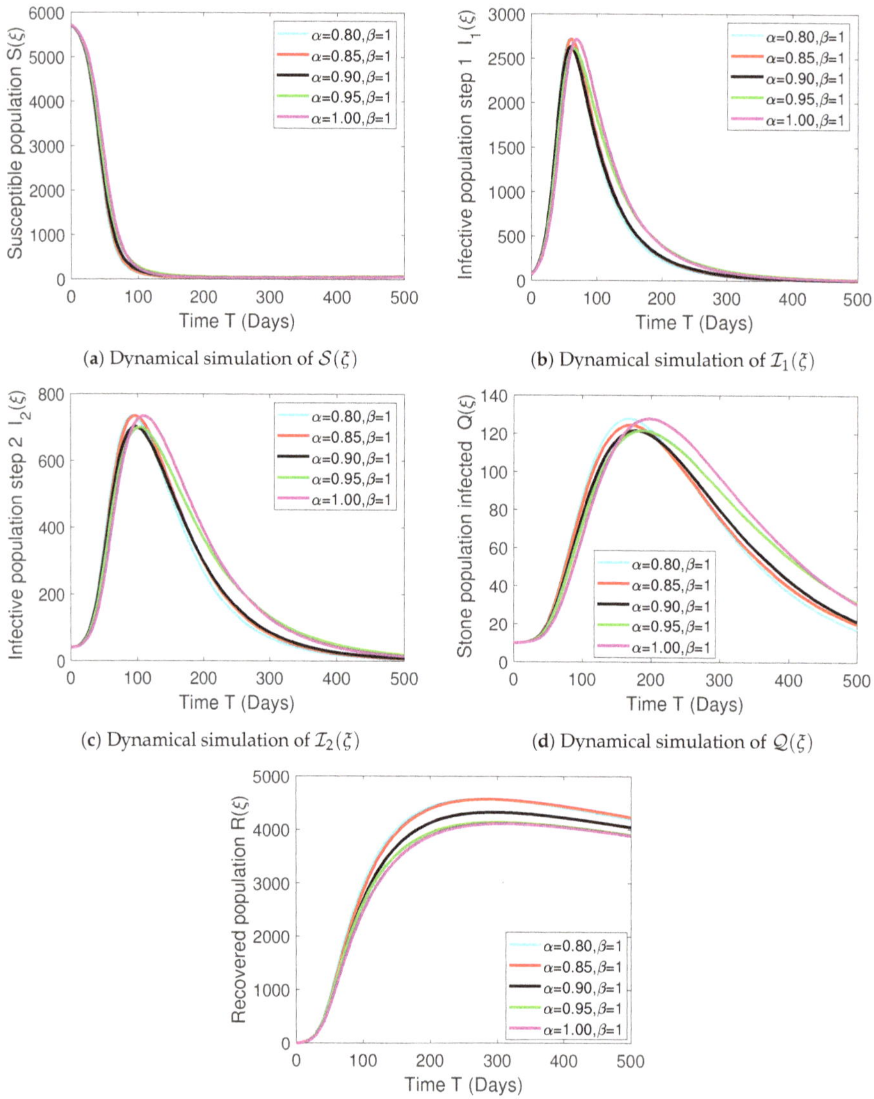

(**a**) Dynamical simulation of $\mathcal{S}(\xi)$ (**b**) Dynamical simulation of $\mathcal{I}_1(\xi)$

(**c**) Dynamical simulation of $\mathcal{I}_2(\xi)$ (**d**) Dynamical simulation of $\mathcal{Q}(\xi)$

(**e**) Dynamical simulation of $\mathcal{R}(\xi)$

Figure 2. The numerical simulations illustrate the behaviors of all compartments in the devised model, specifically by varying the fractional order α while keeping β constant at a value of 1.

In the third exploration case, the model dynamics are analyzed by varying the fractal dimension ($\beta = 0.80, 0.85, 0.90, 0.95$, and 1.00), while keeping the fractional order fixed at $\alpha = 1$. By examining the impact of changing fractal dimensions on HIV transmission dynamics, the study aims to isolate the effects of β while holding α constant. Results depicted in Figure 3a–e illustrate how altering β influences the number of HIV cases across different compartments of the model ($\mathcal{S}$, $\mathcal{I}_1$, $\mathcal{I}_2$, $\mathcal{Q}$, and $\mathcal{R}$), providing insights into the intricate dynamics of HIV spread. The curves resulting from fractional differential equations (2) clearly demonstrate a notably slower rise or decay over prolonged periods compared to those derived from a classical model with $\alpha = 1$. Across all figures, the dynamics tend toward a stable state as the fractional order decreases from 1 to 0.80 or lower. This indicates that a smaller fractional value leads to a more effective solution.

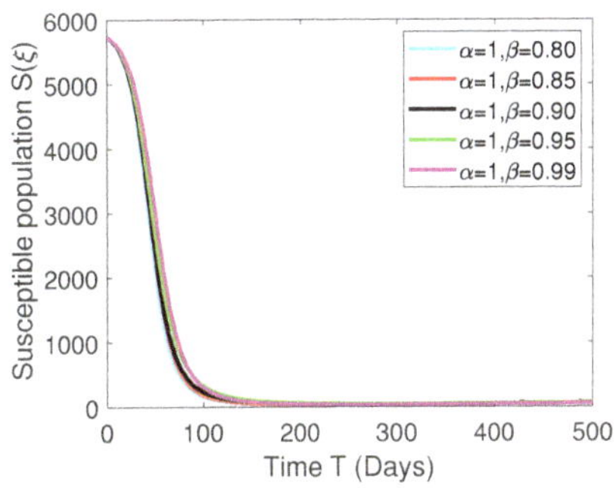

(**a**) Dynamical simulation of $\mathcal{S}(\xi)$

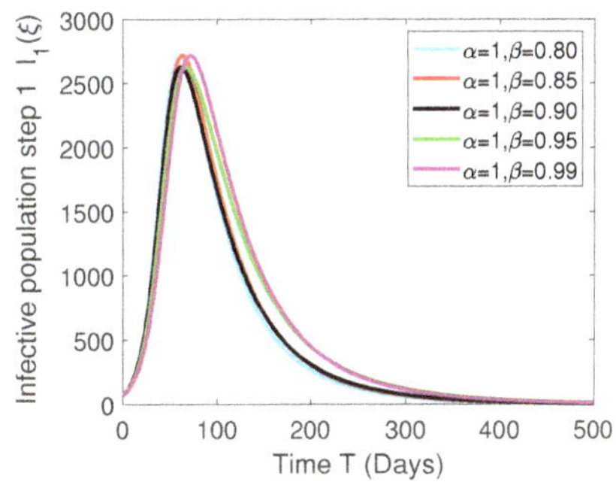

(**b**) Dynamical simulation of $\mathcal{I}_1(\xi)$

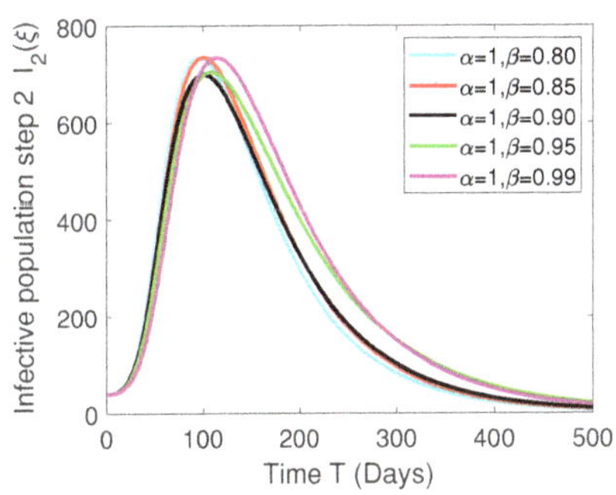

(**c**) Dynamical simulation of $\mathcal{I}_2(\xi)$

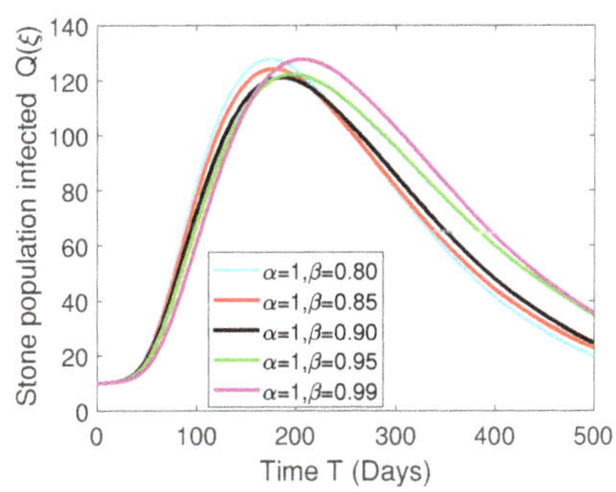

(**d**) Dynamical simulation of $\mathcal{Q}(\xi)$

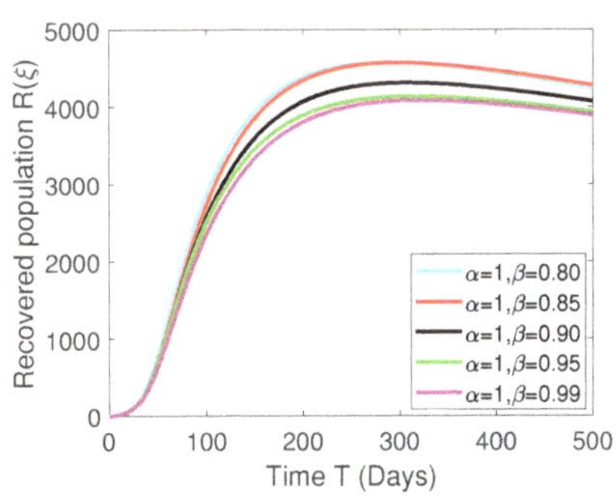

(**e**) Dynamical simulation of $\mathcal{R}(\xi)$

Figure 3. The numerical simulations showcase the behaviors of all compartments in the devised model by varying the fractal dimensions while keeping the fractional order α fixed at 1.

In Figure 4a–e, we plot approximate solutions against different fractional orders at a fractional dimension of $\beta = 0.7$, covering fractional orders of $\alpha = 0.80, 0.85, 0.90, 0.95$, and 1.00. In Figure 5a–e, we investigate model dynamics by varying the fractional order

($\beta = 0.80, 0.85, 0.90, 0.95$, and 1.00) while maintaining a constant fractal dimension of $\beta = 0.9$. This case uniquely explores the influence of changing fractional orders on HIV model dynamics, impacting the reduction in deaths and HIV transmission. Additionally, we derive significant insights from the model's compartments ($\mathcal{S}$, $\mathcal{I}_1$, $\mathcal{I}_2$, $\mathcal{Q}$, and $\mathcal{R}$), revealing the intricate dynamics of HIV spread. Observing Figures 4 and 5, we note that at a large value of fractal dimension, the graphs tend to reach a steady state more rapidly compared to a small value.

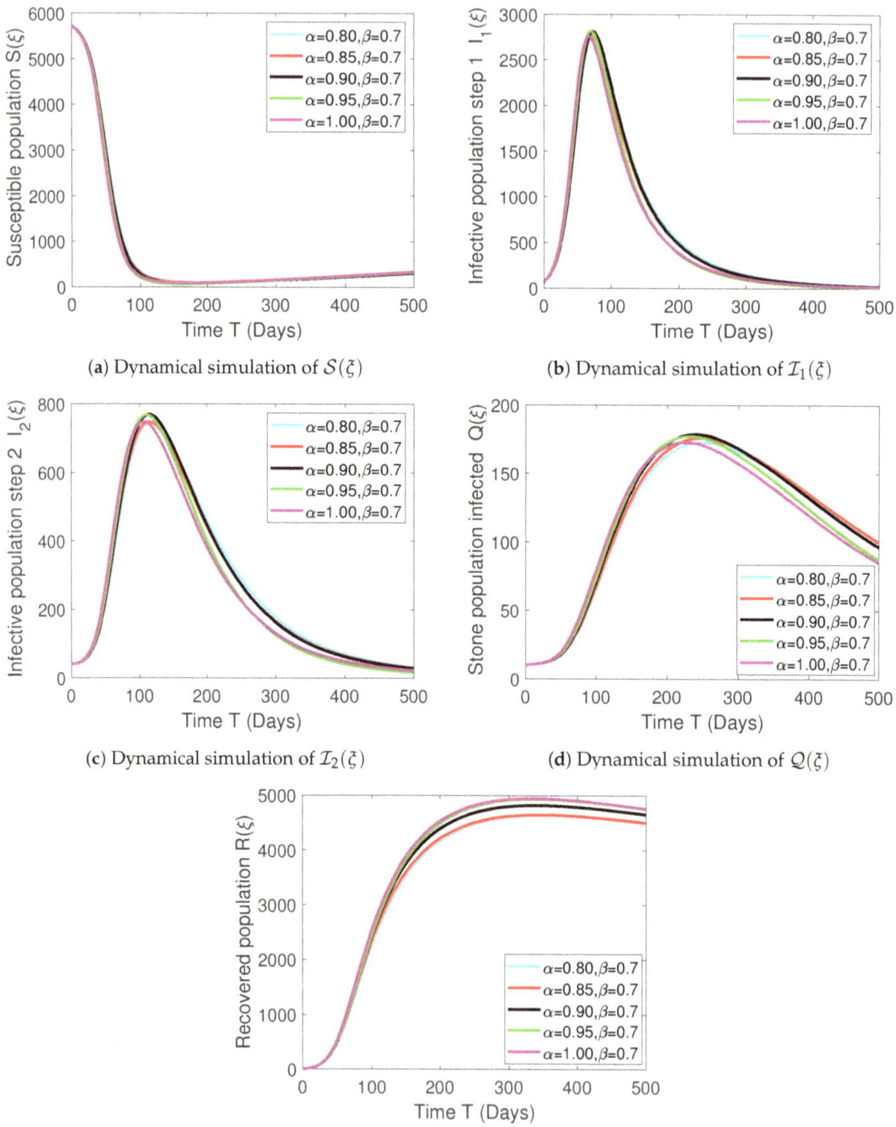

(**a**) Dynamical simulation of $\mathcal{S}(\xi)$

(**b**) Dynamical simulation of $\mathcal{I}_1(\xi)$

(**c**) Dynamical simulation of $\mathcal{I}_2(\xi)$

(**d**) Dynamical simulation of $\mathcal{Q}(\xi)$

(**e**) Dynamical simulation of $\mathcal{R}(\xi)$

Figure 4. The numerical simulations display how the compartments in the model respond over time, varying the fractional order α while maintaining a fixed dimension $\beta = 0.7$.

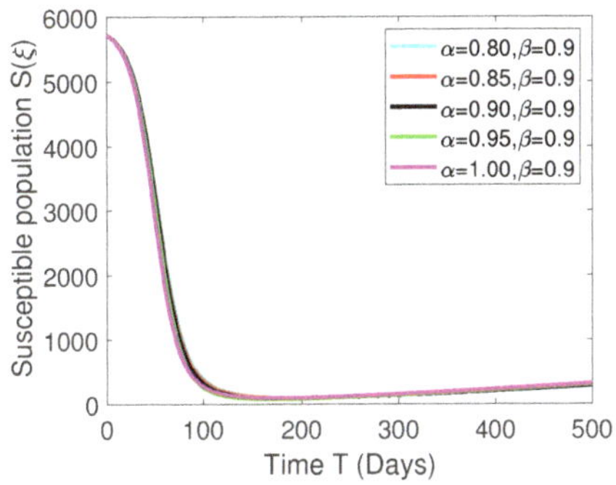

(**a**) Dynamical simulation of $\mathcal{S}(\xi)$

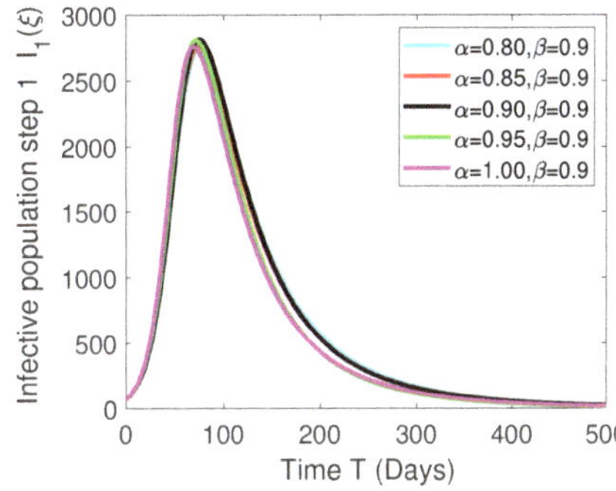

(**b**) Dynamical simulation of $\mathcal{I}_1(\xi)$

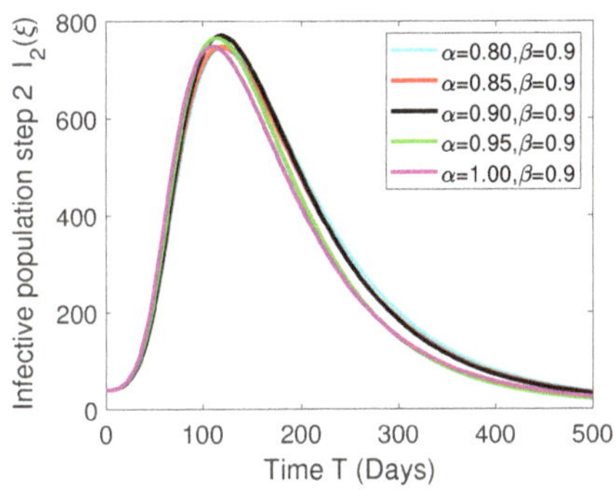

(**c**) Dynamical simulation of $\mathcal{I}_2(\xi)$

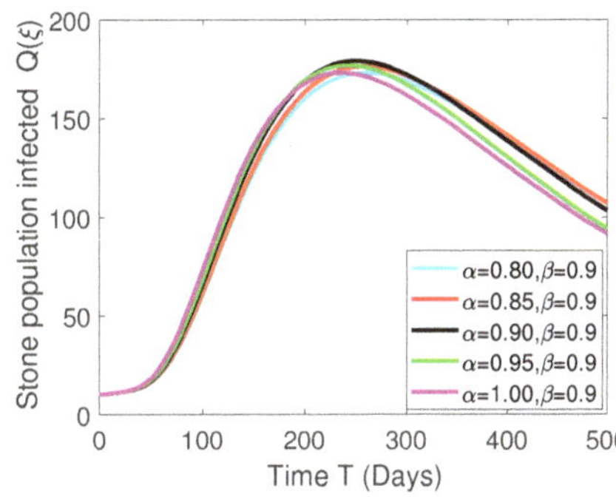

(**d**) Dynamical simulation of $\mathcal{Q}(\xi)$

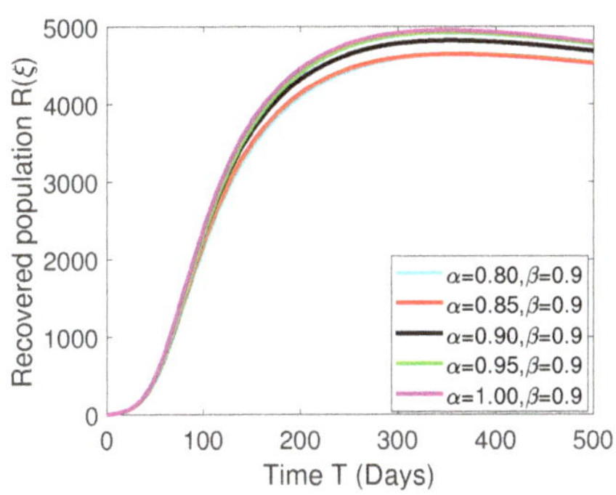

(**e**) Dynamical simulation of $\mathcal{R}(\xi)$

Figure 5. The simulations show how the model's compartments respond over time, changing the fractional order α while holding the dimension $\beta = 0.9$ constant.

The newly generated fractal-fractional derivative model with the power-law kernel allows for the consideration of anomalous spread, similar to infection biological models. This new model avoids the inclusion of artificial singularities seen in the Riemann-Liouville-Caputo case, providing a more accurate description of the biological process's history. Non-local operators, a powerful mathematical tool for describing non-local phenomena following the power-law, have been utilized in this context. Numerical simulations depicted in the figures show significant differences from those generated by the standard HIV/AIDS model proposed by [2,48] for classical derivatives. Across all figures, dynamics reach a steady state as the fractional order decreases from 1 to 0.80 or lower, indicating that smaller fractional values lead to more efficient solutions. The study's numerical scheme accurately captures the system's dynamics, with each solution approaching a steady-state boundary. These variables exhibit relationships with fluctuating fractional order α and fractal dimension β, demonstrating the influence of fractal features on the dynamics. Such features are absent in integer-order derivatives, highlighting the impact of utilizing fractal-fractional approaches for epidemic models. The findings suggest that slight changes in fractal dimensions and fractional orders only manifest in numerical simulations, with solutions for all compartments achieving the required accuracy and reliability as fractional values decrease. This underscores the effectiveness of fractal-fractional systems, compared to fractional systems [49], in investigating epidemic models and predicting asymptotic behavior around endemic equilibrium.

The fractional operator utilized in the study satisfies all the required theoretical conditions for the considered model, with the parameters demonstrating a substantial influence on the ecological system's stability. Even a slight variation in fractal-fractional orders causes a minor change in the model's behavior, highlighting the importance of fractional derivatives in capturing complex HIV transmission dynamics and enhancing the validity and applicability of the findings compared to classical derivatives. Furthermore, the study emphasizes the system's long-term memory effect, as fractional derivatives exhibit a decrease when the fractional order α approaches 1, further enhancing the accuracy and realism of the suggested HIV disease model. In summary, our considered fractal-fractional order HIV epidemic model offers significant advantages, being more realistic, effective, and efficient than the classical model by improving precision through increased flexibility, resulting in better outcomes. By considering long-term dependencies, non-local impacts, persistence, and recurrence, the model provides valuable insights into HIV transmission dynamics, aiding the public health sector in curbing the disease's spread. Simulations also offer relevant data on how infected patients' circumstances evolve over time, supporting informed decision-making. The study also proposes effective strategies to reduce HIV spread and anticipates future developments in this critical field.

7. Conclusions

Mathematical modeling is instrumental in understanding and managing infectious diseases like HIV. In contrast to classical models, nonlinear compartmental models offer a more nuanced view of disease spread. Our study presents a nonlinear deterministic mathematical model incorporating fractal-fractional order derivatives, specifically in the Caputo sense, to capture HIV infection dynamics. This model integrates three infection levels and delineates transitions between various stages for infected individuals, dividing the population into five compartments. We highlight the model's memory effect, which enriches the understanding of disease spread by incorporating fractional derivatives. To validate the model, we conducted a thorough analysis establishing the existence and uniqueness of solutions using fixed-point methods. Ulam-Hyer's stability was assessed through nonlinear functional analysis, affirming the stability of the model's solutions. Numerical solutions were obtained using the fractal-fractional Adam Bashforth iterative scheme in fractional order, validated through MATLAB simulations. Our numerical simulations explored a range of fractional orders and fractal dimensions, revealing how these parameters influence the model's dynamics. Comparisons with integer-order models were made to evaluate stability and convergence, showing the impact of arbitrary order parameters on model dynamics. Overall, utilizing fractal-fractional derivatives enhances the realism of modeling complex events like HIV spread.

The graphical results further illustrate how variations in fractional orders and fractal dimensions impact the dynamics of HIV spread. The analysis reveals that susceptibility dynamics exhibit an initial decline followed by stabilization, with all compartments of the model converging to the true endemic equilibrium point. Higher fractional orders suggest a more intricate interplay of factors affecting susceptibility, indicating a more efficient utilization of historical data or long-term memory in the transmission process. The infected populations at stages 1 and 2 show rapid growth as the fractional order α increases, followed by a decline as the fractional order decreases, leading each solution towards a steady-state boundary. Conversely, populations under treatment exhibit a gradual decline as fractional orders increase, emphasizing the sensitivity of dynamics to parameter settings. Additionally, the recovered population increases rapidly with lower fractional orders and declines more noticeably with higher fractional orders. In all figures, the dynamics reach a steady state as the fractional order decreases from 1 to 0.80 or lower, suggesting that smaller fractional values lead to more efficient solutions. Reducing fractional values enhances the accuracy and reliability of solutions across all compartments. This observation highlights the importance of fractal-fractional derivatives in capturing the complex dynamics of HIV transmission, providing more valid and applicable findings compared to fractional and integer order derivatives. The results emphasize the significance of regulating the effective transmission rate to mitigate fatalities, contain HIV transmission, and increase the number of recoveries. Overall, the proposed novel fractal-fractional derivative technique offers more precise measures and may be better suited for deciphering complex phenomena compared to fractional and integer-order operators.

Our research yields invaluable insights for future scientific endeavors. The use of fractal-fractional derivatives uncovers intricate dynamics in viral disease models, surpassing the capabilities of integer-order derivatives. Mathematical modeling encapsulates certain physical phenomena where the classical derivative only captures dynamics in one direction, whereas the fractional operator enables continuous monitoring of infectious diseases. The fractional order allows analysis of infection from its initial point when infected individuals first carry the infection and begin spreading it, until its culmination. This comprehensive approach aids in understanding the complete behavior of infection and the impact of control strategies through modeling. It enhances our comprehension of the disease's complexities and improves predictions of its behavior over time. This analytical approach is instrumental in future research and control plans aimed at mitigating the effects of the disease. It contributes significantly to HIV transmission management and community-level understanding. Future directions include optimizing control strategies, integrating behavioral dynamics into the model with real-world data validation, exploring the application of fractal-fractional derivatives in neural networks, and enhancing the numerical framework by incorporating fractional dimensions into the independent variable ξ. These efforts hold promise in improving the model's applicability and robustness in capturing the dynamics of HIV transmission.

Author Contributions: All authors made equal contributions to the writing of this paper. All authors have accepted responsibility for the entire content of this manuscript and approved its submission. Conceptualization, R.T.A. and Y.N.A.; methodology, N.H.A. and R.T.A.; software, Y.N.A.; validation, N.H.A., Y.N.A. and R.T.A.; formal analysis, S.T.; investigation, R.T.A.; resources, N.H.A. and R.T.A.; writing—original draft preparation, Y.N.A.; review and editing, R.T.A., Y.N.A., N.H.A. and S.T.; visualization, N.H.A. and Y.N.A.; supervision, R.T.A.; project administration, R.T.A.; funding acquisition, N.H.A. and R.T.A. All authors have read and agreed to the published version of the manuscript.

Funding: This work was supported and funded by the Deanship of Scientific Research at Imam Mohammad Ibn Saud Islamic University (IMSIU) (grant number IMSIU-RPP2023126).

Data Availability Statement: No new data have been created for this study.

Conflicts of Interest: The authors declare no conflict of interest.

References

1. Anderson, R.M. The role of mathematical models in the study of HIV transmission and the epidemiology of AIDS. *J. Acquir. Immune Defic. Syndr.* **1988**, *1*, 241–256. [PubMed]
2. Sakkoum, A.; Lhous, M.; Magri, E.M. A mathematical simulation and optimal control of a VIH model with different infectious level. *J. Math. Comput. Sci.* **2022**, *12*, 117.

3. Anderson, R.M.; Blythe, S.P.; Gupta, S.; Konings, E. The transmission dynamics of the human immunodeficiency virus type 1 in the male homosexual community in the United Kingdom: The influence of changes in sexual behaviour. *Philos. Trans. R. Soc. Lond. B Biol. Sci.* **1989**, *325*, 45–98. [PubMed]
4. Nisar, K.S.; Farman, M.; Abdel-Aty, M.; Cao, J. A review on epidemic models in sight of fractional calculus. *Alex. Eng. J.* **2023**, *75*, 81–113. [CrossRef]
5. Chen, Y.; Liu, F.; Yu, Q.; Li, T. Review of fractional epidemic models. *Appl. Math. Model.* **2021**, *97*, 281–307. [CrossRef]
6. Ngina, P.; Mbogo, R.W.; Luboobi, L.S. Modelling optimal control of in-host HIV dynamics using different control strategies. *Comput. Math. Methods Med.* **2018**, *2018*, 9385080. [CrossRef] [PubMed]
7. Silva, C.J.; Torres, D.F. Modeling and optimal control of HIV/AIDS prevention through PrEP. *Discret. Contin. Dyn. Syst.-S* **2018**, *11*, 119–141. [CrossRef]
8. Shirazian, M.; Farahi, M.H. Optimal control strategy for a fully determined HIV model. *Intell. Control. Autom.* **2010**, *1*, 15–19. [CrossRef]
9. Li, Z.; Teng, Z.; Miao, H. Modeling and control for HIV/AIDS transmission in China based on data from 2004 to 2016. *Comput. Math. Methods Med.* **2017**, *2017*, 8935314. [CrossRef]
10. Shen, M.; Xiao, Y.; Rong, L. Global stability of an infection-age structured HIV-1 model linking within-host and between-host dynamics. *Math. Biosci.* **2015**, *263*, 37–50. [CrossRef]
11. Shi, S.; Nguyen, P.K.; Cabral, H.J.; Diez-Barroso, R.; Derry, P.J.; Kanahara, S.M.; Kumar, V.A. Development of peptide inhibitors of HIV transmission. *Bioact. Mater.* **2016**, *1*, 109–121. [CrossRef] [PubMed]
12. Huo, H.F.; Chen, R.; Wang, X.Y. Modelling and stability of HIV/AIDS epidemic model with treatment. *Appl. Math. Model.* **2016**, *40*, 6550–6559. [CrossRef]
13. Zhai, X.; Li, W.; Wei, F.; Mao, X. Dynamics of an HIV/AIDS transmission model with protection awareness and fluctuations. *Chaos Solitons Fractals* **2023**, *169*, 113224. [CrossRef]
14. Zafar, Z.U.A.; Ali, N.; Younas, S.; Abdelwahab, S.F.; Nisar, K.S. Numerical investigations of stochastic HIV/AIDS infection model. *Alex. Eng. J.* **2021**, *60*, 5341–5363. [CrossRef]
15. Wang, J.; Zhang, R.; Kuniya, T. Global dynamics for a class of age-infection HIV models with nonlinear infection rate. *J. Math. Anal. Appl.* **2015**, *432*, 289–313. [CrossRef]
16. Singh, R.; Ali, S.; Jain, M. Epidemic model of HIV/AIDS transmission dynamics with different latent stages based on treatment. *Am. J. Appl. Math.* **2016**, *4*, 222–234. [CrossRef]
17. Alyobi, S.; Jan, R. Qualitative and quantitative analysis of fractional dynamics of infectious diseases with control measures. *Fractal Fract.* **2023**, *7*, 400. [CrossRef]
18. Anjam, Y.N.; Yavuz, M.; ur Rahman, M.; Batool, A.Analysis of a fractional pollution model in a system of three interconnecting lakes. *AIMS Biophys.* **2023**, *10*, 220–240. [CrossRef]
19. Qureshi, S.; Atangana, A. Fractal-fractional differentiation for the modeling and mathematical analysis of nonlinear diarrhea transmission dynamics under the use of real data. *Chaos Solitons Fractals* **2020**, *136*, 109812. [CrossRef]
20. Anjam, Y.N.; Shahid, I.; Emadifar, H.; Arif Cheema, S.; ur Rahman, M. Dynamics of the optimality control of transmission of infectious disease: A sensitivity analysis. *Sci. Rep.* **2024**, *14*, 1041. [CrossRef]
21. Anjam, Y.N.; Shafqat, R.; Sarris, I.E.; Ur Rahman, M.; Touseef, S.; Arshad, M. A fractional order investigation of smoking model using Caputo-Fabrizio differential operator. *Fractal Fract.* **2022**, *6*, 623. [CrossRef]
22. Caputo, M.; Fabrizio, M. On the singular kernels for fractional derivatives. Some applications to partial differential equations. *Progr. Fract. Differ. Appl.* **2021**, *7*, 79–82.
23. Caputo, M.; Fabrizio, M. A new definition of fractional derivative without singular kernel. *Prog. Fract. Differ. Appl.* **2015**, *1*, 73–85.
24. Atangana, A. Fractal-fractional differentiation and integration: Connecting fractal calculus and fractional calculus to predict complex system. *Chaos Solitons Fractals* **2017**, *102*, 396–406. [CrossRef]
25. ur Rahman, M.; Ahmad, S.; Matoog, R.T.; Alshehri, N.A.; Khan, T. Study on the mathematical modelling of COVID-19 with Caputo-Fabrizio operator. *Chaos Solitons Fractals* **2021**, *500*, 111121. [CrossRef]
26. Zhang, T.; Zhao, Y.; Xu, X.; Wu, S.; Gu, Y. Solution and dynamics analysis of fractal-fractional multi-scroll Chen chaotic system based on Adomain decomposition method. *Chaos, Solitons Fractals* **2024**, *178*, 114268. [CrossRef]
27. Almutairi, N.; Saber, S. Application of a time-fractal fractional derivative with a power-law kernel to the Burke-Shaw system based on Newton's interpolation polynomials. *MethodsX* **2024**, *12*, 102510. [CrossRef] [PubMed]
28. Asifa; Anwar, T.; Kumam, P.; Sitthithakerngkiet, K.; Muhammad, S. A fractal-fractional model-based investigation of shape influence on thermal performance of tripartite hybrid nanofluid for channel flows. *Numer. Heat Transf. Part A Appl.* **2024**, *85*, 155–186. [CrossRef]
29. Adom-Konadu, A.; Bonyah, E.; Sackitey, A.L.; Anokye, M.; Asamoah, J.K.K. A fractional order Monkeypox model with protected travelers using the fixed point theorem and Newton polynomial interpolation. *Healthc. Anal.* **2023**, *3*, 100191. [CrossRef]
30. Atangana, A.; Qureshi, S. Modeling attractors of chaotic dynamical systems with fractal–fractional operators. *Chaos Solitons Fractals* **2019**, *123*, 320–337. [CrossRef]
31. Li, Z.; Liu, Z.; Khan, M.A. Fractional investigation of bank data with fractal-fractional Caputo derivative. *Chaos Solitons Fractals* **2020**, *131*, 109528. [CrossRef]

32. Owolabi, K.M.; Shikongo, A. Fractal fractional operator method on HER2+ breast cancer dynamics. *Int. J. Appl. Comput. Math.* **2021**, *7*, 85. [CrossRef]
33. Ahmad, S.; Ullah, A.; Abdeljawad, T.; Akgül, A.; Mlaiki, N. Analysis of fractal-fractional model of tumor-immune interaction. *Results Phys.* **2021**, *25*, 104178. [CrossRef]
34. Anjam, Y.N.; Arshad, A.; Alqahtani, R.T.; Arshad, M. Unveiling the dynamics of drug transmission: A fractal-fractional approach integrating criminal law perspectives. *AIMS Math.* **2024**, *9*, 13102–13128. [CrossRef]
35. Liu, X.; ur Rahmamn, M.; Ahmad, S.; Baleanu, D.; Nadeem Anjam, Y. A new fractional infectious disease model under the non-singular Mittag–Leffler derivative. *Waves Random Complex Media* **2022**, 1–27. [CrossRef]
36. Ali, Z.; Rabiei, F.; Shah, K.; Khodadadi, T. Qualitative analysis of fractal-fractional order COVID-19 mathematical model with case study of Wuhan. *Alex. Eng. J.* **2021**, *60*, 477–489. [CrossRef]
37. Qureshi, S.; Rangaig, N.A.; Baleanu, D. New numerical aspects of Caputo-Fabrizio fractional derivative operator. *Mathematics* **2019**, *7*, 374. [CrossRef]
38. Atangana, A. Modelling the spread of COVID-19 with new fractal-fractional operators: Can the lockdown save mankind before vaccination? *Chaos Solitons Fractals* **2020**, *136*, 109860. [CrossRef] [PubMed]
39. Farman, M.; Sarwar, R.; Akgul, A. Modeling and analysis of sustainable approach for dynamics of infections in plant virus with fractal fractional operator. *Chaos Solitons Fractals* **2023**, *170*, 113373. [CrossRef]
40. Granas, A.; Dugundji, J. *Fixed Point Theory*; Springer: New York, NY, USA, 2003; Volume 14, pp. 15–16.
41. Kongson, J.; Sudsutad, W.; Thaiprayoon, C.; Alzabut, J.; Tearnbucha, C. On analysis of a nonlinear fractional system for social media addiction involving Atangana-Baleanu-Caputo derivative. *Adv. Differ. Equ.* **2021**, *2021*, 356. [CrossRef]
42. Kreyszig, E. *Introductory Functional Analysis with Applications*; John Wiley Sons: Hoboken, NJ, USA, 1991; Volume 17.
43. Huo, H.F.; Feng, L.X. Global stability for an HIV/AIDS epidemic model with different latent stages and treatment. *Appl. Math. Model.* **2013**, *37*, 1480–1489. [CrossRef]
44. Alizon, S.; Magnus, C. Modelling the course of an HIV infection: Insights from ecology and evolution. *Viruses* **2012**, *4*, 1984–2013. [CrossRef] [PubMed]
45. Yusuf, T.T.; Benyah, F. Optimal strategy for controlling the spread of HIV/AIDS disease: A case study of South Africa. *J. Biol. Dyn.* **2012**, *6*, 475–494. [CrossRef] [PubMed]
46. Arruda, E.F.; Dias, C.M.; de Magalhã, C.V.; Pastore, D.H.; Thomé, R.C.; Yang, H.M. An optimal control approach to HIV immunology. *Appl. Math.* **2015**, *6*, 1115–1130. [CrossRef]
47. Kumar, S.; Chauhan, R.P.; Osman, M.S.; Mohiuddine, S.A. A study on fractional HIV-AIDs transmission model with awareness effect. *Math. Methods Appl. Sci.* **2023**, *46*, 8334–8348. [CrossRef]
48. Cai, L.; Li, X.; Ghosh, M.; Guo, B. Stability analysis of an HIV/AIDS epidemic model with treatment. *J. Comput. Appl. Math.* **2009**, *229*, 313–323. [CrossRef]
49. Khan, A.; Gómez-Aguilar, J.F.; Khan, T.S.; Khan, H. Stability analysis and numerical solutions of fractional order HIV/AIDS model. *Chaos Solitons Fractals* **2019**, *122*, 119–128. [CrossRef]

fractal and fractional

MDPI

Article

Conformal and Non-Minimal Couplings in Fractional Cosmology

Kevin Marroquín [1], Genly Leon [1,2,*], Alfredo D. Millano [1], Claudio Michea [3] and Andronikos Paliathanasis [1,2]

[1] Departamento de Matemáticas, Universidad Católica del Norte, Avenida Angamos 0610, Casilla 1280, Antofagasta 1270709, Chile; kevin.marroquin@alumnos.ucn.cl (K.M.); alfredo.millano@alumnos.ucn.cl (A.D.M.); anpaliat@phys.uoa.gr (A.P.)
[2] Institute of Systems Science, Durban University of Technology, P.O. Box 1334, Durban 4000, South Africa
[3] Departamento de Física, Universidad Católica del Norte, Avenida Angamos 0610, Casilla 1280, Antofagasta 1270709, Chile; claudio.ramirez@ce.ucn.cl
* Correspondence: genly.leon@ucn.cl

Abstract: Fractional differential calculus is a mathematical tool that has found applications in the study of social and physical behaviors considered "anomalous". It is often used when traditional integer derivatives models fail to represent cases where the power law is observed accurately. Fractional calculus must reflect non-local, frequency- and history-dependent properties of power-law phenomena. This tool has various important applications, such as fractional mass conservation, electrochemical analysis, groundwater flow problems, and fractional spatiotemporal diffusion equations. It can also be used in cosmology to explain late-time cosmic acceleration without the need for dark energy. We review some models using fractional differential equations. We look at the Einstein–Hilbert action, which is based on a fractional derivative action, and add a scalar field, ϕ, to create a non-minimal interaction theory with the coupling, $\xi R\phi^2$, between gravity and the scalar field, where ξ is the interaction constant. By employing various mathematical approaches, we can offer precise schemes to find analytical and numerical approximations of the solutions. Moreover, we comprehensively study the modified cosmological equations and analyze the solution space using the theory of dynamical systems and asymptotic expansion methods. This enables us to provide a qualitative description of cosmologies with a scalar field based on fractional calculus formalism.

Keywords: fractional calculus; dynamical systems; asymptotic solutions; cosmology

1. Introduction

Fractional differential calculus is a mathematical tool that has found applications in the study of social and physical behaviors considered "anomalous". These phenomena are often described empirically using the power law, which is universal. However, some of the mathematical models that use integer derivatives, including nonlinear models, need to work better in many cases where the power law is observed. Alternative tools like fractional calculus must be introduced to accurately reflect power-law phenomena' non-local, frequency- and history-dependent properties [1–12].

Fractional calculus has found critical applications in fractional mass conservation. In such cases, a fractional mass conservation equation is needed to model fluid flow when the control volume is not large enough compared to the scale of heterogeneity and when the flow within the volume control is not linear [13]. Other areas where fractional calculus is useful include electrochemical analysis [14,15] and groundwater flow problems [16,17]. In the latter references, Darcy's classical law is generalized by considering the water flow as a function of a non-integer-order derivative of the piezometric height. This generalized law and the law of conservation of mass are then used to derive a new equation for groundwater flow [16,17]. There are various practical applications of fractional calculus, including the fractional advection-dispersion equation [18–20] and fractional spatiotemporal diffusion equations [21,22]. An extension of the fractional derivative is the fractional derivative of variable order, which is helpful in defining anomalous diffusion processes in complex media [23–25]. Fractional derivatives simulate viscoelastic damping in materials such as polymers [26]. In quantum theory, the fractional Schrödinger equation [27,28] and its variations, such as the variable order fractional Schrödinger equation [29], are significant examples of fractional calculus.

Recent studies have shown that fractional calculus is also helpful in modeling fractional derivatives and quantum fields [30,31], quantum gravity and cosmology [32–37], black holes [38,39], fractional dynamics and fractional action cosmology [40–47], non-minimal coupling in fractional cosmology [37,48,49], fractal universe and quantum cosmology [50,51], multiscale gravity [52], classical and quantum gravity with fractional operators [53,54], multi-fractional spacetimes [55], quantum gravity and gravitational-wave astronomy [56], cosmic microwave background and inflation [57], fractional dynamics from Einstein gravity [39,58], and fractional cosmology [49,59–62] and dark energy, among others [63–70].

Some important research questions in this field include the following: Can we use a combination of local and global variables to qualitatively describe scalar field cosmologies based on fractional calculus formalism? Additionally, can we develop precise schemes for finding analytical and numerical approximations to solutions by selecting various approaches? To answer these questions, we present a new formulation of gravity with a scalar field that exhibits non-minimal or, more generally, conformal coupling to gravity. The new action includes the Ricci scalar, R, the scalar field, ϕ, with its potential $V(\phi)$, the coupling constant, ξ, the matter Lagrangian, L_m, the scale factor, a, and the lapse function, N. The Gamma function, $\Gamma(\mu)$, the fractional parameter, μ, and the equation of state parameter of matter, w, are also included. We utilize Caputo's derivative and the formalism of fractional calculus to modify the Friedmann and Klein–Gordon equations. This approach has many applications in describing natural phenomena, making it a unique and compelling framework.

Our research is comprehensive, encompassing a review of the state of the art and confirming that dynamical systems theory, methods of perturbation theory, and the main tools of fractional calculus can be combined to implement a qualitative analysis of gravity models with fractional derivatives. This comprehensive approach is particularly beneficial in cosmologies with scalar fields, conformal coupling, and non-minimal coupling to gravity, broadening previous studies' scope. Our paper thoroughly analyzes the findings from cosmologies involving scalar fields and gravity models with fractional derivatives, specifically focusing on a scalar field with conformal or, generically, non-minimal gravitational coupling. We comment on the use of dynamical systems theory and the tools of fractional calculus in the analysis of cosmological models and propose new cosmologies with scalar fields that have conformal or, in general, non-minimal coupling to gravity within the framework of fractional calculus. Using dynamical systems and asymptotic methods, our qualitative analysis of the models further enhances our understanding. It allows us to draw comprehensive and robust conclusions, instilling confidence in the validity of our findings. Our research goes beyond theory and has significant practical implications. We start with a thorough literature review that serves as a theoretical framework. We then formulate a research hypothesis that suggests the possibility of using qualitative techniques to obtain relevant information on the flow properties associated with an autonomous system of ordinary differential equations in the cosmological context. This approach, enabled by dynamical systems theory, provides qualitative descriptions of cosmologies with a scalar field in fractional calculus, which can be a valuable tool for future cosmological studies. We also offer schemes for finding analytical approximations of solutions and exact solutions by selecting various approaches, providing a practical guide for researchers in the field. In the fractional context, we analyze cosmologies with a scalar field coupled to gravity with conformal and, generally, a non-minimal coupling. We aim to generalize previous results within the framework of the fractional formulation of gravity and describe the phase space of the models. We obtain qualitative results and explicit and approximate exact solutions with high numerical precision from a mathematical point of view.

Our methodology first involves reviewing the literature on fractional calculus methods, solution of fractional differential equations, and their applications. The current literature on applying fractional differential calculus to theories of gravity will also be studied, obtaining modifications. The differential equations that describe the dynamics of the different models are to be derived and well-posed for mathematical analysis and physical interpretation. At this point, it is expected to select the work tools and become familiar with Caputo's fractional derivative and its application in formulating a fractional cosmological action and its respective variational calculation. Secondly, systems of ordinary differential equations will be derived and analyzed from a mathematical point of view. This analysis consists of several steps: finding equilibrium points and invariant sets; defining a linearization matrix for each system and evaluating it at each critical point to calculate the eigenvalues; classifying the stability of the points; generating phase space diagrams and numerical solutions for each system for appropriate values of the coupling and fractional parameters. It is expected that we will find each system's future and past attractors and classify each critical point according to its stability and asymptotic behavior. The dynamical behavior of the systems will also be described graphically by plotting orbits that illustrate the qualitative analysis, which allows the description of the cosmological evolution. Finally, we generalize previous results by considering a conformal and non-minimal coupling to gravity.

The paper is organized as follows. Section 2 covers the primary outcomes of fractional calculus, including different approaches to possible fractional derivatives such as Grünwald–Letnikov, Riemann–Liouville, and Caputo derivatives. The emphasis is on defining fractional integration and the fractional derivative. We discuss fractional differential equations and use Wolfram Language 13.3 [71] to solve physical problems formulated. We also explore the quantum version of the fractional harmonic oscillator and the relation between fractional calculus and q-deformed Lie algebras.

In Section 3, we explore fractional cosmologies with non-minimal coupling ($\xi \neq 0$), building upon previous results with minimal coupling. By studying different dynamical systems, including the invariant set $\Omega_\Lambda = 0$, we utilize numerical integration methods to analyze the behavior of solutions to differential equations from the cosmological model. We also investigate the stability of critical points. Our conclusions are presented in Section 4. In Appendix A, we define several special functions that recurrently appear in these topics.

2. Theoretical Framework

Fractional calculus is a field of study that deals with the extension of derivatives and integrals to fractional orders. It also focuses on the methods for solving differential equations that involve these fractional derivatives and fractional integrals. It was developed by Newton and Leibniz in the 17th century and involves two fundamental operations—differentiation and integration. These fractional operators have memory and are more flexible when describing the dynamic behavior of phenomena and systems using fractional differential equations. On the other hand, the description with integer differential equations uses local operators and is limited in the differentiation order to a constant. Consequently, the resulting models must be sufficiently accurate in many cases [72].

Although many contributions have been made to this topic over the years, it has not been applied directly for centuries. However, in recent years, its applications have grown tremendously, and it is now used universally as an empirical description of complex social and physical phenomena. Research on fractional differentiation spans multiple disciplines and has various applications, such as fractional spacetime in quantum mechanics and gravity and fractional quantum field theory [30–34,38,41,50,51]. This branch of mathematics is gaining more popularity in fluid dynamics, control theory, and signal processing. Due to the importance and potential of this topic, support for fractional derivatives and fractional integrals has been added to the Wolfram Language since the release of Version 13.1 https://blog.wolfram.com/2022/08/12/fractional-calculus-in-wolfram-language-13-1/ (revised on 20 February 2024). This paper will be using Wolfram Language 13.3 [71].

Niels Henrik Abel is known for contributing to fractional calculus in the early 19th century. He introduced the integration and differentiation of fractional order and their inverse relationship. Abel also unified the notation for differentiation and integration of arbitrary real order in the "differintegral" operation. Abel considered the generalized version of the tautochrone problem, formulated as the following integral equation:

$$f(x) = \int_0^x \frac{\phi(s)}{\sqrt{x-s}}\,ds, \tag{1}$$

for the unknown function, $\phi(x)$. After several algebraic manipulations, this integral equation could be rewritten in the following form:

$$\phi(x) = \frac{1}{\pi}\left(\frac{f(0)}{\sqrt{x}} + \int_0^x \frac{f'(\tau)}{\sqrt{x-\tau}}\,d\tau\right), \tag{2}$$

which is what we now call Caputo's fractional derivative of $f(x)$ with respect to x.

Scientists from various areas and backgrounds have been working on fractional calculus theory, approaching it from different perspectives. Some approaches define a fractional differentiation operation. In contrast, others consider a unified differentiation/integration operation, known as the fractional differintegral of order μ, with respect to x and a lower limit, a. Differintegrals depend on the function's value at point a, $f(a)$, using the function's "history". In practice, the lower limit is generally taken as 0.

Summarizing, in fractional calculus, the traditional derivatives and integrals of the integer order have been generalized to derivatives and integrals of arbitrary order. This concept is presented in various sources, including [1–12]. The idea is that a derivative operator of order n, which is a natural number, has been generalized to a derivative of order μ, which can be a complex number or even a complex function. The three most popular and influential definitions widely used in practice are the Grünwald–Letnikov differintegral, the Riemann–Liouville fractional derivative, and Caputo's fractional derivative.

2.1. Grünwald–Letnikov Approach

The Grünwald–Letnikov differintegral provides the basic extension of classical derivatives/integrals and is based on the following limits:

$$_0D_x^\mu f(x) = \lim_{h\to 0} h^{-\mu}\sum_{r=0}^{\infty}(-1)^r\binom{\mu}{r}f(x-rh). \tag{3}$$

In practice, this approach is useless since it contains infinite approximations of the function at different points.

2.2. Riemann–Liouville Approach

The definition of the Riemann–Liouville fractional derivative is as follows:

$$^{\mathrm{RL}}_{\ 0}D_x^\mu f(x) = \frac{1}{\Gamma(n-\mu)}\frac{d^n}{dx^n}\left(\int_0^x (x-\tau)^{n-\mu-1}f(\tau)d\tau\right), \tag{4}$$

where $n = \max\{0, \lfloor\mu\rfloor\}$, where $\lfloor x\rfloor$ denotes the floor function, $\lfloor x\rfloor = \max\{m \in \mathbb{Z} : m \le x\}$.

It is based on a solid and strict mathematical theory of fractional calculus. This theory is well developed, but the Riemann–Liouville approach has some limitations that make it less suitable for applications in real-world problems.

For example, the derivative of a constant is not zero:

$$^{\mathrm{RL}}_{\ 0}D_x^\mu \text{constant} = \frac{\text{constant}}{\Gamma(1-\mu)}x^{-\mu}. \tag{5}$$

Table 1 shows the μ-th fractional derivatives and n-th ordinary derivatives for some standard functions (see Appendix A for definitions of special functions).

Table 1. The μ-th fractional derivatives of Riemann–Liouville and the n-th ordinary derivatives for some common functions.

$f(x)$	$D_x^{\mu}(f(x))$	$f^{(n)}(x)$
e^x	$-e^x(Q(-\mu,x)-1)$	e^x
x^2	$\frac{2x^{2-\mu}}{\Gamma(3-\mu)}$	$\frac{2x^{2-n}}{(2-n)!}$
$\log(x)$	$\begin{cases} -(-1)^{\mu}(\mu-1)!x^{-\mu} & \mu\in\mathbb{Z}\wedge\mu>0 \\ -\frac{x^{-\mu}\left(\psi^{(0)}(1-\mu)-\log(x)+\gamma\right)}{\Gamma(1-\mu)} & \text{True} \end{cases}$	$\begin{cases} -(-1)^{n}(n-1)!x^{-n} & n\geq 1 \\ \log(x) & \text{True} \end{cases}$
$\sin(x)$	$\sqrt{\pi}\,2^{\mu-1}x^{1-\mu}\,{}_1\tilde{F}_2\left(1;1-\frac{\mu}{2},\frac{3-\mu}{2};-\frac{x^2}{4}\right)$	$\sin\left(\frac{\pi n}{2}+x\right)$
$\tan^{-1}(x)$	$\sqrt{\pi}\,2^{\mu-1}x^{1-\mu}\,{}_3\tilde{F}_2\left(\frac{1}{2},1,1;1-\frac{\mu}{2},\frac{3-\mu}{2};-x^2\right)$	$\sqrt{\pi}\,2^{n-1}x^{1-n}\,{}_3\tilde{F}_2\left(\frac{1}{2},1,1;1-\frac{n}{2},\frac{3-n}{2};-x^2\right)$
$J_0(x)$	$\sqrt{\pi}\,2^{\mu}x^{-\mu}\,{}_1\tilde{F}_2\left(\frac{1}{2};\frac{1-\mu}{2},1-\frac{\mu}{2};-\frac{x^2}{4}\right)$	$2^{-n}\sum_{K_1=0}^{n}(-1)^{K_1}J_{2K_1-n}(x)\binom{n}{K_1}$
${}_1F_1(a;b;x)$	$\Gamma(b)x^{-\mu}{}_2\tilde{F}_2(1,a;1-\mu,b;x)$	$\begin{cases} \Gamma(b)x^{-n}{}_2\tilde{F}_2(1,a;1-n,b;x) & n\geq 1 \\ {}_1F_1(a;b;x) & \text{True} \end{cases}$

2.2.1. Caputo's Approach

Caputo's definition of fractional derivative is as follows:

$$ {}_0^C D_x^{\mu} f(x) = \frac{1}{\Gamma(n-\mu)} \int_0^x (x-\tau)^{n-\mu-1} \frac{d^n}{d\tau^n} f(\tau) d\tau, \quad n = \begin{cases} \lfloor \mu \rfloor + 1 & \mu \notin \mathbb{N} \\ \mu & \mu \in \mathbb{N} \end{cases}. \tag{6} $$

There is some similarity between this and the Riemann–Liouville differintegral; in fact, the Caputo differintegral can be defined via the Riemann–Liouville differintegral by the follwing:

$$ {}_0^C D_x^{\mu} f(x) = {}_0^{RL} D_x^{\mu} - \sum_{k=0}^{\lfloor \mu \rfloor - 1} \frac{x^{k-\mu}}{\Gamma(k-\mu+1)} \frac{d^k}{dx^k} f(0). \tag{7} $$

Caputo's definition of fractional and integral derivatives has many advantages compared to those of Riemann–Liouville or Grünwald–Letnikov: first, it takes into account the values of the function and its derivatives at the origin (or, in general, at any lower or upper bound a), which automatically makes it suitable for solving fractional order initial value problems using Laplace transforms. Furthermore, the Caputo fractional derivative of a constant is 0. Therefore, it is more consistent with the classical calculation.

The Riemann–Liouville fractional differintegral has been implemented in the Wolfram Language, using the Wolfram Language Version 13.3 [71] function **FractionalD**. This function calculates the Riemann–Liouville fractional derivative of order μ of the function $f(x)$; the lower limit of the integral is considered 0.

The Caputo fractional differential integral is **CaputoD** in Wolfram Language 13.1, which gives the Caputo fractional derivative of order μ of a function $f(x)$. For negative orders of μ, the output of **CaputoD** matches **FractionalD**.

Table 2 presents the half-order Caputo fractional derivatives of some common mathematical functions.

Table 2. Half-order Caputo fractional derivatives of some common mathematical functions.

$f(x)$	$D_x^{\frac{1}{2}}(f(x))$
e^x	$e^x \operatorname{erf}(\sqrt{x})$
x^2	$\frac{8x^{\frac{3}{2}}}{3\sqrt{\pi}}$
$\log(x)$	$\frac{\log(4)}{\sqrt{\pi}\sqrt{x}}$
$\sin(x)$	$\frac{2\sqrt{x}\,{}_1F_2\left(1;\frac{3}{4},\frac{5}{4};-\frac{x^2}{4}\right)}{\sqrt{\pi}}$
$\tan^{-1}(x)$	$\frac{2\sqrt{x}\,{}_2F_3\left(\frac{1}{2},1,1;\frac{3}{4},\frac{5}{4};-x^2\right)}{\sqrt{\pi}}$
$J_0(x)$	$\frac{{}_1F_2\left(\frac{1}{2};\frac{1}{4},\frac{3}{4};-\frac{x^2}{4}\right)-1}{\sqrt{\pi}\sqrt{x}}$
${}_1F_1(a;b;x)$	$\frac{{}_2F_2\left(1,a;\frac{1}{2},b;x\right)-1}{\sqrt{\pi}\sqrt{x}}$

2.2.2. Rule for Successive Fractional Derivatives

The Caputo fractional derivative for an arbitrary c is as follows: [5]

$$ {}_c^C D_x^{\mu} f(t) = \frac{1}{\Gamma(n-\mu)} \int_c^x \frac{d^n f(\tau)}{d\tau^n} (x-\tau)^{n-\mu-1} d\tau, \quad n = \begin{cases} \lfloor \mu \rfloor + 1 & \mu \notin \mathbb{N} \\ \mu & \mu \in \mathbb{N} \end{cases}. \tag{8} $$

Given the square function, i.e., $f(x) = x^2/2$, choosing $c = 0$, removing the subindex 0, and applying the derivative of order $1/2$ twice, it results in the following: $\mu = 1/2 \Rightarrow n := \lfloor \mu \rfloor + 1 = 1$,

$$ {}^C D_x^{1/2}\left(x^2/2\right) = \frac{1}{\Gamma(\frac{1}{2})} \int_0^x \frac{d}{dt}\left[\frac{t^2}{2}\right](x-t)^{-\frac{1}{2}} dt = \frac{1}{\sqrt{\pi}} \frac{4}{3} x^{\frac{3}{2}}, $$

$$ {}^C D_x^{1/2}\left(\frac{1}{\sqrt{\pi}}\frac{4}{3}x^{\frac{3}{2}}\right) = \frac{1}{\sqrt{\pi}}\frac{4}{3}\frac{1}{\Gamma(\frac{1}{2})} \int_0^x \frac{d}{dt}\left[t^{\frac{3}{2}}\right](x-t)^{-\frac{1}{2}} dt = \frac{1}{\sqrt{\pi}}\frac{4}{3}\frac{1}{\sqrt{\pi}}\frac{3\pi x}{4} = x. $$

The first derivative of the square function is obtained through two "half-order fractional differentiation" procedures. One could easily verify that two similar half-order integration procedures can obtain the anti-derivative of the square function. So, with this example, we show what fractional calculus is and how it relates to and generalizes the classical version. However, this result is based on the choice, $c = 0$. In general, the rule for successive derivatives for fractional calculus is as follows:

$$ D_x^{\mu}\left[D_x^{\beta} f(x)\right] = D_x^{\mu+\beta} f(x) - \sum_{j=1}^{n} D_x^{\beta-j} f(c_+) \frac{(x-c)^{-\mu-j}}{\Gamma(1-\mu-j)}. \tag{9} $$

2.2.3. Fractional Derivatives as Generalizations of Integer-Order Derivatives

From now on, we follow the exposition of [2]. We have the formulas for the n-th derivatives,

$$ \frac{d^n}{dx^n} e^{kx} = k^n e^{kx}, \quad \frac{d^n}{dx^n} \sin(kx) = k^n \sin\left(kx + \frac{\pi}{2} n\right), \quad \frac{d^n}{dx^n} x^k = \frac{k!}{(k-n)!} x^{k-n}, \tag{10} $$

for $n \in \mathbb{N}$ can be extended for real and complex μ numbers,

$$ D_x^{\mu} e^{kx} = k^{\mu} e^{kx}, \qquad k \geq 0, \tag{11} $$

$$ D_x^{\mu} \sin(kx) = k^{\mu} \sin\left(kx + \frac{\pi}{2}\mu\right), \qquad k \geq 0, \tag{12} $$

$$ D_x^{\mu} x^k = \frac{\Gamma(k+1)}{\Gamma(k+1-\mu)} x^{k-\mu}, \qquad x \geq 0, k \neq -1, -2, -3, \dots . \tag{13} $$

The definition of the fractional derivative of the exponential function was given by Liouville in 1832; those of trigonometric functions were proposed by Fourier in 1822, and those of powers were systematically studied by Riemann in 1847. Still, the first attempts at the latter were made by Leibniz and Euler, the latter in 1738. The Riemann–Liouville fractional derivative of a constant is given by (13), setting $k = 0$, we obtain unexpected behavior, as follows:

$$D_x^\mu 1 = D_x^\mu x^0 = \frac{1}{\Gamma(1-\mu)} x^{-\mu}.$$

Therefore, as an additional postulate, Caputo in 1967 introduced the following condition: $D_x^\mu 1 = 0$.

These four definitions of fractional derivatives (11)–(13) and Caputo's share several aspects. On the one hand, they satisfy the following correspondence principle:

$$\lim_{\mu \to n} D_x^\mu f(x) = \frac{d^n}{dx^n} f(x), \quad n = 0, 1, 2, \ldots \;. \tag{14}$$

And the following rules apply:

$$D_x^\mu c f(x) = c D_x^\mu f(x), \quad D_x^\mu [f(x) + g(x)] = D_x^\mu f(x) + D_x^\mu g(x). \tag{15}$$

Therefore, the fractional derivative of an analytic function can be calculated to its series. According to Liouville, we have the following:

$$f(x) = \sum_{k=0}^{\infty} a_k e^{kx} \implies D_x^\mu f(x) = \sum_{k=0}^{\infty} a_k k^\mu e^{kx}. \tag{16}$$

According to Fourier, we have the following:

$$f(x) = a_0 + \sum_{k=1}^{\infty} a_k \sin(kx) + \sum_{k=1}^{\infty} b_k \cos(kx), \tag{17}$$

$$D_x^\mu f(x) = \sum_{k=1}^{\infty} a_k k^\mu \sin\left(kx + \frac{\pi}{2}\mu\right) + \sum_{k=1}^{\infty} b_k k^\mu \cos\left(kx + \frac{\pi}{2}\mu\right). \tag{18}$$

According to Riemann, we have the following:

$$f(x) = x^{\mu-1} \sum_{k=0}^{\infty} a_k x^{k\mu}, \tag{19}$$

$$D_x^\mu f(x) = x^{\mu-1} \sum_{k=0}^{\infty} a_{k+1} \frac{\Gamma((k+2)\mu)}{\Gamma((k+1)\mu)} x^{k\mu}. \tag{20}$$

According to Caputo, we have the following:

$$f(x) = \sum_{k=0}^{\infty} a_k x^{k\mu}, \tag{21}$$

$$D_x^\mu f(x) = \sum_{k=0}^{\infty} a_{k+1} \frac{\Gamma(1+(k+1)\mu)}{\Gamma(1+k\mu)} x^{k\mu}. \tag{22}$$

Calculating the Caputo fractional derivative of order μ to the exponential function, we have the following:

$$D_x^\mu e^x = D_x^\mu \sum_{n=0}^{\infty} \frac{x^n}{n!} = \sum_{n=1}^{\infty} \frac{x^{n-\mu}}{\Gamma(1+n-\mu)} = x^{1-\mu} E(1, 2-\mu, x). \tag{23}$$

So, in contrast to Liouville's definition (16), Caputo's definition is not obviously in terms of an exponential, but in terms of a generalized Mittag-Leffler function (A14).

2.2.4. Leibniz's Rule for the Fractional Derivative of the Product

Let us now analyze whether all the techniques of ordinary differential calculus can be transferred to the field of fractional calculus [2]. For example, if we take the ordinary Leibniz rule, as follows:

$$\frac{d}{dx}(\psi\chi) = \left(\frac{d}{dx}\psi\right)\chi + \psi\left(\frac{d}{dx}\chi\right), \tag{24}$$

it could be carelessly inferred that the relation

$$D_x^\mu(\psi\chi) = \left(D_x^\mu\psi\right)\chi + \psi\left(D_x^\mu\chi\right), \tag{25}$$

remains in the fractional calculus. However, using Liouville's definition of a fractional derivative, we have the following:

$$D_x^\mu(e^{k_1x}e^{k_2x}) = D_x^\mu e^{(k_1+k_2)x} = (k_1+k_2)^\mu e^{(k_1+k_2)x}. \tag{26}$$

While using (25), we obtain the following:

$$D_x^\mu(e^{k_1x}e^{k_2x}) = (k_1^\mu + k_2^\mu)(e^{k_1x}e^{k_2x}). \tag{27}$$

Therefore, Leibniz's rule (25) is not valid for fractional derivatives.

We start from the rule for successive non-negative integer orders to extend Leibniz's rule to be valid for fractional calculus.

$$\begin{aligned}
\frac{d}{dx}(\psi\chi) &= \left(\frac{d}{dx}\psi\right)\chi + \psi\left(\frac{d}{dx}\chi\right),\\
\frac{d^2}{dx^2}(\psi\chi) &= \left(\frac{d^2}{dx^2}\psi\right)\chi + 2\left(\frac{d}{dx}\psi\right)\left(\frac{d}{dx}\chi\right) + \psi\left(\frac{d^2}{dx^2}\chi\right),\\
\frac{d^3}{dx^3}(\psi\chi) &= \left(\frac{d^3}{dx^3}\psi\right)\chi + 3\left(\frac{d^2}{dx^2}\psi\right)\left(\frac{d}{dx}\chi\right) + 3\left(\frac{d}{dx}\psi\right)\left(\frac{d^2}{dx^2}\chi\right) + \psi\left(\frac{d^3}{dx^3}\chi\right),
\end{aligned} \tag{28}$$

et cetera. We have the following formula for an arbitrary integer, as follows:

$$\frac{d^n}{dx^n}(\psi\chi) = \sum_{j=0}^{n}\binom{n}{j}\left(\frac{d^{n-j}}{dx^{n-j}}\psi\right)\left(\frac{d^j}{dx^j}\chi\right), \qquad n \in \mathbb{N}. \tag{29}$$

According to (A5), this expression can be extended to an arbitrary μ:

$$D_x^\mu(\psi\chi) = \sum_{j=0}^{\infty}\frac{\Gamma(\mu+1)}{\Gamma(j+1)\Gamma(\mu-j+1)}(D_x^{\mu-j}\psi)(D_x^j\chi), \tag{30}$$

So, this form of the Leibniz product rule is also valid for fractional derivatives.

2.3. *Fractional Integral*

The Cauchy formula for successive integrations, which can be extended to fractional integrals, is used as the first step. A satisfactory definition of a fractional derivative can be obtained after appropriately deriving a fractional integral, I^μ. If we assume the following:

$$D_x^\mu = I^{-\mu}, \tag{31}$$

this implies that a fractional derivative is the inverse of a fractional integral, and conversely, a fractional integral is the inverse of a fractional derivative.

If ${}_aI$ is used for the integration operator, it is defined as follows:

$${}_aIf(x) = \int_a^x f(\xi)\,d\xi, \tag{32}$$

It is observed that the multiple integral is as follows:

$$ {}_aI^n f(x) = \int_a^x \int_a^{x_{n-1}} \cdots \int_a^{x_1} f(x_0)\, dx_0 \cdots dx_{n-1}, \tag{33} $$

which, using Cauchy's repeated integration formula, can be reduced to a single integral, as follows:

$$ {}_aI^n f(x) = \frac{1}{(n-1)!} \int_a^x (x-\xi)^{n-1} f(\xi)\, d\xi. \tag{34} $$

This formula can be easily extended to the fractional case, as follows:

$$ {}_aI_+^{\mu} f(x) = \frac{1}{\Gamma(\mu)} \int_a^x (x-\xi)^{\mu-1} f(\xi)\, d\xi, \qquad x > a, \tag{35} $$

$$ {}_bI_-^{\mu} f(x) = \frac{1}{\Gamma(\mu)} \int_x^b (\xi-x)^{\mu-1} f(\xi)\, d\xi, \qquad x < b. \tag{36} $$

Constants a and b determine the lower and upper limits of the integral, respectively, and can initially be chosen arbitrarily. The two cases are denoted as the left and right, respectively. This can be understood because the left case deals with values $\xi < x$, values to the left of x. The right case deals with values $\xi > x$, values to the right of x. If x is a time-type coordinate, then the integral of the left case is causal, and that of the right case is anti-causal.

The value of the integral depends on the specific choice of the constants (a, b). This will be the notable difference between the two most widely used definitions of a fractional integral, the so-called Liouville fractional integral and the Riemann fractional integral, which are discussed below.

2.3.1. Liouville Fractional Integral

The Liouville fractional integral is defined by making $a = -\infty$ and $b = +\infty$ in (35) and (36):

$$ {}_{\mathrm{L}}I_+^{\mu} f(x) = \frac{1}{\Gamma(\mu)} \int_{-\infty}^x (x-\xi)^{\mu-1} f(\xi)\, d\xi, \tag{37} $$

$$ {}_{\mathrm{L}}I_-^{\mu} f(x) = \frac{1}{\Gamma(\mu)} \int_x^{+\infty} (\xi-x)^{\mu-1} f(\xi)\, d\xi. \tag{38} $$

2.3.2. Riemann Fractional Integral

The fractional Riemann integral is defined by making $a = 0$ and $b = 0$ in (35) and (36), as follows:

$$ {}_{\mathrm{R}}I_+^{\mu} f(x) = \frac{1}{\Gamma(\mu)} \int_0^x (x-\xi)^{\mu-1} f(\xi)\, d\xi, \tag{39} $$

$$ {}_{\mathrm{R}}I_-^{\mu} f(x) = \frac{1}{\Gamma(\mu)} \int_x^0 (\xi-x)^{\mu-1} f(\xi)\, d\xi. \tag{40} $$

To see the difference between Liouville's definitions, (37) and (38), and Riemann's definitions, (39) and (40), we apply both definitions to $f(x) = e^{kx}$, as follows:

$$ {}_{\mathrm{L}}I_+^{\mu} e^{kx} = k^{-\mu} e^{kx}, x > 0, \quad {}_{\mathrm{L}}I_-^{\mu} e^{kx} = (-k)^{-\mu} e^{kx}, k < 0, $$

$$ {}_{\mathrm{R}}I_+^{\mu} e^{kx} = k^{-\mu} e^{kx}\left(1 - \frac{\Gamma(\mu, kx)}{\Gamma(\mu)}\right), x > 0, \quad {}_{\mathrm{R}}I_-^{\mu} e^{kx} = (-k)^{-\mu} e^{kx}\left(1 - \frac{\Gamma(\mu, kx)}{\Gamma(\mu)}\right), x < 0, $$

where $\Gamma(\mu, x)$ is the incomplete Gamma function. Using Liouville's definition, the function e^{kx} vanishes for $k > 0$ in the lower limit of the domain of the integral, so there is no additional contribution. On the other hand, when using the Riemann definition, an additional contribution is obtained because, at $a = 0$, the exponential function does not vanish [2].

2.4. Link between Integration and Fractional Differentiation

We use the following abbreviation:

$$D_x^{\mu} = D^{\mu}, \tag{41}$$

It is shown that the concepts of fractional integration and fractional differentiation are closely related. Separating the fractional derivative operator into factors, we have the following:

$$D^{\mu} = D^m D^{\mu-m} = \frac{d^m}{dx^m}{}_a I^{m-\mu}, \qquad m \in \mathbb{N}. \tag{42}$$

A fractional derivative can be interpreted as a fractional integral followed by an ordinary derivative. Once the fractional integral is specified, the fractional derivative is automatically determined. We can also reverse the sequence of the operators, resulting in an alternative decomposition, as follows:

$$D^{\mu} = D^{\mu-m} D^m = {}_a I^{m-\mu} \frac{d^m}{dx^m}, \qquad m \in \mathbb{N}. \tag{43}$$

Decompositions (42) and (43) lead to different results. Thus, we can understand the mechanism by which non-locality enters fractional calculus. The standard derivative, of course, is a local operator, but the fractional integral certainly is not. The fractional derivative should be understood as the inverse of fractional integration, a non-local operation. Consequently, fractional differentiation and integration produce the same difficulty [2].

In the previous section, two different definitions of the fractional integral have been given, the Liouville and the Riemann. For each of these definitions, according to the two different decompositions given above, four different realizations follow for the fractional derivative definition, which are presented below.

2.4.1. Liouville Fractional Derivative

For the simple case of $0 < \mu < 1$, using the Liouville definitions (37) and (38), and the sequence of operators, (42), we have the following:

$$_{\mathrm{L}}D_+^{\mu} f(x) = \frac{d}{dx}{}_{\mathrm{L}}I_+^{1-\mu} f(x) = \frac{1}{\Gamma(1-\mu)} \frac{d}{dx} \int_{-\infty}^{x} (x-\xi)^{-\mu} f(\xi)\, d\xi, \tag{44}$$

$$_{\mathrm{L}}D_-^{\mu} f(x) = \frac{d}{dx}{}_{\mathrm{L}}I_-^{1-\mu} f(x) = \frac{1}{\Gamma(1-\mu)} \frac{d}{dx} \int_{x}^{+\infty} (\xi-x)^{-\mu} f(\xi)\, d\xi. \tag{45}$$

2.4.2. Fractional Riemann Derivative

Using (39) and (40), and the sequence of operators, (42), we have the following Riemann fractional derivative:

$$_{\mathrm{R}}D_+^{\mu} f(x) = \frac{d}{dx}{}_{\mathrm{R}}I_+^{1-\mu} f(x) = \frac{1}{\Gamma(1-\mu)} \frac{d}{dx} \int_{0}^{x} (x-\xi)^{-\mu} f(\xi)\, d\xi, \tag{46}$$

$$_{\mathrm{R}}D_-^{\mu} f(x) = \frac{d}{dx}{}_{\mathrm{R}}I_-^{1-\mu} f(x) = \frac{1}{\Gamma(1-\mu)} \frac{d}{dx} \int_{x}^{0} (\xi-x)^{-\mu} f(\xi)\, d\xi. \tag{47}$$

2.4.3. Liouville–Caputo Fractional Derivative

In the case that the sequence of operators is inverted according to (43), it is based on the definition of the Liouville fractional integrals (37) and (38), as follows:

$$_{\mathrm{LC}}D_+^{\mu} f(x) = {}_{\mathrm{L}}I_+^{1-\mu} \frac{d}{dx} f(x) = \frac{1}{\Gamma(1-\mu)} \int_{-\infty}^{x} (x-\xi)^{-\mu} \frac{df(\xi)}{d\xi}\, d\xi, \tag{48}$$

$$_{\mathrm{LC}}D_-^{\mu} f(x) = {}_{\mathrm{L}}I_-^{1-\mu} \frac{d}{dx} f(x) = \frac{1}{\Gamma(1-\mu)} \int_{x}^{+\infty} (\xi-x)^{-\mu} \frac{df(\xi)}{d\xi}\, d\xi. \tag{49}$$

It has been observed that, for a function $f(x) = \text{constant}$, the definition of the Liouville fractional derivative (44) leads to a divergent result, while with the Liouville–Caputo definition (48), the result is zero. The conditions for the Liouville fractional derivative to converge are more restrictive than for the Liouville–Caputo counterpart [2].

2.4.4. Caputo Fractional Derivative

The inverted sequence of operators (43), the definition of the Riemann fractional integrals (39) and (40), leads to the following:

$$ {}^{C}D^{\mu}_{+}f(x) = {}_{R}I^{1-\mu}_{+}\frac{d}{dx}f(x) = \frac{1}{\Gamma(1-\mu)}\int_{0}^{x}(x-\xi)^{-\mu}\frac{df(\xi)}{d\xi}\,d\xi, \tag{50} $$

$$ {}^{C}D^{\mu}_{-}f(x) = {}_{R}I^{1-\mu}_{-}\frac{d}{dx}f(x) = \frac{1}{\Gamma(1-\mu)}\int_{x}^{0}(\xi-x)^{-\mu}\frac{df(\xi)}{d\xi}\,d\xi. \tag{51} $$

Then, for $f(x) = \text{constant}$, the Riemann fractional derivative is ${}_{R}D^{\mu}_{+}\text{constant} = \frac{\text{constant}}{\Gamma(1-\mu)}x^{-\mu}$, while when applying the Caputo derivative, we have ${}^{C}D^{\mu}_{+}\text{constant} = 0$. Therefore, in this section, we present the standard definitions of a fractional derivative, which satisfy the following condition:

$$ \lim_{\mu\to 1} D^{\mu}f(x) = \frac{df(x)}{dx}. \tag{52} $$

Multiple applications of the first-order derivative can generate higher-order derivatives, as follows:

$$ \frac{d^n}{dx^n} = \frac{d}{dx}\frac{d}{dx}\cdots\frac{d}{dx} \qquad n \text{ times.} \tag{53} $$

After applying different definitions of the fractional derivative to the same function, it has been found that they do not give the same result. This can be non-comforting, but all these definitions are equally well-founded. Therefore, physicists can test different definitions of the fractional derivative by comparing theoretical results with experimental data. Depending on the specific problem, one of the definitions will show the most significant agreement with the experiment.

2.5. Fractional Differential Equations

Fractional differential equations (FDEs), which involve fractional derivatives and generalize ordinary differential equations (ODEs), have received much attention. FDEs have been widely used in engineering, physics, chemistry, biology, and other fields involving relaxation and oscillation models.

Let us consider, for example, the FDE, as follows:

$$ {}^{C}_{0}D^{\frac{21}{10}}_{t}y(t) + 10y(t) = 0, \quad y(0) = 1, \quad y'(0) = 0, \quad y''(0) = 0. \tag{54} $$

Solving (54) using the Wolfram Language 13.3 [71] function **DSolve**, we obtain the following:

$$ y(t) = E\left(\frac{21}{10}, -10t^{21/10}\right). \tag{55} $$

The solution presented in Figure 1 is given in terms of the **MittagLefflerE** function, the primary function for fractional calculus applications. Its role in FDE solutions is similar in importance to the **Exp** function for ODE solutions: any FDE with constant coefficients can be solved in terms of Mittag-Leffler functions.

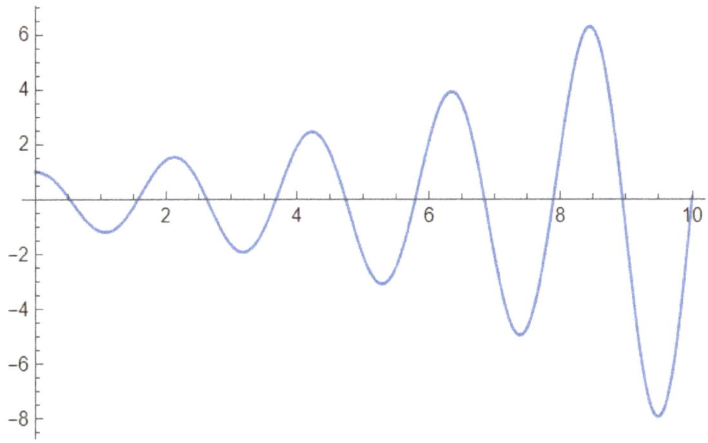

Figure 1. Solution (55) of the fractional harmonic oscillator of order 2.1 given by (54). For $\mu > 2$, the fractional harmonic oscillator mimics an excited oscillator.

An interesting example is the solution of a fractional harmonic oscillator of order 1.9, as follows:

$$ {}_0^C D_t^{\frac{19}{10}} x(t) + x(t) = 0, \quad x(0) = 1, \quad x'(0) = 0. \tag{56} $$

Solving (56) using the Wolfram Language 13.3 [71] function **DSolve**, we obtain the following solution:

$$ \textbf{fracOsc}: \; x(t) = E\left(\frac{19}{10}, -t^{19/10}\right). \tag{57} $$

This type of oscillator behaves similarly to the ordinary damped harmonic oscillator, as follows:

$$ x''(t) + \frac{3}{20}x'(t) + x(t) = 0, \quad x(0) = 1, \quad x'(0) = 0, \tag{58} $$

with the following solution:

$$ \textbf{dampedOsc}: \; x(t) = \frac{e^{-3t/40}\left(3\sqrt{1591}\sin\left(\frac{\sqrt{1591}t}{40}\right) + 1591\cos\left(\frac{\sqrt{1591}t}{40}\right)\right)}{1591}. \tag{59} $$

This example highlights how the order of an FDE can act as a control parameter to model complex systems.

Figure 2 shows a comparison between the solution of the fractional oscillator (57) and the damping oscillator (59). The error function is drawn in the bottom plot.

As a final example of FDE, we consider the fractional friction model, as follows:

$$ \ddot{x}(t) + \frac{1}{4}\, {}_0^C D_t^{\frac{1}{2}} x(t) = 0, \quad x(0) = x_0, \quad x'(0) = v_0 \tag{60} $$

involving the Caputo fractional differintegral of order $1/2$. Solving (60) using the Wolfram Language 13.3 [71] function **DSolve**, we obtain the following solution:

$$ x(t) = x_0 + tv_0 E\left(\frac{3}{2}, 2, -\frac{1}{4}t^{3/2}\right). \tag{61} $$

This solution is given using the **MittagLefflerE** functions and is represented in Figure 3 by a blue line. The pink line corresponds to the following solution:

$$x(t) = \frac{1}{192}(t-24)t^2 + t \tag{62}$$

of the classical Newtonian equation with a friction term, as follows:

$$\ddot{x} = -\frac{1}{4}\dot{x}^{\frac{1}{2}}, \dot{x} > 0, \tag{63}$$

which determines the motion of a point particle influenced by a velocity-dependent force. The thick lines describe the valid motion until the body stops ($v = \dot{x} = 0$). The interval is extended to values beyond the physical region (thin lines) for both solutions.

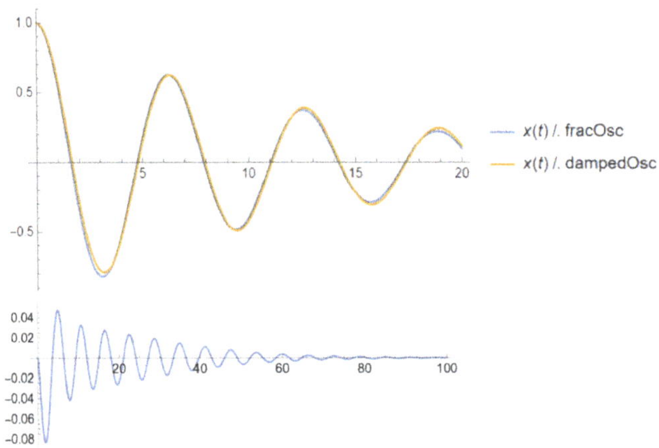

Figure 2. Comparison between the fractional oscillator (57), which satisfies the equation of a fractional harmonic oscillator of order 1.9 (56) with the damping oscillator (59). The error function is drawn in the bottom plot. This shows that the error between both solutions goes to zero as t becomes large.

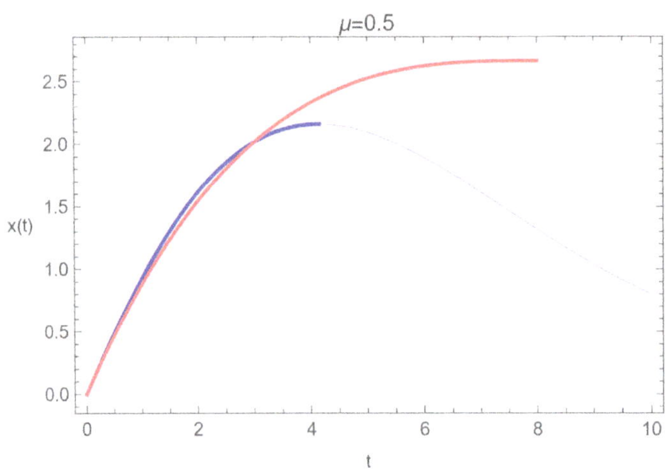

Figure 3. Solution of the FDE (60) for the Caputo derivative for $\mu = 1/2$, $x_0 = 0$, and $v_0 = 1$ (blue line), and a comparison with the solution (134), which gives the position of a point particle under the influence of a velocity-dependent force (pink line).

The fractional equivalent of the Newtonian equation of motion, combined with a classical friction term, allows for a broader range of applications than the classical approach. Damped oscillations can be accurately described with a suitable set of fractional initial conditions. From the perspective of fractional calculus, the harmonic oscillator is an example of a fractional friction phenomenon. This implies that friction and damping, described using separate approaches in a classical context, can be combined in the fractional approach. This feature is widespread in the fractional approach and can be applied to various phenomena [2].

2.6. *Fractional Harmonic Oscillator*

This section shows the behavior of fractional derivatives with the property.

$$\lim_{\mu\to 2} D^{\mu} = \frac{d^2}{dx^2}. \tag{64}$$

In classical mechanics, the equation that describes free oscillations is as follows:

$$\left(\frac{d^2}{dt^2} + \frac{k}{m}\right)x(t) = 0, \tag{65}$$

whose solution is well-known, as follows:

$$x(t) = c_1 \cos(wt) + c_2 \sin(wt), \quad w = \sqrt{k/m}. \tag{66}$$

The fractional formulation of the harmonic oscillator is given by the following:

$$\left(\frac{d^{2\mu}}{dt^{2\mu}} + \frac{k}{m}\right)x(t) = 0. \tag{67}$$

the second-order derivative was directly replaced by one order, 2μ, where μ is a fractional number and the standard harmonic oscillator for $\mu = 1$ is recovered.

The solutions of this fractional differential equation for different types of fractional derivatives are presented below, and the specific differences of the solutions obtained are shown.

2.6.1. Harmonic Oscillator According to Fourier

When the typical *ansatz* is proposed for this type of equation [2], as follows:

$$x(t) = e^{wt}, \tag{68}$$

the solution to the fractional harmonic oscillator reduces to examining the zeros of the polynomial, as follows:

$$w^{2\mu} + \frac{k}{m} = 0. \tag{69}$$

In the region, $1/2 < \mu \leq 3/2$, there are exactly two complex conjugate solutions, as follows:

$$w_{1,2} = \left|\frac{k}{m}\right|^{\frac{1}{2\mu}} \left[\cos\left(\frac{\pi}{2\mu}\right) \pm i \sin\left(\frac{\pi}{2\mu}\right)\right] = \left|\frac{k}{m}\right|^{\frac{1}{2\mu}} e^{\pm i\left(\frac{\pi}{2\mu}\right)}. \tag{70}$$

For $\mu = 1$, two pure imaginary solutions are obtained, which correspond to a free and undamped oscillation. If μ begins to decrease, an increasing negative real part occurs, which, from a classical point of view, can be interpreted as increasing damping. For $\mu > 1$, we have an increasing positive real part corresponding to increasing excitation [2].

On the other hand, the ordinary differential equation for a damped harmonic oscillator is as follows:

$$m\ddot{x}(t) = -kx(t) - \gamma\dot{x}(t), \tag{71}$$

where m is the mass, k is the spring constant, and γ is the damping coefficient.

With (68), we have a quadratic equation for the frequency, w, as follows:

$$w^2 = -\frac{\gamma}{m}w - \frac{k}{m}, \tag{72}$$

Hence, we have two solutions, as follows:

$$w_{1,2} = -\frac{\gamma}{2m} \pm \sqrt{\frac{\gamma^2}{4m^2} - \frac{k}{m}}. \tag{73}$$

Compared with (70), we have the following:

$$-\frac{\gamma}{2m} = \left|\frac{k}{m}\right|^{\frac{1}{2\mu}} \cos\left(\frac{\pi}{2\mu}\right), \tag{74}$$

and with a Taylor series expansion for $\cos(\pi/2\mu)$ around $\mu = 1$, we have the following:

$$-\frac{\gamma}{2m} \approx \left|\frac{k}{m}\right|^{\frac{1}{2\mu}} \frac{1}{2}\pi(\mu - 1). \tag{75}$$

Near $\mu = 1/2$, there is no longer any oscillating contribution. The time evolution of this system is dominated by exponential decay. On the other hand, $\mu > 1$ corresponds to a negative classical friction coefficient. Consequently, we have the surprising result that the behavior of the solutions of the fractional harmonic oscillator under the variation of the fractional derivative parameter, μ, can be interpreted from a classical point of view as damping and excitation phenomena, respectively [2].

The following initial conditions are introduced, as follows:

$$x(t=0) = x_0, \tag{76}$$

$$D^{\mu}x(t)|_{t=0} = \tilde{v}(t=0) = \tilde{v}_0 \tag{77}$$

to compare solutions for different types of fractional derivatives.

Only for $\mu = 1$ do these initial conditions correspond to the classical initial conditions. For all other cases, the physical interpretation of a fractional velocity remains open.

The solutions of the fractional harmonic oscillator can be reformulated: A first set with the fractional initial conditions, $x_0 = 1, \tilde{v}_0 = 0$, can be considered as a fractional extension of the standard cosine function, while the fractional initial conditions, $x_0 = 0, \tilde{v}_0 = 1$, characterize the fractional extension of the sine function, as follows:

$${}_{\mathrm{F}}\sin(\mu, t) = \frac{1}{2i}\left[e^{\frac{1}{2}(e^{\frac{i\pi}{2\mu}})\pi t} - e^{\frac{1}{2}(e^{-\frac{i\pi}{2\mu}})\pi t}\right], \tag{78}$$

$${}_{\mathrm{F}}\cos(\mu, t) = \frac{1}{2}\left[e^{\frac{1}{2}(e^{\frac{i\pi}{2\mu}})\pi t} + e^{\frac{1}{2}(e^{-\frac{i\pi}{2\mu}})\pi t}\right]. \tag{79}$$

An appropriately chosen linear combination of these two extended trigonometric functions will again satisfy the classical initial conditions, $x(t=0) = x_0$ and $v(t=0) = v_0$. A graphical representation of these solutions, (78) and (79), for different μ values, is shown in Figure 4.

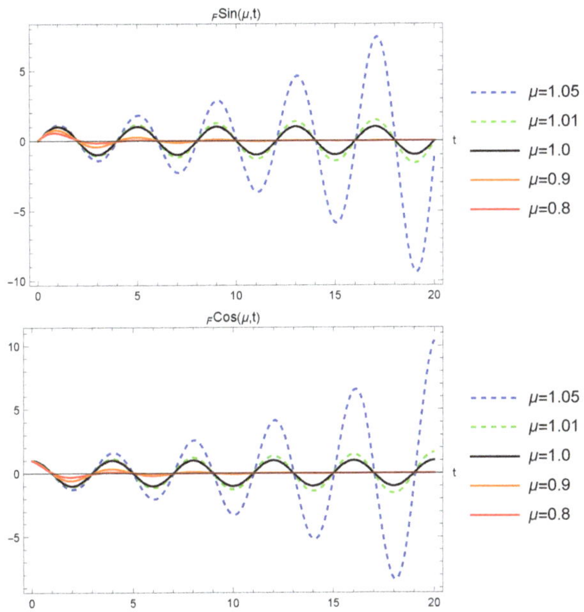

Figure 4. Solutions ${}_{\mathrm{F}}\sin(\mu,t)$ and ${}_{\mathrm{F}}\cos(\mu,t)$ of the fractional harmonic oscillator using the Fourier derivative with different values of μ.

2.6.2. Harmonic Oscillator According to Riemann

To solve the differential equation of the harmonic oscillator, based on the Riemann fractional derivative, a series expansion is used according to (19), as follows:

$$ {}_{\mathrm{R}}D^{\mu}t^{n\mu} = \frac{\Gamma(1+n\mu)}{\Gamma(1+(n-1)\mu)}t^{(n-1)\mu}, \tag{80} $$

there are two linearly independent solutions, which are called ${}_{\mathrm{R}}\sin(\mu,t)$ and ${}_{\mathrm{R}}\cos(\mu,t)$, in analogy to trigonometric functions:

$$ {}_{\mathrm{R}}\sin(\mu,t) = t^{\mu-1}\sum_{n=0}^{\infty}(-1)^n\frac{t^{(2n+1)\mu}}{\Gamma((2n+2)\mu)}, \tag{81} $$

$$ {}_{\mathrm{R}}\cos(\mu,t) = t^{\mu-1}\sum_{n=0}^{\infty}(-1)^n\frac{t^{2n\mu}}{\Gamma((2n+1)\mu)}, \tag{82} $$

with the property

$$ {}_{\mathrm{R}}D^{\mu}{}_{\mathrm{R}}\sin(\mu,wt) = w^{\mu}{}_{\mathrm{R}}\cos(\mu,wt), \tag{83} $$

$$ {}_{\mathrm{R}}D^{\mu}{}_{\mathrm{R}}\cos(\mu,wt) = -w^{\mu}{}_{\mathrm{R}}\sin(\mu,wt). \tag{84} $$

These functions are related to the Mittag-Leffler function (A14), as follows:

$$ {}_{\mathrm{R}}\sin(\mu,t) = t^{2\mu-1}E(2\mu,2\mu,-t^{2\mu}), \tag{85} $$

$$ {}_{\mathrm{R}}\cos(\mu,t) = t^{\mu-1}E(2\mu,\mu,-t^{2\mu}). \tag{86} $$

For $\mu < 1$, the following holds:

$$ \lim_{t\to 0}{}_{\mathrm{R}}\cos(\mu,wt) = \infty, \tag{87} $$

which means that a non-singular solution that satisfies the general initial conditions (76) cannot be given. At first glance, this seems to be a serious drawback for practically applying the fractional Riemann derivative. Nevertheless, it must be considered that the solutions presented can be useful for problems not determined by the initial conditions but are formulated in terms of boundary conditions, as is the case with the solutions of a wave equation [2].

Solutions ${}_{\mathrm{R}}\sin(\mu, t)$ and ${}_{\mathrm{R}}\cos(\mu, t)$ to the fractional harmonic oscillator using the Riemann derivative are presented in Figure 5 for different values of μ.

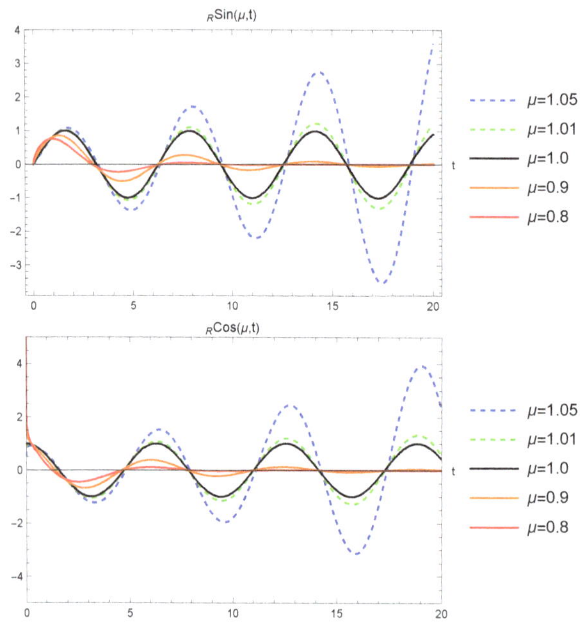

Figure 5. Solutions ${}_{\mathrm{R}}\sin(\mu, t)$ and ${}_{\mathrm{R}}\cos(\mu, t)$ of the fractional harmonic oscillator using the Riemann derivative for different values of μ.

2.6.3. Harmonic Oscillator According to Caputo

This solution can be written as a series according to (21). The Caputo derivative for a power is given by the following:

$$ {}^{\mathrm{C}}D^{\mu} t^{n\mu} = \begin{cases} \frac{\Gamma(1+n\mu)}{\Gamma(1+(n-1)\mu)} t^{(n-1)\mu}, & n > 0, \\ 0, & n = 0. \end{cases} \tag{88} $$

Therefore, we have two linearly independent solutions, which are called ${}_{\mathrm{C}}\sin(\mu, t)$ and ${}_{\mathrm{C}}\cos(\mu, t)$, in analogy to trigonometric functions, as follows:

$$ {}_{\mathrm{C}}\sin(\mu, t) = \sum_{n=0}^{\infty} (-1)^n \frac{t^{(2n+1)\mu}}{\Gamma(1+(2n+1)\mu)}, \tag{89} $$

$$ {}_{\mathrm{C}}\cos(\mu, t) = \sum_{n=0}^{\infty} (-1)^n \frac{t^{2n\mu}}{\Gamma(1+2n\mu)}. \tag{90} $$

The most important property of this series is as follows:

$$^{C}D^{\mu}{}_{C}\sin(\mu, wt) = w^{\mu}{}_{C}\cos(\mu, wt), \tag{91}$$

$$^{C}D^{\mu}{}_{C}\cos(\mu, wt) = -w^{\mu}{}_{C}\sin(\mu, wt). \tag{92}$$

Solutions ${}_{C}\sin(\mu, t)$ and ${}_{C}\cos(\mu, t)$ of the fractional harmonic oscillator using the Caputo derivative are presented in Figure 6 for different values of μ.

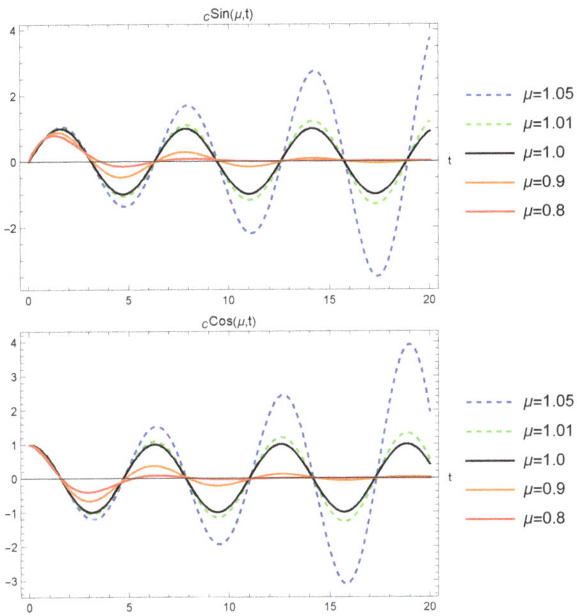

Figure 6. Solutions ${}_{C}\sin(\mu, t)$ and ${}_{C}\cos(\mu, t)$ of the fractional harmonic oscillator using the Caputo derivative for different values of μ.

Upon comparing the solutions obtained from different definitions of the fractional derivative for the differential equation of the harmonic oscillator, we notice a remarkable similarity among the presented solutions. They all display oscillatory behavior with exponential decay when $\mu < 1$, which can be interpreted as a classical damping phenomenon. Conversely, for $\mu > 1$, the fractional harmonic oscillator acts as an excited oscillator. The damping and excitation properties are inherent to the fractional oscillator and do not stem from external factors. In a study by Stanislavsky (2004) [73], a multi-particle statistical interpretation was proposed to physically explain the fractional harmonic oscillator.

Furthermore, the frequency of these damped oscillations is quite similar for the various definitions of fractional derivatives presented, especially for a value of μ approximating 1. Therefore, it can be regarded as an independent property of the definition [2].

2.7. *q*-Deformed Lie Algebras and Fractional Calculus

The combination and integration of ideas and techniques developed across various domains of physics and mathematics have always led to new perspectives and improvements. Lie algebras are mathematical structures used to study symmetries in various branches of mathematics and physics, particularly in the realm of symmetry groups and transformation groups. *q*-deformed Lie algebras, also known as quantum deformations of Lie algebras, are generalizations of classical Lie algebras that arise in the context of quantum groups and non-commutative geometry. See, for example [74–76]. The *q*-deformed Lie algebras theory allows for generalizations of classical symmetry groups and a broader description of natural phenomena. In what follows, we will briefly illustrate the strong relationship between fractional calculus and q-deformed Lie algebras. This relationship arises from the fact that both theories are based on a generalized derivative definition. It has been shown that fractional q-deformed Lie algebras can describe small deviations from classical Lie symmetries and bridge different Lie symmetries. See, for example, [2].

2.7.1. q-Deformed Lie Algebras

Following reference [2], section 18.1, a q-deformed Lie algebra is described by a parameter, q (do not confuse the q-deformation parameter with the deceleration parameter in Cosmology) and define the mapping from ordinary real numbers, x, to q-numbers, by the following:

$$[x]_q = \frac{q^x - q^{-x}}{q - q^{-1}}, \tag{93}$$

which has a limit

$$\lim_{q \to 1} [x]_q = x. \tag{94}$$

By definition, we have $[0]_q = 0$. Now, a q-derivative may be defined as follows:

$$D_x^q f(x) = \frac{f(qx) - f(q^{-1}x)}{(q - q^{-1})x}. \tag{95}$$

This particular definition is chosen such that the q-derivative of the function $f(x) = x^n$ has a similar form to its counterpart in ordinary calculus; that is,

$$D_x^q x^n = [n]_q x^{n-1}. \tag{96}$$

This is the first common aspect of q-deformation and fractional calculus: they introduce a generalized derivative operator. As an example of q-deformed Lie algebras, we shall review the q-deformed harmonic oscillator. The creation and annihilation operators, $a^\dagger$ and a, and the number operator, N, generate the algebra, as follows:

$$\left[N, a^\dagger\right] = a^\dagger, \tag{97}$$

$$[N, a] = -a, \tag{98}$$

$$aa^\dagger - q^{\pm 1} a^\dagger a = q^{\mp N}. \tag{99}$$

According to definition (93), we also have the following:

$$a^\dagger a = [N]_q \qquad \text{and} \qquad aa^\dagger = [N+1]_q. \tag{100}$$

Defining a vacuum state with $a\,|0\rangle = 0$, the action of the operators a, $a^\dagger$, and N, on the basis $|n\rangle$ of a Fock space, defined by the repeated action of the creation operator on the vacuum state, is given by the following:

$$N\,|n\rangle = n\,|n\rangle, \tag{101}$$

$$a^\dagger\,|n-1\rangle = \sqrt{[n]_q}\,|n\rangle, \tag{102}$$

$$a\,|n\rangle = \sqrt{[n]_q}\,|n-1\rangle. \tag{103}$$

Since the q-deformed algebras (97)–(99) have the same form as the non-deformed counterpart, the Hamiltonian for the q-deformed harmonic oscillator remains unchanged; that is,

$$H = \frac{\hbar\omega}{2}\left(aa^\dagger + a^\dagger a\right), \tag{104}$$

however, its eigenvalues in the $|n\rangle$ basis are the q-numbers:

$$E^q(n) = \frac{\hbar\omega}{2}\left([n]_q + [n+1]_q\right). \tag{105}$$

There is a common aspect in the concepts of fractional calculus and q-deformed Lie algebras; they both extend the definition of the standard derivative operator.

In the following, we establish a connection between the q-derivative (95) and the fractional derivative definition. Consider the Caputo definition of the fractional derivative given in the following form:

$$D_x^\alpha f(x) = \begin{cases} \frac{1}{\Gamma(1-\alpha)} \int_0^x (x-\xi)^{-\alpha} \frac{\partial}{\partial\xi} f(\xi) d\xi, & 0 \le \alpha < 1 \\ \frac{1}{\Gamma(2-\alpha)} \int_0^x (x-\xi)^{1-\alpha} \frac{\partial^2}{\partial\xi^2} f(\xi) d\xi, & 1 \le \alpha < 2 \end{cases}. \tag{106}$$

For a function set, $f(x) = x^{n\alpha}$, we obtain the following:

$$D_x^\alpha f(x) = \begin{cases} \frac{\Gamma(1+n\alpha)}{\Gamma(1+(n-1)\alpha)} x^{(n-1)\alpha}, & n > 0 \\ 0, & n = 0 \end{cases}. \tag{107}$$

Now, according to Equation (96) and the fact that $[0]_q = 0$, we can interpret the fractional derivative parameter, α, as a deformation parameter in the sense of q-deformed Lie algebras. Setting $|n\rangle = x^{n\alpha}$, we define the following:

$$[n]_\alpha |n\rangle = \begin{cases} \frac{\Gamma(1+n\alpha)}{\Gamma(1+(n-1)\alpha)} |n\rangle, & n > 0 \\ 0, & n = 0 \end{cases}. \tag{108}$$

Indeed, we have the following:

$$\lim_{\alpha\to 1} [n]_\alpha - n. \tag{109}$$

The more-or-less abstract q-number is now interpreted within the mathematical context of fractional calculus as the fractional derivative parameter α with a well-understood meaning. Definition (108) looks like one more definition for a q-deformation. However, a significant difference makes the definition based on fractional calculus unique. Standard q numbers are usually defined in a heuristic manner. No physical or mathematical framework exists that determines their explicit structure. Consequently, many different definitions have been proposed in the literature [76]. In contrast to this diversity, the q-deformations based on the definition of the fractional derivative are uniquely determined once a set of basis functions is given. As an example, we will briefly illustrate how to derive the q-numbers for the quantum version of the fractional harmonic oscillator in the next subsection. For further details, the reader should check the reference [2].

2.7.2. The Fractional q-Deformed Quantum Harmonic Oscillator

It is well-known that in quantum mechanics, the classical conjugated observables x and p are replaced by quantum mechanical observables $\hat{x}$ and $\hat{p}$, which are introduced as derivative operators on a Hilbert space of square-integrable wave functions. The space coordinate representations of these operators are as follows:

$$\hat{x} f(x) = x f(x), \tag{110}$$
$$\hat{p} f(x) = -i\hbar\partial_x f(x), \tag{111}$$

which satisfies the commutation relation, as follows:

$$[\hat{x}, \hat{p}] = i\hbar. \tag{112}$$

Now, we consider a derivative of an arbitrary (fractional) order α. Then, we are introduced to two canonically conjugated operators in space representation, as follows:

$$\hat{X}f(\hat{x}^{\alpha}) = \left(\frac{\hbar}{mc}\right)^{(1-\alpha)} \hat{x}^{\alpha} f(\hat{x}^{\alpha}) \tag{113}$$

$$\hat{P}f(\hat{x}^{\alpha}) = -i\left(\frac{\hbar}{mc}\right)^{\alpha} mc\hat{D}^{\alpha} f(\hat{x}^{\alpha}). \tag{114}$$

which recover (110) and (111) as $\alpha \to 1$.

The classical nonrelativistic, N, particle Hamilton function is as follows:

$$H_c = \sum_{j=1}^{3N} \frac{p_j^2}{2m} + V(x^1, \ldots, x^j, \ldots, x^{3N}) \tag{115}$$

it is, therefore, replaced by the fractional version, as follows:

$$H^{\alpha} = \sum_{j=1}^{3N} \frac{\hat{P}_j^2}{2m} + V(\hat{X}^1, \ldots, \hat{X}^j, \ldots, \hat{X}^{3N}) \tag{116}$$

$$= \underbrace{-\frac{1}{2}mc^2\left(\frac{\hbar}{mc}\right)^{2\alpha} \hat{D}^{\alpha j}\hat{D}_j^{\alpha} + V(\hat{X}^1, \ldots, \hat{X}^j, \ldots, \hat{X}^{3N})}_{\text{Using Einstein's summation convention } \sum_{j=1}^{N} x_j^2 = x^j x_j.}, \tag{117}$$

by following the canonical quantization method.

The time-dependent Schrödinger type equation for fractional derivatives operators is as follows:

$$H^{\alpha}\Psi = i\hbar\frac{\partial}{\partial t}\Psi \tag{118}$$

$$= \underbrace{\left(-\frac{1}{2}mc^2\left(\frac{\hbar}{mc}\right)^{2\alpha} \hat{D}^{\alpha j}\hat{D}_j^{\alpha} + V(\hat{X}^1, \ldots, \hat{X}^j, \ldots, \hat{X}^{3N})\right)\Psi}_{\text{Using Einstein's summation convention } \sum_{j=1}^{N} x_j^2 = x^j x_j.}. \tag{119}$$

In the limit, $\alpha \to 1$, the classical Schrödinger equation is recovered.

Now, we apply the above arguments to the classical Hamilton function of the one-dimensional quantum harmonic oscillator (see section 19.1 of [2]), as follows:

$$H_{\text{class}} = \frac{p^2}{2m} + \frac{1}{2}m\omega^2 x^2. \tag{120}$$

Following the canonical quantization procedure, we replace the classical observables $\{x, p\}$ with the fractional derivative operators $\{\hat{X}, \hat{P}\}$ according to (113) and (114). Hence, the quantized Hamilton operator is given by the following:

$$H^{\alpha} = \frac{\hat{P}^2}{2m} + \frac{1}{2}m\omega^2\hat{X}^2. \tag{121}$$

The stationary Schrödinger equation is given by the following:

$$H^{\alpha}\Psi = \left(-\frac{1}{2m}\left(\frac{\hbar}{mc}\right)^{2\alpha} m^2c^2 D_x^{\alpha} D_x^{\alpha} + \frac{1}{2}m\omega^2\left(\frac{\hbar}{mc}\right)^{2(1-\alpha)} x^{2\alpha}\right)\Psi = E\Psi. \tag{122}$$

To simplify the notation, we introduce the variable ξ and the scaled energy, E, as follows:

$$\xi^\alpha = \sqrt{\frac{m\omega}{\hbar}} \left(\frac{\hbar}{mc}\right)^{1-\alpha} x^\alpha \qquad \text{and} \qquad E = \hbar\omega E' \tag{123}$$

are introduced. Finally, the stationary Schrödinger equation for the fractional harmonic oscillator in the canonical form then reads as follows:

$$H^\alpha \Psi_n(\xi) = \frac{1}{2}\left(-D_\xi^{2\alpha} + |\xi|^{2\alpha}\right)\Psi_n(\xi) = E'(n,\alpha)\Psi_n(\xi). \tag{124}$$

In contrast to the classical harmonic oscillator, this fractional Schrödinger equation has not been solved analytically until now. Nevertheless, an approximation procedure based on the Sommerfeld quantization rule [28] can be performed to obtain an analytical expression for the energy levels. The result is as follows:

$$E'(n,\alpha) = \left(\frac{1}{2} + n\right)^\alpha \pi^{\alpha/2} \left(\frac{\alpha\Gamma\left(\frac{1+\alpha}{2\alpha}\right)}{\Gamma\left(\frac{1}{2\alpha}\right)}\right)^\alpha, \qquad n = 0,1,2,\ldots. \tag{125}$$

This is an analytically derived approximation of the energy spectrum for the fractional harmonic oscillator. Additionally, this equation is not dependent on a particular definition of the fractional derivative. Considering the q-deformed Lie algebras, we can use this analytical result to calculate the corresponding q-number. Using (105), the q-number is defined by the recursion relation, with the appropriate initial condition:

$$[n+1]_\alpha = 2E'(n,\alpha) - [n]_\alpha. \tag{126}$$

This recurrence relation is fulfilled in the case of $\alpha \in \mathbb{N}$ by the Euler polynomials (A18). Consequently, we have to extend their definition reasonably to the fractional case. The initial condition $[0]_\alpha = 0$ leads to oscillatory behavior for $\alpha < 1$. Another choice, say,

$$[0]_\alpha = 2^{1+\alpha}\pi^{\alpha/2}\left(\frac{\alpha\Gamma\left(\frac{1+\alpha}{2\alpha}\right)}{\Gamma\left(\frac{1}{2\alpha}\right)}\right)^\alpha \left(\zeta\left(-\alpha,\frac{1}{4}\right) - \zeta\left(-\alpha,\frac{3}{4}\right)\right)$$

leads to

$$\begin{aligned}
[n]_\alpha &= 2^{1+\alpha}\pi^{\alpha/2}\left(\frac{\alpha\Gamma\left(\frac{1+\alpha}{2\alpha}\right)}{\Gamma\left(\frac{1}{2\alpha}\right)}\right)^\alpha \left(\zeta\left(-\alpha,\frac{1}{4}+\frac{n}{2}\right) - \zeta\left(-\alpha,\frac{3}{4}+\frac{n}{2}\right)\right) \\
&= \pi^{\alpha/2}\left(\frac{\alpha\Gamma\left(\frac{1+\alpha}{2\alpha}\right)}{\Gamma\left(\frac{1}{2\alpha}\right)}\right)^\alpha E_\alpha\left(n+\frac{1}{2}\right),
\end{aligned}$$

where the Hurwitz ζ function is given by (A26) and the ad hoc extension of the Euler polynomials to the fractional case is (A25).

2.8. Fractional Friction

The evolution of the position $x(t)$ and the velocity $v(t) = \dot{x}(t) = \frac{d}{dt}x(t)$ of a point particle over time, influenced by an external force, F, is determined by Newton's second law, as follows:

$$F = ma = m\ddot{x}(t) = m\frac{d^2}{dt^2}x(t). \tag{127}$$

In the absence of external forces, the solution continues to integrate twice from $\ddot{x} = 0$, as follows:

$$x(t) = x_0 + v_0 t, \tag{128}$$

where the constants of integration are the position $x(0) = x_0$ and initial velocities, $v(0) = v_0$ and $\dot{x}(t) = v_0$, for all t values. This means the point mass maintains its initial velocity forever without external forces. This is what is known as Newton's first law. However, the daily experience of movement contradicts this result. Sooner or later, without external intervention, all types of movement end at rest. Within the framework of Newtonian theory, all these observed phenomena are due to friction forces, F_R.

All friction forces point in the opposite direction of the particle's speed. Empirically, a power-law function can be proposed as follows:

$$F_R = -\alpha \text{sgn}(v)|v|^{\mu}, \tag{129}$$

where μ is an arbitrary real exponent. Some special cases are $\mu \approx 0$, which is observed for static and kinetic pressure in solids, while $\mu = 1$ corresponds to the Stokes friction in a liquid with high viscosity, and $\mu = 2$ is indicative of a general trend toward high speed [2].

Let us consider the following differential equation:

$$m\ddot{x} = -\alpha \text{sgn}(v)|v|^{\mu}, \tag{130}$$

where the mass, m, is measured in kilogram [kg], and the friction coefficient, α, is measured in $\text{kg/s}^{2-\mu}$, which describes the dynamics of a point particle under the effect of a friction force of the type (129).

Assuming that the velocity is positive, we have the following:

$$m\ddot{x} = -\alpha \dot{x}^{\mu}, \dot{x} > 0. \tag{131}$$

Imposing the following initial conditions:

$$x(t = 0) = x_0, \tag{132}$$

$$v(t = 0) = v_0, \tag{133}$$

we obtain the general solution of (131) given by the following:

$$x(t) = x_0 + \frac{m v_0^{2-\mu}}{\alpha(2-\mu)} - \frac{m\left[(\mu-1)(-\frac{v_0^{1-\mu}}{1-\mu} + \frac{\alpha}{m}t)\right]^{\frac{2-\mu}{1-\mu}}}{\alpha(2-\mu)}. \tag{134}$$

Equation (134) determines the motion of a point particle under the influence of a velocity-dependent force for an arbitrary μ.

Special cases $\mu = 0$, $\mu = 1$, and $\mu = 2$ are included as special limits [2], as follows:

$$\lim_{\mu \to 0} x(t) = x_0 + v_0 t - \frac{1}{2}\frac{\alpha}{m}t^2, \tag{135}$$

$$\lim_{\mu \to 1} x(t) = x_0 + \frac{m}{\alpha} v_0 \left(1 - e^{-\frac{\alpha}{m}t}\right), \tag{136}$$

$$\lim_{\mu \to 2} x(t) = x_0 + \frac{m}{\alpha} \ln\left(1 + \frac{\alpha}{m} v_0 t\right). \tag{137}$$

Finally, the modification of Newton's Equation (131) is studied according to [2] where the friction force $F_R(\dot{x}) = -\alpha \dot{x}(t)^{\mu}$ has been replaced by the fractional friction force, as follows:

$$F_R = -\alpha D_t^{\mu} x(t), \qquad \dot{x}(t) > 0, \tag{138}$$

where μ is the order of the fractional derivative. For $\mu \neq 1$ and $t > 0$, we have the following:

$$\dot{x}^{\mu} = \left(\frac{d}{dt}x(t)\right)^{\mu} \neq D_t^{\mu} x(t), \tag{139}$$

so it is expected that the solutions of the fractional equation

$$m\ddot{x}(t) + \alpha D_t^{\mu} x(t) = 0 \tag{140}$$

have behaviors different from the standard. Note that, to compare with the classical damped harmonic oscillator given by (71), we renamed the friction constant, α.

Replacing the *ansatz* $x(t) = e^{wt}$ into (140), and applying Liouville's definition, we have the following:

$$D_t^{\mu} e^{wt} = w^{\mu} e^{wt}. \tag{141}$$

Therefore, the characteristic polynomial of (140) is as follows:

$$w^2 = -\frac{\alpha}{m} w^{\mu}. \tag{142}$$

In addition to the trivial solution, we have the following solution:

$$w = (-1)^{\frac{1}{2-\mu}} \left|\frac{\alpha}{m}\right|^{\frac{1}{2-\mu}}. \tag{143}$$

For $0 < \mu < 1$, we use the following abbreviation:

$$\kappa = \left|\frac{\alpha}{m}\right|^{\frac{1}{2-\mu}}, \tag{144}$$

There are two complex conjugate solutions, as follows:

$$w_{1,2} = \kappa \left[\cos\left(\frac{\pi}{2-\mu}\right) \pm i \sin\left(\frac{\pi}{2-\mu}\right)\right]. \tag{145}$$

So, the general solution of (140) is as follows:

$$x(t) = c_1 + c_2 e^{w_1 t} + c_3 e^{w_2 t}, \qquad 0 < \mu < 1. \tag{146}$$

It is observed that there are three different constants, c_i, two of which can be determined using the initial conditions, $x(t=0) = x_0$ and $v(t=0) := \dot{x}(0) = v_0$. Consequently, the freedom to specify an additional reasonable initial condition indicates that the fractional differential Equation (140) describes a broader range of phenomena than the classical equation [2].

Starting from (140), the condition can be considered as follows:

$$\ddot{x}(t=0) = -\frac{\alpha}{m} v_0^{\mu}. \tag{147}$$

Therefore, the set of equations is obtained as follows:

$$\begin{pmatrix} 1 & 1 & 1 \\ 0 & w_1 & w_2 \\ 0 & w_1^2 & w_2^2 \end{pmatrix} \begin{pmatrix} c_1 \\ c_2 \\ c_3 \end{pmatrix} = \begin{pmatrix} x_0 \\ v_0 \\ -\frac{\alpha}{\mu} v_0^{\mu} \end{pmatrix}. \tag{148}$$

Then, the solution of the fractional differential Equation (140) is as follows:

$$x(t) \approx x_0 + v_0 t - \frac{1}{2}\frac{\alpha}{\mu} v_0^{\mu} t^2 - \frac{t^3 \left(2\alpha \cos\left(\frac{\pi}{\mu-2}\right) v_0^{\mu} \left|\frac{\alpha}{m}\right|^{\frac{1}{2-\mu}} + m v_0 \left|\frac{m}{\alpha}\right|^{\frac{2}{\mu-2}}\right)}{6m} + o(t^4). \tag{149}$$

If the condition is chosen, i.e.,

$$\ddot{x}(t=0) = 0, \tag{150}$$

then the set of equations is obtained, as follows:

$$\begin{pmatrix} 1 & 1 & 1 \\ 0 & w_1 & w_2 \\ 0 & w_1^2 & w_2^2 \end{pmatrix} \begin{pmatrix} c_1 \\ c_2 \\ c_3 \end{pmatrix} = \begin{pmatrix} x_0 \\ v_0 \\ 0 \end{pmatrix}, \tag{151}$$

and in this case, the complete solution is as follows:

$$x(t) = x_0 + \frac{v_0}{\kappa \sin\left(\frac{\pi}{2-\mu}\right)} \left[e^{\kappa \cos\left(\frac{\pi}{2-\mu}\right) t} \sin\left(\frac{2\pi}{2-\mu} - \kappa \sin\left(\frac{\pi}{2-\mu}\right) t\right) - \sin\left(\frac{2\pi}{2-\mu}\right)\right], \tag{152}$$

which is valid from $t = 0$ until a final time, t_f, in which the mass comes to rest, which is determined by the following equation:

$$t_f = \frac{\pi}{(2-\mu)\kappa \sin\left(\frac{\pi}{2-\mu}\right)}. \tag{153}$$

Let us compare the classical damped harmonic oscillator given by (71). The two solutions of the classical damped harmonic oscillator are as follows:

$$w_{1,2} = -\frac{\gamma}{2m} \pm \sqrt{\frac{\gamma^2}{4m^2} - \frac{k}{m}}, \tag{154}$$

where γ is the damping coefficient in (71). By comparing the w_i of (145) and (154), the relations are obtained, as follows:

$$\frac{k}{m} = \left(\frac{\alpha}{\mu}\right)^{\frac{2}{2-\mu}} \tag{155}$$

and

$$\frac{\gamma}{m} = -2\left(\frac{\alpha}{\mu}\right)^{\frac{1}{2-\mu}} \cos\left(\frac{\pi}{2-\mu}\right). \tag{156}$$

These relations describe the behavior of the solutions to the fractional friction differential equation, as investigated in [2].

In Figure 7, different solutions to the fractional friction Equation (140) and the solution in the classical equation (pink) $m\ddot{x} = -\alpha\dot{x}^{\mu}$ given by (134) are presented. In red (up to order 2) and black (up to order 3), the solutions to the fractional friction Equation (140), given by Equation (149), are presented. The blue line represents the solution (152) with the initial condition, $\ddot{x}(0) = 0$ [2].

It is observed that the classical solution and the corresponding fractional solution with the initial condition (147) coincide up to the second order in t, and there is a difference only at the end of the movement. The thick lines describe the valid motion until the body stops ($v = \dot{x} = 0$). Furthermore, for both fractional solutions, the plot interval is extended to values $t > t_f$ (thin lines) beyond the physical region.

When the fractional parameter, μ, approaches zero, the behavior approaches that of damping. Near $\mu = 2$, the fractional friction acts as an acceleration term, and for the ideal case, $\mu = 2$, the differential equation for a free particle is recovered.

Using fractional calculus, we can expand beyond the classical approach by combining the fractional equivalent of the Newtonian equation of motion with a classical friction term. This allows us to describe a broader range of phenomena, including damped oscillations with fractional initial conditions. The harmonic oscillator is an example of a fractional friction phenomenon, where friction and damping can be unified.

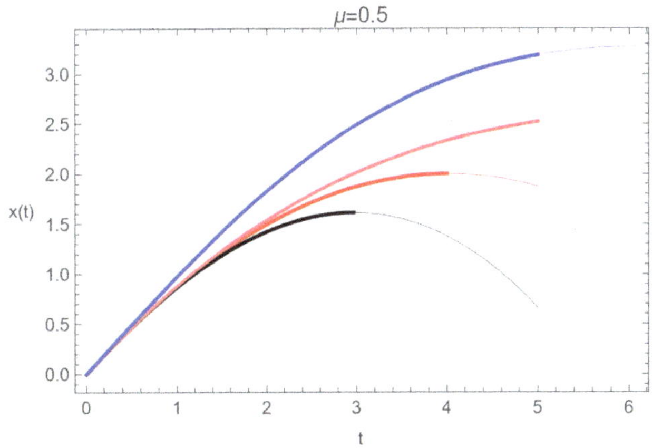

Figure 7. Different solutions of the equation of motion (140) with $\mu = 0.5$, $x_0 = 0$, $v_0 = 1$, $m = 1$, $\alpha = 0.25$ [2].

It is important to note that the fractional differential equation represented by (140) combines two different types of classical differential equations. Nonlinear differential equations generally have complex solutions, whereas a simple second-order differential equation with constant coefficients can be solved using the same fractional equation. This observation suggests that a wide range of complex problems can be solved analytically using fractional calculus with minimal effort. On the other hand, a solution obtained from a classical theory may be more complicated.

In this section, we build upon previous research in the field [2] and emphasize the importance of fractional calculus in explaining physical phenomena. We then explore the applications of this concept in theories of gravity to provide a better understanding of the complex mathematical structure of the universe. The next section aims to use advanced mathematical techniques to create new formulations and tools, which will help us better comprehend the cosmos. This is a crucial aspect of our research.

3. Gravity Models with Fractional Derivatives

In the previous section, we discussed the importance of fractional calculus in understanding physical phenomena. Now, we will focus on its applications to gravity theories to better understand the universe's mathematical structure.

Fractional derivative cosmology has been established using two methods in the classical regime. The first method is called the last-step modification method, where the fractional field equations replace the given cosmological field equations for a specific model. An example of this method is explained in [77]. On the other hand, the second method is called the first-step modification method, which is a more fundamental approach. In this method, a fractional derivative geometry is first established, and then the variational principle for fractional action is applied to derive a modified cosmological model. This method involves defining the fractional derivative and establishing the variational principle of fractional action [44,59,78] to obtain a modified cosmological model. For example, a fractional theory of gravitation has been developed for fractional spacetime, leading to new classes of cosmological models. These models have been studied in great detail [35–68].

It is possible to create fractional versions of Newtonian mechanics and Friedman–Robertson–Walker cosmology by replacing partial and fractional derivatives in familiar equations. In cosmology, the fractional order of differentiation (represented by the symbol μ) itself could be considered a variable that changes with time, although this concept has yet to be explored. The results obtained using fractional derivatives are what one might have expected, but for consistency, it is necessary to start with fractional derivatives at the first step. This leads to the subject of fractional derivative geometry. What fractional derivative geometry should look like needs to be clarified. In [59], a first attempt was made to guess what curvature and line elements might look like in two dimensions. It was found that this leads to a line element that depends on the Gamma function. In such a framework, fractional calculus defines Riemann curvature and the Einstein tensor, dependent on the fractional parameter, μ. The fractional Einstein tensor equation, $G_{\alpha\beta}(\mu) = 8\pi G T_{\alpha\beta}(\mu)$, where $G_{\alpha\beta}(\mu)$ is the fractional Einstein tensor, was modified to study various cosmological events.

In this section, we introduce the concept of fractional differential calculus for computing specific physical quantities. Of particular importance are the applications of these techniques to cosmology. Instead of using covariant fractional derivatives to replace the usual covariant derivatives, we will use the point-like Lagrangian formulation of cosmology in the flat FLRW metric and then generalize such action to the fractional framework. Obtaining specific approximate values for cosmological quantities is not surprising, assuming this can be defined. This is because the fractional modification of the concept of derivative can be manipulated to yield results that can be compared to cosmological measurements. The Lagrangian density is a mathematical tool used to model the dynamic properties of fields [79–85]. Fractional Lagrangian densities have gained popularity in addressing cosmological problems.

In reference [64], a joint analysis was performed using cosmic chronometers and type Ia supernovae data. This comparison with observational tests was used to find the best-fit values for the fractional order of the derivative. These methods are a robust scheme to investigate the physical behavior of cosmological models [64,86–89]. They can be used in new contexts, such as [68], where dynamical systems were used to analyze a fractional cosmology for different matter contents, obtaining a cosmology with late acceleration without including dark energy. References [64,69,70] have explored the potential of fractional cosmology to address the H_0 tension [90,91] from the Supernova data and the Planck value for $z < 1.5$ and have reported a trend of H_0 that aligns with these values. However, a discrepancy exists between the $1.5 < z < 2.5$ range values, indicating that the tension H_0 has not been entirely resolved.

Based on the work presented in [64], two research paths were identified for the cosmological model without a scalar field. The first path involves comparison with the standard model, assuming that the Universe's components are cold dark matter and radiation. The second path entails deducing the equation of state for one of the matter sources based on compatibility conditions [68], which had not been previously analyzed in [64].

3.1. Cosmological Model in the Fractional Formulation of Gravity

Given the fractional integral action,

$$S(\tau) = \frac{1}{\Gamma(\mu)} \int_0^{\tau} \mathcal{L}(\theta, q_i(\theta), \dot{q}_i(\theta), \ddot{q}_i(\theta))(\tau - \theta)^{\mu-1} d\theta, \tag{157}$$

where $\Gamma(\mu)$ is the Gamma function, $\mathcal{L}$ is the Lagrangian, μ is the constant fractional parameter, and τ and θ are the physical and intrinsic times, respectively. Varying the action (157) with respect to q_i, we obtain the Euler–Poisson equations [78]:

$$\begin{aligned} &\frac{\partial \mathcal{L}(\theta, q_i(\theta), \dot{q}_i(\theta), \ddot{q}_i(\theta))}{\partial q_i} - \frac{d}{d\theta}\frac{\partial \mathcal{L}(\theta, q_i(\theta), \dot{q}_i(\theta), \ddot{q}_i(\theta))}{\partial \dot{q}_i} + \frac{d^2}{d\theta^2}\frac{\partial \mathcal{L}(\theta, q_i(\theta), \dot{q}_i(\theta), \ddot{q}_i(\theta))}{\partial \ddot{q}_i} \\ &= \frac{1-\mu}{\tau-\theta}\left(\frac{\partial \mathcal{L}(\theta, q_i(\theta), \dot{q}_i(\theta), \ddot{q}_i(\theta))}{\partial \dot{q}_i} - 2\frac{d}{d\theta}\frac{\partial \mathcal{L}(\theta, q_i(\theta), \dot{q}_i(\theta), \ddot{q}_i(\theta))}{\partial \ddot{q}_i}\right) - \frac{(1-\mu)(2-\mu)}{(\tau-\theta)^2}\frac{\partial \mathcal{L}(\theta, q_i(\theta), \dot{q}_i(\theta), \ddot{q}_i(\theta))}{\partial \ddot{q}_i}. \end{aligned} \tag{158}$$

In cosmology, it is assumed that the flat Friedmann–Lemaître–Robertson–Walker (FLRW) metric,

$$ds^2 = -N^2(t)dt^2 + a^2(t)(dx^2 + dy^2 + dz^2), \tag{159}$$

is the spacetime metric, where $a(t)$ denotes the scale factor and $N(t)$ is the lapse function. This result is supported observationally with data from the Planck's [92] probe. For the metric (159), the Ricci scalar depends on (up to) second derivatives of a and first derivatives of N, written as follows:

$$R(t) = 6\left(\frac{\ddot{a}(t)}{a(t)N^2(t)} + \frac{\dot{a}^2(t)}{a^2(t)N^2(t)} - \frac{\dot{a}(t)\dot{N}(t)}{a(t)N^3(t)}\right). \tag{160}$$

Thus, we can consider the integral action in units where $8\pi G = c = 1$:

$$S(\tau) = \int_0^\tau \left[\frac{R(\theta)}{2} + \frac{\dot{\phi}^2(\theta)}{2N^2(\theta)} - V(\phi(\theta)) + \xi R(\theta)\phi^2(\theta) + L_{\text{matter}}(\theta)\right] a^3(\theta)N(\theta)d\theta, \tag{161}$$

where $R(\theta)$ is the Ricci scalar (160). In cosmology, the Einstein–Hilbert Lagrangian density is related to the Ricci scalar. Generically, integration by parts is taken so that a total derivative in the action is eliminated, as well as the derivatives $\ddot{a}(t)$ and $\dot{N}(t)$. However, since we will use a fractional version of the Lagrangian (161), we will not follow the standard procedure and will keep the higher-order derivatives. Using the formulation (157), the Euler–Poisson Equation (158) is obtained, which involves fractional variational calculus with classical and Caputo derivatives. If $L_{\text{matter}}(\theta) = -\rho_0 a(\theta)^{-3(1+w)}$ for $w \neq -1$, we recover the usual Lagrangian density of matter of a perfect fluid as in [93–95] containing derivatives of the integer order in the Lagrangian. To extend the theory given by the effective fractional action used in [64], we can assume the Einstein–Hilbert action and add a scalar field ϕ to create a scalar field theory with coupling $\xi R\phi^2$ between gravity and the scalar field, with ξ being the coupling constant. The simplest and most natural case is the minimal coupling, where $\xi = 0$. Another viable option is $\xi = 1/6$, known as conformal coupling because the action does not change under conformal transformations of the metric. Any value of the coupling parameter, $\xi \neq 0$, is a non-minimal coupling.

The resulting action is

$$S_{\text{eff}}(\tau) = \frac{1}{\Gamma(\mu)} \int_0^\tau \mathcal{L}(\theta, N(\theta), \dot{N}(\theta), a(\theta), \dot{a}(\theta), \ddot{a}(\theta), \phi(\theta), \dot{\phi}(\theta))(\tau-\theta)^{\mu-1} d\theta, \tag{162}$$

where $\Gamma(\mu)$ is the Gamma function, and the Lagrangian density is as follows:

$$\begin{aligned}\mathcal{L}(\theta, N(\theta), \dot{N}(\theta), a(\theta), \dot{a}(\theta), \ddot{a}(\theta)) :=& \frac{3a(\theta)\left(N(\theta)\left(a(\theta)\ddot{a}(\theta) + \dot{a}^2(\theta)\right) - a(\theta)\dot{a}(\theta)\dot{N}(\theta)\right)}{N^2(\theta)} + a^3(\theta)N(\theta)\left(\frac{\dot{\phi}^2(\theta)}{2N^2(\theta)} - V(\phi(\theta))\right) \\ &- \rho_0 N(\theta)a(\theta)^{-3w}(\tau-\theta)^{-(\mu-1)(w+1)} - \frac{3\xi\phi^2(\theta)a(\theta)\left(N(\theta)\left(a(\theta)\ddot{a}(\theta) + \dot{a}^2(\theta)\right) - a(\theta)\dot{a}(\theta)\dot{N}(\theta)\right)}{N^2(\theta)},\end{aligned} \tag{163}$$

$w = p/\rho$ is a constant state equation parameter for matter, ϕ is the scalar field, and V is its interaction potential, depending on the scalar field.

The Euler–Poisson Equation (158) is derived after varying the action (162) with respect to $q_i \in \{N, a, \phi\}$, obtaining the equations, as follows:

$$\begin{aligned}\left(1-\xi\phi^2(\theta)\right)\left[\left(\frac{\dot{a}(\theta)}{a(\theta)}\right)^2 + \left(\frac{\dot{a}(\theta)}{a(\theta)}\right)\left(\frac{1-\mu}{\tau-\theta}\right)\right] =& \frac{1}{3}\rho_{m0}a(\theta)^{-3w-3}(\tau-\theta)^{-(\mu-1)(w+1)} + \frac{1}{6}\left(\dot{\phi}^2(\theta) + 2V(\phi(\theta))\right) \\ &+ 2\xi\frac{\dot{a}(\theta)\phi(\theta)\dot{\phi}(\theta)}{a(\theta)},\end{aligned} \tag{163}$$

$$\begin{aligned}\left(1-\xi\phi^2(\theta)\right)\left[\frac{\ddot{a}(\theta)}{a(\theta)} + \frac{1}{2}\left(\frac{\dot{a}(\theta)}{a(\theta)}\right)^2 + \frac{(1-\mu)}{(t-\theta)}\frac{\dot{a}(\theta)}{a(\theta)} + \frac{(\mu-2)(\mu-1)}{2(\tau-\theta)^2}\right] =& -\frac{1}{2}\rho_0 w a(\theta)^{-3(1+w)}(\tau-\theta)^{-(\mu-1)(w+1)} - \frac{1}{4}\dot{\phi}^2(\theta) + \frac{1}{2}V(\phi(\theta)) \\ &+ \xi\left[\frac{2\phi(\theta)\dot{a}(\theta)\dot{\phi}(\theta)}{a(\theta)} + \frac{2(1-\mu)\phi(\theta)\dot{\phi}(\theta)}{\tau-\theta} + \phi(\theta)\ddot{\phi}(\theta) + \dot{\phi}^2(\theta)\right],\end{aligned} \tag{164}$$

$$\ddot{\phi}(\theta) + \frac{3\dot{a}(\theta)\dot{\phi}(\theta)}{a(\theta)} + \frac{(1-\mu)\dot{\phi}(\theta)}{\tau-\theta} + V'(\phi(\theta)) = -6\xi\phi(\theta)\left[\frac{\ddot{a}(\theta)}{a(\theta)} + \left(\frac{\dot{a}(\theta)}{a(\theta)}\right)^2\right], \tag{165}$$

and the conservation of matter equation as follows:

$$\dot{\rho}(\theta) = -3\left(\frac{\dot{a}(\theta)}{a(\theta)} + \frac{1-\mu}{3(\tau-\theta)}\right)(\rho(\theta) + p(\theta)), \tag{166}$$

where we replaced $N = 1$ after the variation in the action (162).

For fixed τ, the expressions

$$\rho(\theta) = \rho_0 a(\theta)^{-3(1+w)}(\tau-\theta)^{-(\mu-1)(w+1)}, \tag{167}$$

and

$$p(\theta) = w\rho_0 a(\theta)^{-3(1+w)}(\tau-\theta)^{-(\mu-1)(w+1)}, \tag{168}$$

define the energy density and isotropic pressure of matter fields.

To designate the temporal independent variables, the rule $(\tau,\theta) \mapsto (2t,t)$ is applied, where the new cosmological time, t, [60] is used. Hereafter, dots mean derivatives with respect to t. Furthermore, the parameter Hubble is $H \equiv \dot{a}/a$. Therefore, Equations (163) and (164), the modified Klein–Gordon Equation (165), and the conservation Equation (166) can be written as follows:

$$\begin{aligned}\left(1-\xi\phi^2(t)\right)\left(\dot{H}(t) + \frac{(1-\mu)H(t)}{t} + \frac{3H^2(t)}{2} + \frac{(\mu-2)(\mu-1)}{2t^2}\right) &= -\frac{1}{2}p(t) - \frac{1}{4}\dot{\phi}(t)^2 + \frac{1}{2}V(\phi(t)) \\ &+ \xi\phi(t)\left(2H(t)\dot{\phi}(t) - \frac{2(\mu-1)\dot{\phi}(t)}{t} + \ddot{\phi}(t) + \dot{\phi}(t)\right),\end{aligned} \tag{169}$$

$$\left(1-\xi\phi^2(t)\right)\left(H^2(t) + \frac{(1-\mu)H(t)}{t}\right) = \frac{1}{3}\rho(t) + \frac{1}{6}\dot{\phi}^2(t) + \frac{1}{3}V(\phi(t)) + 2\xi H(t)\phi(t)\dot{\phi}(t), \tag{170}$$

$$\ddot{\phi}(t) + 3H(t)\dot{\phi}(t) - \frac{(\mu-1)\dot{\phi}(t)}{t} + V'(\phi(t)) = -\xi\phi(t)\left(6\dot{H}(t) + 12H(t)^2\right), \tag{171}$$

$$\dot{\rho}(t) = -3\left(H(t) + \frac{(1-\mu)}{3t}\right)(p(t) + \rho(t)). \tag{172}$$

By comparing Equations (171) and (172) with the conservation equations of general relativity for a non-minimally coupled scalar field to gravity, $\xi \neq 0$, we observe the following:

$$\ddot{\phi}(t) + 3H(t)\dot{\phi} + V'(\phi(t)) = -\xi\phi(t)\left(6\dot{H}(t) + 12H(t)^2\right), \tag{173}$$

$$\dot{\rho}(t) = -3H(\rho(t) + p(t)), \tag{174}$$

The extra terms $-\frac{(1-\mu)\dot{\phi}(t)}{t}$ and $-\left(\frac{1-\mu}{t}\right)(\rho(t) + p(t))$, which are nontrivial for $\mu \neq 1$, can be interpreted as non-conservation equations. However, for $\mu = 1$, the standard conservation equations are restored. In the general case, $\mu \neq 1$, the non-conservation equations imply the following:

$$\frac{d}{dt}\left[\left(1-\xi\phi^2\right)\left(H^2 + \frac{(1-\mu)H}{t}\right) - \frac{1}{3}\rho - \frac{1}{6}\dot{\phi}^2 - \frac{1}{3}V(\phi) - 2\xi H\phi\dot{\phi}\right] \neq 0. \tag{175}$$

This feature of fractional cosmology leads to some constraints on the matter fields in the universe that were explored in [68,69] when $\xi = 0$.

We observe that Equation (172) is satisfied for any value of the equation of state of the matter parameter. Furthermore, by eliminating the higher-order derivatives, we obtain Equation (172), and have the following:

$$\dot{H} = H\left(\frac{(1-\mu)(\xi\phi^2-1)}{\xi(6\xi-1)t\phi^2+t} - \frac{\xi\phi\dot{\phi}}{\xi(6\xi-1)\phi^2+1}\right) + \frac{H^2(3(1-8\xi)\xi\phi^2-3)}{2\xi(6\xi-1)\phi^2+2} - \frac{p}{2\xi(6\xi-1)\phi^2+2}$$
$$+ \frac{(\mu-2)(\mu-1)(\xi\phi^2-1)}{2t^2(\xi(6\xi-1)\phi^2+1)} + \frac{\dot{\phi}((4\xi-1)t\dot{\phi}-4(\mu-1)\xi\phi)}{4(\xi(6\xi-1)t\phi^2+t)} - \frac{\xi\phi V'(\phi)}{\xi(6\xi-1)\phi^2+1} + \frac{V(\phi)}{2\xi(6\xi-1)\phi^2(t)+2}, \tag{176}$$

$$\ddot{\phi} = H\left(\frac{6(\mu-1)\xi\phi(\xi\phi^2-1)}{\xi(6\xi-1)t\phi^2+t} - \frac{3(\xi(4\xi-1)\phi^2+1)\dot{\phi}}{\xi(6\xi-1)\phi^2+1}\right)$$
$$+ \frac{3\xi H^2\phi(\xi\phi^2-1)}{\xi(6\xi-1)\phi^2+1} + \frac{3\xi p\phi}{\xi(6\xi-1)\phi^2+1} - \frac{3(\mu-2)(\mu-1)\xi\phi(\xi\phi^2-1)}{t^2(\xi(6\xi-1)\phi^2+1)}$$
$$+ \frac{\dot{\phi}(2(\mu-1)+\xi\phi(2(\mu-1)(12\xi-1)\phi+3(1-4\xi)t\dot{\phi}))}{2(\xi(6\xi-1)t\phi^2+t)} + \frac{(\xi\phi^2-1)V'(\phi)}{\xi(6\xi-1)\phi^2+1} - \frac{3\xi\phi V(\phi)}{\xi(6\xi-1)\phi^2+1}. \tag{177}$$

Solving (170) for ρ, we obtain the following:

$$\rho = \frac{3H(-tH+\mu-1)(\xi\phi^2-1)}{t} - 6\xi H\phi\dot{\phi} - V(\phi) - \frac{1}{2}\dot{\phi}^2. \tag{178}$$

In [68], Equations (169)–(172) for $\xi = 0$ were studied. Using a procedure similar to that of RG, (170) is required to be conserved over time, i.e.,

$$\frac{d}{dt}\left[\left(1-\xi\phi^2\right)\left(H^2+\frac{(1-\mu)H}{t}\right) - \frac{1}{3}\rho - \frac{1}{6}\dot{\phi}^2 - \frac{1}{3}V(\phi) - 2\xi H\phi\dot{\phi}\right] = 0. \tag{179}$$

Calculating the corresponding derivatives and substituting (172) and (176)–(178), we obtain the following:

$$\frac{(\mu-1)}{12t^3(\xi(6\xi-1)\phi^2+1)}\left[-6t^2H^2\left(\xi\phi^2-1\right)^2 + \left(\xi\phi^2-1\right)\left(-12tH(-\mu+\xi\phi((\mu+12\xi-3)\phi+t\dot{\phi})+3)\right.\right.$$
$$\left. -12\xi t^2\phi V'(\phi) + t\dot{\phi}(-12(\mu-1)\xi\phi - t\dot{\phi})\right) - 2t^2p\left(\xi(12\xi+1)\phi^2-1\right) - 12\xi t^2\dot{\phi}^2$$
$$\left. +2t^2\left(\xi(12\xi+1)\phi^2-1\right)V(\phi) + 6(\mu-2)(\mu-1)\left(\xi\phi^2-1\right)^2\right] = 0. \tag{180}$$

This equation is an identity for $\mu = 1$, as expected, in standard cosmology. However, for $\mu \neq 1$, we acquire the new relation for the fluid pressure, as follows:

$$p = -\frac{1}{2t^2(\xi(12\xi+1)\phi^2-1)}\left[6t^2H^2\left(\xi\phi^2-1\right)^2 - t\left(\xi\phi^2-1\right)\left(-12H(-\mu+\xi\phi((\mu+12\xi-3)\phi+t\dot{\phi})+3)\right.\right.$$
$$\left.\left. -12\xi\phi((\mu-1)\dot{\phi}+tV'(\phi)) - t\dot{\phi}^2\right) + 12\xi t^2\dot{\phi}^2 - 2t^2\left(\xi(12\xi+1)\phi^2-1\right)V(\phi) - 6(\mu-2)(\mu-1)\left(\xi\phi^2-1\right)^2\right]. \tag{181}$$

Then, using a procedure similar to GR, a new Equation (181) is obtained, demonstrating that two of the three equations are independent. This characteristic of fractional cosmology imposes certain constraints on the matter fields in the Universe, as explored in [68]. Therefore, the equation of state is modified

$$w(t) = \frac{p(t)}{\rho(t)}. \tag{182}$$

Replacing the expression for p given by (181) into (176), (177), and (172), we obtain the following:

$$\dot{H} = \left(\xi\phi^2 - 1\right)\left(\frac{(\mu-2)(\mu-1)}{t^2(\xi(12\xi+1)\phi^2-1)} - \frac{2(\mu-4)H}{t(\xi(12\xi+1)\phi^2-1)}\right)$$
$$- \frac{2\xi H\phi\dot{\phi}}{\xi(12\xi+1)\phi^2-1} + \frac{H^2(3-3\xi(8\xi+1)\phi^2)}{\xi(12\xi+1)\phi^2-1} + \frac{2\xi t\dot{\phi}^2 - 2\xi\phi((\mu-1)\dot{\phi}+tV'(\phi))}{t(\xi(12\xi+1)\phi^2-1)}, \quad (183)$$

$$\ddot{\phi} = \left(\xi\phi^2 - 1\right)\left[\frac{12(\mu-4)\xi H\phi}{t(\xi(12\xi+1)\phi^2-1)} + \frac{6\xi H^2\phi}{\xi(12\xi+1)\phi^2-1} - \frac{t^2V'(\phi)+6(\mu-2)(\mu-1)\xi\phi}{t^2(\xi(12\xi+1)\phi^2-1)}\right]$$
$$- \frac{3H(\xi(8\xi+1)\phi^2-1)\dot{\phi}}{\xi(12\xi+1)\phi^2-1} + \frac{\dot{\phi}(-\mu+\xi\phi((\mu-1)(24\xi+1)\phi-12\xi t\dot{\phi})+1)}{t(\xi(12\xi+1)\phi^2-1)}, \quad (184)$$

This leads to the auxiliary equation, as follows:

$$\dot{\rho} = \left(\xi\phi^2-1\right)\left[\frac{3H}{t^2(\xi(12\xi+1)\phi^2-1)}\Big((\mu-5)(\mu-1)+\xi\phi\Big((\mu-1)(12(\mu-3)\xi-\mu+5)+6t((\mu-1)\dot{\phi}+tV'(\phi))\Big)\Big)\right.$$
$$\left. + \frac{H^2(-3\mu+3\xi(-48\mu\xi+\mu+120\xi-13)\phi^2+39)}{t(\xi(12\xi+1)\phi^2-1)} + \frac{18H^3(\xi(6\xi+1)\phi^2-1)}{\xi(12\xi+1)\phi^2-1} - \frac{6(\mu-1)\xi\phi((\mu-1)\dot{\phi}+tV'(\phi))}{t^2(\xi(12\xi+1)\phi^2-1)}\right]$$
$$+ \left(\xi\phi^2-1\right)^2\left(\frac{3(\mu-2)(\mu-1)^2}{t^3(\xi(12\xi+1)\phi^2-1)} - \frac{9(\mu-2)(\mu-1)H}{t^2(\xi(12\xi+1)\phi^2-1)}\right) + \frac{3H\dot{\phi}(t(6\xi+\xi(6\xi+1)\phi^2-1)\dot{\phi}-4(\mu-1)\xi\phi(\xi(6\xi+1)\phi^2-1))}{t(\xi(12\xi+1)\phi^2-1)}$$
$$+ \frac{36\xi H^2\phi(\xi(6\xi+1)\phi^2-1)\dot{\phi}}{\xi(12\xi+1)\phi^2-1} - \frac{(\mu-1)(6\xi+\xi(6\xi+1)\phi^2-1)\dot{\phi}^2}{t(\xi(12\xi+1)\phi^2-1)}. \quad (185)$$

These equations allow one to deduce an effective equation of state for matter without imposing equations of state on each matter field. In the case of a minimal coupling, $\xi = 0$, this allows the system to be investigated as follows:

$$\dot{H} = \frac{2(4-\mu)H}{t} - 3H^2 + \frac{(\mu-2)(\mu-1)}{t^2}, \quad (186)$$

$$\ddot{\phi} = -3H\dot{\phi} + \frac{(\mu-1)\dot{\phi}}{t} - V'(\phi). \quad (187)$$

The Equation (186) is the Riccati ordinary differential equation for $\mu \neq 1$ and $\xi = 0$. The analytical solution of (186) is (for an analogous case, see Equation (36) in [61]):

$$H(t) = \frac{1}{3t}\left[\frac{9-2\mu+r}{2} - \frac{cr\alpha_0^r}{c\alpha_0^r + (H_0t)^r}\right], \quad (188)$$

where

$$c = \frac{-2\mu+r-6\alpha_0+9}{2\mu+r+6\alpha_0-9}, \quad r = \sqrt{8\mu(2\mu-9)+105}, \quad (189)$$

and $\alpha_0 = H_0t_0$, where t_0 is the value of t today. H_0 is the current value of the Hubble factor, and α_0 is the current age parameter, for which we obtain the best-fit values. For large t, the asymptotic scaling factor can be expressed as follows:

$$a(t) \simeq t^{\frac{1}{6}(+9-2\mu+r)}, \quad (190)$$

Thus, the acceleration of the late universe can be obtained with a power-law scale factor without a cosmological constant. These results are independent of the matter source and anisotropy.

3.2. Minimal Coupling

In this section, we discuss the results of [69] for minimal coupling ($\xi = 0$) and a constant potential $V(\phi) = \Lambda$.

Introducing the logarithmic independent variable, $\tau = -\ln(1+z) = \ln a$, with $\tau \to -\infty$ when $z \to \infty$, $\tau \to 0$ when $z \to 0$, and $\tau \to \infty$ when $z \to -1$, and defining the age parameter of the universe as $\alpha = tH$, we obtain the initial value problem, i.e.,

$$\alpha'(\tau) = 9 - 2\mu - 3\alpha(\tau) + \frac{(\mu-2)(\mu-1)}{\alpha(\tau)}, \tag{191}$$

$$t'(\tau) = t(\tau)/\alpha(\tau), \tag{192}$$

$$\alpha(0) = t_0 H_0, t(0) = t_0, \tag{193}$$

plus the auxiliary equation, as follows:

$$\phi''(\tau) = -\frac{(\mu-1)\phi'(\tau)(\mu - t(\tau)\phi(\tau) - 2)}{\alpha(\tau)^2} - \frac{\phi'(\tau)(-2\mu + 3t(\tau)\phi(\tau) + 8)}{\alpha(\tau)} + 3\phi'(\tau). \tag{194}$$

Equation (191) gives a one-dimensional dynamical system analyzed in [68]. There is an asymptotic behavior for large τ, which is consistent with [68], in which the attractor solution has an asymptotic age parameter $\lim_{t\to\infty} tH = \frac{1}{6}(9 - 2\mu + r)$.

The exact solution of this system is as follows:

$$t(\tau) = t_0 \exp\left(\frac{2\left(\tan^{-1}\left(\frac{6H_0t_0+2\mu-9}{\sqrt{8(9-2\mu)\mu-105}}\right) - \tan^{-1}\left(\frac{6\alpha(\tau)+2\mu-9}{\sqrt{8(9-2\mu)\mu-105}}\right)\right)}{\sqrt{8(9-2\mu)\mu-105}} \right), \tag{195}$$

where α is obtained implicitly from the following:

$$\begin{aligned} &\frac{1}{6}\ln\Big(-2\mu\alpha(\tau) - 3\alpha(\tau)^2 + 9\alpha(\tau) + \mu^2 - 3\mu + 2\Big) - \frac{(2\mu-9)\tan^{-1}\left(\frac{6\alpha(\tau)+2\mu-9}{\sqrt{-16\mu^2+72\mu-105}}\right)}{3\sqrt{-16\mu^2+72\mu-105}} \\ &= \frac{1}{6}\left(\ln\Big(-2H_0\mu t_0 - 3H_0t_0(H_0t_0-3) + \mu^2 - 3\mu + 2\Big) + \frac{2(9-2\mu)\tan^{-1}\left(\frac{6H_0t_0+2\mu-9}{\sqrt{8(9-2\mu)\mu-105}}\right)}{\sqrt{8(9-2\mu)\mu-105}} - 6\tau \right), \end{aligned} \tag{196}$$

where the parameter ϵ_0 is introduced, such that we have the following:

$$\epsilon_0 = \frac{1}{2}\lim_{t\to\infty}\left(\frac{t_0H_0 - tH}{tH}\right), \quad \alpha_0 = \frac{1}{6}\left(9 - 2\mu + \sqrt{8\mu(2\mu-9)+105}\right)(1+2\epsilon_0). \tag{197}$$

ϵ_0 is a measure of the limiting value of the relative error in the age parameter tH when approximated by t_0H_0.

In a recent study [69], we investigated the potential of using fractional cosmology to account for the universe's accelerated expansion without the requirement of exotic fluids in the model. We found self-accelerated solutions where the matter–energy density is zero. In this article, we will provide an overview of how a model with cold dark matter incorporates these possibilities following the previous reference.

3.2.1. Model with Cold Dark Matter

Assume

$$H(t) = \frac{\alpha}{t}, \tag{198}$$

where α is a constant and $\mu > 1$. If $\alpha = \mu - 1$, we have a power-law solution, as follows:

$$H(t) = \frac{\mu-1}{t} \implies a(t) = \left(\frac{t}{t_0}\right)^{\mu-1}. \tag{199}$$

The conservation equation for matter, as described in (172), applies to cold dark matter ($p_{\text{CDM}} = w_{\text{CDM}}\rho_{\text{CDM}}$, and $w_{\text{DM}} = 0$); when H is defined by (198), this equation simplifies to the following:

$$\dot{\rho}_{\text{CDM}} + \frac{(3\alpha - \mu + 1)\rho_{\text{CDM}}}{t} = 0. \tag{200}$$

Hence, for the matter–energy density, we have the following:

$$\rho_{\text{CDM}} = \rho_{CDM(0)}(t/t_0)^{-3\alpha+\mu-1}. \tag{201}$$

Choosing

$$\alpha = \frac{\mu+1}{3}, \tag{202}$$

we obtain the following:

$$\rho_{\text{CDM}} = \rho_{CDM(0)}(t/t_0)^{-2}. \tag{203}$$

Then, from Equation (178), we obtain the following:

$$\rho_{CDM(0)} = \frac{2(2-\mu)(\mu+1)}{3t_0^2}. \tag{204}$$

Using the redshift parameter, $1+z = 1/a$, we obtain the following:

$$H(t) = \frac{\alpha}{t} \Longrightarrow a(t) = \left(\frac{t}{t_0}\right)^{\alpha}, \tag{205}$$

$$\text{and } 1+z = \frac{1}{a} \Longrightarrow \left(\frac{t}{t_0}\right) = (1+z)^{-\frac{1}{\alpha}}, \tag{206}$$

then, we have the following:

$$\rho_{\text{CDM}}(z) = \rho_{\text{CDM}}(0)(1+z)^{\frac{2}{\alpha}} \text{ and } H(z) = H_0(1+z)^{\frac{1}{\alpha}}, \tag{207}$$

where α is defined by (202). EoS w_{eff} is defined through

$$\rho_{\text{CDM}}(z) = \rho_{\text{CDM}}(0)(1+z)^{3(1+w_{\text{eff}})}, \tag{208}$$

we have the following:

$$w_{\text{eff}} = -1 + \frac{2}{3\alpha} = -1 + \frac{2}{\mu+1} \text{ and } q = -1 + \frac{1}{\alpha} = -1 + \frac{3}{\mu+1}. \tag{209}$$

Similar to GR, we have the usual relation, $q = \frac{1}{2}(1+3w_{\text{eff}})$. Therefore, in fractional cosmology, we have an acceleration ($\ddot{a} > 0, q < 0$) as is present in GR when the effective fluid has $w_{\text{eff}} < -1/3$. Hence,

$$\ddot{a}(t) < 0, q > 0, w_{\text{eff}} > -1/3 \Longleftrightarrow 1 < \mu < 2, \tag{210}$$

and

$$\ddot{a}(t) > 0, q < 0, w_{\text{eff}} < -1/3 \Longleftrightarrow \mu > 2. \tag{211}$$

Finally, we have an accelerated expansion if $\mu > 2$, caused by the fractional derivative correction, and not by the matter content. That is the powerful advantage of fractional cosmology over GR. This is consistent as $\rho_{\text{CDM}} \to 0$ with the asymptotic solution $H(t) = \frac{\mu-1}{t}$, where $q = -\frac{\mu-2}{\mu-1}$, which is a power-law solution $a(t) = (t/t_0)^{\mu-1}$. It is accelerated if $\mu > 2$ and decelerated if $1 < \mu < 2$, as proven in [64].

3.2.2. Interpretation of the Fractional Term as a Dark Energy Source

We write (170) as follows:

$$3H^2 = \rho_{\text{CDM}} + \rho_{\text{frac}}, \tag{212}$$

$$\text{where } \rho_{\text{CDM}}(z) = \rho_{\text{CDM}}(0)(1+z)^{\frac{2}{\alpha}} = \frac{2(2-\mu)(\mu+1)}{3t_0^2}(1+z)^{\frac{6}{1+\mu}}, \tag{213}$$

$$\text{where } \rho_{\text{frac}}(t) = \frac{3(\mu-1)}{t}H \underbrace{\Longrightarrow}_{\text{using (198) and (206)}} \rho_{\text{frac}}(z) = \rho_{\text{frac}}(0)(1+z)^{\frac{2}{\alpha}}, \tag{214}$$

$$\text{and } \rho_{\text{frac}}(0) = \frac{3(\mu-1)}{t_0}H_0 = \frac{(\mu-1)}{t_0 H_0}3H_0^2. \tag{215}$$

Using $H = d\ln a/dt$ and $1+z = 1/a$, we obtain the following:

$$t_0 H_0 = \int_0^\infty \frac{dz}{(1+z)E(z)}. \tag{216}$$

Substituting (see Equation (198)), we have the following:

$$E(z) = (1+z)^{\frac{1}{\alpha}} = (1+z)^{\frac{3}{1+\mu}}, \tag{217}$$

with α defined by (202), we obtain the following:

$$H_0 t_0 = (1+\mu)/3. \tag{218}$$

On the other hand, using (212), (214), and (215), we obtain the following:

$$E^2(z) = \frac{3H^2(z)}{3H_0^2} = \frac{\rho_{\text{CDM}}(z)}{3H_0^2} + \frac{\rho_{\text{frac}}(z)}{3H_0^2} \Longleftrightarrow E^2(z) - \Omega_{\text{DM}}(z) + \Omega_{\text{frac}}(z), \tag{219}$$

$$\Longrightarrow \Omega_{\text{frac}}(0) = 1 - \Omega_{\text{DM}}(0) = \frac{\mu-1}{t_0 H_0} = \frac{3(\mu-1)}{\mu+1} \sim 0.744\%, \ \mu \sim 1.65957, \tag{220}$$

where $\Omega_{\text{DM}}(0) \sim 0.256\%$. We compare the value $\mu \sim 1.66$, with the observational tests performed in [64] for a flat prior $1 < \mu < 3$, where the best-fit value for μ is $\mu^* = 1.71$.

We will inspect the nature of ρ_{frac} as an effective fluid in GR, i.e.,

$$\rho_{\text{frac}} = \frac{3(\mu-1)}{t}H, \ q = -1 - \frac{\dot{H}}{H^2} \Longrightarrow \dot{\rho}_{\text{frac}} = -H\left(1+q+\frac{1}{Ht}\right)\rho_{\text{frac}}, \tag{221}$$

$$\Longrightarrow \dot{\rho}_{\text{frac}} + 3H(1+w_{\text{frac}})\rho_{\text{frac}} = 0, \tag{222}$$

where $w_{\text{frac}} = \frac{1}{3}\left(q - 2 + \frac{1}{\alpha}\right)$. According to (209), we again deduce (208),

$$w_{\text{frac}} = -1 + \frac{2}{3\alpha}, \tag{223}$$

corresponding to the quintessence ($-1 < w_{\text{frac}} < -1/3$) if $\mu > 2$.

3.2.3. Tests against Cosmological Observations

The observational tests performed in [64] were improved in [69]. In this reference, the (theoretical) Hubble parameter as a function of redshift is tested against cosmological observations. Therefore, for the adjustment, systems (191) and (192) are numerically integrated, representing a system for the variables (α, t) as a function of $\tau = -\ln(1+z)$, and for which we consider the initial conditions $\alpha(\tau = 0) \equiv \alpha_0 = t_0 H_0$ and $t(\tau = 0) \equiv t_0 = \alpha_0/H_0$. Then, the parameter Hubble is obtained numerically by $H_{th}(z) = \alpha(z)/t(z)$.

Furthermore, for a better comparison, the free parameters of the ΛCDM model are also fitted, whose Hubble parameter as a function of redshift is given by [69], as follows:

$$H(z) = H_0\sqrt{\Omega_{m,0}(1+z)^3 + 1 - \Omega_{m,0}}. \tag{224}$$

The free parameters of the fractional cosmological model are $\theta = \{h, \mu, \epsilon_0\}$ and the free parameters of the ΛCDM model are $\theta = \{h, \Omega_{m,0}\}$. For the free parameters, μ, ϵ_0 and $\Omega_{m,0}$, we consider the following flat priors: $\mu \in F(1,4)$, $\epsilon_0 \in F(-0.1, 0.1)$ and $\Omega_{m,0} \in F(0,1)$. It is important to mention that, due to a degeneracy between H_0 and $\mathcal{M}$, the SNe Ia data cannot constrain the free parameter, h (as a reminder, $H_0 = 100\frac{\mathrm{km/s}}{\mathrm{Mpc}}h$), contrary to the case of OHD and, consequently, in the joint analysis. Therefore, the posterior distribution of h for the SNe Ia data is expected to cover all prior distributions. On the other hand, the prior is chosen as $\epsilon_0 = 0$, which is a measure of the limiting value of the relative error in the age parameter, tH, when approximated by t_0H_0, according to Equation (197). For the mean value of $\epsilon_0 = 0$, $\alpha_0 = \frac{1}{6}(-2\mu + r + 9)$ was acquired, which implies $c = 0$.

The analysis of the SNe Ia, OHD data, and the joint analysis with SNe Ia plus OHD data lead, respectively, to $h = 0.696^{+0.302}_{-0.295}$, $\mu = 1.340^{+2.651}_{-0.339}$ and $\epsilon_0 = \left(1.976^{+1.709}_{-2.067}\right) \times 10^{-2}$, $h = 0.675^{+0.041}_{-0.021}$, $\mu = 2.239^{+1.386}_{-1.190}$, and $\epsilon_0 = \left(0.865^{+0.793}_{-0.773}\right) \times 10^{-2}$, and $h = 0.84^{+0.031}_{-0.027}$, $\mu = 1.840^{+1.446}_{-0.773}$, and $\epsilon_0 = \left(1.213^{+0.482}_{-1.057}\right) \times 10^{-2}$, where best-fit values are calculated at 3σ CL.

In this model, the deceleration parameter is calculated using specific values for $\alpha(\tau)$ and μ, in closed form, as follows:

$$q(\alpha(\tau)) = 2 + \frac{2(\mu-4)}{\alpha(\tau)} - \frac{(\mu-2)(\mu-1)}{\alpha^2(\tau)}. \tag{225}$$

Using best-fit estimates from Table 3, we show a transition at $z_t \gtrapprox 1$, with a larger transition redshift than the ΛCDM model. The current deceleration parameter for the fractional cosmological model is $q_0 = -0.37^{+0.08}_{-0.11}$ at 3σ CL.

Table 3. The best-fit values and criteria χ^2_{min} for the ΛCDM model with free parameters h and $\Omega_{m,0}$ for the fractional cosmological model (dust plus radiation) [64] and the fractional cosmological model with free parameters h, μ, and ϵ_0 [69]. Using the MCMC analysis [96], the best-fit values and their joint analysis were obtained from the SNe Ia and OHD (or CC) data. The ΛCDM model was used as a reference model (taken from [70]).

Data	Best-Fit Values				χ^2_{min}
	h	$\Omega_{m,0}$	μ	$\epsilon_0 \times 10^2$	
		ΛCDM **Model**			
SNe Ia	$0.692^{+0.209\ +0.296\ +0.307}_{-0.120\ -0.278\ -0.292}$	$0.299^{+0.022\ +0.046\ +0.068}_{-0.021\ -0.042\ -0.059}$	...	...	1026.9
OHD	$0.706^{+0.012\ +0.024\ +0.035}_{-0.012\ -0.024\ -0.036}$	$0.259^{+0.018\ +0.038\ +0.059}_{-0.017\ -0.033\ -0.047}$	...	...	27.5
SNe Ia plus OHD	$0.696^{+0.010\ +0.020\ +0.029}_{-0.010\ -0.020\ -0.029}$	$0.276^{+0.014\ +0.030\ +0.043}_{-0.014\ -0.027\ -0.040}$	...	...	1056.3
Fractional cosmological model (dust plus radiation) [64] (The uncertainties presented correspond to $1\sigma(68.3\%)$ CL)					
SNe Ia	$0.599^{+0.275}_{-0.269}$	$0.160^{+0.050}_{-0.072}$	$2.771^{+0.161}_{-0.214}$	...	54.83
CC	$0.629^{+0.027}_{-0.027}$	$0.399^{+0.093}_{-0.122}$	$2.281^{+0.492}_{-0.433}$	...	16.14
SNe Ia plus CC	$0.692^{+0.019}_{-0.018}$	$0.228^{+0.035}_{-0.040}$	$2.839^{+0.117}_{-0.193}$	...	78.69
Fractional cosmological model [69] (The uncertainties presented correspond to $1\sigma(68.3\%)$, $2\sigma(95.5\%)$, and $3\sigma(99.7\%)$ CL)					
SNe Ia	$0.696^{+0.215\ +0.293\ +0.302}_{-0.204\ -0.284\ -0.295}$	...	$1.340^{+0.492\ +2.447\ +2.651}_{-0.245\ -0.328\ -0.339}$	$1.976^{+0.599\ +1.133\ +1.709}_{-0.905\ -1.848\ -2.067}$	1028.1
OHD	$0.675^{+0.013\ +0.029\ +0.041}_{-0.008\ -0.015\ -0.021}$	...	$2.239^{+0.449\ +0.908\ +1.386}_{-0.457\ -0.960\ -1.190}$	$0.865^{+0.395\ +0.650\ +0.793}_{-0.407\ -0.657\ -0.773}$	29.7
SNe Ia plus OHD	$0.684^{+0.011\ +0.021\ +0.031}_{-0.010\ -0.020\ -0.027}$	...	$1.840^{+0.343\ +1.030\ +1.446}_{-0.298\ -0.586\ -0.773}$	$1.213^{+0.216\ +0.383\ +0.482}_{-0.310\ -0.880\ -1.057}$	1061.1

We use the jerk to determine the type of dark energy in the fractional cosmological model. Its formula is based on the value of q in (225) using equation $j(\tau) = q(\tau)(2q(\tau) + 1) - \frac{dq(\tau)}{d\tau}$. Entering $\alpha(\tau)$, we obtain the following:

$$j(\alpha(\tau)) = \frac{12(\mu-4)}{\alpha(\tau)} + \frac{(\mu-21)\mu+50}{\alpha(\tau)^2} - \frac{2(\mu-3)(\mu-2)(\mu-1)}{\alpha(\tau)^3} + 10. \tag{226}$$

If j deviates from unity, this may suggest a different cosmology with a dynamical equation of state during the late times.

The matter density parameter in the fractional cosmological model has significant uncertainties due to the absence of the matter equation of the state parameter in the Hubble parameter used for the reconstruction. The current value of this parameter is $\Omega_{m,0} = 0.531^{+0.195}_{-0.260}$ at 1σ CL, which aligns with the asymptotic value $\Omega_{m,t\to\infty} = 0.519^{+0.199}_{-0.262}$ determined at the same confidence level through joint analysis.

The fractional cosmological model suggests that a larger $\Omega_{m,0}$ could explain the smaller deceleration parameter q_0 and the excess matter at $\rho_{\text{frac}} = 3(\mu-1)t^{-1}H$ with $\Omega_{\text{frac}}(\alpha(\tau)) = (\mu-1)/\alpha(\tau)$. The current value of $\Omega_{\text{frac},0}$ is 0.469, which satisfies $\Omega_{m,0} + \Omega_{\text{frac},0} = 1$ and potentially alleviates the problem of coincidence. On the other hand, these best-fit values lead to an age of the universe with a value of $t_0 = \alpha_0/H_0 = 25.62^{+6.89}_{-4.46}$ Gyrs [69].

In this case, the expressions (178) and (181) are used to calculate $\rho(t)$ and $p(t)$. Substituting all expressions in system (176)–(178) leads to identities. There is an arbitrary constant of integration, and the equations are satisfied identically (no compatibility equations are required). Therefore, this is the general solution of the system. This result is generic since it does not require specifying the equation of the state parameter of matter. Therefore, Equation (188) provides a family of one-parameter solutions that are complete and independent of matter content.

The results in Table 3 are for the minimally coupled case ($\xi = 0$). The test against cosmological data of the non minimally coupled case has not yet been performed. The analysis is complicated and out of the scope of the present research.

3.2.4. Dynamical Systems Analysis

This section presents new findings and an alternative approach to the dynamical system previously developed in [64,68,69]. Through analyzing dynamical systems, we can identify the model's asymptotic states and explore the phase space for different fractional derivative orders and matter models [97–102]. This allows us to classify the equilibrium points and determine the fractional derivative order to produce a power-law-accelerated late-time solution for the scale factor.

With this objective in mind, we introduce the new variables, as follows:

$$x_1 = \frac{t(\tau)\phi'(\tau)}{\sqrt{6}\alpha(\tau)}, \quad x_2 = t(\tau)\phi(\tau), \quad x_3 = \alpha(\tau), \tag{227}$$

that satisfy

$$\rho + \Lambda = -\frac{3x_2^2 x_3\left(-\mu\xi + \xi + x_3\left(\xi + x_1^2 + 2\sqrt{6}\xi x_1\right)\right)}{t(\tau)^4} + \frac{3x_3(-\mu + x_3 + 1)}{t(\tau)^2}, \tag{228}$$

and define the new time variable, as follows:

$$f' \equiv \alpha^2 \frac{df}{d\tau}, \tag{229}$$

and, thus, we obtain the dynamical system, as follows:

$$x_1' = -2\mu^2 x_1 + \mu x_1(x_2 + 4x_3 + 6) - x_1(3x_2x_3 + x_2 + 2(8 - 3x_3)x_3 + 4), \quad (230)$$

$$x_2' = x_3\left(\sqrt{6}x_1x_3^2 + x_2\right), \quad (231)$$

$$x_3' = x_3\left(\mu^2 - 3\mu - 2\mu x_3 - 3(x_3 - 3)x_3 + 2\right). \quad (232)$$

The equilibrium points of (230)–(232) are as follows:

1. $P_1 : (x_1, x_2, x_3) := (0, x_{2c}, 0)$. The eigenvalues are $\{0, (\mu-1)(-2\mu + x_{2c} + 4), (\mu-2)(\mu-1)\}$. It is normally hyperbolic with a stable 2D manifold for $1 < \mu < 2, x_{2c} < 2\mu - 4$, an unstable 2D manifold for $\mu < 1, x_{2c} < 2\mu - 4$, or $\mu > 2, x_{2c} > 2\mu - 4$. This point is a saddle for $\mu < 1, x_{2c} > 2\mu - 4$, or $1 < \mu < 2, x_{2c} > 2\mu - 4$, or $\mu > 2, x_{2c} < 2\mu - 4$.
2. $P_2 : (x_1, x_2, x_3) := (x_{1c}, 2(\mu-2), 0)$. The eigenvalues are $\{0, 0, (-2+\mu)(-1+\mu)\}$, indicating that the system is non-hyperbolic.
3. $P_3 : (x_1, x_2, x_3) := \left(0, 0, \frac{1}{6}(-2\mu - r + 9)\right)$, with $r = \sqrt{8\mu(2\mu - 9) + 105}$. The eigenvalues are $\left\{\frac{1}{3}(-2\mu - r + 9), \frac{1}{6}(-2\mu - r + 9), \frac{1}{6}(-2\mu(8\mu + r - 36) + 9r - 105)\right\}$. The conditions are as follows:
   (a) Source for $1 < \mu < 2$.
   (b) Sink for $\mu < 1$ or $\mu > 2$.
4. $P_4 : (x_1, x_2, x_3) := \left(\frac{\mu(-12\mu+3r+65)-2(5r+51)}{4\sqrt{6}(\mu-2)(\mu-1)^2}, \frac{1}{12}(4\mu - r - 3), \frac{1}{6}(-2\mu - r + 9)\right)$.
   The eigenvalues are $\left\{\frac{1}{6}(-2\mu(8\mu + r - 36) + 9r - 105),\right.$
   $\frac{1}{12}\left(-2\mu - 3\sqrt{2}\sqrt{2\mu(5\mu - 27) + (2\mu - 9)r + 93} - r + 9\right),$
   $\left.\frac{1}{12}\left(-2\mu + 3\sqrt{2}\sqrt{2\mu(5\mu - 27) + (2\mu - 9)r + 93} - r + 9\right)\right\}$. This point is a saddle for all $\mu \neq 1$ and $\mu \neq 2$.
5. $P_5 : (x_1, x_2, x_3) := \left(0, 0, \frac{1}{6}(-2\mu + r + 9)\right)$. The eigenvalues are $\left\{\frac{1}{6}(-2\mu + r + 9), \frac{1}{3}(-2\mu + r + 9), \frac{1}{6}(2\mu(-8\mu + r + 36) - 3(3r + 35))\right\}$. This point is a saddle for all $\mu \in \mathbb{R}$.
6. $P_6 : (x_1, x_2, x_3) := \left(\frac{\mu(-12\mu-3r+65)+2(5r-51)}{4\sqrt{6}(\mu-2)(\mu-1)^2}, \frac{1}{12}(4\mu + r - 3), \frac{1}{6}(-2\mu + r + 9)\right)$.
   The eigenvalues are $\left\{\frac{1}{6}(2\mu(-8\mu + r + 36) - 3(3r + 35)),\right.$
   $\frac{1}{12}\left(-2\mu - 3\sqrt{20\mu^2 - 4\mu(r + 27) + 6(3r + 31)} + r + 9\right),$
   $\left.\frac{1}{12}\left(-2\mu + 3\sqrt{20\mu^2 - 4\mu(r + 27) + 6(3r + 31)} + r + 9\right)\right\}$.
   This point is a saddle for all $\mu \neq 1$ and $\mu \neq 2$.

3.3. Non-Minimal Coupling

In this section, we present the new results of the thesis for the most general case $\xi \neq 0$ corresponding to non-minimal coupling. For this analysis, we will use the age parameter given by $\alpha = tH$, and we will use the rules

$$\frac{d}{dt} = H\frac{d}{d\tau}, \quad \frac{d^2}{dt^2} = H^2\left(\frac{d^2}{d\tau^2} - (1+q)\frac{d}{d\tau}\right), \quad q := -1 - \frac{\dot{H}}{H^2}, \quad (233)$$

to introduce a new derivative.

Thus, systems (183) and (184) are as follows:

$$
\begin{aligned}
\alpha'(\tau) &= \frac{(\mu-2)(\mu-1)(\xi\phi^2-1)}{\alpha(\xi(12\xi+1)\phi^2-1)} + \frac{\alpha(3-3\xi(8\xi+1)\phi^2)}{\xi(12\xi+1)\phi^2-1} + \frac{\xi(-2\mu+12\xi+9)\phi^2+2\mu-9}{\xi(12\xi+1)\phi^2-1} + \frac{2\xi t^2\phi^2\phi'^2}{\alpha(\xi(12\xi+1)\phi^2-1)} \\
&\quad + \phi'\left(-\frac{2(\mu-1)\xi t\phi^2}{\alpha(\xi(12\xi+1)\phi^2-1)} - \frac{2\xi t\phi^2}{\xi(12\xi+1)\phi^2-1}\right),
\end{aligned} \tag{234}
$$

$$
\begin{aligned}
\phi''(\tau) &= \frac{12(\mu-4)\xi\phi(\xi\phi^2-1)}{\alpha(\xi(12\xi+1)\phi^2-1)} - \frac{6(\mu-2)(\mu-1)\xi\phi(\xi\phi^2-1)}{\alpha^2(\xi(12\xi+1)\phi^2-1)} + \frac{6\xi\phi(\xi\phi^2-1)}{\xi(12\xi+1)\phi^2-1} \\
&\quad + \phi'^2\left(\frac{\frac{2(\mu-1)\xi t\phi^2}{\xi(12\xi+1)\phi^2-1} - \frac{12\xi^2t^2\phi^3}{\xi(12\xi+1)\phi^2-1}}{\alpha^2} + \frac{2\xi t\phi^2}{\alpha(\xi(12\xi+1)\phi^2-1)}\right) - \frac{2\xi t^2\phi^2\phi'^3}{\alpha^2(\xi(12\xi+1)\phi^2-1)} \\
&\quad + \phi'\left(\frac{3(\xi(8\xi+1)\phi^2-1)}{\xi(12\xi+1)\phi^2-1} + \frac{\frac{(\mu-1)t\phi(\xi(24\xi+1)\phi^2-1)}{\xi(12\xi+1)\phi^2-1} - \frac{(\mu-2)(\mu-1)(\xi\phi^2-1)}{\xi(12\xi+1)\phi^2-1}}{\alpha^2} + \frac{\frac{2(\mu-4)(\xi\phi^2-1)}{\xi(12\xi+1)\phi^2-1} + \frac{t(3\phi-3\xi(8\xi+1)\phi^3)}{\xi(12\xi+1)\phi^2-1}}{\alpha}\right),
\end{aligned} \tag{235}
$$

$$
t'(\tau) = t(\tau)/\alpha(\tau), \tag{236}
$$

$$
\alpha(0) = t_0H_0, \quad \phi(0) = \phi_0, \quad \phi'(0) = {\phi'}_0, \quad t(0) = t_0, \tag{237}
$$

and for the initial conditions for the scalar field and the speed of the scalar field, we consider a model with dust-like matter ($p = 0$), and we evaluate at $\tau = 0$ (today) the expressions (178) and (181) to obtain the following:

$$
-\frac{\phi_0^2{\phi_0'}^2}{6H_0^2} - \frac{\mu+\xi\phi_0^2(-\mu+2t_0\phi_0'+1)-1}{H_0t_0} - \xi\phi_0^2 - \Omega_{\Lambda 0} - \Omega_{m0} + 1 = 0, \tag{238}
$$

$$
\begin{aligned}
&-6H_0^2t_0^2\Omega_{\Lambda 0}\left(\xi(12\xi+1)\phi_0^2-1\right) + 6H_0^2t_0^2\left(\xi\phi_0^2-1\right)^2 + 12H_0t_0\left(\xi\phi_0^2-1\right)\left(\mu\left(\xi\phi_0^2-1\right)+\xi\phi_0^2(12\xi+t_0\phi_0'-3)+3\right) \\
&-6(\mu-2)(\mu-1)\left(\xi\phi_0^2-1\right)^2 + t_0^2\phi_0^2\left(\xi\left(\phi_0^2+12\right)-1\right){\phi_0'}^2 + 12(\mu-1)\xi t_0\phi_0^2\left(\xi\phi_0^2-1\right)\phi_0' = 0.
\end{aligned} \tag{239}
$$

3.3.1. Dynamical Systems Analysis

In [49], the assumption $H = H(\phi, \dot{\phi}) = \varepsilon\dot{\phi}/\phi$ was explored, corresponding to $\phi'(\tau)/\phi(\tau) = \varepsilon$, and $\alpha = t\varepsilon\dot{\phi}/\phi$.

In this paper, we consider a more general case where the new variables are introduced as follows:

$$
x_1 = \frac{t(\tau)\phi'(\tau)}{\sqrt{6}\alpha(\tau)}, \quad x_2 = t(\tau)\phi(\tau), \quad x_3 = \alpha(\tau), \quad x_4 = \frac{1}{t(\tau)^2(\xi(12\xi+1)\phi(\tau)^2-1)}, \tag{240}
$$

that satisfy

$$
\rho + \Lambda = -\frac{3x_3x_4\left(-\mu + x_2^2x_4\left(x_1^2x_3 + 2\sqrt{6}\xi x_1x_3 - 12\xi^2(-\mu+x_3+1)\right) + x_3 + 1\right)}{\left(\xi(12\xi+1)x_2^2x_4-1\right)^2}, \tag{241}
$$

and the new time, as follows:

$$
f' \equiv \alpha^3\frac{df}{d\tau}, \tag{242}
$$

which preserves the arrow of time ($\alpha \geq 0$), obtaining the dynamical system, as follows:

$$
\begin{aligned}
x_1' &= -24\xi x_1^3x_2^2x_3^3x_4 + 4\sqrt{6}\xi x_1^2x_2^2x_3^2x_4(\mu-3\xi x_2+x_3-1) \\
&\quad + x_1x_3\Big[-2\mu^2+6\mu+12\xi^2x_2^2x_4\left(2\mu^2-6\mu+x_2(\mu+x_3-1)-4\mu x_3-2(x_3-8)x_3+4\right) \\
&\quad + \mu x_2 - 3x_2x_3 - x_2 + 6x_3^2 + 4\mu x_3 - 16x_3 - 4\Big] \\
&\quad - \sqrt{6}\xi x_2\left(-(\mu-2)(\mu-1)+x_3^2+2(\mu-4)x_3\right)\left(12\xi^2x_2^2x_4-1\right),
\end{aligned} \tag{243}
$$

$$x_2' = x_3^2\left(\sqrt{6}x_1x_3^2 + x_2\right), \quad (244)$$

$$x_3' = x_3^2\Big[\mu^2 - 3\mu + 2\xi x_1 x_2^2 x_3 x_4\left(6x_1x_3 - \sqrt{6}(\mu + x_3 - 1)\right) + 12\xi^2 x_2^2 x_4\left(-(\mu-2)(\mu-1) + x_3^2 + 2(\mu-4)x_3\right) - 3x_3^2 - 2\mu x_3 + 9x_3 + 2\Big], \quad (245)$$

$$x_4' = -2x_3^2 x_4\left(\sqrt{6}\xi(12\xi+1)x_1x_2x_3^2x_4 + 1\right). \quad (246)$$

1. The set $x_3 = 0$ is an invariant set of (243)–(246) when

$$\sqrt{6}(\mu-2)(\mu-1)\xi x_2\left(12\xi^2 x_2^2 x_4 - 1\right) = 0. \quad (247)$$

   That is, when
   (a) $\mu \in \{1,2\}$ o
   (b) $\xi = 0$ o
   (c) $x_2 = 0$ o
   (d) $x_4 x_2^2 = \frac{1}{12\xi^2}$.

2. Taking $x_4 = 0$, we obtain the dynamical system, as follows:

$$x_1' = x_1x_3(6\mu + x_2(\mu - 3x_3 - 1) + 2(3x_3 - \mu)(\mu + x_3) - 16x_3 - 4) + \sqrt{6}\xi x_2\left(-(\mu-2)(\mu-1) + x_3^2 + 2(\mu-4)x_3\right), \quad (248)$$

$$x_2' = x_3^2\left(\sqrt{6}x_1x_3^2 + x_2\right), \quad (249)$$

$$x_3' = x_3^2\left(\mu^2 - 3\mu - 2\mu x_3 - 3(x_3-3)x_3 + 2\right), \quad (250)$$

   Systems (248)–(250) support the following equilibrium points:
   (a) $Q_1 : (x_1, x_2, x_3) := (x_{1c}, 0, 0)$, which is a non-hyperbolic critical point curve.
   (b) $Q_2 : (x_1, x_2, x_3) := \left(0, 0, \frac{1}{6}(-r - 2\mu + 9)\right)$, where $r = \sqrt{8\mu(2\mu-9)+105}$ with eigenvalues $\{\frac{f_1(\mu,\xi)}{36}, \frac{f_2(\mu,\xi)}{108}, \frac{f_3(\mu,\xi)}{108}\}$, where f_i are complicated expressions that depend on μ and ξ. Since $x_3 \geq 0$, this point only exists for $1 \leq \mu \leq 2$. In Figure 8, the point can show source or saddle behavior.
   (c) $Q_3 : (x_1, x_2, x_3) := \left(0, 0, \frac{1}{6}(r - 2\mu + 9)\right)$ with eigenvalues $\{\frac{g_1(\mu,\xi)}{36}, \frac{g_2(\mu,\xi)}{108}, \frac{g_3(\mu,\xi)}{108}\}$, where g_i are complicated expressions that depend on μ and ξ. In Figure 8, the point is a saddle.
   (d) $Q_4 : (x_1, x_2, x_3) := \Big(\frac{\xi\left((\mu-2)(\mu-1)(2\mu-5)r + (2-\mu)(\mu-1)\left(8\mu^2 - 26\mu + 39\right)\right)}{4\sqrt{6}(\mu-2)(\mu-1)^2} + \frac{3\mu r - 10r - 12\mu^2 + 65\mu - 102}{4\sqrt{6}(\mu-2)(\mu-1)^2},$ $\frac{1}{36}\xi\left((-\mu(2\mu-15) - 57)r + \mu\left(8\mu^2 + 30\mu - 279\right) + 549\right) + \frac{1}{36}(-3r + 12\mu - 9),$ $\frac{1}{6}(-r - 2\mu + 9)\Big)$, with eigenvalues $\{\frac{h_1(\mu,\xi)}{36}, \frac{h_2(\mu,\xi)}{108(\mu-2)(\mu-1)^2}, \frac{h_3(\mu,\xi)}{108(\mu-2)(\mu-1)^2}\}$, where, again, h_i are complicated expressions that depend on μ and ξ. Since $x_3 \geq 0$, this point only exists for $1 \leq \mu \leq 2$. In Figure 9, the point can show source or saddle behavior.
   (e) $Q_5 : (x_1, x_2, x_3) := \Big(\frac{\xi\left(-\mu(\mu(2\mu-11)+19)r + 10r + (2-\mu)(\mu-1)\left(8\mu^2 - 26\mu + 39\right)\right)}{4\sqrt{6}(\mu-2)(\mu-1)^2} + \frac{-3\mu r + 10r - 12\mu^2 + 65\mu - 102}{4\sqrt{6}(\mu-2)(\mu-1)^2},$ $\frac{1}{36}\xi\left((\mu(2\mu-15) + 57)r + \mu\left(8\mu^2 + 30\mu - 279\right) + 549\right) + \frac{1}{36}(3r + 12\mu - 9),$ $\frac{1}{6}(r - 2\mu + 9)\Big)$, with eigenvalues $\{\frac{l_1(\mu,\xi)}{36}, \frac{l_2(\mu,\xi)}{108(\mu-2)(\mu-1)^2}, \frac{l_3(\mu,\xi)}{108(\mu-2)(\mu-1)^2}\}$, where l_i are complicated expressions that depend on μ and ξ. In Figure 9, the point is a saddle.

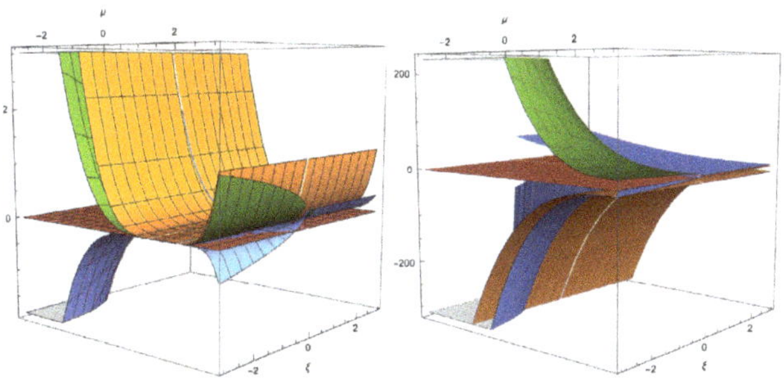

Figure 8. Real parts of the eigenvalues of Q_2 (**left**) and Q_3 (**right**). Q_2 can exhibit source or saddle behavior and Q_3 is a saddle. For reference, the red plane corresponds to the value zero, and the other colors denote the three real parts of the eigenvalues.

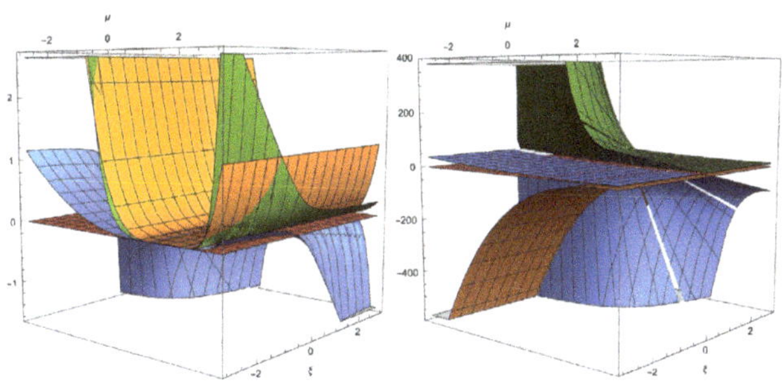

Figure 9. Real parts of the eigenvalues of Q_4 (**left**) and Q_5 (**right**). Q_4 can exhibit either source or saddle behavior and Q_5 is a saddle. For reference, the red plane corresponds to the value zero, and the other colors denote the three real parts of the eigenvalues.

In Figure 10 we present some phase space orbits for systems (248)–(250) for $\xi = 4$ and $\mu = \frac{1}{2}(7 \pm \sqrt{17})$. The red line denotes the non-hyperbolic set of points, Q_1. Since $x_3 \geq 0$, only two equilibrium points appear in the right-hand graph.

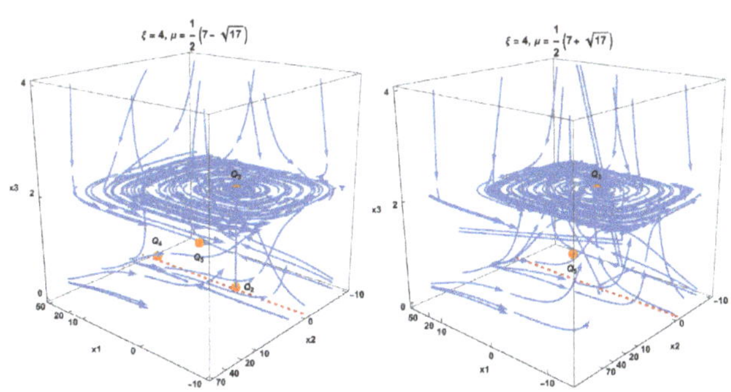

Figure 10. Phase space for systems (248)–(250) for $\xi = 4$ and $\mu = \frac{1}{2}(7 \pm \sqrt{17})$. The red line denotes the non-hyperbolic set of points, Q_1. Since $x_3 \geq 0$, only two equilibrium points appear in the right-hand graph.

The Figure 11 displays the projection of the flow of equations (248)–(250) for $\xi = 4$ and $\mu = \frac{1}{2}(7 \pm \sqrt{17})$ on the plane $x_3 = 2$, highlighted in pink. In the plot, the yellow sphere represents the projection of the point $Q_3 = (0, 0, \frac{1}{6}(r - 2\mu + 9))$, which lies on the plane $(x_1, x_2) = (0, 0)$. As depicted in the figure, Q_3 is an unstable focus. The spiral is constructed from the initial conditions $A = (0.1, 0.1)$, $B = (0.1, 0.1, 4)$, and $C = (1.9, -0.5, 1)$.

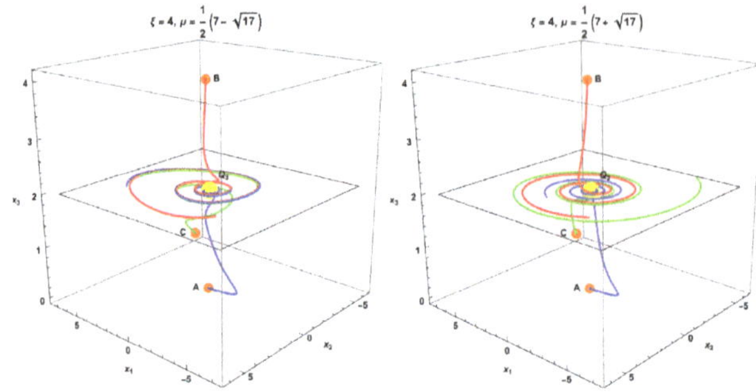

Figure 11. Projection of the flow of (248)–(250) in the plane $x_3 = 2$ for $\mu = \frac{1}{2}(7 \pm \sqrt{17})$ and $\xi = 4$. the yellow sphere represents the projection of the point $Q_3 = (0, 0, \frac{1}{6}(r - 2\mu + 9))$, which lies on the plane $(x_1, x_2) = (0, 0)$. As depicted in the figure, Q_3 is an unstable focus. The spiral is constructed from the initial conditions $A = (0.1, 0.1)$, $B = (0.1, 0.1, 4)$, and $C = (1.9, -0.5, 1)$.

3.3.2. Alternative Formulation of the Dynamical System

We define the following variables:

$$x = \frac{\dot{\phi}(t)}{\sqrt{6}H(t)}, \quad y = \phi(t), \quad \Omega_\Lambda = \frac{\Lambda}{3H^2(t)}, \tag{251}$$

that satisfy

$$(x + \sqrt{6}\xi y)^2 + \xi y^2(1 - 6\xi) + \frac{(\mu - 1)(1 - \xi y^2)}{\alpha} + \Omega_\Lambda + \Omega_m = 1, \tag{252}$$

where

$$\Omega_m = \frac{\rho_m}{3H^2}, \tag{253}$$

which is the dimensionless energy density of matter, and Ω_Λ is interpreted as the energy density of the cosmological constant. The equation of state parameter of matter can be expressed in terms of these variables as follows:

$$\begin{aligned} w = &\left\{\alpha\left(\xi(12\xi + 1)y^2 - 1\right)\left(-\alpha + \mu + \alpha x^2 + \xi y\left(2\sqrt{6}\alpha x + y(\alpha - \mu + 1)\right) + \alpha\Omega_\Lambda - 1\right)\right\}^{-1} \\ &\times \left\{\alpha^2\left[x^2\left(\xi\left(y^2 + 12\right) - 1\right) + 2\sqrt{6}\xi xy\left(\xi y^2 - 1\right) + \xi y^2\left(-(12\xi + 1)\Omega_\Lambda + \xi y^2 - 2\right) + \Omega_\Lambda + 1\right]\right. \\ &\left. + 2\alpha\left(\xi y^2 - 1\right)\left[\mu\left(\xi y\left(\sqrt{6}x + y\right) - 1\right) + \xi y\left(-\sqrt{6}x + 12\xi y - 3y\right) + 3\right] - (\mu - 2)(\mu - 1)\left(\xi y^2 - 1\right)^2\right\}. \end{aligned} \tag{254}$$

Introducing the new time derivative, i.e.,

$$\frac{df}{d\tau} \equiv \frac{1}{H}\frac{df}{dt}, \tag{255}$$

we obtain the four-dimensional dynamical system, as follows:

$$\begin{aligned} \alpha^2 G\frac{dx}{d\tau} = &-12\alpha^2\xi x^3 + 2\sqrt{6}\alpha\xi x^2 y(-6\alpha\xi + \alpha + \mu - 1) \\ &+ x\left(3\alpha\left(-\mu + 8(\mu - 1)\xi^2 y^2 + (\mu - 3)\xi y^2 + 3\right) - (\mu - 2)(\mu - 1)\left(\xi y^2 - 1\right)\right) \\ &+ \sqrt{6}\xi y\left(\alpha^2 + 2\alpha(\mu - 4) - (\mu - 2)(\mu - 1)\right)\left(\xi y^2 - 1\right), \end{aligned} \tag{256}$$

$$\frac{dy}{d\tau} = \sqrt{6}x, \tag{257}$$

$$\alpha^2 G \frac{d\Omega_\Lambda}{d\tau} = 2\Omega_\Lambda \Big\{ \alpha^2 \Big(-12\xi x^2 + 2\sqrt{6}\xi xy + 3\xi(8\xi+1)y^2 - 3 \Big) + 2\alpha \Big(\sqrt{6}(\mu-1)\xi xy + (\mu-4)\Big(\xi y^2 - 1\Big) \Big) - (\mu-2)(\mu-1)\Big(\xi y^2 - 1\Big) \Big\}, \tag{258}$$

$$\alpha G \frac{d\alpha}{d\tau} = 3\alpha^2 + 2\alpha\mu - 9\alpha - \mu^2 + 3\mu + \xi\Big(12\alpha^2 x^2 - 2\sqrt{6}\alpha xy(\alpha+\mu-1) + y^2\Big(-2\alpha\mu - 3(\alpha-3)\alpha + \mu^2 - 3\mu + 2\Big)\Big) + 12(1-2\alpha)\alpha\xi^2 y^2 - 2, \tag{259}$$

where

$$G := (\xi(12\xi+1)y^2 - 1), \tag{260}$$

is defined in the phase space, i.e.,

$$(x + \sqrt{6}\xi y)^2 + \xi y^2(1-6\xi) + \frac{(\mu-1)(1-\xi y^2)}{\alpha} + \Omega_\Lambda \leq 1 \tag{261}$$

which corresponds to $\Omega_m \geq 0$.

We introduce temporal rescaling:

$$f' := \alpha^2 \frac{df}{d\tau}, \tag{262}$$

this preserves the arrow of time. Sometimes, we use the time variable $\tau = \ln(a/a_0)$, which is more convenient.

We obtain the equilibrium points with coordinates $(x, y, \Omega_\Lambda, \alpha)$, as follows:

1. The line of equilibrium points $P_1(y_c)$ with coordinates $\Big(-\sqrt{6}\xi y_c, y_c, 0, 0\Big)$ parameterized by $y_c \in \mathbb{R}$. The equation of state parameter is complex infinity. The eigenvalues are as follows: $\Big\{0, -\frac{2(\mu-2)(\mu-1)(\xi y_c^2 \ 1)}{\xi(12\xi+1)y_c^2-1}, -\frac{(\mu-2)(\mu-1)(\xi y_c^2-1)}{\xi(12\xi+1)y_c^2-1}, \frac{(\mu-2)(\mu-1)(\xi y_c^2-1)}{\xi(12\xi+1)y_c^2-1}\Big\}$. The curve is a saddle because it has at least two eigenvalues with different signs.
2. The equilibrium point, $P_2 : \Big(0, 0, 0, \frac{1}{6}(9-2\mu-r)\Big)$. The equation of state parameter is $w = \frac{r+7}{4-4\mu}$. The eigenvalues are as follows: $\{\frac{1}{3}(9-2\mu-r), \frac{1}{6}(-2\mu(8\mu+r-36)+9r-105), \frac{1}{36}(9(21-4\mu)\mu - 9(\mu-3)r - 279 - s_-), \frac{1}{36}(9(21-4\mu)\mu - 9(\mu-3)r - 279 + s_-)\Big\}$ where $r = \sqrt{8\mu(2\mu-9)+105}$, and s_- is the positive square root of $s_-^2 = 81(\mu(4\mu-21)+(\mu-3)r+31)^2 - 48\xi(\mu(\mu(2\mu(82\mu-933)+8355)-17{,}361) + (\mu(5\mu(8\mu-75)+1209)-1413)r+14{,}481)$. This is a saddle for the following: $\Psi := \Big\{\mu \leq 0.463848, 0 < \xi \leq \frac{\mu(32\mu^3 - 8\mu^2(r+24) + 6\mu(5r+83) - 51r - 567) + 18(r+17)}{48(\mu-2)(\mu-1)(4(\mu-4)\mu+23)}\Big\} \cup \Big\{0.463848 < \mu < 1, 0 < \xi \leq \frac{\mu(2\mu(4\mu(4\mu+r-24)-15r+249)+51r-567)-18(r-17)}{48(\mu-2)(\mu-1)(4(\mu-4)\mu+23)}\Big\} \cup \Big\{\mu > 2, 0 < \xi \leq \frac{\mu(2\mu(4\mu(4\mu+r-24)-15r+249)+51r-567)-18(r-17)}{48(\mu-2)(\mu-1)(4(\mu-4)\mu+23)}\Big\}$. This is a source for the following: $\frac{1}{48}\Big(-\frac{\sqrt{8\mu(2\mu-9)+105}(\mu(8\mu^2-30\mu+51)-18)}{(\mu-2)(\mu-1)(4(\mu-4)\mu+23)} + \frac{38-20\mu}{4(\mu-4)\mu+23} + \frac{20}{\mu-2} - \frac{7}{\mu-1} + 8\Big) \leq \xi < 0$. This case is discarded under the assumption $\xi \geq 0$. Figure 12 presents the real parts of the eigenvalues associated with P_2. This shows that the point is well for $(\mu, \xi) \in \Psi$, or a saddle (assuming $\xi \geq 0$).

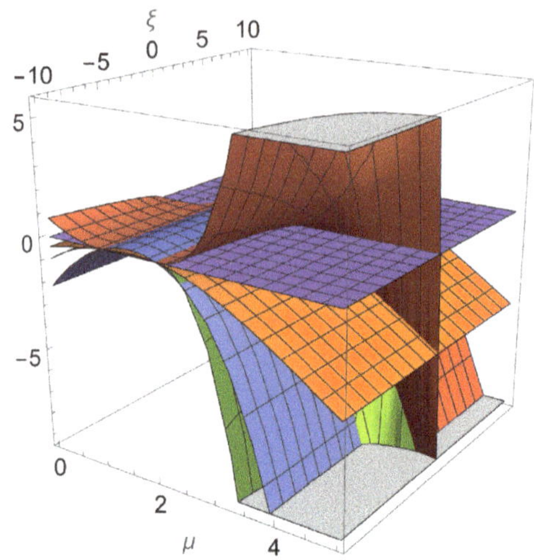

Figure 12. Real parts of the eigenvalues associated with P_2. This shows that the point is a sink if $(\mu, \xi) \in \Psi$, or a saddle (assuming $\xi \geq 0$). For reference, the magenta-colored plane corresponds to the value zero, and the other colors denote the real parts of the four eigenvalues.

3. The equilibrium point $P_3 : \left(0, 0, 0, \frac{1}{6}(9 - 2\mu + r)\right)$. The equation of state parameter is $w = \frac{r-7}{4(\mu-1)}$. The eigenvalues are as follows:
$\left\{\frac{1}{3}(9 - 2\mu + r), \frac{1}{6}(2\mu(-8\mu + r + 36) - 3(3r + 35)), \frac{1}{36}(9(21 - 4\mu)\mu + 9(\mu - 3)r - 279 - s_+),\right.$
$\left.\frac{1}{36}(9(21 - 4\mu)\mu + 9(\mu - 3)r - 279 + s_+)\right\}$ where $r = \sqrt{8\mu(2\mu - 9) + 105}$, and s_+ is the positive square root of $s_+^2 = 81((21 - 4\mu)\mu + (\mu - 3)r - 31)^2 + 48\xi(\mu(\mu(2(933 - 82\mu)\mu - 8355) + 17{,}361) + (\mu(5\mu(8\mu - 75) + 1209) - 1413)r - 14{,}481)$. The point is always saddle, as shown in Figure 13.

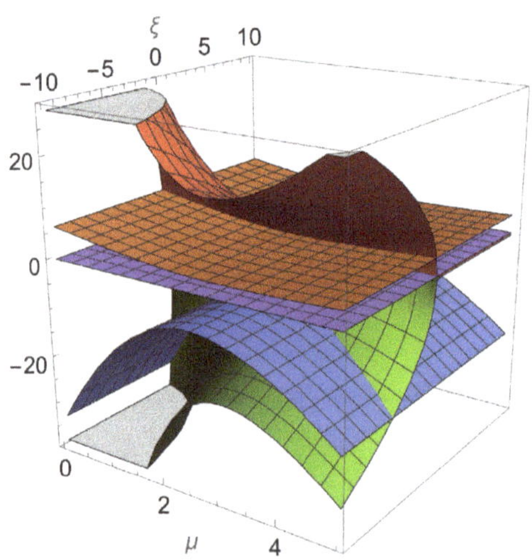

Figure 13. Real parts of the eigenvalues associated with P_3. Hence, the point is a saddle. For reference, the magenta-colored plane corresponds to the value zero, and the other colors denote the real parts of the four eigenvalues.

4. The equilibrium point $P_4 : \left(0, -\frac{1}{\sqrt{\xi}}, 0, \frac{1}{2}\right)$. The equation of state parameter is indeterminate. The eigenvalues are

$\left\{-\frac{1}{2}, 1, \frac{1}{4}\left(2\mu - \sqrt{8\mu - 19} - 2\right), \frac{1}{4}\left(2\mu + \sqrt{8\mu - 19} - 2\right)\right\}$. Eigenvalue 1 corresponds to the coordinate Ω_Λ. This point is always a saddle when $\Omega_\Lambda \neq 0$. In the invariant set $\Omega_\Lambda = 0$, they can be attractors if $\mu < 1$. For $\mu = 1$, the eigenvalues reduce to $-\frac{1}{2}, \pm i\frac{\sqrt{11}}{4}$, and as shown in the lower panel of Figure 14, we see spiral attractors. The analysis of this invariant set is presented in Section 3.3.3.

5. The equilibrium point $P_5 : \left(0, \frac{1}{\sqrt{\xi}}, 0, \frac{1}{2}\right)$. The equation of state parameter is indeterminate. The eigenvalues are $\left\{-\frac{1}{2}, 1, \frac{1}{4}\left(2\mu - \sqrt{8\mu - 19} - 2\right), \frac{1}{4}\left(2\mu + \sqrt{8\mu - 19} - 2\right)\right\}$. Eigenvalue 1 corresponds to the coordinate Ω_Λ. This point is always a saddle when $\Omega_\Lambda \neq 0$. In the invariant set where $\Omega_\Lambda = 0$, they can be attractors if $\mu < 1$. For $\mu = 1$, the eigenvalues reduce to $-\frac{1}{2}, \pm i\frac{\sqrt{11}}{4}$, and as shown in the lower panel in Figure 14, are spiral attractors. The analysis of this invariant set is presented in Section 3.3.3.

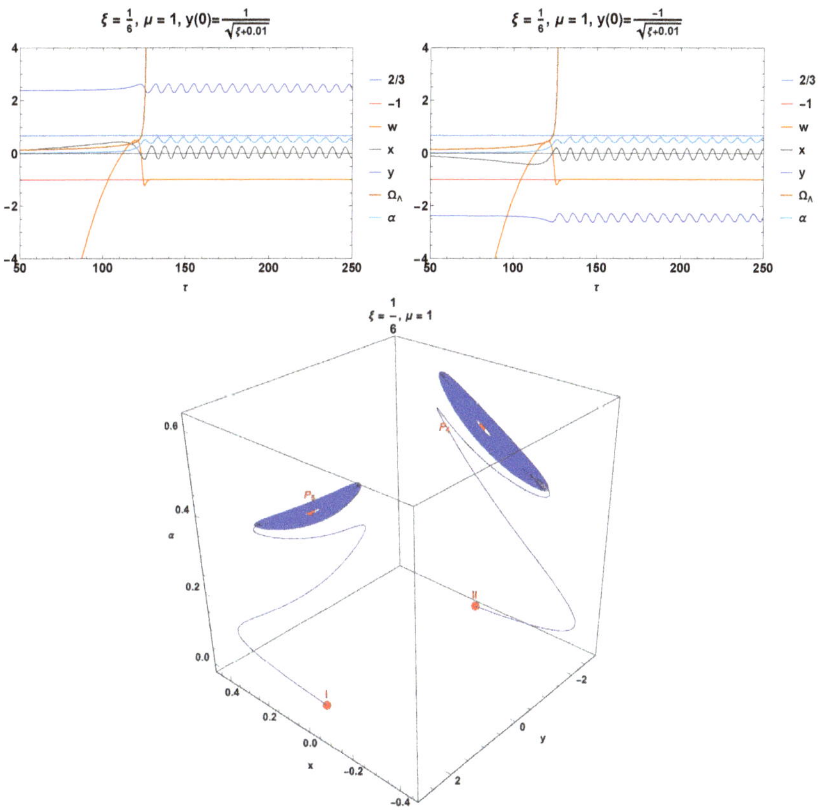

Figure 14. The upper panels show the numerical solutions $x(\tau)$, $y(\tau)$, $\Omega_\Lambda(\tau)$, and $\alpha(\tau)$ of systems (256)–(259), as well as the effective equation of the state of matter $w(\tau)$ defined in (254) for $\mu = 1$. Two spiral orbits of the system, starting at the initial conditions labeled I and II in Table 4, asymptotically tend to the equilibrium points P_4 and P_5.

There are additional points that cancel out the numerator and denominator, such as the following:

6. The set $P_6(x_c) : \left(x_c, -\frac{1}{\sqrt{\xi}}, \Omega_{\Lambda 0}, 0\right)$.
7. The line $P_7(x_c) : \left(x_c, -\frac{1}{\sqrt{\xi}}, 0, 0\right)$. In both cases, the stability analysis of these point curves will be left for future research since it cannot be implemented with the techniques developed in this paper.

8. The line $P_8 : \left(0, -\frac{1}{\sqrt{\xi}}, \Omega_{\Lambda 0}, 0\right)$. The eigenvalues are $\left\{-2, 4, \frac{\mu-\sqrt{\mu-1}-1}{\alpha} + o(1), \frac{\mu+\sqrt{\mu-1}-1}{\alpha} + o(1)\right\}$ when $\alpha \to 0$. Therefore, this point is a saddle.
9. The point $P_9 : \left(0, -\frac{1}{\sqrt{\xi}}, 0, 0\right)$. The eigenvalues are $\left\{-2, 4, \frac{\mu-\sqrt{\mu-1}-1}{\alpha} + o(1), \frac{\mu+\sqrt{\mu-1}-1}{\alpha} + o(1)\right\}$ when $\alpha \to 0$. Therefore, this point is a saddle.
10. The set $P_{10}(x_c) : \left(x_c, \frac{1}{\sqrt{\xi}}, \Omega_{\Lambda 0}, 0\right)$.
11. The line $P_{11}(x_c) : \left(x_c, \frac{1}{\sqrt{\xi}}, 0, 0\right)$. In both cases, the stability analysis of these point curves will be left for future research since it cannot be implemented with the techniques developed in this paper.
12. The line $P_{12} : \left(0, \frac{1}{\sqrt{\xi}}, \Omega_{\Lambda 0}, 0\right)$. The eigenvalues are $\left\{-2, 4, \frac{\mu-\sqrt{\mu-1}-1}{\alpha} + o(1), \frac{\mu+\sqrt{\mu-1}-1}{\alpha} + o(1)\right\}$ when $\alpha \to 0$. Therefore, this point is a saddle.
13. The point $P_{13} : \left(0, \frac{1}{\sqrt{\xi}}, 0, 0\right)$. The eigenvalues are $\left\{-2, 4, \frac{\mu-\sqrt{\mu-1}-1}{\alpha} + o(1), \frac{\mu+\sqrt{\mu-1}-1}{\alpha} + o(1)\right\}$ when $\alpha \to 0$. Therefore, this point is a saddle. All have indeterminate parameters of the equation of the state of matter.
14. The line $\left(0, -\frac{1}{\sqrt{\xi(12\xi+1)}}, \Omega_{\Lambda 0}, -\mu - \sqrt{\mu(2\mu-11)+18} + 4\right)$.
15. The line $\left(0, -\frac{1}{\sqrt{\xi(12\xi+1)}}, \Omega_{\Lambda 0}, -\mu + \sqrt{\mu(2\mu-11)+18} + 4\right)$.
16. The line $\left(0, \frac{1}{\sqrt{\xi(12\xi+1)}}, \Omega_{\Lambda 0}, -\mu - \sqrt{\mu(2\mu-11)+18} + 4\right)$.
17. The line $\left(0, \frac{1}{\sqrt{\xi(12\xi+1)}}, \Omega_{\Lambda 0}, -\mu + \sqrt{\mu(2\mu-11)+18} + 4\right)$. Stability can be determined numerically since the Jacobian matrix has infinite entries.

In these four cases, the stability analysis of these curves/sets of points will be left for future research since it cannot be implemented with the techniques developed in this paper. They all have infinitely complex parameters of the equation of the state of matter.

In Figure 14, the top panels show the numerical solutions $x(\tau)$, $y(\tau)$, $\Omega_\Lambda(\tau)$, and $\alpha(\tau)$ of systems (256)–(259), as well as the effective equation of the state of matter $w(\tau)$ defined in (254). The values of the parameters ξ and μ are shown in the figure. In both cases, the equation of state $w(\tau)$ begins in a phantom regime ($w < -1$), crosses the matter-dominated region ($w = 0$), and tends asymptotically toward a de Sitter regime ($w = -1$). Two spiral orbits of the system starting at the initial conditions labeled I and II in Table 4 asymptotically tend to the equilibrium points P_4 and P_5.

The upper panels of Figure 15 show the numerical solutions $x(\tau)$, $y(\tau)$, $\Omega_\Lambda(\tau)$, and $\alpha(\tau)$ of systems (256)–(259), as well as the effective equation of the state of matter $w(\tau)$ defined in (254) for $\mu < 1$. Two spiral orbits of the system, starting at the initial conditions labeled I and II in Table 4, asymptotically tend the equilibrium points, P_4 and P_5.

Table 4. List of initial conditions used in the numerical integration of systems (256)–(259). The values of ξ and μ considered are the following: (a) $\xi = 1/6$ and $\mu = 1.0$ in Figure 14, (b) $\xi = 1/6$ and $\mu = 0.9$ in Figure 15, (c) $\xi = 1/6$ and $\mu = 1.1$ in Figure 16 and (d) $\xi = 4$ and $\mu = 1.1$ in Figure 17.

Sol.	$x(0)$	$y(0)$	$\Omega_\Lambda(0)$	$\alpha(0)$
$I.$	0.01	$\frac{1}{\sqrt{\xi}+0.01}$	0.1	0.01
II	0.01	$\frac{-1}{\sqrt{\xi}+0.01}$	0.1	0.01

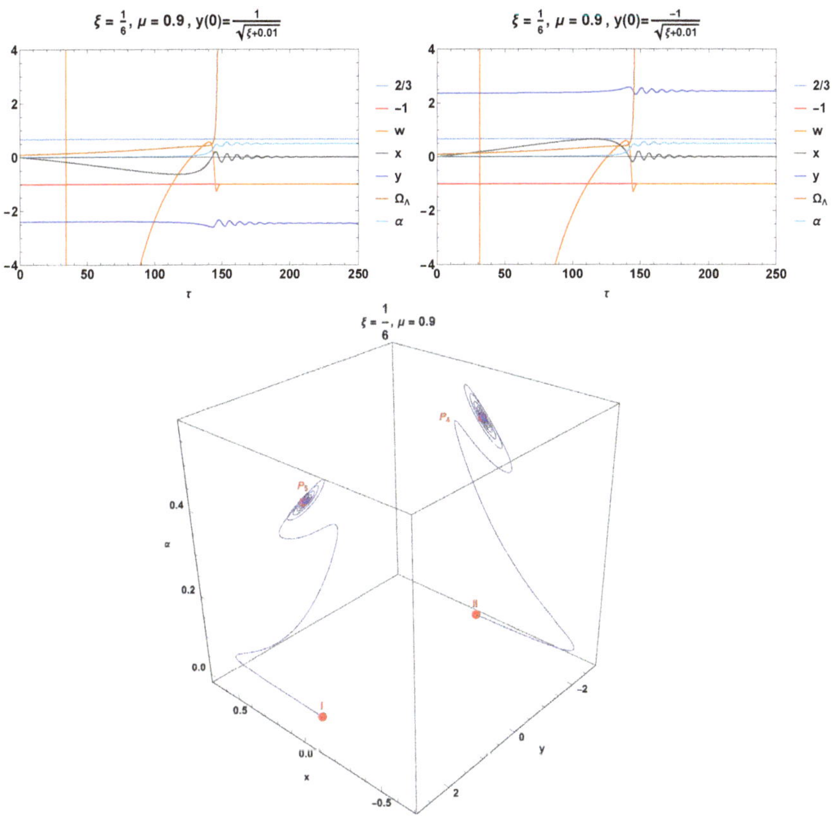

Figure 15. The upper panels show the numerical solution $x(\tau)$, $y(\tau)$, $\Omega_\Lambda(\tau)$ and $\alpha(\tau)$ of systems (256)–(259), as well as the effective equation of the state of matter $w(\tau)$ defined in (254) for $\mu < 1$. Two spiral orbits of the system, starting at the initial conditions labeled I and II in Table 4, asymptotically tend the equilibrium points P_4 and P_5.

In Figure 16, the top panels show the numerical solutions $x(\tau)$, $y(\tau)$, $\Omega_\Lambda(\tau)$, and $\alpha(\tau)$ of systems (256)–(259), as well as the effective equation of state $w(\tau)$ defined in (254). The values of the parameters ξ and μ are shown in the figure. In both cases, the equation of state $w(\tau)$ begins in a phantom regime ($w < -1$), crosses the matter-dominated region ($w = 0$), and tends asymptotically toward a de Sitter regime ($w = -1$). The oscillating behavior of the functions $x(\tau)$, $y(\tau)$, $\Omega_\Lambda(\tau)$ and $\alpha(\tau)$ is still present but exhibits a greater amplitude compared to that shown in Figure 14. Two orbits starting at the initial conditions labeled I and II in Table 4 tend asymptotically to a limit cycle.

Figure 17 presents the dynamics in the invariant set $\Omega_\Lambda = 0$ of systems (256)–(259) for the values of the parameters $\xi = 4$ and $\mu = 1.1$. Two orbits that begin at the initial conditions labeled I and II in Table 4 tend to the saddle points P_4 and P_5 and then form an unstable spiral centered on said points.

Finally, in Figure 18, phase diagrams are presented for the (256)–(259) systems for different values of the parameters ξ and μ.

In this section, we numerically examined the invariant set $\Omega_\Lambda = 0$ of the (256)–(259) systems. However, to characterize such an invariant set analytically, we will present a comprehensive analysis of dynamical systems in Section 3.3.3.

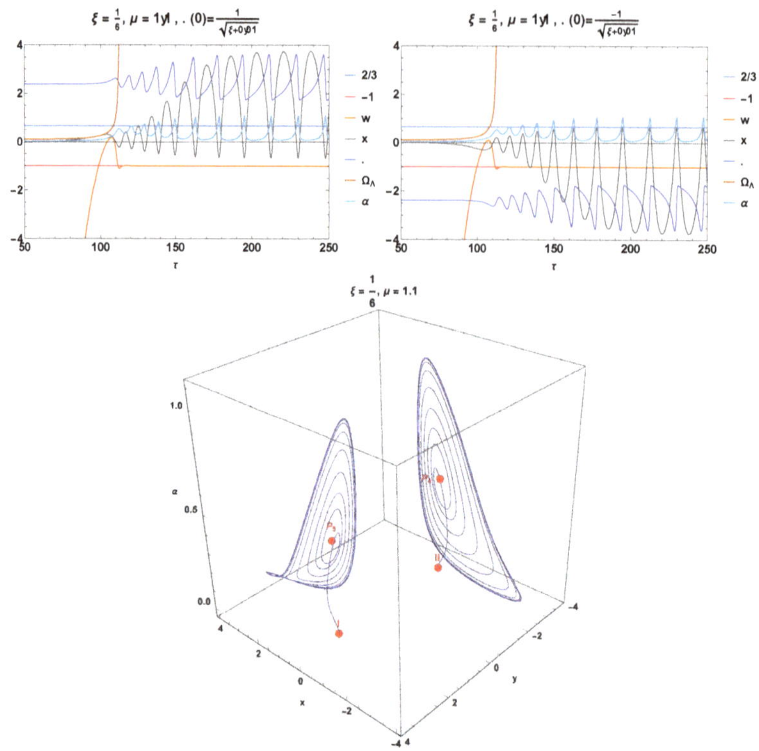

Figure 16. The upper panels show the numerical solutions $x(\tau)$, $y(\tau)$, $\Omega_\Lambda(\tau)$, and $\alpha(\tau)$ of systems (256)–(259), as well as the effective state equation $w(\tau)$ defined in (254) for $\mu > 1$. Two orbits starting at the initial conditions labeled I and II in Table 4 asymptotically tend to a limit cycle.

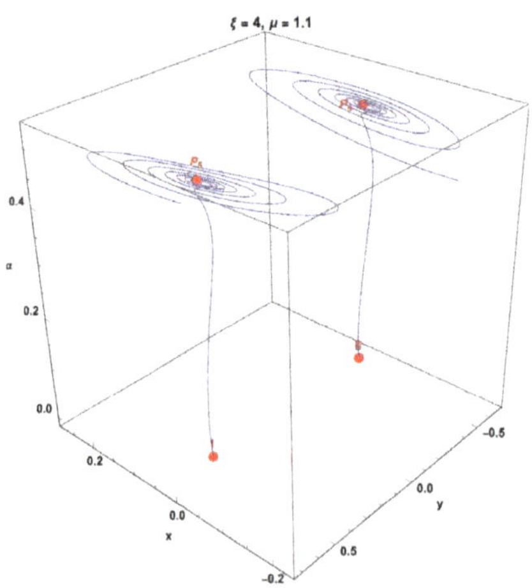

Figure 17. Dynamics in the invariant set $\Omega_\Lambda = 0$ of systems (256)–(259) for the values of the parameters $\xi = 4$ and $\mu = 1.1$. Two orbits that begin at the initial conditions labeled I and II in Table 4 tend to the saddle points P_4 and P_5 and then form an unstable spiral centered on said points.

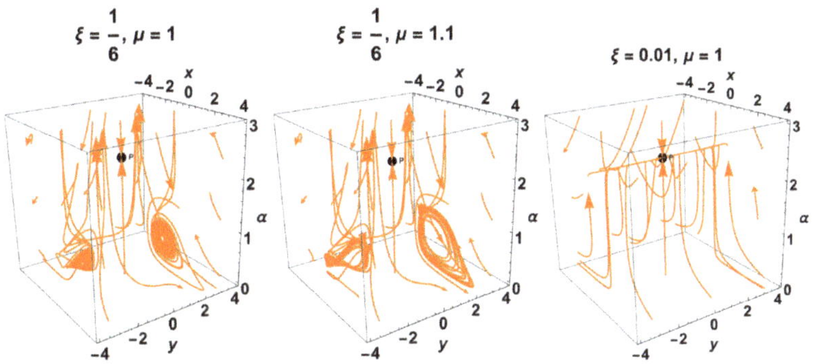

Figure 18. Phase diagrams for systems (256)–(259) for different values of the parameters ξ and μ.

3.3.3. Invariant Set $\Omega_\Lambda = 0$

Replacing $\Omega_\Lambda = 0$ in (251), and defining the new variables, we have the following:

$$x = \frac{\dot{\phi}(t)}{\sqrt{6}H(t)}, \quad y = \phi(t), \tag{263}$$

which satisfies

$$(x + \sqrt{6}\xi y)^2 + \xi y^2(1 - 6\xi) + \frac{(\mu - 1)(1 - \xi y^2)}{\alpha} + \Omega_m = 1, \tag{264}$$

where

$$\Omega_m = \frac{\rho_m}{3H^2} \tag{265}$$

is the dimensionless energy density of matter; we obtain an alternative formulation, which describes the dynamics on the invariant set $\Omega_\Lambda = 0$. The equation of state parameter of matter can be expressed in terms of the new variables as follows:

$$\begin{aligned} w = &\left\{\alpha\left(\xi(12\xi+1)y^2 - 1\right)\left(-\alpha + \mu + \alpha x^2 + \xi y\left(2\sqrt{6}\alpha x + y(\alpha - \mu + 1)\right) - 1\right)\right\}^{-1} \\ &\times \left\{\alpha^2\left[x^2\left(\xi\left(y^2 + 12\right) - 1\right) + 2\sqrt{6}\xi x y\left(\xi y^2 - 1\right) + \xi y^2\left(\xi y^2 - 2\right) + 1\right]\right. \\ &\left. + 2\alpha\left(\xi y^2 - 1\right)\left[\mu\left(\xi y\left(\sqrt{6}x + y\right) - 1\right) + \xi y\left(-\sqrt{6}x + 12\xi y - 3y\right) + 3\right] - (\mu - 2)(\mu - 1)\left(\xi y^2 - 1\right)^2\right\}. \end{aligned} \tag{266}$$

Introducing the derivative (255), we obtain the three-dimensional dynamical system as follows:

$$\begin{aligned} \alpha^2 G \frac{dx}{d\tau} = &-12\alpha^2\xi x^3 + 2\sqrt{6}\alpha\xi x^2 y(-6\alpha\xi + \alpha + \mu - 1) \\ &+ x\left(3\alpha\left(-\mu + 8(\mu - 1)\xi^2 y^2 + (\mu - 3)\xi y^2 + 3\right) - (\mu - 2)(\mu - 1)\left(\xi y^2 - 1\right)\right) \\ &+ \sqrt{6}\xi y\left(\alpha^2 + 2\alpha(\mu - 4) - (\mu - 2)(\mu - 1)\right)\left(\xi y^2 - 1\right), \end{aligned} \tag{267}$$

$$\frac{dy}{d\tau} = \sqrt{6}x, \tag{268}$$

$$\begin{aligned} \alpha G \frac{d\alpha}{d\tau} = &\, 3\alpha^2 + 2\alpha\mu - 9\alpha - \mu^2 + 3\mu + \xi\left(12\alpha^2 x^2 - 2\sqrt{6}\alpha x y(\alpha + \mu - 1)\right. \\ &\left. + y^2\left(-2\alpha\mu - 3(\alpha - 3)\alpha + \mu^2 - 3\mu + 2\right)\right) + 12(1 - 2\alpha)\alpha\xi^2 y^2 - 2, \end{aligned} \tag{269}$$

where

$$G := (\xi(12\xi + 1)y^2 - 1), \tag{270}$$

is defined on the phase space

$$(x+\sqrt{6}\xi y)^2+\xi y^2(1-6\xi)+\frac{(\mu-1)(1-\xi y^2)}{\alpha}\leq 1 \tag{271}$$

which corresponds to $\Omega_m \geq 0$.

Introducing the time-rescaling (262), which preserves the arrow of time, we obtain the system, as follows:

$$\begin{aligned} x' = & \frac{1}{\xi(12\xi+1)y^2-1}\Bigg[-12\alpha^2\xi x^3+2\sqrt{6}\alpha\xi x^2y(-6\alpha\xi+\alpha+\mu-1) \\ & +x\Big(3\alpha\Big(-\mu+8(\mu-1)\xi^2y^2+(\mu-3)\xi y^2+3\Big)-(\mu-2)(\mu-1)\Big(\xi y^2-1\Big)\Big) \\ & +\sqrt{6}\xi y\Big(\alpha^2+2\alpha(\mu-4)-(\mu-2)(\mu-1)\Big)\Big(\xi y^2-1\Big)\Bigg], \end{aligned} \tag{272}$$

$$y' = \sqrt{6}\alpha^2 x, \tag{273}$$

$$\begin{aligned} \alpha' = & \frac{\alpha}{\xi(12\xi+1)y^2-1}\Bigg[3\alpha^2+2\alpha\mu-9\alpha-\mu^2+3\mu+12(1-2\alpha)\alpha\xi^2y^2-2 \\ & +\xi\Big(12\alpha^2x^2-2\sqrt{6}\alpha xy(\alpha+\mu-1)+y^2\Big(-2\alpha\mu-3(\alpha-3)\alpha+\mu^2-3\mu+2\Big)\Big)\Bigg]. \end{aligned} \tag{274}$$

sometimes it is more useful to use the time variable $\tau=\ln(a/a_0)$.

The equilibrium points of systems (272), (273), and (274) in the coordinates (x,y,α) are as follows:

1. The equilibrium point curve $P_1:\left(-\sqrt{6}\xi y_c, y_c, 0\right)$ parameterized by $y_c\in\mathbb{R}$. The equation of state parameter is complex infinity. The eigenvalues are $\left\{0,-\frac{(\mu-2)(\mu-1)\left(\xi y^2-1\right)}{\xi(12\xi+1)y^2-1},\frac{(\mu-2)(\mu-1)\left(\xi y^2-1\right)}{\xi(12\xi+1)y^2-1}\right\}$. The curve is a saddle because it has at least two eigenvalues with different signs.
2. The equilibrium point $P_2:\left(0,0,\frac{1}{6}(9-2\mu-r)\right)$. There exists $(\alpha>0)$ for $1\leq\mu\leq 2$. The eigenvalues are $\Big\{\frac{1}{6}(-2\mu(8\mu+r-36)+9r-105)$, $\frac{1}{72}\left(-72\mu^2-u_--18r\mu+378\mu+54r-558\right)$, $\frac{1}{72}\left(-72\mu^2+u_--18r\mu+378\mu+54r-558\right)\Big\}$, where $r=\sqrt{8\mu(2\mu-9)+105}$ and u_- are the positive square roots of $u_-^2=324(\mu(4\mu+r-21)-3r+31)^2$ $-192(\mu(3(403r-5787)+\mu(2\mu(82\mu+20r-933)-375r+8355))-1413r+14,481)\xi$. The critical point is a saddle in its existence interval, as shown in Figure 19. The equation of state parameter is $w=\frac{-2\mu(r+9)+3r+35}{4\mu(2\mu-3)-4}$.
3. The equilibrium point $P_3:\left(0,0,\frac{1}{6}(9-2\mu+r)\right)$. The eigenvalues are $\Big\{\frac{1}{6}(2\mu(-8\mu+r+36)-3(3r+35))$, $\frac{1}{72}\left(-u_+-72\mu^2+18r\mu+378\mu-54r-558\right)$, $\frac{1}{72}\left(u_+-72\mu^2+18r\mu+378\mu-54r-558\right)\Big\}$, where $r=\sqrt{8\mu(2\mu-9)+105}$ and u_+ are the positive square roots of the following: $u_+^2=324\left(4\mu^2-(r+21)\mu+3r+31\right)^2$ $+192(\mu(3(403r+5787)+\mu(2\mu(-82\mu+20r+933)-15(25r+557)))-9(157r+1609))\xi$. P_3 is a sink for $\left\{\mu>2, 0<\xi\leq\frac{1}{48}\right\}\cup\left\{\mu=1, 0<\xi\leq\frac{27}{154}\right\}\cup\left\{\mu=2, 0<\xi\leq\frac{27}{280}\right\}$ $\cup\left\{\mu+\frac{1}{4}\left(-5-\frac{9}{\sqrt[3]{58+\sqrt{4093}}}+\sqrt[3]{58+\sqrt{4093}}\right)=0, 0<\xi\leq-\frac{27(\mu-3)}{4(2\mu^3-3\mu^2-12\mu+90)}\right\}$

$$\cup\left\{0<\mu<\frac{1}{4}\left(5-\frac{9}{\sqrt[3]{\sqrt{4093}-58}}+\sqrt[3]{\sqrt{4093}-58}\right),0<\xi\leq\frac{1}{48}\right\}$$
$$\cup\left\{\frac{1}{4}\left(5-\frac{9}{\sqrt[3]{\sqrt{4093}-58}}+\sqrt[3]{\sqrt{4093}-58}\right)<\mu<1,0<\xi\leq\frac{1}{48}\right\}.$$

It is a saddle otherwise.
The equation of state parameter is $w=\frac{2\mu(r-9)-3r+35}{4\mu(2\mu-3)-4}$.

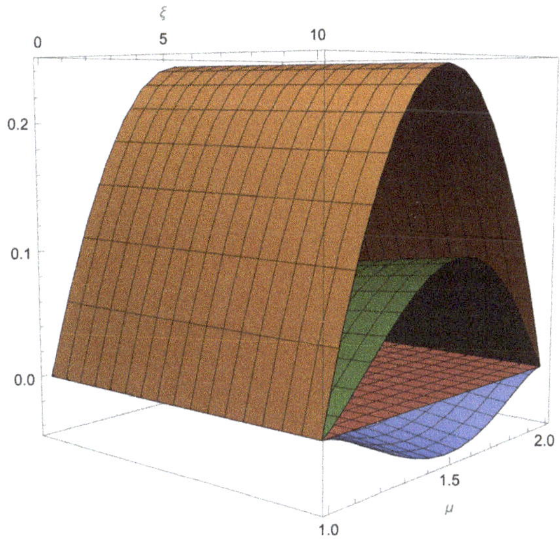

Figure 19. Eigenvalues of P_2 show that the point is a saddle. For reference, the red plane corresponds to the value zero, and the other colors denote the three eigenvalues; two are non-negative, and one is non-positive.

4. The equilibrium point $P_4:\left(0,-\frac{1}{\sqrt{\xi}},\frac{1}{2}\right)$. The eigenvalues are $\left\{-\frac{1}{2},\frac{1}{4}(2\mu-\sqrt{8\mu-19}-2),\frac{1}{4}(2\mu+\sqrt{8\mu-19}-2)\right\}$. The equation of state parameter is $w=\frac{1}{24\left(\xi^{3/2}+\xi\right)}$. The point is a sink for $0<\mu<1$ and $\xi>0$ and becomes a saddle for $\mu>1$, as shown in Figure 17.
5. The equilibrium point $P_5:\left(0,\frac{1}{\sqrt{\xi}},\frac{1}{2}\right)$. The eigenvalues are $\left\{-\frac{1}{2},\frac{1}{4}(2\mu-\sqrt{8\mu-19}-2),\frac{1}{4}(2\mu+\sqrt{8\mu-19}-2)\right\}$. The equation of state parameter is $w=\frac{1}{24\left(\xi^{3/2}+\xi\right)}$. The point is a sink for $0<\mu<1$ and $\xi>0$ and is a saddle for $\mu>1$, as shown in Figure 17.
6. The equilibrium point $P_7:\left(x_c,-\frac{1}{\sqrt{\xi}},0\right)$.
7. The equilibrium point $P_9:\left(0,-\frac{1}{\sqrt{\xi}},0\right)$. The equation of state parameter is $w=0$.
8. The equilibrium point $P_{11}:\left(x_c,\frac{1}{\sqrt{\xi}},0\right)$.
9. The equilibrium point $P_{13}:\left(0,\frac{1}{\sqrt{\xi}},0\right)$. The equation of state parameter is $w=0$.
   Due to the complexity of the stability analysis of these four points, it will be left for future research since it cannot be implemented with the techniques developed in this paper.
10. The equilibrium points $\left(0,-\frac{1}{\sqrt{\xi(12\xi+1)}},-\mu-\sqrt{\mu(2\mu-11)+18}+4\right)$.
11. The equilibrium points $\left(0,-\frac{1}{\sqrt{\xi(12\xi+1)}},-\mu+\sqrt{\mu(2\mu-11)+18}+4\right)$.

12. The equilibrium points $\left(0, \frac{1}{\sqrt{\xi(12\xi+1)}}, -\mu - \sqrt{\mu(2\mu - 11) + 18} + 4\right)$.
13. The equilibrium points $\left(0, \frac{1}{\sqrt{\xi(12\xi+1)}}, -\mu + \sqrt{\mu(2\mu - 11) + 18} + 4\right)$.

In all four cases, the equation of state parameter is complex and infinite. Due to the complexity of the stability analysis of this set of equilibrium points, numerical solution methods can be used. Since the stability analysis of these four points is very complex, it will be left for future research since it cannot be implemented with the techniques developed in this paper.

3.3.4. Asymptotic Expansions for $\varepsilon := \mu - 1 \to 0$

Next, we will study the perturbation problem related to the study of the phase portrait of a system of differential equations, as follows:

$$\dot{x} = X(x;\varepsilon), \quad x \in \mathbb{R}^3, \quad \varepsilon \sim 0 \tag{275}$$

in a neighborhood of the origin, where the unperturbed vector field is as follows: $X(x;0)$ [103–109].

To obtain asymptotic expansions for $\mu \to 1$, the reparametrization $\varepsilon := \mu - 1$ is introduced and the limit $\varepsilon \to 0$ is analyzed using the asymptotic expansion, as follows:

$$\rho = \rho_0 + \varepsilon\rho_1 + \mathcal{O}(\varepsilon^2), \; p = p_0 + \varepsilon p_1 + \mathcal{O}(\varepsilon^2), \; H = H_0 + \varepsilon H_1 + \mathcal{O}(\varepsilon^2), \; \phi = \phi_0 + \varepsilon\phi_1 + \mathcal{O}(\varepsilon^2).$$

After making the substitution in the field equations and comparing the coefficients with equal powers of ε, the following is obtained.

At **order** 0, we have the following equations:

$$\dot{H}_0 = \frac{2t\xi\dot{\phi_0}^2 - 2t\xi H_0\phi_0\dot{\phi}_0 + 3H_0\left(-\xi((8\xi t + t)H_0 - 2)\phi_0^2 + tH_0 - 2\right)}{t\left(\xi(12\xi + 1)\phi_0^2 - 1\right)}, \tag{276}$$

$$\ddot{\phi}_0 = \frac{-12t\xi^2\phi_0\dot{\phi_0}^2 - 3tH_0\left(\xi(8\xi + 1)\phi_0^2 - 1\right)\dot{\phi}_0 + 6\xi H_0(tH_0 - 6)\phi_0\left(\xi\phi_0^2 - 1\right)}{t\left(\xi(12\xi + 1)\phi_0^2 - 1\right)}, \tag{277}$$

and the auxiliary equation is as follows:

$$\begin{aligned}\dot{\rho}_0 = {}& \frac{3H_0}{t\left(\xi(12\xi + 1)\phi_0^2 - 1\right)}\left[t\left(\xi(6\xi + 1)\phi_0^2 + 6\xi - 1\right)\dot{\phi_0}^2 + 12t\xi H_0\phi_0\left(\xi(6\xi + 1)\phi_0^2 - 1\right)\dot{\phi}_0\right. \\ & \left. + 6H_0\left(\xi\phi_0^2 - 1\right)\left(\xi(12\xi + (6\xi t + t)H_0 - 2)\phi_0^2 - tH_0 + 2\right)\right],\end{aligned} \tag{278}$$

and the constraints are as follows:

$$\rho_0 = 3\left(1 - \xi\phi_0^2\right)H_0^2 - 6\xi\phi_0\dot{\phi}_0 H_0 - \frac{1}{2}\dot{\phi_0}^2 - \Lambda, \tag{279}$$

$$\begin{aligned}p_0 = {}& -\frac{1}{2t\left(\xi(12\xi + 1)\phi_0^2 - 1\right)}\left[6tH_0^2\left(\xi\phi_0^2 - 1\right)^2 + 12H_0(\xi\phi_0(2(6\xi - 1)\phi_0 + t\dot{\phi}_0) + 2)\left(\xi\phi_0^2 - 1\right)\right. \\ & \left. + t\left(\xi\phi_0^2 + 12\xi - 1\right)\dot{\phi_0}^2 + 2t\Lambda\left(1 - \xi(12\xi + 1)\phi_0^2\right)\right].\end{aligned} \tag{280}$$

At **order** 1, we have the following equations:

$$
\begin{aligned}
\dot{H}_1 = & \frac{1}{t^2\left(\xi(12\xi+1)\phi_0^2-1\right)^2}\Bigg[-24\xi^2 H_0^2\phi_0\phi_1 t^2 + 4\xi\left(\xi(12\xi+1)\phi_0^2-1\right)\dot{\phi}_0\dot{\phi}_1 t^2 \\
& - 2H_1\left(\xi(12\xi+1)\phi_0^2-1\right)(\xi\phi_0(t\dot{\phi}_0-3\phi_0)+3)t \\
& + 2H_0\Bigg(3tH_1\left(\xi\phi_0^2\left(-\xi(8\xi+1)(12\xi+1)\phi_0^2+20\xi+2\right)-1\right) \\
& + \xi\Big\{-\xi(12\xi+1)\phi_0^4 - t\xi(12\xi+1)\dot{\phi}_1\phi_0^3 + (t(12\xi+1)\phi_1\dot{\phi}_0\xi+12\xi+2)\phi_0^2 \\
& + (72\xi\phi_1+t\dot{\phi}_1)\phi_0 + t\phi_1\dot{\phi}_0\Big\} - 1\Bigg)t \\
& + 2\xi(6\xi+1)\phi_0^2 + \xi\phi_0\left(2t\dot{\phi}_0 - \xi(12\xi+1)\left(\phi_0^3+2t\dot{\phi}_0\phi_0^2+4t^2\phi_1\dot{\phi}_0{}^2\right)\right) - 1\Bigg],
\end{aligned}
\tag{281}
$$

$$
\begin{aligned}
\dot{\phi}_1 = & \frac{1}{t^2\left(\xi(12\xi+1)\phi_0^2-1\right)^2}\Bigg[6\xi^3(12\xi+1)(2t(H_0+(tH_0-3)H_1)+1)\phi_0^5 \\
& + t\xi^2(12\xi+1)\left(6t\xi\phi_1 H_0^2 - 36\xi\phi_1 H_0 - 3t(8\xi+1)\dot{\phi}_1 H_0 + (24\xi-3t(8\xi+1)H_1+1)\dot{\phi}_0\right)\phi_0^4 \\
& + 12\xi^2\left(-2\xi(12\xi+1)\dot{\phi}_0\dot{\phi}_1 t^2 - (6\xi+1)(2t(H_0+(tH_0-3)H_1)+1)\right)\phi_0^3 \\
& + 2t\xi\Big\{6t\xi(6\xi-1)\phi_1 H_0^2 + 3(12(1-6\xi)\xi\phi_1 + t(10\xi+1)\dot{\phi}_1)H_0 \\
& + \dot{\phi}_0\left(6t(12\xi+1)\phi_1\dot{\phi}_0\xi^2 - 18\xi + 3t(10\xi+1)H_1 - 1\right)\Big\}\phi_0^2 \\
& + 6\xi(2t(-3H_1+H_0(tH_1-2t\xi\phi_1\dot{\phi}_0+1)+2t\xi\dot{\phi}_0\dot{\phi}_1)+1)\phi_0 \\
& + t\left(6t\xi\phi_1 H_0^2 - 3(12\xi\phi_1+t\dot{\phi}_1)H_0 + \dot{\phi}_0\left(12t\phi_1\dot{\phi}_0\xi^2 - 3tH_1 + 1\right)\right)\Bigg],
\end{aligned}
\tag{282}
$$

and the auxiliary equation is as follows:

$$\dot{\rho_1} = \frac{1}{t^2(\xi(12\xi+1)\phi_0^2-1)^2}\Bigg[36t^2\xi\phi_0\Big(\xi(6\xi+1)\Big(\xi(12\xi+1)\phi_0^2-2\Big)\phi_0^2-6\xi+1\Big)\phi_1 H_0^3$$
$$+3t\Bigg(18tH_1\Big(\xi\phi_0^2-1\Big)\Big(\xi(6\xi+1)\phi_0^2-1\Big)\Big(\xi(12\xi+1)\phi_0^2-1\Big)$$
$$+\xi\Big\{\xi^2(1-36\xi(16\xi+1))\phi_0^6+12\xi^2(12\xi+1)(2(6\xi-1)\phi_1+t(6\xi+1)\dot{\phi_1})\phi_0^5$$
$$+3\xi(24\xi(8\xi+1)+4t\xi(6\xi+1)(12\xi+1)\phi_1\dot{\phi_0}-1)\phi_0^4$$
$$-24\xi(2(6\xi-1)\phi_1+t(9\xi+1)\dot{\phi_1})\phi_0^3-3(8t(3\xi+1)\phi_1\dot{\phi_0}\xi+12\xi-1)\phi_0^2$$
$$+12((36\xi-2)\phi_1+t\dot{\phi_1})\phi_0+12t\phi_1\dot{\phi_0}\Big\}-1\Bigg)H_0^2$$
$$+3\Bigg(2\Big(\xi(6\xi+1)\phi_0^2+6\xi-1\Big)\Big(\xi(12\xi+1)\phi_0^2-1\Big)\dot{\phi_0}\dot{\phi_1}t^2$$
$$+24H_1\Big(\xi(12\xi+1)\phi_0^2-1\Big)\Big(\xi\phi_0\Big(\phi_0\Big(\xi(6\xi-1)\phi_0^2-6\xi+2\Big)+t\Big(\xi(6\xi+1)\phi_0^2-1\Big)\dot{\phi_0}\Big)-1\Big)t$$
$$+\xi\phi_0\Big\{\xi^2(12(5-24\xi)\xi+7)\phi_0^5+3\xi(8\xi(12\xi-5)-7)\phi_0^3+3(20\xi+7)\phi_0$$
$$-144t^2\xi^2\phi_1\dot{\phi_0}^2+2t\Big(\xi\Big(\Big(\xi-144\xi^3\Big)\phi_0^2-2\Big)\phi_0^2+1\Big)\dot{\phi_0}\Big\}-7\Bigg)H_0$$
$$+t(3tH_1-1)\Big(\xi(6\xi+1)\phi_0^2+6\xi-1\Big)\Big(\xi(12\xi+1)\phi_0^2-1\Big)\dot{\phi_0}^2\Bigg], \tag{283}$$

and the constraints are as follows:

$$\rho_1 = -6\xi\phi_0\phi_1 H_0^2 - \frac{3(2tH_1-1)(\xi\phi_0^2-1)H_0}{t} - 6\xi(H_1\phi_0+H_0\phi_1)\dot{\phi_0} - (6\xi H_0\phi_0+\dot{\phi_0})\dot{\phi_1}, \tag{284}$$

$$p_1 = -\frac{1}{t^2(\xi(12\xi+1)\phi_0^2-1)^2}\Bigg[-144t^2\phi_0\phi_1\dot{\phi_0}^2\xi^3+6t^2H_0^2\phi_0\Big(\xi\phi_0^2-1\Big)\Big(\xi(12\xi+1)\phi_0^2+12\xi-1\Big)\phi_1\xi$$
$$+6t\phi_0\Big(\xi\phi_0^2-1\Big)\Big(\xi(12\xi+1)\phi_0^2-1\Big)\dot{\phi_0}\xi+3\Big(\xi\phi_0^2-1\Big)^2\Big(\xi(12\xi+1)\phi_0^2-1\Big)$$
$$+6tH_1\Big(\xi\phi_0^2-1\Big)\Big(\xi(12\xi+1)\phi_0^2-1\Big)(\xi\phi_0(2(6\xi-1)\phi_0+t\dot{\phi_0})+2)$$
$$+t^2\Big(\xi\phi_0^2+12\xi-1\Big)\Big(\xi(12\xi+1)\phi_0^2-1\Big)\dot{\phi_0}\dot{\phi_1}+6tH_0\Big\{tH_1\Big(\xi(12\xi+1)\phi_0^2-1\Big)\Big(\xi\phi_0^2-1\Big)^2$$
$$+\xi\Big(\xi^2(12\xi+1)\phi_0^6+\xi^2(12\xi+1)(4(6\xi-1)\phi_1+t\dot{\phi_1})\phi_0^5+\xi(t\xi(12\xi+1)\phi_1\dot{\phi_0}-3(8\xi+1))\phi_0^4$$
$$-2\xi(4(6\xi-1)\phi_1+t(6\xi+1)\dot{\phi_1})\phi_0^3+(2t(6\xi-1)\phi_1\dot{\phi_0}\xi+12\xi+3)\phi_0^2$$
$$+((72\xi-4)\phi_1+t\dot{\phi_1})\phi_0+t\phi_1\dot{\phi_0}\Big)-1\Big\}\Bigg]. \tag{285}$$

For simplicity, we will solve the $\xi = 0$ case.
At **order** 0, we have the following equations:

$$\dot{H_0} = -\frac{3H_0(-2+tH_0)}{t}, \tag{286}$$
$$\dot{\rho_0} = -\frac{3H_0(-6H_0(2-tH_0)-t\dot{\phi}^2)}{t}, \tag{287}$$
$$\ddot{\phi_0} = -3H_0\dot{\phi_0}. \tag{288}$$

and the constraints are as follows:

$$\rho_0 = 3H_0^2 - \Lambda - \frac{1}{2}\dot{\phi_0}^2, \tag{289}$$

$$p_0 = \frac{6tH_0^2 - 24H_0 + 2\Lambda t - t\dot{\phi_0}^2}{2t}. \tag{290}$$

At **order** 1, we have the following equations:

$$\dot{H_1} = \frac{-1 + 6tH_1 + 2tH_0(-1 - 3tH_1)}{t^2}, \tag{291}$$

$$\dot{\rho_1} = \frac{1}{t^2}\left(3tH_0^2(-1 - 18tH_1) + t(-1 + 3tH_1)\dot{\phi_0}^2 + 3H_0\left(-7 + 24tH_1 + 2t^2\dot{\phi_0}\dot{\phi_1}\right)\right), \tag{292}$$

$$\ddot{\phi_1} = \frac{(1 - 3tH_1)\dot{\phi_0} - 3tH_0\dot{\phi_1}}{t}. \tag{293}$$

and the constraints are as follows:

$$\rho_1 = \frac{3H_0(2tH_1 - 1)}{t} - \dot{\phi_0}\dot{\phi_1}, \tag{294}$$

$$p_1 = -\frac{6tH_0(-tH_1 - 1) + 12tH_1 + t^2\dot{\phi_0}\dot{\phi_1} - 3}{t^2}. \tag{295}$$

Solving the resulting systems, we obtain the following:

$$H_0(t) = \frac{7t^6}{3t^7 + 7c_1}, \tag{296}$$

$$H_1(t) = \frac{-51t^{14} + 7c_2t^7 - 980c_1\ln(t)t^7 + 49c_1^2}{7t(3t^7 + 7c_1)^2}, \tag{297}$$

$$\rho_0(t) = \frac{147t^{12}}{(3t^7 + 7c_1)^2} - \frac{c_3^2}{2(3t^7 + 7c_1)^2} + c_4, \tag{298}$$

where c_1, c_2, c_3 and c_4 are integration constants.

$$\begin{aligned}
\phi_0(t) = c_5 + \frac{c_3}{7\sqrt[7]{3}7^{\frac{6}{7}}c_1^{\frac{6}{7}}}\Bigg[& -2\sin\left(\frac{\pi}{7}\right)\tan^{-1}\left(\cot\left(\frac{\pi}{7}\right) - \frac{\sqrt[7]{\frac{3}{7}}t\csc\left(\frac{\pi}{7}\right)}{\sqrt[7]{c_1}}\right) \\
&+ \ln\left(\sqrt[7]{3}7^{\frac{6}{7}}t + 7\sqrt[7]{c_1}\right) - \cos\left(\frac{\pi}{7}\right)\ln\left(3^{\frac{2}{7}}7^{\frac{5}{7}}t^2 - 2\sqrt[7]{3}7^{\frac{6}{7}}\sqrt[7]{c_1}\cos\left(\frac{\pi}{7}\right)t + 7c_1^{\frac{2}{7}}\right) \\
&+ \ln\left(3^{\frac{2}{7}}7^{\frac{5}{7}}t^2 + 2\sqrt[7]{3}7^{\frac{6}{7}}\sqrt[7]{c_1}\sin\left(\frac{3\pi}{14}\right)t + 7c_1^{\frac{2}{7}}\right)\sin\left(\frac{3\pi}{14}\right) \\
&- \ln\left(3^{\frac{2}{7}}7^{\frac{5}{7}}t^2 - 2\sqrt[7]{3}7^{\frac{6}{7}}\sqrt[7]{c_1}\sin\left(\frac{\pi}{14}\right)t + 7c_1^{\frac{2}{7}}\right)\sin\left(\frac{\pi}{14}\right) \\
&+ 2\tan^{-1}\left(\frac{\sqrt[7]{\frac{3}{7}}\sec\left(\frac{3\pi}{14}\right)t}{\sqrt[7]{c_1}} + \tan\left(\frac{3\pi}{14}\right)\right)\cos\left(\frac{3\pi}{14}\right) \\
&+ 2\tan^{-1}\left(\frac{\sqrt[7]{\frac{3}{7}}t\sec\left(\frac{\pi}{14}\right)}{\sqrt[7]{c_1}} - \tan\left(\frac{\pi}{14}\right)\right)\cos\left(\frac{\pi}{14}\right)\Bigg],
\end{aligned} \tag{299}$$

$$\begin{aligned}
\rho_1(t) = -\frac{1}{7(3t^7 + 7c_1)^3}\Bigg[& -189c_7t^{21} + 3465t^{19} - 1323c_1c_7t^{14} + 294(21c_1 - c_2)t^{12} \\
&+ 21\left(c_3c_6 - 147c_1^2c_7\right)t^7 + 5145c_1^2t^5 + 14c_1c_3^2 + c_2c_3^2 + 49c_1c_3c_6 - 2401c_1^3c_7 \\
&+ 4\left(10290c_1t^{12} + 18c_3^2t^7 + 7c_1c_3^2\right)\ln(t)\Bigg],
\end{aligned} \tag{300}$$

where c_5, c_6 and c_7 are integration constants.

Finally,

$$
\begin{aligned}
\phi_1(t) = &-\frac{9c_3\,{}_3F_2\left(\frac{8}{7},\frac{8}{7},2;\frac{15}{7},\frac{15}{7};-\frac{3t^7}{7c_1}\right)t^8}{2744{c_1}^2}+\frac{9c_3\,{}_2F_1\left(\frac{8}{7},2;\frac{15}{7};-\frac{3t^7}{7c_1}\right)\ln(t)t^8}{343{c_1}^2}+\frac{c_2c_3t}{343c_1\left(3t^7+7c_1\right)}+\frac{2c_3t}{49\left(3t^7+7c_1\right)}\\
&-\frac{4c_3\,{}_3F_2\left(\frac{1}{7},\frac{1}{7},2;\frac{8}{7},\frac{8}{7};-\frac{3t^7}{7c_1}\right)t}{49c_1}+\frac{4c_3\,{}_2F_1\left(\frac{1}{7},2;\frac{8}{7};-\frac{3t^7}{7c_1}\right)\ln(t)t}{49c_1}+c_8+\frac{2\left(\frac{3}{7}\right)^{\frac{6}{7}}c_2c_3\ln\left(\sqrt[7]{3}\,7^{\frac{6}{7}}t+7\sqrt[7]{c_1}\right)}{2401{c_1}^{\frac{13}{7}}}\\
&+\frac{4\left(\frac{3}{7}\right)^{\frac{6}{7}}c_3\ln\left(\sqrt[7]{3}\,7^{\frac{6}{7}}t+7\sqrt[7]{c_1}\right)}{343{c_1}^{\frac{6}{7}}}+\frac{c_6\ln\left(\sqrt[7]{3}\,7^{\frac{6}{7}}t+7\sqrt[7]{c_1}\right)}{7\sqrt[7]{3}\,7^{\frac{6}{7}}{c_1}^{\frac{6}{7}}}-\frac{2\left(\frac{3}{7}\right)^{\frac{6}{7}}c_2c_3\cos^2\left(\frac{\pi}{14}\right)\ln\left(3^{\frac{2}{7}}7^{\frac{5}{7}}t^2-2\sqrt[7]{3}\,7^{\frac{6}{7}}\sqrt[7]{c_1}\cos\left(\frac{\pi}{7}\right)t+7{c_1}^{\frac{2}{7}}\right)}{2401{c_1}^{\frac{13}{7}}}\\
&-\frac{4\left(\frac{3}{7}\right)^{\frac{6}{7}}c_3\cos^2\left(\frac{\pi}{14}\right)\ln\left(3^{\frac{2}{7}}7^{\frac{5}{7}}t^2-2\sqrt[7]{3}\,7^{\frac{6}{7}}\sqrt[7]{c_1}\cos\left(\frac{\pi}{7}\right)t+7{c_1}^{\frac{2}{7}}\right)}{343{c_1}^{\frac{6}{7}}}-\frac{c_6\cos^2\left(\frac{\pi}{14}\right)\ln\left(3^{\frac{2}{7}}7^{\frac{5}{7}}t^2-2\sqrt[7]{3}\,7^{\frac{6}{7}}\sqrt[7]{c_1}\cos\left(\frac{\pi}{7}\right)t+7{c_1}^{\frac{2}{7}}\right)}{7\sqrt[7]{3}\,7^{\frac{6}{7}}{c_1}^{\frac{6}{7}}}\\
&+\frac{3\left(\frac{3}{7}\right)^{\frac{6}{7}}c_2c_3\csc\left(\frac{\pi}{14}\right)\ln\left(3^{\frac{2}{7}}7^{\frac{5}{7}}t^2+2\sqrt[7]{3}\,7^{\frac{6}{7}}\sqrt[7]{c_1}\sin\left(\frac{3\pi}{14}\right)t+7{c_1}^{\frac{2}{7}}\right)\sin^2\left(\frac{\pi}{7}\right)}{4802{c_1}^{\frac{13}{7}}}\\
&+\frac{3\left(\frac{3}{7}\right)^{\frac{6}{7}}c_3\csc\left(\frac{\pi}{14}\right)\ln\left(3^{\frac{2}{7}}7^{\frac{5}{7}}t^2+2\sqrt[7]{3}\,7^{\frac{6}{7}}\sqrt[7]{c_1}\sin\left(\frac{3\pi}{14}\right)t+7{c_1}^{\frac{2}{7}}\right)\sin^2\left(\frac{\pi}{7}\right)}{343{c_1}^{\frac{6}{7}}}\\
&-\frac{4\left(\frac{3}{7}\right)^{\frac{6}{7}}\tan^{-1}\left(\cot\left(\frac{\pi}{7}\right)-\frac{\sqrt[7]{\frac{3}{7}}t\csc\left(\frac{\pi}{7}\right)}{\sqrt[7]{c_1}}\right)c_2c_3\sin\left(\frac{\pi}{7}\right)}{2401{c_1}^{\frac{13}{7}}}-\frac{8\left(\frac{3}{7}\right)^{\frac{6}{7}}\tan^{-1}\left(\cot\left(\frac{\pi}{7}\right)-\frac{\sqrt[7]{\frac{3}{7}}t\csc\left(\frac{\pi}{7}\right)}{\sqrt[7]{c_1}}\right)c_3\sin\left(\frac{\pi}{7}\right)}{343{c_1}^{\frac{6}{7}}}\\
&-\frac{2\tan^{-1}\left(\cot\left(\frac{\pi}{7}\right)-\frac{\sqrt[7]{\frac{3}{7}}t\csc\left(\frac{\pi}{7}\right)}{\sqrt[7]{c_1}}\right)c_6\sin\left(\frac{\pi}{7}\right)}{7\sqrt[7]{3}\,7^{\frac{6}{7}}{c_1}^{\frac{6}{7}}}-\frac{2\left(\frac{3}{7}\right)^{\frac{6}{7}}c_2c_3\ln\left(3^{\frac{2}{7}}7^{\frac{5}{7}}t^2+2\sqrt[7]{3}\,7^{\frac{6}{7}}\sqrt[7]{c_1}\sin\left(\frac{3\pi}{14}\right)t+7{c_1}^{\frac{2}{7}}\right)\sin^3\left(\frac{\pi}{14}\right)}{2401{c_1}^{\frac{13}{7}}}\\
&-\frac{4\left(\frac{3}{7}\right)^{\frac{6}{7}}c_3\ln\left(3^{\frac{2}{7}}7^{\frac{5}{7}}t^2+2\sqrt[7]{3}\,7^{\frac{6}{7}}\sqrt[7]{c_1}\sin\left(\frac{3\pi}{14}\right)t+7{c_1}^{\frac{2}{7}}\right)\sin^3\left(\frac{\pi}{14}\right)}{343{c_1}^{\frac{6}{7}}}-\frac{c_6\ln\left(3^{\frac{2}{7}}7^{\frac{5}{7}}t^2+2\sqrt[7]{3}\,7^{\frac{6}{7}}\sqrt[7]{c_1}\sin\left(\frac{3\pi}{14}\right)t+7{c_1}^{\frac{2}{7}}\right)\sin^3\left(\frac{\pi}{14}\right)}{7\sqrt[7]{3}\,7^{\frac{6}{7}}{c_1}^{\frac{6}{7}}}\\
&+\frac{2\left(\frac{3}{7}\right)^{\frac{6}{7}}c_2c_3\ln\left(3^{\frac{2}{7}}7^{\frac{5}{7}}t^2-2\sqrt[7]{3}\,7^{\frac{6}{7}}\sqrt[7]{c_1}\cos\left(\frac{\pi}{7}\right)t+7{c_1}^{\frac{2}{7}}\right)\sin^2\left(\frac{\pi}{14}\right)}{2401{c_1}^{\frac{13}{7}}}\\
&+\frac{4\left(\frac{3}{7}\right)^{\frac{6}{7}}c_3\ln\left(3^{\frac{2}{7}}7^{\frac{5}{7}}t^2-2\sqrt[7]{3}\,7^{\frac{6}{7}}\sqrt[7]{c_1}\cos\left(\frac{\pi}{7}\right)t+7{c_1}^{\frac{2}{7}}\right)\sin^2\left(\frac{\pi}{14}\right)}{343{c_1}^{\frac{6}{7}}}+\frac{c_6\ln\left(3^{\frac{2}{7}}7^{\frac{5}{7}}t^2-2\sqrt[7]{3}\,7^{\frac{6}{7}}\sqrt[7]{c_1}\cos\left(\frac{\pi}{7}\right)t+7{c_1}^{\frac{2}{7}}\right)\sin^2\left(\frac{\pi}{14}\right)}{7\sqrt[7]{3}\,7^{\frac{6}{7}}{c_1}^{\frac{6}{7}}}\\
&-\frac{12\left(\frac{3}{7}\right)^{\frac{6}{7}}\tan^{-1}\left(\frac{\sqrt[7]{\frac{3}{7}}\sec\left(\frac{3\pi}{14}\right)t}{\sqrt[7]{c_1}}+\tan\left(\frac{3\pi}{14}\right)\right)c_2c_3\cos\left(\frac{\pi}{14}\right)\sin^2\left(\frac{\pi}{14}\right)}{2401{c_1}^{\frac{13}{7}}}-\frac{24\left(\frac{3}{7}\right)^{\frac{6}{7}}\tan^{-1}\left(\frac{\sqrt[7]{\frac{3}{7}}\sec\left(\frac{3\pi}{14}\right)t}{\sqrt[7]{c_1}}+\tan\left(\frac{3\pi}{14}\right)\right)c_3\cos\left(\frac{\pi}{14}\right)\sin^2\left(\frac{\pi}{14}\right)}{343{c_1}^{\frac{6}{7}}}\\
&-\frac{2\left(\frac{3}{7}\right)^{\frac{6}{7}}\tan^{-1}\left(\frac{\sqrt[7]{\frac{3}{7}}\sec\left(\frac{3\pi}{14}\right)t}{\sqrt[7]{c_1}}+\tan\left(\frac{3\pi}{14}\right)\right)c_6\cos\left(\frac{\pi}{14}\right)\sin^2\left(\frac{\pi}{14}\right)}{7{c_1}^{\frac{6}{7}}}-\frac{2\left(\frac{3}{7}\right)^{\frac{6}{7}}c_2c_3\ln\left(3^{\frac{2}{7}}7^{\frac{5}{7}}t^2-2\sqrt[7]{3}\,7^{\frac{6}{7}}\sqrt[7]{c_1}\sin\left(\frac{\pi}{14}\right)t+7{c_1}^{\frac{2}{7}}\right)\sin\left(\frac{\pi}{14}\right)}{2401{c_1}^{\frac{13}{7}}}\\
&-\frac{4\left(\frac{3}{7}\right)^{\frac{6}{7}}c_3\ln\left(3^{\frac{2}{7}}7^{\frac{5}{7}}t^2-2\sqrt[7]{3}\,7^{\frac{6}{7}}\sqrt[7]{c_1}\sin\left(\frac{\pi}{14}\right)t+7{c_1}^{\frac{2}{7}}\right)\sin\left(\frac{\pi}{14}\right)}{343{c_1}^{\frac{6}{7}}}-\frac{c_6\ln\left(3^{\frac{2}{7}}7^{\frac{5}{7}}t^2-2\sqrt[7]{3}\,7^{\frac{6}{7}}\sqrt[7]{c_1}\sin\left(\frac{\pi}{14}\right)t+7{c_1}^{\frac{2}{7}}\right)\sin\left(\frac{\pi}{14}\right)}{7\sqrt[7]{3}\,7^{\frac{6}{7}}{c_1}^{\frac{6}{7}}}\\
&+\frac{\left(\frac{3}{7}\right)^{\frac{6}{7}}c_6\cos^2\left(\frac{\pi}{14}\right)\ln\left(3^{\frac{2}{7}}7^{\frac{5}{7}}t^2+2\sqrt[7]{3}\,7^{\frac{6}{7}}\sqrt[7]{c_1}\sin\left(\frac{3\pi}{14}\right)t+7{c_1}^{\frac{2}{7}}\right)\sin\left(\frac{\pi}{14}\right)}{7{c_1}^{\frac{6}{7}}}\\
&+\frac{4\left(\frac{3}{7}\right)^{\frac{6}{7}}\tan^{-1}\left(\frac{\sqrt[7]{\frac{3}{7}}\sec\left(\frac{3\pi}{14}\right)t}{\sqrt[7]{c_1}}+\tan\left(\frac{3\pi}{14}\right)\right)c_2c_3\cos^3\left(\frac{\pi}{14}\right)}{2401{c_1}^{\frac{13}{7}}}+\frac{8\left(\frac{3}{7}\right)^{\frac{6}{7}}\tan^{-1}\left(\frac{\sqrt[7]{\frac{3}{7}}\sec\left(\frac{3\pi}{14}\right)t}{\sqrt[7]{c_1}}+\tan\left(\frac{3\pi}{14}\right)\right)c_3\cos^3\left(\frac{\pi}{14}\right)}{343{c_1}^{\frac{6}{7}}}\\
&+\frac{2\tan^{-1}\left(\frac{\sqrt[7]{\frac{3}{7}}\sec\left(\frac{3\pi}{14}\right)t}{\sqrt[7]{c_1}}+\tan\left(\frac{3\pi}{14}\right)\right)c_6\cos^3\left(\frac{\pi}{14}\right)}{7\sqrt[7]{3}\,7^{\frac{6}{7}}{c_1}^{\frac{6}{7}}}+\frac{4\left(\frac{3}{7}\right)^{\frac{6}{7}}\tan^{-1}\left(\frac{\sqrt[7]{\frac{3}{7}}t\sec\left(\frac{\pi}{14}\right)}{\sqrt[7]{c_1}}-\tan\left(\frac{\pi}{14}\right)\right)c_2c_3\cos\left(\frac{\pi}{14}\right)}{2401{c_1}^{\frac{13}{7}}}\\
&+\frac{8\left(\frac{3}{7}\right)^{\frac{6}{7}}\tan^{-1}\left(\frac{\sqrt[7]{\frac{3}{7}}t\sec\left(\frac{\pi}{14}\right)}{\sqrt[7]{c_1}}-\tan\left(\frac{\pi}{14}\right)\right)c_3\cos\left(\frac{\pi}{14}\right)}{343{c_1}^{\frac{6}{7}}}+\frac{2\tan^{-1}\left(\frac{\sqrt[7]{\frac{3}{7}}t\sec\left(\frac{\pi}{14}\right)}{\sqrt[7]{c_1}}-\tan\left(\frac{\pi}{14}\right)\right)c_6\cos\left(\frac{\pi}{14}\right)}{7\sqrt[7]{3}\,7^{\frac{6}{7}}{c_1}^{\frac{6}{7}}},
\end{aligned}
\tag{301}
$$

where c_8 is an integration constant.

In Figure 20, $H(t)$, $\phi(t)$, and ρ are presented vs. the asymptotic expansions $H_0(t)$, $\phi_0(t)$, and ρ_0, defined, respectively, by (296), (299), and (298) for the initial conditions $\rho_m(0.1) = 1, H(0.1) = 1, \dot{\phi}(0.1) = 1, \phi(0.1) = 1$ (arbitrarily chosen), and the parameter values $c_1 = 9.571429 \times 10^{-7}$, $c_3 = 7 \times 10^{-6}$, $c_4 = -1.5$, $c_5 = 0.881801$, $\mu = 1.1, \xi =$

$\frac{1}{6}, V(\phi) = \Lambda = 1$ for $\varepsilon = 0.1$. The accuracy of the asymptotic approximation when $\varepsilon \to 0$ is illustrated as follows:

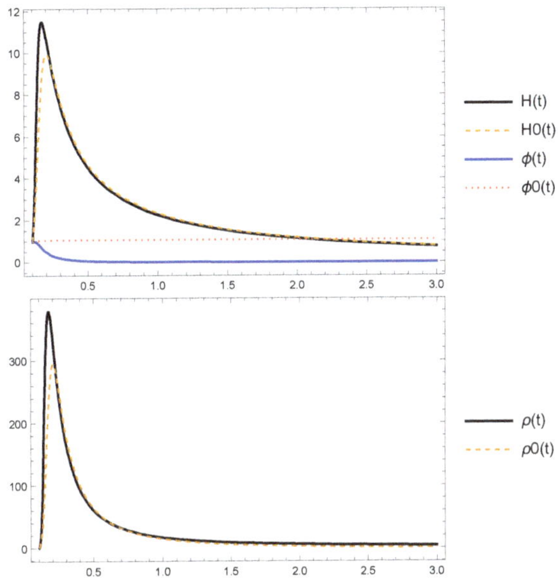

Figure 20. Numerical solutions $H(t)$, $\phi(t)$, and ρ vs. the asymptotic expansions $H_0(t)$, $\phi_0(t)$, and $\rho_0(t)$, defined, respectively, by (296), (299), and (298) (valid for $\xi = 0$) for the initial conditions $\rho_m(0.1) = 1, H(0.1) = 1, \dot{\phi}(0.1) = 1, \phi(0.1) = 1$, and the parameter values $c_1 = 9.571429 \times 10^{-7}$, $c_3 = 7 \times 10^{-6}, c_4 = -1.5, c_5 = 0.881801, \mu = 1.1, \xi = \frac{1}{6}, V(\phi) = \Lambda = 1$ for $\varepsilon = 0.1$. The accuracy of the asymptotic approximation is illustrated when $\varepsilon \to 0$, even though the analytical solutions are calculated for $\xi = 0$.

3.3.5. Asymptotic Expansions for $\xi \to 0$

We consider the following expansions:

$$\rho = \rho_0 + \xi\rho_1 + \mathcal{O}(\xi^2),\ H = H_0 + \xi H_1 + \mathcal{O}(\xi^2),\ \phi = \phi_0 + \xi\phi_1 + \mathcal{O}(\xi^2),$$

where we assume that the non-minimal coupling parameter is a perturbation parameter, $0 < \xi \ll 1$.

Replacing them in (183)–(185), we have the following:

$$\begin{aligned}
&-\frac{1}{t^3}\Big[-3t^3H_0\dot{\phi_0}^2 + 18t^3H_0^3 + 3\mu t^2H_0^2 - 39t^2H_0^2 - 3(\mu-1)(4\mu-11)tH_0 \\
&+3(\mu-2)(\mu-1)^2 + t^3\dot{\rho}_0 + \mu t^2\dot{\phi_0}^2 - t^2\dot{\phi_0}^2\Big] \\
&-\frac{\xi}{t^3}\Big[54t^3H_0^2H_1 + 6(\mu-13)^2H_0H_1 - 6t^3H_0\dot{\phi}_0\dot{\phi}_1 + 18t^3H_0\dot{\phi_0}^2 \\
&-18t^3H_0^3\phi_0^2 - 3t^2H_0^2\phi_0((\mu-13)\phi_0 + 12t\dot{\phi}_0) \\
&-6t^2H_0\phi_0((\mu-1)\dot{\phi}_0 + 3tV'(\phi_0)) \\
&+3(\mu-1)(4\mu-11)tH_0\phi_0^2 - 3tH_1\Big((\mu-1)(4\mu-11) + t^2\dot{\phi_0}^2\Big) \\
&+t^3\dot{\rho}_1 + 2(\mu-1)t^2\dot{\phi}_0\dot{\phi}_1 - 6\mu t^2\dot{\phi_0}^2 + 6\mu\phi_0V'(\phi_0) \\
&-6t^2\phi_0V(\phi_0) + 6t^2\dot{\phi_0}^2 - 3\mu^3\phi_0^2 + 6\mu^2t\phi_0\dot{\phi}_0 + 12\mu^2\phi_0^2 \\
&-12\mu t\phi_0\dot{\phi}_0 - 15\mu\phi_0^2 + 6t\phi_0\dot{\phi}_0 + 6\phi_0^2\Big] = 0,
\end{aligned} \tag{302}$$

$$
\begin{aligned}
&\frac{1}{t^2}\Big[-t^2\dot{H}_0-3t^2H_0^2-2\mu tH_0+8tH_0+(\mu-2)(\mu-1)\Big]\\
&+\frac{\xi}{t^2}\Big[-6t^2H_0H_1+2t^2H_0\phi_0\dot{\phi}_0\\
&-t^2\dot{H}_1-2(\mu-4)tH_1+2t^2\phi_0V'(\phi_0)-2t^2\dot{\phi_0}^2+2(\mu-1)t\phi_0\dot{\phi}_0\Big]=0, && (303)\\
&-\frac{1}{t^2}\Big[3t^2H_0\dot{\phi}_0+t^2V'(\phi_0)+t^2\ddot{\phi}_0-\mu t\dot{\phi}_0+t\dot{\phi}_0\Big]\\
&-\frac{\xi}{t^2}\Big[3t^2H_0\dot{\phi}_1+6\phi_0((\mu-2)(\mu-1)-tH_0(tH_0+2\mu-8))\\
&+3t^2H_1\dot{\phi}_0+t^2\phi_1V''(\phi_0)+t^2\ddot{\phi}_1-\mu t\dot{\phi}_1+t\dot{\phi}_1\Big]=0. && (304)
\end{aligned}
$$

Assuming a constant potential $V(\phi)=\Lambda$, the zeroth and first-order equations are as follows:

Zero order, $\mathcal{O}(\xi^0)$, as follows:

$$
\begin{aligned}
\dot{\rho}_0&=-\frac{(-3tH_0+\mu-1)\Big(t\Big(t\dot{\phi_0}^2-3H_0(2tH_0+\mu-5)\Big)+3(\mu-2)(\mu-1)\Big)}{t^3}, && (305)\\
\dot{H}_0&=\frac{tH_0(-3tH_0-2\mu+8)+(\mu-2)(\mu-1)}{t^2}, && (306)\\
\ddot{\phi}_0&=\frac{(-3tH_0+\mu-1)\dot{\phi}_0}{t}, && (307)
\end{aligned}
$$

with the constraint to order zero specified as follows:

$$
-\frac{(\mu-1)H_0}{t}+H_0^2+\frac{1}{6}\Big(-2(\Lambda+\rho_0)-\dot{\phi_0}^2\Big)=0. \tag{308}
$$

The last two equations have the general solution, as follows:

$$
\begin{aligned}
H_0(t)&=\frac{-2\mu-\frac{2c_1rt_0^r}{t^r+c_1t_0^r}+r+9}{6t}, && (309)\\
\phi_0(t)&=\frac{2c_2\left(\frac{t}{t_0}\right)^{\frac{1}{2}(4\mu+r-9)}{}_2F_1\left(1,\frac{r+4\mu-9}{2r};\frac{3r+4\mu-9}{2r};-\frac{\left(\frac{t}{t_0}\right)^r}{c_1}\right)}{c_1(4\mu+r-9)}+\phi_c, && (310)
\end{aligned}
$$

where c_1, c_2, and ϕ_c are integration constants. Therefore, the first equation reduces to the following:

$$
\begin{aligned}
\dot{\rho}_0=&-\frac{\left(2\mu+r\left(-\frac{1}{2}+\frac{c_1t_0^r}{t^r+c_1t_0^r}\right)-\frac{11}{2}\right)}{6t^3}\\
&\times\left(20\mu^2-75\mu-\frac{r^2(t^r-c_1t_0^r)^2}{(t^r+c_1t_0^r)^2}+\frac{(\mu-3)r(t^r-c_1t_0^r)}{t^r+c_1t_0^r}+\frac{6{c_2}^2t^{4\mu+r-9}t_0^{-4\mu+r+9}}{(t^r+c_1t_0^r)^2}+90\right), && (311)
\end{aligned}
$$

which is integrable, giving us the following solution:

$$
\begin{aligned}
\rho_0(t)=&\frac{r^3}{24t^2}+\frac{r^2\left(-5\mu-\frac{8c_1t^rt_0^r}{(t^r+c_1t_0^r)^2}+14\right)}{24t^2}-\frac{{c_2}^2t^{4\mu+r-11}t_0^{-4\mu+r+9}}{2(t^r+c_1t_0^r)^2}\\
&-\frac{r\left(16\mu^2-92\mu+\frac{8(5\mu-12)t^r}{t^r+c_1t_0^r}+153\right)}{24t^2}+\frac{5(4\mu-11)(\mu(4\mu-15)+18)}{24t^2}-\Lambda. && (312)
\end{aligned}
$$

where $c_3 = -\Lambda$ is an integration constant.

First order, $\mathcal{O}(\xi)$:

$$\dot{\rho_1} = \frac{1}{t^3}\Bigg[3tH_1\Big(t\Big(t\dot{\phi_0}^2 - 2H_0(9tH_0(t) + \mu - 13)\Big) + (\mu-1)(4\mu-11)\Big) + (-3tH_0 + \mu - 1)\Big(-6t\phi_0(2tH_0 + \mu - 1)\dot{\phi_0} + 3\phi_0^2((\mu-2)(\mu-1) - tH_0(2tH_0 + \mu - 5)) + 2t^2\dot{\phi_0}(3\dot{\phi_0} - \dot{\phi_1})\Big)\Bigg], \tag{313}$$

$$\dot{H_1} = -\frac{2\Big(H_1(3tH_0 + \mu - 4) - \phi_0(tH_0 + \mu - 1)\dot{\phi_0} + t\dot{\phi_0}^2\Big)}{t}, \tag{314}$$

$$\ddot{\phi_1} = -\frac{t((3tH_0 - \mu + 1)\dot{\phi_1} + 3tH_1\dot{\phi_0}) + 6\phi_0((\mu-2)(\mu-1) - tH_0(tH_0 + 2\mu - 8))}{t^2}, \tag{315}$$

with the restriction in the first order, as follows:

$$\rho_1 = \frac{H_1(6tH_0 - 3\mu + 3) - 3H_0\dot{\phi_0}(\phi_0(tH_0 - \mu + 1) + 2t\dot{\phi_0}) - t\dot{\phi_0}\dot{\phi_1}}{t}. \tag{316}$$

This expression can be used to define ρ_1, such that Equation (313) is a compatibility condition that is satisfied for all t. Hence, we have a reduced system, as follows:

$$\begin{aligned}\ddot{\phi_1} = &-\frac{6c_2H_1t^{\frac{1}{2}(4\mu+r-9)}t_0^{\frac{1}{2}(-4\mu+r+9)} + \dot{\phi_1}((-4\mu+r+11)t^r - c_1(4\mu+r-11)t_0^r)}{2t(t^r + c_1t_0^r)} \\ &+ \frac{c_2t^{\frac{1}{2}(4\mu+r-9)-2}t_0^{-2\mu-\frac{r}{2}}\,{}_2F_1\left(1, \frac{r+4\mu-9}{2r}; \frac{3r+4\mu-9}{2r}; -\frac{t^rt_0^{-r}}{c_1}\right)}{3c_1(4\mu+r-9)(t^r+c_1t_0^r)^2} \\ &\times\Bigg(t_0^{9/2}\Big(4(69-14\mu)\mu + r^2 + (8\mu-30)r - 423\Big)t^{2r} \\ &- 2c_1\Big(4\mu(14\mu-69) + r^2 + 423\Big)t^rt_0^{r+\frac{9}{2}} + c_1^2\Big(4(69-14\mu)\mu + r^2 + (30-8\mu)r - 423\Big)t_0^{2r+\frac{9}{2}}\Bigg) \\ &+ \frac{\Lambda t_0^2\left(56\mu^2 - 276\mu - \frac{4r^2t^{2r}}{(t^r+c_1t_0^r)^2} - r^2 + 8\mu r + \frac{4r(-4\mu+r+15)t^r}{t^r+c_1t_0^r} - 30r + 423\right)}{6t^2},\end{aligned} \tag{317}$$

$$\begin{aligned}\dot{H_1} = &\frac{H_1\left(-1 + r\left(-1 + \frac{2c_1t_0^r}{t^r+c_1t_0^r}\right)\right)}{t} \\ &+ \frac{2c_2^2t_0^{9-4\mu}t^{4\mu+r-11}((4\mu+r+3)t^r - c_1(-4\mu+r-3)t_0^r)\,{}_2F_1\left(1, \frac{r+4\mu-9}{2r}; \frac{3r+4\mu-9}{2r}; -\frac{t^rt_0^{-r}}{c_1}\right)}{3c_1(4\mu+r-9)(t^r+c_1t_0^r)^2} \\ &- \frac{c_2\Lambda t^{\frac{1}{2}(4\mu+r)-\frac{13}{2}}t_0^{\frac{1}{2}(-4\mu+r+13)}((4\mu+r+3)t^r - c_1(-4\mu+r-3)t_0^r)}{3(t^r+c_1t_0^r)^2} - \frac{2c_2^2t^{4\mu+r-11}t_0^{-4\mu+r+9}}{(t^r+c_1t_0^r)^2}.\end{aligned} \tag{318}$$

The second equation is integrable, giving us the following:

$$
\begin{aligned}
H_1(t) = &-\frac{c_2{}^2(-4\mu+r-3)(4\mu+r-9)\Gamma\left(\frac{4\mu-9}{r}\right)t^{4\mu+r-10}t_0{}^{-4\mu-r+9}\,{}_2\tilde{F}_1\left(1,\frac{4\mu-9}{r};\frac{r+4\mu-9}{r};-\frac{\left(\frac{t}{t_0}\right)^r}{c_1}\right)}{36r\left(\left(\frac{t}{t_0}\right)^r+c_1\right)^2} \\
&-\frac{c_2{}^2(-4\mu+r+11)\Gamma\left(\frac{r+4\mu-9}{r}\right)t^{2(2\mu+r)-10}t_0{}^{-4\mu-2r+9}\,{}_2\tilde{F}_1\left(1,\frac{r+4\mu-9}{r};\frac{2r+4\mu-9}{r};-\frac{\left(\frac{t}{t_0}\right)^r}{c_1}\right)}{3c_1r\left(\left(\frac{t}{t_0}\right)^r+c_1\right)^2} \\
&+\frac{c_2t^{\frac{1}{2}(4\mu+r)-10}t_0{}^{-2(2\mu+r)}}{36\left(\left(\frac{t}{t_0}\right)^r+c_1\right)^2}\left[\frac{2c_2t_0^9t^{\frac{1}{2}(4\mu+r)}\left(12(-4\mu+r+11)t^r+c_1(-4\mu+r-3)(4\mu+r-9)t_0^r\right)}{c_1(4\mu+r-9)}\right. \\
&\times{}_2F_1\left(1,\frac{r+4\mu-9}{2r};\frac{3r+4\mu-9}{2r};-\frac{\left(\frac{t}{t_0}\right)^r}{c_1}\right)-12\Lambda(-4\mu+r+11)t^{r+\frac{9}{2}}t_0^{\frac{1}{2}(4\mu+r+13)} \\
&\left.+12c_1\Lambda t^{9/2}(4\mu+r-11)t_0^{\frac{1}{2}(4\mu+3r+13)}+\frac{72c_2t_0^{r+9}t^{\frac{1}{2}(4\mu+r)}}{9-4\mu}\right]+c_4\left(1+\frac{\left(\frac{t}{t_0}\right)^r}{c_1}\right)^{-\frac{r+1}{r}}\left(1+c_1\left(\frac{t_0}{t}\right)^r\right)^{\frac{1}{r}-1}, \quad (319)
\end{aligned}
$$

where c_4 is a constant of integration.

The equation for ϕ_1 can be solved in quadratures, as follows:

$$
\begin{aligned}
\phi_1(t) = &\int_1^t e^{\left(\int_1^{\mu_3}\left(\frac{\mu-1}{\mu_1}-3H_0(\mu_1)\right)d\mu_1\right)}\times\left[c_5+\int_1^{\mu_3}\frac{e^{\left(-\int_1^{\mu_2}\left(\frac{\mu-1}{\mu_1}-3H_0(\mu_1)\right)d\mu_1\right)}}{\mu_2^2}\Bigg(-3H_1(\mu_2)\dot{\phi}_0(\mu_2)\mu_2^2\right. \\
&\left.-6((\mu-2)(\mu-1)-H_0(\mu_2)\mu_2(2\mu+H_0(\mu_2)\mu_2-8))\phi_0(\mu_2)\Bigg)d\mu_2\right]d\mu_3+c_6, \quad (320)
\end{aligned}
$$

where c_5 and c_6 are integration constants and $H_0(\mu_1)$ is calculated using (309); $\dot{\phi}_0(\mu_2)$ is calculated by taking the derivative with respect to t in (310), and $\phi_0(\mu_2)$ is evaluated using (310). Finally, the expression for $H_1(\mu_2)$ is (319).

4. Conclusions

In this paper, we studied corrections to the Friedman and Klein–Gordon equations based on the formalism of fractional calculus using Caputo's derivative. Thus, we presented fractional calculus as a viable and attractive option for applications to the theory of gravity. Based on the diverse applications of fractional calculus in physics and engineering as shown in the paper, this work presents a didactic exposition of the main aspects of fractional calculus, showing the different approaches that exist and definitions of fractional derivatives.

This paper analyzes the fractional theory in cosmological models with a scalar field with a coupling constant, ξ. We qualitatively analyze the case of $\xi = 0$ and the general case of $\xi \neq 0$. Using different formulations of dynamical systems, we examine their equilibrium points and determine how the fractional term affects their stability—exposing the complex behavior presented by specific equilibrium points in the system's phase space and numerical solutions to different values of ξ and μ. We use methods from perturbation theory to analyze the cosmological behavior, obtaining solutions through two asymptotic expansions proposed for the system functions around the parameters $\mu = 1$ and $\xi = 0$. In these cases, the model recovers standard cosmology and the theory of minimal coupling to gravity, with an excellent approximation to the numerical solutions of the system.

In the paper's introductory Section 1, we discuss the challenges of traditional calculations in modeling power-law phenomena. We then present the various applications of fractional calculus, highlighting its effectiveness in recent studies in cosmology. This makes it a viable option to explore gravity theory further. We also introduce the research questions, pose the fractional formulation of the gravity problem, and outline the paper's general and specific objectives. We then describe the methodology used to develop the paper. Finally, we emphasize the scientific novelty of this research. Specifically, we mention that our analysis of cosmology with a scalar field with conformal and non-minimal coupling to gravity in the fractional context seeks to generalize previous results in the framework of the fractional formulation of gravity, making it a novel contribution.

Section 2 summarizes the main results of fractional calculus, mentioning some approaches to possible fractional derivatives, such as Grünwald–Letnikov, Riemann–Liouville and Caputo. We review the known rules of differentiation in the fractional context under the different approaches and show the fractional derivative of known functions. Emphasis is placed on viewing integration as the inverse operation of differentiation, which facilitates the definition of fractional integration. This is achieved by generalizing Cauchy's formula for iterated integrals, thereby enabling us to define the fractional derivative. The Liouville, Riemann, Liouville–Caputo, and Caputo derivatives are defined. Finally, we discuss what fractional differential equations are, using the Wolfram Language 13.3 tools [71], and we solve the classical problem of the harmonic oscillator. We also explore its quantum version and the relation between fractional calculus and q-deformed Lie algebras. We solve a physical problem of a point particle that moves under the effect of a friction force in the fractional context from different approaches using Wolfram Language 13.3 [71].

It is important to emphasize that fractional differential equations, which involve fractional derivatives, generalize ordinary differential equations. Fractional differential equations have been widely used in engineering, physics, chemistry, biology, and other fields involving relaxation and oscillation models. Recently, they have been used in cosmology. For this reason, since the version of Wolfram Language 13.1, two basic operators for fractional calculation were implemented, the functions **FractionalD** and **CaputoD**. The algorithms of the **MittagLefflerE** functions have been updated, as they are of crucial importance in the theory of fractional calculus, and the powerful **DSolve** function was heavily updated in version 13.1 to support FDE. This paper solves several fractional differential equations using the **DSolve** function of Wolfram Language 13.3 [71]. The solutions to such equations are generally given in terms of the function **MittagLefflerE** and the primary function for fractional calculus applications. Its role in fractional differential equation solutions is similar in importance to the **Exp** function for ODE solutions: any ODE with constant coefficients can be solved in terms of Mittag-Leffler functions.

According to the analysis carried out in this paper, the behavior of the fractional harmonic oscillator is very similar to the behavior of the ordinary damped harmonic oscillator. These examples demonstrate that the order of a fractional differential equation can be used as a control parameter to model some complicated systems.

In Section 3, cosmological models are introduced within the fractional formulation of the gravity framework, and previous results are discussed where the coupling is minimal, $\xi = 0$. The paper's main result is the application of the tools defined in Section 2 to fractional cosmologies with non-minimal coupling $\xi \neq 0$. Different dynamical systems and relevant cases, such as the invariant set $\Omega_\Lambda = 0$, are studied. Some numerical integration methods from the specialized Mathematica software (Version 13.3) [71] are used to study the behavior of the solutions of the systems of differential equations coming from the cosmological model, and the stability of the critical points is studied using appropriate tools.

In Sections 3.3.2 and 3.3.3, we found a great technical difficulty when analyzing the stability of the curves and critical points $P_6(x_c) : \left(x_c, -\frac{1}{\sqrt{\xi}}, \Omega_{\Lambda 0}, 0\right)$, $P_7(x_c) : \left(x_c, -\frac{1}{\sqrt{\xi}}, 0, 0\right)$, $P_8 : \left(0, -\frac{1}{\sqrt{\xi}}, \Omega_{\Lambda 0}, 0\right)$, $P_9 : \left(0, -\frac{1}{\sqrt{\xi}}, 0, 0\right)$, $P_{10}(x_c) : \left(x_c, \frac{1}{\sqrt{\xi}}, \Omega_{\Lambda 0}, 0\right)$, $P_{11}(x_c) : \left(x_c, \frac{1}{\sqrt{\xi}}, 0, 0\right)$, $P_{12} : \left(0, \frac{1}{\sqrt{\xi}}, \Omega_{\Lambda 0}, 0\right)$, $P_{13} : \left(0, \frac{1}{\sqrt{\xi}}, 0, 0\right)$. Due to the complexity of the stability analysis of these sets of equilibrium points, numerical solution methods have to be used. However, partial stability information can be obtained by computing the eigenvalues using the time variable $\tau = \ln(a/a_0)$ and taking the limit when $\alpha \to 0$.

In the study of curves, $\left(0, -\frac{1}{\sqrt{\xi(12\xi+1)}}, \Omega_{\Lambda 0}, -\mu \mp \sqrt{\mu(2\mu - 11) + 18} + 4\right)$ and $\left(0, \frac{1}{\sqrt{\xi(12\xi+1)}}, \Omega_{\Lambda 0}, -\mu \mp \sqrt{\mu(2\mu - 11) + 18} + 4\right)$ The technical difficulties lie in the parameter of the equation for the state of matter, which is complex and infinite. Furthermore, stability has to be determined numerically since the Jacobian matrix has infinite entries. These situations are due to the non-differentiability of the flow when $\alpha \to 0$ and $G := (\xi(12\xi + 1)y^2 - 1) \to 0$. The last case is even more complex since, in a neighborhood of $G \equiv 0$, the direction of the flow changes, entering the context of non-smooth mechanics. In all these cases, the stability analysis of these curves/sets will be left for future research since they cannot be implemented with the techniques developed in this paper.

Non-smooth mechanics is a modeling approach that does not require the temporal evolution of positions and velocities to be smooth functions. Due to potential impacts, the speeds of the mechanical system may experience sudden jumps at certain moments to comply with kinematic restrictions. Consider, for example, a rigid model of a ball falling to the ground. Just before the impact between the ball and the ground, the ball has a pre-impact velocity that does not disappear. At the instant of impact, the velocity must jump to a post-impact velocity of at least zero, or penetration will occur. Non-smooth mechanical models are often used in contact dynamics.

A review of research on non-smooth dynamical systems from the point of view of applications is provided in reference [110]. Two types of lack of smoothness are considered: impact and friction. A list of basic models is provided for each type, application areas are specified, and research results are reviewed. The literature on non-smooth dynamical systems will be reviewed in future work to resolve the difficulties above.

Research hypotheses are implemented in this research, and the paper's general and specific objectives are satisfactorily addressed. It is possible to obtain relevant information on the flow properties associated with several autonomous systems of ordinary differential equations from a cosmological context through qualitative techniques from the dynamical systems theory. The review of the literature on dynamical systems and fractional calculus is exhaustive. The work tools used in the paper were appropriately selected, identifying the use of the Caputo fractional derivative and its application in formulating a fractional cosmological action and its respective variational calculation. The main results of fractional calculus for the qualitative analysis of cosmological models are presented in a didactic manner.

The analysis of cosmologies featuring a scalar field with conformal and non-minimal coupling to gravity within a fractional context is novel, generalizing previous results within the framework of the fractional formulation of gravity. From a mathematical point of view, this approach describes the phase space of the models, obtaining qualitative results and explicit and approximated exact solutions with high numerical precision. This represents a different and attractive scenario due to its high level of applicability in describing natural phenomena.

Author Contributions: Conceptualization, K.M., A.D.M. and G.L.; methodology, G.L.; software, K.M., A.D.M. and G.L.; validation, K.M., A.D.M. and G.L.; formal analysis, K.M., A.D.M., G.L., C.M. and A.P.; investigation, K.M., A.D.M., G.L., C.M. and A.P.; resources, G.L., C.M. and A.P.; writing—original draft preparation, G.L.; writing—review and editing, G.L., C.M. and A.P.; visualization, K.M., A.D.M. and G.L.; supervision, G.L. and A.D.M. ; project administration, G.L. and K.M.; funding acquisition, K.M., A.D.M., G.L., C.M. and A.P. All authors have read and agreed to the published version of the manuscript.

Funding: K.M. and G.L. were funded by Vicerrectoría de Investigación y Desarrollo Tecnológico (VRIDT) at Universidad Católica del Norte (UCN) through Concurso Fondo de Tesis 2023 UCN, Resolución VRIDT N°063/2023. VRIDT-UCN funded G.L. through Resolución VRIDT No. 026/2023, Resolución VRIDT No. 027/2023, Proyecto de Investigación Pro Fondecyt Regular 2023 (Resolución VRIDT N°076/2023) and Resolución VRIDT N°09/2024. A.D.M. was supported by Agencia Nacional de Investigación y Desarrollo—ANID Subdirección de Capital Humano/Doctorado Nacional/año 2020 folio 21200837, Gastos operacionales proyecto de Tesis/2022 folio 242220121 and VRIDT-UCN. C. M. was supported by ANID Subdirección de Capital Humano/Doctorado Nacional/año 2021- folio 21211604. A.P. acknowledges the funding of VRIDT-UCN through Resolución VRIDT No. 096/2022 and Resolución VRIDT No. 098/2022. G.L., A.D.M., and A.P. have the financial support of ANID through Proyecto Fondecyt Regular 2024, Folio 1240514, Etapa 2024.

Data Availability Statement: No new data were created or analyzed in this study. Data sharing is not applicable to this article.

Acknowledgments: We are thankful for the support of Núcleo de Investigación Geometría Diferencial y Aplicaciones, Resolución VRIDT No. 096/2022. A.P. thanks Nikolaos Dimakis and the Universidad de La Frontera for the hospitality provided while part of this work was carried out. We thank Bayron Micolta-Riascos, Antonella Cid, and Juan Magaña for their helpful comments and suggestions. G.L. would like to express his gratitude toward faculty member Alan Coley and staff members Anna Maria Davis, Nora Amaro, Jeanne Clyburne, and Mark Monk for their warm hospitality during the implementation of the final details of the research in the Department of Mathematics and Statistics at Dalhousie University.

Conflicts of Interest: We declare no conflicts of interest. The funders had no role in the design of the study; in the collection, analyses, or interpretation of data; in the writing of the manuscript; or in the decision to publish the results.

Appendix A. Special Functions

This appendix presents several special functions that appear recurrently in these topics.

Appendix A.1. Gamma Function

The Gamma function extends the factorial function; that is, it extends a function of integers to a function of real or complex numbers. Namely, for natural numbers, the factorial of n is defined as follows:

$$n! = 1 \times 2 \times 3 \times \cdots \times n = \prod_{j=1}^{n} j. \tag{A1}$$

On the other hand, the Gamma function can be written as follows:

$$\Gamma(z) = \int_0^\infty t^{z-1} e^{-t}\, dt, \tag{A2}$$

which works for values of the complex number z with $\Re(z) > 0$. The following can be observed:

$$\Gamma(z+1) = z\Gamma(z), \tag{A3}$$

and also

$$\Gamma(n+1) = n!. \tag{A4}$$

Additionally, one can write the binomial coefficient in terms of the Gamma function, as follows:

$$\binom{z}{v} = \frac{z!}{v!(z-v)!} = \frac{\Gamma(z+1)}{\Gamma(v+1)\Gamma(z+1-v)}. \tag{A5}$$

This is added to the reflection formula, as follows:

$$\Gamma(z)\Gamma(1-z) = \frac{\pi}{\sin(\pi z)}, \tag{A6}$$

and to the incomplete gamma function, as follows:

$$\Gamma(a,z) = \int_z^{\infty} t^{a-1} e^{-t} dt, \tag{A7}$$

where

$$\Gamma(a,0) = \Gamma(a). \tag{A8}$$

Appendix A.2. Mittag-Leffler Functions

From the Maclaurin series expansion of the exponential, we have the following:

$$e^z = \sum_{n=0}^{\infty} \frac{z^n}{n!}, \tag{A9}$$

We can replace the factorial with the Gamma function, as follows:

$$e^z = \sum_{n=0}^{\infty} \frac{z^n}{\Gamma(n+1)}. \tag{A10}$$

This can then be extended as follows:

$$E(\alpha,z) = \sum_{n=0}^{\infty} \frac{z^n}{\Gamma(\alpha n+1)}, \tag{A11}$$

where α is an arbitrary real number that is greater than zero.

In fractional calculus, this function is of similar importance to the exponential function in standard calculus. For some values of α and functions of z, already-known functions can be obtained, as follows:

$$E(2,-z^2) = \cos z, \qquad E(1/2,z^{1/2}) = e^z\left[1+\text{erf}(z^{1/2})\right], \tag{A12}$$

where the error function, $\text{erf}(z)$, is given by

$$\text{erf}(z) = \frac{2}{\sqrt{\pi}} \int_0^z e^{-t^2} dt. \tag{A13}$$

The Mittag-Leffler function can also be extended as follows:

$$E(\alpha,\beta,z) = \sum_{n=0}^{\infty} \frac{z^n}{\Gamma(\alpha n+\beta)}, \tag{A14}$$

which is known as the generalized Mittag-Leffler function and has several special cases, such as the following:

$$E(1,2,z) = (e^z-1)/z, \qquad E(2,2,z^2) = \sinh(z)/z. \tag{A15}$$

Appendix A.3. Hypergeometric Functions

These functions contain many particular cases of special functions and are widely used in fractional calculus. From the following definition:

$${}_pF_q(\{a_i\};\{b_j\};z) = \frac{\prod_{j=1}^{q}\Gamma(b_j)}{\prod_{i=1}^{p}\Gamma(a_i)} \sum_{n=0}^{\infty} \frac{\prod_{i=1}^{p}\Gamma(a_i+n)z^n}{\prod_{j=1}^{q}\Gamma(b_j+n)n!}, \tag{A16}$$

It follows that the derivative with respect to z is as follows:

$$\frac{d}{dz}\left[{}_pF_q(\{a_i\};\{b_j\};z)\right] = \frac{\prod_{i=1}^{p}\Gamma(a_i)}{\prod_{j=1}^{q}\Gamma(b_j)}\left[{}_pF_q(\{a_i+1\},\{b_j+1\};z)\right]. \tag{A17}$$

Appendix A.4. Euler Polynomials: Incomplete Riemann or Hurwitz Zeta Function

The Euler polynomials, E_n, are generated by (see (23.1.1), [111]), as follows:

$$E_n(z) = \lim_{w\to 0} D_w^n \left(\frac{2e^{2zw}}{1+e^w} \right), \tag{A18}$$

where the first few are given as follows:

$$E_0(z) = 1, \tag{A19}$$
$$E_1(z) = z - 1/2, \tag{A20}$$
$$E_2(z) = z^2 - z. \tag{A21}$$

The Euler polynomials fulfill the following relation:

$$E_n(1+z) + E_n(z) = 2z^n. \tag{A22}$$

Extending the definition of the Euler polynomials from $n \in \mathbb{N}$ to the fractional case, $\alpha \in \mathbb{R}$, can be conducted easily, interpreting the generating function of the Euler polynomials as the sum of a geometric series, as follows:

$$\sum_{n=0}^{\infty} q^n = \frac{1}{1-q}, \qquad |q| < 1, \tag{A23}$$

to obtain

$$E_n(z) = \lim_{w\to 0} 2 \sum_{n=0}^{\infty} (-1)^n D_w^n e^{(z+n)w}, \qquad w < 0, \quad z \geq 0. \tag{A24}$$

This rule may now easily be extended to the non-integer case by replacing $n \mapsto \alpha$. The ad hoc extension of the Euler polynomials to the fractional case is given by the following:

$$E_\alpha(z) = 2^{1+\alpha}(\zeta(-\alpha, z/2) - \zeta(-\alpha, (1+z)/2)). \tag{A25}$$

where the Hurwitz ζ function is given by the following:

$$\zeta(s,z) = \sum_{n=0}^{\infty} (n+z)^{-s}. \tag{A26}$$

This ad hoc extension of the Euler polynomials to the fractional case corresponds to the use of the Liouville fractional derivative. Furthermore, the following relation has been confirmed:

$$E_\alpha(1+z) + E_\alpha(z) = 2z^\alpha \tag{A27}$$

independently of the fractional derivative.

References

1. Bandyopadhyay, B.; Kamal, S. *Stabilization and Control of Fractional Order Systems: A Sliding Mode Approach*; Lecture Notes in Electrical Engineering; Springer International Publishing: Berlin/Heidelberg, Germany , 2014.
2. Herrmann, R. *Fractional Calculus: An Introduction for Physicists*, 2nd ed.; World Scientific Publishing Company: Singapore, 2014.
3. Klafter, J.; Lim, S.C.; Metzler, R. *Fractional Dynamics: Recent Advances*; World Scientific: Singapore, 2012.
4. Lorenzo, C.F.; Hartley, T.T. *The Fractional Trigonometry: With Applications to Fractional Differential Equations and Science*; Wiley: Hoboken, NJ, USA, 2016.
5. Malinowska, A.B.; Odzijewicz, T.; Torres, D.F.M. *Advanced Methods in the Fractional Calculus of Variations*; Springer briefs in applied sciences and technology; Springer International Publishing: Berlin/Heidelberg, Germany, 2015.
6. Monje, C.A.; Chen, Y.Q.; Vinagre, B.M.; Xue, D.; Feliu-Batlle, V. *Fractional-Order Systems and Controls: Fundamentals and Applications*; Advances in Industrial Control; Springer: London, UK, 2010.
7. Padula, F.; Visioli, A. *Advances in Robust Fractional Control*; Springer International Publishing: Berlin/Heidelberg, Germany, 2014.
8. Tarasov, V.E. Review of some promising fractional physical models. *Int. J. Mod. Phys. B* **2013**, *27*, 1330005. [CrossRef]
9. Tarasov, V.E. *Applications in Physics, Part A*; De Gruyter Reference; De Gruyter: Berlin, Germany, 2019.
10. Kilbas, A.; Srivastava, H.; Trujillo, J. Theory and applications of fractional differential equations. In *North Holland Mathematical Studies*; Elsevier: Amsterdam, The Netherlands, 2006; Volume 204.

11. Podlubny, I. *Fractional Differential Equations*; Elsevier: Amsterdam, The Netherlands, 1998; Volume 198
12. Uchaikin, V.V. *Fractional Derivatives for Physicists and Engineers*; Higher Education Press: Beijing, China, 2013.
13. Wheatcraft, S.W.; Meerschaert, M.M. Fractional conservation of mass. *Adv. Water Resour.* **2008**, *31*, 1377–1381. [CrossRef]
14. Oldham, K.B. Signal-independent electroanalytical method. *Anal. Chem.* **1972**, *44*, 196–198. [CrossRef]
15. Pospíšil, L.; Hromadová, M.; Sokolová, R.; Lanza, C. Kinetics of radical dimerization. Simple evaluation of rate constant from convolution voltammetry and faradaic phase angle data. *Electrochim. Acta* **2019**, *300*, 284–289. [CrossRef]
16. Atangana, A.; Bildik, N. The use of fractional order derivative to predict the groundwater flow. *Math. Probl. Eng.* **2013**, *2013*, 543026. [CrossRef]
17. Atangana, A.; Vermeulen, P.D. Analytical solutions of a space-time fractional derivative of groundwater flow equation. In *Abstract and Applied Analysis*; Hindawi Limited: London, UK, 2014; Volume 2014, pp. 1–11.
18. Benson, D.A.; Wheatcraft, S.W.; Meerschaert, M.M. Application of a fractional advection-dispersion equation. *Water Resour. Res.* **2000**, *36*, 1403–1412. [CrossRef]
19. Benson, D.A.; Wheatcraft, S.W.; Meerschaert, M.M. The fractional-order governing equation of Lévy motion. *Water Resour. Res.* **2000**, *36*, 1413–1423. [CrossRef]
20. Benson, D.A.; Schumer, R.; Meerschaert, M.M.; Wheatcraft, S.W. Fractional dispersion, Lévy motion, and the MADE tracer tests. *Transp. Porous Media* **2001**, *42*, 211–240. [CrossRef]
21. Metzler, R.; Klafter, J. The random walk's guide to anomalous diffusion: A fractional dynamics approach. *Phys. Rep.* **2000**, *339*, 1–77. [CrossRef]
22. Mainardi, F.; Luchko, Y.; Pagnini, G. The fundamental solution of the space-time fractional diffusion equation. *arXiv* **2007**, arXiv:cond-mat/0702419.
23. Atangana, A.; Kilicman, A. On the generalized mass transport equation to the concept of variable fractional derivative. *Math. Probl. Eng.* **2014**, *2014*, 542809. [CrossRef]
24. Gorenflo, R.; Mainardi, F. Fractional diffusion processes: Probability distributions and continuous time random walk. In *Processes with Long-Range Correlations: Theory and Applications*; Springer: Berlin/Heidelberg, Germany, 2003; pp. 148–166.
25. Colbrook, M.J.; Ma, X.; Hopkins, P.F.; Squire, J. Scaling laws of passive-scalar diffusion in the interstellar medium. *Mon. Not. R. Astron. Soc.* **2017**, *467*, 2421–2429. [CrossRef]
26. Mainardi, F. *Fractional Calculus and Waves in Linear Viscoelasticity: An Introduction to Mathematical Models*; World Scientific: Singapore, 2022.
27. Laskin, N. Fractional quantum mechanics. *Phys. Rev. E* **2000**, *62*, 3135. [CrossRef]
28. Laskin, N. Fractional schrödinger equation. *Phys. Rev. E* **2002**, *66*, 056108. [CrossRef] [PubMed]
29. Bhrawy, A.H.; Zaky, M. An improved collocation method for multi-dimensional space–time variable-order fractional Schrödinger equations. *Appl. Numer. Math.* **2017**, *111*, 197–218. [CrossRef]
30. Lim, S.C. Fractional derivative quantum fields at positive temperature. *Phys. A* **2006**, *363*, 269–281. [CrossRef]
31. Lim, S.C.; Eab, C.H. *Fractional Quantum Fields*; De Gruyter: Berlin, Germany, 2019; pp. 237–256.
32. Moniz, P.V.; Jalalzadeh, S. From Fractional Quantum Mechanics to Quantum Cosmology: An Overture. *Mathematics* **2020**, *8*, 313. [CrossRef]
33. Rasouli, S.M.M.; Jalalzadeh, S.; Moniz, P.V. Broadening quantum cosmology with a fractional whirl. *Mod. Phys. Lett. A* **2021**, *36*, 2140005. [CrossRef]
34. Moniz, P.V.; Jalalzadeh, S. *Challenging Routes in Quantum Cosmology*; World Scientific Publishing: Singapore, 2020.
35. Calcagni, G.; Kuroyanagi, S. Stochastic gravitational-wave background in quantum gravity. *J. Cosmol. Astropart. Phys.* **2021**, *3*, 019. [CrossRef]
36. El-Nabulsi, R.A. Fractional derivatives generalization of Einstein's field equations. *Indian J. Phys.* **2013**, *87*, 195–200. [CrossRef]
37. El-Nabulsi, R.A. Non-minimal coupling in fractional action cosmology. *Indian J. Phys.* **2013**, *87*, 835–840. [CrossRef]
38. Jalalzadeh, S.; da Silva, F.R.; Moniz, P.V. Prospecting black hole thermodynamics with fractional quantum mechanics. *Eur. Phys. J. C* **2021**, *81*, 632. [CrossRef]
39. Vacaru, S.I. Fractional Dynamics from Einstein Gravity, General Solutions, and Black Holes. *Int. J. Theor. Phys.* **2012**, *51*, 1338–1359. [CrossRef]
40. Vacaru, S.I. Fractional Nonholonomic Ricci Flows. *Chaos Solitons Fractals* **2012**, *45*, 1266–1276. [CrossRef]
41. Rami, E.N.A. Fractional dynamics, fractional weak bosons masses and physics beyond the standard model. *Chaos Solitons Fractals* **2009**, *41*, 2262–2270. [CrossRef]
42. Debnath, U.; Jamil, M.; Chattopadhyay, S. Fractional Action Cosmology: Emergent, Logamediate, Intermediate, Power Law Scenarios of the Universe and Generalized Second Law of Thermodynamics. *Int. J. Theor. Phys.* **2012**, *51*, 812–837. [CrossRef]
43. Debnath, U.; Chattopadhyay, S.; Jamil, M. Fractional action cosmology: Some dark energy models in emergent, logamediate, and intermediate scenarios of the universe. *J. Theor. Appl. Phys.* **2013**, *7*, 25. [CrossRef]
44. El-Nabulsi, R.A. Cosmology with a fractional action principle. *Rom. Rep. Phys.* **2007**, *59*, 763–771.
45. El-Nabulsi, R.A. Fractional Lagrangian Formulation of General Relativity and Emergence of Complex, Spinorial and Noncommutative Gravity. *Int. J. Geom. Methods Mod. Phys.* **2009**, *6*, 25–76. [CrossRef]
46. Jamil, M.; Momeni, D.; Rashid, M.A. Fractional Action Cosmology with Power Law Weight Function. *J. Phys. Conf. Ser.* **2012**, *354*, 012008. [CrossRef]

47. Shchigolev, V.K. Testing Fractional Action Cosmology. *Eur. Phys. J. Plus* **2016**, *131*, 256. [CrossRef]
48. Giusti, A. MOND-like Fractional Laplacian Theory. *Phys. Rev. D* **2020**, *101*, 124029. [CrossRef]
49. Rami, E.-N.A. Fractional action oscillating phantom cosmology with conformal coupling. *Eur. Phys. J. Plus* **2015**, *130*, 102. [CrossRef]
50. Calcagni, G. Fractal universe and quantum gravity. *Phys. Rev. Lett.* **2010**, *104*, 251301. [CrossRef] [PubMed]
51. Calcagni, G. Quantum field theory, gravity and cosmology in a fractal universe. *J. High Energy Phys.* **2010**, *3*, 120. [CrossRef]
52. Calcagni, G. Multi-scale gravity and cosmology. *J. Cosmol. Astropart. Phys.* **2013**, *12*, 041. [CrossRef]
53. Calcagni, G. Quantum scalar field theories with fractional operators. *Class. Quantum Gravity* **2021**, *38*, 165006. [CrossRef]
54. Calcagni, G. Classical and quantum gravity with fractional operators. *Class. Quantum Gravity* **2021**, *38*, 165005; Erratum in *Class. Quantum Gravity* **2021**, *38*, 169601. [CrossRef]
55. Calcagni, G.; De Felice, A. Dark energy in multifractional spacetimes. *Phys. Rev. D* **2020**, *102*, 103529. [CrossRef]
56. Calcagni, G.; Kuroyanagi, S.; Marsat, S.; Sakellariadou, M.; Tamanini, N.; Tasinato, G. Quantum gravity and gravitational-wave astronomy. *J. Cosmol. Astropart. Phys.* **2019**, *10*, 012. [CrossRef]
57. Calcagni, G.; Kuroyanagi, S.; Tsujikawa, S. Cosmic microwave background and inflation in multi-fractional spacetimes. *J. Cosmol. Astropart. Phys.* **2016**, *8*, 039. [CrossRef]
58. Vacaru, S.I. New Classes of Off-Diagonal Cosmological Solutions in Einstein Gravity. *Int. J. Theor. Phys.* **2010**, *49*, 2753–2776. [CrossRef]
59. Roberts, M.D. fractional derivative Cosmology. *SOP Trans. Theor. Phys.* **2014**, *1*, 310. [CrossRef]
60. Shchigolev, V.K. Cosmological Models with fractional derivatives and Fractional Action Functional. *Commun. Theor. Phys.* **2011**, *56*, 389–396. [CrossRef]
61. Shchigolev, V.K. Cosmic Evolution in Fractional Action Cosmology. *Discontinuity Nonlinearity Complex.* **2013**, *2*, 115–123. [CrossRef]
62. Shchigolev, V.K. Fractional Einstein-Hilbert Action Cosmology. *Mod. Phys. Lett. A* **2013**, *28*, 1350056. [CrossRef]
63. Shchigolev, V.K. Fractional-order derivatives in cosmological models of accelerated expansion. *Mod. Phys. Lett. A* **2021**, *36*, 2130014. [CrossRef]
64. García-Aspeitia, M.A.; Fernandez-Anaya, G.; Hernández-Almada, A.; Leon, G.; Magaña, J. Cosmology under the fractional calculus approach. *Mon. Not. R. Astron. Soc.* **2022**, *517*, 4813–4826. [CrossRef]
65. Jalalzadeh, S.; Costa, E.W.O.; Moniz, P.V. de Sitter fractional quantum cosmology. *Phys. Rev. D* **2022**, *105*, L121901. [CrossRef]
66. Landim, R.G. Fractional dark energy: Phantom behavior and negative absolute temperature. *Phys. Rev. D* **2021**, *104*, 103508. [CrossRef]
67. Landim, R.G. Fractional dark energy. *Phys. Rev. D* **2021**, *103*, 083511. [CrossRef]
68. Micolta-Riascos, B.; Millano, A.D.; Leon, G.; Erices, C.; Paliathanasis, A. Revisiting fractional cosmology. *Fractal Fract.* **2023**, *7*, 149. [CrossRef]
69. González, E.; Leon, G.; Fernandez-Anaya, G. Exact solutions and cosmological constraints in fractional cosmology. *Fractal Fract.* **2023**, *7*, 368. [CrossRef]
70. Leon, G.; García-Aspeitia, M.A.; Fernandez-Anaya, G.; Hernández-Almada, A.; Magaña, J.; González, E. Cosmology under the fractional calculus approach: A possible H_0 tension resolution? *PoS* **2023**, *CORFU2022*, 248. [CrossRef]
71. Wolfram Research. *Mathematica*; Version 13.3; Wolfram Research: Champaign, IL, USA, 2023.
72. West, B.J. Fractional Calculus and the Future of Science. *Entropy* **2021**, *23*, 1566. [CrossRef] [PubMed]
73. Stanislavsky, A. Fractional oscillator. *Phys. Rev. E* **2004**, *70*, 051103. [CrossRef]
74. Arraut, I.; Segovia, C. A q-deformation of the Bogoliubov transformations. *Phys. Lett. A* **2018**, *382*, 464–466. [CrossRef]
75. Hou, B.Y.; Xu, L.C. The Hopf algebraic structure of q-deformed Heisenberg algebra when q is a root of unity. *Commun. Theor. Phys.* **1995**, *24*, 481. [CrossRef]
76. Bonatsos, D.; Daskaloyannis, C. Quantum groups and their applications in nuclear physics. *Prog. Part. Nucl. Phys.* **1999**, *43*, 537–618. [CrossRef]
77. Barrientos, E.; Mendoza, S.; Padilla, P. Extending Friedmann equations using fractional derivatives using a Last Step Modification technique: The case of a matter dominated accelerated expanding Universe. *Symmetry* **2021**, *13*, 174. [CrossRef]
78. Frederico, G.S.F.; Torres, D.F.M. Necessary optimality conditions for fractional action-like problems with intrinsic and observer times. *WSEAS Trans. Math.* **2008**, *7*, 6–11.
79. Agrawal, O.P. Fractional variational calculus in terms of Riesz fractional derivatives. *J. Phys. A Math. Theor.* **2007**, *40*, 6287. [CrossRef]
80. Baleanu, D.; Muslih, S. Lagrangian formulation of classical fields within Riemann-Liouville fractional derivatives. *Phys. Scr.* **2005**, *72*, 119–121. [CrossRef]
81. Baleanu, D.; Trujillo, J. A new method of finding the fractional Euler-Lagrange and Hamilton equations within caputo fractional derivatives. *Commun. Nonlinear Sci. Numer. Simul.* **2010**, *15*, 1111–1115. [CrossRef]
82. El-Nabulsi, R.A.; Torres, D.F. Fractional action-like variational problems. *J. Math. Phys.* **2008**, *49*, 053521. [CrossRef]
83. Odzijewicz, T.; Malinowska, A.; Torres, D. Generalized fractional calculus with applications to the calculus of variations. *Comput. Math. Appl.* **2012**, *64*, 3351–3366. [CrossRef]

84. Odzijewicz, T.; Malinowska, A.; Torres, D. Noether's theorem for fractional variational problems of variable order. *Open Phys* **2013**, *11*, 691–701. [CrossRef]
85. Odzijewicz, T.; Malinowska, A.; Torres, D. Variable order fractional variational calculus for double integrals. In Proceedings o the 2012 IEEE 51st IEEE Conference on Decision and Control (CDC), Maui, HI, USA, 10–13 December 2012; IEEE: Piscataway, NJ USA, 2013; pp. 6873–6878.
86. Hernández-Almada, A.; Leon, G.; Magaña, J.; García-Aspeitia, M.A.; Motta, V. Generalized Emergent Dark Energy: Observationa Hubble data constraints and stability analysis. *Mon. Not. R. Astron. Soc.* **2020**, *497*, 1590–1602. [CrossRef]
87. Hernández-Almada, A.; Leon, G.; Magaña, J.; García-Aspeitia, M.A.; Motta, V.; Saridakis, E.N.; Yesmakhanova, K. Kaniadakis holographic dark energy: Observational constraints and global dynamics. *Mon. Not. R. Astron. Soc.* **2022**, *511*, 4147–4158 [CrossRef]
88. Hernández-Almada, A.; Leon, G.; Magaña, J.; García-Aspeitia, M.A.; Motta, V.; Saridakis, E.N.; Yesmakhanova, K.; Millano, A.D Observational constraints and dynamical analysis of Kaniadakis horizon-entropy cosmology. *Mon. Not. R. Astron. Soc.* **2021**, *512* 5122–5134. [CrossRef]
89. Leon, G.; Magaña, J.; Hernández-Almada, A.; García-Aspeitia, M.A.; Verdugo, T.; Motta, V. Barrow Entropy Cosmology: An observational approach with a hint of stability analysis. *J. Cosmol. Astropart. Phys.* **2021**, *12*, 032. [CrossRef]
90. Di Valentino, E.; Mena, O.; Pan, S.; Visinelli, L.; Yang, W.; Melchiorri, A.; Mota, D.F.; Riess, A.G.; Silk, J. In the realm of the Hubble tension—A review of solutions. *Class. Quantum Gravity* **2021**, *38*, 153001. [CrossRef]
91. Efstathiou, G. To H0 or not to H0? *Mon. Not. R. Astron. Soc.* **2021**, *505*, 3866–3872. [CrossRef]
92. Aghanim, N.; Akrami, Y.; Ashdown, M.; Aumont, J.; Baccigalupi, C.; Ballardini, M.; Banday, A.J.; Barreiro, R.B.; Bartolo, N.; Basak S.; et al. Planck 2018 results. VI. Cosmological parameters. *Astron. Astrophys.* **2020**, *641*, A6; Erratum in *Astron. Astrophys.* **2021** *652*, C4.
93. Carroll, S.; Addison-Wesley. *Spacetime and Geometry: An Introduction to General Relativity*; Addison Wesley: Boston, MA, USA 2004.
94. Carroll, S.M. *Spacetime and Geometry*; Cambridge University Press: Cambridge, UK, 2019.
95. Wald, R.M. *General Relativity*; University of Chicago Press: Chicago, IL, USA, 2010.
96. Foreman-Mackey, D.; Hogg, D.W.; Lang, D.; Goodman, J. emcee: The MCMC hammer. *Publ. Astron. Soc. Pac.* **2013**, *125*, 306–312 [CrossRef]
97. Tavakol, R. *Introduction to Dynamical Systems, Ch 4. Part One*; Cambridge University Press: Cambridge, UK, 1997; pp. 84–98.
98. Wainwright, J.; Ellis, G.F.R. (Eds.) *Dynamical Systems in Cosmology*; Cambridge University Press: Cambridge, UK, 1997.
99. Perko, L. *Differential Equations and Dynamical Systems*; 3rd ed.; Springer: Berlin/Heidelberg, Germany, 2001.
100. Coley, A. *Dynamical Systems and Cosmology*; Kluwer: Dordrecht, The Netherlands, 2003; Volume 291.
101. Hirsch, M.W.; Smale, S.; Devaney, R. *Differential Equations, Dynamical Systems, and An Introduction to Chaos*; Academic Press London, UK; San Diego, CA, USA, 2004.
102. Wiggins, S. *Introduction to Applied Nonlinear Dynamical Systems and Chaos*; Texts in Applied Mathematics; Springer Berlin/Heidelberg, Germany, 2006.
103. Berglund, N.; Gentz, B.B. *Noise-Induced Phenomena in Slow-Fast Dynamical Systems*; Series: Probability and Applications; Springer London, UK, 2006.
104. Fenichel, N. Geometric singular perturbation theory for ordinary differential equations. *J. Differ. Equ.* **1979**, *31*, 53–98. [CrossRef]
105. Fusco, G.; Hale, J.K. Slow-motion manifolds, dormant instability, and singular perturbations. *J. Dyn. Differ. Equ.* **1989**, *1*, 75–94 [CrossRef]
106. Dumortier, F.; Roussarie, R. Canard Cycles and Center Manifolds. *Mem. Am. Math. Soc.* **1996**, *121*, 577. [CrossRef]
107. Holmes, M.H. *Introduction to Perturbation Methods*; Springer Science+Business Media: New York, NY, USA, 2013; ISBN 978-1-4614-5477-9. [CrossRef]
108. Kevorkian, J., Cole, J.D. *Perturbation Methods in Applied Mathematics*; Applied Mathematical Sciences Series; Springer: New York NY, USA, 1981; Volume 34, ISBN 978-1-4757-4213-8. [CrossRef]
109. Verhulst, F. *Methods and Applications of Singular Perturbations: Boundary Layers and Multiple Timescale Dynamics*; Springer: New York, NY, USA, 2000; ISBN 978-0-387-22966-9. [CrossRef]
110. Popp, K. Non-smooth mechanical systems. *J. Appl. Math. Mech.* **2000**, *64*, 765–772. [CrossRef]
111. Abramowitz, M.; Stegun, I.A. *Handbook of Mathematical Functions*; Dover Publications: New York, NY, USA , 1965; Volume 361.

fractal and fractional

MDPI

Article

Fundamental Matrix, Integral Representation and Stability Analysis of the Solutions of Neutral Fractional Systems with Derivatives in the Riemann—Liouville Sense

Hristo Kiskinov [1], Mariyan Milev [2], Slav Ivanov Cholakov [1] and Andrey Zahariev [1,*]

[1] Faculty of Mathematics and Informatics, University of Plovdiv Paisii Hilendarski, 24 Tzar Asen, 4000 Plovdiv, Bulgaria; kiskinov@uni-plovdiv.bg (H.K.); cholakovs@uni-plovdiv.bg (S.I.C.)
[2] Faculty of Economics and Business Administration, Sofia University "St. Kliment Ohridski", 15 Tsar Osvoboditel Blvd., 1504 Sofia, Bulgaria; m.milev@feb.uni-sofia.bg
* Correspondence: zandrey@uni-plovdiv.bg

Abstract: The paper studies a class of nonlinear disturbed neutral linear fractional systems with derivatives in the the Riemann–Liouville sense and distributed delays. First, it is proved that the initial problem for these systems with discontinuous initial functions under some natural assumptions possesses a unique solution. The assumptions used for the proof are similar to those used in the case of systems with first-order derivatives. Then, with the obtained result, we derive the existence and uniqueness of a fundamental matrix and a generalized fundamental matrix for the homogeneous system. In the linear case, via these fundamental matrices we obtain integral representations of the solutions of the homogeneous system and the corresponding inhomogeneous system. Furthermore, for the fractional systems with Riemann–Liouville derivatives we introduce a new concept for weighted stabilities in the Lyapunov, Ulam–Hyers, and Ulam–Hyers–Rassias senses, which coincides with the classical stability concepts for the cases of integer-order or Caputo-type derivatives. It is proved that the zero solution of the homogeneous system is weighted stable if and only if all its solutions are weighted bounded. In addition, for the homogeneous system it is established that the weighted stability in the Lyapunov and Ulam–Hyers senses are equivalent if and only if the inequality appearing in the Ulam–Hyers definition possess only bounded solutions. Finally, we derive natural sufficient conditions under which the property of weighted global asymptotic stability of the zero solution of the homogeneous system is preserved under nonlinear disturbances.

Keywords: fractional derivatives; neutral fractional systems; distributed delay; integral representation

MSC: 34A08; 34A12

1. Introduction

Practically, it has been shown that many real-world phenomena in various fields of science can be represented more accurately through mathematical models, including fractional differential equations [1–3]. More detailed information on fractional calculus theory and fractional differential equations can be seen in the monographs of Kilbas et al. [4] and Podlubny [5]. Compared to fractional equations with Caputo-type derivatives, the fractional equations with Riemann–Liouville-type derivatives have been studied significantly less. The first obstacle was the lack of meaningful geometric and physical interpretations of the Riemann–Liouville type of integration and differentiation, which was overcome with the appearance of Ref. [6]. The other problem was to derive an appropriate formulation of the initial conditions for the initial problem. Some considerations about them are given in [7,8], but as was mentioned in [9] "The initial value problem is a subject that remains quite up-to-date".

It is well known that the existence of explicit solutions or an integral representation (variation of constants formula) of the solutions of linear fractional differential equations and/or systems (ordinary or delayed) is a main tool in executing their qualitative analysis. That is why establishing either explicit solutions (see [10]) or integral representation, for which existence of a fundamental matrix is needed (see [11]), are important tasks for stability analysis, especially in the case of equations with Riemann–Liouville derivatives. But it is surprising that there are not many articles devoted to this problem. As far as we know, a survey concerning stability results for retarded and neutral fractional differential equations with Riemann–Liouville-type derivatives does not exist. In general, partially this gap can be fulfilled by reading the overview [12] and the references therein. From the recent works devoted to the discussed themes concerning fractional differential equations with Riemann–Liouville-type derivatives we refer to [13] for equations, to [14–16] where retarded fractional differential equations are considered, and to [17,18] where the neutral case is considered. We suppose that the mentioned works with their references give a good enough picture of the studies in this area.

In the present article, we study a class of nonlinear disturbed neutral linear fractional systems with derivatives in the the Riemann–Liouville sense and distributed delay. We first study the important problem of the existence and uniqueness of the solutions of an initial problem (IP) for these systems in the case of discontinuous initial functions. As far as we know, there are no results devoted to the initial problem with discontinuous initial functions for neutral differential equations with derivatives in the Riemann–Liouville sense. Since the classically stability concepts are not directly applicable to systems with derivatives with the property that the derivative of a constant is not equal to zero (like the Riemann–Liouville fractional derivative, for example), we introduce a new concept for weighted stabilities in the Lyapunov, Ulam–Hyers, and Ulam–Hyers–Rassias senses, which coincides with the classical stability concepts for the cases of integer-order or Caputo-type derivatives.

The following abbreviations will be used in this manuscript: BV—bounded variation; GAS—globally asymptotically stable; UH—Ulam–Hyers; LAS—locally asymptotically stable; LT—Laplace transform; UHR—Ulam–Hyers–Rassias; IP—initial problem; PC—piecewise continuous; RL—Riemann–Liouville; WML—weighted Mittag–Leffler.

The paper is organized as follows: Section 2 presents the necessary definitions and properties concerning the RL and Caputo fractional derivatives, the problem statement, and the needed auxiliary definitions and facts for our exposition. Section 3 is devoted to the existence and the uniqueness of the solutions of the initial problem (IP) for the studied class of nonlinear neutral systems in the case when the initial function is discontinuous. In Section 4, as a consequence of the derived result we prove the existence and uniqueness of a fundamental matrix and a generalized fundamental matrix for the linear homogeneous system, as well as establishing an integral representation of the solutions of the IP for the homogeneous system and the corresponding inhomogeneous system. Section 5 is devoted to a new concept for weighted stabilities in the Lyapunov, UH, and UHR senses, the definition of which coincides with the classical stability concepts for the cases of integer-order or Caputo-type derivatives. It is proved that the zero solution of the homogeneous system is weighted stable if and only if all its solutions are weighted bounded. In addition, it is established that the weighted stabilities in the Lyapunov and UH senses are equivalent if and only if the inequality appearing in the UH definition possesses only bounded solutions. In Section 6, natural sufficient conditions are obtained under which the property of weighted global asymptotic stability of the zero solution of the homogeneous system is preserved under nonlinear disturbances. Finally, in Section 7 an illustrative example is presented. In the last Section 8, we summarize some conclusions concerning the obtained results and propose some open problems.

2. Preliminaries and Problem Statement

As is standard to avoid possible misunderstandings, we recall some properties concerning the RL-type derivatives, as well as the needed definitions, conditions, and auxiliary results necessary for the exposition below. For more comprehensive information on fractional calculus we refer to Refs. [4,5].

For a function $g\colon \mathbb{R} \to \mathbb{R}$, we will say that some property holds locally if it is fulfilled on every compact subinterval $[b,c] \subset \mathbb{R}$. We will use the following notation for the real linear spaces: $L_1^{loc}(\mathbb{R},\mathbb{R})$ consists of all locally Lebesgue integrable functions, $BL_1^{loc}(\mathbb{R},\mathbb{R}) \subset L_1^{loc}(\mathbb{R},\mathbb{R})$ and $BV^{loc}(\mathbb{R},\mathbb{R}) \subset BL_1^{loc}(\mathbb{R},\mathbb{R})$ are, respectively, the subspaces of all functions which are locally bounded and of all functions which have locally bounded variation.

We define the left-sided fractional RL integral operator of arbitrary order $\alpha \in (0,1)$ with lower limit $a \in \mathbb{R}$ for any $g \in L_1^{loc}(\mathbb{R},\mathbb{R})$, via the relation

$$(I_{a+}^{\alpha}g)(t) = \frac{1}{\Gamma(\alpha)} \int\limits_{a}^{t} (t-s)^{\alpha-1} g(s)ds.$$

The corresponding left-hand side RL and Caputo fractional derivatives of arbitrary order $\alpha \in (0,1)$ with lower limit a are defined for any $t > a$ by

$$\left({}^{RL}D_{a+}^{\alpha}g\right)(t) = \frac{d}{dt}(I_{a+}^{1-\alpha}g(t)),$$

$$\left({}^{C}D_{a+}^{\alpha}g\right)(t) = \left({}^{RL}D_{a+}^{\alpha}g\right)(t) - \left({}^{RL}D_{a+}^{\alpha}g\right)(a).$$

For shortness, we will use the notation $D_{a+}^{\alpha} = {}^{RL}D_{a+}^{\alpha}$.

Consider the neutral fractional nonlinear system with RL-type derivatives of order $\alpha \in (0,1)$ with lower limit $a \in \mathbb{R}$ and distributed delays in the following general form:

$$D_{a+}^{\alpha}\left(X(t) - \int\limits_{-h}^{0}[d_\theta V(t,\theta)]X(t+\theta)\right) = \int\limits_{-h}^{0}[d_\theta U(t,\theta)]X(t+\theta) + \mathfrak{F}(t, X_\tau^T(\theta)), \quad (1)$$

where $h > 0$, $J = [a,\infty)$, $\mathbb{R}_+ = [0,\infty)$, $J^0 = (a,\infty)$, $\mathbb{R}_+^0 = (0,\infty)$, $\langle n\rangle = \{1,2,\ldots,n\}$, $\langle m\rangle_0 = \langle m\rangle \bigcup\{0\}$, $X(t) = col(x_1(t),\ldots,x_n(t))\colon J^0 \to \mathbb{R}^n$, $\mathfrak{F}(t,X_t^T) = col(f_1(t,X_t^T),\ldots,f_n(t,X_t^T))\colon J \times PC \to \mathbb{R}^n$, (the notation col means column and superscript ^{T} denotes the transposed vector), $U(t,\theta) = \{u_k^j(t,\theta)\}_{k,j=1}^n\colon J\times\mathbb{R} \to \mathbb{R}^{n\times n}$, $V(t,\theta) = \{v_k^j(t,\theta)\}_{k,j=1}^n\colon J\times\mathbb{R} \to \mathbb{R}^{n\times n}$, $D_{a+}^{\alpha}X(t) = col(D_{a+}^{\alpha}x_1(t),\ldots,D_{a+}^{\alpha}x_n(t))$, and $X_t(\theta) = X(t+\theta)$ (Krasovskii-type functional) for $t \in J$ and $\theta \in [-h,0]$. In addition, $\mathbf{I},\mathbf{\Theta} \in \mathbb{R}^{n\times n}$ denote the identity and the zero matrices, $\mathbf{0} \in \mathbb{R}^n$ denotes the zero vector, and $I_\gamma((t-a)) = (t-a)^\gamma\mathbf{I}$, $\gamma \in [-1,1]$.

For $Y\colon J\times\mathbb{R} \to \mathbb{R}^{n\times n}$, $Y(t,\theta) = \{y_k^j(t,\theta)\}_{k,j=1}^n$, we use the norm

$$|Y(t,\theta)| = \sum_{k,j=1}^{n} |y_k^j(t,\theta)|, \quad Var_{[b,c]}Y(t,\cdot) = \{Var_{[b,c]}y_k^j(t,\cdot)\}_{k,j=1}^n,$$

$PC([-h,0],\mathbb{R}^n) = \{\Phi = (\phi_1,\ldots,\phi_n)^T\colon [-h,0] \to \mathbb{R}^n \mid \Phi \text{ is piecewise continuous}\}$ and S_Φ denotes the set of all jump points for any $\Phi(t) \in PC([-h,0],\mathbb{R}^n)$. We will use the following Banach spaces of initial functions:

$$\mathbf{PC} = \{\Phi(t) = col(\varphi_1(t),\ldots,\varphi_n(t))\colon [-h,0] \to \mathbb{R}^n \mid \Phi(t) \in PC([-h,0],\mathbb{R}^n)\},$$
$$\mathbf{PC}^* = PC \cap BV([-h,0],\mathbb{R}^n) \quad \text{and} \quad \mathbf{C}([-h,0],\mathbb{R}^n),$$

endowed with the norm $||\Phi|| = \sum\limits_{k\in\langle n\rangle} \sup\limits_{s\in[-h,0]} |\phi_k(s)| < \infty$. In addition, we assume that in all spaces the functions $\Phi(t)$ are right continuous at $t \in S_\Phi$ (for $\Phi \in \mathbf{C}$ this assumption ultimately holds).

For any $\Phi \in \mathbf{PC}$ we define the initial condition for the system (1) as follows:

$$X(t) = \Phi(t-a)\ t \in [a-h, a], D_{a+}^{\alpha-1}X(a+0) = \Phi(0),\ h > 0. \tag{2}$$

More details concerning other types of initial conditions are given in [8] for the case when the initial functions are continuous.

Let us introduce the auxiliary integral system (whose system is considered in detail in Lemma 4 below) for any $\Phi \in \mathbf{PC}$ and $t \in J^0$:

$$\begin{aligned} X(t) &= \Phi(0)(t-a)^{\alpha-1} + \int_{-h}^{0} [d_\theta V(t,\theta)]X(t+\theta) \\ &+ I_{-1}(\Gamma(\alpha)) \int_a^t I_{\alpha-1}(t-\tau) \left(\int_{-h}^{0} [d_\theta U(\tau,\theta)]X(\tau+\theta) + \mathfrak{F}(\tau, X_\tau^T) \right) d\tau. \end{aligned} \tag{3}$$

Let $b > a$ and $\gamma \in [0,1]$ be arbitrary.

Definition 1 ([4]). *The function $G(t) = (g_1(t), \ldots, g_n(t)) \in C(J^0, \mathbb{R}^n)$, $\gamma \in [0,1]$ will be called right γ-continuous at a if the function $I_\gamma(t-a)G(t) = col((t-a)^\gamma g_1(t), \ldots, (t-a)^\gamma g_n(t)) \in C([a,\infty), \mathbb{R}^n)$, i.e., the function $I_\gamma(t-a)G(t)$ is right continuous at a. By $\mathbf{C}^\gamma$ we denote the real linear space of all right γ-continuous-at-a functions and for any $b \in \mathbb{R}_+$ by $\mathbf{C}_b^\gamma$ the real Banach space*

$$\mathbf{C}_b^\gamma = \{R(t) \in C((a,b], \mathbb{R}^n)\,|R(t) = G(t)|_{(a,b]},\ G(t) \in \mathbf{C}^\gamma\}$$

with norm $\|R\|_b^\gamma = \sum_{k\in\langle n\rangle} \sup_{t\in[a,b]} (t-a)^\gamma |r_k(t)|$.

Definition 2 ([11]). *The vector function $colX(t) = (x_1(t), \ldots, x_n(t))$ is a solution of IP (1), (2) in $(a,b](J^0)$ if $X(t) \in \mathbf{C}_b^{1-\alpha}(\mathbf{C}^{1-\alpha})$ satisfies the system (1) for all $t \in (a,b](J^0)$ and the initial condition (2) too.*

Definition 3 ([11]). *The vector function $colX(t) = (x_1(t), \ldots, x_n(t))$ is a solution of IP (3), (2) in $(a,b](J^0)$ if $X(t) \in \mathbf{C}_b^{1-\alpha}(\mathbf{C}^{1-\alpha})$ satisfies system (3) for all $t \in (a,b](J^0)$ and initial condition (2) too.*

The hypotheses $(\mathfrak{S})$ stated below in Definition 4, as in the cases of systems with derivatives of integer order or Caputo-type fractional order, will play a major role in the solvability of IP (1), (2) (IP (3), (2)) (see [19–21]).

Definition 4 ([19–21]). *We say that for the kernels $U, V\colon J \times \mathbb{R} \to \mathbb{R}^{n\times n}$ the hypotheses $(\mathfrak{S})$ hold if the following conditions are fulfilled for any $i \in \langle m\rangle_0$ and $q \in \langle l\rangle$, $l, m \in \mathbb{N}$:*

($\mathfrak{S}$1) *The functions $(t,\theta) \to U(t,\theta)$, $(t,\theta) \to V(t,\theta)$ are measurable in $(t,\theta) \in J \times \mathbb{R}$ and normalized so that $U(t,\theta) = 0$, $V(t,\theta) = 0$ for $\theta \geq 0$, $U(t,\theta) = U(t,-\sigma)$ for $\theta \leq -\sigma$, $V(t,\theta) = V(t,-\tau)$ for $\theta \leq -\tau$, $\sigma, \tau > 0$, $h = \max(\sigma,\tau)$ for any $t \in J$.*

($\mathfrak{S}$2) *For any fixed $t \in J$ the kernels $U(t,\theta)$ and $V(t,\theta)$ are left continuous in θ on $(-\sigma,0)$ and $(-\tau,0)$, $U(t,\cdot), V(t,\cdot) \in BV_0^{loc}(J \times \mathbb{R}, \mathbb{R}^{n\times n})$ and $Var_{[-h,0]}U(t,\cdot), Var_{[-h,0]}V(t,\cdot) \in BL_1^{loc}(J, \mathbb{R}_+)$, $Var_{[-h,0]}V(t,\cdot)$ is uniformly bounded in $t \in J$ and is uniformly nonatomic at zero [21] (i.e., for every $\epsilon > 0$, there exists $\delta(\epsilon) > 0$ such that for any $t \in J$, we have that $Var_{[-\delta,0]}V(t,\cdot) < \epsilon$).*

($\mathfrak{S}$3) *For any fixed $t \in J$, the Lebesgue decomposition of the kernels $U(t,\theta)$ and $V(t,\theta)$ has the form:*

$$U(t,\theta) = U_j(t,\theta) + U_{ac}(t,\theta) + U_s(t,\theta),\ V(t,\theta) = V_j(t,\theta) + V_{ac}(t,\theta) + V_s(t,\theta),$$
$$U_j(t,\theta) = \sum_{i\in\langle m\rangle} A^i(t)H(\theta + \sigma^i(t)),\ A^i(t) = \{a_{kj}^i(t)\}_{k,j=1}^n \in BL_1^{loc}(J, \mathbb{R}^{n\times n}),$$

$$V_j(t,\theta) = \sum_{l\in\langle r\rangle} \overline{A}^l(t)H(\theta+\tau^l(t)),\ \overline{A}^l(t) = \{\overline{a}^l_{kj}(t)\}^n_{k,j=1} \in C(J,\mathbb{R}^{n\times n}),$$

$\sigma^0(t) \equiv 0$, $\sigma^i(t), \tau^l(t) \in C(J,[0,h])$, $U_{ac}(t,\cdot), V_{ac}(t,\cdot) \in AC([-h,0],\mathbb{R}^{n\times n})$, $U_s(t,\cdot)$, $V_s(t,\cdot) \in C([-h,0],\mathbb{R}^{n\times n})$ *and* $H(t)$ *is the Heaviside function.*

($\mathfrak{S}4$) *The sets* $S^i_\Phi = \{t \in J \,|\, t-\sigma^i(t) \in S_\Phi, i \in \langle m\rangle\}$, $S^l_\Phi = \{t \in J \,|\, t-\tau^l(t) \in S_\Phi, l \in \langle r\rangle\}$ *do not have limit points and the relations*

$$\lim_{t\to t_*}\int_{-h}^{0} |U^i(t,\theta) - U^i(t_*,\theta)|d\theta = 0\,, \quad \lim_{t\to t_*}\int_{-h}^{0} |V^l(t,\theta) - V^l(t_*,\theta)|d\theta = 0$$

hold for any $t_* \in J$.

Definition 5 ([20,21]). *We say that the vector-valued functional* $\mathfrak{F}(t,Y)\colon J\times PC \to \mathbb{R}^n$ *satisfies the modified Caratheodory conditions* ($\mathfrak{C}$) *if the following conditions hold:*

($\mathfrak{C}1$) *For almost all fixed* $t\in J$ *the functional* $(t,Y)\to\mathfrak{F}(t,Y)$ *is continuous in arbitrary* $Y \in \mathbf{PC}(\mathbf{PC}^*)$ *and for each fixed function* $Y\in\mathbf{PC}(\mathbf{PC}^*)$ *the function* $\mathfrak{F}(t,Y)\in BL^{loc}_1(J,\mathbb{R}^n)$.

($\mathfrak{C}2$) *(Local Lipschitz-type condition) For any* $(t,Y)\in J\times\mathbf{PC}$ *and for some its vicinity* $O(t,Y)\subset J\times PC$, *there exists a function* $\ell(t)\in BL^{loc}_1(J,\mathbb{R}_+)$ *such that the inequalities*

$$|\mathfrak{F}(t,Y_1)-\mathfrak{F}(t,Y_2)| \le \ell(t)|Y_1(t)-Y_2(t)|$$

hold for every $(t,Y_1),(t,Y_2)\in O(t,Y)$.

In our investigations below, we will use the following auxiliary result:

Lemma 1 ([4]). *Let* $\alpha\in(0,1)$ *and let* $y(t)$ *be a Lebesgue measurable function on* J.

(a) *If there exists a.e. (almost everywhere) the limit* $\lim_{t\to a+0}[(t-a)^{1-\alpha}y(t)] = c\in\mathbb{R}$, *then there also exists a.e. the limit* $(D^{\alpha-1}_a y)(a+0) = (I^{1-\alpha}_a y)(a+0) = \lim_{t\to a+0}(I^{1-\alpha}_a y)(t) = c\Gamma(\alpha)$.

(b) *If there exist a.e. the limit* $\lim_{t\to a+0}[(t-a)^{1-\alpha}y(t)]$ *and* $\lim_{t\to a+0}(I^{1-\alpha}_a y)(t) = c^*$, *then we have that* $\lim_{t\to a+0}[(t-a)^{1-\alpha}y(t)] = \dfrac{c^*}{\Gamma(\alpha)}$.

Definition 6 ([22]). *The low terminal a will be called a noncritical point (noncritical jump point) for some initial function* $\Phi\in\mathbf{PC}$ *relative to the delay* $\tau^l(t)$, $l\in\langle r\rangle$ *if the equality* $\tau^l(a)=0$ *implies that there exists a constant* $b_0>a$ *(eventually depending on* $\tau^l(t)$*) such that* $t-\tau^l(t)<a$ *for* $t\in(a,b_0]$.

Definition 7 ([22]). *The low terminal a for a function* $\Phi\in\mathbf{PC}$ *with* $a\notin S^\Phi$ $(a\in S^\Phi)$ *will be called a critical point (critical jump point) relative to some delay* $\tau^l(t), l\in\langle r\rangle$ *if the equality* $\tau^l(a)=0$ *implies that there exists a constant* $b_0>a$ *(eventually depending on* $\tau^l(t)$*) such that* $t-a\ge\tau^l(t)$ *for* $t\in(a,b_0]$.

Lemma 2 ([22]). *Let the hypotheses* ($\mathfrak{S}$) *hold and* $\prod_{l\in\langle r\rangle}\tau_l(a)>0$. *Then, there exists* $b\in(a,a+h]$ *(eventually depending from* τ_l*), such that* $\Phi(t-\tau_l(t))$ *is continuous for* $t\in(a,b]$.

Lemma 3 ([22]). *Let the hypotheses* ($\mathfrak{S}$) *hold and* $\prod_{l\in\langle r\rangle}\tau_l(a)=0$.

Then, for any initial function $\Phi\in\mathbf{PC}$ *with* $S^\Phi=\{a\}$, *one of the following statements holds:*

(i) *The statement of Lemma 2 holds.*

(ii) *The low terminal a is a critical jump point for* Φ *relative to the kernel* $V(t,\theta)$ *for some* $l_0\in\langle r\rangle$.

Theorem 1 ([23], Krasnosel'skii's fixed point theorem). *Let $(\mathfrak{E}, \|\cdot\|_{\mathfrak{E}})$ be a Banach space, $H \subset \mathfrak{E}$ be a nonempty, closed, and convex subset of $\mathfrak{E}$ and the maps $\mathfrak{T}, \mathfrak{N}\colon H \to \mathfrak{E}$ satisfy the following conditions:*

(i) The operator $\mathfrak{T}$ is a contraction with constant $\gamma \in (0,1)$;
(ii) The operator $\mathfrak{K}$ is continuous and the set $\mathfrak{K}(\mathfrak{B})$ is contained in a compact set;
(iii) For any $x, y \in H$, we have that $\mathfrak{T}x + \mathfrak{K}y \in H$.

Then, there exists a $z \in H$ with $\mathfrak{T}z + \mathfrak{K}z = z$.

Theorem 2 ([24], Corollary 2). *Suppose that $\alpha \in (0,1)$ and the following conditions hold:*

1. *The functions $a(t), g(t), y(t) \in L_1^{loc}(J, \mathbb{R}_+)$.*
2. *The functions $a(t), g(t)$ are nondecreasing, $g(t)$ is bounded on J, and $y(a) = 0$.*
3. *The inequality $y(t) \le a(t) + g(t)\int_a^t (t-s)^{\beta-1} y(s)ds$ holds for $t \in J$.*

Then, for any $t \in J$ we have that $y(t) \le a(t)E_\alpha(g(t)\Gamma(\alpha)t^\alpha)$.

Remark 1. *The main difference between the systems (even in the linear case) with different types of fractional derivatives from the point of view of their applicability as model tools of real-world phenomena is the answer for a concrete type of derivative, whether the derivative of a constant is identically equal to zero or not. Typical representatives of these two classes are the fractional derivatives of Caputo and RL types. So, for the study of retarded and neutral systems with Caputo derivatives a lot of the ideas and techniques known from the systems with integer-order derivatives can be used, because of the continuity of the corresponding Krasovskii functional. Note that in some important special cases it is possible that the Krasovskii functional can have a jump only of the first kind at the initial point, but this obstacle can be overcome with the help of some variants of Banach's contraction principle. In contrast, for retarded and neutral systems with RL derivatives we have at least in the technical aspect several complications, mainly based on the availability of a discontinuity (jump of second kind) of the solutions at the low terminal, a fact which greatly complicates the use of the Riesz theorem for the representation of linear continuous functionals (Krasovskii functionals) on* **C** *via a Lebesgue–Stieltjes integral. Even for the retarded systems with RL derivatives, more sophisticated techniques such as Weissinger theorem combined with application of the Mittag–Lafleur function must be used. We emphasize that the important neutral case with RL derivatives, the study of which is the aim of this article, is essentially more complicated even in comparison with the retarded systems with the same kind of derivatives, not only in the technical aspects, but in their applications as models.*

3. The Initial Problem (1), (2) with Discontinuous Initial Functions

The next Lemma is well known for the case of systems with Caputo-type derivatives and for delayed systems with RL-type derivatives, and therefore, we will sketch only the differences appearing in the neutral case with RL-type derivatives and distributed delays.

Lemma 4. *Let the following conditions be fulfilled:*

1. *The hypotheses $\mathfrak{S}$ hold.*
2. *For any $\Phi \in$ **PC**, the vector-valued functional $\mathfrak{F}\colon J \times$ **PC** $\to \mathbb{R}^n \in BL_1^{loc}(J, \mathbb{R}^n)$.*

Then, every solution $X(t)$ of IP (1), (2) is a solution of IP (3), (2) and vice versa.

Proof. Let $\Phi \in$ **PC** be arbitrary and $X(t)$ be the corresponding solution of IP (1), (2). Then, according to formula 2.1.40 in [5], we have

$$I_{a+}^{\alpha}D_{a+}^{\alpha}\left(X(t)-\int_{-h}^{0}[d_{\theta}V(t,\theta)]X(t+\theta)\right)=X(t)-\int_{-h}^{0}[d_{\theta}V(t,\theta)]X(t+\theta)$$

$$-\lim_{t\to a+0}I_{a+}^{1-\alpha}\left(X(t)-\left(\int_{-h}^{0}[d_{\theta}V(t,\theta)]X(t+\theta)\right)\right)=X(t)-\int_{-h}^{0}[d_{\theta}V(t,\theta)]X(t+\theta)$$

$$-\Phi(0)(t-a)^{\alpha-1}+\lim_{t\to a+0}I_{a+}^{1-\alpha}\left(\int_{-h}^{0}[d_{\theta}V(t,\theta)]X(t+\theta)\right).$$

Then, obviously $X(t)$ will be a solution of IP (3), (2) if we prove

$$\lim_{t\to a+0}I_{a+}^{1-\alpha}\left(\int_{-h}^{0}[d_{\theta}V(t,\theta)]X(t+\theta)\right)=\mathbf{0}.$$

Condition ($\mathfrak{S}2$) implies that there exists a constant $V^h>0$ such that $|Var_{\theta\in[-h,0]}V(t,\theta)|\leq V^h$ for $t\in[a,a+h]$, and since $Var_{\theta\in[-h,0]}V(t,\theta)$ is uniformly nonatomic at zero in t, then for any $\epsilon>0$ there exists $\delta\in(0,\epsilon)$ such that $|Var_{\theta\in[-h,0]}V(t,\theta)|<\dfrac{\epsilon\Gamma(\alpha)}{2||\Phi||}$ uniformly for $t\in[a,a+h]$. Then, for $t\in[a,a+\delta]$ we have

$$\begin{aligned}
&\left|\lim_{t\to a+0}I_{a+}^{1-\alpha}\left(\int_{-h}^{0}[d_{\theta}V(t,\theta)]X(t+\theta)\right)\right|\\
&=\frac{1}{\Gamma(\alpha)}\lim_{t\to a+0}(t-a)^{1-\alpha}\left|\int_{-h}^{a-t}[d_{\theta}V(t,\theta)]\Phi(t+\theta)+\int_{a-t}^{0}[d_{\theta}V(t,\theta)]X(t+\theta)\right|\\
&\leq\frac{1}{\Gamma(\alpha)}\lim_{t\to a+0}(t-a)^{1-\alpha}||\Phi|||Var_{\theta\in[-h,0]}V(t,\theta)|\\
&+\frac{1}{\Gamma(\alpha)}\lim_{t\to a+0}(t-a)^{1-\alpha}\sup_{\theta\in[-\delta,0]}|X(t,\theta)|Var_{\theta\in[-\delta,0]}V(t,\theta)
\end{aligned}\tag{4}$$

and, hence, for the first addend on the right-hand side of (4) the relation

$$\lim_{t\to a+0}(t-a)^{1-\alpha}||\Phi|||Var_{\theta\in[-h,0]}V(t,\theta)|=\mathbf{0}$$

holds. Since $X(t)\in\mathbf{C}^{1-\alpha}$, then there exists $\overline{\delta}\in(0,\delta)$ such that for $t\in[a,a+\delta]$ and any $\theta\in[-h,0]$ we have that $|X(t+\theta)|\leq|X(t+\theta)-X(t)|+|X(t)|\leq 2|X(t)|$. Then, for the second addend on the right-hand side of (4) for $t\in[a,a+\delta]$ we obtain that

$$\begin{aligned}
&\frac{1}{\Gamma(\alpha)}\lim_{t\to a+0}(t-a)^{1-\alpha}\sup_{\theta\in[-\delta,0]}|X(t,\theta)|Var_{\theta\in[-\delta,0]}V(t,\theta)\\
&\leq\frac{2}{\Gamma(\alpha)}\lim_{t\to a+0}(t-a)^{1-\alpha}|X(t)|\frac{\epsilon\Gamma(\alpha)}{2||\Phi||}\leq 2\Phi(0)\frac{\epsilon}{2||\Phi||}<\epsilon,
\end{aligned}$$

which implies that

$$\lim_{t\to a+0}(t-a)^{1-\alpha}\sup_{\theta\in[-\delta,0]}|X(t,\theta)|Var_{\theta\in[-\delta,0]}V(t,\theta)=\mathbf{0}.$$

Thus, $X(t)$ is a solution of IP (3), (2).

Let $X(t)$ is a solution of IP (3), (2), and then, applying the operator D_{a+}^{α} to both sides of (3) we obtain immediately the opposite statement. □

Modifying the approach in [11], for an arbitrary fixed number $\alpha \in (0,1)$ we introduce the following real linear space:

$$\begin{aligned}\mathfrak{E} =&\{G : [a-h,\infty)|G(t)|_{[a-h,a]} = \Phi(t-a), \Phi \in \mathbf{PC};\\ &G|_{J^0} \in \mathbf{C}^{1-\alpha}(J^0,\mathbb{R}^n), \lim_{t\to a+0}(t-a)^{1-\alpha}G(t) = \Phi(0)\}\end{aligned}$$

and for any $b > a$ introduce the linear subspaces:

$$\mathfrak{E}_b = \{R : [a-h,b]|R(t) = G|_{[a-h,b]}, G \in \mathfrak{E}\}$$

endowed with the norm $||R||_b = ||\Phi|| + ||G|_{(a,b]}||_b^{1-\alpha}$.

Let $\Phi_0 \in \mathbf{PC}$ with $S^{\Phi_0} = \{a\}$ be arbitrary fixed and define the nonempty, closed, and convex subset $\mathfrak{E}_b^{\Phi_0} \subset \mathfrak{E}_b$ as follows:

$$\mathfrak{E}_b^{\Phi_0} = \{R \in \mathfrak{E}_b|R(t)|_{[a-h,a]} = \Phi_0(t-a), \lim_{t\to a+0}(t-a)^{1-\alpha}R(t) = \Phi_0(0)\}.$$

It is simple to see that for any $R \in \mathfrak{E}_b$ we have that the norms $||R||_b = ||\Phi_0||+||R||_b^{1-\alpha}$ and $||R||_b = ||R||_b^{1-\alpha}$ are equivalent.

For any $b > a, t \in (a,b]$ and $R \in \mathfrak{E}_b$ define the operator $\mathfrak{R}$: $\mathfrak{E}_b^{\Phi_0} \to \mathfrak{E}_b$ as follows:

$$\begin{aligned}(\mathfrak{R}R)(t) &= \Phi(0)(t-a)^{\alpha-1} + \int_{-h}^{0} [d_\theta V(t,\theta)]R(t+\theta)\\ &+I_{-1}(\Gamma(\alpha))\left(\int_a^t I_{\alpha-1}(t-s)\int_{-h}^{0}[dU(s,\theta)]R(s+\theta)ds + \int_a^t I_{\alpha-1}(t-s)\mathfrak{F}(t,R_s)ds\right),\end{aligned} \tag{5}$$

with the additional conditions

$$(\mathfrak{R}R)(t) = \Phi_0(t-a), t \in [a-h,a]; \lim_{t\to b-0}(\mathfrak{R}R)(t) = (\mathfrak{R}R)(b). \tag{6}$$

In addition, for arbitrary $b>h$, $t \in (a,b]$ and $R\in \mathfrak{E}_b$ we define the operators $\mathfrak{T}, \mathfrak{K}$: $\mathfrak{E}_b^{\Phi_0} \to \mathfrak{E}_b$ as follows:

$$\begin{aligned}(\mathfrak{T}R)(t) &= \Phi_0(0)(t-a)^{\alpha-1} + \int_{-h}^{0} [d_\theta V(t,\theta)]R(t+\theta)\\ (\mathfrak{T}R)(t) &= \Phi_0(t-a), t \in [a-h,a]; \lim_{t\to b-0}(\mathfrak{T}R)(t) = (\mathfrak{T}R)(b),\end{aligned} \tag{7}$$

$$\begin{aligned}&(\mathfrak{K}R)(t) = I_{-1}(\Gamma(\alpha))\\ &\left(\int_a^t I_{\alpha-1}(t-s)\left(\int_{-h}^{0}[d_\theta U(s,\theta)]R(s+\theta)\right)ds + \int_a^t I_{\alpha-1}(t-s)\mathfrak{F}(s,R_s)ds\right)\\ &(\mathfrak{K}R)(t) = \mathbf{0}, t \in [a-h,a]; \lim_{t\to b-0}(\mathfrak{K}R)(t) = (\mathfrak{K}R)(b).\end{aligned} \tag{8}$$

Then, the operator $\mathfrak{R}$, defined via (5), (6), for any $R \in \mathfrak{E}_b^{\Phi_0}$ has the form

$$(\mathfrak{R}R)(t) = (\mathfrak{T}R)(t) + (\mathfrak{K}R)(t). \tag{9}$$

The next technical lemma is an immediate generalization of Theorem 4 in [25]. The lemma below is more appropriate for applications and can be used in the cases of RL derivatives too. For simplicity we will consider only the case when the initial function

$\Phi \in \mathbf{PC}$ has only one jump point, but it is simple to see that the proof provided below can be used in the case of an arbitrary but finite number of jumps too.

Lemma 5. *Let the following conditions be fulfilled:*

1. *The hypotheses* $(\mathfrak{S})$ *hold and* $\Phi \in \mathbf{PC}$ *with* $S^{\Phi} = \{t^{jump}\}, t^{jump} \in (a-h, a]$ *are arbitrary.*
2. *The low terminal* a *is a jump point for* Φ *relative to the delay* $\tau^{l_0}(t)$ *for some* $l_0 \in \langle r \rangle$.

Then, $\lim\limits_{t \to a+0} \overline{A}^{l_0}(t) = \Theta, l_0 \in \langle r \rangle$.

Proof. We will consider the more complicated case when $S^{\Phi} = \{t^{jump} = a\}$ and a is a critical jump point. Then, since $\tau^{l}(t) \in C(J,[0,h])$ for all $l \in \langle r \rangle$ we have that $\lim\limits_{t \to a+0} t - \tau^{l_0}(t) = a$. Let assume that there exists a sequence $\{t_i\}_{i=1}^{\infty} \subset (a, b_0)$ such that $t_i - \tau^{l_0}(t_i) = a$, and hence, the set S^{Φ} has a limit point which contradicts condition $(\mathfrak{S}4)$. Then, there exists $b_0 \in (a, a+h)$ such that $t - \tau^{l_0}(t) > a$ for any $t \in (a, b_0]$. Let us assume that $\left|\overline{A}^{l_0}(a)\right| > 0$, $\epsilon \in \left(0, \dfrac{\left|\overline{A}^{l_0}(a)\right|}{4}\right)$ and $\delta \in (o, \epsilon)$ is the number existing according to condition $(\mathfrak{S}2)$ such that $Var_{[-\delta,0]} V(t, \cdot) < \epsilon$ for any $t \in J$. Then, for any $t \in J$ $\theta \in (0, \delta]$ with $t + \theta \geq a$

$$\left|\overline{A}^{l_0}(a)H(a)\right| = \left|\overline{A}^{l_0}(a)\right| \leq |V_d(t,\theta)| \leq |V_d(t,0)| + \left|Var_{\theta \in [-\delta,0]} V_d(t,\theta)\right|$$

$$= \left|Var_{\theta \in [-\delta,0]} V_d^{l}(t,\theta)\right| < \epsilon < \frac{\left|\overline{A}^{l_0}(a)\right|}{4},$$

which is impossible. Thus, we have that $\left|\overline{A}^{l_0}(a)\right| = 0$, and hence, $\lim\limits_{t \to a+0} = \left|\overline{A}^{l_0}(t)\right| = 0$.

The proofs of the cases when a is a noncritical jump point and when $t^{jump} \neq a$ are simpler versions of the proof in the case when $t^{jump} = a$ (a is a critical jump point), and therefore, will be omitted. □

It is clear that without loss of generality it is possible to renumber all concentrated delays in the jump part $V_j(t,\theta) = \sum\limits_{l \in \langle r \rangle} \overline{A}^{l}(t) H(\theta + \tau^{l}(t))$ and give the first $\bar{l}$ numbers, $0 \leq \bar{l} \leq r$ of these delays, relative to which a is a critical jump point. Everywhere below we will assume that this renumbering is made.

Theorem 3. *Let the following conditions be fulfilled:*

1. *The conditions of Lemma 4 hold.*
2. $\sup\limits_{\theta \in [-h,0]} |\partial V_{\theta}(t,\theta)|, \sup\limits_{\theta \in [-h,0]} |\partial U_{\theta}(t,\theta)| \in BL_1^{loc}(J, \mathbb{R}^{n \times n})$, *where* $\partial V_{\theta}, \partial U_{\theta}$ *denote the partial derivatives with respect to* θ.
3. *The condition* $(\mathfrak{C})$ *holds.*

Then, for any $\Phi_0 \in \mathbf{PC}$ *with* $S^{\Phi} = \{t^{jump}\}, t^{jump} \in (a-h, a]$ *there exists* $b_0 > a$ *such that IP* (3), (2) *has at least one solution* $X(t) \in \mathfrak{C}_b^{\Phi_0}$ *with an interval of existence* $(a, b_0]$.

Proof. As above, we will consider the more complicated case when $\Phi \in \mathbf{PC}$ with $S^{\Phi} = \{a\}$. Let $b \in (a, a+h)$ is arbitrary. As a first step we will prove that $\mathfrak{T}(\mathfrak{C}_b^{\Phi_0}) \subseteq \mathfrak{C}_b^{\Phi_0}$.

For any $R \in \mathfrak{C}_b^{\Phi_0}$ from (6) and Lemmas 2 and 3 it follows that

$$(\mathfrak{T}R)(t) = \Phi_0(0)(t-a)^{\alpha-1} + \int_{-h}^{a-t} [d_\theta V(t,\theta)]\Phi_0(t-a+\theta) + \int_{a-t}^{0} [d_\theta V(t,\theta)]R(t+\theta)$$

$$= \Phi_0(0)(t-a)^{\alpha-1} + \int_{-h}^{a-t} [d_\theta V(t,\theta)]\Phi_0(t-a+\theta)$$

$$+ \sum_{l=\bar{l}+1}^{r} \overline{A}^l(t)\Phi_0(t-\tau^l(t)-a) + \sum_{l=1}^{\bar{l}} \overline{A}^l(t)R(t-\tau^l(t)) + \int_{a-t}^{0} [d_\theta V_c(t,\theta)]R(t+\theta), \tag{10}$$

where $V_c(t,\theta) = V_{ac}(t,\theta) + V_s(t,\theta)$, and $t \in (a,b]$.

The first addend on the right-hand side of (10) is continuous for any $t \in J^0$, and hence, belongs to $\mathbf{C}^{1-\alpha}$. Since

$$\lim_{t\to a+0} (t-a)^{1-\alpha}\Phi_0(0)(t-a)^{\alpha-1} = \Phi_0(0),$$

we can prolong $\Phi_0(0)(t-a)^{\alpha-1}$ as a function from $\mathfrak{E}_b^{\Phi_0}$. According to Lemma 1 in [11] and Lemma 4 in [22], since the initial function $\Phi_0(t-a)$ is a continuous function for $t \in [a-h,a)$, the second and the third addends on the right-hand side of (10) are continuous functions at $t \in (a,b]$. Taking into account that a is a critical jump point relative to the delays with numbers $l \in \langle \bar{l} \rangle$, we conclude that the fourth addend is a continuous function at $t \in (a,b]$ too. For the fifth addend, via the substitution $t+\theta = s$ we obtain

$$\int_{a-t}^{0} [d_\theta V_c(t,\theta)]R(t+\theta) = \int_{a}^{t} [d_s V_c(t,s-t)]R(s). \tag{11}$$

Because $V_c(t,s-t)$ and $R(s)$ for any $t \in (a,b]$ are continuous at $s \in (a,t]$, then the fifth addend is a continuous function at $t \in (a,b]$ by virtue of lemma 1 in [19]. Since the right-hand side of (10) is a continuous function at $t = b$, then the second additional relation in (7) holds too, and hence, from (7) it follows that $\mathfrak{T}(\mathfrak{E}_b^{\Phi_0}) \in \mathfrak{E}_b^{\Phi_0}$. Thus, $\mathfrak{T}(\mathfrak{E}_b^{\Phi_0}) \subseteq \mathfrak{E}_b^{\Phi_0}$.

As a second step we will prove that the operator $\mathfrak{T}$ is a contraction. Denote $L_b = \sup_{t\in[a,b]} \ell(t)$,

$$V_b = \max\left(\sup_{\substack{t\in[a,b],\\ \theta\in[-h,0]}} |\partial_\theta V(t,\theta)|, \sup_{t\in[a,b]} \left| \underset{\theta\in[-h,0]}{Var} V(t,\theta) \right| \right)$$

and

$$U_b = \max\left(\sup_{t\in[a,a+b]} \left| \underset{\theta\in[-h,0]}{Var} U(t,\theta) \right|, \sup_{\substack{t\in[a,b],\\ \theta\in[-h,0]}} |\partial_\theta U(t,\theta)| \right).$$

Then, for arbitrary $R, \overline{R} \in \mathfrak{E}_b^{\Phi_0}$ from (7) and Lemmas 2 and 3 it follows that

$$|(\mathfrak{T}(R))(t) - (\mathfrak{T}(\overline{R}))(t)| = \left| \int_{-h}^{0} [d_\theta V(t,\theta)](R(t+\theta) - \overline{R}(t+\theta)) \right|$$

$$\leq \left| \int_{-h}^{0} [d_\theta V_j(t,\theta)](R(t+\theta) - \overline{R}(t+\theta)) \right| + \left| \int_{-h}^{0} [d_\theta V_c(t,\theta)](R(t+\theta) - \overline{R}(t+\theta)) \right|$$

$$\leq \left|\sum_{l=1}^{\bar{l}} \overline{A}^l(t)(R(t-\tau^l(t)) - \overline{R}(t-\tau^l(t)))\right|$$
$$+\left|\sum_{l=\bar{l}}^{l=r} \overline{A}^l(t)(\Phi_0(t-a-\tau^l(t)) - \overline{\Phi_0}(t-a-\tau^l(t)))\right|$$
$$+\left|\int_{a-t}^{0} [d_\theta V_c(t,\theta)](R(t+\theta) - \overline{R}(t+\theta))\right|$$
$$\leq \left|\sum_{l=1}^{\bar{l}} \overline{A}^l(t)(R(t-\tau^l(t)) - \overline{R}(t-\tau^l(t)))\right| \overset{t+\theta=s}{+} \left|\int_a^t [d_s V(t,s-t)](R(s) - \overline{R}(s))\right|. \tag{12}$$

For the first addend on the right-hand side of (12), since $\tau^l(a) = 0$ and the low terminal a is a critical jump point for Φ relative to the delays $\tau^l(t), l \in \langle \bar{l} \rangle$, by virtue of Lemma 5 there exists $b_1 \in (a,b]$ such that for any $t \in (a,b_1]$ we have the estimation

$$\left|\sum_{l=1}^{\bar{l}} \overline{A}^l(t)(R(t-\tau^l(t)) - \overline{R}(t-\tau^l(t)))\right|$$
$$\leq (t-a)^{\alpha-1}\left|\sum_{l=1}^{\bar{l}} \overline{A}^l(t)(t-a)^{1-\alpha}(R(t-\tau^l(t)) - \overline{R}(t-\tau^l(t)))\right|$$
$$\leq \frac{(t-a)^{1-\alpha}}{6} \sup_{s\in(a,t]} (s-a)^{1-\alpha}|R(s) - \overline{R}(s)|. \tag{13}$$

Hypothesis ($\mathfrak{S}2$) implies that for $\epsilon = \dfrac{1}{6}$ there exists $\delta \in (0,\epsilon)$ such that

$$\left|\underset{\theta\in[-\delta,0]}{Var} V_c(t,\theta)\right| < \frac{1}{6}$$

for any $t \in (a,b_2]$, where $b_2 = \min(b_1, a+\delta)$, we obtain

$$|V(t,s-t)| \leq |V(t,0)| + \left|Var_{s-t\in[-\delta,0]} V_c(t,s-t)\right| \leq \frac{1}{6}.$$

Then, the second addend in (12) for any $t \in (a,b_2]$ has the estimation

$$\left|\int_a^t [d_s V(t,s-t)](R(s) - \overline{R}(s))\right|$$
$$= \left|\int_a^t [\partial_s V(t,s-t)](s-a)^{\alpha-1}(s-a)^{1-\alpha}(R(s) - \overline{R}(s))ds\right|$$
$$\leq \frac{(t-a)^\alpha V_b}{\alpha} \sup_{s\in(a,t]} (s-a)^{1-\alpha}|R(s) - \overline{R}(s)|$$

and, hence, for $t \in (a,b_3]$, where $b_3 \in \left(a, \min\left(1, b_2, a + \left(\frac{\alpha}{6V_b}\right)^{\frac{1}{\alpha}}\right)\right]$ we obtain that

$$\left|\int_a^t [d_s V(t,s-t)](R(s) - \overline{R}(s))\right| \leq \frac{1}{6} \sup_{s\in[a,t]} (s-a)^{1-\alpha}|R(s) - \overline{R}(s)|. \tag{14}$$

Multiplying both sides of (12) by $(t-a)^{1-\alpha}$ and then from (12), (13), and (14) it follows that for any $t \in (a, b_3]$ we obtain that $\|\mathfrak{T}(R) - \mathfrak{T}(\overline{R})\|_{b_3}^{\Phi_0} \leq \frac{1}{3}\|R - \overline{R}\|_{b_3}^{\Phi_0}$ and, hence, $\mathfrak{T}$ is a contraction operator in $\mathfrak{E}_{b_3}^{\Phi_0}$.

For arbitrary $R, \overline{R} \in \mathfrak{E}_{b_3}^{\Phi_0}$, from (7) we obtain that

$$
\begin{aligned}
|(\mathfrak{K}R)(t) - (\mathfrak{K}\overline{R})(t)| &\leq \frac{n}{\Gamma(\alpha)}\left|\int_a^t I_{\alpha-1}(t-s)\left(\int_{-h}^0 [d_\theta U(s,\theta)](R(s+\theta) - \overline{R}(s+\theta))\right)ds\right| \\
&+\frac{n}{\Gamma(\alpha)}\left|\int_a^t I_{\alpha-1}(t-s)(\mathfrak{F}(s,R_s) - \mathfrak{F}(s,\overline{R}_s))ds\right| \\
&\leq \frac{n^2}{\Gamma(\alpha)}\int_a^t (t-s)^{\alpha-1}\left|\int_{a-s}^0 [d_\theta U(s,\theta)](R(s+\theta) - \overline{R}(s+\theta))\right|ds \\
&+\frac{n^2}{\Gamma(\alpha)}\int_a^t (t-s)^{\alpha-1}|\mathfrak{F}(s,R_s) - \mathfrak{F}(s,\overline{R}_s)|ds \\
&\leq \frac{n^2}{\Gamma(\alpha)}\int_a^t (t-s)^{\alpha-1}\int_{a-s}^0 |\partial_\theta U(s,\theta)||R(s+\theta) - \overline{R}(s+\theta)|ds \\
&+\frac{n^2}{\Gamma(\alpha)}\int_a^t (t-s)^{\alpha-1}\ell(s)|R(s) - \overline{R}(s)|ds \\
&\leq \frac{n^2 U_b}{\Gamma(\alpha)}\left(\int_a^t (t-s)^{\alpha-1}\left(\int_a^s |R(\eta) - \overline{R}(\eta)|d\eta\right)ds + L_b\int_a^t (t-s)^{\alpha-1}|R(s) - \overline{R}(s)|ds\right).
\end{aligned}
\tag{15}
$$

For the first addend on the right-hand side of (15), for any $t \in (a, b_3]$ the following estimation holds:

$$
\begin{aligned}
&\frac{n^2 U_b}{\Gamma(\alpha)}\left|\int_a^t (t-s)^{\alpha-1}\left(\int_a^s |R(\eta) - \overline{R}(\eta)|d\eta\right)ds\right| = \frac{n^2 U_b}{\Gamma(\alpha)}\left|\int_a^t \left(\int_a^s |R(\eta) - \overline{R}(\eta)|d\eta\right)d(t-s)^\alpha\right| \\
&\frac{n^2 U_b}{\Gamma(\alpha)}\left|\int_a^t (t-s)^\alpha |R(s) - \overline{R}(s)|ds\right| \\
&\overset{t-s=y-a}{=} \frac{n^2 U_b}{\Gamma(\alpha)}\left|\int_a^t (y-a)^\alpha (y-a)^{\alpha-1}(y-a)^{1-\alpha}|R(t-y+a) - \overline{R}(t-y+a)|dy\right| \\
&\leq (2\alpha)^{-1}\frac{n^2 U_b}{\Gamma(\alpha)}(t-a)^{2\alpha}\sup_{s\in[a,t]}(s-a)^{1-\alpha}|R(s) - \overline{R}(s)| \\
&\leq \frac{n^2 U_b}{2\Gamma(1+\alpha)}\sup_{s\in[a,t]}(s-a)^{1-\alpha}|R(s) - \overline{R}(s)|
\end{aligned}
\tag{16}
$$

and analogously, for the second one we obtain

$$\frac{n^2L_b}{\Gamma(\alpha)}\int_a^t (t-s)^{\alpha-1}|R(s)-\overline{R}(s)|ds = \frac{n^2L_b}{\Gamma(1+\alpha)}\int_a^t |R(s)-\overline{R}(s)|d(t-s)^\alpha$$
$$\leq \frac{n^2L_b}{\Gamma(1+\alpha)}\int_a^t (t-s)^\alpha d|R(s)-\overline{R}(s)|$$
$$\leq \frac{n^2L_b(t-a)^{2\alpha-1}}{\Gamma(1+\alpha)} \sup_{s\in[a,t]} (s-a)^{1-\alpha}|R(s)-\overline{R}(s)|. \tag{17}$$

Multiplying both sides of (15) by $(t-a)^{1-\alpha}$, and then, from (15), (16), and (17), it follows that for any $t \in (a, b_3]$ we obtain that

$$\|\mathfrak{K}(R)-\mathfrak{K}(\overline{R})\|_{b_3}^{\Phi_0} \leq \frac{n^2}{2\Gamma(1+\alpha)}(U_b + 2L_b(b_3-a)^\alpha)\|R-\overline{R}\|_{b_3}^{\Phi_0} \tag{18}$$

and, hence, $\mathfrak{K}\colon \mathfrak{C}_{b_3}^{\Phi_0} \to \mathfrak{C}_{b_3}$ is a continuous operator.

Let $r_0 \in \mathbb{R}_+^0$ and $R_0 \in \mathfrak{C}_{b_3}^{\Phi_0}$ be arbitrary fixed and consider the ball

$$\mathfrak{B}(R_0, r_0) = \{R \in \mathfrak{C}_{b_3}^{\Phi_0} \mid \|R_0 - R\|_{b_3}^{\Phi_0} \leq r_0\} \subset \mathfrak{C}_{b_3}^{\Phi_0}.$$

For any $R \in \mathfrak{B}(R_0, r_0)$, from (18) it follows that

$$\|\mathfrak{K}(R)\|_{b_3}^{\Phi_0} \leq \|\mathfrak{K}(R_0)\|_{b_3}^{\Phi_0} + \|\mathfrak{K}(R)-\mathfrak{K}(R_0)\|_{b_3}^{\Phi_0}$$
$$\leq \frac{n^2}{2\Gamma(1+\alpha)}(U_b + 2L_b(b_3-a)^\alpha)\|R-R_0\|_{b_3}^{\Phi_0} + \|\mathfrak{N}(R_0)\|_{b_3}^{\Phi_0}$$
$$\leq \frac{n^2 r_0}{2\Gamma(1+\alpha)}(U_b + 2L_b(b_3-a)^\alpha) + \|\mathfrak{N}(R_0)\|_{b_3}^{\Phi_0} = C(r_0, b_3) \tag{19}$$

and, hence, the set $\mathfrak{K}(\mathfrak{B}(R_0, r_0))$ is uniformly bounded.

To apply Theorem 1 we must prove that the set $\mathfrak{N}(\mathfrak{B}(R_0, r_0))$ is equicontinuous, and hence, it is at least relative compact. For any $R \in \mathfrak{B}(R_0, r_0)$ and arbitrary $t_1, t_2 \in (a, b_3]$ we have the estimation

$$|(\mathfrak{K}R)(t_2) - (\mathfrak{K}R)(t_1)|$$
$$\leq \frac{n^2}{\Gamma(\alpha)}\left|\int_a^{t_1} ((t_2-s)^{\alpha-1} - (t_1-s)^{\alpha-1})\left(\int_{-h}^0 [d_\theta U(s,\theta)]R(s+\theta) + \mathfrak{F}(s, R_s)\right)ds\right|$$
$$+\frac{n^2}{\Gamma(\alpha)}\left|\int_{t_1}^{t_2} (t_2-s)^{\alpha-1}\left(\int_{-h}^0 [d_\theta U(s,\theta)]R(s+\theta) + \mathfrak{F}(s, R_s)\right)ds\right|$$
$$\leq \frac{n^2}{\Gamma(\alpha)}\int_a^{t_1} \left|(t_2-s)^{\alpha-1} - (t_1-s)^{\alpha-1}\right|\left|\int_{-h}^0 [d_\theta U(s,\theta)]R(s+\theta) + \mathfrak{F}(s, R_s)\right|ds$$
$$+\frac{n^2}{\Gamma(\alpha)}\int_{t_1}^{t_2} (t_2-s)^{\alpha-1}\left|\int_{-h}^0 [d_\theta U(s,\theta)]R(s+\theta) + \mathfrak{F}(s, R_s)\right|ds. \tag{20}$$

Since for $t \in (a, b_3]$ from conditions $(\mathfrak{C})$ and (19) we have that

$$\left|\int_{-h}^0 [d_\theta U(s,\theta)]R(s+\theta) + \mathfrak{F}(s, R_s)\right| \leq (U_b + L_b)C(r_0, b_3), \tag{21}$$

then from (20) and (21) for any $t \in (a, b_3]$ we obtain

$$\begin{aligned}
&|(\mathfrak{K}R)(t_2) - (\mathfrak{K}R)(t_1)| \\
&\leq \frac{n^2 C(r_0, b_3)(U_b + L_b)}{\Gamma(\alpha)} \left(\int_a^{t_1} \left|(t_2 - s)^{\alpha-1} - (t_1 - s)^{\alpha-1}\right| ds + \int_{t_1}^{t_2} (t_2 - s)^{\alpha-1} ds \right) \\
&\leq \frac{n^2 C(r_0, b_3)(U_b + L_b)}{\alpha\Gamma(\alpha)} (2(t_2 - t_1)^{\alpha} + (t_1 - a)^{\alpha} - (t_2 - a)^{\alpha}) \\
&\leq \frac{n^2 C(r_0, b_3)(U_b + L_b)}{\Gamma(1+\alpha)} (2(t_2 - t_1)^{\alpha} + |(t_1 - a)^{\alpha} - (t_2 - a)^{\alpha}|). \qquad (22)
\end{aligned}$$

Then, since $(t-a)^{\alpha}$ is uniformly continuous at $t \in [a, a+h]$, for any $\epsilon > 0$ there exists $\delta \in (0, \epsilon)$ such that if $|t_2 - t_1| < \delta$ we have that

$$|(t_1 - a)^{\alpha} - (t_2 - a)^{\alpha}| < \epsilon \frac{\Gamma(1+\alpha)}{n^2 C(r_0, b_3)(U_b + L_b)}$$

and, hence, from (22) it follows that the set $\mathfrak{K}(\mathfrak{B}(R_0, r_0))$ is equicontinuous. Thus, by virtue of the Arzella–Ascoli theorem, $\mathfrak{K}(\mathfrak{B}(R_0, r_0))$ is at least relative compact. For arbitrary $R, \overline{R} \in \mathfrak{C}_{b_3}^{\Phi_0}$ we consider the sum $(\mathfrak{T}R)(t) + (\mathfrak{K}\overline{R})(t)$. Taking into account that $\lim_{t \to a+0} (\mathfrak{K}\overline{R})(t) = \mathbf{0}$ and can be prolonged as $\mathbf{0}$ for any $t \in [a-h, a]$, from (7) it follows that $(\mathfrak{T}R)(t) + (\mathfrak{K}\overline{R})(t) = \Phi_0(t-a)$. Since $\lim_{t \to a+0} (\mathfrak{K}\overline{R})(t) = \mathbf{0}$, then $\lim_{t \to a+0} (t-a)^{1-\alpha} (\mathfrak{K}\overline{R})(t) = \mathbf{0}$ too. Considering the fact that

$$\lim_{t \to a+0} (t-a)^{1-\alpha} (\mathfrak{T}R)(t) = \Phi_0(0) + \lim_{t \to a+0} \left((t-a)^{1-\alpha} \int_{-h}^{0} [d_\theta V(t, \theta)] R(t+\theta) \right) = \Phi_0(0),$$

then, we obtain that

$$\lim_{t \to a+0} (t-a)^{1-\alpha} ((\mathfrak{T}R)(t) + (\mathfrak{K}\overline{R})(t)) = \Phi_0(t-a)$$

and, hence, $(\mathfrak{T}R)(t) + (\mathfrak{K}\overline{R})(t) \in \mathfrak{C}_{b_3}^{\Phi_0}$. Applying Theorem 1, we obtain that there exists at least one fixed point $R^* \in \mathfrak{C}_{b_0}^{\Phi_0}$, i.e., $R^*(t) = (\mathfrak{T}R^*)(t) + (\mathfrak{K}R^*)(t)$, $t \in (a, b_0]$, $b_0 = b_3$. □

Theorem 4. *Let the conditions of Theorem 3 be fulfilled.*

*Then, for any $\Phi_0 \in$ **PC** with $S^{\Phi} = \{t^{jump}\}$, $t^{jump} \in (a-h, a]$ the solution $X(t) \in \mathfrak{C}_{b_0}^{\Phi_0}$ of IP (3), (2) is unique in the interval of its existence $(a, b_0]$.*

Proof. Assume the contrary, that IP (3), (2) possess two different solutions $X^1(t), X^2(t) \in \mathfrak{C}_b^{\Phi_0}$. Then, from (3) for any $t \in (a, b_0]$ we obtain that

$$\begin{aligned}
&\left|X^1(t) - X^2(t)\right| = |Y(t)| \leq |(\mathfrak{T}Y)(t) + (\mathfrak{K}Y)(t)| \leq |(\mathfrak{T}Y)(t)| + |(\mathfrak{K}Y)(t)| \leq q|Y(t)| \\
&+ \frac{n^2}{\Gamma(\alpha)} \int_a^t (t-\tau)^{\alpha-1} \left(\left| \int_{-h}^{0} \partial_\theta U(\tau, \theta) Y(\tau+\theta) d\theta \right| + \left| \mathfrak{F}(\tau, X_\tau^{1,T}) - \mathfrak{F}(\tau, X_\tau^{2,T}) \right| \right) d\tau \\
&\leq q|Y(t)| + \frac{n^2 (b_0 - a)^{1-\alpha} U_{b_0}}{\Gamma(\alpha)} \int_a^t (t-\tau)^{\alpha-1} \left((\sup_{s \in [a,\tau]} |Y(s)| + \ell(\tau)|Y(s)|) d\tau \right). \qquad (23)
\end{aligned}$$

Since (2) implies that $|Y(a)| = 0$, then from (23) it follows that

$$\sup_{s\in[a,t]} |Y(s)| \leq \frac{n^2(b_0-a)^{1-\alpha}U_{b_0}}{\Gamma(\alpha)(1-q)} \int_a^t (t-\tau)^{\alpha-1}\left((\sup_{s\in[a,\tau]} |Y(s)| + \ell(\tau)|Y(s)|)d\tau \right)$$

$$\leq \frac{n^2(b_0-a)^{1-\alpha}U_{b_0}(1+L_{b_0})}{\Gamma(\alpha)(1-q)} \int_a^t (t-\tau)^{\alpha-1} \sup_{s\in[a,\tau]} |Y(s)|d\tau.$$

Denoting $g(t) = g_0 = \dfrac{n^2(b_0-a)^{1-\alpha}U_{b_0}(1+L_{b_0})}{\Gamma(\alpha)(1-q)}, a(t) \equiv 0$ and applying Theorem 2, we obtain for $t \in (a, b_0]$ the estimation $\sup_{s\in[a,t]} |Y(s)| \leq a(t)E_\alpha(g_0\Gamma(\alpha)t^\alpha) \equiv 0$ which contradicts our assumption. The proof of the case when $t^{jump} \neq a$ is almost the same as the proof in the case when $t^{jump} = a$, and therefore, will be omitted. □

Definition 8. *We say that the solution of IP* (3), (2) $X^2(t) \in \mathfrak{C}_{b_2}^{\Phi_0}$ *is a continuation of a solution* $X^1(t) \in \mathfrak{C}_{b_1}^{\Phi_0}$ *of IP* (3), (2) *if* $(a, b_1] \subset (a, b_2]$ *and* $X^2(t) \equiv X^1(t)$ *on* $(a, b_1]$. *The solution* $X^{Max}(t) \in \mathfrak{C}_{b_{Max}}^{\Phi_0}$ *of IP* (3), (2) *which coincides with all of its continuations will be called the maximal solution.*

Theorem 5. *Let the conditions of Theorem 3 be fulfilled.*

Then, for any $\Phi_0 \in \mathbf{PC}$ *with* $S^\Phi = \{t^{jump}\}, t^{jump} \in (a-h, a]$ *the unique solution* $X(t) \in \mathfrak{C}_{b_0}^{\Phi_0}$ *with interval of existence* $(a, b_0]$ *of IP* (3), (2) *can be continued as a unique solution* $X(t) \in \mathfrak{C}$ *of IP* (3), (2) *with interval of existence* J^0.

Proof. Assume the contrary, that there exists a maximal solution $X^{Max}(t) \in \mathfrak{C}_{b_{Max}}^{\Phi_0}$ of IP (3), (2) with the interval of its existence $(a, b_{Max}]$ (which is closed from the right), $b_{Max} < \infty$, and define the operator $\mathfrak{R}\colon \mathfrak{C}_b^{\Phi_0} \to \mathfrak{C}_b$ with $b > b_{Max}$ via (5) with the additional conditions $(\mathfrak{R}R)(t) = X^{Max}(t), t \in [a-h, a]$; $\lim_{t\to b-0}(\mathfrak{R}R)(t) = (\mathfrak{R}R)(b)$. Then, we can prove, fully analogous to the proof of Theorem 3, that for any $\Phi_0 \in \mathbf{PC}$ with $S^\Phi = \{t^{jump}\}, t^{jump} \in (a-h, a]$ there exists $\bar{b} > b_{Max}$ such that IP (3), (2) has at least one solution $X^{\bar{b}}(t) \in \mathfrak{C}_{\bar{b}}^{\Phi_0}$ with interval of existence $(a, \bar{b}]$, and obviously, $X^{\bar{b}}(t) \equiv X^{Max}(t)$ for any $t \in (a-h, b_{Max}]$. Thus, we obtain that $X^{\bar{b}}(t)$ is a continuation of $X^{Max}(t)$, which is impossible.

Let assume that that there exists a maximal solution $X^{Max}(t)$ of IP (3), (2) and its interval of existence is open and finite, i.e., $(a, b_{Max}), b_{Max} < \infty$. Then, since $X^{Max}(t)$ satisfies (3) for any $t \in (a, b_{Max})$ and the additional condition $\lim_{t\to b_{Max}-0}(\mathfrak{R}R)(t) = (\mathfrak{R}R)(b)$ too, we conclude that $X^{Max}(t)$ satisfies (3) for any $t \in (a, b_{Max}]$, which contradicts our assumption. Thus, we have that $b_{Max} = \infty$, which completes the proof. □

Remark 2. *We note that from Theorems 3–5 it follows that the requirement in Theorem 2 [11], that in the Lebesgue decomposition of* $U(t, \theta)$ *a singular part does not exist, is unnecessary. So, the results proved in Theorems 3–5 generalize the statement of Theorem 2 [11] even in the retarded case.*

4. The Linear Case $\mathfrak{F}(t, X_t^T) = F(t)$ – Fundamental Matrices and Integral Representation of the Solutions

In this section, we establish the existence of two different types of fundamental matrices and of their bases; we obtain two types integral representations for the solutions of IP (24), (2) for different kinds of initial functions. In the case when $\mathfrak{F}(t, X_t^T) = F(t)$, system (1) becomes an inhomogeneous linear system and has the following form:

$$D^{\alpha}_{a+}\left(Y(t)-\int\limits_{-h}^{0}[d_\theta V(t,\theta)]Y(t+\theta)\right)=\int\limits_{-h}^{0}[d_\theta U(t,\theta)]Y(t+\theta)+F(t), \tag{24}$$

where $Y(t)=(y_1(t),\dots,y_n(t))^T: J\to\mathbb{R}^n$ and $F(t)=(f_1(t),\dots,f_n(t))^T\in BL_1^{loc}(J,\mathbb{R}^n)$. Consider the corresponding homogeneous linear system of (1) and (24):

$$D^{\alpha}_{a+}\left(Y(t)-\int\limits_{-h}^{0}[d_\theta V(t,\theta)]Y(t+\theta)\right)=\int\limits_{-h}^{0}[d_\theta U(t,\theta)]Y(t+\theta), \tag{25}$$

and following [11] introduce for any $j\in\langle n\rangle$ and $\bar{s}\in J$ the initial function

$$Y^j(t,\bar{s})=\mathbf{0},t\in[\bar{s}-h,\bar{s});\quad Y(t,\bar{s})=I^j,t=\bar{s}, \tag{26}$$

where I^j denotes the j-th column of the identity matrix $\mathbf{I}$.

From Theorem 5 it follows that for any $j\in\langle n\rangle$ and $\bar{s}\in J$ IP (25), (2) has a unique solution $\mathfrak{H}^j(t,s)$, which satisfies (25) for any $t\in(\bar{s},\infty)$ and the initial condition (2) with the initial function (26) too. Then, the matrix $\mathfrak{H}(t,s)=(\mathfrak{H}^1(t,s),\dots,\mathfrak{H}^n(t,s))$ will be called fundamental matrix of the system (25).

Additionally, we introduce the following initial function for any $j\in\langle n\rangle$ and $\bar{s}\in[a-h,a]$:

$$Y^j(t,\bar{s})=I^j,a-h\le\bar{s}\le t\le a;\quad Y(t,\bar{s})=\mathbf{0},t<\bar{s};Y(t,\bar{s})=\mathbf{0},\bar{s}<a-h. \tag{27}$$

As above, for any $j\in\langle n\rangle$ and $\bar{s}\in J$ we can conclude that IP (24), (2) has a unique solution $\mathfrak{Q}^j(t,s)$ which satisfies (24) for any $t\in J^0$ and the initial condition (2) with the initial function (27) too. The matrix $\mathfrak{Q}(t,s)=(\mathfrak{Q}^1(t,s),\dots,\mathfrak{Q}^n(t,s))$ we will call the generalized fundamental matrix.

Both matrices play crucial roles in the construction of different kinds of integral representations of the solutions of IP (24), (2) and IP (25), (2), having a lot of applications in the qualitative theory of the fractional systems.

It is clear that $\mathfrak{H}(t,a)\equiv\mathfrak{Q}(t,a)$ if and only if $s=a$. First, we will establish some analytical properties of the matrices $\mathfrak{Q}(t,a)$ and $\mathfrak{H}(t,a)$, needed to obtain appropriate integral representations of the solutions of (24) and (25).

As in the case of Caputo-type derivatives [26], for any $\Phi\in\mathbf{PC}^*$ we define the function

$$\tilde{X}(t)=\int\limits_{a-h}^{a}[d_s\tilde{\Phi}(s-a)]\mathfrak{Q}(t,s), \tag{28}$$

where $\tilde{\Phi}(s-a)=\Phi(s-a),s\in(a-h,a]$, and $\tilde{\Phi}(-h)=\mathbf{0},s=a-h$. It is necessary to establish for any $j\in\langle n\rangle$ that the solutions $\mathfrak{Q}^j(t,s)$ to IP (25), (2) are Lebesgue integrable in s on $s\in[a-h,a]$ for any fixed $t\in J^0$.

Remark 3. *Note that to prove the statement that $\mathfrak{Q}^j(t,s),j\in\langle n\rangle$ are Lebesgue integrable in s on $s\in[a-h,a]$ for any fixed $t\in J^0$ is not trivial, in contrast with the Caputo case where this fact can be proved via elementary application of a generalized Bellman–Gronwall inequality (see Theorem 2). The main tool in all these proofs of theorems devoted to integral representations of the solutions of fractional systems with Caputo-type derivatives is the Fubini theorem. Thus, from our point of view it is important to justify its correct application. The greatest obstacle in the neutral case with RL derivatives is the problem with the integrability of the integrands relative to the product measures, which are defined as the products of two Lebesgue–Stieltjes measures. Note that this problem arises in our case, since the integrand is with a singularity of order $1-\alpha$ at the point a in contrast to the case of neutral systems with Caputo-type fractional derivatives, in which case the integrand is a Lebesgue measurable and locally bounded function. This difference leads at least to some additional technical complications, but not only that.*

To overcome this obstacle, we need the statements of the next two lemmas.

Lemma 6. *Let the following conditions be fulfilled:*

1. *Conditions 1 and 2 of Theorem 3 hold.*
2. $\sup_{t\in J^0}\left|Var_{\theta\in[-h,0]}V(t,\theta)\right| < 1$

Then, for any compact interval $[\bar{a},b]\subset J^0, t\in[\bar{a},b]$, *and* $j\in\langle n\rangle$ *we have that*

$$\mathfrak{Q}^j(t,\cdot)\in BL_1^{loc}([a-h,a],\mathbb{R}^n).$$

Proof. Let $t\in J^0$ and $j\in\langle n\rangle$ be arbitrary fixed. Then, from (25), since $\mathfrak{F}(\tau,X_\tau^T)\equiv\mathbf{0}$ we have

$$\begin{aligned}|\mathfrak{Q}^j(t,s)| &\le |I^j\mathbf{1}_{[s,a]}(t-a)|(t-a)^{\alpha-1}+\left|\int_{-h}^{0}[d_\theta V(t,\theta)]\mathfrak{Q}^j(t,s)\right|\\ &+\frac{n^2}{\Gamma(\alpha)}\int_a^t(t-\tau)^{\alpha-1}\left|\int_{-h}^{0}[d_\theta U(\tau,\theta)]\mathfrak{Q}^j(\tau+\theta,s)\right|d\tau\\ &|I^j\mathbf{1}_{[s,a]}(t-a)|(t-a)^{\alpha-1}+V\sup_{\eta\in(a,t]}\left|\mathfrak{Q}^j(t,s)\right|\\ &=\frac{n^2U_b}{\Gamma(\alpha)(1-V)}\left|\int_a^t(t-\tau)^{\alpha-1}\sup_{\eta\in(a,\tau]}\left|\mathfrak{Q}^j(\eta,s)\right|\right|d\tau\end{aligned}$$

and, hence, by virtue of Theorem 2 we obtain

$$\begin{aligned}\sup_{s\in[-h,0]}\left(\sup_{\eta\in(a,t]}\left|\mathfrak{Q}^j(\eta,s)\right|\right) &\le |I^j\mathbf{1}_{[s,a]}(t-a)|\frac{(t-a)^{\alpha-1}}{1-V}\\ &+\frac{n^2U_b}{\Gamma(\alpha)(1-V)}\left|\int_a^t(t-\tau)^{\alpha-1}\sup_{s\in[-h,0]}\left(\sup_{\eta\in(a,\tau]}\left|\mathfrak{Q}^j(\eta,s)\right|\right)\right|d\tau\\ &\le |I^j\mathbf{1}_{[s,a]}(t-a)|\frac{(t-a)^{\alpha-1}}{1-V}E_\alpha\left(\frac{n^2U_b(t-a)^\alpha}{(1-V)}\right),\end{aligned}\tag{29}$$

where in (29) $E_\alpha(z)=\sum_{k=1}^{\infty}\frac{z^k}{\Gamma(\alpha k+1)}$ is the one-parameter Mittag–Laffler function. This completes the proof. □

By virtue of Lemma 6 we can state that the integral on the right-hand side of (28) is correctly defined.

Corollary 1. *Let the conditions of Lemma 6 hold.*

Then, for arbitrary fixed $\bar{s}\in[-h,0)$, $\mathfrak{Q}(t,s)$ *is continuous in* t *for* $t-a\in[-h,\bar{s})\cup(\bar{s},0)$ *or when* $\bar{s}=0$ *for* $t-a\in[-h,0)$. *At* $t-a=\bar{s}$, $\mathfrak{Q}(t,s)$ *has a first-kind jump.*

Lemma 7. *Let the conditions of Lemma 6 hold.*

Then, for any $t\in J^0$ *we have that* $\mathfrak{Q}(t,\cdot)\in BV([a-h,a],\mathbb{R}^{n\times n})$.

Proof. Let $\Phi^*(s)=(\varphi_1^*(s),\dots,\varphi_n^*(s))^T\in\mathbf{PC}^*$ with $\inf_{s\in[a-h,a]}\varphi_j^*(s)\ge c_0>0, j\in\langle n\rangle$. Then, integrating by parts formally the integral in (28) we have that

$$\int_{a-h}^{a} [d_s\tilde{\Phi}^*(s-a)]\mathfrak{Q}(t,s)$$

$$= \tilde{\Phi}^*(0)\mathfrak{Q}(t,a) - \tilde{\Phi}(-h)]\mathfrak{Q}(t,a-h) - \int_{a-h}^{a} [d_s\mathfrak{Q}(t,s)]\tilde{\Phi}^*(s-a), \quad (30)$$

and since the integral on the left-hand side of (30) exists, then the integral on the right-hand side exists too (see [27], point 5, page 229). Let $t \in J^0$ be arbitrary, $\epsilon > 0$ and $\prod_q = \{s_0 = a-h, s_1, \ldots, s_q = a\} \subset [a-h,a]$ be an arbitrary partition. Then, there exists a number $q_\epsilon \in \mathbb{N}$ such that for any $q \geq q_\epsilon$ we have that

$$\left| \int_{a-h}^{a} [d_s\mathfrak{Q}(t,s)]\tilde{\Phi}^*(s-a) - \sum_{k=1}^{q} \tilde{\Phi}^*(s_k-a)\left|\mathfrak{Q}^j(t,s_k) - \mathfrak{Q}^j(t,s_{k-1})\right| \right| < \epsilon,$$

and hence,

$$0 \leq c_0 \sum_{k=1}^{q} \left|\mathfrak{Q}^j(t,s_k) - \mathfrak{Q}^j(t,s_{k-1})\right| \leq \inf_{s\in[a-h,a]} |\tilde{\Phi}^*(s-a)| \sum_{k=1}^{q} \left|\mathfrak{Q}^j(t,s_k) - \mathfrak{Q}^j(t,s_{k-1})\right|$$

$$\leq \sum_{k=1}^{q} \tilde{\Phi}^*(s_k)\left|\mathfrak{Q}^j(t,s_k) - \mathfrak{Q}^j(t,s_{k-1})\right| \leq \int_{a-h}^{a} [d_s\mathfrak{Q}(t,s)]\tilde{\Phi}^*(s-a) + \epsilon.$$

Thus, $\mathfrak{Q}(t,\cdot) \in BV([a-h,a],\mathbb{R}^{n\times n})$. □

Theorem 6. *Let the conditions of Lemma 6 hold.*

Then, for arbitrary initial function $\Phi \in \mathbf{PC}^*$ the function $\tilde{X}(t)$, defined via (28), is the unique solution of IP (25), (2) with interval of existence $t \in J^0$.

Proof. The proof is based on ideas used in [22]. Thereupon, we will emphasize in detail those differences that arise from the influence on the neutral system of the Riemann–Liouville-type derivatives.

Theorem 5 implies that $\mathfrak{Q}(\cdot,s) \in C(J^0,\mathbb{R}^{n\times n})$ for any $s \in [a-h,a]$. Then, for the function $\tilde{X}(t)$, defined via (28), by virtue of Lemma 1 in [22] we have that $\tilde{X}(t) \in C(J^0,\mathbb{R}^n)$ too.

More concretely, for arbitrary fixed $t \in J^0$ the kernels $V(t,\theta)$ of $U(t,\theta)$ define two Lebesgue–Stieltjes measures $\mu_V^\theta = \mu_V((\theta_1,\theta_2]) = V(t,\theta_2) - V(t,\theta_1)$ and $\mu_U^\theta = \mu_U((\theta_1,\theta_2]) = U(t,\theta_2) - U(t,\theta_1)$ for any $(\theta_1,\theta_2] \subset [-h,0]$, as well as the function $\overline{\Phi}(s)$ defining a measure $\mu_{\overline{\Phi}}^s = \mu_{\overline{\Phi}}((s_1,s_2]) = \overline{\Phi}(s_1) - \overline{\Phi}(s_2)$ for any $(s_1,s_2] \subset [a-h,a]$. We introduce the product measures

$$(\mu_V^\theta \times \mu_{\overline{\Phi}}^s)((\theta_1,\theta_2] \times (s_1,s_2]) = \mu_V((\theta_1,\theta_2]\mu_{\overline{\Phi}}((s_1,s_2])$$

and

$$(\mu_U^\theta \times \mu_{\overline{\Phi}}^s)((\theta_1,\theta_2] \times (s_1,s_2]) = \mu_U((\theta_1,\theta_2]\mu_{\overline{\Phi}}((s_1,s_2])$$

of the rectangles in $\mathbf{P} = [-h,0] \times [a-h,a]$. Then, to use the proposition 5.15 in [28] we need to prove that the relations $\left|\iint_P \mathfrak{Q}(t+\theta,s)\mu_U^\theta \times \mu_{\overline{\Phi}}^s\right| < \infty$ and $\left|\iint_P \mathfrak{Q}(t+\theta,s)\mu_V^\theta \times \mu_{\overline{\Phi}}^s\right| < \infty$ hold. Since according to Lemmas 5 and 6 we have $\mathfrak{Q}(t,\cdot) = BV([a-h,a],\mathbb{R}^{n\times n})$ and $\mathfrak{Q}(t+\theta,\cdot) = L_1^{loc}([a-h,\infty),\mathbb{R}^{n\times n})$ for any $t \in J^0$ and $\theta \in [-h,0]$ concerning the first argument, then taking into account that $\mu_V^\theta \times \mu_{\overline{\Phi}}^s = \mu_{\overline{\Phi}}^s \times \mu_V^\theta$ and $\mu_U^\theta \times \mu_{\overline{\Phi}}^s = \mu_{\overline{\Phi}}^s \times \mu_U^\theta$ we obtain

$$\left|\iint\limits_{P}\Omega(t+\theta,s)\mu_U^\theta\times\mu_{\overline{\Phi}}^s\right|=\left|\int\limits_{-h}^{0}[d_\theta U(t,\theta)]\left(\int\limits_{a-h}^{a}[d_s\Phi(s-a)]\Omega(t+\theta,s)\right)\right|<\infty,$$

$$\left|\iint\limits_{P}\Omega(t+\theta,s)\mu_V^\theta\times\mu_{\overline{\Phi}}^s\right|=\left|\int\limits_{-h}^{0}[d_\theta V(t,\theta)]\left(\int\limits_{a-h}^{a}[d_s\Phi(s-a)]\Omega(t+\theta,s)\right)\right|<\infty.$$

Then, applying proposition 5.15 in [28] we have for $t \in J^0$ that

$$\int\limits_{-h}^{0}[d_\theta V(t,\theta)]\tilde{X}(t+\theta)=\int\limits_{-h}^{0}[d_\theta V(t,\theta)]\left(\int\limits_{a-h}^{a}[d_s\Phi(s-a)]\Omega(t+\theta,s)\right)$$
$$=\int\limits_{a-h}^{a}[d_s\Phi(s-a)]\left(\int\limits_{-h}^{0}[d_\theta V(t,\theta)]\Omega(t+\theta,s)\right) \tag{31}$$

and in the same way we obtain

$$\int\limits_{-h}^{0}[d_\theta U(t,\theta)]\tilde{X}(t+\theta)=\int\limits_{a-h}^{a}[d_s\Phi(s-a)]\left(\int\limits_{-h}^{0}[d_\theta U(t,\theta)]\Omega(t+\theta,s)\right). \tag{32}$$

From (25) and (31) via the Fubini theorem it follows that

$$D_{a+}^{\alpha}\left(\tilde{X}^j(t)-\int\limits_{-h}^{0}[d_\theta V(t,\theta)]\tilde{X}^j(t+\theta)\right)$$
$$=\frac{1}{\Gamma(1-\alpha)}\frac{d}{dt}\int\limits_{a}^{t}(t-\eta)^{-\alpha}\left(\int\limits_{a-h}^{a}[d_s\tilde{\Phi}(s-a)]\Omega(\eta,s)\right)d\eta$$
$$-\frac{1}{\Gamma(1-\alpha)}\frac{d}{dt}\int\limits_{a}^{t}(t-\eta)^{-\alpha}\int\limits_{-h}^{0}[d_\theta V(\eta,\theta)]\left(\int\limits_{a-h}^{a}[d_s\tilde{\Phi}(s-a)]\Omega(\eta+\theta,s)\right)d\eta$$
$$=\int\limits_{a-h}^{a}[d_s\tilde{\Phi}(s-a)]\left(\frac{1}{\Gamma(1-\alpha)}\frac{d}{dt}\int\limits_{a}^{t}(t-\eta)^{-\alpha}\Omega(\eta,s)d\eta\right)$$
$$-\int\limits_{a-h}^{a}[d_s\tilde{\Phi}(s-a)]\left(\frac{1}{\Gamma(1-\alpha)}\frac{d}{dt}\int\limits_{a}^{t}(t-\eta)^{-\alpha}\left(\int\limits_{-h}^{0}[d_\theta V(\eta,\theta)]\Omega(\eta+\theta,s)\right)d\eta\right)$$
$$=\int\limits_{a-h}^{a}[d_s\tilde{\Phi}(s-a)]D^{\alpha}\left(\Omega(t,s)-\int\limits_{-h}^{0}[d_\theta V(t,\theta)]\Omega(t+\theta,s)\right). \tag{33}$$

Hence, from (25), (32), and (33) it follows that $\tilde{X}(t)$, defined via (28), satisfies (25) for any $t \in J^0$.

Let $\tilde{s} \in [a-h,a]$ be an arbitrary number, and then, from (28) when $t=\tilde{s}$, it follows that

$$\tilde{X}(\tilde{s})=\int\limits_{a-h}^{a}[d_s\tilde{\Phi}(s-a)]\Omega(t,s)=\int\limits_{a-h}^{\tilde{s}}[d_s\tilde{\Phi}(s-a)]\Omega(t,s)+\int\limits_{\tilde{s}}^{a}[d_s\tilde{\Phi}(s-a)]\Omega(t,s)$$
$$=\int\limits_{a-h}^{\tilde{s}}[d_s\tilde{\Phi}(s-a)]\mathbf{I}=\tilde{\Phi}(\tilde{s})-\tilde{\Phi}(a-h)=\tilde{\Phi}(\tilde{s}),$$

i.e., $\tilde{X}(t)$ satisfies the initial condition (2), and hence, it is the unique solution of the IP (25), (2) with interval of existence $t \in J^0$. □

Following the idea in [22], we introduce

$$\mathfrak{X}(t) = \int_a^t \mathfrak{H}(t,s) D_{a+}^{1-\alpha} F^0(s) ds, \tag{34}$$

where $F^0(t) \equiv F(t), t \in J^0$, and $F^0(0) = \mathbf{0}$.

Theorem 7. *Let the conditions of Lemma 6 hold.*

Then, the function $\mathfrak{X}(t)$ introduced via (34) *is the unique solution of IP* (24), (2) *for the initial function $\Phi(t-a) \equiv \mathbf{0}, t \in [a-h, a]$ and interval of existence $t \in J^0$.*

Proof. As in the theorem above, the proof is based on some ideas used in [15]. Therefore, we will only sketch the similar parts and we will emphasize in detail those differences that arise from the influence on the neutral system of the Riemann–Liouville-type derivatives.

For any $t \in J^0$ and $\theta \in [-h, 0]$, since $\mathfrak{H}(t,s) = 0$ when $t < s$, we have that

$$\int_{t+\theta}^t \mathfrak{H}(t+\theta, s) D_{a+}^{1-\alpha} F^0(s) ds = \mathbf{0}. \tag{35}$$

Then, substituting $\mathfrak{X}(t)$ on the left-hand side of (24) for any $t \in J^0$ via the Fubini theorem and using formula (2.211) in [5] and (35) we obtain that

$$\begin{aligned}
&D_{a+}^{\alpha}\left(\mathfrak{X}(t) - \int_{-h}^{0} [d_\theta V(t,\theta)]\mathfrak{X}(t+\theta)\right) \\
&= \frac{1}{\Gamma(1-\alpha)} \frac{d}{dt} \int_a^t (t-\eta)^{-\alpha} \left(\int_a^{\eta} \mathfrak{H}(\eta, s) \left(D_{a+}^{1-\alpha} F^0\right)(s) ds \right) d\eta \\
&- \frac{1}{\Gamma(1-\alpha)} \frac{d}{dt} \int_a^t (t-\eta)^{-\alpha} \left(\int_{-h}^{0} [d_\theta V(\eta,\theta)] \left(\int_a^{\eta+\theta} \mathfrak{H}(\eta+\theta, s) \left(D_{a+}^{1-\alpha} F^0\right)(s) ds \right) \right) d\eta \\
&= \frac{1}{\Gamma(1-\alpha)} \frac{d}{dt} \int_a^t \left(\int_s^t (t-\eta)^{-\alpha} \mathfrak{H}(\eta, s) d\eta \right) \left(D_{a+}^{1-\alpha} F^0\right)(s) ds \\
&- \frac{1}{\Gamma(1-\alpha)} \frac{d}{dt} \int_a^t (t-\eta)^{-\alpha} \left(\int_{-h}^{0} [d_\theta V(\eta,\theta)] \left(\int_a^{\eta} \mathfrak{H}(\eta+\theta, s) \left(D_{a+}^{1-\alpha} F^0\right)(s) ds \right) \right) d\eta \\
&= \frac{1}{\Gamma(1-\alpha)} \frac{d}{dt} \int_a^t \left(\int_a^t (t-\eta)^{-\alpha} \mathfrak{H}(\eta, s) d\eta \right) \left(D_{a+}^{1-\alpha} F^0\right)(s) ds \\
&- \frac{1}{\Gamma(1-\alpha)} \frac{d}{dt} \int_a^t \left(\int_a^t (t-\eta)^{-\alpha} \left(\int_{-h}^{0} [d_\theta V(\eta,\theta)] \mathfrak{H}(\eta+\theta, s) \right) d\eta \right) \left(D_{a+}^{1-\alpha} F^0\right)(s) ds \\
&= \int_a^t \left(D_{a+}^{1-\alpha} F^0\right)(s) D_{a+}^{\alpha}(\mathfrak{H}(t,s)) ds - \int_a^t \left(D_{a+}^{1-\alpha} F^0\right)(s) D_{a+}^{\alpha} \left(\int_{-h}^{0} [d_\theta V(t,\theta)] \mathfrak{H}(t+\theta, s) \right) ds \\
&+ \lim_{s \to t-0} {}^{RL}D_{a+}^{\alpha-1} \left(\left(D_{a+}^{1-\alpha} F^0\right)(s) \mathfrak{H}(t,s) \right) \\
&- \lim_{s \to t-0} {}^{RL}D_{a+}^{\alpha-1} \left(\left(D_{a+}^{1-\alpha} F^0\right)(s) \left(\int_{-h}^{0} [d_\theta V(t,\theta)] \mathfrak{H}(t+\theta, s) \right) \right).
\end{aligned} \tag{36}$$

For the third addend on the right-hand side of (36), we have that

$$
\begin{aligned}
&\lim_{s\to t-0} {}^{RL}D_{a+}^{\alpha-1}\left(\left(D_{a+}^{1-\alpha}F^0\right)(s)(\mathfrak{H}(t,s))\right)\\
&= \lim_{s\to t-0}\frac{1}{\Gamma(\alpha)}\int_a^t (t-\tau)^{-\alpha}\mathfrak{H}(\tau,s)\left(D_{a+}^{1-\alpha}F^0\right)(s)d\tau\\
&= \frac{1}{\Gamma(\alpha)}\int_a^t (t-\tau)^{-\alpha}\lim_{s\to t-0}\left(\mathfrak{H}(\tau,s)\left(D_{a+}^{1-\alpha}F^0\right)(s)\right)d\tau\\
&= \left|\frac{1}{\Gamma(\alpha)}\int_a^t (t-\tau)^{-\alpha}\mathfrak{H}(\tau,\tau)\left(D_{a+}^{1-\alpha}F^0\right)(\tau)d\tau\right|\\
&= \frac{1}{\Gamma(\alpha)}\int_a^t (t-\tau)^{-\alpha}\mathbf{I}\left(D_{a+}^{1-\alpha}F^0\right)(\tau)d\tau\\
&= \left({}^{RL}D_{a+}^{\alpha-1}\,{}^{RL}D_{a+}^{1-\alpha}F^0\right)(t) = F^0(t) - F^0(0) = F^0(t).
\end{aligned}
\tag{37}
$$

Since $V(\tau,0)=\Theta$ and $\mathfrak{H}(t+\theta,t)=\mathbf{0}$, for any $t\in J^0$ and $\theta\in[-h,0)$ we obtain

$$
\begin{aligned}
&\lim_{s\to t-0} {}^{RL}D_{a+}^{\alpha-1}\left(\left(D_{a+}^{1-\alpha}F^0\right)(s)\int_{-h}^{0}[d_\theta V(\tau,\theta)]\mathfrak{H}(\tau+\theta,s)\right)\\
&= \lim_{s\to t-0}\frac{1}{\Gamma(\alpha)}\int_a^t (t-\tau)^{-\alpha}\left(\left(D_{a+}^{1-\alpha}F^0\right)(s)\int_{-h}^{0}[d_\theta V(\tau,\theta)]\mathfrak{H}(\tau+\theta,s)\right)d\tau\\
&= \frac{1}{\Gamma(\alpha)}\int_a^t (t-\tau)^{-\alpha}\left(D_{a+}^{1-\alpha}F^0\right)(\tau)\int_{-h}^{0}[d_\theta V(\tau,\theta)]\mathfrak{H}(\tau+\theta,\tau)d\tau = \mathbf{0},
\end{aligned}
\tag{38}
$$

and hence, from (36), (37), and (38) it follows that

$$
\begin{aligned}
&D_{a+}^{\alpha}\left(\mathfrak{X}(t) - \int_{-h}^{0}[d_\theta V(t,\theta)]\mathfrak{X}(t+\theta)\right)\\
&= \int_a^t \left(D_{a+}^{1-\alpha}F^0\right)(s)D_{a+}^{\alpha}\left(\mathfrak{H}(t,s) - \int_{-h}^{0}[d_\theta V(t,\theta)]\mathfrak{H}(t+\theta,s)\right)ds + F^0(t).
\end{aligned}
\tag{39}
$$

Similarly as above, for the right-hand side of (24) we obtain

$$
\begin{aligned}
&\int_{-h}^{0}[d_\theta U(t,\theta)]\mathfrak{X}(t+\theta) + F^0(t)\\
&= \int_{-h}^{0}[d_\theta U(t,\theta)]\left(\int_a^{t+\theta}\mathfrak{H}(t+\theta,s)\left(D_{a+}^{1-\alpha}F^0\right)(s)ds\right) + F^0(t)\\
&= \int_a^t \left(D_{a+}^{1-\alpha}F^0\right)(s)\int_{-h}^{0}([d_\theta U(t,\theta)]\mathfrak{H}(t,s))ds + F^0(t),
\end{aligned}
\tag{40}
$$

and since $\mathfrak{H}(t,s)$ is a fundamental matrix, then the statement of the theorem follows from (39) and (40). □

Corollary 2. *Let the following conditions be fulfilled:*

1. *The conditions of Lemma 6 hold.*
2. *For any initial function $\Phi \in PC^*$ and $F(t) \in BL_1^{loc}(J, \mathbb{R}^n)$, the functions $\tilde{X}(t)$ and $\mathfrak{X}(t)$ are defined via* (28) *and* (34)*, respectively.*

Then, the function $X(t) = \tilde{X}(t) + \mathfrak{X}(t)$ is the unique solution of IP (24), (2) *and has the following representation for any $t \in J^0$:*

$$X(t) = \int_a^t \mathfrak{H}(t,s) D_{a+}^{1-\alpha} F(s) ds + \int_{a-h}^a \mathfrak{Q}(t,s) d_s \tilde{\Phi}(s-a), \tag{41}$$

where $\tilde{\Phi}(s-a) \equiv \Phi(s-a)$ for $s \in [a-h, a)$ and $\tilde{\Phi}(a-h) = \mathbf{0}$.

Proof. It follows from the superposition principle and Theorems 5 and 6. □

5. Weighted Stabilities

It is worth noting that the standard definitions for stability in the Lyapunov or Ulam–Hyers senses introduced for the systems with integer-order derivatives (without or with delays) are applicable directly for systems with fractional derivatives only when the fractional derivative of a constant is equal to zero (as Caputo-type derivatives, etc.). As we have mentioned previously [11], in general when the fractional derivative of a constant is not equal to zero (as for RL-type derivatives), then the standard definitions are not applicable since the solutions of the systems with RL-type derivatives have singularity at $a+0$ (the low terminal) of power order $\alpha - 1$. That is why new types of definitions for the different kinds of stabilities applicable to systems with RL-type derivatives are needed. The aim of this section is to introduce definitions of weighted stability in the Lyapunov sense, as well as UH and UHR weighted stabilities for fractional systems (equations) with RL-type derivatives and to study the relations with the classical definitions and with the concept "stability in time" in the Lyapunov sense, introduced in [9].

Let assume that $\mathfrak{F}(t, \mathbf{0}) \equiv \mathbf{0}$ for any $t \in J$. Below, we recall the classical definitions for Lyapunov stability, applicable only for the case when the fractional derivatives are, in the Caputo sense, of order $\alpha \in (0, 1]$ (and not applicable for RL derivatives):

Definition 9 ([29])**.** *The zero solution of IP* (1), (2) *(with derivatives in the Caputo sense!) is said to be:*

(a) *Stable if for a given low terminal $a \in \mathbb{R}$ and any $\epsilon > 0$ there is a $\delta(\epsilon, a) > 0$ such that for each initial function $\Phi \in \mathbf{PC}(\mathbf{PC}^*)$ with $\|\Phi\| < \delta$ the corresponding solution $X(t)$ satisfies for each $t \in J$ the inequality $|X(t)| \le \epsilon$.*

(b) *Stable (uniformly) if for a given low terminal $a \in \mathbb{R}$ and any $\epsilon > 0$ there is a $\delta(\epsilon) > 0$ such that for every initial function $\Phi \in \mathbf{PC}(\mathbf{PC}^*)$, with $\|\Phi\| < \delta$ the corresponding solution $X(t)$ satisfying for each $t \in J$ the inequality $|X(t)| \le \epsilon$.*

(c) *Locally asymptotically stable (LAS) if for a given low terminal $a \in \mathbb{R}$ there is a $\Delta(a) > 0$ such that for every initial function $\Phi \in \mathbf{PC}(\mathbf{PC}^*)$ with $\|\Phi\| < \Delta$ the corresponding solution $X(t)$ is stable and $\lim_{t\to\infty} |X(t)| = 0$.*

(d) *Globally asymptotically stable (GAS) if for every for every initial function $\Phi \in \mathbf{PC}(\mathbf{PC}^*)$ the corresponding solution $X(t)$ is stable and $\lim_{t\to\infty} |X(t)| = 0$.*

Both definitions below are applicable not only for initial problems with Caputo-type derivatives, but also for initial problems with fractional derivatives in the RL sense.

Define for any $\Phi \in \mathbf{PC}$ the weighted function $w(t) \colon J \to \mathbb{R}$ as follows:

$$w(t)=\begin{cases}1, & t=a,\\ (t-a)^{1-\alpha}, & t\in(a,a+1],\\ 1, & t>a+1.\end{cases}$$

Definition 10. *The zero solution of IP (1), (2) is said to be weighted stable (W-stable), weighted uniformly stable (W-uniformly stable), weighted locally asymptotically stable (W-LAS stable), or weighted globally asymptotically stable (W-GAS stable) if for the corresponding solution $X(t)$ the product $w(t)X(t)$ satisfies the conditions (a), (b), (c), or (d) from Definition 9.*

Definition 11 ([9])**.** *The zero solution of IP (1), (2) is said to be:*

(i) Stable in time (Lyapunov in time stable) if for an arbitrary $\epsilon>0$ there exists a point $t_\epsilon\in J^0$ and number $\delta(\epsilon,t_\epsilon)>0$ such that for any initial function $\Phi\in\mathbf{PC}(\mathbf{PC}^*)$ with $\|\Phi\|<\delta$, the corresponding solution $X(t)$ satisfies for each $t\geq t_\epsilon$ the inequality $|X(t)|\leq\epsilon$.

(ii) Asymptotically stable in time if for any initial function $\Phi\in\mathbf{PC}(\mathbf{PC}^*)$ the corresponding solution $X(t)$ is stable in time and additionally $\lim_{t\to\infty}|X(t)|=0$.

Remark 4. *It is simple to see that if $\alpha=1$ (the order of differentiation) then Definition 10 for the weighted stability coincides with the classical one. In addition, when a solution is weighted stable then we can take $t_\epsilon=a+1$ for any $\epsilon>0$ in Definition 11, and hence, the weighted stability implies stability in time, as well as the weighted global asymptotically stability implying asymptotic stability in time.*

Let $\epsilon>0$ be an arbitrary number and consider the inequality

$$\left|D^{\alpha}_{a+}\left(X(t)-\int_{-h}^{0}[d_\theta V(t,\theta)]X(t+\theta)\right)\int_{-h}^{0}[d_\theta U(t,\theta)]X(t+\theta)+\mathfrak{F}(t,X^T_\tau(\theta))\right|\leq\epsilon. \quad (42)$$

Definition 12. *The function $Y(t)\colon[a-h,\infty)\to\mathbb{R}^n$ is a solution of IP (42), (2) in J^0 if $Y(t)|_{t\in J^0}\in\mathbf{C}^{1-\alpha}$ satisfies the inequality (42) for $t\in J^0$ and the condition (2) for $t\in[a-h,a]$, with initial function $Y(t-a)=\Phi^Y(t-a)\in\mathbf{PC}(\mathbf{PC}^*)$.*

Definition 13. *The system (1) is said to be Ulam–Hyers weighted stable in J^0 if for any $\epsilon>0$ there exists a number $\delta\in(0,\epsilon)$ and constant $C_\epsilon>0$ such that for any solution $Y(t)$ of (42) there exists an initial function $\Phi(t)\in\mathbf{PC}(\mathbf{PC}^*)$, with $|\Phi^Y(t-a)-\Phi(t-a)|\leq\delta$ for $t\in[a-h,a]$ and for the corresponding unique solution $X(t)$ of IP (1), (2), with initial function $\Phi(t)$, the inequality*

$$w(t)\big|Y(t)|_J-X(t)\big|\leq C_\epsilon\epsilon \quad (43)$$

holds for any $t\in J^0$.

The first result in this section clarifies the relations between the boundedness of all solutions and the weighted stabilities in the Lyapunov sense.

Theorem 8. *Let the conditions of Lemma 6 hold.*

Then, the zero solution of the system (25) is W-stable in the Lyapunov sense if and only if for all solutions $X(t)$ of IP (25), (2) with initial function $\Phi(t)\in\mathbf{PC}$, the product $w(t)X(t)$ is bounded in J^0.

Proof. Necessity: Let us assume that the zero solution is W-stable in the Lyapunov sense. Assume the contrary, that there exists $\overline{\Phi}(t)\in\mathbf{PC}$ such that for the existing, according to Theorem 3, unique solution $\overline{X}(t)$ of IP (25), (2) we have that $w(t)\overline{X}(t)$ is unbounded in J^0. Since the zero solution is W-stable, then for any $\epsilon>0$ there exists a number $\delta\in(0,\epsilon)$ such that for any $\Phi(t)\in\mathbf{PC}$ with $\|\Phi\|<\delta$ we have that the corresponding solution $X(t)$ satisfies the inequality $|w(t)X(t)| \leq \epsilon$ for any $t \in J^0$. Consider the following initial function $\Phi^* = \dfrac{\delta\overline{\Phi}}{2\|\overline{\Phi}\|}$ with norm $\|\Phi^*\| = \left\|\dfrac{\delta\overline{\Phi}}{2\|\overline{\Phi}\|}\right\| = \dfrac{\delta}{2} < \delta$. Then, since the system (25) is a linear system the function $X^*(t) = \dfrac{\delta}{2\|\overline{\Phi}\|}\overline{X}(t)$ is the corresponding solution of IP (25) (2) for the initial function $\Phi^*(t) \in \mathbf{PC}$, and hence, for $t \in J^0$ we have that $|w(t)X^*(t)| = \left|\dfrac{\delta}{2\|\overline{\Phi}\|}w(t)X(t)\right| \leq \epsilon$, which implies that $|w(t)\overline{X}(t)| \leq \dfrac{2\|\overline{\Phi}\|\epsilon}{\delta}$ for $t \in J^0$, which contradicts our assumption.

Sufficiency: Let for any $\Phi(t) \in \mathbf{PC}$ the product $w(t)X(t)$ be bounded in J^0, where $X(t)$ is the corresponding solution of IP (25), (2) with this initial function, and hence, according to Lemma 4, we have that $X(t)$ satisfies IP (3), (2) with $\mathfrak{F}(t, X_t^T) \equiv \mathbf{0}$ for $t \in J$ and vice versa. Let $t^* \in J^0$ be arbitrary and let $b > a^* > a$ be fixed numbers with $t^* \in [a^*, b]$. Then, for arbitrary initial functions $\overline{\Phi}, \Phi \in \mathbf{PC}$, their corresponding unique solutions of IP (3), (2) are $\overline{X}(t), X(t)$, respectively, and for any $t^* \in [a^*, b]$ we have

$$
\begin{aligned}
|\overline{X}(t) - X(t)| &\leq (\overline{\Phi}(0) - \Phi(0))(t-a)^{\alpha-1} + \left|\int_{-h}^{0}[d_\theta V(t,\theta)](\overline{X}(t+\theta) - X(t+\theta))\right| \\
&+ \frac{n}{\Gamma(\alpha)}\left|\int_a^t (t-\tau)^{1-\alpha}\left(\int_{-h}^{0}[d_\theta U(\tau,\theta)](\overline{X}(\tau+\theta) - X(\tau+\theta))\right)d\tau\right| \\
&\leq \|\overline{\Phi} - \Phi\|(t-a)^{\alpha-1} + V\sup_{s\in[a,t]}|\overline{X}(s) - X(s)| + V\|\overline{\Phi} - \Phi\| \\
&+ \frac{n}{\Gamma(\alpha)}\left|\int_a^t (t-\tau)^{\alpha-1}\left(\int_{-h}^{0}[\partial_\theta U(\tau,\theta)](\overline{X}(\tau+\theta) - X(\tau+\theta))d\theta\right)d\tau\right| \\
&\leq V\sup_{s\in[a,t]}|\overline{X}(s) - X(s)| + \|\overline{\Phi} - \Phi\|\left((t-a)^{\alpha-1} + V\right) \\
&+ \frac{nU_b}{\Gamma(1+\alpha)}\int_a^t (t-\tau)^{\alpha-1}\sup_{\eta\in[a,\tau]}|\overline{X}(\eta) - X(\eta)|d\tau + \frac{nU_b(t-a)^\alpha}{\Gamma(1+\alpha)}\|\overline{\Phi} - \Phi\| \\
&\leq V\sup_{s\in[a,t]}|\overline{X}(s) - X(s)| + \|\overline{\Phi} - \Phi\|\left((t-a)^{\alpha-1} + \frac{nU_b(t-a)^\alpha}{\Gamma(1+\alpha)} + V\right) \\
&+ \frac{nU_b}{\Gamma(1+\alpha)}\int_a^t (t-\tau)^{\alpha-1}\sup_{\eta\in[a,\tau]}|\overline{X}(\eta) - X(\eta)|d\tau.
\end{aligned}
\tag{44}
$$

From (44), for any $t \in [a^*, b]$ it follows that

$$
\begin{aligned}
&\sup_{s\in[a,t]} w(t)|\overline{X}(s) - X(s)| \\
&\leq \|\overline{\Phi} - \Phi\|\left(\frac{\sup_{s\in[a,t]} w(s)(s-a)^{\alpha-1}}{1-V} + \frac{nU_b b^\alpha}{(1-V)\Gamma(1+\alpha)} + \frac{V}{(1-V)}\right) \\
&+ \frac{nU_b}{\Gamma(1+\alpha)}\int_a^t (t-\tau)^{\alpha-1}\sup_{\eta\in[a-h,\tau]}|\overline{X}(\eta) - X(\eta)|d\tau.
\end{aligned}
\tag{45}
$$

Then, applying corollary 2 in [24] to (45), we obtain for any $t \in [a^*, b]$ the estimation

$$\sup_{s\in[a,t]} |\overline{X}(s) - X(s)| \\ \leq ||\overline{\Phi} - \Phi|| \left(\frac{\sup_{s\in[a,t]} w(s)(s-a)^{\alpha-1}}{1-V} + \frac{nU_b(b-a)^{\alpha}}{(1-V)\Gamma(1+\alpha)} + \frac{V}{(1-V)} \right) (E_\alpha(nU_b t^\alpha)). \quad (46)$$

Let us define for any $t \in J^0$ a family of functionals $\aleph_t \colon \mathbf{PC} \to \mathbb{R}^n$ via the equality $\aleph_t(\Phi) = w(t)X(t)$, where $X(t)$ denotes the corresponding solution of IP (25),(2) for initial function $\Phi(t) \in \mathbf{PC}$. From (46), it follows that $\aleph_t(\Phi)$ is a continuous functional at any $\Phi(t) \in \mathbf{PC}$ for any $t \in J^0$ i.e., for every $\Phi(t) \in \mathbf{PC}$ we have that $|\aleph_t(\Phi)| \leq ||\aleph_t|| \, ||\Phi||$, where $||\aleph_t||$ denotes the norm of the functional. Then applying the Banach–Steinhaus theorem we obtain that the norms of all functionals are uniformly bounded, i.e., there exists a constant $||\aleph|| > 0$ such that $||\aleph_t|| \leq ||\aleph||$ for any $t \in J$. Let $\epsilon > 0$ be arbitrary and choose $\delta = \frac{\epsilon}{2||\aleph||} > 0$. Then, for any $\Phi(t) \in \mathbf{PC}$ with $||\Phi|| < \delta$ for the corresponding solution $X(t)$ we have that $|w(t)X(t)| = |\aleph_t(\Phi)| \leq ||\aleph|| \, ||\Phi|| = ||\aleph|| \frac{\epsilon}{2||\aleph||} < \epsilon$ for any $t \in J^0$, which implies that the zero solution is W-stable in the Lyapunov sense. □

Remark 5. *It is worth emphasizing that the result from the application of any kind of stability definitions concerning the differential equation (system) with all types of derivatives (integer or fractional order) essentially depends on the functional type of the set of all solutions of the studied object. As an example, for equations (systems) with first-order derivatives the solutions are usually either continuous differentiable or absolutely continuous functions. So, the conclusions could be true for all solutions which are absolutely continuous or only for these solutions which are continuous differentiable. For retarded or neutral equations (systems) the situation is more complicated. The space of the initial functions plays a leading role in its functional type, because the analytical type of the solutions essentially depends on them. This is very important for the stability in the Ulam–Hyers sense for the following reason: the functional type of the initial function and the solutions of system* (1) *must be the same for the corresponding inequality* (42), *since all solutions of* (1) *are solutions of inequality* (42) *too.*

As a consequence, from the proved results, we obtain two necessary conditions for W-stability of the zero solution of the system (25).

Theorem 9. *Let the following conditions be fulfilled:*

1. *The conditions of Lemma 6 hold.*
2. *The zero solution of the system* (25) *is W-stable in the Lyapunov sense.*

Then, the following relations hold:

$$\mathfrak{Q}^\infty = \sup_{t\in J^0} |w(t)\mathfrak{Q}(t)| < \infty, \mathfrak{H}^\infty = \sup_{t\in J^0} |\mathfrak{H}(t)| < \infty,$$

where $\mathfrak{Q}(t) = Var_{s\in[a-h,a]}\mathfrak{Q}(t,s)$ *and* $\mathfrak{H}(t) = \sup_{s\in[a,t]} |w(t)\mathfrak{H}(t,s)|$.

Proof. Let us, as above for $\Phi(t) \in \mathbf{PC}^*$ and any $t \in J^0$, define a family of functionals $\aleph_t \colon \mathbf{PC} \to \mathbb{R}^n$ via the equality $\aleph_t(\Phi) = w(t)X(t)$, where $X(t)$ denotes the corresponding solution of IP (25), (2) for this initial function. Then, according Theorem 6 and Lemma 6, for any $t \in J^0$ we have that

$$|\aleph_t(\Phi)| = |w(t)X(t)| = \left| w(t) \int_{a-h}^{a} [d_s\tilde{\Phi}(s-a)]\mathfrak{Q}(t,s) \right|$$
$$\leq \sup_{s\in[-h,0]} \mathfrak{Q}(t,s)\|\Phi\| \leq \mathfrak{Q}(t)\|\Phi\| \leq Var_{s\in[-h,0]}|\mathfrak{Q}(t,s)|\|\Phi\|,$$

and hence, $\aleph_t(\Phi)$ is a continuous functional at any $\Phi(t) \in \mathbf{PC}^*$ for any $t \in J^0$ with norm $\|\aleph_t\| = Var_{s\in[-h,0]}|\mathfrak{Q}(t,s)|$. Then, by virtue of the Banach-Steinhaus theorem we have that there exists a constant $\|\aleph\| > 0$ such that $\|\aleph_t\| \leq \|\aleph\|$ for any $t \in J^0$. Thus, we have that the W-boundedness ($\sup_{t\in J^0}(Var_{s\in[-h,0]}|\mathfrak{Q}(t,s)|) < \infty$) of the matrix $w(t)\mathfrak{Q}(t)$ is a necessary condition for the W-stability of the zero solution of system (25).

By virtue of Theorem 8 we have that for any $s \in J^0$ and $j \in \langle n\rangle$, the relation $\sup_{s\in[a,t]}|w(t)\mathfrak{H}^j(t,s)| < \infty$ holds, and taking into account that $|w(t)\mathfrak{H}^j(t,s)| = 0$ when $t < s$, we can conclude that $\mathfrak{H}^\infty = \sup_{t\in J^0}|\mathfrak{H}(t)| < \infty$. □

Corollary 3. *Let the following conditions be fulfilled:*

1. *The conditions of Lemma 6 hold.*
2. *The zero solution of the system* (25) *is W-GAS stable in the Lyapunov sense.*

Then, the following relations

$$\lim_{t\to\infty}|\mathfrak{Q}(t)| = 0, \lim_{t\to\infty}|\mathfrak{H}(t)| = 0$$

hold, where $\mathfrak{H}(t) = \sup_{s\in[a,t]}|w(t)\mathfrak{H}(t,s)|$.

Proof. The statement follows immediately from Theorem 9, since according to condition 2 of Corollary 3, for any $j \in \langle n\rangle$ we have $\lim_{t\to\infty}|\mathfrak{Q}^j(t,s)| = \mathbf{0}$ for $s \in [a-h,a]$ and $\lim_{t\to\infty}|\mathfrak{H}^j(t,s)| = \mathbf{0}$ for any $s \in [a,t]$. □

Remark 6. *Note that the differences in the proofs of Theorems 8 and 9 are caused from the differences in the spaces of the initial functions* $\Phi(t) \in \mathbf{PC}$ *and* $\Phi(t) \in \mathbf{PC}^*$*, respectively.*

The next theorem makes clear the relation between the W-stability in the Lyapunov sense and Ulam–Hyers W-stability.

Theorem 10. *Let the following conditions be fulfilled:*

1. *The conditions of Lemma 6 hold.*
2. *The system* (25) *is Ulam–Hyers W-stable for any initial functions* $\Phi(t) \in \mathbf{PC}$.

Then, the zero solution of the system (25) *is stable in the Lyapunov sense if and only if for any* $\Phi(t) \in \mathbf{PC}$ *and arbitrary* $\epsilon > 0$ *IP* (42), (2) *has only W-bounded solutions.*

Proof. Necessity: Let the zero solution of the system (25) be stable in the Lyapunov sense and assume that IP (42), (2) has a W-unbounded solution $Y(t)|_{t\in J^0} \in \mathbf{C}^{1-\alpha}$ for some $\Phi^Y \in \mathbf{PC}$ and $\epsilon > 0$. Then, since (25) is Ulam–Hyers W-stable for any $\epsilon > 0$, there exists $\delta = \delta(\epsilon) > 0$ and $\Phi^*(t) \in \mathbf{C}$ with $|\Phi^*(t) - \Phi^Y(t)| < \delta$ for $t \in [a-h,a]$ such that for $t \in J^0$ inequality (43) holds for $Y(t)|_{t\in J^0}$ and $X^*(t)$, where $X^*(t)$ is the corresponding solution of IP (25), (3) with initial function $\Phi^*(t)$. On the other hand, since according to Theorem 8 the function $X^*(t)$ is a W-bounded solution of IP (25), (3), and since $Y(t)|_{t\in J^0}$ is a W-unbounded solution of (42) according to our assumption, we conclude that inequality (43) is impossible to be fulfilled for $Y(t)|_{t\in J^0}$ and $X^*(t)$, which contradicts our assumption. Thus, all solutions of the inequality (43) are W-bounded.

Sufficiency: Let IP (42), (2) have only bounded solutions. Then, IP (25), (2) has, for any $\Phi \in \mathbf{PC}$, only W-bounded solutions. Then, by virtue of Theorem 8, the zero solution of system (25) is W-stable in the Lyapunov sense. □

6. On the Preservation of the Stability Properties

The aim of this section is, based on the obtained results in the previous sections, to make clear the preservation of the W-stability properties of the system (25) under nonlinear disturbances.

Definition 14. *The function $X \in \mathbf{C}^{1-\alpha}$ will be called weighted Mittag–Leffler bounded (WML-bounded) of order $\omega \in \mathbb{R}_+$ if there exist $t_0 \in J^0$, a constant $C_X > 0$, and a function $a(t) \in PC(J^0, \mathbb{R}_+)$ with $a(t) = O(t^\alpha)$ such that $|w(t)X(t)| \le a(t)E_\omega(C_X\Gamma(\omega)t^\omega)$ for $t \ge t_0$. By WML_ω, we denote the subset of all WML-bounded functions of order ω in $\mathbf{C}^{1-\alpha}$.*

Definition 15. *We say that the vector-valued functional $\mathfrak{F}: J \times PC \to \mathbb{R}^n$ is a damper of order ω for system (1) if for any $X(t) \in WML_\omega$ for the function $F^X(t) = (F_1^X(t), \dots, F_n^X(t))^T = \mathfrak{F}(t, X_t^T)$ there exist a point $t_0 \in J^0$ and a constant $C^0 = C^0(t_0, X) > 0$ such that the following estimation $|F^X(t)| \le C^0 t^{-(\omega+1)}$ holds for $t \ge t_0$.*

The next theorem establishes an a priori estimate of the solutions of IP (1), (2) with initial functions $\Phi(t) \in \mathbf{PC}$.

Theorem 11. *Let the following conditions be fulfilled.*

1. *The conditions of Lemma 6 hold.*
2. *The conditions $\mathfrak{C}$ hold.*
3. *$\mathfrak{F}(t, \mathbf{0}) = \mathbf{0}$ and $\sup\limits_{t \in J} |\ell(t)| = L^\infty < \infty$.*

Then, any solution $X \in \mathbf{C}^{1-\alpha}$ of IP (3), (2) with initial function $\Phi(t) \in \mathbf{PC}$ is WML-bounded of order α.

Proof. Let $\Phi(t) \in \mathbf{PC}$ be an arbitrary initial function and $X \in \mathbf{C}^{1-\alpha}$ be the corresponding unique solution of IP (3), (2). Then, for $t \in J^0$ from (3) we obtain that

$$\begin{aligned}
|X(t)| &\le \|\Phi\|(t-a)^{\alpha-1} + \left| \int_{-h}^{0} [d_\theta V(t,\theta)]X(t+\theta) \right| \\
&+ \frac{n}{\Gamma(\alpha)} \int_a^t (t-\tau)^{1-\alpha} \left| \int_{-h}^{0} [d_\theta U(\tau,\theta)]X(t+\theta) + \mathfrak{F}(\tau, X_\tau^T) \right| d\tau \\
&\le \|\Phi\|(t-a)^{\alpha-1} + V \sup_{s\in[a,t]} |X(s)| + V\|\Phi\| \\
&+ \frac{n}{\Gamma(\alpha)} \left| \int_a^t (t-\tau)^{\alpha-1} \left(\left| \int_{-h}^{0} [\partial_\theta U(\tau,\theta)]X(t+\theta)d\theta \right| + \left| \mathfrak{F}(\tau, X_\tau^T) \right| \right) d\tau \right| \\
&\le V \sup_{s\in[a,t]} |X(s)| + \|\Phi\|((t-a)^{\alpha-1} + V) + \frac{n(U_b + L^\infty)}{\Gamma(\alpha)} \int_a^t (t-\tau)^{\alpha-1} \sup_{s\in[a-h,\tau]} |X(s)| d\tau \\
&\le V \sup_{s\in[a,t]} |X(s)| + \|\Phi\|((t-a)^{\alpha-1} + V) \\
&+ \frac{n(U_b + L^\infty)}{\Gamma(\alpha)} \left(\int_a^t (t-\tau)^{\alpha-1} \sup_{s\in[a,\tau]} |X(s)| d\tau (t-a)^\alpha \|\Phi\| \right) \\
&\le V \sup_{s\in[a,t]} |X(s)| + \|\Phi\| \left((t-a)^{\alpha-1} + \frac{n(U_b + L^\infty)(t-a)^\alpha}{\Gamma(\alpha)} + V \right) \\
&+ \frac{n(U_b + L^\infty)}{\Gamma(\alpha)} \int_a^t (t-\tau)^{\alpha-1} \sup_{s\in[a,\tau]} |X(s)| d\tau.
\end{aligned} \tag{47}$$

Without loss of generality, we can assume that $\frac{\sup_{s\in[a,a+1]} X(s)}{\alpha\|\Phi\|} = C^* \geq 1$ when $\|\Phi\| > 0$. Then, from (47) we have

$$
\begin{aligned}
|X(t)| &\leq \|\Phi\|\Big(\frac{(t-a)^{\alpha-1}}{(1-V)} + \frac{V\Gamma(1+\alpha)+n(U_b+L^\infty)(t-a)^\alpha}{(1-V)\Gamma(\alpha)}\Big) \\
&= \frac{n(U_b+L^\infty)}{(1-V)\Gamma(\alpha)}\int_a^{a+1}(t-\tau)^{\alpha-1}\sup_{s\in[a,\tau]}|X(s)|d\tau \\
&+ \int_{a+1}^{t}(t-\tau)^{\alpha-1}\sup_{s\in[a,a+1]}|X(s)|d\tau + \int_{a+1}^{t}(t-\tau)^{\alpha-1}\sup_{s\in[a+1,\tau]}|X(s)|d\tau \\
&\leq |\Phi\|\Big(\frac{(t-a)^{\alpha-1}}{(1-V)} + \frac{V\Gamma(1+\alpha)+n(U_b+L^\infty)(t-a)^\alpha}{(1-V)\Gamma(\alpha)}\Big) \\
&+ \frac{n(U_b+L^\infty)}{(1-V)\Gamma(\alpha)}\left(\alpha^{-1}\sup_{s\in[a,a+1]}X(s)(t-a)^\alpha + \int_{a+1}^{t}(t-\tau)^{\alpha-1}\sup_{s\in[a+1,\tau]}|X(s)|d\tau\right) \\
&\leq |\Phi\|\Big(\frac{(t-a)^{\alpha-1}}{(1-V)} + \frac{n(U_b+L^\infty)(1+C^*)(t-a)^\alpha + V\Gamma(1+\alpha)}{(1-V)\Gamma(\alpha)}\Big) \\
&+ \frac{n(U_b+L^\infty)}{(1-V)\Gamma(\alpha)}\int_{a+1}^{t}(t-\tau)^{\alpha-1}\sup_{s\in[a+1,\tau]}|X(s)|d\tau.
\end{aligned}
$$

Since $(t-a)^{\alpha-1}$ is monotone decreasing for $t \in (a, a+1]$, then $\sup_{s\in[a+1,t]}|X^*(s)| \leq \sup_{s\in[a,t]} w(s)|X^*(s)|$, and hence,

$$
\begin{aligned}
\sup_{s\in[a+1,t]}|X(s)| &\leq \|\Phi\|\left(\frac{\sup_{t\geq a+1}(t-a)^{\alpha-1}}{(1-V)} + \frac{n(U_b+L^\infty)(1+C^*)(t-a)^\alpha + V\Gamma(\alpha)}{(1-V)\Gamma(\alpha)}\right) \\
&+ \frac{n(U_b+L^\infty)}{(1-V)\Gamma(\alpha)}\int_{a+1}^{t}(t-\tau)^{\alpha-1}\sup_{s\in[a+1,\tau]}|X(s)|d\tau \\
&\leq \|\Phi\|\Big(\frac{1+V}{(1-V)} + \frac{n(U_b+L^\infty)(1+C^*)(t-a)^\alpha}{(1-V)\Gamma(\alpha)}\Big) \\
&+ \frac{n(U_b+L^\infty)}{(1-V)\Gamma(\alpha)}\int_{a+1}^{t}(t-\tau)^{\alpha-1}\sup_{s\in[a+1,\tau]}|X(s)|d\tau
\end{aligned}
$$

$$
\sup_{s\in[a+1,t]}|X(s)| \leq \|\Phi\|\Big(\frac{1+V}{1-V} + \frac{n(U_b+L^\infty)(1+C^*)(t-a)^\alpha}{(1-V)\Gamma(\alpha)}\Big)E_\alpha\Big(\frac{n(U_b+L^\infty)}{(1-V)}t^\alpha\Big). \tag{48}
$$

Applying to (48) Theorem 2, we obtain that

$$
\sup_{s\in[a+1,t]}|X(s)| \leq \|\Phi\|\Big(\frac{1+V}{(1-V)} + \frac{n(U_b+L^\infty)(1+C^*)(t-a)^\alpha}{(1-V)\Gamma(\alpha)}\Big)E_\alpha\Big(\frac{n(U_b+L^\infty)}{(1-V)}t^\alpha\Big),
$$

which completes the proof. □

Remark 7. *We note that Theorem 11 establishes that for Lipschitz-type nonlinear disturbances, all solutions of IP* (3), (2) *with initial functions* $\Phi(t) \in \mathbf{PC}$ *are WML-bounded of order* α.

The proof of the next theorem is based on the following practical variant of the well-known Barbalat's lemma.

Lemma 8 ([30]). *Let $f \in L_1^{loc}(\mathbb{R}_+, \mathbb{R}_+)$ be a bounded function and $\lim_{t\to\infty} \int_0^t f(s)ds < \infty$. Then, the relation $\lim_{t\to\infty} f(t) = 0$ holds.*

Theorem 12. *Let the following conditions be fulfilled:*

1. *The conditions of Theorem 11 hold.*
2. *The zero solution of system* (25) *is W-GAS.*
3. *There exists $\omega > \alpha$ such that the vector-valued functional $\mathfrak{F}\colon J \times PC \to \mathbb{R}^n$ is a damper of order ω.*

Then, the zero solution of IP (1), (2) *(or IP* (3), (2)*) with initial function $\Phi(t) \in \mathbf{PC}^*$ is W-GAS.*

Proof. Let $\Phi^*(t) \in \mathbf{PC}^*$ be arbitrary and $X^*(t)$ be the corresponding unique solution of IP (1), (2) (or (3), (2)). By virtue of Theorem 11 we have that $X^*(t)$ is WML-bounded of order α. We introduce the function $F^*(t) \equiv \mathfrak{F}(t, X_t^{*T})$, $t \in J^0$, and using (28) and (34) define the functions $\tilde{X}(t)$ and $\mathfrak{X}(t)$ as follows:

$$\tilde{X}(t) = \int_{a-h}^{a} [d_s\tilde{\Phi}^*(s-a)]\mathfrak{Q}(t,s), \tag{49}$$

$$\mathfrak{X}(t) = \int_{a}^{t} \mathfrak{H}(t,s)D_{a+}^{1-\alpha}F^*(s)ds. \tag{50}$$

Then, from Theorem 6 it follows that $\tilde{X}(t)$ is the unique solution of IP (25), (2) with initial function $\Phi^*(t)$, and by virtue of Theorem 7 the function $\mathfrak{X}(t)$ is the unique solution of IP (24), (2) with $F(t) \equiv F^*(t)$ and initial function $Z(t-a) \equiv 0$, $t \in [a-h, a]$. Thus, $\tilde{X}(t) + \mathfrak{X}(t)$ is a solution of IP (2), (1) (IP (3), (2)), and hence, we have that

$$X^*(t) = \tilde{X}(t) + \mathfrak{X}(t) = \int_{a-h}^{a} [d_s\tilde{\Phi}(s-a)]\mathfrak{Q}(t,s) + \int_{a}^{t} \mathfrak{H}(t,s)D_{a+}^{1-\alpha}F^*(s)ds. \tag{51}$$

From (49) and Corollary 3 it follows that

$$\lim_{t\to\infty} |\tilde{X}(t)| = \lim_{t\to\infty}\left|\int_{a-h}^{a} [d_s\tilde{\Phi}(s-a)]\mathfrak{Q}(t,s)\right| \leq \lim_{t\to\infty} (\|\tilde{\Phi}\|)|\mathfrak{Q}(t)| \leq \|\Phi\| \lim_{t\to\infty} |\mathfrak{Q}(t)| = 0. \tag{52}$$

Consideringthe function

$$G(t) = \int_{a}^{t}\left(\int_{a}^{\tau} \mathfrak{H}(\tau,s)D_{a+}^{1-\alpha}F^*(s)ds\right)d\tau, \tag{53}$$

obviously the integrand $\mathfrak{X}(\tau) = \int_{a}^{\tau} \mathfrak{H}(\tau,s)D_{a+}^{1-\alpha}F^*(s)ds$ is a continuous function at any $\tau \in J^0$, and hence, $\frac{d}{dt}G(t) = \mathfrak{X}(t)$ for $t \in J^0$ too. From (53) it follows that

$$|\mathfrak{X}(\tau)| \leq \left| \int_b^\tau \mathfrak{H}(\tau,s) D_{a+}^{1-\alpha} F^*(s) ds \right| \leq \Gamma^{-1}(\alpha) |\mathfrak{H}(t)| \left| \int_a^\tau \left(\frac{d}{ds} \int_a^s (s-\eta)^{\alpha-1} F^*(\eta) d\eta \right) ds \right|$$
$$= \Gamma^{-1}(\alpha) |\mathfrak{H}(\tau)| \left| \int_a^\tau (\tau-\eta)^{\alpha-1} F^*(\eta) d\eta \right| \leq (\alpha\Gamma(\alpha)^{-1}) |\mathfrak{H}(\tau)| \int_a^\tau |F^*(\eta)| d(\tau-\eta)^\alpha$$
$$\leq \Gamma^{-1}(1+\alpha) |\mathfrak{H}(\tau)| \sup_{s\in[a,\tau]} (|F^*(s)| s^\alpha)$$
$$\leq \Gamma^{-1}(1+\alpha) |\mathfrak{H}(\tau)| \left(\sup_{s\in[a,b]} (|F^*(s)| s^\alpha) + \sup_{s\in[b,\tau]} (|F^*(s)| s^\alpha) \right)$$
$$\leq \Gamma^{-1}(1+\alpha) |\mathfrak{H}(\tau)| \left(\sup_{s\in[a,b]} (|F^*(s)| s^\alpha) + \sup_{s\in[b,\tau]} (C^0 s^{-(\omega+1)} s^\alpha) \right). \tag{54}$$

Since $\omega > \alpha$ and the zero solution of the system (25) is W-GAS, then by virtue of Theorem 9 we have that $\mathfrak{H}^\infty = \sup_{t\in J^0} |\mathfrak{H}(t)| < \infty$, and hence, $|g(\tau)|$ is bounded on J^0. Then, from (53) and (54) it follows that

$$\Gamma^{-1}(1+\alpha) |\mathfrak{H}(\tau)| \left(\sup_{s\in[a,b]} (|F^*(s)| s^\alpha) + \sup_{s\in[b,\tau]} (C^0 s^{-(\omega+1)} s^\alpha) \right)$$

$$|G(t)| = \left| \int_a^t \left(\int_b^\tau \mathfrak{H}(\tau,s) D_{a+}^{1-\alpha} F^*(s) ds \right) d\tau \right| \leq \Gamma^{-1}(1+\alpha) \int_a^t |\mathfrak{H}(\tau)| \sup_{s\in[a,\tau]} (|s^\alpha F^*(s)|) d\tau$$

$$\leq \Gamma^{-1}(1+\alpha) b^\alpha \sup_{s\in[a,b]} |\mathfrak{H}(\tau)| |F^*(s)| (b-a) + \Gamma^{-1}(1+\alpha) \int_b^t |\mathfrak{H}(\tau)| \sup_{s\in[b,\tau]} (C^0 s^{-(\omega+1)} s^\alpha) d\tau$$
$$\leq \Gamma^{-1}(1+\alpha) b^\alpha \sup_{s\in[a,b]} |\mathfrak{H}(\tau)| |F^*(s)| (b-a) + \Gamma^{-1}(1+\alpha) \mathfrak{H}^\infty C^0 t^{-(\omega+1)+\alpha+1}$$

and, hence, $\lim_{t\to\infty} |G(t)| < \infty$. Then, by virtue of Lemma 8 we have that $\lim_{t\to\infty} |\mathfrak{X}(\tau)| = 0$, and thus, from (51) and (52) it follows that $\lim_{t\to\infty} |X^*(t)| = 0$, which completes the proof. □

7. An Example

Example 1. *Let* $n = 1$, *the lower terminal* $a = 0$, $\alpha \in (0,1)$, $h > 0$, $p, b, c \in \mathbb{R}$, $U(t,\theta) = aH(t) + bH(t-h)$, $V(t,\theta) = pH(t-h)$, *and* $\phi \in PC([-h,0])$. *Then, IP* (25), (2) *obtains the following form:*

$$D_{a+}^\alpha (x(t) + px(t-h)) = cx(t) + bx(t-h),\ t \in (0,\infty), \tag{55}$$

$$x(t) = \phi(t),\ t \in [-h,0],\ D_{a+}^{\alpha-1} x(0+) = \phi(0). \tag{56}$$

According to the results obtained by us in Section 3, IP (55), (56) *has a unique solution, which we will find an explicit representation of in this example.*

To obtain an explicit representation of the solution we will use the approach based on the Laplace transform (LT) introduced in [31] for the case of Caputo-type derivatives. Below, we assume that $|p| < 1$, *and then, by virtue of theorem 3 in [17] the LT can be applied correctly to Equation* (55). *Denote the LT of* $x(t)$ *by*

$$\hat{x}(s) = L(x(t);s) = \int_0^\infty e^{-st} x(t) dt,\ \hat{\phi}(s) = \int_{-h}^0 e^{-st} \phi(t) dt.$$

Applying the LT to both sides of (55) *and taking into account* (56) *we have*

$$s^{\alpha}\hat{x}(s)+s^{\alpha}e^{-sh}p(\hat{x}(s)+\hat{\phi}(s))-(\phi(0)+p\phi(-h))=c\hat{x}(s)+be^{-sh}(\hat{x}(s)+\hat{\phi}(s)),$$

and hence,

$$\hat{x}(s)\left(1-\frac{b-ps^{\alpha}}{s^{\alpha}-c}e^{-sh}\right)=\frac{\phi(0)+p\phi(-h)}{s^{\alpha}-c}+\frac{b-ps^{\alpha}}{s^{\alpha}-c}e^{-sh}\hat{\phi}(s). \tag{57}$$

For any $s\in\mathbb{C}$ *with* $|s|^{\alpha}>|c|$, *we have the series expansion*

$$\left(1-\frac{b-ps^{\alpha}}{s^{\alpha}-c}e^{-sh}\right)^{-1}=\sum_{k=0}^{\infty}\frac{(b-ps^{\alpha})^{k}}{(s^{\alpha}-c)^{k}}e^{-ksh}$$

and then, from (57) *it follows that*

$$\hat{x}(s)=(\phi(0)+p\phi(-h))\sum_{k=0}^{\infty}\frac{(b-ps^{\alpha})^{k}}{(s^{\alpha}-c)^{k+1}}e^{-ksh}+\hat{\phi}(s)\sum_{k=0}^{\infty}\frac{(b-ps^{\alpha})^{k}}{(s^{\alpha}-c)^{k}}e^{-ksh}. \tag{58}$$

Substituting into (58) *the expression* $(b-ps^{\alpha})^{k}=\sum_{i=0}^{k}\binom{k}{i}(-1)^{i}p^{i}s^{i\alpha}b^{k-i}$ *we obtain that the LT of* $\hat{x}(s)$ *has the following form:*

$$\begin{aligned}\hat{x}(s)&=(\phi(0)+p\phi(-h))\sum_{k=0}^{\infty}\left(\sum_{i=0}^{k}\binom{k}{i}(-p)^{i}b^{k-i}\frac{s^{i\alpha}}{(s^{\alpha}-c)^{k+1}}\right)\\&+\hat{\phi}(s)\sum_{k=0}^{\infty}\left(\sum_{i=0}^{k}\binom{k}{i}(-p)^{i}b^{k-i}\frac{s^{i\alpha}}{(s^{\alpha}-c)^{k}}\right).\end{aligned} \tag{59}$$

For simplicity we will assume that $\phi(t)\equiv\phi^{0}\in\mathbb{R}$, $t\in[-h,0]$, *and then, we have that*

$$\hat{\phi}(s)=\phi^{0}s^{-1}(e^{-sh}-1). \tag{60}$$

Consider the three-parameter Mittag–Leffler (Prabhakar) function

$$E^{\gamma}_{\alpha,\beta}(z)=\Gamma^{-1}(\gamma)\sum_{j=0}^{\infty}\frac{\Gamma(j+\gamma)z^{j}}{j!\Gamma(\alpha j+\beta)}$$

introduced in [32], where $\beta,\gamma\in\mathbb{R}$. *For* $z=ct^{\alpha}$, $t\geq 0$, $Re\,s>0$ *with* $|s|^{\alpha}>|c|$ *the LT of the function* $e^{\gamma}_{\alpha,\beta}(t;c)=t^{\beta-1}E^{\gamma}_{\alpha,\beta}(ct^{\alpha})$ *is* $L(e^{\gamma}_{\alpha,\beta}(t;c);s)=\dfrac{s^{\alpha\gamma-\beta}}{(s^{\alpha}-c)^{\gamma}}$ *and when* $h\geq 0$ *(see theorem 1.31 in [33]) we have that the following relation holds:*

$$L^{-1}\left(\frac{s^{\alpha\gamma-\beta}}{(s^{\alpha}-c)^{\gamma}}e^{-sh},t\right)=\begin{cases}e^{\gamma}_{\alpha,\beta}(t-h;c), & t\geq h,\\ 0, & t<h.\end{cases} \tag{61}$$

Denoting as usual by $[t]$ *the greatest integer number less or equal to* t *for any* $t\in\mathbb{R}$, *from* (59), (60), *and* (61), *it follows that the solution* $x(t)$ *of IP* (55), (56) *possess the representation*

$$\begin{aligned}x(t)&=\phi^{0}(1+c)\sum_{k=0}^{[\frac{t}{h}]}\left(\sum_{i=0}^{k}\binom{k}{i}(-p)^{i}b^{k-i}e^{k+1}_{\alpha,\alpha(k-i)+1}(t-hk;c)\right)\\&-\phi^{0}\sum_{k=0}^{[\frac{t}{h}]}\left(\sum_{i=0}^{k}\binom{k}{i}(-p)^{i}b^{k-i}e^{k}_{\alpha,\alpha(k-i)+1}(t-hk;c)\right)\\&+\phi^{0}\sum_{k=0}^{[\frac{t}{h}]+1}\left(\sum_{i=0}^{k}\binom{k}{i}(-p)^{i}b^{k-i}e^{k}_{\alpha,\alpha(k-i)+1}(t-hk+h;c)\right).\end{aligned} \tag{62}$$

Remark 8. *Note that the approach used by the presentation of the solution $x(t)$ of IP* (55), (56) *can be extended to obtain a presentation of the solutions with step functions (with one jump of the first kind in the interval $[-h, 0]$) as initial functions, and hence, as a consequence, a presentation of the generalized fundamental matrix $\Omega(t,s)$ can be obtained. But this idea, as well as a numerical simulation via the methods developed in [34–37], is beyond the area of this article and can be a theme for future research.*

8. Conclusions and Comments

In this paper, we have studied a general class of nonlinear disturbed neutral linear fractional systems with derivatives in the Riemann–Liouville sense and distributed delays. As motivation for this study we can refer to the meaningful physical interpretations of models with these Riemann–Liouville fractional derivatives presented in [7]. Mainly, we have studied the most important, from the point of view of applications, and the technically more complicated case, when the lower terminal of the Riemann–Liouville derivatives coincides with the end point of the initial interval. First, it was proved that the initial problem for these systems with discontinuous initial functions possesses a unique solution under some natural assumptions. It is worth mentioning that the assumptions used to derive this result are similar to those used in the case of systems with first-order derivatives, and as far as we know this is the first result on this theme. Then, as a consequence of the obtained result, we have proved the existence and uniqueness of a fundamental matrix and a generalized fundamental matrix for the studied neutral linear homogeneous system. The existence of the fundamental matrices have allowed us to establish an integral representation for the solutions of the initial problem for the homogeneous system and also for the corresponding inhomogeneous system. Furthermore, for fractional systems with Riemann–Liouville derivatives we have introduced a new concept for weighted stabilities in the Lyapunov, Ulam–Hyers and Ulam–Hyers–Rassias senses. Note that the introduced concept coincides with the classical stability concept for the cases of integer-order or Caputo-type derivatives. To prove the applicability of the introduced concept it was proved that the zero solution of the homogeneous system is weighted stable if and only if all its solutions are weighted bounded; this result is well known for systems with first-order derivatives and is also established for the case of systems with Caputo-type derivatives in our former works. In addition, for the homogeneous system it was established that the weighted stability in the Lyapunov sense and weighted stability in the Ulam–Hyers sense are equivalent if and only if the inequality appearing in the Ulam–Hyers definition possesses only bounded solutions. Finally, we have derived natural sufficient conditions under which the property of weighted global asymptotic stability of the zero solution of the homogeneous system is preserved under appropriate nonlinear disturbances.

In our point of view the main contributions in the article can be highlighted as follows:

- A new concept was introduced for weighted stabilities in the Lyapunov, Ulam–Hyers and Ulam–Hyers–Rassias senses; it coincides with the classical stability concept for the cases of integer-order or Caputo-type fractional derivatives.
- Sufficient conditions have been obtained which guarantee that the weighted stability in the Lyapunov sense and the weighted stability in the Ulam–Hyers sense are equivalent.
- Sufficient conditions have been given under which the property of weighted global asymptotic stability of the zero solution of the homogeneous system is preserved under appropriate nonlinear disturbances.

As a future perspective for research we think that it will be important from the point of view of applications to establish explicit-type sufficient conditions which guarantee weighted stability in the Lyapunov or Ulam–Hyers senses.

Author Contributions: Conceptualization, H.K., M.M., S.I.C. and A.Z.; methodology, H.K., M.M., S.I.C. and A.Z.; validation, H.K., M.M., S.I.C. and A.Z.; formal analysis, H.K., M.M., S.I.C. and A.Z.; investigation, H.K., M.M., S.I.C. and A.Z.; resources, H.K., M.M., S.I.C. and A.Z.; data curation, H.K., M.M., S.I.C. and A.Z.; writing—original draft preparation, H.K., M.M., S.I.C. and A.Z.; writing—review and editing; supervision and project administration, H.K., M.M., S.I.C. and A.Z. All authors have read and agreed to the published version of the manuscript.

Funding: The authors of this research have been partially supported as follows: Hristo Kiskinov by the Bulgarian National Science Fund, Grant KP-06-N52/9, Mariyan Milev by EU-NextGeneration, through the NRRPlan of Bulgaria, SUMMIT BG-RRP-2.004-0008-C01 and Andrey Zahariev by the Bulgarian National Science Fund under Grant KP-06-N52/4, 2021.

Data Availability Statement: No new data were created or analyzed in this study. Data sharing is not applicable to this article.

Conflicts of Interest: The authors declare no conflicts of interest.

References

1. Hilfer, R. *Applications of Fractional Calculus in Physics*; World Scientific: Singapore, 2000.
2. Saxena, R.K.; Kalla, S.L. On the solutions of certain fractional kinetic equations. *Appl. Math. Comput.* **2008**, *199*, 504–511. [CrossRef]
3. Li, C.; Qian, D.; Chen, Y.Q. On Riemann-Liouville and Caputo derivatives. *Discret. Dyn. Nat. Soc.* **2011**, *2011*, 562494. [CrossRef]
4. Kilbas, A.A.; Srivastava, H.M.; Trujillo, J.J. *Theory and Applications of Fractional Differential Equations*; Elsevier Science B.V: Amsterdam, The Netherlands, 2006.
5. Podlubny, I. *Fractional Differential Equation*; Academic Press: San Diego, CA, USA, 1999.
6. Podlubny, I. Geometric and physical interpretation of fractional integration and fractional differentiation. *Fract. Calc. Appl. Anal.* **2002**, *5*, 367–386.
7. Podlubny, I. Physical interpretation of initial conditions for fractional differential equations with Riemann-Liouville fractional derivatives. *Rheol. Acta* **2006**, *46*, 765–771.
8. Kiskinov, H.; Zahariev, A. On fractional systems with Riemann-Liouville derivatives and distributed delays-Choice of initial conditions, existence and uniqueness of the solutions—Choice of initial conditions, existence and uniqueness of the solutions. *Eur. Phys. J. Spec. Top.* **2017**, *9*, 3473–3487. [CrossRef]
9. Agarwal, R.; Hristova, S.; O'Regan, D. Stability concepts of Riemann-Liouville fractional-order delay nonlinear systems. *Mathematics* **2021**, *9*, 435. [CrossRef]
10. Agarwal, R.; Hristova, S.; O'Regan, D. Explicit solutions of initial value problems for linear scalar Riemann-Liouville fractional differential equations with a constant delay. *Mathematics* **2020**, *8*, 32. [CrossRef]
11. Kiskinov, H.; Madamlieva, E.; Zahariev, A. Hyers–Ulam and Hyers–Ulam–Rassias stability for linear fractional systems with Riemann–Liouville derivatives and distributed delays. *Axioms* **2023**, 12, 637. [CrossRef]
12. Li, C.P.; Zhang, F.R. A survey on the stability of fractional differential equations. *Eur. Phys. J. Spec. Top.* **2011**, *193*, 27–47. [CrossRef]
13. Liu, S.; Wu, X.; Zhou, X.F.; Jiang, W. Asymptotical stability of Riemann-Liouville fractional nonlinear systems. *Nonlinear Dyn.* **2016**, *86*, 65–71. [CrossRef]
14. Li, M.; Wang, J. Representation of solution of a Riemann–Liouville fractional differential equation with pure delay. *Appl. Math. Lett.* **2018**, *85*, 118–124. [CrossRef]
15. Liang, C.; Wang, J.; O'Regan, D. Representation of a solution for a fractional linear system with pure delay. *Appl. Math. Lett.* **2018**, *77*, 72–78. [CrossRef]
16. Agarwal, R.; Hristova, S.; O'Regan, D. Existence and Ulam type stability for nonlinear Riemann–Liouville fractional differential equations with constant delay. *Electron. J. Qual. Theory Differ. Equ.* **2020**, *67*, 1–18. [CrossRef]
17. Veselinova, M.; Kiskinov, H.; Zahariev, A. Explicit conditions for stability of neutral linear fractional system with distributed delays. *AIP Conf. Proc.* **2016**, *1789*, 040005. [CrossRef]
18. Chartbupapan, W.; Bagdasar, O.; Mukdasai, K. A novel delay-dependent asymptotic stability conditions for differential and Riemann-Liouville fractional differential neutral systems with constant delays and nonlinear perturbation. *Mathematics* **2020**, *8*, 82. [CrossRef]
19. Myshkis, A. *Linear Differential Equations with Retarded Argument*; Nauka: Moscow, Russia, 1972. (In Russian)
20. Hale, J.; Lunel, S. *Introduction to Functional Differential Equations*; Springer: New York, NY, USA, 1993.
21. Kolmanovskii, V.; Myshkis, A. *Introduction to the Theory and Applications of Functional Differential Equations*; Kluwer Academic Publishers: Dordrecht, The Netherlands, 1999.
22. Kiskinov, H.; Madamlieva, E.; Veselinova, M.; Zahariev, A. Integral representation of the solutions for neutral linear fractional system with distributed delays. *Fractal Fract.* **2021**, *5*, 222. [CrossRef]
23. Krasnosel'skii, M.A. Some problems of nonlinear analysis. *Am. Math. Soc. Transl. Ser.* **1958**, *2*, 10.
24. Ye, H.; Gao, J.; Ding, Y. A generalized Gronwall inequality and its application to a fractional differential equations. *J. Math. Anal. Appl.* **2007**, *328*, 1075–1081. [CrossRef]
25. Madamlieva, E.; Milev, M.; Stoyanova, T. On stability criteria induced by the resolvent kernel for a fractional neutral linear system with distributed delays. *Mathematics* **2023**, *11*, 626. [CrossRef]

26. Kiskinov, H.; Milev, M.; Veselinova, M.; Zahariev, A. Continuous dependence on the initial functions and stability properties in Hyers–Ulam–Rassias sense for neutral fractional systems with distributed delays. *Fractal Fract.* **2023**, *7*, 742. [CrossRef]
27. Natanson, I.P. *Theory of Functions of a Real Variable*, 5th ed.; Frederick Ungar Publishing Co.: New York, NY, USA, 1983.
28. Reitano, R.R. *Foundations of Quantitative Finance: 5. General Measure and Integration Theory*; Brandeis International Business School: Waltham, MA, USA, 2018.
29. Madamlieva, E.; Kiskinov, H.; Petkova, M.; Zahariev, A. On the preservation with respect to nonlinear perturbations of the stability property for nonautonomous linear neutral fractional systems with distributed delays. *Mathematics* **2022**, *10*, 2642. [CrossRef]
30. Sun, Z. A gathering of Barbalat's lemmas and their (unsung) cousins. *arXiv* **2023**. [CrossRef]
31. Tuan, H.T.; Thai, H.D.; Garrappa, R. An analysis of solutions to fractional neutral differential equations with delay. *Commun. Nonlinear Sci. Numer. Simul.* **2021**, *100*, 105854. [CrossRef]
32. Prabhakar, T.R. A singular integral equation with a generalized Mittag Leffler function in the kernel. *Yokohama Math. J.* **1971**, *19*, 7–15.
33. Schiff, J.L. *The Laplace Transform: Theory and Applications*; Springer: New York, NY, USA, 1999.
34. Garrappa, R.; Popolizio, M. Computing the matrix Mittag-Leffler function with applications to fractional calculus. *J. Sci. Comput.* **2018**, *77*, 129–153. [CrossRef]
35. Micula, S. An iterative numerical method for fractional integral equations of the second kind. *J. Comput. Appl. Math.* **2018**, *339*, 124–133. [CrossRef]
36. Jafari, H.; Tuan, N.A.; Ganji, R.M. A new numerical scheme for solving pantograph type nonlinear fractional integro-differential equations. *J. King Saud Univ.-Sci.* **2021**, *33*, 101185. [CrossRef]
37. Moumen, A.; Mennouni, A.; Bouye, M. A novel Vieta–Fibonacci projection method for solving a system of fractional integrodifferential equations. *Mathematics* **2023**, *11*, 3985. [CrossRef]

fractal and fractional

MDPI

Article

Some Results on Fractional Boundary Value Problem for Caputo-Hadamard Fractional Impulsive Integro Differential Equations

Ymnah Alruwaily [1,*], Kuppusamy Venkatachalam [2] and El-sayed El-hady [1,*]

[1] Mathematics Department, College of Science, Jouf University, Sakaka, P.O. Box 2014, Saudi Arabia
[2] Department of Mathematics, Nandha Engineering College (Autonomous), Erode 638052, India; venkatachalam.k@nandhaengg.org
* Correspondence: ymnah@ju.edu.sa (Y.A.); eaelhady@ju.edu.sa (E.-s.E.-h.)

Abstract: The results for a new modeling integral boundary value problem (IBVP) using Caputo-Hadamard impulsive fractional integro-differential equations (C-HIFI-DE) with Banach space are investigated, along with the existence and uniqueness of solutions. The Krasnoselskii fixed-point theorem (KFPT) and the Banach contraction principle (BCP) serve as the basis of this unique strategy, and are used to achieve the desired results. We develop the illustrated examples at the end of the paper to support the validity of the theoretical statements.

Keywords: impulsive; integro differential equations; Caputo-Hadamard fractional derivative; boundary value problems

MSC: 26A33; 34A09; 34A12; 47H10

1. Introduction

In engineering, physics, chemistry, control theory, signal, image processing, and biology, the study of fractional differential equations (FDE) (see e.g., [1–4]), which is connected to fractional calculus (FC), is significant. The integer-order derivatives are less helpful and useful for characterizing the memory and heredity characteristics of various materials and processes than the fractional derivatives and integrals of arbitrary order; see [5–12].

The investigation of IBVP has advanced in the past few decades. It has also been extremely useful to develop a variety of applied mathematical models of actual processes in applied sciences and engineering. Tian and Bai in [12] stated a few existing findings from IBVP involving fractional derivatives of the Caputo type. Using the fixed-point theorem (FPT), existence and uniqueness results (E-UR) have been developed. Recently, it has been noted that many of the materials on the subject focus on FDEs of the Caputo and Riemann-Liouville types with various situations, including time delays, impulses, and boundary value conditions (BVC) [5,10,13–25].

Along with the Riemann-Liouville and Caputo derivatives, another kind of FD that is mentioned in the literature is the Hadamard FD, which first appeared in 1892; see e.g., [26]. It differs from the previous ones in that it includes an arbitrary logarithm function; see [13–15] for additional details.

The fundamental fractional calculus theorem was subsequently included in the C-H in [16], wher they also suggested a Caputo-type version of the Hadamard FD. Impulsive differential equations with Hadamard and C-H derivatives have been the focus of recent studies (see [11,17–20] and the references therein).

The authors of [20] discussed the following form of the C-H FDE with the impulsive boundary condition:

$$\begin{aligned} &{}^{\mathscr{CH}}\mathscr{D}^{\alpha}_{\tau_{\mathscr{M}}}\mathscr{X}(\tau) = \mathscr{F}(\tau,\mathscr{X}(\tau)),\ \tau,\tau_{\mathscr{M}} \in [1,\mathscr{E}],\ \tau \neq \tau_{\mathscr{M}},\\ &\Delta\mathscr{X}(\tau_{\mathscr{M}}) = \mu_{\mathscr{M}}(\mathscr{X}(\tau_{\mathscr{M}})), \mathscr{K} = 1,2,...,\mathscr{M},\\ &\Delta\delta\mathscr{X}(\tau_{\mathscr{M}}) = \mu^{-}_{\mathscr{M}}(\mathscr{X}(\tau_{\mathscr{M}})), \mathscr{K} = 1,2,...,\mathscr{M},\\ &\mathscr{X}(1) = \mathscr{H}(\mathscr{X}),\ \mathscr{X}(\mathscr{E}) = \mathscr{G}(\mathscr{X}), \end{aligned}$$

In [24], the authors investigated the following FDEs

$$\begin{aligned} &{}^{\mathscr{C}}\mathscr{D}^{\alpha}_{a^+}\varpi(\tau) = \mathscr{F}(\tau,\varpi(\tau),\mathscr{I}^{\alpha}_{a^+}\varpi(\tau)),\ \ \tau \in [a,b]\\ &\varpi(b) = \varpi_b. \end{aligned}$$

The E-UR of the solution of some fractional integro differential equations involving non-instantaneous impulsive boundary conditions have been studied in [27] by some FPTs. See also [28], where the sequential Caputo-Hadamard FDE with fractional boundary conditions have been examined using FPTs.

In [29], W. Yukunthorn et.al. studied the H-FDEs for impulsive multi-order form,

$$\begin{aligned} &{}^{\mathscr{C}}\mathscr{D}^{\mathscr{Q}\mathscr{K}}_{\tau_{\mathscr{K}}}\varpi(\tau) = \mathscr{F}(\tau,\varpi(\tau)),\ \ \tau \in \mathscr{J}_{\mathscr{K}} \subset [\tau_0,\mathscr{T}],\ \tau \neq \tau_{\mathscr{K}},\\ &\Delta_1\varpi(\tau_{\mathscr{K}}) = \phi 1_{\mathscr{K}}(\varpi(\tau_{\mathscr{K}})), \mathscr{K} = 1,2,...,M,\\ &\alpha_1\varpi(\tau_0) + \beta_1\varpi(\mathscr{T}) = \sum_{i=0}^{\mathscr{M}} \gamma 1_i\, \mathscr{J}^{\mathscr{R}_i}_{\tau_i}\varpi(\tau_{i+1}), \end{aligned}$$

In [30], W. Benhamida et.al. discussed the BVP,

$$\begin{aligned} &{}^{\mathscr{C}}_{\mathscr{H}}\mathscr{D}^{\alpha_1}\varpi(\tau) = \mathscr{F}(\tau,\varpi(\tau)),\ \tau \in [1,\mathscr{T}],\ \ 0 < \alpha_1 \leq 1,\\ &\mathscr{A}\mathscr{Y}(1) + \mathscr{B}\mathscr{Y}(\mathscr{T}) = \mathscr{C}, \end{aligned}$$

The literature described above served as our inspiration as we considered a C-HIF I-DE which involves fractional BCs:

$$ {}^{\mathscr{CH}}\mathscr{D}^{\mathscr{P}}\varpi(\tau) = \mathscr{F}(\tau,\varpi(\tau),\mathscr{B}\varpi(\tau)),\ \tau \in \mathscr{J} : [1,\mathscr{T}], 1 < \mathscr{P} \leq 2 \quad (1)$$

$$ \varpi(\tau^{+}_{\mathscr{K}}) = \varpi(\tau^{-}_{\mathscr{K}}) + \mathscr{Y}_{\mathscr{K}},\ \mathscr{Y}_{\mathscr{K}} \in \mathbb{R},\ \mathscr{K} = 1,2,...,\mathscr{M}, \quad (2)$$

$$ \varpi(1) = 0, \alpha_{\mathscr{H}}\mathscr{I}^{\mathscr{Q}}\varpi(\eta) + \beta^{\mathscr{C}}_{\mathscr{H}}\mathscr{D}^{\mathscr{R}}\varpi(\mathscr{T}) = \lambda,\ \ \mathscr{Q},\gamma \in (0,1], \quad (3)$$

where ${}^{\mathscr{CH}}\mathscr{D}(.)$ is the C-H FD. ${}_{\mathscr{H}}\mathscr{I}^{\mathscr{Q}}$ is the standard Hadamard fractional integral. $\mathscr{F} : \mathscr{J} \times \mathbb{R} \times \mathbb{R} \to \mathbb{R}$ is a given continuous function. α, β, λ are real constants and $\eta \in (1,\mathscr{T})$, where $\mathscr{B}\varpi(\tau) = \int_0^{\tau} \mathscr{K}(\tau,s,\varpi(s))ds$, $\mathscr{K} : \Delta \times [1,\mathscr{T}] \to \mathbb{R}, \Delta = \{(\tau,s) : 1 \leq s \leq \tau \leq \mathscr{T}\}, 1 = \tau_0 < \tau_1 < \tau_2 ... < \tau_m = \mathscr{T}$, $\Delta\varpi = \varpi(\tau^{+}_{\mathscr{K}}) - \varpi(\tau^{-}_{\mathscr{K}})$, $\varpi(\tau^{+}_{\mathscr{K}}) = \lim_{\mathscr{H}\to 0^+}\varpi(\tau_{\mathscr{K}} + \mathscr{H})$ and $\varpi(\tau^{-}_{\mathscr{K}}) = \lim_{\mathscr{H}\to 0^-}\varpi(\tau_{\mathscr{K}} + \mathscr{H})$ represent the right and left limits of $\varpi(\tau)$ at $\tau = \tau_{\mathscr{K}}$.

Motivations:

1. This study uses the C-HFD to develop a new class of impulsive C-HIFI-DE with BCs.
2. We additionally verify the E-UR of the solutions to Equations (1)–(3) using BCP and KFPT, respectively.
3. We extend the C-HFD, nonlinear integral terms, and impulsive conditions to the results discussed in [25].

The rest of the paper is organized as follows. Section 2 discusses the basic concepts and lemmas that will be used to support findings. In Section 3, we prove the uniqueness of solutions (1)–(3) and the existence of the system under suitable assumptions. Applications are also presented in Section 4.

2. Supporting Notes

Let the space $\mathscr{PC}(\mathscr{J},\mathbb{R}) = \{\varpi : \mathscr{J} \to \mathbb{R} : \varpi \in \mathscr{PC}(\tau_{\mathscr{K}}, \tau_{\mathscr{K}+1}], \mathbb{R}\}, \mathscr{K} = 1,2,...,\mathscr{M}$ and there $\varpi(\tau_{\mathscr{K}}^-)$ and $\varpi(\tau_{\mathscr{K}}^+)$ exist with $\varpi(\tau_{\mathscr{K}}^-) = \varpi(\tau_{\mathscr{K}}^+)$ and endowed with the norm

$$\|\varpi\|_{\mathscr{PC}} = \sup\{|\varpi(\tau)| : 0 \leq \tau \leq 1\}.$$

Definition 1. *Given a continuous function $\mathscr{G} : [1, +\infty) \to \mathbb{R}$, its Hadamard fractional integral of order $\alpha_1 > 0$, is as follows:*

$$_{\mathscr{H}}\mathscr{I}^{\alpha_1}\mathscr{G}(\tau) = (\Gamma(\alpha_1))^{-1} \int_1^\tau \left(\log \frac{\tau}{s}\right)^{\alpha_1 - 1} \mathscr{G}(s) \frac{ds}{s}$$

where Γ is the Euler gamma function and $\log(.) = \log_e(.)$

Definition 2. *Given a function $\mathscr{G} \in \mathscr{PC}([a,b],\mathbb{R})$the C-HFD of order α_1 is follows:*

$$^{\mathscr{C}}_{\mathscr{H}}\mathscr{D}_1^{\alpha_1}\mathscr{G}(\tau) = \frac{1}{\Gamma(\pi - \alpha_1)} \left(\tau \frac{d}{d\tau}\right)^\pi \int_a^\tau \left(\log \frac{\tau}{s}\right)^{\pi - \alpha_1 - 1} \mathscr{G}(s) \frac{ds}{s}, \ \pi - 1 < \alpha < \pi,$$

where $\delta^\pi = \left(\tau \frac{d}{d\tau}\right)^\pi, \pi = [\alpha_1] + 1$ and $[\alpha_1]$ is the integer part of α_1.

Lemma 1. *Let $\mathscr{G} \in \mathscr{PC}_\delta^\pi[a,b]$ (or)$\mathscr{G} \in \mathscr{PC}_\delta^\pi[a,b]$ and $\alpha_1 \in \mathbb{R}$. Then*

$$_{\mathscr{H}}\mathscr{I}_a^{\alpha_1}(^{\mathscr{C}}_{\mathscr{H}}\mathscr{D}_a^{\alpha_1}\mathscr{G})(\tau) = \mathscr{G}(\tau) - \sum_{\mathscr{K}=0}^{\pi-1} \frac{\delta(\mathscr{K})\mathscr{G}(a)}{\mathscr{K}!}(\log \frac{\tau}{a})^{\mathscr{K}}.$$

Proof. Let $\alpha_1 > 0, \beta_1 > 0, \pi = [\alpha_1] + 1$ and $a > 0$, then

$$_{\mathscr{H}}\mathscr{I}_{a^+}^{\alpha_1}(\log \frac{\varpi}{a})^{\beta_1 - 1}(\varpi) = \frac{\Gamma(\beta_1)}{\Gamma(\beta_1 + \alpha_1)}(\log \frac{\varpi}{a})^{\beta_1 + \alpha_1 - 1},$$
$$^{\mathscr{C}}_{\mathscr{H}}\mathscr{D}_{a^+}^{\alpha_1}(\log \frac{\varpi}{a})^{\beta_1 - 1}(\varpi) = \frac{\Gamma(\beta_1)}{\Gamma(\beta_1 - \alpha_1)}(\log \frac{\varpi}{a})^{\beta_1 - \alpha_1 - 1}, \ \beta_1 > \alpha_1.$$

□

Lemma 2. *The function ϖ is a solution of the BVP*

$$^{\mathscr{CH}}\mathscr{D}^{\mathscr{P}}\varpi(\tau) = \mathscr{H}(\tau), \ \mathscr{J} : [1, \mathscr{T}], 1 < \mathscr{P} \leq 2 \tag{4}$$
$$\varpi(\tau_{\mathscr{K}}^+) = \varpi(\tau_{\mathscr{K}}^-) + \mathscr{Y}_{\mathscr{K}}, \ \mathscr{Y}_{\mathscr{K}} \in \mathbb{R}, \ \mathscr{K} = 1,2,...,M,, \tag{5}$$
$$\varpi(1) = 0, \alpha\, _{\mathscr{H}}\mathscr{I}^{\mathscr{Q}}\varpi(\eta) + \beta\, ^{\mathscr{C}}_{\mathscr{H}}\mathscr{D}^{\mathscr{R}}\varpi(\mathscr{T}) = \lambda, \ \mathscr{Q}, \gamma \in (0,1], \tag{6}$$

if and only if

$$\omega(\tau)=\begin{cases}\frac{1}{\Gamma\mathscr{P}}\int_1^\tau\left(\log\frac{\tau}{s}\right)^{\mathscr{P}-1}\mathscr{H}(s)\frac{ds}{s}+\frac{\log\tau}{\Lambda}[\lambda-\alpha(\Gamma(\mathscr{P}+\mathscr{Q}))^{-1}\int_1^\eta\left(\log\frac{\eta}{s}\right)^{\mathscr{P}+\mathscr{Q}-1}\mathscr{H}(s)\frac{ds}{s}]\\ -\frac{\beta}{\Gamma(\mathscr{P}-\gamma)}\int_1^{\mathscr{T}}\left(\log\frac{\mathscr{T}}{s}\right)^{\mathscr{P}-\gamma-1}\mathscr{H}(s)\frac{ds}{s},\ for\ \tau\in(1,\tau_1]\\ \mathscr{Y}_1+\frac{1}{\Gamma(\mathscr{P})}\int_1^\tau\left(\log\frac{\tau}{s}\right)^{\mathscr{P}-1}\mathscr{H}(s)\frac{ds}{s}+\frac{\log\tau}{\Lambda}[\lambda-\frac{\alpha}{\Gamma(\mathscr{P}+\mathscr{Q})}\int_1^\eta\left(\log\frac{\eta}{s}\right)^{\mathscr{P}+\mathscr{Q}-1}\mathscr{H}(s)\frac{ds}{s}]\\ -\frac{\beta}{\Gamma(\mathscr{R}-\gamma)}\int_1^{\mathscr{T}}\left(\log\frac{\mathscr{T}}{s}\right)^{\mathscr{R}-\gamma-1}\mathscr{H}(s)\frac{ds}{s},\ for\ \tau\in(\tau_1,\tau_2)\\ \cdot\\ \cdot\\ \cdot\\ \sum_{\mathscr{K}=1}^{\mathscr{M}}\mathscr{Y}_i+(\Gamma(\mathscr{P}))^{-1}\int_1^\tau\left(\log\frac{\tau}{s}\right)^{\mathscr{P}-1}\mathscr{H}(s)\frac{ds}{s}\\ +\log\tau(\Lambda)^{-1}[\lambda-\frac{\alpha}{\Gamma(\mathscr{P}+\mathscr{Q})}\int_1^\eta\left(\log\frac{\eta}{s}\right)^{\mathscr{P}+\mathscr{Q}-1}\mathscr{H}(s)\frac{ds}{s}]\\ -\frac{\beta}{\Gamma(\mathscr{R}-\gamma)}\int_1^{\mathscr{T}}\left(\log\frac{\mathscr{T}}{s}\right)^{\mathscr{R}-\gamma-1}\mathscr{H}(s)\frac{ds}{s},\ for\ \tau\in(\tau_{\mathscr{M}},\mathscr{T}]\end{cases}$$

where

$$\Lambda=\frac{\alpha(\log\eta)^{\mathscr{Q}+1}}{\Gamma(\mathscr{Q}+2)}+\frac{\beta(\log\mathscr{T})^{1-\gamma}}{\Gamma(2-\gamma)}$$

Proof. Assume that ω satisfies (4)–(6). If $\tau\in[0,\tau_1)$,

$$^{\mathscr{CH}}\mathscr{D}^{\mathscr{P}}\omega(\tau)=\mathscr{H}(\tau),\quad \mathscr{J}:[1,\mathscr{T}],$$
$$\omega(1)=0,\alpha_{\mathscr{H}}\mathscr{I}^{\mathscr{Q}}\omega(\eta)+\beta^{\mathscr{C}}_{\mathscr{H}}\mathscr{D}^{\mathscr{R}}\omega(\mathscr{T})=\lambda,\quad \mathscr{Q},\gamma\in(0,1].$$

We can obtain

$$\begin{aligned}\omega(\tau)=&\Gamma(\mathscr{P})^{-1}\int_1^\tau\left(\log\frac{\tau}{s}\right)^{\mathscr{P}-1}\mathscr{H}(s)\frac{ds}{s}\\&+\frac{\log\tau}{\Lambda}[\lambda-\frac{\alpha}{\Gamma(\mathscr{P}+\mathscr{Q})}\int_1^\eta\left(\log\frac{\eta}{s}\right)^{\mathscr{P}+\mathscr{Q}-1}\mathscr{H}(s)\frac{ds}{s}]\\&-\frac{\beta}{\Gamma(\mathscr{R}-\gamma)}\int_1^{\mathscr{T}}\left(\log\frac{\mathscr{T}}{s}\right)^{\mathscr{P}-\gamma-1}\mathscr{H}(s)\frac{ds}{s}.\end{aligned}$$

If $\tau\in(\tau_1,\tau_2)$, then

$$^{\mathscr{CH}}\mathscr{D}^{\mathscr{P}}\omega(\tau)=\mathscr{H}(\tau),\ \omega(\tau^+_{\mathscr{K}})=\omega(\tau^-_{\mathscr{K}})+\mathscr{Y}_{\mathscr{K}},$$

we have

$$\begin{aligned}
\varpi(\tau) =& \mathscr{Y}(\tau_1^+) - \Gamma(\mathscr{R})^{-1}\int_1^{\tau_1}\left(\log\frac{\tau}{s}\right)^{\mathscr{R}-1}\mathscr{H}(s)\frac{ds}{s} + \int_1^{\tau}\left(\log\frac{\tau}{s}\right)^{\mathscr{P}-1}\mathscr{H}(s)\frac{ds}{s}\\
&+\frac{\log\tau}{\Lambda}[\lambda - \frac{\alpha}{\Gamma(\mathscr{P}+\mathscr{Q})}\int_1^{\eta}\left(\log\frac{\eta}{s}\right)^{\mathscr{P}+\mathscr{Q}-1}\mathscr{H}(s)\frac{ds}{s}]\\
&-\frac{\beta}{\Gamma(\mathscr{P}-\gamma)}\int_1^{\mathscr{T}}\left(\log\frac{\mathscr{T}}{s}\right)^{\mathscr{P}-\gamma-1}\mathscr{H}(s)\frac{ds}{s},\\
&= \mathscr{Y}(\tau_1^+) + \mathscr{Y}_1 - \frac{1}{\Gamma(\mathscr{R})}\int_1^{\tau_1}\left(\log\frac{\tau}{s}\right)^{\mathscr{R}-1}\mathscr{H}(s)\frac{ds}{s} + \int_1^{\tau}\left(\log\frac{\tau}{s}\right)^{\mathscr{P}-1}\mathscr{H}(s)\frac{ds}{s}\\
&+\frac{\log\tau}{\Lambda}[\lambda - \frac{\alpha}{\Gamma(\mathscr{P}+\mathscr{Q})}\int_1^{\eta}\left(\log\frac{\eta}{s}\right)^{\mathscr{P}+\mathscr{Q}-1}\mathscr{H}(s)\frac{ds}{s}]\\
&-\frac{\beta}{\Gamma(\mathscr{P}-\gamma)}\int_1^{\mathscr{T}}\left(\log\frac{\mathscr{T}}{s}\right)^{\mathscr{P}-\gamma-1}\mathscr{H}(s)\frac{ds}{s},\\
&= \mathscr{Y}_1 - \frac{1}{\Gamma(\mathscr{R})}\int_1^{\tau_1}\left(\log\frac{\tau}{s}\right)^{\mathscr{R}-1}\mathscr{H}(s)\frac{ds}{s} + \int_1^{\tau}\left(\log\frac{\tau}{s}\right)^{\mathscr{P}-1}\mathscr{H}(s)\frac{ds}{s}\\
&+\frac{\log\tau}{\Lambda}[\lambda - \frac{\alpha}{\Gamma(\mathscr{P}+\mathscr{Q})}\int_1^{\eta}\left(\log\frac{\eta}{s}\right)^{\mathscr{P}+\mathscr{Q}-1}\mathscr{H}(s)\frac{ds}{s}]\\
&-\frac{\beta}{\Gamma(\mathscr{P}-\gamma)}\int_1^{\mathscr{T}}\left(\log\frac{\mathscr{T}}{s}\right)^{\mathscr{P}-\gamma-1}\mathscr{H}(s)\frac{ds}{s}.
\end{aligned}$$

If $\tau \in (\tau_2, \tau_3)$, then

$$\begin{aligned}
\varpi(\tau) =& \mathscr{Y}(\tau_2^+) - (\Gamma(\mathscr{R}))^{-1}\int_1^{\tau_2}\left(\log\frac{\tau}{s}\right)^{\mathscr{R}-1}\mathscr{H}(s)\frac{ds}{s} + \int_1^{\tau}\left(\log\frac{\tau}{s}\right)^{\mathscr{P}-1}\mathscr{H}(s)\frac{ds}{s}\\
&+\frac{\log\tau}{\Lambda}[\lambda - \frac{\alpha}{\Gamma(\mathscr{P}+\mathscr{Q})}\int_1^{\eta}\left(\log\frac{\eta}{s}\right)^{\mathscr{P}+\mathscr{Q}-1}\mathscr{H}(s)\frac{ds}{s}]\\
&-\frac{\beta}{\Gamma(\mathscr{P}-\gamma)}\int_1^{\mathscr{T}}\left(\log\frac{\mathscr{T}}{s}\right)^{\mathscr{P}-\gamma-1}\mathscr{H}(s)\frac{ds}{s},
\end{aligned}$$

$$\begin{aligned}
&= \mathscr{Y}(\tau_2^+) + \mathscr{Y}_2 - \frac{1}{\Gamma(\mathscr{R})}\int_1^{\tau_2}\left(\log\frac{\tau}{s}\right)^{\mathscr{R}-1}\mathscr{H}(s)\frac{ds}{s} + \int_1^{\tau}\left(\log\frac{\tau}{s}\right)^{\mathscr{P}-1}\mathscr{H}(s)\frac{ds}{s}\\
&+\frac{\log\tau}{\Lambda}[\lambda - \frac{\alpha}{\Gamma(\mathscr{P}+\mathscr{Q})}\int_1^{\eta}\left(\log\frac{\eta}{s}\right)^{\mathscr{P}+\mathscr{Q}-1}\mathscr{H}(s)\frac{ds}{s}]\\
&-\frac{\beta}{\Gamma(\mathscr{P}-\gamma)}\int_1^{\mathscr{T}}\left(\log\frac{\mathscr{T}}{s}\right)^{\mathscr{P}-\gamma-1}\mathscr{H}(s)\frac{ds}{s},\\
&= \mathscr{Y}_1 + \mathscr{Y}_2 + \frac{1}{\Gamma(\mathscr{R})}\int_1^{\tau_2}\left(\log\frac{\tau}{s}\right)^{\mathscr{R}-1}\mathscr{H}(s)\frac{ds}{s} + \int_1^{\tau}\left(\log\frac{\tau}{s}\right)^{\mathscr{P}-1}\mathscr{H}(s)\frac{ds}{s}\\
&+\frac{\log\tau}{\Lambda}[\lambda - \frac{\alpha}{\Gamma(\mathscr{P}+\mathscr{Q})}\int_1^{\eta}\left(\log\frac{\eta}{s}\right)^{\mathscr{P}+\mathscr{Q}-1}\mathscr{H}(s)\frac{ds}{s}]\\
&-\frac{\beta}{\Gamma(\mathscr{P}-\gamma)}\int_1^{\mathscr{T}}\left(\log\frac{\mathscr{T}}{s}\right)^{\mathscr{P}-\gamma-1}\mathscr{H}(s)\frac{ds}{s}.
\end{aligned}$$

If $\tau \in [\tau_{\mathscr{M}}, \mathscr{T}]$,

$$\begin{aligned}\varpi(\tau) = &\sum_{\mathscr{K}=1}^{\mathscr{M}} \mathscr{Y}_i + \frac{1}{\Gamma(\mathscr{P})} \int_1^{\tau} \left(\log \frac{\tau}{s}\right)^{\mathscr{P}-1} \mathscr{H}(s) \frac{ds}{s} \\ &+ \frac{\log \tau}{\Lambda} [\lambda - \frac{\alpha}{\Gamma(\mathscr{P}+\mathscr{Q})} \int_1^{\eta} \left(\log \frac{\eta}{s}\right)^{\mathscr{P}+\mathscr{Q}-1} \mathscr{H}(s) \frac{ds}{s}] \\ &- \frac{\beta}{\Gamma(\mathscr{R}-\gamma)} \int_1^{\mathscr{T}} \left(\log \frac{\mathscr{T}}{s}\right)^{\mathscr{R}-\gamma-1} \mathscr{H}(s) \frac{ds}{s}. \end{aligned} \tag{7}$$

Suppose that ϖ fulfills the impulsive FBC of (7). □

3. Main Results

The following hypotheses are needed for the main results.

Hypothesis 1. *$\exists$ a constant $\mathscr{L}_1 > 0,\ 0 < \mathscr{L}_2 < 1$:*

$$|\mathscr{F}(\tau, \iota, v) - \mathscr{F}(\tau, \iota_1, v_1)| \leq \mathscr{L}_1 |\iota - \iota_1| + \mathscr{L}_2 |v - v_1|$$

for $\iota, v, \iota_1, v_1 \in \mathbb{R}$ and $\tau \in \mathscr{J}$.

Hypothesis 2. *A constant $\mathscr{G}_1 > 0$ exists:*

$$|\mathscr{K}(\tau, \nu, \mathscr{U}) - \mathscr{K}(\tau, \nu, \mathscr{V})| \leq \mathscr{G}_1 |\mathscr{U} - \mathscr{V}|.$$

For $\mathscr{U} - \mathscr{V} \in \mathbb{R}$ and $\tau, \nu \in \mathscr{J}$.

Hypothesis 3. *Let $\mathscr{F} : \mathscr{J} \times \mathbb{R} \times \mathbb{R} \to \mathbb{R}$ a function and $\exists$ a function $\mu \in \mathscr{PC}([1, \mathscr{T}], \mathbb{R})$:*

$$|\mathscr{F}(\tau, \varpi, \mathscr{Y})| \leq \mu(\tau), \ \ for\ any\ (\tau, \varpi, \mathscr{Y}) \in [1, \mathscr{T}] \times \mathbb{R}.$$

Hypothesis 4. *$\exists$ a constant $\mathscr{M}^* > 0$: $\sum_{i=1}^{m} |\mathscr{Y}_i| \leq \mathscr{M}^*$.*

Theorem 3. *If Hypothesis 1 and 2 are satisfied and if*

$$(\mathscr{L}_1 \models +\mathscr{L}_2\mathscr{G}_1)\left[\frac{(\log \mathscr{T})^{\mathscr{P}}}{\Gamma(\mathscr{P}+1)} + \frac{|\alpha|(\log \mathscr{T})(\log \eta)^{\mathscr{P}+\mathscr{Q}}}{|\Lambda|\Gamma(\mathscr{P}+\mathscr{Q}+1)} + \frac{|\beta|(\log \mathscr{T})^{\mathscr{P}-\gamma+1}}{|\Lambda|(\mathscr{P}-\gamma+1)}\right] < 1 \tag{8}$$

then the problems (1)–(3) have a unique solution on $[1, \mathscr{T}]$.

Proof. Take a look at the following operator $\mathscr{W} : \mathscr{PC}(\mathscr{J}, \mathbb{R}) \to \mathscr{PC}(\mathscr{J}, \mathbb{R})$ defined by

$$\begin{aligned}\mathscr{W}\varpi(\tau) = &\sum_{\mathscr{K}=1}^{\mathscr{M}} \mathscr{Y}_i + \frac{1}{\Gamma(\mathscr{P})} \int_1^{\tau} (\log \frac{\tau}{s})^{\mathscr{P}-1} \mathscr{F}(s, \varpi(s), \mathscr{B}(\varpi(s)))) \frac{ds}{s} \\ &+ \frac{\log \tau}{\Lambda} [\lambda - \frac{\alpha}{\Gamma(\mathscr{P}+\mathscr{Q})} \int_1^{\eta} (\log \frac{\eta}{s})^{\mathscr{P}+\mathscr{Q}-1} \mathscr{F}(s, \varpi(s), \mathscr{B}(\varpi(s))) \frac{ds}{s}] \\ &- \frac{\beta}{\Gamma(\mathscr{P}-\gamma)} \int_1^{\mathscr{T}} (\log \frac{\mathscr{T}}{s})^{\mathscr{P}-\gamma-1} \mathscr{F}(s, \varpi(s), \mathscr{B}(\varpi(s))) \frac{ds}{s}.\end{aligned}$$

Use the BCP to demonstrate that $\mathscr{W}$ is contraction.
Let $(\varpi, \mathscr{Y}) \in \mathscr{PC}_1^{\vartheta}([1, \mathscr{T}], \mathbb{R})$, we have

$$|(\mathscr{W}\varpi)\tau-(\mathscr{W}\mathscr{Y})(\tau)|\leq\frac{1}{\Gamma(\mathscr{P})}\int_{1}^{\tau}(\log\frac{\tau}{\mathtt{s}})^{\mathscr{P}-1}|\mathscr{F}(\mathtt{s},\varpi(\mathtt{s}),\mathscr{B}(\varpi(\mathtt{s}))).\mathscr{F}(\mathtt{s},\mathscr{Y}(\mathtt{s}),\mathscr{B}(\mathscr{Y}(\mathtt{s})))|\frac{\mathtt{ds}}{\mathtt{s}}$$
$$+\frac{\log\tau}{\Lambda}[\lambda-\frac{\alpha}{\Gamma(\mathscr{P}+\mathscr{Q})}\int_{1}^{\eta}(\log\frac{\eta}{\mathtt{s}})^{\mathscr{P}+\mathscr{Q}-1}|\mathscr{F}(\mathtt{s},\varpi(\mathtt{s}),\mathscr{B}(\varpi(\mathtt{s})))-\mathscr{F}(\mathtt{s},(\mathtt{s}),\mathscr{B}\mathscr{Y}((\mathtt{s})))|\frac{\mathtt{ds}}{\mathtt{s}}]$$
$$-\frac{\beta}{\Gamma(\mathscr{P}-\gamma)}\int_{1}^{\mathscr{T}}(\log\frac{\mathscr{T}}{\mathtt{s}})^{\mathscr{P}-\gamma-1}|\mathscr{F}(\mathtt{s},\varpi(\mathtt{s}),\mathscr{B}\varpi((\mathtt{s})))-\mathscr{F}(\mathtt{s},\mathscr{Y}(\mathtt{s}),\mathscr{B}\mathscr{Y}((\mathtt{s})))|\frac{\mathtt{ds}}{\mathtt{s}},$$
$$\leq\frac{(\log\mathscr{T})^{\mathscr{P}}}{\Gamma(\mathscr{P})+1}(\mathscr{L}_1+\mathscr{L}_2\mathscr{G}_1)|\varpi(\mathtt{s})-\mathscr{Y}(\mathtt{s})|+\frac{|\alpha|(\log\mathscr{T})(\log\eta)^{\mathscr{P}+\mathscr{Q}}}{|\Lambda|\Gamma(\mathscr{P}+\mathscr{Q}+1)}(\mathscr{L}_1+\mathscr{L}_2\mathscr{G}_1)|\varpi(\mathtt{s})-\mathscr{Y}(\mathtt{s})|$$
$$+\frac{|\beta|(\log\mathscr{T})^{\mathscr{P}-\gamma+1}}{|\Lambda|\Gamma(\mathscr{P}-\gamma+1)}|\varpi(\mathtt{s})-\mathscr{Y}(\mathtt{s})\leq(\mathscr{L}_1+\mathscr{L}_2\mathscr{G}_1)|\Bigg[\frac{(\log\mathscr{T})^{\mathscr{P}}}{\Gamma(\mathscr{P}+1)}+\frac{|\alpha|(\log\mathscr{T})(\log\eta)^{\mathscr{P}+\mathscr{Q}}}{|\Lambda|\Gamma(\mathscr{P}+\mathscr{Q}+1)}$$
$$+\frac{|\beta|(\log\mathscr{T})^{\mathscr{P}-\gamma+1}}{|\Lambda|(\mathscr{P}-\gamma+1)}\Bigg]||\varpi(\mathtt{s})-\mathscr{Y}(\mathtt{s})|$$
$$\leq(\mathscr{L}_1+\mathscr{L}_2\mathscr{G}_1)\Theta|\varpi(\mathtt{s})-\mathscr{Y}(\mathtt{s})|\,.$$

where

$$\Theta=\left[\frac{(\log\mathscr{T})^{\mathscr{P}}}{\Gamma(\mathscr{P}+1)}+\frac{|\alpha|(\log\mathscr{T})(\log\eta)^{\mathscr{P}+\mathscr{Q}}}{|\Lambda|\Gamma(\mathscr{P}+\mathscr{Q}+1)}+\frac{|\beta|(\log\mathscr{T})^{\mathscr{P}-\gamma+1}}{|\Lambda|(\mathscr{P}-\gamma+1)}\right].$$

By (3), consequences are expressed as $\mathscr{W}$, a contraction. As a result of the Banach FPT, we obtain the result that $\mathscr{W}$ has a FP that is a solution to the problem (1)–(3). □

Theorem 4 ((Krasnoselkii's FPT) [31,32]). *Let a bounded, closed, and convex set $\emptyset\neq\mathbb{M}_1\subset\mathbb{M}$ with Banach space $\mathbb{M}$. Take operators Γ and Δ: (a) $\Gamma x_1+\Delta x_2\in\mathbb{M}_1$, x_1,$x_2\in\mathbb{M}_1$; (b) Γ is compact and continuous; (c) Δ is a contraction mapping. Therefore, $\exists$ $z\in\mathbb{M}_1$: $z=\Gamma z+\Delta z$.*

The following Theorem is based on existence results.

Theorem 5. *If Hypothesis 3 and 4 hold, then the problem (1)–(3) has at least one solution for on $[1,\mathscr{T}]$.*

Proof. Introduce the new operator $\mathscr{E}_1$ and $\mathscr{E}_2$ are

$$(\mathscr{E}_1\varpi)(\tau)=\frac{1}{\Gamma(\mathscr{P})}\int_{1}^{\tau}(\log\frac{\tau}{\mathtt{s}})^{\mathscr{P}-1}\mathscr{F}(\mathtt{s},\varpi(\mathtt{s}),\mathscr{B}(\varpi(\mathtt{s}))))\frac{\mathtt{ds}}{\mathtt{s}}\tag{9}$$

and

$$(\mathscr{E}_2\varpi)(\tau)=\sum_{\mathscr{K}=1}^{\mathscr{M}}\mathscr{Y}_{\mathtt{i}}+\frac{\log\tau}{\Lambda}[\lambda-\frac{\alpha}{\Gamma(\mathscr{P}+\mathscr{Q})}\int_{1}^{\eta}(\log\frac{\eta}{\mathtt{s}})^{\mathscr{P}+\mathscr{Q}-1}\mathscr{F}(\mathtt{s},\varpi(\mathtt{s}),\mathscr{B}(\varpi(\mathtt{s})))\frac{\mathtt{ds}}{\mathtt{s}}]$$
$$-\beta(\Gamma(\mathscr{P}-\gamma))^{-1}\int_{1}^{\mathscr{T}}(\log\frac{\mathscr{T}}{\mathtt{s}})^{\mathscr{P}-\gamma-1}\mathscr{F}(\mathtt{s},\varpi(\mathtt{s}),\mathscr{B}(\varpi(\mathtt{s})))\frac{\mathtt{ds}}{\mathtt{s}}.\tag{10}$$

Consider

$$\mathscr{B}_{\mathtt{d}}=\{\varpi\in\mathscr{PC}:||\varpi||<\mathtt{d}\}.$$

For any $\varpi,\mathscr{Y}\in\mathscr{B}_{\mathtt{d}}$ the $\mathscr{E}_1\varpi+\mathscr{E}_2\mathscr{Y}\in\mathscr{B}_{\mathtt{d}}$ where $\mathscr{E}_1$and $\mathscr{E}_2$ is denoted by (3.2) and (3.3).

$$
\begin{aligned}
\mathscr{E}_1\varpi + \mathscr{E}_2\mathscr{Y}| = & |\frac{1}{\Gamma(\mathscr{P})}\int_1^{\tau}(\log\frac{\tau}{\mathrm{s}})^{\mathscr{P}-1}\mathscr{F}(\mathrm{s},\varpi(\mathrm{s}),\mathscr{B}(\varpi(\mathrm{s}))))\frac{\mathrm{ds}}{\mathrm{s}} \\
& + \frac{\log\tau}{\Lambda}[\lambda - \frac{\alpha}{\Gamma(\mathscr{P}+\mathscr{Q})}\int_1^{\eta}(\log\frac{\eta}{\mathrm{s}})^{\mathscr{P}+\mathscr{Q}-1}\mathscr{F}(\mathrm{s},\varpi(\mathrm{s}),\mathscr{B}(\varpi(\mathrm{s})))\frac{\mathrm{ds}}{\mathrm{s}}] \\
& - \frac{\beta}{\Gamma(\mathscr{P}-\gamma)}\int_1^{\mathscr{T}}(\log\frac{\mathscr{T}}{\mathrm{s}})^{\mathscr{P}-\gamma-1}\mathscr{F}(\mathrm{s},\varpi(\mathrm{s}),\mathscr{B}(\varpi(\mathrm{s})))\frac{\mathrm{ds}}{\mathrm{s}}| + \sum_{\mathscr{K}=1}^{\mathscr{M}}\mathscr{Y}_{\mathrm{i}} \\
& \leq |\frac{1}{\Gamma(\mathscr{P})}\int_1^{\tau}(\log\frac{\tau}{\mathrm{s}})^{\mathscr{P}-1}\mathscr{F}(\mathrm{s},\varpi(\mathrm{s}),\mathscr{B}(\varpi(\mathrm{s}))))\frac{\mathrm{ds}}{\mathrm{s}}| \\
& + |\frac{\log\tau}{\Lambda}[\lambda - \frac{\alpha}{\Gamma(\mathscr{P}+\mathscr{Q})}\int_1^{\eta}(\log\frac{\eta}{\mathrm{s}})^{\mathscr{P}+\mathscr{Q}-1}\mathscr{F}(\mathrm{s},\varpi(\mathrm{s}),\mathscr{B}(\varpi(\mathrm{s})))\frac{\mathrm{ds}}{\mathrm{s}}] \\
& - \frac{\beta}{\Gamma(\mathscr{P}-\gamma)}\int_1^{\mathscr{T}}(\log\frac{\mathscr{T}}{\mathrm{s}})^{\mathscr{P}-\gamma-1}\mathscr{F}(\mathrm{s},\varpi(\mathrm{s}),\mathscr{B}(\varpi(\mathrm{s})))\frac{\mathrm{ds}}{\mathrm{s}}| + \sum_{\mathscr{K}=1}^{\mathscr{M}}\mathscr{Y}_{\mathrm{i}}, \\
& \leq \frac{1}{\Gamma(\mathscr{P})}\int_1^{\tau}(\log\frac{\tau}{\mathrm{s}})^{\mathscr{P}-1}|\mathscr{F}(\mathrm{s},\varpi(\mathrm{s}),\mathscr{B}\varpi((\mathrm{s})))|\frac{ds}{s} \\
& + \frac{\log\tau}{\Lambda}[\lambda - \frac{\alpha}{\Gamma(\mathscr{P}+\mathscr{Q})}\int_1^{\eta}(\log\frac{\eta}{\mathrm{s}})^{\mathscr{P}+\mathscr{Q}-1}|\mathscr{F}(\mathrm{s},\varpi(\mathrm{s}),\mathscr{B}\varpi((\mathrm{s})))|\frac{\mathrm{ds}}{\mathrm{s}}] \\
& - \frac{\beta}{\Gamma(\mathscr{P}-\gamma)}\int_1^{\mathscr{T}}(\log\frac{\mathscr{T}}{\mathrm{s}})^{\mathscr{P}-\gamma-1}|\mathscr{F}(\mathrm{s},\varpi(\mathrm{s}),\mathscr{B}\varpi((\mathrm{s})))|\frac{\mathrm{ds}}{\mathrm{s}} + \sum_{\mathscr{K}=1}^{\mathscr{M}}\mathscr{Y}_{\mathrm{i}}, \\
& \leq \frac{1}{\Gamma(\mathscr{P}+1)}(\log\mathscr{T})^{\mathscr{P}}\mu(\tau)\frac{\mathrm{ds}}{\mathrm{s}} + \frac{\log\mathscr{T}}{|\Lambda|} \\
& \left[\lambda - \frac{|\alpha|}{\Gamma(\mathscr{P}+\mathscr{Q}+1)}(\log\eta)^{\mathscr{P}+\mathscr{Q}}\mu(\tau)\frac{\mathrm{ds}}{\mathrm{s}} + \frac{\beta}{\Gamma(\mathscr{P}-\gamma+1)}(\log\mathscr{T})^{\mathscr{P}-\gamma}\mu(\tau)\frac{\mathrm{ds}}{\mathrm{s}}\right] + \mathscr{M}^*, \\
& \leq \mu(\tau)\frac{1}{\Gamma(\mathscr{P}+1)}(\log\mathscr{T})^{\mathscr{P}} + \frac{\log\mathscr{T}}{|\Lambda|}[\lambda - \frac{|\alpha|}{\Gamma(\mathscr{P}+\mathscr{Q}+1)} + \frac{\beta}{\Gamma(\mathscr{P}-\gamma+1)}] + \mathscr{M}^*, \\
& \leq \mathrm{d}.
\end{aligned}
$$

Thus

$$
\mathscr{E}_1\varpi + \mathscr{E}_2\mathscr{Y} \in \mathscr{B}_{\mathrm{d}},
$$

using $\mathscr{H}_4$, $\mathscr{E}_2$ is a contraction, and when using $\mathscr{E}_1$ the operator $(\mathscr{E}_1\varpi)(\tau)$ is continuous. Additionally, we notice

$$
\begin{aligned}
(\mathscr{E}_1\varpi)(\tau) &= \frac{1}{\Gamma(\mathscr{P})}\int_1^{\tau}(\log\frac{\tau}{\mathrm{s}})^{\mathscr{P}-1}|\mathscr{F}(\mathrm{s},\varpi(\mathrm{s}),\mathscr{B}\varpi((\mathrm{s})))\mathrm{ds}(\mathrm{s})^{-1} \\
&\leq (\Gamma(\mathscr{P}+1))^{-1}(\log\mathscr{T})^{\mathscr{P}}\mu(\tau).
\end{aligned}
$$

$\mathscr{E}_1$ is uniformly bounded on $\mathscr{B}_{\mathrm{d}}$. Let us now demonstrate that the function $(\mathscr{A}_1\varpi)(\tau)$ is equicontinuous.

$$
\sup_{(\tau,\varpi,\mathscr{Y})} \in [1,\mathscr{T}] \times \mathscr{B}_{\mathrm{d}}|\mathscr{F}(\tau,\varpi(\tau),\mathscr{B}(\varpi(\tau)))| < \mathscr{C}_0 < \infty,
$$

We will obtain

$$
\begin{aligned}
|(\mathscr{E}_1\varpi)(\tau_2)+(\mathscr{E}_2\mathscr{Y})(\tau_1)| &= |\frac{1}{\Gamma(\mathscr{P})}\int_1^{\tau_1}(\log\frac{\tau_1}{\mathrm{s}})^{\mathscr{P}-1}\mathscr{G}(\mathrm{s})\frac{\mathrm{ds}}{\mathrm{s}} - \frac{1}{\Gamma(\mathscr{P})}\int_1^{\tau_2}(\log\frac{\tau_2}{\mathrm{s}})^{\mathscr{P}-1}\mathscr{G}(\mathrm{s})\frac{\mathrm{ds}}{\mathrm{s}}| \\
&\le \frac{1}{\Gamma(\mathscr{P})}\int_1^{\tau_1}[(\log\frac{\tau_2}{\mathrm{s}})^{\mathscr{P}-1} - (\log\frac{\tau_1}{\mathrm{s}})^{\mathscr{P}-1}]|\mathscr{G}(\mathrm{s})\frac{\mathrm{ds}}{\mathrm{s}}| \\
&+ \frac{1}{\Gamma(\mathscr{P})}\int_{\tau_2}^{\tau_1}(\log\frac{\tau_2}{\mathrm{s}})^{\mathscr{P}-1}|\mathscr{G}(\mathrm{s})\frac{\mathrm{ds}}{\mathrm{s}}| \\
&\le \frac{\mathscr{C}_0}{\Gamma(\mathscr{P}+1)}[|(\log\tau_1)^{\mathscr{P}} + \log(\frac{\tau_2}{\tau_1})^{\mathscr{P}} - (\log\tau_2)^{\mathscr{P}}| + |\log(\frac{\tau_2}{\tau_1})^{\mathscr{P}}|] \\
&\le \frac{\mathscr{C}_0}{\Gamma(\mathscr{P}+1)}[|(\log\tau_1)^{\mathscr{P}} - (\log\tau_2)^{\mathscr{P}}|].
\end{aligned}
$$

Consequently, $\mathscr{E}_1(\mathscr{B}_{\mathrm{d}})$ is relatively compact. Therefore, according to the Ascoli-Arzela theorem, $\mathscr{E}_1$ is compact. Therefore, the problems (1)–(3) under consideration have at least one FP on $\mathscr{J}$. □

4. Example

Consider the following BVP:

$$
{}^{\mathscr{CH}}\mathscr{D}^{\frac{3}{2}}\varpi(\tau) = \frac{\cos^2\tau}{(\mathrm{e}^{-\tau+2})^2|\varpi(\tau)|} + \int_0^{\tau}\frac{(\mathrm{s}+|\varpi(\mathrm{s})|)}{(2+\tau)^2(1+|\varpi(\mathrm{s})|)}\mathrm{ds}, \tag{11}
$$

$$
\varpi(\tau_{\mathscr{K}}^{+}) = \varpi(\tau_{\mathscr{K}}^{-}) + \frac{1}{6}, \tag{12}
$$

$$
\varpi(1) = 0, \ \frac{1}{2}{}_{\mathscr{H}}\mathscr{I}^{\frac{1}{2}}\varpi(2) + 2^{\mathscr{CH}}\mathscr{D}^{\frac{1}{3}}\varpi(\mathrm{e}) = \frac{3}{4}, \tag{13}
$$

$$
\begin{aligned}
\mathscr{F}(\tau,\iota,v) &= \frac{\cos^2\tau}{(\mathrm{e}^{-\tau+2})^2|\varpi(\tau)|} \\
\mathscr{K}(\tau,\mathrm{s},\varpi) &= \int_0^{\tau}\frac{(\mathrm{s}+|\varpi(\mathrm{s})|)}{(2+\tau)^2(1+|\varpi(\mathrm{s})|)}\mathrm{ds},
\end{aligned}
$$

where $\mathscr{P}=\frac{3}{2}$, $\mathscr{Q}=\frac{1}{2}$, $\gamma=\frac{1}{3}$, $\eta=2$, $\alpha=\frac{1}{2}$, $\beta=2$, $\lambda=\frac{3}{4}$, $\mathscr{T}=\mathrm{e}$, $\mathscr{L}_1+\mathscr{L}_2=\frac{1}{9}$, $\mathscr{G}_1=\frac{1}{9}$. Hence Hypothesis 1 and 2 hold. We check the condition

$$
(\mathscr{L}_1+\mathscr{L}_2\mathscr{G}_1)\left[\frac{(\log\mathscr{T})^{\mathscr{P}}}{\Gamma(\mathscr{P}+1)} + \frac{|\alpha|(\log\mathscr{T})(\log\eta)^{\mathscr{P}+\mathscr{Q}}}{|\Lambda|\Gamma(\mathscr{P}+\mathscr{Q}+1)} + \frac{|\beta|(\log\mathscr{T})^{\mathscr{P}-\gamma+1}}{|\Lambda|(\mathscr{P}-\gamma+1)}\right] \approx 0.047509 < 1
$$

Hence, problems (11)–(13) have a unique solution $[1,\mathscr{T}]$.

Proof. Using Theorem 3 to derive a unique solution, since Hypothesis 1 and 2 are satisfied. Then Theorem 3 implies the uniqueness solution. □

5. Conclusions

In this work, results for a new modeling of IBVP using C-HIFI-DE with Banach space are investigated, along with the E-UR of solutions. The KFPT and the BCP serve as the basis of this unique strategy, and are used to achieve the desired results. We develop the illustrated examples at the end of the paper to support the validity of the theoretical statements. Potential future works could be to examine much more complicated fractional systems and employ some other tools.

Author Contributions: Conceptualization, E.-s.E.-h., K.V. and Y.A.; methodology, E.-s.E.-h. and K.V.; software, E.-s.E.-h., K.V. and Y.A.; validation, E.-s.E.-h., K.V. and Y.A.; formal analysis, E.-s.E.-h., K.V. and Y.A.; investigation, E.-s.E.-h., K.V. and Y.A.; data curation, E.-s.E.-h., K.V. and Y.A.; writing—original draft preparation, E.-s.E.-h. and K.V.; writing—review and editing, E.-s.E.-h.; visualization, E.-s.E.-h., K.V. and Y.A.; supervision, E.-s.E.-h. and K.V.; project administration, E.-s.E.-h., K.V. and Y.A. All authors have read and agreed to the published version of the manuscript.

Funding: This work was funded by the Deanship of Scientific Research at Jouf University through the Fast-track Research Funding Program.

Institutional Review Board Statement: Not applicable.

Informed Consent Statement: Not applicable.

Data Availability Statement: Data are contained within the article

Conflicts of Interest: The author declares he has not used Artificial Intelligence (AI) tools in the creation of this article.

References

1. Oldham, K.B.; Spanier, J. *The Fractional Calculus*; Academic Press: Newyork, NY, USA, 1974.
2. Kilbas, A.A. Hadamard type fractional calculus. *J. Korean Math. Soc.* **2001**, *38*, 1191–1204.
3. Kilbas, A.A.; Srivastava, H.M.; Trujillo, J.J. *Theory and Applications of Fractional Differential Equations*; North-Holland Mathematics Studies 204; Elsevier Science, B.V.: Amsterdam, The Netherlands, 2006.
4. Podlubny, I. *Fractional Differential Equations*; Academic Press: Nweyork, NY, USA, 1999.
5. Agarwal, R.P.; Meehan, M.; O'Regan, D. *Fixed Point Theory and Applications*; Cambridge University Press: Cambridge, UK, 2017
6. Hamoud, A.A.; Abdo, M.S.; Ghadle, K.P. Existence and uniqueness results for Caputo fractional integro-differential equations. *J Korean Soc. Ind. App. Math.* **2018**, *22*, 163–177.
7. Benchora, M.; Hamani, S.; Ntouyas, S.K. Boundary value problems for differential equations with fractional order. *Surv. Math Appl.* **2008**, *3*, 1–12.
8. Benhamida, W.; John, R.; Hamani, S. Boundary value problems for Hadamard fractional differential equations with nonlocal multi-point boundary conditions. *Frac. Diff. Calc.* **2018**, *8*, 165–176. [CrossRef]
9. Boutiara, A.; Guerbati, K.; Benbachir, M. Caputo-Hadamard fractional differential equation with three-point boundary conditions in Banach spaces. *AIMS Math.* **2019**, *5*, 259–272.
10. Derbazi, C.; Hammouche, H. Existence and uniqueness results for a class of nonlinear fractional differential equations with nonlocal boundary conditions. *Jordan J. Math. Stat.* **2020**, *13*, 341–361.
11. Thiramanus, P.; Ntouyas, S.K.; Tariboon, J. Existence and uniqueness results for Hadamard type fractional differential equations with nonlocal fractional integral boundary conditions. *Abstr. Appl. Anal.* **2014**, *2014*, 902054. [CrossRef]
12. Tian, Y.; Bai, Z. Impulsive boundary value problem for differential equations with fractional order. *Differ. Equ. Dyn. Syst.* **2013**, *21* 253–260. [CrossRef]
13. Butzer, P.L.; Kilbas, A.A.; Trujillo, J.J. Compositions of Hadamard type fractional integration operators and the Semigroup property. *J. Math. Anal. Appl.* **2002**, *269*, 387–400. [CrossRef]
14. Butzer, P.L.; Kilbas, A.A.; Trujillo, J.J. Mellin transform analysis and integration by parts for Hadamard type fractional integrals. *J Math. Anal. Appl.* **2002**, *270*, 1–15. [CrossRef]
15. Butzer, P.L.; Kilbas, A.A.; Trujillo, J.J. Fractional calculus in the mellin setting and Hadamard type fractional integrals. *J. Math Anal. Appl.* 2002, 269, 1–27. [CrossRef]
16. Jarad, F.; Baleanu, D.; Abdeljawad, T. Caputo-type modification of the Hadamard fractional derivatives. *Adv. Differ. Equ.* **2012** *2012*, 1–142. [CrossRef]
17. Hamani, S.; Hammou, A.; Henderson, J. Impulsive fractional differential equations involving the Hadamard fractional derivative *Commun. Appl. Nonlinear Anal.* **2017**, *24*, 48–58.
18. Hamani, S.; Hammou, A.; Henderson, J. Impulsive Hadamard fractional differential equations in Banach spaces. *Commun. Appl Nonlinear Anal.* **2018**, *28*, 52–62.
19. Hamani, S.; Hammou, A.; Henderson, J. Initial value problems for impulsive Caputo-Hadamard fractional differential inclusions *Commun. Appl. Nonlinear Anal.* **2019**, *22*, 17–35.
20. Nain, A.K.; Vats, R.K.; Kumar, A. Caputo-Hadamard fractional differential equation with impulsive boundary conditions. *J. Math Model.* **2021**, *9*, 93–106.
21. Arioua, Y.; Basti, B.; Benhamidouche, N. Boundary value problem for Caputo-Hadamard fractional differential equations. *Surv Math. Appl.* **2017**, *12*, 103–115.
22. Irguedi, A.; Nisse, K.; Haman, S. Functional impulsive fractional differential equations involving the Caputo-Hadamard derivative and integral boundary conditions. *Int. J. Anal. Appl.* **2023**, *21*, 1–14. [CrossRef]

23. Wafa, S.M. A Study of Caputo-Hadamard type fractional differential equations with nonlocal boundary conditions. *J. Funct. Spaces* **2016**, *2016*, 1–14.
24. Bai, Y.; Kong, H. Existence of solutions for nonlinear Caputo-Hadamard fractional differential equations via the method of upper and lower solutions. *J. Nonlinear Sci. Appl.* **2017**, *10*, 5744–5752. [CrossRef]
25. Derdar, N. Nonlinear implicit Caputo-Hadamard fractional differential equations with fractional boundary conditions. *Jordan J. Math. Stat.* **2022**, *15*, 999–1014.
26. Hadamard, J. Essai sur l'etude des fonctions donnees par leur development de Taylor. *J. Math. Appl.* **1892**, *8*, 101–186.
27. Arul, R.; Karthikeyan, P.; Karthikeyan, K.; Geetha, P.; Alruwaily, Y.; Almaghamsi, L.; El-hady, E.S. On Nonlinear Ψ-Caputo Fractional Integro Differential Equations Involving Non-Instantaneous Conditions. *Symmetry* **2022**, *15*, 5. [CrossRef]
28. Arul, R.; Karthikeyan, P.; Karthikeyan, K.; Alruwaily, Y.; Almaghamsi, L.; El-hady, E.S. Sequential Caputo-Hadamard Fractional Differential Equations with Boundary Conditions in Banach Spaces. *Fractal Fract.* **2022**, *6*, 730.
29. Yukunthorn, W.; Suantai, S.; Ntouyas, S.K.; Tariboon, J. Boundary value problems for impulsive multi-order Hadamard fractional differential equations. *Bound. Value Probl.* **2015**, *148*, 1–13. [CrossRef]
30. Benhamida, W.; Hamani, S.; Henderson, J. Boundary value problems for Caputo-Hadamard fractional differential equations. *Adv. Theory Nonlinear Anal. Its Appl.* **2018**, *2*, 138–145.
31. Burton, T.A. A fixed-point theorem of Krasnoselskii. *Appl. Math. Lett.* **1998**, *11*, 85–88. [CrossRef]
32. Granas, A.; Dugundji, J. *Fixed Point Theory;* Springer: New York, NY, USA, 2003.

fractal and fractional

MDPI

Article

Approximation of Caputo Fractional Derivative and Numerical Solutions of Fractional Differential Equations

Yuri Dimitrov [1,2,*], Slavi Georgiev [2,3] and Venelin Todorov [2,4]

1 Department of Mathematics, Physics and Informatics, University of Forestry, 1756 Sofia, Bulgaria
2 Department of Informational Modeling, Institute of Mathematics and Informatics, Bulgarian Academy of Sciences, 1113 Sofia, Bulgaria; sggeorgiev@math.bas.bg (S.G.); vtodorov@math.bas.bg (V.T.)
3 Department of Applied Mathematics and Statistics, University of Ruse, 7017 Ruse, Bulgaria
4 Department of Parallel Algorithms, Institute of Information and Communication Technologies, Bulgarian Academy of Sciences, 1113 Sofia, Bulgaria
* Correspondence: yuri.dimitrov@ltu.bg; Tel.: +359-2-979-28-40

Abstract: In this paper, we consider an approximation of the Caputo fractional derivative and its asymptotic expansion formula, whose generating function is the polylogarithm function. We prove the convergence of the approximation and derive an estimate for the error and order. The approximation is applied for the construction of finite difference schemes for the two-term ordinary fractional differential equation and the time fractional Black–Scholes equation for option pricing. The properties of the approximation are used to prove the convergence and order of the finite difference schemes and to obtain bounds for the error of the numerical methods. The theoretical results for the order and error of the methods are illustrated by the results of the numerical experiments.

Keywords: fractional derivative; approximation; numerical solution; convergence

1. Introduction

Fractional differential equations are an essential means of modeling complex processes in different fields of science [1–5]. The Riemann–Liouville fractional integral of order $\alpha > 0$ is defined as as follows:

$$ {}_aI_x^\alpha f(x) = \frac{1}{\Gamma(\alpha)} \int_a^x (x-t)^{\alpha-1} f(t) \mathrm{d}t. $$

When n is a positive integer and $0 < \alpha < 1$, the Caputo and Riemann–Liouville fractional derivatives of order α are defined as follows:

$$ {}_a^C D_x^{n+\alpha} f(x) = I^{1-\alpha} D^{n+1} f(x) = \frac{1}{\Gamma(1-\alpha)} \int_a^x \frac{f^{(n+1)}(t)}{(x-t)^\alpha} \mathrm{d}t, $$
$$ {}_a^{RL} D_x^{n+\alpha} f(x) = D^{n+1} I^{1-\alpha} f(x) = \frac{1}{\Gamma(1-\alpha)} \frac{\mathrm{d}^{n+1}}{\mathrm{d}x^{n+1}} \int_a^x \frac{f(t)}{(x-t)^\alpha} \mathrm{d}t. $$

The Caputo and Riemann–Liouville fractional derivatives are related as

$$ {}_a^{RL} D_x^{n+\alpha} f(x) = {}_a^C D_x^{n+\alpha} f(x) + \sum_{k=0}^{n} \frac{f^{(k)}(0) x^{k-n-\alpha}}{\Gamma(k-\alpha-n+1)}. \quad (1) $$

In this paper, we considered the case when the order of fractional differentiation is between zero and one. In the remainder of the paper, the parameter $\alpha \in (0,1)$. Without loss of generality, the lower limit of the integral in the definition of the fractional derivative is zero. The Caputo fractional derivative of order α is defined as follows:

$$f^{(\alpha)}(x) = D_x^\alpha f(x) = \frac{1}{\Gamma(1-\alpha)} \int_0^x \frac{f'(t)}{(x-t)^\alpha} dt.$$

Fractional derivatives and integrals are nonlocal and have a singularity at the endpoint. The properties of the fractional derivatives make them an important tool for describing memory processes. The exponential, sine, and cosine functions have Caputo derivatives:

$$D_x^\alpha e^x = x^{1-\alpha} E_{1,2-\alpha}(x), \quad D_x^\alpha \sin x = x^{1-\alpha} E_{2,2-\alpha}(-x^2), \quad D_x^\alpha \cos x = -x^{2-\alpha} E_{2,3-\alpha}(-x^2),$$

where $E_{\beta_1,\beta_2}(x)$ is the Mittag–Leffler function:

$$E_{\beta_1,\beta_2}(x) = \sum_{k=0}^{\infty} \frac{x^k}{\Gamma(\beta_1 k + \beta_2)}.$$

Approximations of fractional derivatives involve the use of special functions. The Riemann zeta function is an analytic function that is defined for complex numbers with the real part greater than one as follows:

$$\zeta(x) = \sum_{n=1}^{\infty} \frac{1}{n^x}.$$

The polylogarithm function of order β is defined as follows:

$$\mathrm{Li}_\beta(x) = \sum_{n=1}^{\infty} \frac{x^n}{n^\beta}$$

and $\mathrm{Li}_\beta(e^{-x})$ has a series expansion:

$$\mathrm{Li}_\beta(e^{-x}) = \Gamma(1-\beta)x^{\beta-1} + \sum_{n=0}^{\infty} \frac{\zeta(\beta-n)}{n!}(-x)^n. \quad (2)$$

Finite difference schemes for the numerical solution of fractional differential equations use discretizations of the fractional derivative. Two important discretizations of the Caputo fractional derivative are the Grünwald difference approximation and the L1 approximation [6–10]. The Grünwald difference approximation has a first-order accuracy and a generating function $(1-x)^\alpha$. Central difference approximations of integer-order derivatives have a second-order accuracy. Grünwald difference approximation is a second-order shifted approximation of the fractional derivative with a shift parameter $\alpha/2$, and it is a generalization of finite difference approximations of integer-order derivatives [11,12].

Let n be a positive integer, $h = x/n$, and $y_k = y(kh)$ for $k = 0, 1, \cdots, n$. The L1 approximation has an order $2-\alpha$ and is defined as follows:

$$\frac{h^{-\alpha}}{\Gamma(2-\alpha)} \sum_{k=0}^{m} \sigma_k^{(\alpha)} f_{n-k} = f_n^{(\alpha)} + O\left(h^{2-\alpha}\right), \quad (3)$$

where $\sigma_0^{(\alpha)} = 1$, $\sigma_n^{(\alpha)} = (n-1)^{1-\alpha} - n^{1-\alpha}$ and

$$\sigma_k^{(\alpha)} = (k-1)^{1-\alpha} - k^{1-\alpha} + (k+1)^{1-\alpha}, \quad (k = 1, \cdots, n-1).$$

The L1 approximation has a generating function $\frac{(x-1)^2 \mathrm{Li}_{\alpha-1}(x)}{x\Gamma(2-\alpha)}$ and a second-order expansion formula [13]:

$$\frac{h^{-\alpha}}{\Gamma(2-\alpha)} \sum_{k=0}^{m} \sigma_k^{(\alpha)} f_{n-k} = f_n^{(\alpha)} + \frac{\zeta(\alpha-1)}{\Gamma(2-\alpha)} f_n'' h^{2-\alpha} + O\left(h^2\right), \quad (4)$$

The construction of the L1 approximation uses central difference approximations of the first derivative on a uniform net. Over the past few decades, there has been an increasing interest in developing efficient numerical techniques for solving fractional differential equations. The growing interest in this field has resulted in the development of high-order approximations for fractional derivatives and innovative methods for investigating their properties and practical applications. Approximations of the fractional derivative of order $3-\alpha$, which are called the $L1-2$ and $L1-2_\sigma$ formulas, were constructed by Alikhanov [14] and Gao et al. [15]. In [13,16], we used the L1 approximation and approximations of the second derivative for the construction of second-order approximations of the fractional derivative. Finite difference schemes using L2 formula approximations of the fractional derivative of order $3-\alpha$ and their convergence were studied by Alikhanov [17], Lv and Xu [18], and Wong and Ren [19]. High-order approximations of the fractional derivative and difference schemes for fractional differential equations were constructed in [20–27]. Navot [28] used Taylor polynomials to deal with the singularity of the fractional integral $\int_0^1 t^\alpha f(t)\mathrm{d}t$. He derived the asymptotic formula for Riemann sums on a uniform net, called the extended Euler–Maclaurin summation formula. The formula was extended by Navot [29] to functions with a logarithmic singularity. In [30], we derived the asymptotic formula of the Riemann sum of the fractional integral using the series expansion Formula (2) of the generating function $\mathrm{Li}_{1-\alpha}(x)$. Many of the techniques, originally formulated for ordinary and partial differential equations, have been modified and extended to address fractional differential equations. Spectral methods employ orthogonally based functions such as the Jacobi and Chebyshev polynomials to approximate solutions of fractional differential equations [31,32]. Fractional multistep methods, which can be viewed as an extension of classical multistep methods, were studied in [33,34]. Methods using spline interpolation were presented in [35,36]. Numerical methods using fractional wavelets were explored in [37,38].

This paper is a continuation of the work in [39]. In the paper, we study the properties of an approximation of order $2-\alpha$ of the Caputo derivative and the convergence of the corresponding difference schemes for the two-term ordinary fractional differential equation and the time fractional Black–Scholes equation for options pricing. A main approach for constructing approximations of fractional derivatives involves interpolating the function f in the definitions of fractional derivatives over a suitable stencil on a uniform grid. Using this method, formulas for L1 and L2 approximations are derived, as well as high-order approximations of fractional derivatives. The approximations obtained in this way have generating functions that include the polylogarithm function, and their expansion formulas are derived using (2). The direct application of this method leads to the construction of approximations of fractional derivatives with weights whose exponents are greater than -1, as the fractional integral of a negative order is divergent. Naturally, the question arises of constructing and studying the properties of approximations whose weights contain terms with exponents smaller than -1. A direct application of (2) for the function $\mathrm{Li}_{1+\alpha}(e^{-x})$ leads to the construction of an approximation of the fractional derivative and its expansion formula, which has weights of $1/k^{1+\alpha}$. The construction of this approximation and the corresponding approximations of order $2-\alpha$ were presented in [39]. The comparison performed with the L1 approximation shows that these approximations have the same order, similar properties of the weights, and comparable performance for the numerical solution of fractional differential equations. In this paper, we derive an estimate for the error of the approximation of order $2-\alpha$ of the fractional derivative with a generating function $\mathrm{Li}_{1+\alpha}(x)$ and the corresponding difference schemes for the numerical solution of fractional differential equations. The motivation of the study this approximation stems from the simpler formulas of its weights, its mathematical properties and applications, and for constructing efficient methods for numerically solving fractional differential equations.

In [39], we constructed an approximation of the Caputo fractional derivative and its asymptotic formula of order $2-\alpha$:

$$\frac{1}{h^{\alpha}}\sum_{k=1}^{n-1}\frac{f_{n-k}}{k^{1+\alpha}}=\Gamma(-\alpha)f_n^{(\alpha)}+\frac{\zeta(1+\alpha)}{h^{\alpha}}f_n-\zeta(\alpha)f_n'h^{1-\alpha}+O\left(h^{2-\alpha}\right). \tag{5}$$

Approximation (5) has a generating function $\mathrm{Li}_{1+\alpha}(x)$. By substituting the derivative in the right-hand side of (1) using the first-order backward difference $(f_n-f_{n-1})/h$, we find an approximation of the fractional derivative:

$$\mathcal{L}_n f(x)=\frac{h^{-\alpha}}{\Gamma(-\alpha)}\sum_{k=0}^{m}\sigma_k^{(\alpha)}f_{n-k}=f_n^{(\alpha)}+O\left(h^{2-\alpha}\right), \tag{6}$$

$$\sigma_0^{(\alpha)}=\zeta(\alpha)-\zeta(1+\alpha),\quad \sigma_1^{(\alpha)}=1-\zeta(\alpha),\quad \sigma_k^{(\alpha)}=\frac{1}{k^{1+\alpha}},\quad (2\leq k\leq n).$$

Approximations (5) and (6) have an order $2-\alpha$ when the function f satisfies the condition $f(0)=f'(0)=0$. In [39], we extended the approximation (6) to all functions in the class $C^2[0,x]$ by assigning the values of the last two weights.

$$\mathcal{A}_n f(x)=\frac{h^{-\alpha}}{\Gamma(-\alpha)}\sum_{k=0}^{n}\sigma_k^{(\alpha)}f_{n-k}=f_n^{(\alpha)}+O\left(h^{2-\alpha}\right), \tag{7}$$

$$\sigma_0^{(\alpha)}=\zeta(\alpha)-\zeta(1+\alpha),\quad \sigma_1^{(\alpha)}=1-\zeta(\alpha),\quad \sigma_k^{(\alpha)}=\frac{1}{k^{1+\alpha}},\quad (2\leq k\leq n-2), \tag{8}$$

$$\sigma_{n-1}^{(\alpha)}=\frac{1}{(n-1)^{1+\alpha}}-nS_n[1+\alpha]+S_n[\alpha]-\frac{n^{1-\alpha}}{\alpha(1-\alpha)}, \tag{9}$$

$$\sigma_n^{(\alpha)}=(n-1)S_n[1+\alpha]-S_n[\alpha]+\frac{n^{1-\alpha}}{\alpha(1-\alpha)}, \tag{10}$$

where $S_n[\alpha]=\sum_{k=1}^{n-1}k^{-\alpha}-\zeta(\alpha)$. In this paper, we investigate the properties of the approximations (6) and (7) and applications of the approximations for the numerical solution of ordinary and partial fractional differential equations. The outline of the paper is as follows. In Section 2, we study the properties of the weights of the approximation (7) and we derive the following inequality:

$$\sum_{k=1}^{n-1}\frac{(n-k)^{\alpha}}{k^{1+\alpha}}<\zeta(1+\alpha)n^{\alpha}-2. \tag{11}$$

In Section 3, we derive estimates for the errors of the approximations (6) and (7). In Sections 4 and 5, we construct finite difference schemes for numerically solving the two-term ordinary fractional differential equation and the time fractional Black–Scholes equation for option pricing. The convergence of the finite difference schemes is proven, and bounds for the errors of the methods are derived using Inequality (11) and the estimate for the truncation error of the approximation.

The approximation (5) is constructed using the series expansion Formula (2) of the function $\mathrm{Li}_{1+\alpha}(x)$ and can be extended to arbitrary orders. Equation (2) holds for any value of β that is not an integer. This indicates that the approximations (5)–(7) also apply to fractional derivatives of order greater than one. One direction for future work related to the paper is to consider applications of the discussed approximations for numerically solving fractional differential equations of orders greater than one. The L1 approximation (4) and the approximation (7) have an order $2-\alpha$ and similar performance and properties of the weights [39]:

$$\sigma_0^{(\alpha)}>0,\quad \sigma_1^{(\alpha)}<\sigma_2^{(\alpha)}<\cdots<\sigma_{n-1}^{(\alpha)}<0. \tag{12}$$

The properties of the L1 approximation and the approximation (7) presented in Section 2 enable an efficient analysis of the convergence and error of difference schemes for fractional differential equations. One approach for constructing approximations of integer-order and fractional derivatives was presented in [16]. Another direction for future work is constructing high-order approximations for fractional derivatives that have the properties (12) of the weights, investigating the properties of the constructed high-order approximations, and analyzing the convergence of the difference schemes for fractional differential equations. Additionally, it is important to examine the behavior of the numerical solution for values of the parameters where the denominator has a small value.

2. Properties of the Weights

Approximation (7) has the property that the values of $\mathcal{A}_n 1$ and $\mathcal{A}_n x$ are equal to the fractional derivatives of the functions:

$$\mathcal{A}_n 1 = D_x^\alpha 1 = 0, \quad \mathcal{A}_n x = D_x^\alpha x = \frac{x^{1-\alpha}}{\Gamma(2-\alpha)}.$$

The values of the weights of $\sigma_{n-1}^{(\alpha)}$ and $\sigma_n^{(\alpha)}$ are computed from the system of equations:

$$\sum_{k=0}^{n} \sigma_k^{(\alpha)} = 0, \quad \sum_{k=0}^{n} k\sigma_k^{(\alpha)} = \frac{n^{1-\alpha}}{\Gamma(2-\alpha)}.$$

In this section, we prove Inequality (11) and we derive an estimate for the weight $\sigma_{n-1}^{(\alpha)}$ of Approximation (6). The proof uses the inequalities in Claims 1 and 2.

Claim 1. *Let $0 < \alpha < 1$ and $1 \le k \le n$. Then,*

$$(n-k)^\alpha < n^\alpha - \frac{\alpha k}{n^{1-\alpha}}. \tag{13}$$

Proof. From the binomial formula,

$$(n-k)^\alpha = n^\alpha \left(1 - \frac{k}{n}\right)^\alpha = n^\alpha \sum_{i=0}^{\infty} (-1)^i \binom{\alpha}{i} \left(\frac{k}{n}\right)^i.$$

The numbers $(-1)^i \binom{\alpha}{i}$ are negative for $i \ge 1$. Then,

$$(n-k)^\alpha - n^\alpha + \frac{\alpha k}{n^{1-\alpha}} = n^\alpha \sum_{i=2}^{\infty} (-1)^i \binom{\alpha}{i} \left(\frac{k}{n}\right)^i < 0.$$

□

Claim 2. *Let $0 < \alpha < 1$. Then,*

$$\frac{1-\alpha+\alpha^2}{\alpha(1-\alpha)} + \frac{\alpha\zeta(\alpha)}{2^{1-\alpha}} > 2. \tag{14}$$

Proof. The Riemann zeta function has a series expansion [40]:

$$\zeta(\alpha) = \frac{1}{\alpha-1} + \gamma + \sum_{k=1}^{\infty} \frac{\gamma_n}{n!}(1-\alpha)^n, \tag{15}$$

where γ is an Euler constant and γ_n are generalized Euler constants:

$$\gamma_n = \lim_{N\to\infty} \left(\sum_{k=1}^{N} \frac{\log^n k}{k} - \frac{\log^{n+1} k}{n+1} \right),$$

$$\gamma = 0.5772157, \quad \gamma_1 = -0.0728158, \quad \gamma_2 = -0.0096904, \quad \gamma_3 = 0.0020538.$$

Then,

$$\zeta(\alpha) > \frac{1}{\alpha-1} + \gamma + (1-\alpha)\gamma_1 + \frac{(1-\alpha)^2}{2}\gamma_2 > \frac{1}{\alpha-1} + 0.49 + 0.08\alpha. \tag{16}$$

The value of $\ln 2 = 0.693147 < 0.7$. From Taylor's Theorem,

$$\begin{aligned} 2^{-(1-\alpha)} = e^{-(1-\alpha)\ln 2} &< 1 - (1-\alpha)\ln 2 + (1-\alpha)^2 \frac{\ln^2 2}{2} \\ &< 1 - \left(\ln 2 - \frac{\ln^2 2}{2}\right)(1-\alpha) \\ &< 1 - 0.45(1-\alpha) = 0.55 + 0.45\alpha. \end{aligned} \tag{17}$$

From (16) and (17),

$$\begin{aligned} \frac{1-\alpha+\alpha^2}{\alpha(1-\alpha)} + \frac{\alpha\zeta(\alpha)}{2^{1-\alpha}} &> \frac{1-\alpha+\alpha^2}{\alpha(1-\alpha)} + \alpha\left(\frac{1}{\alpha-1} + 0.497 + 0.08\alpha\right)(0.55 + 0.45\alpha) \\ &> \frac{1}{\alpha} + 0.036a^3 + 0.26765a^2 + 0.72335\alpha. \end{aligned}$$

Inequality (14) holds when

$$\frac{1}{\alpha} + 0.036\alpha^3 + 0.26765\alpha^2 + 0.72335\alpha > 2,$$

$$0.036a^4 + 0.26765a^3 + 0.72335\alpha^2 - 2\alpha + 1 > 0.$$

The function $f(\alpha) = 0.036a^4 + 0.26765a^3 + 0.72335\alpha^2 - 2\alpha + 1$ has a first derivative:

$$f'(\alpha) = 0.144\alpha^3 + 0.80295\alpha^2 + 1.4467\alpha - 2$$

and a minimum value $f(0.882) = 0.00414$. Therefore, $f(\alpha)$ is positive on $[0,1]$. □

Lemma 1. *Let $n \geq 2$. Then*

$$\sum_{k=1}^{n-1} \frac{(n-k)^\alpha}{k^{1+\alpha}} < \zeta(1+\alpha)n^\alpha - 2. \tag{18}$$

Proof. From Inequality (13),

$$\sum_{k=1}^{n-1} \frac{(n-k)^\alpha}{k^{1+\alpha}} < \sum_{k=1}^{n-1} \frac{1}{k^{1+\alpha}}\left(n^\alpha - \frac{\alpha k}{n^{1-\alpha}}\right) < n^\alpha \sum_{k=1}^{n-1} \frac{1}{k^{1+\alpha}} - \frac{\alpha}{n^{1-\alpha}} \sum_{k=1}^{n-1} \frac{1}{k^\alpha}.$$

The sum of the α-th powers of the first $n-1$ integers has an asymptotic formula [41]:

$$\sum_{k=1}^{n-1} k^\alpha = \zeta(-\alpha) + \frac{n^{1+\alpha}}{1+\alpha} \sum_{p=1}^{\infty} \binom{1+\alpha}{p} \frac{b_p}{n^p}, \tag{19}$$

where b_p are the Bernoulli numbers. Equation (19) is derived using the Euler–Maclaurin formula, and the actual value of $\sum_{k=1}^{n-1} k^\alpha$ lies between two consecutive partial sums [41]. Then,

$$\sum_{k=1}^{n-1} \frac{1}{k^{1+\alpha}} < \zeta(1+\alpha) - \frac{1}{\alpha n^\alpha} - \frac{1}{2n^{1+\alpha}} - \frac{1+\alpha}{12n^{2+\alpha}} + \frac{(1+\alpha)(2+\alpha)(3+\alpha)}{720n^{4+\alpha}},$$

$$\sum_{k=1}^{n-1} \frac{1}{k^\alpha} > \frac{n^{1-\alpha}}{1-\alpha} + \zeta(\alpha) - \frac{1}{2n^\alpha} - \frac{\alpha}{12n^{1+\alpha}}$$

and

$$n^\alpha \sum_{k=1}^{n-1} \frac{1}{k^{1+\alpha}} < \zeta(1+\alpha)n^\alpha - \frac{1}{\alpha} - \frac{1}{2n} - \frac{1+\alpha}{12n^2} + \frac{1}{30n^4},$$

$$\frac{\alpha}{n^{1-\alpha}} \sum_{k=1}^{n-1} \frac{1}{k^\alpha} > \frac{\alpha}{1-\alpha} + \frac{\alpha\zeta(\alpha)}{n^{1-\alpha}} - \frac{\alpha}{2n} - \frac{\alpha^2}{12n^2}.$$

Therefore,

$$\begin{aligned}
\sum_{k=1}^{n-1} \frac{(n-k)^\alpha}{k^{1+\alpha}} &< n^\alpha \sum_{k=1}^{n-1} \frac{1}{k^{1+\alpha}} - \frac{\alpha}{n^{1-\alpha}} \sum_{k=1}^{n-1} \frac{1}{k^\alpha} \\
&< \zeta(1+\alpha)n^\alpha - \frac{1-\alpha+\alpha^2}{\alpha(1-\alpha)} - \frac{\alpha\zeta(\alpha)}{n^{1-\alpha}} - \frac{1-\alpha}{2n} - \frac{1+\alpha-\alpha^2}{12n^2} + \frac{1}{30n^4} \\
&< \zeta(1+\alpha)n^\alpha - \frac{1-\alpha+\alpha^2}{\alpha(1-\alpha)} - \frac{\alpha\zeta(\alpha)}{n^{1-\alpha}} - \frac{1}{12n^2} + \frac{1}{30n^4} \\
&< \zeta(1+\alpha)n^\alpha - \frac{1-\alpha+\alpha^2}{\alpha(1-\alpha)} - \frac{\alpha\zeta(\alpha)}{n^{1-\alpha}}.
\end{aligned}$$

From Claim 2, it follows that

$$\sum_{k=1}^{n-1} \frac{(n-k)^\alpha}{k^{1+\alpha}} < \zeta(1+\alpha)n^\alpha - 2.$$

□

Now, we derive an estimate for the weight $\sigma_{n-1}^{(\alpha)}$ of Approximation (7). Denote

$$\bar{\sigma}_{n-1}^{(\alpha)} = \sigma_{n-1}^{(\alpha)} - \frac{1}{(n-1)^{1+\alpha}} = S_n[\alpha] - nS_n[1+\alpha] - \frac{n^{1-\alpha}}{\alpha(1-\alpha)}.$$

Claim 3. *Let $n \geq 2$. Then*

$$\left|\bar{\sigma}_{n-1}^{(\alpha)}\right| < \frac{1+2\alpha}{12n^{1+\alpha}}.$$

Proof. From (19),

$$S_n[\alpha] = \frac{n^{1-\alpha}}{1-\alpha} - \frac{1}{2n^\alpha} + R_1, \quad nS_n[\alpha+1] = -\frac{n^{1-\alpha}}{\alpha} - \frac{1}{2n^\alpha} + R_2,$$

where

$$|R_1| < \frac{1+\alpha}{12n^{1+\alpha}}, \quad |R_2| < \frac{\alpha}{12n^{1+\alpha}}.$$

Then,

$$\left|\bar{\sigma}_{n-1}^{(\alpha)}\right| = \left|S_n[\alpha] - nS_n[1+\alpha] - \frac{n^{1-\alpha}}{\alpha(1-\alpha)}\right| < |R_1| + |R_2| < \frac{1+2\alpha}{12n^{1+\alpha}}$$

□

3. Estimate for the Error

In this section, we use the method from [28] to derive estimates for the errors of Approximations (6) and (7). Let $0 < t < x$ and

$$g(t) = f(t) - f(x) + (x-t)f'(x) - \frac{(x-t)^2}{2} f''(x). \tag{20}$$

The function $g(t)$ satisfies $g(x) = g'(x) = g''(x) = 0$. From Taylor's Theorem,

$$g(t) = \frac{(t-x)^3}{6} f'''(\xi_{0,t}),\ g'(t) = \frac{(t-x)^2}{2} f'''(\xi_{1,t}),\ g''(t) = (t-x) f'''(\xi_{2,t})$$

where $t < \xi_{i,t} < x$ for $i = 0, 1, 2$. Let

$$M_i = \max_{0<t<x} |f^{(i)}(t)|, \qquad (i = 0, 1, 2, 3).$$

Then,

$$|g(t)| < \frac{M_3}{6}(x-t)^3,\ |g'(t)| < \frac{M_3}{2}(x-t)^2,\ |g''(t)| < M_3(x-t).$$

Denote $G(t) = g(t)/(x-t)^{1+\alpha}$. The function $G(t)$ satisfies $G(x) = G'(x) = 0$, and its second derivative is not defined at the point x.

Claim 4. *Let $0 < t < x$. Then,*

$$|G'(t)| < \frac{5}{6} M_3 (x-t)^{1-\alpha}, \quad |G''(t)| < \frac{4M_3}{(x-t)^\alpha}.$$

Proof.

$$G'(t) = \frac{(x-t)g'(x) + (1+\alpha)g(t)}{(x-t)^{2+\alpha}},$$

$$G''(t) = \frac{(x-t)^2 g''(t) + 2(\alpha+1)(x-t)g'(t) + (\alpha+1)(\alpha+2)g(t)}{(x-t)^{3+\alpha}}.$$

Therefore,

$$|G'(t)| < \frac{1}{2} M_3 (x-t)^{1-\alpha} + \frac{1+\alpha}{6} M_3 (x-t)^{1-\alpha} < \frac{5}{6} M_3 (x-t)^{1-\alpha},$$
$$|G''(t)| < \left((2+\alpha)(1+\alpha)\frac{M_3}{6} + (1+\alpha)M_3 + M_3\right)(x-t)^{-\alpha} < \frac{4M_3}{(x-t)^\alpha}.$$

□

Lemma 2. *Let $f(0) = f'(0) = 0$. Then,*

$$\int_0^x G(t)\mathrm{d}t = \Gamma(-\alpha) f^{(\alpha)}(x) + \frac{f(x)}{\alpha x^\alpha} + \frac{f'(x) x^{1-\alpha}}{1-\alpha} - \frac{f''(x) x^{2-\alpha}}{2(2-\alpha)}.$$

Proof.

$$\begin{aligned}
\int_0^x G(t)\mathrm{d}t &= \int_0^x \frac{g(t)}{(x-t)^{1+\alpha}} \mathrm{d}t = \int_0^x g(t) d\frac{(x-t)^{-\alpha}}{\alpha} \\
&= g(t) \frac{(x-t)^{-\alpha}}{\alpha}\Big|_0^x - \frac{1}{a} \int_0^x \frac{g'(t)}{(x-t)^\alpha} \mathrm{d}t \\
&= -\frac{g(0)}{\alpha x^\alpha} + \frac{\Gamma(-\alpha)}{\Gamma(1-\alpha)} \int_0^x \frac{g'(t)}{(x-t)^\alpha} \mathrm{d}t.
\end{aligned}$$

The function $g(t)$ satisfies

$$g(0) = -f(x) + f'(x)x - \frac{f''(x)}{2} x^2.$$

Hence,

$$\int_0^x \frac{g(t)}{(x-t)^{1+\alpha}}\mathrm{d}t = \Gamma(-\alpha)g^{(\alpha)}(x) + \frac{1}{\alpha}\left(\frac{f(x)}{x^\alpha} - x^{1-\alpha}f'(x) + \frac{x^{2-\alpha}}{2}f''(x)\right). \quad (21)$$

In view of Equation (20), the fractional derivative of the function $g(x)$ satisfies

$$g^{(\alpha)}(x) = f^{(\alpha)}(x) - \frac{x^{1-\alpha}f'(x)}{(1-\alpha)\Gamma(1-\alpha)} + \frac{x^{2-\alpha}f''(x)}{(2-\alpha)\Gamma(1-\alpha)},$$

which can be written in the form:

$$\Gamma(-\alpha)g^{(\alpha)}(x) = \Gamma(-\alpha)f^{(\alpha)}(x) + \frac{x^{1-\alpha}f'(x)}{\alpha(1-\alpha)} - \frac{x^{2-\alpha}f''(x)}{\alpha(2-\alpha)}. \quad (22)$$

From (21) and (22), it follows that

$$\int_0^x \frac{g(t)}{(x-t)^{1+\alpha}}\mathrm{d}t = \Gamma(-\alpha)f^{(\alpha)}(x) + \frac{f(x)}{\alpha x^\alpha} + \frac{f'(x)x^{1-\alpha}}{1-\alpha} - \frac{f''(x)x^{2-\alpha}}{2(2-\alpha)}.$$

□

The trapezoidal rule of a function $F(t)$ has a second-order accuracy when $F \in C^2[0,x]$. The error of the trapezoidal rule E_T^F satisfies [42]

$$|E_T^F| < \frac{1}{12}h^2x^3 \max_{0<t<x}|F''(t)|.$$

The second derivative of the function $G(t)$ is undefined at the point x, which leads to a lower order of accuracy of the trapezoidal rule in the interval $[0,x]$. Now, we estimate the error of the trapezoidal rule of the function $G(t)$. Let $h = x/n$ and T_n be the error of the trapezoidal rule of $G(t)$ in the interval $[0,x]$.

Lemma 3.

$$|T_n| \leq \frac{1}{3}M_3x(x^2+1)h^{2-\alpha}.$$

Proof. Let T_n^1 be the of trapezoidal rule of $G(t)$ in the interval $[0, x-h]$.

$$\left|T_n^1\right| \leq \frac{1}{12}h^2(x-h)^3 \max_{0<t<x-h}|G''(t)| \leq \frac{1}{12}h^2x^3\frac{4M_3}{h^\alpha} \leq \frac{1}{3}M_3x^3h^{2-\alpha}. \quad (23)$$

Let T_n^2 be the error of the trapezoidal rule of $G(t)$ in the interval $[x-h, x]$.

$$\int_{x-h}^x G(t)\mathrm{d}t = \int_{x-h}^x G(t)\mathrm{d}\left(t+\frac{h}{2}-x\right) = \frac{h}{2}G(x-h) - \int_{x-h}^x\left(t+\frac{h}{2}-x\right)G'(t)\mathrm{d}t.$$

The error T_n^2 satisfies

$$T_n^2 = \int_{x-h}^x\left(t+\frac{h}{2}-x\right)G'(t)\mathrm{d}t,$$

$$|T_n^2| < \int_{x-h}^x\left|t+\frac{h}{2}-x\right||G'(t)|\mathrm{d}t < \frac{5}{6}M_3h^{1-\alpha}\int_{x-h}^x\left|t+\frac{h}{2}-x\right|\mathrm{d}t < \frac{5}{24}M_3h^{3-\alpha}. \quad (24)$$

From Equations (23) and (24), we obtain a bound for the error $T_n = T_n^1 + T_n^2$ of the function $G(t)$ in the interval $[0,x]$:

$$|T_n| \le |T_n^1| + |T_n^2| < \frac{1}{3}M_3 x^3 h^{2-\alpha} + \frac{5}{24}M_3 h^{3-\alpha}$$
$$< \frac{1}{3}M_3\left(x^3 + h\right)h^{2-\alpha} < \frac{1}{3}M_3 x(x^2+1)h^{2-\alpha}.$$

□

The trapezoidal rule of the function $G(t)$ satisfies

$$\frac{1}{h^\alpha}\left(\sum_{k=1}^{n-1}\frac{g_{n-k}}{k^{1+\alpha}} + \frac{g_0}{2n^{1+\alpha}}\right) = \int_0^x \frac{g(t)}{(x-t)^{1+\alpha}}\mathrm{d}t + T_n$$

The function $g(t)$ has a value at zero:

$$\frac{g(0)}{2n^{1+\alpha}h^\alpha} = -\frac{f(x)}{2n^{1+\alpha}h^\alpha} + \frac{f'(x)x}{2n^{1+\alpha}h^\alpha} - \frac{f''(x)x^2}{4n^{1+\alpha}h^\alpha} = \frac{h}{2}\left(-\frac{f(x)}{x^{1+\alpha}} + \frac{f'(x)}{x^\alpha} - \frac{f''(x)x^{1-\alpha}}{2}\right).$$

Therefore,

$$\frac{1}{h^\alpha}\sum_{k=1}^{n-1}\frac{g_{n-k}}{k^{1+\alpha}} = \Gamma(-\alpha)f^{(\alpha)}(x) + \frac{f(x)}{\alpha x^\alpha} + \frac{f(x)h}{2x^{1+\alpha}} + \frac{x^{1-\alpha}f'(x)}{1-\alpha} - \frac{f'(x)h}{2x^\alpha}$$
$$+\frac{x^{1-\alpha}f''(x)h}{4} - \frac{x^{2-\alpha}f''(x)}{2(2-\alpha)} + T_n.$$

Let E_n be the error of Approximation (5).

$$\frac{1}{h^\alpha}\sum_{k=1}^{n-1}\frac{f_{n-k}}{k^{1+\alpha}} = \Gamma(-\alpha)f_n^{(\alpha)} + \frac{\zeta(1+\alpha)}{h^\alpha}f_n - \zeta(\alpha)f'_n h^{1-\alpha} + E_n.$$

Theorem 1. *Let $f(0) = f'(0) = 0$ and $f \in C^3[0, x_n]$. Then,*

$$|E_n| < \frac{2M_3 x(x^2+1) + M_2}{6}h^{2-\alpha}.$$

Proof. From the definition (20) of the function $g(t)$,

$$\frac{1}{h^\alpha}\sum_{k=1}^{n-1}\frac{g_{n-k}}{k^{1+\alpha}} = \frac{1}{h^\alpha}\sum_{k=1}^{n-1}\frac{f_{n-k}}{k^{1+\alpha}} - \frac{f(x)}{h^\alpha}\sum_{k=1}^{n-1}\frac{1}{k^{1+\alpha}} + f'(x)h^{1-\alpha}\sum_{k=1}^{n-1}\frac{1}{k^\alpha} - \frac{f''(x)}{2}h^{2-\alpha}\sum_{k=1}^{n-1}k^{1-\alpha}.$$

From Equation (19), we find

$$\sum_{k=1}^{n-1}\frac{1}{k^{1+\alpha}} = \zeta(1+\alpha) - \frac{1}{\alpha n^\alpha} - \frac{1}{2n^{1+\alpha}} + R_1, \quad \sum_{k=1}^{n-1}\frac{1}{k^\alpha} = \frac{n^{1-\alpha}}{1-\alpha} + \zeta(\alpha) - \frac{1}{2n^\alpha} + R_2,$$

$$\sum_{k=1}^{n-1}k^{1-\alpha} = \frac{n^{2-\alpha}}{2-\alpha} - \frac{n^{1-\alpha}}{2} + \zeta(\alpha-1) + R_3,$$

where

$$|R_1| < \frac{1+\alpha}{12n^{2+\alpha}}, \quad |R_2| < \frac{\alpha}{12n^{1+\alpha}}, \quad |R_3| < \frac{1-\alpha}{12n^\alpha}.$$

Then,

$$\frac{f(x)}{h^\alpha}\sum_{k=1}^{n-1}\frac{1}{k^{1+\alpha}} = \zeta(1+\alpha)\frac{f(x)}{h^\alpha} - \frac{f(x)}{\alpha n^\alpha h^\alpha} - \frac{f(x)}{2n^{1+\alpha}h^\alpha} + R_1\frac{f(x)}{h^\alpha}$$
$$= \zeta(1+\alpha)\frac{f(x)}{h^\alpha} - \frac{f(x)}{\alpha x^\alpha} - \frac{f(x)h}{2x^{1+\alpha}} + R_1\frac{f(x)}{h^\alpha}.$$

Similarly,

$$f'(x)h^{1-\alpha}\sum_{k=1}^{n-1}\frac{1}{k^{\alpha}} = f'(x)h^{1-\alpha}\zeta(\alpha) + \frac{f'(x)x^{1-\alpha}}{1-\alpha} - \frac{f'(x)h}{2x^{\alpha}} + f'(x)h^{1-\alpha}R_2,$$

$$\frac{f''(x)}{2}h^{2-\alpha}\sum_{k=1}^{n-1}k^{1-\alpha} = \zeta(\alpha-1)\frac{f''(x)}{2}h^{2-\alpha} + \frac{f''(x)x^{2-\alpha}}{2-\alpha} - \frac{f''(x)x^{1-\alpha}h}{4} + R_3\frac{f''(x)}{2}h^{2-\alpha}.$$

Hence,

$$\frac{1}{h^{\alpha}}\sum_{k=1}^{n-1}\frac{f_{n-k}}{k^{1+\alpha}} = \Gamma(-\alpha)f^{(\alpha)}(x) + \frac{f(x)}{h^{\alpha}}\zeta(1+\alpha) - f'(x)h^{1-\alpha}\zeta(\alpha) + \frac{f''(x)}{2}h^{2-\alpha}\zeta(\alpha-1) + E_n,$$

where

$$E_n = T_n + R_1\frac{f(x)}{h^{\alpha}} - f'(x)h^{1-\alpha}R_2 + R_3\frac{f''(x)}{2}h^{2-\alpha},$$

$$|E_n| < |T_n| + |R_1\frac{f(x)}{h^{\alpha}}| + |f'(x)h^{1-\alpha}R_2| + |R_3\frac{f''(x)}{2}h^{2-\alpha}|. \tag{25}$$

From Taylor's Theorem,

$$f(x) = \frac{1}{2}f''(\xi_1)x^2, \qquad f'(x) = f''(\xi_2)x,$$

where $0 < \xi_2 < x$ for $i = 1, 2$. Therefore,

$$M_0 \leq \frac{1}{2}M_2x^2, \qquad M_1 \leq M_2x.$$

The terms on the right-hand side of (25) satisfy the estimates:

$$|R_1f(x)h^{-\alpha}| < \frac{(1+\alpha)M_0h^{-\alpha}}{12n^{2+\alpha}} = \frac{(1+\alpha)M_0h^2}{12x^{2+\alpha}} < \frac{(1+\alpha)M_2h^{2-\alpha}}{24},$$
$$|R_2f'(x)h^{1-\alpha}| < \frac{\alpha M_1h^{1-\alpha}}{12m^{1+\alpha}} = \frac{\alpha M_1h^2}{12x^{1+\alpha}} < \frac{\alpha M_2h^2}{12x^{\alpha}} < \frac{\alpha M_2h^{2-\alpha}}{12},$$
$$|R_3\frac{f''(x)}{2}h^{2-\alpha}| < \frac{(1-\alpha)M_2h^{2-\alpha}}{24n^{\alpha}} = \frac{(1-\alpha)M_2h^2}{24x^{\alpha}} < \frac{(1-\alpha)M_2h^{2-\alpha}}{24}.$$

Hence,

$$|E_n| < \frac{1}{3}M_3x(x^2+1)h^{2-\alpha} + \frac{(1+\alpha)M_2h^{2-\alpha}}{12} < \frac{2M_3x(x^2+1)+M_2}{6}h^{2-\alpha}.$$

□

Let L_n be the error of Approximation (6).

$$\mathcal{L}_nf(x) = \frac{h^{-\alpha}}{\Gamma(-\alpha)}\sum_{k=1}^{m}\sigma_k^{(\alpha)}f_{n-k} = f_n^{(\alpha)} + L_n,$$

$$\sigma_0^{(\alpha)} = \zeta(\alpha) - \zeta(1+\alpha), \quad \sigma_1^{(\alpha)} = 1 - \zeta(\alpha), \quad \sigma_k^{(\alpha)} = \frac{1}{k^{1+\alpha}}, \quad (2 \leq k \leq n).$$

Approximation (6) is constructed from Approximation (5) by substituting f'_n with first-order backward difference approximation $(f_n - f_{n-1})/h$.

Claim 5. *Let $f \in C^3[0,x]$ and $f(0) = f'(0) = 0$. Then,*

$$|L_n| < \frac{2M_3 x(x^2+1) + (1+3|\zeta(\alpha)|)M_2}{6|\Gamma(-\alpha)|} h^{2-\alpha}.$$

Proof. From Taylor's Theorem,

$$f_{n-1} = f_n - hf'_n + \frac{h^2}{2} f''(\xi),$$

$$\left| f'_n - \frac{f_n - f_{n-1}}{h} \right| < \frac{h}{2} |f''(\xi)|,$$

where $\xi \in (x_{n-1}, x_n)$. The error L_n of Approximation (6) satisfies

$$L_n = \frac{1}{\Gamma(-\alpha)} \left(E_n - \frac{1}{2}\zeta(\alpha) f''(\xi) h^{2-\alpha} \right),$$

$$\begin{aligned} |L_n| &< \frac{1}{|\Gamma(-\alpha)|} \left(\frac{2M_3 x(x^2+1) + M_2}{6} h^{2-\alpha} + \frac{|\zeta(\alpha)| M_2}{2} h^{2-\alpha} \right) \\ &< \frac{2M_3 x(x^2+1) + (1+3|\zeta(\alpha)|)M_2}{6|\Gamma(-\alpha)|} h^{2-\alpha}. \end{aligned}$$

□

Let A_n be the error of Approximation (7).

$$\mathcal{A}_n f(x) = \frac{h^{-\alpha}}{\Gamma(-\alpha)} \sum_{k-1}^{n} \sigma_k^{(\alpha)} f_{n-k} = f_n^{(\alpha)} + A_n.$$

The weights of Approximation (7) are defined with (8)–(10). Denote

$$\tilde{f}(t) = f(t) - f(0) - f'(0)t.$$

The function $\tilde{f}$ satisfies $\tilde{f}(0) = \tilde{f}'(0) = 0$, and the second and third derivatives of f and $\tilde{f}$ are equal. Therefore,

$$\max_{0 \le t \le x} |\tilde{f}''(t)| = M_2, \quad \max_{0 \le t \le x} |\tilde{f}'''(t)| = M_3.$$

Lemma 4. *Let $f \in C^3[0,x]$. Then,*

$$|A_n| < \frac{4M_3 x(x^2+1) + 3(1+2|\zeta(\alpha)|)M_2}{12|\Gamma(-\alpha)|} h^{2-\alpha}.$$

Proof.

$$\begin{aligned} \mathcal{A}_n f(x) &= \mathcal{A}_n \tilde{f}(x) + \mathcal{A}_n[f(x) - \tilde{f}(x)] \\ &= \mathcal{L}_n \tilde{f}(x) + \frac{\bar{\sigma}_{n-1}^{(\alpha)} \tilde{f}_1}{\Gamma(-\alpha) h^\alpha} + D_x^\alpha [f(x) - \tilde{f}(x)]. \end{aligned}$$

From Claim 3,

$$\left| \bar{\sigma}_{n-1}^{(\alpha)} \right| < \frac{1+2\alpha}{12 n^{1+\alpha}} < \frac{1}{4n} < \frac{1}{8}.$$

From Taylor's Theorem,

$$|\tilde{f}_1| = \frac{h^2}{2} |\tilde{f}''(\xi)| \le \frac{h^2 M_2}{2}.$$

Then,

$$|A_n| < |L_n| + \frac{1}{|\Gamma(-\alpha)|h^\alpha} \left|\bar{\sigma}_{n-1}^{(\alpha)}\right| |\tilde{f}_1|$$
$$< \left(\frac{2M_3x(x^2+1) + (1+3|\zeta(\alpha)|)M_2}{6|\Gamma(-\alpha)|} + \frac{M_2}{16\Gamma(-\alpha)}\right)h^{2-\alpha}$$
$$< \frac{4M_3x(x^2+1) + 3(1+2|\zeta(\alpha)|)M_2}{12|\Gamma(-\alpha)|}h^{2-\alpha}.$$

□

4. Numerical Solution of Two-Term Equation

The two-term equation is an ordinary fractional differential equation in the form:

$$y^{(\alpha)}(t) + Dy(t) = F(t), \qquad y(0) = y_0. \tag{26}$$

Numerical and analytical solutions of ordinary fractional differential equations were studied in [43–48].In this section, we construct the numerical solution of the two-term Equation (26), which uses the approximation (7) of the fractional derivative, and prove its convergence and order. Let $h = x/N$ and $x_n = nh$ for $n = 0, \cdots, N$. By approximating the fractional derivative at the point x_n, we find

$$\frac{1}{\Gamma(-\alpha)h^\alpha} \sum_{k=0}^{n} \sigma_k^{(\alpha)} y_{n-k} + Dy_n = F_n + A_n,$$

$$\left(\sigma_0^{(\alpha)} + \Gamma(-\alpha)Dh^\alpha\right)y_n + \sum_{k=1}^{n} \sigma_k^{(\alpha)} y_{n-k} + Dy_n = \Gamma(-\alpha)h^\alpha F_n + B_n h^2,$$

where $B_n = \Gamma(-\alpha)A_n h^{\alpha-2}$.

$$(\zeta(\alpha) - \zeta(1+\alpha) + \Gamma(-\alpha)Dh^\alpha)y_n - \zeta(\alpha)y_{n-1} + \sum_{k=1}^{n} \frac{y_{n-k}}{k^{1+\alpha}} - \bar{\sigma}_{n-1}^{(\alpha)}u_1 = \Gamma(-\alpha)h^\alpha F_n + B_n h^2.$$

The numerical solution $\{u_n\}_{n=2}^N$ of Equation (26) is computed as

$$(\zeta(\alpha) - \zeta(1+\alpha) + \Gamma(-\alpha)Dh^\alpha)u_n - \zeta(\alpha)u_{n-1} + \sum_{k=1}^{n} \frac{u_{n-k}}{k^{1+\alpha}} + \bar{\sigma}_{n-1}^{(\alpha)}u_1 + Du_n = \Gamma(-\alpha)h^\alpha F_n,$$

$$u_n = \frac{1}{\zeta(\alpha) - \zeta(1+\alpha) + \Gamma(-\alpha)Dh^\alpha}\left(\Gamma(-\alpha)h^\alpha F_n + \zeta(\alpha)u_{n-1} - \sum_{k=1}^{n} \frac{u_{n-k}}{k^{1+\alpha}} - \bar{\sigma}_{n-1}^{(\alpha)}u_1\right). \tag{27}$$

The value of the numerical solution u_1 in the first step is computed with the following approximation [39]:

$$y_1^{(\alpha)} = \frac{y_1 - y_0}{\Gamma(2-\alpha)h^\alpha} + a_1 h^{2-\alpha}. \tag{28}$$

From the estimate for the error of the L1 approximation [6],

$$|a_1| < \frac{1}{\Gamma(2-\alpha)}\left(\frac{2+\alpha}{2^\alpha(2-\alpha)} - \frac{11+\alpha}{12}\right) \max_{0\le t\le h}|y''(t)| < \frac{2M_2}{\Gamma(2-\alpha)}, \tag{29}$$

where $M_2 = \max_{0\le t\le x}|y''(t)|$. The numerical solution (27) has initial conditions [39]:

$$u_0 = y(0), \quad u_1 = \frac{y(0) + \Gamma(2-\alpha)F(h)h^\alpha}{1 + D\Gamma(2-\alpha)h^\alpha}.$$

When the solution of two-term Equation (26) satisfies the condition $y(0) = y'(0) = 0$, both Approximations (6) and (7) can be used for the computation of the numerical solution (27).

4.1. Convergence and Error Estimates

Denote by $e_n = y_n - u_n$ the error of the numerical solution (27) at the point $x_n = nh$, where $n = 0, 1, \cdots, N$. The errors e_n satisfy

$$e_n = \frac{1}{\zeta(\alpha) - \zeta(1+\alpha) + \Gamma(-\alpha)Dh^\alpha} \left(\zeta(\alpha)e_{n-1} - \sum_{k=1}^{n-1} \frac{e_{n-k}}{k^{1+\alpha}} - \tilde{\sigma}_{n-1}^{(\alpha)} e_1 + B_n h^2 \right), \tag{30}$$

$$e_0 = 0, \qquad e_1 = \frac{\Gamma(2-\alpha)a_1 h^2}{1 + D\Gamma(2-\alpha)h^\alpha}.$$

In Theorems 2 and 3, we prove the convergence of the numerical solution (27) of two-term Equation (26) and derive estimates for the error, depending on the value of the parameter D. The proofs use induction on n, where $n = 1, 2, \cdots, N$.

Theorem 2. *Let* $D \in \left(-\infty, -\frac{2}{h^\alpha}\frac{\zeta(\alpha)-\zeta(1+\alpha)}{\Gamma(-\alpha)}\right) \cup (0, \infty)$ *and* $y \in C^2[0,1]$. *Then,*

$$|e_n| < Ch^2 n^\alpha, \qquad (1 \le n \le N), \tag{31}$$

where $C = 2M_2 + \frac{1}{2} \max_{1 \le n \le N} |B_n|$.

Proof. The value of the error e_1 in the first step satisfies

$$|e_1| = \frac{\Gamma(2-\alpha)|a_1|h^2}{|1 + D\Gamma(2-\alpha)h^\alpha|} < \frac{2M_2 h^2}{|1 + D\Gamma(2-\alpha)h^\alpha|}. \tag{32}$$

When $D > 0$, the denominator $|1 + D\Gamma(2-\alpha)h^\alpha| > 1$ and

$$|e_1| < 2M_2 h^2 < Ch^2.$$

Now, we estimate the error e_1 when the parameter $D < -\frac{2}{h^\alpha}\frac{\zeta(\alpha)-\zeta(1+\alpha)}{\Gamma(-\alpha)}$.

$$D\Gamma(-\alpha)h^\alpha > 2(|\zeta(\alpha)| + \zeta(1+\alpha)),$$

$$|D|\Gamma(2-\alpha)h^\alpha > 2\alpha(1-\alpha)(|\zeta(\alpha)| + \zeta(1+\alpha)).$$

From (15),

$$\zeta(1+\alpha) > \frac{1}{\alpha} + \gamma, \quad |\zeta(\alpha)| > \frac{1}{1-\alpha} - \gamma,$$

$$|\zeta(\alpha)| + \zeta(1+\alpha) > \frac{1}{1-\alpha} + \frac{1}{\alpha} = \frac{1}{\alpha(1-\alpha)}.$$

Hence, $|D|\Gamma(2-\alpha)h^\alpha > 2$. In this case, the denominator of (32) is again greater than one, $|1 + D\Gamma(2-\alpha)h^\alpha| > 1$, and the error e_1 satisfies

$$|e_1| < 2M_2 h^2 < Ch^2.$$

Suppose that Inequality (31) holds for all $n = 1, \cdots, m-1$. The values of $\zeta(\alpha)$ and $\Gamma(-\alpha)$ are negative. In both cases, $D > 0$ and $D < -\frac{2}{h^\alpha}\frac{\zeta(\alpha)-\zeta(1+\alpha)}{\Gamma(-\alpha)}$, the following estimate holds:

$$|\zeta(\alpha) - \zeta(1+\alpha) + \Gamma(-\alpha)Dh^\alpha| > |\zeta(\alpha)| + \zeta(1+\alpha).$$

From (30) and Claim 3,

$$
\begin{aligned}
|e_m| &< \frac{1}{|\zeta(\alpha)|+\zeta(1+\alpha)}\left(|\zeta(\alpha)|e_{m-1}+\sum_{k=1}^{m-1}\frac{|e_{m-k}|}{k^{1+\alpha}}+\left|\bar{\sigma}_{m-1}^{(\alpha)}e_1\right|h^2+|B_m|h^2\right)\\
&< \frac{1}{|\zeta(\alpha)|+\zeta(1+\alpha)}\left(|\zeta(\alpha)|e_{m-1}+\sum_{k=1}^{m-1}\frac{|e_{m-k}|}{k^{1+\alpha}}+\frac{M_2}{4}h^2+|B_m|h^2\right)\\
&< \frac{1}{|\zeta(\alpha)|+\zeta(1+\alpha)}\left(|\zeta(\alpha)|e_{m-1}+\sum_{k=1}^{m-1}\frac{|e_{m-k}|}{k^{1+\alpha}}+2Ch^2\right).
\end{aligned}
$$

By the induction hypothesis,

$$
|e_m| < \frac{Ch^2}{|\zeta(\alpha)|+\zeta(1+\alpha)}\left(|\zeta(\alpha)|(m-1)^\alpha+\sum_{k=1}^{m-1}\frac{(m-k)^\alpha}{k^{1+\alpha}}+2\right).
$$

From Inequality (11),

$$
|e_m| < \frac{Ch^2}{|\zeta(\alpha)|+\zeta(1+\alpha)}\left(|\zeta(\alpha)|m^\alpha+(\zeta(1+\alpha)m^\alpha-2)+2\right)=Ch^2m^\alpha.
$$

□

Theorem 3. *Let* $\frac{1}{\Gamma(-\alpha)} < D < 0$ *and* $y \in C^2[0,1]$. *Then,*

$$
|e_n| < Kh^2n^\alpha, \qquad (1 \le n \le N), \tag{33}
$$

where $K = 3M_2 + \max_{1\le n\le N}|B_n|$.

Proof. The error e_1 in the first step satisfies the bound:

$$
|e_1| < \frac{2M_2h^2}{1-\alpha(1-\alpha)D\Gamma(-\alpha)h^\alpha} < \frac{2M_2h^2}{1-\alpha(1-\alpha)} \le \frac{8}{3}M_2h^2.
$$

Assume that (33) holds for all $n = 1,\cdots,m-1$. Then,

$$
\begin{aligned}
|e_m| &< \frac{1}{|\zeta(\alpha)|+\zeta(1+\alpha)-\Gamma(-\alpha)Dh^\alpha}\left(|\zeta(\alpha)|e_{m-1}+\sum_{k=1}^{m-1}\frac{|e_{m-k}|}{k^{1+\alpha}}+\left|\bar{\sigma}_{m-1}^{(\alpha)}e_1\right|h^2+|B_m|h^2\right)\\
&< \frac{1}{|\zeta(\alpha)|+\zeta(1+\alpha)-h^\alpha}\left(|\zeta(\alpha)|Kh^2(m-1)^\alpha+Kh^2\sum_{k=1}^{m-1}\frac{(m-k)^\alpha}{k^{1+\alpha}}+Kh^2\right)\\
&< \frac{Kh^2}{|\zeta(\alpha)|+\zeta(1+\alpha)-h^\alpha}\left(|\zeta(\alpha)|m^\alpha+\zeta(1+\alpha)m^\alpha-1\right)\\
&< \frac{Kh^2m^\alpha}{|\zeta(\alpha)|+\zeta(1+\alpha)-h^\alpha}\left(|\zeta(\alpha)|+\zeta(1+\alpha)-\frac{1}{m^\alpha}\right) \le Kh^2m^\alpha.
\end{aligned}
$$

□

From Theorems 2 and 3, the errors e_n of the numerical solution (27) of the two-term equation in the interval $[0,1]$ satisfy the estimate:

$$
|e_n| < Kh^2n^\alpha \le Kh^{2-\alpha} \tag{34}
$$

for all $n = 1,\cdots,N$. Now, we generalize the results of Theorems 2 and 3 to an arbitrary interval $[a,b]$. Consider the two-term equation:

$$y^{(\alpha)}(t) + Dy(t) = F(t), \quad y(a) = y_0, \quad t \in [a, b]. \tag{35}$$

Substitute $t = a + (b-a)s$ and $z(s) = y(t) = y(a + (b-a)s)$. The function $z(s)$ satisfies a two-term equation:

$$z^{(\alpha)}(s) + (b-a)^\alpha Dz(s) = G(s) = (b-a)^\alpha F(a + (b-a)s), \quad z(0) = y_0, \quad s \in [0, 1] \tag{36}$$

Let $\mathcal{E} = \{e_n\}_{n=1}^N$ be an N-dimensional vector with the errors of the numerical solution (27) of Equation (35). The L_∞ (maximum) norm of a vector is the maximum of the absolute values of its elements. From Theorems 2 and 3, we obtain the conditions for the convergence and a bound of the error of the numerical solution (27) of two-term Equations (35) and (36).

Corollary 1. *The maximum error of the numerical solution* (27) *of two-term Equation* (35) *satisfies*

$$\|\mathcal{E}\| < K(b-a)^\alpha h^{2-\alpha}$$

when the solution $y \in C^2[a, b]$ and $h = (b-a)/N$:

$$D \in \left(-\infty, -\frac{2(\zeta(\alpha) - \zeta(1+\alpha))}{\Gamma(-\alpha)h^\alpha}\right) \cup \left(\frac{1}{\Gamma(-\alpha)(b-a)^\alpha}, \infty\right)$$

4.2. Numerical Examples

The numerical results for the error and order of the numerical solution (27) of two-term Equation (26) are given below.

Example 1. *Consider the following two-term equation:*

$$y^{(\alpha)} + Dy = -\alpha^2 t^{2-\alpha} E_{2,3-\alpha}\left(-(\alpha t)^2\right) + D(\cos(\alpha t) - 1), \quad y_0 - 0. \tag{37}$$

Two-term Equation (37) has a solution $y(x) = \cos(\alpha t) - 1$, which satisfies $y(0) = y'(0) = 0$. The experimental results for the error and order of the numerical solution (27) of Equation (37), which uses the approximation (6) of the fractional derivative, are given in Tables 1 and 2.

Example 2.

$$y^{(\alpha)} + Dy = \alpha t^{1-\alpha} E_{1,2-\alpha}(\alpha t) + De^{\alpha t}, \quad y_0 = 1. \tag{38}$$

Equation (38) has a solution, $y(t) = e^{\alpha t}$. The experimental results for the maximum error and order of the numerical solution (27) of Equation (38) are given in Tables 3 and 4. The experimental results in Tables 1–4 are consistent with the theoretical results from Theorems 2 and 3.

Table 1. Error and order of the numerical solution (27) of Equation (37) in $[0, 1]$.

h	$\alpha = 0.25, D = 1$		$\alpha = 0.75, D = 100$		$\alpha = 0.4, D = -1$	
	Error	Order	Error	Order	Error	Order
0.005	5.10×10^{-9}	1.704	1.02×10^{-8}	1.245	6.00×10^{-5}	1.574
0.0025	1.37×10^{-9}	1.713	3.09×10^{-9}	1.2473	3.42×10^{-5}	1.581
0.00125	3.7×10^{-10}	1.720	9.4×10^{-10}	1.2484	2.12×10^{-6}	1.586

Table 2. Error and order of the numerical solution (27) of Equation (37) in $[0,2]$.

h	$\alpha = 0.7, D = -10$		$\alpha = 0.9, D = -20$		$\alpha = 0.5, D = -1000$	
	Error	**Order**	**Error**	**Order**	**Error**	**Order**
0.005	2.08×10^7	3.174	3.67×10^8	4.225	1.69×10^{-8}	1.493
0.0025	5.18×10^6	2.005	7.07×10^7	2.378	6.01×10^{-9}	1.490
0.00125	1.74×10^6	1.577	2.23×10^7	1.663	2.15×10^{-9}	1.486

Table 3. Error and order of the numerical solution (27) of Equation (38) in $[0,1]$.

h	$\alpha = 0.2, D = 1$		$\alpha = 0.4, D = 100$		$\alpha = 0.6, D = -0.1$	
	Error	**Order**	**Error**	**Order**	**Error**	**Order**
0.005	9.62×10^{-8}	1.799	6.35×10^{-8}	1.599	2.16×10^{-4}	1.398
0.0025	2.76×10^{-8}	1.799	2.09×10^{-8}	1.599	8.21×10^{-5}	1.399
0.00125	7.93×10^{-9}	1.799	6.91×10^{-9}	1.599	3.11×10^{-5}	1.399

Table 4. Error and order of the numerical solution (27) of Equation (38) in $[0,2]$.

h	$\alpha = 0.8, D = -20$		$\alpha = 0.5, D = -50$		$\alpha = 0.5, D = -1000$	
	Error	**Order**	**Error**	**Order**	**Error**	**Order**
0.005	7.05×10^{34}	15.733	4.65×10^{46}	27.426	4.24×10^{-8}	1.498
0.0025	7.98×10^{32}	6.466	4.98×10^{43}	9.864	1.50×10^{-8}	1.499
0.00125	7.87×10^{31}	3.342	2.07×10^{42}	4.586	5.31×10^{-9}	1.499

5. Time Fractional Black–Scholes Equation

The time fractional Black–Scholes equation is a fractional partial differential equation, which is used for modeling the prices of the options [49–55].

$$\frac{\partial^\alpha C(S,t)}{\partial t^\alpha} + \frac{1}{2}\sigma^2 S^2 \frac{\partial^2 C(S,t)}{\partial S^2} + rS\frac{\partial C(S,t)}{\partial S} - rC(S,t) = 0, \tag{39}$$

where C is the options price, T is the expiry time, r is the risk-free rate, σ is the volatility, and S is the underlying stock price. Fractional Black–Scholes Equation (39) has terminal and boundary conditions:

$$C(S,T) = C_0(S), \quad C(0,t) = C_1(t), \quad C(\infty,t) = C_2(t)$$

and the fractional derivative is

$$\frac{\partial^\alpha C(S,t)}{\partial t^\alpha} = \frac{1}{\Gamma(1-\alpha)}\frac{\mathrm{d}}{\mathrm{d}t}\int_t^T \frac{C(S,\xi) - C(S,T)}{(\xi - z)^\alpha}\mathrm{d}\xi. \tag{40}$$

The terminal condition is transformed to an initial condition with the substitution [55]:

$$t = T - z, \quad \eta = T - \xi, \quad v(S,\mu) = C(S,\xi) = C(S,t-\mu).$$

By applying the substitution to (40), we find [55]

$$\begin{aligned}\frac{\partial^\alpha C(S,t)}{\partial t^\alpha} &= -\frac{1}{\Gamma(1-\alpha)}\frac{\mathrm{d}}{\mathrm{d}z}\int_z^T \frac{C(S,\xi) - C(S,T)}{(\xi - z)^\alpha}\mathrm{d}\xi \\ &= -\frac{1}{\Gamma(1-\alpha)}\frac{\mathrm{d}}{\mathrm{d}z}\int_0^z \frac{v(S,\mu) - v(S,0)}{(z-\mu)^\alpha}\mathrm{d}\mu\end{aligned}$$

In view of the definitions of the Riemann–Liouville and Caputo fractional derivatives and (1)

$$\frac{\partial^\alpha C(S,t)}{\partial t^\alpha} = -{}_0^{RL}D_z^\alpha v(S,z) + \frac{v(S,0)z^{1-\alpha}}{\Gamma(2-\alpha)} = -D_z^\alpha v(S,z).$$

The function $v(S,z)$ satisfies the partial fractional differential equation:

$$D_z^\alpha v(S,z) = \frac{1}{2}\sigma^2 S^2 \frac{\partial^2 v(S,z)}{\partial S^2} + rS\frac{\partial v(S,z)}{\partial S} - rv(S,z). \tag{41}$$

The substitution $u(x,t) = v(e^x,z)$ transforms (41) into a linear partial fractional differential equation [55]:

$$D_t^\alpha u(x,t) = \frac{1}{2}\sigma^2 \frac{\partial^2 u(x,t)}{\partial x^2} + \left(r - \frac{\sigma^2}{2}\right)\frac{\partial u(x,t)}{\partial x} - ru(x,t). \tag{42}$$

Finite difference schemes for the time fractional Black–Scholes equation were constructed in [55–58]. Now, we construct an implicit finite difference scheme, which uses the approximation (7) of the fractional derivative and central difference approximations of the partial derivatives for the following time fractional Black–Scholes equation:

$$D_t^\alpha u(x,t) = \frac{1}{2}\sigma^2 \frac{\partial^2 u(x,t)}{\partial x^2} + \left(r - \frac{\sigma^2}{2}\right)\frac{\partial u(x,t)}{\partial x} - ru(x,t) + F(x,t), \tag{43}$$

where $(x,t) \in \mathcal{R} = [B_l, B_r] \times [0,T]$. Equation (43) has initial and boundary conditions:

$$u(x,0) = u_0(x), \quad u(B_l,t) = u_1(t), \quad u(B_r,t) = u_2(t).$$

Let M and N be positive integers and $\mathcal{G}$ be a rectangular grid on $\mathcal{R}$, which has a step size $h = (B_r - B_l)/N$ in space and $\tau = T/M$ in time:

$$\mathcal{G} = \{(nh, m\tau) | 0 \leq n \leq N, 0 \leq m \leq M\}.$$

Denote $u_n^m = u(nh, m\tau)$. The central difference approximations of the partial derivatives of Equation (43) have second-order accuracy:

$$\frac{\partial u(nh,m\tau)}{\partial x} = \frac{u_{n+1}^m - u_{n-1}^m}{2h} + e_{n,m}^1 h^2,$$

$$\frac{\partial^2 u(nh,m\tau)}{\partial x^2} = \frac{u_{n+1}^m - 2u_n^m + u_{n-1}^m}{h^2} + e_{n,m}^2 h^2,$$

where $\left|e_{n,m}^1\right| < \bar{M}_3/3$ and $\left|e_{n,m}^2\right| < \bar{M}_4/12$. The numbers $\bar{M}_3$ and $\bar{M}_4$ are the bounds for the third- and fourth-order partial derivatives:

$$\bar{M}_3 = \max_{(x,t)\in\mathcal{R}} \left|\frac{\partial^3 u(x,t)}{\partial x^3}\right|, \quad \bar{M}_4 = \max_{(x,t)\in\mathcal{R}} \left|\frac{\partial^4 u(x,t)}{\partial x^4}\right|.$$

The numerical solution $\{U_n^m\}_{n=1}^{N-1}$ of Equation (43) on layer m of the grid $\mathcal{G}$ satisfies

$$\frac{\tau^{-\alpha}}{\Gamma(-\alpha)} \sum_{k=0}^{m} \sigma_k^{(\alpha)} U_n^{m-k} = \frac{\sigma^2}{2h^2}\left(U_{n+1}^m - 2U_n^m + U_{n-1}^m\right)$$
$$+ \frac{1}{2h}\left(r - \frac{\sigma^2}{2}\right)\left(U_{n+1}^m - U_{n-1}^m\right) - rU_n^m + F_n^m$$

for $m = 2, \cdots, M$ and has has initial conditions:

$$U_n^0 = u_0(nh), \quad U_0^m = u_1(m\tau), \quad U_N^m = u_2(m\tau).$$

Denote $\eta = \Gamma(-\alpha)\tau^\alpha/h^2$ and

$$K_1 = -\left(\frac{\sigma^2}{2} - \left(r - \frac{\sigma^2}{2}\right)h\right)\eta, \quad K_2 = \sigma_0^{(\alpha)} + \sigma^2\eta + rh^2\eta, \quad K_3 = -\left(\frac{\sigma^2}{2} + \left(r - \frac{\sigma^2}{2}\right)h\right)\eta.$$

The numerical solution of the time fractional Black–Scholes Equation (43) is a solution of the system of linear equations:

$$K_1 U_{n-1}^m - K_2 U_n^m + K_3 U_{n+1}^m = -\sum_{k=1}^{m} \sigma_k^{(\alpha)} U_n^{m-k} + h^2\eta F_n^m. \tag{44}$$

Denote by $E_n^m = U_n^m - u_n^m$ the error of the finite difference scheme (44) at the point $(nh, m\tau)$ and by $A_n^m\tau^{2-\alpha}$ and $B_n^m h^2$ the the truncation errors of the approximations of the left-hand and right-hand sides of (43). The errors E_n^m on row $m \geq 2$ of the grid $\mathcal{G}$ satisfy

$$K_1 E_{n-1}^m + K_2 E_n^m + K_3 E_{n+1}^m = -\sum_{k=1}^{m} \sigma_k^{(\alpha)} E_n^{m-k} + \Gamma(-\alpha)\tau^\alpha\left(A_n^m\tau^{2-\alpha} + B_n^m h^2\right).$$

The errors are equal to zero, $E_n^0 = E_0^m = E_N^m = 0$ at the boundary points of $\mathcal{G}$. Let $\mathcal{K}$ be the $(N-1)$-dimensional tridiagonal matrix with entries K_2 on the main diagonal and K_1 and K_3 below and above the main diagonal. The error vector $\mathcal{E}^m$ of row m is a solution of the matrix equation:

$$\mathcal{K}\mathcal{E}^m = \mathcal{Q}^m; \qquad \mathcal{E}^m = \mathcal{K}^{-1}\mathcal{Q}^m,$$

where

$$Q_n^m = \zeta(\alpha)E_n^{m-1} - \sum_{k=1}^{m} \frac{E_n^{m-k}}{k^{1+\alpha}} - \bar{\sigma}_{m-1}^{(\alpha)} E_n^1 + \Gamma(-\alpha)\tau^\alpha\left(A_n^m\tau^{2-\alpha} + B_n^m h^2\right). \tag{45}$$

The numerical solution on the first row of $\mathcal{G}$ is computed with Approximation (28):

$$\frac{U_n^1 - U_n^0}{\Gamma(2-\alpha)\tau^\alpha} = \frac{\sigma^2}{2h^2}\left(U_{n+1}^1 - 2U_n^1 + U_{n-1}^1\right) + \frac{1}{2h}\left(r - \frac{\sigma^2}{2}\right)\left(U_{n+1}^1 - U_{n-1}^1\right) - rU_n^1 + F_n^1.$$

Denote $\tilde{\eta} = \Gamma(2-\alpha)\tau^\alpha/h^2$. Then,

$$\tilde{K}_1 U_{n-1}^1 + \tilde{K}_2 U_n^1 + \tilde{K}_3 U_{n+1}^1 = U_n^0 + h^2\eta F_n^1,$$

where $1 \leq n \leq N$ and

$$\tilde{K}_1 = -\left(\frac{\sigma^2}{2} - \left(r - \frac{\sigma^2}{2}\right)h\right)\tilde{\eta}, \quad \tilde{K}_2 = 1 + \sigma^2\tilde{\eta} + rh^2\tilde{\eta}, \quad \tilde{K}_3 = -\left(\frac{\sigma^2}{2} + \left(r - \frac{\sigma^2}{2}\right)h\right)\tilde{\eta}.$$

The errors of the numerical solution of the fractional Black–Scholes Equation (43) on the first row of $\mathcal{G}$ are the solutions of the system of linear equations:

$$\tilde{K}_1 E_{n-1}^1 + \tilde{K}_2 E_n^1 + \tilde{K}_3 E_{n+1}^1 = \Gamma(2-\alpha)\tau^\alpha\left(A_n^1\tau^{2-\alpha} + B_n^1 h^2\right).$$

Let $\tilde{\mathcal{K}}$ be the $(N-1)$-dimensional tridiagonal matrix with elements $\tilde{K}_1, \tilde{K}_2$, and $\tilde{K}_3$. The error vector for the first row satisfies

$$\tilde{\mathcal{K}}\mathcal{E}^1 = \mathcal{Q}^1; \qquad \mathcal{E}^1 = \tilde{\mathcal{K}}^{-1}\mathcal{Q}^1,$$

where

$$Q_n^1 = \Gamma(2-\alpha)\tau^\alpha\left(A_n^1\tau^{2-\alpha} + B_n^1 h^2\right).$$

5.1. Convergence and Error Estimate

Let $C = \max_{n,m}\{|A_n^m|, |B_n^m|\}$ for all $n = 1, \cdots, N$; $m = 1, \cdots, M$ and $K = |\Gamma(-\alpha)C|$. The L_∞ norm of a matrix is the maximum of the absolute row sums.

Theorem 4. *Let $u \in C^4[B_l, B_r] \times C^2[0, T]$ and $r < \frac{\sigma^2}{2h}$. Then,*

$$\|\mathcal{E}^m\| < Km^\alpha \tau^\alpha \left(h^2 + \tau^{2-\alpha}\right) \tag{46}$$

for all $m = 1, \cdots M$.

Proof. When $0 < \alpha < 1$, the gamma function satisfies [59]

$$0.88 < \Gamma(2-\alpha) < 1,$$

$$|\Gamma(-\alpha)| = \frac{\Gamma(2-\alpha)}{\alpha(1-\alpha)} > 3.$$

Then,

$$\|Q^1\| < C\Gamma(2-\alpha)\tau^\alpha\left(\tau^{2-\alpha} + h^2\right) < C\tau^\alpha\left(\tau^{2-\alpha} + h^2\right).$$

When $r < \sigma^2/(2h)$, we have that

$$|K_1| + |K_3| = \left|\frac{\sigma^2}{2} - \left(r - \frac{\sigma^2}{2}\right)h\right||\eta| + \left|\frac{\sigma^2}{2} + \left(r - \frac{\sigma^2}{2}\right)h\right||\eta| \le \sigma^2|\eta|,$$

$$|K_2| - |K_1| - |K_3| > |\sigma_0^{(\alpha)}|.$$

Similarly,

$$\left|\tilde{K}_2\right| - \left|\tilde{K}_1\right| - |\tilde{K}_3| > 1.$$

The matrices $\mathcal{K}$ and $\tilde{\mathcal{K}}$ are M-matrices. From the Ahlberg–Nilson–Varah bound [60,61],

$$\|\tilde{\mathcal{K}}^{-1}\| < 1, \qquad \|\mathcal{K}^{-1}\| < \frac{1}{|\sigma_0^{(\alpha)}|} = \frac{1}{|\zeta(\alpha)| + \zeta(1+\alpha)}.$$

The L_∞ norm of the error vector of the first row of $\mathcal{G}$ satisfies the bound:

$$\|\mathcal{E}^1\| \le \|\tilde{\mathcal{K}}^{-1}\|\|\mathcal{Q}^1\| < C\tau^\alpha\left(\tau^{2-\alpha} + h^2\right) < K\tau^\alpha\left(\tau^{2-\alpha} + h^2\right).$$

Suppose that Inequality (46) holds for all $m = 1, \cdots, p-1$. From (45),

$$\begin{aligned}
\left|Q_n^p\right| &< |\zeta(\alpha)|\|\mathcal{E}^{p-1}\| + \sum_{k=1}^{p} \frac{\|\mathcal{E}^{p-k}\|}{k^{1+\alpha}} + \left|\bar{\sigma}_{p-1}^{(\alpha)} E_n^1\right| + \Gamma(-\alpha)C\tau^\alpha\left(h^2 + \tau^{2-\alpha}\right) \\
&< K\tau^\alpha\left(h^2 + \tau^{2-\alpha}\right)\left(|\zeta(\alpha)|p^\alpha + \sum_{k=1}^{p} \frac{(p-k)^\alpha}{k^{1+\alpha}} + \frac{1}{8|\Gamma(-\alpha)|} + 1\right) \\
&< K\tau^\alpha\left(h^2 + \tau^{2-\alpha}\right)\left(|\zeta(\alpha)|p^\alpha + \zeta(1+\alpha)p^\alpha - 1 + \frac{1}{8|\Gamma(-\alpha)|}\right).
\end{aligned}$$

Therefore,

$$\|\mathcal{Q}^p\| < (|\zeta(\alpha)| + \zeta(1+\alpha))Kp^\alpha\tau^\alpha\left(h^2 + \tau^{2-\alpha}\right),$$

$$\|\mathcal{E}^p\| < \|\mathcal{K}^{-1}\|\|\mathcal{Q}^p\| < Kp^\alpha\tau^\alpha\left(h^2 + \tau^{2-\alpha}\right).$$

□

Corollary 2. *Let $r < \frac{\sigma^2}{2h}$. Then,*

$$\|\mathcal{E}^m\| < KT^\alpha\left(h^2 + \tau^{2-\alpha}\right)$$

for all $m = 1, 2, \cdots, M$.

Proof. From Theorem 4,

$$\|\mathcal{E}^m\| < Km^\alpha\tau^\alpha\left(h^2 + \tau^{2-\alpha}\right) \leq KM^\alpha\tau^\alpha\left(h^2 + \tau^{2-\alpha}\right) = KT^\alpha\left(h^2 + \tau^{2-\alpha}\right).$$

□

5.2. Numerical Examples

Numerical results for the error and order of the numerical solution of time fractional Black–Scholes Equation (43) are given below.

Example 3. *Consider the following time fractional Black–Scholes equation:*

$$\begin{cases} D_t^\alpha u(x,z) = \frac{1}{2}\sigma^2\frac{\partial^2 u(x,t)}{\partial S^2} + \left(r - \frac{\sigma^2}{2}\right)\frac{\partial u(x,t)}{\partial S} - ru(x,t) + t^{1-\alpha}e^x E_{1,2-\alpha}(t), \\ u(x,0) = e^x, \quad u(0,t) = e^t, \quad u(1,t) = e^{1+t}. \end{cases} \tag{47}$$

Equation (47) has a solution $u(x,t) = e^{t+x}$. The experimental results of the numerical solution of Equation (47) with parameters $\sigma = 0.35, r = 0.05$ are given in Tables 5 and 6. The orders of convergence of the finite difference scheme are $\log_{\frac{\tau_1}{\tau_2}} \frac{\text{error}_1}{\text{error}_2}$ in time and $\log_{\frac{h_1}{h_2}} \frac{\text{error}_1}{\text{error}_2}$ in space.

Table 5. Error and order of the numerical solution of Equation (47) and $N = 100$.

τ	$\alpha = 0.25$		$\alpha = 0.5$		$\alpha = 0.75$	
	Error	Order	Error	Order	Error	Order
1/10	8.12×10^{-5}		2.02×10^{-3}		1.94×10^{-2}	
1/20	2.47×10^{-5}	1.719	7.47×10^{-4}	1.435	8.68×10^{-3}	1.162
1/40	7.40×10^{-6}	1.736	2.69×10^{-4}	1.472	3.75×10^{-3}	1.212
1/80	2.21×10^{-6}	1.744	9.61×10^{-5}	1.487	1.59×10^{-3}	1.232
1/160	6.58×10^{-7}	1.748	3.42×10^{-5}	1.493	6.75×10^{-4}	1.241

Table 6. Error and order of the numerical solution of Equation (47) and $M = 1000$.

h	$\alpha = 0.2$		$\alpha = 0.5$		$\alpha = 0.8$	
	Error	Order	Error	Order	Error	Order
1/4	5.48×10^{-4}		5.32×10^{-4}		6.59×10^{-4}	
1/8	1.49×10^{-4}	1.878	1.58×10^{-4}	1.750	2.14×10^{-4}	1.620
1/16	3.82×10^{-5}	1.965	4.46×10^{-5}	1.824	6.69×10^{-5}	1.681
1/32	9.63×10^{-6}	1.987	1.21×10^{-5}	1.888	1.95×10^{-5}	1.780
1/64	2.42×10^{-6}	1.992	3.10×10^{-6}	1.962	5.32×10^{-6}	1.873

The order of the error of the finite difference scheme for the fractional Black-Scholes equation (47) in space is greater than the order in time. When the step size h is small, the errors in the temporal direction dominate the errors in space. The errors of the numerical solution to (47) for different values of N and M are plotted in Figure 1.

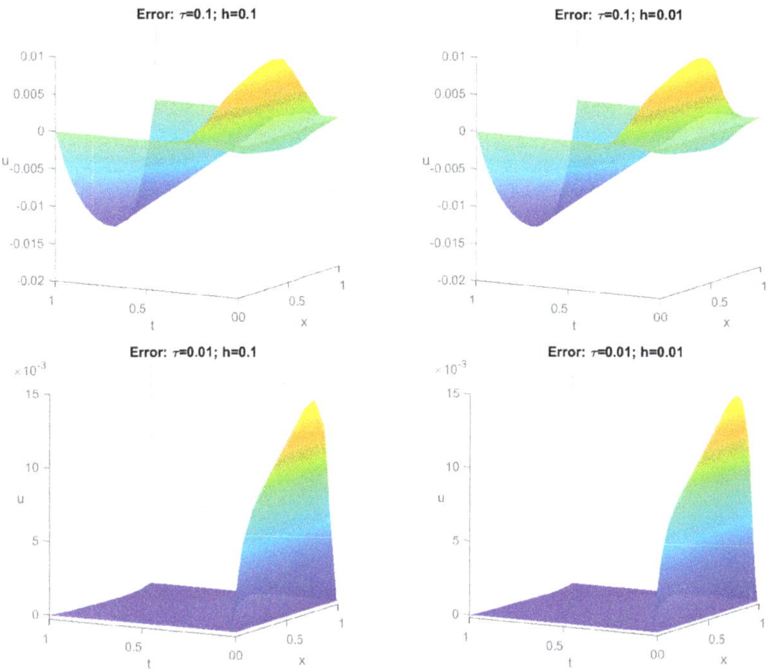

Figure 1. Numerical solution to (47) for $\alpha = 0.5$.

Example 4. *Consider the time fractional Black–Scholes Equation* (41) *for pricing European call options, with a source term $F(x,t) = 0$ and initial and boundary conditions:*

$$u_0(x) = (e^x - K)^+, \quad u_1(t) = 0, \quad u_2(t) = e^{B_r} - Ke^{-rt}.$$

The European call option premium curves for different values of α are given in Figure 2, for values of the parameters $r = 2\%$, $\sigma = 30\%$, $B_l = 0$, $B_r = 200$, $T = 1$ (year), and strike price $K = 100$. Regarding near-the-money options, lower values of α price them lower and evaluate higher out-of-the-money and in-the-money options, compared to the classical Black–Scholes dynamics.

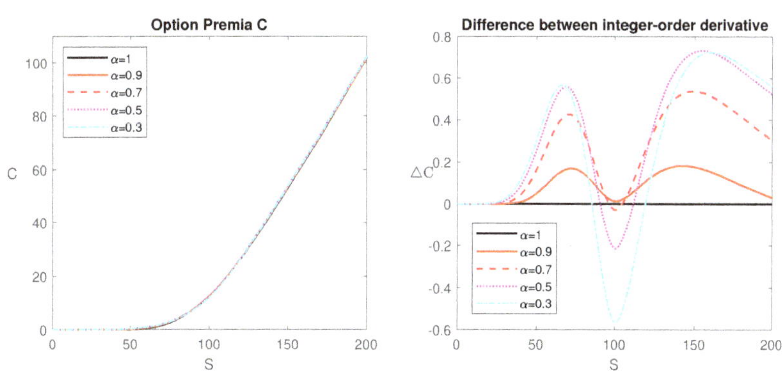

Figure 2. Option premia for various α (**left**) and the difference between them and the option premium for the integer-order model (**right**).

The graphs of the call options and put options premiums for $\alpha = 0.7$ and all t are given in Figures 3 and 4. To conclude the section with computational simulations, we compare the numerical solutions to (41), using the scheme explained in the paper (7)–(10) and the L1 scheme, as defined, for example, in [55]. We plot the difference as the solution for $\alpha = 0.7$, obtained from the L1 scheme, subtracted from the solution, obtained by the $\mathcal{A}_n$ scheme (7). The results for $t = T$ and for all t are given on Figure 5.

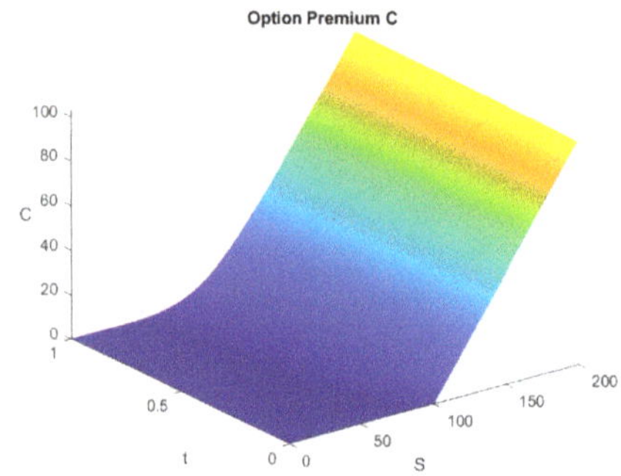

Figure 3. Call options premiums for all t.

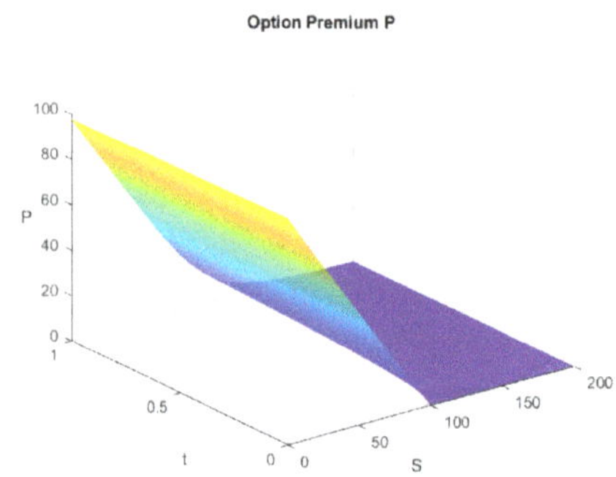

Figure 4. Put options premiums for all t.

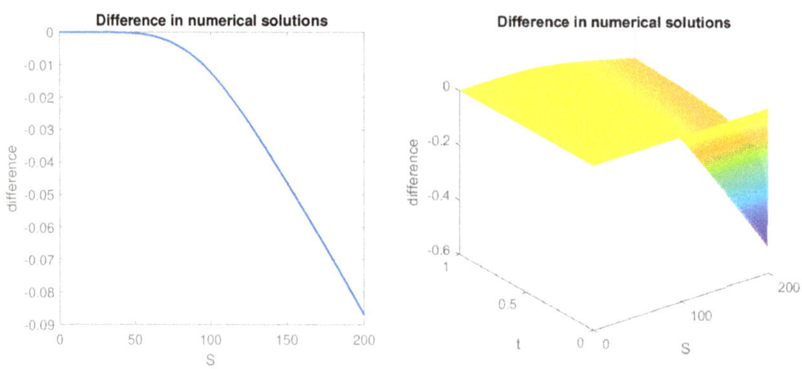

Figure 5. Difference in the numerical solution at $t = T$ (**left**) and for all t (**right**).

6. Conclusions

In this paper, we studied the convergence and order of the numerical solutions of ordinary and partial fractional differential equations, which use the approximation (7) of the fractional derivative. The results of the numerical experiments given in the paper illustrated the theoretical results. In future work, we will use the method from [16] for the construction of second-order and high-order approximations of the fractional derivative. We will consider applications of approximations for numerical solutions of linear and nonlinear fractional differential equations and analyze their convergence.

Author Contributions: Conceptualization, Y.D. and V.T.; data curation, S.G.; formal analysis, Y.D.; funding acquisition, S.G.; investigation, Y.D.; methodology, Y.D. and S.G.; project administration, Y.D. and V.T.; resources, S.G.; software, S.G.; supervision, V.T.; validation, V.T.; visualization, S.G.; writing—original draft, Y.D. and S.G.; writing—review and editing, Y.D. and V.T. All authors have read and agreed to the published version of the manuscript.

Funding: This study is supported by the Project BG05M2OP001-1.001-0004 UNITe: "Virtualization, Digitization and Prototyping", funded by the Operational Programme "Science and Education for Smart Growth", co-funded by the European Union trough the European Structural and Investment Funds, by the Bulgarian National Science Fund under Project KP-06-M62/1 "Numerical deterministic, stochastic, machine and deep learning methods with applications in computational, quantitative, algorithmic finance, biomathematics, ecology and algebra" from 2022, and by the National Program "Young Scientists and Postdoctoral Researchers-2"—Bulgarian Academy of Sciences.

Data Availability Statement: The data presented in this study are available on request from the corresponding author.

Acknowledgments: The authors are grateful to the anonymous referees for the useful suggestions and comments.

Conflicts of Interest: The authors declare no conflict of interest.

References

1. Acay, B.; Bas, E.; Abdeljawad, T. Fractional economic models based on market equilibrium in the frame of different type kernels. *Chaos Solit. Fract.* **2020**, *130*, 109438. [CrossRef]
2. Cardone, A.; Donatelli, M.; Durastante, F.; Garrappa, R.; Mazza, M.; Popolizio, M. *Fractional Differential Equations "Modeling, Discretization, and Numerical Solvers"*; Springer: Singapore, 2023.
3. Singh, H.; Kumar, D.; Baleanu, D. *Methods of Mathematical Modelling "Fractional Differential Equations"*; CRC Press, Taylor & Francis: Boca Raton, FL, USA, 2019.
4. Shams, M.; Kausar, N.; Samaniego, C.; Agarwal, P.; Ahmed, S.F.; Momani, S. On efficient fractional Caputo-type simultaneous scheme for finding all roots of polynomial equations with biomedical engineering applications. *Fractals* **2023**, *31*, 2340075. [CrossRef]
5. Sun, D.; Liu, J.; Su, X.; Pei, G. Fractional differential equation modeling of the HBV infection with time delay and logistic proliferation. *Front. Public Health* **2022**, *10*, 1036901. [CrossRef] [PubMed]
6. Cai, M.; Li, C. Numerical approaches to fractional integrals and derivatives: A review. *Mathematics* **2020**, *8*, 43. [CrossRef]
7. Jin, B.; Lazarov, R.; Zhou, Z. An analysis of the L1 scheme for the subdiffusion equation with nonsmooth data. *IMA J. Numer. Anal.* **2016**, *36*, 197–221. [CrossRef]
8. Lin, Y.; Xu, C. Finite difference/spectral approximations for the time fractional diffusion equation. *J. Comput. Phys.* **2007**, *225*, 1533–1552. [CrossRef]
9. Mascarenhas, P.V.S.; Moraes, R.M.; Cavalcante, A.L.B. Using a shifted Grünwald–Letnikov scheme for the Caputo derivative to study anomalous solute transport in porous medium. *Int. J. Numer. Anal. Methods Geomech.* **2019**, *43*, 1956–1977. [CrossRef]
10. Scherer, R.; Kalla, S.L.; Tang, Y.; Huang, J. The Grünwald–Letnikov method for fractional differential equations. *Comput. Math. Appl.* **2011**, *62*, 902–917. [CrossRef]
11. Nasir, H.M.; Nafa, K. A new second order approximation for fractional derivatives with applications. *SQUJS* **2018**, *23*, 43–55.
12. Zeng, F.; Li, C.; Liu, F.; Turner, I. Numerical algorithms for time fractional subdiffusion equation with second-order accuracy. *SIAM J. Sci. Comput.* **2015**, *37*, A55–A78. [CrossRef]
13. Dimitrov, Y. A second order approximation for the Caputo fractional derivative. *J. Fract. Calc. Appl.* **2016**, *7*, 175–195.
14. Alikhanov, A.A. A new difference scheme for the time fractional diffusion equation. *J. Comput. Phys.* **2015**, *280*, 424–438. [CrossRef]
15. Gao, G.-H.; Sun, Z.-Z.; Zhang, H.-W. A new fractional numerical differentiation formula to approximate the Caputo fractional derivative and its applications. *J. Comput. Phys.* **2014**, *259*, 33–50. [CrossRef]
16. Apostolov, S.; Dimitrov, Y.; Todorov, V. Constructions of second order approximations of the Caputo fractional derivative. *Lect. Notes Comput. Sci.* **2022**, *13127*, 31–39.

17. Alikhanov, A.A.; Huang, C. A high-order L2 type difference scheme for the time fractional diffusion equation. *Appl. Math. Comput.* **2021**, *411*, 1–19. [CrossRef]
18. Lv, C.; Xu, C. Error analysis of a high order method for time fractional diffusion equations. *SIAM J. Sci. Comput.* **2016**, *38*, A2699–A2724. [CrossRef]
19. Wang, Y.-M.; Ren, L. A high-order L2-compact difference method for Caputo-type time fractional sub-diffusion equations with variable coefficients. *Appl. Math. Comput.* **2019**, *342*, 71–93. [CrossRef]
20. Chen, M.H.; Deng, W.H. Fourth order accurate scheme for the space fractional diffusion equations. *SIAM J. Numer. Anal.* **2014**, *52*, 1418–1438. [CrossRef]
21. Cao, J.; Cai, Z. Numerical analysis of a high-order scheme for nonlinear fractional differential equations with uniform accuracy. *Numer. Math. Theory Methods Appl.* **2020**, *14*, 71–112. [CrossRef]
22. Dehghan, M.; Safarpoor, M.; Abbaszadeh, M. Two high-order numerical algorithms for solving the multi-term time fractional diffusion-wave equations. *J. Comput. Appl. Math.* **2015**, *290*, 174–195. [CrossRef]
23. Li, L.; Zhao, D.; She, M.; Chen, X. On high order numerical schemes for fractional differential equations by block-by-block approach. *Appl. Math. Comput.* **2022**, *425*, 127098. [CrossRef]
24. Lubich, C. Discretized fractional calculus. *SIAM J. Math. Anal.* **1986**, *17*, 704–719. [CrossRef]
25. Ramezani, M.; Mokhtari, R.; Haase, G. Some high order formulae for approximating Caputo fractional derivatives. *Appl. Numer. Math.* **2020**, *153*, 300–318. [CrossRef]
26. Roul, P.; Rohil, V. A novel high-order numerical scheme and its analysis for the two-dimensional time fractional reaction-subdiffusion equation. *Numer. Algor.* **2022**, *90*, 1357–1387. [CrossRef]
27. Wu, R.F.; Ding, H.F.; Li, C.P. Determination of coefficients of high-order schemes for Riemann–Liouville derivative. *Sci. World J.* **2014**, *2014*, 402373. [CrossRef] [PubMed]
28. Navot, I. An extension of the Euler-Maclaurin summation formula to functions with a branch singularity. *J. Math. Phys.* **1961**, *40*, 271–276. [CrossRef]
29. Navot, I. A further extension of the Euler–Maclaurin summation formula. *J. Math. Phys.* **1962**, *41*, 155–163. [CrossRef]
30. Dimitrov, Y. Approximations of the fractional integral and numerical solutions of fractional integral equations. *Commun. Appl. Math. Comput.* **2021**, *3*, 545–569. [CrossRef]
31. Doha, E.H.; Bhrawy, A.H.; Baleanu, D.; Ezz-Eldien, S.S. On shifted Jacobi spectral approximations for solving fractional differential equations. *Appl. Math. Comput.* **2013**, *219*, 8042–8056. [CrossRef]
32. Youssri, Y.H.; Abd-Elhameed, W.M.; Ahmed, H.M. New fractional derivative expression of the shifted third-kind Chebyshev polynomials: Application to a type of nonlinear fractional pantograph differential equations. *J. Funct. Spaces* **2022**, *2022*, 3966135. [CrossRef]
33. Lubich, C. Fractional linear multistep methods for Abel-Volterra integral equations of the second kind. *Math. Comp.* **1985**, *45*, 463–469. [CrossRef]
34. Marasi, H.; Derakhshan, M.H.; Joujehi, A.S.; Kumar, P. Higher-order fractional linear multi-step methods. *Phys. Scr.* **2023**, *98*, 024004. [CrossRef]
35. Abbas, M.; Bibi, A.; Alzaidi, A.S.M.; Nazir, T.; Majeed, A.; Akram, G. Numerical solutions of third-order time fractional differential equations using cubic B-spline functions. *Fractal Fract.* **2022**, *6*, 528. [CrossRef]
36. Duan, J.-S.; Li, M.; Wang, Y.; An, Y.-L. Approximate solution of fractional differential equation by quadratic splines. *Fractal Fract.* **2022**, *6*, 369. [CrossRef]
37. Ray, S.S.; Gupta, A.K. *Wavelet Methods for Solving Partial Differential Equations and Fractional Differential Equations*; Chapman and Hall/CRC: Boca Raton, FL, USA, 2018. [CrossRef]
38. Ur Rehman, M.; Baleanu, D.; Alzabut, J.; Saeed, I. Green–Haar wavelets method for generalized fractional differential equations. *Adv. Differ. Equ.* **2020**, *515*, 2020.
39. Dimitrov, Y. Approximations for the Caputo derivative (I). *J. Fract. Calc. Appl.* **2018**, *9*, 15–44. [CrossRef]
40. Matsuoka, Y. On the power series coefficients of the Riemann zeta function. *Tokyo J. Math.* **1989**, *12*, 49–58.
41. Edwards, H.M. *Riemann's Zeta Function*; Academic Press: New York, NY, USA, 1974. [CrossRef]
42. Weideman, J.A.C. Numerical integration of periodic functions: A few examples. *Am. Math. Mon.* **2002**, *109*, 21–36.
43. Anjara, F.; Solofoniaina, J. Solution of general fractional oscillation relaxation equation by Adomian's method. *Gen. Math. Notes* **2014**, *20*, 1–11. [CrossRef]
44. Güulsu, M.; Öztürk, Y.; Anapalı, A. Numerical approach for solving fractional relaxation-oscillation equation. *Appl. Math. Model.* **2013**, *37*, 5927–5937.
45. Hu, Y.; Luo, Y.; Lu, Z. Analytical solution of the linear fractional differential equation by Adomian decomposition method. *J. Comput. Appl. Math.* **2008**, *215*, 220–229. [CrossRef]
46. Odibat, Z.M.; Momani, S.M. An algorithm for the numerical solution of differential equations of fractional order. *J. Appl. Math. Inform.* **2008**, *26*, 15–27. [CrossRef]
47. Podlubny, I. *Fractional Differential Equation*; Academic Press: Princeton, NJ, USA, 1999.
48. Ray, S.S.; Bera, R.K. Analytical solution of the Bagley Torvik equation by Adomian decomposition method. *Appl. Math. Comput.* **2005**, *168*, 398–410.

49. Nuugulu, S.M.; Gideon, F.; Patidar, K.C. A robust numerical solution to a time fractional Black–Scholes equation. *Adv. Differ. Equ.* **2021**, *2021*, 123. [CrossRef]
50. Cen, Z.; Huang, J.; Xu, A.; Le, A. Numerical approximation of a time fractional Black–Scholes equation. *Comput. Math. Appl.* **2018**, *75*, 2874–2887. [CrossRef]
51. Abdi, N.; Aminikhah, H.; Sheikhani, A.H.R. High-order compact finite difference schemes for the time fractional Black–Scholes model governing European options. *Chaos Solit. Fract.* **2022**, *162*, 112423. [CrossRef]
52. Chen, X.; Xu, X.; Zhu, S.-P. Analytically pricing double barrier options based on a time fractional Black–Scholes equation. *Comput. Math. Appl.* **2015**, *69*, 1407–1419. [CrossRef]
53. Wang, X.-T. Scaling and long-range dependence in option pricing I: Pricing European option with transaction costs under the fractional Black–Scholes model. *Phys. A Stat. Mech.* **2010**, 389, 438–444. [CrossRef]
54. Kumar, S.; Kumar, D.; Singh, J. Numerical computation of fractional Black–Scholes equation arising in financial market. *Egypt. J. Basic Appl. Sci.* **2014**, *1*, 177–183. [CrossRef]
55. Zhang, H.; Liu, F.; Turner, I.; Yang, Q. Numerical solution of the time fractional Black–Scholes model governing European options. *Comput. Math. Appl.* **2016**, *71*, 1772–1783. [CrossRef]
56. Grzegorz Krzyżanowski, G.; Magdziarz, M.; Plociniczak, L. A weighted finite difference method for subdiffusive Black–Scholes model. *Comput. Math. Appl.* **2020**, *80*, 653–670. [CrossRef]
57. Dimitrov, Y.; Vulkov, L. Three-point compact finite difference scheme on non-uniform meshes for the time fractional Black–Scholes equation. *AIP Conf. Proc.* **2015**, *1690*, 040022. [CrossRef]
58. Song, L.; Wang, W. Solution of the fractional Black–Scholes option pricing model by finite difference method. *Abstr. Appl. Anal.* **2013**, *2013*, 194286.
59. Deming, W.; Colcord, C. The minimum in the gamma function. *Nature* **1935**, *135*, 917. [CrossRef]
60. Kolotilina, L.Y. Bounds for the infinity norm of the inverse for certain M- and H-matrices. *Linear Algebra Appl.* **2009**, *430*, 692–702. [CrossRef]
61. Nilson, E.N.; Ahlberg, J.H. Convergence properties of the spline fit. *J. SIAM* **1963**, *11*, 95–104. [CrossRef]

fractal and fractional

MDPI

Article

On Stability of a Fractional Discrete Reaction–Diffusion Epidemic Model

Omar Alsayyed [1], Amel Hioual [2,*], Gharib M. Gharib [3], Mayada Abualhomos [4], Hassan Al-Tarawneh [5], Maha S. Alsauodi [6], Nabeela Abu-Alkishik [7], Abdallah Al-Husban [8] and Adel Ouannas [9]

1 Department of Mathematics, Faculty of Science, The Hashemite University, Zarqa 13133, Jordan; omarm_re@hu.edu.jo
2 Laboratory of Dynamical Systems and Control, University of Oum EL Bouaghi, Oum El Bouaghi 04000, Algeria
3 Department of Mathematics, Faculty of Science, Zarqa University, Zarqa 13110, Jordan; ggharib@zu.edu.jo
4 Applied Science Research Center (ASRC), Applied Science Private University, Amman 11931, Jordan; abuhomos@asu.edu.jo
5 Department of Data Sciences and Artificial Intelligence, Al-Ahliyya Amman University, Amman 19111, Jordan; h.altarawneh@ammanu.edu.jo
6 Department of Basic Scientific Sciences, Applied Science Private University, Amman 11931, Jordan; m_alsoudi@asu.edu.jo
7 Department of Mathematics, Jerash University, Jerash 26150, Jordan; nabeelakishik@yahoo.com
8 Department of Mathematics, Faculty of Science and Technology, Irbid National University, Irbid 2600, Jordan; dralhosban@inu.edu.jo
9 Department of Mathematics and Computer Science, University of Oum EL Bouaghi, Oum El Bouaghi 04000, Algeria; ouannas.adel@univ-oeb.dz
* Correspondence: amel.hioual@univ-oeb.dz

Abstract: This paper considers the dynamical properties of a space and time discrete fractional reaction–diffusion epidemic model, introducing a novel generalized incidence rate. The linear stability of the equilibrium solutions of the considered discrete fractional reaction–diffusion model has been carried out, and a global asymptotic stability analysis has been undertaken. We conducted a global stability analysis using a specialized Lyapunov function that captures the system's historical data, distinguishing it from the integer-order version. This approach significantly advanced our comprehension of the complex stability properties within discrete fractional reaction–diffusion epidemic models. To substantiate the theoretical underpinnings, this paper is accompanied by numerical examples. These examples serve a dual purpose: not only do they validate the theoretical findings, but they also provide illustrations of the practical implications of the proposed discrete fractional system.

Keywords: fractional discrete epidemic reaction–diffusion model; local stability; Lyapunov function; global stability

1. Introduction

In recent decades, fractional differential equation models have gained extensive attention within research fields. The prevalence of these models across a wide spectrum of applications, encompassing fields like biological mathematics, physics, and biology, has significantly motivated their exploration. Notably, the domain of nonlinear dynamics has increasingly turned its focus to fractional models, inspiring a surge of relevant research pursuits. For those intrigued by these developments, valuable insights can be gleaned from references such as [1–8].

Fractional reaction–diffusion order models are a generalization of traditional integer reaction–diffusion order models. It must be emphasized that they have benefits over standard integer-order reaction–diffusion models due to the fact that they have memory and genetic qualities that these latter models, which are commonly used by many biological systems, do not have. In addition, these models describe models of population with greater precision than integer-order models [9–13].

In reality, the transmission of infectious illnesses is affected not just by their present condition, but also by their former status. Since each fractional derivative comprises a kernel function, it is possible to conclude that the present state of fractional epidemic systems is dependent on previous data [14]. More notably, Angstmann et al. introduced an infectiousness fractional SIR system and demonstrated how fractional derivatives automatically arise from continuous random walks [15]. Hethcote presented a fractional SIR system with a constant population as a generalization of traditional integer ones [16]. The local stability of both equilibriums of a fractional SEIR epidemic system was then investigated in [17].

Except in rare instances where obtaining an explicit solution for diffusion fractional differential equations proves challenging, the possibilities extend to the study of both numerical and exact solutions based on the partial differential equation. In scenarios where the exact solution is elusive, recourse to the numerical solution remains a viable approach. Not only that, but discrete models have a unique physical process. [18–22]. In particular, infectious illness data are not continuous; however, they cover a specific time period. Furthermore, because the discrete representation of infectious illnesses can be in any time step for the unit, the continuous model is appropriate for easier and more efficient data following the discretization of the epidemic model (see [23–26]). Nonetheless, previous research on discrete epidemic systems either did not account for any types of diffusion or exclusively studied conventional diffusion. A noteworthy observation relates to the exploration of fractional discrete models coupled with diffusion, which has accumulated significant attention in the research fields. For instance, the work presented in [27] explores the advancement of a fractional discrete reaction–diffusion Lengyel–Epstein system, as well as a detailed examination of its asymptotic stability. Furthermore, the literature includes the presentation of a fractional discrete diffusion equation in [28], providing a unique path for further exploration. An intriguing work explores the chaotic dynamics of a variable-order fractional diffusion equation across non-continuous time scales, as detailed in [29]. The area of epidemic systems with discrete fractions combined with reaction–diffusion processes has been comprehensively explored in [30], uncovering the complexities of their behavior. These efforts together enhance our grasp of the interaction between fractional dynamics and diffusion phenomena. For a more comprehensive exploration into the dynamics of fractional discrete reaction–diffusion models, one can find additional insights in [31–33].

Inspired by prior research, we conduct a detailed study of a discrete fractional epidemic system with reaction–diffusion, featuring a generalized incidence rate. In this study, we uncover essential insights that play a key role in our investigation:

- At the core of our investigation is the introduction of a new discrete fractional epidemic model. This model is created by skillfully combining the L1 scheme and the second-order central difference scheme, which effectively transforms the continuous model into its discrete form. This transformation results in a carefully crafted discrete model, laying the foundation for our subsequent analyses.
- Central to our study is a thorough examination of both the local and global asymptotic stability within the proposed fractional discrete reaction–diffusion epidemic model. We employ a powerful linearization technique to analyze the complex stability characteristics near equilibrium points. To establish global stability, we utilize a Lyapunov function that effectively captures historical data, strengthening the reliability of our findings.
- The theoretical framework resulting from our analyses strongly aligns with real-world dynamics. This alignment is robustly confirmed through a series of simulations, where the practical significance of our theoretical discoveries becomes evident. The simulations clearly validate the substantial influence of our findings on the complex network of disease transmission dynamics.

Below is a detailed elaboration of how our work is organized, including every crucial aspect: Within Section 2, we start an important step by generating the discrete form of the fractional reaction–diffusion epidemic system. This process is achieved through the skillful application of the second-order central difference scheme and the L1 scheme. This section is fundamental for the following analyses and investigations that will take place. Section 3 represents a crucial point where we start identifying equilibrium points within the investigated epidemic system. Moreover, we introduce and compute the fundamental reproduction number—an essential metric that Describes how the system spreads. This section sets the foundation for our subsequent explorations of stability. Our investigation advances to Section 4, where we engage in a detailed analysis of the local asymptotic stability. We explore various scenarios both with and without diffusion, all centered around the fundamental reproduction number. This section dissects the stability properties of equilibrium points under varying conditions, enriching our understanding of the system's dynamics. In Section 5, our attention turns to the global stability analysis of the system. We utilize a well-suited Lyapunov functional to unravel the stability of both the disease-free and epidemic equilibrium points. This section offers a profound perspective on the long-term behavior of the system, highlighting its lasting characteristics. Section 6 connects theory with real-world application through the presentation of examples and simulations. Through these illustrative instances, we illustrate the theoretical ideas in real-world situations, allowing readers to see how they work. This section demonstrates the practical utility of our approach. In Section 7, to conclude, we review our research path and summarize the key insights gathered from each preceding section. We also offer insights into potential directions for future research, providing a comprehensive conclusion that covers both the outcomes of our work and its potential implications.

2. A Novel Fractional Discrete-Time Reaction–Diffusion Epidemic Model

Numerous studies on fractional anomalous diffusion models of infectious diseases have been published [14–17]. In particular, Zhen et al. examined a class of reaction–diffusion by generalizing the incidence rate fractional-order SIR epidemic model in [34] as follows:

$$\begin{cases} {}_0^C D_t^\alpha S = k_1 \Delta S + \theta - \gamma S \psi(I) - \epsilon S, \quad t > 0, \quad x \in \Omega, \\ {}_0^C D_t^\alpha I = k_2 \Delta I + \gamma S \psi(I) - (\nu + \sigma) I, \quad t > 0, \quad x \in \Omega, \\ {}_0^C D_t^\alpha R = k_3 \Delta R + \sigma I - \delta R, \quad t > 0, \quad x \in \Omega, \end{cases} \tag{1}$$

where the investigated population includes both vulnerable individuals S and infected individuals I. θ reflects the flow rate of recently exposed persons; the symbol ϵ is the mortality rate; the parameter γ defines the rate of disease prevalent within individuals per unit time; and the constant σ is provided by $\sigma = \epsilon + \nu$, where $\frac{1}{\nu}$ is the mean length of a sexual encounter among affected individuals.

k_1 and k_2 represent the diffusion coefficients, and Δ is the Laplacian operator on Ω, where $\Omega \in \mathbb{R}^n$ is a bounded subset of $\mathbb{R}^n$ with a smooth border $\partial\Omega$ and with homogeneous Neumann boundary conditions and initial conditions.

$$S(x,0) = S_0(x), \quad I(x,0) = I_0(x), \quad R(x,0) = R_0(x). \tag{2}$$

It goes without saying that the nonlinearity ψ is a positive and continuously differentiable functional on $\mathbb{R}^+$ such that

$$\psi(0) = 0, \tag{3}$$

and

$$0 < I\psi'(I) \leq \psi(I), \quad I > 0. \tag{4}$$

However, it has been reported that the recovered class R of System (1) has no effect on the susceptible class S or the infected class I. As a result, the study in [34] concentrated on the following reduced system:

$$\begin{cases} {}_0^C D_t^\alpha S = k_1 \Delta S + \theta - \gamma S \psi(I) - \epsilon S, & t > 0, \quad x \in \Omega, \\ {}_0^C D_t^\alpha I = k_2 \Delta I + \gamma S \psi(I) - (\nu + \sigma) I, & t > 0, \quad x \in \Omega. \end{cases} \tag{5}$$

Hence, the discretization and dynamics in this work are based on the epidemic model (5). Because real-world data are discrete, the discrete system is better suited to simulating the spread of disease, based on System (5) and the discretization approach used in [28]. When $x \in [0, L]$, we obtain $x_{i+1} = x_i + d_x, \quad i = 0, \ldots, m$, and by using the central difference formula for x, $\frac{\partial^2 S(x,t)}{\partial x^2}$ and $\frac{\partial^2 I(x,t)}{\partial x^2}$ are estimated by

$$\begin{cases} \dfrac{\partial^2 S(x,t)}{\partial x^2} \approx \dfrac{S_{i+1}(t) - 2S_i(t) + S_{i-1}(t)}{d_{x^2}}, \\ \dfrac{\partial^2 I(x,t)}{\partial x^2} \approx \dfrac{I_{i+1}(t) - 2I_i(t) + I_{i-1}(t)}{d_{x^2}}. \end{cases} \tag{6}$$

Considering the definition of the second-order difference operator of S_i and I_i described in [35,36] by

$$\Delta^2 \mathfrak{y}(\mathfrak{r}) = \mathfrak{y}(\mathfrak{r}+2) - 2\mathfrak{y}(\mathfrak{r}+1) + \mathfrak{y}(\mathfrak{r}), \quad \mathfrak{r} \in \mathbb{N}. \tag{7}$$

We obtain the following approximations:

$$\begin{cases} \dfrac{\partial^2 S(x,t)}{\partial x^2} \approx \dfrac{\Delta^2 S_{i-1}(t)}{d_{x^2}}, \\ \dfrac{\partial^2 I(x,t)}{\partial x^2} \approx \dfrac{\Delta^2 I_{i-1}(t)}{d_{x^2}}. \end{cases} \tag{8}$$

Consequently, we take into consideration the following discrete fractional reaction–diffusion epidemic model:

$$\begin{cases} {}_\hbar^C\Delta_{t_0}^\xi S_i(t) = \dfrac{k_1}{d_{x^2}} \Delta^2 S_{i-1}(t + \hbar\xi) + \theta - \gamma S_i(t + \hbar\xi) \psi(I_i(t + \hbar\xi)) - \epsilon S_i(t + \hbar\xi), \\ {}_\hbar^C\Delta_{t_0}^\xi I_i(t) = \dfrac{k_2}{d_{x^2}} \Delta^2 I_{i-1}(t + \hbar\xi) + \gamma S_i(t + \hbar\xi) \psi(I_i(t + \hbar\xi)) - (\nu + \sigma) I_i(t + \hbar\xi). \end{cases} \tag{9}$$

To simplify our simulations and ensure that edge effects do not interfere with our results, we will utilize periodic boundary conditions, following the approach outlined in [28].

$$\begin{cases} S_0(t) = S_m(t), \quad S_1(t) = S_{m+1}(t), \\ I_0(t) = I_m(t), \quad I_1(t) = I_{m+1}(t), \end{cases} \tag{10}$$

and the initial condition

$$S_i(t_0) = \Phi_1(x_i) \geq 0, \quad I_i(t_0) = \Phi_2(x_i) \geq 0.$$

while the definition of the Caputo $\hbar$-difference operator is as follows:

Definition 1 ([37,38]). *The Caputo $\hbar$-difference operator is denoted by*

$${}_\hbar^C\Delta_a^\alpha \mathfrak{y}(t) = {}_\hbar\Delta_{\mathfrak{a}}^{-(n-\alpha)} \Delta_\hbar^n \mathfrak{y}(t), \quad t \in (\hbar\mathbb{N})_{\mathfrak{a}+\alpha\hbar}, \quad 0 < \alpha < 1, \tag{11}$$

and the α-th order ℏ-sum is described by

$$ {}_{\hbar}\Delta_{\mathfrak{a}}^{-\alpha}\mathfrak{y}(t) = \frac{\hbar}{\Gamma(\alpha)} \sum_{\frac{t}{\hbar}-\alpha}^{s=\frac{\mathfrak{a}}{\hbar}} (t-\sigma(s\hbar))^{(\alpha-1)}\mathfrak{y}(s\hbar), \quad \sigma(s\hbar) = (s+1)\hbar, \tag{12} $$

with the set $(\hbar\mathbb{N})_{\mathfrak{a}+\alpha\hbar}$ *defined by*

$$ (\hbar\mathbb{N})_{\mathfrak{a}+\alpha\hbar} = \{\mathfrak{a}+(1-\alpha)\hbar, \mathfrak{a}+(2-\alpha)\hbar, \ldots\}. $$

3. Fixed Points and Basic Reproduction Number

3.1. Fixed Points

Identifying the fixed points is a prerequisite for studying the dynamics of System (9), and the following nonlinear system needs to be solved in order to do so:

$$ \begin{cases} \theta - \gamma S_i(t+\hbar\xi)\psi(I_i(t+\hbar\xi)) - \epsilon S_i(t+\hbar\xi) = 0, \\ \gamma S_i(t+\hbar\xi)\psi(I_i(t+\hbar\xi)) - (\nu+\sigma)I_i(t+\hbar\xi) = 0. \end{cases} \tag{13} $$

The point $E_0 = \left(\frac{\theta}{\epsilon}, 0\right)$ is a solution to the previous system. Since the disease is nonexistent, E_0 is referred to as the disease-free fixed point.

Now, considering that $I > 0$, we have

$$ S^* = \frac{\theta}{\epsilon} - \frac{(\nu+\sigma)I^*}{\epsilon}. \tag{14} $$

The point $E^* = (S^*, I^*)$ is called the epidemic equilibrium point; its existence may be explored numerically.

3.2. Basic Reproduction Number

For the purpose of understanding how epidemic systems behave, the fundamental reproduction number is crucial. Ref. [39] states that the fundamental reproduction number is the spectral radius of the subsequent generation matrix $\mathbb{F}\mathbb{V}^{-1}$, wherein F and V are the Jacobian matrices for $\mathbb{F}$ and $\mathbb{V}^{-1}$, respectively, at the disease-free fixed point, and where $\mathbb{F}$ is the rate at which new infections appear:

$$ \mathbb{F} = \begin{pmatrix} \gamma S\psi(I) \\ 0 \end{pmatrix}, \tag{15} $$

and $\mathbb{V}$, the infection disappearance rate:

$$ \mathbb{V} = \begin{pmatrix} (\nu+\sigma)I \\ -\theta + \gamma S\psi(I) + \epsilon S \end{pmatrix}. \tag{16} $$

Hence, the Jacobite matrices at the disease-free equilibrium E_0 are as follows:

$$ F = \begin{pmatrix} \frac{\theta}{\epsilon}\gamma\psi'(0) & 0 \\ 0 & 0 \end{pmatrix}, \quad V = \begin{pmatrix} \nu+\sigma & 0 \\ \frac{\theta}{\epsilon}\gamma\psi'(0) & \epsilon \end{pmatrix}, \tag{17} $$

The fundamental reproductive number, based on the Jacobite matrices, is provided by:

$$ R_0 = \frac{\gamma\theta}{\epsilon(\nu+\sigma)}\psi'(0). \tag{18} $$

4. Local Stability

4.1. Local Stability of the Free Diffusion Epidemic Model

We now provide adequate requirements for the local asymptotic stability of the two equilibriums of the following system:

$$\begin{cases} {}^{C}_{\hbar}\Delta^{\xi}_{t_0} S(t) = \theta - \gamma S(t+\hbar\xi)\psi(I(t+\hbar\xi)) - \epsilon S(t+\hbar\xi), \\ {}^{C}_{\hbar}\Delta^{\xi}_{t_0} I(t) = \gamma S(t+\hbar\xi)\psi(I(t+\hbar\xi)) - (\nu+\sigma)I(t+\hbar\xi). \end{cases} \tag{19}$$

with the initial conditions

$$S(t_0) = S_0 > 0, \quad I(t_0) = I_0 > 0. \tag{20}$$

We require the following theorem before we can investigate local stability:

Theorem 1 ([40]). *Let (S^*, I^*) represent the equilibrium point of (19). If all of the eigenvalues of J_{E^*} are in $S^{\alpha}_{\hbar}$, then (S^*, I^*) is asymptotically stable.*
where

$$S^{\alpha}_{\hbar} = \left\{ w \in \mathbb{C} : |Arg(w)| > \frac{\alpha\pi}{2} \quad or \quad |w| > \frac{2^{\alpha}}{\hbar^{\alpha}} \cos^{\alpha}\left(\frac{Arg(w)}{\alpha}\right) \right\}. \tag{21}$$

Theorem 2.
- *If $R_0 < 1$, the disease-free fixed point E_0 is asymptotically stable.*
- *If $R_0 > 1$, the epidemic equilibrium point E^* is asymptotically stable.*

Proof. First, we establish the Jacobian matrix of System (19)

$$J = \begin{pmatrix} -\gamma\psi(I(t+\hbar\xi)) - \epsilon & -\gamma S(t+\hbar\xi)\psi'(I(t+\hbar\xi)) \\ \gamma\psi(I(t+\hbar\xi)) & \gamma S(t+\hbar\xi)\psi'(I(t+\hbar\xi)) - (\nu+\sigma) \end{pmatrix}. \tag{22}$$

- The Jacobian matrix at the free disease point E_0

$$J_{E_0} = \begin{pmatrix} -\epsilon & \frac{\theta}{\epsilon}\psi'(0)\gamma \\ 0 & \frac{\theta}{\epsilon}\psi'(0)\gamma - (\nu+\sigma) \end{pmatrix} = \begin{pmatrix} -\epsilon & (\nu+\sigma)R_0 \\ 0 & (\nu+\sigma)(R_0-1) \end{pmatrix}. \tag{23}$$

The Jacobian matrix's eigenvalues associated with E_0 are

$$\lambda_1 = -\epsilon, \quad \lambda_2 = (\nu+\sigma)(R_0-1), \tag{24}$$

System (19) is asymptotically stable if $Arg(\lambda_i) \leq \frac{\alpha\pi}{2}, i = 1,2$. Clearly, the eigenvalues are reel and $\lambda_1 < 0$, if $R_0 < 1$. This implies $\lambda_2 < 0$. Hence, $Arg(\lambda_1) = Arg(\lambda_2) = \pi \leq \frac{\alpha\pi}{2}$.

- The Jacobian matrix at the free disease point E^*

$$J_{E^*} = \begin{pmatrix} -\gamma\psi(I^*) - \epsilon & -\gamma S^*\psi'(I^*) \\ \gamma\psi(I^*) & \gamma S^*\psi'(I^*) - (\nu+\sigma) \end{pmatrix}. \tag{25}$$

$$\begin{aligned} \mathrm{tr}(J_{E^*}) &= -\gamma\psi(I^*) + \gamma S^*\psi'(I^*) - (\nu+\sigma+\epsilon), \\ &= \gamma S^*\psi'(I^*) - \frac{\gamma S^*\psi(I^*)}{I^*} - \frac{\theta}{S^*}, \\ &= -\frac{\theta}{S^*} - \gamma S^*\left(\frac{\psi(I^*)}{I^*} - \psi'(I^*)\right), \end{aligned}$$

and

$$\det(J_{E^*}) = \gamma\psi(I^*)(\nu+\sigma) - \epsilon\gamma S^*\psi'(I^*) + \epsilon(\nu+\sigma),$$
$$= \epsilon\gamma S^*\left(\frac{\psi(I^*)}{I^*} - \psi'(I^*)\right) + \frac{\gamma S^*\psi(I^*)}{I^*}\gamma\psi(I^*),$$

Clearly, $\mathrm{tr}(J_{E^*}) < 0$ and $\det(J_{E^*}) > 0$.
Now, we have the following discriminant

$$\mathfrak{D}_\lambda = \mathrm{tr}^2(J_{E^*}) - 4\det(J_{E^*})$$
$$= \left(\frac{\theta}{S^*} - \gamma S^*\left(\frac{\psi(I^*)}{I^*} - \psi'(I^*)\right)\right)^2 - 4\left(\epsilon\gamma S^*\left(\frac{\psi(I^*)}{I^*} - \psi'(I^*)\right) + \frac{\gamma S^*\psi(I^*)}{I^*}\gamma\psi(I^*)\right).$$

The eigenvalues of the Jacobian matrix J_{E^*} are obviously dependent on the sing of $\mathfrak{D}_\lambda$; therefore, we may analyze the stability in the following situations:

- If $\mathfrak{D}_\lambda > 0$ and since $\det(J_{E^*}) > 0$. As a consequence, the negativity of the eigenvalues is determined by the sign of $\mathrm{tr}(J_{E^*})$, and as $\mathrm{tr}(J_{E^*}) < 0$, the eigenvalues λ_1 and λ_2 are real, and we have

$$\lambda_1 = \frac{\mathrm{tr}(J_{E^*}) - \sqrt{\mathfrak{D}_\lambda}}{2} < 0. \tag{26}$$

  As a consequence of this, $Arg(\lambda_1) = \pi$. It is self-evident that $Arg(\lambda_1) = Arg(\lambda_2) = \pi$. As a result, according to Theorem 1, the equilibrium E^* is asymptotically stable.
- If $\mathfrak{D}_\lambda < 0$, then

$$\lambda_1 = \frac{\mathrm{tr}(J_{E^*}) - i\sqrt{-\mathfrak{D}_\lambda}}{2}, \qquad \lambda_2 = \frac{\mathrm{tr}(J_{E^*}) + i\sqrt{-\mathfrak{D}_\lambda}}{2}. \tag{27}$$

  Because $\mathrm{tr}(J_{E^*}) < 0$, System (19) is then asymptotically stable, based on the identical situation studied before.
- If $\mathfrak{D}_\lambda = 0$, $\mathrm{tr}(J_{E^*})$ cannot have a value of zero. The sign of the eigenvalues corresponds to the sign of $\mathrm{tr}(J_E^*)$.. Consequently, E^* is asymptotically stable for all $\alpha \in (0,1]$.

We can conclude that if $R_0 > 1$, E^* is locally asymptotically stable regardless of the sign of $\mathfrak{D}_\lambda$

□

4.2. Local Stability of the Diffusion Epidemic Model

In this section, we will show that the steady state can be stable in the presence of diffusion under certain variable circumstances. To accomplish this, we will use the same method as in [41], and we start by computing the eigenvalues of the following equation:

$$\begin{cases} \Delta^2\mathfrak{y}_{i-1}(t) + \theta_i\mathfrak{y}_i(t) = 0, & t \in \mathbb{N}, \\ \mathfrak{y}_0(t) = \mathfrak{y}_1(t), & t \in \mathbb{N}, \\ \mathfrak{y}_N(t) = \mathfrak{y}_{N-1}(t), & t \in \mathbb{N}, \end{cases} \tag{28}$$

then, we obtain

$$\begin{cases} {}^{C}_{\hbar}\Delta^{\xi}_{t_0} S_i(t) = -\frac{k_1}{d_{x^2}}\theta_i S_i(t+\hbar\xi) + \theta - \gamma S_i(t+\hbar\xi)\psi(I_i(t+\hbar\xi)) - \epsilon S_i(t+\hbar\xi), \\ {}^{C}_{\hbar}\Delta^{\xi}_{t_0} I_i(t) = -\frac{k_2}{d_{x^2}}\theta_i I_i(t+\hbar\xi) + \gamma S_i(t+\hbar\xi)\psi(I_i(t+\hbar\xi)) - (\nu+\sigma)I_i(t+\hbar\xi) \end{cases} \tag{29}$$

When linearizing the reaction–diffusion system (9) with respect to the steady state, we arrive at the following:

$$J_i = \begin{pmatrix} -\frac{k_1}{d_{x^2}}\theta_i - \gamma\psi(I(t+\hbar\xi)) - \epsilon & \gamma S(t+\hbar\xi)\psi'(I(t+\hbar\xi)) \\ \gamma\psi(I(t+\hbar\xi)) & -\frac{k_2}{d_{x^2}}\theta_i + \gamma S(t+\hbar\xi)\psi'(I(t+\hbar\xi)) - (\nu+\sigma) \end{pmatrix}. \tag{30}$$

Theorem 3.
- *If $R_0 < 1$, E^0 is locally asymptotically stable.*
- *If $R_0 > 1$, we suppose that*
$\left(\frac{\theta}{S^*} - \gamma S^*\left(\frac{\psi(I^*)}{I^*} - \psi'(I^*)\right)\right)^2 > 4\left(\epsilon\gamma S^*\left(\frac{\psi(I^*)}{I^*} - \psi'(I^*)\right) + \frac{\gamma S^*\psi(I^*)}{I^*}\gamma\psi(I^*)\right),$
System (9) is asymptotically stable at the steady state (E^*) if the following hold:
  - *If $k_1 < k_2$ and* $-\frac{k_1}{d_{x^2}}\theta_i \geq \gamma\psi(I(t+\hbar\xi)) + \epsilon.$
  - *If $k_1 > k_2$ and* $-\frac{k_1}{d_{x^2}}\theta_i \geq \gamma\psi(I(t+\hbar\xi)) + \epsilon$, *in addition the eigenvalues*

$$\lambda_j(\theta_i) = \frac{\mathrm{tr}(J_{i(E^*)}) \pm \sqrt{\mathrm{tr}(J_{i(E^*)})^2 - 4\det(J_{i(E^*)})}}{2}, \quad j = 1, 2,$$

satisfy $Arg(\lambda_j(\theta_i)) > \frac{\alpha\pi}{2}.$

Proof. In order to discuss the stability of E_0, we evaluate $J_i(E_0)$

$$J_i(E_0) = \begin{pmatrix} -\frac{k_1}{d_{x^2}}\theta_i - \epsilon & \frac{\theta}{\epsilon}\gamma\psi'(I(0)) \\ 0 & -\frac{k_2}{d_{x^2}}\theta_i + \frac{\theta}{\epsilon}\gamma\psi'(I(0)) - (\nu+\sigma) \end{pmatrix} = J_{E_0} - \lambda(\theta_i)I. \tag{31}$$

The eigenvalues of the Jacobian matrix $J_i(E_0)$ associated with E_0 are

$$\lambda_1(\theta_i) = -\frac{k_1}{d_{x^2}}\theta_i - \epsilon, \quad \lambda_2(\theta_i) = -\frac{k_2}{d_{x^2}}\theta_i + (\nu+\sigma)(R_0 - 1), \tag{32}$$

If $R_0 < 1$, it is evident that $\lambda_1(\theta_i) < 0$ and $\lambda_2(\theta_i) < 0$, which means that $Arg(\lambda_1(\theta_i)) = Arg(\lambda_2(\theta_i)) = \pi > \frac{\alpha\pi}{2}$. Thus, E_0 is asymptotically stable.

Now, we suppose that $R_0 > 1$, clearly E_0 is unstable. Hence, we are interested in this case in the stability of E^* and we have

$$J_i(E^*) = \begin{pmatrix} -\frac{k_1}{d_{x^2}}\theta_i - \gamma\psi(I^*) - \epsilon & -\gamma S^*\psi'(I^*) \\ \gamma\psi(I^*) & -\frac{k_2}{d_{x^2}}\theta_i + \gamma S^*\psi'(I^*) - (\nu+\sigma) \end{pmatrix}. \tag{33}$$

Then, we define the characteristic equation associated with the Jacobian matrix (33):

$$\lambda^2(\theta_i) - \mathrm{tr}(J_i(E^*))\lambda(\theta_i) + \det(J_i(E^*)) = 0. \tag{34}$$

and we have

$$\mathrm{tr}(J_i(E^*)) = -\left(\frac{k_1}{d_{x^2}} + \frac{k_2}{d_{x^2}}\right)\theta_i + \mathrm{tr}(J_{E^*}), \tag{35}$$

$$\det(J_i(E^*)) = \frac{k_1k_2}{d_x^4}\theta_i^2 + \left(-\frac{k_1}{d_{x^2}}(\gamma S^*\psi'(I^*) - (\nu+\sigma)) + \frac{k_2}{d_{x^2}}(\gamma\psi(I^*) + \epsilon)\right)\theta_i + \det(J_{E^*}), \tag{36}$$

and the discriminant is defined by

$$\mathfrak{D}_i = \left(\frac{k_1}{d_{x^2}} - \frac{k_2}{d_{x^2}}\right)^2 \theta_i^2 + 4\left(\frac{k_1}{d_{x^2}}(\gamma S^* \psi'(I^*) - (\nu + \sigma)) - \frac{k_2}{d_{x^2}}(\gamma\psi(I^*) + \epsilon)\right)\theta_i + \mathfrak{D}$$

We need to evaluate the sign of $\mathfrak{D}_i$. Therefore, we calculate the discriminant of $\mathfrak{D}_i$ in relation to θ_i as follows:

$$\begin{aligned}\mathfrak{D}_{\theta_i} &= \left(\left(\frac{k_1}{d_{x^2}}(\gamma S^* \psi'(I^*) - (\nu + \sigma)) - \frac{k_2}{d_{x^2}}(\gamma\psi(I^*) + \epsilon)\right)\theta_i\right)^2 - \left(\frac{k_1}{d_{x^2}} - \frac{k_2}{d_{x^2}}\right)^2 \lambda_i^2 \Delta, \\ &= 4\left(\frac{k_1}{d_{x^2}} - \frac{k_2}{d_{x^2}}\right)^2 (\gamma\psi(I^*) + \epsilon)\gamma S^* \psi'(I^*).\end{aligned}$$

Clearly, $\mathfrak{D}_{\theta_i} > 0$ because $k_1 \neq k_2$, and we distinguish two cases,

- If $k_1 < k_2$, then $\left(\frac{\theta}{S^*} - \gamma S^*\left(\frac{\psi(I^*)}{I^*} - \psi'(I^*)\right)\right)^2 > 4\left(\epsilon\gamma S^*\left(\frac{\psi(I^*)}{I^*} - \psi'(I^*)\right)\right.$ $\left.+\frac{\gamma S^* \psi(I^*)}{I^*}\gamma\psi(I^*)\right)$, the two solutions of the equation $\mathfrak{D}_{\theta_i} = 0$ are both negative. Thus, $\mathfrak{D}_i > 0$, and the roots of (34) are

$$\begin{cases} \lambda_1(\theta_i) = \dfrac{\mathrm{tr}(J_i(E^*)) + \sqrt{\mathrm{tr}(J_i(E^*))^2 - 4\det(J_i(E^*))}}{2} \\ \lambda_2(\theta_i) = \dfrac{\mathrm{tr}(J_i(E^*)) - \sqrt{\mathrm{tr}(J_i(E^*))^2 - 4\det(J_i(E^*))}}{2}. \end{cases} \quad (37)$$

  Note that the solutions are real, and $\lambda_1(\theta_i) < 0$. In addition, $-\frac{k_1}{d_{x^2}}\theta_i \geq \gamma\psi(I(t + \hbar\xi)) + \epsilon$. This leads to

$$|Arg(\lambda_1(\theta_i))| = |Arg(\lambda_2(\theta_i))| = \pi, \quad (38)$$

  which ensures E^* is asymptotic stability.
- If $k_1 > k_2$, we have $(\gamma - \epsilon)^2 > 4\epsilon\gamma$. This returns us to the previous scenario Again, for $-\frac{k_1}{d_{x^2}}\theta_i \geq \gamma\psi(I(t + \hbar\xi)) + \epsilon$, $det(J_i(E^*)) > 0$, and hence, $\lambda_1(\theta_i)$ and $\lambda_2(\theta_i)$ are negative and must meet the conditions of Theorem 1.

□

5. Global Stability

We examine here the global stability of both stable states E_0 and E^*. We have chosen to handle the cases $R_0 > 1$ and $R_0 < 1$ independently since global stability relies on the reproduction number R_0. First, we provide the following theorem with regard to the global stability of fractional discrete systems:

Theorem 4 ([42]). *Let $(S^*, I^*) = 0$ be the system's equilibrium point (9). The equilibrium point is asymptotically stable if there exists a positive definite and declining scalar function such that:* ${}^{C}_{\hbar}\Delta^{\alpha}_{\mathfrak{a}} V(t) \leq 0$.

We also have the following important inequality:

Lemma 1 ([42]). *The following inequality holds*

$${}^{C}_{\hbar}\Delta^{\alpha}_{\mathfrak{a}}\mathfrak{y}^2(t) \leq 2\mathfrak{y}(t + \alpha\hbar)\,{}^{C}_{\hbar}\Delta^{\alpha}_{\mathfrak{a}}\mathfrak{y}(t), \quad t \in (\hbar\mathbb{N})_{\mathfrak{a}+\alpha\hbar}, \quad (39)$$

Theorem 5 ([43]). *The summation by parts formulas for two functions $\mathfrak{y}$ and $\mathfrak{z}$ defined on $\mathbb{N}$ and $\mathfrak{a}; \mathfrak{b} \in \mathbb{N}$ are given by:*

$$\sum_{\mathfrak{r}=\mathfrak{a}}^{\mathfrak{b}-1} \mathfrak{y}(\mathfrak{r})\Delta\mathfrak{z}(\mathfrak{r}) = \mathfrak{y}(\mathfrak{r})\mathfrak{z}(\mathfrak{r})|_{\mathfrak{a}}^{\mathfrak{b}} - \sum_{\mathfrak{r}=\mathfrak{a}}^{\mathfrak{b}-1} \mathfrak{z}(\mathfrak{r}+1)\Delta\mathfrak{y}(\mathfrak{r}), \tag{40}$$

$$\sum_{\mathfrak{r}=\mathfrak{a}}^{\mathfrak{b}-1} \mathfrak{y}(\mathfrak{r}+1)\Delta\mathfrak{z}(\mathfrak{r}) = \mathfrak{y}(\mathfrak{r})\mathfrak{z}(\mathfrak{r})|_{\mathfrak{a}}^{\mathfrak{b}} - \sum_{\mathfrak{r}=\mathfrak{a}}^{\mathfrak{b}-1} \mathfrak{z}(\mathfrak{r})\Delta\mathfrak{y}(\mathfrak{r}). \tag{41}$$

while the forward difference operator Δ is defined by

$$\Delta\mathfrak{y}(\mathfrak{r}) = \mathfrak{y}(\mathfrak{r}+1) - \mathfrak{y}(\mathfrak{r}). \tag{42}$$

5.1. Global Stability of E_0

Theorem 6. *If $R_0 < 1$, E_0 is globally asymptotically stable for $\xi \in (0,1)$.*

Proof. We start by selecting the following Lyapunov function

$$Ł(t) = \sum_{i=1}^{m} S_i(t) - \frac{\theta}{\epsilon} - \frac{\theta}{\epsilon}\ln\left(\frac{\epsilon}{\theta}S_i(t)\right) + \frac{1}{2}I_i^2(t). \tag{43}$$

Employing the Caputo $\hbar$-difference operator and Lemma 1, we have

$$\begin{aligned}
{}_{\hbar}^{C}\Delta_{\mathfrak{a}}^{\alpha}Ł(t) &= \sum_{i=1}^{m} {}_{\hbar}^{C}\Delta_{\mathfrak{a}}^{\alpha}\left(S_i(t) - \frac{\theta}{\epsilon} - \frac{\theta}{\epsilon}\ln\left(\frac{\epsilon}{\theta}S_i(t)\right)\right) + \frac{1}{2}{}_{\hbar}^{C}\Delta_{\mathfrak{a}}^{\alpha}I_i^2(t),\\
&\leq \sum_{i=1}^{m}\left(1 - \frac{1}{S_i(t+\alpha\hbar)}\frac{\theta}{\epsilon}\right){}_{\hbar}^{C}\Delta_{\mathfrak{a}}^{\alpha}S_i(t) + I_i(t+\hbar\xi){}_{\hbar}^{C}\Delta_{\mathfrak{a}}^{\alpha}I_i(t),\\
&= \sum_{i=1}^{m}\left(1 - \frac{1}{S_i(t+\alpha\hbar)}\frac{\theta}{\epsilon}\right)\left(\frac{k_1}{d_{x^2}}\Delta^2 S_{i-1}(t+\hbar\xi) + \theta - \gamma S_i(t+\hbar\xi)\psi(I_i(t+\hbar\xi))\right.\\
&\quad \left.-\epsilon S_i(t+\hbar\xi)\right)\\
&\quad + I_i(t+\hbar\xi)\left(\frac{k_2}{d_{x^2}}\Delta^2 I_{i-1}(t+\hbar\xi) + \gamma S_i(t+\hbar\xi)\psi(I_i(t+\hbar\xi)) - (\nu+\sigma)I_i(t+\hbar\xi)\right),\\
&\leq \sum_{i=1}^{m}\frac{k_1}{d_{x^2}}\left(1 - \frac{1}{S_i(t+\alpha\hbar)}\frac{\theta}{\epsilon}\right)\Delta^2 S_{i-1}(t+\hbar\xi)\\
&\quad + \left(1 - \frac{1}{S_i(t+\alpha\hbar)}\frac{\theta}{\epsilon}\right)(\theta - \gamma S_i(t+\hbar\xi)\psi(I_i(t+\hbar\xi)) - \epsilon S_i(t+\hbar\xi))\\
&\quad + \frac{k_2}{d_{x^2}}I_i(t+\hbar\xi)\left(\Delta^2 I_{i-1}(t+\hbar\xi)\right) + I_i(t+\hbar\xi)(\gamma S_i(t+\hbar\xi)\psi(I_i(t+\hbar\xi))\\
&\quad -(\nu+\sigma)I_i(t+\hbar\xi)),\\
&= J_1(t) + J_2(t),
\end{aligned}$$

where

$$J_1(t) = \sum_{i=1}^{m}\frac{k_1}{d_{x^2}}\left(1 - \frac{1}{S_i(t+\alpha\hbar)}\frac{\theta}{\epsilon}\right)\Delta^2 S_{i-1}(t+\hbar\xi) + \frac{k_2}{d_{x^2}}I_i(t+\hbar\xi)\left(\Delta^2 I_{i-1}(t+\hbar\xi)\right),$$

and

$$\begin{aligned}
J_2(t) &= \sum_{i=1}^{m}\left(1 - \frac{1}{S_i(t+\alpha\hbar)}\frac{\theta}{\epsilon}\right)(\theta - \gamma S_i(t+\hbar\xi)\psi(I_i(t+\hbar\xi)) - \epsilon S_i(t+\hbar\xi))\\
&\quad + I_i(t+\hbar\xi)(\gamma S_i(t+\hbar\xi)\psi(I_i(t+\hbar\xi)) - (\nu+\sigma)I_i(t+\hbar\xi)),
\end{aligned}$$

We evaluate $J_1(t)$

$$
\begin{aligned}
J_1(t) \leq & \sum_{i=1}^{m} \frac{k_1}{d_{x^2}}\left(1-\frac{1}{S_i(t+\alpha\hbar)}\frac{\theta}{\epsilon}\right)(S_{i+1}(t+\alpha\hbar)-2S_i(t+\alpha\hbar)+S_{i-1}(t+\alpha\hbar)) \\
& -\frac{k_2}{d_{x^2}}(\Delta I_{i-1}(t+\hbar\xi))^2+\frac{k_2}{d_{x^2}}I_i(t+\hbar\xi)\Delta I_{i-1}(t+\hbar\xi)|_1^{m+1}, \\
\leq & \sum_{i=1}^{m}\frac{k_1}{d_{x^2}}(S_{i+1}(t+\alpha\hbar)-2S_i(t+\alpha\hbar)+S_{i-1}(t+\alpha\hbar)) \\
& -\frac{k_1}{d_{x^2}}\left(\frac{S_{i+1}(t+\alpha\hbar)}{S_i(t+\alpha\hbar)}+\frac{S_{i-1}(t+\alpha\hbar)}{S_i(t+\alpha\hbar)}-2\right)-\frac{k_2}{d_{x^2}}(\Delta I_{i-1}(t+\hbar\xi))^2, \\
\leq & \sum_{i=1}^{m}\frac{k_1}{d_{x^2}}(S_{m+1}(t+\alpha\hbar)-2S_m(t+\alpha\hbar)+S_0(t+\alpha\hbar)-S_1(t+\alpha\hbar)) \\
& -\frac{k_1}{d_{x^2}}\left(\frac{S_{i+1}(t+\alpha\hbar)}{S_i(t+\alpha\hbar)}-2+\frac{S_{i-1}(t+\alpha\hbar)}{S_i(t+\alpha\hbar)}\right)-\frac{k_2}{d_{x^2}}(\Delta I_{i-1}(t+\hbar\xi))^2
\end{aligned}
$$

According to [32], we have

$$
\frac{S_{i+1}(t+\alpha\hbar)}{S_i(t+\alpha\hbar)}-2+\frac{S_{i-1}(t+\alpha\hbar)}{S_i(t+\alpha\hbar)} \geq 0,
$$

which means $J_1(t) \leq 0$.

Now, we have

$$
\begin{aligned}
J_2(t) \leq & \sum_{i=1}^{m}\left(1-\frac{1}{S_i(t+\alpha\hbar)}\frac{\theta}{\epsilon}\right)(\theta-\epsilon S_i(t+\hbar\xi))-\gamma\left(1-\frac{1}{S_i(t+\alpha\hbar)}\frac{\theta}{\epsilon}\right)S_i(t+\hbar\xi)\psi(I_i(t+\hbar\xi)) \\
& +\gamma S_i(t+\hbar\xi)I_i(t+\hbar\xi\psi(I_i(t+\hbar\xi))-(\nu+\sigma)I_i^2(t+\hbar\xi), \\
\leq & \sum_{i=1}^{m}-\epsilon\left(\frac{S_i(t+\alpha\hbar)-\frac{\theta}{\epsilon}}{S_i(t+\alpha\hbar)}\right)\left(S_i(t+\hbar\xi)-\frac{\theta}{\epsilon}\right)+\frac{\theta}{\epsilon}\gamma\psi(I_i(t+\hbar\xi)))-(\nu+\sigma)I_i^2(t+\hbar\xi), \\
\leq & \sum_{i=1}^{m}-\epsilon\frac{\left(S_i(t+\alpha\hbar)-\frac{\theta}{\epsilon}\right)^2}{S_i(t+\alpha\hbar)}+\frac{\theta}{\epsilon}\gamma I_i^2(t+\hbar\xi)\psi'(I_i(0))-(\nu+\sigma)I_i^2(t+\hbar\xi), \\
\leq & (\nu+\sigma)\left(\frac{\theta\gamma}{\epsilon((\nu+\sigma))}\psi'(I_i(0))-1\right)\sum_{i=1}^{m}I_i^2(t+\hbar\xi), \\
= & (\nu+\sigma)(R_0-1)\sum_{i=1}^{m}I_i^2(t+\hbar\xi).
\end{aligned}
$$

Therefore, if $R_0-1<0$, then $J_2(t)<0$. Hence, ${}_{\hbar}^{C}\Delta_{\mathfrak{a}}^{\alpha}Ł(t) \leq 0$, and according to Theorem 6, E_0 is globally asymptotically stable. □

5.2. Global Stability of E^*

Theorem 7. *If $R_0>1$, E^* is globally asymptotically stable for $\xi \in (0,1)$.*

Proof. We use the exact same Lyapunov function as in [44] to show this result. For this, we take into consideration the following function:

$$
ł(z)=z-1-\ln(z),
$$

where $ł(1)=0$, and this function has a global minimum. Consider the non-negative function:

$$
Ł(t)=Ł_1(t)+Ł_2(t), \tag{44}
$$

where

$$Ł_1(t) = S^* ł\left(\frac{S_i(t)}{S^*}\right), \quad Ł_2(t) = I^* ł\left(\frac{I_i(t)}{I^*}\right) \tag{45}$$

First, we calculate ${}^{C}_{\hbar}\Delta^{\alpha}_{\mathfrak{a}} Ł_1(t)$

$$\begin{aligned}
{}^{C}_{\hbar}\Delta^{\alpha}_{\mathfrak{a}} Ł_1(t) &= \sum_{i=1}^{m} {}^{C}_{\hbar}\Delta^{\alpha}_{\mathfrak{a}} S^* ł\left(\frac{S_i(t)}{S^*}\right), \\
&\leq \sum_{i=1}^{m}\left(1 - \frac{S^*}{S_i(t+\hbar\xi)}\right) {}^{C}_{\hbar}\Delta^{\alpha}_{\mathfrak{a}} S_i(t), \\
&\leq \sum_{i=1}^{m}\left(1 - \frac{S^*}{S_i(t+\hbar\xi)}\right)\left(\frac{k_1}{d_{x^2}}\Delta^2 S_{i-1}(t+\hbar\xi) + \theta - \gamma S_i(t+\hbar\xi)\psi(I_i(t+\hbar\xi))\right. \\
&\left. -\epsilon S_i(t+\hbar\xi)\right), \\
&\leq \sum_{i=1}^{m} \frac{k_1}{d_x^2}(S_{m+1}(t+\alpha\hbar) - 2S_m(t+\alpha\hbar) + S_0(t+\alpha\hbar) - S_1(t+\alpha\hbar)) \\
&- \frac{k_1}{d_{x^2}}\left(\frac{S_{i+1}(t+\alpha\hbar)}{S_i(t+\alpha\hbar)} - 2 + \frac{S_{i-1}(t+\alpha\hbar)}{S_i(t+\alpha\hbar)}\right) \\
&+ \gamma S^*\psi(I^*)\left(1 - \frac{S^*}{S_i(t+\hbar\xi)}\right)\left(1 - \frac{S_i(t+\hbar\xi)\psi(I_i(t+\hbar\xi))}{S^*\psi(I^*)}\right) \\
&+ \epsilon S^*\left(1 - \frac{S^*}{S_i(t+\hbar\xi)}\right)\left(1 - \frac{S_i(t+\hbar\xi)}{S^*}\right), \\
&\leq \sum_{i=1}^{m} -\frac{k_1}{d_{x^2}}\left(\frac{S_{i+1}(t+\alpha\hbar)}{S_i(t+\alpha\hbar)} - 2 + \frac{S_{i-1}(t+\alpha\hbar)}{S_i(t+\alpha\hbar)}\right) \\
&- \gamma S^*\psi(I^*)\left(ł\left(\frac{S^*}{S_i(t+\alpha\hbar)}\right) - ł\left(\frac{\psi(I_i(t+\hbar\xi))}{\psi(I^*)}\right) + ł\left(\frac{S_i(I_i(t+\hbar\xi)\psi(I_i(t+\hbar\xi))}{S^*\psi(I^*)}\right)\right) \\
&- \epsilon S^*\left(ł\left(\frac{S^*}{S_i(t+\alpha\hbar)}\right)\right) + ł\left(\frac{S_i(t+\alpha\hbar)}{S^*}\right)
\end{aligned}$$

Now, we have

$$\begin{aligned}
{}^{C}_{\hbar}\Delta^{\alpha}_{\mathfrak{a}} Ł_2(t) &= \sum_{i=1}^{m} {}^{C}_{\hbar}\Delta^{\alpha}_{\mathfrak{a}} I^* ł\left(\frac{I_i(t)}{I^*}\right), \\
&\leq \sum_{i=1}^{m}\left(1 - \frac{I^*}{I_i(t+\hbar\xi)}\right) {}^{C}_{\hbar}\Delta^{\alpha}_{\mathfrak{a}} I_i(t), \\
&\leq \sum_{i=1}^{m}\left(1 - \frac{I^*}{I_i(t+\hbar\xi)}\right)\left(\frac{k_2}{d_{x^2}}\Delta^2 I_{i-1}(t+\hbar\xi) + \gamma S_i(t+\hbar\xi)\psi(I_i(t+\hbar\xi))\right. \\
&\left. -(\nu+\sigma)I_i(t+\hbar\xi)\right), \\
&\leq \sum_{i=1}^{m} \frac{k_2}{d_{x^2}}\left(1 - \frac{I^*}{I_i(t+\hbar\xi)}\right)(I_{i+1}(t+\hbar\xi) - 2I_i(t+\hbar\xi) + I_{i-1}(t+\hbar\xi)) \\
&+ \left(1 - \frac{I^*}{I_i(t+\hbar\xi)}\right)\left(\gamma S_i(t+\hbar\xi)\psi(I_i(t+\hbar\xi)) - \frac{\gamma S^*\psi(I^*)}{I^*}I_i(t+\hbar\xi)\right), \\
&\leq \sum_{i=1}^{m} \frac{k_2}{d_{x^2}}(I_{m+1}(t+\alpha\hbar) - 2I_m(t+\alpha\hbar) + I_0(t+\alpha\hbar) - I_1(t+\alpha\hbar)) \\
&- \frac{k_2}{d_{x^2}}\left(\frac{I_{i+1}(t+\alpha\hbar)}{I_i(t+\alpha\hbar)} - 2 + \frac{I_{i-1}(t+\alpha\hbar)}{I_i(t+\alpha\hbar)}\right) \\
&+ \gamma S^*\psi(I^*)\left(1 - \frac{I^*}{I_i(t+\hbar\xi)}\right)\left(\frac{S_i(t+\hbar\xi)\psi(I_i(t+\hbar\xi)}{S^*\psi(I^*)} - \frac{I_i(t+\hbar\xi)}{I^*}\right),
\end{aligned}$$

$$\leq \sum_{i=1}^{m} -\frac{k_2}{d_{x^2}}\left(\frac{I_{i+1}(t+\alpha\hbar)}{I_i(t+\alpha\hbar)} - 2 + \frac{I_{i-1}(t+\alpha\hbar)}{I_i(t+\alpha\hbar)}\right)$$
$$+\gamma S^*\psi(I^*)(\text{ł}\left(\frac{\psi(I_i(t+\hbar\xi)}{\psi(I^*)}\right) - \text{ł}\left(\frac{S^*}{S_i(t+\hbar\xi)}\right) - \text{ł}\left(\frac{I_i(t+\hbar\xi)}{I^*}\right)$$
$$-\text{ł}\left(\frac{I^*S_i(t+\hbar\xi)\psi(I_i(t+\hbar\xi)}{S^*\psi(I^*)I_i(t+\hbar\xi)}\right)).$$

We conclude that

$$
\begin{aligned}
{}^{C}_{\hbar}\Delta^{\alpha}_{a}\text{Ł}(t) &= {}^{C}_{\hbar}\Delta^{\alpha}_{a}\text{Ł}_1(t) + {}^{C}_{\hbar}\Delta^{\alpha}_{a}\text{Ł}_2(t),\\
&\leq \sum_{i=1}^{m} -\gamma S^*\psi(I^*)\left(\text{ł}\left(\frac{S^*}{S_i(t+\alpha\hbar)}\right) - \text{ł}\left(\frac{\psi(I_i(t+\hbar\xi))}{\psi(I^*)}\right) + \text{ł}\left(\frac{S_i(I_i(t+\hbar\xi)\psi(I_i(t+\hbar\xi))}{S^*\psi(I^*)}\right)\right)\\
&-\epsilon S^*\left(\text{ł}\left(\frac{S^*}{S_i(t+\alpha\hbar)}\right)\right) + \text{ł}\left(\frac{S_i(t+\alpha\hbar)}{S^*}\right) + \gamma S^*\psi(I^*)(\text{ł}\left(\frac{\psi(I_i(t+\hbar\xi)}{\psi(I^*)}\right)\\
&-\text{ł}\left(\frac{S^*}{S_i(t+\hbar\xi)}\right) - \text{ł}\left(\frac{I_i(t+\hbar\xi)}{I^*}\right) - \text{ł}\left(\frac{I^*S_i(t+\hbar\xi)\psi(I_i(t+\hbar\xi)}{S^*\psi(I^*)I_i(t+\hbar\xi)}\right)) < 0.
\end{aligned}
$$

As a result, the proof is complete. □

6. Numerical Simulations

In this section, we provide illustrative simulations that demonstrate the theoretical aspects related to stability of the discrete fractional epidemic reaction–diffusion system. Moreover, we explore the characteristics of solutions for the epidemiological fractional discrete reaction–diffusion systems (9) across various fractional-order values. These simulations have been conducted using the finite difference approach within the MATLAB software framework.

Example 1. *First, we consider the bilinear incidence rate $\psi(I) = I$, and System (9) becomes*

$$
\begin{cases}
{}^{C}_{\hbar}\Delta^{\xi}_{t_0} S_i(t) = \dfrac{k_1}{d_{x^2}}\Delta^2 S_{i-1}(t+\hbar\xi) + \theta - \gamma S_i(t+\hbar\xi)I_i(t+\hbar\xi) - \epsilon S_i(t+\hbar\xi),\\
{}^{C}_{\hbar}\Delta^{\xi}_{t_0} I_i(t) = \dfrac{k_2}{d_{x^2}}\Delta^2 I_{i-1}(t+\hbar\xi) + \gamma S_i(t+\hbar\xi)I_i(t+\hbar\xi) - (\nu+\sigma)I_i(t+\hbar\xi).
\end{cases}
\quad (46)
$$

We employ the following numerical solution, and System (46) seems to be as follows:

$$
\begin{cases}
S_i(\mathrm{n}\hbar) = \psi_1(x_i) + \dfrac{\hbar^{\alpha}}{\Gamma(\alpha)}\sum_{\mathrm{r}=1}^{\mathrm{n}}\dfrac{\Gamma(\mathrm{n}-\mathrm{r}+\alpha)}{\Gamma(\mathrm{n}-\mathrm{r}+1)}[\dfrac{S_{i+1}((\mathrm{r}-1)\hbar) - 2S_i((\mathrm{r}-1)\hbar) + S_{i-1}((\mathrm{r}-1)\hbar)}{d_{x^2}}\\
\qquad +\theta - \gamma S_i((\mathrm{r}-1)\hbar)I_i((\mathrm{r}-1)\hbar) - \epsilon S_i((\mathrm{r}-1)\hbar)],\\
I_i(\mathrm{n}\hbar) = \psi_2(x_i) + \dfrac{\hbar^{\alpha}}{\Gamma(\alpha)}\sum_{\mathrm{r}=1}^{n}\dfrac{\Gamma(\mathrm{n}-\mathrm{r}+\alpha)}{\Gamma(\mathrm{n}-\mathrm{r}+1)}[\dfrac{I_{i+1}((\mathrm{r}-1)\hbar) - 2I_i((\mathrm{r}-1)\hbar) + I_{i-1}((\mathrm{r}-1)\hbar)}{k^2}\\
\qquad +\gamma S_i((\mathrm{r}-1)\hbar)I_i((\mathrm{r}-1)\hbar) - (\nu+\sigma)I_i((\mathrm{r}-1)\hbar)],\\
1 \leq i \leq m,\\
n > 0.
\end{cases}
\quad (47)
$$

We provide the following parameters for System (46)

$$k_1 = 5, \quad k_2 = 2, \quad \theta = \frac{3}{5}, \quad \gamma = \frac{1}{2}, \quad \epsilon = \frac{2}{7}, \quad \nu = 0.2, \sigma = 0.7. \quad (48)$$

It is easy to see that R_0 stands at 0.6, a value below the limit of 1. In accordance with the principles outlined in Theorem 6, the disease-free equilibrium point $E_0 = (0.5, 0)$ within the *framework of System (46) is endowed with global stability, a substantiated assertion illustrated by Figures 1–3. Additionally, for the following parameters:*

$$k_1 = 2, \quad k_2 = 1, \quad \theta = 5, \quad \gamma = 1, \quad \epsilon = 2, \quad \nu = 0.2, \sigma = 0.3. \tag{49}$$

Within System (46), a single equilibrium point denoted as E^* prevails. The calculation of R_0 yields a value of 10, surpassing the threshold of 1 as prescribed by Equation (46). It is noteworthy that the endemic equilibrium point E^* within System (46), as substantiated by the aforementioned investigation, enjoys global stability, a conclusion supported by the evidence presented in Figure 4 stable.

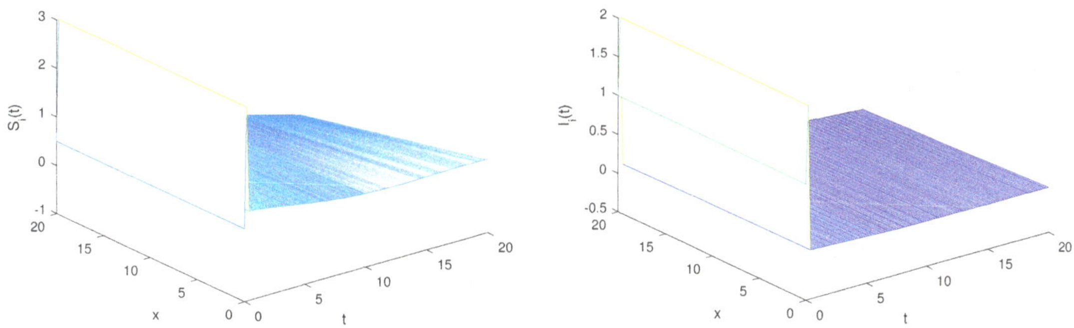

Figure 1. Dynamic behaviors of $S_i(t)$ and $I_i(t)$ for $N = 110$ and the periodic boundary condition $(S_0, I_0) = (3, 2)$ and the fractional order $\alpha = 0.8$.

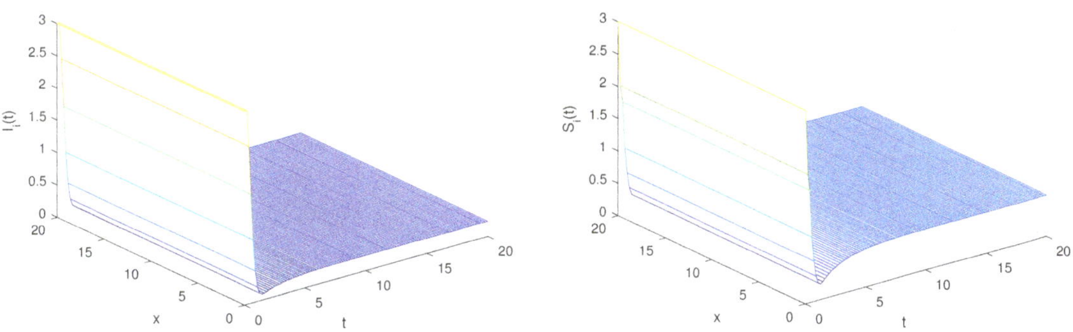

Figure 2. Dynamic behaviors of $S_i(t)$ and $I_i(t)$ for $N = 110$ and the periodic boundary condition $(S_0, I_0) = (3, 3)$ and the fractional order $\alpha = 0.5$.

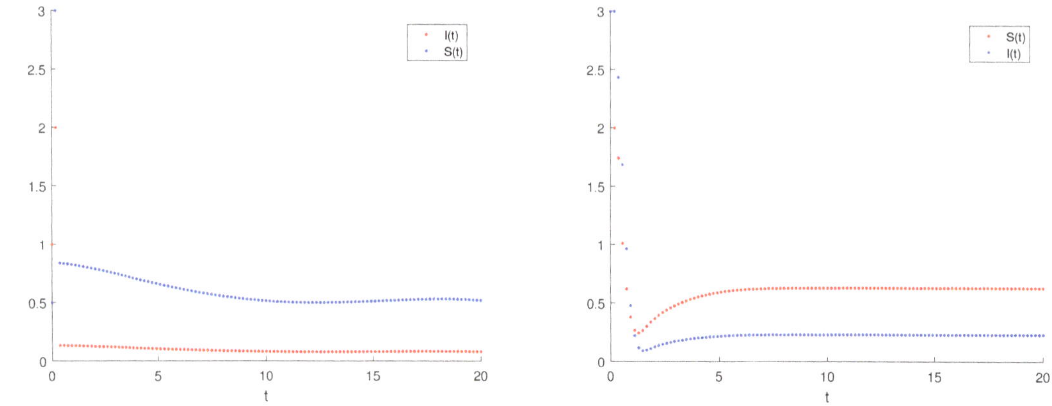

Figure 3. State trajectories of $S_i(t)$ and $I\_i(t)$ for $N = 110$.

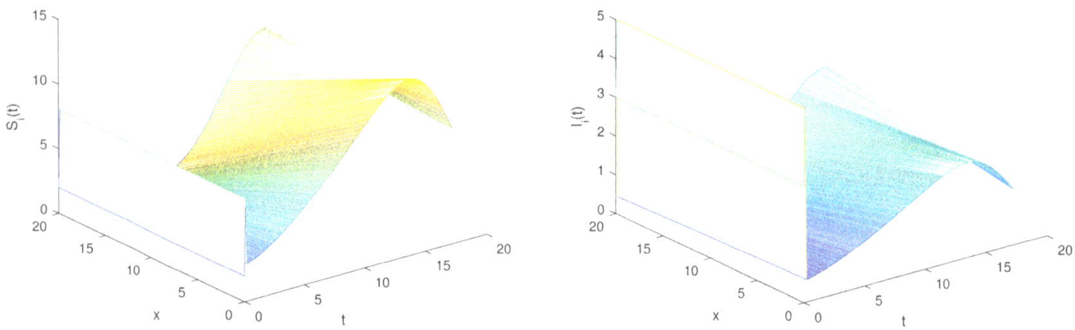

Figure 4. Dynamic behaviors of $S_i(t)$ and $I_i(t)$ for $N = 200$ and the periodic boundary condition $(S_0, I_0) = (6, 5)$ and the fractional order $\alpha = 0.1$.

Example 2. *We use the following incidence rate as an illustration:*

$$\psi(I) = \frac{I}{1 + \delta I}, \tag{50}$$

where δ is a positive parameter measuring the psychological or inhibitory effect. System (9) is expressed as follows:

$$\begin{cases} {}^{C}_{\hbar}\Delta^{\xi}_{t_0} S_i(t) = \dfrac{k_1}{d_{x^2}}\Delta^2 S_{i-1}(t + \hbar\xi) + \theta - \gamma \dfrac{S_i(t + \hbar\xi) I_i(t + \hbar\xi)}{1 + \delta I_i(t + \hbar\xi)} - \epsilon S_i(t + \hbar\xi), \\ {}^{C}_{\hbar}\Delta^{\xi}_{t_0} I_i(t) = \dfrac{k_2}{d_{x^2}}\Delta^2 I_{i-1}(t + \hbar\xi) + \gamma \dfrac{S_i(t + \hbar\xi) I_i(t + \hbar\xi)}{1 + \delta I_i(t + \hbar\xi)} - (\nu + \sigma) I_i(t + \hbar\xi). \end{cases} \tag{51}$$

and the numerical solution of System (51) is provided by

$$\begin{cases} S_i(n\hbar) = \psi_1(x_i) + \dfrac{\hbar^{\alpha}}{\Gamma(\alpha)} \sum_{\mathfrak{r}=1}^{n} \dfrac{\Gamma(n-\mathfrak{r}+\alpha)}{\Gamma(n-\mathfrak{r}+1)} [\dfrac{S_{i+1}((\mathfrak{r}-1)\hbar) - 2S_i((\mathfrak{r}-1)\hbar) + S_{i-1}((^{j}-1)\hbar)}{d_{x^2}} \\ \quad +\theta - \gamma \dfrac{S_i((\mathfrak{r}-1)\hbar) I_i((\mathfrak{r}-1)\hbar)}{1+\delta I_i((\mathfrak{r}-1)\hbar)} - \epsilon S_i((\mathfrak{r}-1)\hbar)], \\ I_i(n\hbar) = \psi_2(x_i) + \dfrac{\hbar^{\alpha}}{\Gamma(\alpha)} \sum_{\mathfrak{r}=1}^{n} \dfrac{\Gamma(n-\mathfrak{r}+\alpha)}{\Gamma(n-\mathfrak{r}+1)} [\dfrac{I_{i+1}((\mathfrak{r}-1)\hbar) - 2I_i((\mathfrak{r}-1)\hbar) + I_{i-1}((\mathfrak{r}-1)\hbar)}{k^2} \\ \quad +\gamma \dfrac{S_i((\mathfrak{r}-1)\hbar) I_i((\mathfrak{r}-1)\hbar)}{1+\delta I_i((\mathfrak{r}-1)\hbar)} - (\nu+\sigma) I_i((\mathfrak{r}-1)\hbar)], \\ 1 \le i \le m, \\ n > 0. \end{cases} \tag{52}$$

We supply the system with the following settings:

$$k_1 = 3, \quad k_2 = 2, \quad \theta = \frac{1}{2}, \quad \gamma = \frac{1}{2}, \quad \epsilon = \frac{2}{7}, \quad \nu = 0.2, \sigma = 0.7. \tag{53}$$

Computing R_0 *as* 0.9, *which is less than* 1, *is a straightforward task. It is noteworthy that the disease-free equilibrium point* $E_0 = (1, 0)$ *of System (51) exhibits global stability, as evidenced in Figures 5 and 6.*

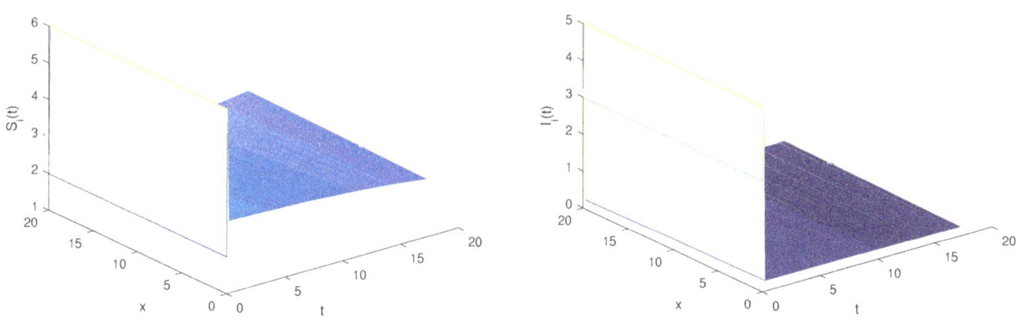

Figure 5. Dynamic behaviors of $S_i(t)$ and $I_i(t)$ for $N = 200$ and the periodic boundary condition $(S_0, I_0) = (6, 5)$ and the fractional order $\alpha = 0.7$.

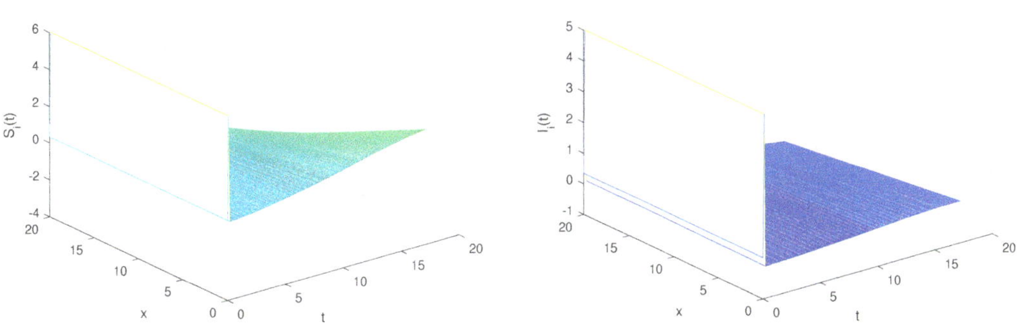

Figure 6. Dynamic behaviors of $S_i(t)$ and $I_i(t)$ for $N = 200$ and the periodic boundary condition $(S_0, I_0) = (6, 5)$ and the fractional order $\alpha = 0.2$.

7. Conclusions

This study explores the discrete version of the fractional reaction–diffusion epidemic system featuring a generalized incidence rate. Notably, when the fractional order approaches unity, the system naturally transitions into its discrete form through the use of the forward difference scheme. The core of our investigation lies in the analysis of the asymptotic stability of this discretized system. The conclusions drawn are in line with those of the corresponding continuous system, suggesting a compelling alignment between discrete and continuous dynamics. This insight emphasizes the capacity of a discrete system, precisely formulated using an L1 finite difference scheme and a second-order central difference scheme, to acquire key characteristics from the continuous version, including positivity, boundedness, and global stability of equilibrium points. Enhancing this theoretical investigation, our numerical simulations validate the proposed approach's efficiency and applicability. These simulations not only validate the feasibility of our methodology but also highlight its practical effectiveness in capturing system dynamics.

Author Contributions: Conceptualization, H.A.-T.; Methodology, A.A.-H.; Software, M.A.; Validation, O.A.; Formal analysis, M.S.A.; Investigation, A.H.; Writing—original draft, A.H.; Writing—review & editing, A.O.; Visualization, G.M.G. and N.A.-A.; Supervision, A.O. All authors have read and agreed to the published version of the manuscript.

Funding: This research received no external funding.

Institutional Review Board Statement: Not applicable.

Informed Consent Statement: Not applicable.

Data Availability Statement: Not applicable.

Conflicts of Interest: The authors declare no conflict of interest.

References

1. El-Saka, H.A.A. The fractional-order SIS epidemic model with variable population size. *J. Egypt. Math. Soc.* **2014**, *22*, 50–54. [CrossRef]
2. Vargas-De-León, C. Volterra-type Lyapunov functions for fractional-order epidemic systems. *Commun. Nonlinear Sci. Numer. Simul.* **2015**, *24*, 75–85. [CrossRef]
3. Ahmed, E.; Elgazzar, A.S. On fractional order differential equations model for nonlocal epidemics. *Phys. A Stat. Mech. Its Appl.* **2007**, *379*, 607–614. [CrossRef]
4. Rihan, F.A.; Al-Mdallal, Q.M.; AlSakaji, H.J.; Hashish, A. A fractional-order epidemic model with time-delay and nonlinear incidence rate. *Chaos Solitons Fractals* **2019**, *126*, 97–105. [CrossRef]
5. He, Z.Y.; Abbes, A.; Jahanshahi, H.; Alotaibi, N.D.; Wang, Y. Fractional-order discrete-time SIR epidemic model with vaccination: Chaos and complexity. *Mathematics*, **2022**, *10*, 165. [CrossRef]
6. Can, N.H.; Nikan, O.; Rasoulizadeh, M.N.; Jafari, H.; Gasimov, Y.S. Numerical computation of the time non-linear fractional generalized equal width model arising in shallow water channel. *Therm. Sci.* **2020**, *24*, 49–58. [CrossRef]
7. Asaduzzaman, M.; Kilicman, A.; Ali, M.Z. Presence and diversity of positive solutions for a Caputo-type fractional order nonlinear differential equation with an advanced argument. *J. Math. Comput. Sci* **2021**, **23**, 230–244. [CrossRef]
8. AlAhmad, R.; AlAhmad, Q.; Abdelhadi, A. Solution of fractional autonomous ordinary differential equations. *J. Math. Comput. Sci.* **2022**, *27*, 59–64. [CrossRef]
9. Henry, B.I.; Wearne, S.L. Fractional reaction–diffusion. *Phys. A Stat. Mech. Its Appl.* **2000**, *276*, 448–455. [CrossRef]
10. Seki, K.; Wojcik, M.; Tachiya, M. Fractional reaction-diffusion equation. *J. Chem. Phys.* **2003**, *119*, 2165–2170. [CrossRef]
11. Gafiychuk, V.; Datsko, B.; Meleshko, V. Mathematical modeling of time fractional reaction–diffusion systems. *J. Comput. Appl. Math.* **2008**, *220*, 215–225. [CrossRef]
12. Owolabi, K.M.; Atangana, A.; Akgul, A. Modelling and analysis of fractal-fractional partial differential equations: Application to reaction-diffusion model. *Alex. Eng. J.* **2020**, *59*, 2477–2490. [CrossRef]
13. Akram, T.; Abbas, M.; Ali, A. A numerical study on time fractional Fisher equation using an extended cubic B-spline approximation. *J. Math. Comput. Sci.* **2021**, *22*, 85–96. [CrossRef]
14. Zhou, P.; Ma, J.; Tang, J. Clarify the physical process for fractional dynamical systems. *Nonlinear Dyn.* **2020**, *100*, 2353–2364. [CrossRef]
15. Angstmann, C.N.; Henry, B.I.; McGann, A.V. A fractional-order infectivity SIR model. *Phys. A Stat. Mech. Appl.* **2016**, *452*, 86–93. [CrossRef]
16. Hethcote, H.W. The mathematics of infectious diseases. *SIAM Rev.* **2000**, *42*, 599–653. [CrossRef]

17. Almeida, R. Analysis of a fractional SEIR model with treatment. *Appl. Math. Lett.* **2018**, *84*, 56–62. [CrossRef]
18. Angstmann, C.N.; Donnelly, I.C.; Henry, B.I.; Jacobs, B.A.; Langlands, T.A.M.; Nichols, J.A. From stochastic processes to numerical methods: A new scheme for solving reaction subdiffusion fractional partial differential equations. *J. Comput. Phys.* **2016**, *307*, 508–534. [CrossRef]
19. Angstmann, C.N.; Donnelly, I.C.; Henry, B.I.; Nichols, J.A. A discrete time random walk model for anomalous diffusion. *J. Comput. Phys.* **2015**, *293*, 53–69. [CrossRef]
20. Angstmann, C.N.; Henry, B.I.; McGann, A.V. A fractional order recovery SIR model from a stochastic process. *Bull. Math. Biol.* **2016**, *78*, 468–499. [CrossRef]
21. Dababneh, A.; Djenina, N.; Ouannas, A.; Grassi, G.; Batiha, I.M.; Jebril, I.H. A new incommensurate fractional-order discrete COVID-19 model with vaccinated individuals compartment. *Fractal Fract.* **2022**, *6*, 456. [CrossRef]
22. Saadeh, R.; Abbes, A.; Al-Husban, A.; Ouannas, A.; Grassi, G. The Fractional Discrete Predator–Prey Model: Chaos, Control and Synchronization. *Fractal Fract.* **2023**, *7*, 120. [CrossRef]
23. Yi, N.; Liu, P.; Zhang, Q. Bifurcations analysis and tracking control of an epidemic model with nonlinear incidence rate. *Appl. Math. Model.* **2012**, *36*, 1678–1693. [CrossRef]
24. Chen-Charpentier, B.M.; Dimitrov, D.T.; Kojouharov, H.V. Numerical simulation of multi-species biofilms in porous media for different kinetics. *Math. Comput. Simul.* **2009**, *79*, 1846–1861. [CrossRef]
25. Jang, S.; Elaydi, S. Difference equations from discretization of a continuous epidemic model with immigration of infectives. *Math. Fac. Res.* **2003**, *11*, 93–105.
26. Sekiguchi, M.; Ishiwata, E. Global dynamics of a discretized SIRS epidemic model with time delay. *J. Math. Anal. Appl.* **2010**, *371*, 195–202. [CrossRef]
27. Almatroud, O.A.; Hioual, A.; Ouannas, A.; Grassi, G. On Fractional-Order Discrete-Time Reaction Diffusion Systems. *Mathematics* **2023**, *11*, 2447. [CrossRef]
28. Wu, G.C.; Baleanu, D.; Zeng, S.D.; Deng, Z.G. Discrete fractional diffusion equation. *Nonlinear Dyn.* **2015**, *80*, 281–286. [CrossRef]
29. Wu, G.C.; Baleanu, D.; Xie, H.P.; Zeng, S.D. Discrete fractional diffusion equation of chaotic order. *Int. J. Bifurc. Chaos* **2016**, *26*, 1650013. [CrossRef]
30. Lu, Z.; Yu, Y.; Xu, W.; Ren, G.; Meng, X. Global dynamics for a class of discrete fractional epidemic model with reaction-diffusion. *arXiv* **2022**, arXiv:2208.06548.
31. Abu Falahah, I.; Hioual, A.; Al-Qadri, M.O.; AL-Khassawneh, Y.A.; Al-Husban, A.; Hamadneh, T.; Ouannas, A. Synchronization of Fractional Partial Difference Equations via Linear Methods. *Axioms* **2023**, *12*, 728. [CrossRef]
32. Hamadneh, T.; Hioual, A.; Alsayyed, O.; AL-Khassawneh, Y.A.; Al-Husban, A.; Ouannas, A. Local Stability, Global Stability, and Simulations in a Fractional Discrete Glycolysis Reaction–Diffusion Model. *Fractal Fract.* **2023**, *7*, 587. [CrossRef]
33. Hamadneh, T.; Hioual, A.; Alsayyed, O.; Al-Khassawneh, Y.A.; Al-Husban, A.; Ouannas, A. The FitzHugh–Nagumo Model Described by Fractional Difference Equations: Stability and Numerical Simulation. *Axioms* **2023**, *12*, 806. [CrossRef]
34. Lu, Z.; Yu, Y.; Ren, G.; Xu, C.; Meng, X. Global dynamics for a class of reaction–diffusion multigroup SIR epidemic models with time fractional-order derivatives. *Nonlinear Anal. Model. Control.* **2022**, *27*, 142–162. [CrossRef]
35. Kelley, W.G.; Peterson, A.C. *Difference Equations: An Introduction with Applications*; Academic Press: Cambridge, MA, USA, 2001.
36. Sharkovsky, A.N.; Maistrenko, Y.L.T.; Romanenko, E.Y. *Difference Equations and Their Applications*; Springer Science & Business Media: Berlin/Heidelberg, Germany, 2012; Volume 250.
37. Baleanu, D.; Wu, G.C.; Bai, Y.R.; Chen, F.L. Stability analysis of Caputo–like discrete fractional systems. *Commun. Nonlinear Sci. Numer. Simul.* **2017**, *48*, 520–530. [CrossRef]
38. Hioual, A.; Ouannas, A.; Oussaeif, T.E.; Grassi, G.; Batiha, I.M.; Momani, S. On variable-order fractional discrete neural networks: Solvability and stability. *Fractal Fract.* **2022**, *6*, 119. [CrossRef]
39. Van den Driessche, P.; Watmough, J. Reproduction numbers and sub-threshold endemic equilibria for compartmental models of disease transmission. *Math. Biosci.*, **2002**, *180*, 29–48. [CrossRef]
40. Čermák, J.; Nechvátal, L. On a problem of linearized stability for fractional difference equations. *Nonlinear Dyn.* **2021**, *104*, 1253–1267. [CrossRef]
41. Xu, L.; Zhao, L.J.; Chang, Z.X.; Feng, J.T.; Zhang, G. Turing instability and pattern formation in a semi-discrete Brusselator model. *Mod. Phys. Lett. B* **2013**, *27*, 1350006. [CrossRef]
42. Franco-Perez, L.; Fernandez-Anaya, G.; Quezada-Téllez, L. A. On stability of nonlinear nonautonomous discrete fractional Caputo systems. *J. Math. Anal. Appl.*, **2020**, *487*, 124021. [CrossRef]
43. Elaydi, S. *An Introduction to Difference Equations*; Springer: San Antonio, TX, USA, 2015
44. Anakira, N.; Hioual, A.; Ouannas, A.; Oussaeif, T.E.; Batiha, I.M. Global Asymptotic Stability for Discrete-Time SEI Reaction-Diffusion Model. In *International Conference on Mathematics and Computations*; Springer Nature: Singapore, 2022; pp. 345–357.

fractal and fractional

Article

A Study on Generalized Degenerate Form of 2D Appell Polynomials via Fractional Operators

Mohra Zayed [1,*,†] **and Shahid Ahmad Wani** [2,*,†]

[1] Mathematics Department, College of Science, King Khalid University, Abha 61413, Saudi Arabia
[2] Department of Applied Sciences, Symbiosis Institute of Technology, Symbiosis International (Deemed) University, Pune 412115, Maharashtra, India
* Correspondence: mzayed@kku.edu.sa (M.Z.); shahidwani177@gmail.com or shahid.wani@sitpune.edu.in (S.A.W.)
† These authors contributed equally to this work.

Abstract: This paper investigates the significance of generating expressions, operational principles, and defining characteristics in the study and development of special polynomials. The focus is on a novel generalized family of degenerate 2D Appell polynomials, which were defined using a fractional operator. Motivated by inquiries into degenerate 2D bivariate Appell polynomials, this research reveals that well-known 2D Appell polynomials and simple Appell polynomials can be regarded as specific instances within this new family for certain values. This paper presents the operational rule, generating relation, determinant form, and recurrence relations for this generalized family. Furthermore, it explores the practical applications of these degenerate 2D Appell polynomials and establishes their connections with equivalent results for the generalized family of degenerate 2D Bernoulli, Euler, and Genocchi polynomials.

Keywords: fractional operators; Euler's integral; degenerate special polynomials; 2D Appell polynomials; determinant representation; operational connection; applications

1. Introduction

Special polynomials form a distinct group of mathematical functions known for their exceptional and valuable properties, rendering them indispensable and captivating across diverse domains such as mathematics, physics, engineering, and other scientific disciplines. What sets these polynomials apart from regular ones is their distinct attributes, including specific generating expressions, operational rules, and other defining characteristics. Special polynomials and fractional operators have a noteworthy relationship within the realm of mathematics. Fractional operators introduce a new dimension for ordinary differentiation and integration by extending these operations to non-integer orders, which are often represented by fractional exponents. Special polynomials, on the other hand, are a class of mathematical functions with unique properties and generated expressions. The combination of special polynomials with fractional operators leads to the development of more sophisticated and versatile mathematical tools. By applying fractional operators to special polynomials, researchers can create new families of fractional special polynomials, which can offer enhanced capabilities in solving complex mathematical problems and the modeling of various phenomena. This synergy has proven valuable in numerous fields, including mathematical physics, signal processing, and control theory. Fractional special polynomials provide a powerful framework for addressing problems involving fractional calculus and fractional differential equations, offering insights and solutions beyond what traditional integer-order polynomials can achieve. As a result, the study of special polynomials in conjunction with fractional operators continues to be an active and fruitful area of research in mathematics and its applications.

The idea of fractional calculus, which includes integrating non-integral orders, has a long history. Its roots may be found in the beginnings of differential calculus when, in the late 17th century, the renowned mathematician and philosopher Leibniz—who competed with Newton—offered the idea and possibility of a fractional derivative of order 1/2. But it was not until Liouville produced a devoted effort on this matter that a careful and full investigation of this subject was made, thus producing accurate and rigorous research. Both differential and integral equations can be solved with the use of integral transforms. As seen in the works of Oldham and Widder [1,2], fractional operators have long piqued the curiosity of mathematicians and engineers. According to the academic publications of [1,2], the use of integral transforms to solve fractional derivatives may be traced back to the contributions of Riemann and Liouville. The synergistic utilization of integral transformations and specialized polynomials offers a powerful approach in dealing with fractional derivatives. This strategy has been acknowledged as a potent instrument; see, for instance [3,4], where the authors of those studies underline the importance of this combination strategy and give further information about the real-world uses and theoretical developments made possible by the use of integral transformations and specific polynomials when dealing with fractional derivatives. The advantages of this technique have been thoroughly investigated by researchers and practitioners, thus contributing to a greater knowledge of fractional calculus and its wide variety of applications.

A reliable and efficient method for managing fractional derivatives is provided by the combination of integral transformations and special polynomials. This strategy has drawn a lot of interest and is recognized as a potent instrument in the industry. Researchers and practitioners can develop effective techniques for analyzing and resolving fractional differential equations by combining integral transforms, such as Laplace or Fourier transforms, with unique polynomials, such as Hermite, Laguerre, or Chebyshev polynomials. These methods have proven useful in a variety of industries, including engineering, banking, and signal processing, as well as in physics.

In [3], Dattoli and coauthors explored the potential of using integral transforms in a wider context. In their research, they examine using Euler's integral to extend the use of integral transforms beyond their typical limitations. A comprehensive foundation for increasing the applicability and efficiency of integral transformations in numerous domains is provided by Euler's integral:

$$\sigma^{-\mu} = \frac{1}{\Gamma(\mu)} \int_0^\infty e^{-\sigma u} u^{\mu-1} du, \tag{1}$$

where σ and μ are complex numbers with positive real parts and satisfy $\min\{\mathrm{Re}(\mu), \mathrm{Re}(\sigma)\} > 0$. Researchers may tackle a larger range of issues by bringing Euler's integral within the framework of integral transformations, enabling for the study and solution of challenging mathematical equations found in a variety of domains. This broader framework allows for novel perspectives in terms of investigating fractional derivatives and the implications that they have, thus producing original ideas and approaches to tackling problems. This study shows the potential for further advancement in this area, and provides both researchers and practitioners with a useful tool for solving difficult issues involving fractional derivatives in a broader context.

Further, in [3], it is evident that, for derivatives of a first and second order, the listed axioms hold:

$$\left(\beta - \frac{\partial}{\partial p}\right)^{-\mu} g(p) = \frac{1}{\Gamma(\mu)} \int_0^\infty e^{-\beta t} t^{\mu-1} e^{u\frac{\partial}{\partial p}} g(p) du = \frac{1}{\Gamma(\mu)} \int_0^\infty e^{-\beta t} u^{\mu-1} g(p+u) du \tag{2}$$

$$\left(\beta - \frac{\partial^2}{\partial p^2}\right)^{-\mu} g(p) = \frac{1}{\Gamma(\mu)} \int_0^\infty e^{-\beta u} u^{\mu-1} e^{u\frac{\partial^2}{\partial p^2}} g(p) du, \tag{3}$$

A synergistic combination of exponential operators and suitable integral representations may be used to efficiently address fractional operators. Researchers and practitioners can efficiently handle fractional operators in a streamlined manner by making use of the characteristics of exponential operators and by choosing appropriate integral representations. This method makes it possible to explore cutting-edge mathematical ideas and makes it easier to accurately and quickly analyze fractional derivatives. A strong foundation for handling fractional operators is provided by the use of exponential operators and specialized integral representations, which leads to improved approaches and solutions across a range of mathematical and scientific areas.

The Appell polynomials [5] find numerous applications in diverse fields of mathematics and physics, including algebraic geometry, differential equations, and quantum mechanics. They demonstrate significant connections with other special function families, such as hypergeometric functions and Jacobi polynomials. When two Appell polynomials are composed, they yield another Appell polynomial, thereby forming an abelian group under composition. This group property arises due to the Appell polynomials' differential equation being a specific case of the Heun equation, known for its Galois group being an abelian extension of the differential field generated by the equation's solutions.

Precisely speaking, the sequences of Appell polynomials form an abelian group when composed, which is where the constant polynomial sequence serves as the identity element. The commutativity of this group arises from the inherent symmetry of the Appell polynomials. The group property of the Appell polynomials carries significant implications across various fields of mathematics and physics, particularly in the realms of differential equation theory and integrable systems research. By leveraging this group property, one can derive recursion relations for the coefficients of Appell polynomials, which prove valuable in computing special polynomial values. Furthermore, this property allows for the construction of novel families of Appell polynomials by composing existing ones, leading to the exploration and discovery of new intriguing mathematical structures.

Appell [5] in the 19th century presented a family of polynomials known as the Appell polynomial family. It is given by $\mathbb{R}_k(p),\ p \in \mathbb{C}$, which satisfies the following differential equation:

$$\frac{d}{dp}\mathbb{R}_k(p) = k\,\mathbb{R}_{k-1}(p), \qquad k \in \mathbb{N}_0 \tag{4}$$

and generates the following relation expression:

$$\mathbb{R}(u)\,e^{pu} = \sum_{k=0}^{\infty} \mathbb{R}_k(p)\frac{u^k}{k!}, \tag{5}$$

where $\mathbb{R}(u)$ is represented by

$$\mathbb{R}(u) = \sum_{k=0}^{\infty} \mathbb{R}_k \frac{u^k}{k!}, \tag{6}$$

which is a formal power series with complex coefficients $\mathbb{R}_k$, $k = 0, 1, 2, \cdots, \mathbb{R}_0 \neq 0$.

These polynomials were introduced by the French mathematician Paul Appell in his research on elliptic functions. The generating relation (5) offers a method through which to represent the exponential function e^{pu} as an infinite sum of the polynomials $\mathbb{R}_k(p)$, which are multiplied by powers of u. This relation proves useful in simplifying certain integrals and in evaluating specific functions. In mathematical physics, the Appell polynomials find numerous applications, particularly in the study of quantum mechanics, electromagnetism, and fluid dynamics. They play a significant role in these fields, enhancing our understanding, and facilitating calculations in various contexts.

Recently, the 2D Appell polynomials [6] have been represented by the following generating relation:

$$\sum_{l=0}^{\infty} {}_{\mathbb{G}}\mathbb{R}_l^{(j)}(p,q)\frac{u^l}{l!} = \mathbb{R}(u)\exp(pt+qt^j), \quad p,q \in \mathbb{C} \tag{7}$$

where $\mathbb{R}(u)$ is given by (6), and acts as a solution of the following heat equation:

$$\begin{aligned} \frac{\partial}{\partial q}\{{}_{\mathbb{G}}\mathbb{R}_l^{(j)}(p,q)\} &= \frac{\partial^j}{\partial p^j}\{{}_{\mathbb{G}}\mathbb{R}_l^{(j)}(p,q)\} \\ \text{and} \qquad {}_{\mathbb{G}}\mathbb{R}_l^{(j)}(p,0) &= R_l(p). \end{aligned} \tag{8}$$

These polynomials are significant in numerous branches of mathematics, such as enumerative combinatorics, algebraic combinatorics, and applied mathematics. These polynomials are employed to solve certain ordinary differential equations in approximation theory and physics. Hermite polynomials are a noteworthy subgroup of these polynomial sequences. The group of orthogonal polynomials known as Hermite polynomials was first developed by Hermite himself [7]. Numerous mathematical, physics, engineering, and computer science problems may be solved using these polynomials. Harmonic oscillator wave functions are described by Hermite polynomials. The quantum theory of light and research on the hydrogen atom both heavily rely on them. Additionally, the probability distribution function of the kinetic energy of gas molecule molecules is derived using these polynomials. They are also employed to examine the energy distribution of a harmonic oscillator.

Many writers are interested in developing and discovering various properties of degenerate special polynomials (for instance [8–13]). Wani and colleagues recently produced several doped polynomials of a certain type, as well as identified their different traits and behaviors, which are crucial from an engineering perspective (for example [14–18]). Examples of these significant properties involve determinant forms, operational formalism, approximation properties, poly forms, degenerate forms, summation formulas, approximation quality, explicit and implicit formulae, generating expressions, etc.

The study of degenerate forms of special functions is crucial for understanding the mathematical foundations of many physical phenomena. The degenerate polynomials are used to describe the behavior of quantum systems, such as the quantum harmonic oscillator. These functions have found wide-ranging applications in various fields of science and engineering, and their significance has been acknowledged in both pure mathematics and practical contexts. Future discoveries and breakthroughs are anticipated as the theory of special functions continues to progress (see for instance [9,10]).

Recently, Shahid et al. [19] introduced 2-variable degenerate Appell polynomials by generating the following expression:

$$\sum_{s=0}^{\infty} \mathbb{G}_s^{[j]}(p,q;\lambda)\frac{u^s}{s!} = \mathbb{R}(u)(1+\lambda)^{(\frac{pu+qu^j}{\lambda})}, \ \lambda \in \mathbb{C} \tag{9}$$

and the operational representation as follows:

$$\exp\left(q\frac{\lambda}{log(1+\lambda)}\frac{\partial^j}{\partial p^j}\right)\mathbb{R}_s(p;\lambda) = \mathbb{G}_s^{[j]}(p,q;\lambda). \tag{10}$$

It is evident that degenerate 2D bivariate Appell polynomials reduce to degenerate Appell polynomials [20], which are provided by $v \ \rightarrow 0$ as follows:

$$\sum_{s=0}^{\infty} \mathbb{G}_m^{[j]}(p,0;\lambda)\frac{u^s}{s!} = \mathbb{R}(u)(1+\ \lambda)^{\frac{pu}{\lambda}} = \sum_{s=0}^{\infty} \mathbb{R}_s(p;\lambda)\frac{u^s}{s!}. \tag{11}$$

Also, if $(1+\lambda)^{\frac{pu}{\lambda}} \rightarrow \exp(pu)$, then Expression (11) reduces to (5).

Moreover, as $(1+\lambda)^{\frac{pu}{\lambda}} \rightarrow \exp(pu)$ and $(1+\lambda)^{\frac{qu^j}{\lambda}} \rightarrow \exp(qu^j)$, then (9) reduces to (7).

In the area of mathematical analysis, fractional calculus is one of the most swiftly developing areas. Applications in a wide range of fields, including biology, physics, electrochemistry, economics, probability theory, and statistics, are possible. Fractional operators provide a more precise depiction of intricate systems that cannot be adequately represented by derivatives of an integer order. Consequently, they find extensive use across various disciplines, including multiple branches of mathematics, physics [21] engineering [22], and finance [23]. For instance, fractional operators are employed to describe the characteristics of viscoelastic materials, biological systems, and electrical networks [24]. Moreover, in the realm of electromagnetics, fractional operators play a crucial role in elucidating the behavior of electromagnetic waves within media that possess fractional-order dielectric and magnetic properties [25]. Further applications of fractional calculus can be observed in [26].

The research conducted in this paper draws inspiration and motivation from the groundbreaking work of Dattoli and colleagues [3] as well as from Wani et al. [19], who highlighted the immense significance of fractional operators. In this study, we construct the generalized form of a degenerate special polynomial family by utilizing the fractional operator known as Euler's integral (1). We introduce the generalized degenerate 2D Appell polynomial family, denoted as ${}_{\mathbb{G}}\mathbb{R}^{[j]}_{s,\mu}(p,q;\lambda,\beta)$, through the generating expression given in the form of the following definition:

Definition 1.

$$\frac{\mathbb{R}(u)(1+\lambda)^{\frac{pu}{\lambda}}}{\left[\beta - \frac{(qu^j)}{\lambda}\, log(1+\lambda)\right]^{\mu}} = \sum_{s=0}^{\infty} {}_{\mathbb{G}}\mathbb{R}^{[j]}_{s,\mu}(p,q;\lambda,\beta)\frac{u^s}{s!}. \tag{12}$$

The application of these degenerate special polynomials extends to image processing and computer vision, thereby facilitating tasks such as image enhancement and feature extraction. Additionally, they find utility in financial mathematics, providing models to analyze the behavior of stock prices, interest rates, and other financial variables.

The purpose of this article is to carry out a comprehensive analysis of the properties of the generalized versions of degenerate special polynomials that are associated with 2D Appell polynomials. This research makes extensive use of integral transformations and operational ideas. This paper's major contributions are included in Sections 2 and 3, which follow an extensive introduction that highlights significant data that were previously known. In Section 2, the novelty of the discovery is demonstrated by using fractional operators to build a generalized version of degenerate 2D Appell polynomials in the form of operational formulae and generating functions. Further study of these established polynomials led to the development of a summation formula and recurrence relations. In Section 3, the determinant form for these polynomials and their special cases are deduced. This article explores the potential applications for exceptional outcomes in Section 4 along with the generalized degenerate 2D Appell polynomials; furthermore, these applications also contain comparable results for degenerate 2D-Bernoulli and 2D-Euler polynomials. By looking at various applications, this article demonstrates the broad applicability and relevance of the discovered results in several disciplines of mathematics and beyond.

2. Generalized Degenerate 2D Appell Polynomials

This section examines the newly discovered class of generalized degenerate 2D Appell polynomials. Moreover, these polynomials are also produced with a number of properties. First, we derive the operational connection of the generalized degenerate 2D Appell polynomials by demonstrating the following result:

Theorem 1. *The generalized degenerate 2D Appell polynomials* ${}_{\mathbb{G}}\mathbb{R}^{[j]}_{s,\mu}(p,q;\lambda,\beta)$ *satisfy the following operational connection:*

$$\left(\beta - q\frac{\lambda}{\log(1+\lambda)}\frac{\partial^j}{\partial p^j}\right)^{-\mu}\mathbb{R}_s(p;\lambda) = {}_{\mathbb{G}}\mathbb{R}^{[j]}_{s,\mu}(p,q;\lambda,\beta). \tag{13}$$

Proof. On substituting σ by $\left(\beta - \frac{\lambda}{log(1+\lambda)}\frac{\partial^j}{\partial p^j}\right)$ in Expression (1) of Euler's integral, and then operating the resultant equation on $\mathbb{R}_s(p;\lambda)$, we find

$$\left(\beta - \frac{\lambda}{log(1+\lambda)}\frac{\partial^j}{\partial p^j}\right)^{-\mu}\mathbb{R}_s(p;\lambda) = \frac{1}{\Gamma(\mu)}\int_0^\infty e^{-\beta u}u^{\mu-1}\exp\left(qu\frac{\lambda}{log(1+\lambda)}\frac{\partial^j}{\partial q^j}\right)\mathbb{R}_s(p;\lambda)du. \tag{14}$$

It is clear from Equation (10) that the following outcome is attained from the following (14):

$$\left(\beta - \frac{\lambda}{log(1+\lambda)}\frac{\partial^j}{\partial p^j}\right)^{-\mu}\mathbb{R}_s(p;\lambda) = \frac{1}{\Gamma(\mu)}\int_0^\infty e^{-\beta u}u^{\mu-1}{}_{\mathbb{G}}\mathbb{R}^{[j]}_s(p,qu;\lambda)du. \tag{15}$$

By applying the transformation described on the right-hand side of Equation (15), a novel set of polynomials is introduced. These polynomials are denoted by ${}_{\mathbb{G}}\mathbb{R}^{[j]}_{s,\mu}(p,q;\lambda;\beta)$, and are referred to as the generalized degenerate 2D Appell polynomials. Thus, we establish the following relationship:

$$\frac{1}{\Gamma(\mu)}\int_0^\infty e^{-\beta u}u^{\mu-1}{}_{\mathbb{G}}\mathbb{R}^{[j]}_s(p,qu;\lambda)du = {}_{\mathbb{G}}\mathbb{R}^{[j]}_{s,\mu}(p,q;\lambda;\beta). \tag{16}$$

Therefore, on consideration of Expressions (15) and (16), Assertion (13) is established. □

Remark 1. *The generalized degenerate 2D Appell polynomials can be reduced to the generalized degenerate 2-variable Hermite–Appell polynomials if* $j = 2$*. As a result, the following operational connection is established by replacing* $j = 2$ *in the left-hand side of Equation* (13) *and representing the resulting generalized degenerate 2-variable Hermite–Appell polynomials on the right-hand side as* ${}_{\mathbb{G}}\mathbb{R}^{[2]}_{s,\mu}(p,q;\lambda,\beta)$*, which are expressed as follows:*

$$\left(\beta - q\frac{\lambda}{\log(1+\lambda)}\frac{\partial^2}{\partial p^2}\right)^{-\mu}\mathbb{R}_s(p;\lambda) = {}_{\mathbb{G}}\mathbb{R}^{[2]}_{s,\mu}(p,q;\lambda,\beta).$$

Remark 2. *The generalized degenerate 2D Appell polynomials can be reduced to the generalized 2D Appell polynomials if* $\lambda \to 0$*. As a result, the following operational connection is established by replacing* $\lambda \to 0$ *in the left-hand side of Equation* (13) *and representing the resulting generalized Appell polynomials on the right-hand side as* ${}_{\mathbb{G}}\mathbb{R}_{s,\mu}(p;q;\beta)$*, which are expressed as follows:*

$$\left(\beta - q\frac{\partial^j}{\partial p^j}\right)^{-\mu}\mathbb{R}_s(p) = {}_{\mathbb{G}}\mathbb{R}^{[j]}_{s,\mu}(p,q;\beta).$$

Theorem 2. *For the generalized degenerate 2D Appell polynomials* ${}_{\mathbb{G}}\mathbb{R}^{[j]}_{s,\mu}(p,q;\lambda;\beta)$*, the listed generating expression holds true:*

$$\frac{\mathbb{R}(u)(1+\lambda)^{\frac{pu}{\lambda}}}{\left[\beta - \frac{qu^j}{\lambda}\,log(1+\lambda)\right]^{\mu}} = \sum_{s=0}^{\infty}{}_{\mathbb{G}}\mathbb{R}^{[j]}_{s,\mu}(p,q;\lambda,\beta)\frac{u^s}{s!}. \tag{17}$$

Proof. On multiplication of Expression (16) on b/s with $\frac{u^s}{s!}$, and by subsequently summing over all values of s, it follows that

$$\sum_{s=0}^{\infty}\frac{1}{\Gamma(\mu)}\int_0^\infty e^{-\beta u}u^{\mu-1}{}_{\mathbb{G}}\mathbb{R}^{[j]}_s(p,qu;\lambda)du\frac{u^s}{s!} = \sum_{s=0}^{\infty}{}_{\mathbb{G}}\mathbb{R}^{[j]}_{s,\mu}(p,q;\lambda;\beta)\frac{u^s}{s!}. \tag{18}$$

Thus, in view of Expression (9) on the l.h.s. of the previous equation, we find

$$\frac{1}{\Gamma(\mu)}\int_0^\infty \mathbb{R}(u)(1+\lambda)^{\frac{pu}{\lambda}} e^{-\left(\beta-\frac{qu^j}{\lambda}\, log(1+\lambda)\right)u} u^{\mu-1}du = \sum_{s=0}^{\infty} {}_{\mathbb{G}}\mathbb{R}^{[j]}_{s,\mu}(p,q;\lambda;\beta)\frac{u^s}{s!}. \tag{19}$$

on consideration of the integral Expression (1), Assertion (17) is deduced. □

Remark 3. *The generalized degenerate 2D Appell polynomials can be reduced to the generalized degenerate 2-variable Hermite–Appell polynomials if $j=2$. As a result, the following generating expression is established by replacing $j=2$ on the left-hand side of Equation (13) and by representing the resulting generalized degenerate 2-variable Hermite–Appell polynomials on the right-hand side as ${}_{\mathbb{G}}\mathbb{R}^{[2]}_{s,\mu}(p,q;\lambda,\beta)$, which are expressed as follows:*

$$\frac{\mathbb{R}(u)(1+\lambda)^{\frac{pu}{\lambda}}}{\left[\beta-\frac{qu^2}{\lambda}\,\log(1+\lambda)\right]^\mu} = \sum_{s=0}^{\infty} {}_{\mathbb{G}}\mathbb{R}^{[2]}_{s,\mu}(p,q;\lambda,\beta)\frac{u^s}{s!}. \tag{20}$$

Remark 4. *The generalized degenerate 2D Appell polynomials can be reduced to the generalized 2D Appell polynomials if $\lambda \to 0$. As a result, the following generating expression is established by replacing $\lambda \to 0$ on the left-hand side of Equation (13) and by representing the resulting generalized Appell polynomials on the right-hand side as ${}_{\mathbb{G}}\mathbb{R}_{s,\mu}(p;q;\beta)$, which are expressed as follows:*

$$\frac{\mathbb{R}(u)e^{pu}}{\left[\beta-qu^j\right]^\mu} = \sum_{s=0}^{\infty} {}_{\mathbb{G}}\mathbb{R}^{[j]}_{s,\mu}(p,q;\beta)\frac{u^s}{s!}. \tag{21}$$

Remark 5. *The generalized degenerate 2D Appell polynomials can be reduced to the generalized degenerate Gould-Hopper polynomials if $\mathbb{R}(u)=1$. As a result, the following generating expression is established by taking $\mathbb{R}(u)=1$ on the left-hand side of Equation (13) and by representing the resulting generalized degenerate Gould-Hopper polynomials on the right-hand side as $\mathbb{G}^{[j]}_{s,\mu}(p,q;\lambda,\beta)$, which are expressed as follows:*

$$\frac{(1+\lambda)^{\frac{pu}{\lambda}}}{\left[\beta-\frac{(qu^j)}{\lambda}\, log(1+\lambda)\right]^\mu} = \sum_{s=0}^{\infty} \mathbb{G}^{[j]}_{s,\mu}(p,q;\lambda,\beta)\frac{u^s}{s!}. \tag{22}$$

Next, in view of the above Expression (22), the following generated expression holds true for the generalized degenerate 2D Appell polynomials ${}_{\mathbb{G}}\mathbb{R}^{[j]}_{s,\mu}(p,q;\lambda,\beta)$ in terms of the generalized degenerate degenerate Gould-Hopper polynomials $\mathbb{G}^{[j]}_{s,\mu}(p,q;\lambda,\beta)$, which are expressed as follows:

Theorem 3. *For the generalized degenerate 2D Appell polynomials ${}_{\mathbb{G}}\mathbb{R}^{[j]}_{s,\mu}(p,q;\lambda,\beta)$, the succeeding generating expression holds true:*

$${}_{\mathbb{G}}\mathbb{R}^{[j]}_{s,\mu}(p,q;\lambda,\beta) = \sum_{k=0}^{s}\binom{s}{k}\mathbb{R}_k\mathbb{G}^{[j]}_{s-k,\mu}(p,q;\lambda,\beta). \tag{23}$$

Proof. Expression (12), in terms of Expressions (6) and (22), can be written as

$$\frac{\mathbb{R}(u)(1+\lambda)^{\frac{pu}{\lambda}}}{\left[\beta-\frac{(qu^j)}{\lambda}\, log(1+\lambda)\right]^\mu} = \sum_{k=0}^{\infty}\mathbb{R}_k\frac{u^k}{k!}\sum_{s=0}^{\infty} {}_{\mathbb{G}}\mathbb{R}^{[j]}_{s,\mu}(p,q;\lambda,\beta)\frac{u^s}{s!}. \tag{24}$$

Therefore, in view of the Cauchy product rule [27] (p. 85, Equation (5)), Assertion (23) is established. □

Next, by taking into account the generating relation of generalized degenerate 2D Appell polynomials ${}_{\mathbb{G}}\mathbb{R}^{[j]}_{s,\mu}(p,q;\lambda,\beta)$, the recurrence relations for these polynomials can be deduced. Equations that recursively specify the terms of the sequence or array can be used to build recurrence relations for a sequence or multidimensional array of values. These relationships enable us to express each subsequent term in relation to the preceding ones. When we wish to construct the values of a sequence or array iteratively, beginning with one or more initial terms, recurrence relations come in extremely handy. By taking derivatives with respect to p, q, and the β for generating Expression (17), the succeeding recurrence relations of polynomials ${}_{\mathbb{G}}\mathbb{R}^{[j]}_{s,\mu}(p,q;\lambda,\beta)$ are deduced as follows:

$$\begin{aligned}\frac{\lambda}{\log(1+\lambda)}\frac{\partial}{\partial p}\left({}_{\mathbb{G}}\mathbb{R}^{[j]}_{s,\mu}(p,q;\lambda,\beta)\right) &= s\,{}_{\mathbb{G}}\mathbb{R}^{[j]}_{s-1,\mu}(p,q;\lambda,\beta),\\ \frac{\lambda}{\log(1+\lambda)}\frac{\partial}{\partial q}\left({}_{\mathbb{G}}\mathbb{R}^{[j]}_{s,\mu}(p,q;\lambda,\beta)\right) &= \mu\, s(s-1)\cdots(s-j+1)\,{}_{\mathbb{G}}\mathbb{R}^{[j]}_{s-j,\mu}(p,q;\lambda,\beta),\\ \frac{\partial}{\partial \beta}\left({}_{\mathbb{G}}\mathbb{R}^{[j]}_{s,\mu}(p,q;\lambda,\beta)\right) &= -\mu\,{}_{\mathbb{G}}\mathbb{R}^{[j]}_{s,\mu}(p,q;\lambda,\beta).\end{aligned} \tag{25}$$

In consideration of the above relations, the succeeding expression holds true:

$$\left(\frac{\lambda}{\log(1+\lambda)}\right)^{j-1}\frac{\partial}{\partial q}\left({}_{\mathbb{G}}\mathbb{R}^{[j]}_{s,\mu}(p,q;\lambda,\beta)\right) = -\frac{\partial^{j+1}}{\partial p^j\partial\beta}\,{}_{\mathbb{G}}\mathbb{R}^{[j]}_{s,\mu}(p,q;\lambda,\beta). \tag{26}$$

3. Determinant Forms

Determinants play a significant role in many branches of mathematics and its applications. Determinants are used to create the orthogonality connections between the functions, which are necessary for many applications in mathematics and physics. They also help in normalizing the functions, ensuring that their squared magnitudes integrate into unity. They are utilized to create generating functions for special functions. They act as a powerful method for obtaining difference equations, recursion relations, and other properties of special functions. Determinants commonly appear in the generating functions as coefficients.

Here, we establish the determinant form for the generalized degenerate 2D Appell polynomials ${}_{\mathbb{G}}\mathbb{R}^{[j]}_{s,\mu}(p,q;\lambda,\beta)$, which are given by Expression (17) in the form of the following result:

Theorem 4. *The generalized degenerate 2D Appell polynomials ${}_{\mathbb{G}}\mathbb{R}^{[j]}_{s,\mu}(p,q;\lambda,\beta)$ give rise to the determinant of the following form:*

$${}_{\mathbb{G}}\mathbb{R}^{[j]}_{s,\mu}(p,q;\lambda,\beta) = \frac{(-1)^s}{(\gamma_0)^{s+1}}\begin{vmatrix} 1 & \mathbb{G}^{[j]}_{1,\mu}(p,q;\lambda,\beta) & \mathbb{G}^{[j]}_{2,\mu}(p,q;\lambda,\beta) & \cdots & \mathbb{G}^{[j]}_{s-1,\mu}(p,q;\lambda,\beta) & \mathbb{G}^{[j]}_{s,\mu}(p,q;\lambda,\beta)\\ \gamma_0 & \gamma_1 & \gamma_2 & \cdots & \gamma_{s-1} & \gamma_s\\ 0 & \gamma_0 & \binom{2}{1}\gamma_1 & \cdots & \binom{s-1}{1}\gamma_{s-2} & \binom{s}{1}\gamma_{s-1}\\ 0 & 0 & \gamma_0 & \cdots & \binom{s-1}{2}\gamma_{s-3} & \binom{s}{2}\gamma_{s-2}\\ . & . & . & \cdots & . & .\\ . & . & . & \cdots & . & .\\ 0 & 0 & 0 & \cdots & \gamma_0 & \binom{s}{s-1}\gamma_1\end{vmatrix}, \tag{27}$$

where γ_s, $s=0,1,\cdots$ are the coefficients of Maclaurin's series $\frac{1}{\mathbb{R}(u)}$.

Proof. In multiplying both sides of Equation (17) by $\frac{1}{\mathbb{R}(u)} = \sum_{k=0}^{\infty} \gamma_k \frac{u^k}{k!}$, we find

$$\sum_{s=0}^{\infty} \mathbb{G}_{s,\mu}^{[j]}(p,q;\lambda,\beta)\frac{u^s}{s!} = \sum_{k=0}^{\infty} \gamma_k \frac{u^k}{k!} \sum_{s=0}^{\infty} {}_{\mathbb{G}}\mathbb{R}_{s,\mu}^{[j]}(p,q;\lambda,\beta)\frac{u^s}{s!}. \tag{28}$$

By using the Cauchy product rule in Equation (28), we have

$$\mathbb{G}_{s,\mu}^{[j]}(p,q;\lambda,\beta) = \sum_{k=0}^{s} \binom{s}{k} \gamma_k \, {}_{\mathbb{G}}\mathbb{R}_{s,\mu}^{[j]}(p,q;\lambda,\beta). \tag{29}$$

The system of $s-$ equations with unknown ${}_{\mathbb{G}}\mathbb{R}_{s,\mu}^{[j]}(p,q;\lambda,\beta)$, $s = 0,1,2,\cdots$ is produced as a result of this equality. Cramer's rule is used to solve this system, and by using the fact that the denominator is the determinant of the lower triangular matrix with determinant $(\gamma_0)^{s+1}$, as well as by taking the transpose of the numerator, then replacing the $i-th$ row by $(i+1)-th$ position for $i = 1,2,\cdots s-1$ gives the desired result. □

Remark 6. *The generalized degenerate 2D Appell polynomials can be reduced to the generalized degenerate 2-variable Hermite–Appell polynomials if $j = 2$. As a result, the following determinant representation is established by replacing $j = 2$ in Expression (27) and by representing the resulting generalized degenerate 2-variable Hermite–Appell polynomials on the right-hand side as ${}_{\mathbb{G}}\mathbb{R}_{s,\mu}^{[2]}(p,q;\lambda,\beta)$, which are expressed as follows:*

$$ {}_{\mathbb{G}}\mathbb{R}_{s,\mu}^{[2]}(p,q;\lambda,\beta) = \frac{(-1)^s}{(\gamma_0)^{s+1}} \begin{vmatrix} 1 & \mathbb{R}_{1,\mu}^{[2]}(p,q;\lambda,\beta) & \mathbb{R}_{2,\mu}^{[2]}(p,q;\lambda,\beta) & \cdots & \mathbb{R}_{s-1,\mu}^{[2]}(p,q;\lambda,\beta) & \mathbb{R}_{s,\mu}^{[2]}(p,q;\lambda,\beta) \\ \gamma_0 & \gamma_1 & \gamma_2 & \cdots & \gamma_{s-1} & \gamma_s \\ 0 & \gamma_0 & \binom{2}{1}\gamma_1 & \cdots & \binom{s-1}{1}\gamma_{s-2} & \binom{s}{1}\gamma_{s-1} \\ 0 & 0 & \gamma_0 & \cdots & \binom{s-1}{2}\gamma_{s-3} & \binom{s}{2}\gamma_{s-2} \\ . & . & . & \cdots & . & . \\ . & . & . & \cdots & . & . \\ 0 & 0 & 0 & \cdots & \gamma_0 & \binom{s}{s-1}\gamma_1 \end{vmatrix}, $$

Remark 7. *The generalized degenerate 2D Appell polynomials can be reduced to the generalized 2D Appell polynomials if $\lambda \to 0$. As a result, the following determinant representation is established by replacing $\lambda \to 0$ in Expression (27) and by representing the resulting generalized Appell polynomials on the right-hand side as ${}_{\mathbb{G}}\mathbb{R}_{s,\mu}(p;q;\beta)$, which are expressed as follows:*

$$ {}_{\mathbb{G}}\mathbb{R}_{s,\mu}^{[j]}(p,q;\beta) = \frac{(-1)^s}{(\gamma_0)^{s+1}} \begin{vmatrix} 1 & \mathbb{G}_{1,\mu}^{[j]}(p,q;\beta) & \mathbb{G}_{2,\mu}^{[j]}(p,q;\beta) & \cdots & \mathbb{G}_{s-1,\mu}^{[j]}(p,q;\beta) & \mathbb{G}_{s,\mu}^{[j]}(p,q;\beta) \\ \gamma_0 & \gamma_1 & \gamma_2 & \cdots & \gamma_{s-1} & \gamma_s \\ 0 & \gamma_0 & \binom{2}{1}\gamma_1 & \cdots & \binom{s-1}{1}\gamma_{s-2} & \binom{s}{1}\gamma_{s-1} \\ 0 & 0 & \gamma_0 & \cdots & \binom{s-1}{2}\gamma_{s-3} & \binom{s}{2}\gamma_{s-2} \\ . & . & . & \cdots & . & . \\ . & . & . & \cdots & . & . \\ 0 & 0 & 0 & \cdots & \gamma_0 & \binom{s}{s-1}\gamma_1 \end{vmatrix}. $$

4. Applications

The Appell polynomial family is a vast collection of polynomials that can be constructed by selecting the appropriate functions $\mathbb{R}(u)$. Table 1 provides a list of the various members of the Appell polynomial family along with their corresponding names, generating functions, series definitions, and related numbers.

The Bernoulli, Euler, and Genocchi numbers hold immense significance in mathematics, thus finding numerous applications in various fields. For example, the Bernoulli numbers are frequently employed in diverse mathematical formulas, such as the Bernoulli polynomials and the Euler–Maclaurin formula. They have practical uses in number theory, numerical analysis, and combinatorics, and they are also closely related to representation theory and algebraic geometry.

Table 1. Expressions for certain Appell family members.

S. No.	Name of The Polynomials and Related Numbers	$\mathbb{R}(u)$	Generating Expression	Series Representation
I.	Bernoulli polynomials and numbers [28]	$\left(\frac{u}{e^u-1}\right)$	$\left(\frac{u}{e^u-1}\right)e^{uj_1} = \sum\limits_{k=0}^{\infty} \mathbb{B}_k(j_1)\frac{u^k}{k!}$ $\left(\frac{u}{e^u-1}\right) = \sum\limits_{k=0}^{\infty} \mathbb{B}_k\frac{u^k}{k!}$ $\mathbb{B}_k := \mathbb{B}_k(0)$	$\mathbb{B}_k(j_1) = \sum\limits_{m=0}^{k} \binom{k}{m}\mathbb{B}_m u^{k-m}$
II.	Euler polynomials and numbers [28]	$\left(\frac{2}{e^u+1}\right)$	$\left(\frac{2}{e^u+1}\right)e^{j_1 u} = \sum\limits_{k=0}^{\infty} \mathbb{E}_k(j_1)\frac{u^k}{k!}$ $\frac{2e^u}{e^{2u}+1} = \sum\limits_{k=0}^{\infty} \mathbb{E}_k\frac{u^s}{s!}$ $\mathbb{E}_k := 2^k\mathbb{E}_k\left(\frac{1}{2}\right)$	$\mathbb{E}_k(j_1) =$ $\sum\limits_{m=0}^{k} \binom{k}{m}\frac{\mathbb{E}_m}{2^m}\left(j_1 - \frac{1}{2}\right)^{k-m}$
III.	Genocchi polynomials and numbers [29]	$\left(\frac{2u}{e^u+1}\right)$	$\left(\frac{2u}{e^u+1}\right)e^{j_1 u} = \sum\limits_{k=0}^{\infty} \mathbb{G}_k(j_1)\frac{u^k}{k!}$ $\frac{2u}{e^u+1} = \sum\limits_{k=0}^{\infty} \mathbb{G}_k\frac{u^s}{s!}$ $\mathbb{G}_k := \mathbb{G}_k(0)$	$\mathbb{G}_k(j_1) = \sum\limits_{m=0}^{k} \binom{k}{m}\mathbb{G}_m\, {j_1}^{k-m}$

Similarly, the integer sequence of Euler numbers plays a vital role in different mathematical domains, including algebraic topology, geometry, and number theory. These numbers are essential in the study of elliptic curves and the theory of modular forms, which find applications in cryptography and coding theory.

On the other hand, the Genocchi numbers, which also form an integer sequence, are applied to various combinatorial problems, including the counting of labeled rooted trees and up–down sequences. They are linked to the Riemann zeta function and prove useful in graph theory and automata theory.

Moreover, the trigonometric and hyperbolic secant functions are closely connected to the Euler numbers. The Taylor series expansions of these functions involve Euler numbers and their derivatives, making them valuable in many areas of mathematics and physics, such as signal processing and quantum field theory.

Therefore, by replacing $\mathbb{R}(u)$ with $\mathbb{B}(u)$, $\mathbb{E}(u)$, and $\mathbb{G}(u)$ in Expressions (13) and (17), the listed expression's for the operational connection and generating function for the generalized degenerate 2D Bernoulli, Euler, and Genocchi polynomials are established as follows:

Corollary 1. *The generalized degenerate 2D Bernoulli* ${}_{\mathbb{G}}\mathbb{B}^{[j]}_{s,\mu}(p,q;\lambda,\beta)$, *Euler* ${}_{\mathbb{G}}\mathbb{E}^{[j]}_{s,\mu}(p,q;\lambda,\beta)$, *and Genocchi* ${}_{\mathbb{G}}\mathbb{G}^{[j]}_{s,\mu}(p,q;\lambda,\beta)$ *polynomials satisfy the following operational connection:*

$$\left(\beta - q\frac{\lambda}{\log(1+\lambda)}\frac{\partial^j}{\partial p^j}\right)^{-\mu}\mathbb{B}_s(p;\lambda) = {}_{\mathbb{G}}\mathbb{B}^{[j]}_{s,\mu}(p,q;\lambda,\beta),$$
$$\left(\beta - q\frac{\lambda}{\log(1+\lambda)}\frac{\partial^j}{\partial p^j}\right)^{-\mu}\mathbb{E}_s(p;\lambda) = {}_{\mathbb{G}}\mathbb{B}^{[j]}_{s,\mu}(p,q;\lambda,\beta),$$
$$\left(\beta - q\frac{\lambda}{\log(1+\lambda)}\frac{\partial^j}{\partial p^j}\right)^{-\mu}\mathbb{B}_s(p;\lambda) = {}_{\mathbb{G}}\mathbb{G}^{[j]}_{s,\mu}(p,q;\lambda,\beta). \quad (30)$$

Corollary 2. *The generalized degenerate 2D Bernoulli* ${}_{\mathbb{G}}\mathbb{B}^{[j]}_{s,\mu}(p,q;\lambda,\beta)$, *Euler* ${}_{\mathbb{G}}\mathbb{E}^{[j]}_{s,\mu}(p,q;\lambda,\beta)$, *and Genocchi* ${}_{\mathbb{G}}\mathbb{G}^{[j]}_{s,\mu}(p,q;\lambda,\beta)$ *polynomials satisfy the following generating relations:*

$$\frac{\mathbb{B}(u)(1+\lambda)^{\frac{pu}{\lambda}}}{\left[\beta - \frac{(qu^j)}{\lambda}\,log(1+\lambda)\right]^{\mu}} = \sum_{s=0}^{\infty} {}_{\mathbb{G}}\mathbb{B}^{[j]}_{s,\mu}(p,q;\lambda,\beta)\frac{u^s}{s!},$$
$$\frac{\mathbb{E}(u)(1+\lambda)^{\frac{pu}{\lambda}}}{\left[\beta - \frac{(qu^j)}{\lambda}\,log(1+\lambda)\right]^{\mu}} = \sum_{s=0}^{\infty} {}_{\mathbb{G}}\mathbb{E}^{[j]}_{s,\mu}(p,q;\lambda,\beta)\frac{u^s}{s!},$$
$$\frac{\mathbb{G}(u)(1+\lambda)^{\frac{pu}{\lambda}}}{\left[\beta - \frac{(qu^j)}{\lambda}\,log(1+\lambda)\right]^{\mu}} = \sum_{s=0}^{\infty} {}_{\mathbb{G}}\mathbb{G}^{[j]}_{s,\mu}(p,q;\lambda,\beta)\frac{u^s}{s!}. \quad (31)$$

Next, we establish the determinant representation for these polynomials:

Corollary 3. *The generalized degenerate 2D Bernoulli polynomials* ${}_{\mathbb{G}}\mathbb{B}^{[j]}_{s,\mu}(p,q;\lambda,\beta)$ *give rise to the determinant of the following form:*

$${}_{\mathbb{G}}\mathbb{B}^{[j]}_{s,\mu}(p,q;\lambda,\beta) = \frac{(-1)^s}{(\gamma_0)^{s+1}}\begin{vmatrix} 1 & \mathbb{B}^{[j]}_{1,\mu}(p,q;\lambda,\beta) & \mathbb{B}^{[j]}_{2,\mu}(p,q;\lambda,\beta) & \cdots & \mathbb{B}^{[j]}_{s-1,\mu}(p,q;\lambda,\beta) & \mathbb{B}^{[j]}_{s,\mu}(p,q;\lambda,\beta) \\ \gamma_0 & \gamma_1 & \gamma_2 & \cdots & \gamma_{s-1} & \gamma_m \\ 0 & \gamma_0 & \binom{2}{1}\gamma_1 & \cdots & \binom{s-1}{1}\gamma_{s-2} & \binom{s}{1}\gamma_{s-1} \\ 0 & 0 & \gamma_0 & \cdots & \binom{s-1}{2}\gamma_{s-3} & \binom{s}{2}\gamma_{s-2} \\ \vdots & \vdots & \vdots & \cdots & \vdots & \vdots \\ 0 & 0 & 0 & \cdots & \gamma_0 & \binom{s}{s-1}\gamma_1 \end{vmatrix}.$$

Corollary 4. *The generalized degenerate 2D Euler polynomials* ${}_{\mathbb{G}}\mathbb{E}^{[j]}_{s,\mu}(p,q;\lambda,\beta)$ *give rise to the determinant of the following form:*

$$
{}_{\mathbb{G}}\mathbb{E}^{[j]}_{s,\mu}(p,q;\lambda,\beta) = \frac{(-1)^s}{(\gamma_0)^{s+1}} \begin{vmatrix} 1 & \mathbb{E}^{[j]}_{1,\mu}(p,q;\lambda,\beta) & \mathbb{E}^{[j]}_{2,\mu}(p,q;\lambda,\beta) & \cdots & \mathbb{E}^{[j]}_{s-1,\mu}(p,q;\lambda,\beta) & \mathbb{E}^{[j]}_{s,\mu}(p,q;\lambda,\beta) \\ \gamma_0 & \gamma_1 & \gamma_2 & \cdots & \gamma_{s-1} & \gamma_m \\ 0 & \gamma_0 & \binom{2}{1}\gamma_1 & \cdots & \binom{s-1}{1}\gamma_{s-2} & \binom{s}{1}\gamma_{s-1} \\ 0 & 0 & \gamma_0 & \cdots & \binom{s-1}{2}\gamma_{s-3} & \binom{s}{2}\gamma_{s-2} \\ . & . & . & \cdots & . & . \\ . & . & . & \cdots & . & . \\ 0 & 0 & 0 & \cdots & \gamma_0 & \binom{s}{s-1}\gamma_1 \end{vmatrix}.
$$

Corollary 5. *The generalized degenerate 2D Genocchi polynomials ${}_{\mathbb{G}}\mathbb{G}^{[j]}_{s,\mu}(p,q;\lambda,\beta)$ give rise to the determinant of the following form:*

$$
{}_{\mathbb{G}}\mathbb{G}^{[j]}_{s,\mu}(p,q;\lambda,\beta) = \frac{(-1)^s}{(\gamma_0)^{s+1}} \begin{vmatrix} 1 & \mathbb{G}^{[j]}_{1,\mu}(p,q;\lambda,\beta) & \mathbb{G}^{[j]}_{2,\mu}(p,q;\lambda,\beta) & \cdots & \mathbb{G}^{[j]}_{s-1,\mu}(p,q;\lambda,\beta) & \mathbb{G}^{[j]}_{s,\mu}(p,q;\lambda,\beta) \\ \gamma_0 & \gamma_1 & \gamma_2 & \cdots & \gamma_{s-1} & \gamma_m \\ 0 & \gamma_0 & \binom{2}{1}\gamma_1 & \cdots & \binom{s-1}{1}\gamma_{s-2} & \binom{s}{1}\gamma_{s-1} \\ 0 & 0 & \gamma_0 & \cdots & \binom{s-1}{2}\gamma_{s-3} & \binom{s}{2}\gamma_{s-2} \\ . & . & . & \cdots & . & . \\ . & . & . & \cdots & . & . \\ 0 & 0 & 0 & \cdots & \gamma_0 & \binom{s}{s-1}\gamma_1 \end{vmatrix}.
$$

5. Conclusions

This study builds on the previous work by [19] on degenerate 2D Appell polynomials; moreover, it introduces a new family of generalized degenerate 2D Appell polynomials with the notation of ${}_{\mathbb{G}}\mathbb{R}^{[j]}_{s,\mu}(p,q;\lambda,\beta)$. In Section 2 of this research, the operational rule in terms of Theorem 1, and the generating expression in terms of Theorem 2, for these polynomials are provided together with an inference of their special cases in the form of remarks. In Section 3, the explicit summation formula for ${}_{\mathbb{G}}\mathbb{R}^{[j]}_{s,\mu}(p,q;\lambda,\beta)$ is firmly established, and the determinant form for the generalized family is generated. Further, the recurrence relations of the generalized degenerate 2D Appell polynomials are also obtained. In Section 4, the paper demonstrates the broad applicability of the results obtained in Section 2. It presents equivalent results for degenerate 2D Bernoulli, 2D Euler, and 2D Genocchi polynomials. These generalized degenerate special polynomials, which are associated with Appell polynomials, find extensive applications in the fields of mathematics and physics. Notably, they have natural connections to quantum mechanics and probability theory, where they can be linked to the normal distribution—a fundamental concept in probability theory. Furthermore, these polynomials serve as a basis for approximating the functions in approximation theory, thereby making them valuable in numerical analysis. Moreover, in the realm of statistical mechanics, Hermite polynomials—which are a special case of these polynomials—play a crucial role in calculating the partition function and thermodynamic properties of ideal gases. Additionally, they find utility in Fourier analysis for decomposing functions into orthogonal functions.

Operational techniques are vital in the development of novel families of functional equations and for gaining insights into their characteristics; thus, they encompass both regular and generalized special functions. Scholars, including Dattoli and various others, have emphasized the significance of employing operational methods, particularly when addressing the explicit solutions for families of partial differential equations such as the Heat and D'Alembert types, as well as in exploring their wide-ranging applications. For the notable contributions by researchers like Dattoli and others see, for instance [3,30,31]. These studies serve to illustrate the essential role of operational methods in the analysis of special functions and their practical implications.

Future research endeavors can focus on the exploration of symmetric identities and the investigation of the Δ_h properties of the aforementioned polynomials. Additionally, delving into implicit summation equations as potential avenues for obtaining additional data could prove to be beneficial for further analysis. Further, the verification of the monomiality principle and a sequence of upward and downward operators may also be taken as worthy offuture observation.

Author Contributions: Conceptualization, M.Z. and S.A.W.; validation, M.Z. and S.A.W.; formal analysis, M.Z. and S.A.W.; investigation, S.A.W.; writing—original draft preparation, S.A.W.; writing—review and editing, M.Z. and S.A.W.; visualization, M.Z.; funding acquisition, M.Z. All authors have read and agreed to the published version of the manuscript.

Funding: This research work was funded by the Deanship of Scientific Research at King Khalid University through the Large Group Research Project, under grant number RGP2/237/44.

Acknowledgments: M. Zayed extends her appreciation to the Deanship of Scientific Research at King Khalid University, Saudi Arabia, for funding this work through the Large Group Research Project under grant number RGP2/237/44.

Conflicts of Interest: The authors declare no conflict of interest.

References

1. Oldham, H.; Spanier, N. *The Fractional Calculas*; Academic Press: San Diego, CA, USA, 1974.
2. Widder, D.V. *An Introduction to Ttransform Theory*; Academic Press: New York, NY, USA, 1971.
3. Dattoli, G.; Ricci, P.E.; Cesarano, C.; Vâzquez, L. Special polynomials and fractional calculus. *Math. Comput. Model.* **2003**, *37*, 729–733. [CrossRef]
4. Assante, D.; Cesarano, C.; Fornaro, C.; Vazquez, L. Higher order and fractional diffusive equations. *J. Eng. Sci. Technol. Rev.* **2015**, *8*, 202–204. [CrossRef]
5. Appell, P. Sur une classe de polynômes. *Ann. Sci. École. Norm. Sup.* **1880** , *9*, 119–144. [CrossRef]
6. Khan, S.; Raza, N. General-Appell Polynomials within the Context of Monomiality Principle. *Int. J. Anal.* **2013**, *2013*, 328032. [CrossRef]
7. Hermite, C. Sur un nouveau dévelopment en séries de functions. *Compt. Rendus Acad. Sci. Paris* **1864**, *58*, 93–100.
8. Ryoo, C.S. Notes on degenerate tangent polynomials. *Glob. J. Pure Appl. Math.* **2015**, *11*, 3631–3637.
9. Hwang, K.W.; Ryoo, C.S. Differential equations associated with two variable degenerate Hermite polynomials. *Mathematics* **2020**, *8*, 228. [CrossRef]
10. Hwang, K.W.; Seoul, Y.; Ryoo, C.S. Explicit Identities for 3-Variable Degenerate Hermite Kampe deFeriet Polynomials and Differential Equation Derived from Generating Function. *Symmetry* **2021**, *13*, 7. [CrossRef]
11. Kim, T. A Note on the Degenerate Type of Complex Appell Polynomials. *Symmetry* **2019**, *11*, 1339. [CrossRef]
12. Kim, T.; Yao, Y.; Kim, D.S.; Jang, G.-W. Degenerate r-Stirling numbers and r-Bell polynomials. *Russ. J. Math. Phys.* **2018**, *25*, 44–58. [CrossRef]
13. Kim, D.S.; Kim, T.; Lee, H. A note on degenerate Euler and Bernoulli polynomials of complex variable. *Symmetry* **2019**, *11*, 1168. [CrossRef]
14. Wani, S.A.; Khan, S.; Naikoo, S. Differential and integral equations for the Laguerre-Gould-Hopper based Appell and related polynomials. *Bol. Soc. Mat. Mex.* **2020**, *26*, 617–646. [CrossRef]
15. Khan, S.; Wani, S.A. Fractional calculus and generalized forms of special polynomials associated with Appell sequences. *Georgian Math. J.* **2021**, *28*, 261–270. [CrossRef]
16. Khan, S.; Wani, S.A. Extended Laguerre-Appell polynomials via fractional operators and their determinant forms. *Turk. J. Math.* **2018**, *42*, 1686–1697. [CrossRef]
17. Wani, S.A.; Nisar, K.S. Quasi-monomiality and convergence theorem for Boas-Buck-Sheffer polynomials. *Mathematics* **2020**, *5*, 4432–4453. [CrossRef]
18. Khan, W.A.; Muhyi, A.; Ali, R.; Alzobydi, K.A.H.; Singh, M.; Agarwal, P. A new family of degenerate poly-Bernoulli polynomials of the second kind with its certain related properties. *AIMS Math.* **2021**, *6*, 12680–12697. [CrossRef]
19. Wani, S.A.; Warke, A.; Dar, J. Degenerate 2D bivariate Appell polynomials: Properties and applications. *Appl. Math. Sci. Eng.* **2023**, *31*, 2194645. [CrossRef]
20. Riyasat, M.; Nahid, T.; Khan, S. An Algebraic Approach to Degenerate Appell Polynomials and Their Hybrid Forms via Determinants. *Acta Math. Sci.* **2023**, *43*, 719–735. [CrossRef]
21. Kumar, D.; Baleanu, D. Fractional calculus and its applications in physics. *Front. Phys.* **2019**, *7*, 81. [CrossRef]

2. Sun, H.; Zhang, Y.; Baleanu, D.; Chen, W.; Chen, Y. A new collection of real world applications of fractional calculus in science and engineering. *Commun. Nonlinear Sci. Numer. Simul.* **2018**, *64*, 213–231. [CrossRef]
3. Farman, M.; Akgül, A.; Baleanu, D.; Imtiaz, S.; Ahmad, A. Analysis of Fractional Order Chaotic Financial Model with Minimum Interest Rate Impact. *Fractal Fract.* **2020**, *4*, 43. [CrossRef]
4. Patnaik, S.; Hollkamp, J.P.; Semperlotti, F. Applications of variable-order fractional operators: A review. *Proc. R. Soc. A* **2020**, *476*, 20190498. [CrossRef] [PubMed]
5. Kachhia, K.B.; Atangana, A. Electromagnetic waves described by a fractional derivative of variable and constant order with non singular kernel. *Discret. Contin. Dyn. Syst. S* **2021**, *14*, 2357–2371. [CrossRef]
6. Qiao, L.; Xu, D.; Qiu, W. The formally second-order BDF ADI difference/compact difference scheme for the nonlocal evolution problem in three-dimensional space. *Appl. Numer. Math.* **2022**, *172*, 359–381. [CrossRef]
7. Srivastava, H.M.; Manocha, H.L. *A Treatise on Generating Functions*; Halsted Press: New York, NY, USA, 1984.
8. Erdélyi, A.; Magnus, W.; Oberhettinger, F.; Tricomi, F.G. *Higher Transcendental Functions*; McGraw-Hill Book Company: New York, NY, USA; Toronto, ON, Canada; London, UK, 1955.
9. Sandor, J.; Crstici, B. *Handbook of Number Theory*; Kluwer Academic Publishers: Dordrecht, The Netherlands; Boston, MA, USA; London, UK, 2004.
0. Dattoli, G. Generalized polynomials operational identities and their applications. *J. Comput. Appl. Math.* **2000**, *118*, 111–123. [CrossRef]
1. Dattoli, G. Hermite-Bessel and Laguerre-Bessel functions: A by-product of the monomiality principle, Advanced Special functions and applications. *Adv. Spec. Funct. Appl.* **2000**, *1*, 147–164.

fractal and fractional

MDPI

Article

A Physical Phenomenon for the Fractional Nonlinear Mixed Integro-Differential Equation Using a Quadrature Nystrom Method

A. R. Jan [1], M. A. Abdou [2] and M. Basseem [3,*]

[1] Department of Mathematics, Faculty of Applied Science, Umm Al-Qura University, Makkah P.O. Box 715, Saudi Arabia; arjaan@uqu.edu.sa
[2] Department of Mathematics, Faculty of Education, Alexandria University, Alexandria 21544, Egypt; abdella_777@yahoo.com
[3] Department of Mathematics, Faculty of Engineering, Sinai University, El Arish 16020, Egypt
* Correspondence: basseem777@yahoo.com

Abstract: In this work, the existence and uniqueness solution of the fractional nonlinear mixed integro-differential equation (**FrNMIoDE**) is guaranteed with a general discontinuous kernel based on position and time-space $L_2[\Omega] \times C[0,T]$, $T < 1$. The **FrNMIoDE** conformed to the Volterra-Hammerstein integral equation (**V-HIE**) of the second kind, after applying the characteristics of a fractional integral, with a general discontinuous kernel in position for the Hammerstein integral term and a continuous kernel in time to the Volterra integral (**VI**) term. Then, using a separation technique methodology, we developed **HIE**, whose physical coefficients were time-variable. By examining the system's convergence, the product Nystrom technique (**PNT**) and associated schemes were employed to create a nonlinear algebraic system (**NAS**).

Keywords: fractional nonlinear (linear) integro-differential equation; discontinuous kernel; nonlinear algebraic system; Nystrom method; the rate of convergence error

MSC: 45B05; 65H10; 65R20; 45G10

1. Introduction

Due to the vast number of applications that can be found for fractional nonlinear/linear integro-differential equations **FrNIoEs/FrLIoEs** containing time-dependent coefficients in physics, engineering, and other scientific domains, their significance has been growing steadily over the past several decades. These equations are ideal for accurately representing a variety of events that occur in the real world because they capture both the non-local and local behavior of a large number of complex systems. Hermann [1] introduced some applications of fractional calculus to the field of physics. Oyedepo et al. [2] presented a numerical solution to the linear **FrLIoDE** problem by employing the method of standard least squares. Bernstein piecewise polynomials were exploited by Osama and Sarmad [3] in order to find an approximate solution to the **FrLIoDE** problem. In Daşcıoğlu and Bayram [4], approximate solutions to **FrLIoDEs** were found by using Laguerre polynomials. Mohammed [5] utilized the approach of least squares in conjunction with a shifted Chebyshev polynomial in order to solve the **FrLIoDE** problem. In [6], Mahdy et al. investigated the numerical solution of **FrLIoDE** by employing the least squares approach and supplementing it with a shifted Laguerre polynomial. In order to locate the numerical solution of **FrLIoDE** with the Caputo derivative, Nanware et al. [7] used the Bernstein polynomial to solve it. The least square technique and the homotopy perturbation method were both proposed by Oyedepo et al. [8] to discuss the solution to the **FrIDE** problem. Several techniques are used in efficient ways to solve **IE** and **FrIE.** For instance, Basseem and Alayani [9] solved a nonlinear quadratic mixed IE of the second kind with a singular kernel by employing the Toeplitz matrix method in conjunction with the **PNT**. A quadrature scheme was implemented by I. Katani [10] for the numerical outcomes of the second type of the Fredholm integral (**FI**) model. Al-Bugami [11] employed the Simpson and Trapezoidal methods to perform numerical representations based on an integral model that utilized 2D surface crack layers. In order to obtain numerical computing results for the second kind of nonlinear integral model that has a continuous kernel, Brezinski and Zalglia [12] employed the extrapolation method. Baksheesh [13] suggested making use of the Galerkin scheme in order to find the approximate solution for the **VIEs** of the second kind. The sinc-collocation method was utilized by Alkan and Hatipoglu [14] to find solutions of **V-FIDEs** of fractional order. Mosa et al. [15] researched the semigroup scheme to evaluate uniqueness and existence based on the partial and fractional integro models of heat performance in the Banach space using the Adomian decomposition scheme. An effective methodology for finding an approximate solution using the wavelet collocation method to **FrFIDEs** was proposed by Bin Jebreen and Dassios [16]. Using the extended cubic B-spline, Akram et al. [17] interpreted the collocation strategy in order to solve the fractional partial integro-differential problem. After employing the Riemann–Liouville fractional integral and fractional derivative, Abdelkawy et al. [18] used the Jacobi–Gauss collocation method to achieve an approximate solution for a variable-order of **FrLIoDE** with a weakly singular kernel. This was accomplished by applying the Jacobi–Gauss collocation method. Khalil [19] used a Jacobi polynomial for a solution of coupled system of fractional differential equations. Some different numerical methods for **NLIoEs** are introduced in Abdou [20].

This paper is divided into 12 sections. In Section 2, we derive the fractional mixed integral equation from the phase lag mixed integral equation. In Section 3, using a mixed **NIE** of the second kind with local conditions, we establish **FrNIoDE,** using the Caputo-fractional integral. In addition, the existence of a unique solution is guaranteed. In Section 4, the convergence of this solution is established and proved. In Section 5, the technique of separation variables method is applied to change the problem to **HNIE** of the second kind where its coefficients are parameters of time. **PNT** is employed in Section 6 to obtain the **NAS**. Then, we discuss the existence and uniqueness solution of **NAS** in Section 7. While the convergence system is considered in Section 8, the estimated error of **PNT** is discussed in Section 9. Illustrative numerical examples are involved to demonstrate the propriety and effectuality of the technique and some conclusions are stated in Sections 10 and 11. In Section 12, we propose some parameters for our future work.

2. Time Fractional and Phase Lag Integral Equation

The integral equations play an important role in the phase-lag problems with local conditions. Consider, in the time fractional calculus, the phase lag integral equation:

$$\varphi(x,t+q) = \\ f(x,t)+\lambda\int_0^t\int_\Omega k(|x-y|)G(t,\tau)\gamma(y,\tau,\varphi(y,\tau))dyd\tau, (0\leq q\ll 1), \tag{1}$$

with conditions

$$\varphi(x,0)=V_1(x), \frac{\partial}{\partial t}[\varphi(x,t)]_{t=0}=V_2(x), \tag{2}$$

where $f(x,\ t)$ is a known function in the space $L_2[\Omega]\times C[0,T],\ T<1$ represents the free term of the problem, λ is a constant that depends on the kind of material (in applied mathematics and has many physical meanings). The function $G(t,\tau)$ is a smooth kernel in time, while $k(|x-y|)$ is a singular kernel in position, which will be taken as a logarithmic form and Carleman function, $\gamma(x,t,\varphi(x,t))$ is a known nonlinear function of the unknown function $\varphi(x,t)$, $V_1(x)$ and $V_2(x)$ are two given initial position functions, the constant q is a small quantity that represents the delay of time.

Here, the aim of this research is to predict the near future, by studying fractional derivatives, and using the initial conditions, where it is known that the differential derivatives express the breaking of the ionic bond between the particles of the substance, and that the use of fractional time enables the researcher to deepen this study. The past time is studied when q is negative.

Abdou and Raad [21] and Mosal et al. [22] discussed the solution of mixed IE with nonlocal conditions. However, in this research, the above is developed by studying the fractional delay over time for a local phase-lag problem of a **FrNMIoDE** with continuous kernel in time and singular kernel in position.

Using Taylor's expansion, in the fractional calculus, to have

$$\begin{aligned}\varphi(x,t+q) \cong \varphi(x,t) + \tfrac{q^{\alpha}}{\Gamma(\alpha+1)}\tfrac{\partial^{\alpha}}{\partial t^{\alpha}}\varphi(x,t) + \tfrac{q^{\alpha+1}}{\Gamma(\alpha+2)}\tfrac{\partial^{\alpha+1}}{\partial t^{\alpha+1}}\varphi(x,t) + \\ \tfrac{q^{\alpha+2}}{\Gamma(\alpha+3)}\tfrac{\partial^{\alpha+1}}{\partial t^{\alpha+1}}\varphi(x,t) + ,\ldots, \quad (n-1) < \alpha < n.\end{aligned} \tag{3}$$

In this work, we have focused on $n = 2$

$$\varphi(x,t+q) = \varphi(x,t) + \frac{q^{\alpha}}{\Gamma(\alpha+1)}\frac{\partial^{\alpha}}{\partial t^{\alpha}}\varphi(x,t) + \frac{q^{\alpha+1}}{\Gamma(\alpha+2)}\frac{\partial^{\alpha+1}}{\partial t^{\alpha+1}}\varphi(x,t). \tag{4}$$

Using the basic formula of the Caputo-fractional integral

$$I_a^{\alpha} f(x) = \frac{1}{\Gamma(\alpha)}\int_a^x (x-t)^{\alpha-1} f(t)dt, \tag{5}$$

$$\left(\left(I_a^{\alpha} I_a^{\beta}\right) f\right)(x) = \left(I_a^{\alpha+\beta} f\right)(x) = \frac{1}{\Gamma(\alpha+\beta)}\int_a^x (x-t)^{\alpha+\beta-1} f(t)dt, \tag{6}$$

and

$$\int_0^t \int_0^{\tau_{n-1}} \cdots \int_0^{\tau_2}\int_0^{\tau_1} f(\tau)d\tau d\tau_1 \ldots d\tau_{n-2}d\tau_{n-1} = \frac{1}{\Gamma(n)}\int_0^t (t-\tau)^{n-1} f(\tau)d\tau. \tag{7}$$

In the view of Equations (1) and (4), we have

$$\begin{aligned}&\tfrac{q^{\alpha+1}}{\Gamma(\alpha+2)}\left(\tfrac{\partial^{\alpha}}{\partial t^{\alpha}}\varphi(x,t) - \tfrac{\partial}{\partial t}\varphi(x,0)\right) + \tfrac{q^{\alpha}}{\Gamma(\alpha+1)} I^{1-\alpha}\varphi(x,t) + \textstyle\int_0^t \varphi(x,\tau)d\tau \\ &-\lambda \textstyle\int_0^t \int_0^{\tau_1} \int_{\Omega} G(t,\tau)k(|x-y|)\gamma(y,\tau,\varphi(y,\tau))dyd\tau_1 d\tau = \int_0^t f(x,\tau)d\tau.\end{aligned} \tag{8}$$

Applying Equations (5)–(7) in Equation (8), we obtain

$$\begin{aligned}&\mu_1\varphi(x,t) + \mu_2 \textstyle\int_0^t \left(1 + \tfrac{\alpha}{q^{\alpha}}(t-\tau)^{\alpha}\right)\varphi(x,\tau)d\tau \\ &+\mu_3 \textstyle\int_0^t \int_{\Omega} (t-\tau)^{\alpha+1} G(t,\tau)k(|x-y|)\gamma(y,\tau,\varphi(y,\tau))dyd\tau = F(x,t),\end{aligned}$$

where

$$\begin{aligned}&\mu_1 = \tfrac{q^{\alpha+1}}{\Gamma(\alpha+2)}, \mu_2 = \tfrac{q^{\alpha}}{\Gamma(\alpha+1)}, \mu_3 = -\tfrac{\lambda}{2\Gamma(\alpha)} \\ &F(x,t) = \tfrac{1}{\Gamma(\alpha)}\textstyle\int_0^t (t-\tau)^{\alpha} f(x,\tau)d\tau + \tfrac{q^{\alpha+1}V_1(x)}{\Gamma(\alpha+2)\Gamma(\alpha+1)}t^{\alpha} + \tfrac{q^{\alpha+1}}{\Gamma(\alpha+2)}V_2(x).\end{aligned} \tag{9}$$

In order to guarantee the existence of a unique solution of the considered problem of Equation (1) or its equivalent in Equation (9), we assume the following conditions:

(i) The unknown function $\varphi(x,t)$ and its derivatives are in the space $L_2(\Omega) \times C[0,T]$ and its norm is defined as

$$\|\varphi(x,t)\| = \max_{0\le t\le T}\int_0^t \left\{\int_{\Omega} \varphi^2(x,\tau)dx\right\}^{1/2} d\tau.$$

(ii) For the constant Q, the known function $\gamma(x,t,\varphi)$ satisfies the following conditions:

$$\|\gamma(x,t,\varphi)\| \le Q\|\varphi(x,t)\|.$$
$$\|\gamma(x,t,\varphi_1) - \gamma(x,t,\varphi_2)\| \le Q\|\varphi_1(x,t) - \varphi_2(x,t)\|$$

(iii) The given function $f(x,t)$ satisfies

$$\|f(x,t)\| = \max_{0\le t\le T}\int_0^t \left\{\int_\Omega f^2(x,\tau)dx\right\}^{1/2} d\tau \le B, \ \ B \text{ is a constant.}$$

(iv) The two functions $V_i(x)$ for the constants D_i , $i = \{1, 2\}$ satisfy the following:

$$|V_1(x)| \le D_1 \text{ and } |V_2(x)| \le D_2.$$

(v) The position kernel in the space $L_2(\Omega)$ satisfies

$$\|k(|x-y|)\| = \left\{\int_\Omega\int_\Omega k^2(|x-y|)dxdy\right\}^{1/2} = C, \ \ C \text{ is a constant.}$$

(vi) The continuous function $G(t,\tau)$ in time satisfies

$$\max_{0\le t\le T}|G(t,\tau)| = E, \ \ E \text{ is a constant.}$$

3. Existence and Uniqueness

To prove the existence and uniqueness of Equation (9), it can be written in the following integral operator form

$$\begin{aligned} \chi\varphi(x,t) - \chi_1\varphi(x,t) - \chi_2\varphi(x,t) + V_2(x) \\ +\tfrac{V_1(x)}{\Gamma(\alpha)}\int_0^t (t-\tau)^{\alpha-1}d\tau + \tfrac{\alpha(\alpha+1)}{q^{\alpha+1}}\int_0^t (t-\tau)^{\alpha} f(x,\tau)d\tau. \\ \chi_1\varphi(x,t) = \tfrac{(\alpha+1)}{q}\int_0^t \varphi(x,\tau)d\tau + \tfrac{\alpha(\alpha+1)}{q^{\alpha+1}}\int_0^t (t-\tau)^{\alpha}\varphi(x,\tau)d\tau \\ \chi_2\varphi(x,t) = \tfrac{\lambda\alpha(\alpha+1)}{2q^{\alpha+1}}\int_0^t\int_\Omega (t-\tau)^{\alpha+1}G(t,\tau)k(|x-y|)\gamma(y,\tau,\varphi(y,\tau))dyd\tau. \end{aligned} \tag{10}$$

Theorem 1. *The solution of Equation (9) exists and is unique under the condition:*

$$(\alpha+1)Tq^{\alpha} + \alpha T^{\alpha+1} + \frac{\lambda\alpha(\alpha+1)T^{\alpha+2}}{2(\alpha+2)}ECQ < q^{\alpha+1}. \tag{11}$$

The following lemmas must be proved to satisfy the above theorem.

Lemma 1. *The operator χ maps the space $L_2(\Omega)\times C[0,T]$ onto itself under the conditions (i)–(vi).*

Proof. From Equation (10), we obtain

$$\begin{aligned} \|\chi\varphi(x,t)\| \le \|\chi_1\varphi(x,t)\| + \|\chi_2\varphi(x,t)\| + |V_2(x)| \\ +\tfrac{|V_1(x)|}{\Gamma(\alpha)}\left|\int_0^t (t-\tau)^{\alpha-1}d\tau\right| \\ +\tfrac{\alpha(\alpha+1)}{q^{\alpha+1}}\left|\int_0^t (t-\tau)^{\alpha} f(x,\tau)d\tau\right| \end{aligned} \tag{12}$$

Using conditions (i)–(v) and Cauchy–Schwartz inequality, we have

$$\|\chi\varphi(x,t)\| \le \delta\|\varphi(x,t)\| + \frac{D_1T^{\alpha}}{\Gamma(\alpha+1)} + D_2 + \frac{\alpha BT^{\alpha+1}}{q^{\alpha+1}} \tag{13}$$

where

$$\delta = \frac{(\alpha+1)Tq^{\alpha} + \alpha T^{\alpha+1} + \frac{\lambda\alpha(\alpha+1)T^{\alpha+2}}{2(\alpha+2)}ECQ}{q^{\alpha+1}}. \quad (14)$$

It is obvious that the operator χ maps the ball $B_r \in L_2[-1, 1] \times C[0, T]$ onto itself where

$$r = \frac{\sigma}{1-\delta}, \ \sigma = \frac{D_1 T^{\alpha}}{\Gamma(\alpha+1)} + D_2 + \frac{\alpha B T^{\alpha+1}}{q^{\alpha+1}}.$$

The inequality (13) involves the boundedness of the operator χ under the condition $\delta < 1$. □

In the previous Lemma, we considered that the discontinuous kernel $(t-\tau)^{\alpha-1}$, for all t, $\tau \in [0, T]$, satisfies for every continuous function $h(t,\tau), |h(t,\tau)| \leq$ constants, the following $\int_0^t (t-\tau)^{\alpha-1} h(t,\tau)d\tau$ or $\int_{t_1}^{t_2} (t-\tau)^{\alpha-1} h(t,\tau)d\tau, 0 < t_1 \leq t_2 \leq t, \max_t \int_0^t (t-\tau)^{\alpha-1} d\tau$, exists.

Lemma 2. *If conditions (i)–(vi) are satisfied, then χ is a contraction operator in Banach space $L_2[-1, 1] \times C[0, T]$.*

Proof. Let two functions $\varphi_1(x,t)$ and $\varphi_2(x,t)$ be two solutions of (9), and then, the Formula (10) leads to the

$$\|\chi\varphi_1(x,t) - \chi\varphi_2(x,t)\| \leq \|\chi_1(\varphi_1(x,t) - \varphi_2(x,t))\| + \|\chi_2(\varphi_1(x,t) - \varphi_2(x,t))\|.$$

Using conditions (i)–(iv) and Cauchy–Schwarz inequality, we deduce that

$$\|\chi\varphi_1(x,t) - \chi\varphi_2(x,t)\| \leq \delta\|\varphi_1(x,t) - \varphi_2(x,t)\| \quad (15)$$

It follows that for $\delta < 1$, χ is a contraction operator of Equation (10). Hence, there exists a unique solution in $L_2[\Omega]$ by a Banach fixed point theorem for every $t \in C[0, T], T < 1$. □

4. Convergence of Solution

For this aim, take the straightforward iteration $\{\varphi_1(x, t), \varphi_2(x, t), \ldots, \varphi_n(x, t), \ldots\} \subset \varphi(x, t)$. Then, use Equation (9), to have

$$\begin{aligned} &\tfrac{q^{\alpha+1}}{\Gamma(\alpha+2)}(\varphi_n(x,t) - \varphi_{n-1}(x,t)) + \tfrac{q^{\alpha}}{\Gamma(\alpha+1)}\int_0^t (\varphi_{n-1}(x,\tau) - \varphi_{n-2}(x,\tau))d\tau \\ &+\tfrac{1}{\Gamma(\alpha)}\int_0^t (t-\tau)^{\alpha}(\varphi_{n-1}(x,\tau) - \varphi_{n-2}(x,\tau))d\tau \\ &= \tfrac{\lambda}{2\Gamma(\alpha)}\int_0^t\int_{\Omega}(t-\tau)^{\alpha+1}G(t,\tau)k(|x-y|)(\gamma_n(y,\tau,\varphi_{n-1}(y,\tau)) - \\ &\qquad \gamma_n(y,\tau,\varphi_{n-2}(y,\tau)))dyd\tau, \end{aligned} \quad (16)$$

let

$$\varphi_n(x,t) = \sum_{i=0}^{n} \psi_i(x,t),$$

where

$$\begin{aligned} \psi_n(x,t) &= \varphi_n(x,t) - \varphi_{n-1}(x,t), \\ \psi_0(x,t) &= \tfrac{1}{\Gamma(\alpha)}\int_0^t (t-\tau)^{\alpha} f(x,\tau)d\tau.(n \geq 1). \end{aligned} \quad (17)$$

Lemma 3. *A sequence $\{\varphi_n(x, t)\}$ of Equation (17) is uniformly convergent under the condition $\delta < 1$.*

Proof. By applying Cauchy–Schwarz and using (17) in (16), we obtain

$$\begin{aligned}\frac{q^{\alpha+1}}{\Gamma(\alpha+2)}\|\psi_n(x,t)\| \leq \left|\frac{q^{\alpha}}{\Gamma(\alpha+1)}\int_0^t d\tau\right|\|\psi_{n-1}(x,t)\| + \left|\frac{1}{\Gamma(\alpha)}\int_0^t (t-\tau)^{\alpha}d\tau\right|\times \\ \|\psi_{n-1}(x,t)\| + \frac{\lambda N}{2\Gamma(\alpha)}\left|\int_0^t \int_\Omega (t-\tau)^{\alpha+1}G(t,\tau)k(|x-y|)dyd\tau\right|\|\psi_{n-1}(x,t)\|\end{aligned} \tag{18}$$

Taking $n = 1$, the above formula becomes

$$\|\psi_n(x,t)\| \leq \delta\frac{T^{\alpha+1}B}{\Gamma(\alpha+1)},$$

and then

$$\|\psi_n(x,t)\| \leq \delta^n\frac{T^{\alpha+1}B}{\Gamma(\alpha+1)}, \delta < 1. \tag{19}$$

The sequence $\{\psi_n(x,t)\}$ is uniformly convergent by Equation (19). Additionally, it gives the sequence's $\varphi_n(x,t) = \sum_{i=0}^{n}\psi_i(x,t)$ convergent solution.

As $n \to \infty$, $\varphi_n(x,t) \to \varphi(x,t)$, hence the solution $\varphi(x,t)$ is uniformly convergent under the condition $\delta < 1$. This demonstrates the lemma. □

5. Separation of Variables Technique

We discover that researchers are drawn to the unknown potential function, which is connected to time and place, in the issues of mathematical physics. The unknown function can be obtained using a variety of approaches. Time division is one of these techniques, converting the mixed integral problem into an algebraic system of integral equations.

Some researchers use the separation technique method which is a powerful mathematical tool that allows us to transform **FrNIoE** with time-dependence into a class of integral equations with coefficients on time only. This technique simplifies the problem by separating the time-dependent part from the integral part, enabling us to handle the integral equations more efficiently. The unknown and well-known functions are shown in the separation form as

$$\begin{aligned}\varphi(x,t) = N(t)\psi(x), f(x,t) = g(x)M(t), \\ \gamma(x,t,\varphi(x,t)) = \gamma_1(t,N(t))\gamma_2(x,\psi(x)).\end{aligned} \tag{20}$$

Hence, after using (20), the Formula (9) yields,

$$\begin{aligned}\mu_1(t)\psi(x) - \mu_2(t)\int_\Omega k(|x-y|)\gamma_2(\psi(y),y)dy = \mu_3(t)g(x) \\ +q^{\alpha+1}\frac{V_1(x)}{\Gamma(\alpha)}\int_0^t (t-\tau)^{\alpha-1}d\tau + q^{\alpha+1}V_2(x),\end{aligned} \tag{21}$$

where

$$\begin{aligned}\mu_1(t) = q^{\alpha+1}N(t) + (\alpha+1)q^{\alpha}\int_0^t N(\tau)d\tau + \alpha(\alpha+1)\int_0^t (t-\tau)^{\alpha}N(\tau)d\tau. \\ \mu_2(t) = \tfrac{\lambda}{2}\alpha(\alpha+1)\int_0^t (t-\tau)^{\alpha+1}G(t,\tau)\gamma_1(\tau,N(\tau))d\tau, \\ \mu_3(t) = \alpha(\alpha+1)\int_0^t (t-\tau)^{\alpha}M(\tau)d\tau.\end{aligned} \tag{22}$$

Equation (21) considers **HIE** of the second kind with coefficients specifying the time domain $\mu_i(t)$, $i = \{1, 2, 3\}$. Here, $\mu_1(t)$ and $\mu_2(t)$ indicate the time term of the unknown function $\varphi(x,t)$. Meanwhile, $\mu_3(t)$ describes the time in the free term $f(x,t)$.

6. Product Nystrom Technique (PNT)

To solve integral equations with continuous or disconnected kernels, several numerical approaches have been utilized. The PNT is the best approach for solving singular integral equations for the following reasons: the singular term vanishes instantly, turned into simple integrals that can be solved rapidly, and then creates a NAS. The relative error approach has a lower degree of convergence than the other methods.

Here, by using the product integration, we approximate the integral part of Equation (21) by a suitable Lagrange interpolation polynomial. For this, let $x = x_m$ and the integral part can be written as

$$\begin{aligned} \int_{\Omega} k(|x_m - y|)\gamma_2(\psi(y), y)dy &= \sum_{n=0}^{N} \Im_{m,n}\gamma_2(\psi(y_n), y_n) \\ &= \sum_{n=0}^{\frac{N-2}{2}} \int_{y_{2n}}^{y_{2n+2}} k(|x_m - y|)\gamma_2(\psi(y), y)dy. \end{aligned} \tag{23}$$

Without sacrificing generality, we take $\Omega = [-1, 1]$, $x_m = y_m = -1 + mh$, $m = 1, 2, 3, \ldots, N$ where $h = \frac{2}{N}$ and N is an even number.

The Lagrange interpolation polynomial is used to approximate the nonsingular component of the integral throughout each interval $[y_{2n}, y_{2n+2}]$ at the points $2n$, $2n+1$ and $2n+2$. As a result, the integral term of (23) becomes

$$\int_{-1}^{1} k(|x_m - y|)\gamma_2(\psi(y), y)dy =$$

$$\sum_{n=0}^{\frac{N-2}{2}} \int_{y_{2n}}^{y_{2n+2}} k(|x_m - y|) \begin{bmatrix} \frac{(y_{2n+1}-y)(y_{2n+2}-y)}{(y_{2n+1}-y_{2n})(y_{2n+2}-y_{2n})}\gamma_2(\psi(y_{2n}), y_{2n}) \\ +\frac{(y_{2n}-y)(y_{2n+2}-y)}{(y_{2n}-y_{2n+1})(y_{2n}-y_{2n+1})}\gamma_2(\psi(y_{2n+1}), y_{2n+1}) \\ +\frac{(y_{2n}-y)(y_{2n+1}-y)}{(y_{2n}-y_{2n+2})(y_{2n+1}-y_{2n+2})}\gamma_2(\psi(y_{2n+2}), y_{2n+2}) \end{bmatrix} dy. \tag{24}$$

Comparing Equations (23) and (24), we deduce

$$\begin{aligned} \Im_{m,0} &= \frac{1}{2h^2}\int_{y_0}^{y_2} k(|x_m - y|)(y_1 - y)(y_2 - y)dy, \\ \Im_{m,2n+1} &= \frac{1}{h^2}\int_{y_{2n}}^{y_{2n+2}} k(|x_m - y|)(y - y_{2n})(y_{2n+2} - y)dy, \\ \Im_{m,2n} &= \frac{1}{2h^2}\begin{bmatrix} \int_{y_{2n}}^{y_{2n+2}} k(|x_m - y|)(y_{2n+1} - y)(y_{2n+2} - y) \\ +\int_{y_{2n-2}}^{y_{2n}} k(|x_m - y|)(y - y_{2n-1})(y - y_{2n-2})dy \end{bmatrix}, \\ \Im_{m,N} &= \frac{1}{2h^2}\int_{y_{N-2}}^{y_N} k(|x_m - y|)(y - y_{N-2})(y - y_{N-1})dy. \end{aligned} \tag{25}$$

Introduce the following notations

$$\alpha_n(y_m) = \frac{1}{2h^2}\int_{y_{2n-2}}^{y_{2n}} k(|x_m - y|)(y - y_{2n-2})(y - y_{2n-1})dy,$$

$$\beta_n(y_m) = \frac{1}{2h^2}\int_{y_{2n-2}}^{y_{2n}} k(|x_m - y|)(y_{2n-1} - y)(y_{2n} - y)dy,$$

and

$$\zeta_n(y_m) = \frac{1}{2h^2}\int_{y_{2n-2}}^{y_{2n}} k(|x_m - y|)(y - y_{2n-2})(y_{2n} - y)dy, \tag{26}$$

then

$$\begin{aligned} \Im_{m,0} &= \beta_1(x_m), \\ \Im_{m,2n+1} &= 2\zeta_{n+1}(x_m), \\ \Im_{m,2n} &= \alpha_n(x_m) + \beta_{n+1}(x_m), \\ \Im_{m,N} &= \alpha_{N/2}(x_m). \end{aligned} \tag{27}$$

By substituting in Equation (21), we obtain

$$\begin{aligned} \mu_1(t)\psi(x_m) - \mu_2(t)\sum_{n=0}^{N} \Im_{m,n}\gamma_2(\psi(y_n), y_n) = \mu_3(t)g(x_m) \\ +\frac{q^{\alpha+1}}{\Gamma(\alpha+1)}\{V_1(x_m)t^{\alpha} + V_2(x_m)\Gamma(\alpha+1)\}. \end{aligned} \tag{28}$$

Equation (28) represents the NAS which gives an approximate solution of Equation (4) in a certain domain of time.

7. The Existence of a Unique Solution of NAS

To prove the existence of a unique solution of Equation (28), we write it in the following operator form

$$\|\overline{\chi}\psi(x_m)\| = \frac{\mu_2(t)}{\mu_1(t)}\sum_{n=0}^{N}\Im_{m,n}\gamma_2(\psi(y_n),y_n) + \frac{\mu_3(t)}{\mu_1(t)}g(x_m) + \frac{q^{\alpha+1}}{\mu_1(t)\Gamma(\alpha+1)}\{V_1(x_m)t^{\alpha} + V_2(x_m)\Gamma(\alpha+1)\}, \tag{29}$$

where the following assumptions are held:

(a) The parameters $\mu_i(t)$ satisfy $\max_t|\mu_i(t)| \le A_i \forall t \in [0,T], T < 1, i = \{1,2,3\}$ where A_i are constants.

(b) $\|g(x_m)\|_{l_2} = \left[\sum_{m=0}^{\infty}|g(x_m)|^2\right]^{\frac{1}{2}} \le \overline{B}$.

(c) $\sup_m|V_i(x_m)| \le \overline{D_i}, i = \{1,2\}$ where $\overline{D_i}$ are constants.

(d) $\|\Im_{m,n}\|_{l_2} = \left[\sum_{n=0}^{\infty}\sum_{m=0}^{\infty}\Im^2(|x_m - x_n|)\right]^{\frac{1}{2}} \le \overline{C}$.

(e) The unknown function $\psi(x_m)$ is in the space l_2 and its norm is defined as

$$\|\psi(x_m)\| = \left[\sum_{m=0}^{\infty}|\psi(x_m)|^2\right]^{\frac{1}{2}}$$

(f) For the constant $\overline{Q}$, the known function $\gamma_2(x_m,\psi(x_m))$ satisfies the following conditions:

$$\|\gamma_2(x_m,\psi(x_m))\| \le \overline{Q}\|\psi(x_m)\|$$

and

$$\|\gamma_2(x_m,\psi_1(x_m)) - \gamma_2(x_m,\psi_2(x_m))\| \le \overline{Q}\|\psi_1(x_m) - \psi_2(x_m)\|.$$

Theorem 2. *The approximate solution of the NAS of Equation (28) exists and unique under the condition*

$$A_2\overline{C}\,\overline{Q} < A_1. \tag{30}$$

The following lemmas must be proved to satisfy the above theorem.

Lemma 4. *The operator $\overline{\chi}$ maps the space l_2 onto itself under the conditions (a)–(f).*

Proof. From Equation (29), applying Cauchy–Minkowski inequality, we obtain

$$\|\overline{\chi}\psi(x_m)\| \le \left|\frac{\mu_2(t)}{\mu_1(t)}\right|\|\gamma_2(\psi(y_m),y_m)\|\left[\sum_{n=0}^{\infty}\sum_{m=0}^{\infty}\Im^2(|x_m - x_n|)\right]^{\frac{1}{2}} + \left|\frac{\mu_3(t)}{\mu_1(t)}\right|\|g(x_m)\| + \frac{q^{\alpha+1}}{|\mu_1(t)|\Gamma(\alpha+1)}\{|V_1(x_m)|T^{\alpha} + \Gamma(\alpha+1)|V_2(x_m)|, \tag{31}$$

using the conditions (a)–(f), we obtain

$$\|\overline{\chi}\psi(x_m)\| \le \frac{A_2}{A_1}\overline{Q}\|\psi(x_m)\|\overline{C} + \frac{A_3}{A_1}B^* + \frac{q^{\alpha+1}}{A_1\Gamma(\alpha+1)}[D_1T^{\alpha} + D_2\Gamma(\alpha+1)], \tag{32}$$

so, we have

$$\|\overline{\chi}\psi(x_m)\| \le \delta^*\|\psi(x_m)\| + \sigma^* \tag{33}$$

where

$$\delta^* = \frac{A_2}{A_1}\overline{Q}\,\overline{C}. \tag{34}$$

It is obvious that the operator $\overline{\chi}$ maps the ball $B_r^* \in l_2 \times C[0, T]$ onto itself where

$$r = \frac{\sigma^*}{1-\delta^*},\ \sigma^* = \frac{A_3}{A_1}B^* + \frac{q^{\alpha+1}}{A_1\Gamma(\alpha+1)}[D_1T^\alpha + D_2\Gamma(\alpha+1)].$$

The inequality (33) involves the boundedness of the operator $\overline{\chi}$ under the assumption $\delta^* < 1$. □

Lemma 5. *If conditions (a)–(f) are satisfied, then $\overline{\chi}$ is a contraction operator in Banach space l_2.*

Proof. Let two functions $\psi_1(x_m)$ and $\psi_2(x_m)$ be two solutions of (29), and then, the Formula (31) leads to

$$\|\overline{\chi}\psi_1(x_m) - \overline{\chi}\psi_2(x_m)\| \le \left|\frac{\mu_2(t)}{\mu_1(t)}\right|\left|\sum_{n=0}^{N}\Im_{m,n}\begin{bmatrix}\gamma_2(x_m,\psi_1(x_m))\\ -\gamma_2(x_m,\psi_2(x_m))\end{bmatrix}\right|. \tag{35}$$

Using conditions (a)–(f) and Cauchy–Minkowski inequality, we obtain

$$\|\overline{\chi}\psi_1(x_m) - \overline{\chi}\psi_2(x_m)\| \le \delta^*\|\psi_1(x_m) - \psi_2(x_m)\|. \tag{36}$$

It follows that for $\delta^* < 1$, $\overline{\chi}$ is a contraction operator of a system (36). Hence, there exists a unique solution in l_2 by a Banach fixed point theorem for every $t \in C[0, T]$.

8. Convergence of the Approximate Solution of NAS

To discuss the convergence of the system (28), we state the following theorem.

Theorem 3. *The NAS (28) for all values of time $t \in [0, T]$, $T < 1$ is convergent in the Banach space l_2 under the condition $\delta^* < 1$.*

Proof. We construct the sequence $\{\psi_z(x_m)\}$, and using Equation (29), we have

$$\mu_1(t)(\psi_z(x_m) - \psi_{z-1}(x_m)) = \mu_2(t)\sum_{n=0}^{N}\Im_{m,n}\begin{bmatrix}\gamma_2(\psi_{z-1}(y_n),y_n)\\ -\gamma_2(\psi_{z-2}(y_n),y_n)\end{bmatrix}, \tag{37}$$

consider

$$\psi_z(x_m) = \sum_{s=0}^{z}\eta_s(x_m),$$

where

$$\eta_z(x_m) = \psi_z(x_m) - \psi_{z-1}(x_m), \eta_0(x_m) = \mu_3(t)g(x_m).(z \ge 1). \tag{38}$$

By applying Cauchy–Schwarz and using (38) in (37), we obtain

$$A_1\|\eta_z(x_m)\| \le A_2\overline{CQ}\|\psi_{n-1}(x,t)\|.$$

Taking $n = 1$, the above formula becomes

$$\|\eta_1(x_m)\| \le \delta^* A_3\overline{B},$$

and then

$$\|\eta_z(x_m)\| \le (\delta^*)^z A_3\overline{B}, \delta^* < 1. \tag{39}$$

The sequence $\{\eta_z(x_m)\}$ is uniformly convergent by Equation (39). Additionally, it gives the sequence's $\psi_z(x_m) = \sum_{s=0}^{z}\eta_z(x_m)$ convergent solution.

As $z \to \infty$, $\psi_z(x_m) \to \psi(x_m)$, hence the solution $\psi(x_m)$ is uniformly convergent under the condition $\delta^* < 1$. This demonstrates the lemma. □

9. The Error of the Product Nystrom Technique

The following two definitions are used to calculate the error of this technique:

Definition 1. *The Nystrom method is said to be convergent of order r in the interval [−1, 1], if and only if, for N sufficient large, there exists a constant K > 0 independent of N such that*

$$\|\psi(x) - \psi_N(x)\| \leq KN^{-r} \tag{40}$$

Definition 2. *The estimated error of this method can be calculated in the form*

$$R_N = \left| \int_{-1}^{1} k(|x_m - y|)\gamma_2(\psi(y), y)dy - \sum_{n=0}^{N} \Im_{m,n}\gamma_2(\psi(y_n), y_n) \right|, \tag{41}$$

As $N \to \infty,\ R_N \to 0$. In this case, the approximate solution of (28) is equivalent to the exact solution of (21) in the space $L_2[-1,1] \times C[0,T],\ T < 1$.

10. Numerical Results

In this section, some numerical applications are considered to show the accuracy and applicable of the proposed methods.

Example 1.

$$\varphi(x, t + 0.03) = f(x,t) + 0.01\int_0^t \int_{-1}^{1} k(|x-y|)\tau^3 t^3 \varphi^2(y,\tau)dyd\tau, \tag{42}$$

with conditions

$$\varphi(x,0) = x, \frac{\partial\varphi(x,0)}{\partial t} = 0.5x^2. \tag{43}$$

Then, by taking

$$\varphi(x,t+0.03) = \varphi(x,t) + \frac{0.03^{0.75}}{\Gamma(1.75)}\frac{\partial^{0.75}}{\partial t^{0.75}}\varphi(x,t) + \frac{0.03^{1.75}}{\Gamma(2.75)}\frac{\partial^{1.75}}{\partial t^{1.75}}\varphi(x,t),$$

and $k(|x-y|) = |x-y|^{-v}$, we obtain

$$\begin{aligned}
&\tfrac{0.03^{1.75}}{\Gamma(2.75)}\left(\varphi(x,t) - 0.5x^2\right) - \tfrac{0.03^{1.75}x}{\Gamma(2.75)\Gamma(0.75)}\int_0^t (t-\tau)^{-0.25}d\tau \\
&\quad + \tfrac{0.03^{0.75}}{\Gamma(1.75)}\int_0^t \varphi(x,\tau)d\tau + \tfrac{1}{\Gamma(0.75)}\int_0^t (t-\tau)^{\alpha}\varphi(x,\tau)d\tau \\
&\quad - \tfrac{\lambda}{2\Gamma(0.75)}\int_0^t\int_{-1}^{1} (t-\tau)^{1.75}|x-y|^{-v}\tau^3 t^3\varphi^2(y,\tau)dyd\tau \\
&\quad = \tfrac{1}{\Gamma(0.75)}\int_0^t (t-\tau)^{\alpha} f(x,\tau)d\tau,
\end{aligned} \tag{44}$$

where $f(x,t)$ is given by putting $\varphi(x,t) = X(x)N(t), X = x^2, N(t) = t + 0.5$ as an exact value. We have the following two cases:

Case (i): if $f(x,t)$ and the unknown function $\varphi(x,t)$ have the same function of time where $M(t) = t + 0.5$.

Case (ii): if $f(x,t)$ and the unknown function $\varphi(x,t)$ have different time function in which $M(t) = 0.7e^t$.

The absolute errors in case (i) with some values of $x \in [-1,\ 1]$ are shown in Table 1 and the approximate solution $\varphi(x,t) = (t + 0.5)x^2$ is represented by Figure 1 while the errors for different T are shown by Figures 2–6. The errors in case (ii) are shown in Table 2 and Figures 7 and 8.

Table 1. The error for different. ν. of the approximate solution in case (i) in which $X(x) = [0.5625, 0.2500, 0.0625, 0.2500, 0.5625]$ at the given points above reduced to 10^{-5}.

T	X	Error (ν=0.01)	Error (ν=0.47)
	−0.75	2.000×10^{-10}	2.000×10^{-10}
	−0.5	1.000×10^{-10}	1.000×10^{-10}
0.0	0.25	1.000×10^{-11}	1.000×10^{-11}
	0.5	0.000	0.000
	0.75	0.000	0.000
	−0.75	0.000	0.000
	−0.5	1.000×10^{-10}	1.000×10^{-10}
0.1	0.25	1.000×10^{-11}	1.000×10^{-11}
	0.5	1.000×10^{-10}	1.000×10^{-10}
	0.75	0.000	0.000
	−0.75	8.000×10^{-10}	1.200×10^{-9}
	−0.5	9.000×10^{-10}	1.300×10^{-9}
0.5	0.25	8.400×10^{-10}	1.400×10^{-10}
	0.5	9.000×10^{-10}	1.200×10^{-9}
	0.75	9.000×10^{-10}	1.200×10^{-9}
	−0.75	8.770×10^{-8}	1.294×10^{-7}
	−0.5	8.460×10^{-8}	1.326×10^{-7}
0.9	0.25	8.533×10^{-8}	1.337×10^{-8}
	0.5	8.480×10^{-8}	1.327×10^{-7}
	0.75	8.750×10^{-8}	1.293×10^{-7}

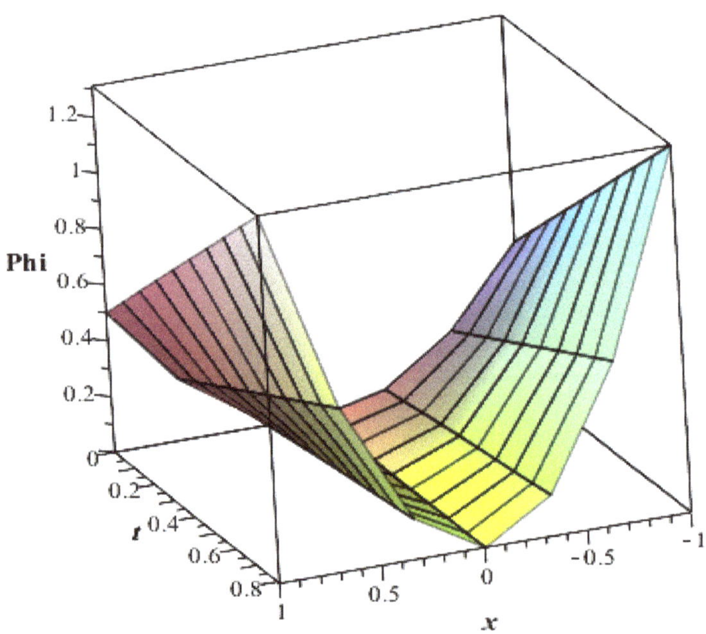

Figure 1. Approximate solution $\varphi(x,t) = (\mathrm{t}+0.5)x^2$ where $T = 0.9$.

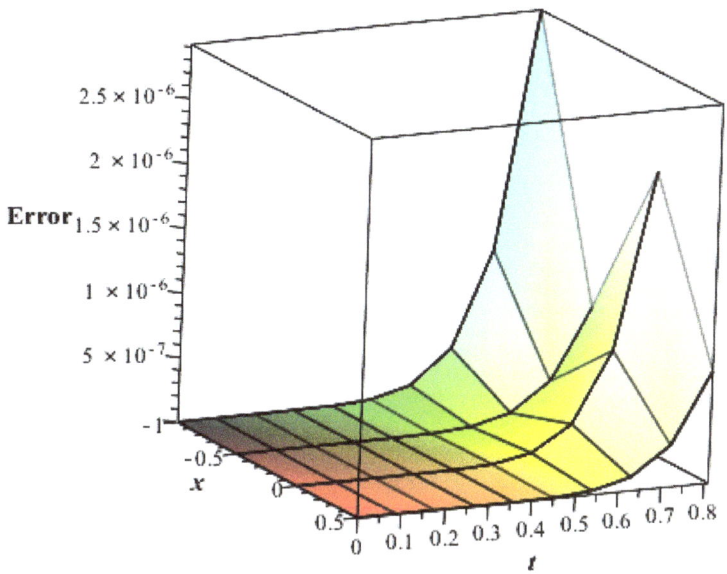

Figure 2. The error of example 1, case (i), where $N = 4$, $T = 0.9$.

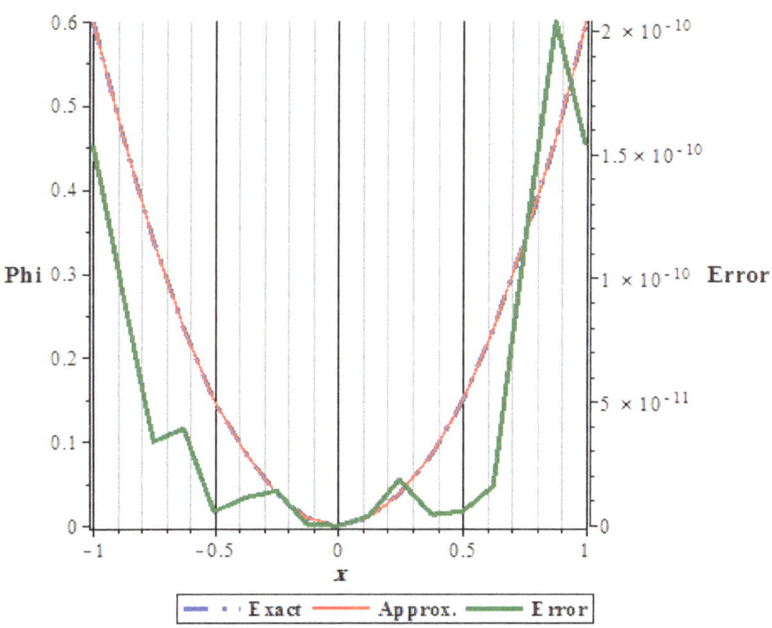

Figure 3. The error of example 1, case (i), where $N = 16$, $T = 0.1$.

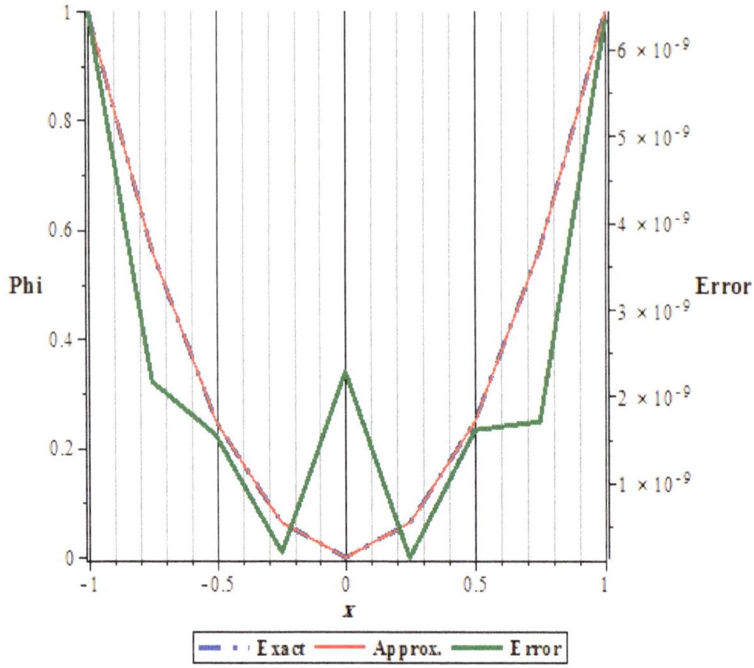

Figure 4. The error of example 1, case (i), where $N = 8$, $T = 0.5$.

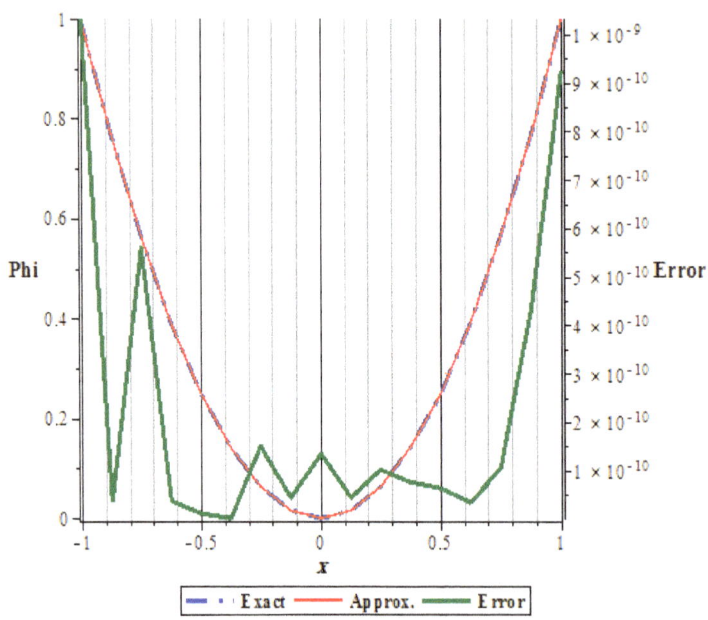

Figure 5. The error of example 1, case (i), where $N = 16$, $T = 0.5$.

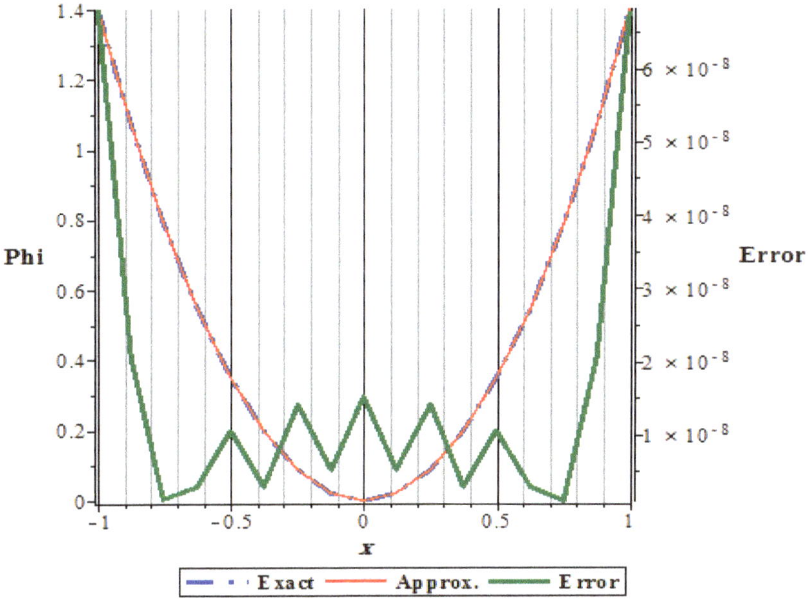

Figure 6. The error of example 1, case (i), where $N = 16,\ T = 0.9$.

Table 2. The error for different. ν. of the approximate solution in case (ii).

T	X	Error (ν = 0.01)	Error (ν = 0.47)
0.0	−0.75	0.000	0.000
	−0.5	1.000×10^{-10}	1.000×10^{-10}
	0.25	0.000	0.000
	0.5	0.000	0.000
	0.75	1.000×10^{-10}	1.000×10^{-10}
0.1	−0.75	2.000×10^{-10}	2.000×10^{-10}
	−0.5	$1.000 \times 10^{-1}0$	1.000×10^{-10}
	0.25	1.000×10^{-11}	1.000×10^{-11}
	0.5	0.000	0.000
	0.75	2.000×10^{-10}	2.000×10^{-10}
0.5	−0.75	9.000×10^{-10}	1.300×10^{-9}
	−0.5	9.000×10^{-10}	1.400×10^{-9}
	0.25	8.400×10^{-10}	$1.300 \times 10^{-1}0$
	0.5	1.000×10^{-9}	1.200×10^{-9}
	0.75	9.000×10^{-10}	1.300×10^{-9}
0.9	−0.75	8.770×10^{-8}	1.293×10^{-7}
	−0.5	8.460×10^{-8}	1.326×10^{-7}
	0.25	8.532×10^{-8}	1.337×10^{-8}
	0.5	8.480×10^{-8}	1.326×10^{-7}
	0.75	8.740×10^{-8}	1.293×10^{-7}

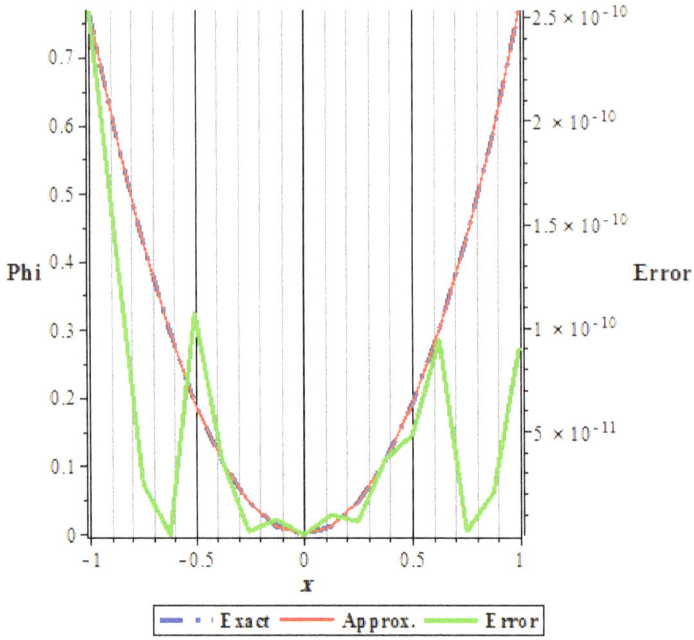

Figure 7. The error of example 1, case (ii), where $N = 16,\ \ T = 0.27$.

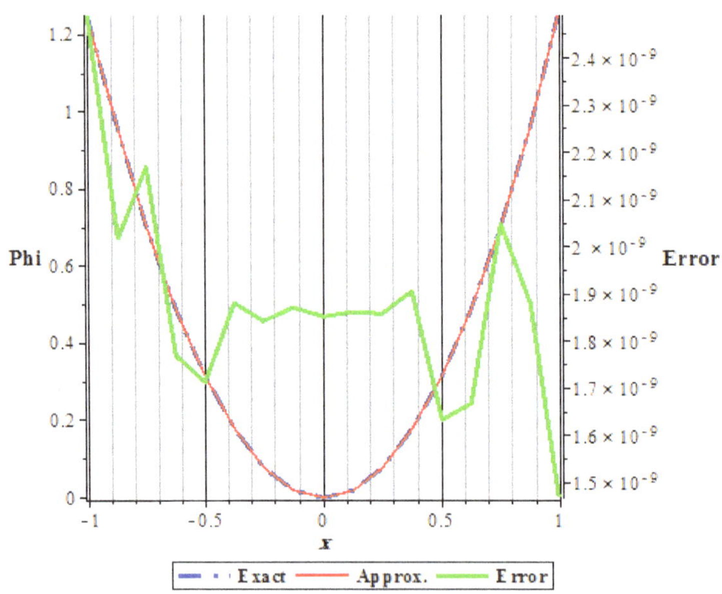

Figure 8. The error of example 1, case (ii), where $N = 16,\ \ T = 0.75$.

The error increases with time and decreases by increasing the number of iterations, see Figures 3–8.

Example 2. *Consider Equation (41) with $k(|x-y|) = ln|x-y|$, we obtain*

$$\begin{aligned}\frac{0.03^{1.75}}{\Gamma(2.75)}\left(\varphi(x,t)-0.5x^2\right)-\frac{0.03^{1.75}x}{\Gamma(2.75)\Gamma(0.75)}\int_0^t(t-\tau)^{-0.25}d\tau+\frac{0.03^{0.75}}{\Gamma(1.75)}\int_0^t\varphi(x,\tau)d\tau\\ +\frac{1}{\Gamma(0.75)}\int_0^t(t-\tau)^{\alpha}\varphi(x,\tau)d\tau\\ -\frac{\lambda}{2\Gamma(0.75)}\int_0^t\int_{-1}^1(t-\tau)^{1.75}\ln|x-y|\tau^3t^3\varphi^2(y,\tau)dyd\tau\\ =\frac{1}{\Gamma(0.75)}\int_0^t(t-\tau)^{\alpha}f(x,\tau)d\tau.\end{aligned} \quad (45)$$

Here, $f(x,t) = (0.1+\sin t)g(x)$ is given by putting $\varphi(x,t) = X(x)N(t), X = x^3$, $N(t) = 0.3\cos t$ as an exact value.

The rate of errors is evaluated using the following formula: $Rate = \left|\log_2 \frac{Error(2N)}{Error(N)}\right|$.

By increasing N, the error decreases and the rate of convergence is given below, see Tables 3–6.

Table 3. Convergence rate in both methods with fixed time $T = 0.0$.

N	Mean Error	Rate
4	2.4×10^{-10}	0.49
8	1.7×10^{-10}	0.79
16	9.8×10^{-11}	0.16
32	8.8×10^{-11}	---

Table 4. Convergence rate in both methods with fixed time $T = 0.3$.

N	Mean Error	Rate
4	4.8×10^{-10}	0.94
8	2.5×10^{-10}	1.32
16	1.0×10^{-10}	0.12
32	9.2×10^{-11}	---

Table 5. Convergence rate in both methods with fixed time $T = 0.6$.

N	Mean Error	Rate
4	5.8×10^{-8}	0.16
8	6.5×10^{-8}	3.92
16	4.3×10^{-9}	2.10
32	1.0×10^{-9}	---

Table 6. Convergence rate in both methods with fixed time $T = 0.9$.

N	Mean Error	Rate
4	8.9×10^{-7}	2.89
8	1.2×10^{-7}	3.79
16	8.7×10^{-9}	1.92
32	2.3×10^{-9}	---

The approximate solution is shown in Figure 9, and the absolute errors with different time are shown in Figures 10 and 11.

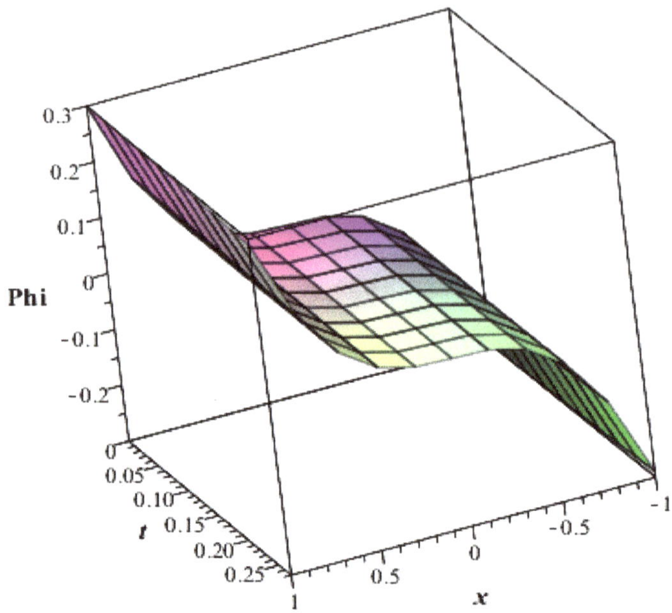

Figure 9. Approximate solution $\varphi(x,t) = (0.3 \cos t)X$.

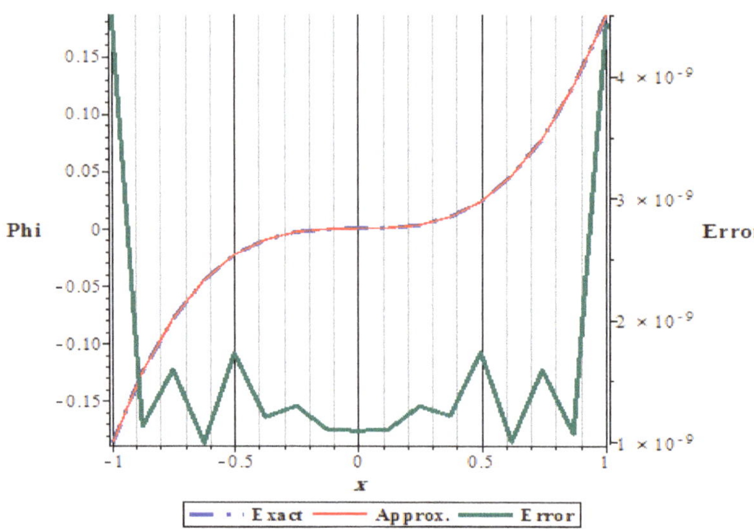

Figure 10. The error of example 2, where $T = 0.9$.

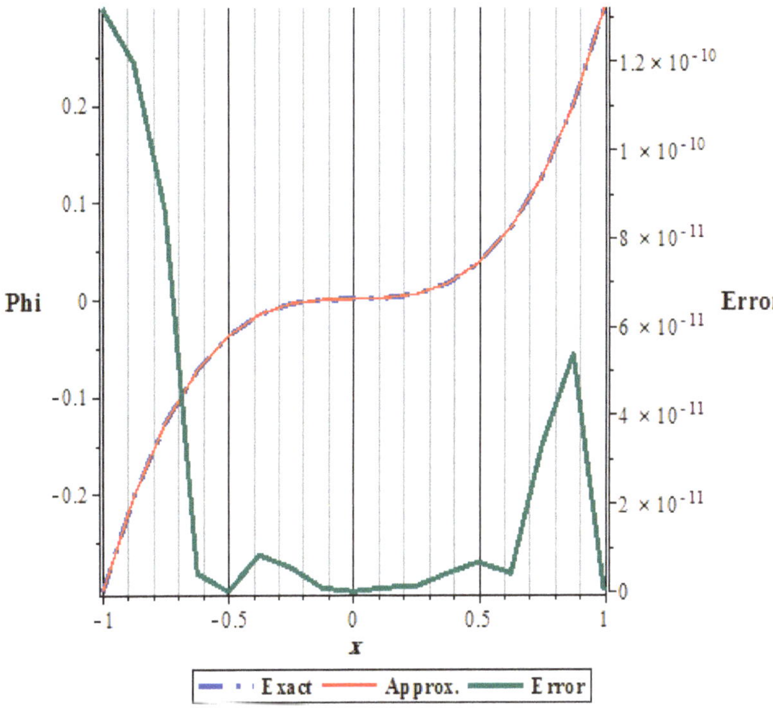

Figure 11. The error of example 2, where $T = 0.03$.

11. Conclusions

Fractional calculus has proved to be a valuable tool for modeling and analyzing numerous phenomena with non-local and memory-dependent characteristics. In this research, we focus on the study of fractional nonlinear integral equations with a time-dependent coefficient using the separation technique method. By employing this approach, we aim to transform the integral equation into a class of integral equations with coefficients on time, which can be subsequently solved using the Nystrom method. From the previous work and discussion, we can establish the following:

- The separation technique method is a powerful mathematical tool that allows us to transform fractional nonlinear integral equations with time-dependent coefficients into a class of integral equations with coefficients on time only. This technique simplifies the problem by separating the time-dependent part from the integral part, enabling us to handle the integral equations more efficiently.
- We present the Nystrom method as a numerical scheme to solve the sub-equations derived from the separation process. The Nystrom method efficiently discretizes the integral equation using a set of points and exploits the smoothness of the kernel functions to achieve high accuracy and computational efficiency. We discuss the convergence analysis and error estimates associated with the Nystrom method for the proposed fractional integral equations.
- In the Carleman kernel, when decreasing ν, the solution becomes better, see Table 1.
- The error increases with time, see Figures 3–8.
- The error decreases by increasing the number of iterations, see Tables 3–6.
- CPU Time for Intel® Core(TM) i7 CPU M 620 @ 2.67 GHz (64-bit Operating system) in example 2 takes the following:

N	Time in Seconds	Memory
4	10.4	59 M.
8	14.34	219.19 M.
16	34.32	215.9 M.

- The error is the same to an extreme degree between positive and negative values for x in the region of integration. We note that the maximum error occurs at the ends of x values while it takes the minimum in the middle, see Figure 2.

12. Future Work

We will attempt to solve Equation (1) as a phase-lag problem with a history memory function in the sense of general form of fractional calculus and differ between the three following cases of time: terrestrial ($T < 1$), eternal ($T > 1$), and isthmus lives ($T = 1$).

Author Contributions: Conceptualization, M.A.A.; Methodology, A.R.J. and M.B.; Software, M.B.; Validation, M.A.A.; Formal analysis, A.R.J., M.A.A. and M.B.; Writing—original draft, A.R.J. and M.B.; Writing—review & editing, M.A.A. and M.B.; Supervision, M.A.A.; Funding acquisition, A.R.J. All authors have read and agreed to the published version of the manuscript.

Funding: This research received no external funding.

Data Availability Statement: No instructional records have been created or comfortable with the ongoing assessment data in the original copy.

Conflicts of Interest: The authors declare no conflict of interest.

References

1. Herrmann, R. *Fractional Calculus: An Introduction for Physicists*; World Scientific: Singapore, 2014.
2. Oyedepo, T.; Taiwo, O.A. Numerical Studies for Solving Linear Fractional Integro-differential Equations Based on Constructed Orthogonal Polynomials. *ATBU J. Sci. Technol. Educ.* **2019**, *7*, 1–13.
3. Mohammed, O.H.; Altaie, S.A. Approximate solution of Fractional Integro-Differential Equations by using Bernstein polynomials. *Eng. Technol. J.* **2012**, *30*, 1362–1373. [CrossRef]
4. Daşcıoğlu, A.; Bayram, D.V. Solving Fractional Fredholm Integro-Differential Equations by Laguerre Polynomials. *Sains Malays.* **2019**, *48*, 251–257. [CrossRef]
5. Mohammed, D.S. Numerical solution of Fractional Integro-differential Equations by least squares method and shifted Chebyshev polynomial. *Comp. Methods Eng. Sci.* **2014**, *2014*, 431965. [CrossRef]
6. Mahdy, A.M.S.; Mohamed, E.M.H.; Marai, G.M.A. Numerical solution of fractional integro-differential Equations by least squares method and shifted Chebyshev polynomials of the third kind method. *Theor. Math. Appl.* **2016**, *6*, 87–101.
7. Nanware, J.A.; Goud, P.M.; Holambe, T.L. Solution of Fractional Integro-differential Equations by Bernstein Polynomials. *Malaya. J. Mat.* **2020**, *1*, 581–586. [CrossRef]
8. Oyedepo, T.; Taiwo, O.A.; Adebisi, A.F.; Ishola, C.Y.; Faniyi, O.E. Least Squares Method and Homotopy Perturbation Method for Solving Fractional Integro-Differential Equations. *Pac. J. Sci. Technol.* **2019**, *20*, 86–95.
9. Basseem, M.; Alalyani, A. On the Solution of Quadratic Nonlinear Integral Equation with Different Singular Kernels. *Math. Probl. Eng.* **2020**, *2020*, 7856207. [CrossRef]
10. Katani, R. Numerical solution of the Fredholm integral Equations with a quadrature method. *SeMA J.* **2018**, *76*, 271–276. [CrossRef]
11. Al-Bugami, A.M. Numerical Treating of Mixed Integral Equation Two-Dimensional in Surface Cracks in Finite Layers of Materials. *Adv. Math. Phys.* **2022**, *2022*, 3398175. [CrossRef]
12. Brezinski, C.; Redivo-Zaglia, M. Extrapolation methods for the numerical solution of nonlinear Fredholm integral Equations. *J. Integral Equ. Appl.* **2019**, *31*, 29–57. [CrossRef]
13. Bakhshayesh, S.J. Discontinuous Galerkin Approximations for Volterra Integral Equations of the First Kind with Convolution Kernel. *Indian J. Sci. Technol.* **2015**, *8*, 33. [CrossRef]
14. Alkan, S.; Hatipoglu, V.F. Approximate solutions of Volterra-Fredholm integro-differential Equations of fractional order. *Tbil. Math. J.* **2017**, *10*, 1–13. [CrossRef]
15. Mosa, G.A.; Abdou, M.A.; Gawish, F.A.; Abdalla, M.H. On the behavior solutions of fractional and partial integro differential heat Equations and its numerical solutions. *Math. Slovak* **2022**, *72*, 397–410. [CrossRef]
16. Jebreen, H.B.; Dassios, I. On the Wavelet Collocation Method for Solving Fractional Fredholm Integro-Differential Equations. *Mathematics* **2022**, *10*, 1272. [CrossRef]
17. Akram, T.; Ali, Z.; Rabiei, F.; Shah, K.; Kumam, P. A Numerical Study of Nonlinear Fractional Order Partial Integro-Differential Equation with a Weakly Singular Kernel. *Fractal Fract.* **2021**, *5*, 85. [CrossRef]

8. Abdelkawy, M.A.; Amin, A.Z.M.; Lopes, A.M.; Hashim, I.; Babatin, M.M. Shifted Fractional-Order Jacobi Collocation Method for Solving Variable-Order Fractional Integro-Differential. *Fractal Fract.* **2021**, *6*, 19. [CrossRef]
9. Khalil, H. The use of Jacobi polynomials in the numerical solution of coupled system of fractional differential Equation. *Int. J. Comput. Math.* **2014**, *92*, 1452–1472. [CrossRef]
0. Abdou, M.A. On the solution of linear and nonlinear integral Equation. *J. App. Math. Comp.* **2014**, *146*, 857–871. [CrossRef]
1. Abdou, M.A.; Raad, S.A. Nonlocal solution of a nonlinear partial differential Equation and its equivalent of nonlinear integral Equation. *Inter. J. Comp. Math.* **2014**, *92*, 1452–1472. [CrossRef]
2. Mosal, G.A.; Abdou, M.A.; Rahby, A.S. Numerical solutions for nonlinear Volterra-Fredholm integral equations of the second kind with a phase lag. *AIMS Math* **2021**, *6*, 8525–8543. [CrossRef]

fractal and fractional

Article

Dynamical Behaviour, Control, and Boundedness of a Fractional-Order Chaotic System

Lei Ren [1], Sami Muhsen [2], Stanford Shateyi [3,*] and Hassan Saberi-Nik [4,*]

1 School of Mathematics and Statistics, Shangqiu Normal University, Shangqiu 476000, China; math@sqnu.edu.cn
2 Air Conditioning and Refrigeration Techniques Engineering Department, College of Engineering and Technologies, Al-Mustaqbal University, Babylon 51001, Iraq; samimuhsen.1950@uomus.edu.iq
3 Department of Mathematics, University of Venda, Private Bag X5050, Thohoyandou 0950, South Africa
4 Department of Mathematics and Statistics, University of Neyshabur, Neyshabur 9319774446, Iran
* Correspondence: stanford.shateyi@univen.ac.za (S.S.); saberi_hssn@yahoo.com (H.S.-N.)

Abstract: In this paper, the fractional-order chaotic system form of a four-dimensional system with cross-product nonlinearities is introduced. The stability of the equilibrium points of the system and then the feedback control design to achieve this goal have been analyzed. Furthermore, further dynamical behaviors including, phase portraits, bifurcation diagrams, and the largest Lyapunov exponent are presented. Finally, the global Mittag–Leffler attractive sets (MLASs) and Mittag–Leffler positive invariant sets (MLPISs) of the considered fractional order system are presented. Numerical simulations are provided to show the effectiveness of the results.

Keywords: fractional-order hyperchaotic system; global Mittag–Leffler attractive sets (MLASs); Mittag–Leffler positive invariant sets (MLPISs); chaos control

1. Introduction

In recent years, fractional-order calculus has become a prominent part of applied research. Since applied sciences are naturally related to systems with memory, which dominates most physical and scientific systems, modeling with fractional order equations has been an undeniable necessity [1–5]. Fractional-order differential equations, which are actually generalizations of integer order calculus, deal with derivatives and integrals with non-integer orders. These equations have a unique feature which is the description of the memory effect [6–8]. Fractional derivative chaotic systems are now an important topic of study in nonlinear dynamics. The fractional-order chaotic system is considered a new alternative for which significant attention has been focused on developing techniques for modelling, synchronization, and control of the generalized dynamical systems [9–13]. Recently, fractional-order calculus has been applied to financial market changes. Investigations have indicated that economics and finance are extremely complex nonlinear systems involving many subjective factors, and there are many characteristics that cannot be modeled by integer-order calculus. Therefore, it is necessary to try to use the bifurcation and chaos of fractional nonlinear dynamics [14–16].

A chaotic system is a bounded nonlinear deterministic system with a long-term nature depending on the initial condition. The importance of the boundedness of a dynamical system can be found from the definition of chaos. Therefore, estimating the ultimate bound and positive invariant set of a chaotic system plays an important role in predicting its behavior, controlling chaos and preventing possible failures in physical and engineering systems. It can be clearly seen that the existence of the global attractor set for a system means the absence of hidden attractors outside this set [17–20].

By studying the ultimate bound of chaotic systems by Leonov [18], a new direction for research in this field was introduced. Many efforts have been made to develop methods for estimating the ultimate bound and the global attractive set of chaotic systems [21–24]. Despite many problems in determining the ultimate bound of some dynamical systems, various methods were presented that generally used optimization and the method of Lagrange coefficients [25–27]. Among the interesting studies that have been carried out so far, we can mention the calculation of the ultimate bound for various classical and generalized Lorenz systems [28], autonomous high-dimensional systems [29], complex Lorenz system [30], financial risk system [14], etc.

The four-dimensional autonomous system that indicates the equations related to the laser is defined as follows:

$$\begin{aligned} \dot{y_1} &= -ky_1 + ky_2, \\ \dot{y_2} &= ry_1 - y_2 - ey_3 - y_1y_4, \\ \dot{y_3} &= ey_2 - y_3, \\ \dot{y_4} &= -by_4 + y_1y_2, \end{aligned} \tag{1}$$

where k, r, b, e are real system parameters. The dynamical behaviour of this system such as stability of equilibria, Hopf bifurcations and randomness of multistability regions were studied by Natiq et al. [31]. One of the subjects that is necessary to investigate for this system is the estimation of the bound set. Of course, the ultimate bound set for system (1) has not been taken into account neither in the integer-order nor fractional-order. In order to develop methods for fractional-order systems, in this article we introduce the four-dimensional fractional-order chaotic system.

In this paper, a four-dimensional fractional-order system with cross-product nonlinearities has been introduced and analyzed. Using the concept of stability in fractional-order systems, the stability of equilibrium points and chaos control are performed theoretically and numerically. Furthermore, the dynamical characteristics of the considered system, such as the existence or absence of chaos, bifurcation diagrams, and Lyapunov exponents are investigated. The calculation of the ultimate bound called Mittag–Leffler bound set for chaotic dynamical systems has been implemented for a small number of systems. The MLASs and MLPISs for the chaotic fractional systems have been estimated so far [32–34]. The main contribution of this research work is to estimate the MLASs and MLPISs for a fractional system that belongs to a special class of nonlinear systems with only cross-product nonlinearities. By constructing a suitable generalized Lyapunov function and using the extremum principle of function, we obtain the new 3D ellipsoid estimations of the bounds for the presented fractional system, which improve the earlier publications and can deduce some new estimations.

This article is organized in the following sections. Section 2 presents a fractional-order chaotic system and its dynamical behaviors are theoretically and numerically investigated. In Section 3, we apply the feedback control method to study chaos control. In Section 4, we will study the Mittag–Leffler attractive sets (MLASs) and Mittag–Leffler positive invariant sets (MLPISs) of the fractional-order chaotic system. Conclusions are drawn in Section 5.

2. Fractional-Order Chaotic System

In this section, we present a fractional-order system derived from system (1). This four-dimensional system has nonlinear terms in the product form, which we define in a special class of chaotic systems. The new fractional-order chaotic system can be expressed as follows:

$$\begin{aligned} D_t^q y_1(t) &= -ky_1 + ky_2, \\ D_t^q y_2(t) &= ry_1 - y_2 - ey_3 - y_1y_4, \\ D_t^q y_3(t) &= ey_2 - y_3, \\ D_t^q y_4(t) &= -by_4 + y_1y_2, \end{aligned} \tag{2}$$

where D_t^q is q-order Caputo differential operator and q is the derivative order:

$$D_t^q y_i(t) = \frac{1}{\Gamma(n-q)} \int_0^t (t-s)^{n-q-1} y_i^{(n)}(s) ds, \ i = 1,2,3. \tag{3}$$

Definition 1 ([32])**.** *The Mittag–Leffler function $E_{\eta_1,\eta_2}(.)$ with two parameters is defined as*

$$E_{\eta_1,\eta_2}(c) = \sum_{i=0}^{\infty} \frac{c^i}{\Gamma(i\eta_1 + \eta_2)}, \tag{4}$$

where $\eta_1 > 0, \eta_2 > 0$, and c is a complex number. Obviously,

$$E_{\eta_1}(c) = E_{\eta_1,1}(c), E_{0,1}(c) = \frac{1}{1-c}, E_{1,1}(c) = e^c.$$

2.1. Stability Analysis of Equilibrium Points

Here, we consider the stability of the fractional-order nonlinear system (2). The equilibrium points of fractional-order system (2) can be obtained by solving

$$\begin{aligned} &-ky_1 + ky_2 = 0, \\ &ry_1 - y_2 - ey_3 - y_1y_4 = 0, \\ &ey_2 - y_3 = 0, \\ &-by_4 + y_1y_2 = 0. \end{aligned} \tag{5}$$

If selecting the parameters as $k = 4, e = 0.5, r = 27$, and $b = 1$, there are three equilibrium points of system (2), which as follows:

$$\begin{aligned} E_1 &= \Big(0,0,0,0\Big), \\ E_2 &= \Big(5.074445783, 5.074445783, 2.537222891, 25.75\Big), \\ E_3 &= \Big(-5.074445783, -5.074445783, -2.537222891, 25.75\Big). \end{aligned} \tag{6}$$

Then, we have the following conclusions for the stability of these equilibrium points.

Theorem 1 ([4])**.** *Consider the fractional-order nonlinear dynamical system*

$$D_t^q y(t) = f(y(t)), \ 0 < q < 1, \tag{7}$$

where $f = [f_1, f_2, \cdots, f_n]^T$, is a vector function and $f_i (i = 1, 2, \cdots, n)$ are continuous differential nonlinear functions. The equilibrium points E^* of system (7) are asymptotically stable if all the eigenvalues $\lambda_i (i = 1, 2, \cdots, n)$ of the Jacobian matrix $J = \frac{\partial f}{\partial y}$, satisfy the following condition:

$$|\arg(\lambda_i)| > \frac{q\pi}{2} (i = 1, 2, \cdots, n).$$

The Jacobian matrix of the system (2) at the equilibrium point of E^* is

$$J(E^*) = \begin{bmatrix} -k & k & 0 & 0 \\ r - y_4^* & -1 & -e & -y_1^* \\ 0 & e & -1 & 0 \\ y_2^* & y_1^* & 0 & -b \end{bmatrix}.$$

The characteristic equation of the Jacobian matrix $J(E^*)$ is given by

$$C(\lambda) = \begin{vmatrix} \lambda+k & -k & 0 & 0 \\ y_4^*-r & \lambda+1 & e & y_1^* \\ 0 & -e & \lambda+1 & 0 \\ -y_2^* & -y_1^* & 0 & \lambda+b \end{vmatrix}$$

$$\begin{aligned} &= \lambda^4 + (b+k+2)\lambda^3 + \Big((b-r+y_4^*+2)k + e^2 + y_1^{*2} + 2b + 1\Big)\lambda^2 \\ &+ \Big(\Big((-r+y_4^*+2)b + e^2 + y_1^{*2} + y_2^* y_1^* - r + y_4^* + 1\Big)k + e^2 b + y_1^{*2} + b\Big)\lambda \\ &+ k\Big(\Big(e^2 - r + y_4^* + 1\Big)b + y_1^*(y_1^* + y_2^*)\Big) = 0. \end{aligned}$$

At the equilibrium point E_1 and parameters $k = 4, e = 0.5, r = 27$, and $b = 1$ the characteristic equation, becomes

$$C(\lambda) = \lambda^4 + 7\lambda^3 + 36\lambda^2 + 236\lambda + 206 = 0, \tag{8}$$

and eigenvalues of Equation (10) are

$$\begin{aligned} &\lambda_1 = 0.1842463692 - 5.68443459i, \ \lambda_2 = -1, \\ &\lambda_3 = 0.1842463692 + 5.684434590i, \ \lambda_4 = -6.368492738. \end{aligned}$$

Since,

$$\begin{aligned} &|\arg(\lambda_1)| = 1.538395235, \quad |\arg(\lambda_2)| = \pi, \\ &|\arg(\lambda_3)| = 1.538395235, \quad |\arg(\lambda_4)| = 1.538395235, \end{aligned}$$

by Theorem 1, equilibrium point E_1 is asymptotically stable, when $q < \frac{2|\arg(\lambda_{1,4})|}{\pi} = 0.9793$.

2.2. Dynamical Behaviors

In this section, the basic dynamical properties such as phase portraits, bifurcation diagram, Lyapunov exponents and chaos diagram of the fractional-order chaotic system (2) are presented.

Selecting the parameters $k = 4, e = 0.5, r = 27$, and $b = 1$, Figure 1 depicts Lyapunov exponents. When $q = 0.999$, the values of Lyapunov exponents at 500th second are $L_1 = 0.5291$, $L_2 = -0.0022$, $L_3 = -0.9789$, and $L_4 = -4.7122$.

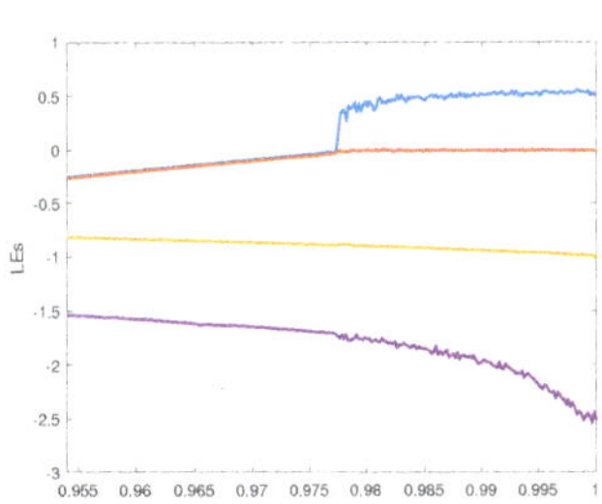

Figure 1. Lyapunov exponent spectra for system (2) with $k = 4$, $e = 0.5$, $r = 27$, and $b = 1$.

The Benettin–Wolf algorithm to determine all Lyapunov exponents for the fractional-order systems modeled by Caputo's derivative is used [35]. The values of Lyapunov exponents at 500th second are obtained as $L_1 = -0.0783$, $L_2 = -0.0839$, $L_3 = -0.9501$, and $L_4 = -2.9103$. As it is clear from Figures 1 and 2, for some values of q, system (2) has positive Lyapunov exponent and therefore is in a chaotic state and for different values of q, system (2) converges to the equilibrium point.

The bifurcation diagram of system (2) is drawn based on the change of the derivative order parameter and by fixing the values of other parameters as $k = 4, e = 0.5, r = 27$, and $b = 1$. Figure 3, shows the effect of varying parameter q in the interval $(0.954, 1)$. It is obvious that with different values of the derivative order of q, the system (2) is in stable, periodic and chaotic state and the bifurcation diagram is well consistent with the Lyapunov exponent spectrum. The system is stable in $q \in (0.954, 0.978)$ and the system exhibits chaotic behavior when $q \in (0.978, 1)$.

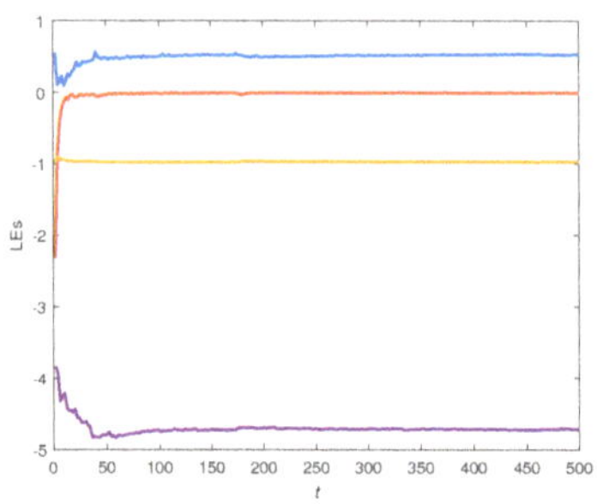

(**a**) $q = 0.99$

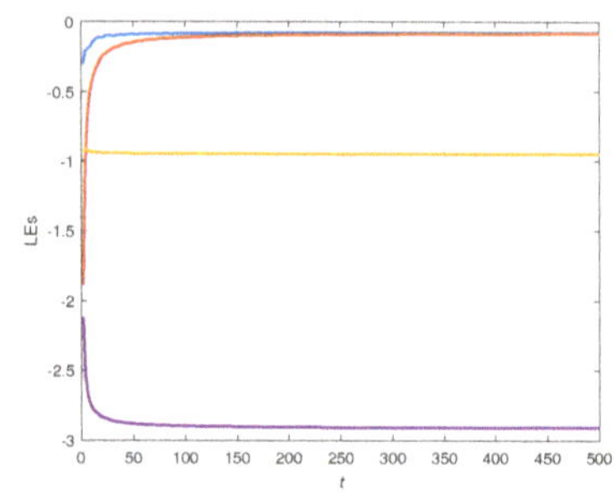

(**b**) $q = 0.97$

Figure 2. Lyapunov exponent spectra for system (2) with $k = 4$, $e = 0.5$, $r = 27$, and $b = 1$.

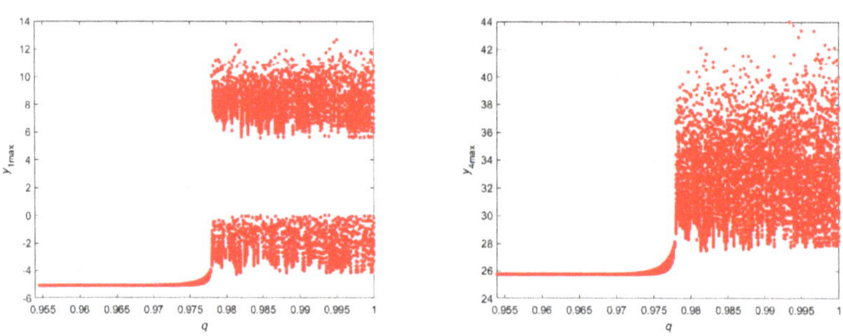

Figure 3. Bifurcation diagram with fixed values $k = 4$, $e = 0.5$, $r = 27, b = 1$, and $q \in (0.954, 1)$.

When $k = 4$, $e = 0.5$, $r = 27$, and $b = 1$, the phase portraits of system (2) are shown in Figure 4, that indicates for the value of $q = 0.97$, the trajectories of the system converge to the equilibrium point.

When $q = 0.99$, $k = 4$, $e = 0.5$, $r = 27$, and $b = 1$, the phase portraits of system (2) are shown in Figure 5. The system exhibits the chaotic behavior and the equilibrium point is not stable.

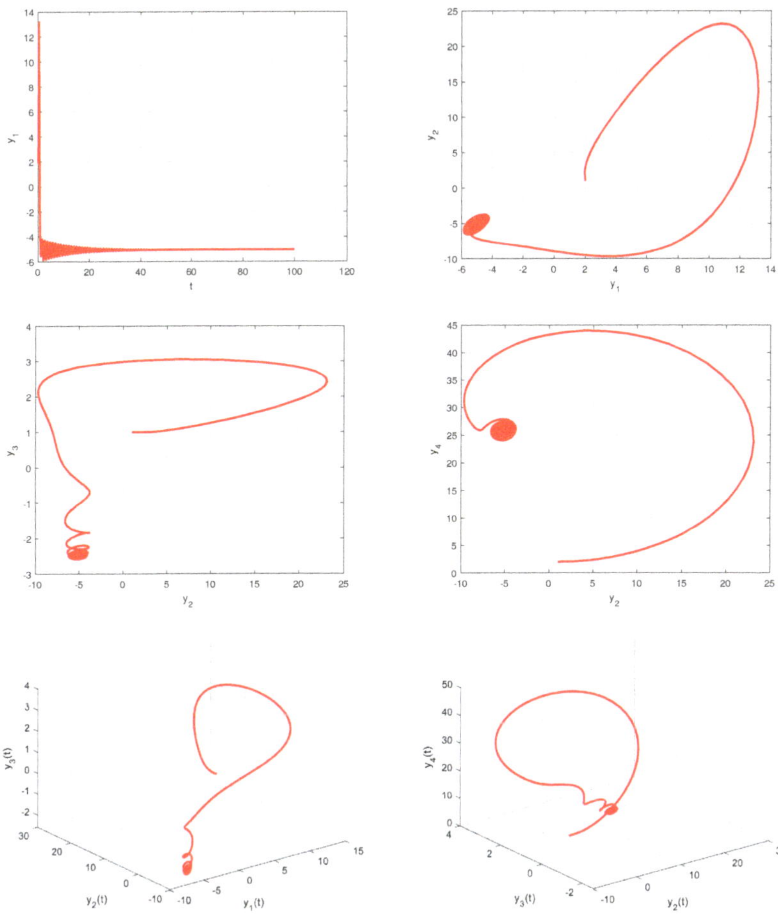

Figure 4. Phase portraits for (2) with $q = 0.97,\ k = 4,\ e = 0.5, r = 27$, and $b = 1$.

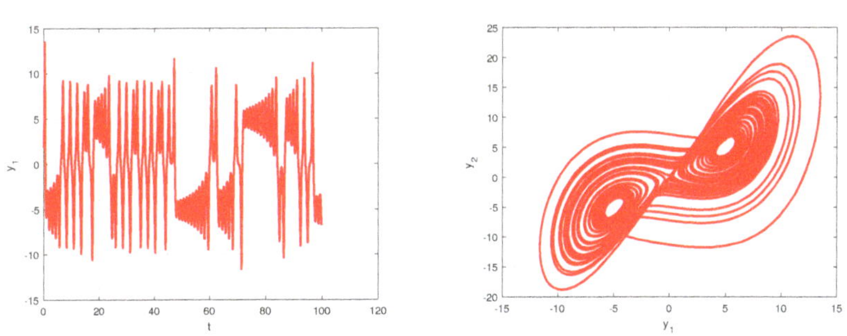

Figure 5. *Cont.*

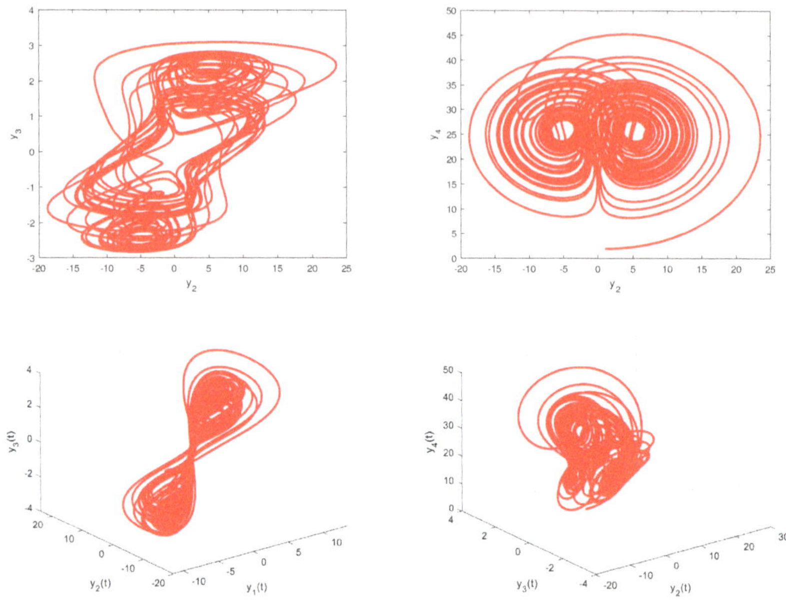

Figure 5. Phase portraits for (2) with $q = 0.99, k = 4, e = 0.5, r = 27$, and $b = 1$.

3. Chaos Control

In this section, we apply the linear feedback control method to stabilize system (2) to its equilibrium points. Let consider the following controlled form of fractional-order system (2):

$$\begin{aligned} D_t^q y_1(t) &= -ky_1 + ky_2 - w_1(y_1 - y_1^*), \\ D_t^q y_2(t) &= ry_1 - y_2 - ey_3 - y_1y_4 - w_2(y_2 - y_2^*), \\ D_t^q y_3(t) &= ey_2 - y_3 - w_3(y_3 - y_3^*), \\ D_t^q y_4(t) &= -by_4 + y_1y_2 - w_4(y_4 - y_4^*), \end{aligned} \tag{9}$$

where w_1, w_2, w_3, w_4 are control parameters and E^* is the equilibrium point of the system (2).

The Jacobian matrix at E^* for the system (9) is obtained as

$$J(E^*) = \begin{bmatrix} -k - w_1 & k & 0 & 0 \\ r - y_4^* & -1 - w_2 & -e & -y_1^* \\ 0 & e & -1 - w_3 & 0 \\ y_2^* & y_1^* & 0 & -b - w_4 \end{bmatrix}.$$

The characteristic equation of the Jacobian matrix $J(E^*)$ is given by

$$f(\lambda) = \begin{vmatrix} \lambda + k + w_1 & -k & 0 & 0 \\ y_4^* - r & \lambda + 1 + w_2 & e & y_1^* \\ 0 & -e & \lambda + 1 + w_3 & 0 \\ -y_2^* & -y_1^* & 0 & \lambda + b + w_4 \end{vmatrix} = 0.$$

Selecting $k_1 = 1, k_2 = 2, k_3 = 3$ and $k_4 = 4$, the characteristic polynomial of for the equilibrium point E_1 with the parameters $k = 4, e = 0.5, r = 27$, and $b = 1$ is given as

$$C(\lambda) = \lambda^4 + 17\lambda^3 + 128\lambda^2 + 587.25\lambda + 1133.25 = 0, \tag{10}$$

and the characteristic roots of Equation (10) are calculated as

$$\lambda_1 = -2.539703887 - 5.413874345i, \ \lambda_2 = -7.918563161,$$
$$\lambda_3 = -4.002029066, \ \lambda_4 = -2.539703887 + 5.413874345i.$$

Since, all the eigenvalues of Equation (10) are negative real numbers and complex numbers with negative real parts, therefore the equilibrium point E_1 is asymptotically stable for all $0 < q < 1$. When $q = 0.99, k = 4, e = 0.5, r = 27$, and $b = 1$, the phase portraits and time series of the controlled system (9) are shown in Figure 6.

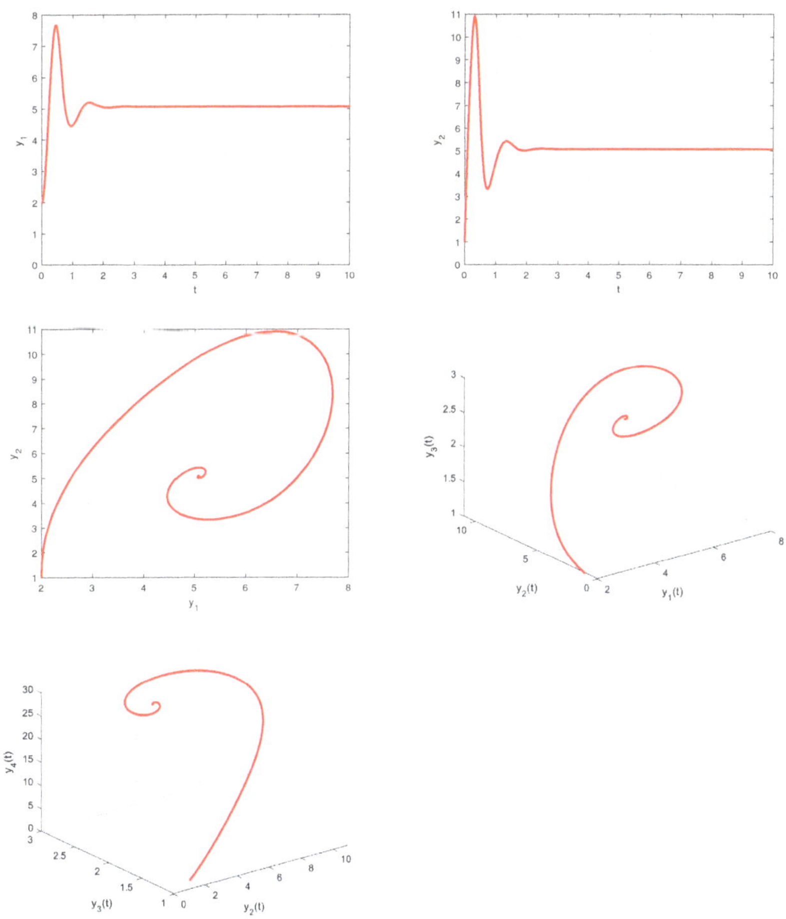

Figure 6. Phase portraits and time series of the controlled system (9) with $q = 0.99, k = 4, e = 0.5, r = 27$, and $b = 1$.

4. Global Mittag–Leffler Attractive Sets

In this section, our main aim is to estimate the global Mittag–Leffler attractive sets (MLASs) and Mittag–Leffler positive invariant sets (MLPISs) for the fractional-order chaotic system (2). Firstly, we introduce some definitions for calculating the MLAS and MLPIS of fractional-order systems with only cross-product nonlinearities.

Lemma 1 ([32]). *Let $y(t) \in \mathbb{R}$, is the continuous and differentiable functions, then*

$$\frac{1}{2}D^q(y^2(t)) \leq y(t)D^q(y(t)), \tag{11}$$

Lemma 2 ([32]). *For $q \in (0,1)$ and constant $\gamma \in \mathbb{R}$, if a continuous function $y(t)$ meets*

$$D^q(y(t)) \leq \gamma y(t), \quad t \geq 0, \tag{12}$$

then

$$y(t) \leq y(0)E_q(\gamma t^q), \quad t \geq 0. \tag{13}$$

Definition 2 ([32]). *Let us consider the following fractional-order system*

$$D_t^q y_i = f(y_i), \quad y_i(t_0) = y_{i,0}, \ i = 1,2,\cdots,n, \tag{14}$$

where $y_i \in \mathbb{R}^n$, $f : \mathbb{R}^n \to \mathbb{R}^n$ is sufficiently smooth, and $y_i(t,t_0,y_{i,0})$ is the solution.

For a given Lyapunov function $\mathcal{L}(Y(t))$, if there exist constants $\mathcal{K}_\gamma > 0$ and $\gamma > 0$ for all $Y_0 \in \mathbb{R}^n$ such that

$$\mathcal{L}(Y(t)) - \mathcal{K}_\gamma \leq (\mathcal{L}(Y(t_0)) - \mathcal{K}_\gamma)E_q(-\gamma(t-t_0)^q), \ t \geq t_0, \tag{15}$$

for $\mathcal{L}(Y(t)) > \mathcal{K}_\gamma$, then $\mathcal{G} = \{(y_1,y_2,\cdots,y_n)|\mathcal{L}(Y(t)) \leq \mathcal{K}_\gamma\}$ is said to be the global Mittag–Leffler attractive sets (MLASs) of system (14). If for any $Y_0 \in \mathcal{G}$ and any $t > t_0$, $Y(t,t_0,Y_0) \in \mathcal{G}$, then $\mathcal{G}$ is said to be a Mittag–Leffler positive invariant sets (MLPISs).

4.1. Main Results

Here we will discuss the ultimate bound of a class of the fractional-order chaotic systems with only cross-product nonlinearities:

$$\begin{aligned}
D_t^q y_1(t) &= \sum_{j=1}^{4} \alpha_{1j} y_j + \sum_{j=1}^{4}\sum_{k=1}^{4} \beta_{1jk} y_j y_k + r_1, \\
D_t^q y_2(t) &= \sum_{j=1}^{4} \alpha_{2j} y_j + \sum_{j=1}^{4}\sum_{k=1}^{4} \beta_{2jk} y_j y_k + r_2, \\
D_t^q y_3(t) &= \sum_{j=1}^{4} \alpha_{3j} y_j + \sum_{j=1}^{4}\sum_{k=1}^{4} \beta_{3jk} y_j y_k + r_3,
\end{aligned} \tag{16}$$

$$D_t^q y_4(t) = \sum_{j=1}^{4} \alpha_{4j} y_j + \sum_{j=1}^{4}\sum_{k=1}^{4} \beta_{4jk} y_j y_k + r_4. \tag{17}$$

The candidate Lyapunov function for this problem is defined as follows

$$\mathcal{L}(Y(t)) = \frac{1}{2}(\omega_1 y_1 - s_1)^2 + \frac{1}{2}(\omega_2 y_2 - s_2)^2 + \frac{1}{2}(\omega_3 y_3 - s_3)^2 + \frac{1}{2}(\omega_4 y_4 - s_4)^2, \tag{18}$$

where $\omega_i, s_i, i = 1,2,3,4$ are known parameters. The function $h(Y,\delta)$ is considered as follows

$$\begin{aligned} h(Y,\delta) = {} & \omega_1(\omega_1 y_1 - s_1)\left(\sum_{j=1}^{4}\alpha_{1j}y_j + \frac{\delta_1}{\omega_1}(\omega_1 y_1 - s_1) + \sum_{j=1}^{4}\sum_{k=1}^{4}\beta_{1jk}y_j y_k + r_1\right) \\ & + \omega_2(\omega_2 y_2 - s_2)\left(\sum_{j=1}^{4}\alpha_{2j}y_j + \frac{\delta_2}{\omega_2}(\omega_2 y_2 - s_2) + \sum_{j=1}^{4}\sum_{k=1}^{4}\beta_{2jk}y_j y_k + r_2\right) \\ & + \omega_3(\omega_3 y_3 - s_3)\left(\sum_{j=1}^{4}\alpha_{3j}y_j + \frac{\delta_3}{\omega_3}(\omega_3 y_3 - s_3) + \sum_{j=1}^{4}\sum_{k=1}^{4}\beta_{3jk}y_j y_k + r_3\right) \\ & + \omega_4(\omega_4 y_4 - s_4)\left(\sum_{j=1}^{4}\alpha_{4j}y_j + \frac{\delta_4}{\omega_4}(\omega_4 y_4 - s_4) + \sum_{j=1}^{4}\sum_{k=1}^{4}\beta_{4jk}y_j y_k + r_4\right), \end{aligned} \tag{19}$$

where $\delta = (\delta_1, \delta_2, \delta_3, \delta_4)$.

Theorem 2. *Let $h(Y_0,\delta) > 0$ is the supremum of function $h(Y,\delta)$ on $Y \in \mathbb{R}^4$ defined in (19), $\gamma = \min\{\delta_1, \delta_2, \delta_3, \delta_4\}$. Then the following inequality is fulfilled:*

$$\mathcal{L}(Y(t)) - \frac{1}{2\gamma}h(Y_0,\delta) \le \left(\mathcal{L}(Y(t_0)) - \frac{1}{2\gamma}h(Y_0,\delta)\right)E_q(-2\gamma(t-t_0)^q), \ t \ge t_0. \tag{20}$$

Furthermore,

$$\begin{aligned} \mathcal{G} &= \{Y|\mathcal{L}(Y(t)) \le \frac{1}{2\gamma}h(Y_0,\delta)\} \\ &= \{Y|(\omega_1 y_1 - s_1)^2 + (\omega_2 y_2 - s_2)^2 + (\omega_3 y_3 - s_3)^2 + (\omega_4 y_4 - s_4)^2 \le \frac{1}{\gamma}h(Y_0,\delta)\}, \end{aligned} \tag{21}$$

is the Mittag–Leffler attractive sets (MLASs) and Mittag–Leffler positive invariant sets (MLPISs) of system (2).

Proof. Computing the fractional derivative of $\mathcal{L}(Y(t))$ along the trajectory of system (16) and using Lemma 1, we have

$$\begin{aligned} D^q\mathcal{L}(Y(t)) \le {} & (\omega_1 y_1 - s_1)D^q\omega_1 y_1 + (\omega_2 y_2 - s_2)D^q\omega_2 y_2 + (\omega_3 y_3 - s_3)D^q\omega_3 y_3 \\ & + (\omega_4 y_4 - s_4)D^q\omega_4 y_4 \\ & = \omega_1(\omega_1 y_1 - s_1)\left(\sum_{j=1}^{4}\alpha_{1j}y_j + \sum_{j=1}^{4}\sum_{k=1}^{4}\beta_{1jk}y_j y_k + r_1\right) \\ & + \omega_2(\omega_2 y_2 - s_2)\left(\sum_{j=1}^{4}\alpha_{2j}y_j + \sum_{j=1}^{4}\sum_{k=1}^{4}\beta_{2jk}y_j y_k + r_2\right) \\ & + \omega_3(\omega_3 y_3 - s_3)\left(\sum_{j=1}^{4}\alpha_{3j}y_j + \sum_{j=1}^{4}\sum_{k=1}^{4}\beta_{3jk}y_j y_k + r_3\right) \\ & + \omega_4(\omega_4 y_4 - s_4)\left(\sum_{j=1}^{4}\alpha_{4j}y_j + \sum_{j=1}^{4}\sum_{k=1}^{4}\beta_{4jk}y_j y_k + r_4\right) \\ & = -\delta_1(\omega_1 y_1 - s_1)^2 - \delta_2(\omega_2 y_2 - s_2)^2 - \delta_3(\omega_3 y_3 - s_3)^2 - \delta_4(\omega_4 y_4 - s_4)^2 \\ & + h(Y,\delta) \le -\gamma\sum_{j=1}^{4}(\omega_j y_j - s_j)^2 + h(Y,\delta) \\ & \le -\gamma\sum_{j=1}^{4}(\omega_j y_j - s_j)^2 + h(Y_0,\delta). \end{aligned} \tag{22}$$

From there we have

$$D^q \mathcal{L}(Y(t)) \leq -2\gamma \mathcal{L}(Y(t)) + h(Y_0, \delta), \tag{23}$$

i.e.,

$$D^q \Big(\mathcal{L}(Y(t)) - \frac{1}{2\gamma} h(Y_0, \delta) \Big) \leq -2\gamma \Big[\mathcal{L}(Y(t)) - \frac{1}{2\gamma} h(Y_0, \delta) \Big]. \tag{24}$$

According to Lemma 2, we obtain

$$\mathcal{L}(Y(t)) - \frac{1}{2\gamma} h(Y_0, \delta) \leq (\mathcal{L}(Y_0) - \frac{1}{2\gamma} h(Y_0, \delta)) E_q(-2\gamma t^q), \ t \geq 0. \tag{25}$$

Finally, Definition 2, indicates that the ellipsoid $\mathcal{G}$ is the Mittag–Leffler attractive sets (MLASs) and Mittag–Leffler positive invariant sets (MLPISs) of the system (2). □

4.2. MLAS and MLPIS for the Fractional-Order System (2)

To investigate the correctness of Theorem 4.1, we consider the calculation of the bound set for the fractional-order system (2). The following theorem determines the necessary conditions for estimating the MLAS and MLPIS for the system (2).

Theorem 3. *Let consider $\delta_1 < k, \delta_2 < 1, \delta_3 < 1, \delta_4 < b$, and $E_0 = (y_1^0, y_2^0, y_3^0, y_4^0)$ be the stable point of $h(Y, \delta)$ defined by (19). Moreover, the Hessian Matrix of $h(Y, \delta)$ is a negative definite matrix on E_0. Then,*

$$\mathcal{G} = \Big\{ Y(t) \in \mathbb{R}^4 \mid \omega_1 y_1^2 + \omega_2 y_2^2 + \omega_3 y_3^2 + \omega_2 (y_4 - \frac{k\omega_1 + r\omega_2}{\omega_2})^2 \leq \frac{b^2 (k\omega_1 + r\omega_2)^2}{4\gamma (b - \delta_4)} \Big\}, \tag{26}$$

is the Mittag–Leffler attractive sets (MLASs) and Mittag–Leffler positive invariant sets (MLPISs) of the system (2).

Proof. Let $\alpha_{11} = -k, \alpha_{12} = k, \alpha_{21} = r, \alpha_{22} = -1, \alpha_{23} = -e, \alpha_{32} = e, \alpha_{33} = -1, \alpha_{44} = -b, \beta_{214} = -1, \beta_{412} = 1, r_1 = r_2 = r_3 = r_4 = 0$, else $\alpha_{ij} = 0, \beta_{ijk} = 0$, and $s_1 = s_2 = s_3 = 0, s_4 = k\omega_1 + r\omega_2$.

Thus, $\mathcal{L}(Y(t))$ can be rewritten as:

$$\mathcal{L}(Y(t)) = \frac{1}{2}\omega_1 y_1^2 + \frac{1}{2}\omega_2 y_2^2 + \frac{1}{2}\omega_3 y_3^2 + \frac{1}{2}\omega_2 (y_4 - \frac{k\omega_1 + r\omega_2}{\omega_2})^2, \tag{27}$$

and

$$\begin{aligned} h(Y, \delta) = {} & \omega_1^2 y_1 \Big(-k y_1 + k y_2 + \delta_1 y_1 \Big) + \omega_2^2 y_2 \Big(r y_1 - y_2 - e y_3 - y_1 y_4 + \delta_2 y_2 \Big) \\ & + \omega_3^2 y_3 \Big(e y_2 - y_3 + \delta_3 y_3 \Big) + \omega_2 \Big(\omega_2 y_4 - (k\omega_1 + r\omega_2) \Big) \\ & \Big(-b y_4 + y_1 y_2 + \frac{\delta_4}{\omega_2} (\omega_2 y_4 - (k\omega_1 + r\omega_2)) \Big). \end{aligned}$$

Since E_0 is the stable point of the $h(Y, \delta)$, we have

$$\nabla(h)_{E_0} = (h'_{y_1}, h'_{y_2}, h'_{y_3}, h'_{y_4}) = 0. \tag{28}$$

and the Hessian Matrix H of the $h(Y, \delta)$ is a negative definite matrix. Therefore,

$$h'_{y_1} = \omega_1^2(-ky_1 + ky_2 + \delta_1 y_1) + \omega_1^2 y_1(-k + \delta_1) + \omega_2^2 y_2(r - y_4) + \omega_2(-k\omega_1 - r\omega_2 + \omega_2 y_4)y_2,$$

$$h'_{y_2} = \omega_1^2 y_1 k + \omega_2^2(-ey_3 + ry_1 + \delta_2 y_2 - y_1 y_4 - y_2) + \omega_2^2 y_2(\delta_2 - 1) + \omega_3^2 y_3 e + \omega_2(-k\omega_1 - r\omega_2 + \omega_2 y_4)y_1,$$

$$h'_{y_3} = -\omega_2^2 y_2 e + \omega_3^2(ey_2 + \delta_3 y_3 - y_3) + \omega_3^2 y_3(\delta_3 - 1),$$

$$\begin{aligned} h'_{y_4} &= -\omega_2^2 y_2 y_1 + \omega_2^2(-by_4 + y_1 y_2 + \delta_4(-k\omega_1 - r\omega_2 + \omega_2 y_4)/\omega_2) \\ &\quad + \omega_2(-k\omega_1 - r\omega_2 + \omega_2 y_4)(-b + \delta_4), \\ h''_{y_1y_1} &= 2\omega_1^2(-k + \delta_1), \\ h''_{y_2y_2} &= 2\omega_2^2(\delta_2 - 1), \\ h''_{y_3y_3} &= 2\omega_3^2(\delta_3 - 1), \\ h''_{y_4y_4} &= 2\omega_2^2(-b + \delta_4), \\ h''_{y_1y_2} &= h''_{y_2y_1} = k\omega_1^2 - k\omega_1\omega_2, \end{aligned}$$

$$\begin{aligned} h''_{y_1y_3} &= h''_{y_3y_1} = 0, \\ h''_{y_1y_4} &= h''_{y_4y_1} = 0, \\ h''_{y_2y_3} &= h''_{y_3y_2} = -e\omega_2^2 + e\omega_3^2, \\ h''_{y_2y_4} &= h''_{y_4y_2} = 0, \\ h''_{y_3y_4} &= h''_{4y_3} = 0, \end{aligned}$$

$$\begin{vmatrix} h''_{y_1y_1} & h''_{y_1y_2} \\ h''_{y_2y_1} & h''_{y_2y_2} \end{vmatrix} = \begin{vmatrix} 2\omega_1^2(-k + \delta_1) & k\omega_1^2 - k\omega_1\omega_2 \\ k\omega_1^2 - k\omega_1\omega_2 & 2\omega_2^2(\delta_2 - 1) \end{vmatrix} > 0,$$

$$\begin{vmatrix} h''_{y_1y_1} & h''_{y_1y_2} & h''_{y_1y_3} \\ h''_{y_2y_1} & h''_{y_2y_2} & h''_{y_2y_3} \\ h''_{y_3y_1} & h''_{y_3y_2} & h''_{y_3y_3} \end{vmatrix} = \begin{vmatrix} 2\omega_1^2(-k + \delta_1) & k\omega_1^2 - k\omega_1\omega_2 & 0 \\ k\omega_1^2 - k\omega_1\omega_2 & 2\omega_2^2(\delta_2 - 1) & -e\omega_2^2 + e\omega_3^2 \\ 0 & -e\omega_2^2 + e\omega_3^2 & 2\omega_3^2(\delta_3 - 1) \end{vmatrix} < 0.$$

And

$$\begin{vmatrix} h''_{y_1y_1} & h''_{y_1y_2} & h''_{y_1y_3} & h''_{y_1y_4} \\ h''_{y_2y_1} & h''_{y_2y_2} & h''_{y_2y_3} & h''_{y_2y_4} \\ h''_{y_3y_1} & h''_{y_3y_2} & h''_{y_3y_3} & h''_{y_3y_4} \\ h''_{y_4y_1} & h''_{y_4y_2} & h''_{y_4y_3} & h''_{y_4y_4} \end{vmatrix} = \begin{vmatrix} 2\omega_1^2(-k + \delta_1) & k\omega_1^2 - k\omega_1\omega_2 & 0 & 0 \\ k\omega_1^2 - k\omega_1\omega_2 & 2\omega_2^2(\delta_2 - 1) & -e\omega_2^2 + e\omega_3^2 & 0 \\ 0 & -e\omega_2^2 + e\omega_3^2 & 2\omega_3^2(\delta_3 - 1) & 0 \\ 0 & 0 & 0 & 2\omega_2^2(-b + \delta_4) \end{vmatrix} > 0.$$

By solving the following system we will have

$$\begin{cases} h'_{y_1} = 0, \\ h'_{y_2} = 0, \\ h'_{y_3} = 0, \\ h'_{y_4} = 0. \end{cases} \tag{29}$$

$y_1 = y_2 = y_3 = 0,\ y_4 = \frac{(b-2\delta_4)(k\omega_1+r\omega_2)}{2\omega_2(b-\delta_4)}$, and $h(Y,\delta) \le \sup_{Y\in\mathbb{R}^4} h(Y,\delta) = \frac{b^2(k\omega_1 + r\omega_2)^2}{4(b-\delta_4)}$.

Using Lemma 2, gives the following result

$$\mathcal{L}(Y(t)) - \frac{b^2(k\omega_1 + r\omega_2)^2}{8\gamma(b-\delta_4)} \le \left[\mathcal{L}(Y(0)) - \frac{b^2(k\omega_1 + r\omega_2)^2}{8\gamma(b-\delta_4)}\right] E_q(-2\gamma t^q),\ t \ge 0.$$

and the Mittag–Leffler attractive sets (MLASs) and Mittag–Leffler positive invariant sets (MLPISs) of the system (2) is

$$\mathcal{G} = \left\{Y(t) \in \mathbb{R}^4 \mid \omega_1 y_1^2 + \omega_2 y_2^2 + \omega_3 y_3^2 + \omega_2 (y_4 - \frac{k\omega_1 + r\omega_2}{\omega_2})^2 \le \frac{b^2(k\omega_1 + r\omega_2)^2}{4\gamma(b-\delta_4)}\right\}, \quad (30)$$

□

Remark 1. *It is obvious that by changing the parameters $\omega_1, \omega_2, \omega_3, \delta_1, \delta_2, \delta_3$, and δ_4, different estimates of the global attractive set and the positive reliable set for system (2) can be obtained.*

Let us take $\omega_1 = \omega_2 = \omega_3 = 1, \delta_1 = 1, \delta_2 = \delta_3 = \delta_4 = 0.999,\ q = 0.99, k = 4$, $e = 0.5, r = 27$, and $b = 1$. Then

$$\mathcal{G} = \left\{(y_1, y_2, y_3, y_4)|y_1^2 + y_2^2 + y_3^2 + (y_4 - 31)^2 \le (31)^2\right\}.$$

is the Mittag–Leffler MLAS and Mittag–Leffler MLPIS of system (2). Figure 7 shows the Mittag–Leffler MLAS and phase portrait of system (2).

When $q = 0.9, k = 4, e = 0.5, r = 27$, and $b = 1$, Figure 8 shows the phase portrait and Mittag–Leffler MLAS of system (2).

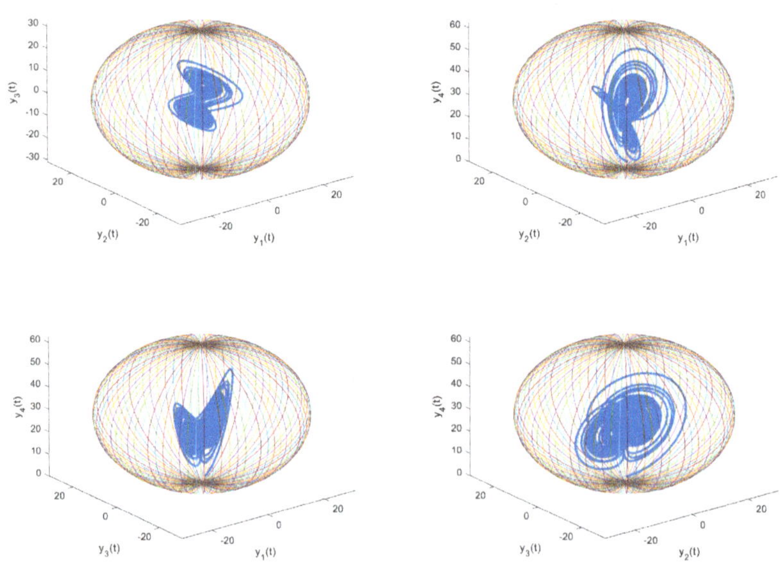

Figure 7. The estimated Mittag–Leffler MLAS of system (2), where $q = 0.99, k = 4, e = 0.5, r = 27$, and $b = 1$.

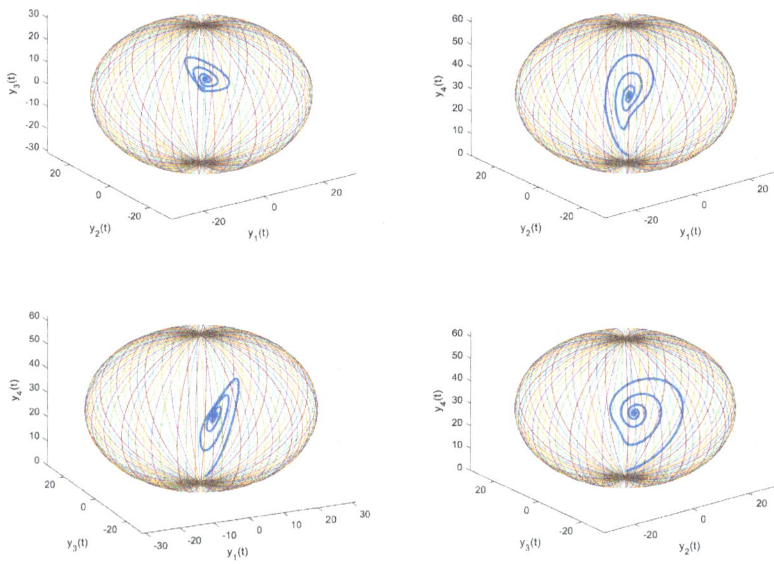

Figure 8. The estimated Mittag–Leffler MLAS of system (2), where $q = 0.9, k = 4, e = 0.5, r = 27$, and $b = 1$.

5. Conclusions

In this paper, we present a four-dimensional fractional-order system with cross-product nonlinearities. Using the concept of stability in fractional-order systems, the stability of equilibrium points and chaos control were performed theoretically and numerically. Furthermore, the dynamical characteristics of the considered system, such as the existence or absence of chaos, bifurcation diagrams, and Lyapunov exponents are investigated. Finally, the estimation of the MLASs and MLPISs for a fractional system that belongs to a special class of nonlinear systems is presented.

Author Contributions: L.R., S.M., S.S., H.S.-N., contributed equally to conceptualization, formal analysis, writing—original draft preparation, methodology, software, and numerical simulation. All authors have read and agreed to the published version of the manuscript.

Funding: This research received no external funding.

Institutional Review Board Statement: Not applicable.

Informed Consent Statement: Not applicable.

Data Availability Statement: Not applicable.

Acknowledgments: The second author extends her appreciation to the Al Mustaqbal University College for supporting this work for grant number (MUCE0122).

Conflicts of Interest: The authors declare that there is no conflict of interests regarding the publication of this article.

References

1. Hilfer, R. *Applications of Fractional Calculus in Physics*; World Scientific: Singapore, 2000.
2. Tavazoei, M.S; Haeri, M. Synchronization of chaotic fractional-order systems via active sliding mode controller. *Physica A* **2008**, *387*, 57–70. [CrossRef]
3. He, Y.; Peng, J.; Zheng, S. Fractional-order financial system and fixed-time synchronization. *Fractal Fract.* **2022**, *6*, 507. [CrossRef]

4. Ahmed, E.; El-Sayed, A.M.A.; El-Saka, H.A.A. On some Routh-Hurwitz conditions for fractional order differential equations and their applications in Lorenz, Rössler, Chua and Chen systems. *Phys. Lett. A* **2006**, *358*, 1–4. [CrossRef]
5. He, Y.; Zheng, S.; Yuan, L. Dynamics of fractional-order digital manufacturing supply chain system and its control and synchronization. *Fractal Fract.* **2021**, *5*, 128. [CrossRef]
6. Zhou, P.; Ma, J.; Tang, J. Clarify the physical process for fractional dynamical systems. *Nonlinear Dyn.* **2020**, *100*, 2353–2364. [CrossRef]
7. Aghababa, M.P. Comments on "H_∞ synchronization of uncertain fractional order chaotic systems: Adaptive fuzzy approach" [ISA Trans 50, 548–556 (2011)]. *ISA Trans.* **2012**, *51*, 11–12. [CrossRef]
8. Chen, Y.; Wang, B.; Chen, Y.; Wang, Y. Sliding mode control for a class of nonlinear fractional order systems with a fractional fixed-time reaching law. *Fractal Fract.* **2022**, *6*, 678. [CrossRef]
9. Mahmoud, G.M.; Arafa, A.A.; Abed-Elhameed, T.M.; Mahmoud, E.E. Chaos control of integer and fractional orders of chaotic Burke–Shaw system using time delayed feedback control. *Chaos Solitons Fractals* **2017**, *104*, 680–692. [CrossRef]
10. Pham, V.T.; Kingni, S.T.; Volos, C.; Jafari, S.; Kapitaniak, T. A simple three-dimensional fractional-order chaotic system without equilibrium: Dynamics, circuitry implementation, chaos control and synchronization. *Int. J. Electron. Commun.* **2017**, *78*, 220–227. [CrossRef]
11. Wang, S.; He, S.; Yousefpour, A.; Jahanshahi, H.; Repnik, R.; Perc, M. Chaos and complexity in a fractional-order financial system with time delays. *Chaos Solitons Fractals* **2020**, *131*, 109521. [CrossRef]
12. Sayed, W.S.; Roshdy, M.; Said, L.A.; Herencsar, N.; Radwan, A.G. CORDIC-based FPGA realization of a spatially rotating translational fractional-order multi-scroll grid chaotic system. *Fractal Fract.* **2022**, *6*, 432. [CrossRef]
13. Qi, F.; Qu, J.; Chai, Y.; Chen, L.; Lopes, A.M. Synchronization of incommensurate frractional-order chaotic systems based on linear feedback control. *Fractal Fract.* **2022**, *6*, 221. [CrossRef]
14. Gao, W.; Yan, L.; Saeedi, M.H.; Saberi Nik, H. Ultimate bound estimation set and chaos synchronization for a financial risk system. *Math. Comput. Simul.* **2018**, *154*, 19–33. [CrossRef]
15. Lin, Z.; Wang, H. Modeling and application of fractional-order economic growth model with time delay. *Fractal Fract.* **2021**, *5*, 74. [CrossRef]
16. Wen, C.; Yang, J. Complexity evolution of chaotic financial systems based on fractional calculus. *Chaos Solitons Fractals* **2019**, *128*, 242–251. [CrossRef]
17. Kuznetsov, N.; Leonov, G. Hidden attractors in dynamical systems: Systems with no equilibria, multistability and coexisting attractors. *IFAC Proc.* **2014**, *47*, 5445–5454. [CrossRef]
18. Leonov, G.; Kuznetsov, N. Hidden attractors in dynamical systems. From hidden oscillations in Hilbert-Kolmogorov, Aizerman, and Kalman problems to hidden chaotic attractor in Chua circuits. *Int. J. Bifurc. Chaos* **2013**, *23*, 1330002. [CrossRef]
19. Ouannas, A.; Khennaoui, A.A.; Momani, S.; Pham, V.T.; El-Khazali, R. Hidden attractors in a new fractional-order discrete system: Chaos, complexity, entropy, and control. *Chin. Phys. B* **2022**, *29*, 050504. [CrossRef]
20. Leonov, G.; Bunin, A.; Koksch, N. Attractor localization of the Lorenz system. *Z. Angew. Math. Mech.* **1987**, *67*, 649–656. [CrossRef]
21. Liao, X.; Fu, Y.; Xie, S. On the new results of global attractive set and positive invariant set of the Lorenz chaotic system and the applications to chaos control and synchronization. *Sci. China Ser. F-Inf. Sci.* **2005**, *48*, 304–321. [CrossRef]
22. Li, D.; Lu, J.A.; Wu, X.; Chen, G. Estimating the bounds for the Lorenz family of chaotic systems. *Chaos Solitons Fractals* **2005**, *23*, 529–534. [CrossRef]
23. Zhao, X.; Jiang, F.; Hu, J. Globally exponentially attractive sets and positive invariant sets of three-dimensional autonomous systems with only cross-product nonlinearities. *Int. J. Bifurc. Chaos* **2013**, *23*, 1350007. [CrossRef]
24. Kumar, D.; Kumar, S. Ultimate numerical bound estimation of chaotic dynamical finance model. In *Modern Mathematical Methods and High Performance Computing in Science and Technology*; Springer: Singapore, 2016; pp. 71–81.
25. Chien, F.; Chowdhury, A.R.; Saberi-Nik, H. Competitive modes and estimation of ultimate bound sets for a chaotic dynamical financial system. *Nonlinear Dyn.* **2021**, *106*, 3601–3614. [CrossRef]
26. Wang, H.; Dong, G. New dynamics coined in a 4-D quadratic autonomous hyper-chaotic system. *Appl. Math. Comput.* **2019**, *346*, 272–286. [CrossRef]
27. Chien, F.; Inc, M.; Yosefzade, H.R.; Saberi Nik, H. Predicting the chaos and solution bounds in a complex dynamical system. *Chaos Solitons Fractals* **2021**, *153*, 111474. [CrossRef]
28. Zhang, F.; Liao, X.; Chen, Y.A. On the dynamics of the chaotic general Lorenz system. *Int. J. Bifurc. Chaos.* **2017**, *27*, 1750075. [CrossRef]
29. Wang, P.; Zhang, Y.; Tan, S.; Wan, L. Explicit ultimate bound sets of a new hyper-chaotic system and its application in estimating the Hausdorff dimension. *Nonlinear Dyn.* **2013**, *74*, 133–142. [CrossRef]
30. Saberi Nik, H.; Effati, S.; Saberi-Nadjafi, J. New ultimate bound sets and exponential finite-time synchronization for the complex Lorenz system. *J. Complex.* **2015**, *31*, 715–730. [CrossRef]
31. Natiq, H.; Said, M.R.M.; Al-Saidi, N.M.G.; Kilicman, A. Dynamics and complexity of a new 4D chaotic Laser system. *Entropy* **2019**, *21*, 34. [CrossRef]
32. Jian, J.; Wu, K.; Wang, B. Global Mittag–Leffler boundedness and synchronization for fractional-order chaotic systems. *Phys. A Stat. Mech. Appl.* **2020**, *540*, 123166. [CrossRef]

3. Peng, Q.; Jian, J. Estimating the ultimate bounds and synchronization of fractional-order plasma chaotic systems. *Chaos Solitons Fractals* **2021**, *150*, 111072. [CrossRef]
4. Huang, M.; Lu, S.; Shateyi, S.; Saberi-Nik, H. Ultimate boundedness and finite time stability for a high dimensional fractional-order Lorenz model. *Fractal Fract.* **2022**, *6*, 630. [CrossRef]
5. Danca, M.; Kuznetsov, N. Matlab code for Lyapunov exponents of fractional-order systems. *Int. J. Bifurc. Chaos* **2018**, *28*, 1850067. [CrossRef]

fractal and fractional

MDPI

Article

A Hybrid Local Radial Basis Function Method for the Numerical Modeling of Mixed Diffusion and Wave-Diffusion Equations of Fractional Order Using Caputo's Derivatives

Raheel Kamal [1], Kamran [1,*], Saleh M. Alzahrani [2] and Talal Alzahrani [2,*]

[1] Department of Mathematics, Islamia College Peshawar, Peshawar 25120, Khyber Pakhtunkhwa, Pakistan; 2019-icp-5120@icp.edu.pk

[2] Mathematics Department, Al-Qunfudhah University College, Umm Al-Qura University, Al-Qunfudhah 28821, Saudi Arabia; salzahrani@uqu.edu.sa

* Correspondence: kamran.maths@icp.edu.pk (K.); tazahrani@uqu.edu.sa (T.A.)

Abstract: This article presents an efficient method for the numerical modeling of time fractional mixed diffusion and wave-diffusion equations with two Caputo derivatives of order $0 < \alpha < 1$, and $1 < \beta < 2$. The numerical method is based on the Laplace transform technique combined with local radial basis functions. The method consists of three main steps: (i) first, the Laplace transform is used to transform the given time fractional model into an equivalent time-independent inhomogeneous problem in the frequency domain; (ii) in the second step, the local radial basis functions method is utilized to obtain an approximate solution for the reduced problem; (iii) finally, the Stehfest method is employed to convert the obtained solution from the frequency domain back to the time domain. The use of the Laplace transform eliminates the need for classical time-stepping techniques, which often require very small time steps to achieve accuracy. Additionally, the application of local radial basis functions helps overcome issues related to ill-conditioning and sensitivity to shape parameters typically encountered in global radial basis function methods. To validate the efficiency and accuracy of the proposed method, several test problems in regular and irregular domains with uniform and non-uniform nodes are considered.

Keywords: mixed diffusion and wave diffusion equation; Caputo derivative; Laplace transform; local radial basis function method; convergence; stability; Stehfest method

1. Introduction

Fractional order calculus (FOC) has not been explored in engineering and other sciences, due to its inherent complexity, as well as the fact that it lacks a completely valid geometric or physical interpretation [1]. However, some natural behaviors related to different fields of engineering are more accurately represented by using it; now, it is a promising tool used in physics [2], fluid mechanics [3], signal processing [4], thermal diffusion phenomenon [5], botanical electrical impedances [6], robotics [7], etc. Various analytical and numerical methods have been developed for fractional order differential equations (FODEs). For instance, in [8], the authors derived the analytic solution of the fractional diffusion wave equation using the Wright function. Liu et al. [9] obtained the complete solution of the time fractional advection–dispersion equation by employing Mellin and Laplace transforms as well as the properties of H functions. Mainardi [10] obtained the fundamental solution of the fractional diffusion-wave equation using an auxiliary function. Wyss [11] obtained the solution of the fractional diffusion equation using Fox functions. Some notable works have been done on the theoretical analysis of FODEs (see [12–14] and references therein).

Fractional partial differential equations (FPDEs) in mathematical models have experienced significant growth in recent years, establishing them as one of the most crucial topics in the field of fractional order calculus (FOC). Several FPDE-based models have been proposed [15–17], and various analytical and numerical schemes have been developed to solve them. Numerous authors have studied the numerical solution of FPDEs. For instance, Liu et al. [18] employed a first-order finite difference scheme for both time and space derivatives, deriving stability conditions in the process. Zhao et al. [19] used the finite element method to solve the multi-term time fractional mixed diffusion and diffusion-wave equation with a variable coefficient. In [20], an ADI spectral method based on the Legendre spectral approximation in space and finite difference method in time was developed to obtain the solution of wave-diffusion equations. Agrawal [21] obtained the general solution of wave-diffusion equations using the Laplace transform and finite sine transform. Tadjeran et al. [22] obtained the solution of the fractional diffusion equation using the Crank–Nicholson technique combined with the spatial extrapolation method. Li and Chen [23] employed three methods: finite difference methods, Galerkin finite element methods, and spectral methods, for numerical simulations of FPDEs. Lie et al. [24] utilized the fully discrete spectral method to solve multi-term fractional mixed diffusion and diffusion wave equations. Dehgan et al. [25] applied the homotopy analysis method to study the numerical solutions of various nonlinear FPDEs.

Different types of meshless methods are rapidly gaining popularity due to their meshless nature and ease of implementation for multi-dimensional problems on a set of uniform or non-uniform nodes in regular and irregular domains. Numerous meshless methods have been developed for the numerical modeling of partial differential equations (PDEs). For instance, Liu et al. [26] proposed an implicit meshless approach based on radial basis functions for solving fractional diffusion equations. Chen et al. [27] solved the time fractional diffusion equation using the Kansa method. Shivanian and Jafarbadi [28] employed the spectral meshless radial point interpolation technique coupled with finite difference discretization for the numerical simulation of fractional diffusion equations. Meshless methods can be categorized into two types: global meshless methods (GMMs) and local meshless methods (LMMs). A GMM has two major disadvantages, namely a dense ill-conditioned interpolation matrix and sensitivity to shape parameters. To overcome these issues, the LMM was developed in [29].

In an LMM, collocation is performed over small overlapping domains of influence. This approach allows for solving small systems of linear equations, with dimensions equal to the number of nodes in each domain of influence, for each node individually. LMMs have found applications in various scientific and engineering problems. For instance, in [30], the authors proposed an efficient local meshless upwind method based on radial basis functions (RBFs) for the numerical simulation of the time fractional advection–diffusion equation. Kumar and Bhardwaj [31] developed a local meshless method for the numerical solution of the nonlinear time fractional diffusion wave equation. Bhardwaj and Kumar [32] introduced an efficient local RBF-based meshless method for the numerical simulation of Tricomi-type equations of fractional order. The authors of [33,34] obtained the numerical solutions of linear and nonlinear time fractional diffusion waves and the telegraph equation using local RBFs. Hosseini et al. [35] obtained the approximate solution of the time fractional diffusion wave equation with damping via an efficient meshless local radial point interpolation method. Salehi [36] used a meshless point collocation method to solve the multi-term fractional diffusion wave equation. An RBF-based meshless technique was proposed in [37] for the approximate solution of the time fractional diffusion-wave equation. Yang et al. [38] employed the moving least squares approximation method for the numerical approximation of fractional diffusion wave equations. Other works on the applications of RBF-based local meshless methods can be found in the references (see [39–42] and the references therein).

Many researchers have investigated the time fractional mixed diffusion and wave diffusion equation. Sun et al. [43] obtained the solution of the fractional mixed diffusion and wave diffusion equation using an L-type difference scheme. The authors of [19] proposed a linear triangle finite element method for the numerical simulation of the multi-term fractional mixed diffusion and wave diffusion equation. Feng et al. [44] obtained the solution of the 2D multi-term fractional mixed sub-diffusion and wave-diffusion equation using finite difference and finite element methods. Liu et al. [24] proposed an efficient fully discrete spectral method for the numerical modeling of the fractional mixed diffusion and diffusion wave equations. Bhardwaj and Kumar [45] obtained the numerical solution of the fractional mixed diffusion and wave diffusion equation using an efficient local RBF-based meshless method. The authors used the finite difference method for time discretization; for space discretization, an RBF-based local collocation method was used.

In this work, our aim is to approximate the solution of fractional mixed diffusion and wave diffusion equations using an RBF-based local meshless method coupled with Laplace transform. The RBF-based local meshless methods are easy to implement for solving problems in irregular and complex geometries and offer high accuracy at a low computational cost. Additionally, the Laplace transform is employed to overcome stability limitations associated with finite difference temporal discretization techniques. To the best of our knowledge, this is the first attempt to utilize the RBF-based local meshless method coupled with Laplace transform for the numerical modeling of time fractional mixed diffusion and wave diffusion problems. In this study, we consider a fractional mixed diffusion and wave diffusion problem of the following form:

$$\begin{cases} {}_0^cD_t^{\alpha}u(\bar{\theta},t) + {}_0^cD_t^{\beta}u(\bar{\theta},t) = \Delta u(\bar{\theta},t) + f(\bar{\theta},t), (\bar{\theta},t) \in \Omega \times [0,T], \\ u(\bar{\theta},0) = \xi(\bar{\theta}), \frac{\partial u(\bar{\theta},0)}{\partial t} = \eta(\bar{\theta}), \bar{\theta} \in \Omega, \\ \mathcal{L}_b u(\bar{\theta},t) = \beta(\bar{\theta},t), \bar{\theta} \in \partial\Omega, \end{cases} \tag{1}$$

where $0< \alpha < 1, 1< \beta < 2$ and $\xi(\bar{\theta})$, $\eta(\bar{\theta})$, and $f(\bar{\theta},t)$ are sufficiently smooth functions on domain Ω, with its boundary $\partial\Omega$, and the Caputo derivatives ${}_0^cD_t^{\alpha}u(\bar{\theta},t)$ and ${}_0^cD_t^{\beta}u(\bar{\theta},t)$ of order α and β are defined by

$${}_0^cD_t^{\alpha}u(\bar{\theta},t) = \frac{1}{\Gamma(1-\alpha)}\int_0^t \frac{\partial u(\bar{\theta},\tau)}{\partial \tau}(t-\tau)^{-\alpha}d\tau, 0 < \alpha < 1,$$

and

$${}_0^cD_t^{\beta}u(\bar{\theta},t) = \frac{1}{\Gamma(2-\beta)}\int_0^t \frac{\partial^2 u(\bar{\theta},\tau)}{\partial \tau^2}(t-\tau)^{1-\beta}d\tau, 1 < \beta < 2.$$

The rest of the paper is organized as follows: Section 2.1 discusses the time discretization through Laplace transform. Section 2.2 discusses spatial discretization using the local RBF method. Section 2.3 explains the Stehfest method for the numerical inversion of the Laplace transform. Section 2.4 focuses on the error analysis of the method. Section 3 addresses the stability of the method. Section 4 presents numerical examples to demonstrate the effectiveness of the proposed method. Finally, Section 5 provides the conclusions.

2. Proposed Numerical Method

In our proposed numerical method, there are three main steps: (i) time discretization via the Laplace transform, (ii) spatial discretization via the local RBF method, and (iii) a numerical inversion of the Laplace transform via the Stehfest method.

2.1. (i) Time Discretization via the Laplace Transform

In this section, we use the Laplace transform to transform the problem into an equivalent time-independent problem and avoid the time stepping technique. The Laplace transform of a $u(\bar{\theta},t)$ is defined as

$$\mathscr{L}\{u(\bar{\theta},t)\} = \widehat{u}(\bar{\theta},z) = \int_0^{\infty} e^{-zt}u(\bar{\theta},t)dt,$$

the Laplace transform of the Caputo derivative ${}_0^cD_t^\alpha u(\bar{\theta},t)$ is defined as

$$\mathscr{L}\{{}_0^cD_t^\alpha u(\bar{\theta},t)\} = z^\alpha \widehat{u}(\bar{\theta},z) - z^{\alpha-1}u(\bar{\theta},0),$$

and the Laplace transform of the Caputo derivative ${}_0^cD_t^\beta u(\bar{\theta},t)$ is defined as

$$\mathscr{L}\left\{{}_0^cD_t^\beta u(\bar{\theta},t)\right\} = z^\beta \widehat{u}(\bar{\theta},z) - z^{\beta-1}u(\bar{\theta},0) - z^{\beta-2}u_t(\bar{\theta},0).$$

Applying the Laplace transform to the model defined in (1), we have

$$\mathscr{L}\left[{}_0^cD_t^\alpha u(\bar{\theta},t) + {}_0^cD_t^\beta u(\bar{\theta},t)\right] = \mathscr{L}\left[\Delta u(\bar{\theta},t) + f(\bar{\theta},t)\right],$$

and

$$\mathscr{L}\left[\mathcal{L}_b u(\bar{\theta},t)\right] = \mathscr{L}\left[\beta(\bar{\theta},t)\right],$$

which implies

$$z^\alpha \widehat{u}(\bar{\theta},z) - z^{\alpha-1}u(\bar{\theta},0) + z^\beta \widehat{u}(\bar{\theta},z) - z^{\beta-1}u(\bar{\theta},0) - z^{\beta-2}u_t(\bar{\theta},0) = \Delta\widehat{u}(\bar{\theta},z) + \widehat{f}(\bar{\theta},z),$$

and

$$\mathcal{L}_b\widehat{u}(\bar{\theta},z) = \beta(\bar{\theta},z),$$

simplifying the above equations, we obtain the following system

$$(z^\alpha I + z^\beta I - \mathcal{L}_g)\widehat{u}(\bar{\theta},z) = \widehat{F}(\bar{\theta},z), \tag{2}$$

$$\mathcal{L}_b\widehat{u}(\bar{\theta},z) = \beta(\bar{\theta},z), \tag{3}$$

where $\widehat{F}(\bar{\theta},z) = z^{\alpha-1}\xi(\bar{\theta}) + z^{\beta-1}\varsigma(\bar{\theta}) - z^{\beta-2}\eta(\bar{\theta}) + \widehat{f}(\bar{\theta},z)$ and $\mathcal{L}_g = \Delta$, where I denotes the identity operator, $\mathcal{L}_g$ is the linear differential operator, and $\mathcal{L}_b$ is the boundary differential operator. In order to obtain the solutions of the systems in (2) and (3), first, we use the local RBF method to discretize the operators $\mathcal{L}_g$ and $\mathcal{L}_b$, then systems (2) and (3) are solved in parallel for each point z in the complex plane (see, e.g., [46]). Finally, the solution of the original problem (1) is obtained using the inverse Laplace transform. The local RBF method is described in the next section.

2.2. (ii) Spatial Discretization via Local RBF Method

In the local RBF method, the problem and its corresponding boundary are interpolated on n_g nodes that can be distributed regularly or irregularly. For each node $\bar{\theta}_j (j = 1,2,3,\ldots,n_g)$, there is a local domain $\Omega_j = \{\bar{\theta}_i^j\}_{j=1}^{n_l} (i = 1,2,3,\ldots,n_g)$, where n_l denotes the number of nodes in the local domain Ω_j. Thus, the local RBF interpolant of $\hat{u}(\bar{\theta})$ is of the form,

$$\widehat{u}(\bar{\theta}_j) = \sum_{i=1}^{n_l} \lambda_i^j \varphi(\|\bar{\theta}_j - \bar{\theta}_i^j\|), \tag{4}$$

where the vector $\lambda^j = \{\lambda_i^j\}_{i=1}^{n_g}$ is a vector of unknown expansion coefficients, $\varphi(r)$ is a RBF and $r = \|\bar{\theta}_j - \bar{\theta}_i^j\|$ denotes the distance between $\bar{\theta}_j$ and $\bar{\theta}_i^j$. In the literature, there are several RBFs. Some commonly used RBFs are listed in Table 1 and the corresponding graphs are shown in Figure 1.

Table 1. Different types of finite and infinite smooth RBFs.

Multiquadric (MQ)	$\phi(r) = \sqrt{1+\varepsilon^2 r^2}$
Inverse multiquadric (IMQ)	$\phi(r) = \frac{1}{\sqrt{1+\varepsilon^2 r^2}}$
Gaussian (GA)	$\phi(r) = e^{-(\varepsilon r)^2}$
Wendlan	$\phi(r) = (1-r)_+^k p(r)$, $p(r)$ is a polynomial, $k \in \mathbb{N}$
Duchon spline	$\phi(r) = r^{2k} log(r), k \in \mathbb{N}$
Thin Plate Spline (TPS)	$\phi(r) = r^2 log(r)$,

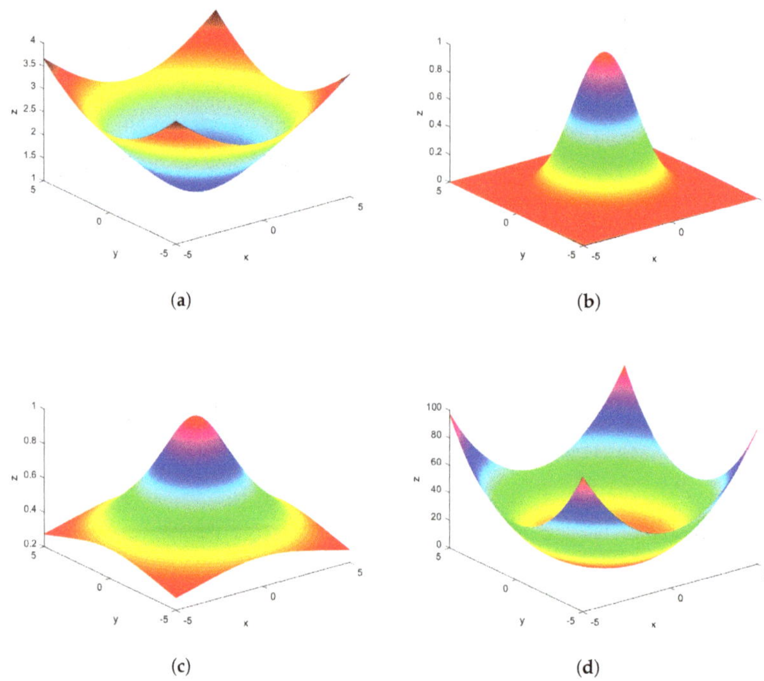

Figure 1. (**a**) The MQ RBF plot in the domain $[-5,5]$ with $\varepsilon = 0.5$; (**b**) the GA RBF plot in the domain $[-5,5]$ with $\varepsilon = 0.5$; (**c**) the IMQ RBF plot in the domain $[-5,5]$ with $\varepsilon = 0.5$; (**d**) the TPS RBF plot in the domain $[-5,5]$ with $\varepsilon = 0.5$.

In this study, we select MQ RBF and GA RBF, which are defined as

$$\varphi(\|\bar{\theta}_j - \bar{\theta}_i^j\|) = \sqrt{1+\varepsilon^2\|\bar{\theta}_j - \bar{\theta}_i^j\|^2},$$

and

$$\varphi(\|\bar{\theta}_j - \bar{\theta}_i^j\|) = exp(-\varepsilon^2\|\bar{\theta}_j - \bar{\theta}_i^j\|^2),$$

where ε denotes the shape parameter. Each node $\bar{\theta}_i^j$ and its $n_l - 1$ neighbors are referred to as a stencil. A typical stencil is shown in Figure 2.

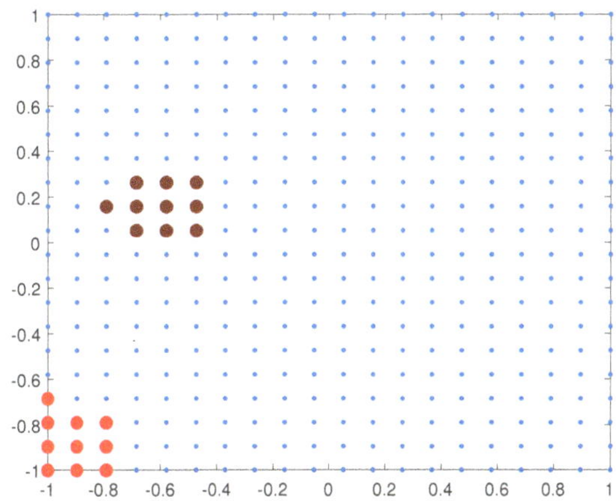

Figure 2. A stencil for $n_l = 10$, red corresponds to the boundary node and brown to the interior node.

At each stencil, we obtain the $n_l \times n_l$ matrix, given as

$$\widehat{\boldsymbol{u}}^j = \boldsymbol{B}^j \boldsymbol{\lambda}^j, \tag{5}$$

where $\widehat{\boldsymbol{u}}^j = [u(\bar{\theta}_1^j), u(\bar{\theta}_2^j), \dots, u(\bar{\theta}_{n_l}^j)]^T$, $\boldsymbol{B}^j = [\phi(\|\bar{\theta}_k^j - \bar{\theta}_i^j\|)]_{1\le k,i\le n_l}$, and $\boldsymbol{\lambda}^j = [\lambda_1^j, \lambda_2^j, \dots, \lambda_{n_l}^j]^T$. The invertibility of the system (5) requires the following definitions

Definition 1 ([47]). *A function $\zeta(r)$ is completely monotone on $[0,\infty)$, if*

1. $\zeta(r) \in C[0,\infty)$.
2. $\zeta(r) \in C^\infty[0,\infty)$.
3. $(-1)^m \zeta^{(m)}(r) \ge 0$, *for* $m = 1,2,3,\dots$

Theorem 1 ([47]). *If $\zeta(r) = \varphi(\sqrt{r}) \in C[0,\infty)$ and $\zeta(r) > 0$ for $r > 0$. Let $\zeta'(r)$ be completely monotone and non-constant on $(0,\infty)$, then for any set of n_g distinct centers $\bar{\theta}_j (j = 1,2,3,\dots,n_g)$, the interpolation matrix $\boldsymbol{B}^j$ is invertible.*

The unknown coefficients $\boldsymbol{\lambda}^j$ in Equation (5) can be computed as

$$\boldsymbol{\lambda}^j = (\boldsymbol{B}^j)^{-1} \widehat{\boldsymbol{u}}^j, \tag{6}$$

whose entries are

$$\begin{pmatrix} \lambda_1^j \\ \lambda_2^j \\ \cdot \\ \cdot \\ \cdot \\ \lambda_{n_l}^j \end{pmatrix} = \begin{pmatrix} \varphi(\|\bar{\theta}_1^j - \bar{\theta}_1^j\|) & \varphi(\|\bar{\theta}_1^j - \bar{\theta}_2^i\|) & \cdot\ \cdot\ \cdot & \varphi(\|\bar{\theta}_1^j - \bar{\theta}_{n_l}^j\|) \\ \varphi(\|\bar{\theta}_2^j - \bar{\theta}_1^j\|) & \varphi(\|\bar{\theta}_2^j - \bar{\theta}_2^i\|) & \cdot\ \cdot\ \cdot & \varphi(\|\bar{\theta}_2^j - \bar{\theta}_{n_l}^j\|) \\ \cdot & \cdot & \cdot\ \cdot\ \cdot & \cdot \\ \cdot & \cdot & \cdot\ \cdot\ \cdot & \cdot \\ \cdot & \cdot & \cdot\ \cdot\ \cdot & \cdot \\ \varphi(\|\bar{\theta}_{n_l}^j - \bar{\theta}_1^j\|) & \varphi(\|\bar{\theta}_{n_l}^j - \bar{\theta}_2^i\|) & \cdot\ \cdot\ \cdot & \varphi(\|\bar{\theta}_{n_l}^j - \bar{\theta}_{n_l}^j\|) \end{pmatrix}^{-1} \begin{pmatrix} \widehat{u}(\bar{\theta}_1^j) \\ \widehat{u}(\bar{\theta}_2^j) \\ \cdot \\ \cdot \\ \cdot \\ \widehat{u}(\bar{\theta}_{n_l}^j) \end{pmatrix}.$$

The differential operator $\mathcal{L}_g$ can be approximated as

$$\mathcal{L}_g \widehat{u} = \sum_{i=1}^{n_l} \lambda_i^j \mathcal{L}\varphi(\|\bar{\theta}_i - \bar{\theta}_i^j\|),$$

which can be written as

$$\mathcal{L}_g\widehat{u} = \boldsymbol{\psi}^j(\boldsymbol{B}^j)^{-1}\widehat{\boldsymbol{u}}^j,$$

where $\boldsymbol{\psi}^j = [\mathcal{L}\phi(\|\bar{\theta}^j_k - \bar{\theta}^j_i\|)]_{1\le k,i\le n_l}$. Hence, we have

$$\mathcal{L}_g\widehat{u} = \boldsymbol{\Psi}^j\widehat{\boldsymbol{u}}^j, \tag{7}$$

where $\boldsymbol{\Psi}^j = \boldsymbol{\psi}^j(\boldsymbol{B}^j)^{-1}$. Equation (7), is the local form; the global form can be obtained by expanding $\boldsymbol{\Psi}^j$ to $\mathbf{Y}$ by inserting zeros into each row in corresponding positions. Therefore, the approximation of the differential operator $\mathcal{L}$ at each $\bar{\theta}_j$ is given as

$$\mathcal{L}_g\widehat{u} = \mathbf{Y}\widehat{u}. \tag{8}$$

The matrix $\mathbf{Y}$ is sparse, having $n_g - n_l$ zero entries and n_l non-zero entries. The boundary differential operator $\mathcal{L}_b$ can be approximated in a similar way

$$\mathcal{L}_b\widehat{u} = \boldsymbol{\Phi}\widehat{u}, \tag{9}$$

using Equations (8) and (9) in Equations (2) and (3), we obtained the following fully discrete system

$$(z^\alpha I + z^\beta I - \mathbf{Y})\widehat{u}(\bar{\theta}, z) = \widehat{F}(\bar{\theta}, z), \tag{10}$$

$$\boldsymbol{\Phi}\widehat{u}(\bar{\theta}, z) = \beta(\bar{\theta}, z). \tag{11}$$

Now, solving the system defined in Equations (10) and (11) for each point z in the complex plan will give us the solution $\widehat{u}(\bar{\theta}, z)$.

Selection: Good Value of the Shape Parameter

We utilized MQ RBF and GA RBF in our numerical experiments. These RBFs contain parameter ε; for optimal accuracy of the numerical solution, the value of ε varies. The condition number C_d of the matrix $\boldsymbol{B}^j$ is used to quantify the sensitivity to perturbation of the linear system. In this work, the uncertainty principle [48] is used for the best shape parameter ε.

The necessary steps for obtaining the optimal value of shape parameter ε are presented in the following Algorithm 1.

Algorithm 1 : Optimal Shape Parameter

1: **Input:** $C_{dmin}, C_{dmax}, \varepsilon_{Increment}$.
2: **Step 1:** $C_d = 1$
3: **Step 2:** select $10^{+12} < C_d < 10^{+16}$
4: **Step 3:** while $C_d > C_{dmax}$ and $C_d < C_{dmin}$
5: **Step 4:** Construct the matrix $\boldsymbol{B}^j$
6: **Step 5:** $\mathbf{E}, \mathbf{S}, \mathbf{P} = svd(\boldsymbol{B}^j)$
7: **Step 6:** $C_d = \frac{\rho_{max}}{\rho_{min}}$
8: **Step 7:** if $C_d < C_{dmin}, \varepsilon = \varepsilon - \varepsilon_{Increment}$
9: **Step 8:** if $C_d > C_{dmax}, \varepsilon = \varepsilon + \varepsilon_{Increment}$
10: **Output:** $\varepsilon(\text{optimal}) = \varepsilon$.

After obtaining the best value of the shape parameter, we compute $(\boldsymbol{B}^j)^{-1}$ using svd as $(\boldsymbol{B}^j)^{-1} = (\mathbf{ESP}^{\mathrm{T}})^{-1} = \mathbf{PS}^{-1}\mathbf{E}^{\mathrm{T}}$ (see [49]). Hence, we can calculate $\boldsymbol{\Psi}^j$ in (7).

2.3. (iii) Stehfest Method

In this section, we utilize the Stehfest algorithm for numerically inverting the Laplace transform. It is one of the most important algorithms used for the numerical inversion of the Laplace transform. This method was developed in the late 1960s [50,51]. Due to its simplicity and performance, it is becoming popular in many areas, such as economics, geophysics, financial mathematics, chemistry, and computational physics. This method is fast and gives good results for smooth functions. The solution $u(\bar{\theta}, t)$ can be retrieved via the Stehfest method, as

$$u(\bar{\theta}, t) = \frac{ln2}{t}\sum_{i=1}^{N} \rho_i \widehat{u}(\bar{\theta}, z), \tag{12}$$

where the weights ρ_i are given by

$$\rho_i = (-1)^{\frac{N}{2}+i} \sum_{p=\lfloor \frac{i+1}{2} \rfloor}^{min(i,\frac{N}{2})} \frac{p^{\frac{N}{2}}(2p!)}{(\frac{N}{2}-p)!p!(p-1)!(i-p)!(2p-i)!}. \tag{13}$$

Here, N, refers to the Stehfest number, which should be even. Solving (10) and (11) for parameters $z = \frac{ln2}{t}i, i = 1, 2, 3, \ldots, N$ in the LT space. Using (12), the original solution can be obtained.

The Gaver–Stehfest algorithm possesses several attractive properties. Firstly, the approximations of any function using this algorithm are linear in the values of the transform. Secondly, it only requires the values of the transform function for real z. Thirdly, the computation of the coefficients is straightforward. Lastly, the approximations obtained using this algorithm are exact for constant functions. The Gaver–Stehfest algorithm has been extensively studied by various authors, as documented in [52,53]. These studies have demonstrated that this method has very fast convergence for non-oscillatory functions.

2.4. Error Analysis

Here, we discuss the error analysis of the proposed method. In step (a), we employ the LT, which is analytic; thus, no error occurs in this step. The error of the method arises in steps (b) and (c). In step (b), we utilize the RBF-based local meshless method, which has an error estimate of order $O(\sigma^{\frac{1}{\varepsilon H_d}}), 0 < \sigma < 1$, where H_d denotes the fill distance and ε is the shape parameter [47]. In step (c), the Stehfest method is employed for the numerical inversion of the LT. The error analysis of this method has been studied in [54,55], where the authors conducted various numerical experiments to investigate the effects of the involved parameters on the accuracy and efficiency of the method. They noted that "If β significant digits are required, suppose $N = \lceil 2.2\beta \rceil$ positive integer. Set the precision of the system at $\nu = \lceil 1.1N \rceil$. Then for the argument t and $\widehat{u}(\bar{\theta}, z)$, calculate $u(\bar{\theta}, t)$ in (12)." According to these observations, the following error estimation is obtained.

Remark 1 ([56]). *If the error of input data satisfies* $10^{-(\nu+1)} \leq \frac{\|\widehat{u}-u\|}{\|u\|} \leq 10^{-\nu}$, *where N is a positive even integer via* $\nu = \lceil 1.1N \rceil$, *then the error is* $10^{-(\beta+1)} \leq \frac{\|\widehat{u}-u\|}{\|u\|} \leq 10^{-\beta}$, *where* $N = \lceil 1.1\beta \rceil$.

3. Stability

Here, we discuss the stability of the fully discrete systems (10) and (11). We express the system in the following form

$$\boldsymbol{C}\widehat{\boldsymbol{u}} = \boldsymbol{R}, \tag{14}$$

the coefficient matrix $\boldsymbol{C}$ is obtained using the local meshless method. The constant for the stability of the system (14) is defined as

$$\delta = \sup_{\widehat{u} \neq 0} \frac{\|\widehat{\boldsymbol{u}}\|}{\|\boldsymbol{C}\widehat{\boldsymbol{u}}\|}, \tag{15}$$

δ has a finite value for any norm $||.||$ defined in $\mathbb{R}^N$. From Equation (15), we obtain

$$||\mathcal{C}||^{-1} \leq \frac{||\widehat{u}||}{||\mathcal{C}\widehat{u}||} \leq \delta. \tag{16}$$

Moreover, we can write

$$||\mathcal{C}^{\dagger}|| = \sup_{v \neq 0} \frac{||\mathcal{C}^{\dagger} v||}{||v||}. \tag{17}$$

where $\mathcal{C}^{\dagger}$ is the pseudoinverse of $\mathcal{C}$. Therefore,

$$||\mathcal{C}^{\dagger}|| \geq \sup_{v=\mathcal{C}\widehat{u}\neq 0} \frac{||\mathcal{C}^{\dagger}\mathcal{C}\widehat{u}||}{||\mathcal{C}\widehat{u}||} = \sup_{\widehat{u}\neq 0} \frac{||\widehat{u}||}{||\mathcal{C}\widehat{u}||} = \delta. \tag{18}$$

Equations (16) and (17) give the bounds for the constant δ. For system (14), the pseudoinverse may be hard to compute, but by using it, stability is guaranteed. The MATLAB condest function can be used for evaluating $||\mathcal{C}^{-1}||_{\infty}$ as

$$\delta = \frac{condest(\mathcal{C}')}{||\mathcal{C}||_{\infty}} \tag{19}$$

4. Applications

This section focuses on presenting numerical results and discussions. The performance, efficiency, accuracy, and convergence of the proposed method are tested and validated using five test problems in one and two dimensions. For two-dimensional problems, six different sets of regular and irregular domains with uniform and non-uniform points are selected. Three error norms are utilized: the maximum absolute error, the relative error, and the root mean square error, which are denoted and defined as follows:

$$Error_1 = \max_{1\leq j\leq n_g} |u(\zeta_j,t) - u_k(\zeta_j,t)|,$$

$$Error_2 = \sqrt{\frac{\sum_{j=1}^{n_g}(u(\bar{\zeta}_j,t) - u_k(\bar{\zeta}_j,t))^2}{n_g}},$$

$$Error_3 = \sqrt{\frac{\sum_{j=1}^{n_g}(u(\zeta_j,t) - u_k(\zeta_j,t))^2}{\sum_{j=1}^{n_g}(u(\zeta_j,t))^2}},$$

where n_g represents the total number of points, n_l represents the points in the sub-domain, and N represents the points used in the Stehfest method. $u(\zeta j,t)$ denotes the analytic solution, and $uk(\zeta_j,t)$ denotes the numerical solution. The numerical experiments are conducted using MQ and GA RBFs. In all experiments, the initial conditions, boundary conditions, and source terms are calculated based on the analytic solutions. All of the numerical experiments are performed with a final time of $T = 1$.

Problem 1. *Consider the following one-dimensional test problem*

$${}_0^cD_t^{\alpha}u(x,t) + {}_0^cD_t^{\beta}u(x,t) = \Delta u(x,t) + f(x,t), 0 \leq x \leq 1, \tag{20}$$

with the exact solution

$$u(x,t) = t^3\sin(\pi x).$$

The errors of the proposed method for problem 1 with $\alpha = 0.5$, $\beta = 1.1$, and different values of n_g, n_l, and N using MQ RBF are presented in Table 2, while the errors using GA RBF are presented in Table 3. It is observed that the performance of MQ RBF is better than GA RBF. The results demonstrate that the proposed numerical method is efficient and reliable. Figure 3a,b depict the numerical and analytic solutions of problem 1 with $\alpha = 0.5$ and $\beta = 1.6$. The surface plots of $Error_1$ and $Error_2$ with $n_g = 70$, $n_l = 10$, $N = 16, \alpha = 0.5$, and $\beta = 1.9$ using MQ RBF are presented in Figure 4a,b; using GA RBF with $n_g = 70, n_l = 10, N = 16, \alpha = 0.5$, and $\beta = 1.7$, they are presented in Figure 5a,b. The surface plots of $Error_3$ of the proposed method corresponding to problem 1 with $n_g = 90, n_l = 6, N = 18, \alpha = 0.5, \beta = 1.9$ using MQ RBF and GA RBF are presented in Figure 6a,b. The plots of $Error_1$, $Error_2$, and $Error_3$ using MQ RBF for different values of α with $\beta = 1.6, n_g = 120, n_l = 5, N = 16$ are depicted in Figure 7a and for different values of β with $\alpha = 0.5, n_g = 120, n_l = 5, N = 16$ are presented in Figure 7b. The plots of $Error_1$, $Error_2$, and $Error_3$ for various values of α and β with the same parameters using GA RBF are shown in Figure 8a,b, respectively. The plots of $Error_1$, $Error_2$, and $Error_3$ for different values of N with $\alpha = 0.5, \beta = 1.9, n_g = 120, n_l = 5$ using MQ RBF are shown in Figure 9a; using GA RBF, they are presented in Figure 9b. Similarly, the plots of $Error_1$, $Error_2$, and $Error_3$ for different values of t with $N = 16, \alpha = 0.7, \beta = 1.4, n_g = 120, n_l = 5$ using MQ RBF are shown in Figure 10a; using GA RBF, they are shown in Figure 10b. From the data reported in the figures and tables, it is evident that the numerical solution is in good agreement with the analytic solution.

Table 2. The errors obtained using the proposed method for problem 1 using MQ RBF.

$\alpha = 0.5$, $\beta = 1.1$	n_g	n_l	N	$Error_1$	$Error_2$	$Error_3$	C.Time(s)
	95	10	16	2.72×10^{-4}	2.79×10^{-5}	3.97×10^{-5}	0.132263
		15		8.99×10^{-5}	9.22×10^{-6}	1.31×10^{-5}	0.183286
		20		7.34×10^{-5}	7.53×10^{-6}	1.07×10^{-5}	0.228481
		22		6.32×10^{-5}	6.48×10^{-6}	9.22×10^{-6}	0.258556
	120	21	12	9.12×10^{-4}	8.32×10^{-5}	1.18×10^{-4}	0.242945
			14	4.59×10^{-4}	4.19×10^{-5}	5.95×10^{-5}	0.248445
			16	1.74×10^{-4}	1.59×10^{-5}	2.26×10^{-5}	0.238210
			18	8.95×10^{-5}	8.17×10^{-6}	1.16×10^{-5}	0.237966
	82	21	16	9.20×10^{-5}	1.01×10^{-5}	1.44×10^{-5}	0.226662
	85			8.70×10^{-5}	9.44×10^{-6}	1.34×10^{-5}	0.227972
	88			7.08×10^{-5}	7.55×10^{-6}	1.07×10^{-5}	0.234824
	95			6.88×10^{-5}	7.06×10^{-6}	1.00×10^{-5}	0.239582
[32]				1.69×10^{-4}			

Table 3. The errors obtained using the proposed method for problem 1 using GA RBF.

$\alpha = 0.5$, $\beta = 1.6$	n_g	n_l	N	$Error_1$	$Error_2$	$Error_3$	C.Time(s)
	115	10	12	9.86×10^{-4}	9.19×10^{-5}	1.30×10^{-4}	0.188929
	125			6.69×10^{-4}	5.98×10^{-5}	8.50×10^{-5}	0.185436
	130			5.69×10^{-4}	4.99×10^{-5}	7.09×10^{-5}	0.223009
	135			4.92×10^{-5}	4.23×10^{-5}	6.01×10^{-5}	0.213365
	95	8	12	7.69×10^{-4}	7.89×10^{-5}	1.12×10^{-5}	0.173427
		13		3.06×10^{-4}	3.14×10^{-5}	4.47×10^{-5}	0.220220
		14		2.92×10^{-4}	3.00×10^{-5}	4.27×10^{-5}	0.202532
		15		1.08×10^{-4}	1.11×10^{-5}	1.58×10^{-5}	0.196352
	74	10	12	6.84×10^{-4}	7.95×10^{-5}	1.13×10^{-4}	0.102373
			14	4.09×10^{-4}	4.75×10^{-5}	6.77×10^{-5}	0.136801
			16	2.01×10^{-4}	2.33×10^{-5}	3.33×10^{-5}	0.129105
			18	1.73×10^{-4}	2.01×10^{-5}	2.87×10^{-5}	0.148823
[32]				9.47×10^{-4}			

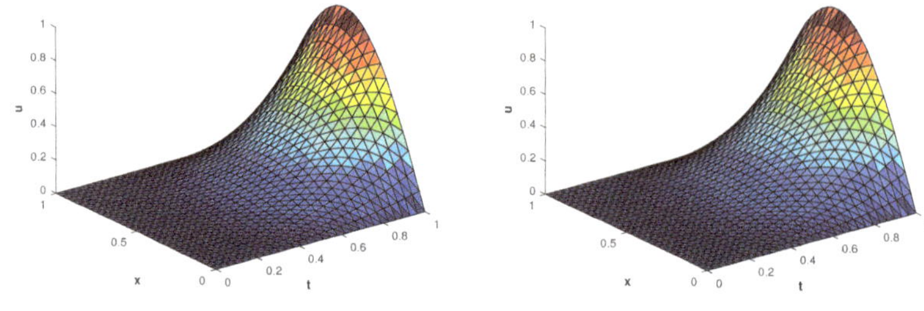

(a) (b)

Figure 3. (**a**) The numerical solution of problem 1 with $\alpha = 0.5, \beta = 1.6$. (**b**) The exact solution of problem 1 with $\alpha = 0.5, \beta = 1.6$.

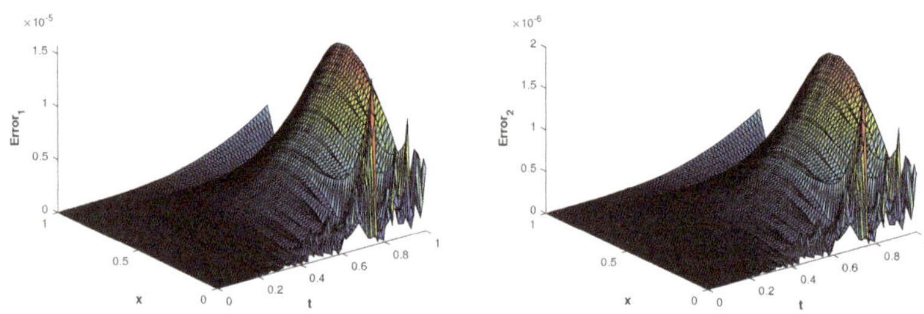

(a) (b)

Figure 4. (**a**) The surface plot of $Error_1$ of the proposed method corresponding to problem 1 with $n_g = 70, n_l = 10, N = 16, \alpha = 0.5, \beta = 1.9$ using MQ RBF. (**b**) The surface plot of $Error_2$ of the proposed method corresponding to problem 1 with $n_g = 70, n_l = 10, N = 16, \alpha = 0.5, \beta = 1.9$ using MQ RBF.

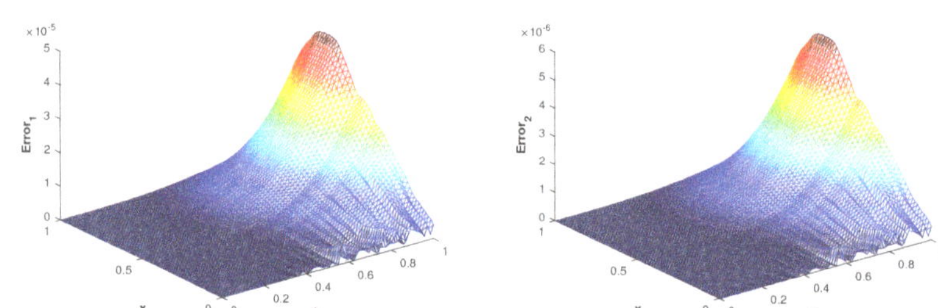

(a) (b)

Figure 5. (**a**) The mesh plot of $Error_1$ of the proposed method corresponding to problem 1 with $n_g = 70, n_l = 10, N = 16, \alpha = 0.5, \beta = 1.7$ using GA RBF. (**b**) The mesh plot of $Error_2$ of the proposed method corresponding to problem 1 with $n_g = 70, n_l = 10, N = 16, \alpha = 0.5, \beta = 1.7$ using GA RBF.

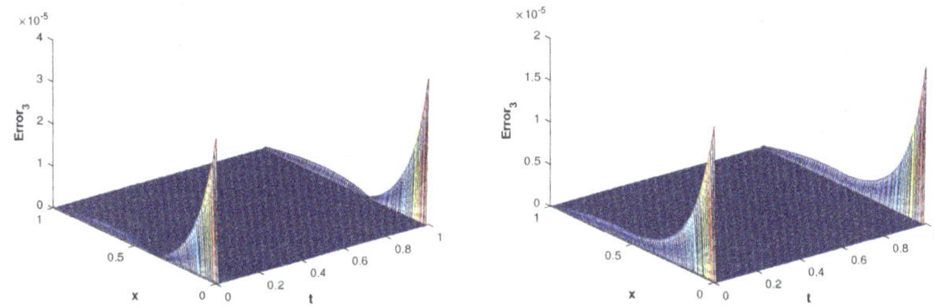

(**a**) (**b**)

Figure 6. (**a**) The surface plot of $Error_3$ of the proposed method corresponding to problem 1 with $n_g = 90, n_l = 6, N = 18, \alpha = 0.5, \beta = 1.9$ using MQ RBF. (**b**) The surface plot of $Error_3$ of the proposed method corresponding to problem 1 with $n_g = 90, n_l = 6, N = 18, \alpha = 0.5, \beta = 1.9$ using GA RBF.

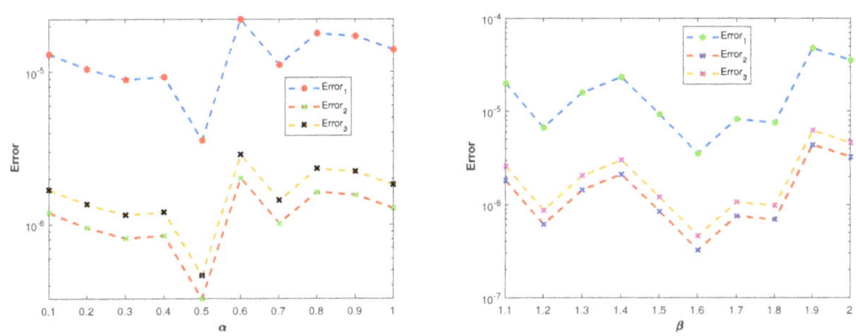

(**a**) (**b**)

Figure 7. (**a**) The plots of $Error_1$, $Error_2$, and $Error_3$ of the proposed method corresponding to problem 1 with various values of α and $\beta = 1.6, n_g = 120, n_l = 5, N = 16$ using the MQ RBF. (**b**) The plots $Error_1$, $Error_2$, and $Error_3$ of the proposed method corresponding to problem 1 with various values of β and $\alpha = 0.5, n_g = 120, n_l = 5, N = 16$ using the MQ RBF.

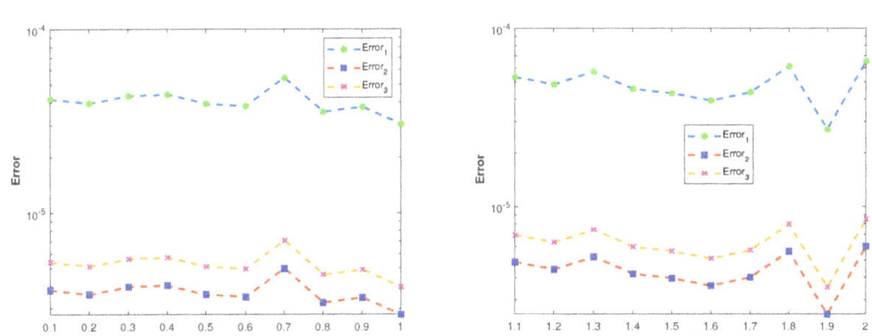

(**a**) (**b**)

Figure 8. (**a**) The plots of $Error_1$, $Error_2$, and $Error_3$ of the proposed method corresponding to problem 1 with various values of α and $\beta = 1.6, n_g = 120, n_l = 5, N = 16$ using the GA RBF. (**b**) The plots $Error_1$, $Error_2$, and $Error_3$ of the proposed method corresponding to problem 1 with various values of β and $\alpha = 0.5, n_g = 120, n_l = 5, N = 16$ using the GA RBF.

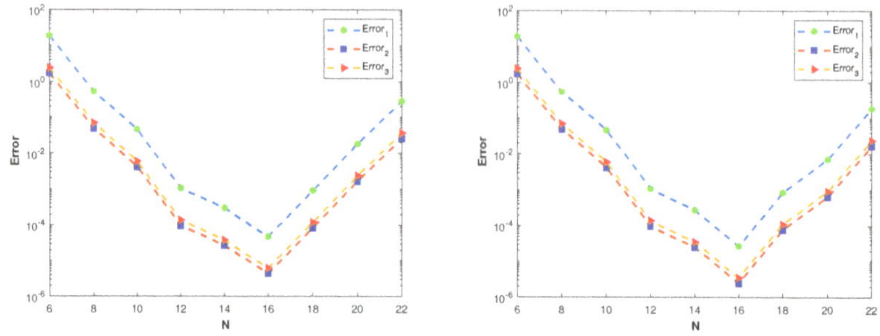

(a) (b)

Figure 9. (**a**) The plots of $Error_1$, $Error_2$, and $Error_3$ of the proposed method corresponding to problem 1 with various values of N and $\alpha = 0.5, \beta = 1.9, n_g = 120, n_l = 5$ using the MQ RBF. (**b**) The plots $Error_1$, $Error_2$, and $Error_3$ of the proposed method corresponding to problem 1 with various values of N and $\alpha = 0.5, \beta = 1.9, n_g = 120, n_l = 5$ using the GA RBF.

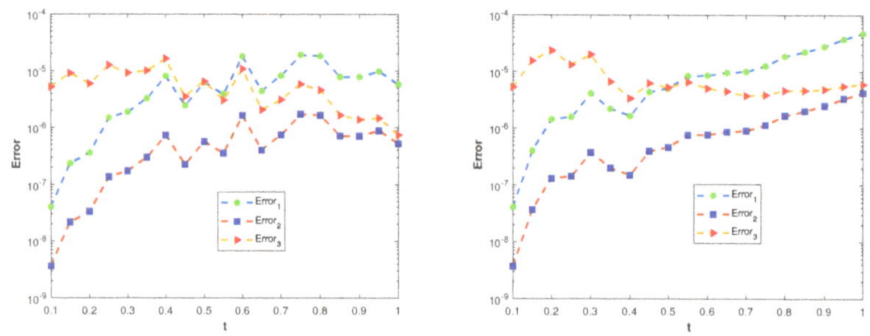

(a) (b)

Figure 10. (**a**) The plots of $Error_1$, $Error_2$, and $Error_3$ of the proposed method corresponding to problem 1 with various values of t and $N = 16, \alpha = 0.7, \beta = 1.4, n_g = 120, n_l = 5$ using the MQ RBF. (**b**) The plots $Error_1$, $Error_2$, and $Error_3$ of the proposed method corresponding to problem 1 with various values of t and $N = 16, \alpha = 0.7, \beta = 1.4, n_g = 120, n_l = 5$ using the GA RBF.

Problem 2. *Consider the following one-dimensional test problem*

$$ {}_0^cD_t^{\alpha} u(x,t) + {}_0^cD_t^{\beta} u(x,t) = \Delta u(x,t) + f(x,t), 0 \leq x \leq 1, \tag{21} $$

with the exact solution

$$ u(x,t) = t^{(3+\alpha+\beta)} exp(-x^2). $$

The errors of the proposed method for problem 2 with $\alpha = 0.5, \beta = 1.5$, and different values of n_g, n_l, and N using MQ RBF are presented in Table 4; using the GA RBF, they are presented in Table 5. We can see that the method has produced accurate and stable results. The numerical and analytic solutions of problem 2 with $\alpha = .5$ and $\beta = 1.1$ are depicted in Figure 11a,b; a nice agreement between the numerical and analytic solutions is observed. The surface plots of $Error_1$ and $Error_2$ with $n_g = 90, n_l = 20, N = 18, \alpha = 0.9$ and $\beta = 1.3$ using MQ RBF are presented in Figure 12a,b. The surface plots of $Error_1$ and $Error_2$ with $n_g = 70, n_l = 10, N = 16, \alpha = 0.2$, and $\beta = 1.6$ using GA RBF are presented in Figure 13a,b. The surface plot of $Error_3$ with $n_g = 90, n_l = 10, N = 18, \alpha = 0.2$ and $\beta = 1.6$ using MQ RBF is presented in Figure 14a and surface plot of $Error_3$ with $n_g = 90, n_l = 10, N = 18, \alpha = 0.2$ and $\beta = 1.6$ using GA RBF is presented in Figure 14b. The plots of $Error_1$, $Error_2$, and $Error_3$ using MQ RBF for different values of α with $\beta = 1.1, n_g = 120, n_l = 6, N = 18$ are depicted in Figure 15a, and for different values of β with $\alpha = 0.9, n_g = 120, n_l = 5, N = 18$ are presented in Figure 15b. The plots of $Error_1$, $Error_2$, and $Error_3$ using GA RBF for different values of α with $\beta = 1.6, n_g = 450, n_l = 5, N = 18$ are depicted in Figure 16a, and for different values of β with $\alpha = 0.2, n_g = 450, n_l = 5, N = 18$, are presented in Figure 16b. The plots of $Error_1$, $Error_2$, and $Error_3$ using MQ RBF for different values of N with $\alpha = 0.9, \beta = 1.6, n_g = 450, n_l = 6$ are shown in Figure 17a; using GA RBF, they are presented in Figure 17b. The plots of $Error_1$, $Error_2$, and $Error_3$ using MQ RBF for different values of t with $N = 18, \alpha = 0.9, \beta = 1.1, n_g = 450, n_l = 5$ are depicted in Figure 18a; using GA RBF, they are presented in Figure 18b. From the data presented in the tables and figures, it is observed that the proposed method has produced accurate and stable results, and can handle such types of problems efficiently.

Table 4. The errors obtained using the proposed method for problem 2 using MQ RBF.

$\alpha = 0.5$, $\beta = 1.5$	n_g	n_l	N	$Error_1$	$Error_2$	$Error_3$	C.Time(s)
	120	15	18	3.76×10^{-4}	3.44×10^{-5}	4.45×10^{-5}	0.203494
		16		3.34×10^{-4}	3.05×10^{-5}	3.95×10^{-5}	0.216352
		17		1.65×10^{-4}	1.51×10^{-5}	1.95×10^{-5}	0.198863
		18		1.15×10^{-4}	1.05×10^{-5}	1.36×10^{-5}	0.259377
	90	16	14	9.20×10^{-3}	9.64×10^{-4}	1.20×10^{-3}	0.193569
			16	2.10×10^{-3}	2.22×10^{-4}	2.87×10^{-4}	0.199498
			18	2.65×10^{-4}	2.79×10^{-5}	3.62×10^{-5}	0.188744
			20	1.98×10^{-4}	2.08×10^{-5}	2.70×10^{-5}	0.202167
	110	18	18	2.38×10^{-4}	2.27×10^{-5}	2.94×10^{-5}	0.232646
	112			9.76×10^{-5}	9.22×10^{-6}	1.19×10^{-5}	0.228243
	115			9.75×10^{-5}	9.09×10^{-6}	1.17×10^{-5}	0.223190
	116			4.45×10^{-5}	4.13×10^{-6}	5.34×10^{-5}	0.233154
[32]				4.38×10^{-5}			

Table 5. The errors obtained using the proposed method for problem 2 using GA RBF.

$\alpha = 0.5$, $\beta = 1.5$	n_g	n_l	N	$Error_1$	$Error_2$	$Error_3$	C.Time(s)
	80	11	18	3.42×10^{-4}	3.83×10^{-5}	4.95×10^{-5}	0.147621
	90			2.53×10^{-4}	2.66×10^{-5}	3.44×10^{-5}	0.148642
	100			1.26×10^{-4}	1.26×10^{-5}	1.63×10^{-5}	0.161187
	101			8.43×10^{-5}	8.39×10^{-6}	1.08×10^{-5}	0.156145
	99	10	14	9.20×10^{-3}	9.87×10^{-4}	1.30×10^{-3}	0.206573
			16	2.40×10^{-3}	2.46×10^{-4}	3.18×10^{-4}	0.272171
			18	5.02×10^{-4}	5.05×10^{-5}	6.53×10^{-5}	0.225353
			20	4.87×10^{-4}	4.90×10^{-5}	6.33×10^{-5}	0.247079
	95	10	18	4.94×10^{-4}	5.07×10^{-5}	6.56×10^{-5}	0.205846
		11		4.22×10^{-4}	4.33×10^{-5}	5.60×10^{-5}	0.200952
		12		3.22×10^{-4}	3.30×10^{-5}	4.27×10^{-5}	0.216622
		15		2.33×10^{-4}	2.39×10^{-5}	3.09×10^{-5}	0.201578
[32]				5.72×10^{-6}			

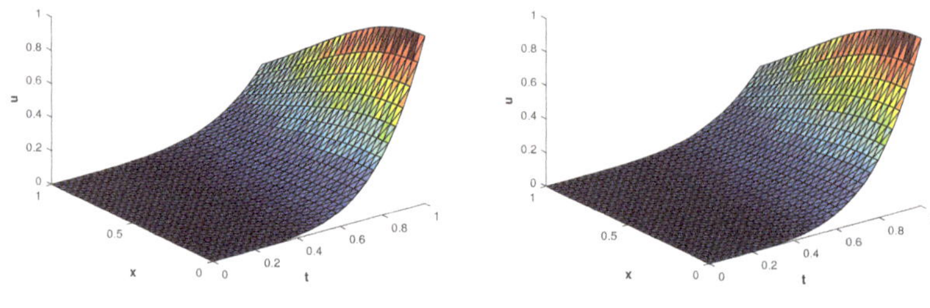

(**a**) (**b**)

Figure 11. (**a**) The numerical solution of problem 2 with $\alpha = 0.5, \beta = 1.1$. (**b**) The exact solution of problem 2 with $\alpha = 0.5, \beta = 1.1$.

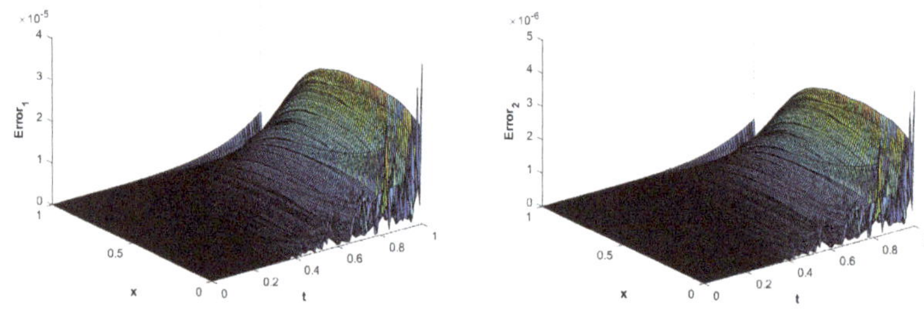

(**a**) (**b**)

Figure 12. (**a**) The surface plot of $Error_1$ of the proposed method corresponding to problem 2 with $n_g = 90, n_l = 20, N = 18, \alpha = 0.9, \beta = 1.3$ using MQ RBF. (**b**) The surface plot of $Error_2$ of the proposed method corresponding to problem 2 with $n_g = 90, n_l = 20, N = 18, \alpha = 0.9, \beta = 1.3$ using MQ RBF.

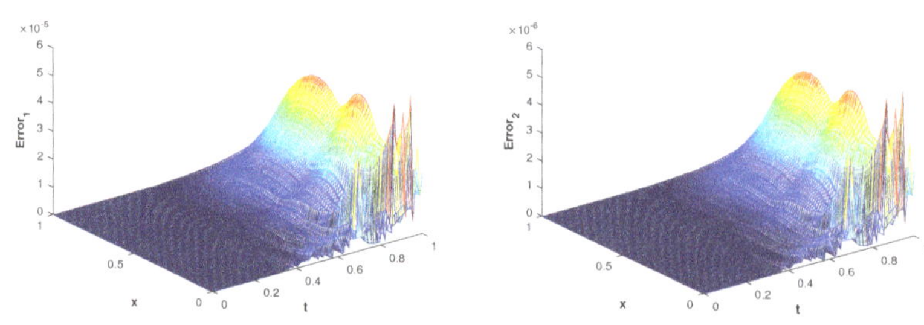

(**a**) (**b**)

Figure 13. (**a**) The mesh plot of $Error_1$ of the proposed method corresponding to problem 2 with $n_g = 90, n_l = 10, N = 18, \alpha = 0.2, \beta = 1.6$ using GA RBF. (**b**) The mesh plot of $Error_2$ of the proposed method corresponding to problem 2 with $n_g = 90, n_l = 10, N = 18, \alpha = 0.2, \beta = 1.6$ using GA RBF.

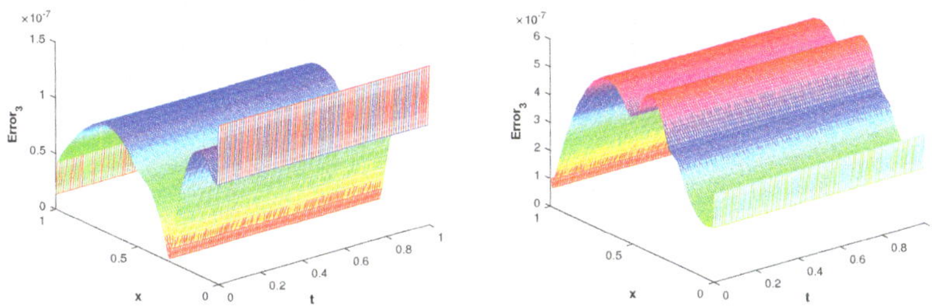

(a) (b)

Figure 14. (**a**) The surface plot of $Error_3$ of the proposed method corresponding to problem 2 with $N = 18, \alpha = 0.2, \beta = 1.6, n_g = 90, n_l = 10$ using MQ RBF. (**b**) The surface plot of $Error_3$ of the proposed method corresponding to problem 2 with $N = 18 \alpha = 0.2, \beta = 1.6, n_g = 90, n_l = 10$ using GA RBF.

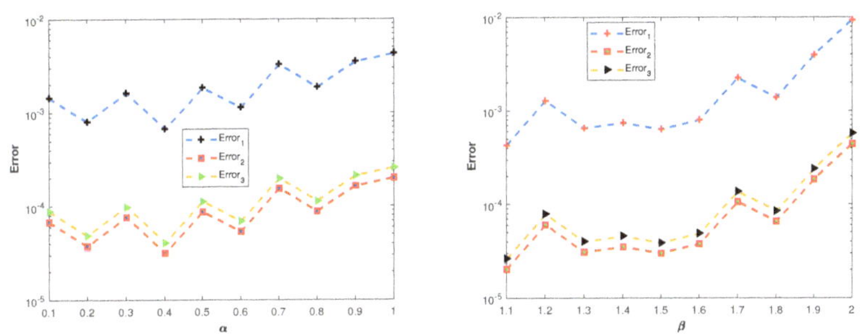

(a) (b)

Figure 15. (**a**) The plots of $Error_1$, $Error_2$, and $Error_3$ of the proposed method corresponding to problem 2 with various values of α and $\beta = 1.1, n_g = 120, n_l = 6, N = 18$ using MQ RBF. (**b**) The plots $Error_1$, $Error_2$, and $Error_3$ of the proposed method corresponding to problem 2 with various values of β and $\alpha = 0.9, n_g = 120, n_l = 6, N = 18$ using MQ RBF.

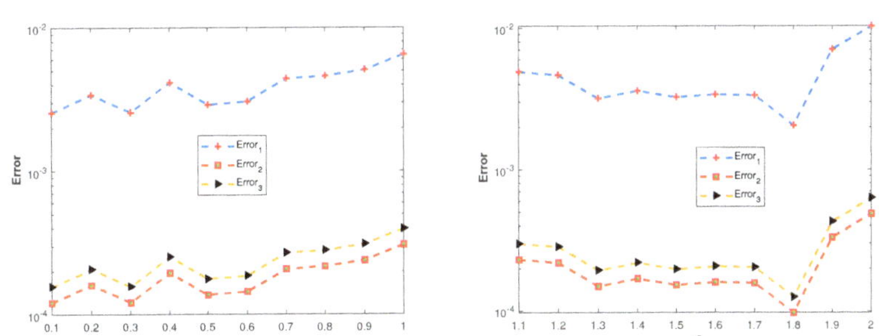

(a) (b)

Figure 16. (**a**) The plots of $Error_1$, $Error_2$, and $Error_3$ of the proposed method corresponding to problem 2 with various values of α and $\beta = 1.6, n_g = 450, n_l = 5, N = 18$ using GA RBF. (**b**) The plots $Error_1$, $Error_2$, and $Error_3$ of the proposed method corresponding to problem 2 with various values of β and $\alpha = 0.2, n_g = 450, n_l = 5, N = 18$ using GA RBF.

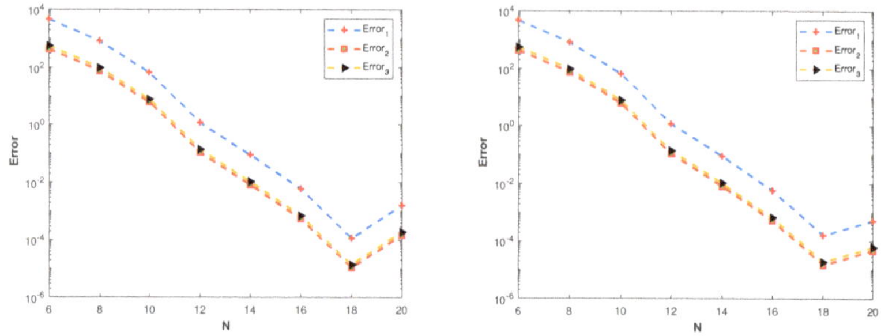

(**a**) (**b**)

Figure 17. (**a**) The plots of $Error_1$, $Error_2$, and $Error_3$ of the proposed method corresponding to problem 2 with various values of N and $\alpha = 0.5, \beta = 1.6, n_g = 120, n_l = 5$ using MQ RBF. (**b**) The plots $Error_1$, $Error_2$, and $Error_3$ of the proposed method corresponding to problem 2 with various values of N and $\alpha = 0.5, \beta = 1.6, n_g = 120, n_l = 5$ using GA RBF.

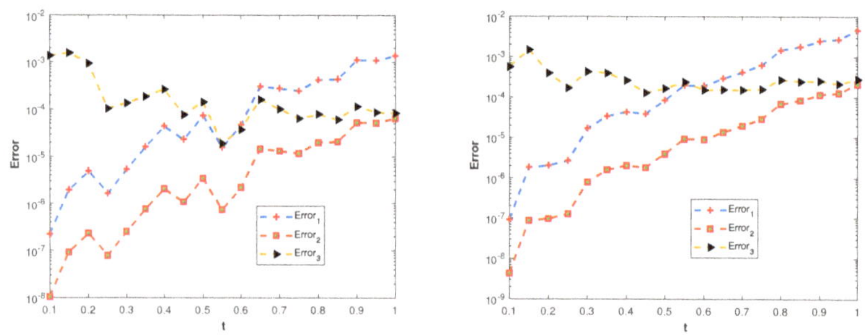

(**a**) (**b**)

Figure 18. (**a**) The plots of $Error_1$, $Error_2$, and $Error_3$ of the proposed method corresponding to problem 2 with various values of t and $N = 18, \alpha = 0.9, \beta = 1.1, n_g = 450, n_l = 5$ using MQ RBF. (**b**) The plots $Error_1$, $Error_2$, and $Error_3$ of the proposed method corresponding to problem 2 with various values of t and $N = 18\alpha = 0.9, \beta = 1.1, n_g = 450, n_l = 5$ using GA RBF.

Problem 3. *Consider the following two-dimensional test problem*

$$ {}_0^cD_t^{\alpha} u(x,y,t) + {}_0^cD_t^{\beta} u(x,y,t) = \Delta u(x,y,t) + f(x,y,t), 0 \le x,y \le \pi, \tag{22} $$

with analytic solution

$$ u(x,y,t) = t^4 \sin(\pi x) \sin(\pi y). \tag{23} $$

This problem is considered for validating the numerical scheme on domains Ω_1 and Ω_6 as shown in Figure 19a and Figure 19f, respectively. The errors of the proposed method for problem 3 using the MQ RBF on domain Ω_1 are presented in Table 6; using the GA RBF on domain Ω_6, they are presented in Table 7. It is observed that the method has produced results with acceptable accuracy. The numerical and analytic solutions of problem 3 on domain Ω_1 are depicted in Figure 20a,b, a good agreement between the numerical and analytic solutions is observed. The mesh plots of $Error_1$ and $Error_2$ on domain Ω_1 using MQ RBF with $n_g = 6400, n_l = 35, N = 18, \alpha = 0.4, \beta = 1.7$ are presented in Figure 21a,b. The mesh plots of $Error_1$ and $Error_2$ on domain Ω_6 using MQ RBF with $n_g = 1225, n_l = 35$, $N = 18$, $\alpha = 0.4, \beta = 1.7$ are presented in Figure 22a,b. The mesh plots of $Error_1$ and $Error_2$ on domain Ω_1 using GA RBF with $n_g = 2500, n_l = 35, N = 18, \alpha = 0.9, \beta = 1.1$ are presented in Figure 23a,b. The mesh plots of $Error_1$ and $Error_2$ on domain Ω_6 using

GA RBF with $n_g = 1600, n_l = 35, N = 18, \alpha = 0.5, \beta = 1.5$ are depicted in Figure 24a,b. The surface plots of $Error_3$ on domain Ω_1 using MQ RBF with $n_g = 1600, n_l = 30, N = 16$, $\alpha = 0.5, \beta = 1.5$ are depicted in Figure 25a and the surface plots of $Error_3$ on domain Ω_6 using GA RBF with $n_g = 1600, n_l = 30, N = 16, \alpha = 0.5, \beta = 1.5$ are depicted in Figure 20b. From the obtained results, it is evident that the proposed method can efficiently solve problems with both uniform and non-uniform node distributions.

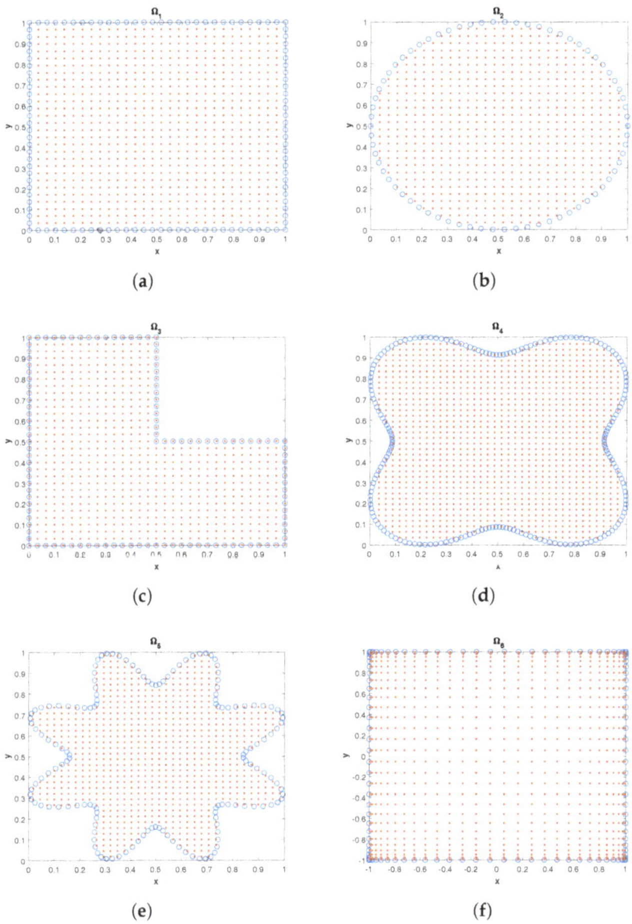

Figure 19. (**a**) Uniform nodes distribution in the square domain; (**b**) Uniform nodes distribution in the circular domain; (**c**) Uniform nodes distribution in the L shaped domain; (**d**) Uniform nodes distribution in the nut shaped domain; (**e**) Uniform nodes distribution in the star shaped domain; (**f**) Chebyshev nodes distribution in the square domain.

Table 6. The errors obtained using the proposed method for problem 3 on domain Ω_1 using MQ RBF.

$\alpha = 0.50$, $\beta = 1.50$	n_g	n_l	N	$Error_1$	$Error_2$	$Error_3$	C.Time(s)
	4624	13	14	1.27×10^{-2}	1.86×10^{-4}	3.78×10^{-4}	28.244165
			16	9.32×10^{-4}	1.37×10^{-5}	2.78×10^{-5}	21.367193
			18	3.91×10^{-4}	5.75×10^{-6}	1.16×10^{-5}	25.048697
			20	3.62×10^{-4}	5.33×10^{-6}	1.08×10^{-5}	25.466929
	4225	13	16	1.20×10^{-3}	1.82×10^{-5}	3.71×10^{-5}	24.562205
		14		9.56×10^{-4}	1.47×10^{-5}	2.99×10^{-5}	25.343475
		15		4.42×10^{-4}	6.80×10^{-6}	1.38×10^{-5}	25.994300

Table 6. *Cont.*

$\alpha = 0.50$, $\beta = 1.50$	n_g	n_l	N	$Error_1$	$Error_2$	$Error_3$	C.Time(s)
		17		4.16×10^{-4}	6.40×10^{-6}	1.30×10^{-5}	26.284367
	4096	16	16	5.86×10^{-4}	9.16×10^{-6}	1.86×10^{-5}	26.098623
	4356			5.84×10^{-4}	8.85×10^{-6}	1.79×10^{-5}	27.673088
	4761			5.51×10^{-4}	7.99×10^{-6}	1.62×10^{-5}	31.860493
	4900			5.30×10^{-4}	7.58×10^{-6}	1.53×10^{-5}	37.681474
[32]				1.44×10^{-4}			

Table 7. The errors obtained using the proposed method for problem 3 on domain Ω_6 using GA RBF.

$\alpha = 0.50$, $\beta = 1.50$	n_g	n_l	N	$Error_1$	$Error_2$	$Error_3$	C.Time(s)
	1600	15	16	6.10×10^{-3}	1.51×10^{-4}	3.98×10^{-4}	10.247910
			18	5.90×10^{-3}	1.47×10^{-4}	3.87×10^{-4}	10.275675
			20	5.80×10^{-3}	1.45×10^{-4}	3.83×10^{-4}	10.530108
			22	5.70×10^{-3}	1.43×10^{-4}	3.78×10^{-4}	13.210822
	1521	13	16	8.00×10^{-3}	2.04×10^{-4}	5.38×10^{-4}	6.366293
		14		6.30×10^{-3}	1.61×10^{-4}	4.25×10^{-4}	6.503034
		15		6.20×10^{-3}	1.59×10^{-4}	4.18×10^{-4}	7.186865
		18		6.18×10^{-3}	1.58×10^{-4}	4.17×10^{-4}	8.509750
	1600	13	18	8.30×10^{-3}	2.08×10^{-4}	5.48×10^{-4}	7.300554
	1764			6.80×10^{-3}	1.62×10^{-4}	4.26×10^{-4}	8.319459
	1936			6.60×10^{-3}	1.49×10^{-4}	3.91×10^{-4}	9.356419
	2401			6.30×10^{-3}	1.28×10^{-4}	3.36×10^{-4}	12.664379
[32]				1.98×10^{-3}			

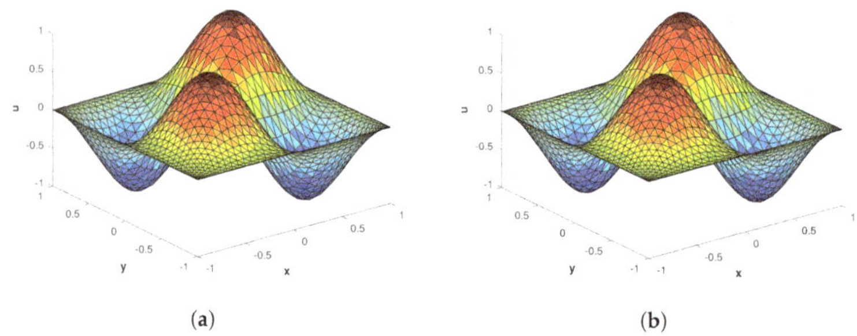

Figure 20. (**a**) The numerical solution of problem 3 on Ω_1. (**b**) The exact solution of problem 3 on Ω_1.

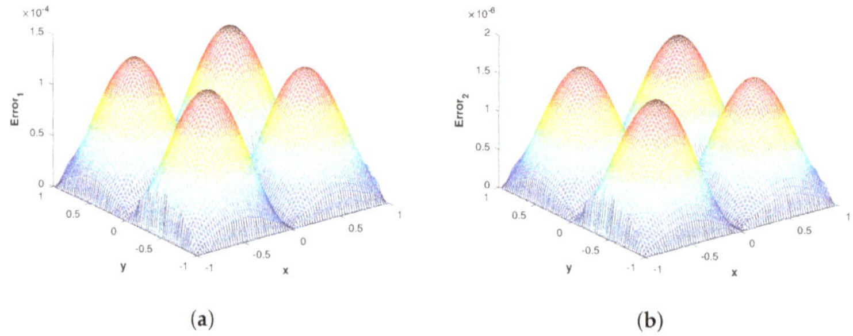

Figure 21. (**a**) The mesh plot of $Error_1$ of the proposed method corresponding to problem 3 using MQ RBF on Ω_1 with $n_g = 6400, n_l = 35, N = 18, \alpha = 0.4, \beta = 1.7$. (**b**) The mesh plot of $Error_2$ of the proposed method corresponding to problem 3 using MQ RBF on Ω_1 with $n_g = 6400, n_l = 35, N = 18$, $\alpha = 0.4, \beta = 1.7$.

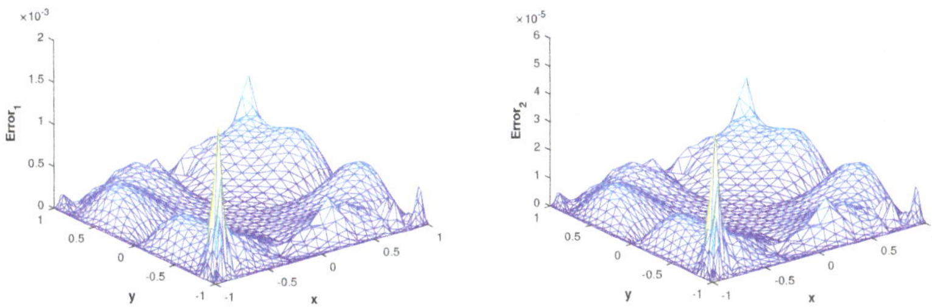

(**a**) (**b**)

Figure 22. (**a**) The mesh plot of $Error_1$ of the proposed method corresponding to problem 3 using MQ RBF on Ω_6 with $n_g = 1225, n_l = 35, N = 18, \alpha = 0.4, \beta = 1.7$. (**b**) The mesh plot of $Error_2$ of the proposed method corresponding to problem 3 using MQ RBF on Ω_6 with $n_g = 1225, n_l = 35$, $N = 18$, $\alpha = 0.4, \beta = 1.7$.

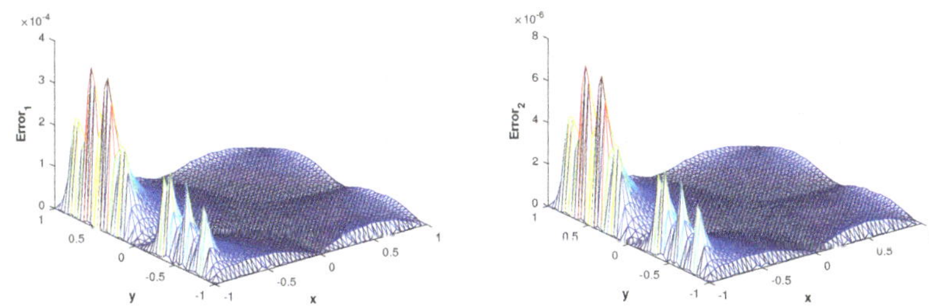

(**a**) (**b**)

Figure 23. (**a**) The mesh plot of $Error_1$ of the proposed method corresponding to problem 3 using GA RBF on Ω_1 with $n_g = 2500, n_l = 35, N = 18, \alpha = 0.9, \beta = 1.1$. (**b**) The mesh plot of $Error_2$ of the proposed method corresponding to problem 3 using GA RBF on Ω_1 with $n_g = 2500, n_l = 35$, $N = 18$, $\alpha = 0.9, \beta = 1.1$.

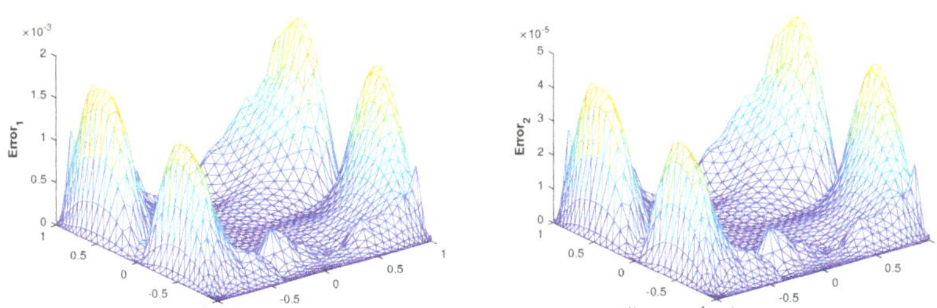

(**a**) (**b**)

Figure 24. (**a**) The mesh plot of $Error_1$ of the proposed method corresponding to problem 3 using GA RBF on Ω_6 with $n_g = 1600, n_l = 35, N = 18, \alpha = 0.5, \beta = 1.5$. (**b**) The mesh plot of $Error_2$ of the proposed method corresponding to problem 3 using GA RBF on Ω_6 with $n_g = 1600, n_l = 35$, $N = 18$, $\alpha = 0.5, \beta = 1.5$.

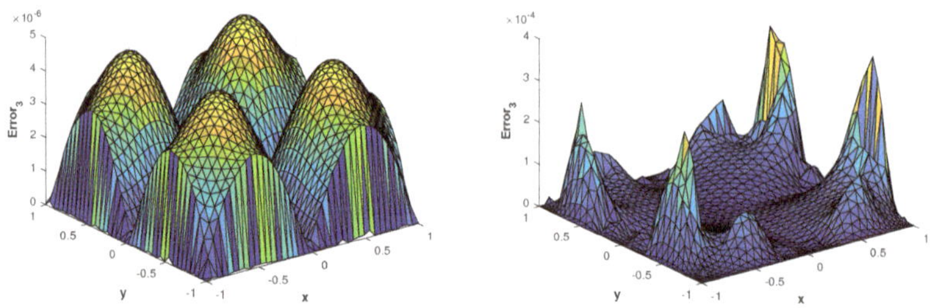

(**a**) (**b**)

Figure 25. (**a**) The surface plot of $Error_3$ of the proposed method corresponding to problem 3 using MQ RBF on Ω_1 with $n_g = 1600, n_l = 30, N = 16, \alpha = 0.5, \beta = 1.5$. (**b**) The surface plot of $Error_3$ of the proposed method corresponding to problem 3 using GA RBF on Ω_6 with $n_g = 1600, n_l = 30$, $N = 16$, $\alpha = 0.5, \beta = 1.5$.

Problem 4. *Consider the following two-dimensional test problem*

$$ {}_0^C D_t^{\alpha} u(x,y,t) + {}_0^C D_t^{\beta} u(x,y,t) = \Delta u(x,y,t) + f(x,y,t), 0 \le x, y \le 1, \tag{24} $$

with analytic solution

$$ u(x,y,t) = (1+t^3)(1-x^2-y^2) \tag{25} $$

This problem serves to validate the numerical scheme on domains Ω_1, Ω_3, and Ω_5 as illustrated in Figure 19a, Figure 19c and Figure 19e, respectively. The errors of the proposed method for problem 4 in domain Ω_1 using MQ RBF are presented in Table 8, while the errors using GA RBF are presented in Table 9. In Table 10 the errors of the proposed method on domain Ω_3 using MQ RBF are presented; in Table 11, the errors on domain Ω_5 using GA RBF are shown. We can see that the proposed method has efficiently solved the considered problem of regular and irregular domains. Figure 26a,b shows the numerical and exact solutions of problem 4 on domain Ω_1. It is observed that the numerical solution agrees well with the analytic solution. In Figure 27a,b the surface plots of $Error_1$ and $Error_2$ using MQ RBF on domain Ω_1 with $n_g = 4225, n_l = 40$, $N = 16, \alpha = 0.7, \beta = 1.9$ are depicted. The surface plots of $Error_1$ and $Error_2$ using GA RBF on domain Ω_1 with $n_g = 6400, n_l = 30, N = 16, \alpha = 0.2, \beta = 1.8$ are shown in Figure 28a,b. The scatter plots of $Error_1$ and $Error_2$ using MQ RBF on domain Ω_3 with $n_g = 1281, n_l = 40, N = 16, \alpha = 0.7, \beta = 1.9$ are depicted in Figure 29a,b; using GA RBF, they are presented in Figure 30a,b. The scatter plots of $Error_1$ and $Error_2$ using MQ RBF on domain Ω_5 with $n_g = 3069, n_l = 80, N = 16, \alpha = 0.3, \beta = 1.6$ are shown in Figure 31a,b; using GA RBF with $n_g = 3069, n_l = 30, N = 16, \alpha = 0.3, \beta = 1.6$, they are displayed in Figure 32a,b. The scatter plots of $Error_3$ of the proposed method corresponding to problem 4 using MQ RBF on Ω_3 with $n_g = 1875, n_l = 30, N = 18, \alpha = 0.7, \beta = 1.9$ are shown in Figure 33a. Similarly, the scatter plots of $Error_3$ using GA RBF on Ω_5 with $n_g = 2259, n_l = 30, N = 18, \alpha = 0.7, \beta = 1.9$ are shown in Figure 33b. It can be seen that the performance of the method is excellent for irregular domains as well.

Table 8. The errors obtained using the proposed method for problem 4 on domain Ω_1 using MQ RBF.

$\alpha = 0.7$, $\beta = 1.6$	n_g	n_l	N	$Error_1$	$Error_2$	$Error_3$	C.Time(s)
	625	40	20	9.75×10^{-4}	3.90×10^{-5}	2.29×10^{-4}	5.780576
	676			8.36×10^{-4}	3.21×10^{-5}	1.88×10^{-4}	5.887121
	729			7.78×10^{-4}	2.88×10^{-5}	1.69×10^{-4}	6.109537

Table 8. *Cont.*

$\alpha = 0.7$, $\beta = 1.6$	n_g	n_l	N	$Error_1$	$Error_2$	$Error_3$	C.Time(s)
	784			7.69×10^{-4}	2.74×10^{-5}	1.60×10^{-4}	6.602348
	1444	55	12	8.18×10^{-4}	2.15×10^{-5}	1.24×10^{-4}	18.340002
			14	7.57×10^{-4}	1.99×10^{-5}	1.15×10^{-4}	18.271623
			16	6.07×10^{-4}	1.59×10^{-5}	9.26×10^{-5}	18.396910
			18	5.87×10^{-4}	1.54×10^{-5}	8.96×10^{-5}	19.094877
	841	50	22	1.10×10^{-3}	3.84×10^{-5}	2.24×10^{-4}	9.939883
		51		1.00×10^{-3}	3.55×10^{-5}	2.07×10^{-4}	10.480804
		52		6.16×10^{-4}	2.12×10^{-5}	1.24×10^{-4}	10.572760
		53		5.45×10^{-4}	1.88×10^{-5}	1.09×10^{-4}	10.763141
[32]				9.54×10^{-6}			

Table 9. The errors obtained using the proposed method for problem 4 on domain Ω_1 using GA RBF.

$\alpha = 0.7$, $\beta = 1.90$	n_g	n_l	N	$Error_1$	$Error_2$	$Error_3$	C.Time(s)
	1444	10	16	9.00×10^{-3}	2.36×10^{-4}	2.18×10^{-4}	3.095921
	1521			8.70×10^{-3}	2.22×10^{-4}	2.05×10^{-4}	3.330961
	1600			8.60×10^{-3}	2.14×10^{-4}	1.98×10^{-4}	3.742602
	1764			8.50×10^{-3}	2.03×10^{-4}	1.87×10^{-4}	4.456763
	2025	11	18	7.90×10^{-3}	1.75×10^{-4}	1.62×10^{-4}	5.512489
		17		7.60×10^{-3}	1.69×10^{-4}	1.56×10^{-4}	6.991000
		18		5.60×10^{-3}	1.24×10^{-4}	1.15×10^{-4}	6.989841
		19		3.30×10^{-3}	7.36×10^{-5}	6.81×10^{-5}	6.974949
	676	19	14	3.40×10^{-3}	1.29×10^{-4}	1.19×10^{-4}	2.241376
		51	16	3.10×10^{-3}	1.17×10^{-4}	1.07×10^{-4}	3.233400
		52	18	3.00×10^{-3}	1.15×10^{-4}	1.06×10^{-4}	2.891570
		53	20	2.80×10^{-3}	1.08×10^{-4}	9.96×10^{-5}	2.693629
[32]				8.90×10^{-5}			

Table 10. The errors obtained using the proposed method for problem 4 on domain Ω_3 using MQ RBF.

$\alpha = 0.5$, $\beta = 1.50$	n_g	n_l	N	$Error_1$	$Error_2$	$Error_3$	C.Time(s)
	560	23	18	9.91×10^{-4}	4.19×10^{-5}	3.59×10^{-5}	2.342120
		30		8.62×10^{-4}	3.64×10^{-5}	3.13×10^{-5}	3.562138
		31		8.49×10^{-4}	3.58×10^{-5}	3.08×10^{-5}	3.845987
		32		8.27×10^{-4}	3.49×10^{-5}	3.00×10^{-5}	4.054985
	481	65	12	1.60×10^{-3}	7.47×10^{-5}	6.41×10^{-5}	10.473426
			14	1.00×10^{-3}	4.71×10^{-5}	4.04×10^{-5}	10.964542
			16	7.50×10^{-4}	3.42×10^{-5}	2.93×10^{-5}	10.637479
			18	7.48×10^{-4}	3.41×10^{-5}	2.93×10^{-5}	10.676450
	481	74	18	8.04×10^{-4}	3.66×10^{-5}	3.15×10^{-5}	13.894779
	560			7.56×10^{-4}	3.19×10^{-5}	2.74×10^{-5}	15.420818
	645			7.28×10^{-4}	2.87×10^{-5}	2.46×10^{-5}	16.253816
	736			7.11×10^{-4}	2.62×10^{-5}	2.25×10^{-5}	17.652880
[32]				6.22×10^{-6}			

Table 11. The errors obtained using the proposed method for problem 4 on domain Ω_5 using GA RBF.

$\alpha = 0.7$, $\beta = 1.90$	n_g	n_l	N	$Error_1$	$Error_2$	$Error_3$	C.Time(s)
	800	70	18	4.70×10^{-3}	1.65×10^{-4}	1.59×10^{-4}	16.835572
	805			3.60×10^{-3}	1.26×10^{-4}	1.21×10^{-4}	18.014559
	819			1.90×10^{-3}	6.54×10^{-5}	6.31×10^{-5}	17.489709
	839			1.70×10^{-3}	5.80×10^{-5}	5.59×10^{-5}	17.416943
	905	38	16	4.70×10^{-3}	1.56×10^{-4}	1.50×10^{-3}	8.011904
		39		3.40×10^{-3}	1.13×10^{-4}	1.09×10^{-4}	8.525006
		40		2.80×10^{-3}	9.44×10^{-5}	9.08×10^{-5}	6.758216
		41		2.20×10^{-3}	7.23×10^{-5}	6.95×10^{-5}	6.854242
	824	58	10	8.91×10^{-2}	3.10×10^{-3}	3.00×10^{-3}	8.248187
			12	3.10×10^{-3}	1.07×10^{-4}	1.03×10^{-4}	9.049039

Table 11. *Cont.*

$\alpha = 0.7$, $\beta = 1.90$	n_g	n_l	N	$Error_1$	$Error_2$	$Error_3$	C.Time(s)
			14	2.40×10^{-3}	8.23×10^{-5}	7.93×10^{-5}	9.104889
			16	2.30×10^{-3}	7.95×10^{-5}	7.67×10^{-5}	9.238572
[32]				3.19×10^{-5}			

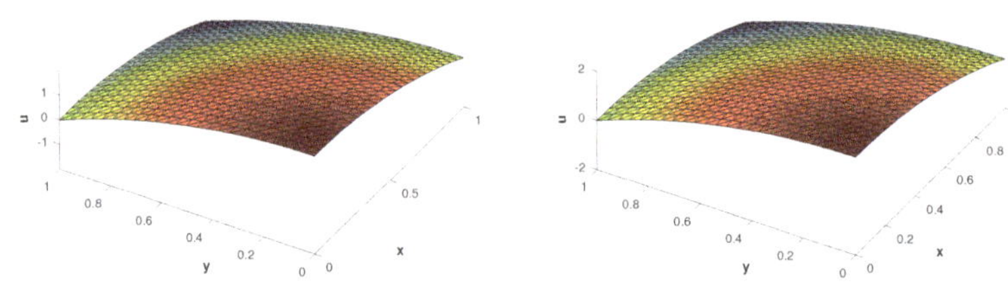

(a) (b)

Figure 26. (**a**) The numerical solution of problem 4 on Ω_1. (**b**) The exact solution of problem 4 on Ω_1.

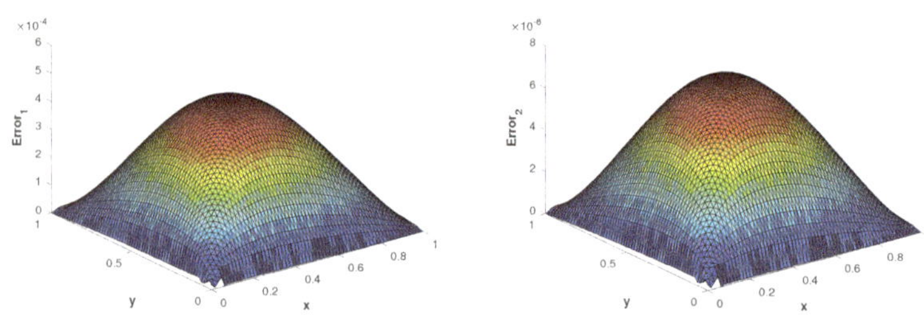

(a) (b)

Figure 27. (**a**) The surface plot of $Error_1$ of the proposed method corresponding to problem 4 using MQ RBF on Ω_1 with $n_g = 4225, n_l = 40, N = 16, \alpha = 0.7, \beta = 1.9$. (**b**) The surface plot of $Error_2$ of the proposed method corresponding to problem 4 using MQ RBF on Ω_1 with $n_g = 4225, n_l = 40$, $N = 16, \alpha = 0.7, \beta = 1.9$.

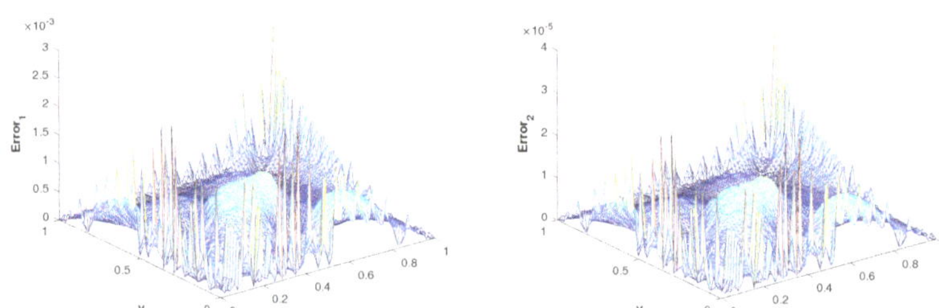

(a) (b)

Figure 28. (**a**) The surface plot of $Error_1$ of the proposed method corresponding to problem 4 using GA RBF on Ω_1 with $n_g = 6400, n_l = 30, N = 16, \alpha = 0.2, \beta = 1.8$. (**b**) The surface plot of $Error_2$ of the proposed method corresponding to problem 4 using GA RBF on Ω_1 with $n_g = 6400, n_l = 30$, $N = 16$, $\alpha = 0.2, \beta = 1.8$.

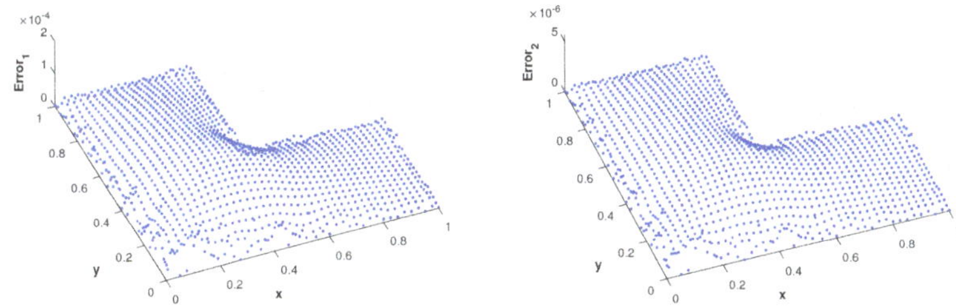

(a) (b)

Figure 29. (**a**) The scatter plot of $Error_1$ of the proposed method corresponding to problem 4 using MQ RBF on Ω_3 with $n_g = 1281, n_l = 40, N = 16, \alpha = 0.7, \beta = 1.9$. (**b**) The scatter plot of $Error_2$ of the proposed method corresponding to problem 4 using MQ RBF on Ω_3 with $n_g = 1281, n_l = 40$, $N = 16, \alpha = 0.7, \beta = 1.9$.

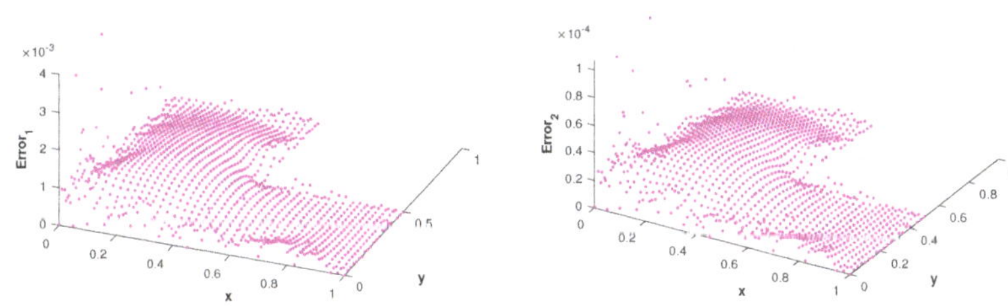

(a) (b)

Figure 30. (**a**) The scatter plot of $Error_1$ of the proposed method corresponding to problem 4 using GA RBF on Ω_3 with $n_g = 1281, n_l = 40, N = 16, \alpha = 0.7, \beta = 1.9$. (**b**) The scatter plot of $Error_2$ of the proposed method corresponding to problem 4 using GA RBF on Ω_3 with $n_g = 1281, n_l = 40$, $N = 16$, $\alpha = 0.7, \beta = 1.9$.

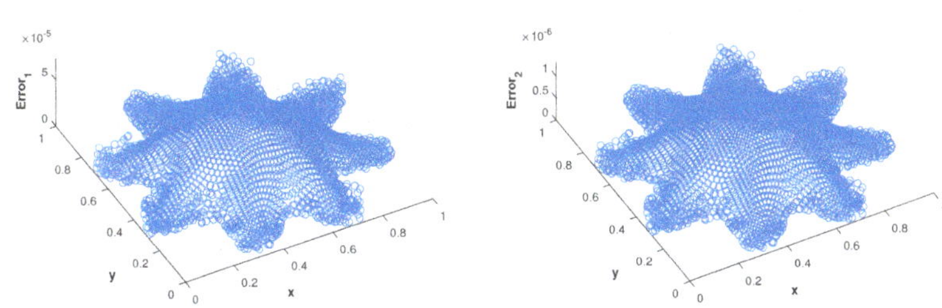

(a) (b)

Figure 31. (**a**) The scatter plot of $Error_1$ of the proposed method corresponding to problem 4 using MQ RBF on Ω_5 with $n_g = 3069, n_l = 80, N = 16, \alpha = 0.3, \beta = 1.6$. (**b**) The scatter plot of $Error_2$ of the proposed method corresponding to problem 4 using MQ RBF on Ω_5 with $n_g = 3069, n_l = 80$, $N = 16, \alpha = 0.3, \beta = 1.6$.

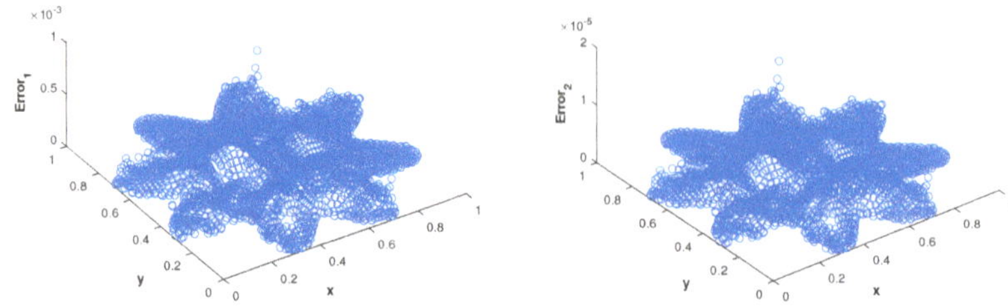

(**a**) (**b**)

Figure 32. (**a**) The scatter plot of $Error_1$ of the proposed method corresponding to problem 4 using GA RBF on Ω_5 with $n_g = 3069, n_l = 30, N = 16, \alpha = 0.3, \beta = 1.6$. (**b**) The scatter plot of $Error_2$ of the proposed method corresponding to problem 4 using GA RBF on Ω_5 with $n_g = 3069, n_l = 30$, $N = 16$, $\alpha = 0.3, \beta = 1.6$.

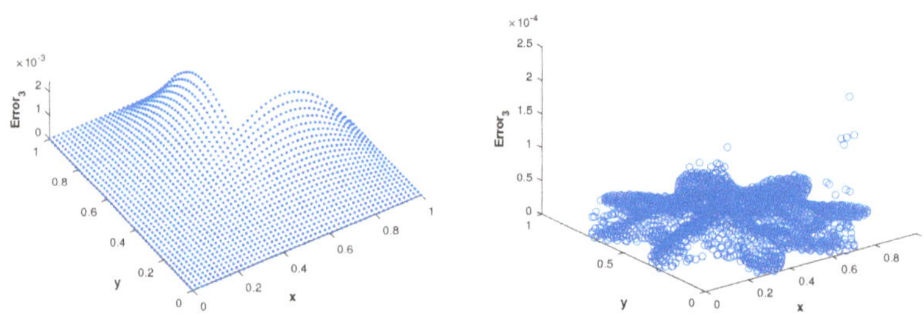

(**a**) (**b**)

Figure 33. (**a**) The scatter plot of $Error_3$ of the proposed method corresponding to problem 4 using MQ RBF on Ω_3 with $n_g = 1875, n_l = 30, N = 18, \alpha = 0.7, \beta = 1.9$. (**b**) The scatter plot of $Error_3$ of the proposed method corresponding to problem 4 using GA RBF on Ω_5 with $n_g = 2259, n_l = 30$, $N = 18$, $\alpha = 0.7, \beta = 1.9$.

Problem 5.

$$ {}_0^C D_t^{\alpha} u(x,y,t) + {}_0^C D_t^{\beta} u(x,y,t) = \Delta u(x,y,t) + f(x,y,t), 0 \leq x,y \Longleftrightarrow 1, \tag{26} $$

with analytic solution

$$ u(x,y,t) = t^3 \left(\frac{(x-0.5)^2}{\gamma} + \frac{(y-0.5)^2}{\gamma} \right). $$

This problem is considered for validating the numerical scheme on domains Ω_1, Ω_2 and Ω_4, as shown in Figure 19a, Figure 19b and Figure 19d, respectively. The errors of the proposed method on domain Ω_1 for problem 5 using MQ RBF are presented in Table 12; using GA RBF, they are presented in Table 13. The errors obtained using MQ RBF on domain Ω_2 are presented in Table 14; using GA RBF on domain Ω_4, they are presented in Table 15. The proposed method produced accurate and stable results on regular as well as irregular domains. The numerical and exact solutions of problem 5 on domain Ω_1 are shown in Figure 34a,b; a nice agreement is observed. The surface plots of $Error_1$ and $Error_2$ on domain Ω_1 using MQ RBF with $n_g = 4900, n_l = 35, N = 18, \alpha = 0.7, \beta = 1.6$ are shown in Figure 35a,b. The surface plots of $Error_1$ and $Error_2$ using GA RBF on

Ω_1 with $n_g = 8100, n_l = 35, N = 18, \alpha = 0.7, \beta = 1.6$ are shown in Figure 36a,b. The mesh plots of $Error_1$ and $Error_2$ using MQ RBF on domain Ω_2 with $n_g = 5064, n_l = 30$, $N = 18$, $\alpha = 0.9, \beta = 1.3$ are depicted in Figure 37a,b; using GA RBF, they are presented in Figure 38a,b. The scatter plots of $Error_1$ and $Error_2$ using MQ RBF on domain Ω_4 with $n_g = 6393, n_l = 35, N = 16, \alpha = 0.7, \beta = 1.6$ are displayed in Figure 39a,b; using GA RBF, they are presented in Figure 40a,b. The mesh plot of $Error_3$ using MQ RBF on domain Ω_2 with $n_g = 5064, n_l = 35, N = 18, \alpha = 0.7, \beta = 1.6$ is presented in Figure 41a; the scatter plot of $Error_3$ using GA RBF on domain Ω_4 with $n_g = 6393, n_l = 35, N = 18, \alpha = 0.7, \beta = 1.6$ is presented in Figure 41b. It is observed that the method can solve these types of problems efficiently on regular as well as irregular domains.

Table 12. The errors obtained using the proposed method for problem 5 on domain Ω_1 using MQ RBF.

$\alpha = 0.60$, $\beta = 1.50$	n_g	n_l	N	$Error_1$	$Error_2$	$Error_3$	C.Time(s)
	1296	18	20	7.11×10^{-4}	1.97×10^{-5}	1.14×10^{-4}	4.254578
	1369			6.30×10^{-4}	1.70×10^{-5}	9.87×10^{-5}	4.517336
	1444			6.03×10^{-4}	1.58×10^{-5}	9.20×10^{-5}	5.330350
	1600			5.92×10^{-4}	1.48×10^{-5}	8.57×10^{-5}	5.933110
	2304	15	12	1.10×10^{-3}	2.38×10^{-5}	1.37×10^{-4}	6.226840
			14	4.60×10^{-4}	9.58×10^{-6}	5.52×10^{-5}	6.486711
			16	2.86×10^{-4}	5.96×10^{-6}	3.43×10^{-5}	7.310871
			18	2.81×10^{-4}	5.85×10^{-6}	3.37×10^{-5}	7.713956
	1600	13	18	6.47×10^{-4}	1.61×10^{-5}	9.36×10^{-5}	3.810299
		14		5.98×10^{-4}	1.49×10^{-5}	8.66×10^{-5}	4.302964
		15		5.94×10^{-4}	1.48×10^{-5}	8.59×10^{-5}	4.404455
		16		5.03×10^{-4}	1.25×10^{-5}	7.28×10^{-5}	4.543246
[32]				1.01×10^{-4}			

Table 13. The errors obtained using the proposed method for problem 5 on domain Ω_1 using GA RBF.

$\alpha = 0.70$, $\beta = 1.60$	n_g	n_l	N	$Error_1$	$Error_2$	$Error_3$	C.Time(s)
	2025	16	18	3.33×10^{-4}	7.42×10^{-6}	4.28×10^{-5}	6.454437
	2500			1.98×10^{-4}	3.97×10^{-6}	2.28×10^{-5}	8.824310
	3025			1.25×10^{-4}	2.28×10^{-6}	1.31×10^{-5}	11.457521
	3600			1.06×10^{-4}	1.77×10^{-6}	1.02×10^{-5}	15.700804
	3969	12	18	9.70×10^{-3}	1.53×10^{-4}	8.80×10^{-4}	21.993975
		13		1.49×10^{-4}	2.37×10^{-6}	1.36×10^{-5}	24.161273
		14		1.48×10^{-4}	2.35×10^{-6}	1.34×10^{-5}	23.322577
		16		1.16×10^{-4}	1.85×10^{-6}	1.06×10^{-5}	24.757581
	3721	16	12	1.40×10^{-3}	2.35×10^{-5}	1.35×10^{-4}	16.911628
			14	4.58×10^{-4}	7.52×10^{-6}	4.31×10^{-5}	18.235145
			16	1.10×10^{-4}	1.80×10^{-6}	1.03×10^{-5}	20.645716
			18	9.52×10^{-5}	1.56×10^{-6}	8.95×10^{-6}	21.862306
[32]				1.01×10^{-4}			

Table 14. The errors obtained using the proposed method for problem 5 on domain Ω_2 using MQ RBF.

$\alpha = 0.70$, $\beta = 1.60$	n_g	n_l	N	$Error_1$	$Error_2$	$Error_3$	C.Time(s)
	718	53	23	3.90×10^{-4}	1.45×10^{-5}	7.60×10^{-5}	9.462843
	822			2.99×10^{-4}	1.04×10^{-5}	5.44×10^{-5}	10.868986
	893			2.62×10^{-4}	8.77×10^{-6}	4.62×10^{-5}	11.586178
	1115			2.61×10^{-4}	7.83×10^{-6}	4.10×10^{-5}	13.733598
	1286	50	12	7.92×10^{-4}	2.21×10^{-5}	1.14×10^{-4}	13.692401
			14	6.78×10^{-4}	1.89×10^{-5}	9.81×10^{-5}	13.796613
			16	4.95×10^{-4}	1.38×10^{-5}	7.16×10^{-5}	14.059077
			18	4.70×10^{-4}	1.31×10^{-5}	6.81×10^{-5}	14.525208
	1357	45	18	5.19×10^{-4}	1.41×10^{-5}	7.33×10^{-5}	14.082632
		46		4.68×10^{-4}	1.27×10^{-5}	6.61×10^{-5}	13.687417
		47		4.03×10^{-4}	1.09×10^{-5}	5.68×10^{-5}	14.141039
		48		1.96×10^{-5}	5.33×10^{-6}	2.77×10^{-5}	14.555474
[32]				1.01×10^{-4}			

Table 15. The errors obtained using the proposed method for problem 5 on domain Ω_4 using GA RBF.

$\alpha = 0.70$, $\beta = 1.60$	n_g	n_l	N	$Error_1$	$Error_2$	$Error_3$	C.Time(s)
	1765	28	18	2.70×10^{-3}	6.32×10^{-5}	3.48×10^{-4}	12.738675
		29		7.78×10^{-4}	1.85×10^{-5}	1.02×10^{-4}	12.319389
		30		7.03×10^{-4}	1.67×10^{-5}	9.23×10^{-5}	12.649178
		32		5.20×10^{-4}	1.23×10^{-5}	6.82×10^{-5}	13.501318
	2031	15	16	8.69×10^{-4}	1.93×10^{-5}	1.06×10^{-4}	10.713900
	2108			7.38×10^{-4}	1.60×10^{-5}	8.80×10^{-5}	6.853962
	2292			5.97×10^{-4}	1.24×10^{-5}	6.81×10^{-5}	7.950902
	2367			3.93×10^{-4}	8.09×10^{-6}	4.39×10^{-5}	8.201278
	2460	15	12	9.49×10^{-4}	1.91×10^{-5}	1.03×10^{-4}	7.867139
			14	8.75×10^{-4}	1.76×10^{-5}	9.56×10^{-5}	7.951785
			16	5.96×10^{-4}	1.20×10^{-5}	6.52×10^{-5}	8.449387
			18	5.57×10^{-4}	1.12×10^{-5}	6.09×10^{-5}	8.862747
[32]				1.01×10^{-4}			

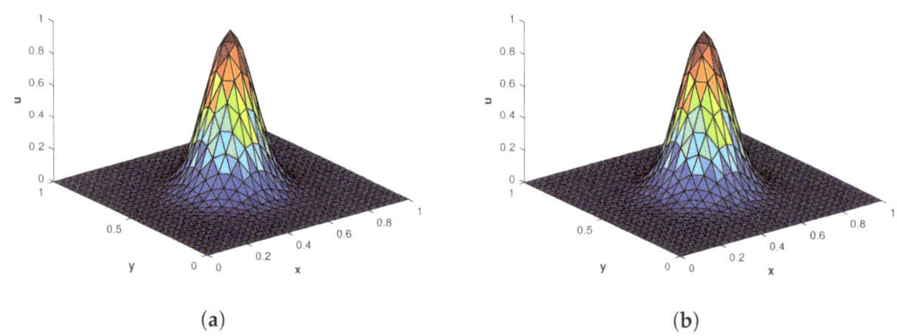

Figure 34. (**a**) The numerical solution of problem 5 on domain Ω_1. (**b**) The exact solution of problem 5 on domain Ω_1.

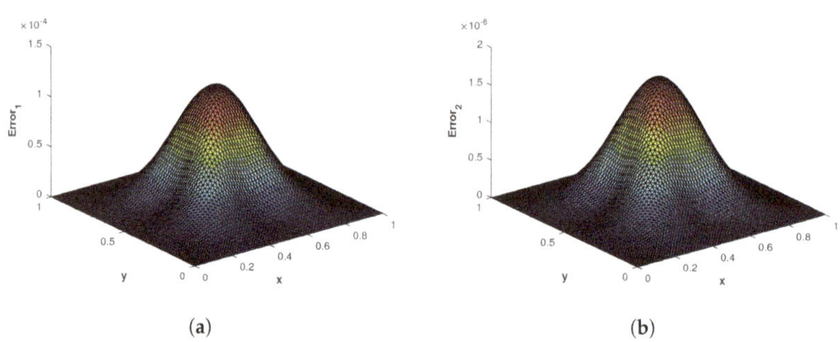

Figure 35. (**a**) The surface plot of $Error_1$ of the proposed method corresponding to problem 5 on Ω_1 with $n_g = 4900, n_l = 35, N = 18, \alpha = 0.7, \beta = 1.6$ using MQ RBF. (**b**) The surface plot of $Error_2$ of the proposed method corresponding to problem 5 on Ω_1 with $n_g = 4900, n_l = 35, N = 18, \alpha = 0.7, \beta = 1.6$ using MQ RBF.

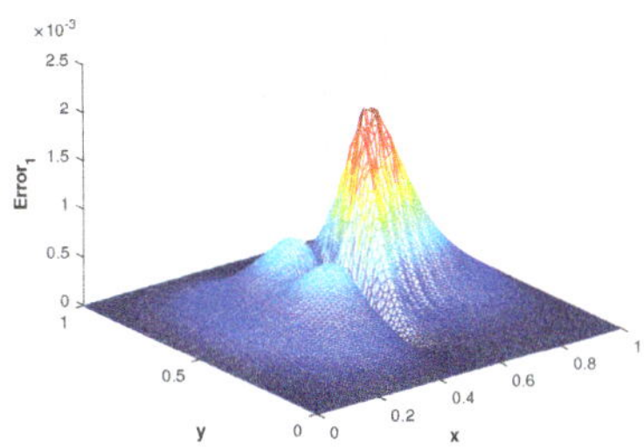

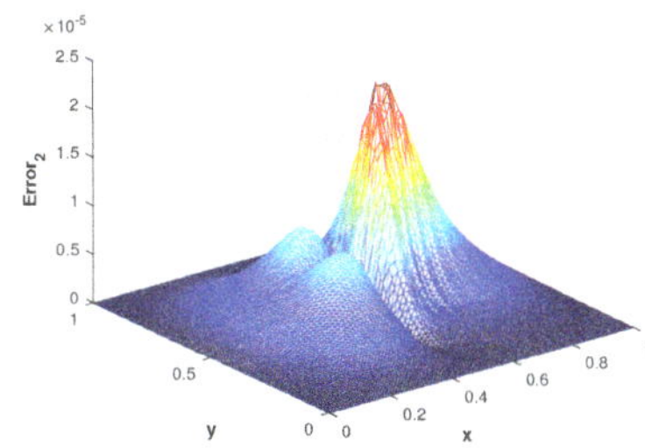

(**a**) (**b**)

Figure 36. (**a**) The surface plot of $Error_1$ of the proposed method corresponding to problem 5 using GA RBF on domain Ω_1 with $n_g = 8100, n_l = 35, N = 18, \alpha = 0.7, \beta = 1.6$. (**b**) The surface plot of $Error_2$ of the proposed method corresponding to problem 5 using GA RBF on domain Ω_1 with $n_g = 8100, n_l = 35, N = 18, \alpha = 0.7, \beta = 1.6$.

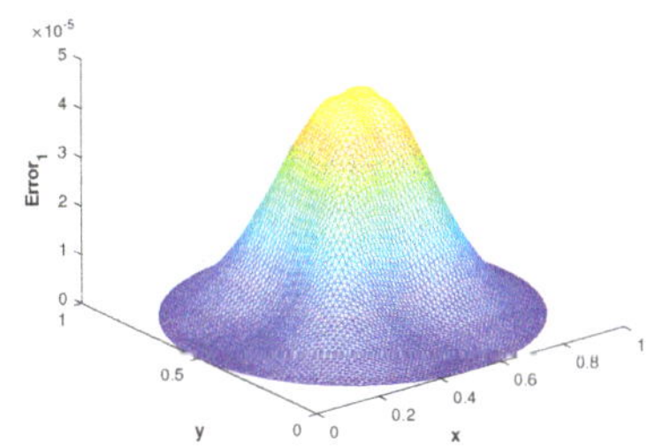

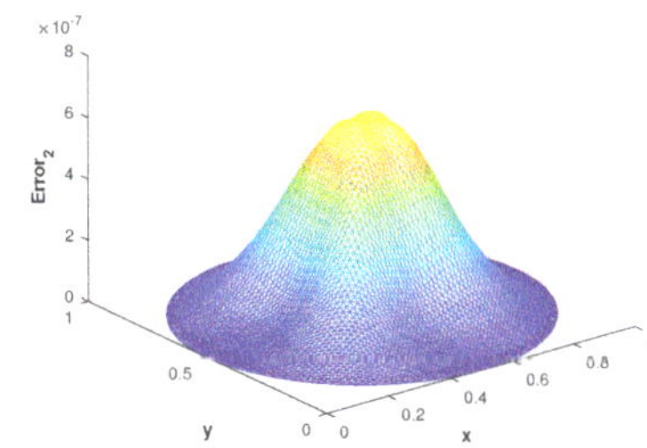

(**a**) (**b**)

Figure 37. (**a**) The mesh plot of $Error_1$ of the proposed method corresponding to problem 5 using MQ RBF on Ω_2 with $n_g = 5064, n_l = 30, N = 18, \alpha = 0.9, \beta = 1.3$. (**b**) The mesh plot of $Error_2$ of the proposed method corresponding to problem 5 using MQ RBF on Ω_2 with $n_g = 5064, n_l = 30$, $N = 18$, $\alpha = 0.9, \beta = 1.3$.

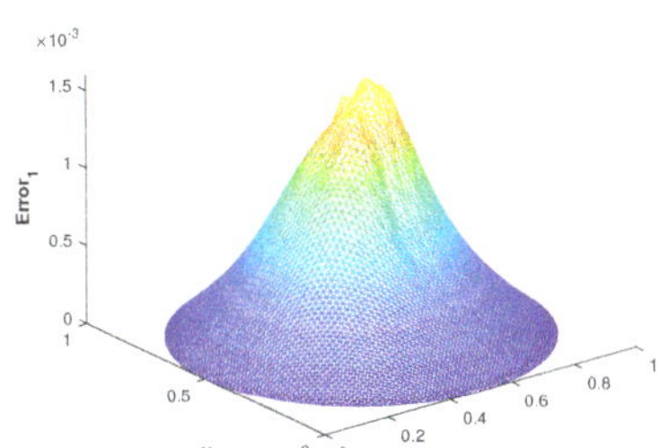

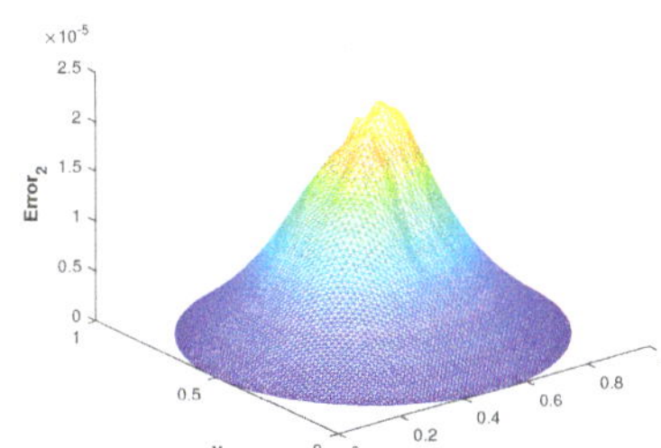

(**a**) (**b**)

Figure 38. (**a**) The mesh plot of $Error_1$ of the proposed method corresponding to problem 5 using GA RBF on Ω_2 with $n_g = 5064, n_l = 30, N = 18, \alpha = 0.9, \beta = 1.3$. (**b**) The mesh plot of $Error_2$ of the proposed method corresponding to problem 5 using GA RBF on Ω_2 with $n_g = 5064, n_l = 30$, $N = 18$, $\alpha = 0.9, \beta = 1.3$.

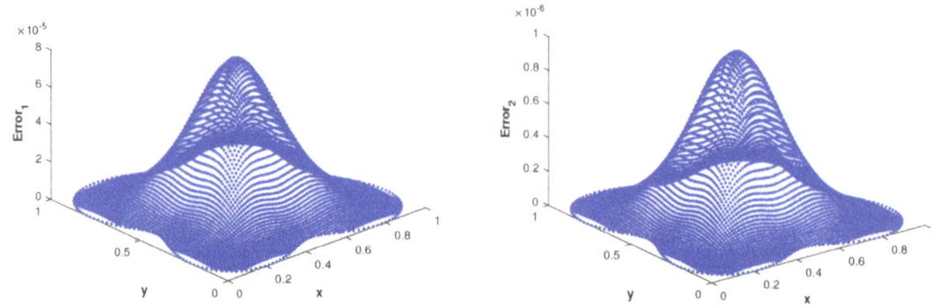

(**a**) (**b**)

Figure 39. (**a**) The scatter plot of $Error_1$ of the proposed method corresponding to problem 5 using MQ RBF on Ω_4 with $n_g = 6393, n_l = 35, N = 16, \alpha = 0.7, \beta = 1.6$. (**b**) The scatter plot of $Error_2$ of the proposed method corresponding to problem 5 using MQ RBF on Ω_4 with $n_g = 6393, n_l = 35$, $N = 16, \alpha = 0.7, \beta = 1.6$.

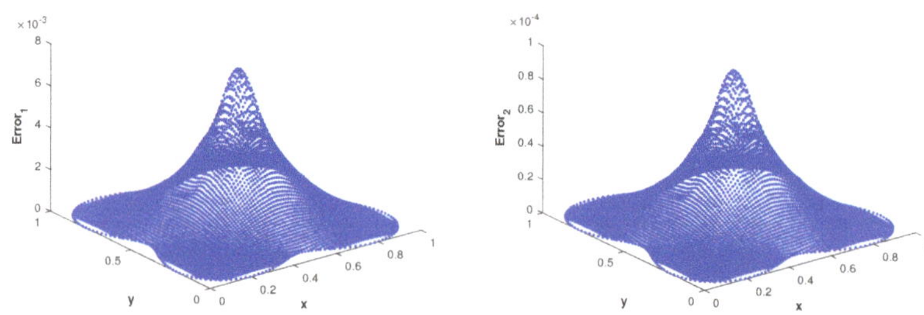

(**a**) (**b**)

Figure 40. (**a**) The scatter plot of $Error_1$ of the proposed method corresponding to problem 5 using GA RBF on Ω_4 with $n_g = 6393, n_l = 35, N = 16, \alpha = 0.7, \beta = 1.6$. (**b**) The scatter plot of $Error_2$ of the proposed method corresponding to problem 5 using GA RBF on Ω_4 with $n_g = 6393, n_l = 35, N = 16$, $\alpha = 0.7, \beta = 1.6$.

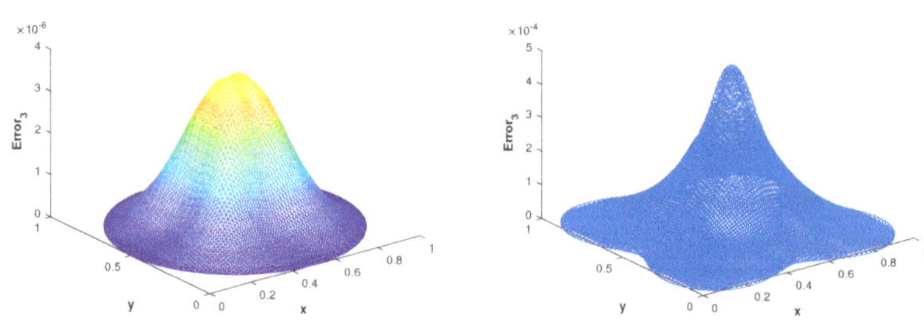

(**a**) (**b**)

Figure 41. (**a**) The mesh plot of $Error_3$ of the proposed method corresponding to problem 5 using MQ RBF on Ω_2 with $n_g = 5064, n_l = 35, N = 18, \alpha = 0.7, \beta = 1.6$. (**b**) The scatter plot of $Error_3$ of the proposed method corresponding to problem 5 using GA RBF on Ω_4 with $n_g = 6393, n_l = 35, N = 18$, $\alpha = 0.7, \beta = 1.6$.

5. Conclusions

In this article, an efficient numerical method based on Laplace transform and local radial basis functions for the numerical modeling of fractional mixed diffusion and wave diffusion equations with two Caputo derivatives of order $0 < \alpha < 1$ and $1 < \beta < 2$ is proposed. Numerical experiments were conducted in regular and irregular domains with uniform and non-uniform nodes. It is observed that the proposed method effectively solves problems defined on regular and irregular domains with a large number of nodes, requiring less computational time without experiencing any time instability. The results lead to the conclusion that the proposed method is an efficient and reliable technique for the considered problem in all types of domains. However, implementing this computational framework in coupled multi-component systems of partial differential equations remains an open problem. Successful implementation of such a framework could pave the way for further mathematical and biological applications. In future work, we will aim to extend our numerical method to include multiple components of the differential operator of order 2, as introduced in [57]. This will allow us to compare the impact of the errors of the proposed method and the validity of the model with clinical outcomes, thereby facilitating the understanding of complex phenomena.

Author Contributions: Conceptualization, K. and R.K.; methodology, K.; software, R.K. and K.; validation, R.K., K. and S.M.A.; formal analysis, T.A.; investigation, K.; resources, S.M.A.; data curation, S.M.A.; writing—original draft preparation, K.; writing—review and editing, S.M.A. and K.; visualization, R.K.; supervision, K.; project administration, T.A.; funding acquisition, T.A. All authors have read and agreed to the published version of the manuscript.

Funding: This research received no external funding.

Data Availability Statement: All data generated or analyzed during this study are included in this article.

Conflicts of Interest: The authors declare that they have no conflict of interest.

References

1. Tenreiro Machado, J.A. A probabilistic interpretation of the fractional-order differentiation. *Fract. Calc. Appl. Anal.* **2003**, *6*, 73–79.
2. Sun, H.; Chen, W.; Chen, Y. Variable-order fractional differential operators in anomalous diffusion modeling. *Phys. Stat. Mech. Its Appl.* **2009**, *388*, 4586–4592. [CrossRef]
3. Torvik, P.J.; Bagley, R.L. On the appearance of the fractional derivative in the behavior of real materials. *J. Appl. Mech.* **1984**, *51*, 294–298. [CrossRef]
4. Panda, R.; Dash, M. Fractional generalized splines and signal processing. *Signal Process.* **2006**, *86*, 2340–2350. [CrossRef]
5. Benchellal, A.; Poinot, T.; Trigeassou, J.C. Fractional modelling and identification of a thermal process. *IFAC Proc. Vol.* **2006**, *39*, 248–253. [CrossRef]
6. Jesus, I.S.; Machado, J.T.; Cunha, J.B. Fractional electrical dynamics in fruits and vegetables. *IFAC Proc. Vol.* **2006**, *39*, 308–313. [CrossRef]
7. Lima, M.F.; Tenreiro Machado, J.A.; Crisóstomo, M. Experimental signal analysis of robot impacts in a fractional calculus perspective. *J. Adv. Comput. Intell. Intell. Inform.* **2007**, *11*, 1079–1085. [CrossRef]
8. Gorenflo, R.; Luchko, Y.; Mainardi, F. Wright functions as scale-invariant solutions of the diffusion-wave equation. *J. Comput. Appl. Math.* **2000**, *118*, 175–191. [CrossRef]
9. Liu, F.; Anh, V.V.; Turner, I.; Zhuang, P. Time fractional advection-dispersion equation. *J. Appl. Math. Comput.* **2003**, *13*, 233–245. [CrossRef]
10. Mainardi, F. The fundamental solutions for the fractional diffusion-wave equation. *Appl. Math. Lett.* **1996**, *9*, 23–28. [CrossRef]
11. Wyss, W. The fractional diffusion equation. *J. Math. Phys.* **1986**, *27*, 2782–2785. [CrossRef]
12. Jiang, H.; Liu, F.; Turner, I.; Burrage, K. Analytical solutions for the multi-term time-fractional diffusion-wave/diffusion equations in a finite domain. *Comput. Math. Appl.* **2012**, *64*, 3377–3388. [CrossRef]
13. Momani, S.; Odibat, Z.M. Fractional green function for linear time-fractional inhomogeneous partial differential equations in fluid mechanics. *J. Appl. Math. Comput.* **2007**, *24*, 167–178. [CrossRef]
14. Lv, X.; Feng, X. Identifying a Space-Dependent Source Term and the Initial Value in a Time Fractional Diffusion-Wave Equation. *Mathematics* **2023**, *11*, 1521. [CrossRef]
15. Diethelm, K.; Ford, J. Numerical solution of the Bagley-Torvik equation. *BIT Numer. Math.* **2002**, *42*, 490–507. [CrossRef]
16. Liu, L.; Zhang, S.; Chen, S.; Liu, F.; Feng, L.; Turner, I.; Zhu, J. An Application of the Distributed-Order Time-and Space-Fractional Diffusion-Wave Equation for Studying Anomalous Transport in Comb Structures. *Fractal Fract.* **2023**, *7*, 239. [CrossRef]

17. Atta, A.G.; Abd-Elhameed, W.M.; Youssri, Y.H. Shifted fifth-kind Chebyshev polynomials Galerkin-based procedure for treating fractional diffusion-wave equation. *Int. J. Mod. Phys. C* **2022**, *33*, 2250102. [CrossRef]
18. Liu, F.; Shen, S.; Anh, V.; Turner, I. Analysis of a discrete non-Markovian random walk approximation for the time fractional diffusion equation. *Anziam J.* **2004**, *46*, C488–C504. [CrossRef]
19. Zhao, Y.; Wang, F.; Hu, X.; Shi, Z.; Tang, Y. Anisotropic linear triangle finite element approximation for multi-term time-fractional mixed diffusion and diffusion-wave equations with variable coefficient on 2D bounded domain. *Comput. Math. Appl.* **2019**, *78* 1705–1719. [CrossRef]
20. Liu, Z.; Liu, F.; Zeng, F. An alternating direction implicit spectral method for solving two dimensional multi-term time fractional mixed diffusion and diffusion-wave equations. *Appl. Numer. Math.* **2019**, *136*, 139–151. [CrossRef]
21. Agrawal, O.P. Solution for a fractional diffusion-wave equation defined in a bounded domain. *Nonlinear Dyn.* **2002**, *29*, 145–155 [CrossRef]
22. Tadjeran, C.; Meerschaert, M.M.; Scheffler, H.P. A second-order accurate numerical approximation for the fractional diffusion equation. *J. Comput. Phys.* **2006**, *213*, 205–213. [CrossRef]
23. Li, C.; Chen, A. Numerical methods for fractional partial differential equations. *Int. J. Comput. Math.* **2018**, *95*, 1048–1099 [CrossRef]
24. Liu, Y.; Sun, H.; Yin, X.; Feng, L. Fully discrete spectral method for solving a novel multi-term time-fractional mixed diffusion and diffusion-wave equation. *Z. Angew. Math. Und Phys.* **2020**, *71*, 1–19. [CrossRef]
25. Dehghan, M.; Manafian, J.; Saadatmandi, A. Solving nonlinear fractional partial differential equations using the homotopy analysis method. *Numer. Methods Partial. Differ. Equ. Int. J.* **2010**, *26*, 448–479. [CrossRef]
26. Liu, Q.X.; Gu, Y.; Zhuang, P.; Liu, F.; Nie, Y. An implicit RBF meshless approach for time fractional diffusion equations. *Comput Mech.* **2011**, *48*, 1–12. [CrossRef]
27. Chen, W.; Ye, L.; Sun, H. Fractional diffusion equations by the Kansa method. *Comput. Math. Appl.* **2010**, *59*, 1614–1620. [CrossRef]
28. Shivanian, E.; Jafarabadi, A. The spectral meshless radial point interpolation method for solving an inverse source problem of the time-fractional diffusion equation. *Appl. Numer. Math.* **2018**, *129*, 1–25. [CrossRef]
29. Shu, C.; Ding, H.; Yeo, K.S. Local radial basis function-based differential quadrature method and its application to solve two-dimensional incompressible Navier-Stokes equations. *Comput. Methods Appl. Mech. Eng.* **2003**, *192*, 941–954. [CrossRef]
30. Abbaszadeh, M.; Dehghan, M. Meshless upwind local radial basis function-finite difference technique to simulate the time fractional distributed-order advection-diffusion equation. *Eng. Comput.* **2021**, *37*, 873–889. [CrossRef]
31. Kumar, A.; Bhardwaj, A. A local meshless method for time fractional nonlinear diffusion wave equation. *Numer. Algorithms* **2020** *85*, 1311–1334. [CrossRef]
32. Bhardwaj, A.; Kumar, A. Numerical solution of time fractional tricomi-type equation by an RBF based meshless method. *Eng Anal. Bound. Elem.* **2020**, *118*, 96–107. [CrossRef]
33. Kumar, A.; Bhardwaj, A.; Kumar, B.R. A meshless local collocation method for time fractional diffusion wave equation. *Comput Math. Appl.* **2019**, *78*, 1851–1861. [CrossRef]
34. Kumar, A.; Bhardwaj, A.; Dubey, S. A local meshless method to approximate the time-fractional telegraph equation. *Eng. Comput* **2021**, *37*, 3473–3488. [CrossRef]
35. Hosseini, V.R.; Shivanian, E.; Chen, W. Local radial point interpolation (MLRPI) method for solving time fractional diffusion-wave equation with damping. *J. Comput. Phys.* **2016**, *312*, 307–332. [CrossRef]
36. Salehi, R. A meshless point collocation method for 2-D multi-term time fractional diffusion-wave equation. *Numer. Algorithms* **2017**, *74*, 1145–1168. [CrossRef]
37. Aslefallah, M.; Shivanian, E. An efficient meshless method based on RBFs for the time fractional diffusion-wave equation. *Afr Mat.* **2018**, *29*, 1203–1214. [CrossRef]
38. Yang, J.Y.; Zhao, Y.M.; Liu, N.; Bu, W.P.; Xu, T.L.; Tang, Y.F. An implicit MLS meshless method for 2-D time dependent fractional diffusion-wave equation. *Appl. Math. Model.* **2015**, *39*, 1229–1240. [CrossRef]
39. Wei, S.; Chen, W.; Zhang, Y.; Wei, H.; Garrard, R.M. A local radial basis function collocation method to solve the variable-order time fractional diffusion equation in a two-dimensional irregular domain. *Numer. Methods Partial. Differ. Equ.* **2018**, *34*, 1209–1223 [CrossRef]
40. Kamran, K.; Shah, Z.; Kumam, P.; Alreshidi, N.A. A meshless method based on the laplace transform for the 2D multi-term time fractional partial integro-differential equation. *Mathematics* **2020**, *8*, 1972. [CrossRef]
41. Kamran; Ali, A.; Gómez-Aguilar, J.F. A transform based local RBF method for 2D linear PDE with Caputo-Fabrizio derivative Comptes Rendus. *Mathématique* **2020**, *358*, 831–842.
42. Sarra, S.A. A local radial basis function method for advection-diffusion-reaction equations on complexly shaped domains. *Appl. Math. Comput.* **2012**, *218*, 9853–9865. [CrossRef]
43. Sun, Z.Z.; Ji, C.C.; Du, R. A new analytical technique of the L-type difference schemes for time fractional mixed sub-diffusion and diffusion-wave equations. *Appl. Math. Lett.* **2020**, *102*, 106115. [CrossRef]
44. Feng, L.; Liu, F.; Turner, I. Finite difference/finite element method for a novel 2D multi-term time-fractional mixed sub-diffusion and diffusion-wave equation on convex domains. *Commun. Nonlinear Sci. Numer. Simul.* **2019**, *70*, 354–371. [CrossRef]
45. Bhardwaj, A.; Kumar, A. A numerical solution of time-fractional mixed diffusion and diffusion-wave equation by an RBF-based meshless method. *Eng. Comput.* **2020**, *38*, 1883–1903. [CrossRef]

6. Gu, X.M.; Wu, S.L. A parallel-in-time iterative algorithm for Volterra partial integro-differential problems with weakly singular kernel. *J. Comput. Phys.* **2020**, *417*, 109576. [CrossRef]
7. Sarra, S.A.; Kansa, E.J. Multiquadric radial basis function approximation methods for the numerical solution of partial differential equations. *Adv. Comput. Mech.* **2009**, *2*, 220.
8. Schaback, R. Error estimates and condition numbers for radial basis function interpolation. *Adv. Comput. Math.* **1995**, *3*, 251–264. [CrossRef]
9. Trefethen, L.N.; Bau, D., III. *Numerical Linear Algebra*; Siam: Philadelphia, PA, USA, 1997; Volume 50.
0. Stehfest, H. Algorithm 368: Numerical inversion of Laplace transforms [D5]. *Commun. ACM* **1970**, *13*, 47–49. [CrossRef]
1. Stehfest, H. Remark on algorithm 368: Numerical inversion of Laplace transforms. *Commun. ACM* **1970**, *13*, 624. [CrossRef]
2. Davies, B.; Martin, B. Numerical inversion of the Laplace transform: A survey and comparison of methods. *J. Comput. Phys.* **1979**, *33*, 1–32. [CrossRef]
3. Kuznetsov, A. On the Convergence of the Gaver–Stehfest Algorithm. *SIAM J. Numer. Anal.* **2013**, *51*, 2984–2998. [CrossRef]
4. Abate, J.; Valkó, P.P. Multi-precision Laplace transform inversion. *Int. J. Numer. Methods Eng.* **2004**, *60*, 979–993. [CrossRef]
5. Abate, J.; Whitt, W. A unified framework for numerically inverting Laplace transforms. *INFORMS J. Comput.* **2006**, *18*, 408–421. [CrossRef]
6. Fu, Z.J.; Chen, W.; Yang, H.T. Boundary particle method for Laplace transformed time fractional diffusion equations. *J. Comput. Phys.* **2013**, *235*, 52–66. [CrossRef]
7. Alzahrani, T. Spatio-temporal modeling of immune response to SARS-CoV-2 infection. *Mathematics* **2021**, *9*, 3274. [CrossRef]

MDPI AG
Grosspeteranlage 5
4052 Basel
Switzerland
Tel.: +41 61 683 77 34

Fractal and Fractional Editorial Office
E-mail: fractalfract@mdpi.com
www.mdpi.com/journal/fractalfract

www.ingramcontent.com/pod-product-compliance
Lightning Source LLC
Chambersburg PA
CBHW061506220926
51850CB00004B/185
9783725879816